P9-DGQ-524

Encyclopedia of the United States in the Twentieth Century

Editorial Board

ENCYCLOPEDIA OF THE UNITED STATES IN THE TWENTIETH CENTURY

Stanley I. Kutler
Editor in Chief

Robert Dallek
David A. Hollinger
Thomas K. McCraw
Associate Editors

Judith Kirkwood
Assistant Editor

Volume I

CHARLES SCRIBNER'S SONS
Macmillan Library Reference USA
Simon & Schuster Macmillan
New York

SIMON & SCHUSTER AND PRENTICE HALL INTERNATIONAL
London Mexico City New Delhi Singapore Sydney Toronto

Charles Scribner's Sons
An imprint of Simon & Schuster Macmillan
1633 Broadway
New York, New York 10019

Library of Congress Cataloging-in-Publication Data

Encyclopedia of the United States in the twentieth century / Stanley I. Kutler, editor in chief; Robert Dallek, David A. Hollinger, Thomas K. McCraw, associate editors; Judith Kirkwood, assistant editor.

p. cm.

Includes bibliographical references and index.

ISBN 0-13-210535-7 (set: hc: alk. paper). — 0-13-307190-1 (vol. 1: hc: alk. paper). — 0-13-307208-8 (vol. 2: hc: alk. paper). — 0-13-307216-9 (vol. 3: hc: alk. paper). — 0-13-307224-X (vol. 4: hc: alk. paper).

1. United States—Encyclopedias. I. Kutler, Stanley I. E740.7.E53 1996
973'.003–dc20
95-22696 CIP

5 7 9 11 13 15 17 19 20 18 16 14 12 10 8 6 4

PRINTED IN THE UNITED STATES OF AMERICA

The paper in this publication meets the requirements of ANSI/NISO Z39.48-1992 (Permanence of Paper)

Editorial and Production Staff

Managing Editor
Stephen Wagley

Assistant Managing Editor
Sarah Gardner Cunningham

Manuscript Editors
Judith Kirkwood
Grace Burford　John W. Hopper
James Waller　Cecile Watters

Illustration Editor
Michael A. Ross

Proofreaders
Rachel Benzaquen　Mary Flower　Adrian Saich
David Sassian　David Shapiro

Compositor
Atlis Graphics, Inc.

Cartographer
Donald S. Frazier

Indexer
Katharyn Dunham
ParaGraphs

Production Manager
Rose Capozzelli

Publisher, Charles Scribner's Sons
Karen Day

President, Macmillan Library Reference USA
Gordon Macomber

Contents

Volume I

Part 1

THE AMERICAN PEOPLE

Part 2

POLITICS

CONTENTS

VOLUME II

Part 3

GLOBAL AMERICA

Part 4

SCIENCE, TECHNOLOGY, AND MEDICINE

VOLUME III

Part 5

THE ECONOMY

Alphabetical Table of Contents

ALPHABETICAL TABLE OF CONTENTS

List of Maps

General Introduction

STANLEY I. KUTLER

Eighty distinguished historians have contributed to this volume, narrating and analyzing the major topics and themes of the twentieth century, ranging from definitions of the American people, their politics and government, their society and its cultural expressions, to American economic life and institutions, the effect of science and technology, and America's place in the world. As best they can, historians deal with the past on its own terms, but inevitably they interpret it from the perspective of their own day, with its concerns reflected in their choice of topics and the questions they ask of the past. An encyclopedia of twentieth-century America written a generation ago would not have explored religion beyond the bounds of Protestantism, Catholicism, and Judaism. Here, one will find a significant contribution describing "nontraditional" religions, ranging from Buddhism, Islam, and "New Age" movements. Similarly, a generation ago, the role of labor unions would have been the focus of a major essay dealing with society and the economy; here labor organization is treated as part of the larger phenomenon of "work." Considerations of race and gender here figure more prominently than they would have been earlier, not as a reflection of turbulent current issues, but rather as an attempt to recover their prominence and significance throughout the century.

The twentieth century is not self-contained nor can it be isolated from the preceding four centuries of American history. Still, historians find it useful and convenient to isolate this slice of time—the twentieth century—and relate it to some understanding of who and what Americans are in the present. Of course, as a construct of American history, the "twentieth century" is not neatly coterminous with the years 1900 to 2000. Arguments could be made for dating the century from 1898 when the United States defeated Spain and became a major player in world affairs. Future historians might want to consider the end of the Cold War in 1991 or the nation's re-emergence as a debtor nation and the rise of new, powerful world economic rivals in the mid-1980s as an endpoint to the century. Certainly, the grandiose concept of the "American Century" no longer has any reality. The American preeminence—whether diplomatic, military, or economic—that characterized much of the century was severely challenged as the century drew to a close. This reality, together with a variety of other considerations, has tempered some of the traditional optimism that envisioned ever-greater material prosperity and national power. Diminished expectations dominated society's outlook as the twentieth century ended. From a perspective shrouded in pessimism and uncertainty, we like to think that optimism reigned at some earlier, ideal time in the past. But, in fact, nostalgia is our greatest barrier to historical understanding. Life's trials seemed at least as gloomy and contentious to the people of past generations as they are to many Americans today.

As we cross into a new period for American life, we recognize that the enormous changes the nation experienced over the past century have produced new dimensions of old problems for the nation to confront in the twenty-first century: new variants of old questions involving race, gender, class, health, prosperity, the environment, technology, and world power. The work of the twentieth century will, in large part, determine how we approach and react to those questions in the next century.

The *Encyclopedia of the United States in the*

Twentieth Century takes stock of the political, economic, social, cultural, and technological developments that have marked the century. The Austrian-born social scientist, Peter F. Drucker, noted that "no century in recorded history has experienced so many social transformations and such radical ones as the twentieth century."

Drucker observed that it has not been the century's dramatic political events of wars, civil wars, and revolutions that transformed the world. True, those events left indelible marks of cruelty, evil, and devastation, but they resulted in little permanent or ongoing change. Colonialism was abandoned, but the traumatic events of the century now seem so remote. The Soviet Union no longer exists; the Chinese Revolution has gone through so many convulsions as to be almost unrecognizable today, and World War II, however traumatic, resulted in little permanent alteration of political arrangements. But that war accelerated profound economic and social transformations, with enormous consequences for the rest of the century. In the United States the war of the 1940s and the subsequent Cold War stimulated an explosion of technology that dramatically transformed the lives of almost everyone. The ideological crusades in behalf of "democracy" further undermined the logic of legally imposed race discrimination. The winds of change irrevocably altered the role of people of color, in the United States and throughout the world.

For certain, the United States is a vastly different nation from a century ago. Current vocabulary would describe the United States then as a developing nation, however we characterize it physically, politically, socially, or economically. In 1900, only the Northeast had any pockets of settlement containing more than ninety inhabitants per square mile. The portrait of Americans was dramatically changing. By 1910, more than 70 percent of European immigrants came from southern and eastern Europe, about the proportion that had come from western and northern Europe two decades earlier. The new immigrants brought with them new languages, new cultures, and multitudes of adherents to religions that had been marginalized in American life.

Nearly 20 percent of Americans lived or worked on farms, down some 4 percent from a decade earlier, and heralding a similar decline by 1910. Slightly more than 35 percent of Americans were industrial wage-earners, up more than 3 percent from 1890 and destined to rise another 3 percent in the next decade. The 1900 census classified 5 percent of the populace as servants, a figure steadily in decline by about 1 percent each decade. On the other hand, the Census Bureau noted an expanding middle class, particularly among "proprietors and managers." Material changes were startling. Gross national product rose from $37 billion in 1901 to more than $55 billion in the next five years, while the per capita share of GNP rose more than 20 percent in the same period.

The United States in 1990 was a world with only a few hundred automobiles, but no airplanes, television, computers, social security, female senators, AIDS, or any mastery of the science of genetics. Except for a handful of doctors, hardly anyone had heard of Sigmund Freud, whose *Interpretation of Dreams* was published in Europe that year. Albert Einstein, a young patent clerk in Switzerland, had yet to introduce relativity into physical theory. Theodore Dreiser's *Sister Carrie* was banned for suggesting that the social conditions spawned by industrial capitalism made it almost reasonable for a woman to sell her body. Mandatory school attendance laws, though commonplace, were laxly enforced; the temptation to use child labor in factories and mines enticed employers and families alike. College education existed only for a wealthy elite.

The people of the United States openly spoke of a "color line." African Americans, 10 percent of all Americans, were supposedly equal citizens under the law, but in fact held second-class citizenship. They lived a segregated life enforced by law in the South and by custom in significant parts of the North. In the South, only 5 percent of eligible blacks voted and fewer than 1 percent attended high school.

What Americans did abroad reflected what they did at home. The United States had taken over the Spanish empire after 1898 and American soldiers spent the next three years suppressing an indigenous rebellion in the Philippine Islands. Many Americans bitterly opposed the acquisition of empire. They regarded it as a betrayal of their own heritage of a domestic empire conceived in liberty. Others blithely rationalized American imperialism as the fulfillment of the English poet Rudyard Kipling's plea that the great western nations take up the "white man's burden." That burden, it seemed, was to bring the blessings of American liberty, democracy, and Christianity to "our little brown brothers," no matter the human costs to both sides, and no matter their standards of civilizations and religious belief.

What Americans later praised as the "American Century," with the United States as the dominant, hegemonic power, indeed was remote in 1900.

Whatever American claims to world power, the United States had only junior status in an imposing club of great imperial nations. The "sun never set on the British Empire," so the saying went, as London's writ ran throughout east and south Asia, Africa, and on the high seas. Queen Victoria was in the sixty-third year of her reign and her empire seemed indestructible. The Manchu dynasty still ruled China, and the Russian, German, Austrian, and Dutch empires, while not a match for the British, provided significant influence and grandeur to the mother countries.

As the twentieth century opened, the United States had attained unprecedented levels as an industrialized, urbanized, commercial, and military power. Still, those levels seemed trifling by century's end. Certainly, the United States of George Bush and Bill Clinton, of Martin Luther King and the National Organization of Women, and of computers and lasers is far different than the world of William McKinley and Theodore Roosevelt, of the genteel, middle-class reformers of the Progressive era, and of a society largely dependent upon horses and steam power.

A hundred years ago, aside from New York and Chicago, Americans measured large cities in hundreds of thousands of persons; today, we count in millions and speak about urban sprawl and metropolitan areas. The nation moved from a rural to an urbanized to a suburbanized, and even edge-city demographic pattern. In 1900 voluntarism and private charity had been the primary means for ameliorating the hardships of life. By the 1990s, the welfare state was a fact of life, despite enormous political pressures to dismantle or diminish it. Politically, Americans have watched the presidency, with its accompanying executive bureaucracy, move to the forefront of governmental power. Complex administrative arrangements have surpassed simple statutes for creating the necessary elements of coercion and sanction for effective governance. The operation and clash of competing interest groups have taken us far beyond the idealized conflict that James Madison and the framers of the Constitution envisioned in a day of less sophisticated communication.

As the nation approached the year 2000, the functions and activities of American society were spread more evenly throughout the land, with perhaps an edge to the southern and western "rims" for political influence, resources, and even population. The 1990 Census recognized that California controls 20 percent of the electoral vote and 12 percent of the seats in the House of Representatives, or one out of eight seats. In 1994, Texas replaced New York as the second most populous state. The so-called Sun Belt has fifty percent of the representatives, and its interests in water, environment, public power, immigration, and infrastructures are quite different from those of other areas. White, Protestant, European-based stock, and rural or small-town men dominated society in 1900. A century later, notions of diversity and multiculturalism, present in American life since the seventeenth century but always muted and subsumed under the banner of unity and "Americanism," were celebrated as preferable norms.

Agriculture remains important, but genetic and mechanistic innovations have further accelerated the decline in the number of agrarian workers, leaving the nation with an agricultural component that comprises about 2 percent of the total labor force. Americans nostalgically celebrate the family farm, but in truth, that farm more likely is part of the vast complex known as agribusiness. Industrial workers, the fastest-growing class of the early twentieth century, rapidly dwindled in number at a breathtaking pace in the last twenty years of the century. Unions and traditional industrial workers have been marginalized in the nation's economy. In their stead, there developed what many commentators have called knowledge workers, a group that has been the fastest growing sector in the work force since 1980. These "technologists" work with their hands and with specialized, theoretical knowledge, such as the vast array of computer and medical technicians.

American society and culture, too, have grown more complex and diverse. A half century ago, Americans spoke optimistically of a "triple melting pot" that eventually would obliterate religious and ethnic conflict. It was rooted in the traditional interplay between European-oriented Protestantism, Catholicism, and Judaism. By the end of the twentieth century, nontraditional religions have emerged as a force in their own right and American society again has been infused with waves of immigrants, creating what has been described as the "first universal nation." New peoples have arrived from Asia, Africa, and Latin America, while the flow of newcomers from Europe (aside from those from the former Soviet Union) has been reduced to a trickle. The prospect of an integrated, "color-blind" society has yielded to empowerment of racial and ethnic groups, desirous of greater separation and preservation of cultural uniqueness.

Social change, economic progress, cultural conflict, and technological innovations have always characterized American history. The twentieth century witnessed those phenomena, to be sure, in a heightened and accelerated fashion. But if any characteristic of the United States in the twentieth century is strikingly different from that of earlier periods, it is the nation's world role, military and economically. The triumph over Spain in 1898 traditionally marks the emergence of the United States as a world power. Appearance became reality in less than two decades as the United States contributed men, materiél, and, above all, wealth to the triumph of the Allies in World War I. Despite internal resistance, the United States was in the world to stay, and for the rest of the century, it was preoccupied with determining and fulfilling its commitments to that role.

America's world role alternated between conflict and cooperation. At century's end, talk of a global economy is commonplace. A hundred years ago, the nation sought overseas markets, fearing that domestic ones were saturated and victimized by overproduction. The American search for global economic success has often produced conflict, ranging from tariff wars to causing (in part) full-scale wars such as that with Japan and Germany in the 1940s and the long twilight struggle with the Soviet Union and the battle to thwart communist expansion. The Cold War, spanning half the century, influenced much more than diplomacy and military development. The domestic costs, whether to civil liberties or to the skewing of the nation's commitment to industrial research, were very significant. The Cold War required regimen, conformity, and an extraordinary expenditure of resources. Defense-oriented industries profited enormously from a peculiar form of the "welfare state," while other economic sectors, such as consumer electronics, were left to wither and fall to foreigners. The demands for loyalty and conformity, particularly from the 1940s to the 1960s, affected all aspects of life from politics to education to culture.

The post-Cold War period has been celebrated by some as "the end of history," meaning an end to ideology and issue-conflict in American society and the world. But we well know that the world remains a fragile, unstable place in which new rivalries and new interests have supplanted the bipolar struggle of more than seventy years between capitalism and communism. The time may come when we look back nostalgically on the Cold War as a relatively simple conflict. Now, the United States must compete for world markets with a reunified Europe and trading blocs of emergent, dynamic Asian nations. Both at home and abroad, the nation must confront the challenge of depleting resources, a fragile environment, and an exploding population. Within the society itself, we face new challenges to old institutions and processes which, under the glare of modern communications, increasingly are vulnerable to cynicism and contempt. Ideologies and issues continue to generate controversy and division.

The one certainty in history is change.

ACKNOWLEDGMENTS

Associate Editors Robert Dallek, David A. Hollinger, and Thomas K. McCraw—valued and old friends—were indispensable collaborators on this project. Their commitment, energy, and imagination are reflected throughout the work, both in concept and execution. Assistant Editor Judith Kirkwood, who has worked with me for more than a decade, performed her editorial magic with distinction and flair. Various members of the editorial board provided helpful readings and criticism. Sam Daniel of the Prints and Photographs Division at the Library of Congress helped with the illustrations.

The project originated at Johns Hopkins University Press. Former Director Jack Goellner and Executive Editor Henry Tom solidly backed the enterprise, but Jackie Wehmueller gave us invaluable conceptual advice and, most of all, uncommon common sense. For various reasons, the project had to be moved. Charles E. Smith brought it to Simon & Schuster. But the crucial final stages have been in the eminently capable and gentle hands of Karen Day, our publisher at Charles Scribner's Sons, and Stephen Wagley, Senior Editor *extraordinaire*.

Common Abbreviations Used in This Work

Ala.	Alabama
Ariz.	Arizona
Ark.	Arkansas
Art.	Article
b.	born
c.	*circa*, about, approximately
Calif.	California
cf.	*confer*, compare
chap.	chapter (plural, chaps.)
Colo.	Colorado
Cong.	Congress
Conn.	Connecticut
d.	died
D	Democrat, Democratic
D.C.	District of Columbia
Del.	Delaware
diss.	dissertation
ed.	editor (plural, eds); edition
e.g.	*exempli gratia*, for example
enl.	enlarged
esp.	especially
et al.	*et alii*, and others
etc.	*et cetera*, and so forth
exp.	expanded
f.	and following (plural, ff.)
Fla.	Florida
Ga.	Georgia
ibid.	*ibidem*, in the same place (as the one immediately preceding)
Ida.	Idaho
i.e.	*id est*, that is
Ill.	Illinois
Ind.	Indiana
Kan.	Kansas
Ky.	Kentucky
La.	Louisiana
M.A.	Master of Arts
Mass.	Massachusetts
Md.	Maryland
Me.	Maine
Mich.	Michigan
Minn.	Minnesota
Miss.	Mississippi
Mo.	Missouri
Mont.	Montana
n.	note
N.C.	North Carolina
n.d.	no date
N.D.	North Dakota
Neb.	Nebraska
Nev.	Nevada
N.H.	New Hampshire
N.J.	New Jersey
N.Mex.	New Mexico
no.	number (plural, nos.)
n.p.	no place
n.s.	new series
N.Y.	New York
Okla.	Oklahoma
Oreg.	Oregon
p.	page (plural, pp.)
Pa.	Pennsylvania
P.L.	Public Law
pt.	part (plural, pts.)
R	Republican
Rep.	Representative
rev.	revised
R.I.	Rhode Island
S.C.	South Carolina
S.D.	South Dakota
sec.	section (plural, secs.)
Sen.	Senator
ser.	series
ses.	session
supp.	supplement
Tenn.	Tennessee
Tex.	Texas
UN	United Nations

U.S.	United States
U.S.S.R.	Union of Soviet Socialist Republics
v.	versus
Va.	Virginia
vol.	volume (plural, vols.)
Vt.	Vermont
Wash.	Washington
Wis.	Wisconsin
W.Va.	West Virginia
Wyo.	Wyoming

CHRONOLOGY

CHRONOLOGY

Year	The American People	Politics	Global America
1898			Spanish-American War; Spain cedes Puerto Rico and Guam, and surrenders the Philippines, to the United States
1899	W. E. B. Du Bois, *The Philadelphia Negro*		Beginning of Philippine insurrection; first Hague Peace Conference on arms limitations
1900	Census counts 75,994,575 Americans	William McKinley reelected president	
1901		Assassination of McKinley; Theodore Roosevelt becomes president	
1902			End of Philippine insurrection
1903	Bureau of the Census established	Joseph Cannon becomes Speaker of the House of Representatives	United States recognizes independence of Panama; Canal Zone established; first Dick (Militia) Act
1904	Chinese Exclusion Act	Theodore Roosevelt elected president; Lincoln Steffens, *The Shame of the Cities*	Construction of Panama Canal begins
1905			Treaty of Portsmouth (N.H.) ends Russo-Japanese War
1906	Naturalization Act; San Francisco earthquake		The Navy's "White Fleet" sails around the world; Theodore Roosevelt receives Nobel Prize for peace
1907	Oklahoma admitted to the Union		Second Hague Peace Conference on arms limitations
1908		William Howard Taft elected president; Bureau of Investigation created	Second Dick (Militia) Act

CHRONOLOGY

Science, Technology, and Medicine	The Economy	Culture	Year
	U.S. Industrial Commission established	Charlotte Perkins Gilman, *Women and Economics*	1898
Guglielmo Marconi makes first wireless broadcast	Thorstein Veblen, *The Theory of the Leisure Class*	Kate Chopin, *The Awakening* (novel); John Dewey *School and Society*; Scott Joplin, "Maple Leaf Rag"	1899
	Negro Business League founded; Gold Standard Act	Ellis Island reception center (Boring & Tilton) completed; Charles W. Chesnutt, *The House behind the Cedars;* Theodore Dreiser, *Sister Carrie* (novel)	1900
	First Oldsmobile; U.S. Steel founded	American Philosophical Association founded; Jewish Theological Seminary (New York City) founded; Frank Norris, *The Octopus* (novel); American League (baseball) established	1901
	Reclamation Act; anthracite coal strike	John Dewey, *The Child and the Curriculum*; Carson Pirie Scott department store (Chicago; Louis Sullivan) and New York Public Library (Carrère and Hastings) completed; first Rose Bowl football game	1902
Wright brothers' first flight	Department of Commerce and Labor established	Enrico Caruso debuts at the Metropolitan Opera; W. E. B. Du Bois, *The Souls of Black Folk;* Henry James, *The Ambassadors* (novel); Edwin S. Porter, *The Great Train Robbery* (movie); first World Series	1903
Mount Wilson Solar Observatory established; first New York City subway opens	*Northern Securities* v. *U.S.*; Robert Hunter, *Poverty*	George M. Cohan, *Little Johnny Jones* (musical); Lincoln Steffens, *The Shame of the Cities*; Wisconsin state capitol (George B. Post) completed	1904
	Industrial Workers of the World founded; U.S. Forest Service established; *Swift* v. *U.S.*	Thomas Dixon, *The Clansman* (novel); Edith Wharton, *The House of Mirth* (novel)	1905
	Meat Inspection Act; Pure Food and Drugs Act	Beginnings of Pentecostalism; American Jewish Committee founded; Charles Ives, *The Unanswered Question* (orchestral piece); Upton Sinclair, *The Jungle* (novel)	1906
	Panic of 1907	Russell Sage Foundation established; William James, *Pragmatism*; Walter Rauschenbusch, *Christianity and the Social Crisis*	1907
	General Motors founded; Ford introduces the Model T		1908

CHRONOLOGY

Year	The American People	Politics	Global America
1909	National Association for the Advancement of Colored People (NAACP) founded	Herbert Croly, *The Promise of American Life*	Payne-Aldrich Tariff
1910	Census counts 91,972,266 Americans; *The Crisis* (NAACP magazine) founded	Edwin D. White becomes chief justice; House of Representatives revolts against Speaker Cannon	
1911			
1912	Arizona and New Mexico admitted to the Union	Woodrow Wilson elected president	
1913		Seventeenth Amendment (direct election of senators); Walter Lippmann, *A Preface to Politics*	Underwood Tariff reduces rates
1914	Marcus Garvey founds Universal Negro Improvement Association		World War I begins; Panama Canal opens; Mexican border conflict
1915			
1916		Woodrow Wilson reelected president	National Defense Act; second Mexican border conflict; Reserve Officers Training Corps (ROTC) established

CHRONOLOGY

Science, Technology, and Medicine	The Economy	Culture	Year
Sigmund Freud's trip to the United States		Beginning of "The Fundamentals" tracts; Scofield Reference Bible; Israel Zangwill, *The Melting Pot* (play; premiere, 1908)	1909
	Mann-Elkins Act	Jane Addams, *Twenty Years at Hull House;* Victor Herbert, *Naughty Marietta* (operetta); Horatio Parker, *Mona* (opera); Edward E. Slosson, *Great American Universities*; Jack Johnson wins heavyweight boxing championship; Grand Central Terminal (New York; Warren and Wetmore) and Pennsylvania Station (New York; McKim, Mead and White) completed	1910
American Psychoanalytic Association founded	Triangle Shirtwaist Company fire; *Standard Oil Company of New Jersey* v. *United States*; Supreme Court announces "rule of reason" for antitrust suits	Irving Berlin, "Alexander's Ragtime Band"; Scott Joplin, *Treemonisha* (opera); Carnegie Corporation founded	1911
	Pujo Committee investigates securities industry	Hadassah (Jewish women's service organization) founded; *Titanic* sinks; James Weldon Johnson, *Autobiography of an Ex-Colored Man*; L. L. Bean begins its mail-order clothing business	1912
	Recession (to 1914); Sixteenth Amendment (income tax); Federal Reserve System established; Department of Commerce and Labor split into Department of Commerce and Department of Labor; Ford establishes moving assembly line	Anti-Defamation League of B'nai B'rith founded; Rockefeller Foundation established; Woolworth Building (New York; Cass Gilbert) completed; Charles Beard, *An Economic Interpretation of the Constitution;* Eleanor Hodgman Porter, *Pollyanna* (novel); Edward L. Thorndike, *Educational Psychology*	1913
First long-distance telephone connection	Agricultural Extension (Smith-Lever) Act; Clayton Antitrust Act; Federal Trade Commission Act; Hetch Hetchy water project	First issue of the *New Republic;* W. C. Handy, "St. Louis Blues"; Charles Ives, *Three Places in New England* (orchestral piece); Walter Lippmann, *Drift and Mastery;* Walter Rauschenbusch, *Christianizing the Social Order*	1914
		Palace of the Fine Arts (San Francisco; Bernard Maybeck) completed; John Dewey and Evelyn Dewey, *Schools for Tomorrow;* D. W. Griffith, *Birth of a Nation* (movie)	1915
	American Institute of Accountants founded; National Park Service established; Federal Aid Road Act	Roy Wood Sellars, *Critical Realism*	1916

CHRONOLOGY

Year	The American People	Politics	Global America
1917			United States enters World War I (April); Selective Service Act; Espionage Act; Soviet Union established
1918			Sedition Act (May); armistice ends World War I (11 November)
1919	Eighteenth Amendment (prohibition); Chicago race riot	Red Scare; Boston police strike	Paris Peace Conference; Senate rejects Versailles Treaty
1920	Census counts 105,710,620 Americans; 51 percent live in urban areas; Nineteenth Amendment (women's suffrage)	Warren G. Harding elected president	Senate again rejects Versailles Treaty; National Defense Act creates modern U.S. Army and National Guard; *Missouri* v. *Holland*
1921		Budget and Accounting Act; William Howard Taft becomes chief justice	Beginning of Washington Naval Conference
1922			Fordney-McCumber Tariff; Treaty of Washington
1923		Harding dies; Calvin Coolidge becomes president; Teapot Dome scandal	
1924	National Origins Act	Calvin Coolidge elected president	Dawes Plan for reparations and war debt payments
1925		First national convention of Ku Klux Klan	Geneva Protocol bans chemical weapons
1926			
1927	Sacco and Vanzetti executed		Beginning of Sandinista war in Nicaragua
1928		Herbert Hoover elected president	Kellogg-Briand Pact

CHRONOLOGY

Science, Technology, and Medicine	The Economy	Culture	Year
		National Catholic War Council founded	1917
Influenza pandemic (to 1919); William I. Thomas and Florian Znaniecki, *The Polish Peasant in Europe and America*		Willa Cather, *My Ántonia* (novel)	1918
	Steelworkers' strike; first commercial radio station, KDKA (Pittsburgh) established; Radio Corporation of America (RCA) formed	National Catholic Welfare Conference established; first major mosque opens at Highland Park, Mich.; United Artists formed; Sherwood Anderson, *Winesburg, Ohio* (novel)	1919
	First commercial radio broadcast (KDKA, Pittsburgh)	John Dewey, *Reconstruction in Philosophy;* Sinclair Lewis, *Main Street* (novel); Edith Wharton, *The Age of Innocence* (novel); Babe Ruth joins New York Yankees; American Professional Football Association (later National Football League) formed	1920
	Recession (to 1922)	Sheppard-Towner Maternity and Infancy Protection Act	1921
Insulin introduced		First issue of *Reader's Digest;* Sinclair Lewis, *Babbitt*	1922
		Henry Luce founds *Time*	1923
John B. Watson, *Behaviorism*		George Gershwin, *Rhapsody in Blue*; first issue of *Commonweal* magazine	1924
Bell Laboratories established	Kelly (Air Mail) Act	Scopes trial; Theodore Dreiser, *An American Tragedy;* F. Scott Fitzgerald, *The Great Gatsby* (novel); Sinclair Lewis *Arrowsmith* (novel); first issue of *The New Yorker*; Chicago Tribune Tower (John Mead Howells and Raymond Hood) completed	1925
Robert Goddard launches first liquid-propellant rocket	National Broadcasting Company (NBC) formed	Book-of-the-Month Club founded; Dale Carnegie, *How to Win Friends and Influence People*; Ernest Hemingway, *The Sun Also Rises* (novel); Lewis Mumford, *The Golden Day*	1926
Charles Lindbergh makes first solo flight across the Atlantic	Columbia Broadcasting System (CBS) formed	Willa Cather, *Death Comes for the Archbishop* (novel); Sinclair Lewis, *Elmer Gantry* (novel); *The Jazz Singer* (first sound movie)	1927
			1928

CHRONOLOGY

Year	The American People	Politics	Global America
1929	League of United Latin American Citizens founded		Young Plan for war debt payment
1930	Census counts 122,775,046 Americans; "Star-spangled Banner" becomes national anthem	Charles Evans Hughes becomes chief justice	Smoot-Hawley Tariff
1931		Scottsboro case	Japan seizes Manchuria from China
1932		Bonus Army march on Washington; Franklin D. Roosevelt elected president	End of Sandinista war in Nicaragua
1933	Twenty-first Amendment (repeal of prohibition)	Twentieth Amendment (presidential and congressional terms; presidential election and vacancy); New Deal begins; Tennessee Valley Authority established	Adolf Hitler becomes chancellor of Germany; U.S. recognizes USSR
1934	Wheeler-Howard Indian Reorganization Act	Dr. Francis Townsend proposes Old Age Revolving Pensions plan; Huey Long establishes Share Our Wealth Society; Rev. Charles Coughlin establishes National Union for Social Justice	

CHRONOLOGY

Science, Technology, and Medicine	The Economy	Culture	Year
E. O. Lawrence develops first cyclotron	Stock market crash	William Faulkner, *The Sound and the Fury* (novel); Ernest Hemingway, *A Farewell to Arms* (novel); Walter Lippmann, *A Preface to Morals;* Robert Lynd and Helen Merrell Lynd, *Middletown*; Museum of Modern Art (New York) opens	1929
	First King Kullen supermarket opens	John Dewey, *Individualism Old and New;* William Faulkner, *As I Lay Dying* (novel); Twelve Southerners, *I'll Take My Stand;* Sinclair Lewis, first American to win Nobel Prize for literature; McGraw-Hill Building (New York; Raymond Hood) completed; movie-industry Production Code established	1930
		Nevada legalizes gambling; Duke Ellington, *Creole Rhapsody*; Edmund Wilson, *Axel's Castle*; Empire State Building (New York; Shreve, Lamb and Harmon) completed	1931
Beginning of Tuskegee syphilis study	Reconstruction Finance Corporation and Home Loan Bank System established	James T. Farrell, *Young Lonigan* (novel); William Faulkner, *Light in August* (novel); Reinhold Niebuhr, *Moral Man and Immoral Society*; Philadelphia Savings Fund Society building (William Lescaze and George Howe) completed	1932
	National Industrial Recovery Act; Agricultural Adjustment Act; Farm Credit Act; Glass-Steagall Act; Public Works Administration and Civil Works Administration established	Civilian Conservation Corps created	1933
Invention of nylon	National Labor Relations Board, Securities and Exchange Commission, Federal Communications Commission established	Malcolm Cowley, *Exile's Return;* T. S. Eliot, *After Strange Gods;* Zora Neale Hurston, *Mules and Men;* Henry Roth, *Call It Sleep* (novel); first issue of *Partisan Review;* first comic book, *Famous Funnies;* Legion of Decency established; motion-picture Production Code Administration established	1934

CHRONOLOGY

Year	The American People	Politics	Global America
1935		Bureau of Investigation renamed Federal Bureau of Investigation; assassination of Huey Long	Italy invades Ethiopia; Neutrality Act
1936	John Dollard, *Class and Caste in a Southern Town*	Franklin D. Roosevelt reelected president; *U.S.* v. *Curtiss Wright*	German troops occupy the Rhineland
1937		Court-packing controversy; Brownlow Committee report on government organization	Beginning of war between Japan and China; Roosevelt's "Quarantine Speech"
1938		House Un-American Activities Committee formed	Germany annexes Austria and Czech Sudentenland; Munich Conference
1939	E. Franklin Frazier, *The Negro Family*		Pact between Germany and Soviet Union; alliance of Italy and Germany; World War II begins
1940	Census counts 131,669,275 Americans; Alien Registration Act	Franklin D. Roosevelt reelected president (third term)	Selective Service and Training Act; destroyers-for-bases agreement with Britain
1941	A. Philip Randolph leads March on Washington Movement; Fair Employment Practice Committee established; Allison Davis et al., *Deep South*	Harlan F. Stone becomes chief justice	Lend-Lease Act; Pearl Harbor (7 December); United States enters World War II
1942	Internment of Japanese Americans		Formation of Joint Chiefs of Staff

CHRONOLOGY

Science, Technology, and Medicine	The Economy	Culture	Year
	Committee for Industrial Organization (CIO) splits from American Federation of Labor (AFL); Wagner National Labor Relations Act; Connally Hot Oil Act; *Schechter* v. *U.S.*; Resettlement Administration, Rural Electrification Administration, Works Progress Administration, National Youth Administration established	Social Security Act; National Housing Act; Kirsten Flagstad debuts at Metropolitan Opera	1935
Radiation Laboratory (Berkeley, Calif.) established; Ralph Linton, *The Study of Man*	First sit-down strike	Ford Foundation established; William Faulkner, *Absalom, Absalom!* (novel); Jesse Owens wins four gold medals at Berlin Olympics; Fallingwater and Johnson Wax Administrative Building (Frank Lloyd Wright) completed	1936
Talcott Parsons, *The Structure of Social Action;* first television broadcasts	Farm Security Administration established; Supreme Court reverses itself on minimum-wage and labor legislation cases	Zora Neale Hurston, *Their Eyes Were Watching God;* Robert Lynd and Helen Merrell Lynd, *Middletown Revisited*	1937
	CIO renamed Congress of Industrial Organizations; Fair Labor Standards Act; second Farm Security Act; Civil Aeronautics Authority established	Louis Mumford, *The Culture of Cities;* Benny Goodman plays jazz in Carnegie Hall	1938
Albert Einstein's letter to President Roosevelt		Marian Anderson's Washington, D.C., recital; John Steinbeck, *The Grapes of Wrath* (novel); first scheduled television broadcast; *Gone with the Wind* (movie); Museum of Modern Art building (New York; Philip L. Goodwin and Edward Durell Stone) completed	1939
National Defense Research Committee established		Richard Wright, *Native Son* (novel)	1940
	3.8 million passenger cars produced	James Agee and Walker Evans, *Let Us Now Praise Famous Men;* F. O. Matthiessen, *American Renaissance*	1941
Beginning of Manhattan Project; Enrico Fermi produces first controlled chain reaction; Kaiser Permanente health-care plan established	War Production Board, War Manpower Commission established	National Association of Evangelicals founded; Alfred Kazin, *On Native Grounds*	1942

CHRONOLOGY

Year	The American People	Politics	Global America
1943			Teheran Conference (Roosevelt, Churchill, Stalin)
1944	Gunnar Myrdal, *An American Dilemma*	Franklin D. Roosevelt reelected president (fourth term)	D-Day invasion of Normandy (6 June); Bretton Woods accords
1945	Horace Cayton and St. Clair Drake, *Black Metropolis*	Roosevelt dies; Harry S. Truman becomes president	End of World War II; Yalta Conference; Potsdam Conference; United Nations, World Bank, International Monetary Fund founded
1946	Benjamin Spock, *Baby and Child Care*	Administrative Procedure Act; Fred F. Vinson becomes chief justice	NSC-68 (national security policy statement); Philippine independence; first portrayals of kisses in Japanese movies (*A Certain Night Kiss* and *Twenty-year-old Youth*)
1947		Americans for Democratic Action formed	Truman Doctrine pledges aid to countries threatened by communism; George Kennan's "X" article; Central Intelligence Agency, National Security Council, and National Military Establishment (by merger of War and Navy departments) created
1948	Displaced Persons Act	Harry S. Truman elected president	Rio Pact; Marshall Plan established; Berlin airlift begins
1949		First Hoover Commission report on government organization	North Atlantic Treaty Organization (NATO) established; National Military Establishment renamed Department of Defense; Berlin airlift ends; first Soviet atomic test; communist victory in China
1950	Census counts 150,697,361 Americans	Joseph McCarthy charges communist influence in State Department	Korean War begins; General Agreement on Tariffs and Trade (GATT) founded; Alger Hiss convicted of perjury
1951		Twenty-second Amendment (president limited to two terms); Kefauver Committee investigates organized crime	Truman dismisses MacArthur

CHRONOLOGY

Science, Technology, and Medicine	The Economy	Culture	Year
	Smith-Connally Labor Relations Act	T. S. Eliot, *Four Quartets* (poetry); Duke Ellington, *Black, Brown, and Beige* (jazz suite); Rogers and Hammerstein, *Oklahoma!* (musical); All-American Girls Professional Baseball League formed; zoot-suit riots in California	1943
	610 passenger cars produced	Serviceman's Readjustment Act (GI Bill of Rights); Aaron Copland, "Appalachian Spring" (dance suite); Reinhold Niebuhr, *The Children of Light and the Children of Darkness*	1944
First atomic bomb detonated at Alamagordo, N.M.		First issue of *Commentary* magazine	1945
Brookhaven National Laboratory established; atomic bombs tested at Bikini Atoll	Employment Act	Robert Penn Warren, *All the King's Men* (novel)	1946
Atomic Energy Commission established	Taft-Hartley Labor-Management Relations Act	Levittown, Long Island, established; House Un-American Activities Committee investigation in Hollywood; Christian Dior's "New Look" in women's clothing; Jackie Robinson joins Brooklyn Dodgers	1947
	4 million passenger cars produced	James Gould Cozzens, *Guard of Honor* (novel); Norman Mailer, *The Naked and the Dead* (novel); Thomas Merton, *The Seven Storey Mountain* (autobiography); B. F. Skinner, *Walden Two; Paramount* decision	1948
	First Diners Club credit cards	Housing Act; Ezra Pound, *Pisan Cantos* (poetry); Aldo Leopold, *Sand County Almanac*	1949
National Science Foundation established		First broadcast of Billy Graham's *Hour of Decision*; David Riesman, *The Lonely Crowd*	1950
Talcott Parsons, *The Social System;* UNIVAC computer	Du Pont begins manufacturing Dacron polyester	Hannah Arendt, *The Origins of Totalitarianism;* W. V. O. Quine, "Two Dogmas of Empiricism"; J. D. Salinger, *The Catcher in the Rye* (novel)	1951

CHRONOLOGY

Year	The American People	Politics	Global America
1952	Puerto Rico becomes a U.S. commonwealth; McCarran-Walter Immigration and Nationality Act	Dwight D. Eisenhower elected president; *Youngstown* v. *Sawyer*	Construction of first atom-powered submarine, *Nautilus*
1953	Termination policy for Native Americans	Department of Health, Education, and Welfare established; Earl Warren becomes chief justice	Korean War ends; establishment of U.S. Information Agency; Julius and Ethel Rosenberg executed
1954	*Brown* v. *Board of Education*	Army-McCarthy hearings; Senate censures McCarthy	Southeast Asia Treaty Organization (SEATO) established; Vietnamese defeat French at Dien Bien Phu
1955	Rosa Parks begins Montgomery, Ala., bus boycott	Second Hoover Commission report on government organization	
1956	Little Rock desegregation crisis	Dwight D. Eisenhower reelected president	Suez Crisis; USSR invades Hungary
1957	Southern Christian Leadership Conference established		European Economic Community (Common Market) founded
1958			
1959	Alaska and Hawaii admitted to the Union		Nixon-Khrushchev kitchen debate; Castro comes to power in Cuba; Central Treaty Organization (CENTO) established
1960	Census counts 178,464,236 Americans	John F. Kennedy elected president	
1961		Twenty-third Amendment (District of Columbia residents vote in presidential elections)	Bay of Pigs invasion of Cuba fails; Soviets build Berlin Wall; Peace Corps established

CHRONOLOGY

Science, Technology, and Medicine	The Economy	Culture	Year
Livermore Laboratory established; United States explodes first hydrogen bomb	Truman seizes steel mills; J. K. Galbraith, *American Capitalism*	Federation of Islamic Associations founded; first issue of *Mad* magazine; John Cage, *4′33″*; Ralph Ellison, *Invisible Man* (novel); Ernest Hemingway, *The Old Man and the Sea* (novel); Reinhold Niebuhr, *The Irony of American History;* Norman Vincent Peale, *The Power of Positive Thinking*; 860–880 North Lake Shore Drive (Chicago; Ludwig Mies van der Rohe) completed	1952
B. F. Skinner, *Science and Human Behavior*	Submerged Lands Act	James Baldwin, *Go Tell It on the Mountain* (novel); Saul Bellow, *The Adventures of Augie March* (novel); United Nations headquarters (New York) completed	1953
Bell Telephone Co. develops solar battery	Agricultural Trade Development and Assistance Act	Wallace Stevens, *Collected Poems; On the Waterfront* (movie)	1954
Distribution of Salk polio vaccine; first atomic-generated electric power in United States; Herbert Marcuse, *Eros and Civilization*	Ray Kroc franchises McDonald's; AFL and CIO reunite	Daniel Bell, "The End of Ideology" (article); Will Herberg, *Protestant, Catholic, Jew*; first issue of *National Review*; Disneyland opens	1955
	Interstate Highway Act; William H. Whyte, *The Organization Man*	C. Wright Mills, *The Power Elite*; Elvis Presley records "Heartbreak Hotel"; *Invasion of the Body Snatchers* (movie)	1956
Beginning of International Geophysical Year; Soviet Union launches *Sputnik*	McClellan Committee investigates labor unions	Leonard Bernstein, *West Side Story* (musical); Vladimir Nabokov, *Pnin* (novel); Vance Packard, *The Hidden Persuaders*; Brooklyn Dodgers move to Los Angeles, New York Giants move to San Francisco	1957
First U.S. satellite launched; National Aeronautics and Space Administration (NASA) established	J. K. Galbraith, *The Affluent Society*	National Defense Education Act; John Barth, *The End of the Road* (novel); Seagram Building (New York, Ludwig Mies van der Rohe and Philip Johnson) completed	1958
C. Wright Mills, *The Sociological Imagination*	Landrum-Griffin Labor-Management Reporting and Disclosure Act	William Burroughs, *Naked Lunch* (novel); Lorraine Hansberry, *A Raisin in the Sun* (play); José Antonio Villarreal, *Pocho* (novel)	1959
FDA approves birth control pill			1960
Erving Goffman, *Asylums*		Joseph Heller, *Catch-22* (novel); Jane Jacobs, *The Death and Life of Great American Cities*	1961

CHRONOLOGY

Year	The American People	Politics	Global America
1962		Students for a Democratic Society issue Port Huron Statement	Cuban missile crisis
1963	Civil rights march on Washington; Betty Friedan, *The Feminine Mystique*	Assassination of Kennedy; Lyndon Johnson becomes president; *Gideon* v. *Wainwright*	Nuclear test ban treaty
1964		Lyndon B. Johnson elected president; Warren Commission report; Twenty-fourth Amendment (prohibition of poll tax); Civil Rights Act; *New York Times* v. *Sullivan*	Gulf of Tonkin Resolution
1965	Immigration Act; *Griswold* v. *Connecticut*; Daniel P. Moynihan, *The Negro Family*	Voting Rights Act; assassination of Malcolm X; Watts riot in Los Angeles	American combat troops first sent to Vietnam; United States invades Dominican Republic
1966	National Organization for Women founded	*Miranda* v. *Arizona*	
1967	*Loving* v. *Virginia*	Twenty-fifth Amendment (presidential disability); Thurgood Marshall appointed to Supreme Court (first African American)	Six-day War in Middle East
1968	Bilingual Education Act; widespread urban riots; Kerner Commission report on violence	Assassinations of Robert F. Kennedy and Martin Luther King, Jr.; Richard M. Nixon elected president	Tet Offensive in Vietnam; USSR invades Czechoslovakia; Outer Space Treaty; *Pueblo* incident
1969	Stonewall riot	Warren E. Burger becomes chief justice	
1970	Census counts 203,302,031 Americans; suburbanites outnumber city dwellers	Ash Council report on government organization	United States invades Cambodia; Kent State and Jackson State shootings
1971		Twenty-sixth Amendment (voting age lowered to eighteen); U.S. Postal Service established	Nixon ends convertibility of dollars to gold; Pentagon Papers published
1972	Equal Rights Amendment approved by Congress and sent to the states	Richard M. Nixon reelected president; Watergate break-in; Revenue Sharing Act	Antiballistic Missile (ABM) Treaty (SALT I treaty) with Soviet Union; Nixon visits People's Republic of China

CHRONOLOGY

Science, Technology, and Medicine	The Economy	Culture	Year
Rachel Carson, *Silent Spring*; Du Pont begins manufacturing Lycra spandex fiber	Kennedy forces rollback of steel prices; Michael Harrington, *The Other America*	Daniel Bell, *The End of Ideology* (book); Clark Kerr, *The Uses of the University*; Thomas Kuhn, *The Structure of Scientific Revolutions*	1962
			1963
Herbert Marcuse, *One-dimensional Man*	Wilderness Act	Model Cities program established; Saul Bellow, *Herzog* (novel); Ken Kesey, *Sometimes a Great Notion* (novel); *The Autobiography of Malcolm X*; Beatles' American tour	1964
Medicare established	Department of Housing and Urban Development established; Ralph Nader, *Unsafe at Any Speed*	Higher Education Act; Elementary and Secondary Education Act; National Endowment for the Arts established; Pope Paul VI visits United States	1965
Barrington Moore, Jr., *Social Origins of Dictatorship and Democracy*	Department of Transportation established; first BankAmericards (later VISA) issued	Super Bowl I	1966
	First microwave oven introduced	Corporation for Public Broadcasting established; first issue of *Rolling Stone;* Donald Barthelme, *Snow White* (novel); William Styron, *The Confessions of Nat Turner* (novel)	1967
Garrett Hardin, "The Tragedy of the Commons"; first heart transplant (South Africa)		Marshall McLuhan, *The Gutenburg Galaxy;* motion-picture rating system established	1968
Neil Armstrong walks on the moon	National Environmental Policy Act	Philip Roth, *Portnoy's Complaint* (novel); Jonas Salk Institute buildings (La Jolla, Cal.; Louis I. Kahn) completed; Woodstock music festival	1969
			1970
	Nixon imposes wage and price controls	Disney World opens near Orlando, Fla.; John Rawls, *A Theory of Justice*	1971
Fermilab opens; Endangered Species Act		Supplemental Security Income (SSI) established; Indian Education Act; first woman Reform Jewish rabbi ordained; Richard Rorty, "A World Well Lost"; Transamerica Pyramid (San Francisco; William Pereria) completed; Pruitt-Igoe Houses (Saint Louis) dynamited	1972

CHRONOLOGY

Year	The American People	Politics	Global America
1973	*Roe* v. *Wade*; Rehabilitation Act ("Civil Rights Act for the Handicapped"); standoff at Wounded Knee		End of fixed currency-exchange rates; Paris Peace Accords between United States, North Vietnam, and South Vietnam; end of draft; War Powers Act; Organization of Petroleum Exporting Countries (OPEC) quadruples oil prices
1974	Education for All Handicapped Act	Nixon resigns; Gerald Ford becomes president; Congressional Budget and Impoundment Control Act	
1975			Saigon falls to North Vietnamese Offensive; *Mayaguez* incident
1976	Bicentennial of the Declaration of Independence; Hyde Amendment	Jimmy Carter elected president; *National League of Cities* v. *Usery*	
1977			
1978	*Bakke* v. *University of California*		
1979			SALT II treaty with Soviet Union; Soviet Union invades Afghanistan; Tehran embassy crisis
1980	Census counts 226,542,199 Americans; Refugee Act; Mariel boatlift	Ronald Reagan elected president; Paperwork Reduction Act	
1981		Sandra Day O'Connor appointed to Supreme Court (first woman)	
1982	Equal Rights Amendment defeated		
1983		*INS* v. *Chadha*	United States invades Grenada
1984		Ronald Reagan reelected president	
1985			Mikhail Gorbachev becomes general secretary of Soviet Communist party
1986	Immigration Reform and Control Act	William H. Rehnquist becomes chief justice	Iran-Contra controversy
1987			Intermediate-range Nuclear Forces (INF) Treaty with Soviet Union
1988		George Bush elected president	Department of Veterans Affairs established
1989			United States invades Panama; communist regimes collapse in central and eastern Europe
1990	Census counts 248,709,873 Americans		

CHRONOLOGY

Science, Technology, and Medicine	The Economy	Culture	Year
Clifford Geertz, *The Interpretation of Cultures*			1973
		Sears Tower (Chicago; Skidmore, Owens and Merrill) completed	1974
E. O. Wilson, *Sociobiology*	First videocassette recorder (VCR) introduced	Maxine Hong Kingston, *The Woman Warrior* (novel)	1975
Viking II lands space probe on Mars; Apple II computer introduced			1976
Clean Air Act	Department of Energy established		1977
	Airline Deregulation Act; Humphrey-Hawkins Full-Employment Act	*Roots* television series	1978
Three Mile Island nuclear reactor accident		Department of Education established	1979
Department of Health, Education, and Welfare renamed Health and Human Services	Beginning of deregulation of savings-and-loan industry	Cable News Network (CNN) established; Maxine Hong Kingston, *China Men* (novel)	1980
First space shuttle flight; IBM personal computer introduced; acquired immune deficiency syndrome (AIDS) identified	Economic Recovery Tax Act	Richard Rodriquez, *Hunger of Memory* (autobiography)	1981
		First issue of *USA Today*	1982
		"A Nation at Risk" report on education	1983
	Breakup of Bell System		1984
	Gramm-Rudman-Hollings balanced budget act		1985
Space shuttle *Challenger* explodes	Tax Reform Act		1986
	Stock market crash	Allan Bloom, *The Closing of the American Mind*	1987
DNA fingerprinting introduced			1988
First human gene therapy experiment; cold fusion scandal	Savings-and-loan bailout enacted; Time-Warner communications corporation formed; *Exxon Valdez* oil spill	David Harvey, *The Condition of Postmodernity*	1989
Hubble Space Telescope launched	Clean Air Act	Ramon Saldívar, *Chicano Narratives*	1990

Year	The American People	Politics	Global America
1991	Tailhook scandal		Persian Gulf War; START I treaty with Soviet Union; Soviet Union dissolved; end of Cold War
1992	Los Angeles riots	Bill Clinton elected president; Twenty-seventh Amendment (congressional pay raises)	Euro Disneyland opens
1993			START II treaty with Russia
1994	Proposition 187 approved in California		
1995	Oklahoma City bombing		

CHRONOLOGY

Science, Technology, and Medicine	The Economy	Culture	Year
IBM-Apple cooperation agreement	Pan American Airways goes out of business		1991
Food and Drug Administration restricts breast implants			1992
		Martin Scorsese, *The Age of Innocence* (movie)	1993
		Baseball players strike	1994
			1995

Part 1

THE AMERICAN PEOPLE

INTRODUCTION

Stanley I. Kutler

"What then is the American," the French observer J. Hector St. John de Crèvecoeur asked just prior to the American Revolution. Ever since, Americans have grappled with that question, and with mixed results. The scale of the land, the size, and the diversity of the population make the task formidable indeed. Crèvecoeur recognized that a new person had been created out of nearly two centuries of migration and colonial development, and he apparently anticipated an evolving homogeneity of Americans. But two centuries later, the people of the United States still can be described only from a model of diversity, of ongoing change and newness, and always conditioned and varied by regional allegiances, race, religion, ethnicity, gender, class, and family.

The articles in this part consider these characteristics and how they have evolved throughout the twentieth century. The essays are offered both as conceptual modes of analysis and as particular descriptions of the American people.

John Thomas's survey of persistent regionalism in the twentieth century begins with the ideas of Frederick Jackson Turner and his concept of regions as a brake on the political, economic, and cultural aggrandizing tendencies of the national state. Turner, of course, celebrated the agrarian ideal and made it the focus of his social and economic determinism. For him and his followers, cultural and political impulses flowed from the margins. But by the mid-twentieth century, reality dictated a different understanding: central place theory argued that metropolitan centers dictated the relationship between themselves and their outlying areas. By century's end, edge cities had become the new frontier, a commercial and consumer enterprise that in many areas had displaced the primacy of older central cities.

Thomas's analysis is followed by a quartet of articles dealing with particular sections. Despite enormous population movements and transfers, and despite the ongoing revolution in transportation and communications, regional patterns remain important, from economic focus to politics to cultural behavior. The lines are blurred, to be sure; they have been smoothed from the classic pre–Civil War image of two sharply defined nations, North and South, with distinctive economic and social foundations. But the journey has been long since 1900, when a dominant Northeast prevailed over the semicolonial status of the South and the West. Furthermore, each section has undergone sharp change within itself during the century. Is Texas a southern or a western state? Is California more akin to New York than to bordering western states such as Nevada, Arizona, and Oregon? In essays on the East, the Midwest, the South, and the West, the contributors sense the sharp changes resulting from advancing or declining fortunes within various regions or parts of them during the century. Despite the difficulty of carefully delineating regions, the writers discern differences between them and important unifying traits within them. Furthermore, the regions still mark an important means for defining the countervailing balance of resources, people, and power that always has characterized the American nation—almost, one might say, in a Turnerian sense.

Yet it seems clear that Americans no longer define themselves with the same degree of regional or state loyalties as their ancestors did earlier in the twentieth century and before. The ease of mobility, for one, has made such attachments far more tenuous. But other considerations compete for a more prominent place in the way people define and see themselves. By the late twentieth century, divining American society and interpreting its history became heavily focused on emphasizing the roles of race, gender, and class.

The essays that follow on those subjects are discrete and self-standing, but they should be read for their linkages as well. Race, gender, and class condition and temper each other. Each has an element of cohesion, and each has its own divisiveness and internal conflicts. Racial unity is qualified by gender and class differences; similarly, gender or class unity are strained by differences in the other identifying characteristics.

Gender understanding and analysis are integral to any understanding of American society. In simplest terms, we ask: What has it meant to be a man? What has it meant to be a woman? Throughout the century, there have been striking, even dramatic, shifts that make the answers complex and ever evolving. Lizabeth Cohen and Mark Tebeau consider these questions in their examination of gender roles and relationships within the family, at work, at leisure and in consumption, and in politics and public policy. While they emphasize the sharp changes that have occurred in this area, the authors underscore the significant continuity as well. Gender segmentation and discrimination, for example, persist in many areas of American life. Interest in this subject, of course, has been sparked by the women's movement of the last third of the twentieth century. We have learned a great deal about a subject that only a generation ago attracted our attention largely through such questions as voting patterns and factory conditions. While gender-based studies have substantially enhanced an understanding of women and their role, work similarly focused on men is only beginning.

Race, Earl Lewis writes, has been our "greatest fiction, greatest fascination, and greatest 'truth.' " Which is, perhaps, another way of saying that it has been a subject for endless inquiry and debate. In his article, Lewis nicely balances the concept of race as a social construction—one that functioned both as an idea and an ideology—with the role of race as a social reality. But ideas and concepts inevitably collide with public policy, and Lewis properly assesses the role of public or government practices that influenced the ideological dimensions of race.

The United States has been described as a nation of immigrants. Ethnic-group identity and solidarity has always been a powerful force in shaping society, but especially so in the twentieth century. Rudolph J. Vecoli, our leading historian of ethnicity, has defined ethnicity as "a form of collective consciousness that presumes a common past and prospective future with 'one's own kind.' " Ethnicity has influenced public and private life, from foreign policy to choices of marriage partners. Social scientists have persistently believed that ethnic attachments would dissolve in the wake of assimilation of succeeding generations. But in the United States—and in the world, as late-twentieth-century events have dramatically shown—ethnicity has retained its force and appeal.

Throughout the twentieth century, ethnic attachments have been at war with the notions of the "melting pot" and ideas of "Americanism." By the 1990s, the conflict expanded to politics, the culture, and the marketplace, and perhaps more than ever, it was sharpened by heightened clashes between cultural nationalists and advocates of multiculturalism. Each has seen the other as a threat to the existing order of pluralism, and each, as Vecoli has noted, has "carried its own ideological freight; each [is] committed to its own vision of American society." By century's end, the United States found itself confronting questions similar to those it had confronted at the beginning: did the new and persistent diversity of Americans threaten national unity and order?

Class is always is a difficult term to define, especially throughout the American experience. People readily respond that they belong to the middle class, but the term is devoid of precision given the disparity in income and style between, for example, a stockbroker and a skilled craftsman. Yet both undoubtedly would insist that they belong to the "middle class." Self-perception as well as the perception of others are two valid forms of definition. Olivier Zunz examines the American social fabric through four broad categories: the middle class, the working class, the elites, and the underclass. He also ties the essays in this part of the Encyclopedia together by noting the intersection of class debates and concerns with those of ethnicity, race, and gender.

The debate over class reflects the concerns of pluralists who wish to maximize freedom of association, those who emphasize individual opportunity, and those who wish to guarantee social justice. Class wars in this country have largely been muted as Americans have maintained a balance and a mix of all these concerns. Zunz notes that the last third of the century has seen a new obstacle to class mobility. The decline of manufacturing and blue collar enterprises and the resulting collapse of organized labor and its successful struggle for high wages have meant the loss of the kind of jobs that provided entrée to the "middle class," characterized by heavy consumption, improved education, and home investment, or some other "stake in society."

Finally, the article on the family ties together many of the concerns discussed in the preceding essays on gender, race, ethnicity, and class. The perception of the family and the way in which it functions have undergone significant changes, but, again, continuity over the course of the century is an important line for understanding the family. Arguably, public rhetoric has focused on "the family" and "family values" on a par with gender, race, or class.

Too often, the debate has revolved around those advocating the defense of "traditional" values to combat the nation's ills, while demonizing those who practiced or accepted anything different. But as Steven Mintz shows, this phenomenon does not reflect a "crisis" of contemporary American life. In 1900, public debate over rising divorce rates, declining population, increasing juvenile delinquency, the social mores and values of new immigrants or of varying races, centered on some alleged collapse of family values. Those dissatisfied with their lot or with contemporary society regularly revert to some mythical golden age, and try to resurrect some standard from the past. But in the light of long-term historical analysis, it is difficult to find an absolute, prevalent, stable family standard. Throughout the century, as always, the family has been an institution constantly in change, affected by or responding to major social events—including depression, war, heightened mobility, gender roles, and the influx of new groups into American society. The challenge is to acknowledge and deal with family changes based on current and long-term realities rather than on the imagined past.

REGIONALISM

John L. Thomas

The story of twentieth-century regionalism properly begins with Frederick Jackson Turner and his mixed legacy to a generation of regional writers, artists, critics, and planners who came of intellectual age in the twenty years between the two world wars. It was Turner who, in the decades following his pathbreaking essay in 1893, built the commanding interpretation of frontier and section bequeathed to his younger followers who, in their turn, questioned, qualified, or applied it with energy and ingenuity until the middle of the century when it was challenged and then quickly supplanted by a competing paradigm. In "The Significance of the Frontier in American History" (1893) Turner offered the sweeping hypothesis that "the existence of an area of free land, its continuous recession, and the advance of American settlement westward, explain American development." Convinced that the frontier was now closed, he turned, in subsequent essays, to defining the role of the region in checking the aggrandizing power of the national industrial state.

TURNER'S LEGACY

Turner himself was the legatee of a regionalist geographical tradition stretching back to the middle of the eighteenth century when British geographers and travel writers first began to explore the idea that North America's varied landscape and peoples could best be encompassed by tracing patterns of soil, climate, and topographic features. Daniel Fenning and Joseph Collyer's *A New System of Geography* (1764–1765) was more or less typical in its use of implicit sectional divisions, separating the lands bordering Hudson Bay from the Maritimes, New England, and New York together with the Middle Colonies, and these in turn from Virginia, the Carolinas, and Florida, as well as from the "Back Settlements" along the Mississippi. After the Revolution the concept of region gained clarity and precision in the successive editions of pioneer American geographer Jedidiah Morse's *The American Geography*, in which a growing number of sections formed the organizing principle of his ongoing surveys. Throughout the nineteenth century, school geographies, travel accounts, and promotional pamphlets solidified popular notions of natural "divisions" and then of cultural "sections," notions that derived from amateur efforts lacking analytical rigor, even as their designers agreed that somehow soils, climate, crops, and, increasingly, cultural traits and political preferences played sharply differentiating roles in American life.

By the time Turner advanced his frontier hypothesis in 1893, however, two developments had given the concept of region a measure of precision. The first was the use of statistical cartography introduced in the Ninth Census (1870) by Francis Walker and expanded in the Tenth by Henry Gannett, who explained his "three great divisions" of continental United States—the Atlantic Region, the Region of the Great Valley, and the Western or Cordilleran Region—as corresponding to the three primary topographical contours of the country. In drawing a line approximating the Mason-Dixon Line through his Atlantic division so as to distinguish peoples and social conditions as well as climate and soil, and then in extending that line out to the Great Valley, Gannett in effect added a temporal dimension to his spatial coordinates—an innovation which Turner soon adapted to his own purposes. "From a historical point of view," Gannett explained in the Tenth Census, "the divisions are characteristically different." The two regions along the Atlantic littoral had been settled in the colonial period "and may be said to represent that stage of our progress." The two regions comprising the Great Valley and settled since the Revolution "may properly be regarded as representing the stage of our progress from the time of independence up to the present day; while the West is still, as far as development goes, in its infancy, and may properly represent the development of the future."

A second major contributor to Turner's thinking

on sections and regions was John Wesley Powell, whose approach was primarily physiographic. After publishing his classic *Report upon the Lands of the Arid Regions of the United States* in 1878, Powell as head of the United States Geological Survey answered his own call for a systematic classification of American lands according to soil coverage and the availability of water. In 1895, two years after Turner had presented his groundbreaking argument on the significance of the frontier, Powell published his monograph *Physiographic Regions of the United States.* In it he defined the four main slopes of the country—Atlantic, Great Lakes, Gulf, and Pacific—and identified each of their contrasting characteristics, principally rainfall, which accounted for desert, prairie, and forest. Each of the slopes on Powell's physiographic map was made up of particular regions, stretching from the Atlantic plains and Piedmont plateau in the East through prairie plains and Ozark mountains beyond the Mississippi, out to the Stony mountains, Columbia plateau, Basin ranges and Pacific mountains. Here, Powell concluded, were the primal "natural divisions" of the United States, products of a common geological history that accounted for their varying physiographic features and, ultimately, their several cultural traits.

Turner studied both Gannett's and Powell's analyses as he proceeded to elaborate his own regional model based on the insights contained in his original essay on the significance of the frontier. Both the limitations of a purely scientific functionalist approach and the imaginative possibilities in a multifactor cultural scheme became clear to Turner as he began to construct his own model of regional analysis. "There has been a good deal done upon the *resources* of different states or cities, but of the *spirit* of various sections, nothing of importance has been said, so far as I am aware," he wrote to Walter Hines Page of the *Atlantic Monthly* in 1896, adding that "the time is ripe for some such survey, if my view that we have reached a turning point in our national life—with the exhaustion of the supply of free land—is correct." For Turner the question posed to twentieth-century Americans concerned the very identity of American society: what made America different from the Old World and how did it depart from patterns of Europe's historical development? "What is this United States—at the end of the movement of colonization—the colonization of the interior, with all the forces of city making, railroad building, immigration, sectional expansion, etc., involved in the movement?" The answer, he argued, could be found only in a combination of different modes of analysis that would uncover "the natural non-State areas of the country." The physiographic would constitute only one of many modes of attack. Others would include crop areas, manufacturing clusters, commercial territories staked out by competing business firms, congressional voting patterns, immigration charts and maps, and newspaper circulation. Carefully coordinated, these several "tests" would enable the social historian "to divide the West into its proper regions, and describe the spirit of each."

Turner's model of regional analysis is at once evolutionary, incremental, progressive, and phased. American development begins with empty land—the open quarter lying just beyond successive lines of settlement—and is quickly marked by the inpouring of sequential waves of explorers, trappers, settlers, and developers, all of them dreaming of "continental conquest" and fashioning out of their confrontations with primitive conditions those individualist, democratic, and nationalist traits that "powerfully affect" the settled East and beyond it the Old World. For a brief moment along each segment of the receding frontier the bonds of custom are broken, new fields of opportunity open, the burdens of the past are cast aside, and vital democratic institutions are built by rejuvenated peoples responding to the challenges of unfenced land.

The second phase in Turner's linear model of national development arrives with the appearance of the self-conscious section, a cultural as well as political entity in which he discovered the "shadowy image" of the European national state fortunately "denatured of its toxic qualities." Each section, Turner explains in naming them—New England, the Middle States, the Southeast, the Southwest, the Great Plains, Mountain States, and Pacific Coast—developed its own identifying qualities, resources, capacities, and ultimately "its own rival interests." Sectionalism, as it matures rapidly in the wake of receding frontiers, takes different forms: a "sectionalism of material interests" that generates intense political rivalries with more settled regions of the country, but also an assertive "sectionalism of culture . . . a real consciousness of sectional solidarity . . . a special flavor" at once social, literary, and "even religious." "Each region," Turner concludes, "reached in the process of expansion from the coast had its frontier experience . . . and when the frontier passed on to new regions, it left behind, in the older areas, memories, traditions, and inherited attitudes towards life, that persisted long after the frontier had passed by."

The Civil War, in Turner's reading, was only the most "drastic" and "tragic" of sectional struggles between North and South for dominance of the growing West—in essence, "a contest for empire." The victory of the North closes the second chapter in Turner's account of American development, for by the end of Reconstruction the imminent triumph of urbanism, consolidating corporate capitalism, and the powerful nation-state is all too clear. The age of sectional independence and cultural exclusivity is over.

The twentieth century, Turner predicted, would witness the coming of regional maturity with the transformation of a now discredited political sectionalism into a widening social and cultural regionalism. Although Turner generally limited his use of the word *region* to geographical and areal characteristics, frequently employing it interchangeably with "province" while continuing to refer to new cultural units as "sections," he nevertheless foresaw a coming age of regional diversity needed to check the aggrandizing power of the national state. "There is a sense in which sectionalism is inevitable and desirable," he explained as he watched with apprehension the consolidation of national power following World War I. Accordingly, there would be a commensurate need for a "sectional geography"—one "based upon geographic regions"—which would draw on political habit, social opinion, cultural grammar, and material interests to counter the expanding power of the national state. There was always a slight danger that the provincial would seek to displace the cosmopolitan world, that, as Turner put it wryly, "the province or section shall think of itself naively as the nation . . . and then proceed to denounce the sections that do not perceive the accuracy of this view as wicked or ignorant or un-American." Much more threatening, however, was the overweening power of the imperial industrial state that necessitated "the vigorous development of a highly organized provincial life to serve as a check upon the mob psychology on a national scale, and to furnish that variety which is essential to vital growth and originality." American ingenuity, Turner warned, would be sorely tested in a commercialized postfrontier world rapidly filling with industrial cities and saturated with new immigrant peoples.

With this apprehensive assessment Turner formulated the regionalist agenda for a younger generation of intellectuals equally convinced that an agrarian age was passing and conservation and preservation would be the order of the new day. "The vast public domain, so far as it is suited to agriculture, is taken up." Only yesterday Americans considered their resources inexhaustible. "Now we are told by high authority that we shall feel the pinch of timber shortage in less than fifteen years. The free lands are no longer free; the boundless resources are no longer boundless." Here lay the primary challenge to Turner and the twentieth-century regionalists who read him: to devise the means and create the agencies to conserve, preserve, and stabilize American life in a delicate balance of resources, people, and power. To what end this regional dispersal of culture and authority? "Restraints upon a deadly uniformity . . . breakwaters against overwhelming surges of national emotion . . . fields for experiment in the growth of different types of society, political institutions, and ideals . . . an impelling force for progress along the diagonal of contending varieties. . . ." In short, an open, diffuse, participatory culture of the American folk as an alternative to the false values of the monolithic corporate industrial state.

EARLY TWENTIETH-CENTURY REGIONALISTS

The first-generation regionalists, who arrived at intellectual maturity in the 1920s, shared Turner's concerns and followed some of his directives even as many of them jettisoned his frontier thesis and rejected his claims for the pioneer as the provider of democratic virtue. Regionalism, as it spread in the two decades between the world wars, constituted a movement rather than a party, a loose confederation of the like-minded rather than a political cadre with a shared program. In their variety and contentiousness regionalists practiced what they preached—the virtues of widely dispersed economic power, participatory politics, the importance of place, and, above all, the therapeutic value of vigorous dissent. Regional writers, critics, planners, and reformers admitted to being cautious conservatives in several senses: they hated corporate capitalism and its centralizing tendencies; they feared the results of rampant industrialization; they loathed the wasteland that unchecked development was making of the American landscape; and they fought against the commercialized mass civilization that the United States had become. Their frequently declared preference for small scale, measured pace, neighborhood communities, artisanal values and indigenous culture made the regionalists seem at first country bumpkins and cranks to their city cousins, ghosts at the promotional and developmental banquets of the twenties. But the regionalists also considered themselves true cultural radicals—believers in the power of social criticism, preachers of a civic religion of social responsibility, prophet-educators with a lineage running back to Emerson and William Lloyd Garrison. "We are not in a political sense a group, and never can be," John Crowe Ransom, poet, editor, critic, and for a time a leading Nashville Agrarian, admitted, "too many individuals, all up in years and positions and advanced in different styles of individualism." Fellow Agrarian Robert Penn Warren agreed that "certainly no program or dogma has emerged . . . [and] no political party stands behind the regional writer."

The list of major regionalist texts is nevertheless varied and impressive: Benton MacKaye's pioneer regional planning tract, *The New Exploration* (1928); Twelve Southerners' *I'll Take My Stand* (1930), the Nashville Agrarians' indictment of corporatism and industrialism; Walter Prescott Webb's magisterial *The Great Plains* (1931); *The Southwest Scene* (1931), the first volume of Benjamin Botkin's mammoth folk history of American regions; Lewis Mumford's *The Culture of Cities* (1938), the regionalists' enchiridion; Mari Sandoz's prize-winning *Old Jules* (1935), the opening autobiographical account in her regional tale of the trans-Mississippi West; Donald Davidson's angry *The Attack on Leviathan* (1938); and Howard Odum's massive compilation *American Regionalism*; William Faulkner's *Absalom, Absalom* (1937), his great epic of the Black Belt; and John Steinbeck's regional saga of forced migration, *The Grapes of Wrath* (1940); *Let Us Now Praise Famous Men* (1941), the transcendent regional documentary fashioned by James Agee and Walker Evans; David Lilienthal's hymn to regionalist achievements, *TVA: Democracy on the March* (1941).

The regionalists held their conferences and gathered their forces in a series of provincial centers spread across the American map—in Taos and Santa Fe, New Mexico; Nashville, Tennessee; Norman, Oklahoma; Chapel Hill, North Carolina; Lincoln, Nebraska; Iowa City, Iowa; Charlottesville, Virginia; Missoula, Montana. Many of these centers of regionalist activity were university sites or cultural collecting-points, small towns clustered around land-grant colleges and state universities, still compact enough to provide a sense of community without seeming claustrophobic. Some of the regionalists, like the folklorist Benjamin Botkin and Lewis Mumford, were fugitives from the metropolis; others, like Willa Cather and Mari Sandoz, were country recruits to the big city; and still others were returnees to their roots following years spent in eastern academia or Europe, such displaced inhabitants of the shifting cultural middle ground as Sherwood Anderson, Thomas Hart Benton, and Henry Nash Smith.

Regionalists came in all cultural shapes and intellectual sizes—from major novelists like William Faulkner, Willa Cather, and Robert Penn Warren to innovative modernist poets like Allen Tate and John Crowe Ransom. There were sharp-eyed regionalist editors like William T. Couch at the University of North Carolina Press and Stringfellow Barr at Charlottesville or T. M. Pearce at the *New Mexico Quarterly.* There were the regional artists and muralists Thomas Hart Benton and Grant Wood; historians Walter Prescott Webb, Frank Owsley, Bernard DeVoto, and Wallace Stegner; regional sociologists Howard Odum and his students at Chapel Hill, Rupert Vance and Arthur Raper; folklorists Benjamin Botkin, Constance Rourke, and J. Frank Dobie; feisty freelancers, polemicists, and perpetual nay-sayers Donald Davidson and John Gould Fletcher.

Western regionalists tended to follow Turner in identifying their democratic credo with the frontier as the source of a premodern purity. Southern regionalists generally took their stand with the Nashville Agrarians in defining the South as a problem even though they differed dramatically on just what the problem was or how best to solve it. Common to regionalist enterprises in both South and West, however, was a belief in the preservation of the folk and what the regional planner Benton MacKaye called the "indigenous landscape" as the only alternative to a capitalist empire of paper and power. This conviction led naturally to an urge to name the sins of corporate-financed capitalism, chief among which, Donald Davidson told his readers, was that it "abstracted the economic function from its old place in the complex of human activities and made it the chief, and almost the only important member of the hierarchy of social functions." In this sense the defense of the region involved a "battle of cultures" over "how people ought to live." The Texas historian Walter Prescott Webb added a specifically political warning: if not countered by a revived adversarial force, corporatism would quickly triumph and the United States would come to be governed by an executive office "headed by the most powerful financial organization or firm in America, a Congress composed exclusively of the representatives of America's two hundred top corporations, and a pliant Supreme Court." In calling for a first-class provincial revolt Bernard DeVoto denounced his own native Mountain West as a "plundered province" that harvested only a crop of grievances: water monopolies, rigged bankruptcies, crooked mortgage companies, extortionate interest rates. Early on, DeVoto declared, the West had learned a salutary lesson: "the wealth of a country belongs to the owners, and the owners are not the residents, or even the stockholders, but the manipulators." Regionalism everywhere, its practitioners agreed, involved a militant defense of the middle ground of the American mind lying somewhere between modernist and traditionalist worlds.

ODUM AND MUMFORD

This middle ground lay open to two quite different explorations, one conducted by the social scientist Howard Odum at Chapel Hill, the other by the prophet-historian of American regionalism, Lewis Mumford. Odum and Mumford traced routes to the regional synthesis along divergent paths: Odum in a journey from a poor-boy upbringing in rural Georgia via progressive training at Clark and Columbia universities to the University of North Carolina, where he built his community of regional investigators; Mumford moving from a childhood on New York's Upper West Side out to satellite garden cities and then up the Hudson Valley to a rural retreat in the town of Amenia. Admirers of each other's work, Odum and Mumford agreed on the need for a new equilibrium of man, nature, and community to be sketched out in programs for cultural regeneration but embodied finally in the designs of regional planners prepared to play a new kind of educational politics. In the combined writings of the two men the regionalist project received its fullest statement.

Lewis Mumford. In *The Golden Day* (1926), a seminal work in American Civilization and an important piece of regional history, Mumford supplied the philosophical justification for the regionalist movement he sought to lead. Regionalism, he argued, meant first and foremost the recovery of a cultural legacy to serve as a model for the twentieth century's task of reconstruction. For Mumford regionalism involved a *specific time* and a *definite place,* the precise point at which past and present collide and in so doing fracture a particular culture along temporal and spatial lines, thus opening the possibility for a new synthesis. The first regional moment in America, he argued, was quite literally a day in the life of nineteenth-century New England. Emerson, in Mumford's account of the American Renaissance, is the "morning star" of the golden day that follows, a figure rising on the horizon of a recovered past who also portends new cultural achievements. What Emerson promises in the first light of a predawn, Thoreau fulfills at sunrise, and Whitman celebrates at high noon. For if Emerson surveys a symbolic New England cultural landscape, Thoreau inhabits a real one. "As for his country," Mumford explains, "he loved the land too well to confuse it with the shifting territorial boundaries of the National State. In this he had that vital regional consciousness which every New Englander shared." In his turn Whitman visualizes—even in the midst of a fratricidal war—a renewed pluralist America emerging from sectional strife, a vision quickly demolished by Gilded Age hucksters yet surviving as a legacy of idealism to be repossessed by twentieth-century regionalists.

In *The Golden Day* Mumford also defined for his regionalist colleagues in the 1920s the cultural motive he discerned at the center of their movement to rebuild twentieth-century American society. This task he performed in a series of linked propositions. "Human culture is a continuous process of choosing, selecting, nurturing." This weeding process involves the thoughtful assimilation of the past and its transformation into new cultural growths and social forms. A genuine culture is nurtured by a constituent people and takes root and flourishes in their locale. When a culture like that of New England's renaissance breaks with its past, having acquired the needed nurture from it, that culture becomes indigenous to a place. In this sense, Mumford insisted, all vital cultures grow in regional soils. It was already past time for the regionalist generation of the 1920s to pick up on that "first exploration" of regional culture and launch another renewal, one that would cross the boundaries of high culture and invade the recesses of postfrontier America.

Regionalism, as Mumford and his friend Benton MacKaye, a forester turned regional planner, conceived of it, was intended to disperse Americans and resettle them in orderly patterns outside the metropolis. There had already been three migrations in American history, they argued. The first of them was the transatlantic migration from Europe beginning in the seventeenth century that distributed settlers haphazardly and wastefully across the land. The second migration was the result of nineteenth-century technological developments that collected Americans in industrial cities and railhead towns that provided work and business opportunity but very little genuine culture. Then with the turn of the century there arose giant cities—New York, Chicago, San Francisco—the overcrowded, unhealthy, dysfunctional financial centers of the new American empire of paper and power. After that, Mumford and MacKaye agreed, a new technological revolution based on electricity and light alloys began to decentralize industry and propel people out of dinosaur cities and into the supporting regional environs in a "fourth migration."

Here in the indigenous world Americans could "remold themselves and their institutions" in integrated functional communities ringing the metropolis. These garden cities, modeled on Ebenezer Howard's original English examples of Letchworth and Welwyn, would be no mere bedroom towns but vital working communities with cooperative economies serving regional markets—full-blown alternatives to metropolitan financial capitalism with its national market and exploitative tendencies.

Mumford's regional polity, both his idealized version of nineteenth-century New England and its predicted reappearance in satellite garden cities rested securely on an economy of small property, diffused wealth, and participatory politics. Its architectural form was the scaled community—whether remembered New England village or Clarence Stein's Radburn, New Jersey—sensibly planned to take advantage of new kinds of building materials provided by a neotechnic age in order to adapt them to universal social needs. At the center of Mumford's regional utopia stands the village square or town commons, a public space landscaped for communal dramas and civic functions—iconographic "places" which he would describe in an enlarged historical context a decade later in *The Culture of Cities*.

Regional Planning. By the time Mumford undertook *The Culture of Cities*, the detailed assessment of regionalism he had outlined in the twenties, an entire system of thought and language had been developed with which to inform the idea of "regional planning." The two conceptual sources of regional planning in its early phase were an established and widely accepted idea of the "watershed," traceable to the pioneer ecological work of George Perkins Marsh and W J McGee, and the concept of the "valley section," adapted from the Scottish urban planner Patrick Geddes. The first was essentially a forester's formulation more purely natural and environmental; the second was a sociologist's model, quasi-historical and mythic. The watershed idea, so crucial to regional planners, postulated a linkage between upstream sources and downstream flow, between forest cover and flood control and the prevention of erosion. It was MacKaye who borrowed Geddes's Comtean coinage "geotechnics" to explain his own integrated idea of a regional watershed. "For a great river is more than a river, it's a matrix of rivers like a leaf ending in a stem, or a bowl with a thousand rivers draining to one mouth. Looked at this way, a river is part of a whole which consists of water-oozing land." Watersheds were divided by a natural boundary-line running along the ridge that separated two or more drainages and appeared to fit within each other like a set of Chinese boxes, the largest of which made up the region—"the Allegheny inside the Ohio and the Ohio inside the Mississippi."

Patrick Geddes's "valley section," substituting the relief model for the map, formed a huge saucer rising from regional cities and surrounding staple-crop farms in the bottomlands up the sides to small farms and diversified agriculture and further to pastoral slopes and wilderness along the rim. MacKaye employed both the watershed and the valley section models in his "visualization" of the regional city as the solution to the major problem of the twentieth century, which he defined as "the contact of the indigenous with the metropolitan world" and the resultant need to contain the urban outflow. Realizing that much of what went by the name of regional planning was only rationalization of unchecked metropolitan expansion, MacKaye reversed this approach by beginning at the other end with the preservation of wilderness. MacKaye's regional world consisted of three genuine communities and one false one. The "primeval," "rural," and "cosmopolitan" communities and the natural balance among them was threatened by a bastard form of urbanism, a "metropolitan" "super-city" spreading across all natural barriers and flooding the whole countryside with mass-produced ugliness.

MacKaye's solution to the problem of metropolitan spread was the "indigenous mold," containing the regional city of ideally no more than 40,000 people, ringed with up to twenty outlying villages in a pattern strikingly similar to Ebenezer Howard's Garden City complex. Beyond the villages lies the natural countryside stretching away to upland wilderness. Each segment of MacKaye's ecological whole has its symbolic center—campfire, village green, and wayside—which are connected by limited access "townless highways" and ribbons of public land serving as levees to contain the flood from the "thousand ruptured reservoirs" of metropolitanism. This regional system MacKaye saw as the only alternative to a dreaded "roadtown," whose substance consisted of tenements, cheap bungalows, stores, factories, billboards, filling stations, and eateries—"the slum of commerce." Flanking the townless highway and checking the metropolitan flood stand all the natural barriers of MacKaye's indigenous regional world, the escarpments, canyons, river bottoms, and swamps that act as a natural boundary running beneath the mountain crestline that is the backbone of regional America. These "open ways" paralleling and bisecting the townless highways save both the rural and village segments of the valley section from the developers as Mumford and MacKaye's regional planner helps nature recover rural and primeval territory by planting publicly owned and communally maintained havens from rapacious commercialism.

By the mid-1920s, as Mumford and MacKaye surveyed the regional route out of a congested New York City and visualized clusters of garden cities on its peripheries, another group of planners was busy advertising a competing brand of metropolitan regionalism, the "Regional Plan of New York." The metropolitan regionalists were led by the respected British planner Thomas Adams, and would eventually publish a two-volume report in making their case for what Adams called the "city efficient." Metropolitan regionalism, which would rise to dominance in the second half of the twentieth century, proceeded from a different set of assumptions about the relationship between the modern metropolis and its regional environs. Adams and his staff were thoroughly versed in the new European regional theory, in particular the German analysis of the metropolis as the continually expanding center of a regional complex of people, markets, and services. The urban challenge, according to Adams and the metropolitanists, was "to so direct urban growth in the future that the greatest practicable measure of health, safety, convenience and general welfare will be secured for its inhabitants." Like the European urban planners, Adams drew on massive compilations of scientific data in making his forecasts and supporting his conclusions that "we cannot overcome the economic forces that make cities as large as New York" and that "there is nothing to be gained by conceiving the impossible." Like Mumford, Adams realized that the abandonment of the city for its outlying suburbs had been proceeding for over half a century and had recently been given renewed impetus by the advent of the automobile. But unlike his adversaries, he called for the "recentralization" of the city to be achieved through zoning and slum clearance coupled with arterial highways and mass transit leading to the outlying bedroom suburbs.

In a decade of financial boom and seemingly endless prosperity neither Mumford and MacKaye's tiny adversarial Regional Planning Association of America nor Thomas Adams's subsidized investigators enjoyed much success in convincing the politicians and the developers of the need for an integrated plan for regional development. Serious regional planning awaited the onset of the Depression and the initiative of another group of regionalists, this one situated in Chapel Hill, North Carolina, directing their attention to the urgent needs of an impoverished South and its peoples, black and white.

Odum and the Agrarians. If Mumford served the early-twentieth-century regionalist movement as its prophet and Benton MacKaye as its chief planner, Howard Odum was its principal entrepreneur and an academic empire-builder without peer. Odum, who was born in the tiny Georgia town of Bethlehem in 1884, was trained in the North as a progressive social investigator with an obsessive belief in the power of scientific fact to tell the would-be reformer what to do. Odum remained true to this simple faith throughout a long and illustrious career at the University of North Carolina where he founded the Institute of Research in the Social Sciences, edited the influential *Journal of Social Forces*, and recruited and trained dozens of young social scientists in what by the mid-1930s was the busiest and most productive regionalist laboratory in the country. The master and his students, the most talented of whom were Rupert Vance and Arthur Raper, specialized in "fact-gathering"—compiling indices, figuring percentages, drawing bar graphs, making inventories—as a means of providing their native South with a science of regional resource management. Collaborating with W. T. Couch, the adventurous editor of the University of North Carolina Press, Odum and his students published an entire library of important regional studies in the 1920s and 1930s, among them Rupert Vance's *Human Geography of the South* (1932), Arthur Raper's comparative analysis of two Georgia Black Belt counties, *Preface to Peasantry* (1936), and Margaret J. Hagood's *Mothers of the South* (1939), a study of gender roles and childrearing among tenant-farm women. These, together with useful surveys of mill-town housing, public health in rural North Carolina, and inadequate social-welfare services in the state, made Chapel Hill the regionalist publishing center of the country. Odum's own contributions to this impressive collection were two huge tomes, *Southern Regions of the United States* (1936) and, with Harry Estill Moore, *American Regionalism: A Cultural-Historical Approach to National Integration* (1938), two heavily fact-laden and stylistically dense inventories and summaries.

Odum considered regionalism simply a tool for analysis, an instrument for studying the entirety of what he called the "folk-regional society" with a method "in which all factors are sought out and interpreted in their proper perspective." Or, as Rupert Vance explained more succinctly, regionalism was "a case for analysis and a cause for social action."

The two constants in Odum's social equation were the fixed universals in his folk-regional society and the dynamic "social forces" set in motion by modern technology that would, he hoped, correct "deficiencies" and eliminate "differentials" without upsetting the "folkways" on which the regional culture rested. The result of this balancing act, Odum devoutly believed, would be a self-perpetuating equilibrium of "common traditions," on the one side, and controlled developmental forces, on the other. Such a balance of forces, once acknowledged and legitimated, would cure the "pathological conditions"—endemic poverty, deep-seated racism, dysfunctional communities, and weak institutions—besetting the South.

In their attack on the South's problems Odum and his students were led ever further from Turner's original characterization of the frontier as the cradle of democracy and of the pioneer as its favored child. Just as Lewis Mumford, in compiling his regional history of New England, came to denounce the frontiersman as restless and unheeding, wasteful and greedy, so the Chapel Hill school was driven by massive collections of data to question the frontier thesis, at least as applied to the South before the Civil War. These findings set a collision course with another and contrary-minded band of regionalists in the late 1920s and 1930s, the so-called Nashville Agrarians, whose romantically indulgent reading of the antebellum South Odum and his young sociologists were determined to correct.

The regionalist manifesto of the Nashville Agrarians was a set of polemical essays, *I'll Take My Stand* (1930), written by "Twelve Southerners," as they styled themselves, searching for a way to dethrone modern industrialism. The group formed around four poets—John Crowe Ransom, Allen Tate, Donald Davidson, and the young Robert Penn Warren—who earlier in the 1920s had attracted attention by publishing a magazine of poetry and criticism, the *Fugitive,* at Vanderbilt. These four were joined by novelists Stark Young and Andrew Nelson Lytle, another poet and radical regionalist, John Gould Fletcher, two historians, a journalist, and a psychologist, all of whom agreed on repudiating industrialism as the source of overproduction, unemployment, and economic inequality, demanding a return to the remembered ways of an agrarian Old South.

The image of the Old South, variously rendered by individual Agrarians, was nevertheless composed of a set of propositions not fully harmonious but together depicting a spiritually satisfying way of life now on the verge of destruction. There was, first of all, John Crowe Ransom's picture of slavery as "monstrous enough in theory, but, more often than not, humane in practice," on which judgment Robert Penn Warren set a defense of contemporary segregation as the only means of building "an informed and productive negro community." For historian Frank Owsley regional recovery depended on a true understanding of the Civil War as an "irrepressible conflict," a mortal combat between an aggressive industrializing North and an outmanned agrarian South in which slavery "was only one element and not an essential one." Stark Young's patrician Old South was the handiwork of a cotton aristocracy complete with personal honor, mutuality of interests, and "an innate code of obligations," while John Donald Wade's country squire "Cousin Lucius" asked his cotton-infatuated neighbors what they meant "in a land where all delectable fruits would grow for the planting, by planting never a fruit tree?" Allen Tate considered a southern war against capitalist industrialism another Lost Cause, but his friend Donald Davidson insisted that "industrialism can be deposed as the regulating god of modern society." Despite these variant readings of their southern heritage the Nashville Agrarians stood squarely behind their Statement of Principles—"the theory of agrarianism is that the culture of the soil is the best and most sensitive of vocations."

This Agrarian premise Odum and his sociologists dismissed as romantic nonsense, the old self-defeating sectionalism in a new guise. Their corrective followed from Odum's insistence on the "facing of absolute facts rather than substituting rationalizations which grow out of irrelevant comparisons or defense explanations of how things have come to be as they are." Their scrutiny of Nashville nostalgia led Odum and his school to the discovery of a "hidden history" of the region that indicted slavery and its companion cotton culture for sustaining an "immature" frontier society, one now in need, not of repair, but of wholesale replacement. The root cause of southern impoverishment, Odum, Vance, and Raper argued persuasively, was King Cotton, "a hard master over the whole human culture of the region." For every acre of lush bottomland along the Mississippi there were hundreds more in upcountry Georgia and Alabama gullied by cotton and abandoned. Here, according to Vance, the sharpest of Odum's observers, were the effects of frontier development that had survived in the Depression South: exhausted fields, downtrodden tenants, black and white, speculative land usage, absentee ownership—all unmistakable signs of a deeply entrenched colonial economy.

Their impressive compilation of facts demonstrating regional poverty strengthened Chapel Hill's political appeal to President Roosevelt and the New Deal. Their proposals were tactically astute, economically adventurous, and racially timid. Odum explained the southern regionalists' disinclination to meddle with race relations by pointing to the "powerful folkways of long generations" which made it impossible for "a region to change over night." Even Arthur Raper, the boldest of Odum's students on race relations, argued that "first things come first" and that the primary task was to break the grip of the cotton economy on tenant farmers of both races by teaching them to recognize the "common denominators" in their joint "disinheritance."

NEW DEAL REGIONALISM

By the late 1930s it was clear that mechanized agriculture was already making a revolution in the South, pushing tenants back down the agricultural ladder to wage status or forcing them off the land to join the ranks of the urban unemployed. But man is not a machine, Arthur Raper complained, and when mechanized production leads to increased dependency, then mechanical efficiency simply causes social inefficiency. Look at the regional victims of technological revolution, he urged, "and estimate how much it will cost America to restore the resources that have been wasted and reestablish the people who have been disinherited."

Federal response to the southern regionalists' cries for help was well-intentioned but also sporadic and ultimately ineffectual in checking the ravages of the Depression in the rural South and rescuing the dispossessed and the downtrodden. The Farm Security Administration (FSA) was established by New Dealers to provide credit for tenant farmers seeking to purchase the land they were working and to encourage crop diversification and cooperative communities. But the combined opposition of agribusiness and rural elites kept the struggling agency on a short financial tether. Similarly, the Resettlement Administration's proposal for building hundreds of greenbelt towns encountered the stiff resistance of local real estate interests, and the list was promptly reduced to plans for six new towns, only three of which were ever built. The Resettlement Administration, established in 1935, lasted just two years, while the FSA survived the first year of World War II before being dismantled by a hostile Congress. Meanwhile proposals for restructuring federal agencies and strengthening the executive with regional councils and boards in a "third New Deal" also foundered on the rocks of congressional conservatism.

On the other hand, the federal government sponsored a number of successful regional cultural projects, which extended from the document (the WPA State Guide Series) to the photograph (the Farm Security Administration's Historical Division collection) to thousands of murals adorning post office walls across the nation. Holger Cahill's Federal Art Project compiled the Index of American Design, which provided a documentary record of regional art forms from Shaker crafts in upstate New York and New England to the hand tools of Appalachia and the weaving and carving of the Southwest. The Music Project sent collectors scouring the American hinterland, recording Creole songs in Louisiana and the dances of the Five Indian Tribes in Oklahoma, and listening to the "living lore" of Maine clamdiggers and New York City vagrants. The federally funded State Guide series constituted a huge regional sociology with fifty-one state studies, thirty guides to major cities, and twenty excursions into such regional territory as Death Valley and the Oregon Trail—altogether mapping what critic Alfred Kazin called "an America unexampled in density and regional diversity."

The single exception to federal neglect of regional development in the 1930s was the Tennessee Valley Authority (TVA), on which regional planners all across America pinned their hopes for a revival of producerist culture and the renovation of an entire region. For a brief time in the late 1930s, before World War II brought the invasion of war industries and corporate dominance to the valley, the TVA appeared to be fulfilling, at least in part, these hopes for a producerist alternative to business consolidation. Housing units built in vernacular styles, test-demonstration programs, greenbelts to prevent speculative development, small industry and market-garden farming, mobile libraries and educational extension services, appeared to point to the unity of the people with their environment that regional planners since the days of John Wesley Powell had hoped for. For Arthur E. Morgan, the first chairman of the TVA, it was the town of Norris in particular on which he counted to establish the regionalist principle. Twenty miles from Knoxville and hard by the dam site, Norris was intended to be the prototype of a series of planned communities following construction crews down the valley all the way to Kentucky. Morgan touted his town as proof of regionalist principles and the superiority of a cooperative regional culture.

Included in the original plan for Norris was a cooperative barn for livestock, woodworking and electrical shops, and a museum clad in rustic wood shakes for the display of country crafts in a balanced juxtaposing of the traditional and the technological. Planners made blueprints for paired satellite villages on the outskirts of Norris as well as for an encircling "town wood." The community was designed and for a short while actually functioned as a "demonstration"—a key component in regional planning concepts and a substitute for more controlling social theory—a working-model of an open-ended, self-correcting approach to problem solving.

Yet the fate of the town of Norris and the postwar surrender of the valley to giant industry symbolized the defeat of the original regionalist vision of the interwar years. Construction workers soon moved on to another site, and wartime mobility remained high, so that by 1950 there were only three families in town who had been there since 1934. In 1948, TVA sold the land and afterward concentrated on generating atomic power and building coal-fired plants. Norris was finally chartered as a regular municipality by the Tennessee legislature in 1949.

A retrospective account of the flaws in early-twentieth-century regionalism might focus initially on the failure of its practitioners to fashion a workable political program or devise a realistic planning agenda. Seemingly secure in their faith in the power of cultural radicalism, regionalists—so the indictment goes—tended to view moral suasion itself as a form of politics. Their civic republicanism led them to champion decentralization and diffusion of power as an alternative to an increasingly centralized national state. They defined their own collective role as that of the educator-prophet dispensing lessons in citizenship, cultural pluralism, and conservation. At the core of regionalism lay a belief in the energizing power of art to unite people in a transpolitical, noncoercive community. This insistence on aesthetic education, a fear of concentrated power, and a profound distrust of political parties and special interests meant that regionalism in its first American incarnation was a brand of evangelical politics or, more accurately, a form of communitarian antipolitics with deep roots in a nineteenth-century reform tradition. Preach the truth—so the regionalist litany went—and they will come. In this sense the collapse of the TVA, both as cooperative "demonstration" and communitarian vision in the years after World War II, signaled the end of the original regionalist reform project and the belief in American exceptionalism on which it rested.

THE EXPLODING METROPOLIS

The problem, however, was more complicated and deep-seated than this. It lay in that metropolitan outrush that Lewis Mumford had noted twenty years earlier and Thomas Adams had verified with charts, graphs, and statistics, and that by now had become the flood against which Benton MacKaye once warned. With the return of peace and the coming of economic recovery in the decade following World War II middle-class Americans came pouring out of city centers, not flowing, into carefully planned garden cities and new towns, but rushing along arterial "slurbs" into a scattered suburbia in search of the "good life" suddenly available to them. The good life, when translated, meant a two-story Cape Cod cottage on Shady Lane designed for a nuclear family and complete with white picket fence, two-car garage, hollyhocks to tend and a lawn to mow, as well as better schools for the kids and all the amenities and securities increasingly unavailable in central cities, where out-migration and urban blight proceeded apace. Although this process of draining the city center of jobs, people, and wealth had been clearly discernible for some time, by the 1950s the "exploding metropolis" had become a sufficiently dramatic phenomenon to require a new model of the region and its relationship to the central place, an explanation which, with its directives to regional planners, subverted all of the underlying assumptions of the original Turnerian paradigm. This new definition of the region had been formulated in Germany at about the same time that Turner announced his frontier thesis. Central place theory, as it was called, then crossed the Atlantic, found an institutional home at the University of Chicago, and by 1950 was acquiring the dominance it would retain until the end of the century.

The actual origins of metropolitan regionalism lay in the nineteenth-century theory of agricultural markets devised by the Prussian economist J. H. von Thünen, whose early study *The Isolated State* (1825), provided would-be planners with the first abstract model of the regional city based on location theory. Thünen calculated the regional reach of the metropolitan center in terms of agricultural markets and the process of exchange, drawing a series of concentric circles radiating from the central city and delineating zones of influence out to the perimeter of agricultural-industrial exchange. The analytical beauty of Thünen's exposition of what would come to be location theory lay in its dynamism—the way in which it both predicted and accommodated change and shifting patterns of the mutual exchange of goods and people. Turner's account of regional development was linear and sequential, proceeding in time as well as direction from unfenced land inward toward the urban core in a predictable sequence of revitalizing activity. The new location and systems theory which dominated American planning in the second half of the twentieth century built on and extended German location theorists' elaboration of Thünen's original concerns, first with respect to industrial development (Alfred Weber, 1909), then to cities as "central places" generally (Walter Cristaller, 1933), and ultimately to a complete location theory synthesis (August Lösch, 1940).

Deriving its analytical power from new combinations of economics, human geography, demography, and urban and land planning, the new central place theory turned Frederick Jackson Turner's exceptionalist American assumption inside out. In this new regional science it was the dynamic relation between the metropolis and its outlying provinces *everywhere in the world* that finally mattered, a universal reciprocity could be measured, analyzed, regulated, and monitored. Moreover, in this new system of regional exchange that was guided by market forces and shaped by transportation patterns it was the central city—the metropolis—that played a dominant, even imperial, role as it invaded the outlying region, following the directives of a colonizing impulse, as developer and entrepreneur. Finally, in the new central place theory there was an assumed simultaneity—a constant interaction between urban core and rural periphery—that made it impossible any longer to conceive of the region in Turner's terms as undergoing an orderly developmental sequence with the invigorating cultural and political impulses coming from the margins.

An account of the rise and ultimate triumph of metropolitan regionalism in the United States opens in the Progressive years, soon after the turn of the century, with the appearance of a generation of urban sociologists and demographers who looked to Britain and more particularly to Germany for their inspiration and training. Their leader and a major contributor to the field of urban and regional studies was the founder of the Chicago school of sociology, Robert Park, who, in a manner similar to that of Howard Odum at Chapel Hill at about the same time, gathered a group of highly talented colleagues and students at the University of Chicago. Park and his associates combined the survey method so attractive to Progressives with the new German social psychology and demography to study the shifting structure of the twentieth-century metropolis. In a classic series of essays entitled *The City* (1925) Park, together with contributors E. W. Burgess and R. D. McKenzie, constructed a new model of the American city to replace the outworn notion of the neighborhood as the primary building block of the metropolitan community. The Chicago school's model of the city rested on the enduring reality of a money economy, capitalist competition, increasing mobility, advertising, and mass consumerism—all the attributes of twentieth-century American life that the original regionalists deplored.

It was the Chicago school's R. D. McKenzie who, in *The Metropolitan Community* (1933), provided the clearest picture of metropolitan regionalism and predicted its future course with startling accuracy. "The population of the United States," McKenzie observed in his opening pages, "is tending to concentrate more and more in large regional aggregates. In every such aggregate, the population tends to subdivide and become multinucleated in a complex of centers that are economically and socially integrated in a larger regional unity." Noting that these metropolitan regions across the country failed to match political divisions, McKenzie defined his region as "primarily a functional entity" that extends "geographically as far as the city exerts a dominant influence." Here was the application of European location theory to the American scene: the metropolitan region is the product of the transformative effects of urban marketing and the new transportation-communication network that commerce engenders. It consists of centers, routes, and rims, with the several parts of the region clustered around the central city like iron filings around a magnet. Or, as McKenzie himself put it, "Smaller cities and towns tend to group themselves around larger ones somewhat as planets group themselves around a sun." The first half of McKenzie's book neatly summarized the results of the ongoing suburbanization of America, with financial services, merchandising, and some kinds of manufacturing accompanying the American middle class in its exodus from the central city.

Projecting his findings into the future, McKenzie predicted the eventual disappearance of traditional regions as metropolitanism continued to erase indigenous values and undermine their ethnic and cultural foundations. As intensive suburbanization sweeps westward from its eastern and midwestern bases, "the various indices of maturation presented . . . definitely support the hypothesis that the different regions of the country are tending to become more nearly uniform in economic and cultural characteristics." With new belts of suburban settlement springing up in the

South and on the West Coast, McKenzie concluded, future regional supercommunities would become more and more like each other in both economic and social structure.

Seen from the perspective of its central city, the metropolitan region looked less like Turner's seedbed of democracy than the colony of an imperial power vying with its rivals for control of markets both local and foreign. In this process of homogenization, McKenzie announced, old regional distinctions and characteristics would continue to fade. New intraregional "bonds of common interests" will redefine the region as essentially a "commercial province" with colonizing ambitions to annex and control as much surrounding territory as it can. Already, McKenzie notes in the early 1930s, "we can in fact draw a map tentatively allotting the entire territory of the continental United States to a comparatively small number of larger cities."

Using McKenzie's data, an observer of metropolitan regionalism could foresee, in addition, a much less attractive set of consequences: intensive unregulated land use on the city's peripheries; sprawling suburban subdivisions; speculative and wholly destructive commercial development; transportation congestion; underuse of central-city land; increased municipal tax burdens accompanied by mounting revenue shortfalls—in short, all of the problems that Lewis Mumford had pinpointed in his epochal quarrel with the developmentalist planner Thomas Adams over the regional plan for New York City. As Mumford insisted, all these problems highlighted the urgent need for extensive regional planning, but cooperation between politically independent communities would prove difficult to achieve. The pattern for the rest of the twentieth century, as McKenzie acknowledged, seemed set: "It is highly improbable, within the near future at any rate, that any revolutionary changes will occur in population patterning. In all probability our great cities will continue to decentralize in the sense that population and economic functions will become more widely dispersed throughout the metropolitan region."

McKenzie's forecast acquired sharpened spatial definition in a classic article by Chauncy D. Harris and Edward L. Ullman, "The Nature of Cities," which appeared in the *Annals of the American Academy of Political and Social Science* in 1945. Harris and Ullman's model of axial routes, concentric rings, and peripheral nuclei summarized an earlier phase of twentieth-century suburbanization marked by the outward growth of goods-producing and manufacturing economies primarily in the urban Northeast and Midwest. Already, however, with the return of peace and the onset of prosperity, the United States was entering another phase of migration out of the city, this one propelled by a rapidly expanding knowledge industry and an accompanying service economy. Between 1920 and 1970 service industries—chiefly in finance, real estate, insurance, and corporate management—grew from 38 to 63 percent of the American labor force. This economic growth traced a new pattern of national settlement along the receding boundaries of suburbia and exurbia as regional differences became less and less pronounced. Two characteristics distinguished the new migrants: the "high mobiles," as they were called, were younger and better off financially than the "low mobiles," those blue-collar workers increasingly unemployed and the new minority recruits to center cities now left behind. "What has developed," Brian J. L. Berry observed in the mid-1980s,

> is a stratification system cutting across widely varying geographical and cultural sub-regions of the country, creating *national citizens*.

Now, when high mobiles move, Berry added, they need not change their lifestyles:

> there is a tendency to move between near-identical social environments. . . . This attachment to a type of environment that sustains a particular lifestyle is the key to the way contemporary Americans have adjusted the need to retain a locally based sense of security and stability to the emergence of a nationwide highly mobile society.

All contemporary Americans, one might add, except those low-mobile national citizens mired in inner-city ghettos.

McKenzie's prediction was further verified three decades later by the sociologist Jean Gottmann in his massive survey *Megalopolis* (1961), compiled for the Twentieth Century Fund. Gottmann, in effect, completed the analysis of American regionalization undertaken by McKenzie by describing the fusing of formerly distinct metropolitan regions encircling major eastern seaboard cities into one extended megalopolitan corridor running from Boston to Baltimore-Washington and beyond. What was recently a string of separate metropolitan regions, each with its own discernible boundaries marking off competing entities, one from another, had, by the late 1950s, melted into a single giant agglomeration, itself now denoted a region. Subtitled *The Urbanized Northeastern Seaboard of the United States*, Gottmann's study was a 782-page survey of what he termed "the Main Street of the Nation," which traced the growth of "an almost continuous system of deeply interwoven urban and suburban areas" that "straddles state boundaries, stretches across wide estuaries and bays, and encompasses many regional differences."

The direction of Gottmann's process of regional melding is the reverse of Turner's democratic drift in moving from east to west. By 1960, he argued, this developmental thrust had already reached beyond Chicago to Los Angeles and the Bay Area, but nowhere had it attained the density of the megalopolitan corridor stretching from Boston to Washington: "None of them is yet comparable to megalopolis in size of population, density of population, or density of activities, be these expressed in terms of transportation, communications, banking operations, or political conferences." This outward flow from the central city, Gottman agreed with his predecessor McKenzie, will continue unabated. "As this tide reaches more and more cities they will burst out of old bounds to expand and scatter all over the landscape, taking new forms like those already observable throughout Megalopolis." By 1960 the changes being wrought had become so enormous that "an analysis of this region's problems often gives one the feeling of looking at the dawn of a new stage in human civilization."

The "tidal movement" of people, goods, and services, in, out, and across the new megalopolitan region, Gottman warned, involves a total redesigning and reshaping of land use as agricultural land continues to give way to industrial and residential use, and reforestation only partially compensates for the initial loss of trees. By 1960 the effects on central city "downtowns," as they were still called, had already become disastrous: city cores continued to crumble while suburbia, and increasingly exurbia, flourished as they extended the widening band of megalopolis. This increasing inequity in the distribution of amenities, Gottmann insisted in echoing McKenzie's proposals three decades earlier, requires a whole new system of regional management because "the old system of local, state, and national authorities and jurisdictions, which has changed little, is poorly suited to present needs." Gottmann's verdict on megalopolis was an admonitory one:

> In some ways this suburban sprawl may have alleviated a crowding [in central cities] that had threatened to become unbearable, for residential densities of population per square mile have decreased. But new problems have arisen because of activity and of traffic in the central cities and because the formerly rural areas or small towns have been unprepared to cope with the new demands on the resources. New programs are needed to conserve the natural beauty of the landscape and to assure the health, prosperity, and freedom of the people.

NEW REGIONAL PLANNING

Gottman threw down the challenge to a new generation of urban and regional planners who by the time his analysis appeared were already equipping themselves with a new regional planning approach based on systems analysis, a seemingly revolutionary method which was to yield surprisingly meager results. Traditional regional planning as espoused by Lewis Mumford and his generation had been based on fairly simple notions of prediction and control—a two-phase approach involving the preliminary survey and resultant design followed by direct implementation of an essentially static arrangement. The new computer-based systems analysis, by contrast, was dynamic, flexible, complete with "feedback" mechanisms that made the planning model infinitely adjustable, at least in theory. Wedded to location analysis, the new regional planning seemingly answered a whole list of perplexing questions with positivistic assurance: What is a region? How does it come into being? How does it actually function? How can it be most effectively managed? Systems analysis produced a new paradigm in the study of cities and their surrounding regions, one resting not on the Turnerian principles of American exceptionalism and civic republicanism, but rather on abstract spatial models subject to infinite modification and manipulation in the ongoing process of prediction. The exportability of the new metropolitan model internationalized the science of urban planning and supplied a comparative dimension to regional theory as practitioners studied rates and degrees of industrialization and urbanization across the world—in countries as different as Poland and China, Israel and India, Brazil and Tanzania. Ironically this new comparative analysis had the unintended effect of reintroducing Turnerian exceptionalism in a different guise by emphasizing those more purely American "frontier" cultural features—individualism, competitiveness, and faith in the free market—that militated against the whole idea of regional planning.

In effect then, the new regional planning necessarily tied the concept of region tightly to existing modes of transportation and marketing with the discovery that forms of commercial, industrial, and residential use were inextricably bound to rail, automobile, and, increasingly, air traffic patterns. With that recognition, beginning in the 1950s and quickly acquiring dominance, came the engineers with their assurances that, given the basic data on transportation links, employment estimates, and residential density, they could predict, plan, generate, and control regional activities and land use.

Increasingly regional planners and theorists in the United States began to construct multiple-choice plans for community consideration in place of the old "normative" schemes of Lewis Mumford and Benton MacKaye. Now they could offer a range of alternatives tailored to the shifting needs of mobile Americans. One example of this new type of planning was *A Policies Plan for the Year 2000*, compiled by the National Capital Planning Commission in 1961, a hydra-headed report that presented seven different models. "A metropolis can now choose to grow in any one of a variety of ways," the regional planners announced boldly. "New tools are being created continually. . . . Used in concert, the means within our reach can shape the region and each of its parts into the form we desire." Their schemes ranged from a Draconian "restricted growth" plan, rejected as politically unrealistic, to a design for a series of distanced new towns on the far metropolitan rim, an idea quickly abandoned as too expensive. More practical was a model of "Planned Sprawl," providing much encouragement but less guidance in ushering would-be migrants to their proper suburban seats. The planning commission's final nod went to the "Radial Corridor Plan," with "controlled open space"—wedges of open land separating high-density corridors running out to the countryside. All these alternatives, however, seemed superfluous once speculators convinced farmers to sell their land to builders and developers. Wedge boundaries were unenforceable. Government agencies on all levels hesitated to use eminent domain as a device for placing the wedges into public ownership. Americans—if their nation's capital was representative—were not interested in regional planning.

Another example of the broad-gauged regional plan was the Comprehensive General Plan for the Development of the Northeastern Illinois Counties Area of 1968, which, like its Washington progenitor, proffered a variety of land use and transportation options, including satellite cities, peripheral expansion, and what was termed a "finger plan" with digits poking out from a central-city palm and pointing toward wilderness. Once again the result was not what planners had hoped for but instead a mishmash of elements borrowed from competing visions.

In fact, by the last decade of the twentieth century engineers and planners working in concert with blue-sky developers had succeeded in building commercial strips, condominium clusters, industrial parks, and corporate headquarters in mushrooming "technoburbs" or "Edge City," as Joel Garreau calls it in a recent book by that title—outlying urban industrial villages encircling a moribund central city, the destination of young Americans seeking "life on the new frontier."

Edge City is at once the endpoint of metropolitan regionalism, the negation of the civic spirit of the original regionalist reformers, and the beckoning future for legions of commercial expansionists and developers as they invade the hinterland, seize natural preserves, and use them up. Speaking for the earlier generation of regionalists, Frank Lloyd Wright, in a plea for civic republicanism, urged Americans to "try to live deep *in* nature" so as to nurture the "democratic spirit of man." Today, as Garreau points out, Edge City—"the workplace of the Information Age"—consists of any area of pristine land that can promise 5 million square feet of office space, half a million feet of leasable retail space, mammoth plats of upscale housing and eager young professionals to fill it, and a canopied shopping mall complete with entertainment module—altogether a consumer paradise that "has it all."

As an example of the postmodern American region Garreau instances the "Sixty-Mile Circle" surrounding downtown Los Angeles and containing some twenty-six actual or potential Edge Cities. The old Los Angeles downtown, including East LA and Central, now contain less than 5 percent of the region's jobs, which have accompanied the middle-class flight from the city. The Sixty-Mile Circle as a region boasts 139 colleges and universities, an intricate if chaotic automotive transportation system, acres of agribusiness-owned farmland, and hundreds of corporate headquarters complete with de rigueur artificial waterfalls. What this particular Edge City and others like it lack are two critical components: an integrated public planning instrumentality and the will to use it, and the communitarian ethic and civic republicanism on which to construct a regional planning agenda for citizen participation. The first shortcoming leaves the door to Edge City open to private developers practicing a new form of slash-and-burn. And the second leaves an ideological (some would say spiritual) vacuum which is quickly filled with speculative building, drained wetlands, and a burgeoning service sector catering to jaded consumer appetites.

ECOLOGICAL REGIONALISM

Arrayed in a defensive posture against the builders of technoburbia in the last decade of the twentieth century stand the still thin but growing ranks of a new generation of ecological regionalists armed with the communitarian ethic of the early reformers but equipped as well with recently collected scientific data on the state of the environment. Unlike the old regionalism, which was largely anticipatory and preventive, the new ecology-based regionalism specializes in reclamation and repair. In place of the discrete and sharply demarcated land areas visualized by Benton MacKaye earlier in the century the regionalist revival pins its faith on linkage. "Linkage," writes William H. Whyte, the veteran observer and critic of urban and regional planning, "is the key. Most of the big tracts in our metropolitan areas have already been saved, or they have already been lost. The most pressing need now [1968] is to weave together a host of seemingly disparate elements—an experimental farm, a private golf course, a local park, the spaces of a cluster subdivision, the edge of a new freeway right-of-way."

Ecological regionalists today take many of their cues from Ian McHarg of the Department of Landscape Architecture and Regional Planning at the University of Pennsylvania as they discover the basic materials for regional reconstruction ready at hand in the shape and substructure of the land itself. Defining forest land in terms reminiscent of MacKaye as an "upland sponge," McHarg singled out for condemnation those developers who, heedless of ultimate environmental costs, plunge happily into the work of destroying the land. McHarg marks our arrival at the edge of countryside by pointing to the "emblems" of development "the cadavers of old trees piled in untidy heaps at the edge of the razed deserts, the magnificent machines for land despoliation, for felling forests, filling marshes, culverting streams, and sterilizing farmland, making thick brown sediments of the creeks." Here at the edges where public powers are weakest and greed goes unchecked, the erosion of values keeps pace with the erosion of the landscape. "Here are the meek mulcted, and the refugees thwarted."

The prohibitive costs of development can be lowered if not eliminated, McHarg insisted, through the simple process of identifying the natural design of a region or subregion—that system of streams and valleys, aquifers and bedrock, wetlands and wooded slopes—that provide the necessary directives. In 1965 McHarg, together with David Wallace, drew up a plan for adapting settlement to regional imperatives for large landowners in the Spring Green and Worthington Valleys northwest of Baltimore. Their "Plan for the Valleys vs. Spectre of Uncontrolled Growth" embraced some seventy square miles consisting of three valleys, several plateaus, and large farms whose owners had formed a council and hired the planners. "Uncontrolled growth," McHarg warned in the prophetic tones of Benton MacKaye or Patrick Geddes, "occurring sporadically, spreading without discrimination, will surely obliterate the valleys, inexorably cover the landscape with its smear, irrevocably destroy all that is beautiful or memorable. No matter how well-designed each individual sub-division may be, no matter if small parks are interfused with housing, the great landscape will be expunged and remain only as a receding memory." Following nature's directives, instead—down the water courses and along the forest cover on their sides—leads to the solution: to build cluster housing selectively on the plateaus but leave the valleys and their slopes alone.

Ecological regionalists have subsequently followed McHarg's recommendations in seeking to identify "natural corridors" like the Blackstone Valley running from Worcester, Massachusetts, to Providence, Rhode Island—any open passageway of streams and valleys to which can be added man-made links such as abandoned railroad rights-of-way, unused aqueducts, old logging roads— forming altogether a checkerboard-like "linear open-space network" with a greater peripheral perimeter than a solid unbroken tract of land.

At the end of the century, such thinking, together with other ideas for reclaiming and repairing the damage done by unplanned metropolitan expansion, guides the activities of hundreds of nature conservancies, land trusts, shoreline commissions, wilderness groups, park planners, and landowner compacts across the nation. Dimly discernible in these efforts is an emergent philosophy of the *commons*—land set aside for all the people—which admittedly will be a hard sell to a national citizenry divided into high-mobile "haves" and low-mobile "have-nots." What is lacking so far is the engagement of the federal government in promoting the idea of that national commons as it extends from revitalized inner cities out along suburban corridors past exurbia to regional parks and wilderness areas. Without this federal commitment the struggle between ecological regionalists and their powerful enemies is bound to remain an unequal one. If the victories of the regional reformers to date have been partial and quite literally piecemeal, it can nevertheless be said that the communitarian vision of the original regionalists has not been killed or their ongoing war yet lost.

BIBLIOGRAPHY

Two massive surveys of colonial settlement and development provide a needed regional perspective on early American history. Donald W. Meining, *Atlantic America, 1492–1800*, the first volume of his *The Shaping of America: A Geographical Perspective on 500 Years of History* (1986), emphasizes cultural conflict and regional diversity in the Europeanized New World. David Hackett Fisher, *Albion's Seed: Four British Folkways in America* (1989), traces four colonial cultures in North America to their roots in four different regions of Great Britain. Fulmer Mood, "The Origin, Evolution, and Application of the Sectional Concept, 1750–1900," in Merrill Jensen, ed., *Regionalism in America* (1951), provides a highly informative survey of the regional concept from the work of colonial geographers to that of Frederick Jackson Turner. Turner's essays on section and region have been collected in two handy volumes, Max Farrand, ed., *The Significance of Sections in American History* (1950), and Ray Allen Billington, ed., *Selected Essays of Frederick Jackson Turner: Frontier and Section* (1961).

Robert L. Dorman, *Revolt of the Provinces: The Regionalist Movement in America, 1920–1945* (1993), is a masterful survey of the various strands of regionalist thought and activity in the interwar years. For Lewis Mumford's contributions in these same two decades, see his *The Golden Day: A Study in American Experience and Culture* (1926), *Technics and Civilization* (1934), and *The Culture of Cities* (1938, 1970). Mumford's varied contributions are discussed at length in Donald L. Miller, *Lewis Mumford: A Life* (1989); and Thomas P. Hughes and Agatha C. Hughes, eds., *Lewis Mumford: Public Intellectual* (1990). Benton MacKaye's regional planning scheme is detailed in *The New Exploration: A Philosophy of Regional Planning* (1928). The Regional Planning Association of America's regional blueprints first appeared in *Survey Graphic* 7 (May 1925), and are reprinted in Carl Sussman, ed., *Planning the Fourth Migration: The Neglected Vision of the Regional Planning Association of America* (1976).

Howard Odum's multifaceted approach to regionalism and regional planning is contained in his massive compilation of data and quotations, written with Harry Estill Moore, *American Regionalism: A Cultural-Historical Approach to National Integration* (1939). A clearer, as well as more succinct, account of the shifting emphasis of regional analysis as Odum's students registered the conceptual impact of the new demography can be found in John Shelton Reed and Daniel Joseph Singal, eds., *Regionalism and the South: Selected Papers of Rupert Vance* (1982). The central ideas of the variously contributing Nashville Agrarians can be found in Louis D. Rubin, Jr., ed., *I'll Take My Stand: The South and the Agrarian Tradition* (1977).

R. D. McKenzie, *The Metropolitan Community* (1933), retains all the power of prophecy sixty years later, as does Jean Gottmann, *Megalopolis: The Urbanized Northeastern Seaboard of the United States* (1961), after thirty years.

Two good histories of the origins and growth of suburbia are John R. Stilgoe, *Borderland: Origins of the American Suburb, 1820–1939* (1988); and Kenneth Jackson, *Crabgrass Frontier: The Suburbanization of the United States* (1985). Federal urban policy is thoroughly treated in Mark I. Gelfand, *A Nation of Cities: The Federal Government and Urban America, 1933–1965* (1975). Jon C. Teaford, *The Rough Road to Renaissance: Urban Revitalization in America, 1940–1985* (1990), traces the struggles of the nation's major cities to cope with myriad mounting difficulties. Peter Hall, *Cities of Tomorrow: An Intellectual History of Urban Planning and Design in the Twentieth Century* (1988), is a learned and provocative overview.

William H. Whyte, *The Last Landscape* (1968), pioneered in combining urban planning with ecologically sensitive regional analysis, an approach followed on a wider scale by David R. Goldfield, *Cotton Fields and Skyscrapers: Southern City and Region, 1607–1890* (1982). Also see two articles by Goldfield: "The New Regionalism," *Journal of Urban History* (February 1984): 171–186, and "The Urban South: A Regional Framework," *American Historical Review* 86 (December 1981): 1009–1034. For recent regional developments in the West, see Gerald D. Nash, *The American West Transformed: The Impact of the Second World War* (1985). Patricia Nelson Limerick, *The Legacy of Conquest: The Unbroken Past of the American West* (1987), offers a new perspective on the West as a borderland region and in so doing dispenses with the Turner thesis altogether. Joel Farreaus, *Edge City: Life on the New Frontier* (1991), is a lively but even-handed analysis of a disturbing phenomenon. Lee Taylor, *Urbanized Society* (1980), provides a useful comparative perspective on urban and regional planning, as does Michael P. Conzen, ed., *World Patterns of Modern Urban Change: Essays in Honor of Chauncy D. Harris* (1986). Melville C. Branch, ed., *Urban Planning The-*

ory (1975), offers a wide range of selections on various aspects of urban and regional planning theory.

Finally, three books complete a twentieth-century survey of regionalism as idea and fact. William Cronon, *Nature's Metropolis: Chicago and the Great West* (1991), traces the rise and slow decline of the nation's midwestern gateway city. Robert Fishman, *Bourgeois Utopias* (1987), faults the privatized social ideals that led the American middle classes to leave the city for the suburbs. New "green cities" landscapes are discussed from a variety of points of view in David Gordon, ed., *Green Cities: Ecologically Sound Approaches to Urban Space* (1990).

THE EAST

David C. Hammack

Americans have not always agreed that the "East" is a region. Through most of the twentieth century, as through the nineteenth, many westerners and southerners have shared a common set of views of the East—views that seemed simply ill-informed and inconsistent to easterners. On the one hand, the East is seen as powerful, arrogant, controlling—the home of old-rich capitalists who dominate other parts of the United States and the port through which disquieting European ideas and fashions enter to challenge the middle-American heartland. Yet it is also characterized as conflict-ridden, corrupt, and decadent, riven into hostile ethnic and religious minorities, divided into warring classes of "rich" and "poor," lacking a sensible "American" middle class, excessively urban and exurban. Easterners have tended to dismiss such perceptions as provincial carping against the economic and intellectual center of the United States and as ill-informed generalizations that lump "real" regions—Cape Cod, Greater New York, the Catskills, York County—into an artificial whole that is little more than a Census Bureau convenience and a figment of the fevered imaginations of western and southern politicians from William Jennings Bryan to Barry Goldwater to Strom Thurmond.

Given that the boundaries of the East are necessarily contested, in order to make comparative statements about population, urbanization, economic development, and voting patterns, this essay will follow the U.S. Census Bureau's practice of defining regions in terms of states, and group together two census regions plus part of a third: New England, including Maine, New Hampshire, Vermont, Massachusetts, Rhode Island, and Connecticut; the Middle Atlantic states of New York, New Jersey, and Pennsylvania; and Delaware and Maryland.

These census-defined boundaries do, however, lump into a single unit two of the three great regions usually distinguished by historians of the colonial and revolutionary periods: New England and the Middle Colonies. An East that includes two regions whose original cultures, social patterns, governments, and even legal traditions differ so widely is in many ways an awkward and ungainly unit devoid of a coherent history. An East that includes Syracuse, Rochester, Buffalo, New York State's Southern Tier, western Pennsylvania, Pittsburgh, and Erie, extends far into the West or Midwest (a connection suggested by Pennsylvania State University's admission to the Big Ten athletic conference): yet it does not reach far enough to embrace Cleveland, Ohio, which often considers itself to be an eastern city. Western New York and western Pennsylvania form important parts of the agricultural and trading hinterland for New York City, Philadelphia, and other East Coast cities; but so do the Tidewater and the Valley of Virginia, the Carolinas, and Georgia—and the east coast of Florida is often described as New York City's subtropical borough. An East that embraces Delaware, Maryland, and for some purposes the northern counties of Virginia includes a significant portion of the third colonial region, the Chesapeake part of the South. It connects the scrapple-eating and bourbon-drinking areas of eastern Pennsylvania with their counterparts in Maryland and Virginia. And it includes territory that is now an integral part of the Boston-to-Washington megalopolis that has provided the material structure for the largest part of the East since at least 1945.

Thus no single geographical definition of the East in the twentieth century is possible. It is certain, however, that over the course of the century the East has become more and more integrated into what might be called a coherent region, dominated by the vast urban complex of Megalopolis and by great branches that run up the Hudson River to Albany and out along the Erie Canal–New York State Thruway route to Buffalo and Erie, and along the Pennsylvania Railroad-Pennsylvania Turnpike route to Pittsburgh. It is also clear that since World War II, the other regions of the United States—the Upper Midwest, the Pacific Coast, and the South in particular—

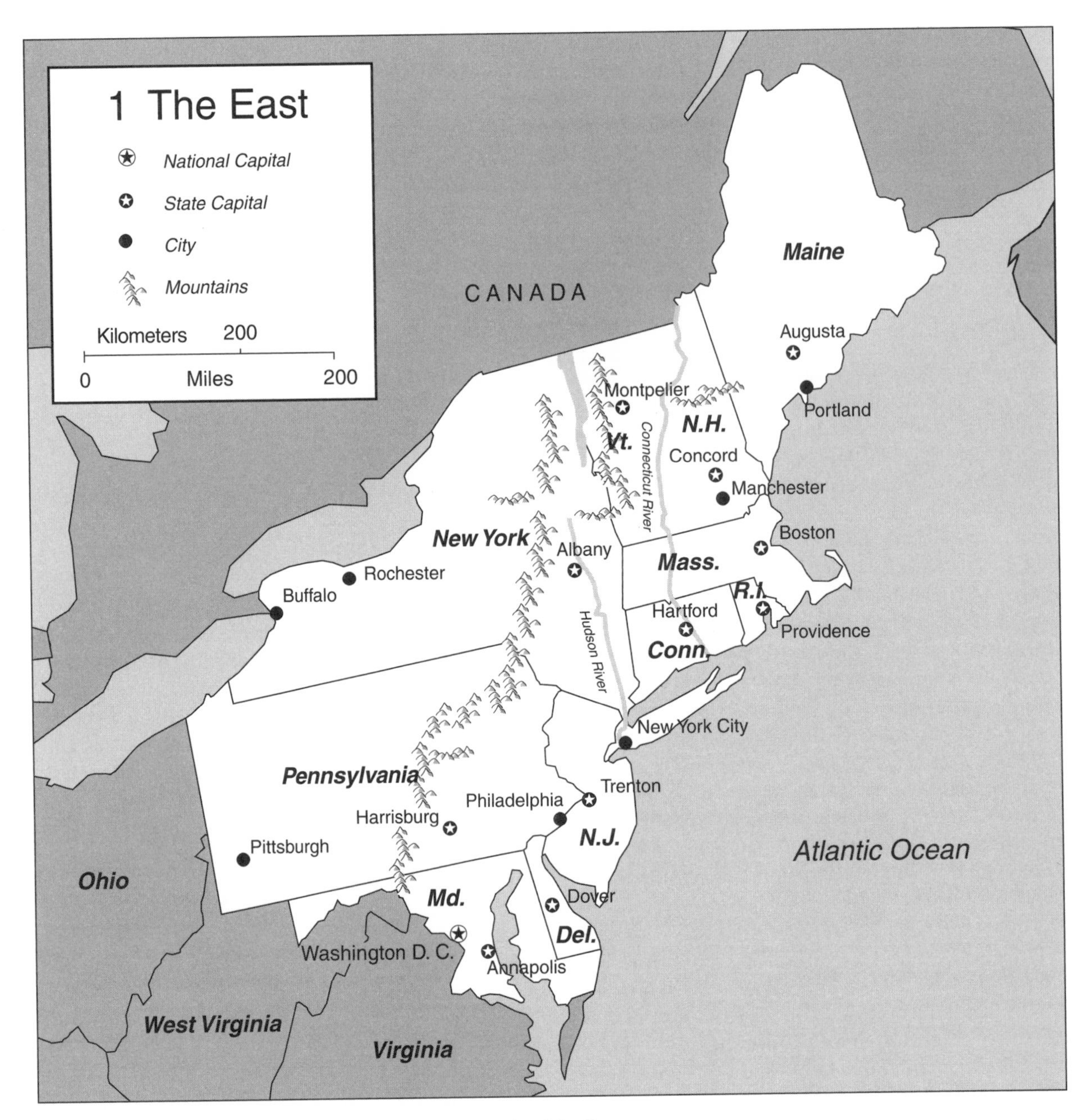

Map 1. The East.

have grown to resemble the East in many respects. As living patterns in the entire nation have grown more similar, the East has also become more unified, more like a single region.

THE MEGALOPOLITAN ECONOMY

Throughout American history, the East has been viewed as the most intensely urbanized region of the United States. Although the cities of the Pacific Coast have in fact held a larger portion of their region's population throughout the twentieth century, the East has consistently contained the nation's largest and most intensively interrelated network of cities. At the start of the twentieth century over two-thirds of the region's people already lived in cities. A substantial majority lived in the biggest cities and in their suburbs. Brookline and Newton, outside of Boston, the towns of Long Island's North Shore and of Westchester County north of New York City, the Oranges west of Newark, and Ardmore, Bryn Mawr, and other towns along the Main Line west of Philadelphia—together they had by the mid-nineteenth century defined the very idea of the affluent American suburb. By 1900 all the large eastern cities were also neighbored by lower-middle-income suburbs and by industrial towns.

The East thus pioneered the politically and socially fragmented metropolitan region that had grown, by the end of the twentieth century, to be the standard American settlement pattern. The U.S. census first devoted special attention to a multistate metropolitan region in its 1880 treatment of New York City. The Boston area managed its water supply, sewage disposal, and park needs through a Metropolitan District Commission after 1890; New York and New Jersey created a joint Port Authority after World War I; by the late 1920s the private Regional Plan Association of New York and New Jersey was seeking to promote cooperation in an area that reached south to Princeton—which was on the northern edge of the region covered by a similar private planning group in Philadelphia. In 1961 regional geographer Jean Gottmann could show that a vast "megalopolis"—a more-or-less unified complex of cities and towns—extended from Concord and Manchester, New Hampshire, through Boston and Worcester, Providence, Hartford and New Haven, New York City, Newark and Trenton, Philadelphia, Harrisburg, and Wilmington all the way to Baltimore, Washington, D.C., and the northern counties of Virginia. This megalopolitan complex has become more tightly intertwined in the succeeding years. Indeed, by the 1990s the East could well be divided into three distinct parts: Megalopolis, associated recreational areas to the north and along the less-populated parts of the Atlantic Coast, and the inland agricultural and manufacturing areas that focus on Albany, Utica, Syracuse, Rochester, Buffalo, and Pittsburgh.

Throughout the twentieth century, both the megalopolitan and the inland portions of the East have been among the most industrialized and prosperous parts of the United States (usually, only California has had a higher per capita income). The East was the nation's first great manufacturing region. Heavy industry—especially the production of iron and steel, rails and girders—and the processing of most agricultural products through meat packing, flour milling, brewing, and sugar refining, had already moved from the East to the Midwest by 1900. But in 1920 the share of New England's labor force engaged in manufacturing was still two-thirds larger than the national average, and the Mid-Atlantic states' share was one-third larger. Each of the great eastern cities contained sprawling industrial districts producing a wide variety of goods. At the beginning of the twentieth century, easterners who did not live in the great commercial and manufacturing centers of Boston, New York, and Philadelphia generally found themselves in the small mill and mining towns that were also typical of the East. Most of the smaller cities featured one or two manufacturing industries whose origins could be traced well back into the nineteenth century: textiles in Manchester, Lowell, Chicopee, Pawtucket, Springfield, Holyoke, and many other places in New England; shoes in Lawrence and Brockton north of Boston; silverware in Newburyport and jewelry in Providence; brass and bronze products, including clocks and guns in Waltham and Springfield, Massachusetts and in Hartford, New Haven, and Connecticut's Naugatuck Valley; men's hats in Danbury; table and sanitary pottery in Trenton; cast iron stoves in Poughkeepsie and Bucks County, Pennsylvania. Other eastern towns depended on a single extractive industry: lumber in Maine and Vermont; fishing on the Maine coast, in Marblehead and Cape Cod, on Maryland's Eastern Shore; bluestone in Kingston, New York; coal in several towns and small cities in Pennsylvania.

Many of the East's smaller cities—like all its large cities—suffered the decline of old established industries throughout the twentieth century. Textiles were already moving south in 1900, shoe and pottery-making were moving west, and Connecticut's buggy-whip industry and New York City's gaslight-fixture industries were shortly to be destroyed by the rise of the automobile and electricity. Poverty on eastern farms and the continuing decline of New England's textile industry and Pennsylvania's coal mines prevented many rural and small-city easterners from participating in the boom of the 1920s—and helped bring about the Great Depression. By mid-century the garment-making industries of New York and Philadelphia had also begun to shift to the Southwest—and to Asia and Central America. Toward the end of the century, New York and other eastern cities were losing many printing-industry jobs to the Southeast. The steadily increasing routinization of manufacturing processes and the steady decline of transportation costs continued, throughout the century, to shift manufacturing jobs away from the region. Put another way, the East lost some of its distinctiveness as the other regions developed their own manufacturing industries and as metropolitan regions throughout the United States came to resemble one another more and more closely.

As the North American center for information-exchange, investment decision making, and fashion, however, the East also continued to play "incubator" and "nursery" roles for new industries, sustaining the growth of its largest cities and creating new manufacturing centers as well. The Boston area, Pittsfield, Syracuse, Schenectady, New York City, Newark, and Philadelphia all became significant centers for the manufacture of electrical equipment early in the twentieth century. Rochester, Waltham, and other cities developed large facilities for the production of scientific and medical equipment. Rochester's Kodak and Boston's Polaroid defined photography in the United States; Xerox built large plants in Rochester, then moved its headquarters to New York's Connecticut suburbs. The Lincoln Laboratories played a key role in developing radar during World War II, and helped create a large computer industry on Boston's circumferential Route 128 freeway—and in Manchester, Nashua, and other places in southern New Hampshire—during the 1970s and 1980s. New Jersey's Bell Laboratories played a similar role in telecommunications after World War II, and industrial research also helped that state expand its pharmaceutical industry and, with Delaware, its concentration in chemical production.

At mid-century optimistic analysts suggested that the entire population of the East was moving toward nicer work and higher incomes. The main eastern centers—New York, Boston, and Philadelphia—continued to play key national and international roles. They mediated trade and financial relations with Europe and much of the rest of the world, managed national markets in money, bonds, and stocks, housed many of the central institutions of the information and entertainment and advertising industries, provided a large share of the managers and white-collar workers for American industry. In all these activities the great eastern cities were supported not only by their rail and water connections with the Midwest and the South, but also by the strength and variety of the manufacturing activities located within their own borders, and in many of the small cities of their region. Their labor forces earned high incomes, and employers saw the East as a region of high wage costs. But it was also a region of highly specialized, highly skilled, and productive workers, and in the cities and suburbs of Megalopolis it led the nation through most of the century in the creation of white-collar, managerial, and professional jobs.

The East retained most of these characteristics into the 1990s, but optimistic mid-century predictions about prospects for its labor force as a whole were not borne out. Throughout the region manufacturing employment fell sharply. New England's textile and shoe industries collapsed during the 1960s, much of New York and Philadelphia's printing followed garment-making south and to Asia, and miscellaneous manufacturing also declined. A smaller share of America's international trade flowed through New York and other eastern harbors, and the trade that remained required far fewer dock workers and generated less and less processing, manufacturing, and packaging work. Booms in computer and office-machine manufacturing and in defense-related industries offset these trends to some extent, especially in New England during the 1980s. But these new industries usually located in suburban and outlying areas, where they failed to provide many jobs for the millions who remained in the older manufacturing districts of many towns and of all the region's big cities.

With the end of the Cold War after 1989 and the maturing of the computer industry, these industries, too, proved vulnerable. White-collar managerial and professional jobs expanded more steadily, providing work for an ever-increasing share of the labor force both in the central cities and in such suburban or "edge city" locations as Stamford, Connecticut; central New Jersey's Route 1 corridor; King of Prussia, Pennsylvania; and Bethesda, Silver Spring, Columbia, and other towns between Baltimore and Washington, D.C. Financial and marketing firms greatly increased the number of their employees in Manhattan, Boston, and Philadelphia during the 1960s and again during the 1980s. After the mid-1970s, however, white-collar workers also ran into busts as well as booms—and many large corporations began to move "back-office" white-collar jobs, such as the processing of credit card bills and insurance claims, to distant locations in the suburbs, in the Dakotas, and even overseas.

PEOPLE AND POLITICS

In 1969 the political analyst Kevin Phillips argued persuasively that the East could be divided broadly into three major political subregions: the "Yankee Northeast" of northern Pennsylvania, western and northern New York, western Massachusetts, and northern New England; Megalopolis; and the "Non-Yankee East" of New York's Hudson Valley, non-Megalopolitan New Jersey, Delaware, and Maryland, and western Pennsylvania. History and economic opportunity provided each of these subregions with a distinctive population mix, and each has its own political history. As Megalopolis grew to embrace a larger and larger share of the East's population by the 1990s (when over three-quarters of the New England population and over four-fifths of the Mid-Atlantic population lived in cities), however, the region took on an increasingly unified quality.

At the beginning of the twentieth century, English Protestants who remained strongly conscious of their colonial origins still dominated the farms, villages, and small manufacturing cities of the Yankee Northeast, although they had been joined by significant numbers of French Canadians along the border with Canada, and by many Irish laborers and German skilled workers. Newcomers from Poland and Italy and Portugal would join them early in the twentieth century, responding to new opportunities offered by the manufacturing industries of Buffalo and other cities. The colonial and nineteenth-century non-Yankee Northeast had been much more diverse; its early settlers included the Dutch, the Scotch-Irish, English Quakers and Catholics, German dissenters, and French Protestants. The nineteenth century brought some Irish Catholics and many Germans; Italians and eastern Europeans followed around the turn of the century.

In 1900 immigrants and their children constituted half of the East's population; by 1930, the proportion had risen to 54 percent. The big cities received the largest share of these immigrants, and even in 1900 they were famous for their distinctive immigrant neighborhoods: Irish Southie and Charlestown in Boston; New York's Little Germany, Irish West Side, Jewish Lower East Side, and Chinatown. As the big cities grew into Megalopolis, they attracted an increasingly diverse array of people. New York, which had been an Irish and German city in 1890, led the way: by 1930 its population contained considerably more Italians, and more eastern European Jews, than either Irish or German immigrants and their children. When the 1980 census asked Americans to describe their own ancestry, easterners were about twice as likely as residents of other regions to say that their forebears had come from Italy, Portugal, Russia, Poland, or Hungary. They were significantly less likely to cite family ties to Scandinavia, and more likely to name Ireland or Wales than England.

In other respects, the East's population became more and more similar to that of the United States as a whole over the course of the twentieth century. The region had been home to a very small share of the nation's African American population in 1900: just 3 percent of the East's people, against the national average of 10 percent. Northward migration steadily raised this figure—to 4 percent in 1930, 7 percent in 1960—until it reached the national average of just over 11 percent in 1990. Hispanic migration, from Puerto Rico and other Caribbean locations far more than from Mexico or the American Southwest, also increased in the second half of the century, so that by 1990 the Hispanic share of the East's population was just under the national average of about 9 percent. The East's Asian population similarly grew to 2.6 percent, just under the national average of 2.9 percent, by 1990.

Eastern cultural traditions combined with economic interests to make the region solidly Republican in presidential elections in the first third of the twentieth century: leaving aside the three-cornered election of 1912, in which Theodore Roosevelt and William Howard Taft split the Republican vote, between 1900 and 1928 Democrats carried only New Hampshire in 1916 and Massachusetts and Rhode Island in 1928. In 1932 Hoover carried just six states, all of them in the East: Delaware, Pennsylvania, Connecticut, Vermont, New Hampshire, and Maine. All eastern states except Maine and Vermont joined the Roosevelt coalition, but all those that had gone for Hoover in 1932, plus New York and New Jersey, returned to the Republican fold in 1948 and remained there through the Eisenhower years.

Congregationalist Yankees, Scotch-Irish Presbyterians, German Protestants, dairy farmers, and, through the first third of the century, most of those engaged in the steel and most other manufacturing industries, tended strongly to vote for the party of the high tariff, Protestant respectability, the Civil War, and a kind of cosmopolitan support for economic opportunity: the Republican party. So, too, did many members of the Italian American and eastern European communities who had found Irish Americans already well-established in the Democratic parties of many eastern cities. In many small manufacturing cities where a few industries dominated by small, self-conscious local elites employed specialized, often skilled, labor forces, labor relations were necessarily intimate. There were bitter strikes after 1900 in the silk mills of Paterson, the textile mills of Lawrence, the coal towns of Pennsylvania. Often, however, factory owners persuaded their workers to support the political campaigns of Republican congressional and presidential candidates who promised to use high tariffs to protect American markets for American manufacturers—and to protect "American" wage levels.

Factory workers, members of most immigrant communities, and farmers moved heavily into the Democratic party after 1932 out of appreciation for Franklin D. Roosevelt's efforts to provide relief and social security, reform the financial markets, open opportunities to many immigrants and some African Americans, and encourage unions. Postwar prosperity enabled vast numbers to move to the new suburbs that grew up around New York, Philadelphia, Baltimore and other cities, however, and new concerns about taxes and about the Soviet Union's domination of Poland, Hungary, and other parts of eastern Europe helped the Republican party regain its eastern dominance in 1948 and to contribute important electoral votes for Eisenhower in 1952 and 1956. Republicans appealed more successfully to workers in the skilled, craft- or trades-union tradition that remained very influential in the East, than to workers organized by the industrial unions that dominated the Midwest's steel and automobile industries from Pittsburgh to Milwaukee.

Despite the influence of suburbanization and prosperity, the eastern states have, since 1960, given Democratic presidential candidates a significant share of their votes, even in years when Republicans have carried the nation. Massachusetts and Rhode Island have been almost "safely" Democratic, with New York close behind. A sort of "Eastern Liberalism" came to be associated with the region and particularly with the residents of Megalopolis, as such diverse senators as Democrats Robert and Edward Kennedy, Claiborne Pell, Daniel Patrick Moynihan, and Bill Bradley—and often such Republicans as Ed Brooke, Lowell Weicker, Jacob Javits, Richard Schweiker, and Arlen Specter—urged an active federal government role in the economy, in social welfare, in education, and even in the arts, while also pressing for government protection of the rights of racial and religious minorities and of women. Liberalism of this kind appealed to several groups that were increasingly well represented in Megalopolis, including unionized government workers, teachers, and health workers, as well as members of racial and religious minorities.

Meanwhile, many cultural issues that had long divided the region into distinct parts faded from memory. Books and movies were no longer frequently "banned in Boston"; it became possible to purchase birth control information and materials in Connecticut; New Jersey abandoned its longstanding prohibition of the dissection of cadavers, allowing Rutgers University to develop the state's first medical school. Part of this convergence among eastern subregions was due to the federalization of much health and cultural policy in the wake of the creation of Medicare, Medicaid, the National Endowment for the Humanities, and the National Endowment for the Arts in the late 1960s. But an important part was due to the economic and social convergence indicated by the rise of Megalopolis, and to the prominence of new African American, Hispanic, and Asian cultural groups, whose presence made old divisions between white Protestants and Catholics—let alone between Yankee Congregationalists and Scotch-Irish Presbyterians—pale by comparison.

For a few years in the mid-1970s some eastern political leaders thought they perceived a clear difference between the national policy interests of the East (and Midwest) and those of the sunbelt states of the South and West. Federal energy policy, they argued, forced Easterners to pay more for oil and gas than necessary, shifting wealth to the South and West. Federal defense policy had placed disproportionately large numbers of military bases and defense plants in southern and western states. And federal education and welfare policies tended to shift some resources from the wealthier eastern and midwestern states to the poorer states of the Southeast, the southern plains, and the Rocky Mountains.

While there was some truth to these generalizations about conflicting regional economic interests, they proved on closer examination to cover many variations and exceptions. It turned out that many eastern and midwestern manufacturers benefited a great deal from their subcontracts with western prime contractors for aircraft and other weapons systems: indeed, in many cases the profits went to the subcontractors. Poor counties both within Megalopolis and outside it benefited from federal education and welfare expenditures, and many northern and oceanside counties competed successfully with Florida for retirees, thus keeping their social security income and their Medicare funds within the region. As the coordinator of much of the nation's economic activity, the East also stood to gain from prosperity in any part of the nation. And when international forces drove oil and gas prices sharply down during the 1980s, a new arms build-up brought prosperity to the high-tech corporations of New England. By the mid-1980s, arguments that the East and the Midwest should mount a comprehensive challenge to the regional economic implications of federal policy all but evaporated. It was not at all clear that federal economic policy uniformly disadvantaged the East. And in any case, Presidents Reagan and Bush worked (however inconsistently) to reduce the federal economic role rather than to direct it to one or another purpose—or region. Notably, with the exception of Rhode Island in 1980 and 1988 and of Massachusetts and New York in 1988, the East joined heartily in the massive Republican presidential majorities of the 1980s. Then in 1992 eastern states gave Bill Clinton pluralities that were only slightly larger than those he received in the Midwest and the Pacific Coast.

PRIVATE INSTITUTIONS

Through the first half of the twentieth century its many great private institutions gave a certain credibility to the notion that "the East" aspired to control the United States as a whole: by the 1970s, however, such institutions were more evenly distributed throughout the nation. New York City has been, as Kenneth Jackson remarked, the "capital of capitalism," the locus of the great markets identified with Wall Street, Madison Avenue, Fifth Avenue and Seventh Avenue, Forty-Seventh Street, Broadway, Tin Pan Alley, Times Square, and Greenwich Village, and home of the national market-making publications in finance and investment *(Wall Street Journal),* advertising *(Advertising Age),* fashion *(Vogue),* clothing *(Women's Wear Daily),* publishing *(Publishers Weekly),* popular culture *(Variety),* and counterculture *(Village Voice).* The East as a whole supported New York's dominant role in business. It has also been distinguished, nationally, for its support of private, nonprofit educational and cultural institutions.

From Andrew Jackson's destruction of the national bank (headquartered in Philadelphia) in the early 1830s to the Great Crash of 1929, the so-called Clearing House Banks of New York City (institutionalized, after 1914, in the New York branch of the Federal Reserve) served as central bank to the United States. "City" and "country" banks alike in other cities had to maintain accounts with the clearing house banks to enable their own depositors to buy and sell in national and international markets. These banks, the New York Stock Exchange, and many related institutions have sustained New York City's role as the great money market of the United States. Boston's State Street banks and trust companies, Hartford and Newark's insurance companies, Philadelphia's investment banks, and New Jersey and Delaware's hospitality to holding companies have further reinforced the East's role as the directing center of the nation's economy. And although the Wall Street lawyer surpassed the Philadelphia lawyer in fame after 1900, the legal communities of both cities have included many graduates of the law schools at Harvard and Yale as well as Columbia and the University of Pennsylvania.

New York City has also been the nation's journalistic center throughout the century, housing newspapers from the *World* to the *Herald Tribune* to the *Nation* to the *New York Times*, as well as the Associated Press and other news services, news and general magazines from *Time* and *Newsweek* to *Reader's Digest,* and the headquarters of the national radio, television, and cable TV systems. New York City's rough-and-tumble publishing market long found a certain degree of support in the more literary publishing houses and periodicals of Boston (home of *Atlantic Monthly*) and in Curtis and other conservative publishing companies of Philadelphia. Similarly, through the first two-thirds of the twentieth century theatrical shows "tried out" in Boston, Hartford, New Haven, and Philadelphia, passed the critical market test on Broadway, then turned into "road shows" to tour through the Midwest, the South, and the West. The production (though not the financial) side of the movie industry had moved from New York to Hollywood by the late 1920s, and after about 1970 theatrical initiative diffused away from New York, as much entertainment television also moved to Southern California, and as new "regional" theaters in Chicago, Los Angeles, Minneapolis, and other cities as well as in New Haven, Brooklyn, and Philadelphia, provided new places to try new shows. In "public" as in commercial television, however, New York's and Boston's broadcasting stations and independent production companies continued to give the East the leading national role.

Its wealth, corporate traditions, and religious diversity combined to make the twentieth-century East home to the nation's largest cluster of cultural institutions, nearly all of which are organized as private nonprofit corporations. The powerful "benevolent empire" of Protestant evangelical institutions long based in New York, Connecticut, Princeton, and Philadelphia was fading by the end of the nineteenth century, although the national headquarters of several mainline Protestant denominations stayed on. But many of their more secular twentieth-century successors also located in the East. Foundations have concentrated in New York from the beginning of the twentieth century, among them the Carnegie Corporation (1911), the Rockefeller (1913), Ford (from 1953), Andrew W. Mellon (1969), and other large foundations, and the Foundation Center (begun by the Russell Sage Foundation, 1907, independent from 1950). Altogether, in 1992 ten of the nation's twenty-five largest private foundations were still located in New York City, five in the Philadelphia-Wilmington-Princeton area, and one in Greenwich, Connecticut. New York was also home to the National Council of Churches, Freedom House, the American Civil Liberties Union, and similar organizations.

The East also holds the largest group of private schools, colleges, and universities that have successfully sought to play national roles even as they moved away from their own once-strong Protestant origins. Most Ivy League universities and "Little Ivy" colleges (Amherst, Bowdoin, Hamilton, Haverford, Swarthmore, Williams, etc.) proudly trace their origins to the colonial period or the early nineteenth century, while most of the colleges for women (Barnard, Bryn Mawr, Pembroke, Radcliffe, Smith, Vassar, Wells, Wellesley, etc.) date from the mid- or late nineteenth century. Although they retain important ties to nearby areas, as a group these private universities and colleges have sought to play a role in the training of the nation's educated elite not unlike the role played by Oxford and Cambridge in Great Britain, or by the University of Paris in France; and for many southern and western students they have provided, throughout the twentieth century, an education "back east" of an intellectual and social quality not to be duplicated anywhere else in the United States. In turn, most midwestern and western cities have long supported such institutions as Harvard and Princeton university clubs, and Williams and Smith college scholarship funds. By the last third of the twentieth century, however, these cities were also supporting comparable private universities and colleges in their own regions (Chicago, Northwestern, Stanford, Cal Tech, Duke, Vanderbilt, Washington University, Emory, Rice, Case Western Reserve, Notre Dame, Oberlin, Kenyon, Carleton, Macalester, Grinnell, Reed, Pomona, Scripps, and many other colleges).

Most of the eastern institutions derived from Protestant origins, but over the course of the twentieth century Catholic and Jewish institutions also developed strong eastern clusters. Nearly all of the nation's major Jewish institutions have been created in the twentieth century and are headquartered in New York City, including the Jewish Theological Seminary (leader of the Conservative movement in religious practice, 1901), Yeshiva University (origins in 1897 as an Orthodox seminary, expanded into a distinguished comprehensive university under Orthodox leadership), and the Council of Jewish Federations and Welfare Funds (1932). Supporting these New York organizations were such other key institutions as the Jewish Publication Society of America (1888) in Philadelphia and Brandeis University (1948) in Waltham, Massachusetts. Catholic institutions are less concentrated in New York or even in the East as a whole. But Boston College, Newton College of the Sacred Heart, Fordham, St. John's, Manhattanville, Villanova, and many other Catholic colleges, together with numerous and distinguished Catholic elementary and secondary schools, seminaries, and many leading Catholic hospitals and welfare institutions, strongly reinforce the East's role as a national center of private educational and cultural institutions.

The elitist reputation of most eastern institutions was tempered in the twentieth century by their increasing religious and ethnic diversity and large financial-aid budgets, as well as by the fact that the East also produced, in the Boston Public Library, the (twentieth-century) New York Public Library, a cluster of famous libraries in Philadelphia, and the many library-building grants of Andrew Carnegie (most of which were made from New York City after 1900), a deeply influential national model for free and open access to learning. Private engineering schools and research universities that cater largely to residents of their own area are not quite so characteristically eastern as the Ivy League institutions, but they have provided national models and been prominent in the region throughout the twentieth century. The Massachusetts Institute of Technology traces its beginnings to the years after the Civil War, but it, like Worcester Polytechnic Institute, Rensselaer Polytechnic Institute in Troy, New York, the Cornell University College of Engineering, Rochester Institute of Technology, the Cooper Union in New York City, Brooklyn Polytechnic Institute, Stevens Institute of Technology in Hoboken, Drexel Institute of Technology in Philadelphia, and the engineering school of Lehigh University, flourished in the twentieth century. Private research universities such as The Johns Hopkins University in Baltimore, Clark and Boston universities in Massachusetts, New York University, Syracuse University, and the University of Rochester also set national standards in the twentieth century. Until the 1960s the East also differed from other regions of the United States in the modesty of its support for state colleges and universities. In this as in other respects the East converged with the other regions of the United States during the 1970s and 1980s, as state governments developed new institutions and assumed financial responsibility for the City University of New York and several private- or city-sponsored institutions in New York, Massachusetts, New Jersey, and Pennsylvania, and built Rutgers and the University of Maryland into major state universities.

Changing patterns of government support have not eroded the East's prominence as the locus of the largest and best-established cluster of private arts organizations in the United States. In music, the New York Philharmonic (dating from 1842), the Metropolitan Opera (1883), and Carnegie Hall (1891) are operated as private nonprofit institutions, as are the Boston Symphony Orchestra (1881), the Philadelphia Orchestra (1900), the orchestras of Pittsburgh and Baltimore, and the Juilliard School, the Curtis Institute, the New England Conservatory, Rochester's Eastman School, and Baltimore's Peabody Conservatory. New York City is far and away the national center for dance. New York City's international art market is complemented by the Metropolitan Museum of Art (1870), Brooklyn Museum (1897), Museum of Modern Art (1929), Morgan Library (1928), Whitney Museum (1931), Frick Collection (1935), and Guggenheim Museum (1959)—and by the great collections of Boston's Museum of Fine Arts (1870), the Philadelphia Museum of Art (1875–1876), and Walters Art Gallery in Baltimore (1931), as well as by the distinguished smaller collections of such institutions as the Isabella Stewart Gardner Museum in Boston, the Wadsworth Atheneum in Hartford, the Clark Museum in Williamstown, the Barnes Collection outside Philadelphia, Winterthur near Baltimore, the Albright-Knox Gallery in Buffalo, the Carnegie Institution in Pittsburgh, and the museums attached to Harvard, Yale, Princeton, and other colleges. Apart from the national museums in Washington, other regions of the United States have been converging with the East by developing their own private institutions for classical music (notably the Cleveland Orchestra, the Chicago Symphony, the Lyric Opera of Chicago, the Houston Grand Opera, the San Francisco and Seattle operas) and the fine arts (the Cleveland Museum of Art, the Art Institute of Chicago, the High Museum of Art in Atlanta, the de Menil Museum in Houston, the Kimball Museum in Fort Worth, the Los Angeles County and Getty Museums in Los Angeles), just as they have also been developing their own private foundations, universities, and religious and welfare agencies.

IMAGES OF "THE EAST": LITERATURE, FILM, LANDSCAPE, ARCHITECTURE

Although it is possible to describe the East as an increasingly unified region whose national economic and cultural dominance began to recede in the last third of the twentieth century, the region has never had a unified self-consciousness and has never been perceived as a unified whole. Is there any such thing as a literature of "the East"? Many twentieth-century writers have offered brilliantly perceptive accounts (if we grant, contrary to some literary theorists, that fictions may have some relation to real places and times) of some of its parts or aspects, and even of connections and conflicts among several of its parts: but there is no easily defined "Eastern school." Cultural historians have written of *The Flowering of New England* (Van Wyck Brooks), of *The Problem of Boston* (Martin Green), of *New York Intellect* (Thomas Bender), of *Philadelphia: Patricians and Philistines, 1900–1950* (John Lukacs), and of *Puritan Boston and Quaker Philadelphia* (E. Digby Baltzell) in efforts to define the peculiarities of distinct parts of the East but there has been no comparable effort to treat the entire East as a single literary unit.

Early in the twentieth century a few great writers did deal ambitiously with large portions of the East. The fact that Mark Twain lived in Connecticut for many years did not make him an "eastern" writer, even though his essays in literary criticism belong at the center of the American literary tradition. William Dean Howells moved from Boston to New York just before the turn of the century and for twenty years wrote expansively of the contrasting literary life of the two places. Edith Wharton wrote brilliantly of the sinister impact on women of the manners and mores of upper-class New York, Connecticut, and Newport—and of impoverished rural northern New England—during the same period. The heroine of Theodore Dreiser's *Sister Carrie* moved from Wisconsin to Chicago but achieved her great success in New York, where Dreiser wrote the classic sketches included in *The Color of a Great City. The Autobiography of Lincoln Steffens,* which has many of the qualities of fiction, is in large part the tale of a California boy's journey to the center of things in Greenwich Village and Hastings-on-Hudson. Such diverse books as Jacob Riis's *The Making of an American,* the autobiographical *Americanization of Edward Bok,* Mary Antin's *The Promised Land,* and Abraham Cahan's fictional *Rise of David Levinsky* all relate encounters of literate European immigrants with eastern cities and suburbs.

Writing in the next generation, F. Scott Fitzgerald described a midwesterner's encounter with the American Dream at Princeton and on Long Island in more than one story, while John Dos Passos sought in *Manhattan Transfer* to cut through many of the social layers that unite and divide New York and its suburbs. Slightly later again, Edmund Wilson's *Memoirs of Hecate County* reflected his own exploration of exclusive suburbs, New York's literary magazines and socialist downtown districts, and the Hudson River Valley, just as Mary McCarthy's *The Group* chronicled the lives of several friends who moved (as she had done) from the West to an eastern women's college to New York City and its suburbs.

Easterners who began life closer to the center of the great cities have also produced a series of major fictions. Alfred Kazin's *Walker in the City* recounted a Jewish boy's encounter with neighborhoods farther and farther from his home; in his essays even more vividly than in his novels James Baldwin took his African American protagonists from their Harlem homes to the difficult territory of New Jersey and Greenwich Village; and Frank O'Connor showed how Boston's ever-increasing social complexity finally defeated a tough Irish American politician in *The Last Hurrah.* Following the theme of encounter between a child of one eastern group and others in the region, Norman Mailer described his own arrival in bohemian Manhattan in *Advertisements for Myself;* Bernard Malamud invented, in *The Assistant,* a rapprochement between an Italian American clerk and the Jewish family that employed him; and Philip Roth, in *Goodbye Columbus,* sent a young Jewish explorer forth from Newark. In more recent years William Kennedy has shown how much of the modern world is reflected in Albany, and Tom Wolfe set *Bonfire of the Vanities,* with its striking images of class, race, and ethnic conflict and confusion, in the many parts of Greater New York.

Those whose work emphasizes a single group, however, are also important contributors to an eastern literature—if there is such a thing. Over the course of the twentieth century writers like John P. Marquand, James Gould Couzzens, and Louis Auchincloss chronicled the efforts of the "Protestant Establishment" to come to grips with the increasingly diverse reality of Boston, New York, and Philadelphia. For writers out of the immigrant experience, it was often the Protestants who seemed diverse and strange, as in *The Rise of David Levinsky, Call It Sleep, A Tree Grows in Brooklyn,* and *Christ in Concrete.* New York in particular is the classic setting for fiction reflecting the Jewish experience in the United States, for central images of African American life from the many authors of the Harlem Renaissance in the 1920s to Ralph Ellison's *Invisible Man* and James Baldwin's *Another Country,* and for the Italian American experience as recorded by Mario Puzo and others. Most recently, New York and other cities of the East have provided the essential settings for a new fiction of independent women by such writers as Tama Janowitz, Laurie Colwin, and Susan Isaacs. Meanwhile, still another identifiable group of writers has portrayed as increasingly alienated and anxious the life of the formerly Protestant outer suburbs and countryside from Pennsylvania to New Hampshire: John Cheever, John O'Hara, Rosellen Brown, John Updike. To judge from celebrated contemporary novels and memoirs, eastern cities and colleges were playing less dominant roles—and attracting smaller shares of those with literary ambitions—by the 1980s.

A similar shift occurred in the portrayal of the East in film. In the first third of the twentieth century, American films portrayed the East, not as a unified region like the plantation or Civil War–ravaged South or the frontier West, but as the national center of entertainment, fashion, publishing, money, urban diversity, and class and ethnic conflict. Among the films that successfully sought large national audiences in the 1920s and 1930s, many were set in New York and its suburbs, along with a few set in Philadelphia and Boston. Their titles illustrate the point: *Lights of New York, Royal Family of Broadway, Forty-Second Street, The Front Page.* The movies are necessarily as conservative as popular taste, and the same themes appear in popular movies of more recent times: show business *(A Chorus Line, Fame)*; money *(Wall Street, Working Girl)*; conflict over ethnicity, race, gender, and class *(On The Waterfront, The Apartment, Rocky, Coming to America, Tootsie, Pink Flamingos).* The greater boldness of the 1970s and 1980s, however, opened the way for some especially harsh films about conflict, crime, and terror in New York and other eastern locales: *Klute, The French Connection, Fort Apache, the Bronx, The Godfather, Goodfellas, New Jack City, Dog Day Afternoon, Three Days of the Condor, Midnight Cowboy.* Collectively, these films surely made eastern cities appear more dangerous, less glamorous and attractive than their counterparts of the twenties and thirties. Many of these films also narrowed their focus—and thus the sense of eastern possibilities—in a way suggested by the contrast between *King Kong* and *Manhattan,* both of which presented classic images of the East as the locus of the big city in America.

Many of the most influential images of any region are those of landscape, perhaps especially the man-made landscape. The movies have reinforced popular perceptions of the East as urban, diverse, commercial, and conflict-ridden. Related images have also been conveyed, throughout the twentieth century, by widely reprinted photographs of the New York City skyline, of the New York and Boston harbors, of great bridges at Philadelphia, New York and Brooklyn, and

The image of the eastern city. The tip of Manhattan around 1915. The Woolworth Building is the tall building to the right; the Brooklyn Bridge is in the foreground. PRINTS AND PHOTOGRAPHS DIVISION, LIBRARY OF CONGRESS

Boston, of the Statue of Liberty and the immigrants flowing through Ellis Island, and of St. Patrick's and the other great Catholic churches that rose in New York and other eastern cities from the middle of the nineteenth century on.

The East (like the midwestern industrial belt that runs along the Great Lakes) was also represented to many Americans, through the first two-thirds of the twentieth century, by innumerable black-and-white photographs of railroad and rapid transit facilities. Just as New York City's Ashcan School of painting replaced the bucolic nineteenth-century Hudson River school at the turn of the century, these railroad images defined an East of tracks, smoking locomotives, suburban stations, city terminals, and sprawling railway yards from the timber country of Maine and New Hampshire to Boston's South Station and New York's Grand Central Terminal and Pennsylvania Station and its elevated railways and subways, through the massed railyards of Newark, Hoboken, and Jersey City to Philadelphia, up the New York Central line to Albany and Buffalo and out the Main Line of the Pennsylvania Railroad toward Harrisburg and the West. Eastern highway engineers pioneered the twentieth-century superhighway as they built the Pennsylvania Turnpike, New Jersey's Garden State Parkway, and the parkways that lead from New York City to the Hudson Valley and Connecticut (although the region is better known west of the Appalachians for the fact that so many of its superhighways are toll roads rather than freeways).

In an explicit effort to counter all these images of modernity and capitalism, influential schools of landscape architecture and historic preservation

The image of eastern city. The tip of Manhattan, 1990. ARCHIVE PHOTOS

sought, beginning in the late nineteenth century but with more and more effectiveness in the twentieth, to create impressions of tradition, order, and stability. These schools were not confined to the East, but their works are especially thick on the ground there, in part because they could build on the long-established districts of rural estates where large houses were set on carefully designed, "natural"-looking lawns and in artfully tended groves of trees, as on the North Shore of Massachusetts, around Narragansett Bay in Rhode Island, on Long Island's North Shore, along the Connecticut and Massachusetts borders with New York, in Westchester County and up the Hudson Valley, and in the Pennsylvania and New Jersey counties west and north of Philadelphia.

Throughout the East, landscape architects and historical preservationists recalled images from the colonial, revolutionary, and early national eras that differ from those evoked by Colonial Williamsburg and the great plantation houses and town squares of the South in that they are free of the disturbing overlay of slavery and the Civil War. In New England these included the structures of Boston's "Freedom Trail"—Paul Revere's house, Faneuil Hall, the Old North Church—as well as Concord and Lexington (valued for their elm- or maple-shaded village greens and white-steepled churches as well as for their associations with the Minute Men). In college towns from Maine to Maryland eighteenth-century college buildings set in grassy grounds are designed to recall a tranquil past—and many more of the impressive "Georgian" buildings of eastern colleges date from the 1920s than from the entire eighteenth century. New York City's Castle Clinton (an 1807 fort at Manhattan's tip) and Trinity Church (1841–1846) date from the era they celebrate, but Fraunces Tavern (1907) and Federal Hall on Wall Street (various dates through 1925) were reconstructed or remodeled in the twentieth century to commemorate the presence of George Washington and to celebrate a set of values that could be attributed to the Revolution. Philadelphia is perhaps richest of all in buildings of this sort, with Independence Hall, Congress Hall—which were repackaged as Independence National Historical Park by the National Park Service in the 1950s—as well as the "Betsy Ross House," the Friends Meeting House, and other structures.

Like historic buildings, village museums are not unique to the East, but several of them convey distinctively eastern images: the Wayside Inn with its associated old mills and shops, set in expansive grounds purchased and restored by Henry Ford in Sudbury, Massachusetts, during the 1920s; Old Sturbridge Village, Massachusetts; Mystic Seaport, in Connecticut; and the Farmers' Museum at Cooperstown, New York. Unlike the shrines of the Revolution, these villages eschewed explicit politics, but they nonetheless advanced political messages through the display of what their sponsors presented as the wholesome work-disciplines of an earlier age.

"Historic" eighteenth- and nineteenth-century buildings and museum villages have provided many twentieth-century tourists with carefully constructed images of an eastern past. They also (like the *Saturday Evening Post* and *Ladies Home Journal,* which were produced in Philadelphia for most of the twentieth century) reflected and helped popularize a taste for "colonial" and Georgian design. Georgian (along with Dutch colonial and Tudor) taste muted the influence of the Beaux Arts style developed in France from classical and renaissance precedents—an influence that in the 1890s had led New York City builders to reject the Romanesque revival and the shingle style, the arts and crafts movement, and Chicago's Louis Sullivan in favor of neoclassical columns and pediments. By the early 1920s public buildings in Boston, Providence, Philadelphia, Wilmington, and Baltimore, as well as houses and shopfronts throughout the East (and indeed in much of the Midwest as well) were sporting red brick, tudor-stone, or half-timbered and high gabled facades. This taste no doubt served a widespread desire to affirm colonial origins in the face of massive immigration from the Continent (as well as an Anglophilia appropriate to an era of world wars with British allies against Germany and Austria)—and no doubt it also appealed to many newcomers eager to fit in.

By the last third of the century, however, eastern clients were quite willing to employ modern architects for expensive houses and college buildings as well as for center-city office towers, and new buildings in the East quickly became identical to new buildings anywhere else in the United States—similar indeed to new buildings anywhere in the world. At the same time, the new fashion for authenticity, and the new assertiveness of the socially or economically disadvantaged, brought challenges to the sanitized images of the past conveyed by the original museum villages. Newer facilities—notably New Hampshire's Strawberry Bank, Plimoth Plantation, the Lowell Historic District, and Hancock Shaker Village in Massachusetts, the redeveloped Brooklyn Historical Society, the Strong Museum in Rochester, Delaware's Hagley Museum—presented more complex, diverse, and accurate images of the past, as did newer exhibits in some of the older facilities. One challenge facing the creators of historical exhibits in the 1990s was the development of effective images of the nineteenth- and early-twentieth-century experiences of immigration, industrialization, and life in African American and Hispanic communities. In all these

The image of New England. East Corinth, Vermont. ARCHIVE PHOTOS/AMERICAN STOCK

respects, however, the late-twentieth-century East was converging with the United States as a whole.

THE END OF REGIONAL DIFFERENCE?

Regional variations of almost every kind were fading rapidly away by the end of the twentieth century. As federal policy eclipsed state and local autonomy in more and more fields after 1936 and again after 1964, regional variations in government services, regulations, and taxes grew less significant. As the mass media embraced national chains of newspapers and national magazines, radio, broadcast television, and then cable television, regional variations in access to political and economic news, to fashion, and to entertainment disappeared. And as the cost of transport declined even more rapidly in the age of automobiles, trucks, container ships, and aircraft than it had in the age of steamships and railroads, regional propinquity affected fewer and fewer decisions about the location of economic activities.

Early in the twentieth century only the East, the Midwest, and California sported fully developed metropolitan regions with a complete array of occupations and of public and private institutions. Only in the metropolitan regions was it possible to find money-center banks, specialized shops of every kind, and large art museums. Ambitious doctors from all over the nation sought residencies available only in the great teaching hospitals in Boston, New Haven, New York, Philadelphia, Baltimore, Pittsburgh, and just a few places in the Midwest and West: Cleveland, Ann Arbor, Chicago, and San Francisco. Major league baseball was played only in the metropolitan regions of the East and the Midwest.

By the last third of the twentieth century, over 80 percent of the U.S. population lived in metropolitan regions that dominated every region. Los Angeles, Dallas, Atlanta, and Miami had joined Chicago, Philadelphia, Boston, and New York as major financial and wholesale centers (although Manhattan continued to dominate international financial relations, generating, for example, well over a majority of the nation's overseas telephone calls through a state-of-the-art fiber-optic telephone system installed in the 1970s, long before other regions had anything like it). Nearly every metropolitan region developed a major medical center (notable postwar examples included the Texas Medical Center in Houston and the federal Centers for Disease Control in Atlanta) and one or more major research universities. Los Angeles gave New York a serious challenge for the prominence of its market for film, television, and popular music. Federal government agencies in Washington, D.C., challenged and even displaced private financial and cultural institutions in New York, Boston, Philadelphia, and Chicago (as well as state capitals throughout the nation) in economic and social decision making—and attracted literally hundreds of new national trade associations. Houston and Seattle developed major opera companies and many metropolitan regions developed first-rate orchestras and art museums. And every metropolitan region had to have at least one or two major league teams in baseball, football, or basketball.

These converging institutional patterns reflected the steady migration of occupational patterns and of income from one metropolitan area, and one region, to another. As late as 1940 it made some sense to speak of the South as agricultural; of the West as devoted to agriculture, mining, forestry, and tourism; and of the Midwest as the land of farms and factories. By the last decade of the twentieth century these differences had largely disappeared. Nationally only 2 or 3 percent of the population was engaged in agriculture, and a good deal of manufacturing had moved from the East and the Midwest to the South and the West—and abroad. Service industries gained prominence everywhere, and every region developed its own tourist trade. Similar work produced similar incomes across the country: whereas easterners had earned 30 or 35 percent more than the national average in 1900, they earned just about 15 percent more in 1990. Through most of the century higher incomes in the East and on the Pacific Coast attracted migrants away from the interior, from agriculture, and from abroad. By 1990, as a result, there was much less variation in the ethnic and racial make-up of the population from one region to another.

Early in the twentieth century the regions of the United States had differed widely in economic activity, occupational mix, income, racial and ethnic make-up, and political inclination. By the 1990s they had become remarkably similar in all these respects. Now, similar economic and social differences could be found within each region—and within each of the large metropolitan areas that together housed well over three-quarters of each region's people. Every metropolitan area had its own prominent financial and cultural institutions. Every metropolitan area was also profoundly, and increasingly, segregated along lines of race, lifestyle, and most of all, along lines of income. The East had pioneered many of these patterns, but by the end of the twentieth century, it was no longer unique.

BIBLIOGRAPHY

That students of social history, language, literature, art, music, and most other phenomena in the United States usually do not treat the "East" as a region is indicated by the brevity and heterogeneity of the works on the "Northeast" included in the bibliographic note provided by Howard W. Odum to his essay, "The Promise of Regionalism," ch. 15 of Merrill Jensen, ed., *Regionalism in America* (1951). Most of the works that Odum includes concern New England, individual states, or parts of states such as Cape Cod, the Berkshires, the Hudson Valley, the Finger Lakes, or the Susquehanna and Brandywine rivers.

One work that does treat the East as a meaningful cultural region is G. E. Kidder Smith's lively, selective, and stimulating *The Architecture of the United States,* vol. 1, *New England and the Mid-Atlantic States* (1981). William R. Taylor, ed., *Inventing Times Square: Commerce and Culture at the Crossroads of the World* (1991), provides a wide range of stimulating perspectives on the images of a key eastern place. The best overview of American landscape architecture, with many eastern examples, is still Norman T. Newton, *Design on the Land: The Development of Landscape Architecture* (1971). Michael Wallace's essays on history museums and historic preservation in Susan Porter Benson, Stephen Brier, and Roy Rosenzweig, eds., *Presenting the Past: Essays on History and the Public* (1986), are particularly stimulating; John R. Stilgoe's *Metropolitan Corridor: Railroads and the American Scene* (1983) provides a vivid description of the East's railroads.

Regionalism in America, like most treatments of regions in the United States, had little to say about cities, yet cities, suburbs, and urban regions have dominated the East over the entire course of the twentieth century. Jean Gottmann, *Megalopolis: The Urbanized Northeast Seaboard of the United States* (1961), offers a brilliant and comprehensive interpretation of the growth of the great unified urban region that stretches from northern Virginia to southern Maine and that has embraced the majority of the people who have lived in the East during the twentieth century. Also broadly useful are the volumes of the New York Metropolitan Region Study commissioned by the Regional Plan Association of New York and New Jersey summarized in Edgar M. Hoover and Raymond Vernon, *Anatomy of a Metropolis* (1959). On the suburbs, see Kenneth T. Jackson, *Crabgrass Frontier: The Suburbanization of the United States* (1985); and Robert Fishman, *Bourgeois Utopias: The Rise and Fall of Suburbia* (1987), which contains useful discussions of early eastern suburbs. Several historians have emphasized contrasts between major cities within the region: Frederic Cople Jaher, *The Urban Establishment: Upper Strata in Boston, New York, Charleston, Chicago, and Los Angeles* (1982); E. Digby Baltzell, *Puritan Boston and Quaker Philadelphia* (1979); David Ward, *Poverty, Ethnicity, and the American City, 1840–1925: Changing Conceptions of the Slum and the Ghetto* (1989); and David C. Hammack, *Power and Society: Greater New York at the Turn of the Century* (1982).

Relevant historical and social studies of individual metropolitan regions and cities include Charles H. Trout, *Boston: The Great Depression and the New Deal* (1977); Geoffrey Blodgett, *The Gentle Reformers: Massachusetts Democrats in the Cleveland Era* (1966); Ronald P. Formisano and Constance K. Burns, eds., *Boston 1700–1980: The Evolution of Urban Politics* (1984); J. Joseph Huthmacher, *Massachusetts People and Politics, 1919–1933* (1959); Irving Howe, *World of Our Fathers: The Journey of the East European Jews to America and the Life They Found and Made* (1976); Nathan Glazer and Daniel Patrick Moynihan, *Beyond the Melting Pot* (1963); Ronald H. Bayor, *Neighbors in Conflict: The Irish, Germans, Jews, and Italians of New York City, 1929–1941* (1978); Jervis Anderson, *This Was Harlem, 1900–1950* (1982); Jonathan Rieder, *Canarsie: The Jews and Italians of Brooklyn Against Liberalism* (1985); Sam Bass Warner, Jr., *The Private City: Philadelphia in Three Periods of Its Growth* (1968); Russell F. Weigley, ed., *Philadelphia: A 300-Year History* (1982); John Lukacs, *Philadelphia: Patricians and Philistines, 1900–1950* (1981); and Carol E. Hoffecker, *Corporate Capital: Wilmington in the Twentieth Century* (1983).

The relative decline in the Northeast and its increasing concern that federal policy and federal subsidies were giving unfair advantages to the Sunbelt produced a good deal of literature. Bernard L. Weinstein, Harold T. Gross, and John Rees, *Regional Growth and Decline in the United States* (1985), is a good example; it pulls together a good deal of economic and population data for the period between 1950 and 1980. Ann R. Markusen's *Regions: The Economics and Politics of Territory* (1987) provides an excellent review and critique of much of this literature and of the political organizations that sponsored much of it.

Kevin R. Phillips, *The Emerging Republican Major-*

ity (1969), provides an excellent discussion of the economic and social changes that lay behind the decline of the majorities enjoyed by Democrats in presidential elections from 1932 to 1964. Several state studies emphasize political and economic developments relevant to the region as a whole. Neal R. Peirce offers a journalist's valuable overview of the individual states in two works, *The Megastates of America* (1972), and *The New England States: People, Politics, and Power* (1976). W. W. Norton and the American Association for State and Local History published a "bicentennial history" for each state; although these volumes tend to slight twentieth-century developments, the volumes *Massachusetts,* by Richard D. Brown, *Rhode Island,* by William G. McLaughlin, and *Pennsylvania,* by Thomas C. Cochran (all published in 1978) were especially useful for this essay.

THE MIDWEST

James H. Madison

At the center of the nation—geographically, historically, culturally—the Midwest is the place where soap, Hollywood films, and presidential candidates must sell. Although some claim it is the most "American" of all regions, its very centrality leads to images of a blandness that includes "unaccented" English and middle-of-the-road politics. Yet the Midwest remains as distinctive at the end of the twentieth century as it had been at the end of the nineteenth century.

There is no clear delineation of where the Midwest actually lies on the map. The easiest definition is that of the Census Bureau, including the East North Central and West North Central states—Ohio, Michigan, Indiana, Illinois, Wisconsin, Minnesota, Iowa, Missouri, Kansas, Nebraska, North Dakota, and South Dakota. All manner of objections can be raised, particularly concerning the edges. Parts of Missouri, Indiana, and Illinois might seem more southern than midwestern, parts of Ohio more eastern. In some ways the Midwest extends northward into Canada. The fuzziest boundary is to the west, where Kansas, Nebraska, and the Dakotas, especially beyond the 98th or 100th meridians, might seem more western.

The Midwest is not uniform but changes over time and space. As one moves from Ohio toward Nebraska, for example, dependence on the federal government, average farm size, and church membership increase, rainfall and population density decline, railroad depots rather than courthouse squares sit at the center of towns, and more retired people spend winters in Arizona rather than Florida, though frequently with other midwesterners. As one moves from the Lower Midwest to the Upper Midwest, humidity decreases, winters extend into April, and politics become more progressive. In the end, the Census Bureau's definition of the twelve-state region is as useful as any.

Americans who do not know the region believe the Midwest is flat. To describe the region thus is usually to say it is boring, simplistic, monotone. This is the Midwest that in the late twentieth century became "flyover" country, depicted as the flat nothingness between the coasts in Saul Steinberg's 1976 *New Yorker* map. In fact, the Midwest is not flat, but is marked by great variation in landscape—with hills, vistas, valleys, Great Lakes, and powerful rivers—and by beautiful undulating fields of planted crops and natural prairies. The sweep of prairie and plain and the vastness of the region offer a perspective that makes "human beings appear as the little bugs they really are," painter Thomas Hart Benton claimed in his autobiography, and thereby had a "releasing effect" that made him want to jump for joy. Or as William Least Heat-Moon wrote in *PrairyErth,* (1991) "Whatever else prairie is—grass, sky, wind—it is most of all a paradigm of infinity, a clearing full of many things except boundaries, and its power comes from its apparent limitlessness."

The sense of openness and opportunity that marked the Midwest from its beginning was never absolute, of course. Natural forces always placed limits. The climate is one of extremes of heat and cold that even domed stadiums, skywalks, and indoor shopping malls cannot conquer. Often there is too little rain, especially on the plains of Kansas and Nebraska, and sometimes there is too much, with the region's major rivers—the Missouri, Mississippi, and Ohio—bringing devastating floods, as in 1913, 1937, and 1993. More than anywhere else on earth, there are disastrous tornadoes, as in the 1925 twister that killed 689 people in Missouri, Illinois, and Indiana.

Nonetheless it was opportunity that pulled hopeful pioneers into the region at the end of the eighteenth century, a migration that continued westward through the nineteenth. The pioneer came to be the Midwest's dominant cultural symbol, an important shared historical memory that shaped the region long after all useful land was settled. Whatever their actual history of success and failure, the pioneers by 1900

Map 2. The Midwest.

had become objects of veneration—people whose hard work, close-knit family attachments, individualism, and honest democracy made this region different from the East or South or Europe. Historian Frederick Jackson Turner gave these notions their scholarly base (to be challenged again and again, of course) but the Midwest's most important celebrants of pioneer democracy were ordinary people who held firm to this pastoral vision long after many scholars had filled it with holes. Twentieth-century state fairs celebrated pioneer days; libraries and historical societies collected relics and documents that told of hardship and achievement; courthouse and statehouse lawns featured statues not only of great men—military heroes, governors, and senators—but also of pioneer families. Even the Midwest's greatest national hero, Abraham Lincoln, was celebrated as representative of ordinary pioneer families and their values. "The sweat of the pioneer," one of Thomas Hart Benton's Indiana history murals proclaimed in 1933, "is salt in the bread we daily eat."

In the early decades of the twentieth century especially, the telling of the pioneer story, with its agrarian traditions and pastoral values, helped to create the Midwest and to make it America's heartland. The pioneer success story was central to this process because it helped transform "the West"—as the region beyond the Appalachians had been labeled—from the backward periphery of the nation into its center. It was important therefore that the pioneer

Balloon-frame house under construction. ARCHIVE PHOTOS/LAMBERT

story was told as a success story, of men and women who conquered the wilderness and the prairies and built a civilization that was politically democratic, economically abundant, and socially stable. It was a society that especially valued, to use Lewis Atherton's term, the "immediately useful and the practical." Its agrarian focus was on producing long rows of corn, fat livestock, and utilitarian goods—all of which the region did exceedingly well by 1900. Midwesterners also valued order, as in the square angles that marked the grid pattern of the landscape or the balloon frame houses that dotted the region. They celebrated rural communities and small towns that were intensely personal, places where even adults had nicknames and where houses were located by family names rather than by road or street addresses.

As powerful as these stories and images are, however, they do not account for the industrial and urban growth that transformed much of the Midwest, or the great diversity of midwesterners, ranging from grandchildren of African American slaves in Chicago, to German American toolmakers in Cincinnati and Jewish seamstresses in Indianapolis. Throughout the twentieth century midwesterners have struggled to reconcile the classic version of their heritage, represented by the white pioneer family bound toward middle-class security, with the reality of racial and ethnic diversity and an increasingly urban and industrial environment. The tension between the two has been fundamental to the history of the last one hundred years, prompting some to redraw the region's boundaries to preserve the classic agrarian, pioneer version, eliminating Detroit or the "Rust Belt" and centering the twentieth-century Midwest in Nebraska and Kansas. Perhaps the Midwest will find new ways of incorporating other aspects of its heritage into its image as the nation's heartland.

CONFIDENT YEARS, 1900–1920

The heart of the heartland in 1900 was the family farm. It was fundamental to the vitality and confidence that prevailed in the region during the first two decades of the century. Prosperous farms suggested that this was the land of milk and honey or, more correctly, corn and hogs. No other place in America, or perhaps even on the face of the earth, could claim such abundance from the soil over such vast distances.

The core of the abundance was corn and hogs, which had their Midwest origins in early-nineteenth-century Ohio and marched steadily westward

A family farm. Swedish farmer in Minnesota, March 1942. Photograph by Jack Delano, Office of War Information. PRINTS AND PHOTOGRAPHS DIVISION, LIBRARY OF CONGRESS

through Indiana and Illinois to Iowa and the eastern parts of Kansas and Nebraska but then halted in the face of inadequate rainfall on the Great Plains. The Corn Belt emerged on this rich, deep soil. Long, hot summers and periodic bursts of heavy rainfall made corn knee high by the Fourth of July. While corn was king in most of the early twentieth century Midwest, wheat was common throughout the region but increasingly on the Great Plains. In much of Kansas, Nebraska, and the Dakotas the droughts of the late 1880s and 1890s halted the westward march of corn and turned farmers to winter wheat.

In the northern parts of the Midwest, in Michigan, Wisconsin, and Minnesota, the advance of corn slowed because of short, cool summers rather than inadequate rainfall. Here mixed farming and especially dairy farming took shape. Even further north, in the forests of the Upper Great Lakes states, lumber operations cut and burned timber so as to leave behind cutover areas of little economic value. Efforts to settle and develop the cutover region brought only limited success.

On the southern edge of the Midwest, in the Ohio Valley, corn's days as king were fading. On hillier land a thinner, less fertile soil had washed and blown away during three or four generations of hard use. By the early twentieth century farmers in southern Ohio, Indiana, and Illinois struggled to produce yields that were competitive with their countrymen to the north and west. Many shifted to a more mixed agriculture, and some abandoned their farms for futures elsewhere.

In the Corn Belt especially, but throughout the Midwest, most farms were family farms. All able-bodied members contributed their labor, and most of the labor on most farms was performed by the family. It was their labor that not only produced the corn that fattened the hogs and the oats and hay that fueled the horses and dairy cattle, but also the eggs, poultry, milk, potatoes, beans, and jams that fed the family. There were few labor-saving devices, so that not only men, but also women and children learned the value of a strong back and a handkerchief to wipe the sweat of the brow.

While farm families produced most of what they needed they were not self-sufficient. Store purchases in town or from the Sears catalog were increasingly common. Nor were midwestern farmers removed from the sellers' market. From the early nineteenth century they had eagerly sought and generally obtained means to sell their surplus off the farm. Farming by 1900 was very much a business in most of the Midwest, but one mixed with family goals and with pastoral values that made it a way of life. In the years from the beginning of the century to 1920 it was a good business, as rising farm prices gave many families more income and opportunity than they had ever imagined in the hard years of the 1890s. For many midwesterners the first two decades of the twentieth century would become the golden age of agriculture.

One of the Midwest's greatest achievements was creating a dense transportation system that penetrated the region and linked it to the nation and the world. The disadvantages of an interior location and of huge geographic space quickly melted away. The river and lake system that had first served Indians and then early pioneers continued to provide efficient, cheap transportation, particularly of high-bulk cargo. On the Great Lakes in the first decades of the twentieth century a fleet of cargo ships moved millions of tons of iron ore, coal, and grain. And on the Mississippi River and its major tributaries, particularly the Ohio and Missouri rivers, barges moved similar cargoes.

Even more important than rivers was the network of rails that spread by 1900 like a spider web over the region. The primary rail center was Chicago, but nearly any city of importance owed its growth to the railroad. In addition to the steam railroad the Midwest profited from an electric interurban network that by the beginning of the twentieth century was the densest in the nation. Interurbans provided quick and inexpensive transportation for passengers and for light freight through much of the region. More than in the Northeast or South, the iron and steel rails made the Midwest what it was.

It was midwestern farmers who were the first major users of the region's transportation facilities. Huge quantities of corn, wheat, and hogs moved off the farm and to national and international markets. Chicago soon emerged as the center of much of this trade. The rails from Windy City grain elevators and stockyards penetrated far into Indiana, Illinois, Iowa, and beyond to gather the abundance of the Corn Belt and make the city the primary regional metropolis. Chicago's South Side stockyards sent out refrigerated cars of dressed beef and pork to dinner tables hundreds of miles away. The city's banking facilities and Board of Trade connected the region to the world economy.

As grain and livestock production increased west of Chicago, new meatpacking and grain centers developed in Kansas City, Omaha, and elsewhere. In the Upper Midwest the Twin Cities (Minneapolis–Saint Paul) became in the early twentieth century the major receivers of agriculture products, particularly the wheat from Minnesota and Dakota farms. Led by Pillsbury and General Mills, Minneapolis became the world's largest flour-manufacturing center.

The Midwest's transportation network was crucial also to the region's increasing industrial strength. Unlike agriculture, which extended from Ohio to Kansas, manufacturing concentrated in the eastern half of the Midwest, particularly in the rapidly growing cities of Ohio, Michigan, Indiana, Illinois, and Wisconsin. Here the Midwest confounded the more common pattern of world economic development in which a nation's coastal regions dominated as the most economically advanced while the interior regions lagged behind as the periphery or colony. Perhaps for the first time in the history of modern nation-states an interior region became in very short order the real core, the industrial heartland.

Production in this industrial heartland was exceedingly diverse, ranging from kitchen cabinets and bicycles to pharmaceuticals and steel. Within this diversity, however, the region developed a critically important strength in metals, machinery, and equipment, leading the nation in these areas by 1900. Heavy industry in which metals were manufactured or shaped would play a central role in the region's ups and downs through the twentieth century.

One of the most impressive examples of midwestern industrial might took form in 1906 on the windy sand dunes along Lake Michigan's southern shore. There United States Steel built the world's greatest steel plant in order to take advantage of Great Lakes' shipping, which provided cheap movement of high quality iron ore from Minnesota's Mesabi Range, and the railroad network, which moved coal from Appalachia. US Steel's Gary Works manufactured its first steel in 1909, using the most modern and efficient equipment and procedures imaginable. By 1910 the new mills employed over 4,000 workers. The numbers increased rapidly thereafter as Midwest farm boys, European immigrants, and African Americans from the South moved to the self-proclaimed "City of the Century."

The demand for steel multiplied rapidly as midwestern shops and factories produced all kinds of machines and equipment. The 1905 manufacturing census showed that the Midwest produced over half the nation's farm equipment, office machines, railway cars, and household appliances, including refrigerators and stoves. The important machines that made machines were increasingly concentrated in the re-

Steel mill in Gary, Indiana, 1952. PRINTS AND PHOTOGRAPHS DIVISION, LIBRARY OF CONGRESS

gion, particularly in Cincinnati, which led the nation in machine-tool production by 1910. The machine that more than any other made the Midwest the nation's industrial heartland, however, was the automobile.

Midwestern tinkerers in machine shops and wagon and bicycle shops quickly became enthralled with the gasoline engine. By the first decade of the century they were producing hundreds of kinds of automobiles, from Cleveland to South Bend to Kenosha. But it was Detroit that would become the auto capital. Numerous explanations have been offered for this concentration, ranging from the city's water access to coal and iron ore to more sympathetic midwestern bankers and a fortuitous gathering of talented mechanics and entrepreneurs.

The most remarkable of the group was Henry Ford, who in many ways was the Midwest's most representative success story. Born on a Michigan farm in 1863, Ford was one of those skilled mechanical men for whom work was play. His genius was expressed in 1908 with the first Model T. This simple black car captured the midwestern values of the immediately useful and practical. Farm boys could drive it hard over bumpy country roads and easily fix it. So could their mothers and sisters. Within two years the "Tin Lizzie" was the nation's best-selling car, recognized everywhere as the choice of the common person and the warm object of vaudeville jokes and folk stories.

Ford's challenge was to produce enough Model T's to meet demand. This he accomplished by introduction of the moving assembly line in 1913, drawing on many examples from elsewhere, including the Cincinnati and Chicago meat packers' disassembly lines. Mass manufacturing of autos immediately proved its value and quickly extended throughout the industry and beyond. It enabled Ford to reduce the price of his Model T's to $490 and in 1914 to startle the nation by paying his workers five dollars a day, twice the going wage in Detroit. By 1920 three-fifths of all automobiles in the country were Model T's. The success of Henry Ford and his car molded a loyalty and mentality that would endure for decades in the minds of midwestern farmers, businessmen, and auto workers. All believed in salvation by the automobile via Henry Ford.

By 1920 two fundamental features of twentieth-century auto manufacturing were apparent. One was oligopoly. Although more than one hundred auto companies were counted in the 1919 manufacturing census, the way was clear for the emergence during the 1920s of the Big Three—Ford, General Motors, and Chrysler. Other companies continued, including Studebaker, which endured until 1963, but the dominance of a handful of mass production, large-scale organizations was the central feature of the American automobile industry.

A second basic feature was midwestern location. By 1920 the five states of Ohio, Michigan, Indiana, Wisconsin, and Illinois accounted for 79 percent of the nation's auto workers and 81 percent of the value added in auto manufacturing. Detroit was clearly the regional and national capital, but there were many other auto towns scattered across the Midwest. They grew rapidly in the early twentieth century. Flint's Buick and Chevrolet plants, for example, caused the town's population to increase from 13,000 in 1900 to 92,000 in 1920. Many towns grew because they became suppliers to the auto industry. Akron, Ohio, was home to the three largest tire manufacturers; Toledo became a major auto glass maker; Dayton an electrical components manufacturer. All cast their fate with Detroit. Into these booming auto towns poured newcomers seeking jobs in the glamorous auto industry—immigrants from Poland who made up one-third of Hamtramck's population by 1920; Appalachian farmers and miners who constituted large proportions of the work force in Akron's tire factories; and large numbers of rural, southern blacks seeking any kind of job in the industrial heartland.

Not every midwestern place became an auto town. Large cities, most notably Chicago and Saint Louis, avoided dependence on the auto and remained diverse in their manufacturing mix. Smaller urban places such as Indianapolis and Columbus also continued with a mixture of enterprises. Nonetheless, the auto industry dominated many communities by the end of World War I, a situation that would only increase thereafter.

No visitor to the Midwest could doubt the region's productivity: from Henry Ford's assembly lines and Chicago's stockyards to Iowa's corn fields and the wheat fields of the Red River Valley material prosperity was the region's clear message. To many midwesterners the dreams of the founding generation of pioneers seemed realized. The booming confidence of the first two decades of the twentieth century suggested that the Midwest was no longer on the periphery of the nation. Carl Sandburg's 1916 poem celebrated Chicago and caught a vitality that extended through the Midwest:

> Laughing the stormy, husky, brawling laughter of
> Youth, half-naked, sweating, proud to be Hog
> Butcher, Tool Maker, Stacker of Wheat, Player
> with Railroads and Freight-handler to the
> Nation.

The Midwest's sense of achievement and confidence was especially evident in its towns and cities. Bustling downtowns showcased their material prosperity in grand department stores and office buildings. No city in America matched Chicago in architecture or planning. Its commercial buildings rose magnificently from the downtown Loop, which from the 1880s onward became America's showcase for skyscraper architecture. And its business and civic leaders united to bring order and beauty to the city on the lake. Chicago's chief planner, Daniel Burnham, set out in 1909 a system of parks, green spaces, forest preserves, boulevards, and highways intended to create an enduring dream city. Never fully realized, the Burnham plan nonetheless suggested the vitality and vision that suffused heartland cities. St. Louis followed its Louisiana Purchase Exposition of 1904 with park, street, and riverfront improvements. Detroit, Milwaukee, Columbus, and others created plans to bring order and beauty to cities that had changed rapidly in the late nineteenth century and that now had sufficient civic pride and business sense to want to show the world their new prosperity.

Residential neighborhoods also displayed the region's prosperity, comfort, and confidence. Although the smoke, smell, and noise of nearby stockyards, factories, and railroad yards might assault the downtown visitor, every city provided easy access to quieter, middle-class and upper-class suburbs. Each had its fancy street—Prospect Avenue in Milwaukee, East Broad Street in Columbus, Euclid Avenue in Cleveland. Even in neighborhoods closer to the downtown or factory areas there were often comfortable single-family homes. Indeed, more than any other region of the country the twentieth-century Midwest was a place of single-family homes rather than apartment or tenement houses. And a larger proportion of midwestern city dwellers, of all classes, owned their homes than in other regions.

Most midwestern city families lived in simple cottages, but a growing number showcased their new prosperity in grander houses, usually designed from European models imported via the East Coast. With Frank Lloyd Wright and his Prairie School, however, came a new regional architecture that expressed a distinctive vision of the Midwest. Wright and other Prairie School architects took their inspiration from the midwestern landscape. Their buildings were flat and horizontal with low, overhanging roofs, earth colors, and simple ornamentation. Prairie School advocates claimed that theirs was a new, more thoroughly American style, one more democratic, one that aggressively rejected imported and aristocratic styles derived from Gothic cathedrals, Tudor country homes, and French chateaus. Accompanying the new domestic architecture was an emerging school of Prairie Style landscape architects. Led by Jens Jensen, a Danish immigrant to Chicago, they urged abandonment of English and Italian gardens for native flora and more natural landscapes that incorporated horizontal forms and prairie grasses and flowers. Here too there was a conscious effort to combine democratic values and simple indigenous styles that expressed the vitality of the heartland. Although these Prairie styles were never widely adopted, they gave to the nation and the world a powerful and enduring expression of regional identity.

By the first decades of the century midwestern city-dwellers could also show their visitors all manner of cultural entertainment. Chicago's great cultural institutions were founded in the 1880s and early 1890s, mostly by the city's business elite, but they developed their full form in the 1900s and 1910s, particularly in their increased openness to modern forms of cultural expression and in their closer identification with the whole city, even its working-class residents. The Art Institute, the Chicago Symphony Orchestra, the Newberry Library, and the Field Museum of Natural History became jewels in the city's crown and began to draw visitors from across the Midwest. Saint Louis, Detroit, and Cleveland also offered museums, symphonies, libraries, and other institutions that proclaimed a new maturity.

Every city also had a sporting district or tenderloin, which provided release from Victorian respectability in saloons, brothels, gambling parlors, and social clubs. At the Maple Leaf Club in Sedalia, Missouri, in 1899, a young black musician created the "Maple Leaf Rag." Scott Joplin became America's most popular ragtime composer. The new music was intensely democratic, growing out of African American traditions and extending to white as well as black audiences and performers and blending across class lines as well. Centered in Saint Louis, where Joplin himself moved in 1900, ragtime spread through the Mississippi Valley and to the nation. Even more enduring music appeared in the form of the blues, played by African Americans in midwestern river cities such as Evansville, Saint Louis, and Kansas City and then moving north to Chicago and Detroit. W. C. Handy's "St. Louis Blues," published in 1914, became America's all-time favorite. From its midwestern base the blues moved into the mainstream of American popular culture.

In midwestern cities residents and rural visitors found an increasing range of commercial entertainment, including flickering nickelodeons, vaudeville houses, amusement parks, and spectator sports, particularly baseball. And there were clubs and social organizations for businessmen, members of ethnic groups, literary women, and nearly every other kind of urban resident. Cities provided daily newspapers, public parks, and the excitement of lighted sidewalks filled with people.

The rural and small-town Midwest could hardly match the excitement of Chicago or even Toledo. Yet the first decades of the century showed numerous examples of increased opportunity that indicated that some of the region's confidence and hopefulness extended far into the countryside. Most notable were the increasing opportunities countryfolk had to communicate with each other and with distant places. Model T Fords zipped over graded and even paved roads, electric interurban cars quietly rolled toward the downtown department stores and theaters, and telephones rang on kitchen walls—all suggesting reductions in the isolation that had always plagued the Midwest's vast spaces. Rural Free Delivery of mail, begun in 1896, brought magazines and newspapers and the consumer world of Sears, Roebuck and Montgomery Ward. Increasingly, public libraries served even rural and small-town midwesterners. The Midwest led the nation in successful grant applications to philanthropist Andrew Carnegie for public library buildings: 792 midwestern communities received Carnegie grants, of a total 1,412 the steel magnate made in the first two decades of the century. By World War I most of the region's county-seat towns boasted a good public library.

Formal entertainment was also increasingly available in the countryside and small towns. Perhaps most notable was the annual itinerant Chautauqua, which reached its peak in midwestern country towns between 1900 and 1925. Usually a week in duration, the traveling Chautauqua provided a mixture of old-time camp meeting and cultural uplift, with an added dollop of wholesome family fun. Programs included theatrical plays, demonstrations of science, folklore, African American spirituals, string quartets, Swiss bell ringers, and lectures by notables. Wholesomeness was essential. When a Chautauqua group in Kansas included scenes from *Carmen* the company had the young women working in a dairy rather than a cigarette factory and Carmen entering the stage carrying a milk pail.

Midwestern county and state fairs also expanded opportunities for entertainment and socializing. From their origins as agricultural exhibitions in the mid-nineteenth century, fairs became multipurpose extravaganzas in the first two decades of the twentieth century. The Minnesota State Fair by 1905 offered seventy-five acres of farm implements and machinery plus exhibition buildings filled with prize-winning jellies, quilts, livestock, and flour. There were also such eye-catching exhibits as a 300-pound loaf of bread made with the state's finest flour, American flags composed of vegetables, and pioneer cabins made of corn. Special features of the Minnesota fair were the butter sculptures of such popular subjects as a seven-foot farm madonna. Across the Midwest state fair entertainment included balloon parachute jumps, auto races, tightrope walkers, and airplane rides. The midway attractions were especially enticing, with their wild animals, fat ladies, two-headed men, games of chance, mechanical rides, and "girlie shows." Frequent morality crusades failed to clean up the midway. And always there was something to eat at the state fair, from the novel hamburger stands introduced just after 1900 to the church tents in which the ladies aid societies sold homemade meals. All this was enjoyed by tens of thousands of people as each Midwest state attempted to provide the biggest and best.

Midwestern confidence and achievement, from farms to courthouse squares to downtown offices, also cast its light into the political arena during the first two decades of the twentieth century. It was during these years that Frederick Jackson Turner's visions of American democracy seemed to many midwesterners most realizable and most threatened. One response was progressivism, a distinctive midwestern blend that built on Jeffersonian agrarianism, Grangerism, and populism combined with an acceptance, if properly regulated, of the industrial and urban changes that were sweeping the nation. Midwestern progressivism came to represent one of the region's strongest claims to heartland status.

Professor Turner's home state led the way and set the standard. The "Wisconsin Idea" assumed a public interest and general welfare that stood above individual or group interests and that could be served by active government in concert with private interests. Progressive Wisconsinites deemed government a positive force to be used by the people for the people. From this "laboratory of democracy" came workmen's compensation, open primaries, civil service, child-labor laws, county schools of agriculture, and state income taxes. And Wisconsin was blessed with exceptional politicians, most notably Robert La Follette, perhaps the nation's greatest Progressive, a man who passionately believed in government as an ally for achieving the common good.

The progressivism that so engulfed Wisconsin in the first decade and a half of the century had its counterparts in other midwestern states. Those of the Upper Midwest entered particularly vigorous reform modes. Minnesota, North Dakota, and Iowa joined Wisconsin in what the political scientist Daniel J. Elazar has labeled a "commonwealth" concept of government—one in which citizens expected efficient, honest government that responded effectively to the general welfare and in which citizens showed a strong sense of civic responsibility. This commonwealth orientation had its primary proponents among former New England and upstate New York populations that settled the Upper Midwest in the nineteenth century, reinforced by some of the northern European immigrant cultures.

In contrast, the states of the lower Midwest, particularly Ohio, Indiana, Illinois, and Missouri (as well as to some extent Nebraska), tended toward a more marketplace or job-oriented politics. Political patronage and interest groups were stronger, as was fear that government would threaten individual liberty. Government was often perceived as an adversary rather than an ally or else as an agent to advance individual interests. Such diminished expectations of government had their primary origins among the Upland South peoples who settled the lower Midwest in the early nineteenth century. Even in the lower Midwest, however, there were many signs of Progressive reform, so that a genuine Midwest progressivism extended across the region.

Progressivism was especially strong in the growing cities, as the Midwest became the nation's center of urban reform. Mayors such as Tom L. Johnson of Cleveland, Hazen Pingree of Detroit, and Samuel M. (Golden Rule) Jones in Toledo led campaigns for honesty, efficiency, and expanded public service that became models for the nation. So too did Dayton's pioneer city-manager plan. This effort to bring business efficiency to city government was especially popular in Michigan, which by 1920 had twenty-three city-manager municipalities (compared to eighteen in the entire Northeast). Perhaps even more important than city government were the social-settlement houses that appeared across the region. Jane Addams's Hull House in Chicago was the best known, but all Midwest cities made similar efforts to help those in need and to extend order and democracy through the community. Midwestern state universities and the newly founded private University of Chicago also took on a more public, service-oriented character as professors and students devoted less attention to Latin or Greek and more to studying taxation and social welfare and to providing extension services off the campus.

Some midwesterners thought the challenges to democracy were so serious as to require a socialist response. In small industrial towns such as Marion, Indiana, Flint, Michigan, and Dayton, Ohio, and in large cities such as Minneapolis and Milwaukee midwesterners elected socialist candidates to local offices. Socialism was more prominent in the Midwest than elsewhere in the nation, but it was a moderate and reformist socialism, focusing less on bitter class conflict and more on public ownership of municipal utilities, aid for dependent people, and honesty in government. Another related and more enduring form of protest was the Nonpartisan League, which in North Dakota achieved some success in the 1910s with a state-owned bank and flour mill.

The confidence and prosperity that marked the first two decades of the century did not touch everyone. Many midwesterners lagged behind, some far behind. In a time of booming agricultural prosperity some farmers struggled mightily just to feed their families. These struggles were particularly evident in southern Ohio, Indiana, and Illinois. Industrial workers too did not all share fully in the region's booming factories. Ford's five dollars a day never became the norm. Moreover, conditions of work often meant long, hard, and dangerous labor. Child labor remained a common feature of the region's factories even though it declined in the face of Progressive reform.

There were many midwesterners whose opportunities were restricted because of race or gender. Women found few opportunities for formal participation in the political sphere, even as they fought mightily for suffrage. Many nonetheless became key agents of Progressive reform, particularly at the local level. Often women's work in clubs and church groups led to the most energetic reform campaigns.

African Americans also faced limitations on their participation in the confident prosperity of the Midwest. Jim Crow segregation was not nearly as extensive as it was in the South. Many southern-born blacks never forgot the joy of being able to move out of the segregated coach as their northward bound train crossed the Ohio River. Settled in their new midwestern homes, they saw many signs that life was better. Even under the more segregated conditions that characterized Lower Midwest cities such as Saint Louis and Evansville possibilities were greater than in Dixie. There were more jobs at higher pay, especially in the growing industrial cities of the Great Lakes area. By the beginning of the century a small black middle class had emerged, extending from Topeka to Cleveland, composed of businessmen, doctors, ministers, teachers, and lawyers. Midwest African Americans also could vote and send their children to public schools. They could create autonomous communities with churches, social clubs, and other institutions. And in many midwestern towns and cities local branches of the National Association for the Advancement of Colored People (NAACP) organized in the second decade of the century to fight for civil rights.

Life had possibilities for many black midwesterners, but the early twentieth century also saw an increase in white racism that often brought a tightening of the color line and even mob violence, which scarred Akron in 1900, Evansville, Indiana, in 1903, Springfield, Illinois, in 1908, East Saint Louis in 1917, and Omaha and Chicago in 1919. Even in North Dakota whites felt sufficiently threatened by blacks among them to pass a state antimiscegenation law in 1909. These tensions seemed to increase with the Great Migration of 1916–1919, when tens of thousands of southern blacks moved to the urban Midwest. While the newcomers often found work it was almost always at the very bottom of the ladder with limited opportunity for movement up. When they found housing it was often in a segregated neighborhood.

For Native Americans conditions were even less satisfactory. The process of removal in the nineteenth century had led to dispersion and sometimes loss of cultural identity but also to concentration on government reservations. The reservation Sioux in South Dakota and the Chippewa in Wisconsin, for example, lived in bleak economic circumstances, and although many resisted pressures for Americanization their economic dependence on the federal government increased substantially in the early twentieth century, as did white antipathy. Few Native Americans knew the full opportunity so often proclaimed by midwestern boosters.

ANXIOUS YEARS, 1920–1940

The sense of prosperity and confidence that marked much of the Midwest in the first two decades of the twentieth century and that underlay its claims to being the nation's heartland came under attack during the 1920s. The earlier optimism, even smugness, was still present but mixed now with a more pronounced anxiety and defensiveness.

The first blow came to the region's farmers. The post–World War I decade saw a significant farm depression that replaced the prewar golden age. As farm prices declined the rural to urban exodus swelled, farm families cut back on store purchases, small-town banks and restaurants closed, and rural schools and churches stood abandoned. There were significant potential improvements in farm productivity in the 1920s: increased use of fertilizers and electrical machinery; adoption of tractors and new mechanical equipment; use of trucks and automobiles; development of hybrid corn, principally by Henry A. Wallace of Iowa and Eugene D. Funk of Illinois; introduction of soybeans to the crop mix. These and other steps toward a more "scientific" agriculture held great promise, as the midwestern land-grant universities tirelessly preached through their missionary-like experiment stations and extension services, but only if agricultural prices were high enough to enable farmers to join in the march toward greater productivity. In the 1920s relatively few could.

The farm depression of the 1920s produced a political response, as had been the case in the late nineteenth century. The difference was that in the 1920s farmers organized intensely in the national political arena. With strong lobbying from the newly organized American Farm Bureau Federation, midwestern political leaders such as Arthur Capper of Kansas, Gilbert N. Haugen of Iowa, and George Norris of Nebraska, often supported by Secretary of Agriculture Henry C. Wallace, publisher of *Wallace's Farmer,* presented a potent political force in Washington. Joined with colleagues from the South, they created a farm bloc in Congress to secure federal aid in raising prices. Farm-bloc politicians argued for parity, that is, for government support to give farmers the purchasing power they had enjoyed in the prosperous period of 1909–1914. Farm-bloc efforts to enact significant legislation failed, but the principle of parity and the notion that the federal government had responsibility to help farmers was significantly advanced in the farm politics of the 1920s.

Along with the economic crisis that faced midwestern farmers in the 1920s came a cultural crisis, a growing suspicion that farm families lagged behind their urban cousins. Farm descendants of pioneer settlers had always had first claim to the region's values and lifestyles. Now they seemed to be hicks and hayseeds or, even worse, fools struggling to maintain a way of life that was no longer sensible, economically or culturally. So bad was their condition that the rural Midwest became the object of reformers' attentions.

The opening round of rural reform was fired by President Theodore Roosevelt's Commission on Country Life. Its 1909 report urged that the efficiency and order of urban Progressive reform be applied to rural America. A host of surveys and reports followed. Many focused on schools and churches. Professional educators, national denominational church leaders, and rural sociologists at the state universities proposed standards that ranged from special training and minimum salaries for country ministers and teachers to sanitary toilets for their worshipers and students. In many instances the reports recommended closing and consolidating the small one-room churches and schools that dotted the Midwest landscape. To many rural midwesterners these reformers attacked the fundamental institutions of their community life.

Other threats to old-fashioned morality seemed to emanate from the city. Cigarette smoking, bootleg liquor, motion pictures, jazz music, and new forms of dancing began to entice farm boys and girls, or so their parents feared. Adults looked with horror on newspaper reports in 1928 that the University of Iowa women's debate club had discussed free love and companionate marriage and was preparing next to debate birth control. Most of these new vices seemed connected to the freedom and privacy given by the automobile, "a house of prostitution on wheels," an Indiana judge thundered.

The distance between urban and rural was most apparent in the scarcity of conveniences in face of the allures of the rapidly growing consumer society. More than four-fifths of Midwest farm homes lacked electricity and running water in 1930. Family members might work from dawn to dusk but rarely could afford the more expensive consumer items advertised in *Wallace's Farmer* or the Sears catalog.

Rural women suffered special challenges. The distances of the Midwest had always meant isolation, particularly on the Great Plains. Most farm women worked as hard as or harder than men, cooking, sewing, caring for children, helping in the fields, tending a garden, feeding chickens. Yet they often lacked the opportunities their husbands, fathers, and brothers had to talk with neighbors or to go to town on business. Home-extension clubs, church missionary societies, automobiles, radios, and Sunday worship could break the isolation, especially in the more densely settled areas, but loneliness, drudgery, and boredom were the lot of most rural midwestern women. Many unhappy farm mothers did not share in the rosy agrarian vision professed by farm-bloc politicians and other men and strongly urged their sons and daughters to leave the farm.

The tribulations of the rural Midwest in the 1920s were not matched in the region's cities. Life there still seemed promising. Automobiles poured from Detroit factories. Steel, rubber, petroleum, and other products supported the region's industrial preeminence. Department stores and movie palaces offered consumer delights and Hollywood entertainment that rivaled that of any East Coast city. And suburbs spread, including elite enclaves such as Cleveland's Shaker Heights and Milwaukee's Shorewood.

Yet there were threats to midwestern confidence in the towns and cities too. One was a wave of corruption and crime that darkened the region. In Chicago Al Capone rather than Jane Addams took center stage. Machine politics and municipal corruption dominated in Kansas City, Detroit, Muncie, and across the region. Critics charged that this urban decay was fed by gambling, bootleg liquor, and prostitution. The Progressive reform spirit that had promised to uplift prewar urban life was spent.

Across the region there were disturbing signs of a narrowing of spirit, a focusing inward, a grim intolerance. The Midwest led the nation during the 1920s in celebrating the comforts of isolation and turning away from Europe and the world. And it led in Ku Klux Klan membership. Klan organizers found willing followers in many midwestern communities: Protestant ministers, shopkeepers, factory workers, insurance agents, and even some former socialists thought they were protecting traditional moral values by parading in white sheets. The Klan twisted those values to attack "others" they saw as threatening—Jews, Catholics, African Americans, as well as bootleggers, prostitutes, adulterers, and all manner of violators of old-fashioned Protestantism. From Klan and non-Klan sources discrimination and segregation seemed more pronounced. In Columbia, Missouri, in 1923 and Marion, Indiana, in 1930, lynching of blacks produced tragedies as stark as any in the South.

Perhaps nowhere else in the 1920s did the Midwest's mixture of pessimism and confidence, of anxiety and optimism appear so clearly as in the region's literature. Midwestern writers and poets came into national prominence during the first three decades of the century. They expressed a newfound sense of power and regional identification, often standing eagerly in opposition to the traditional gentility and stuffy literary grasp of the East, which too often looked to Europe for recognition and certification. They claimed for the Midwest the new voice of America.

Some of the region's most popular authors, best exemplified by the Hoosier writer Booth Tarkington and poet James Whitcomb Riley, celebrated the region's countryside, small towns, and plain-spoken people. Usually Tarkington and Riley looked backward to the nineteenth century, to a time before bustling cities and roaring factories, to an imagined time when there had been no doubt about pioneer achievements and enduring values. Both Hoosiers were popular for a long time—Tarkington won two Pulitzer Prizes and school children from Pennsylvania to Oregon memorized Riley's verses about frost on the pumpkin and corn in shocks—but other midwestern writers made different and, in the end, more lasting contributions.

Sherwood Anderson, Edgar Lee Masters, Sinclair Lewis, Willa Cather, F. Scott Fitzgerald, and Theodore Dreiser were among the large number of writers who drew on their midwestern experiences but were more ambivalent, sometimes more pessimistic and even disparaging about the rural and small-town values Tarkington and Riley so warmly celebrated. There was a tension in their work that recognized both the region's promise and its failure to fulfill that promise and that suggested both attraction and repulsion.

In F. Scott Fitzgerald's *The Great Gatsby* (1925), Nick Carraway left his midwestern home, "the ragged edge of the universe," for the East, yet returned to "the warm center of the world," the Midwest, "borne back ceaselessly into the past." Willa Cather in *O Pioneers* (1913) and *My Ántonia* (1918) conveyed with lyrical affection the passing of the pioneer generation and also with realism the harshness and limitations of ordinary lives in Nebraska. Perhaps the book that suggested to the largest audience the region's vulnerability was *Main Street* (1920). In his fictional village of Gopher Prairie, Sinclair Lewis portrayed not only the kindness and common-sense devotion to duty of Will Kennicott but also, through the eyes of his wife, Carol Kennicott, the town's insular hypocrisy, materialism, and claustrophobia. Rather than opening up new possibilities, the "grasping" prairie that surrounded Carol Kennicott and the town closed in to stifle individualism. *Main Street* was the loudest rallying cry in the revolt against the midwestern village that pervaded the 1920s. Lewis contributed a second blow in *Babbitt* (1922), in which the mindless cry of Zenith's middle-class businessmen was "Don't knock, boost." Lewis's Nobel Prize for literature in 1930 gave international sanction to his ambivalence about the Midwest and helped to enshrine his vision of what was wrong with middle-class life in the middle of America. This more negative side would endure long after the 1920s, representing a fundamental shift in the region's self-conception, from confidence and pride toward defensiveness and lack of fulfillment.

Lewis's Nobel Prize marked the high point of recognition for midwestern literature. Many midwestern writers had made their way hopefully to Chicago in the 1910s and early 1920s. This "Robin's Egg Renaissance," Sherwood Anderson noted, never hatched, because the best of them left the nest by the mid-1920s, moving to New York or Paris. A primary focus of the midwestern literary ascendancy was John T. Frederick's *The Midland: A Magazine of the Middle West,* begun in Iowa City in 1915 and later moved to Chicago. In 1933 *The Midland* ceased publication.

The blows to midwestern confidence in the 1920s were serious, particularly from literary works such as *Main Street* and from the economic troubles of farmers. But the Great Depression of the 1930s struck even harder and more evenly across the region,

Dust storm, Cimarron County, Oklahoma, April 1936. Photograph by Arthur Rothstein.
PRINTS AND PHOTOGRAPHS DIVISION, LIBRARY OF CONGRESS

affecting both farm and factory. Some farm families would later claim that times were so bad during the 1920s that they hardly noticed a downturn during the 1930s. In fact life did get worse. Wheat farmers on the Great Plains suffered most, as the Depression combined with disastrous drought, especially in 1934 and 1936. On "Black Sunday," 9 May 1934, millions of tons of bone-dry topsoil blew off the Great Plains, settling in Chicago and as far east as Boston. Some farmers took direct action against the Depression, such as in the Farmers' Holiday Association strikes organized in Iowa, Nebraska, Minnesota, and the Dakotas in 1932. Farmers also organized to stop foreclosure sales.

Midwest farmers' voices in Congress and the White House were more organized and more powerful in the 1930s than at perhaps any other time. Farm politicians and New Deal sympathies produced the Agricultural Adjustment Act and other legislation that provided aid to farmers who agreed to take land out of production. The New Deal firmly established the principle of parity and left farmers generally convinced that government aid was not charity but a legitimate response to the special challenges of agriculture. The New Deal also provided support for agricultural conservation, rural electrification, and resettlement of marginal farmers. While not all farmers benefited fully, farm conditions generally improved after 1933. Some asserted that these economic changes of the 1930s brought loss of the independence and cultural autonomy farmers had so prized. Others claimed that once again the connection between democracy and midwestern farmers had been demonstrated and expanded, as it had been in the Grange and Populist movements. The political strength of farmers, however, was seldom effectively combined with that of industrial workers, despite some efforts at farmer-labor parties in the Upper Midwest.

Sit-down strike. Strikers guarding a window entrance to the Fisher Body plant, factory no. 3, Flint, Mich., January–February 1937. Photograph by Sheldon Dick, Farm Security Administration. PRINTS AND PHOTOGRAPHS DIVISION, LIBRARY OF CONGRESS

The Depression struck an even greater blow to the midwestern industrial economy. The heavy industries that dominated the region were especially hard-hit as consumers stopped buying automobiles, refrigerators, sewing machines, and other expensive durable goods. Many midwestern industrial cities began to suffer a population decline.

Along with depression came labor unrest. As with most industrial challenges in the region since the early twentieth century it came most forcefully in the auto industry. There had been strikes earlier, difficult ones like the 1913 Calumet copper strike, the 1916 Iron Range strike, the steel strike of 1919, and the soft-coal miners' strikes in the 1920s. In the 1930s the newly formed United Auto Workers won recognition after a massive sit-down strike that began in Flint and spread through General Motors plants. The UAW along with the United Steel Workers and the United Rubber Workers emerged from the Depression as strong industrial unions with their bases firmly in the heartland. They had proven their value to their members by delivering improved conditions of work and higher wages and in giving industrial workers a stronger political voice. But the newly strengthened industrial unions also contributed to a view in more conservative quarters that the Midwest suffered from "poor" labor relations.

While the Midwest struggled under the blows of the Great Depression it also experienced a revival of self identification. Regionalism attracted attention across the nation in the 1930s, but in the Middle West, where fears were growing that a golden age had passed or, even worse, that the promise of pioneer expectations had not been fulfilled, regionalism revived with a special force.

The New Deal provided some of the stimulus for the regionalism of the 1930s. Many New Deal programs were administered along state and regional lines. And several New Deal initiatives directly supported regional expression. New Deal–sponsored historical research, the American Guide Series, and post office murals all stimulated expression of local and regional identity. The Midwest created the largest number of post office murals, many of them depicting a local history that featured virtuous, hardy pioneer farm families as the embodiment of American progress and democracy.

Scholars on state university campuses, sometimes working with New Deal support, contributed to the revived interest, often explicitly rejecting eastern and

European influences. Historians at the University of Wisconsin and elsewhere built on Turner's work. Midwestern writers of fiction also reached large audiences in the 1930s, particularly in those books that romantically celebrated the region's pioneer and rural values, such as Louis Bromfield's *The Farm* (1933), Phil Stong's *State Fair* (1932), and Laura Ingalls Wilder's *Little House* series for children (1932–1943).

Perhaps the most significant expression of Midwest regionalism came from artists, particularly the great regional triumvirate of Grant Wood, John Steuart Curry, and Thomas Hart Benton. Paintings such as Curry's *Baptism in Kansas* (1928) and Wood's *Stone City, Iowa* (1930) were vigorous expressions of affection for the region generally and particularly for the traditional values they attached to its rural people and agricultural landscapes. In 1935 Wood set forth his case in an essay titled "Revolt against the City." Asserting that the Great Depression had produced an introspective rediscovery of America's "old frontier virtues," Wood gloried in the opportunity to turn away from Europe and East Coast cities (which were imitative because they were "still colonies of Europe") and to seek a genuinely American culture in music, theater, literature, and art. This culture would be regional. The Midwest, Wood argued, found its essential character with the farmer and the land, not in "scenes of the picture-postcard type" but rather in art that sought out the "genuineness" and the "extraordinary independence" of midwestern farmers. Here was the region's personality and from it and from competition with other regions "a rich American culture will grow."

Thomas Hart Benton shared many of Wood's hopes. In an interview published in *Art Front* in April 1935, Benton claimed that "The Middle West is the least provincial area of America. It is the least affected, that is, by ideas which are dependent on intellectual dogmas. . . . It has provided the substance of every democratic drive in our history." But Benton, more so than Wood and Curry, vigorously and positively incorporated city and industrial life into his art. Among his most notable achievements in the 1930s were two sets of murals, one telling the history of Missouri, the other the history of Indiana. The latter was the Hoosier state's contribution to the "Century of Progress" exhibition at the Chicago World's Fair of 1933. Benton's 200-foot-long mural depicted not only Indiana's pioneer heritage but also its automobile and steel industries, its unhappy brush with the Ku Klux Klan, and especially its democratic promise in Progressive politics, economic growth, science, and, most unusual of all, racial equality. Benton celebrated midwestern pioneer democracy, but pointedly included laboratory scientists, African American construction workers, and Socialist Eugene V. Debs in that democracy.

Much midwestern regionalism of the 1930s was more nationalistic than separatist, as it often argued the heartland thesis that equated Midwest with nation. Regional distinctiveness was claimed too, however, but less in separating the Midwest from the nation than in separating the nation from the rest of the world, particularly from Europe. Like Grant Wood, many midwesterners believed that Europe had "lost much of its magic." Doubts about entrance into World War I and disillusionment with its aftermath expanded to full-blown isolationism, stronger in the Midwest than in any other region of the nation. The best Europeans had long ago migrated to the Midwest, many believed. Those with ancestral attachments to Germany or Ireland expressed harsh anti-British sentiments. The Senate's leading isolationists included Ohio's Robert A. Taft, Michigan's Arthur H. Vandenberg, and North Dakota's Gerald P. Nye. The isolationist America First Committee, headquartered in Chicago, had its major strength in the Midwest. Chaired by Robert E. Wood, head of Sears, Roebuck, it had strong support from Charles A. Lindbergh and Colonel Robert R. McCormick, publisher of the brash *Chicago Tribune*. Midwestern isolationists had little use for dictators or fascism, despite some support for Michigan's anti-Semitic Father Charles Coughlin.

The Midwest's isolationism was never absolute: the University of Michigan was a mecca for foreign students; Chicago's *Daily News* provided a voice far more favorable to aiding the Allies than the *Tribune;* and Kansas newspaper editor William Allen White headed the Committee to Defend America by Aiding the Allies. With the attack on Pearl Harbor there was little more heard of midwestern isolationism.

DECLINING YEARS, 1940–1990

World War II brought much more than an end to midwestern isolationism. Prosperity returned in nearly unimaginable strength. Farmers planted to the fence rows as prices rose, and factories boomed as the arsenal of democracy filled with Midwestern goods. The strength of the wartime industrial economy was nowhere better displayed than in the auto industry now converted to war production. Henry Ford's Willow Run factory spread over sixty-seven acres and by war's end had produced 8,685 B-24 bombers.

The boom continued into the late 1940s and beyond. The confidence that had marked the Mid-

Changes in the Midwest landscape. Large grain elevators dominate the rural Midwest.
ARCHIVE PHOTOS/LAMBERT

west in the first decades of the century seemed to have returned by 1950. In agriculture, in industry, in respect for the traditional values of the heartland, the Midwest seemed as much as ever to represent the best the nation offered. When the editors of *Look* magazine in 1947 published an illustrated guide titled *The Midwest* they celebrated the region as "perhaps the richest area of its size mankind has ever known." Before the twentieth century was over, however, the Midwest faced challenges as large as any since initial settlement.

Midwestern farmers in the last half of the twentieth century achieved technological and commercial sophistication that enabled them to feed the nation and much of the world. Farmers quickly adopted new means of increasing output: tractors, hybrid corn, soybeans, commercial fertilizers, and grain combines that could pick eight rows of corn in one pass. They increased their acreage and tore out old fences to make longer fields that maximized use of the new equipment. Rather than the diversification that had characterized most farms before World War II midwesterners increasingly specialized in cash grain farming. Soybeans became immensely popular, but corn remained dominant. The Corn Belt expanded west to the High Plains where rainfall was marginal. Massive irrigation projects in Nebraska and Kansas in the 1960s pumped water from the High Plains aquifer to new fields and cattle feedlots. The Corn Belt also moved north as new hybrids met the challenges of shorter and cooler summers. By the 1970s millions of bushels of Midwest corn moved by rail, down the Mississippi River system, and over the Saint Lawrence Seaway to world markets.

As farm size and capitalization increased, small or less efficient family farms began to disappear rapidly. Some farmers hung on part-time, with both husband and wife also working in town, but by 1970 there were about the same number of farms in the Midwest as there had been in 1870. The Midwest rural landscape changed dramatically as a result, for not only did large metal grain bins replace the smaller wooden corn cribs but farm houses, one-room schools, churches, and stores stood abandoned and derelict. Rural and small-town communities withered and disappeared, especially if located off the routes of the new interstate highways. Specialization and high capitalization forced adoption of corporate values that maximized short-term gain rather than stewardship of the land over generations. Understanding agribusiness, government farm programs, credit arrangements, and federal income tax provisions became as important as knowing when to plant corn. Many families survived and even passed their farms to their children, but only by making them more like business than familial operations.

The most successful farmers enjoyed increased output and reasonable prosperity through the 1970s. During the 1970s especially, the lure of high profit induced many farmers to invest heavily in new equipment and more acreage. The 1980s brought a farm crisis of major proportions as exports declined, land prices dropped, and farm debt rose. Foreclosures and bankruptcies produced scenes like those of the 1930s, adversely affecting not only farmers but bankers, merchants, implement dealers, and many others. Responses included stress-counseling hotlines, violence, and grim humor (the Des Moines *Register* reported the latest case of child abuse: the farmer gave the son the farm). There were political responses too, but by this time the farmers' direct political clout had been considerably lessened as the powerful farm bloc of the 1920s and 1930s had withered in the face of declining farm population. Farmers protested their condition directly through tractorcades and Farm Aid concerts. Hollywood films such as *Country* showed a Midwest angst that melted hearts from New York to Los Angeles. Public-opinion polls in the 1980s revealed sympathy for farmers and helped bring significant government aid to rescue the agricultural Midwest. Despite some arguments for free-market agriculture, the government continued farm subsidies and land set-asides to reduce acreage into the 1990s. Nonetheless, the 1980s showed that agriculture, even in the best place in the world, remained as risky as it had ever been.

The struggles of agriculture in the Midwest were more than matched by those in manufacturing in the late twentieth century. The industrial might that won World War II continued into the postwar era. Steel mills, auto factories, and machine shops helped make the region the primary source of the durable consumer goods that anchored the so-called affluent society of the 1950s. Factory jobs continued to pull newcomers, especially from the South, which sent large numbers of African Americans and even larger numbers of whites to the Midwest. Nearly 10 percent of Ohio's and Indiana's populations were southern-born whites by 1970, attracted north by the prospect of a high-paying job in an Akron tire factory or Muncie auto-parts plant. Midwest manufacturers not only appeared rock solid economically at mid-century but also seemed broadly deserving of the sentiment that what was good for General Motors was good for the nation.

By the 1970s conditions had changed so markedly that the terms *Rust Belt* and *decline* were commonly applied to the region. Factories that had provided high pay and job security for several generations closed. Newcomers stopped arriving from the South and elsewhere, and many longtime residents left. Cleveland, Detroit, and Saint Louis suffered population declines of more than 20 percent between 1970 and 1980. The changes were most trying in the auto industry, where foreign competition revealed weaknesses that left the Big Three fighting for survival. Only massive government aid saved Chrysler, after its head, Lee Iacocca, successfully argued in 1979, "My problems are the problems of the country." Workers lost jobs not only in the auto plants but in steel, rubber, and most of the heavy industries that constituted the core of the Midwestern economy. The recession of 1980–1982 hit the region especially hard. Unemployment exceeded 10 percent in many towns, particularly auto parts towns like Anderson, Indiana. Through the 1980s and early 1990s newspaper headlines frequently announced plant closings: "It's not the American Dream anymore," *Roger and Me* filmmaker Michael Moore told the *New York Times* in 1989 after GM's Flint plant closed, "it's the American nightmare."

The Midwest was competing not only internationally with Germany, Japan, and Mexico but also with the American South and West, particularly those Sunbelt areas where wages and taxes were lower and labor unions less powerful. The energy crisis that was so pointedly displayed in the oil embargo of 1973 stimulated further migration of people and capital to the Sunbelt. Nor in the midst of all these challenges did the Midwest have the safety net of federal defense spending: the region received far fewer Cold War defense contracts than the Sunbelt or New England. Companies in Dayton, Detroit, Chicago, and elsewhere had pioneered in military engineering and production and had made overwhelming contributions to victory in World War II, but they failed in the 1950s and after to pursue defense contracts aggressively, preferring to concentrate instead on consumer goods. Defense industries remained important in St. Louis, Wichita, and Minneapolis but less so in other parts of the region. By the 1980s, when military aerospace weapons increasingly relied on electronic and other high-tech features, the Midwest's failure to garner a larger share of defense spending contributed to the relative scarcity of the high-tech corridors found in California and Massachusetts. Midwestern universities continued to educate some of the brightest engineers, computer programmers, and businesspeople but exported them elsewhere. Considerable high-tech and service-industry growth occurred, as with Omaha's success in becoming one of the nation's leading telemarketing and telecommunications centers, but most of the jobs were low paying compared to those of traditional blue-collar factory workers.

Until the 1970s the Midwest lagged behind in forming regional organizations, perhaps because it was sufficiently prosperous and confident of its heartland status to argue in terms of national goals. Even a potentially region-wide economic benefit such as the Saint Lawrence Seaway produced only limited cooperation. Not until 1962 did the Midwest Governors Conference organize, following behind similar groups in the other regions. With emigration of people and jobs and growing fears of economic stagnation, however, midwestern business and political leaders began to unite to appeal to Washington for federal aid. The Midwest's congressional delegation began to argue that the region received far smaller returns on the tax dollars it sent to Washington than other regions. They joined in 1977 with colleagues in the Northeast to form the Northeast-Midwest Congressional Coalition to encourage more federal interest in the nation's Frost Belt and Rust Belt. The "new federalism," which President Ronald Reagan promoted to return tax dollars and power to the states, won anemic support from the Midwest because of fears that other regions would receive even more in grants-in-aid and other federal assistance.

Fears of economic decline also brought backbiting competition within the region, particularly in state and local incentives to lure business. Ohio Governor James Rhodes pioneered such programs, recruiting businesses from Michigan and Indiana as well as overseas. Midwest states also competed aggressively for foreign investment and offered huge incentives to Japanese companies to attract auto parts and assembly plants. Many of these new factories located in small towns or cornfields, where the Japanese owners thought they would avoid labor unions, racial diversity, and other features of the American auto industry.

In seeking their own version of pastoralism in the American heartland the Japanese were doing what many midwesterners were themselves doing in the last decades of the twentieth century. They continued to retain the pioneer family as a strong cultural image, to be celebrated heartily in state centennials and sesquicentennials, state fairs, and the nation's bicentennial in 1976. How to acknowledge the regions's diversity, and so include immigrants, Native Americans, and African Americans along with pioneer traditions remained a question through the end of the century.

The Midwest did not pioneer in civil rights. The region's industrial cities attracted large numbers of black newcomers during the first two-thirds of the twentieth century but seldom provided equal opportunity in jobs, education, or urban services. Housing was highly segregated, and despite some success at suburban integration in Shaker Heights, Ohio, and Oak Park, Illinois, Midwest cities had the most residentially segregated neighborhoods in the nation, with Cleveland, Detroit, Chicago, and Milwaukee leading in 1980. Schools were segregated too, more so than anywhere else. One consequence of this segregation was to make possible election of black mayors, beginning with Richard Hatcher in Gary and Carl Stokes in Cleveland in 1967, followed by Coleman Young in Detroit in 1973, and Harold Washington in Chicago in 1983. Alabama segregationist George Wallace attracted a sizeable number of votes during his presidential campaign forays into the Midwest in the 1960s. Many white midwesterners remained reluctant to consider the rich and abundant evidence of African American contributions to life in the region, from the music of Scott Joplin, Count Basie, and Chuck Berry to the Brown family in Topeka that only wanted its daughter to attend the school in her neighborhood.

The Midwest struggled also to reconcile its pioneer origins and values with preservation of the natural environment. Like nineteenth-century pioneers, many midwesterners continued to act as though the region's resource base was rich enough to support any manner of inefficiency or waste. And they remained firmly attached to pioneer notions of individual property. As the region's most noted conservationist, Aldo Leopold, asserted in his *Sand County Almanac* (1949), "We abuse land because we regard it as a commodity belonging to us," rather than seeing "land as a community to which we belong." Early in the century Minneapolis, Saint Louis, and other river and lake cities dumped their untreated garbage and sewage into the same water from which they took their drinking water. The 1920s brought some signs of a conservation movement: the Izaak Walton League formed in Chicago in 1922 with a strong base among midwestern business and professional men determined to protect rivers and wetlands. But the region's economic growth far outstripped these early efforts. Not until the 1970s did the rising environmental consciousness focus action on such environmental disasters as water quality in Lake Erie and air quality over Gary. Midwestern farmers had contributed to the problem too, polluting the ground water by overusing chemical fertilizers, removing far more water from the High Plains aquifer than nature replaced, and sometimes sending more topsoil than corn down the Mississippi River. The Upper Midwest, particularly Minnesota, Wisconsin, and Michigan, led in environmental regulation, but throughout the region potential and actual environmental damage remained a major challenge.

HOPEFUL YEARS, THE 1990s

There were reasons for midwesterners to be glum as the twentieth century closed. The farmers who had given the region its most distinctive quality were fewer in number and influence and seemed less committed themselves to the pastoral values that had defined the region. The industrial might that had been the envy of the world in the first two-thirds of the century had greatly faded. The region that had always celebrated freedom and the dignity of the individual had failed to pioneer in civil rights. And the region that claimed to love the land was abusing it as much as anyplace on earth. The sense of openness, limitlessness, and opportunity present at the beginning of the century was much harder to find at the end.

Yet in the gloom was hope. The agricultural and industrial economies showed signs of recovery in the late 1980s and early 1990s, though with far fewer jobs. Strength remained in pharmaceutical manufacturing, medical technology, chemicals, machine tools, and even in the restructured steel and auto industries. Indeed, for a time the region did significantly better than other places, including Massachusetts and California, causing a certain smugness to return again. Many midwesterners hoped that with the decline in defense spending in the 1990s the region would compete more successfully for federal dollars. Midwest cities showed some signs of revival of downtown vitality, as in Omaha's Old Market and Chicago's new skyscrapers; some proclaimed a prosperous transition from stockyards and factories to service industries. And suburban malls sprouted, led by the Mall of America near Minneapolis, which covered seventy-eight acres, a bit more than Henry Ford's Willow Run bomber factory. The region's state universities, built by such giants as John Hannah at Michigan State and Herman Wells at Indiana, remained among the best in the world. Even the Prairie Style of architecture seemed more cherished in the late twentieth century. There were still Babbitts, or as Richard Rhodes labeled them, well-scrubbed residents of Cupcake Land. Yet hope persisted that the Midwest still had a claim to its confident status as heartland. In its issue of 19 December 1988, *Newsweek* ran an article titled "The Heartland is Hot: 'Flyover Country' Becomes a Hip Place to Live."

Many midwesterners still thought that way about themselves as the 1980s and 1990s brought signs of growing regional identity and pride. Some of this was artificial or the defensive reaction to feelings that other regions were better off. Even if data suggested that midwestern per capita income was at about the national average, other places had better weather or more national recognition, it seemed. But some of the revived regional pride was genuine, as midwesterners searched for ties that bound them and that separated them from the rest of the nation. They devoted more attention to their history through state and local historical societies, among the strongest in the nation. Their growing interest in historic preservation took deep root not only in large cities but in small towns like Madison, Indiana, and Marshall, Michigan, where Main Street architecture, once considered drab and utilitarian now appeared charming and authentically American—so much so that Walt Disney built a cleaned-up version of his Missouri hometown for Disneyland's Main Street. State humanities and arts councils helped create local and regional forums that encouraged a sense of place. Serious writers derived insight and creativity from their Midwest experiences—writers as diverse as Richard Rhodes, Louise Erdrich, Scott Sanders, Curtis Harnack, Carol Bly, Michael Martone, and William Least Heat-Moon. Even when midwesterners seemed to adopt the lowest national standards they sometimes did it differently: Iowa legalized riverboat gambling in 1991, but its floating casinos had $5 betting limits and posted the number of the gamblers' crisis center.

There remained a tension between past and present, real and ideal, between the pastoralism expressed in William Least Heat-Moon's *PrairyErth,* where the Kansas wind blew clean, and the urban challenges of Detroit, where harsher winds blew, fanned by memories of the 1967 riots; between the visions of small-town security expressed by rock musician John Mellencamp or the film *Hoosiers* and the drab despair of a winter prairie farm auction; between lush cornfields photographed for *Midwest Living,* the glossy regional magazine published in Des Moines, and the Rust Belt factories that dumped out workers as they once dumped out air pollution. Whether pioneer success stories, even in modified form, were still worth telling or whether new stories and new regional identities were to be created remained unclear as the century ended.

BIBLIOGRAPHY

A good foundation for understanding the twentieth-century Midwest is Andrew R. L. Cayton and Peter S. Onuf, *The Midwest and the Nation: Rethinking the History of an American Region* (1990), which examines the region's nineteenth-century development and the relevant historiography. James H. Madison, ed., *Heartland: Comparative Histories of the Midwestern States* (1988), offers historical essays on each of the twelve states and an overview. The important work of geographers is well represented in James R. Shortridge, *The Middle West: Its Meaning in American Culture* (1989); and John Borchert, *America's Northern Heartland* (1987). Two books provide examples of hopeful assessments at mid-century: Graham Hutton, *Midwest at Noon* (1946), an English visitor's informed account; and *The Midwest* (1947), by Louis Bromfield and the editors of *Look.*

The changes in agriculture are surveyed in Gilbert C. Fite, *American Farmers: The New Minority* (1981). Mark Friedberger, *Farm Families and Change in Twentieth-Century America* (1988), examines recent family and community life for Iowa and California farmers; while Deborah Fink, *Agrarian Women: Wives and Mothers in Rural Nebraska, 1880–1940* (1992), uses one Nebraska county to explore the challenges of gender. Karal Ann Marling, *Blue Ribbon: A Social and Pictorial History of the Minnesota State Fair* (1990), examines the cultural meaning of state fairs. The most insightful evocation of small-town life remains Lewis Atherton, *Main Street on the Middle Border* (1954). Jon C. Teaford, *Cities of the Heartland: The Rise and Fall of the Industrial Midwest* (1993), gives special attention to the industrial cities of the Great Lakes area. Ann Markusen et al., *The Rise of the Gunbelt: The Military Remapping of Industrial America* (1991), analyzes regional consequences of federal military expenditures.

An understanding of the ethnic diversity of the Midwest is available in Frederick C. Luebke, ed., *Ethnicity on the Great Plains* (1980). Different regional political cultures are examined in Daniel J. Elazar, *American Federalism: A View From the States,* 3d ed. (1984).

Aldo Leopold, *A Sand County Almanac and Sketches Here and There* (1949), is a classic argument for environmentalism; while Philip V. Scarpino, *Great River: An Environmental History of the Upper Mississippi, 1890–1950* (1985), shows the environmental significance of the river to the region. James M. Dennis, *Grant Wood: A Study in American Art and Culture* (1975), includes Wood's "Revolt against the City" essay. Erika Doss, *Benton, Pollock, and the Politics of Modernism: From Regionalism to Abstract Expressionism* (1991), shows Benton's key role in regional art and culture, while Benton's *An Artist in America,* 4th rev. ed. (1983), is a fascinating autobiography. Ronald Weber, *The Midwestern Ascendancy in American Writing* (1992), identifies the scope and character of the region's literature during the first three decades of the century. Good examples of recent writing include Richard Rhodes, *The Inland Ground: An Evocation of the American Middle West,* rev. ed. (1991); Michael Martone, ed., *A Place of Sense: Essays in Search of the Midwest* (1988); and William Least Heat-Moon, *PrairyErth: (a deep map)* (1991).

THE SOUTH

David R. Goldfield

The South is more than geography. To define the region as the eleven former states of the Confederacy—Alabama, Florida, Georgia, Louisiana, Mississippi, North Carolina, South Carolina, Texas, Arkansas, Tennessee, and Virginia—plus Kentucky, is to give concrete boundaries to an abstraction. Within those borders is a confusing diversity of terrains and people. The South is hills, green and blue, with creeks and valleys hidden among its folds; it is flatness as far as the eye can see and beyond that. The South is rich black soil, easy to till, easier to cultivate; it is sandy ground as easy to plow as the sea. The South is big-shouldered live oaks and knobby-kneed cypress trees; it is thin, shallow-rooted pines and cedars scented of death and closets. The South is gentle breezes, soft summer, and blue-sky winters; it is violent thunderstorms, frenzied rivers, and furnace heat.

Those who inhabit this land are equally difficult to categorize. Southerners are lazy, yet animated and quick-tempered. They live in the past yet are given to periodic enthusiasms for progress at any cost. They can be so future-oriented as to deny this world altogether and await the sweet life of heaven. Southerners claim an almost mystical bond with the land, yet are the most nomadic Americans. They can be flag-waving patriots and fierce provincials simultaneously. Their religion dwells upon the joy of redemption, yet the whites among them have sinned deeply against the blacks. Food, its abundance, and the rituals surrounding it are central to daily life in the South, yet the southerner's diet has produced, for some, disease and incapacity. Southerners have a rich cultural heritage of music and literature, yet have at times vigorously limited creative and independent thinking. Southerners have a penchant for making the abstract concrete, for telling a story to explain an idea, or for translating biblical parables into everyday terms. Yet, they have adhered to an array of myths and theories about races, history, the weather, and the nature of sin that are so abstract as to defy reality and reason. Southerners cherish family reunions, historical legends told and re-told to the point of habit, ties to ancestral homes, church cemeteries, and relatives living and dead—yet if there has been one constant in southern history, it has been change, often wrenching in scope and impact.

With such antithetical attributes in the land and its people, the South seems more a subject for psychologists than historians. But historians have perennially searched for southern identity; the need to define the South is not only a twentieth-century phenomenon. In 1785 Thomas Jefferson set down a list of distinguishing characteristics for North and South: "In the North . . . they are cool, sober, laborious, persevering, independant [sic], jealous of their own liberties, and just to those of others, interested, chicaning, superstitious and hypocritical in their religion"; southerners are "fiery, voluptuary, indolent, unsteady, independant [sic], zealous for their own liberties but trampling on those of others, generous, candid, without attachment or pretentions [sic] to any religion but that of the heart."

Jefferson's list is remarkable because it presages compilations of nineteenth-and twentieth-century observers (religion is a notable exception). In 1962, for example, the Vanderbilt University theologian James Sellers, in *The South and Christian Ethics,* offered the following comparison between North and South: southerners have "a sense of place, contrasted with the northerners' sense of time; [a] high valuation on the rootedness and personalness of man, contrasted with the northerners' high valuation on the equality of man; a passion for concreteness, contrasted with the northerners' thirst for universality in the abstract; a longing for stability, contrasted with northerners' hankering for progress."

If these characterizations are accurate, the question arises, how did southerners get this way? The most promising explanations focus on the distinctiveness of southern history. Other peoples in this country and abroad have a strong sense of the past.

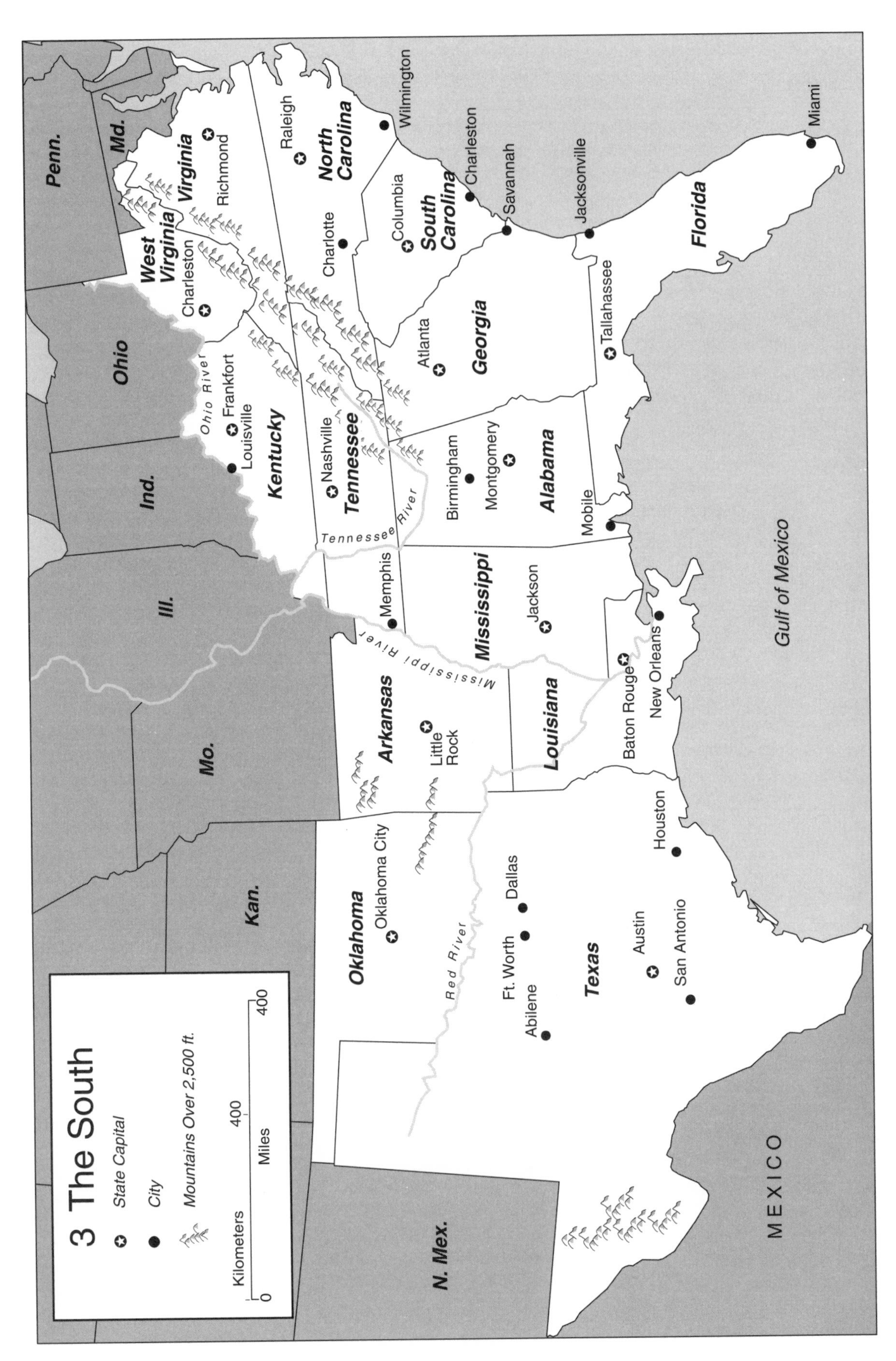

Map 3. The South.

But in the South, history has assumed a power and an intimacy bordering on obsession.

The southerner is born into the past. "I had been born with an intimate feeling for the spirit of the past," writer Ellen Glasgow, who grew to adulthood in the late-nineteenth-century South, explained. The past surrounds southerners: generations, heirlooms, homes, and, above all, customs. The family early forms the most intimate and lasting connection with the past. Not only current family members, but those of preceding generations remain intimate members of the circle long after they have passed on. Southern women especially keep the circle, attending carefully to naming children, keeping genealogies, and remembering birth dates and deaths. "Like any properly brought up southern girl," the writer Shirley Abbott noted of her post–World War II childhood, "I used to spend a lot of time in graveyards. . . . We knew—and thoughtfully made use of—everybody's middle name. We knew who was buried where. We all mattered, and the dead most of all."

The past is a spider web. The family is the center, connecting the southerner to town, county, and region. The boundary between public and private, as between past and present, is as thin as the threads of the web. Movement at the edges of the web is felt and eventually incorporated at the center. And history holds it all together.

Early in this century, the connections to the past were comforting to southerners and afforded security in an unpredictable world. But the web was a trap as well. Its gossamer strands shielded the southerner from reality and exacted heavy burdens in exchange for that protection. That protection served an important purpose. As the historian Arnold Toynbee observed, "the vividness of historical impressions is apt to be proportionate to their violence and painfulness." And southern history has had considerable "violence and painfulness." Slavery, defeat, and poverty were some of the very un-American experiences of black and white southerners. For southerners, history was not learned, it was remembered.

The history of the twentieth-century South is the history of black and white southerners attempting to reconcile the present with their perceptions of the past. Most southerners did not think of how or whether they interpreted their past; they merely accepted it as given and, if necessary, their political leaders reminded them what those givens were. Their evangelical faith taught them great patience. And their chronic poverty taught them not to expect much.

THE SOUTH IN 1900

The South was an American anomaly in 1900: a poor, agricultural region in the midst of an urbanizing industrial nation. Nearly 40 percent of Americans lived in cities in 1900, but only 18 percent of southerners. Lives in the South revolved around crop cycles, the planting and cultivating of such labor-intensive crops as tobacco, a "thirteen-month" crop where farmers prepared for next year's crop while cutting wood for next year's curing and arranging this year's crop for market, and cotton, which required hard work from early spring through July, and then in September and October. In August, the "lay-by" time for cotton, preachers pitched tents and held revivals deep into the humid nights. At other times, men, women, and children spent much of their time out in the fields. Women bore many children, nearly four per family, compared with less than three nationally. The larger the family, the bigger the work force. The fall brought cash for crops, enough, it was hoped, to pay the debt at the local store, a debt carried over to next year's crop sale if necessary, as it often was. A pair of new shoes and a few ribbons for the children became luxuries. One North Carolina study in 1923 revealed that one cotton-cultivating county's farmers earned an average of nine cents a day. If debt became chronic, farmers would lose their land. Increasing numbers of southerners fell into tenancy and sharecropping during the early twentieth century; more than 200,000 of 1.5 million white farmers lost their farms in the 1920s alone.

Subsistence farmers not yet involved in a market economy existed in southern Appalachia. But as the railroad penetrated the hills of Virginia, Kentucky, and North Carolina in the 1870s, timber and then coal-mining interests bought up land and labor and turned a farming region into an industrial district. When the timber played out and the mines lost their productivity by the 1920s, the erstwhile farmers were left with little land to call their own and a blighted environment.

No longer tied to the land by ownership, thousands of southern farmers and their families, both in the lowlands and highlands, took to the road in the early 1900s, moving from farm to farm. For lives that had revolved around family and the country church, such moves were wrenching. By the 1920s, southern white sharecroppers moved at least every other year. Nationally, only two out of ten farmers moved annually. The growing numbers of textile mills in the southern piedmont absorbed some of the rural white population, as did the mines and lumber camps of Appalachia. Mill families re-created as much as possible the kin networks and social life they had built on the farm and, as on the farm, women, children, and men worked together. They often moved back and forth between farm and mill village, sustaining a life in one location to work in another.

White southern landowners, merchants, and industrialists lived in a different world, dependent on agricultural and industrial workers, yet apart from them. Although they may have disagreed among themselves about particulars, most supported white supremacy and one-party rule as the best means to secure their labor force and ensure profits. The agrarian revolt led by the Populist party in the 1890s had threatened these interpretations of southern history. Populist legislatures taxed and regulated railroads, funded education for all children, and lowered interest rates for hard-pressed farmers. White Democratic leaders launched a counter-revolution designed to restore white supremacy and preserve traditional economic relations. The *Charlotte Observer* in 1900 depicted the Democratic insurgency as "a struggle of the white people to rid themselves of the dangers of rule by negroes and the lower class of whites."

A PROGRESSIVE SOUTH, 1900–1920

Democrats framed their arguments in the Progressive rhetoric of the early twentieth century. Progressivism, a national movement that advocated state and federal regulation of corporations, reform of local government, and greater protection for children and laborers, included a limited southern version that linked many of these reforms with white supremacy and one-party political rule. The Democratic party promoted disfranchisement as a method to "purify" the electoral process by ending the manipulation of the black vote by some white employers. Two of the era's major urban political reforms—the commission form of government and the city-manager system—both appeared initially in the South, in Galveston, Texas, and Staunton, Virginia, respectively. Reformers hoped to make local government more efficient by taking urban administration out of the hands of elected officials and placing it with a nonpartisan board of directors, in the case of the commission, or a "neutral" professional city manager. But the reforms did not remove the administrators from politics, although they did deflect the impact of popular democracy.

Southern educational reforms in the early 1900s also reflected racial and class concerns. Decades of tightfisted Democratic rule, an impoverished agricultural economy, and opposition to educating blacks and certain whites had left southern public education a "disgrace," according to a 1901 report issued by Charles Dabney, a North Carolina educator. Less than 30 percent of Tarheel youngsters attended public school regularly, and the average school term lasted only seventy-one days. While all but two states outside the South had enacted compulsory school-attendance laws, Kentucky was the only southern state with such a law. Dabney pitched appeals for more state funding on racial grounds, arguing that new literacy standards required whites to obtain some schooling in order to vote. Southern states increased money for public education, revised curricula, established teacher-education criteria, and built and refurbished physical plants.

Educational reform not only enhanced learning but also reinforced white supremacy. Mississippi, for example, deleted references to voting and democracy in textbooks meant for black schools. Hoke Smith, who became Georgia's governor in 1907 on the Progressive platform of black disfranchisement, railroad regulation, and education reform, advocated a curriculum recognizing that "the large majority of negroes are incapable of anything but manual labor and many taught from books spurn labor and live in idleness." Accordingly, black education should stress menial vocational skills. Smith recommended a similar, though slightly elevated program, for the state's white children as he called for the improvement of white "manual training and agricultural schools." Such curricular changes also saved money. Throughout the South, the funding gap between white and black school systems widened dramatically in the early decades of the twentieth century.

Prohibition also became entwined with racial and class issues. Southern evangelical religious leaders had supported the prohibition of alcohol since the antebellum decades. But only after 1900 did they muster sufficient political support to attain their objectives in several southern states. The unsettling racial and class implications of the populist movement again moved many Democratic leaders to support prohibition statutes. John E. White, a North Carolina prohibitionist, set out the matter plainly for fellow southerners in 1908. He complained that both blacks and lower-class whites had used alcohol irresponsibly and attributed the recent increase in lynchings to alcohol abuse on both sides of the color line. But race collaboration rather than race war concerned him most. "Following the racial lines from top to bottom," he wrote, "it becomes evident to everybody that the lines of both races converged at the saloon. . . . It is the attractive social center for the dangerous elements of our population. At their hearts the intelligent white people of the South are sick of the race issue as a menace to social peace. They are tired of the depraved and criminal negro. They are tired of the irresponsible white man. The Liquor Traffic fostered and encouraged both."

Even as southern reformers advanced programs from purely Christian motives, they felt compelled to include racial arguments to legitimate their cause. Edgar Gardner Murphy, an Episcopal priest from Alabama, led the South's efforts to eliminate child labor, which had become widespread in the region's growing textile industry. Murphy wrote movingly in a letter to the Boston *Evening Transcript* in 1901 about the "heartrending" scenes of children working in the mills until they fell asleep on their feet, and of the "compulsory ignorance" millowners foisted on these youngsters. But he also warned that peaceful race relations depended on educated whites to deal fairly with the Negro, and child labor robbed whites of their education.

The Southern Sociological Congress, an organization formed in 1912 primarily by southern churchmen and churchwomen, was one of the few white Progressive groups that eschewed appeals to racial fears or prejudices. While congress members did not challenge racial segregation at their annual meetings, they advocated mobilizing southern churches "to see that justice is guaranteed to all citizens regardless of race, color, or religion." The congress was the forerunner of another church-inspired organization that opened interracial dialogue in the South for the first time in the twentieth century, the Committee on Interracial Cooperation, founded in 1919 by congress member Will Alexander.

White southern middle-class women also created reform agendas apart from racial and class concerns. The growth of towns and customary strictures against white married middle-class women working outside the home for wages spurred the volunteer movement among white urban women. Beginning in the 1890s, women's clubs and church groups advocated child labor laws, improved education, and city beautification. Methodist women's groups, following the example of secular organizations up North, established settlement houses in southern cities during the 1890s. By 1920, there were twenty-six such homes for whites and blacks in the urban South. Men considered these activities extensions of southern women's domestic responsibilities and promoted and funded them. The men were less enthusiastic about the women's suffrage movement. Engaging in politics, they argued, required women to step across the line separating the domestic sphere from activities that competed with men and sullied the image of women as above reproach. Also, opening up the issue of voting rights so soon after denying them to blacks and some whites threatened both white solidarity and disfranchisement.

Progressive reformers, North and South, hoped to make their societies more orderly and efficient. In the South, order and efficiency meant the elimination of blacks from political life, their restriction to menial positions in the region's economy, and a specific set of rules governing social relations within the framework of segregation. Order and efficiency southern-style also implied fixed and subordinate political and economic roles for working-class whites and the appearance of social solidarity through the ideology of white supremacy. White women also filled subordinate positions. Their vulnerability justified restrictions against blacks. White women were distinguished from each other by whether they worked outside the home. Married elite and middle-class white women did not work; other white women did, and always had, whether in the fields alongside the men or in textile mills. Such distinctions enabled southern men to exploit female labor because chivalry was reserved for a class of women rather than the entire gender. But if married middle-class white women ventured into the public domain, they upset the gender and class hierarchy and threatened racial tenets as well. Their reform efforts, emanating from acceptable women's clubs and churches, had to appear more like charity than work. Race not only circumscribed and defined southern reform, but fixed the places of whites and blacks in southern society.

Blacks participated in Progressive reform, too, but hardening segregation and growing political impotence restricted the reform agenda. Blacks could no longer use the political system to secure more funds for their schools, or improve services in black neighborhoods, or lobby against cheating landlords and merchants. Black men had to take special care not to be too visible or too successful in their reform endeavors since white society reacted sharply against assertive black males. Black women, through their clubs and churches, performed extensive social service work after 1900. They were active in black Young Women's Christian Associations (YWCA) and occasionally met with their white counterparts, something that rarely occurred with black and white men. Black men channeled their efforts to building a black economy in the urban South.

After a bloody race riot in Wilmington, North Carolina, in 1898, where "respectable" whites rampaged through black neighborhoods and unseated the duly-elected Republican city government, John Merrick, a black barber from Durham, North Carolina, concluded that blacks must turn their "attention to making money. The almighty dollar is the magic wand that knocks the bottom out of race prejudice and all the humbugs that fatten on it." Merrick and six other black entrepreneurs and artisans formed the North Carolina Mutual Life Insurance Company, and within two decades it was a multimillion-dollar enterprise with a six-story building in the heart of "the Negro Wall Street of America" in Durham.

Few blacks fared as well as Merrick and his colleagues. But by the second decade of the twentieth century, thriving black business districts had emerged in cities across the South, such as "Sweet Auburn" in Atlanta and "Hayti" in Raleigh. Black-owned businesses catered to a clientele that could not obtain a haircut, a doctor's appointment, a restaurant meal, a drink, or trustworthy legal advice in the whites' downtown.

The church stood prominently in the black neighborhood, both physically and spiritually. White evangelical churches (which accounted for 90 percent of white church membership in the South during the first half of the twentieth century) stressed the relationship of the individual with God and social sins such as dancing, drinking, sex, and Sabbath-breaking. Black churches, however, were more similar to the institutional Protestant churches of the North. They organized social services, built or provided educational facilities, since many southern states failed to fund school buildings for black children, served as community centers, and offered the spiritual sustenance necessary to persist in a segregated society. Although urban black church leaders rarely challenged segregation openly during this era, they often used the Gospel to instill a sense of self-worth and pride among their parishioners.

As nurturing as black communities and churches were, segregation still cut deep into southern black souls. Segregation was not only a system of separating races but also of degrading blacks. As writer and theologian Pauli Murray wrote in her autobiography *Proud Shoes* about her childhood in segregated Durham during the 1920s, "It was never the hardship which hurt so much as the *contrast* between what we had and what the white children had. We got the greasy, torn, dog-eared books; they got the new ones. . . . They got wide mention in the newspaper; we got a paragraph at the bottom." It was easy to see where white neighborhoods ended and black districts began; that was where the pavement ran out. It was easy to tell black waiting rooms at bus and train stations from white waiting rooms; black water fountains from white water fountains; and black restrooms from white restrooms. The labels "White" and "Colored" defined black life in the urban South and were constant reminders of inferiority and second-class citizenship.

Segregation extended to employment after 1900. Black artisans had filled jobs in brickmasonry and carpentry during the slavery era and continued to do so after the Civil War. As the South's agricultural economy faltered during the late nineteenth century, more white southerners left the farm for the city and competed with blacks for artisanal employment. In some cases, as in Atlanta in 1906, the competition turned violent, and a full-scale race riot erupted. In other cases, growing intimidation reduced the numbers of black artisans after 1900 to mostly menial labor. Influential white landowners supported whites' claims to skilled jobs because limiting urban black employment meant a more stable black work force on the farm.

Blacks lost additional economic ground after 1880 as new industries emerged that for the most part excluded blacks. The textile industry was an all-white preserve except for the most menial janitorial and heavy-lifting work in which blacks would not come into contact with the numerous white women who worked in the mills. Also, white entrepreneurs believed that blacks were incapable of operating machinery, a canard that cut blacks out of some of the jobs in the mechanizing tobacco industry, although their representation was better there than in textiles. Increasingly circumscribed from urban and industrial occupations, blacks labored hard for little in the countryside. By 1900, nearly three out of four black southerners worked on a farm as a sharecropper or tenant.

Blacks also went about their communities less secure than at any time since Reconstruction. White political leaders such as James K. Vardaman and Theodore Bilbo in Mississippi, Cole Blease in South Carolina, and Hoke Smith in Georgia had built their political careers on Progressive rhetoric laced with virulent racism. In that charged atmosphere, to look at a white woman, to question a country merchant, to compete for a construction job, or merely to walk down a sidewalk were all fraught with personal danger. When opportunities for advancement opened up for blacks in the North during World War I, they left the South in droves.

Beginning with World War I and continuing for half a century, black southerners abandoned the region of their birth and ancestry. The war in Europe created jobs in northern industry that exceeded the supply of labor. Black southerners took note and streamed northward from the farmlands of the Mississippi Delta to the South Side of Chicago, and from Atlanta, Charlotte, and Richmond to North Philadelphia and Harlem in New York. As many as 700,000 southern blacks migrated to the North during World War I, and the stream continued after the war, subsiding during the Great Depression, but picking up again in the 1940s. By 1970, nearly one-half of the nation's black population resided outside the South, compared with just 10 percent in 1900.

The move was necessary but difficult. White landowners spread rumors about blacks starving and dying of the cold up North; they discouraged distribution of black newspapers such as the *Chicago Defender*, which listed job opportunities and encouraged migration; and they swept through train stations intimidating or cajoling departing blacks to rethink their situation. The black stream continued unabated; on occasion, whole black communities left their sharecropper cabins in the middle of the night. On other occasions, one family member left to get established and later bring the rest of the relatives. Whatever the pattern, the move was difficult on blacks who had built family networks, churches, friendships, and businesses in the South. They also left behind their ancestors, buried in the red Georgia clay or black Alabama loam. That was the most wrenching leaving of all. The South was home, bad as it was, and its sweet fragrances were remembered fondly in the gritty ghettos of the North.

Whites migrated as well. Although overshadowed by the Great Migration of southern blacks, nearly 2.3 million southern whites left for the North between 1900 and 1920, with another million leaving the following decade. Textiles and other southern industries offered insufficient opportunities for ambitious and talented young white southerners. Although regional boosters addressed this problem by holding periodic expositions to entice investment and initiating a good-roads movement to ease farm-to-market travel and attract tourists and businesses, few leaders addressed the need to improve the South's human capital—to improve public education, to provide social and health services, and to end the destructive racial antagonisms and separation. A Mississippi proverb placed the region's Progressive priorities in proper perspective: "Mississippians ride to the poorhouse on the best roads in the country."

NEW REALISM IN SOUTHERN CULTURE, 1920–1933

The South's participation in World War I started the slow process of self-assessment necessary to expose the contradictions between southern rhetoric and southern reality. Potential critics, however, faced serious obstacles. The South's political and economic leaders vigorously protected the principles of white supremacy and one-party rule. Dissenters from either orthodoxy were subject to economic or physical intimidation.

Southerners' defensiveness about their region's distinctive institutions softened a bit after World War I. The Woodrow Wilson administration had welcomed southern politicians into leadership positions to an extent unknown since before the Civil War. Southern lawmakers played a significant role in passing Wilson's Progressive legislation and in supporting the war effort. The war also offered the opportunity for thousands of southerners to leave their towns and counties for the first time in their lives. They returned hoping to change the stagnant economic and educational systems of their region.

Up to that time, southerners' contribution to American mass culture had been confined mostly to music. From the cotton fields of Mississippi in the 1890s came the blues; from the barrelhouses of Louisiana and the brothels of Storyville in New Orleans, the strains of jazz moved up the Mississippi to Memphis, Saint Louis, and Chicago; and, in the 1920s, "hillbilly" music filtered down from the Southern Appalachians to Charlotte, Atlanta, and later to Nashville and the rest of the country. Another form of hillbilly wafted from the West Texas hills, where "cowboy songs" blended with Mexican music, black blues, and gospel. WBAP in Fort Worth aired the musical hybrid in 1923, and Vernon Dalhart, a regular on the show, recorded the first national hillbilly hit, "The Prisoner's Song," the following year. By the late 1920s, Texas singer Jimmie Rogers emerged as the first national country-and-western (the upscale name for "hillbilly" music) star.

Southern output in literature and academic research was slight in extent, influence, and creativity prior to World War I, lending some credence to literary critic H. L. Mencken's depiction of the region as a "Sahara of the Bozart." Such publications as the *Double Dealer* in New Orleans and the *Fugitive* in Nashville provided outlets for poetry, literary criticism, and prose fiction. By the end of the 1920s, two literary giants, Thomas Wolfe and William Faulkner, were publishing their first novels, which were highly critical of southern traditions. By the 1930s, Richard Wright and Eudora Welty, erstwhile Jackson, Mississippi, neighbors, painted haunting portraits of small-town southern life from black and white perspectives, respectively. At the University of North Carolina at Chapel Hill, president Frank Porter Graham hoped to transform the institution from a mediocre state school to a regional leader in social-science research and policy. Howard W. Odum, a Georgia-born sociologist, organized the Institute for Research in the Social Sciences at Graham's university, and established a new journal, *Social Forces,* to provide an outlet for those studying the South's numerous social and economic problems. Odum and his colleagues challenged regional mores by looking critically at fundamentalist religion, lynching, sharecropping, and industrial labor. Chapel Hill sociologist Gerald Johnson threw down the gauntlet in a 1924 issue of *Social Forces:*

> Too much has been said of the South's need for "sympathetic criticism." This demand has resulted in some so-called criticism that is sympathetic, not with the South, but with the South's least admirable traits, with bigotry, intolerance, superstition and prejudice. What the South needs is criticism that is ruthless toward those things . . . and sympathetic only with its idealism, with its loyalty, with its courage and its inflexible determination.

But the South was not yet clear it wanted more candor and an open discussion of its history. Although the Ku Klux Klan revival reached across much of the Midwest and even as far west as Oregon, it was particularly strong in the South. The resurgent Klan marched down Peachtree Street in Atlanta and numerous lesser avenues around the South. In addition, fundamentalists railed against teaching evolution, mill owners brutally quashed strikes, and no political leaders emerged to implement the research findings of Odum and his colleagues. Even intellectuals disputed the wisdom of breaking the South's isolation from new ideas and trends. In 1930, a group of literary critics at Vanderbilt University in Nashville produced a bitter volume, *I'll Take My Stand,* which defended the traditions of the Old South and warned the region's inhabitants away from the twentieth century.

The dialogue about the nature of southern society persisted, however, as the Great Depression and the New Deal set in motion forces that pushed southerners to reassess the burdens of their past and change their lives accordingly. Southern economic and political leaders were well aware of the potential damage federal intrusion could inflict on white supremacy and one-party rule, even if unintended. As historian Bruce J. Schulman noted in *From Cotton Belt to Sunbelt,* "open channels risked both the loss of labor and the inflow of political heresy."

THE NEW DEAL AND WORLD WAR II, 1933–1945

The Roosevelt administration relied on the support of southern congressmen for New Deal legislation and had no intention of upsetting political or racial traditions in the South. But the unintended consequences of federal initiatives, the President's fondness for the southern people, the presence of a persuasive group of young southern white liberals in the administration, and the growing strength of the Democratic party in the North, convinced Roosevelt to take bolder initiatives as the 1930s wore on.

The Agricultural Adjustment Act (AAA; 1933) had a major and unforeseen impact on the South. Crop-reduction plans had been as numerous in the South as June bugs, and about as effective in raising cotton and tobacco prices. The AAA paid landowners to take land out of staple production, and set a floor under staple prices, above the costs of cultivation. By introducing some stability in the staple market, the government enabled farmers to plan their cultivation and their budgets. Cotton prices jumped from 6.5 cents a pound in 1932 to 11.09 cents in 1935, while the amount of land in cotton cultivation plummeted 30 percent. Tobacco prices doubled during this period.

The AAA had the effect of not only taking land out of production but also of taking tenants and sharecroppers off the land. Although the law provided that landowners share their crop-reduction checks with tenants and sharecroppers, many landlords evicted them. An interracial group of tenants in Arkansas organized the Southern Tenant Farmers Union (STFU) in 1934 to stay the evictions. The union spread through the Deep South, but evictions continued. By the end of the 1930s, average farm size increased in the South for the first time in the twentieth century and more machines were evident, as government checks paid for the tractors that replaced farm labor.

Southern industry, although a much smaller sector of the region's economy than agriculture, also experienced upheaval. The National Recovery Administration (NRA), established in 1933, set minimum wages for the nation's industries. The low-wage southern textile industry countered by cutting workers and increasing the workload of remaining employees. A general textile strike in 1934 failed to improve conditions. But the Roosevelt administration did not accept the mill owners' arguments that they needed cheap labor because their white employees "cannot learn to operate complicated machinery like that used in the North." The Fair Labor Standards Act of 1938 fixed wages for southern industry after the Supreme Court declared the NRA unconstitutional. But war mobilization was primarily responsible for the 40 percent increase in real Southern industrial wages between 1939 and 1942.

Rising wages for southern factory workers cut two ways. On the one hand, their standard of living increased; on the other hand, higher labor costs encouraged employers to mechanize and eliminate jobs, many of which were held by blacks and white women. In a Greensboro, Georgia, textile mill, the NRA code raised hourly wages by 500 percent, forcing the owners to install labor-saving machinery that eliminated most of the work force. White labor leaders referred to the NRA as the "National Run Around," while black leaders called it the "Negro Removal Act."

The impact of other New Deal legislation also reflected the distinctive race and class relationships in southern society. Public Works Administration (PWA) projects required states and localities to provide 55 percent of the funding, although they could obtain this sum through a PWA loan. But several states passed on such projects due either to insufficient funds or the efforts of powerful textile, tobacco, and farm lobbies concerned about losing workers to higher-paying PWA jobs.

Despite the auspicious beginning of the federal housing program in Atlanta with the construction of the first two public-housing complexes in the country, Techwood Homes for whites and University Homes for blacks, several other states and localities balked at competing with the private sector. In Winston-Salem, North Carolina, for example, local officials spurned a $1 million slum-clearance grant from the Federal Housing Administration (FHA) because of landlord opposition.

The Wagner Act (1935) strengthened federal support for collective bargaining and established the National Labor Relations Board (NLRB) to guard against antiunion practices by employers. When the Congress of Industrial Organizations (CIO) moved into the South to organize workers, business leaders responded with a frenzy of antiunion rhetoric. In Charlotte, textile propagandist David Clark alluded darkly to alien influences in the CIO leadership, referring especially to Lithuanian-born Sidney Hillman. Clark warned his readers that Hillman "was educated to be a rabbi" and had probably changed his name to confuse his adversaries. Other leaders resorted to more direct scare tactics, such as the Tupelo, Mississippi, editor who warned workers in that city: "If you join the CIO, you will be endorsing the closing of a factory;" or the Greenville, South Carolina, evangelist who advised his followers that "CIO" means "Christ Is Out."

If New Deal legislation was not always able to protect white workers, it fared worse with respect to blacks, as the impact of the AAA and NRA demonstrated. State and local governments manipulated federal relief programs to the detriment of black residents. Although black families outnumbered white families in Jacksonville, Florida, by a three-to-one ratio, blacks received only 45 percent of relief funds. In Atlanta during 1935, relief benefits averaged $32.66 monthly for whites and $19.29 for blacks.

By the late 1930s the sentiment of southern liberals in the Roosevelt administration and the president's own frustration with the growing reluctance of southerners in Congress led to an executive order to prepare a report on economic conditions in the South. Roosevelt hoped that the findings would embarrass his political enemies in the South and lead to a comprehensive policy to improve the southern economy which, in turn, would have positive social and political consequences. The resulting *Report on Economic Conditions in the South* (1938), prepared with the assistance of Howard W. Odum, highlighted the South as "the nation's Number One economic problem." The report focused candidly on the region's economic and educational shortcomings, skirting the race issue. The Fair Labor Standards Act (FLSA) was the first policy outcome of the report. Some southern leaders chafed at the criticism and old historical shibboleths resurfaced to discredit the report. The *Atlanta Constitution,* usually an administration supporter, warned the president that "no new reconstruction government is desired or will be tolerated."

The *Constitution*'s threat aside, the New Deal made inroads into the South, often with the complicity of mayors such as Atlanta's William B. Hartsfield and San Antonio's Maury Maverick and New Deal supporters at the state level. Federal programs built infrastructure in many localities, including water and sewer systems, stadiums, archives, office buildings, and post offices. Wage levels increased for some workers and unions made a little headway, especially in the mining, steel, and rubber industries. For black

The image of the South during the Depression. Floyd Burroughs and the Tengle Children, Hale County, Alabama, Summer 1936. Photograph by Walker Evans, Farm Security Administration. PRINTS AND PHOTOGRAPHS DIVISION, LIBRARY OF CONGRESS

workers on PWA or WPA jobs, receiving a check from the federal government loosened their dependence on local whites. Rural southerners of both races began to close a gap between themselves and their urban colleagues as the Rural Electrification Administration and the Tennessee Valley Authority brightened homes after dark, eased household cooking and cleaning routines, and connected farm families to the wider world with radio. For many southerners, the New Deal put a positive light on the federal government for the first time in memory. It was difficult to travel anywhere in the South during the 1930s without seeing a picture of the President tacked up on the side of a barn, a general store, or hanging in a home.

The New Deal broadened horizons, but World War II shattered boundaries. The federal government pumped $4 billion into southern war plants alone, or more than one-third of the national total. Federal funds also built and renovated training bases (almost 80 percent of the armed forces trained in the South at one time or another during the war), and infrastructure such as housing and roads to accommodate the migration of labor to the cities.

Southern ports sprang alive with infusions of federal money. Naval and private shipyards in Newport News, Norfolk, Charleston, Pensacola, Mobile, Pascagoula, and Houston issued calls for workers and more workers. Interior cities maintained the rapid cadence of wartime development with aircraft plants. Consolidated-Vultee in Fort Worth built B-24 Liberators and Bell Aircraft of Marietta, Georgia, won a contract to assemble the B-29 Superfortress. The armed forces desperately needed large numbers of trained recruits early in 1942, and the South's moderate climate facilitated outdoor maneuvers and training of troops as well as their rapid deployment. Industries that were either small-scale or nonexistent in the South prior to 1940 received a significant boost from federal funds. Texas cities especially benefited from the war effort. New aircraft industries in the Dallas–Fort Worth area and shipyards in Beaumont, Galveston, and Houston, the new synthetic rubber industry along the Texas Gulf Coast, steel mills in Houston, the world's largest tin smelter plant at Texas City, and a revived wood pulp industry in East Texas transformed the Lone Star State into a manufacturing juggernaut. The value added by manufacturing in Texas stood at $453 million in 1939 and at nearly $2 billion five years later.

The establishment of national uniform wages at defense installations proved a bonanza to southern workers. Women, when they worked before the war, typically earned no more than $5 a week; during the war years, $40 a week was the norm. As for men, a cash income of $500 a year would have been considered substantial; now, some men earned that sum in a month.

The employment opportunities generated by war resulted in a mass shuffling of the southern population. Mobility within and out from the region reached an all-time high during the war years and, for the first time in decades, there was a detectable migration into the South. With war industries absorbing so many southern workers, the revolution on the farm accelerated. Shortages, strategic shifts to soybeans, truck crops, and livestock, and a 22 percent decline in the farm population during the war increased mechanization and raised profits.

Equally significant changes occurred in the lives of southern blacks. The American war-propaganda machine produced daily reminders that we were fighting for freedom and liberty against the evils of fascism. Southern blacks easily made the connection and adopted "double victory"—at home and abroad—as their official slogan. Southern blacks pressed for equal employment opportunities and secured the establishment of the Fair Employment Practices Committee (FEPC) in 1941 to ensure that neither labor unions nor firms engaged in defense-related work would discriminate against black workers. The Committee quickly ran afoul of southern racial customs and, in the interests of defense, generally bowed to white pressures to retain segregation. When the FEPC intervened in a dispute at the Alabama Dry Dock and Shipping Company in Mobile, whites rioted against black workers.

The U.S. Supreme Court furthered black political interests in the South with its 1944 ruling in *Smith* v. *Allwright,* which struck down the white primary, enabling blacks to vote in the election that counted most in the South. Although white officials attempted to circumvent the decision, blacks in cities across the South successfully organized to increase registration and to elect a few black local officials in the late 1940s and early 1950s.

If these actions failed to send southern whites the message that blacks were not content within the bounds of a segregated society, then several events during the war removed any ambiguity regarding black aspirations. Blacks and whites held conferences in Durham and Richmond out of which came the interracial Southern Regional Council, headed by Howard W. Odum, in 1944. That same year, the University of North Carolina Press published *What the Negro Wants,* a series of essays edited by Howard University professor Rayford Logan that called for an end to racial segregation in the South and voting rights for blacks.

The assault on white supremacy and one-party rule provoked harsh reactions from white southerners. A race riot erupted in Beaumont, Texas, in June 1943 when a false report circulated that a black man had raped a white woman; whites killed black soldiers in Centerville, Mississippi, and Hampton, Arkansas, for alleged racial slights; and rumors of insolent blacks and plots against whites, especially white women, abounded. In 1942, Virginia Durr, a white woman living in Virginia with her husband, who worked for the Roosevelt Administration, received a letter from her father in Birmingham reporting that "all white people in Alabama are buying pistols and other ammunition in preparation for the race war which is coming."

But for the tens of thousands of white GIs returning from their first experiences outside the South in 1945, the promise of a new era loomed larger in their thoughts than revenge against blacks advocating civil rights. The South was on the move: "Yankees coming South; Negroes going North; cotton going West; livestock coming East; money coming in," wrote Lillian Smith in *Killers of the Dream* (1949). The accelerating tempo of life seemed to portend something good at last for the region. But southern history taught caution. Reaction and reform could work in tandem, as they had in the Progressive era. If it was possible to maintain white supremacy and one-party rule while prospering at the same time, southern leaders would follow that course; if not, then prosperity would have to wait.

POSTWAR ECONOMIC TRANSFORMATION, 1945–1965

Many restless returning veterans, especially blacks, decided not to wait for things to change and headed north. Nearly one out of five southerners left the region during the 1940s, compared with one out of ten during the 1920s. Outmigration was heavy among blacks, who saw ominous signs in white southerners' reactions to their limited freedoms during the war. More than one million blacks left the South in the 1940s.

The outmigration affected rural areas most. Between 1940 and 1960, the southern farm population declined by nearly 60 percent, forcing those farmers who could afford it to mechanize (a mechanical cotton picker became available by the late 1940s), or to switch to crops such as soybeans and peanuts. In 1940 the South had produced 7.6 million bales of cotton and 5.4 million bushels of soybeans; by 1975, those figures were 3 million bales and 523 million bushels, respectively. Agricultural-extension agents typically served mechanized farms rather than marginal family farms unable to compete in the new agribusiness market. Lost in the statistics was a way of life for tens of thousands of southerners who had grown up, several generations deep, on the farm, had held on to their living, perhaps supplementing it with a mill job, and now were finally lured into a new lifestyle of public (off-farm) work and living out of bags (buying groceries at the supermarket).

The green revolution on the farm and the money pumped into the region during the war strengthened the South's anemic consumer purchasing power. Local boosters saw opportunities to attract outside investment. As early as 1936, Mississippi launched its Balance Agriculture with Industry (BAWI) program, complete with tax incentives, land giveaways, and environmental concessions to attract manufacturing plants. The selling of the South began in earnest after the war and each southern state established a recruiting office to tout its nonunion labor, low taxes, cheap land, and the absence of government interference (i.e., the absence of regulations).

Southerners who had made a fetish of scorning any kind of federal assistance, even through the New Deal era, soon learned to belly up to the federal trough. Prominent lawmakers such as Georgia senator Richard B. Russell, chairman of the Senate Appropriations Committee, fellow Georgian Carl Vinson, head of the House Armed Services Committee, and Charleston congressman L. Mendel Rivers funneled federal funds into Georgia and South Carolina for weapons systems, airplanes, and military bases. These southern states rivaled California as defense-industry capitals.

Many of these activities required technically trained personnel and supporting infrastructure. The federal government subsidized research and development firms, and, through the National Defense Education Act of 1957, passed with the leadership of Alabama congressman Carl Elliott, pumped millions of dollars into southern universities and community colleges. With the Airport Act of 1946 and the Interstate Highway Act of 1956, Congress ensured that southern products and managers had easy access into and out of the region. Airports and major roads triggered their own economic activity, including retail shopping malls, light industry, and trucking. In 1940 federal grants made up 14 percent of southern state government revenues; by 1955, that figure surpassed 20 percent and every southern state except Florida exceeded the national average.

Other aspects of the South's postwar economic development required less lobbying and advertising. Climate proved to be a natural attraction for the region. Florida had benefited from its balmy locale since early in the century, but as roads improved and as retirement there became more feasible economically for greater proportions of the population after the war, the Sunshine State enjoyed an unprecedented boom. (See figure 1 for a comparison of the population growth in the South and in other regions of the country.)

Texas followed Florida as the regional pacesetter in economic advance largely on the strength of its growing petrochemical industry. By the mid-1950s the Texas-Louisiana area was producing one-half of the nation's oil. The abundance of oil and gas, sulphur, and fresh water was ideal for the development of petrochemicals in that region.

Florida and Texas were special beneficiaries of the widespread use of air conditioning by the 1950s. The stifling heat and humidity of southern summers had slowed even the most energetic go-getters. The ability to control the summer climate facilitated work in high-rise office buildings, college campuses, shopping malls, and countless small businesses and homes. If new homes featured verandas and high ceilings, they were now more for effect than for climate-control.

Air conditioning and market-oriented economic expansion after the war fueled urban growth. Prior to 1940, the South's small towns had grown at a more rapid rate than its larger cities; the pattern reversed after 1940. Aggressive new leaders, such as Atlanta mayor William B. Hartsfield and New Orleans mayor De Lesseps Morrison, cast aside the traditional political reliance on white supremacy and emphasized consensus politics (including black voters) and economic development. With cities in the lead, per capita income in the South rose from approximately one-half the national average in 1940 to more than two-thirds by 1960. Bank deposits nearly doubled during the 1940s, and real individual income increased by 223 percent in that decade, compared with a 119 percent rise in the North.

But the new economy existed alongside the old race relations. Initial signs after the war implied a positive, gentle transition away from white supremacy. Moderate governors such as Alabama's James E. ("Big Jim") Folsom, Sid McMath in Arkansas, Kerr Scott in North Carolina, and Frank Clement in Ten-

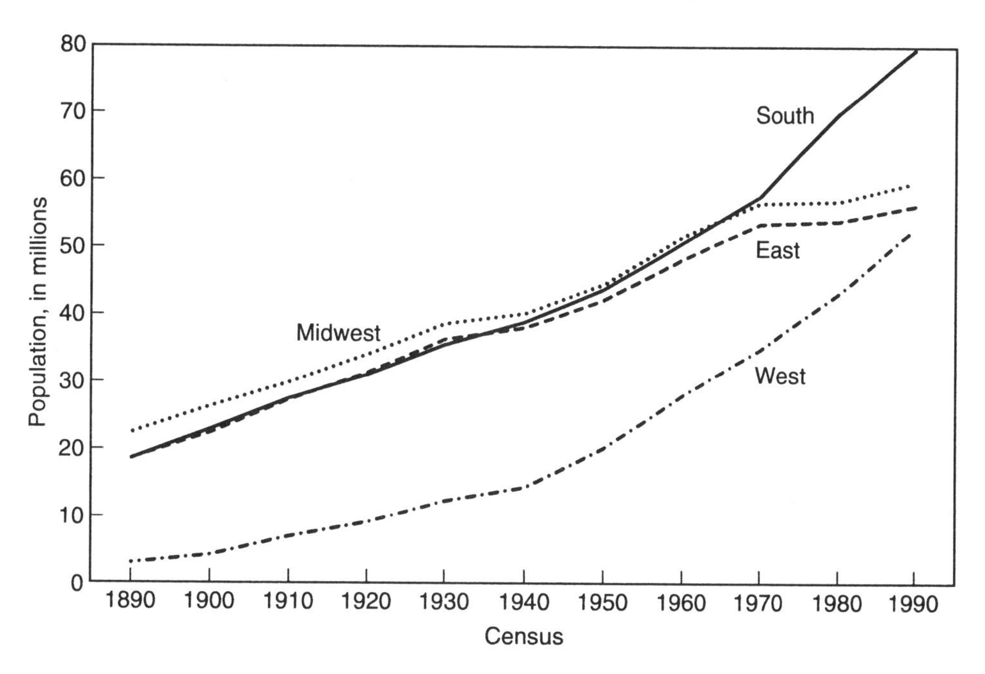

Figure 1. Population of the United States by Region, 1890–1990. (Source: U.S. Bureau of the Census. Figures for 1890–1960 from *Historical Statistics of the United States, Colonial Times to 1970* [1975]; figures for 1970–1990 from *Statistical Abstract of the United States, 1994.*)

nessee led Atlanta editor Ralph McGill to declare in the late 1940s that "the South is freer of ranters and demagogues than it has been for a generation or more." But subsequent events proved that McGill's declaration was premature. The persistence of returning black veterans pushing against the barriers of segregation and disfranchisement, as well as President Truman's civil-rights package and the U.S. Supreme Court decision in *Brown* v. *Board of Education* (1954) provoked hostile white reaction in the South. Race resurfaced as *the* political litmus test. As the Iron Curtain fell in Eastern Europe, southern whites circled their wagons, stifled dissent from within and discredited or blocked ideas from without.

THE CIVIL RIGHTS ERA, 1955–1965

By 1955 southern reaction had become organized and stylized. In the towns and cities, white citizens' councils appeared, disavowing violence but at the same time imposing economic sanctions against white dissenters and black protesters, and creating an atmosphere that implicitly condoned the use of force. Politicians, the more responsible among them, developed a routine that also condemned force but at the same time encouraged constituents to defy the Supreme Court and educate blacks as to their proper place in southern society. White churches reiterated their interest in promoting the relationship between the individual and God for the benefit of the hereafter, but avoiding its implications for the present. In rural areas, especially in the Black Belt regions of Georgia, Alabama, and Mississippi, areas of heavy black concentration and dependency on white employers, whites could be more direct.

While the Eisenhower administration moved with great caution against this reaction, with the notable exception of the school desegregation issue in Little Rock, Arkansas, southern blacks risked their economic and physical well-being to secure their rights. The U.S. Supreme Court continued to chip away at the already shaky foundations of segregation. Southern white youngsters crossed the fading color line to embrace "race" music in a new blend of white hillbilly and black blues called "rock 'n' roll." Sun Recording Studios in Memphis introduced the music to the nation in the mid-1950s, with such stars as Elvis Presley, Johnny Cash, Carl Perkins, and Jerry Lee Lewis often covering black tunes. Southern mayors built airports, office parks, and convention centers, and compromised to avoid racial confrontations detrimental to economic growth. Southern resistance wore thin on Capitol Hill as some lawmakers began to note the irony of accusing the Soviets of using strong-arm tactics in Eastern Europe and Asia while white authorities in the South bullied peaceful blacks.

But rather than wait for history to catch up to their aspirations, blacks seized the moment for themselves. The Montgomery bus boycott of 1955, which brought the Reverend Dr. Martin Luther King, Jr., to national prominence, focused a national audience on segregation in the South. A small group of black Greensboro, North Carolina, college students initiated the sit-in demonstrations in 1960, turning the cause of civil rights into a mass movement. When the movement turned to the Deep South violence erupted. But the attacks by white authorities and civilians during the Freedom Rides in 1961, the demonstrations in Birmingham in 1963, the Mississippi Freedom Summer of 1964, and the Selma voting-rights march of 1965 were instrumental in securing the passage of the 1964 Civil Rights Act and the 1965 Voting Rights Act.

The civil rights movement was a black-led crusade thoroughly rooted in the South's history and culture. The movement initially sprang out of black churches and utilized the familiar regional rhetoric of sin and redemption, not to reify the Lost Cause and white supremacy, but to offer a new interpretation of southern history that included both races. Black southerners sought to exorcise not white sinners, but their sin of race pride. Employing tactics of civil disobedience and nonviolent confrontation, blacks fought for their civil liberties with dignity and civility, a language of manners that white southerners understood as much as the rhetoric of redemption. At the same time, black southerners sought to educate whites about segregation, an institution most southern whites took for granted and assumed everyone, including blacks, accepted. The civil rights movement underscored black discontent with segregation and disfranchisement and it stressed the possibilities of interracial collaboration for the South. Blacks presented a history lesson, challenging the verities of white supremacy, of the Lost Cause, and Reconstruction, and offered a new version of racial harmony and regional prosperity.

Blacks sought not only to redeem whites and the South, but themselves as well. The sit-in demonstrations which spread across the South in 1960 involved a new generation of black southerners, high school and college students who refused to accept the racial status quo or employ the traditional tactics for challenging the system. The movement imparted a sense of dignity to its participants that segregation had assaulted through its daily reminders of inferiority. Franklin McCain, one of the initial sit-in demonstrators in 1960 in Greensboro explained, "I probably felt better that day than I've ever felt in my life. I felt as though I had gained my manhood, so to speak, and not only gained it, but had developed quite a lot of respect for it."

The 1964 Civil Rights Act barred segregation in public accommodations and the 1965 Voting Rights Act afforded blacks access to the political process. These measures were the two immediate results of the movement's efforts. Most cities had abandoned segregated facilities by the time President Lyndon B. Johnson signed the 1964 act into law, but segregation lingered on in smaller communities. As late as 1990, several cases of discrimination at public swimming pools and restaurants surfaced in South Carolina, but such incidents were rare in the cities by then. After the 1965 Voting Rights Act became law, blacks swamped registration offices across the South. In those scattered districts where prospective registrants encountered resistance, federal registrars assumed the responsibility of enrolling voters.

Ironically, when blacks registered to vote, they usually signed up for the party of white supremacy, the Democratic party. But their allegiance was primarily to the national Democratic party that had sponsored most of the civil rights legislation of the 1960s. Black enrollment in the Democratic party triggered a major political reorganization in the one-party South. The Republican party, previously confined to selected mountain and urban areas of the region, surged forward first with the presidential candidacy of conservative Republican Barry Goldwater in 1964, and second as the GOP increasingly identified itself as a party committed to restricting federal involvement in local civil rights issues ranging from school desegregation to affirmative-action programs.

Conservative white Democrats abandoned their ancestral party in droves, especially in presidential voting. Lyndon B. Johnson in 1964 was the last Democratic candidate to receive a majority of the southern white vote. Even native sons Jimmy Carter in 1976 and Bill Clinton in 1992 could not generate a white majority. Democratic candidates fared better in local and statewide elections as they held on to majorities in state legislatures and occupied a majority of the governors' chairs through the early 1990s. Southern white voters rarely turned out incumbents (and most incumbents were Democrats), and generally practiced "friends and neighbors" politics demonstrating a willingness to overlook the occasional liberal stance of a person who had looked after constituents. Even so, statewide Democratic candidates rarely received a majority of white votes. They relied on a close-to-unanimous vote from blacks to attain victory.

The Voting Rights Act has been especially effective in increasing the number of black elected officials in the South, from a trace in 1965 to over three thousand in 1990, the most in the nation. Black mayors led major cities such as Atlanta, Birmingham, Charlotte,

Little Rock, New Orleans, and Houston during the 1970s and 1980s. More typically, black elected officials presided over mostly black and poor small towns and counties with minimal tax bases and heavy reliance on federal and state social-service revenues. In the larger cities, black mayors have improved services in neglected black neighborhoods and established affirmative-action programs in city departments, but they have not made significant inroads in their communities' unemployment and housing problems, which have worsened with federal cutbacks. Black mayors such as Atlanta's Andrew Young and Charlotte's Harvey Gantt succeeded in attracting considerable business investment to their respective cities during the 1980s but made less headway solving their cities' social ills. The trickle-down theory of economics has not worked for the urban South. Economic power remains primarily in the hands of whites, even if political power is increasingly shared with or even is wielded primarily by blacks.

THE SUNBELT, 1965–PRESENT

Federal highway, airport, defense, and research and development programs expanded the southern economy but did not appreciably redistribute regional wealth, nor were they intended to do so. Federal funding enabled state and local authorities to maintain low tax bases, skimp on social services, and offer attractive incentive packages to incoming businesses. By the 1970s the federal government assumed more than 70 percent of the welfare costs in every southern state except Virginia. The national average was 52 percent. As early as 1949, *Business Week* noted that defense spending "doesn't really alter the structure of the economy. It goes through the regular channels. . . . [W]elfare and public works spending . . . does alter the economy. It makes new channels of its own. It creates new institutions. It redistributes income."

Federal pump-priming further boosted consumer spending and attracted branches of northern retail, service, and manufacturing firms. Many of these firms and spin-off activities located in the growing metropolitan areas of the South. By 1970 farm life had not so much changed as diminished in the South. Interurban migration was the most common population movement in the South; farm-to-city migration declined. Newcomers to the region settled in the suburban rings around southern cities as well.

Although southern blacks did not share equally in the South's economic development, the prosperity of the 1960s eased the transition to an integrated society. Black versus white competition for jobs had been a frequent source of interracial conflict since the antebellum era. As more blacks left the South and more employment opportunities appeared, jobs were not major flash points for racial antagonism. When the southern economy slowed in the late 1980s, racial tensions bubbled to the surface again.

But for two decades after 1965, few cared about persistent social and economic disparities. America had fallen in love with the South again. As the rest of urban America battled racial violence in the late 1960s and early 1970s, the South remained relatively calm. The nation's image of a benighted, bigoted, and backward region changed. With substantial black populations of their own, northerners wrestled with their own prejudices. As northern urban economies sunk in a sea of red ink and infrastructure crumbled, the spanking-new airports, roads, and shopping malls of the suburbanized and sanitized South looked almost idyllic by comparison. *Southern Living* rather than *Tobacco Road* became the prevailing image of the South, and southerners did little to disabuse others of its accuracy.

Southerners had full complicity from the national media, including a *New York Times* series in 1976 that dubbed the region the "Sunbelt." Buffeted by Watergate, disintegrating cities, and defeat overseas, the nation needed a refurbished South and the South obliged. Millions of tourists poured in, especially to the beaches and mountains of the region, and millions more decided to retire in the South. Florida led the South and the nation in the mailbox economy, the transfer of Social Security and other pensions from the North to the South. The retirees were part of a larger movement of population back into the South for the first time in over a century. Most came for economic opportunity such as that offered by the Research Triangle Park in North Carolina or the National Aeronautics and Space Administration (NASA) facilities in Huntsville, Alabama, and Houston. Some came for the educational opportunities as the state universities of North Carolina, Virginia, and Texas attained high rank among the nation's public institutions, and Duke, Rice, Vanderbilt, and Emory were widely recognized as among the major private universities in the country. It was a remarkable transition, both in image and in fact, of a region that the federal government had proclaimed just a generation earlier as the "nation's Number One economic problem."

But the South is ever the master of illusion, to itself and to others. From the 1880s to 1930, many southern leaders maintained that the region was the economic wonder of the age, a "new" South replete with industries, paved roads, and shining cities. The

Depression revealed both the fragility of the region's economy and the hyperbole of its boosters. Similarly, southern leaders had touted Dixie's racial harmony and assured those outside the South that white southerners knew best how to handle black southerners. That racial harmony rested on a system of racial oppression did not occur to many white southerners because, given alleged black inferiority and natural instincts (as demonstrated in the Reconstruction era), and given the virulent racism of working-class whites (as indicated by lynchings and the periodic emergence of racial demagogues), law and order required separation and restriction.

The civil rights movement undercut white supremacy because it challenged incontrovertibly many of the premises on which supremacists based their policies. But the Sunbelt economy merely confirmed what many boosters had stated all along: nonunion labor, low taxes, and a weak regulatory state equals a good business climate. The Sunbelt economy also confirmed that investments in primary education, social services, and environmental policies were unnecessary for economic prosperity.

But the history of the twentieth-century South indicated that the region did not move decisively from one era to another; rather it welcomed the new to a place alongside the old. The metropolitan South of the 1980s was the Sunbelt South; the rural South, increasingly the impoverished South. The postindustrial or service economy also created a two-tier employment system: occupations in real estate, insurance, government, accounting, finance, and education, on the one hand, and employment in minimum-wage service industries such as tourism, fast food, and maintenance on the other. Sought-after high-tech electronics industries employed mostly low-skill, low-wage workers. Many of the jobs in the lower tier of the service economy did not pay as well as the old manufacturing jobs in textiles, lumbering, and furniture. And service sector jobs were typically located in the fast-growing suburbs of metropolitan areas far from the residences of inner-city black and Hispanic workers.

For many rural southerners, the Sunbelt phenomenon has been a bitter ruse. Northern firms branched or moved to the rural South during the 1960s to escape higher labor, land, and tax costs in the North. But growing international competition from nations that offered better terms led to the flight of these footloose firms overseas. In addition, traditional rural industries such as textiles mechanized in order to compete with low labor costs abroad. Between 1979 and 1985, the Piedmont textile belt lost 300,000 textile jobs. Many of those workers filtered into the lower tier of service employment, where wages and benefits were even lower than in textiles. And a higher percentage of these workers were black; ironically, the textile industry, under pressure of civil rights legislation, had begun hiring significant numbers of blacks in the late 1960s and early 1970s.

If the rural South could not undersell its foreign competition, it presented an attractive profile for business nobody else wanted, such as toxic waste dumps. In 1990, the Institute for Southern Studies in Durham, North Carolina, devised a "green scorecard" to measure the nation's environmental health. Environmental policies, health, and toxic emissions and storage facilities were among the key indices the institute used to score the states. Southern states accounted for nine of the ten worst environmental offenders. Most of the poisons were located in poor, rural, and heavily black counties: the so-called "Cancer Alley" between New Orleans and Baton Rouge, Louisiana, the radioactive waste dump in Sumter County, Alabama, and various rural locations in South Carolina were some examples the report cited.

For those counties that were poor, but not desperate, the loss of the younger population, the boarding-up of downtown stores, and the inability to compete with more urban counties portended a bleak economic future. At most, if the road system cooperated, a Wal-Mart appeared on the edge of town, benefiting shoppers but further depressing downtown businesses. Health care, life expectancy, and educational levels were likely to be poor in these areas as well. The South continues to rank at the bottom in these categories primarily because of its rural poverty.

For blacks, there has been undeniable progress since 1965. The politically sanctioned daily reminders of inferiority are mostly gone, especially in the cities, and in many areas there is likely as not to be a black elected official at city hall or on the county commission. Equally important, black men and women in business suits are no longer oddities in any downtown. While the black middle class has increased significantly in the South since 1975, black poverty remains endemic. State and local governments have not picked up the federal programs dropped during the 1980s. In rural areas, 80 percent of black children under the age of six in 1988 fell below the poverty line.

Race is a factor not only in poverty, but in politics as well. Although the ranting demagogues have largely disappeared, candidates, especially from the Republican party, couch their racial appeals in phrases and images acceptable to white middle-class sensibilities. The Willie Horton ads in George Bush's 1988 presidential bid were concocted by a southern Republican. Code terms such as "forced busing," "law and order," "workfare," and "welfare mothers" have replaced less subtle race-baiting, but the southern Republican party is more the heir to the party of white supremacy than to the party of Lincoln. Although race relations have changed significantly in the South since 1900, race is still important in defining regional economic and political issues, which is to say that the South is like the rest of the country.

THE SOUTH: AMERICAN REGION, SEPARATE PLACE

Many scholars have argued that the South as a distinctive region is dead or dying. Such arguments have persisted at least since Henry Grady spoke of a New South in 1886, but it may be more true now than at any time in the region's history. Most southerners no longer define their lives by crop cycles. The South now is an urban and suburban region and except for a few architectural fillips here and there, these areas are virtually indistinguishable from areas of California or Kansas. Moreover, millions of "southerners" are not native southerners; the rapid in-migration during the 1970s and 1980s of northerners and foreigners (especially Hispanics) into the metropolitan areas of states such as Florida, Texas, North Carolina, Virginia, and Georgia have imparted a diversity to the southern population unknown since the antebellum era. And even native-born southerners, influenced by the homogenizing efforts of television, magazines, and mail-order catalogs, display consumer habits little different from those of people in other parts of the country. If the South is more a state of mind than states of geography, then the mind of the South has become increasingly American, and all that may be left of the South is the geographic designation valuable for census purposes and little else.

Still, a survey conducted by the *Atlanta Constitution* in 1992 of 1,140 southerners revealed a remarkable self-consciousness about regional heritage. Better than two-thirds interviewed believed that the South was a distinctive region; equally revealing, three-quarters of the white respondents and an equal ratio of blacks identified themselves as southerners. Here is one of the major changes wrought by the civil rights movement: many more blacks now consider themselves southern, thereby reinforcing the distinctive identity of the region. Sociologist John Shelton Reed argued in *Southerners: The Social Psychology of Sectionalism* (1983) that the rise of the metropolitan South, and the middle-class southerner along with it, has not weakened southern identity but has reinforced it. As white-collar southerners have traveled to other parts of the country, they have become more aware and conservative of southern distinctiveness. Finally, the pace of life, the friendliness and civility of the people, as well as the cleanliness, low taxes, and open spaces of their new homes have captivated newcomers from the North and abroad. But regardless of their perspectives, most new residents agree that they have come to a different place. Much as southerners adapted the industrial revolution to their own culture and engaged in a racial accommodation rooted in regional values, so these newcomers are being absorbed into the prevailing culture.

Southerners, especially native southerners, still care a great deal about certain traditions that seem impervious to the changing economy and demography swirling around them. They have discovered that it is possible to be a late-twentieth-century American and a southerner at the same time. The southerner's daily life is no longer circumscribed by the county line or the debt at the country store. Today's typical southerner lives in a suburban home and works at an occupation and enjoys recreation virtually indistinguishable from those of other Americans. But family and church continue to mean a great deal in this still overwhelmingly evangelical Protestant region. And the past remains important through revered ancestors, tales handed down through generations, and memories of momentous family and local events. Family reunions, iced tea, visiting on Sundays, country music, fried everything, collards and kudzu, molasses speech, fishing, hunting, stock-car racing, and down-home religion seem to have well survived massive population exchanges, an economic resurrection, a political upheaval, and dramatic social and racial changes. White supremacy, one-crop agriculture, and one-party politics no longer describe the South; other, and one hopes, more positive definitions will emerge as the South continues to redefine its relationship to its history of slavery, defeat, and reconstruction. The South's history is distinctive and it will remain a distinctive region; how southerners, black and white, native-born and newcomer, interpret that history will help to determine the features of regional distinction for the next century.

BIBLIOGRAPHY

Several works provide overviews of part or most of twentieth-century southern history. W. J. Cash, *The Mind of the South* (1941), is a classic, if incomplete, introduction to southern history from the perspective of the era of segregation and one-party politics. Pete Daniel, *Standing at the Crossroads: Southern Life since 1900* (1986), is a gracefully written account of the twentieth-century South stressing southern cultural contributions and the transformation of southern agriculture. A venerable but still valuable analysis and survey of the period through World War II is George B. Tindall, *The Emergence of the New South, 1913–1945* (1967). David R. Goldfield covers the post–World War II era in *Promised Land: The South since 1945* (1987), emphasizing the racial, political, and economic changes in the recent South and the persistence of a distinctive regional culture.

The standard work on the Progressive era in the South is Dewey W. Grantham, *Southern Progressivism: The Reconciliation of Progress and Tradition* (1983), a balanced survey whose thesis is explicit in the subtitle. The early twentieth century was an era not only of incipient reform in the South but also of industrial development, especially in textiles. Jacqueline Dowd Hall et al., *Like a Family: The Making of a Southern Cotton Mill World* (1987), uses oral testimony from former textile mill workers to present a portrait at odds with the conventional view that management subjugated docile mill workers wrenched away from their rural environment.

Although the South shared in national reform and economic trends, racial patterns skewed the results of regional progress. Joel Williamson, *The Crucible of Race: Black-White Relations in the American South since Emancipation* (1984), is the best general source for explicating the relationship between race and reform, as well as the southern white psyche during the era of segregation. J. Morgan Kousser, *The Shaping of Southern Politics: Suffrage Restriction and the Establishment of the One-Party South, 1880–1910* (1974), connects the restriction of black voting rights to Progressive reform. And Pauli Murray's *Proud Shoes* (1956), presents a searing portrait of her segregated childhood in Durham, North Carolina, and is one of the best reminiscences of southern blacks growing up under segregation.

From within the South during the 1920s and increasingly from outside the region during the Depression and war years, forces of change assaulted racial, political, and economic traditions. The Southern Renaissance that began in the 1920s was one important reflection of regional introspection and self-criticism. Richard H. King, *A Southern Renaissance: The Cultural Awakening of the American South, 1930–1955* (1980), adds social science and journalistic creativity to the more typical discussions of southern literary output and analyzes how novelists and social scientists sought both to come to terms with the southern past and develop new strategies for coping with a struggling region. For an overview of how the New Deal affected the South, see James C. Cobb and Michael Namorato, eds., *The New Deal and the South* (1984), whose essays contend that the New Deal had a significant impact on southern social and economic conditions. Few areas experienced more wrenching change during the 1930s and 1940s than southern agriculture. Pete Daniel, *Breaking the Land: The Transformation of Cotton, Tobacco, and Rice Cultures since 1880* (1985), charges that federal policies, especially in the cotton sector, destroyed the independence of the small farmer, threw the tenant off the land, and severed the strong psychic ties to the soil. Jack Temple Kirby, in *Rural Worlds Lost: The American South, 1920–1960* (1987), shares Daniel's concerns about the disappearing family farm and discusses how the shift to town and "public" work changed farmers, especially since World War II, not only in the staple crop regions but also in marginal farming areas such as Southern Appalachia. World War II both sealed and accelerated many economic and social trends initiated during the twenties and thirties, as Morton Sosna notes in "More Important than the Civil War?: The Impact of World War II on the South," in James C. Cobb and Charles R. Wilson, eds., *Perspectives on the American South: An Annual Review of Society, Politics and Culture* 4 (1987): 145–58. This is the best survey in print of the lightly studied subject of how World War II changed the South.

The postwar South reaped the whirlwind of racial, economic, and political change. Initially, a mass exodus of black southerners to the North occurred, an event chronicled by Nicholas Lemann, *The Promised Land: The Great Black Migration and How It Changed America* (1991), a beautifully written portrait of how southern culture shaped the experience of black migrants to the North and what federal policy has done to address the resulting problems of the northern urban ghettos. Federal policy not only responded to regional migration but also helped to shape southern economic development after the war. Bruce J. Schulman, *From Cotton Belt to Sunbelt: Federal Policy, Economic Development, and the Transformation of the South, 1938–1980* (1991), offers a thorough treatment of how federal grants played a major role in creating the Sunbelt economy without making significant social changes in the South. Although James C. Cobb, *The Selling of the South: The Southern Crusade for Industrial Development, 1936–1980* (1982), does not grant such a major role to the federal government, he also stresses social continuity in the form of land and labor exploitation as southern business and political leaders pursued economic development. In a lighter vein, but no less important to southern economic fortunes after World War II, is Raymond Arsenault, "The End of the Long Hot Summer: The Air Conditioner and Southern Culture," *Journal of Southern History* 50 (1984): 597–628, which presents a brief and informative history of the invention of air conditioning in the South and then makes a strong case for its importance in modifying southern culture.

Perhaps the most significant change in the postwar South occurred in race relations. David R. Goldfield, *Black, White, and Southern: Race Relations and Southern Culture, 1940 to the Present* (1990), argues that the civil rights struggle in the South was a black-led movement that emphasized the commitment of blacks to a new interpretation of southern history and culture without destroying that culture. David Garrow, *Bearing the Cross: Martin Luther King, Jr., and the Southern Christian Leadership Conference* (1986), is the most comprehensive and detailed of the numerous King biographies, and it emphasizes the religious aspect of King's leadership. Religion played an ambiguous role in the civil rights movement. While evangelical Protestantism enabled southern whites to understand and even appreciate black witness, regional theology also contributed to white resistance. For a broad view of this ambiguity, see Samuel S. Hill, *The South and North in American Religion* (1980), which contrasts the style, social impact, and constituencies of religion in the two sections. Early in the civil rights campaigns, white churches were not forthcoming in their support of their black brethren. That episode is told best by James Sellers, *The South and Christian Ethics* (1962), which is both an indictment of white southern evangelical Protestantism and its relation to racial justice and an outline of how southern religion in the hands of black southerners can redeem the region.

The civil rights movement, economic prosperity, and interregional migration patterns transformed the one-party South. V. O. Key, Jr., *Southern Politics in State and Nation* (1949), is the classic study of the one-party South and a prerequisite for understanding the changes that occurred during and after the 1960s. Those changes are analyzed in Earl Black and Merle Black, *Politics and Society in the South* (1987), which covers the rise of the two-party South after the 1965 Voting Rights Act and the persistence of race as a factor in southern politics.

Is the South still the South? There is plenty of evidence in the works of the Blacks, Cobb, Daniel, Goldfield, and Schulman to answer a qualified "yes." Supporting this view is John Shelton Reed, *Southerners: The Social Psychology of Sectionalism* (1983), which makes a strong case for the persistence of southern distinctiveness in the increasingly urban world of the modern South.

THE WEST

Patricia Nelson Limerick and Jon Coleman

The American West—which includes the Pacific Northwest, the Southwest, California, the Rocky Mountain States, and the Great Basin—contains the nation's extremes of geography: the highest and lowest altitudes and the most rugged terrain. The plains, deserts, and mountains of the region have posed a lasting challenge to American notions of a useful, cooperative, properly domesticated landscape. In climate, much of the West has a conspicuously lower rainfall than the rest of the nation, a limit that an enormous campaign for the redistribution of water would ease, but not erase. In human geography, the West also embraces extremes: rural areas with a very low population density, and urban and suburban areas with very concentrated populations. In political geography, the West has, by virtue of its enormous public lands, a particularly intense relationship with the federal government. In many of its activities, the Department of the Interior has functioned as a national agency established with the particular purpose of governing the American West; federal bureaucrats have thus become an influential part of the western population and important shapers of the western landscape.

In its range of cultural groups, the West also has a claim for distinctiveness. The region holds the majority of the nation's Indian people, both on reservations and in cities, as well as a long-standing Hispanic population, descendants of settlers from the 1600s. In Utah, southern Idaho, and northern Arizona, Mormonism gives its particular flavor to local culture. Throughout the region, a range of rural subcultures have their roots in the often precarious economies of mining, ranching, farming, and logging. In contrast to these well-established populations, many more western groups in this century were recent arrivals: health-seekers and tourists who decided to stay; middle-class midwesterners looking for a new way of life in the winter-free areas of Southern California and Arizona; Americans from all over the country responding to the opportunity in defense work during World War II and the Cold War; Asian and Latin American immigrants seeking jobs, opportunity, and often enough, refuge; and more and more "amenity-seekers," enthusiasts for the natural landscapes, recreational options, and appealing "lifestyles" of the region.

In sheer numbers, the westward movement of the twentieth century dwarfed the more celebrated and studied westward movement of the nineteenth century. This continuing migration left the region particularly unsettled on the question of legitimacy. In the midst of ongoing cycles of migration, what was the difference between qualified, deserving, *real* westerners, entitled to the use of the region's resources, and illegitimate intruders? Some based their claim to legitimacy on the number of years of their own, or their family's, residence in the region. Others took money and property as their standard, or the ability to secure one's position by legislation or litigation. Yet another set of claims rested on the proposition that one's own group had invested the most labor and gained the least reward from the development of the region's resources. As issues of environmental limits, especially in water supply, gained more attention in the late twentieth century, this contest for legitimacy took center stage in the region's political and economic life. Environmentalists might see purity and principle in the proposition that growth must be limited and human population kept to the carrying capacity of the land, but the question of how those limits would be defined and enforced remains unresolved.

The struggle over the right to use the region's human and natural resources began centuries ago. Indian groups contested each other's territorial claims before the intrusion of Europeans. When Francisco Vásquez de Coronado in 1540 claimed New Mexico for Spain, the contest became more heated with the entry of agents for European empire. Neither the mid-nineteenth-century conquest of the West by the United States, taking the Pacific Northwest from

Map 4. The West.

England and the Southwest from Mexico, nor the more prolonged American conquest of the West's Indian people, ended the contest for dominance and profit in the region. That contest continued long after formal territorial conquest. Many of the issues and dilemmas of the twentieth-century West grew directly out of events in the previous century.

Despite these links and ties between the centuries, traditional versions of national and regional history offered a different story, one premised on discontinuity. In 1893, Frederick Jackson Turner delivered his famed speech, "The Significance of the Frontier in American History." To Turner and his followers, the terms *frontier* and *West* were interchangeable. Both represented a constantly moving process, not a permanent place. Moreover, following the lead of the director of the 1890 census, Turner declared the frontier closed: "four centuries from the discovery of America, at the end of a hundred years of life under the Constitution, the frontier has gone, and with its going has closed the first period of American history."

The assumption of a closed frontier left the twentieth-century West without a present self-conception. Conventional western historians used the word *postfrontier* to characterize the twentieth-century trans-Mississippi West. "The term *[frontier]*," Turner had written, "is an elastic one, and for our purposes does not need sharp definition." With no clear definition of the concept "frontier," there was not much hope for grounding the meaning of the twentieth-century West in the foggy concept, *postfrontier.* Those historians who relied on it followed an unexamined analogy to the life cycle. In the nineteenth century, the West had been newly born, young, rambunctious; in the twentieth century, the West had become adult, mature, and stable.

Had the frontier West really matured into the postfrontier West? Happily for a clear understanding of the region, this conceptual puzzle came with an easy solution. When historians turned away from the unrewarding effort to define the frontier and to fix its ending, the continuity of western issues across the centuries became instantly apparent. The list of unbroken themes is a long one: the assertion of Indian rights to land, natural resources, religious and cultural freedom, and self-government; unsettled relations between Mexico and the United States, and between citizens of Mexican origin and the Anglo-American majority; the allocation of water; the role of the federal government in supervising public resources and in aiding western economic development; the reorientation of the United States from the Atlantic to the Pacific, with a special focus on the American response to Asian immigration and trade; the tension between urban interests and rural interests; the test posed to transportation systems by the region's vast distances; and the uncertain fortunes of communities relying on extractive economies. On these issues, the history of the twentieth-century West rests firmly on the foundation of the nineteenth century West, despite a widespread belief, held both by scholars and laypeople, in the end of the frontier and the discontinuity of western history. To reckon with these unsettled issues, twentieth-century westerners had to maneuver their way through a confusing web of regional myth and nostalgia.

THE WESTERN MYTH

By 1900, the image of a colorful, quaint, romantic, and wild old West had obscured the actual complexity and seriousness of the region's past. In the last years of the nineteenth century and the first years of the twentieth, an interdisciplinary, multimedia team of image-makers had taken up the task of sprucing up, glorifying, and romanticizing the western past. The artists Charles Russell and Frederic Remington, and the novelist Owen Wister, along with many lesser known allies, offered the public a persuasive image of the West as a place populated by hardy, self-reliant white men who courageously battled Indians, nature, and cattle rustlers. Perhaps most influential was Buffalo Bill Cody, whose Wild West shows were a national and international force for diffusing the colorful and intoxicating pieces and parts of the western myth.

With the foundations of the western myth well-laid by 1900, the movie business finished the construction process, leaving the region tightly fenced in by stereotypes and clichés. Filmmakers began filtering into Hollywood in the first decade of the twentieth century. David Horsley, the head of the Nestor Film Company, built the first studio in Hollywood, a dusty Los Angeles neighborhood, in 1910. Movie directors loved Southern California for its year-round sunshine and its photogenic and accessible mountains, deserts, cities, and coast. The studio moguls loved Southern California for its cheap land, its antiunion tradition, and its distance from the East Coast Edison Trust, which held most of the patents in the motion picture business. The filmmakers brought the Western movie with them from the East. Edwin S. Porter shot the first Western, *The Great Train Robbery* (1903), on the tracks of the Delaware and Lackawanna Railroad outside of Dover, New Jersey. Transplanted westward, the Western blossomed in the California sunshine. In the early twentieth century, stars like William S. Hart and Tom Mix established the Western in American popular culture. In the twenties and thirties, Hoot Gibson, Gene Autry, and Roy Rogers continued the tradition and added the peculiar feature of the "singing cowboy" to the genre. The forties and fifties were the golden age of movie Westerns. At the forefront were directors John Ford *(Stagecoach, My Darling Clementine, Fort Apache, She Wore a Yellow Ribbon, The Man Who Shot Liberty Valance)* and Howard Hawks *(Red River, The Big Sky, Rio Bravo)*. The stars in these films—James Stewart, Henry Fonda, and John Wayne—came to epitomize the West. At mid-century, television perpetuated and embellished the myth of the West with *The Lone Ranger, Gunsmoke, The Rifleman, and Bonanza*.

In the minds of many Americans, indeed, in the minds of many people internationally, the authentic, legitimate westerner was a self-reliant, independent, tough, and well-armed white cowboy, on horseback in the wide open spaces. The project of stretching the image of the *real* westerners to include women, or people of color, or city-dwellers required considerable skills of persuasion. Moreover, beside the myth of the Old West, the twentieth-century West was a tame, dreary, and dull place, only of interest as the stage setting where the legendary figures of the frontier had once lived their colorful lives. By the same terms, the West's contemporary people were diminished and reduced in comparison to their pioneer predecessors. Much of the region's cultural life would involve a wrestling match between the complex, diverse reality of the West and this simple, misleading, and very powerful myth.

THE ROLE OF THE FEDERAL GOVERNMENT

The allocation of power between the federal government and western resource users was a particularly rich source of friction. Always an important force in western development, the federal government at the turn of the century made a major switch in policy. For a century, the government had directed its efforts to the distribution of land, moving land from public to private ownership. Now that pattern shifted dramatically, with the federal government retaining permanent ownership of much of the public domain and taking up a mandate for management. The transition was, however, neither complete nor immediate. While the practice of transferring land to private ownership ended, the extraction of natural resources did not. The federal land-management agencies continued to take the demands and preferences of the local resource users into account in their management plans. While they tried to regulate the extraction of resources, they by no means tried to end it.

The shift to permanent federal ownership stemmed from a variety of events and decisions. In 1891, Congress authorized the president to set aside forest reserves. In 1905, President Theodore Roosevelt and his close friend Gifford Pinchot succeeded in transferring the forest reserves from the Department of the Interior to the Department of Agriculture, where Pinchot could preside over the new agency, the U.S. Forest Service. As Chief Forester, Pinchot sought to balance the interests of loggers and livestock grazers with the requirements of a consistently replanted, croplike forest. On another track entirely, Yellowstone had been made a national park in 1872, and Yosemite followed in 1890. Status as a national park carried no clear meaning until 1916, when Congress created the National Park Service, with the mandate to provide for "the enjoyment of the parks in such a manner and by such means as will leave them unimpaired for the enjoyment of future generations." A third major land-management agency had its origins in the 1930s, when the Dust Bowl dramatized the dangers of overgrazing and won support for the Taylor Grazing Act. That act at long last set up a permit system for grazing on the remaining public lands, supervised by the Grazing Service. In 1946, the Grazing Service was merged with the vestigial General Land Office to form the Bureau of Land Management.

With the U.S. Forest Service, the National Park Service, and the Bureau of Land Management, enormous sections of the West were now in permanent federal custody. Nevada led with 87 percent of its land owned by the federal government; even California registered 45 percent federal ownership. An equally important federal force in western development was at work in water management. In 1902, the Newlands Reclamation Act created the Reclamation Service (later, the Bureau of Reclamation), and placed the federal government in the business of constructing dams and reservoirs. Behind the Reclamation Act was a powerful western hope that aridity would prove to be only a temporary obstacle to agricultural development. With federal support, the heavy spring run-off from melted snow could be captured, held, and released for use in the summer growing season. The deserts would blossom, and western opportunity in farming would get a second wind, as lands once judged to be useless were brought into production.

Along with its bureaucratic rival, the Army Corps of Engineers, the Bureau of Reclamation oversaw an extraordinary transformation of the western landscape. A chain of dams made the wild Colorado River into a tamed supplier of hydroelectric power and water for agricultural and urban use. In the Pacific Northwest, the Columbia River also became a linked chain of reservoirs, with a devastating impact on the once-abundant salmon, but with a great increase in the area's ability to support farms, cities, and industry. In light of periodic bouts of overproduction in agriculture, the federal government's willingness to devote the nation's resources to the cause of increasing opportunity for western farmers was a remarkable act of regional favoritism.

Predictably, the West made the most of the increase in federal resources during the New Deal. As the historian Leonard Arrington put it, the New Deal "benefitted the West more than other sections of the nation. Indeed, when one lists the states in the order of per capita expenditures of the federal economic agencies, the top fourteen states in benefits received were all in the West." By the 1930s, the pattern was well-established: the West would lead the nation in seeking—and, often enough, in securing—federal money, and it would also lead the nation in condemning federal interference, lamenting the growth of big government, and celebrating the region's legendary history of frontier individualism and self-reliance.

World War II drew the ties between the West and the federal government even more tightly. Defense industries and military installations needed places with the very qualities the West had in abundance: open, undeveloped spaces; cheap hydroelectric power; remote locations that would serve the cause of secrecy; and access to Pacific Coast shipping. The result was a great rush of both federal money and hopeful job-seekers to a number of western locations. The Pacific Coast was the particular beneficiary of this military bonanza. In the Seattle area, Boeing employed 40,000 workers to build the B-17 Flying Fortress and the B-29 Superfortress. In California, Lockheed, Hughes, Northrop, North American, and Douglas manufactured aircraft for the war. The West Coast also became a shipbuilding center. Shipyards in Puget Sound and San Francisco refurbished the Pacific Fleet after the Japanese attack at Pearl Harbor and produced countless cargo ships, destroyers, and aircraft carriers. The king of the West Coast shipbuilding industry was Henry J. Kaiser. Kaiser ran shipyards in Bremerton, Washington, and in the San Francisco Bay area. The son of German immigrants, Kaiser created a corporate empire with federal subsidies and a talent for completing enormous jobs with extraordinary speed. Thanks, in part, to Kaiser's energy, California received 10 percent of all government war funding. But other sections of the West also profited from the war. The government financed the largest magnesium plant in the world in Henderson, Nevada; Denver prospered from the Rocky Mountain Arsenal and the Remington Arms Company; and Phoenix received a rubber manufacturing plant.

The development of the atomic bomb had an equally dramatic effect on the region. As chief scientist for the Manhattan Project, J. Robert Oppenheimer consulted memories of his vacations, and selected northern New Mexico for his research laboratory. The mesa of Los Alamos thus became the principal facility for the design of the bomb and a sudden, unexpected home for hundreds of scientists and engineers. Selecting a site for the production of plutonium, the planners of the Manhattan Project chose the desert of eastern Washington; the Hanford Works would have the benefits of remoteness, Columbia River water for cooling nuclear reactors, and hydroelectric power from the Grand Coulee Dam. Here, too, a boom town, created by a wage bonanza, sprang up. In the haste to develop a workable bomb, industrial safety and careful disposal of radioactive and chemical wastes took second place to production.

Successfully tested at Alamogordo in the New Mexico desert, the atomic bomb continued to be a vital factor in western development. After a brief phase of transition, the Cold War took the place of World War II in creating a steady market for weapons development and production. The Los Alamos laboratory became a permanent federal installation for weapons research; in the early 1950s, it was joined by a competitor, the Lawrence Livermore laboratory in California. Hanford, too, continued to be a major center of nuclear engineering and plutonium production. Initially performed at the distant Marshall Islands, nuclear weapons testing moved to the continental United States in 1951, with the creation of the Test Site in southern Nevada. The residents of southern Nevada and southern Utah, located downwind from the Test Site, initially took comfort in their chance to play a part in national defense; over time, that patriotism took second place to concerns over high rates of cancer and leukemia.

The build-up in nuclear weapons gave a new value to the raw material of uranium. The result was a classic resource rush to the Four Corner area, where the states of Colorado, Utah, New Mexico, and Arizona meet, with prospectors and speculators racing in with jeeps, Geiger counters, and stock certificates, hoping to cash in on the high prices for uranium guaranteed by federal purchase. Like other forms of mining, uranium mining also made a quick shift from a fortune-hunting free-for-all to hard, underground wage work under the control of large companies. In the case of uranium, mine work carried the added danger of radioactivity; breathing in radon daughters (lethal byproducts of uranium decay) in unventilated mines, western uranium miners were laying the foundation for a later epidemic of lung cancer in their ranks.

With its testing grounds, missile silos, military bases, weapons assembly plants, and research labs, the West had become the geographical center of gravity of Cold War nuclear activities. In the nineteenth century, western settlement had been heavily dependent on military backing for the enterprise of conquest; in the twentieth century, for very different reasons, the West's economic destiny had once again become intertwined with the military and its abundant funding.

THE ROLE OF NATURAL RESOURCES

Federal money had not, however, stabilized the region's economy and society. Far from entering a "postfrontier" age of stability and maturity, much of the western economy continued to rise and fall with the booms and busts of extractive industry. Precious-metal mining continued in the twentieth century, with ups and downs following changes in federal currency policy and federal purchases of gold and silver. With growing use of electricity, the demand for copper for electrical wire expanded copper mines, especially in Montana, Utah, and Arizona. A number of copper mines—most notably, in Butte, Montana, Bingham Canyon, Utah, and Bisbee, Arizona—shifted from underground to pit configurations, leaving dramatic, deep holes in the landscape. The rewards of western copper mining rose and fell until the 1970s and 1980s, when competition with international copper producers brought the regional operations to a virtual standstill.

Far from being a refuge from industrialization, the mining West had proven to be its forefront. In large-scale mining, the structure of large companies, absentee owners, hard-driving managers, and wage-workers laboring under dangerous and difficult circumstances bore little resemblance to the lore of western individualism and freedom. The harsh working conditions in western mining inspired a radical brand of labor unionism. In 1893, miners in Butte, Montana, founded the Western Federation of Miners. A departure from earlier craft unions, which organized workers according to their skills and concentrated on the length of work days and safety conditions, the WFM was an industry-wide union with increasingly socialist goals. In 1905, leaders of the WFM formed the Industrial Workers of the World, nicknamed the Wobblies. The IWW was to be "one big union," uniting all workers and ushering in a golden age for the working class. While Wobblies were also active in the Northeast and Midwest, the IWW found a particularly receptive audience in the mines, agricultural fields, and logging camps of the West.

Western mineowners countered the efforts of the WFM and the IWW with threats and force. From 1900 to 1920, class warfare erupted throughout the American West. In 1904, miners and smelter workers in Cripple Creek, Colorado, struck the Colorado Reduction and Refining Company when the company refused to allow the WFM to organize its workers. With the aid of the Colorado state militia, the owners broke the strike only after someone blew up a train depot, killing thirteen strikebreakers. In 1914, in the midst of a strike against the Colorado Fuel and Iron Company, the Colorado militia fired on a tent colony of strikers at Ludlow; five men, two women, and eleven children died from bullets, fire, and smoke. In 1916, the police and the IWW clashed in Everett, Washington. Five Wobblies and two deputy sheriffs died, and fifty-one people were injured. In 1917, vigilantes executed IWW leader Frank Little in Butte; in the same year, the Phelps-Dodge company broke a strike of copper miners in Bisbee, Arizona, by rounding up 1,200 union members, placing them on southbound trains, and depositing them in the desert in New Mexico.

Equally industrial in its business organization and labor relations was the western oil industry. In 1901, a gusher at Spindletop, near Beaumont, Texas, dramatically launched the boom in trans-Mississippi oil. Wildcatters, speculators, boosters, and job seekers rushed to the sites of discoveries, and oil boomtowns shared many of the characteristics of early western mining boomtowns. In Texas, Oklahoma, New Mexico, Colorado, Wyoming, and California, oil booms launched a number of powerful competitors to John D. Rockefeller's eastern-based Standard Oil monopoly. The oil fields proved a particularly risky place of employment; combined with the haste of development, the heavy equipment of an oil rig offered many opportunities for serious injury. Like western cowboys and miners before them, western oil workers developed an occupational subculture adapted to risk and transiency.

Oil proved to be a particularly difficult resource to control. Under the law of capture, the person who pumped the oil to the surface was the one who owned it; when a pool of oil lay underground with various claimants at the surface, a cautious operator, who showed restraint and did not keep up with his neighbors in pumping, simply lost his share of the resource. Under these circumstances, conservation was unimaginable, and overproduction—with correspondingly low prices—was a constant threat. Accordingly, by the 1930s, many western oil producers were willing to support government regulation to limit production and thereby to raise and support prices.

Even with regulatory laws, the oil business continued to ride a roller-coaster pattern of ups and downs. Rather than stabilizing over time, the cycles remained quite wild into the late twentieth century. In 1973, when the Organization of Petroleum Exporting Countries (OPEC) refused to sell oil to the United States as a punishment for American support of Israel, the incentives for domestic oil production increased dramatically. Western oil and gas exploration and development boomed; workers flocked to this wage bonanza; the economies of Houston, Dallas, and Denver prospered. But by the early 1980s, the industry had reached the downside of the cycle. The OPEC boycott had been short-lived; Americans renegotiated their peace with dependence on oil imports and oil prices fell sharply. Workers faced sudden terminations as many companies went bankrupt, and cities like Denver found themselves well-supplied with new, virtually empty office buildings.

The most dramatic effect of the oil bust was on the Western Slope of Colorado. In 1980, the federal government created the Synthetic Fuels Corporation, offering financial incentives for the production of synthetic fuels. In western Colorado, the effect was almost immediate, with Exxon and Union Oil of California both setting to work on the problems of bringing the area's abundant oil shale into production. Workers rushed to the area, and confidence in a long-lasting boom took hold. The fall in oil prices alarmed Exxon, and on 2 May 1982, after investing millions in the effort, Exxon abruptly announced the closing of its plant, putting hundreds of people out of work and destroying the local dreams for an economic renaissance.

Riding the same roller coaster of energy development was the western coal industry. Coal mining had taken hold in the Rocky Mountain states and territories in the late nineteenth century. Railroad companies, eager for local sources of fuel, played a central role in opening these operations in areas like southern Wyoming. Worker discontent with the dangers of underground coal mines led to important innovations in state regulation of industry and in compensation for industrial injuries. In the middle of the twentieth century, coal acquired the standing of an environmentally "dirty" fuel, but any slump in western coal mining was reversed in the 1970s energy boom. The sudden resurgence of the industry strained the resources of towns in Montana, Wyoming, and Colorado. Inspired by studies of the boomtown of Gillette, Wyoming, the phrase "Gillette syndrome" came to refer to a set of symptoms of social malaise—alcoholism, drug use, child abuse, depression, and petty violence. The end of the energy boom in the 1980s hit the coal boomtowns hard, leaving many of them with burdensome debts for unneeded roads, schools, sewers, buildings, and city services.

The more traditional western economies were not much more successful at reaching stability. Open-range cattle-raising had undergone a major reorganization with the hard winter of 1886–1887. After thousands of animals died from cold and hunger while trying to find grass on badly overgrazed lands, many ranchers shifted to growing forage crops for winter feeding and supervising the animals more closely. Nonetheless, success in ranching still depended on good weather and good markets. The early years of the twentieth century were fairly prosperous ones, especially with the demand created by World War I. But the years after 1918 were not so prosperous. The national and international depression of the 1930s came early to western ranchers. Drought years in the early 1930s compounded their financial problems. Federal aid during the New Deal—emergency purchases of otherwise unsalable cattle, and limits on overproduction that came through the restricted access to public land imposed by the Taylor Grazing Act—helped cattlemen through the Depression. But a trend toward larger—and fewer—ranches was already well established.

An unexpected frustration for cattle-raisers began to appear in the last half of the century. Alarmed by warnings of cholesterol and the cardiovascular risks of a high-fat diet, Americans began to lose their enthusiasm for red meat, further constricting the market for cattle. Changing popular taste affected ranchers in other ways as well: a growing enthusiasm for outdoor recreation brought hikers and adventurers into opposition with cattle-raisers. To environmentalists, cattle were an intrusive, damaging presence on the public lands, destroying native grasses and competing with wildlife; "Cattle-Free in '93" became the rallying cry for Earth First!, an environmental group lobbying for the removal of cattle from the public lands. With the pressure of debt and a declining market, for many western ranch men and women cattle-raising became less a way of making a living, and more a personal enthusiasm that they supported with jobs in town. Many ranch-owning families were unable to pass their enterprises on to the next generation, as rural children pursued more profitable jobs in cities.

In the twentieth century, western farming followed similar patterns of expansion and contraction, boom and bust, confounding the declarations of an ended and closed frontier. Indeed, more homesteads claims were filed after 1890 than before. Homesteaders swept into eastern Montana in the first two decades of the twentieth century, encouraged by the promises of boosters and by a phase of unusually high rainfall. But bust followed boom rapidly. Similarly, on the southern plains, a great plow-up of open land early in the century rewarded farmers with a few years of fine harvests with good prices. Crop prices declined after World War I, and then the drought and dust storms of the 1930s made prosperity a distant memory. The disaster of the Dust Bowl was the effect of both nature and humanity; nature provided the winds and drought, but human action had loosened the soil and removed the natural grasses that had held it in place for centuries.

Relief from the drought and the adoption of conservation techniques like contour plowing seemed to end the crisis, and Plains farmers returned to many of their old habits. Frequently those habits were supported by a more aggressive pumping of water from the underground aquifers of the Plains. Powered by gasoline engines, the pumps supplied abundant waters for irrigation. But withdrawal considerably surpassed replenishment; natural processes of restoring water could not keep pace with the farmers' pumping, and this method of forcing the semi-arid Plains to produce crops would eventually reach its limits.

Over the twentieth century, western farming followed a pattern, comparable to ranching, of an increasing size of individual farms, a shrinking number of farms, and a diminished rural population. Farming, of course, had been the foundation of the country; farmers were, for the first century and a half of the nation's existence, the majority population. This shrinkage was thus profoundly unsettling for the farmers themselves and for the American public in general. Fond sentiment for the agrarian life gave ideological support for a variety of government programs to aid the farm economy. By the terms of the agrarian myth, farmers were the hardiest and most independent of democratic citizens; in the struggle to maintain that independence in a competitive, commercial world, farmers in the twentieth century needed all the help they could get.

Commercial logging had a relatively slow start in the trans-Mississippi West. Local forests had, of course, been cut for building material, fuel, and timber framing to support underground mines. The commercial possibilities of the enormous forests of the Pacific Northwest had been limited by the difficulty and expense of transportation; San Francisco and a Pacific Coast market dominated the Northwest's timber business until the arrival of transcontinental railroads created other options. At the turn of the century, with midwestern forests much depleted by heavy cutting, the giant Weyerhaeuser Corporation moved into the Northwest. The demand for timber in wartime and the post–World War II housing boom increased the drive to cut western timber. A number of communities, especially in Oregon and Washington, but also in the Rocky Mountain states, became dependent on logging and the manufacturing of wood products. In the late twentieth century, those communities were on a collision course with the rising environmental movement, with its hostility to the commercial exploitation of trees. Protected by federal legislation on behalf of endangered species, the Northwest's spotted owl became the symbolic center of the region's, as well as the nation's, resource conflicts. While local employees of logging companies pushed for continued cutting, environmentalists argued that the loss of forest habitat would be fatal to the spotted owl, and to the wilderness and wildlife values it had come to represent. The quarrels over the line between proper and improper exploitation of timber came to focus, predictably, on the federal government, and particularly on the policy and philosophy of the Forest Service.

URBANIZATION AND WESTERN CITIES

While western rural enterprises struggled with boom-and-bust cycles, uncertain markets, burdens of debt, opposition from environmentalists, the prospect of resource depletion, and a general loss of power

Aerial view of Los Angeles in 1930. PRINTS AND PHOTOGRAPHS DIVISION, LIBRARY OF CONGRESS

and profit, many western cities prospered and grew, sometimes in ways that set precedents for the rest of the country. The phrase "American West" continued to bring to mind images of wide open spaces and vast, untamed wilderness, yet by 1970 the West was established as the region of the country with the highest percentage of the population living in cities.

In urbanization, California led the West and, indeed, the nation. San Francisco grew steadily, but Los Angeles grew explosively. In that growth, William Mulholland, chief engineer for the city's water and power department, played a key role. In the early twentieth century, Mulholland secured the rights to the water of the Owens Valley, on the eastern side of the Sierras, and oversaw the massive project of building an aqueduct to carry the water to Los Angeles. The transfer of resources was an enormous blow to the Owens Valley economy, and a great gain to the residents of Los Angeles. Thanks to Mulholland and his successors in the Los Angeles Power and Water Department, the city spent its formative years with a surplus of water; its residents had no reason to conserve water, or even to recognize that they were living in a desert.

With a major burst of growth in the 1920s, Los Angeles led the way in setting the shape and form for American cities. In dispersed housing and the proliferation of suburbs, Los Angeles gave the term *growth* new meaning. The metropolitan area led the nation in detached housing. One half of the population of Los Angeles lived in detached houses in 1940; Los Angeles's nearest competitor in this category was Chicago, with only 15.9 percent of its population in single-family houses. How were residents to get from these decentralized houses to their places of work and commerce? Increasingly, the answer was the privately owned automobile, but the spread of suburbs initially followed an elaborate system of interurban streetcars,

Aerial view of Los Angeles in the 1960s. ARCHIVE PHOTOS/AMERICAN STOCK

a system undermined, and then eliminated, by the preference for the automobile. Prior to 1950, Los Angeles had the premier public transportation system in the nation. In the 1930s, the Auto Club of Southern California suggested the idea of a network of high-speed roadways, set apart from city streets; with generous state funding, this proposal would eventually bear fruit in the elaborate Los Angeles freeway system.

Urban and industrial growth in Los Angeles took place on such a large scale and at such an accelerated pace that it was logical to wonder if Los Angeles, along with the rest of the state of California, had detached itself from the West and set off on another track of development entirely. No other subregion of the West came near to matching Los Angeles in industrialization; on the contrary, many areas remained tied to the boom-and-bust patterns of extractive economies. While Los Angeles grew by hundreds every week in the early 1940s, the Plains states lost population. As startling as California's urban growth was, much of the interior of the state remained more rural than urban. But here, too, California made a poor fit with patterns familiar from other areas of the West. California agriculture lacked the landmarks of the traditional family farm. Few houses, barns, silos, corrals, or pens stood in California's Central Valley and Imperial Valley. Instead, the land stretched out, completely dominated by crops.

The failure of the Bureau of Reclamation to follow one part of its mandate insured the uninhabited look of California farms. The 1902 Newlands Act had originally directed the Bureau of Reclamation to impose a limit of 160 acres on the size of farms receiving water from the Bureau's projects. In 1935, the Bureau of Reclamation began construction of the massive Central Valley Project to supply water to the San Joaquin Valley. The San Joaquin "farmers" included Standard Oil, the DiGiorgio Corporation, and the Southern Pacific Railroad. The largest landowner, the Southern Pacific, held over 100,000 acres. The corporations created subsidiaries, juggled land titles, and "gave" farms to overseers and family members to dodge the 160-acre restriction. In the Imperial Valley, as well, the Bureau of Reclamation allowed the circumvention of the acreage limit.

Despite the state's distinctive elements, much of California history continued to follow familiar western themes, from the struggle with aridity to the complicated relations between Anglo-Americans and people of Mexican origin. Moreover, precisely because of its advantage in power and prosperity, California had a considerable influence on the rest of the region. When, for instance, California citizens rallied to protect their own natural environment, one common route to that goal was to export the state's environmental problems. In the 1960s, for instance, Californians would continue to use electrical power freely, but they would draw some of that power from coal-fired generating plants in the Four Corners region. The strip-mined sites of coal production and the air pollution from the plants would trouble the interior, not the coast. The relationship between California and its western neighbors might not have been happy, but it was close and consequential.

In the enthusiasm for dispersed housing and for heavy use of the automobile, Los Angeles led both the region and the nation. Developers of cities like Phoenix, Tucson, Albuquerque, and Denver mimicked Los Angeles's suburbs and freeways. The sprawling, decentralized city offered its affluent residents yards, barbecues, and a sense of independence, as well as tiresome commutes, traffic congestion, and smog. Each city followed its own route down the trail blazed by Los Angeles. Albuquerque remained a small railroad town until World War II, but the creation of local air force bases, the proliferation of regional government agency offices, and the growth of the University of New Mexico set off a postwar growth spurt. Like Phoenix and Las Vegas, Albuquerque had a group of satellite suburbs that refused to be annexed to the city and its problems. Sun City, the planned community for senior citizens outside Phoenix, epitomized the annexation anxiety displayed by many suburbs of western cities. Fearing higher taxes and less autonomy, the residents of Sun City overwhelmingly voted against proposals to join Phoenix.

Animosity between suburbs and traditional urban centers reflected the conglomerate nature of western cities in the twentieth century. Unitary names like Denver, Phoenix, Dallas, Fort Worth, and Houston fail to capture the diversity of the places they name. Like solar systems, these cities developed an urban core and numerous satellite suburbs. After World War II, the suburb satellites of many western cities began to dominate the old urban cores. In the Pacific Northwest, Portland and Seattle resisted this trend with varying degrees of success. Extensive urban planning allowed downtown Portland to escape the decline of many western cities. In 1962, Seattle hosted the World's Fair and thereby revitalized its downtown.

Perhaps the most unusual of western cities was Las Vegas, Nevada. In 1931, Nevada legalized gambling. A poor state with far more desert reptiles than people, Nevada turned to gambling, easy divorces, and low taxes to revive its weak economy. The state of Nevada gave Las Vegas permission to gamble; the federal government provided and financed many of the gamblers. In 1931, construction began on Hoover Dam, on the Colorado River, twenty miles south of Las Vegas. While the workers lived at the site, they traveled to Las Vegas on weekends for recreation. During World War II, cheap electricity from the dam and Las Vegas's desert isolation attracted further government expenditures. The federal government financed a magnesium plant at Henderson, built a flying school in the desert, and offered a significant number of jobs at the Nevada Test Site, north of Las Vegas. The federal government provided the infrastructure upon which the tycoons built their neon gambling palaces.

In its devotion to and dependence on tourism, Las Vegas represented one of the most important trends in western economic and social patterns. As extractive industries proved unreliable and vulnerable to sudden slumps, tourism more and more appeared as the region's preferred industry. In national parks and forests, in re-creations of "frontier" towns, in Indian trading posts, in theme parks following the model set by Anaheim's Disneyland, and in a giant web of gas stations, motels, and roadside restaurants, the West turned to tourism as a source of both income and identity. In the nineteenth century, western tourism had been open only to the upper and middle classes; in the twentieth century, tourism became democratized through the automobile and the family vacation.

While tourism had undeniable benefits, it carried costs as well. Most of the jobs supported by tourism were lower-level, blue-collar service jobs; tourist towns thus stood a good chance of dramatic stratification, with workers living in poor housing or trailer parks while the visitors enjoyed their stays in comfortable hotels. Since much of western tourism involved the use and manipulation of the frontier myth, the mandate of the industry required the locals to engage in a certain amount of role-playing, satisfying the tourists' desire to believe that the quaint and romantic West lived. Perhaps most productive of conflict was the growing sense, on the part of western rural people, that they were being asked to sacrifice their own preferences and interests, and to serve, instead, as a kind of Western theme-park cast of characters designed to satisfy tourist expectations. Tourists had a set, and strict, vision of what the rural West should be. When, for instance, local people wanted to cut a forest, and urban outsiders wanted the forest kept uncut and pristine for their hiking and camping interests, the problems posed by tourism came to a sharp focus.

WESTERN CULTURES

The division between the rural West and urban West affected every population, often cutting across lines of ethnicity. By the last decades of the century, half of the western Indian population lived in cities, while half remained on reservations. In the 1930s, under the direction of Commissioner of Indian Affairs John Collier, the Indian New Deal opened new possibilities for reservation self-government and ended the policy, formalized in the Dewes Act of 1887, of dividing up reservations into individual allotments of 160 acres and selling the surplus to non-Indians. Originally from Georgia and New York, Collier had converted to the cause of Indian rights during a visit to New Mexico. The Indian New Deal thus gave reservations a permanence they had not had under the pressures of allotment and forced assimilation. And yet federal Indian policy was neither stable nor consistent; after World War II, Congress and the Bureau of Indian Affairs reversed the policies set by Collier. Pushed with particular vigor by Utah senator Arthur Watkins, the policy of termination offered to set the Indians free of federal supervision, while also setting the federal government free of its obligations to support and aid tribes. The permanence of reservations once again became precarious. In the spirit of termination, the Bureau of Indian Affairs offered a program in relocation, sponsoring the move of Indian people from reservations to cities. Los Angeles emerged as the city with the largest Indian population, with Tulsa and Albuquerque as runners-up. In cities, few tribes were represented in numbers large enough to offer a basis for community defined by tribal identity alone; instead, cities were prime locations for the emergence of a transtribal Indian identity and bases for Indian activism.

Another accompaniment of termination, the Indian Claims Commission, had a similar effect in unintentionally developing sources of Indian self-assertiveness. The ICC was created to hear Indian claims of the unjust appropriation of land, so that this leftover business might be resolved to clear the way for termination. The operations of the ICC proved to be an important training ground for lawyers working in Indian law. Rather than quickly and finally resolving Indian claims, the Commission's proceedings turned out to be a force unleashing a new wave of litigation, as lawyers—increasingly of Indian descent themselves—brought a variety of tribal claims into the federal courts. Through the 1960s and 1970s, the courts proved remarkably receptive to arguments on behalf of Indian treaty rights.

One of the most consequential decisions on behalf of Indian tribes was the Boldt decision of 1974. After a contentious decade in which Pacific Northwest tribes reasserted their fishing rights, set forth in treaties of the 1850s, federal Judge George Boldt ruled in favor of the tribes. By Boldt's determination, the guarantee written into the treaties—the right to fish "in common with all the citizens of the Territory"—gave the tribes the right to half of the annual catch. Likely to be even more consequential was a decision made in the early twentieth century, but only very gradually applied to particular reservations. By the terms of the *Winters* decision of 1908, Indian reservations were understood to have reserved rights to water; since the policymakers who created the reservations intended the Indians to farm, then the reserved right to the necessary water would date from the year of the reservation's founding, whether or not the Indians had put that right to use. Fully applied, *Winters* doctrine rights could have enormous impacts on the distribution of western water.

To the many white Americans of the nineteenth century who had seen Indians as a vanishing race, this resurgence of Indian people and their rights would have been astonishing, even inexplicable. By the 1970s, when President Richard Nixon officially ended the federal commitment to termination and declared, instead, a policy of Indian self-determination, there was no question that Indian people were once again significant and influential players in the various conflicts and struggles over the resources in the western states.

This did not, however, mean that the situation in Indian affairs was either simple or clear. In some cases, as at the troubled situation on the Pine Ridge Reservation in the 1970s, the rise of activism brought a situation close to civil war. The American Indian Movement (AIM), originating largely in urban Indian communities, had forged an alliance with some of the elders on the reservation, and launched a serious, sometimes violent rebellion against the official tribal government, judged by AIM to be a puppet government serving the interests of the federal government and a few, well-connected Indians. This struggle culminated in 1973, in a seventy-one-day siege at Wounded Knee, the site of the grim encounter between the Sioux and the U.S. Army in 1890.

In the Southwest, one of the most complicated and painful dilemmas in the allocation of land emerged in a conflict between the Hopi and the Navajo. Friction between the tribes was an old story. To the Hopi, the Navajo were the late arrivals, seminomadic intruders who sometimes engaged in trade and exchange and sometimes raided and harassed the Hopi. In 1882, with an executive order defining the Hopi reservation, the federal government added a great complication to the situation. The reservation, the order declared, would be set aside for "the use and occupancy of the Moqui [Hopi] and such other Indians as the Secretary of the Interior may see fit to settle thereon." From the ambiguous phrase "such other Indians" would come much confusion and struggle a century later. With livestock-grazing as a key activity, the Navajo had a greater motive for territorial expansion than did the farming Hopi; the Navajo population, moreover, was growing steadily through the twentieth century. Thus the land set aside for the Hopi and "such other Indians" ended up primarily occupied by the Navajo. When the Hopi protested this loss of territory, an extraordinarily complex chain in litigation and legislation began. Both tribes hired, not only lawyers, but also public relations firms. The Navajo gave every sign of winning the media battle, capturing the public's attention and sympathy with the story of Navajo families who would be displaced if the land were restored to the Hopi. But the dispute remained a genuinely intertribal conflict, with powerful arguments on both sides.

The ethnicity of "Indianness" in the twentieth-century West remained a complicated and unsettled matter, a shifting arrangement of tribal identity and pan-Indian identity, of tradition and change. Many white Americans missed these complexities entirely, and continued to think that the only real Indians were the "pure" Indians of the distant, mythic western past. In those terms, these modern-day tribal people driving pickup trucks and wearing Levi's jeans and jackets seemed to be unconvincing imposters. In assembling and valuing the pieces and parts of ethnic identity—biological descent, place of residence, culture, religion, language, politics, and personal loyalty—and in sorting through the issues of tribal identification and pan-Indian identification, tradition and assimilation, continuity and change, twentieth-century Indian people dramatically illustrated the concept of the social construction of ethnicity. Here, too, one could see the concrete impact of myth, as both Indians and non-Indians found their attitudes and behavior shaped by popular images of Indianness. In some cases, where years of government repression had eroded traditional practices, Indian people had to re-create an identity, drawing on the records left by white observers, whether traders, tourists, or anthropologists. And yet, in other cases, traditional ways of passing on knowledge—storytelling, or close relations between grandparents and grandchildren—had proved remarkably effective in transmitting tribal identity.

Surely the West's best example in the various and complex meanings of group identity had its center in Utah. Founded in 1830 by the prophet Joseph Smith, the Church of Jesus Christ of Latter-day Saints had met persecution in the eastern United States and arrived in Utah in 1847. In the last half of the nineteenth century, the Mormons had resisted federal efforts to force them to give up their peculiar institution of polygamy. In 1890, the Mormons relented, and in 1896 they were rewarded with statehood for Utah. This was, however, by no means the end of their distinctiveness as a people. While some splinter groups continued to practice polygamy, the majority of the Mormons found other ways to mark the boundaries of their identity. Along with the other distinctive elements of their theology, a revived respect for Joseph Smith's "Word of Wisdom," forbidding the use of coffee or alcohol, gave Mormons a way of showing their distinctiveness in daily life. By the start of twentieth century, Mormonism had indeed given rise to what might be called its own ethnicity—a historically generated pattern of religious assumptions, work habits, community organization, family structure, and public and private rituals.

The lives of people of Mexican descent in the West demonstrated equally complex patterns of identity. Anglo-Americans in the West were often oblivious to the origin of the West's Hispanic or Latino populations. Some families had resided in the Southwest since the 1600s; others were recent arrivals from

Mexico. The American-born children of Mexican immigrants in the Southwest faced the usual second-generation dilemmas of assimilation and tradition, but they faced them in a particularly complex setting. They lived, after all, in territory that had recently belonged to Mexico. They were separated from their parents' homeland, not by an ocean, but only by the political border running through contiguous terrain. Mexican Americans constantly had to redefine themselves in relation to Mexican immigrants; the common Anglo-American inability or unwillingness to distinguish between Mexican American citizens and Mexican immigrants repeatedly made it clear to both groups that they could not simply declare their independence from each other.

Through the twentieth century, Mexican immigration increased and shrank and increased again; growing or contracting, it never ceased to be a central issue in the American West. In the early years of the century, push and pull factors combined to increase the numbers of Mexicans traveling into the United States. The concentration of landowning oligarchy in Mexico displaced peasants from their farms and villages, and the violence and complicated politics of the Mexican Revolution gave many families a compelling reason to leave home. At the same time, the economic development of the Southwest created a great demand for labor for the construction and maintenance of railroads and the tending and harvesting of new crops made possible by the expansion of irrigated agriculture. Congressional legislation in 1917 made a head tax and a literacy test the requirements for immigration; but enforcement of these regulations on the border was by no means thorough. The Immigration Act of 1924 imposed strict quotas on southern and eastern European immigration, but it left Mexican immigration without a quota, in deference to the interests of good international relations in the Western Hemisphere and the demands of Southwest employers.

Transforming a labor shortage to a labor glut, the onset of the Depression reversed American attitudes toward Mexican immigration. With tacit federal approval, local governments pursued a strategy of repatriation, persuading—in some situations, frightening—Mexican immigrant families to return voluntarily to Mexico. Many of these families had children who held citizenship in the United States by virtue of their American birth. Repatriation thus demonstrated the precarious position of Mexican-descended people in the West.

With the labor shortage of World War II, Mexican immigration accelerated again. In a formal agreement between the United States and Mexico, Mexican workers were formally recruited and imported as *braceros.* The arrangement carried an official promise of fair treatment, guaranteed by the U.S. federal government, but enforcement of that promise remained uneven and unreliable. The end of the war, western farmers insisted, did not relieve the urgency of their labor needs; with the skillful lobbying of farm groups, the *bracero* agreement was extended to 1964.

With or without the agreement, illegal immigration had its own momentum. Regardless of official American border policy, cross-border labor migration continued for two compelling reasons: the Mexican economy remained unstable and often impoverished, with American investors and companies playing their part in the manipulation of Mexican resources; and employers in the United States remained eager to hire illegal Mexican labor, often claiming that they simply could not find American citizens who were willing to take, for instance, the trying stoop labor in California's vast agricultural fields. Without addressing either of those two reasons for immigration, periodic alarms led federal officials to crack down on the border. In 1954, for instance, in an enterprise flavored strongly with Cold War fears of an insidious infiltration of the United States, the Immigration and Naturalization Service conducted Operation Wetback, deporting several hundred thousand illegal Mexican workers, along with a number of Mexican American citizens seized by "mistake."

Political agitation on the subject of Mexican immigration had its major impact on legislation in the Immigration Act of 1986. By this law, illegal aliens who had lived peacefully and productively in the United States, and who could provide documents to prove their continuous, unlawful residence since before 1 January 1982, would receive amnesty and naturalization. In a conspicuous departure from earlier laws, employers who hired illegal aliens would now be subject to sanctions—penalties and fines for their complicity in illegal immigration. Mexican American groups expressed concern that sanctions would lead employers to treat all people of Mexican descent with suspicion. The act seemed to have minimal effect in slowing illegal immigration. With Mexico's economic problems unaddressed and with the impossibility of scrupulously and thoroughly policing a 2,000-mile border, neither amnesty nor sanctions had much of an impact on the ambitions of impoverished and hopeful immigrants.

Within the American West, the population of Mexican descent had a long history of activism on behalf of their rights. Early in the twentieth century, in cooperative organizations called *mutualistas,* Mexican Americans and Mexican immigrants had organized for a combination of social, economic, and political purposes, helping members in hard times and sometimes protesting discrimination. Mexican-origin workers were active in various unions and strikes, especially in the 1930s. Mexican Americans were also earlier advocates of the cause of school desegregation. In Lemon Grove, California, the school district attempted to separate Hispanic children into "Mexican" schools. The Mexican American Lemon Grove parents organized and took the school district to court in 1931. A local judge ruled in favor of the parents and prohibited the creation of separate schools.

Through the middle of the twentieth century, the most visible Mexican American groups, like the League of United Latin American Citizens, advocated both assimilation, stressing the Americanness of their citizenship and character, and an end to discrimination against Americans of Mexican descent. In the 1960s, the tone of Mexican American activism changed notably. In the Chicano movement, students and other participants expressed their reservations about assimilation, took pride in Mexican culture and in the Spanish language, and declared their solidarity with Mexican immigrants. In California, the United Farm Workers movement, led by Cesar Chávez, at last put a national spotlight on the hard lives and minimal rewards of southwestern migrant laborers, while in New Mexico, *La Alianza Federal de Mercedes* (Federal Alliance of Land Grants), led by Reies Tijerina, reasserted Mexican American claims to their traditional land grants.

In a number of ways, Mexican American activism in the American West followed a different timetable and agenda than the much more familiar African American civil rights movement in the South. Indeed, the West had its own story of segregation and of resistance, litigation, and protest against segregation. Perhaps the most important benefit of taking western American history seriously as a part of national history is the realism that the study of the region brings to the complexity of American race relations. American historians have long heard the phrases "race relations" or "civil rights movement" primarily as a reference to the relation between Anglo-Americans and African Americans. While no one would deny the crucial significance of that relation, the history of the West is a reminder that Indians, Hispanic Americans, and Asian Americans have played big roles in the national story of race relations. What often appears in American history textbooks as a confrontation between two groups was, in fact, a multisided encounter, in which relations between, for instance, African Americans and Asian Americans could be as complex and heated as relations between either of those two groups and Anglo Americans.

Just as important, the western version of the African American civil rights movement of the twentieth century has received virtually no attention from historians preoccupied with the compelling events of the South and the Northeast. Demographic patterns shaped the African American civil rights movement in the West. Prior to World War II, the black population in most western cities remained small, and yet blacks in the West fought for and won civil rights victories years before their counterparts in the South and Northeast. In the early twentieth century, for instance, African Americans in San Francisco attended desegregated schools, rode public transportation, and lived anywhere in the city they desired. A harsh economic reality, however, limited the "tolerance" displayed in cities like San Francisco. In western cities, business owners and labor unions collaborated to keep African Americans in unskilled and low-paying jobs. Ironically, economic racism reinforced social "tolerance." Dismal employment prospects discouraged African Americans from the South and Northeast from migrating to western cities. Economic racism ensured that few blacks would travel West to test the magnanimity of white citizens.

During World War II, the demographics of western cities shifted. In 1941, President Franklin Roosevelt issued Executive Order 8802, prohibiting racial discrimination in companies with government contracts. The order and the creation of the Fair Employment Practices Commission (FEPC) opened some higher paying jobs to African Americans in western cities. Although economic discrimination continued unabated in most war-related industries, the promise of good jobs brought thousands of African Americans to the West Coast. During the war years, San Francisco's black population increased by 600 percent. Forty-five thousand African Americans migrated to Seattle alone.

As some employment opportunities brightened for African Americans, the social tolerance that had depended upon a sparse black population eroded. White realtors and "neighborhood organizations" worked to restrict housing. In San Francisco and Seattle, ghettos formed in the Fillmore and Central Districts. Housing discrimination fostered de facto segregation in the public schools. African Americans confronted the changing racial landscape by organizing protest groups. Indeed, the story of their activism in the West is a long one: in the early twentieth century, western branches of the National Association for the Advancement of Colored People (NAACP) and Marcus Garvey's Universal Negro Improvement Association (UNIA) were community watchdogs. In 1915, the NAACP in San Francisco and Seattle pressured the cities' governments to ban the showing of *Birth of a Nation,* D. W. Griffith's epic glorifying the Ku Klux Klan and deriding black slaves. During World War II, the NAACP in San Francisco worked closely with the FEPC and pushed shipyard unions to accept blacks.

By the 1960s, frustration with the disparity between the promise of western opportunity and the reality of discrimination was a daily experience for many black westerners. For young men in ghettos, confrontations with police brought that frustration to a focus. On 11 August 1965, an arrest for drunk driving began a chain of riots in the Los Angeles district of Watts that left thirty-four dead, hundreds injured, and $35 million in property damage.

Western social diversity, and the tensions attached to that diversity, went far beyond the conflicts between blacks and whites. As the section of the nation bordering on the Pacific Ocean, the West has been the place of arrival, as well as residence, for most Asian immigrants. The category Asian American embraces a range of cultures and nationalities, from Chinese to Hmong. Each group has a different immigration history, according to its point of origin and the conditions existing in the West at the time of its arrival. Chinese Americans, for instance, have followed one of the nation's most unusual demographic patterns. With constant obstacles to the immigration of women and with the immigration of workers prohibited in the Chinese Exclusion Act of 1882, the population began to dwindle. By the start of the twentieth century, Chinese American society was primarily a bachelor society of aging men. Japanese aggression against China, Pearl Harbor, and World War II made China into a crucial American ally; under those circumstances, prohibition of Chinese immigration seemed both uncivil and dangerous to international good will. Following the Communist takeover of China, just as the previous bachelor society had come close to disappearing, the numbers of immigrants began to grow again, this time taking shape as a family society with strong anti-Communist sentiments. Once strictly segregated in Chinatowns, a growing middle class of professionals and businesspeople became increasingly visible, especially on the West Coast. With a strong work ethic and a dedication to education, Chinese Americans became a large segment in university student bodies. By the 1970s, administrators, legislators, and taxpayers who had been content to think of universities as meritocracies, admitting students purely on the basis of their academic achievement, began to reject that premise when the meritocracy began to work in the interests of a nonwhite group.

Japanese Americans, as well, challenged Anglo-American notions of the allocation of success. Japanese immigration into the United States began in the last years of the nineteenth century and continued until the Immigration Act of 1924 closed the door to Japanese arrivals. Many immigrants found economic opportunity in farming, especially in fruits and vegetables for urban markets. As aliens ineligible for citizenship, facing a number of state laws prohibiting land-owning by aliens, Japanese immigrants, the *issei* or first generation, had to show considerable enterprise in negotiating alternative forms of land tenure—arranging tenancies and rentals, or placing the property in the name of their American-born, citizenship-holding children, the *nisei.*

Cycles of hostility to the "yellow peril" of Japanese immigration reached their peak in World War II. The surprise attack at Pearl Harbor unleashed a movement to classify all American residents of Japanese origin as potentially dangerous collaborators with the enemy and to remove them from their homes along the West Coast. With Executive Order 9066, President Franklin Roosevelt authorized this dubious exercise in national security. Moved initially to temporary assembly centers along the coast (often at fairgrounds or race tracks, with residents forced to move into buildings that had recently been stables), the Japanese and Japanese Americans were then placed at a number of guarded camps, two in Arkansas, and the rest in arid, remote parts of the West. Forced to move with little time for preparation, the *issei* and *nisei* suffered incalculable property losses. When the Supreme Court, in response to several lawsuits begun in protest against the relocation, ruled in support of the program, American civil liberties in wartime were disturbingly undermined.

Koreans began to emigrate to the United States early in the twentieth century. In 1910, the Japanese conquest of Korea had a profound effect on Koreans in the United States. They organized to promote the Korean independence movement, forming political organizations like the Korean National Association to raise funds and lobby the U.S. government. They also formed Korean language schools to keep the generations born in the United States acquainted with Korean ways and tied to the cause of Korean independence.

Like the Koreans, Asian Indians traveled to the United States in limited numbers in the early twentieth century. Most Asian Indians were men from the Punjab region of India, and most were from the *Jat,* or farmer, caste. Most worked as agricultural laborers on western farms. The Asian Indian immigrants threw a wrench in the racist ideology that governed the western states' policies toward Asian Americans. Asian Indians, unlike the Chinese, Japanese, and Koreans, were classified as Caucasian. In 1923, the Supreme Court in *U.S.* v. *Bhagat Singh Thind* addressed the problem by declaring that while Asian Indians were Caucasians, they were not white. The *Thind* decision ensured that Asian Indians were subject to the same discriminatory laws as other Asian American groups.

Filipino immigration followed a divergent path from other Asian groups. With the American acquisition of the Philippines, the Filipinos were classified as American nationals. Neither citizens of the United States nor foreigners, they were not subject to the same laws as other Asian American groups. While their legal status differed from other Asian groups, however, Filipinos learned quickly that American racism did not observe legal technicalities. They found themselves relegated to agricultural labor and unskilled service jobs. Whatever their occupation, Filipinos suffered harsh racism, which escalated to race riots in Southern California in the 1930s. In 1934, the Tydings-McDuffie Act granted the Philippines the status of a commonwealth. Many western politicians promoted the idea of independence so that they could limit Filipino immigration to the United States.

In April 1975, Saigon, South Vietnam, fell to the North Vietnamese. The inglorious end to the Vietnam War generated a flow of immigrants to the United States. Thousands of Vietnamese, Laotians, and Cambodians fled Southeast Asia in the next decade. Many of the immigrants had been allies of the United States during the war, and were now trying to escape the ramifications of the American defeat. These Asian immigrants had an inclination to political conservatism and support of the Republican party, which distinguished them from other western minorities.

While hostility to Asian immigrants could appear in any part of the nation, it also drew on longstanding western racial hostilities. In national memory, a peculiar kind of alchemy has been at work: the South, in popular understanding, was the center of racial hostility and inequity, while the West was supposed to be a different case entirely—the place where one went to escape the tensions and conflicts of the eastern United States. In fact, the American West has its own distressing history of discrimination, prejudice, segregation, and the exercise of white privilege. With restrictive real estate covenants, white Californians engineered their own system of residential segregation; the California prohibition against interracial marriage was not ended until the 1940s. In the 1920s, both Colorado and Oregon were governed by elected officials who had publicly declared their support for the Ku Klux Klan.

In more recent times, a beautiful section of northern Idaho, Hayden Lake, became the headquarters for Richard Butler's Aryan Nations, a white supremacist group. Affiliates of the Aryan Nations murdered a liberal Jewish talk show host in Denver in 1984 and committed acts of racist harassment in the region. Arizona, meanwhile, remained for a time the only state that refused to approve a holiday in honor of Martin Luther King; after several years of a national boycott against the state, voters in Arizona finally approved the holiday in 1992. A number of western states—California, Colorado, and Arizona—led the nation in the passage of "Official English" laws, laws of limited substance but strong statements that the majority of voters found the English language to be superior to the languages of Latin American and Asian immigrants and their children. In a western state like California, where Spanish had been spoken long before English and where much tourist promotion had involved the glorifying of the Spanish missions, the Official English sentiment seemed particularly puzzling.

In the spring of 1992, the vision of the American West as the place to escape ethnic conflict reached its final collapse. On 3 March 1991, an African American, Rodney King, was taken from his car by Los Angeles police officers and savagely beaten. Caught on videotape by a bystander, the beating shocked Americans everywhere, and deeply angered African Americans. The four officers had their trial moved to the Simi Valley, an almost all-white area north of Los Angeles. On 30 April 1992, the jurors—ten whites, one Asian American, and one Hispanic—acquitted the officers of using excessive force. Violence broke out almost instantly in South Central Los Angeles, as African Americans expressed their rage at the verdict. True to the patterns of western history, this was not simply a confrontation between African Americans and Anglo Americans. Hispanic people also participated in the riots; nearly half of the arrests were of Hispanic people, with a number of accusations raised that the Immigration and Naturalization Service had used this occasion to arrest and deport illegal aliens. Some of the most distressing violence was directed by African Americans at Korean Americans—small-scale shopkeepers who, African Americans felt, had been taking advantage of their economic vulnerability for years. With estimates of property damage as high as $3 billion, the Los Angeles riots in the spring of 1992 were, many commentators remarked, "a wake-up call" to America. The period of alertness, however, seemed extremely brief; within a month or two, the troubled race relations of Los Angeles had moved to the back pages of newspapers, when they appeared at all.

THE LEGACY OF THE MODERN WEST

On two counts—interethnic conflict and rural-urban conflict—the American West seemed to be pulling apart. The context for these conflicts was one of unsettling demographic change, in which the nation's peripheries and centers became more difficult to distinguish. In the 1960s, California passed New York as the nation's most populous state. In the 1980s, the population of the West and the South—the Sunbelt—came to outnumber the population of the Northeast and the Midwest. Over that same period, the rural West lost population as dramatically as the urban West gained it. Beginning, as well, in the 1960s, as a result of changes in immigration law, the points of origin of most American immigrants shifted from Europe to Latin America and Asia. Voters for Official English laws were thus, in some sense, expressing their discontent and disorientation with the turn that events had taken in the American West in their lifetimes. To many, it may well have seemed that the nineteenth century's Manifest Destiny had begun to fall apart in the twentieth century. Won for white Americans a hundred years before, the West seemed to be slipping from their grasp.

The conquest seemed to be unraveling in other ways as well. The reality of plate tectonics was nowhere more noticeable than in California, where a series of earthquakes, and increasing talk of the "Big One," punctuated daily life. Just as alarming, California—traditionally the prosperous part of the American West—entered its own economic slump in the 1990s. The depletion of underground aquifers—in California's Central Valley as well as on the West's Great Plains—intimated an enormous crisis in natural resources; those areas had indeed been abundant producers of food and fiber, but increasingly that productivity appeared to be an achievement that could not be sustained with the dwindling of water resources. Equally unsettling for the western economy was the rising distress over the federal deficit; long sustained by government assistance and subsidy, the West was particularly vulnerable to cutbacks in federal spending. In the same vein, the end of the Cold War alarmed observers and planners of the western economy. For many western defense industries, the urgent spending of World War II had moved easily into the urgent spending of the Cold War. What seemed, at first impression, to be good news—the dissolution of the Soviet Union and the end of a depleting struggle for national security against a Communist enemy—was, for this region, decidedly mixed news, threatening the free flow of federal money that had become an essential element of the western economy. All around the West—at the Los Alamos labs, at the Nevada test site, the weapons-assembly plants at Rocky Flats, Colorado, and Amarillo, Texas, and especially the Hanford Nuclear Reservation—lay the toxic and radioactive leavings of the Cold War. Given the West's long-standing status as the nation's dumping ground, it was hardly surprising that the leading candidates for permanent nuclear-waste disposal were at Carlsbad, New Mexico, and Yucca Mountain, Nevada. The West had long been the region that seemed to offer an escape from the limits, dilemmas, and conflicts of the rest of the nation. On the edge of the twenty-first century, the West had emerged as a dramatic example of the dilemmas facing the nation in environmental affairs and in social relations.

BIBLIOGRAPHY

For a comprehensive view of the twentieth century West, see Richard White, *"It's Your Misfortune and None of My Own": A New History of the American West* (1991); Michael P. Malone and Richard W. Etulain, *The American West: A Twentieth Century History* (1989); Patricia Nelson Limerick, *The Legacy of Conquest: The Unbroken Past of the American West* (1987); and Howard R. Lamar, "Persistent Frontier: The West in the Twentieth Century," *Western Historical Quarterly* 4 (January 1973): 5–25. Richard Slotkin tackles the subject of the western myth in *Gunfighter Nation: The Myth of the Frontier in Twentieth Century America* (1992).

The substantial role of the federal government

in the twentieth-century West is covered by Richard Lowitt in *The New Deal and the West* (1984); Gerald D. Nash in *The American West Transformed: The Impact of the Second World War* (1985); and Peter Wiley and Robert Gottlieb, *Empires in the Sun: The Rise of the New American West* (1982). For a history of water in the West, consult Donald Worster, *Rivers of Empire: Aridity and the Growth of the American West* (1985); and John Opie, *Ogallala: Water for a Dry Land* (1993). Mark S. Foster chronicles the life of Henry Kaiser in *Henry J. Kaiser: Builder in the American West* (1989). The deadly effects of atomic testing in the West are the subject of Howard Ball's *Justice Downwind: America's Atomic Testing Program in the 1950s* (1986); and Philip L. Fradkin, *Fallout: An American Nuclear Tragedy* (1989).

The fickleness of the West's natural-resource-based economy is discussed in Kenny Arthur Franks, *The Oklahoma Petroleum Industry* (1980); Andrew Gulliford, *Boom Town Blues: Colorado Oil Shale, 1885–1985* (1989); Philip O. Foss, *Politics and Grass: The Administration of Grazing on the Public Domain* (1960); Leslie Hewes, *The Suitcase Farming Frontier: A Study in the Historical Geography of the Central Great Plains* (1973); and Ed Marston, ed., *Reopening the Western Frontier* (1989).

William L. Kahrl investigates the fight between Los Angeles and the Owens Valley in *Water and Power: The Conflict over Los Angeles's Water Supply in the Owens Valley* (1982). For the history of cities in the twentieth-century West, see Carl Abbott, *Portland: Planning, Politics, and Growth in a Twentieth-Century City* (1983), and *Metropolitan Frontier: Cities in the Modern American West* (1993); John M. Findlay, *Magic Lands: Western Cityscapes and American Culture after 1940* (1992); and Richard M. Bernard and Bradley R. Rice, ed., *Sunbelt Cities: Politics and Growth since World War II* (1983).

Federal Indian policy is examined by Frederick L. Hoxie in *A Final Promise: The Campaign to Assimilate the Indians, 1820–1920* (1984); and Donald Fixico in *Termination and Relocation: Federal Indian Policy, 1945–1960* (1986). For the history of John Collier and the Indian New Deal, read Kenneth R. Philp, *John Collier's Crusade for Indian Reform, 1920–1954* (1977); Lawrence C. Kelly, *The Assault on Assimilation: John Collier and the Origins of Indian Reform Policy* (1983); and Donald L. Parman, *The Navajos and the New Deal* (1976).

Rudolfo Acuna provides a challenging history of Mexican Americans in *Occupied America: A History of Chicanos* (1981). Mexican immigration is the subject of Lawrence A. Cardoso, *Mexican Emigration in the United States, 1987–1930* (1980); Abraham Hoffman, *Unwanted Mexican Americans in the Great Depression: Repatriation Pressures, 1929–1939* (1974); and Mark Reisler, *By the Sweat of Their Brow: Mexican Immigrant Labor in the United States, 1900–1940* (1976).

For the history of African Americans in the West, see Albert S. Broussard, *Black San Francisco: The Struggle for Racial Equality in the West, 1900–1954* (1993); and Quintard Taylor, *The Forging of a Black Community: A History of Seattle's Central District, 1870–1970* (1994).

For studies in Asian American history, read Ronald Takaki, *Strangers from a Different Shore: A History of Asian Americans* (1989); Sucheng Chan, *Asian Americans: An Interpretive History* (1991); and Victor Nee and Brett de Bary Nee, *Longtime Californ': A Documentary Study of an American Chinatown* (1973).

GENDER ISSUES

Lizabeth Cohen and Mark Tebeau

Before the emergence in the 1960s of "the women's movement," which sparked interest first in women's and then in a more broadly construed gender history, a comprehensive encyclopedia like this one probably would not have included an essay on gender issues. That fact alone marks a change over the course of the twentieth century in attitudes toward gender—by which we mean socially acquired characteristics of femaleness and maleness, in contrast to biological distinctions of sex. Change has not been simply a matter of greater consciousness about the importance of gender roles, identities, and relations in history. The reality of people's experiences as men and women also has changed substantially over the century. In the family, at the workplace, through leisure and material consumption, and as a result of both political movements and state policy, the lives of men and women at the end of the twentieth century were very different than at its start. The gender dimension of people's lives, as well as our understanding of it, have both been transformed.

It is not sufficient, however, to track one course of change for all men and women in the crucial arenas of experience mentioned above. Patterns of femaleness and maleness have varied according to individuals' other social traits, such as social class, race, ethnicity, and religion. To discuss the subject of gender in the twentieth century, then, we must work with a complex matrix that includes historical time, maleness and femaleness, the major arenas of life where gender has been constructed, and diversity in that experience resulting from people's multiple social identities.

Because historians' increased attention to gender grew out of the feminist movement of the 1960s, the existing literature emphasizes the gender experiences of women. Although mainstream history has traditionally been told "from the male point of view" and with a greater emphasis on men's public actions, their more personal lives—including their roles and identities as men—have received little systematic study. Recent efforts by scholars to correct this imbalance have led to several important monographs on the nineteenth century, but the study of male lives in the twentieth century remains for the most part unexplored territory. Ironically, then, we must infer and speculate more about the construction of maleness over the twentieth century. The emphasis on gender, moreover, has reshaped women's history as well as reinvigorated that of men, in that it has broadened the concern from simply documenting women's experiences to reconceptualizing how "female" was socially constructed, in contrast to or in keeping with what was "male."

This essay is organized thematically around analyses of five arenas of twentieth-century life where the meaning of being male and female has undergone significant change and, at times, noteworthy continuity. Within each arena, crucial moments when gender identities and relations were reconfigured or unchanged are discussed, so that the approach is both thematic and chronological. Although for purposes of clarity and organization we have divided our investigation into these discrete arenas of life, it will be clear from our discussion that in reality these various dimensions of men's and women's experiences overlap.

GENDER IN THE FAMILY

At the most intimate level of social life—the family—gender roles and relationships underwent dramatic changes during the course of the twentieth century. Yet, at the century's end, the nuclear family remained the central institution of American social life, and many elements of traditional gender roles persisted. The nineteenth-century Victorian model of the male breadwinner and domesticated wife had all but disappeared by the last years of the twentieth century, as women entered the labor force in increasing numbers and some men returned home to help in childrearing and housekeeping. Sexual relationships within the conjugal bed changed as well, as both partners came to expect sexual satisfaction from marriage. But as marital expectations—sexual and otherwise—rose, so did divorce rates. Nonetheless, despite challenges to nineteenth-century ideals of marriage and family, Americans remained loyal to these institutions, remarrying after divorces and reconstituting nuclear families whenever possible. In fact, even as homosexuality—which might be taken as a fundamental assault on the family—emerged from the shadows in the post–World War II period, many gay and lesbian relationships were modeled on heterosexual marriage. Gender arrangements within the family also remained relatively constant. For instance, women working outside the home continued to shoulder many of the same domestic tasks that they had in the nineteenth century. Although aspects of the family have changed over the past century, commitment to it as the basic way to structure American society has not.

In 1898, Jane Addams wrote that "it has always been difficult for the family to regard the daughter as otherwise than as a family possession." As Addams's statement suggests, in the nineteenth century women were expected to devote themselves to their families and children if they were married, or to their parents and other relatives if they were not. Indeed, the family's claim on women continued to constrain women's lives throughout the twentieth century. Yet in the early years of this century, middle-class and working-class women began to define themselves in new ways that challenged some of the gender assumptions of the nineteenth-century family.

Middle-class "new women" began attending high school and college in rising numbers. Whereas in the 1890s, 35 percent of all undergraduate students were women, by 1920 the proportion had risen to almost 50 percent. At graduation, these women faced a difficult choice between a career and traditional domesticity. As often as not, these women chose to begin careers, typically as teachers and social workers. The result was a dramatic challenge by middle-class women to gender roles within the traditional family. In the early decades of the century, half of all college-educated women never married. In 1914, a study of women graduates of Barnard, Bryn Mawr, Cornell, Mount Holyoke, Radcliffe, Smith, Vassar, Wellesley, and Wells revealed that less than 40 percent had ever married.

During the 1920s, however, middle-class society began to address the needs of women who wanted to marry as well as have careers, making the integration of the two more possible. In 1925, Smith College set up the Institute to Coordinate Women's Interest with the express intent of helping Smith graduates juggle careers and family. In 1932, Barnard College likewise addressed the issue when it implemented a six-month-leave policy for female faculty and staff members who were going to have children. When middle-class women did marry in the twenties, many delayed childbirth and had fewer children. Native-born, educated, middle-class women were not abandoning the family in the 1920s, but they tried to adapt it to new female gender roles and expectations.

Working-class women launched a similar challenge to prescribed gender roles within the traditional family in the early twentieth century when they, too, increasingly left the home for the workplace. But since the factory-bound "working girl" was often seeking to preserve the economic viability of her family, she had less of an impact on restructuring the working-class family than the middle-class new woman had on hers. While the middle-class new woman took great pride in supporting herself, the working girl usually worked to support her family. Typically, an immigrant or daughter of immigrant parents surrendered most of her meager earnings to the family economy. In the 1910s, New York City reformers reported that over 75 percent of all working daughters turned over their full pay to parents. In contrast, the family often claimed less of the wages and labor of male children, who were expected to want things for themselves. Once married, working girls lived lives not very different from their mothers. Despite some variation by ethnicity, working-class women traded the responsibility of contributing financially to the family economy for the task of providing maternal care and managing a productive household. Many supplemented the family income by caring for boarders and taking in home work. Thus, working-class women as daughters expanded their own gender roles and expectations by working, but as wives they retreated from the formal labor force and did little to change the traditional structure of the working-class family.

The vast majority of African American women were working class, but they differed from their white working-class peers in that they continued to work after marriage. For them, gender, race, and class intersected powerfully to shape individuals' experiences. Single and married, black women worked to contribute to their families' support. Like all married women who worked, domestic duties also awaited them at home, but rather than view these as an added burden, historian Jacqueline Jones has suggested that black women found particular pleasure in their domestic responsibilities. "For the outcast group, the preservation of family integrity served as a political statement to the white South. To nurse a child, send a daughter to school, feed a hungry family after a long day at work in the fields, or patch a shirt by the light of a flickering fire—these simple acts of domesticity acquired special significance." Through their labor inside and outside the home, black women worked to defy the multiple economic, social, and political forces conspiring against their families' survival.

The institution of marriage itself changed in the early decades of the twentieth century as gender roles within the family shifted. Middle-class marriage, and to a lesser extent working-class marriage, began to reflect a new ideal: a more egalitarian "companionate marriage" between "new women" and "new men." For a successful marriage, it was no longer considered sufficient for husband and wife to fulfill their respective family responsibilities; rather, both partners came to expect marriage to provide emotional support and companionship previously found in same-sex relationships. This prescription encouraged men to cultivate more emotionally intimate relationships with their families, children as well as wives. Men were urged to be their children's friend as well as parent, to take time to watch their families develop. More attention from their fathers, combined with declining fertility rates which made families smaller, gave children significantly more parental attention by the 1920s than ever before. As the family declined in size during the twentieth century, it grew in emotional intensity.

The companionate marriage also encouraged new assumptions about male and female sexuality in particular and the role of sexuality in marriage more generally. Female sexual desire was recognized as being as strong as, if different from, male desire, and a successful marriage was expected to fulfill the sexual needs of both partners. Middle-class couples may not have worked as hard to achieve sexual pleasure as the new marital-advice manuals advocated, but nonetheless both men and women more often expected sexual fulfillment in marriage. Ernest Burgess and Paul Wallin's study of college-educated couples in the Chicago area during the early 1940s, *Engagement and Marriage* (1953), revealed that most actively sought information about sexuality to improve their dating relationships as well as their marriages. Over 75 percent of men and women said they looked forward to conjugal relations with anticipation. Crucial to the companionate marriage and particularly to these new attitudes toward sexuality was the greater availability of birth control by the 1920s and the legalization of its distribution and advertisement by the 1930s. Contraception gave men and women the opportunity to enjoy sex without fearing unwanted pregnancy, while also indicating that sexuality apart from procreation was not only possible but desirable. Not only had middle-class women's engagement in the world beyond the home begun to change by the twenties, but middle-class men and women were also pioneering new gender roles within marriage that were reshaping their families into smaller, more affective units.

The companionate ideal of marriage and its revised gender prescriptions did not readily trickle down below the middle classes, however. Traditional sexual relationships persisted among men and women of lower economic and educational status, according to sex researcher Alfred Kinsey in his twin studies entitled *The Sexual Behavior of the Human Male* (1948) and *The Sexual Behavior of the Human Female* (1953). Kinsey found that in contrast to better educated men, working-class men avoided extended foreplay and for many, "the more quickly [orgasm] is attained, the more effective the performance is judged to be." In addition, working-class men avoided certain types of sexual contact known to give pleasure to women because they considered these acts "perversions." Not surprisingly, Kinsey found that many more working-class women reported that they did not achieve orgasm during the first years of their marriage than college-educated, middle-class women. Significant gender differences in access to sexual information also affected working-class marriages. Males typically entered marriage with more experience than their wives. Working-class women, on the other hand, were less likely than their husbands, or middle-class women, to approach their weddings with knowledge about sex or contraception.

By the 1920s, new interest in sexual expressiveness led to more openness outside of, not just inside, heterosexual relationships. During the twenties and thirties, the popularization of Freud and other psychological and psychoanalytic concepts, as well as increased sexual experimentation, laid the groundwork for identifying and labeling homosexuality. Although men and women had engaged in homosexual behavior for centuries, until the twentieth century it had been considered an act that might coexist with heterosexual relations, not a distinctive identity. Now, as a freer sexual environment brought homosexuality farther "out of the closet," it also reified it as something different.

Popular culture helped nurture homosexual

identity. Homosexuals could see lesbian relationships openly dealt with in a Broadway play like *The Captive* (1926), and they could find fictional characters to identify with in novels such as *The Well of Loneliness* (1928) and *Strange Brother* (1931). In Harlem, popular black singers sang of same-sex attraction in songs like "Fairey Blues," "Bull Dagger Woman," and "Sissy Man." As homosexual relationships were being more sharply defined and labeled, both world wars—but particularly World War II—offered gay men and women unparalleled opportunities to experience sex and love. Joining the Women's Army Corps during World War II opened up a new world of lesbian companionship. Historian Allan Berube has demonstrated that homosexual men in the military found a unique vehicle to express their identity in the hundreds of theatrical productions produced by and for soldiers. Gay men performed in drag, titillating "straight" audiences while asserting publicly their own sexual identities. Heterosexual male reviewers and GIs in the audience spoke about the sex appeal of the "women" on stage and found that the performances reassured and confirmed their heterosexuality. Meanwhile, for gay men the productions offered a subtext that spoke to their own lives as homosexuals. They could read the play's gender role inversions differently than heterosexual audiences as well as use the performances to connect with the network of homosexual men in the military.

While homosexual relationships threatened many Americans by offering what was perceived as a radical challenge to the traditional family, gay men and women increasingly expressed their homosexuality openly within models of heterosexual gender roles. Among lesbians in the 1940s and 1950s, for example, the masculine partner was called "dyke" or "butch" while the feminine partner was her "lady" or "girlfriend." Although historians are still analyzing the complex relationship between homosexual and heterosexual cultures, it is nonetheless clear that the mores of homosexual subcommunities were not insulated from the mainstream, heterosexual world.

Even though many homosexuals did not necessarily challenge the gender norms of society, they found themselves increasingly labeled as deviant by a society clinging fiercely to normative family values defined by heterosexuality. By the middle of the twentieth century, as homosexuality became perceived as a distinct identity, gay men were more likely to forsake heterosexuality and hence could be portrayed as a threat to the family. In the context of the Cold War, supporters of traditional family norms cast homosexuality as a menace to the American moral order. In their eyes, not only were homosexuals moral perverts, they were also national security risks. Men and women were dismissed from the military for exhibiting homosexual "tendencies." Local police forces picked up on federal repression of homosexuals and continually harassed them. As Barbara Ehrenreich has argued in *The Hearts of Men* (1983), a study of postwar masculinity, "Fear of homosexuality kept heterosexual men in line as husbands and breadwinners. . . . The ultimate reason why a man would not just 'walk out the door' was the taint of homosexuality which was likely to follow him." That stigma only began to lift with the emergence of a gay liberation movement in the 1970s, symbolically born on 27 June 1969 when homosexuals fought back during a police raid of a gay bar, the Stonewall Inn, in New York's Greenwich Village.

The traditional gender ideals that were invoked to label homosexuals as deviant continued to be contested among heterosexuals as well. Not only did the companionate marriage change the expectations of marriage partners by the 1920s, but the Great Depression of the next decade challenged the traditional economic division of labor within the family. While women had long been contributing to family support as wives and daughters, men retained the status of chief breadwinner. Despite this trend—and in fact one might argue because of it—male unemployment in the Depression fueled a conservative ideology that women belonged in the home while their husbands kept the jobs "that rightfully belong to the God-intended providers of the household," in the words of one civic organization in Chicago. Even when the needs of wartime production required more women in the industrial work force, the message conveyed was that this was temporary assistance until men returned from World War II to reclaim their jobs.

The insecurities of the Cold War era only gave further impetus to resurrecting traditional gender role prescriptions, and a renewed focus on family gave new power to them. Beginning in the early 1940s, young people married and had children at record rates, having postponed both due to the economic hard times of the Great Depression and wartime separation. Fertility, which had been declining since the early years of the twentieth century, increased markedly. Suddenly, there were more three- and four-children families than at any other time in this century; baby-boom families of five or six were the norm everywhere one looked, down the street as well as in popular fiction, magazine advertisements, and on television.

Increased attention to family formation and the importance of the home coincided with tremendous growth in the suburbs, at least for white, middle-class Americans living in traditional two-parent households. In the 1950s, 85 percent of all new homes were built in the suburbs, and the proportion of the population residing there grew from 24 percent in 1950 to 35 percent by 1968. The culture of the suburbs revolved around domesticity. Women and men became involved in do-it-yourself crazes centered around remodeling homes, planting gardens, and making clothes. Suburban mothers became chauffeurs for their children, driving them from one enriching activity to another, from scouts to piano lessons to Little League practice. Women were encouraged to feel that their rediscovered domesticity was part of the natural order and that they should make home an oasis for their husbands, "organization men" with ambitions to climb the corporate ladder. Continuing the trend begun by the companionate marriage earlier in the century, husbands and fathers were expected to take their own distinctive kind of responsibility in the home, particularly in raising children. Historian Peter Stearns has argued that while mothers became disciplinarians in the middle of the twentieth century, fathers became their children's playmates. In the rapidly changing and uncertain world of the Cold War, suburban lifestyles offered men and women simplified identities easily accessible through social conformity and material consumption. The historian Elaine May suggests that "domestic containment," with its emphasis on traditional gender roles, mirrored and reinforced the "international containment" of communism, the two thus protecting American families from the threat of internal and external corruption.

The powerful, and gendered, rhetoric of domesticity articulated in the 1950s should not obscure other continuing trends in American life, such as women's increasing participation in the work force. By the 1960s, 30 percent of married women were working, twice as many as in 1940, and nearly 40 percent of all women over the age of sixteen were working outside the home. The powerful ideology of domesticity that prevailed in the 1950s did not keep women out of the labor market, and since the 1960s women's labor force participation has steadily been nearing men's. Divorce rates, too, continued to climb in the postwar period, as they had throughout the century. Whereas in 1940 there was one divorce for every six marriages, by 1980 one out of every two marriages ended in divorce. Between 1960 and 1980 the number of divorced men and women rose by almost 200 percent, the divorce rate itself jumping by 90 percent. Liberalization of divorce laws in the 1970s both resulted from, and further fueled, these increases, as "irreconcilable differences"—not just adultery, abandonment, and cruelty—became just cause. Yet even as divorce rates increased, most people who divorced remarried. Five out of six men and three out of four women married again after a divorce, half of them within three years, though second marriages failed at a higher rate than first marriages. Although it is clear that men and women no longer view marriage as a contract to be observed until "death do us part," by continuing to marry and remarry they have demonstrated confidence in the institution itself.

Despite attempts by couples to construct families with two parents, single parenthood also became increasingly common. Between 1970 and 1991, the proportion of children living in two-parent living arrangements declined from 85 to 72 percent, while the proportion living with one parent more than doubled, from 12 to 26 percent. In some cases, single parenting arose when unmarried women, and occasionally men, chose to become parents, through natural conception or adoption. But far more frequently, it has resulted from separation, divorce, and children born out of wedlock. Among African American families the rates of single parenting are particularly high. In 1991, more than half the nation's black children, 58 percent, were living with one parent, compared with 20 percent of white children.

Some portion of single parenthood can be traced to the growing independence of women arising out of the second wave of feminism in the 1960s and 1970s, which broke the hold of the fifties' ideology of domesticity. Not only did women's entry into the work force become more legitimate, but another sexual revolution took place. More openness about sexuality, much like in the 1920s, became a crucial ingredient of the counterculture of the 1960s. Men and women increasingly sought to fulfill themselves sexually, both inside and outside of marriage. Not only did men and women divorce more frequently, but some lived in "open marriages" tolerant of extramarital affairs, and even more cohabited outside of marriage. By the 1970s cohabitation among unmarried people had tripled in frequency; one study found that nearly one in five men had lived with a woman other than his spouse for at least six months before he was married.

As all these arrangements—divorce, sexual experimentation, living together, and single parenting—have become a part of American life from the

1960s to the 1990s, they have posed important challenges to the survival of the American family and to gender roles within that family. So, too, has Americans' continued tendency to marry later and less often, and to have fewer children; today American women have on the average 1.8 children. The traditional two-parent family with children accounted for only about three-fifths of all living arrangements by 1980, and it describes fewer families all the time.

Yet it is much too soon to proclaim the demise of the American family, or even traditional gender roles within it. Despite the decline in families that resemble the ideal, popular culture such as network television and Hollywood movies continues to reinforce traditional images of the family, thereby stigmatizing families that differ. Americans, moreover, continue to marry in huge numbers, and divorce rates, which peaked in the 1980s, are leveling off. The majority of men, women, and children still live in two-parent households. And the ideology of the traditional family remains so strong that institutional day care continues to be more expensive, scarce, and unpopular than many think it should be. As of 1990, two-thirds of all children were cared for at home or in someone else's home, while less than a quarter were in day care centers or preschools.

One way to explain the current condition of the American family is to view its increasing complexity and greater variation as evidence of the institution's survival, not its demise. With women equal participants in the work force, with men and women both expecting emotional and sexual gratification from their family relationships, with childbearing and childrearing becoming more a choice than an unquestioned assumption, the family has had to change to survive. At the beginning of the twenty-first century, few Americans are calling for alternatives to the nuclear family; rather, they are continuing to innovate within the institution. While politicians compete with each other to be the voice of authentic "family values," what those values are—and what they mean for maleness and femaleness—are constantly being contested.

GENDER IN THE WORKPLACE

As we turn from considering how gender has mattered within family life toward how it has shaped—and been shaped by—the workplace, it is imperative to recognize the links between the two arenas. As we have seen, changes in men's and women's work patterns had a crucial influence on the way the family developed over the century. The exigencies of American capitalism, ranging from the unemployment of the thirties to the need for a larger managerial middle class in the fifties, had clear repercussions for the family. Changes in the family, moreover, such as greater female independence, were impossible without changes at the workplace, in this case increased opportunities for women at work. Likewise, tacit acceptance of traditional gender roles within the family at the beginning of the century encouraged certain distinctively male and female patterns of work, wages, and job assignment, while questioning of those gender expectations in more recent decades has led to challenges to the earlier configuration of gender in the workplace.

As in the case of the family, however, change at work has not been a simple unilinear progression toward more equality for men and women; rather, the workplace has played a complex and paradoxical role in the shaping of gender relations over the twentieth century. It has helped both to equalize power and resources between men and women and to reinforce differences, particularly ones that have discriminated against women as wage earners. At the end of the twentieth century, women are working more, earning more, and gaining more access to the most prestigious and lucrative occupations. Nonetheless, job segmentation by gender continues, particularly within working-class occupations. And in work, as in other arenas of experience, the dynamics of gender have varied according to class, ethnicity, and race. By tracking historically the shifting contours of gender at the workplace for different social groups, we can understand better its paradoxical impact.

From 1900 to 1930, America's mass production economy grew into maturity, along with the jobs—both blue and white collar—needed to support it. In 1910, about 32 percent of all male employees were manual wage laborers, with the most recent immigrants in the lowest paying and least skilled jobs. Although for many workers the industrial economy promised better opportunities than they had had in rural America, Europe, China, or Mexico, work remained seasonal, wages barely kept pace with the cost of living, and technological innovation dislocated workers or diminished their control over production.

In the face of these difficulties, laboring men and women developed a camaraderie and work culture to exert as much control as possible over their labor. Because work tended to be segmented by sex, a distinctive male and female social life shaped these work cultures, which were often based as well on shared ethnicity, race, and class. Native-born skilled workers, for example, inherited the ideal of the "manly skilled worker" from their nineteenth-century forebears, and made the notion of "manly labor" the organizing principle of their trade unions. The exclusivity at the base of this ideology, however, invited conflicts among workers along ethnic, racial, and gender lines. Historian David Montgomery has argued that workers promoted a code of manly behavior usually cast in ethnic and racial terms. A labor poem describing the unity celebration following the late-nineteenth-century signing of a union scale by iron puddlers suggests both the ethnic and racial exclusion built into the concept of manliness:

> There were "Johnny Bulls" and "Paddies," and some sturdy men from Wales
> Who are nicknamed after animals that wear contracted tails;
> Americans from every state took sets 'mongst Dutch and Scotch,
> And all appeared as friendly as if they'd never made a "potch."
> There were no men invited such as Slavs and "Tally Annes,"
> Hungarians and Chinamen with pigtail cues and fans.
> No, every man who go the "pass" a union man should be;
> No blacksheep were admitted to the Puddlers' Jubilee.

Although women workers developed their own culture of the workplace (less often based on skill than men's), and even organized unions in the garment, textile, and shoe industries, where they were well represented in the labor force, they, too, were excluded from the brotherhood of labor. An American Federation of Labor official wrote in 1897 that "the growing demand for female labor . . . is an insidious assault upon the home; it is the knife of the assassin, aimed at the family circle. . . . It debars the man through financial embarrassment from family responsibility, and physically, mentally and socially excludes the woman equally from nature's dearest impulse." In the mind of the manly trade unionist, women should be supported as wives and daughters by an adequate family wage, not encountered as competitors in the labor market. When women joined the union cause, it was to be in a distinctive role. In 1920, a union newspaper in Seattle explained, "The labor man fights at the point of production, where he is robbed; the labor woman fights at the point of consumption, where she is robbed." Many labor organizations, as well as the structure of the workplace, were built on a rhetoric, and reality, of exclusion based on gender, ethnicity, and race.

Despite the demand for a family wage, few industrial workers, particularly immigrants holding the most menial jobs, could live on the male breadwinner's earnings alone. Family survival depended on the economic contributions of other members, particularly women, both married and unmarried. Daughters, for instance, supplemented the family income by working as domestics, in garment sweatshops and in laundries, or in better-paying jobs in offices, department stores, and factories. For many of these young women, their introduction to the work force as teens bridged the gap between youth and adulthood. In New York an astounding 60 percent of women aged sixteen to twenty worked in the early 1900s. After marriage, however, working-class women's labor force participation was often constrained by domestic responsibilities as well as ethnic and cultural heritage. For instance, among Italian immigrants, it was rare for married women to work, unless they assisted their husbands. In 1900 the United States Industrial Commission reported that Italian men often employed their sisters, wives, and daughters. "If he is a pants operator, she is usually his helper, or if he is a cloakmaker, she is his hand-sewer and finisher, and so both labor together to cover the expenses of the family." For the most part, however, immigrant women, once married, left the labor market and contributed to the family economy in informal ways, such as by taking laundry or boarders into the family home. A study of the textile-mill town of Lawrence, Massachusetts, in 1912 found that among families where the husband was the only wage earner, 90 percent took in boarders. In the steel-mill town of Homestead, Pennsylvania, at about the same time, nearly 40 percent of families had at least one boarder, and earnings from their keep often added as much as 25 percent to the family's income.

The mass-production economy of the first third of the twentieth century also created new kinds of work for the middle class. In the early part of the century, men and women began entering corporate offices as clerks, bookkeepers and other white-collar workers in record numbers. Indeed, the number of clerks increased 127 percent in the first decade of the twentieth century. On the surface, the world of white-collar work appeared relatively well integrated along gender lines, but in fact, as historian Olivier Zunz argues in *Making America Corporate* (1990), companies like Metropolitan Life in New York were consciously involved in segregating jobs by sex, and in particular in feminizing office work. Many departments were staffed by only women or men, and in departments where men and women worked together they were assigned different tasks based on their sex. In the actuarial department of Metropolitan, for instance, there were 490 clerks, 70 men and

420 women. While women engaged in menial tasks such as cataloguing cards and recording policy details, men performed computations on the department's adding and division machines. In contrast, the only technology taught to women in the actuarial division was the typewriter. While the expansion of white-collar work gave women more occupational opportunities, with greater status and better pay than at the factory, it still kept them segregated in "female jobs" at wage scales lower than men's. Only the tiny, though growing, number of women entering the professions during the teens and twenties gained access to "male" occupations, but usually they lacked power within the organizations that governed the way a professional practiced.

The paradox of increasing opportunity in the face of continuing job segmentation proved to hold for African Americans as well, but as the historian Jacqueline Jones has pointed out, in distinctive ways, due to racial discrimination. In the early twentieth century, nine out of ten blacks lived in the South, and 80 percent of these resided in rural areas. Much as they had in the nineteenth-century South, blacks constituted 40 percent of the region's farmers and farm laborers. Furthermore, nearly 90 percent of all blacks who earned their living from the land occupied the lowest rungs of that occupational ladder; they were tenant farmers, sharecroppers, and day laborers in a system that perpetuated the economic dependency of blacks on whites that had existed during slavery. In this rural economy, the family was the unit of production, which placed an especially heavy burden on black women. Rising around 4 A.M., before anyone else, they prepared and served breakfast and then joined family members in the fields, where jobs related to planting, cultivating, and picking were assigned by age and sex. Needless to say, many tasks needed to sustain the family labor force also kept black women up late into the night.

Cities, first in the South and then in the North, offered black men and women the opportunity to escape the cycles of poverty and dependency that came with working the land. Here was the promise of wages for their labor. The small but growing number of urban blacks in the South, however, often found a different reality than they expected. By the early twentieth century, the skilled trades had, through unions, locked out black men, leaving them only work as laborers in construction or ditch digging, or unskilled factory work on a temporary or seasonal basis. Long periods of unemployment were common. This discrimination against black men had drastic effects on the black family. In 1897, an Atlanta University study revealed that of 1,100 urban black families, only 24 percent relied exclusively on a male household head's earnings. Working wives, children, and relatives all contributed to sustaining the black household. Although many white working families also depended on multiple earners, the situation proved much more severe for blacks. Indeed, married black women were five times more likely than their white counterparts to enter the work force. Between 50 and 70 percent of black women worked at least part of the year in the largest southern cities, most often as laundresses and servants, since in the urban South nine out of ten domestic servants were black women.

When on rare occasions black women found better paying jobs in the industrial work force, they had as much to fear from their fellow employees as from their employers. In 1897, an Atlanta textile mill hired two black female spinners, setting off a spontaneous protest by white employees. When over 1,400 women of the Textile Workers Union struck "in sympathy," the black women were fired. Thus, blacks in the urban, as in the rural, South found themselves constrained not only by their inferior economic position but also by a racial caste system which kept them in that position. Opportunities were often better in southern cities than the countryside, but the intersection of racial and gender segmentation at the workplace put great pressure on the black family.

The onset of World War I offered southern blacks new employment opportunities in northern cities. As European immigration halted and war put new demands on northern industry, employers faced serious labor shortages. By 1916 the factory gates began to open to white women as well as blacks, who previously had found jobs in northern industry only as strikebreakers. Pulled by the lure of well-paying, year-around employment and pushed by the difficulties of making a decent living in southern agriculture and the tightening of Jim Crow restrictions, black men and women migrated northward.

The Great Migration was a family affair that was often accomplished in a series of moves that slowly expanded the migrants' contact with industrial society. In order to supplement their rural household economy as sharecroppers or tenant farmers, many black men and women migrated to southern cities or logging camps, sawmills, and mines. Having thus been introduced to a world outside the familiar farm and kin, going North was for many the next logical step. The particular industrial economies of northern cities determined the demographic patterns of migration. Black men usually led the migration to cities like Pittsburgh, which offered industrial jobs to men but few positions outside domestic service to women. On the other hand, cities like Chicago with more diversified economies promised women greater job opportunities and hence attracted single women and even wives who preceded their husbands to reconnoiter the economic and general living conditions. Whatever the specific demographic patterns, family and extended kin networks shaped blacks' migration and entry into the northern economy, much as they had within the South. But while black men and women found expanded economic opportunity in northern cities, they soon learned that it was opportunity carefully assigned according to race and gender. It may have been easier to make a living wage in the North, but this "Promised Land" offered little relief from the job segmentation they had encountered in southern cities.

After 1930, the industrial economy went through several stages that changed the nature of work and the job opportunities available to American men and women. Through the Great Depression, World War II, the postwar era of the late 1940s through the 1960s, and finally the 1970s and 1980s, men and women continued to encounter the paradox of expanded opportunity and persistent job segmentation, though how severely and in what ways depended on their class and race.

The stock market crash of 1929 signaled the official beginning of the Great Depression, although working men and women had been encountering more layoffs and longer periods of unemployment for quite some time. Widespread business retrenchment and failure meant the disappearance of many jobs, with great consequences for the way men and women lived and thought of themselves. Many men felt that they had lost their identity along with their job. Unable to provide for their families, they sometimes felt emasculated. As one investigator of unemployed families in Chicago put it: "In his own estimation, he was failing to fulfill the central duty of his life—the very touchstone of his manhood—the role of family provider." Often women had an easier time finding and keeping a job than their husbands and fathers, which further undermined traditional authority relationships within the family. Not surprisingly, a Census Bureau study of Minneapolis–Saint Paul in 1940 found that wives of unemployed men worked much more often than wives of men who remained employed. Whereas in 1930, 28 percent of women wage earners were married, by 1940, 35 percent were.

As community institutions such as churches, neighborhood stores, ethnic benefit societies, and building-and-loan associations failed along with the family economy in the depression, workers turned for security toward new institutional structures, particularly the federal government and labor unions. Stable, effective industrial unions within the Congress of Industrial Organizations (CIO) successfully organized factory workers and increasingly won recognition from employers, thanks to new protections assured by the New Deal. Although women did join CIO unions in many plants, their roles were carefully circumscribed. As the CIO became institutionalized, the labor movement went from being community-based and fairly inclusive of women to being more workplace oriented, more bureaucratically and nationally centralized, and hence more marginalizing of women. Women increasingly found themselves excluded from leadership, labor-movement culture, and even membership. Historian Elizabeth Faue has traced the increasing masculinization of the iconography of labor within the union press over the course of the 1930s. In the symbolic discourse of the labor movement, assertive—even violent—male images represented union solidarity, while female imagery emerged only to depict victimization and to portray need and want.

The labor movement mirrored what was happening in society more broadly. Just as women were gaining importance as wage earners in the family, public opinion was denigrating the woman as wage earner. Historian Barbara Melosh has documented through a careful investigation of painting and plays produced under the New Deal's Works Progress Administration how art supported by state patronage contributed to an ideology antagonistic to women working. Post office wall murals and federal theater productions idealized women as wives and mothers. Even as women were contributing more to the support of their families, their labor continued to be viewed as auxiliary to that of males. One way that unions and management ensured that women would not threaten the job security of men was to implement separate seniority rules, job ladders, and wage scales by sex. Unionization, then, not only protected workers from bosses, but also male workers from the competition of women. The sexual division of labor grew in other fields as well. By 1950 over 62 percent of all clerical workers were women, increasingly isolated in "pink-collar" ghettos. The professions, on the other hand, grew more male dominated beginning in the 1930s, a trend that would not reverse until the 1960s. As in earlier times, the participation of women, particularly married ones, in the labor force grew during the depression years and steadily thereafter, but the opportunities open to them remained restricted.

World War II brought an end to the depression, and, on the surface, it appeared to reshape popular attitudes toward women's work. In fact, for a time, gender almost seemed to lose its salience as a divisive factor in the workplace, even as the sexual division of labor continued within the military. Between 1940 and 1945, about 4.7 million women entered the labor force for the first time, to produce the armaments and supplies needed for the Allied war effort. Not surprisingly, the reasons women offered for taking new jobs resembled the ones they had given a decade earlier: middle-class women increasingly sought work for personal fulfillment while working-class women sought economic security. Black women, long used to working, particularly made gains. Although they were excluded from the best-paying jobs available, the number of black women factory operatives, clerical workers, sales workers, and professionals more than doubled by the war's end, while the number of black women domestic servants declined by 15 percent. Not only were more women working, but their pay rates also increased relative to men's. In 1940 women's average wages were 56 cents per hour, compared to 76 cents for men; in 1944 the rates were 76 cents for women and 89 cents for men.

Despite women's unprecedented participation in the labor force, progress made during the war proved for the most part illusory, as traditional gender boundaries were sharply redrawn in the postwar workplace. Employers, organized labor, and the government had supported women's work only as an emergency measure. At war's end, they all expected women to return home and give their jobs to returning male veterans. It soon became clear that unions such as the United Auto Workers had only supported equal pay for women during the war to insure that women did not undercut men's wages. Following the war, women workers faced massive layoffs and enormous pressure to leave the workplace. In a typical plea, Marynia Farnham and Ferdinand Lundberg, authors of the best-selling *Modern Woman: The Lost Sex* (1947), urged women to "recapture those functions in which they have demonstrated superior capacity. Those are, in general, the nurturing functions around the home."

Some women, particularly those who had never worked before the war, willingly went home because, according to Frieda Miller, director of the Women's Bureau in 1944, they did not want to "get ahead at the expense of veterans." But women who had been employed prior to the war or needed to work did not give up their jobs so easily. Many fought their layoffs and sought to retain gains in wages and job classification won in wartime. In 1945, Mary Norton, Claude Pepper, and Wayne Morse introduced the Women's Equal Pay Act in Congress to try to protect working women. But despite aggressive help from the Women's Bureau of the Labor Department, the Women's Trade Union League, and other supporters of female laborers, the bill failed. The effort to insure equal pay and job opportunity for women could not overcome opposition from special interests as well as a majority of the American public. In 1946, a *Fortune* magazine survey showed that less than 22 percent of men and 29 percent of women thought female workers "should have an equal chance with men." The GI bill, which helped so many postwar families reenter civil society, not only symbolically reinforced the "male breadwinner" family, but it also gave men—and not women—access to the higher education and skill training that would secure their place in the managerial, high-technology economy of the postwar era.

This tension between the reality of women's need to work and the prevailing ideology opposing that work as threatening to the livelihood of men and the survival of the traditional family persisted from the Great Depression and the war into the 1950s. Despite an ideological climate that relentlessly promoted female domestication, women continued to stream into the labor force. Married as well as single women were increasingly living important parts of their lives outside the home, accelerating a trend which had been evident since the turn of the century. Between 1950 and 1960 the portion of married women working increased from 25 to 32 percent; by 1970, 40 percent of all married women worked, and by 1980, 50 percent. For many women in the postwar era, work was an economic necessity. The new suburban lifestyle, with its consumption orientation, was hard to achieve on a man's salary alone, even as his employment opportunities grew with the explosion of white-collar work in the postwar period. But women worked not only to help pay the bills. Some women began working as a way to escape what Betty Friedan, in her best-selling *The Feminine Mystique* (1963), called "the problem that has no name." Friedan articulated the frustration that many women felt with the limitations of their domestic roles as wives and mothers. Working became a way not only of contributing to the family economy, but of developing a more independent sense of self. (See table 1 and figure 1.)

In the postwar period the explosive growth of a managerial white-collar economy contributed to re-

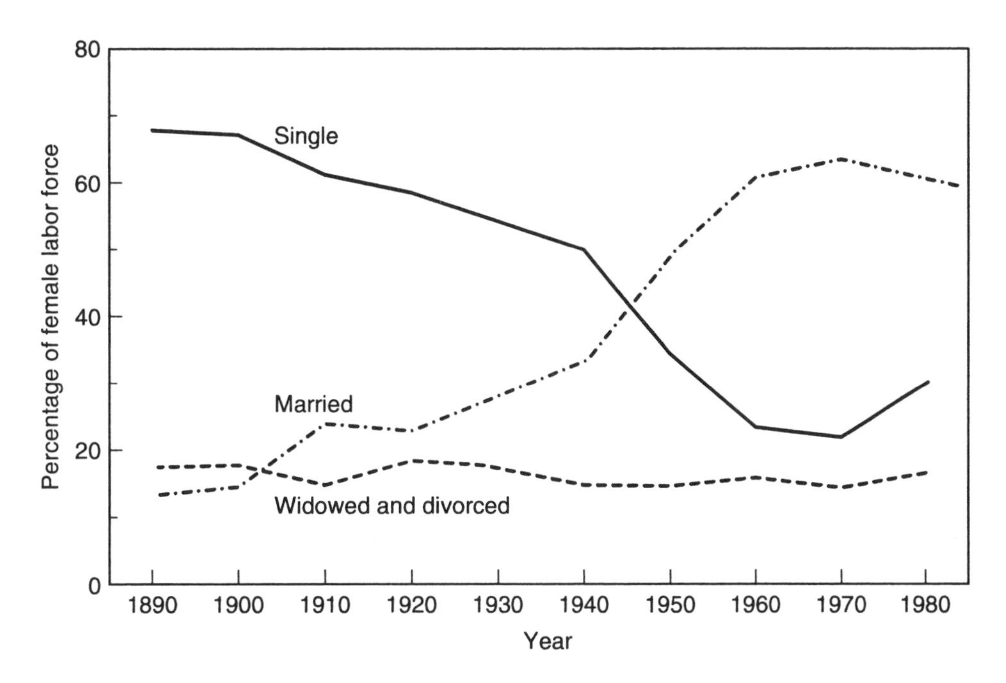

Figure 1. Composition of Female Labor Force by Marital Status, 1890–1980. This graph is based on table 1. (Adapted from Lynn Y. Weiner, *From Working Girl to Working Mother* [1985].)

Table 1. PERCENTAGE OF WOMEN IN THE U.S. LABOR FORCE, BY FAMILY STATUS, 1890–1990

	1890	1900	1910	1920	1930	1940	1950	1960	1970	1980[a]	1990
					Total Female Labor Force						
Single	68	67	61	77[b]	54	49	32	23	22	25	25
Wid.-Div.	18	18	15	—[b]	17	15	16	6	14	15	20
Married	14	15	24	23	29	36	52	61	63	60	55
Mothers[c]	—	—	—	—	—	11	26	27	38	40	38
					Female Labor Force Participation Rate						
Single	41	41	48	44[b]	46	48	51	44	53	62	67
Wid.-Div.	30	33	35	—[b]	34	32	36	13	46	41	47
Married	5	6	11	9	12	17	25	32	41	51	58
Mothers[c]	—	—	—	—	—	28	33	37	43	56	67[d]

[a] Figures for March 1980.
[b] Single women counted with widows and divorced women.
[c] Mothers of children under age 18.
[d] Figure for March 1993.

SOURCES: Adapted from Lynn Y. Weiner, *From Working Girl to Working Mother* (University of North Carolina Press, 1985), p. 6; U.S. Bureau of the Census, *Women at Work,* p. 14, table VII, p. 15, table VIII; U.S. Department of Labor, Women's Bureau, *Employed Mothers and Child Care,* p. 9, table 3; U.S. Department of Labor, Bureau of Labor Statistics, *Working Women: A Databook,* p. 19, table 18; U.S. Department of Labor, Bureau of Labor Statistics, *Marital and Family Statistics of Workers,* p. 5, table 3; U.S. Department of Labor, Bureau of Labor Statistics, *Marital and Family Patterns,* p. 1, table 1, p. 2, table 2, p. 25, table C-1. Figures for 1980 and 1990 from U.S. Bureau of the Census, *Statistical Abstract of the United States 1994,* p. 55, table 59; p. 401, tables 624 and 625; p. 402, table 627; and *1990 Census of Population,* CP-2-1, table 19.

vised ideals of masculinity as well. "The man in the gray flannel suit" and the "organization man"—as these workers were dubbed in popular works of the era—often prized job security with a big, stable corporation over excitement or earning power. Reinforced in popular literature, in movies, and on television, the new middle-class ideal placed more emphasis on reliability and predictability than on economic risk-taking. Middle-class manhood came to be equated not only with rational and steady leadership but also, as historian Roland Marchand has argued, with scientific expertise. One typical advertisement for Gulf Refining

Company, for instance, argued that modern men "bring to their tasks a gift for scientific prophecy and genius for perseverance." Not coincidentally, male scientific expertise was used to legitimate a new kind of sexual division of labor within a postwar corporate world where R&D (research and development) took on new significance and authority.

As more women entered the work force from the 1960s on, class affiliation dictated to a large extent their fates in the labor market. Educated middle-class women gained increased entry into the white-collar male world of business and the professions, albeit in certain kinds of jobs. By the end of the 1970s, for example, women had become 12 percent of lawyers, 35 percent of accountants, and 25 percent of managers. Although the sexual integration of the middle-class workplace was not without discrimination and limitation—popularly known as the "glass ceiling"—tremendous progress was made. Working-class women also broke into traditional male occupations, particularly as a result of equal-opportunity suits by the federal government. By 1980, women made up nearly 50 percent of all bus drivers, and they were also repairing telephones, mining, and doing many other jobs that they would never have been allowed to do a decade earlier. Correspondingly, women increased their share of union membership, from 18 percent in 1960 to 34 percent in 1980, although a large portion of that growth can be attributed to a decline in the number of men employed in the unionized heavy-industry sectors and to the expansion of public-sector unionization where women are well represented. Still, women joined unions to protect themselves from the job segmentation and feminization that in the past led invariably to declines in wages and status when women won access to traditionally male jobs. And they have also pushed the concept of comparable worth at the bargaining table and the courthouse, demanding that women be equitably compensated for skill and responsibility, even when they do different kinds of jobs than men. Where the sexual division of labor could not be broken down, women have tried to minimize its economic penalties.

The greatest challenge to the status quo in the working-class labor market, however, has arisen not so much from changing gender roles and expectations as from the deindustrialization of the American economy since the 1970s. During the decades of prosperity following World War II, American corporations began expanding their operations to other parts of the globe as well as to areas of the United States outside the industrial North. In particular, corporate investment in foreign subsidiaries created the possibility of excess productive capacity in many industries as well as helping to generate international competition. By the 1970s, this new competition came back to haunt major American industries such as steel, electronics, and automobiles. Corporate management, faced with critical choices, often decided to abandon aging and technologically backward facilities in the Northeast and invest elsewhere in the United States and the world. During the 1970s, hundreds of thousands, perhaps even millions, of workers lost their jobs as a result of shop closings and economic restructuring. Needless to say, the deindustrialization of America has had a devastating effect on the economic well-being of the working class, particularly the predominantly male work force that characterized many of these basic industries. The economic and psychological costs of long-term unemployment for steel workers and auto workers can hardly be calculated. In their book *Unwanted Workers: Permanent Layoffs and Long-Term Employment* (1963), Richard Wilcock and W. H. Franke noted that for the typical male worker, the loss of a job meant "not only disappearance of human relationships built up over a period of years, but also the end of a meaningful institutional relationship. When he is severed from his job, he discovers that he has lost, in addition to the income and activity, his institutional base in the economic and social system." African Americans, who built their entry into the stable working class on industrial opportunity, have suffered disproportionately. When a laundry in Saint Louis began decentralizing its operation out of downtown in 1964, 75 percent of its employees were black. Ten years later, after it had opened thirteen suburban facilities, only 5 percent of its work force was black. A similar loss of black jobs occurred in 1976 when a Detroit manufacturer relocated its facilities to rural Ohio. Predominantly white salaried employees were offered assistance in finding new jobs, while the mostly black hourly employees were not. The new facility in Ohio opened with a labor force that was 2 percent nonwhite, while in Detroit minorities had made up 40 percent of the workers. The burden of deindustrialization has fallen particularly hard on black men, as black women have increasingly gained access to low-level service sector jobs since the 1960s. Black women's greater opportunities for employment and social mobility, moreover, have re-created some of the sexual inequities facing urban blacks earlier in the century. The postindustrial economy of the 1980s and 1990s, thus, has placed an undue burden on the black family. (See table 2.)

In places like the Southwest, which benefited from the deindustrialization of the Northeast and Midwest, dramatic growth in the industrial sector has dovetailed

Table 2. PERCENTAGE OF MARRIED WOMEN IN THE LABOR FORCE, BY RACE, SELECTED YEARS, 1890–1990

	1890	1900	1920	1930	1940	1950	1960	1970	1980	1990
All women	5	6	9	12	17	25	32	40	49	56
White	2	3	7	10	14	17	30	39	48	56
Black	23	26	33	33	32	36	47	51	60	63

SOURCES: Adapted from Lynn Y. Weiner, *From Working Girl to Working Mother* (University of North Carolina Press, 1985), p. 89; Brownlee, "Household Values," p. 200, table 1; Durand, *Labor Force in the U.S.*, pp. 216–17, table A-7; U.S. Bureau of the Census, *U.S. Census of Population, 1960,* pp. 501–6, table 196; U.S. Bureau of the Census, *Nineteenth Census of the U.S., 1970,* pp. 688–89, table 216. Figures for 1980 from U.S. Bureau of the Census, *1980 Census of Population,* vol. 1, chap. C, tables 103 and 124. Figures for 1990 from U.S. Bureau of the Census, *1990 Census of Population,* CP-2-1, table 4-1.

with prevailing gender, racial, and ethnic discrimination to restructure the workplace. In Albuquerque, New Mexico, for instance, employment in manufacturing grew over 100 percent between 1969 and 1979, and women workers benefited most from it; between 1970 and 1980 female employment increased by 58 percent while male employment declined by 16 percent. The labor force participation of Hispanic women particularly increased, by 66 percent, in contrast to only 18 percent for Anglo women. "Sunbelt industrialization" occurred at the expense of working-class white men, who lost work elsewhere in the economy. The women employed in new manufacturing jobs were hired because their labor was cheaper and nonunion. In the 1970s, female manufacturing jobs paid only 44 percent of male manufacturing jobs.

Although much has changed over the course of the twentieth century, deindustrialization has perpetuated a longstanding dynamic in the American labor market, of women gaining increasing access to new jobs while those jobs, in turn, are devalued. Women made up 18 percent of the work force in 1900; by the year 2000 half of all workers will be female. Because of persistent, discriminatory ideologies and practices, however, it is unlikely that they will earn half of the total wages (they now earn 70 cents to every dollar earned by males) or gain access to the best jobs available. (See table 3.)

Table 3. NUMBER[a] AND PROPORTION OF WORKING WOMEN IN THE U.S. LABOR FORCE, 1870–1990

Year	Total Labor Force	Working Women	Percent of All Women Who Work	Women as Percent of Labor Force
1870	12,160	1,717	15	14
1880	16,274	2,354	16	14
1890	21,814	3,597	19	16
1900	27,323	4,834	21	18
1910	35,749	7,011	24	20
1920	41,017	8,278	24	20
1930	48,163	10,546	25	22
1940	52,711	12,951	27	25
1950	59,223	16,443	30	28
1960	69,234	22,222	36	32
1970	82,048	30,547	41	37
1980	106,066	44,741	51	42
1990	125,182	56,673	57	45

[a] In thousands.

SOURCES: Adapted from Lynn Y. Weiner, *From Working Girl to Working Mother* (University of North Carolina Press, 1985) p. 4; U.S. Bureau of the Census, *Comparative Statistics for the U.S., 1870–1940,* p. 92, table xv; U.S. Bureau of the Census, *Nineteenth Census of the U.S.,* vol. 1, pt. I, p. 372, table 78; U.S. Bureau of the Census, *1980 Census of Population,* p. 25, table p. 3; U.S. Bureau of the Census, *1990 Census of Population,* CP-2-1, p. 19, table 19.

GENDER IN LEISURE AND CONSUMPTION

Life outside the workplace was as influential as life inside in shaping women's and men's gender identities over the twentieth century. Leisure as well as work, consumption as well as production, played important roles in defining maleness and femaleness. In contrast to work, where people felt compelled to abide by rules made by those in authority, leisure and consumption have had the aura of personal choice. Patterns of gender differentiation in this realm, then, were extremely powerful in defining gender relations more broadly.

The major change in gendered patterns of leisure from the nineteenth century to the twentieth was a different division between single-sex and mixed-sex socializing. In the Victorian culture of the nineteenth century, "separate spheres" characterized social life as well as work and home. Only during courtship and on explicit family occasions after marriage did men and women spend leisure time together. Typically, girls and boys were educated and played separately, and they grew up continuing to spend free time with members of their own sex. Whatever ways men and women socialized in the nineteenth century—whether middle-class men who went to social clubs or working-class men who hung out at the corner saloon, whether middle-class women making social calls or working-class women visiting on the tenement stoop—leisure reinforced other institutional boundaries at home, school, and work that kept the sexes apart.

Over the course of the twentieth century the gender boundaries of leisure were redrawn. In the early years of the century, mixed-sex socializing increased dramatically, revolving around sexually charged imagery and behavior at the increasing number of sites of mass culture, such as dance halls, cabarets, amusement parks, and motion-picture theaters. As historian Kathy Peiss has shown in her study of working women in turn-of-the-century New York, young working-class men and, particularly, women pioneered this break from nineteenth-century patterns of single-sex socializing, promoting "heterosexual companionship" as an expression of their newfound autonomy apart from their families. They developed rituals of dating and treating that put sexuality at the heart of social interaction. Peiss argues convincingly that this social change percolated up from working class to middle class, encouraging in time the creation of a broad-based leisure culture of mixed-sex socializing. By the 1920s, middle-class high school and college students participated in a youth culture built around attracting the attention of the other sex. Young women who bobbed their hair, shortened their skirts, wore makeup, and smoked in public, young men who identified their masculinity with owning an automobile and being a good dancer, and couples who sociologists discovered petted in record numbers—all contributed to a new linking of leisure to sexuality. One could hardly go to the movies, the quintessential twentieth-century entertainment, without observing sexual models in the audience as well as on the screen. As feminist film critics have pointed out, motion pictures contributed to the objectification of women by making them the "to-be-looked-at object" of male desire.

Despite the increase in heterosexual socializing, leisure continued to reinforce the distinctiveness of male and female worlds during the twentieth century. Beginning in childhood, children spent their free time playing with toys, reading books, and participating in organized activities, such as the Boy Scouts and Girl Scouts, specifically designed for their sex. Through this participation, young boys and girls were explicitly and inexplicitly socialized to behaviors, values, and psychological responses considered appropriate for each sex. Even for adults, much leisure was coded male or female, with men, for example, more likely to watch sports and women to attend a ballet or an exhibition at an art museum. Throughout the century, popular literature, too, has been produced for gender-specific markets, whether *Popular Mechanics* and *Ladies Home Journal* early in the century, or *Esquire* or *Working Woman* more recently.

Associational life has also reinforced gender differentiation, with men active in male service and business clubs and women in female community or social organizations. Novelist William Kennedy recalled the centrality of the Knights of Columbus in the lives of the men in his family during the 1930s and 1940s. In this Catholic men's fraternal club in downtown Albany, he learned to bowl, play cards, and shoot pool. When his interest in women grew by late adolescence, he learned quickly that "women came to the Knights only for parties, dances, and bingo; club life excluded them otherwise." Some members, in fact, sent their women friends to the movies across the street, "while the men nightly, every night, hung around the club." Although some of these exclusively male and female bastions have broken down in recent decades due to the challenges to sex discrimination and other social changes, versions of them remain. Peter Stearns has suggested that for men, working out and playing sports have become important compensatory ways of asserting manhood as work has offered fewer opportunities to demonstrate masculine prowess. At the same time, sports have reinforced such traditional male values associated with the workplace as discipline, teamwork, and competition. They have also recreated the class and racial segmentation of the workplace, as certain games and positions have become associated with distinctive social groups. For black athletes in particular sports have become a highly visible vehicle for upward mobility when other career ladders have been hard to climb.

This bifurcation in the gender patterns of leisure has reinforced a social world sharply divided between male-female interactions that are sexually charged and other recreational interactions that are single sex. Only in the very recent past, as girls have won access to Little League teams and boys have been allowed more feminine play, have these boundaries blurred. It is too soon to know what kind of impact more permeable gender socialization in children will have on future adults. Thus, although men and women have spent more leisure time together in the twentieth century than they did in the nineteenth, strong vestiges of separate spheres remain. Leisure has proven a crucial arena for reinforcing stereotypes of the seducer male and seduced female, on the one hand, while reserving less self-conscious, more natural socializing for same-sex relationships, on the other. Leisure patterns thereby have contributed to the persistence of traditional gender roles over the twentieth century, despite the greater integration of women in previously male occupations and their increasing responsibility for supporting families financially.

Another realm of life outside of work where gender roles have been shaped during the twentieth century is that of consumption. Managing individual and family consumption—the purchasing of goods and services in the marketplace—has remained a primary responsibility of women throughout the twentieth century, while men have played the role of dominant economic provider. Typically, wives in working-class and middle-class families—regardless of their financial contribution to the family income, which has grown substantially over the century—have overseen procurement of food, furnishings, clothing, and other staple items, only to bow to the authority of husbands in the case of larger purchases, such as homes, automobiles, and major appliances. These exceptions to what has otherwise been viewed as the feminine act of consumption has served to reinforce a hierarchy of authority in the family and to privilege the power of the chief earner over chief spender.

Women nonetheless have used their power as consumers to exert social and political influence throughout the twentieth century. Beginning in the Progressive Era, women reformers organized female consumers through the Women's Trade Union League and the National Consumers' League and its state affiliates to pressure for better working conditions and wages for employed women. Women bought products manufactured under acceptable conditions and patronized stores with good employer records. During strikes and in cities with strong labor movements, they also used their consumer power to support union demands, union cooperatives, and union-label campaigns. In 1917 working-class Jewish women took to the streets of New York City to protest the high cost of chicken, fish, and vegetables; in 1919 trade union women organized to support Seattle's general strike by boycotting an antiunion leader's department store; at the end of World War II women throughout America refused to buy meat to protest its high cost; in the 1950s and early 1960s African American women in the South initiated boycotts of department stores, bus companies, and other public accommodations until they were racially integrated; and in the 1960s and 1970s women consumers supported a national boycott of table grapes to help the United Farm Workers win contracts from growers. Women were using their power over the purse to support political causes they believed in.

Historians have also identified ways that women have used consumption to express their personal dissatisfactions with the power of patriarchy in their lives. Janice Radway's analysis of women who bought and read popular romance fiction around 1980 suggests that women have used romance reading both to protest and to escape temporarily the limited role prescribed for them by patriarchal culture, even as the romance paradoxically makes that role seem more desirable.

Thus, consumption, much like leisure, has been an arena of experience where women have gained power but in carefully circumscribed ways that have not challenged the fundamental patriarchal structure of society. As production and work have declined in social importance over the century, the more feminized territories of consumption and leisure have grown in influence. Yet within these territories, men and women have continued to compete for influence, so that an increase in female authority has rarely been assured. Interestingly, the growing cultural hegemony of consumption over production in twentieth-century culture has led to popular images not only of the female consumer but also of the ad man and the salesman, men seeking to manage female consumption. In the case of the salesman, masculinity is often at stake with the job. From Bruce Barton's *The Man Nobody Knows* (1925), which depicted Jesus as the original go-getter who built his disciples into the most effective sales organization of all time, to the archetype salesmen in Sinclair Lewis's *Babbitt* (1922) and Arthur Miller's *Death of a Salesman* (1949), to late-twentieth-century versions in David Mamet's play *Glengarry Glen Ross* (1983; movie 1992) and Barry Levinson's popular movie *Tin Men* (1987), men have struggled to prove their manhood as producers on the threatening terrain of consumption.

Although these generalizations about patterns of leisure and consumption apply to a wide cast of Americans, some diversity in experience is worth noting. On the one hand, working-class men and women, who initiated the gender integration of leisure early in the century, have in the recent period been slowest to abandon the single-sex socializing of clubs, bowling leagues, and the like. In the traditional working-class family, moreover, the woman's income is viewed as secondary, and responsibility for everyday consumption does little to challenge male authority. More middle-class professional families, by contrast, have been at the forefront in breaking down barriers to female participation in male leisure activities such as sports teams and business clubs. But in the realm of consumption, although middle-class wives' income often compares favorably with their husbands', it is not clear that women have gained any more authority in the family. Reinforcing sociologist Arlie Hochschild's analysis of what she calls the "second shift"—women's greater responsibility for domestic and child care duties despite their equal labor force participation—middle-class working wives often continue to live with traditional power relations in the family.

African American culture features its own distinctive patterns of leisure and consumption, in that blacks have long been comfortable with mixed-gender informal socializing and have made less of a distinction between heterosocial and homosocial leisure. Perhaps this is so because they have built leisure around mixed-sex institutions such as extended family, neighborhoods, and churches. Among a population where female-headed households have become increasingly prevalent, female independence is often demonstrated through consumer power, although the harsh reality of poverty that disproportionately affects African American households constrains consumption for men and women alike.

GENDER IN POLITICS

Gender has mattered not only as people have lived out their individual lives in families, at work, and while pursuing leisure and consumption. In the more public arena and through the more collective action of politics, gender has been a prime concern. The century began with women's successful struggle to achieve suffrage and is ending in an era when the most intense, divisive political battles are over gender-related issues such as abortion, affirmative action, and sexual harassment. In the intervening years there have been times when gender concerns have mattered politically, and others when they have not. But overall, the twentieth century has been a period during which gender itself has increasingly become a political issue. Ironically, this has become the case even as men and women have moved from participating in the political arena in distinctively gendered ways to engaging in it in far more similar ways. Not only have women gained access to power as organized voters and office holders, but men have responded to calls like President George Bush's to become "a thousand points of light," a revival of the voluntarism that characterized women's political activity before they could vote.

It is first crucial to consider the gendered character of politics as it was practiced when the twentieth century began. During the Progressive Era electoral politics ceased being the exclusive bastion of male prerogative as women gained the vote. As significant as the incorporation of women into the electorate, however, was change in the way politics was practiced. In the nineteenth century, as historian Michael McGerr has argued, electoral politics was male. Men organized, rallied, and voted in ways that affirmed their collective masculinity, often cutting across social class lines. Women, barred from this male political world by their lack of the vote and by conventional notions of respectability, could only participate in electoral politics by performing "appropriate" assigned tasks, such as preparing food, sewing banners, and decorating meeting halls.

By the early twentieth century, masculine popular politics had broken down along class lines. A middle-class reform politics emerged to challenge the old system of political partisanship, now associated with urban working-class and ethnic communities. This new, still masculine political style rejected the rowdy masculinity of nineteenth-century politics for a more reserved style favoring reason, sensibility, and efficiency, a style, it should be noted, that resembled the educational politics pioneered by disenfranchised women in the nineteenth century. Middle-class men in the early twentieth century regarded party bureaucrats and trained experts as the ideal public servants. Alongside this emphasis on education was another innovation, to apply the tools of advertising to politics. Political parties now sought to sell candidates' personalities. Middle-class, experienced advertisers were charged with selling a new product—the candidate—to middle-class consumers—the voters. By World War I, the physical, rough-and-tumble masculine politics of the nineteenth century failed to persuade many middle-class men, who now preferred a more elite and less democratic masculine politics. During the Progressive Era, then, male politics bifurcated along lines of social class, leading ultimately to the victory of a mainstream political culture that rejected mass mobilization in favor of control by an elite.

During the same period that a new form of male politics was taking shape, women were fighting for the right to vote. Their political trajectory differed from men's, however, in that they moved from class-specific public political activity to more cross-class alliances. In the nineteenth century, despite their inability to vote, typically working-class women had organized in labor unions and middle-class women had actively participated in politics through a host of voluntary associations in which they sought to reform society and to educate the public and politicians. Although organizations like the Women's Temperance Crusade staged mass marches against liquor dealers, most middle-class women were reluctant to imitate the mass rituals of male popular politics. This reluctance had notable consequences for the suffrage movement; by 1900, only four states had granted women the right to vote, and the future of the movement seemed bleak.

In a reversal of what happened in male politics, female politics entered a period in the early twentieth century of greater cross-class alliance building and more mass mobilization. The ultimate achievement of the Nineteenth Amendment resulted from the broadening of the constituency for suffrage to include more working-class women. New working-class adherents of suffrage coming from the Women's Trade Union League and the Equality League of Self-Supporting Women, moreover, supported the more militant, less "ladylike" tactics that Alice Paul and her Constitutional Union were pushing and British suffragists had already employed. American suffragists also turned to more open-air meetings, parades, and other attention-getting strategies, such as a "trolley car campaign" between Syracuse and Albany using interurban trolleys to go from town to town.

In reviving some features of nineteenth-century male politics in the early twentieth century, suffragists did not ignore the innovations men were bringing to politics, particularly the use of education and advertising, and they in fact pushed them to new heights. The National American Woman Suffrage Association (NAWSA) and state-level suffrage organizations had their own publicity departments devoted to feeding stories to newspapers and magazines. In 1916, in fact, the *New York Times* noted how well women were using advertising methods in the fight for suffrage: "Every legitimate method of campaigning was used . . . leaflets . . . posters and all kinds of designs; city circularizing of the most thorough kind in many languages; pageants, plays, concerts . . .; the placarding of city billboards over miles of country; advertising of every possible kind; huge electric and other signs." Moreover, from 1912 to 1914 NAWSA and the Women's Political Union (WPU) contracted with movie companies to produce the films *Vote for Women, Your Girl and Mine, 80 Million Women Want —?,* and *Suffrage and Man,* all of which were exhibited to exuberant audiences at nickelodeons, fairs, and churches.

Once women had gained the franchise, however, the class tensions that shaped male politics in the early twentieth century also worked to undermine the solidarity of suffragists. During the struggle for the vote, class-based concerns, such as debates over women's proper role, had been obscured by the groundswell of support. Once women joined men as ordinary political actors, however, women's political participation began to divide along class and racial lines. In the context of national conflicts over strikes, race riots, the Red Scare, and immigration restriction, and in a mainstream political culture where popular voting was losing out to interest-group lobbying, postsuffrage female politics lost its participatory, cross-class character. Women now had the vote, but they disappointed those who had anticipated that an enfranchised female population would transform American politics. Women voted their class and racial interests along with their husbands and fathers and returned to many of the voluntary political activities of the presuffrage era. Conflicts over such issues as social welfare, protective labor legislation, and civil rights divided rather than unified them.

The struggle over an Equal Rights Amendment (ERA) to the United States Constitution serves as a good example of how a feminist issue faltered after the passage of suffrage due to women's conflicting class agendas. Introduced into Congress in 1923 by the National Women's Party (NWP), which had been a crucial base of support for the suffrage movement, the ERA read: "Men and women shall have equal rights throughout the United States and every place subject to its jurisdiction." Rejecting the longstanding female reform agenda of protecting women by legislating for their special treatment, the NWP pushed for total equality before the law. The NWP had come to believe that sameness, not difference, should be women's goal. Protective legislation, the NWP held, did not actually protect female workers. Rather, as Harriot Stanton Blatch argued, "In many highly paid trades women have been pushed into lower grades of work, limited in earning capacity, if not shut out of the trades entirely by so-called protective laws."

Many middle-class reformers and working-class men and women did not agree with the NWP, for different reasons reflecting their different ways of linking class and gender. Some reformers viewed protective legislation as part of a broad strategy for advancing working conditions for both men and women. When Florence Kelley and her National Consumers' League fought for minimum-hour legislation for women, they hoped to extend those protections eventually to men via the court system. Working-class men and women had their own reasons for rejecting the ERA. Working-class men feared that equal access would undermine their exclusive hold on jobs and labor organizations, ultimately undermining the "family wage" they had long sought. To them, women were primarily wives and mothers to be supported by a male wage adequate to feed, clothe, and house a family. Working-class women, meanwhile, feared the loss of their limited stake in the industrial workplace. They also attacked equal-rights legislation for representing a middle-class notion of individual achievement better suited to women in the professions than in the factory. Elisabeth Christman, a former glovemaker and WTUL officer, angrily wished to "put some of the 'equal righters' in a boiler factory or to work at the conveyer belt in a highly speeded-up mass production industry," so that they could understand the benefits of protective legislation.

The NWP and its main agenda item, the ERA, became increasingly isolated from the concerns of the mainstream of women. Not until the 1970s, with its very different political climate, would widespread public support for the ERA emerge. Interestingly, the NWP's criticism of protective legislation was also resurrected in the 1970s by feminist scholars like Heidi Hartmann who rooted it in an agreement between capitalist men and working-class men whose sexual and economic interests converged to exclude women from equal participation in wage labor.

Race, too, divided women in the political sphere, both during the struggle for woman suffrage and afterwards. African American women, like working-class women, had supported the campaign for the vote, but they frequently found themselves banished to the margins of the movement because of their race. Despite rhetoric to the contrary, suffrage organizations from NAWSA to the NWP only reluctantly included black women in their suffrage plans. For instance, in 1916, Carrie Catt, president of NAWSA, argued that NAWSA had to be conciliatory to the South if suffrage were to become a reality and even went so far as to urge southern white women delegates not to attend the NAWSA convention in Chicago that year because the majority of southern NAWSA delegates were black. Given their marginalization by white suffragists, the strength of black women's support for suffrage is impressive and suggests how committed they were to a political agenda that went beyond simply gaining the vote. They hoped to use suffrage to make extensive social reforms, such as abolishing Jim Crow legislation and passing antilynching laws. With nearly 90 percent of all black women living in the South in 1920, in many southern states the enfranchisement of black women would have markedly affected the electoral balance. Many whites, in fact, feared enfranchisement of black women because of their potential power as Republican voters and the precedent it would set for reestablishing the male franchise, which had been effectively eliminated by Jim Crow legislation.

The great hopes of black women for political empowerment with suffrage were soon dispelled throughout the South. In Columbia, South Carolina, when black and white women swarmed the offices of the registrar on the first day of voter registration, black women waited patiently for their turn; racial etiquette dictated that all the white women be registered first. The next morning, surprised by the high turnout among black women the previous day, South Carolina registers implemented a new set of registration rules for black women wanting to vote. Any black woman seeking to register was required to pay a $300 tax, and if she somehow managed to fulfill this requirement, she was required to read and interpret a portion of the state or federal constitution. Needless to say, white women voters did not have to follow the same set of rules. When the NAACP protested restrictions such as these and enlisted the help of the NWP, the NWP responded that because black men and women faced similar restrictions this was a race, not a women's, issue. The adoption of the Nineteenth Amendment, at least for the vast majority of black women remaining in the South, proved more a reminder of their inferior status as blacks than a mark of their equality with men.

It would take more than thirty years for southern blacks to mount successful collective campaigns to demand the rights due them as American citizens. African Americans and their white supporters organized sit-ins and boycotts to win equal access to segregated public accommodations in the 1950s and early 1960s and voter registration drives soon thereafter. Young people were particularly important in the struggle to end a caste system that kept blacks in separate and unequal institutions despite Supreme Court decisions declaring them unconstitutional, and often high schools and colleges were the scene of bitter—and violent—battles.

Although black men and women worked together in the civil rights movement, often their organizing built on separate gender communities and experiences. In a now famous moment, in 1955 Rosa Parks refused to give up her seat on a Montgomery bus to a white person. That act heralded the beginning of a more militant struggle for racial integration, moreover, because networks of women and men immediately went into action. Jo Ann Robinson and the Women's Political Council of Montgomery, an organization of black professional women, began distributing fliers urging local blacks to stay off the city's buses. By the next night, an established male network of Montgomery's black ministers led by Martin Luther King, Jr., joined the boycott, pledging to use the authority of their pulpits to support the boycott. For the entire next year, two gender-based groups—women domestic workers who walked or carpooled to work and the powerful male ministerial establishment—were the bulwark of the boycott, which lasted until December 1956, when the federal courts in Alabama and finally the Supreme Court ruled that Montgomery's Jim Crow law violated the Fourteenth Amendment. In unique ways for men and women, the civil rights movement provided opportunities to assert self-worth on gender as well as racial grounds. Black women in the South were fulfilling a longstanding cultural tradition of defending the rights of their families. For black men, who had often been humiliated—and even physically endangered and lynched—by Jim Crow practices, the civil rights movement offered an important public opportunity to assert their manliness. When James Meredith, for example, stood his ground and demanded admission into all-white Ole Miss, the flagship campus of Mississippi's public colleges and universities, he became an important symbol of black manhood successfully resisting coercive white violence.

These gender differences were complicated by the new kinds of regional, racial, and class bridges that the civil rights movement built. During the Freedom Summers of 1964 and 1965, white students from the North joined southern activists, leaving their comfortable college communities to participate in the direct action tactics of the southern civil rights movement. They were children of the American Dream—college educated and middle-class—and in the South they encountered many unsettling situations, such as extreme poverty, intense racism, and the wariness of black staff members.

Although for a while gender and class divisions seemed inconsequential in the greater quest for racial justice, it did not take long for them to surface. Many women in the movement—white and black—found the dynamics of power frustrating and even discriminatory, but their complaints varied by race. White women pointed out how, as in society as a whole, work in the movement tended to be structured along gender lines. At a Student Nonviolent Coordinating Committee (SNCC) staff retreat in November 1964, an anonymous paper detailed eleven transgressions by men in SNCC, such as excluding women from decision-making bodies, relegating women to office work, and identifying women first as "girls" rather than individuals. In an important conceptual leap linking racism to sexism, the anonymous author argued, "The average white person doesn't realize that he assumes he is superior . . . doesn't understand the problem of paternalism. So too the average SNCC worker finds it difficult to discuss the woman problem because of the assumption of male superiority. Assumptions of male superiority are as widespread and deep rooted and every much as crippling to the woman as the assumptions of white supremacy are to the Negro." The position paper prompted more laughter and ridicule than serious discussion at the SNCC retreat, but activist women nonetheless had made a crucial breakthrough. The civil rights movement and other campaigns for social justice in the 1960s, much like the New Deal and labor organizing earlier in the century, challenged inequities of class and race, but not of gender. Women activists were facing the same kinds of discrimination as those whom they were committed to helping. Black women active in the civil rights movement made their own gender-based critique of these male-dominated organizations. Most of all, they resented the sexual attention that black men paid to the white women workers from the North, perceiving it as an implicit rejection of black womanhood.

Women active in the New Left, particularly in Students for a Democratic Society (SDS), also found themselves making coffee and photocopies while their male counterparts led demonstrations against American capitalism and militarism in Vietnam. And when they challenged the hypocrisy of men in the movement, their concerns were often ridiculed, as in a 1967 cartoon in an SDS publication featuring a girl with earrings, a polka dot minidress and matching panties holding a sign reading "We Want Our Rights and We Want Them Now." But while women active in the New Left, as in the civil rights movement, were understandably frustrated at their experiences, in the end their involvement with the New Left contributed to a rebirth of feminism by altering the shape of the legitimate political arena. Historian Sara Evans has argued that organizations like SDS helped expand society's notion of what was political by including personal relations within the political sphere. Because the private was now understood as part of the larger system of power relations, marriage, family, and sexuality all came to be central political issues. In this new political climate, women drew on their experiences in the New Left as well as in the larger society to challenge entrenched male authority.

Women did not build the new feminist movement as isolated individuals. Rather, they resurrected older models of female politics in an effort to establish gender as a political identity group separate from race and class. Indeed, glaring evidence for the necessity for an independent women's political movement lay in the uneven implementation of the Civil Rights Act of 1964. Although a provision barring discrimination on the basis of sex was added to Title VII of the act, the Equal Employment Opportunity Commission (EEOC), an independent agency charged with enforcement, made it clear that it would not enforce discrimination based on sex. In response, Betty Friedan, author of *The Feminine Mystique* (1963), and a number of other middle-class women joined together to form one of the earliest and most influential feminist organizations, the National Organization for Women (NOW). Dedicated to bringing about "a fully equal partnership of the sexes, as part of the worldwide revolution of human rights," NOW sought to eliminate all practices which, "in the guise of protectiveness, not only deny opportunities but also foster in women self-denigration, dependence, and evasion of responsibility, undermine their confidence in their own abilities and foster contempt for women." According to NOW's agenda, the public and private worlds of women interconnected and mattered politically: a national, government-funded system of day care was advocated alongside a new, more equitable concept of marriage. In politicizing so much of private and public life, however, NOW could not escape serious conflicts within its own ranks, between radical and moderate feminists and lesbian and straight women.

By the 1970s, as more women entered the work force and supported feminist causes in the political arena, gender had become a prominent political issue. Continuing to integrate the private and the public, concerned with identity and home as well as work and community, women developed their own distinctive political strategy of consciousness-raising. In group sessions, feminists pooled their experiences as women, developing both a method for feminist theory as well as an agenda for building a new political movement that would demand not just equal rights but also equal power in every area of society. Knowingly or not, these second-wave feminists were replicating many of the cultural politics of the first wave, born in Greenwich Village during the 1910s. Now, as then, women's economic, domestic, and sexual freedoms were linked, and became topics of intense debate. Interestingly, during the late 1970s and 1980s, some men—often ones personally involved with feminists—created their own men's movement employing the consciousness-raising techniques of the women's movement. As they struggled to relate to their female contemporaries at home and in the workplace, they recognized the necessity of understanding better, and sometimes changing, their own maleness as socialized by families and by the larger society.

Women's political victories during the 1970s reflected the permeability of private and public and the increased importance of gender as an issue in the formal political worlds of electoral politics, legislation, and the courts. In 1972, Congress passed an equal rights amendment and sent it along to the states for ratification. A new coalition of groups that had not previously supported equal-rights legislation, such as the League of Women Voters, Business and Professional Women, the YWCA, the American Association of University Women, Common Cause, and the United Auto Workers, made congressional passage possible. One year later, the Supreme Court upheld *Roe* v. *Wade,* making unconstitutional Texas's criminalization of abortion on the grounds that a woman's right to privacy was violated by restricting her access to medically safe abortions. And in the 1970s, women began to win victories at the workplace based on charges of gender discrimination. When a group of secretaries in Chicago calling themselves Women Employed successfully protested the firing of legal secretary Iris Rivera for refusing to make coffee, they articulated their complaints not in the traditional working-class language of wages and working conditions, but in terms of the gender humiliation of being treated like a maid at work. Nationally, women appealed to the protections of Title VII and affirmative-action legislation to support their demands for equitable treatment.

These successes, ranging from *Roe* v. *Wade* to local campaigns such as the one that saved Iris Rivera's job, did not, however, end the debate over women's rights and power. Rather, they launched a new era of contention over the personal and public rights of women. In the final decades of the century, gender was a more serious political issue than at any time since suffrage. Indeed, it can be argued that recent debates have politicized gender roles more than suffrage ever did, as female suffrage was often defended as the fulfillment of women's traditional role as moral protector of society. The ERA, abortion, affirmative action, parental leaves with job protection, quality child care, and other issues on the feminist agenda have inspired a strong backlash from those committed to preserving traditional female roles. Antifeminists portray themselves as defenders of the family and sometimes even of capitalism and democracy. A leader like Phyllis Schlafly first attacked the ERA by playing on Cold War fears, urging her readers to identify "the unkempt, the lesbians, the radicals, the socialists" in photos of ERA rallies. When this failed, she resorted to arguing that the ERA was "a total assault on the family, marriage, and children." It also, she claimed, would force women into military combat, male working conditions onto females, and the federal government's authority onto terrain reserved for the states. Antifeminist rhetoric of this sort struck a nerve among many Americans and, despite an extension granted by Congress, too few states ratified the ERA amendment to secure its place in the Constitution.

After the ERA was no longer fought over in state legislatures, the battle between those against abortion and those in favor of a woman's right to choose, as well as over other feminist concerns such as sexual harassment and comparable worth, raged on in offices, union halls, state houses, Congress, and the courts. In the early 1990s, the intensity of the contest over competing notions of women's rights and power brought gender issues to the forefront in elections and the largest number of female candidates ever in front of voters. The national elections of 1992 saw 117 women running for seats in the House and Senate, far ahead of the previous record of 77 set in 1990. Twenty-one of the female candidates, moreover, were women of color, up from fourteen in 1990. Still, however, despite historic victories, only 3 percent of the Senate and 6 percent of the House was female as the new session opened. The intense public debate over the proper role for the president's wife, Hillary Rodham Clinton, a lawyer and political activist in her own right, dramatized how divided Americans are about how to balance traditional and feminist gender expectations.

In the early twentieth century, politics became gendered in a new way, as women sought, and won, the right to participate as full-fledged citizens in the electoral process. Although they brought their particular concerns to politics, such as fighting for legislative protections for women and children, their participation for most of the century did not fundamentally challenge the status quo in the two-party system or in their class and racial worlds. In the late twentieth century, however, that situation seemed to be changing. A "gender gap" between male and female voting patterns, absent for so much of the century, reemerged. As distinctions between public and private have blurred, issues such as abortion, affirmative action, child care, and sexual harassment build new bridges between women that transcend traditional partisan politics and possibly even the longstanding divisions of class and race. Indeed, gender polarization over these issues may be creating a more inviolable divide than the contest between the Democrats and Republicans ever did.

GENDER AND STATE POLICY

We live in nation states that have developed increasingly elaborate bureaucracies and regulations in the modern period. Although state policy covers many areas with implications for gender, ranging from the criminal-justice system to the tax system, the most important development during the twentieth century has been the emergence of an American version of the welfare state. A sophisticated gendered analysis of the welfare state has appeared only recently, but even in a short time it has transformed the way we understand the origins, growth, and impact of the American welfare state.

Scholars previously have interpreted the emergence of the welfare state in the late nineteenth and early twentieth centuries in a variety of ways, but most commonly as reflecting a struggle between classes, arguing that an emerging elite sought "social control" over a threatening mass, or as the evolution of an ever more benign, and more bureaucratic, liberal state. To the minimal extent that gender had any place in the discussion of the welfare state's origins, it was in terms of a male effort to take control out of the hands of women and the female-dominated family and give it to a male-dominated state bureaucracy. Recent feminist scholarship has argued instead, however, that the building of the American welfare state was fundamentally a gendered activity, and that women, rather than being victimized by it, played a crucial role in laying its foundation. Led by committed reformers such as Jane Addams, Julia Lathrop, Florence Kelley, and Grace and Edith Abbott, "social feminists" first tried to improve the conditions of life through the traditional voluntarist politics of settlement houses, charities, and organizations like the National Consumers' League. But faced with such powerful opponents as liquor interests and industrial employers, they soon looked to the state to institute reforms, specifically to take new kinds of responsibility for the lives—and livelihoods—of women and children.

In contrast to many European countries, where the welfare state came into being as a result of the pressure of organized labor movements, social feminists and their supporters argued for welfare programs on the basis not of class, but gender. The state needed to protect vulnerable women and children from preying men, exploitative industrialists, and corrupt capitalists, and women reformers who understood their needs were best suited to construct a compassionate and equitable welfare state. Female-led and dominated agencies such as the Children's Bureau, founded in 1912, and the Women's Bureau of the Department of Labor, established in 1920, were at the heart of the early welfare state in lobbying for and monitoring reform programs. Female social workers, the rank-and-file of these agencies as well as other public and private ones at the local, state, and federal level, made up less than 3 percent of the profession in 1889; by 1910, women constituted a majority of the profession. Historian Robyn Muncy has, in fact, identified the women who led the shift, between 1890 and 1935, from voluntarism to statism as the "female dominion." By the New Deal, these women—albeit still in small numbers—were serving in important roles even outside of these female ghettos. Eleanor Roosevelt, Secretary of Labor Frances Perkins, the relief administrator Ellen Woodward, and national Democratic party executive Molly Dewson all played a role in shaping New Deal policies from the highest level of government. These visible women notwithstanding, some historians have argued that the New Deal represented a break with the maternalist state, as men took control of the legislative process and most administrative structures. But even considering this shift, women undeniably played a role in building and monitoring the American welfare state. That does not mean, of course, that they were not victimized in certain ways by its patriarchal structure, but it does make it difficult to sustain the simplistic model of the welfare state as a "male conspiracy."

The policies of the American welfare state as they evolved during the Progressive Era, the 1920s, and the New Deal expanded in ways that supported, rather than undermined, as critics had feared, the traditional family, particularly as defined in white, middle-class terms. Prostitution, drinking, and child labor were to be outlawed. Working women, preferably single, were to be protected at the workplace by legislation that regulated working hours and working conditions. Married women were to be supported by breadwinning husbands, but if they were so unfortunate as to be widowed with children, they were to receive Mothers' Pensions to keep them home and out of the labor market. Men, on the other hand, were expected to earn a wage large enough to support a family and, if injured, would receive workmen's compensation to help the family survive temporarily without its chief breadwinner. One of the Children's Bureau's greatest victories, the 1921 Sheppard-Towner Maternity and Infancy Protection Act, provided federal assistance to the states to set up programs in which public-health nurses, under the supervision of doctors, instructed women in maternal and child care. (The act was revoked by conservative congressmen in 1929 who rejected the state's entry into the provision of medical care.)

The New Deal only perpetuated a welfare state devoted to preserving the traditional family. Employment programs under the Public Works Administration, the Works Progress Administration, and the Civilian Conservation Corps provided men with jobs, while the new Social Security system established Aid to Families with Dependent Children (AFDC) to provide financial support for women and their children who had no male breadwinners. The continued assumption was that women should be supported in dependent familial roles, men as independent wage earners. The Fair Labor Standards Act of 1938, which established minimum wages and maximum hours for workers, even went so far as to exclude from eligibility domestic servants, one of the most common female occupations. As the welfare state has developed in the postwar period, with predominantly female clients of AFDC on the one hand, and male-associated, work-related programs such as unemployment insurance and workmen's compensation, on the other, men and women have become subject to different procedures as clients of the state. While men encounter standardized rules of eligibility in most of the programs they apply for, women are subject to what the political scientist Barbara Nelson calls "moralistic, diffuse decision criteria." The AFDC recipient continually encounters moral scrutiny from her case worker, whose job includes making sure no man is living with her client; receiving benefits requires putting up with a state that behaves much like a possessive husband or father.

Although the intention of the American welfare state has been to preserve the traditional nuclear family, the impact of its policies has often been quite the opposite. Making welfare available only to single women with children has provided few incentives for these women to live with the fathers of their children and, thus, has contributed to the enormous growth in female-headed households, particularly among African Americans. And although welfare benefits keep women and children from starving, they do not keep them out of poverty. The result has been what the sociologist Diana Pearce has termed the feminization of poverty. In 1980, two out of three adults who fit the federal definition of poverty were women, and more than half the families defined as poor were maintained by single women. From the mid-sixties until the mid-seventies, the number of poor adult males actually declined, prompting the National Advisory Council of

Economic Opportunity to predict that "if the proportion of the poor in female householder families were to continue to increase at the same rate as it did from 1967 to 1978, the poverty population would be composed solely of women and their children before the year 2000." The feminization of poverty has extended not only to people traditionally poor, but also to those made poor by reforms in state divorce laws during the 1970s. When no-fault divorce laws made irreconcilable differences legitimate grounds for divorce and repudiated alimony, wives suffered much greater economic penalties from divorce than did husbands. The sociologist Leonore Weitzman studied divorced families in California in the 1970s and discovered that a year after divorce, ex-husbands' standard of living rose on average by 42 percent, while the standard of living of ex-wives and their children fell 73 percent. Although Weitzman's numbers have been criticized as extreme, the point remains that in the case of divorce, as in other areas, changes in state policy have intended and unintended consequences for public welfare and gender roles.

The welfare state's assumption that only women can legitimately be dependent or in need has recently contributed to a new social crisis of male homelessness, men without jobs who fall through the female-oriented safety net. Although it is difficult to compile statistics on the homeless, James Wright, in his book *Address Unknown: The Homeless in America* (1989), has estimated that out of every 1,000 homeless people in America, 120 or so are adults with children, another 100 are children, and the rest are single adults. Out of that number, 156 are single women and 580 are single men. So out of all single homeless adults, 78 percent are men; out of all homeless adults, more than 64 percent are single men. Disqualified in most cases from AFDC and deprived of assistance from localities and states because they are deemed employable, homeless men are victims of a welfare system that denies them the right to be dependent. According to the critic Peter Marin, "They are expected to take care of both others *and* themselves. And when they cannot do it, or will not do it, the built-in assumption at the heart of the culture is that they are *less than men* and therefore unworthy of help. An irony asserts itself: Simply by being in need, men forfeit the right to it."

The welfare state discriminates not only by gender, but also by class and race. Just as men and women are not equal in the eyes of the welfare state, neither are people whose social class and race do not fit the system's white middle-class family ideal. Until the passage of Medicaid and Medicare in 1965, which provided health care for the poor and elderly respectively, most welfare provisions other than AFDC assumed that the recipient had a stable, long-term employer to contribute financially, or would soon get another one. Whereas social insurance in many European countries covers individuals as citizens, the American welfare system of social security, unemployment insurance, and workmen's compensation covers individuals as employees of companies who make contributions to the program. Poor, and even many working people without stable jobs, fall through the cracks. Racial discrimination is also built into the welfare system, because it operates with underlying assumptions about the family that take little notice of African American family patterns of extended kin, surrogate parenting, and female breadwinning. When the historic Fair Labor Standards Act was passed in 1938 with provisions excluding agricultural and domestic workers from coverage, it effectively left a majority of blacks out. As the historian Linda Gordon has argued, "The white vision of public welfare—aid to needy children, replacement of male wages for dependent wives, protection for working women in industrial and urban enterprises—took as given the structures that not only excluded blacks but confirmed them in subordination." The biases of state welfare policy against men and blacks, combined with the huge loss in manufacturing jobs in northern cities where the black population is centered, have led to a devastating crisis among African American males at the end of the twentieth century. With participation in underground economies of drugs and guns often more attainable than good jobs and effective help from the state, young black males are more likely to die from homicide than any other cause.

Since the 1960s, some important alterations in state policy have given more support to women as wage earners. The passage of the Equal Pay Act of 1963, the inclusion of women in Title VII of the Civil Rights Act of 1964 barring discrimination in employment and creating the EEOC to enforce it, and other protections ensured through executive orders, federal agencies, and the courts have all helped women in the labor market. But there have also been defeats, such as President Nixon's veto of the Comprehensive Child Development Bill of 1972, which would have established a national system of day care. These victories and defeats aside, however, the welfare state has not significantly altered over the last thirty years. Despite numerous efforts to get women on welfare to work, the system itself, in its fierce ideological loyalty to the traditional family and ambivalence toward female breadwinning, keeps them dependent on the state in place of being dependent on a husband. Until women have adequate child care, skills training, access to jobs, and incentives to work, the American welfare state will continue to reinforce female dependence, even when traditional male independence through the family wage is becoming increasingly difficult to ensure. Although both liberals and conservatives acknowledge the devastating social effects of the present welfare system, neither side has articulated a viable alternative.

The gender-oriented revision of the history of the American welfare state has made the story of its evolution more complex. What we are living with today is both the product of female vision and agency and a patriarchal system that subordinates women in particular ways. In the light of recent research, it is unimaginable that gender could ever be left out of this story, as it was for so long. Bringing it in ensures a narrative of neither feminist enlightenment nor male conspiracy, but rather a complicated tale where women appear as both actors and victims.

CONTINUITIES AND CHANGES

This essay has charted changes and continuities in the way women and men have experienced their femaleness and maleness over the course of the twentieth century. In five major arenas of life—family, work, leisure and consumption, politics, and state policy—what it has meant to be a female or male, a wife or husband, son or daughter has altered dramatically. Yet, perhaps more surprising given the extent of those changes, important characteristics of gender roles and identities have persisted. Families have become smaller, more vulnerable to divorce and single parenthood, and more burdened with emotional expectations. But these changes notwithstanding, the nuclear family remains the structure within which most Americans still intend to live out their personal lives. Similarly, women's participation in the work force has mushroomed during the twentieth century, until women now make up 47 percent of the work force. Although women have made important strides breaking into professions and jobs previously reserved for men, equally significant has been the persistence of segmentation and discrimination based on gender. The story is much the same in the arena of leisure and consumption. While mixed-sex socializing has come to characterize leisure for most of the century, vestiges of an older pattern of single-sex socializing remained late in the twentieth century. Likewise, while women's power over consumption has grown over the century, it has not kept up with their increasing contribution to the family economy or the expanding importance of consumerism in the postwar world. Gender in twentieth-century politics, moreover, has become a great deal more influential than it proved immediately after women secured the suffrage, yet class and race still divide women and men almost as much as gender unites them. Finally, the American welfare state took on a permanent shape over the twentieth century, through several crucial periods of reform. Nonetheless even as it evolved, it continued to reinforce patterns of female dependence and male independence.

Identifying these continuities, however, does not mean that there has not been a trajectory of change over the course of the twentieth century, with different factors shaping changes in gender identities, roles, and relationships at different times, whether in the economy, war, political pressure, or popular ideology. Change, moreover, has not always been acknowledged while underway. During the 1950s, innovations in gender relations escalated, but the powerful rhetoric of domesticity and conformity obscured the real changes taking place. Since the 1960s, however, new kinds of gender expectations have been powerfully articulated, from the family to the workplace to politics. And as we near the twenty-first century, further change is inevitable.

This essay highlights areas of historical knowledge as well as exposes areas of historical ignorance requiring further research. Unquestionably, we need further investigation of masculinity in the twentieth century. Although men have been actors in the political, social, and intellectual history of the century, how their actions and attitudes have been shaped by male identities or by pressures to conform to standards of masculinity requires much more consideration. Also, although this essay has contended that gender cannot be considered apart from class or race, more work is needed that addresses exactly how gender has reinforced these other social divisions, as well as how class and race have contributed to definitions of gender. The present effort to synthesize what we know about gender in twentieth-century society is as telling for what it leaves out as for what it includes. Nonetheless, by legitimizing gender as a category of analysis requiring primary consideration in the writing of twentieth-century history, we make important progress down what is bound to be a very long and difficult road.

SEE ALSO Gender Theories (volume II); Race; Ethnicity and Immigration; Family; Class (all in this volume).

BIBLIOGRAPHY

A general background on the subject of gender in the twentieth century can be gained from a number of books. Peter Gabriel Filene, *Him/Her/Self: Sex Roles in Modern America* (1974), is an early study that is still useful. Two books provide a broad history of American women, including the pre-twentieth-century period: Sarah Evans, *Born for Liberty: A History of Women in America* (1989); and Ellen Carol DuBois and Vicki L. Ruiz, eds., *Unequal Sisters: A Multi-Cultural Reader in U.S. Women's History* (1990), which brings together many of the most important essays in women's history from the 1970s and 1980s. A sensitive portrait of the lives of African American women over the last two centuries can be found in Jacqueline Jones, *Labor of Love, Labor of Sorrow: Black Women, Work and the Family, from Slavery to the Present* (1985). Rosalind Rosenberg, *Divided Lives: American Women in the Twentieth Century* (1992), and William Chafe, *The Paradox of Change: American Women in the Twentieth Century* (1991), provide invaluable surveys of the history of women in this century, taking full account of recent scholarship. The literature on men is less developed. See Peter N. Stearns, *Be a Man! Males in Modern Society,* 2d ed. (1990), for an interpretation of the changes in ideals and realities of manhood and masculinity for middle-class and working-class men over the nineteenth and twentieth centuries. A fascinating recent study of American men is E. Anthony Rotundo, *American Manhood: Transformations in Masculinity from the Revolution to the Modern Era* (1993). For reflections by major personalities and writers about growing up male in the post–World War II period, see *Esquire, Special Issue on the American Man, 1946–1986* 105 (June 1986).

An overview of the changing American family is provided by Steven Mintz and Susan Kellog, *Domestic Revolutions: A Social History of American Family Life* (1988). A recent book by Robert L. Griswold, *Fatherhood in America: A History* (1993), sheds new light on a poorly understood subject. Three works focus on family roles, particularly parenting, in the years since the Second World War: Elaine Tyler May, *Homeward Bound: American Families in the Cold War Era* (1988), makes an important argument linking the containment of postwar families in domesticated, consumer-oriented suburbs with American foreign policy of containing communism in the world; Barbara Ehrenreich, *The Hearts of Men: American Dreams and the Flight from Commitment* (1983), is a fascinating study of male revolt in the postwar period; and Arlie Hochschild with Anne Machung, *Second Shift: Working Parents and the Revolution at Home* (1989), reveals how many more domestic responsibilities working women shoulder compared to their husbands, despite the so-called feminist revolution.

On the history of sexuality, see John D'Emilio and Estelle B. Freedman, *Intimate Matters: A History of Sexuality in America* (1988) for the best overview. Kathy Peiss and Christina Simmons, eds., *Passion and Power: Sexuality in History* (1989), includes several innovative essays exploring the experiences, ideas, and conflicts that have shaped the emergence of modern sexual identities. Linda Gordon's *Woman's Body, Woman's Right: A Social History of Birth Control in America* (1976, 1990) covers a crucial subject for understanding twentieth-century sexuality. Two recent books make important contributions to the history of homosexuality in the twentieth century: Allan Berube, *Coming Out under Fire: The History of Gay Men and Women in World War Two* (1991), is an excellent treatment of gay men and lesbians in the military; Lillian Faderman, *Odd Girls and Twilight Lovers: A History of Lesbian Life in Twentieth-Century America* (1991), is a good place to start on the history of lesbianism in the twentieth century.

A number of works are helpful in understanding gender and the workplace. A recent collection of essays edited by Ava Baron, *Work Engendered: Toward A New History of American Labor* (1991), includes a number of case studies shedding light on the way the workplace and unionization have been shaped by gender and on how the work environment has affected gender identity. Elizabeth Faue, *Community of Suffering and Struggle: Men, Women, and the Labor Movement in Minneapolis, 1915–1945* (1991), is a fascinating study claiming that the CIO during the 1930s fostered a gender reorientation of the labor movement from grassroots and family-based to national and male. Barry Bluestone and Bennett Harrison, *The Deindustrialization of America: Plant Closings, Community Abandonment, and the Dismantling of Basic Industry* (1982), investigates a recent economic phenomenon with major implications for gender roles in the family and workplace. Several studies deal specifically with women at the workplace. Two good overviews are Alice Kessler-Harris, *Out to Work: A History of Wage-Earning Women in the United States* (1982); and Lynn Y. Weiner, *From Working Girl to Working Mother: The Female Labor Force in the United States, 1920–1980* (1985). Numerous occupational and union case studies have been appearing in recent years. Two of the best are Susan A. Glenn, *Daughters of the Shtetl: Life and Labor in the Immigrant Generation* (1990), which follows Jewish women from the Old World to the urban neighborhoods and garment sweatshops of America; and Nancy Gabin, *Feminism in the Labor Movement: Women and the United Auto Workers, 1935–1975* (1990), which investigates the attitude of the United Auto Workers union and its male and female members toward women workers in auto plants. Although work on women in the professions is not very developed, except for studies of teachers, Barbara Miller Solomon's *In the Company of Educated Women: A History of Women and Higher Education in America* (1985) provides a history of women in higher education. On the subject of masculinity and the workplace, in addition to essays in the Baron collection cited above, consult David Montgomery, *The Fall of the House of Labor* (1987), which investigates the changing work lives of men, and the union organizations they built, from the late nineteenth century through the 1920s.

The gendered character of leisure and consumption in the twentieth century is a new subject for historians, and hence relevant works are just now appearing. Important pioneer efforts include the following. Kathy Peiss, *Cheap Amusements: Working Women and Leisure in Turn-of-the-Century New York* (1986), shows how changes in working women's patterns of leisure transformed gender relations for men and women of all social classes. Janice A. Radway, *Reading the Romance: Women, Patriarchy, and Popular Literature* (1984), is a fascinating study of what reading popular romances means to the women who buy them. Roland Marchand, *Advertising the American Dream: Making Way for Modernity, 1920–1940* (1985), examines how advertising reflected and shaped American values, particularly ones about gender. Also see Dana Frank's essay on how women in Seattle used their consumer power to support the labor movement, in the Baron collection cited above, as well as her "Housewives, Socialists, and the Politics of Food: The 1917 New York Cost-of-Living Protests," *Feminist Studies* 11 (Summer 1985): 255–287, for a case history of women being politicized around their power and responsibilities as consumers.

The literature on women and politics over the course of the twentieth century is best reviewed chronologically. Two important essays situate the struggle for female suffrage in the larger context of distinctive male and female political cultures: Paula Baker, "The Domestication of Politics: Women and American Political Society, 1780–1920," *American Historical Review* 89 (June 1984): 620–647; and Michael McGerr, "Political Style and Women's Power, 1830–1930," *Journal of American History* 77 (December 1990): 865–885. Another essay contributing to a deeper understanding of suffrage is Ellen Carol DuBois, "Working Women, Class Relations, and Suffrage Militants: Harriot Stanton Blatch and the New York Suffrage Movement, 1894–1909," *Journal of American History* 74 (June 1987): 34–58, which explores the interclass alliances within the suffrage movement. Nancy Cott's wonderful book, *The Grounding of Modern Feminism* (1987), is an important study of what happened to early-twentieth-century feminism as the century progressed. Lois Scharf and Joan M. Jensen, eds., *Decades of Discontent: The Women's Movement, 1920–1940* (1983), is a collection of essays examining the women's movement after suffrage. Note in particular Rosalyn Terborg-Penn's contribution, "Discontented Black Feminists: Prelude and Postscript to the Passage of the Nineteenth Amendment," which discusses the experiences of black women. Susan Ware, *Beyond Suffrage: Women in the New Deal* (1981), brings a new dimension to analysis of the New Deal. Two books that investigate women and politics in the postwar era are Sara Evans, *Personal Politics: The Roots of Women's Liberation in the Civil Rights Movement and the New Left* (1979), which argues that feminists of the second wave were politicized by the sexism they encountered working in the civil rights movement and other political causes during the 1960s; and Joan Hoff-Wilson, *Rights of Passage: The Past and Present of the ERA* (1986), which provides valuable background on the century-long struggle for an equal-rights movement.

Finally, readers may learn more about gender and the welfare state—a relatively new subject of analysis—through the following references. Linda Gordon has edited a collection of pathbreaking essays entitled *Women, the State, and Welfare* (1990). Two other essays that place the origins of the American welfare state in comparative perspective are Sonya Michel and Seth Koven, "Womanly Duties: Maternalist Politics and the Origins of the Welfare States in France, Germany, Great Britain, and the United States, 1880–1920," *American Historical Review* 95 (October 1990): 1076–1108; and Miriam Cohen and Michael Hanagan, "The Politics of Gender and the Making of the Welfare State, 1900–1940: A Comparative Perspective," *Journal of Social History* 24 (Spring 1991): 469–484. A useful book that focuses solely on the American case is Robyn Muncy, *Creating a Female Dominion in American Reform, 1890–1935* (1991). To trace gender and the state into the

New Deal era, see Barbara Melosh's beautifully illustrated and imaginative book analyzing the gendered messages embedded in the iconography of New Deal–sponsored murals and plays, *Engendering Culture: Manhood and Womanhood in New Deal Public Art and Theater* (1991). Joan Hoff, *Law, Gender, and Injustice: A Legal History of U.S. Women* (1991), although about a subject not dealt with in this essay, addresses an important aspect of the state's role in shaping gender.

RACE

Earl Lewis

After an exhausting journey, which brought him to town much too late for an evening stroll, John (Walden) Warrick began his morning with a purposeful walk down the time-frozen streets of his old home. The hotel clerk who glimpses his departure figures him, of tall features and straight black hair, a big shot from South Carolina in town for business. Unaware of the clerk's thoughts Warrick exits the hotel. In coming home, he reencounters a world he once rejected. Only this time, he embraces the world on his own terms—as a wealthy and powerful man of standing and influence.

So begins Charles W. Chesnutt's *The House behind the Cedars*, a novel first published in 1900. This important but somewhat forgotten work of fiction is about more than the financial coming of age of another aristocrat in reconstruction America. Chesnutt uses John (Walden) Warrick and his sister Rena Walden to tackle what W. E. B. Du Bois would label one year later, "the problem of the color-line," for they were the products of a union between a mulatto woman and a white man. What made them "black" or "white" challenged the conventions of biology and exposed the role of the state in socially constructing race. As William Andrews notes in an accompanying foreword, Chesnutt, who could have comfortably "passed" as white, recognized racial categorization as a "social fiction." Although Andrews is no doubt correct when he writes, "Chesnutt was convinced that society had no legal right to prevent those who could from crossing America's color line," the characters of John and Rena Walden reveal as few others how race functioned as an ideology and an idea. Thus, what made it possible for some to cross made it impractical or unthinkable for others to so venture.

With growing sophistication, scholars, historians included, have begun to examine the social construction of race. The discussion has been aided by significant changes in the politics of intellectual inquiry. The firm belief in the immutable boundaries of racial classification has mostly disappeared. It has been popularly reported by some physical anthropologists and geneticists that "Eve," symbolic mother of humankind, was most probably African. This being the case, some have reasoned that race truly has no meaning since we are all related; others, as evinced by racially motivated murders in New York City, Los Angeles, Seattle, and Miami, the growth of neo-Nazi propaganda, and attempts to revise the history of the Holocaust, are not as sanguine. Nonetheless, the majority of geneticists concur that when we isolate certain genetic characteristics and thereby create population groupings we call races, we find greater intragroup variation than intergroup variation. As a consequence, race loses its analytical power as a meaningful category since we could as comfortably talk about the blue-eyed "race" and the brown-eyed "race."

When placed in historical context, the concept of race retains its importance as a useful explanatory category. After all, to talk about race is to talk about power. As Winthrop Jordan and George Fredrickson have ably documented, Americans with the power to impose their viewpoints subdivided the overall population into social groupings called races for self-serving purposes. Europeans were created as whites, Africans as blacks, Asians as yellows, Indians as reds, and all others as browns or mongrels. In the social order that followed, those created as whites were always superior; the others jockeyed for the position of the best of the least, although the imprecision in classification made for numerous exceptions and considerable variation.

In the process race ceased to be merely a concept, it became an ideology. Stressing this point, Barbara Fields writes, "Race is not an idea but an ideology. It came into existence at a discernible historical moment for rationally understandable historical reasons and is subject to change for similar reasons." Fields's important argument advances the discussion considerably. Indeed, *race* has assumed all the properties of an ideology: it is the doctrine, myth, and symbol accepted by a large segment of the population—yet, is it not also an idea, an impression, notion, or conception?

Only by considering race as idea and ideology will we have the tools to properly explicate the history of race in twentieth-century America. As an idea, race served to mark difference. In this context, individuals, in open defiance of law and custom, treated race as but one of many distinguishing characteristics. Some intermarried, others supported biracial unionism, while others "passed" from one group to another. By so doing, these historical actors underscored the ways in which race was constructed.

Still, only the most determined individual could ignore the body of doctrine—i.e., customs, laws, cultural forms, and power differences—that endowed difference with meaning. By the late nineteenth century, white, black, brown, yellow, and red meant something particular in the nation's vocabulary of social relations. As a result, the majority of Americans might have agreed that race was a nicely crafted social fiction, but they nonetheless believed that fiction to be their reality, and acted accordingly. To ignore the ideological dimensions of race means that we lose sight of how each social group defined and sought to advantage themselves in relation to the "outsider." Moreover, such a tendency hinders our effort to explain why race functioned as a social construction and much more.

African American fiction and folklore is replete with examples of blacks who were phenotypically white but accepted the prominent social ideologies that defined race as more than the sum of parentage. In *The House behind the Cedars,* for example, John reconstructs himself as a white, landed, gentleman. His sister, Rena, remains attached to the black community, with all too tragic consequences: she dies, unable to reconcile her heritage, her appearance, and her love for a white man who had mistaken her for white. John and Rena are proportionally more "white" than "black." Yet, John, while acknowledging the ideological dimensions of race, sees race as an idea or conception. He challenges the conception by assertion: he is white and not black, period. His sister succumbs to the overpowering features of the doctrinal or ideological aspects of the concept. She is black and not white because the dominant ideology supports this framing.

Cognizant of the multiple meanings of race in a multiracial society, Howard University professor Alain Locke argued in a series of 1916 lectures that "the biological meaning of race has lapsed and the sociological meaning of race is growing in significance." Locke knew race as an "ethnic fiction," but one worth considering for what it reveals about power in the industrial phase of world history. This essay follows Locke's lead. It builds on the work of social constructionists by highlighting race as a socially situated historical phenomenon that functioned as an idea and an ideology. But because I am as interested in examining both dimensions of race as well as the nexus between the two, the essay is also concerned with race as a social reality for generations of Americans. Of course, no understanding of race in the twentieth century is possible without paying special attention to the role of the state. At the local and national levels, state officials, policies, and practices informed if not influenced the ideological dimensions of race on topics from intermarriage to housing, group membership to citizenship. Thus, any attempt to understand this topic dictates the interrelated study of race, social construction, and the state.

RACE AND ETHNICITY: DEVELOPMENT OF AN UNEQUAL IDENTITY

In a recent essay on the problems of racial identities and the potentials for racial understanding, the historian David Hollinger introduced the phrase *racial pentagon.* By using the word *pentagon* rather than *pentagram,* Hollinger conjures an image of a five-sided polygon with little intersection instead of a star-shaped, five-pointed structure with complete intersection. The five elements of this pentagon represented the primary elements of human possibility. In color terms they are white, black, brown, yellow, and red. In the nomenclature of contemporary society the constituent groups are European Americans, African Americans, Latinos and Latinas, Asian Americans, and Native Americans. In the context of twentieth-century United States history, the pentagon connects the broadest societal groupings. How each came to assume unequal shares of the pentagon is part of the history of race in the twentieth century.

By 1900, racial difference had become an accepted and legally sanctioned component of social understanding. Moreover, racial consciousness had given way to racial prejudice and discrimination so that rights, privilege, and power differed depending upon which of the five groups offered you membership. Regional variations in law and practice, however, complicates a strictly drawn interpretation. For example, between 1898 and 1902, across the South white delegates to state constitutional conventions openly connived to strip blacks of the franchise. Lynchburg delegate Carter Glass, who became Virginia's U.S. senator, gleefully claimed various legislative devices would "eliminate the darky as a political factor in this state in less than five years." Hardly a word was spoken about the status of the nation's other nonwhites. At the same time, after a quarter of a century of action to exclude blacks from California, the nineteenth century closed on the ignoble note of anti-Asian agitation, as whites acted to prevent a perceived threat to the sanctity of community.

Rigid, xenophobic responses ostensibly parallel the development of more complex social organizations. For despite obstacles—geographical, topographical, and sociological—considerable intergroup interaction has been a constant of history. Moving out from the Rift Valley of Kenya, early hominids made the slow and awkward advance from hunting and gathering to sedentary societies. As they did, their sense of belonging changed. Anthropologists fix the clan as the primary unit of social affiliation. At this level, each individual has a direct filial relationship to all other members of the group. With the advent of more complex social organizations, one's primary affective ties grew in complexity. Clusters of clans became tribes, groups of tribes organized into empires, and empires gave way to nation states.

These more differentiated, more complex social organizations, worrying that the lines of affiliation would fracture, created more specialized rituals of belonging—citizenship, flags, anthems, parades, titles, and awards. Moreover, membership in the state became all the more important if it became more restrictive. As a result, states developed elaborate rituals of exclusion. Simplified, these rituals underscored that "I am a citizen, and you are not and cannot be." Consequently, the birth of the nation-state as the ultimate form of social organization included as its sine qua non a firm belief in the saliency of near-exclusive fraternity, so much so that provisions for inclusion and exclusion became one of the key functions of the modern nation-state. Different physical characteristics became one of the convenient and portable markers, a means of identifying the "other," the one who did not belong.

This imagined communion keys most contemporary understandings of race, for in most cases it is tied—loosely or explicitly—to the imaginings of a community. Thus Benedict Anderson's lovely phrase "imagined communities" has great importance for a complete understanding of race in the twentieth century. Once created as a distinct group, members of a race created rituals of belonging that distinguished themselves from all others and attached meaning to that membership. In writing about the history of nationalism, Anderson described such communities as imagined and exclusionary "because the members of even the smallest nation will never know most of their fellow-members, meet them, or even hear of them, yet in the minds of each lives the image of their communion." As part of this communion many found comfort in the familiar; they envisioned a community in which other communicants reminded them of themselves.

Failure in this regard prompted poems like the following from the era of the California gold rush:

John Chinaman

John Chinaman, John Chinaman,
But five short years ago,
I welcomed you from Canton, John—
But wished I hadn't though;

For then I thought you honest, John,
Not dreaming but you'd make
A citizen as useful, John,
As any in the State.

I thought you'd open wide your ports,
And let our merchants in,
To barter for their crepes and teas,
Their wares of wood and tin.

I thought you'd cut your queue off, John
And don a Yankee coat,
And a collar high you'd raise, John,
Around your dusky throat.

I imagined that the truth, John,
You'd speak when under oath,
But I find you'll lie and steal too–
Yes, John, you're up to both.

I thought of rats and puppies, John,
You'd eaten your last fill.
But on slimy pot-pies, John,
I'm told you dinner still.

Oh, John, I've been deceived in you
And in all your thieving clan,
For our gold is all you're after John,
To get it as you can.

Although an expression of racist intent, utilizing some of the most offensive stereotypes, this poem is an intriguing example of an attempt to first place a nonwhite inside the boundary of community, and the ultimate decision to place that individual and his or her group well outside of the community. In this instance, the Chinese laborer was given an Anglicized name; yet the process of forced acculturation, the process of inclusion, disintegrated when the mythic laborer refused to become just another would-be Yankee. He held on to patterns of traditional dress and social etiquette, competed as a desired equal and not a supplicant seeking the ultimate prize of citizenship. His "failure" to behave sealed his fate as an undesirable as one who valued his difference. As the poem vividly illustrates, race became the convenient vernacular for expressing difference.

It is nearly impossible to talk about race in the twentieth century without at least passing reference to the nearly three centuries of development of a historical idea and ideology. That which we think we know about the other assumed an important role in framing social relations in the United States from the beginning. British settlers went to great lengths to denote their differences from the Africans and Indians who occupied the same geographic and—occasionally—social spaces. Blackness connoted something sinister, dirty, and vile in the English imagination. English travelers, without rebuke, regaled their country folk with stories linking the African and the ape, the human and the beast. Spanish missionaries and luminaries like Las Casas pondered the makeup of those they encountered, debating whether the other was human enough to possess a soul.

Such sociocultural ruminations hardened into outright prejudice when codified in the mid- to late seventeenth century. As A. Leon Higginbotham carefully outlined in *A Matter of Color,* colonial legislatures throughout British North America felt compelled to distinguish among Africans, Native Americans, and Europeans. By 1693, assemblies in Virginia and Maryland had established a link between permanent bondage and place of origin. Africans, regardless of their mate, produced offspring destined to carry the badge of slavery. Meanwhile, Native Americans, both in the Spanish Southwest and on the British Atlantic seaboard, became the embodiment of heathen lesser beings. In the eyes of some missionaries redemption was possible but in the eyes of many elimination was preferable.

Nonetheless, the direct connection between Africans and slavery was not cemented until other sources of labor were eliminated. Well into the last years of the seventeenth century, European, especially British, indentured servants outnumbered Africans in North America. But (as Menard and Galenson have documented) once the cost of indentured servants rose to a level equaling the costs of purchasing Africans, business acumen dictated a shift in labor. Planters in the West Indies discovered the cruel lessons of profit: it was cheaper to purchase hundreds of Africans and literally work them to death on a sugar plantation because the profits far outnumbered maintenance and replacement costs.

The so-called chicken-and-egg debate—which came first, slavery or race prejudice?—is exposed for what it is: a needless diversion. Without question, perceptions about Africans lessened the moral and psychic anguish of many Europeans affected by the Enlightenment. But by the late seventeenth century, a bevy of laws and intellectual pronouncements defined Africans as physically, morally, and socially different from Europeans. In the Americas few Africans or African Americans had the power to alter the fundamental truth that Europeans were in control. But at the same time, it is also clear that the permanent switch to African labor did not come before experimentation with Europeans and indigenous labor. Moreover, the harsh treatment meted out to them served as a dress rehearsal for the enslavement of Africans. Contemporary scholarship has shown, however, the disjunction between the intended and the actual. Almost from the start, people lived their lives in nonlinear ways, whether in colonial Virginia or the Spanish Southwest. In a stinging critique of the legalistic interpretation T. H. Breen and Stephen Innes complain,

> This form of argumentation creates considerable interpretive problems, not the least of which is that it flies in the face of social reality. . . . [T]he closer we examine specific biracial communities . . . the more we discover that gross generalizations about race are misleading, if not altogether incorrect. We find ourselves with too many exceptions, with blacks and whites who stubbornly refuse to behave as blacks and whites are supposed to behave.

Yet the exceptions, while perhaps numerous, highlight a departure from the main. Why some violated law and defied customs returns us to an examination of the relationship between race as ideology and idea.

Moreover, the story of race in colonial America is too often presented as the reaction of racial minorities to the bold and troublesome actions of whites. The narrative is driven by the story of white racism. Books by Richard White and Ramón Gutiérrez, the former detailing white-Indian relations in the Great Lakes region and the latter a study of the Southwest, paint a much more involved portrait of interracial relations, and those relations should inform any understanding of race in American history. First, the axis of power is balanced in these two accounts. As members of nations who presumed superior power, various Indian peoples viewed various Europeans as outsiders or the other. At the same time, settlers in British North America or the Spanish Southwest, convinced of their own superiority, proclaimed the indigenous peoples the other. This social minuet, characterized by marriage, religious conversions, language appropriations, and land acquisitions, forces us to reconsider the changing role of power in the framing of race.

Second, both books illustrate in poignant terms that race could not exist as a social reality until a vocabulary was created. According to White, the Algonquians, for example, had a fairly longstanding practice of absorbing refugees. With the expansion of the Iroquois in the late seventeenth century, the incorporation of strangers accelerated. White maintains,

> In our attempts to understand these bonds, the conventional units of discourse about Indians—tribes with their distinct territories and their chiefs—are misleading. These people are almost classic examples of the composite groups described by Elman Service as the product of "rapid depopulation by disease which, when combined with the ending of hostilities among the aborigines themselves under the dominance of the common enemy, resulted in the merging of previously unrelated people." At their most enduring, the connections between groups were not so much diplomatic ties between clear political entities as social bonds between much smaller social units.

But what of race? Did these new groupings see themselves through the eyes of Europeans, as a race apart? The literature suggests not. A pan-Indian consciousness was not an immediate part of the incorporation process. Iroquois warriors were outsiders as much as were the French clerics and English traders with whom they came into contact. Tzvetan Todorov may be correct in asserting that Europeans have comforted themselves by forcing the unknown into the known, Native Americans into Indians. But viewed from the perspective of all participants, race must be seen as an evolving vocabulary of social relations rather than a static practice, perception, or conception. The Algonquians remained Algonquians long after others called them Indians.

Even in the more starkly drawn world of black and white, residents of the new nation continued the practice of challenging racial laws and customs. Voluntary interracial unions continued to exist long after the prohibitions enacted by nineteenth-century state legislatures, despite exorbitant penalties. Near Savannah, Georgia, Adele Alexander reports that a prominent white judge openly maintained a relationship with a mixed-raced woman of color. Indian-black or Indian-white unions further confounded social reasoning. The progeny of such liaisons (black-white, white-Indian, Indian-black, or some combination) were in the strictest sense neither black nor white, although few places in the United States adopted the Brazilian practice of acknowledging gradations. Nor did they or those children from more coerced unions follow a predetermined social lesson plan. Race was but one position in the constellation of the self.

Contemporaries born under somewhat similar circumstances, Frederick Douglass and William Ellison, for example, approached the challenge of life in the world of the slaveholders quite differently. Douglass freed himself by running away. Through his writings, public appearances, and general eloquence, he became the embodiment of African American resistance to the peculiar institution. Ellison, on the other hand, purchased his freedom and remained in the restricted world of his birth. Most important, he fought the system by accepting its basic precepts. Rather than call for slavery's abolition, he used his skills to become a slaveowner. Whereas others adopted this guise to secure the freedom of loved ones, Ellison sought to prove himself capable in a world predicated on slave labor and racial difference. Both men symbolized the full range of human reactions to notions of race, reactions that shaped twentieth-century practices and patterns.

As had their parents, Douglass and Ellison also battled a larger society convinced of their inferiority. For a brief moment between the end of the Revolutionary War and the dawning of the new century some blacks and whites thought slavery's death was imminent. Indeed, revolutionary zeal, political and economic factors, and moral suasion resulted in the abolition of slavery in the North (some states like New York and Connecticut would abolish slavery twice) and the manumission of hundreds in the South. The 1793 introduction of the cotton gin, however, made it clear that slavery would survive and thrive. Eventually the expansion of slavery became linked to the claims that it was the nation's Manifest Destiny to dominate the land from the Atlantic to the Pacific Oceans. As a result, the dispersal of slavery and the removal of Native Americans became loosely connected.

The promotion of slavery and the attacks on Indians also unleashed an intellectual apparatus that conflated race as ideology and idea. Even people who never encountered blacks or Indians thought they knew them. They existed for many whites at the level of myth or symbol. As a result, minstrel shows found eager audiences in nineteenth-century northeastern urban centers. The ideological markers worked so well because most Americans remained convinced of race's biological properties. Race after all was an idea of what the other looked like. Americans of all backgrounds took comfort in playing the guessing games because they thought they understood the biological and social parameters; they thought they could single out a black from a red from a white from a yellow from a brown. Thus many whites who favored the abolition of slavery found it difficult to reject the ingrained notions of superiority. Proponents of colonization or the repatriation of African Americans to Africa, for instance, thought blacks too different to find comfort and solace in America. Blacks sardonically joked that the first word immigrants from Germany and Ireland learned to say was "nigger." Some abolitionists even feared that Douglass was too well spoken to be considered an authentic slave. They wanted him to doctor his speech and persona to fit the symbolic and conceptual definitions of blackness and slavery.

Moral arguments and scientific reason fueled the beliefs about the immutable boundaries of race. Slavery apologists, aware of the benefit that they derived from the institution, nonetheless championed theirs as a just cause. For men of Thomas Jefferson's generation, slavery served as a necessary evil; by the 1830s, Thomas Dew, a member of the faculty at William and Mary College, had come to see slavery as a positive good. Dew and his peers positioned themselves as the stewards of a backward race who needed the guidance, forceful hand, and moral teachings of a superior race. He believed that without direct white intervention, blacks, once freed, would devolve into a state of slavery worse than they now endured. After all, polygenists like Josiah Nott argued, blacks hailed from an entirely separate and inferior race. Slavery, therefore, was an act of benevolence.

Others applied the findings of naturalists like Charles Darwin to the cause of white supremacy. Although his findings were not in themselves racist, with the publication of *On the Origin of Species by Means of Natural Selection* (1859), Darwin helped structure the debate by arguing that the natural world is hierarchically arranged. He added that a selection process eliminates the unadaptable; those who survive are deemed more fit. He extended this argument to humans twelve years later in *The Descent of Man* when he wrote: "At some future period, not very distant as measured by centuries, the civilized races of man will almost certainly exterminate and replace the savage races throughout the world." But as John Haller has cautioned, Darwin recognized that human similarity rivaled the obvious differences. Still, Darwin's arguments lent themselves to racist applications. Several generations of social, biological, and pseudo-scientists shrouded their racism under the cover of Darwin's science.

The belief in the irrefutable laws of racial difference affected Indians and Asians as well. Both in the Southeast and the western plains, contact and conflict with native peoples revealed two often contradictory impulses. Racialized images of Indians presented them as primitive and savage. Missionaries among others saw primitiveness or savagery as a stage of development that could be corrected with education, the adoption of Christianity and the English language. Cultural practices were deemed the problem and not some deeper biological predisposition. Others, in an intense battle over land and resources, favored quarantining Indians. The first step was the forceful removal of indigenous adversaries from their traditional homelands. The second step was the creation of a reservation system that ensured native peoples' separation from whites. The latter worked so long as the lands granted Indians in a series of treaties proved valueless; otherwise, their lands were confiscated. This two-pronged strategy of cultural assimilation or military elimination (or quarantine) became part of formal and informal policy. Beginning in the 1820s with forced removal of the Cherokee from the Carolinas and Georgia to what became Oklahoma, through the 1890 battle between federal forces and Lakota people at Wounded Knee, South Dakota, America's aborigines struggled against the twin themes of incorporation and annihilation, both of which proved devastating.

Asians (Chinese, Japanese, Indians, Filipinos, and Koreans) came to the United States at different times under different circumstances, but, as Ronald Takaki notes, they all became in one sense or another "strangers from a different shore." For the better part of the nineteenth century, to speak of Asians was to mean Chinese. The first Chinese immigrants came to California in large numbers during and immediately after the gold rush. Although they would settle in the Northeast, Southwest, and South, three-quarters of the 63,000 lived in California by 1870. This overwhelmingly male population encountered a land desperate for their labor but fellow laborers hostile to their presence.

More important, Asian immigrants entered a social and cultural milieu in which individuals were taught to think in racial terms. As Takaki reminds us, black easily became yellow in the game of identifying and neutralizing the other. Because race was both an ideology and an idea, many felt comfortably justified with their new insertions. Thus, as Takaki quotes from one California newspaper: "Every reason that exists against the toleration of free blacks in Illinois may be argued against that of the Chinese here." Likened to blacks in many instances, and in a region where the African American population remained small through World War II, Chinese men and women symbolized what was not white. Referred to as *nigger, heathen,* and *savage,* through the Chinese Exclusion Act of 1882, in plays like *The Chinese Must Go!,* in labor periodicals, in the California state constitution, and political campaigns, Europeans defined themselves as white by defining Asians as yellow and dangerous. Japanese immigrants who followed the Chinese found little relief. Many non-Asians failed or did not dare to discern a distinction between them: Japanese or Chinese, it seemingly made little difference.

What happened to blacks, Indians, and Asians during the late nineteenth century profoundly shaped the meaning of race in the twentieth century. At the same time, the massive immigration of Europeans from southern and eastern Europe, the continued arrival of immigrants from Asia, new arrivals from U.S. possessions in the Pacific and the West Indies, as well as new relations between the United States and Mexico altered old patterns.

WHO WAS WHITE?

F. James Davis has recently sought to answer the question: who is black? A better question, and the one that shaped the twentieth century was: who was white? Through the 1960s, who was white and who could become white established the parameters of racial understanding in the twentieth century. The answer to this question was not at first glance as easily understood as we assume, looking from the end of the century backward.

The process of counting the American people had become a very complex business by 1900, pushed by a sudden and dramatic surge in population. Between 1880 and 1890 the United States' population grew by nearly 7 million; a decade later, the numbers jumped another 6.5 million. Still the government had no permanent, professional office for surveying the American people. This changed in 1902 after a successful fifteen-year lobbying effort. Frank Merriman, who was hired by President William McKinley to direct the 1900 decennial count of the population for apportionment purposes, combined with others to demonstrate the utility and range of topics that should be counted on a regular basis. Once convinced of this, Congress approved legislation in 1902 and the Bureau of the Census officially opened in 1903.

Counting the American people was other than a "pure" science, however. Through 1950 individuals were seldom free to self-designate; rather, a census enumerator had the godly task of assigning racial membership. From the start the state conflated biology and social practice. In a 1975 volume the bureau advised, "the classification of the population by race reflects common usage rather than an attempt to define biological stock." This claim notwithstanding, sociobiological notions of race informed the counting of the nation's population. (See tables 1 and 2.)

In 1900 the United States had a population of 76,994,575 residents; of this number 66,900,000 were considered white. During a period of intense immigration from Europe, the white proportion of the population increased modestly, from 87.7 percent in 1890 to 88.1 percent in 1900. At the highwater mark of segregation, 1950, nearly nine in ten Americans were considered white by census enumerators. (See table 3.)

These numbers seem quite straightforward, reflecting societal definitions of racial identity. Yet they shield the Census Bureau's role in defining and refining the nation's racial vocabulary. For instance, by the turn of the century the racial classification system included separate categories for citizens of Chinese or Japanese origins. Such ideological remedies, spurred by xenophobic anxieties, actually confused the discussion about race. By this simple act, the government conflated racial and national or ethnic designations. Chinese and Japanese residents were not merely Asian, they were different kinds of Asians. The same reasoning could have been applied to Europeans. For a number of reasons, however, among them a clear link between state action and the social construction of race, this did not occur.

In fact, the process that transformed Potawatomis into Indians made Armenians whites. For some the change started with passage through Ellis Island, when notetakers wittingly and unwittingly Anglicized immigrant names. Other immigrants became aware of the social and financial benefit, and did so later. This little addressed version of racial "passing" made it possible for Doris Kapplehoff to become Doris Day, for Bernie Schwartz to entertain us as Tony Curtis, for red-blooded American men (read "white") to lust after Rita Hayworth because she was not Margarita Carmen Cansino, or for several

Table 1. U.S. CENSUS DESIGNATION OF POPULATION BY RACE AND GENDER, 1880–1930

	Male			Female		
Year	White	Black	Other Races[a]	White	Black	Other Races
1880	22,130,900	3,735,115	134,805	21,272,070	3,327,678	37,215
1890	28,270,379	3,735,603	231,119	26,830,879	3,753,073	126,661
1900	34,201,735	4,386,547	228,166	32,607,461	4,447,447	123,219
1910	42,178,245	4,885,881	268,151	39,553,712	4,941,882	144,395
1920	48,430,655	5,209,436	260,340	46,390,260	5,253,695	166,234
1930	62,137,080	5,855,669	358,883	54,364,212	6,035,474	238,280

[a] "Other Races" includes Indians, Japanese, Chinese, and Filipinos.
SOURCE: U.S. Bureau of the Census. *Historical Statistics of the United States, Colonial Times to 1970, Bicentennial Edition,* Part 1 (1975), p. 14.

Table 2. U.S. CENSUS DESIGNATION OF POPULATION BY RACE AND GENDER, 1940–1990

	Male			Female		
Year	White	Black	Other Races[a]	White	Black	Other Races
1940	59,448,548	6,269,038	344,006	58,766,322	6,596,480	244,881
1950	67,129,192	7,298,722	405,325	67,812,836	7,743,564	307,722
1960	78,153,040	9,105,702	850,937	80,301,916	9,754,415	543,395
1970	86,720,987	10,748,316	1,442,889	91,027,988	11,831,973	1,439,773
1980	91,685,333	12,519,189	5,848,639	96,686,289	13,975,836	5,430,058
1990	97,475,880	14,170,151	9,593,387	102,210,190	15,815,909	9,444,356

[a] "Other Races" includes Indians, Japanese, Chinese, and Filipinos.
SOURCE: U.S. Bureau of the Census, *Historical Statistics of the United States, Colonial Times to 1970, Bicentennial Edition,* Part 1 (1975), p. 14; U.S. Bureau of the Census, *20th Census of the United States: 1980,* vol. I, part I (1983), pp. 1–22; U.S. Bureau of the Census, *21st Census of the United States: 1990,* vol. I, part I (1993), pp. 1–23, 24.

Table 3. FOREIGN-BORN POPULATION BY RACE AND GENDER, 1880–1970

	Male			Female		
Year	White	Black	Other Races[a]	White	Black	Other Races
1880	3,521,635	7,758	101,173	3,038,044	6,259	5,074
1890	4,951,858	[b]	[b]	4,170,009	[b]	[b]
1900	5,515,285	11,829	103,076	4,698,532	8,507	4,047
1910	7,523,788	23,888	120,072	5,821,757	16,451	9,930
1920	7,528,322	42,641	104,472	6,184,432	31,162	29,663
1930	7,502,491	42,641	104,472	6,184,432	31,162	29,663
1940	6,011,015	44,488	66,144	5,408,123	39,453	25,673
1950	5,098,370	[c]	[c]	4,997,045	[c]	[c]
1960	4,507,502	65,952	186,978	4,786,490	59,370	131,799
1970	3,982,797	115,406	305,484	4,750,973	138,052	326,590

[a] "Other Races" includes Indians, Japanese, Chinese, and Filipinos.
[b] Data by gender not available. Total for both genders: Black, 19,979; Other Races, 107,701.
[c] Data for 1950 are unreliable.
SOURCE: U.S. Bureau of the Census: *Historical Statistics of the United States, Colonial Times to 1970, Biocentennial Edition,* Part 1 (1975), p. 14.

generations of Americans to lovingly embrace the comedian Jerry Lewis because they never had to know him as Joseph Levitch.

At the turn of the century, all Europeans were not the same. Hierarchies of inclusion proved quite durable, reflecting a strong need to order, to place, to assign a social position based on physical characteristics. Darwin's notion of phyla and stratum provided the vehicle. The score of tracts that appeared in the middle of the nineteenth century, reaching a state of mature perversity during the Nazi regime, used scientific reasoning to concretize perceptions and old prejudices. It was a long time before we called these works pseudoscientific. Through the early years of the twentieth century a firm belief in innate difference found wide acceptance among all people.

Prominently represented and influential were men of standing and means. The M.I.T. sociologist and Columbia anthropologist William Z. Ripley tackled the thorny question of European races. Acknowledging that which disappeared in the United States, he carefully set out to delineate the broad outlines of racial differences among Europeans. In the process he also upset some of the conventional wisdom. For example, in his 1899 magnum opus he concluded that the innumerable European racial types—Mediterranean, Jewish, Eastern European, Teutonic, Anglo-Saxon, and Aryan, among others—derived from African and Asian intermarriage: "The European races, as a whole, show signs of a secondary or derived origins; certain characteristics, especially the texture of the hair, lead us to class them as intermediate between the extreme primary types of the Asiatic and the negro races respectively." Because he held fast to his period's other beliefs even as he acknowledged the history of intermixture, these "new" groups were unquestionable improvements.

John R. Commons, a noted professor of economics and labor at the University of Wisconsin fused the discussion of race and immigration in a 1907 publication entitled *Races and Immigrants in America*. Somewhat less categorical than Ripley, Commons wrote, "Mankind in general has been divided into five great racial stocks, and one of these stocks, the Aryans or Indo-Germanic, is represented among us by ten or more subdivisions which we term race." While noting long histories of "amalgamation and assimilation," Commons wondered how the various races with their subdivisions would fare in the United States. Democracy, he posited, was an alien concept to many who hailed from Asia, Africa, and large parts of Europe. A few years later the physician M. S. Iseman pondered the "disastrous" consequences of abortions and suppressed fertility among educated and capable whites in a 1912 publication, *Race Suicide*.

American imperialists like Theodore Roosevelt harbored similar thoughts and views about race in general and race suicide in particular. Roosevelt's use of race was anything but tight and consistent, however. At various times, race could denote a particular religious, ethnic, national or social group; in this regard, on several occasions Anglo-Saxons and Germanic people represented both the same race and members of different races. Where he was consistent had to do with a firm belief in the superiority of his race. As a result, he openly worried about threats to the exalted status of his group, including significant demographic changes.

More important to Commons, an unchecked flow of immigrants from Europe threatened the material well-being of native-born white workers, who were his principal concern. Nationality and race functioned synonymously in the minds of many in the early twentieth century. Mediterraneans or Latins were perceived as different from Anglos or Aryans. Nor did such notions disappear with passage through New York's harbor. Ellis Island confirmed difference rather than altered the efficacy of racial thinking.

Nativists, rather than being pacified by promises of immigrant assimilation and amalgamation, raised considerable alarm. Works like *Race Suicide* and Madison Grant's *The Passing of the Great Race* intentionally drew attention to the consequences of unimpeded European immigration to the United States. For Grant, the scion of a well-to-do New York family, Italians, Slavs, and especially Jews threatened the promise of America. He and other architects of restricted immigration publicly worried about the significant waves of European immigration, from the perceived inferior areas of eastern and southern Europe.

Thus, becoming acceptably "white" is a fascinating historical process. In most quarters, for example, the Irish, who in the middle of the nineteenth century had been viewed as a "race apart," had become securely white by the beginning of the twentieth century. Victimized by a blinding ethnocentrism, they had been called "low-browed and savage, grovelling and bestial, lazy and wild, simian and sensual." But, as Kerby Miller has argued, the Irish, to borrow a phrase from Henry Cabot Lodge, became "honorary Anglo-Saxons" because they repositioned themselves as guardians of the citadel of American purity. This process of inclusion was neither fast nor complete. Old prejudices lingered. But in Boston, New York, Chicago, and San Francisco little doubt remained by 1900, the Irish were indeed white. They could "pass."

The process was more arduous for many southern and eastern Europeans. Some groups had a high rate of return migration, which marked them as permanent outsiders. Roughly half of all Italians returned to Italy, for example, during the late nineteenth and early twentieth centuries. This pattern led some to question the newcomers' commitment to their new land. Paradoxically, low rates of return could inflame sensibilities as much as high rates. Jewish immigrants fleeing pogroms in Lithuania, Poland, or Russia had little reason to return. Their 5.2 percent return rate indicated a real desire to find comfort in a new home. Yet their continued presence threatened men like Grant and Iseman more than the actions of Italians. Differences in language, religion, and custom set even the most assimilated apart from the majority.

Fiercely held antipathies could have socially stigmatizing and even deadly consequences. New words appeared that captured the perceived degraded essence of the newcomers. Words like *wop, kike,* and *dago* competed for their place alongside *nigger, jap, chinee,* and *sheenie.* Harsh terms, these disparaging references underscored the subordinate status of the new groups in the larger order. More important, such phrases became part of the vocabulary of social relations, serving to reracialize the new immigrants by setting them apart from more comfortably recognized whites.

Latin, which became a code word for dark, exotic, and, perhaps, not white, complicated matters even more. According to Leonard Dinnerstein, some southern communities considered Italians more colored than white and assigned them to schools with blacks. Perhaps even more ironically, decades before elements of the political elite positioned Greece as the centerpiece of the Western world, some questioned if Greeks were white. Signs appeared with slogans: "John's Restaurant. Pure American. No rats. No Greeks." Meanwhile, the Latin label shrouded other aspects of the conversation about race. As late as the 1940s, major league baseball teams played Latin teams if their players were not too dark. The darker players, despite Latin backgrounds, struggled to evade obscurity in the Negro Leagues.

But intragroup tensions were as profound as interracial differences. In the Tampa area of Florida, Cuban immigrants of African descent uneasily negotiated the interlocking worlds of race and ethnicity. Afro-Cubans separated themselves from African Americans, clinging to claims of Cubanness. Jim Crow policies, which forced them to share segregated public facilities with black Americans, were an imperfect shield for the racial discrimination that occurred within the Cuban community. Cuban social clubs, according to Nancy Mirabal, divided along racial lines during the first decades of the twentieth century, reflecting racial divisions within Cuba as much as social conditions in the United States.

The social melodrama in which this all unfolded could turn violently ugly. Anti-Italian violence marred relations in Pennsylvania in 1874, West Virginia and New Orleans in 1891, and Colorado in 1895. Likewise, the coal mines of western Pennsylvania turned deadly following a series of strikes by Slavs, who were portrayed enduringly as outsiders. Individual acts of violent aggression filled the nation's papers during the first decades of the twentieth century. A few became crowning moments in America's racial reordering, signaling a shift in perspective, if not beliefs.

The trial and subsequent murder of Leo Frank proved an epiphanic event. Frank, college-educated and New York–born, moved to Atlanta during the mature years of the Progressive Era. Atlanta, the epitome of the New South, offered many opportunities for someone of Frank's background. With capital assistance from an uncle, he opened and managed a pencil factory, and became a noted member of the city's Jewish community. Meanwhile, the harshness of farm life that sent thousands of African Americans to the cities ensnared thousands of southern whites, too. One was the family of Mary Phagan. Unable to make a go of it, Phagan's father and siblings entered the urban wage economy, although they did not live in Atlanta, per se. The lives of Mary Phagan and Leo Frank became entangled when she went to work for him, and when he, accused of her murder, was lynched by a vengeful mob.

For some, the fate of the teenaged Mary Phagan captured a general unease about the changing social order. As Jacquelyn Hall reminds us, the New South featured the entrance of more and more young women into the wage economy. Between 1900 and 1920 Atlanta's population more than doubled; concomitantly, the number of white women wage earners nearly quadrupled, far outpacing the employment of black women who had long worked for wages to counter the pervasive problem of male un- or underemployment. From all accounts Mary went to the factory on a Saturday, where she received her weekly pay of $1.20. Later that night the watchman discovered her lifeless and partially unclothed body with a cord around the neck.

After suspicion focused first on the watchman and next on the black janitor, Jim Conley, Leo Frank became the chief suspect. In a society marked by economic dislocation, where families like the Phagans represented the majority, Frank's success fed many prejudices. To some he was "the Jew," forever marked by his religion and customs as a member of another community. Others saw him as the embodiment of capitalism's underbelly: exploitative, exacting, and demeaning. That police beat an incriminating confession from the black suspect fueled rather than dampened these harsh assessments. Conley, who admitted lying repeatedly, accused Frank of using the power of his position to "corrupt" many of the factory's female laborers. Frank never denied that he entered the women's changing area in search of delinquent workers or that he touched his female employees and referred to them in a familiar manner. Nor, writes Nancy MacLean, did Frank or his attorney understand why some would see this as other than an employer's prerogative.

More sensationally, Conley accused Frank of sexual perversions of an unspecified nature. Thus a hostile atmosphere, palpable anti-Semitism, and a key witness who would retract many statements but not the one implicating Frank in the murder, led the jury to recommend the death penalty. After a year and a half of failed appeals, Frank's lawyers ultimately convinced the governor to commute the sentence to life in prison. A broad cross section of men from Phagan's hometown executed the final verdict: they kidnapped Frank from jail, drove him to Mary's place of birth, and lynched him. The erstwhile factory supervisor bled to death when the gnawing rope reopened stitches designed to close an earlier attempt on his life.

Historians generally agree on the details and importance of this case. Previously viewed in racial and class terms, a new consensus is emerging that the case really addresses the complicated interaction among race, class, and gender in the New South. What few have acknowledged is the case's importance for answering the question of who was white. In the forced-choice world of racial identification—black, white, brown, yellow, or red—a son of German parents was white. For most of his life Frank had enjoyed that privilege. Frank's attorney even used this knowledge in his defense: How could anyone trust the word of a black man who was a liar and ex-convict when compared to that of a white man of standing and privilege? Yet such a social and lexical repertoire, based as it was on differences in power and resources, worked as long as one retained the ability to define the terms. Conley's role as the authentic black who indicted Frank filtered through the racial imaginations of Atlanta's white residents. As the genuine other, Conley surely recognized one of his own. Conley's claim of authenticity transfigured Frank, offering new meditations on blackness—and whiteness.

Just as important, ideologically charged inflections of religion, class, and gender modified notions about race. Race was but one position of the self that constituted the individual. In this situation, other elements transformed Leo Frank the white man into Leo Frank the Jewish, exploitative, lewd, bestial, other rapist and murderer. In the words of one contemporary he became a "fiend." Although few white men of any station suffered his fate in the first two decades of the twentieth century, the case dramatized the debate over race, its social construction, and how essential realities were struggled over at the local level.

The argument over racial belonging continued well into the 1960s, kept alive by groups like the Ku Klux Klan. The modern version of the racist, nativist organization reemerged during the 1920s. The 1924 Immigration Act, which established national quotas, halted the flow of immigrants from Europe, but not the fear that "outsiders" threatened America. With opposition to blacks, Catholics, and Jews, among others, as a rallying cry, the Klan infiltrated the political mainstream, winning elections in several states and countless municipalities. Through the rituals of parades and huge public gatherings they etched an image of a country at war with itself and presented themselves as the guardians of the status quo. More important, its members inflamed public discussion about race, nationality, and America.

Ironically, however, their successes galvanized a broader racial consensus. European immigrants worked very hard to counter negative images. Some simply blended into the caldron of the racial mainstream: they Anglicized their names, made exogamous marriages, and dropped hints of their immigrant origins. Others tenaciously claimed their birthrights and their right to be white. Americanization efforts eased the transition.

By the mid-1920s, despite efforts to curb European and Asian immigration, only the most anachronistic denied the equation between European and white. Scores worried that some might evince a stronger attachment to the old country; yet few doubted that other Europeans, regardless of how foreign in dress or custom, were white. Of course intragroup hostilities and antipathies remained. Native-born whites still asserted their superiority, even when they proposed to uplift the others. For example, by mass producing more than 2 million pamphlets on obligations to America, the Daughters of the American Revolution simply used its role as an older group of whites to educate a newer group of whites—nothing more. Ethnicity rather than race separated the communities. This eventual understanding formed the covenant that made white interethnic marriage so prominent by 1990.

For the most part, Native Americans remained in their accustomed place on the American racial landscape. After the 1890 Wounded Knee massacre in South Dakota, they lived apart from most of America.

Fixed as permanent wards, assigned the Bureau of Indian Affairs as guardian, and most of them contained on reservations, they disappeared from the nation's view. Declining numbers and the ravages of grinding poverty and chemical dependency reinforced the pattern of invisibility. As many new western historians maintain, we reintroduced American Indians when we wanted to underscore the triumph of white western ways. Hence, the views of Indians often stood outside of time. Popular media, with few exceptions, ended their story with the closing of the nineteenth century.

Of course this general trend operated at such a grand level that we risk surrendering to caricature. There was no way that American Indians could enter the twentieth century without a powerful understanding of themselves as racial beings. To do so would mean denying the history of American conquest and subjugation. If anything, in much the same way that Europe became equated with whiteness, the coalescence of events would lead native peoples to adopt a pan-Indian consciousness predicated on racial difference.

Also, interracial relations minimized the complete disappearance of American Indians. European immigrants who settled in the Dakotas and were influenced by racial perceptions warned their children against forming romantic relations with Indians. Thus images, families, and customs prohibited the complete erasure of Native Americans from the nation's conscience or the ongoing conversation about race. In contrast to those who sought avoidance, others wanted to make Indians more assimilated. Language, customs, and religion were said to be too Indian. Mission and boarding schools like Carlisle in Pennsylvania tried to drive away this Indianness.

Race occasionally became part of a political agreement more than a social plan. After a period of intense competition over land and political rights, whites and Indians in Oklahoma shared in the political neutering of blacks. When the state joined the nation in 1907, "colored" referred to blacks only. All other residents, including Native peoples, were legally—if not socially—white. With the legal imprimatur of whiteness, Indians could vote. More important, the Oklahoma example highlighted the ways in which the state manufactured racial views and influenced the meaning of race in the twentieth century.

The place of Mexican Americans and Asians both solidified the definition of whiteness and expanded the meaning of race. Following the Treaty of Guadalupe Hidalgo in 1848, which ended hostilities between Mexico and the United States and ceded much of the Southwest to the United States, Mexicans then living in this country were guaranteed the right of citizenship. Yet in the heady days of the early twentieth century, some questioned the racial pedigree of Mexicans and Mexican Americans. Many agreed with one Texan who said, "for Mexican immigrants, there is no congenial social group to welcome them. . . . They are not Negroes. . . . They are not accepted as white men, and between the two there seems to be no midway position." When numerous southern and southwestern communities tried to separate Mexican Americans on the basis of race, elite civil rights groups like the League of United Latin American Citizens (LULAC) voiced their strong opposition.

Founded in 1929, this primarily middle-class organization accepted the principle of racial exceptionalism at the same time that it argued for treatment as whites. As Mario Garcia notes, the organization acknowledged its intent "to maintain a sincere and respectful reverence for our racial origin of which we are proud." Nonetheless, acutely aware of the debilitating consequences of de facto and de jure segregation, members of LULAC vigorously denied that they were colored. Some of this stemmed from an intensely ambivalent relationship with blacks; it also reflected a sensitive understanding of power dynamics. If the state defined them as colored they lost employment, voting, and social opportunities. Given a choice, they declared themselves both white and other. The federal census followed suit. Through the 1950s Mexicans were counted as white, although many communities in Texas and the broader Southwest simply designated them nonwhite—neither white nor colored.

Regional and internal variation among Asians confounded categories even more. Along the West Coast, virulent anti-Asian sentiments persisted well into the early decades of the twentieth century. Some continued to equate Asians and blacks. In San Francisco, for example, school officials tried to segregate Asian and white students in much the same manner as they segregated whites and blacks. Earlier laws had prohibited intermarriage between white and Japanese residents, and from 1907 through 1931 federal law stripped white women who married Asians of their American citizenship. And as late as 1949, federal courts in San Francisco maintained one room for white witnesses and another for black and Asian witnesses. Yet under United States law Asian Indian immigrants had a more ambiguous status.

In the minds of many, Asian Indians had every right to be considered Caucasian. Few disputed their membership in the broad Aryan family. Therefore, the 1924 immigration legislation, which barred Chinese, Japanese, and Korean immigrants because they could not become naturalized citizens, raised the specter of a new status for Asian Indians. In a series of legal renderings beginning in 1907, a new consensus emerged. Because race was both an idea and an ideology, Attorney General Charles Bonaparte insisted that British colonials might be many things, but they were not white. A decade and a half later the Supreme Court ruled that Japanese resident aliens were not Caucasian, and because heretofore the Constitution granted citizenship to whites and blacks, they were excluded. The court's decision in *Ozawa* v. *United States* (1922) prefigured a ruling a year later in *United States* v. *Bhagat Singh Thind* (1923). George Sutherland, writing for the majority, drew a sharp distinction between Caucasian, which Asian Indians might have been, and white. In his words, race derived from the "understanding of the common man." Therefore, despite ancient relations, much had changed in the intervening years. "White person," the Court reasoned, denoted a social as much as legal understanding. Hence, Asian Indians were not white and not eligible for citizenship.

Too often the story of immigration and nativism is told in race-neutral terms. But as the 1923 Supreme Court decision and much of the foregoing discussion suggest, race played a central role in the peopling of America. This convoluted decision, which admitted a divide between science and social practice, narrowed the meaning of race in the United States by clearly outlining who could pass for white. Although at the local level some may have had doubts, as far as the state was concerned all Europeans were not only Caucasian, they were white; at least through World War II, others might be Caucasian but they could not be white. As a result, who became white is as important to the history of race in the United States as the wrongs inflicted upon the nation's racial minorities. Thus the process of making European immigrants white—slow, uneven, and sometimes unpredictable—established other parts of the human rainbow and informed the racial beliefs systems of at least three generations of Americans. But the contestation did not end there. To be labeled white and to benefit from one's whiteness produced a new form of contestation, which framed the meaning of race in the twentieth century.

THE POWER DYNAMICS OF RACE

No discussion of race is complete without an examination of the coercive and discursive aspects of power. Access to and different uses of power provided the context for understanding what transpired between 1900 and 1945. Power in this instance is not restricted to a discussion of the horrors of lynching or the psychological trauma of constant racial harassment. Insofar as possible, we must explore the language, cultural traditions, and artifacts of race as well. After all, Billie Holiday's song, "Strange Fruit," was as powerful a declaration against lynching as the attempts to secure passage of federal antilynching legislation.

In the South, the new century began with the clear intent of disfranchising African Americans. In state conventions from Virginia to Mississippi held between 1890 and 1902, new constitutions restricted the voting prerogatives of the black male electorate. Some states introduced grandfather clauses (restricting the franchise to those whose grandfathers voted in the last election before the Civil War), understanding clauses (requiring potential voters to interpret a passage of the Constitution to the satisfaction of a registrar), and the poll tax (requesting payment of typically three years of cumulative taxes before voting) with the explicit intent of reducing the size and diversity of the electorate. When asked if such measures might inadvertently penalize poor whites, a future Virginia U.S. senator and convention delegate dismissed such concerns as a small price to pay if they succeeded in eliminating "the darky." Carter Glass went on to boldly advertise their larger mission:

> Discrimination! Why, that is exactly what we propose; that exactly is why this convention was elected—to discriminate to the very extremity of permissible action under the limitations of the Federal Constitution with the view to the elimination of every Negro who can be gotten rid of, legally, without materially impairing the strength of the white electorate.

Concern with the voting power of African Americans followed successful political advances in the decades after the Civil War. At the national level, the first African American representatives took their seats in 1869. Between 1869 and 1901 the South sent twenty blacks to Congress. During that period South Carolina sent the most, followed by North Carolina and Alabama. Five other states sent one each. Officially two African Americans became senators during the period, Hiram Revels and Blanche Bruce, both from Mississippi. P. B. S. Pinchback of Louisiana was elected but never served in the Senate.

At the local level, African Americans served in most southern state legislatures and local common or city councils. Nearly three dozen African Americans won election to the city council in Richmond, Virginia, between 1871 and 1898, for example; about

255 blacks joined the South Carolina legislature between 1868 and 1876. Some, like Revels of Mississippi or George Teamoh, who served in the Virginia legislature, had fled the South during slavery, returning after emancipation. Others gained skills and resources during the antebellum period and parlayed those advantages into political capital after the war ended. Nor were they unusual. Participation in the electoral process captivated and motivated many blacks. Thus rank political maneuvering proved so malodorous. In Louisiana, writes John Hope Franklin, "in 1896 there were 130,344 Negroes registered. . . . In 1900, two years after the adoption of the new constitution, only 5,320 Negroes were on the registration books."

The final outcome met challenges along the way. African Americans, heavily outnumbered at all conventions, nonetheless challenged the efficacy of such moves. Yet few could deny the dramatic change in mood. After a series of crippling decisions, in 1896 the Supreme Court issued the ultimate penalty: separate but equal did not violate the Constitution. In a case noted for the manipulation of race, Homer Adolph Plessy, a Louisianan with more white relatives than black, lost his suit against the railroads for discriminatory service. Railroad executives had sided with Plessy, finding the new segregation ordinances a nuisance, an inconvenience, and costly. The same court ruled in 1883 that individuals—not states—had the right to discriminate. Saddened, perplexed, and frustrated, scores of African Americans rejected that ruling and would feel similarly about the 1896 *Plessy* v. *Ferguson* decision. More than any other state action, that verdict forever changed the trajectory of America's racial history, ushering in over sixty years of social protest, protest that eventually challenged the efficacy of the *Plessy* doctrine.

The contest, like the history itself, defies easy categorization. Jim Crow or segregation reached adulthood in a series of fits and starts, not all at once. Mississippi, long considered the most hellish swath of land in America for blacks, proved the rule rather than the exception. During the period when white supremacists asserted their right to everything of value, blacks still held positions as teachers, postal clerks, justices of the peace, and customs collectors. Although a number of blacks lost control of vital offices during the first decade, a few prevailed. On this point Neil McMillan maintained that "in a few relatively tolerant cities along the Gulf Coast black postmasters served without appreciable opposition until at least World War I."

By World War I the full effects of the *Plessy* decision had taken root. Ranging from the pernicious to the silly, municipalities introduced measures to separate the races. On public conveyances and official governmental lists, in toilets, at drinking fountains, churches, schools, theaters, even cemeteries, society divided along racial lines. Such a schema made little room for Asians, American Indians, or Mexican Americans; oddly they were not part of the dominant discourse in many locales. America's dilemma had been shaded in monochrome—that is, in hues of black and white.

Historians disagree about the evolution of Jim Crow. C. Vann Woodward, in his classic statement *The Strange Career of Jim Crow* dated the formal codification of legal segregation to the *Plessy* decision and to the introduction of restrictive municipal ordinances in the 1900s and 1910s. Howard Rabinowitz, Joel Williamson, and others maintain that such restrictions began some time after the abolition of slavery, when the battle began for the mind and soul of the South. Rabinowitz went a step further, suggesting that before segregation there was exclusion, marked by a total disregard for the wants and needs of African Americans. According to him, segregation proved a curious but effective innovation. All agree, however, that by the eve of World War I, in custom and law, blacks had a legal and social status as second-class citizens. Moreover, in spirit this lesser status applied to other nonwhites as well.

Segregation, although often brutal, demeaning, and psychologically troubling, could also be empowering. Against the backdrop of increasing social violence, a hostile Supreme Court, and beginning with Theodore Roosevelt's presidential indifference if not hostility, African, Asian, Indian, and Mexican Americans began a measured assault on the citadels of racial power and privilege. This was possible because race functioned as both an idea and an ideology. In this way men like Theodore Roosevelt, who resolutely believed blacks his inferior, nonetheless invited the famed black educator and leader Booker T. Washington to the White House. Roosevelt never forgot that Washington was black, but he could distinguish between the individual and the group, between race as idea and ideology. Thus the grand accomplishments of a member of a subordinate group, who had overcome group limits to realize individual greatness, justified a presidential invitation. That many saw this gesture of presidential largesse as a direct threat to the racial covenant emerging among whites meant that there was no need to replicate the offer. The episode did highlight the tension between the promise of white supremacy and the threat to that belief system. Few incidents symbolized the crisis of belonging and strategies adopted more than the epic battle between Jack Johnson and Jim Jeffries on 4 July 1910.

Nearly half a century earlier famed abolitionist Frederick Douglass questioned the meaning of Independence Day for the 4 million Americans of African origin who remained enslaved. Douglass drew a clear line between the promise and reality of American democracy. He, like many of his contemporaries, favored the day of Haitian Independence rather than the day would-be Americans declared their independence from their European overlords. But instead of becoming a dismissive attack on the principles of American democracy, Douglass's entreaty invited the republic to broaden its vision of inclusion. Two generations later, Baltimore-born Thurgood Marshall captured the essence of Douglass's intent and championed the battle for equal opportunity. Between Douglass and Marshall others fought both individual and collective battles.

On this particular Fourth of July, Jack Johnson waged his own struggle for inclusion. In the minds of many whites the boxing match should not have been needed. Except for a few exhibitions, no white fighter of any prominence had allowed a black man into the ring for a fight of any consequence. Like other spheres, boxing adopted the wisdom of racial segregation: blacks fought blacks, whites fought whites. Then, in 1908, Tommy Burns, convinced that his racial background produced a shield of invincibility, allowed Jack Johnson into the ring. Johnson towered over the more diminutive Burns, but most who witnessed the fight in Australia figured that Johnson would wilt under the mental and physical assault. Dominant prejudices clouded the judgment of even the most astute observers. Ex-champ John L. Sullivan and his colleagues believed that Johnson, the "brute," "beast," or "ape," certainly lacked the skills to defeat Burns. And then it happened: a black man beat a white man and claimed the prize of virility—heavyweight champion of the world.

Everything about Johnson spoke of race and he, in actions and words, eschewed any acceptance of the evolving social-racial contract. First, his coffee-colored complexion deprived anyone seeking an interracial alibi. Johnson lacked any discernible "white" blood; the age-old practice of attributing accomplishment to European ancestry would not work in this instance. Second, Johnson loved the sporting life, its fast cars, gambling dens, and working women. In a period when antimiscegenation legislation proliferated, he brazenly cavorted with white women, some of whom were prostitutes. Third, Johnson enjoyed beating Burns as much as he had enjoyed beating black opponents. Moreover, he did so with style and flair, with a learned African American cultural imprint. Since that time black youth across urban America have used verbal sparring as a means of modifying conventions of power. Words enabled weaker opponents to defeat ostensibly more powerful rivals. Fifty years later Muhammad Ali (a.k.a. Cassius Clay) gained fame for his ringside verbal assaults as well as his fighting prowess, but it was Johnson who was among those who originated this practice in professional boxing. He loved to use his words as well as his fists to jab opponents. Thus, because of his color, out-of-ring behavior, and in-ring style, Johnson questioned the racial treaty that called for blacks to settle for seconds. Many whites feared that Johnson was not alone.

Jim Jeffries, who retired as the undisputed heavyweight champion more than two years earlier, accepted the task of restoring the dominion of his fraternity and race. He answered Jack London who, in a *New York Herald* account of the Burns fight, pleaded, "Jeff, it's up to you. The White Man must be rescued." Progressive-Era crusaders found boxing a vile and extremely manly undertaking. Some ranted that it defied decency and civilization. Scores, however, saw boxing for what it was: a socially sanctioned act of orchestrated aggression that satisfied some primordial need for men to engage in hand-to-hand combat. For Jeffries the stakes were more simple and eloquent. As a white man he had to put Johnson and all his imitators in their place. Gender and race made this necessity sensible.

Most boxing experts picked Jeffries to win. He had experience, size, a proven record, and certain racial intangibles on his side. Johnson, therefore, took great pleasure in beating and taunting his challenger. Not only did he taunt Jeffries, he taunted his cornerman, the former champion "Gentleman" Jim Corbett, and by extension all whites. The verbal whipping hurt as much as the physical defeat. In a purposeful inversion of the period's social equation, Jack Johnson used the African American word game of signifying or playing the dozens to expose Jeffries as the Great Pretender.

The state rather than an individual proved Johnson's toughest rival. After near invincibility in the ring, government officials charged and convicted him of violating the Mann or White Slave Traffic Act (which prohibited the interstate transport of white women for prostitution). Johnson fled the country, and remained away for several years. Upon returning, he served a prison term. Yet the coalescence of events heightened instead of tarnished his reputation. Thus was born the myth of Johnson the badman, Johnson the "Bad Nigger."

The fight and its riotous aftermath revealed race as both an invention and a variation of the real. Writing a decade after time had erased the bout's anxious moments, W. E. B. Du Bois offered,

> The discovery of personal whiteness among the world's peoples is a very modern thing—a nineteenth and twentieth century matter, indeed. The ancient world would have laughed at such a distinction. The Middle Ages regarded skin color with mild curiosity; and even up into the eighteenth century we were hammering our national manikins into one, great, Universal man, with fine frenzy which ignored color and race even more than birth. Today we have changed all that, and the world in a sudden, emotional conversion has discovered that it is white and by that token, wonderful!

Du Bois joined a chorus of African Americans who exposed the ruse of racial belonging. Given the variety of colors in the black community, ranging from charcoal to chalk, many accepted race as a fiction stemming from broader social claims. Yet once created, race consciousness generated its own reality, a reality that fused memories of shared experiences with present conditions. As a calculated game of power, rewards came to those who understood and played by the rules. After all, the period of redemption showed that individual gains without group guarantees jeopardized the individual.

The riots that followed word of Johnson's victory produced one of those moments of racial identification by interlacing geographically distinct locations into a web of common understanding. In communities as varied as Boston; Pueblo, Colorado; Greenwood, South Carolina; Shreveport, Louisiana; and New York City whites defined themselves in opposition to blacks. In Norfolk, Virginia, a riot started when two black men exclaimed in recognition of the accomplishment, "Oh, you Johnson!" This spontaneous outburst produced a violent reaction from the city's white community, who charged the riot stemmed from the "insolence of Negroes."

Nor were such outbursts read as independent blots on the racial landscape. Between 1900 and 1910 race riots occurred in Wilmington, North Carolina; New Orleans; Atlanta; and Springfield, Illinois. These and future acts of racial violence helped form a collective memory and mold a degree of community on both sides of the color divide, despite innumerable intragroup differences. Recalling the Johnson victory, Benjamin Mays, a noted black educator and longtime president of Morehouse College in Atlanta wrote, "White men in my county could not take it. A few Negroes were beaten up because a Negro had beaten a white man in far-away Nevada. . . . In fact, Johnson's victory was hard on the white man's world."

In Norfolk the riot ended when blacks retreated to their own community and erected a collective wall of defense. The need for collective action reinforced race as more than an idea. Here, race's ideological dimensions spawned deadly consequences. As a result, even Du Bois, whose considerable intellectual gifts enabled him to view race as social creation, recognized that an invention, once informed by clear differentials in power, assumed a certain reality. Most Americans accepted the veracity of this view as they fought over life's other essentials.

The reality of difference could even create a race where one had not existed before. Immigration and Naturalization Service officials, who deported nearly one-third of the Mexican population of Los Angeles during the economic crises of the 1930s, never asked if a Mexican migrant was from Vera Cruz and traced his or her ancestry to Africa, from Mexico City and hailed from a Spanish family, from Tijuana and belonged to a predominantly Indian group, or was the offspring of an American, African, and European union. Noted racial and regional differences disappeared into the vortex of American racialism. Once they moved north they were simply nonwhites.

Crossing the border separating Mexico and the United States, notes George Sánchez, had the added effect of creating a new people—Mexican Americans. Not all Mexican migrants accepted this change right away. The generation born in the late nineteenth century held tenaciously to the idea that they were Mexican, even refusing to seek American citizenship when given the option. Instead, they moved back and forth across the border, adapting to their circumstances in accordance with changes in law and belief. Yet, the border crossing, with the general process of social and cultural adaptation that occurred, produced a change in philosophy and response.

By the 1930s, a new generation schooled in the value of civil rights and protest politics had assumed the leadership of indigenous organizations. Whether they were in the Southwest or Midwest, members of this cohort had become part of America's racial world. In turn, Mexican Americans in Texas founded LULAC, and in Los Angeles they founded the Mexican American Movement (MAM) to protect the vital interests of their communities. These and other groups struggled with what it meant to be Mexican and American. LULAC leaders, for example, vowed to be Mexican in things cultural and social, but American in things political. MAM members, most of whom were second generation, upwardly mobile, and unquestionably American, believed that as a group, Mexican Americans had to seize the right to be treated as citizens. Yet, even in the face of hardening racial attitudes, especially during the 1930s and 1940s, they remained optimistic that they would be included.

In the period that has been called a nadir for African Americans, strategies for empowerment varied with time and place. Individuals like Ida B. Wells-Barnett, Booker T. Washington, W. E. B. Du Bois, and Marcus Garvey illustrated the variety of approaches. Such organizations as the National Baptist Convention, National Association for the Advancement of Colored People, and the National Urban League highlighted the range of institutional options. Although a master narrative emerged, a number of subplots with their own scripts complicates any narration of race in the twentieth century.

Despite claims to the contrary, African Americans never completely agreed on one leader or one approach to their common problems. Booker T. Washington, the founder and head of Tuskegee Institute, came as close as any to a national leader. The 1890s were a heady time, noted in many quarters for the country's retreat from any pretense of racial equality. Washington acquired public fame after his speech at the 1895 Atlanta Exposition, in which he said that blacks and whites could be as separate as the five fingers in things social and like the clenched fist in things economic. Designed to showcase the face of the New South, this event proved the perfect stage for Washington's brand of progressive conservatism. There he invited close interracial economic cooperation at the same time he implicitly endorsed the development of separate social spheres. When he finished the address blacks and whites applauded his judicious reasoning. Soon thereafter the country anointed him successor to Frederick Douglass, and like his predecessor his blood coursed with the streams from two of America's racial rivers.

More significantly, Washington emerged from the period's racial crucible with more influence than any man of color of his generation. During a period when blacks suffered an amazing political decline, he counseled presidents McKinley and Roosevelt. Although he publicly eschewed politics and social activism, he privately protected blacks fleeing vigilante justice, financially supported cases challenging the legality of Jim Crow legislation, and expertly sought the allegiance of the nation's chief capitalists for purposes of advancing the race's interests. Washington achieved many of his feats by playing on the racial arrogance of whites. "Putting on ol' massa" became a staple survival technique during slavery; it proved as effective in the twentieth century. This same man built a network of allegiances by purchasing black newspapers, bestowing patronage, and founding institutions like the Negro Business League (1900). Called many things by his foes and friends, Washington did not shrink from the title of race man; it was a moniker that he and others wore as a badge of achievement.

Washington's ascent did not go unchallenged. By 1910 Du Bois, Monroe Trotter, and Ida B. Wells-Barnett joined the list of Washington's critics. On the outside, the national black community often presented a unified front; internally, petty jealousies and intellectual differences germinated. After praising the deftness of Washington's 1895 address, Du Bois had grown to believe Washington minimized the importance of classical education and traditional routes to black political empowerment. Du Bois and Trotter both believed Washington the boss of an "infernal machine"; they chafed when he chose to use it against them rather than a common adversary. Wells-Barnett, who fled Memphis when her editorials attacking the lynching of black men put her on the wrong side of racial etiquette, was especially rankled by Washington's public finessing of the evils of lynching.

Washington died in 1915, to be replaced in one sense by Marcus Garvey, a Washington devotee who cherished the public features of race. Where Washington built institutions, Garvey built a social movement, one dedicated to the social, economic, and spiritual salvation of the race. Scholars have estimated that perhaps as many as 2 million members of the African diaspora hailed Garvey as their leader. The Jamaican-born Garvey preached a civil religion of triumph. In a language deeply rooted in the vernacular of the black everyday person, he trumpeted "Up You Mighty Race!" He understood that the key to economic and social improvement hinged on psychological betterment. True liberation and empowerment required a revolution of the mind.

Garvey realized the latter through the Universal Negro Improvement Association (UNIA) and its many offshoots. The UNIA had more branches in the southern United States, although most of its members lived north of the Mason-Dixon line. Garvey globalized the condition of black folks. He compared their struggles against racism to colonial struggles in Ireland, Asia, and Palestine. He bridged the distance between black Africans and black Americans in his paper the *Negro World* and his declarations that black salvation and advancement hinged on the reclamation of Africa. When many others rejected Africa, Garvey embraced the "Mother Continent." Still, Garvey was a product of the West. Many of his views of Africa, while romantic, were tinged by Western definitions of progress and civilization. More than anything, however, the UNIA, various business ventures, meetings modeled on church services, and proclamations of black importance, channeled the energies of a people seeking to redirect the disempowering aspects of race in America.

Although Garvey's UNIA survived his deportation for mail fraud, other institutions had the most lasting effects on race in American society. Among African Americans, the National Association for the Advancement of Colored People (NAACP) heads the list. Between 1900 and 1908 groups of African Americans convened several civil rights congresses. In 1905 a group meeting in Niagara Falls championed the most radical steps. Known as the Niagara Movement, it wanted an immediate and enduring end to rank discrimination and the protected integration of blacks into the nation's mainstream. A vicious race riot overwhelmed Abraham Lincoln's hometown of Springfield, Illinois, in 1908, which prompted the meeting of a biracial group the next year. Save for Monroe Trotter, a number of the Niagara Movement leaders, including Du Bois and Wells-Barnett attended. Within a year the conveners had incorporated as the NAACP. With the support of several influential whites and a few select blacks the group launched its steady attack on Jim Crow and racial discrimination.

What the NAACP set out to accomplish in the realm of civil rights, the National Urban League attempted in employment rights. In its early years the NAACP concentrated on housing discrimination. The Urban League stepped into the void in scores of cities, north and south. They helped longtime as well as new residents find jobs in the expanding labor markets. The League offices functioned as a clearinghouse in numerous locales.

The role of the NAACP and National Urban League was hastened by the mass migrations of millions of African Americans between 1900 and 1945. The first of the Great Migrations came between 1900 and 1920, when thousands of blacks used their feet to register their displeasure with southern rural life and racial treatment. Between 1900 and 1920 more than 1.5 million African Americans left the rural South. More than two times that number left between 1940 and 1960.

Throughout the first half of the century the dramatic increase profoundly altered the shape of many cities. For instance, during the period from 1910 to 1920, Chicago's population grew by more than 65,000 blacks, New York's by more than 60,000, and Detroit's by more than 30,000. Percentage-wise, the increase proved even more dramatic. Detroit's black population grew by an amazing 611 percent, Chicago's by 114 percent, and New York's by 66 percent. The growth was just as impressive in Cleveland and Pittsburgh—308 and 87 percent, respectively. Most important, this pattern was repeated in the North, South, and West between 1940 and 1960. (See table 4.)

The reasons for migrating were complex and varied. Most blacks sought better economic opportunity, greater personal freedom, and more material comforts. Others simply wished to escape the harshness of life in the Jim Crow South. Few completely severed ties with kin and kith who remained behind; black newspapers registered the visiting habits of thousands of migrants for the period. Yet in moving from country to city, African Americans continued the process of defining and redefining race in twentieth-century America.

In many respects, the movement was part of a vital interplay between culture, power, and race. For too long we have emphasized the culture of oppression which enveloped southern life. Although perfectly reasonable at one level, that story advantages whites. In such a narrative, whites act and blacks and other nonwhites react. We are only beginning to understand the oppositional culture that oppression engendered. Clearly, however, migration north was a large part of this cultural expression, as excerpts from the poem "Bound for the Promised Land" vividly captured:

Hasten on, my dark brother,
Duck the "Jim Crow" laws.
No "crackers" north to slap your mother
Or knock you in the jaw.
No "Cracker" there to seduce your sister,
Nor hang you to a limb,
And you're not obliged to call them mister,
Nor show your teeth at them.

Now, why should I remain longer south,
To be kicked and dogged around?
"Crackers" to knock me in the mouth
And shoot my brother down.

Table 4. Percentage of Population by Race, for Selected Cities of 100,000 or More, 1920–1980

	1920		1940			1960			1980		
City	White	Black	White	Black	Other Races[a]	White	Black[b]	Other Races	White	Black	Other Races[a]
Atlanta, Ga.	68.7	31.3	65.4	34.6	—	77.2	—	22.8	74.3	24.6	1.1
Baltimore, Md.	85.2	14.8	80.6	19.3	—	77.8	—	22.2	72.8	35.2	1.6
Birmingham, Ala.	60.7	39.3	59.3	40.7	—	65.4	—	34.6	71.3	28.3	0.4
Chicago, Ill.	95.8	4.1	91.7	8.2	0.1	85.2	—	14.8	73.3	20.0	6.7
Dallas, Tex.	84.8	15.1	83.9	17.1	—	85.4	—	14.6	79.8	14.1	6.1
Detroit, Mich.	95.8	4.1	90.7	9.2	1.1	84.9	—	15.1	77.6	20.5	1.9
Los Angeles, Calif.	94.8	2.7	93.5	4.2	2.3	91.2	—	8.8	67.9	12.6	19.5
New York, N.Y.	97.1	2.7	93.6	6.1	—	88.0	—	12.0	67.1	21.3	11.6
Norfolk, Va.	62.4	37.5	68.1	31.8	—	73.6	—	26.4	69.5	27.7	2.8
Oakland, Calif.	94.3	2.5	95.3	2.8	0.1	[c]	—	[c]	[c]	[c]	[c]
Philadelphia, Pa.	92.6	7.4	86.9	13.0	0.1	84.3	—	15.7	78.7	18.7	2.6
San Francisco, Calif.	96.7	0.5	95.0	0.8	4.3	87.5	—	12.5	71.8	12.0	17.0
Seattle, Wash.	96.0	0.9	96.5	1.0	2.8	95.2	—	4.8	90.0	3.6	6.4
Washington, D.C.	74.7	25.1	71.5	28.2	0.2	75.1	—	24.9	67.7	28.9	4.3

[a] "Other Races" includes Indians, Japanese, Chinese and Filipinos.
[b] For 1960, the black population is included in the total given for "Other Races."
[c] Oakland's population is combined with San Francisco's for 1960 and 1980.
SOURCES: U.S. Bureau of the Census, *15th Census of the United States: 1930*, vol. III, part I (1932), p. 61; U.S. Bureau of the Census, *16th Census of the United States: 1940*, vol. II (1943), p. 114; U.S. Bureau of the Census, *18th Census of the United States: 1960*, vol. I, part I (1963), pp. 1, 126–128; U.S. Bureau of the Census, *20th Census of the United States: 1980*, vol. I, part I (1983), pp. 1, 201–211.

No, I won't. I'm leaving today,
No longer can I wait.
If the recruiters fail to take me 'way,
I'm bound to catch a freight.

Such poems enabled African Americans to vent their anger with minimum risk. Oftentimes etched into the sides of northern-bound trains, these public displays reinforced the shared aspects of southern life. They worked as a semipublic transcript. In writing about power, James Scott has argued that both the powerful and the powerless produced hidden and public transcripts that critique and alter the valence of power. Sometimes, however, seemingly public transcripts carried a coded message which made them audible but unintelligible to those outside the circle of community. One could only learn the meanings behind the words if someone else taught their meaning.

Over and over again African Americans testified that race was not a natural condition but a learned location in the global community. Rituals of learning that recounted the deep wrongs of slavery, the capriciousness of life in the segregated South, the violence inherited by all with black skins transformed this public poem into a semipublic transcript that, for purposes of survival, all blacks learned to decode. The language allowed any reader to insert him or herself into the text of "your mother" in the first stanza and "my brother" in the second. In the process, with subtlety and evident care, blacks modified notions about race by empowering themselves to act in their own interests.

Messages could get distorted. Nothing illustrates this point better than conversations about color in the black community. One of the last taboo topics in African American history, color rivalries unsettle the traditional story of racial unity. In some cases individuals paid the price because of light skin; in other instances, dark skin cost them. Moreover, in each version the costs were painful and exacting.

Lillian Smith, a prominent white author, recounts the woes of color consciousness in *Killers of the Dream*. Smith's family agreed to adopt a white baby from a neighboring black family. The black family had adopted the ostensibly white baby as well. But as Smith notes, her family promptly returned the child when they discovered that it was mixed. Race, after all, was not just an idea. Although the child may have looked white, looks were not enough; in that place in those times, one drop was the rule. The child was black.

Helen Jackson Lee came of age in a color-conscious Richmond, Virginia, family. As she recalled, her "mama and her light-skin relatives and friends . . . spent a lot of time making jokes and sly remarks about folks whose skins were duskier than theirs." "From such comments," she insisted, "I learned quickly that the true criterion for social acceptance was light skin. The lighter the skin, the easier it was to make it." Lee's internalization of this lesson caused her considerable pain several years later. As a Virginia State junior she considered running for homecoming queen. During her first year, she defied the odds by defeating a light-skinned sister in a popularity contest. As a result two years later she marveled at her chances of winning the coveted title of homecoming queen. Apparently so did "a group of women faculty members . . . [who] were all members of the graduate chapter of Alpha Kappa Alpha, my sorority," she recalled. They asked her to withdraw so that fellow AKA sister Vickie Meadows could run. When asked why, one of the teachers is remembered to have responded, "You see dear, Vickie is more . . . more representative of what a campus queen looks like." Whether the events happened just as Lee recounted is not as important as what she took from the experience. She later wrote,

> To my shame, I gave in because I wanted to cooperate with my sisterhood. Mostly I gave in because I had little respect for myself and inwardly agreed with the belief that the ideal beauty queen should look like the white girls pictured in white collegiate magazines. It gave me no real satisfaction when Vickie lost the contest, because the girl who was crowned was just as fairskinned as she. So it continued that way for years, with obeisance paid to fair skin. Hail to the Queen, Hail to the Damned-Near-White Queen! The value system had to be upheld.

Alice Dunnigan, the first black woman admitted to the White House Press Corps, had a different experience. Somewhat lighter than her older brother, Alice suffered rejection when her maternal grandmother, who viewed her color as a stamp of the slavemaster's power, denied her love. Although color like race was the gift of birth over which she had no control, Dunnigan felt that she was somehow responsible. This case and countless others underscore the degree to which some blacks willfully inverted notions about color and race with equally painful consequences for those affected. In fact, because most people lived their lives in the shadows of greatness, personal slights and tortured relationships became inflated, allowing race to take on even grander meanings.

Looking white and acting white were different, however. Working-class blacks frequently criticized those among them who acted white. Phrases like "Uncle Tom," and "handkerchief head" captured the devalued status of those who were perceived to excel at the expense of others. Convinced that race was ideologically based, working-class blacks criticized the speech patterns, dress, and education of middle-class blacks—those markers of success and distance. More than that, class position in the black community was part of an intraracial discourse. Teachers, doctors, businesspeople, and others depended on black workers for their economic survival and slightly elevated social position. If the former was denied so too was the latter.

Although we are to assume that acting white carried special meanings among Asians, Native Americans, and Latinos, we do know that all Americans were influenced by the racial structure of the economy. Members of the white majority labeled various aspects of everyday life. Dirty, menial jobs became "nigger work," which signaled a low and degraded status beneath which no self-respecting white person should fall. Throughout the nineteenth century and well into the twentieth—despite regional and temporal variations—jobs such as barbering, hauling, and bricklaying were for blacks only. In places as different as Fargo, North Dakota, and Cleveland, Ohio, black barbers dominated local business as late as 1910. Of course, a lock on these jobs meant that they were excluded from other jobs.

In Pittsburgh, Poles and Italians obtained certain jobs, and once placed, worked very hard to ensure that other members of their family or community benefited. Institutions like the Ateleta Beneficial Association functioned as conduits, funneling information and job prospects between more established Italian residents and new immigrants. As sociologist Carole Marks noted, in 1910, "48 percent of the workers in coal mines were foreign born, 67 percent in iron mines, 76 percent in clothing factories, 76 percent in slaughter and packing houses, and 53 percent in steel mills." More than that, through 1920 labor organizations in places like Pittsburgh became racial and ethnic enclaves, fraternities for "whites" only.

Ironically, at times the racial contours of employment aided nonwhites. In many instances, it allowed them to retain near-exclusive control over certain segments of the labor market. For example, during World War I, when thousands of African Americans migrated to the nation's cities, blacks in Norfolk, Virginia, used their numerical superiority to build a race-conscious labor movement. Starting first with black dockworkers who controlled the Hampton Roads (Virginia) ports, the Transportation Workers Association branched out to include female cigar stemmers, male and female oyster shuckers, and female domestics. State intervention quashed their efforts among the latter groups, but among the longshoremen there was much success. The all-black union successfully negotiated a contract with the shipping lines when government mediators concluded that any closure of the ports jeopardized the war effort. In the end, the men received better pay, improved working conditions, and union recognition. Similar efforts can be documented among Filipino farm workers in California in the 1930s, Chinese laborers who made Chinatowns economic and social islands, and Mexican American agricultural laborers in the 1970s.

Although it is tempting to equate the rise of the United Farm Workers (UFW) with the history of Chicano labor in the twentieth century, the labor market segmentation that made the UFW possible led to labor agitation throughout this century. For example, Mexican and Mexican American laborers in Laredo, Texas, organized an AFL-chartered union in 1905. From 1905 to 1907, members of the union, who worked for the Mexican National railroad, tied worker advancement to group improvement. Primary among their goals was the formation of worker unity on both sides of the borders.

A generation later, Chicano workers in the Southwest turned to the Fair Employment Practices Committee (FEPC) for protection against discrimination. Whites in the region had long held that "I prefer Mexican labor to other classes of labor. It is more humble and you get more for your money." Men like Joe Chavez rejected this cliché; they campaigned for fair labor treatment at the Phelps Dodge mining operations in Arizona. Chicanos would do similarly in the Midwest, joining and promoting labor's causes where and when it made sense. Nor is this history simply the tale of male action. As Vicki Ruiz reminds us, the combined sex and racial segregation of California's food processing industry led many women into the United Cannery, Agricultural, Packing, and Allied Workers of America (UCAPAWA) between 1930 and 1950.

Thus, César Chávez's successful organization of the predominantly Chicano labor force in the California agricultural system should not be viewed as an isolated effort. Mexican and Mexican American workers had a clear history of self-organizing. Moreover, Chávez, who had worked for the Community Service Organization, had a firm understanding of the economics of race. Because most agricultural laborers were Mexican migrants, withholding their labor could bring the agriculture system to its knees and the growers to the bargaining table. Despite grower-supported violence and intimidation, the UFW organized a successful boycott of the grape industry. Because of its success, between 1965 and 1970 a sizable portion of the industry agreed to improving wages and working conditions, and recognizing the UFW.

The confluence of a number of cultural developments expanded the national conversation about race in the 1920s and beyond. Out of the crucible of race emerged new music forms, a renaissance in writing and art, and the genesis of racial image making. The individuals, motifs, forms, and vernaculars became distinctly American.

Nowhere was the racializing of culture more noted than in music. During slavery, music marked important changes in one's life, promised better conditions in heaven, critiqued contemporary conditions, and prefigured the coming of emancipation. Although historians have demarcated the emergence of real divisions between secular and sacred music after emancipation, artists blurred those distinctions in their own lives. The noted gospel singer Mahalia Jackson learned her trade in part by secretly listening to the more bawdy blues songs. Thomas A. Dorsey began his career as a blues pianist in Atlanta and Chicago before he made a lasting contribution as a composer and performer of sacred music like "Precious Lord."

Secular music had only a few locations in which to develop and mature in the early days of the twentieth century. Oftentimes this happened in small clubs or juke joints, cabarets, and brothels. In these venues America first heard ragtime, the blues, and later jazz. With the large commingling of blacks, native whites, and European immigrants in the nation's cities during the 1910s and 1920s, newer and larger clubs appeared in New York, Chicago, Kansas City, and other places with the people and revenue to support them. Usually we associate segregated entertainment with the South, which featured its own racially selective circuit for black entertainers who performed blues and jazz. But even New York clubs like the Cotton Club excluded black would-be patrons, although most performers, dancers, and wait staff were black workers.

Thus the tag of ragtime, the blues, and jazz as "race" music had certain redeeming features when one looks beyond the obviously racist intent. As music designed especially for the black buying audience, estimated at 5 percent in the early 1920s, and based on syncopated polyrhythms, it marked the birth of a truly American art form. Born of the suffering of African Americans, this music also captured the hopes and dreams of those who came of age during the twentieth century. In the progression from rag to blues to jazz to rhythm and blues to soul and then rap, innovation, improvisation, and experimentation became canonized as something distinctly American. In the process, with the aid of radio, the phonograph, and television, a blurring and an understanding occurred. Cross-racial adoption and borrowing became a social mainstay; with it came a certain appreciation and understanding (and occasionally charges of theft).

That is not to say that music lost its racial edge. First it was the blues, then jazz, then R&B and the rock 'n' roll it created; most recently rap and the boombox have become symbols of blackness and danger. But it is not just danger that provokes such strong reactions. These musical forms generated new technologies (choreographed singers, electric guitars, portable stereos) and at a certain level introduced the possibility of racial androgyny. Caught up in the dialectics of racial discourse, most Americans favored certainty to ambiguity because by the 1960s blackness had a value that competed with whiteness. They questioned those things that upset their racial comfort zones. Thus it is all the more ironic that race music evolved into symbols of the "real" America.

The building of this racial comfort zone led to a kind of Mexican American race music as well. For example, during the 1920s and 1930s Mexican American entrepreneurs and musicians brought Mexican folk music to Los Angeles and packaged it for a mass consumer market. On radios and at record shops members of Los Angeles's Chicano community began to hear themselves. Prior to this, it was not uncommon for clubs catering to a Mexican clientele to feature mostly black bands. The mass production of a Chicano sound changed this just as it transformed the sound itself. George Sánchez contends that the *corridos* or folk songs especially appealed to the solidifying Mexican American community because the songs reminded residents of a rural past but reflected an urban present. These songs, much like the African American blues, often commented on the harshness of competing in an urban economy. The first commercially recorded *corrido* was "El Lavaplatos," which detailed the dashed hopes of an immigrant whose dreams of riches never materialized. With middlemen such as Mauricio Calderón connecting talented musicians and record producers, the Mexican American community created its own music form and added immensely to the American cultural mosaic.

Literary artists aided the ongoing discussions, too. Race had been a popular topic in American letters for some time. From James Fenimore Cooper through William Faulkner, whites had sprinkled their stories with the presence of colored others. At times the portrayals were sentimental (for example, Harriet Beecher Stowe); at other times they were unquestionably racist (for example, Thomas Dixon's work). Such writers, satirists, and essayists as H. L. Mencken, Faulkner, and Will Rogers refused to be pigeonholed. Still, race played a prominent role in their critiques and observations.

Perhaps more than any other cultural form, literature obfuscated the connection between race and whiteness. America's so-called race problem always stemmed from the presence of blacks—or Indians, Asians, or Latinos. But as Nobel Prize–winner Toni Morrison observed, even when supposedly ignoring nonwhites, racial conceptions framed narratives. White authors often wrote blacks into spaces ostensibly peopled by whites. Often these dark spots or persons represented anarchy, danger, fear, frivolity, or disease. Whiteness became normative because it had the freedom to appear and develop without paying full attention to the referential other. But as the saying goes, white is significant only if there is black. Race as an idea and ideology functioned well when one could establish contrasts.

America's nonwhites wrote themselves into the nation's literature as well. Nowhere was this more prominent than in the flowering of literary expression among blacks in the 1920s. Known as the Harlem Renaissance, this period produced a cohort of African American men and women like Langston Hughes, Zora Neal Hurston, Countee Cullen, Nella Larson, Jean Toomer, and Claude McKay. As to be expected from a group of such diverse origins and personal histories, for them race had no single meaning. Hughes and Hurston defined themselves as black writers, whereas Cullen and Toomer viewed themselves as writers who happened to be black (Toomer questioned that label). Hughes and Hurston also turned to working-class and poor blacks for inspiration, peopling their stories with individuals seldom heard from before. Although Cullen and Toomer invoked "the folk" as authentic representatives of the race in their works, they both shied away from such affiliations in their personal lives. Larson puzzled through the implications of racial passing and its social and personal consequences, while McKay embraced and rejected nationalism and communism in his lifetime. Collectively, however, this group and its successors introduced an African American vocabulary into the conversation about race. From this point on they demanded a part in the unfolding social construction.

As the dominant purveyors of images, the film industry played a central role in scripting attitudes and opinions about race in the twentieth century. Headed primarily by a mixture of Jewish immigrants and oldtime whites, the major movie studios reflected rather than challenged prevailing assumptions about "good" and "bad." Nowhere was this more obvious than in their generally conservative take on race. Through the 1960s, in films like *Chinatown Nights* or series like *Charlie Chan* (which incidentally featured a white actor in the lead role) Asians frequently appeared as conniving, sneaky, sinister, and dangerous. Blacks figured as either the dutiful, if bumbling, superstitious servant in need of white guidance as in *Gone with the Wind*, or the licentious, dangerous, beast outside the family of humans as in *Birth of a Nation*.

Native and Mexican Americans fared no better. Myth-making about the "taming" of the West depended in large part on the movie industry. Instead of questioning the slaughter of the buffalo, imprisoning of American Indians, and misuse of the environment, Hollywood transformed the human foibles into action-packed adventures. For five cents, millions of American kids watched double features during the Depression that left little doubt about the value of American Indians. Sometimes they were noble but silent savages; other times they were the very antithesis of whiteness. We learned to cheer the cowboys and the cavalry, seldom the movie Indians. As red men and women who spoke funny, dressed peculiarly, practiced pagan rituals, and hampered progress, they were expendable—out of step with a modern world. Stereotyping rather than analyzing became the rule of commercial success. Once the formula proved successful, few defied it.

Hollywood also created definitions of whiteness and stereotyped European immigrants who did not measure up to Anglo standards. Images of the corrupt, clannish Irish hoodlum populated the screen during the 1930s. James Cagney's role in *Public Enemy* solidified his growing reputation as an actor even as it conjured images of criminality in the Irish underworld. Elsewhere films depicting Italians, Jews, and other white ethnics underscored the contestation over the multiple meanings of race in America. Moreover, questions of interethnic marriage, religious difference, and other factors complicated the general storyline by suggesting taboo areas and problematizing the whole meaning of "white." In the process, the manufacturing of an Anglo-Saxon norm became part of a larger Americanization effort.

Racially coded scripts appeared in cartoons, too. For the most part classic productions like *Dumbo* and *The Song of the South,* and even Bugs Bunny played on rather than challenged conventional notions about race. Yet such a declaration assumes an obstructed receipt of transmitted images. We know, however, that individuals often refashioned negatives into positives, as the appropriation and hence neutering of the word *nigger* by blacks suggests. Used as a colloquial expression of fraternity or sorority, the word's negative became a positive. Popular—indeed any—cultural forms could be modified as well.

Yet, even the most innocuous film served as a vehicle for the insidious use of race. In *Dumbo* the main character awakens in a tree after imbibing too much alcohol. Who does he meet but a collection of singing black scarecrows. In obvious black dialect the group breaks into song and dance. Referring to each other as "brothers," the birds offer sentiment in a socially sanctioned style. They also clearly represent blackness in a setting where race is otherwise obscured. The rat who accompanies Dumbo on his drinking binge calls the crows "boys," a clear reference to their subordinate status. Moreover, when they embrace him as a brother, he quickly retorts he "ain't their brother." Subtle to be sure, this exchange was nonetheless very racial. This time, however, it is the birds who assume the role of instructor. Just as Bill "Bojangles" Robinson instructed the child star Shirley Temple to dance without surrendering the facade of subservience, the crows, once established as black boys (read Negroes), teach the seemingly raceless young elephant to fly. They do so, however, by using psychology, telling the beast that a special feather endows him with the power to defy gravity. The psychological ploy becomes a strategy for the crows to demonstrate their superiority without inviting retribution. In many ways the ploy serves as a trope for blacks who claimed a place in an exceedingly race-conscious society. Thus, race was as much a part of the text as it was in movies where Bugs Bunny dressed in blackface and whistled "Dixie."

Before one reads the story of Hollywood and popular culture as one giant conspiracy, it is well worth remembering that individuals who commanded new technologies both anticipated and reflected attitudes. Because race functioned as one constitutive element of the self, the distinction between race as an ideology or idea could be confusing. Through World War II, nothing demonstrated this more than the Amos 'n' Andy radio show. Long before a multitude of African Americans objected to the stereotyped images, many embraced the characters as facsimiles of the real—or at least the plausible. More knowledgeable whites found comfort in the familiar and whites who knew no blacks enjoyed their brief sojourns into a world that was otherwise off limits.

For nearly two decades the radio duo who created the characters negotiated the pitfalls of race by presenting a comfortably human set of characters without requiring a drastic reordering of belief systems. For years white artists had donned blackface and become what they supposedly never wanted to be and what they could not become at one level: black. In the past, however, whites seldom played these roles for blacks. Building on a minstrel and vaudeville tradition, the two white performers, Freeman Gosden and Charles Correll, served up corrupt whites, gullible blacks, man-eating black women, pretentious black men, and a wide assortment of others. Almost daily for more than a decade and a half, and after 1943 weekly, millions of Americans listened to the adventures of Amos, Andy, and their friends. Although the black characters had a depth of humanity generally denied them in other media, little challenged conventions. Thus why blacks enjoyed the show is an interesting question. Certainly some middle-class African Americans abhorred the less than flattering portrait. But in the 1930s, Roy Wilkins, future head of the NAACP and, with his predecessor Walter White, a strong opponent of the television version, endorsed the radio format as harmless entertainment. Nor was Wilkins in the minority. Maybe because blacks knew that whites enlivened the voices they could treat the show as a fiction, a funny one at that. In addition, black comedians had attracted large followings by adopting some of the same routines. Perhaps, too, blacks read the scripts differently. Signs of ineptness registered as veiled protests; assertive women bespoke early brands of feminism; inflated language and exaggerated behavior highlighted the difficulties of migration. Ultimately, many blacks expected no more than tokens of truth from whites; to their credit, Gosden and Correll delivered. In the end, by seeking sanctuary in racially secure spaces, black and white audiences reinforced rather than subverted pre–World War II racial meanings. After the war, the ground rules changed, especially concerning matters of race.

THE NEW POLITICS OF RACE

The confluence of domestic and international events forever modified interpretations about the saliency of race. The atrocities of Nazi Germany confounded those in America who had accepted the basic belief that Europeans were white. Hitler successfully challenged the efficacy of the intraracial covenant. By killing more than six million Jews, gypsies, gays, North Africans, and others in the name of racial purity, he unveiled the true underbelly of a vigorously discriminatory racist belief system. Worse, he demonstrated the horrible capacity of the state to act on race as idea (certain people are different) and ideology (certain differences justify the elimination of the outsider).

The state-approved internment of Japanese Americans because of their difference narrowed the gulf between German atrocities and American practices. To be sure, the American government did not authorize the wholesale slaughter of millions of people because of their race. Yet this same government authorized doctors to infect African Americans in Tuskegee with syphilis for "scientific" benefit, evincing total disregard for the well-being of the expendable patients. Likewise, a series of courts and government bodies upheld the imprisoning of Nisei and Issei generation Japanese and Japanese Americans because many feared that their racial allegiance to a distant homeland overrode their allegiance to America.

Questions of democracy and race reverberated throughout the nation with wildly fascinating results. Concern with India's role in the war led Congress to heed the urging of Mubarak Ali Khan and the Indian Welfare League and open the door for Asian Indians to become citizens in 1946; other bills eased the restrictions on Chinese exclusion. Federal legislation prohibiting racial discrimination in government employment and the endless demand for labor enabled women of all races, and nonwhite men in great numbers, to work in factory settings previously closed to them. For a time the glass ceiling in employment was raised.

More commonly, international animosities spilled over stateside. Korean and Chinese Americans shared their mastery of Japanese with other Americans. Some even formed ethnic military units and volunteered for service abroad. Meanwhile Filipino Americans, upset by Japanese colonialism in Asia, cheered and benefited from the internment of Japanese Americans. By joining the armed forces for nationalist and patriotic reasons, hundreds of Filipinos gained citizenship rights, and the deeds to Japanese-owned property in California.

Still, their roles in the liberation of the Philippines could not erase decades of racial prejudice. To many whites, especially in California, Filipinos remained the "little brown men." Worse, they remained the nonwhite men who lusted after and won the favor of white women. Much of the conversation about race turned on the sexual politics of interracial relations. Uneven sex ratios among most Asian groups had produced decidedly male communities. In California, Asian Indians addressed the difficulties by marrying the most likely and socially feasible group: Mexican Americans. According to Karen Leonard, after ruling out white and black women except in rare instances—the former because of their high status and the latter their low status—Punjabi immigrants formed unions with Mexican Americans, further complicating racial categories.

Filipinos, on the other hand, defied accepted wisdom about the size and makeup of the marriage market. Rejecting notions of racial purity, unhampered by traditions of arranged marriages, many Filipino men believed white women suitable and available partners. The conflict that ensued reminded writers like Philippines-born Carlos Bulosan of the power of race in his adopted land. Even the donning of a military uniform, and the increased possibility of death in the South Pacific did little to mark him as other than a "stranger from a different shore."

As much as anything, however, the war unleashed a number of transformative social forces that brought down the weakened edifice of racial segregation and the accompanying covenant predicated on white superiority. First, the dramatic movement of America's peoples altered urban politics and upset white male control of labor and employment. More than three million blacks left the rural South between 1940 and 1960. Thousands made their way north and west. Thousands of others followed relatives to the urban South. By the middle 1950s cities like Birmingham, Mobile, New Orleans, and Washington, D.C., were between one-third and one-half black. By the 1970s, many of the nation's cities had become more than half black.

Expanded employment opportunities came with this dramatic movement out of the rural South. In large part this was a by-product of inroads made during the war years. With the lukewarm backing of the federal government Asians, blacks, Chicanos, and women of all races entered industrial employment. Although many women lost these jobs to returning GIs when the war ended, black male opportunity contracted partially but not completely. As a result, the income gap between black and white men narrowed during the period from 1940 to 1960. In 1939, black men earned about 41 cents for every dollar earned by a white man. And although parity was never achieved, by 1959 the ratio was 47 cents for every dollar, increasing to 63 cents per dollar by the early 1970s, a pattern repeated for the South and between black and white women.

In addition, the war highlighted the gap between the American ideal and the reality of racial prejudice and discrimination. One-time radical George Schuyler harped, "Our Fight Is Not against the Hitlers Abroad, But the Hitlers at Home." More than a decade before Rosa Parks's heroic action galvanized a community and spawned a national movement, blacks in Birmingham and Norfolk challenged segregation ordinances and the ideologies that supported them. Although their efforts were modest, they signaled a pending change in America's racial history.

Then in November 1954 the United State Supreme Court altered the trajectory of what the Swedish economist Gunnar Myrdal had called America's dilemma. Since the 1920s, blacks and whites affiliated with the NAACP had engineered a careful, yet measured, assault on the legality of "separate but equal." Segregation had functioned as the cornerstone of a racial belief system. It enabled whites to rationalize racism without asking if they were racists. It encouraged nonwhites to settle for a second-class citizenship because the state had deemed it constitutional. Then *Brown* v. *Board of Education,* which ruled separate but equal unconstitutional, cancelled a half-century of negotiated order. Some predicted the immediate downfall of America; others expected a period of immediate reconciliation. Neither happened of course.

Race had been and still is about ordering the disparate parts of one's world. Thus people who deny race as a biological category find themselves playing the racial guessing game. They look at people of ambiguous origins and try and place them in a previously agreed-on box. Through the 1960s, few fretted over the basic outline of this understanding. When doubt had arisen, the state had heretofore stepped in and reestablished order and hierarchy. *Brown,* however, indicated that the state, in a liberal retreat from a racist posture, was about to undo one social construction without constructing a new reality. Aware of its complicated role, the Court eased the shock by allowing the process of school desegregation to take more than twenty years. It was powerless to prevent the bloodshed that resulted.

The mid-1950s through the mid-1970s were some of the most violent years in American history. A lot of that violence grew out of the post-1954 conversation about race. On the heels of the Court decision blacks in countless southern communities engineered campaigns to end all traces of Jim Crowism. Montgomery, which catapulted Dr. Martin Luther King, Jr., into the national spotlight, might be the most well-known site, but similar efforts took place in Baton Rouge, Mobile, Danville, and Greensboro, among others. These hard-won successes were punctuated by scenes of unadulterated brutality. From the murder of Emmett Till for whistling at a white woman, to the murder of civil rights workers Chaney, Goodman, and Schwerner; from the vicious attacks on the Freedom Riders through the bombing deaths of four black girls attending a Birmingham Sunday school; from the riots that rocked Watts in 1965 through the uprising following the initial acquittal of the police batterers of Rodney King; from the death of a child in the spring of life in New York City to the vengeful murder of an innocent rabbinical student a few blocks away—the nation has forged a new link between race and identity, race, and violence.

Students of American history will rightly note that this is nothing new; violence has always been a part of America's racial history. And indeed there is an element of continuity between pre-1954 violence and post-*Brown* violence. What has changed, and what has changed the meaning of violence, has been the shift from the politics of identity—so key to any understanding of race in the twentieth century—to identity politics. By "identity politics" I mean the unerring sense that each individual has only one salient identity, most often a racial or ethnic identity. Proponents of identity politics underscore the ideological dimensions of race even as they come close to speaking of race as a naturalized condition. Identity politics also frequently leads to a kind of racial chauvinism that precludes intergroup coalition building. By contrast, the politics of identity acknowledges the multiplicity of identities (i.e., race, gender, sexual orientation, age, class) that move from the foreground to the background depending on the circumstances. Its proponents are not blind to the ideological dimensions of race, but because race is among a number of factors that explain who they are, they are more inclined to treat race as a notion or idea. They are also more likely to seek and sustain intergroup cooperation.

No one event produced the change and no one moment captures the full effects of the change. Much of what transpired between 1954 and 1968 was quite subtle. For instance, increased numbers and expanded buying power bolstered the power and effectiveness of economic boycotts in space and time from Montgomery to Memphis—1954 to 1968. As part of the process, a cross section of African Americans experienced a revolution of the mind. Sit-ins, voter registration campaigns, education camps, and militant action empowered a generation to demand the unthinkable: equality and equity.

Meanwhile, television seared the cruelties of southern and northern racism into the consciousness of a nation better than Richard Wright's *Native Son* or Ralph Ellison's *Invisible Man*. Only the most hardened supremacist could sanction the hosing of young children in 1963 Birmingham or the beating of schoolchildren in Boston a decade later. The news upset the facade of a complacent America where everyone was happy and knew their place. After all, this was the age of *Father Knows Best*. On television only Desi Arnaz, the "hot blooded Cuban," violated social strictures, and even here gender perceptions made his actions tolerable. Whereas Jackie Gleason's working-class character promised to belt his television wife, he never did. Physical assault, while common in America's ethnic enclaves, was not something television producers (and we assume their audiences) wished rehearsed during the entertainment hour. With the pretense of a needed spanking, Desi alone assaulted his wife on a regular basis. He, of course, was not responsible, it was his Latin temper, and in an earlier day, his race.

The period also witnessed the breakup of white ethnic neighborhoods in many cities and the movement of middle- and working-class whites to the suburbs in a volume that outpaced the movement of nonwhites to the cities. Unscrupulous real estate agents, especially after the outbreak of race riots from 1964 to 1968, used the fears of whites to "bust" blocks in places as far removed as the Dorchester section of Boston and North Minneapolis. Sometimes it took the presence of one nonwhite; most often several had to move in before alarmed whites sold property at a bargain before selling, they were told, would be impossible. As a result, between 1970 and 1980 Detroit's population went from 43.6 to 63.1 percent black, Atlanta's from 51.3 to 66.6 percent, and Birmingham's from 42.0 to 55.6 percent.

Thousands moved to the ever-growing suburbs. Postwar suburbanization created islands of homogeneity. Designed for the well-heeled as well as the average worker, these postwar communities were readily available, low in density, familiar in style, and removed from the central city; more important, for nearly two decades they remained racially exclusive. Thus despite the 1948 prohibition against restrictive covenants and the 1968 Fair Housing Act, housing served to racialize space. Ghettos became the places where blacks, Latinos, and a few Asians resided. Ghetto-style became the style of African Americans or Latinos. And once again whites who invaded these spots were slumming, trying to be cool, or liberal do-gooders.

In the meantime, the state confused matters by working at cross purposes. When the Supreme Court ruled in *Loving* v. *Virginia* (1967) that state prohibitions against interracial marriage were unconstitutional, it tackled the last taboo. This was the genie most Americans wanted kept in the bottle. Despite claims to the contrary, chauvinism was not the province of whites exclusively. Interracial marriage remains low in America because of the lessons previously taught and currently retaught. As late as the 1980s, California resident Joyce Hoffman told sociologist Mary Waters: "I always knew that I should not date blacks." And in 1992 novelist Bebe Moore Campbell expressed outrage and a sense of rejection whenever she eyed a black man with a white woman.

The FBI under J. Edgar Hoover was not prepared to take such a hands-off approach. Against the backdrop of African Americans chanting "Black Power," images of gun-toting Black Panthers descending on the California state legislature or students with bandoliers commandeering buildings at Columbia and Cornell, Hoover portrayed black, Chicano, and Indian groups as a dangerous threat. His carefully crafted program of terror designed to eliminate these threats produced quiet indifference in certain quarters and vocal support in others. Most Americans were unaware of the state's full involvement; they were aware of the change in mood, however.

According to public surveys conducted in the early 1960s, race was a major national problem. This had not always been the case. In the 1940s, improved interracial relations ranked low on a list of priorities for whites. But once the breach occurred in 1954, and sensitized by the public education they received, white Americans told pollsters that something must be done. In some respects a consensus had emerged, with national leaders pointing the way. By 1970, most whites had concluded that enough had been done. They cited new federal legislation, court injunctions, and cries of affirmative action to ask, what more do those people want? Far out of proportion with the likelihood of personal danger, they feared these other Americans. Bussing meant that the suburbs or ethnic neighborhoods were no longer safe fortresses. Whites reconstructed themselves as aggrieved white ethnics and a backlash was unleashed.

From the New Deal through 1968, race in America was informed by the politics of identity. Whites and nonwhites struggled against their parochialism and prejudices to form broad alliances where possible and feasible. The labor movement proved an important element. Begrudgingly, the AFL, spurred by the successes of the CIO, opened its doors to blacks and Chicanos in greater numbers. With the merger of the two unions in the 1950s came a greater push. Unions contributed to civil rights campaigns in the South, sponsored broad-based rallies in the North and West. Race, therefore, became just one part of the individual; class, gender, sexual orientation, and age could inflate or deflate race's importance at any moment.

Identity politics, however, turned on race as the fundamental identity. The children of European immigrants, who feared a loss of mobility, redefined themselves as white ethnics. Class, religion, and customs still marked them as non-Anglo. But as the social critic Michael Novak observed, they worried that the new racial dialogue benefited blacks and browns, penalized them, and left the old white elite untouched. They defined themselves in opposition to America's nonwhites. Maude Wiley, a white informant, told the sociologist Bob Blauner and his team of interviewers what many sensed: "They [whites] felt, well, these colored people were just pushing 'em away and trying to take over, you know, and be better than they were!"

Politicians and public commentators capitalized on this anxiety, inflaming public sensibilities, and encouraging the retreat to identity politics. New words with obvious and coded racial meanings—reverse discrimination, welfare queen, quotas, illiberal, affirmative action, and special interests—entered the language system. George Wallace measured the pulse of that portion of the electorate that felt vulnerable. He appealed to their collective anxieties, winning stunning victories or followings in the North and South. According to the historian Dan Carter, he developed a strategy quickly adopted and perfected by the Republican party. Southern white voters shifted to the Republican party faster as nonwhites took their turns as heads of the nation's larger cities. In northern communities like Warren, Michigan, whites who voted Democratic in local elections voted Republican in national elections. Richard Nixon, Ronald Reagan, and George Bush promised to put them first, using messages notable for their racial content.

It is hard, however, to pinpoint the arrows of cause and effect. Nonwhites also practiced identity politics in greater numbers and with more focus. Among African Americans few black power advocates or Afrocentric originists considered the rebukes of Du Bois or Alain Locke. Many viewed race as a primordial condition as much as their white counterpart or adversary. But to argue that black is beautiful was one thing, to argue that only black is beautiful moved the discussion closer to an essentialist logic.

Such an orientation also alienated those who recognized the saliency of racism but questioned the meaning of race. On college campuses the debates raged—and rage. Afro-American and Ethnic Studies units struck some as the ultimate surrender to the logic of race. These charges had some merit. In some cases, obsequious college administrators allowed anyone who professed an experiential or partial knowledge of their subject matter to teach. We can also point to a few examples of individuals promoted from assistant to full professor without accumulating the expected plaudits along the way. Yet by 1980 few nonacademic trained scholars survived. Those who remained earned a reputation as traditional scholars; they researched, footnoted, and critically examined their topic of study, despite continued attacks from social and academic activists on the right and the left.

Yet the racial aspects of identity politics have distorted the record of these scholars and muddled the larger discourse. Exaggerated claims become the focal point of public discussion. Thus Afrocentricity is reduced to the most outrageous statement or specious claims. To be sure, public intellectuals such as Henry Louis Gates, Jr., Cornel West, and Adolph Reed have attacked aspects of identity politics, but their efforts have been outnumbered by those who proclaim it the new truth. As a result, community leaders and educators overstate the redemptive value of "knowing one's history," ignoring in the process the profound structural changes that have occurred since the early 1960s. Young people accept the most vocal as merchants of truth or adopt the latest lesson gleaned from popular culture, without bothering to investigate, interrogate, or interpret.

At the same time, a new vocabulary is introduced that turns on identity politics. Most notable has been the phrase "people of color." Before the 1960s, "colored" pushed one closer to blacks, and Asians, Chicanos, and Native Americans understood the limits of such a strategy. Individuals did form cross-racial alliances, but group mergers came rarely. Then the 1960s gave way to broader pan-racial creations. The American Indian Movement, building on grassroots efforts dating from the 1940s, attempted to forge a common purpose among the country's many Indian people. After the brutal murder of Vincent Chin (a second-generation Chinese American who was perceived to be Japanese) by two unemployed white autoworkers in Detroit, a broad coalition of Asians formed the American Citizens for Justice in recognition of their common plight. Once organized, the other nonwhites insisted on an audience seldom granted them. They understood, however, the politics of race in America. As a result, on college campuses nonwhite students began referring to themselves as students of color, which gave way to people of color. The phrase resonated with the times.

The implied coalition works at the grand level a lot better than it works at the local level. California, the state with the most dramatic demographic transition shows its strengths and weaknesses. Demographers estimate that nonwhites will make up the majority of residents of the state by the second decade of the twenty-first century. At the University of California at Berkeley and at UCLA, that future is reality. Since the fall of 1989, whites have made up a minority of the first-year class. This happened after the Asian community successfully sued the university for discrimination, noting that numerous qualified Asians had been denied admission to protect slots for whites, and by inference blacks and browns. In a less elite setting, raw animosities pepper relations between Korean merchants and their black customers in Los Angeles and New York and between African American and Latino residents in Miami. In the competition over access, mobility, and standing, we are clearly in a profound state of flux. "People of color" works better as a metaphor than as a practical description of a new form of racial politics. It works as a metaphor because we wrestle with identity politics.

Unavoidably, such broad-stroke analysis misses certain nuances and contradictions. For example, middle-class Asians, blacks, and Latinos gained the most from the affirmative action programs. Economics are creating hyper-racial zones. It is not just nonwhites who live in the ghetto, but poor nonwhites, primarily. Their middle-class relatives are often as uncomfortable in these zones as whites. As a result, class, gender, and regional differences crosscut claims of racial belonging. In 1984, a majority of white kids called Bill Cosby their principal hero. Nonwhite authors have experienced a wide public and critical acceptance. Until recently, public bigotry had become anachronistic. And across the South the visible vestiges of the Jim Crow era had all but disappeared. Yet, America is more residentially segregated than ever before. In some big cities nonwhite children are less likely to attend integrated schools than their parents were. And, of course, the most public debate about sexual harassment featured a black woman and a black man (Anita Hill and Clarence Thomas).

It is the Hill-Thomas encounter, more than the neoconservative tracts, violent acts of racism, prominent portraits of nonwhites in the media, or spate of new books about race that define the present moment. No event in the modern history of race in America digs as deep into the nation's history and rushes us as far into the near future as that exchange. More than any event in recent memory it encapsulated the shift from the politics of identity to identity politics—and much more.

Briefly telescoped, the controversy was about gender and sexual discrimination. A credible black woman alleged that her black male superior had used his power to intimidate and harass her. Others contradicted her claim, but her testimony was believable. Women of color had long kept quiet when men in their communities violated their bodies. Some even lost their voices, undergoing a process of dissemblance. Remarkably, after a decade of silence Hill recovered her voice, and in so doing became a symbol of women's struggles for dignity nationwide.

During the course of congressional hearings, Thomas moved the discussion from the abuse of Hill's body to the abuse of his body. The staged shift from a discussion of sexual harassment to lynching brought back a century of memories and images of racial violation. In so doing, Thomas attempted to show that no discussion of sexual harassment could occur without talking about race. African Americans, already tense over the prospects of losing "their" seat on the Supreme Court, ultimately surrendered to this kind of identity politics. Thousands, in fact, may have doubted Thomas's truthfulness but found comfort in the prospect of one of theirs serving on the bench. Never mind the obvious question: What made Clarence Thomas or Anita Hill one of them? The answer to that question returns us to the observation that race is both an idea and an ideology, and underscores the power of the eye to structure a social reality built on the shaky foundation of a shared memory.

Race has been the one thing that we think we know about the other. Stripped of power, presented in such a neutral tone, it is the logical conclusion to the mind's game of ordering and categorizing. Forced back into historical context, race fits neatly into a hierarchy of logic and privilege. It provided the cover for making some Americans slaves and others their masters. It enabled men and women of reason to die because their look differed from what the majority defined as normative. It transformed the states into matchmakers and marriage brokers. More than that it marred the meaning of democracy by limiting its full extension.

Race also filtered into the language, culture, and customs of a people. Despite racial prescriptions and prohibitions, people overcame harsh existences to assert their humanity and right to be heard. Aspects of race introduced new cultural forms and idioms, produced important works of insight and understanding, and transformed dreams into realities. It also tied together groups and created communities of belonging where lines of allegiance were otherwise fragile.

Race is a social construction and much more. Once endowed with a history and meaning, people of all backgrounds built their own reality. Clearly none of this was possible without the able and willing involvement of the state. After all, only the state had the might to tell Asian Indians they were Caucasian but not white. Only the state could code, recode, decode the formal aspects of race, as it did every decennial. Moreover, the state's sudden change of direction in the 1950s and 1960s, and equally puzzling reversal in the 1970s and 1980s led to the breakdown in dialogue. In the struggle to order their world, many Americans substituted the politics of identity with identity politics. The latter treats race as the most important aspect of life, blinding many to other possibilities.

Yet, it is also true that race functioned at many levels and often in unpredictable manners. It is possible to pinpoint trends but equally important to highlight deviations. Because race functioned as an idea and ideology people viewed themselves as active participants in the ongoing dialogue. This dialogue changed with shifts in the political economy. As a result, race remains our greatest fiction, greatest fascination, and greatest "truth." It is what made Arthur Ashe, a few months before his premature death, fret over the color of a doll his daughter held before a national television audience. As he philosophized, it should not have mattered. But it did, of course. Sadly, but too often, race defines a large part of what it means to be an American.

SEE ALSO Gender Issues; Ethnicity and Immigration; Class (all in this volume); African American Cultural Movements (volume IV); Social Welfare (in this volume); Wealth and Poverty (volume III).

BIBLIOGRAPHY

Novelists such as Charles W. Chesnutt, in *The House Behind the Cedars* (1900), and scholars such as Barbara Jeanne Fields, "Ideology and Race in American History," in *Region, Race and Reconstruction,* ed., J. Morgan Kousser and James M. McPherson (1982), and "Slavery, Race and Ideology in the United States of America," *New Left Review* (May/June 1990), discuss the ideological basis of race. Other assessments are offered by Thomas F. Gossett, *Race: The History of an Idea in America* (1965); Ashley Montagu, *Man's*

Most Dangerous Myth: The Fallacy of Race (1974); Stephen Jay Gould, *The Mismeasure of Man* (1981); and Michael Omi and Howard Winant, *Racial Formation in the United States* (1986). These works echo sentiments made by Alain Locke and W. E. B. Du Bois at the turn of the century. For references, see Alain LeRoy Locke, *Race Contacts and Interracial Relations* (1992); and W. E. B. Du Bois, *Darkwater, Voices from Within the Veil* (1920). Henry Louis Gates, ed., *"Race," Writing, and Difference* (1986), helps situate race as a study of difference; as does Abdul R. JanMohamed and David Lloyd, eds., *The Nature and Context of Minority Discourse* (1990).

For a discussion of the relationship between race and ethnicity, see David Hollinger, "Postethnic America," *Contention* (1992). Benedict Anderson, in *Imagined Communities* (1991), draws the implications between group identity and nationalism, which has a bearing on racial thought as well. The historical roots of racial identification and prejudice are discussed in *The Negro in Virginia* (1940); Winthrop Jordan, *White over Black* (1969); George Fredrickson, *The Black Image in the White Mind* (1971); Robert F. Heizer, *The Other Californians: Prejudice and Discrimination under Spain, Mexico, and the United States* (1971); A. Leon Higginbotham, *In the Matter of Color* (1980); and T. H. Breen and Stephen Innes, *Myne Owne Ground* (1980).

On the complicated construction of a pan-Indian identity among the many different Native Americans, read fine studies by Ramón Gutiérrez, *When Jesus Came, the Corn Mothers Went Away* (1991); and Richard White, *The Middle Ground* (1991). On the blurring of race and the connection to gender see June Namias, *White Captives* (1993).

Biracial relations and the complications that resulted are featured in Adele Logan Alexander, *Ambiguous Lives* (1991); Michael Johnson and James Roark, *Black Masters* (1984); and William McFeely, *Frederick Douglass* (1991). Leon Litwack's *North of Slavery* (1961) remains the classic treatment of the subject. And Ira Berlin, *Slaves Without Masters* (1974), offers the best overview of free blacks in the South. In reviewing the literature on race and ideology in the nineteenth century, see Ronald Takaki, *Iron Cages* (1979), and *Strangers from a Different Shore* (1989); Drew Gilpin Faust, ed., *The Ideology of Slavery* (1981); John S. Haller, *Outcasts from Evolution* (1971); and Lawrence H. Fuchs, *The American Kaleidoscope: Race, Ethnicity, and the Civic Culture* (1990). Other useful volumes are Edward Ayers, *The Promise of the New South* (1992); Joel Williamson, *A Rage for Order* (1986); Joseph Boskin, *Sambo* (1986); and C. Vann Woodward, *Origins of the New South, 1877–1913* (1967).

The critical question of who is white is raised in a number of volumes on immigration, Americanization, and race. Consult F. James Davis, *Who Is Black?* (1991), for a discussion of the other side of the issue. The state's role in assigning race is mentioned in Margo J. Anderson, *The American Census* (1988). Stanley Lieberson drew attention to nonethnic naming in *A Piece of the Pie* (1980). Among the studies of immigration, race, and race suicide are William A. Ripley, *The Races of Europe* (1899); John R. Commons, *Races and Immigrants in America* (1907); M. S. Iseman, *Race Suicide* (1912); and Madison Grant, *The Passing of the Great Race* (1921).

For general treatments of individual immigrant groups review the following volumes: Oscar Handlin, *The Uprooted* (1951); John Higham, *Strangers in the Land* (1963); Virginia Yans-McLaughlin, ed., *Immigration Reconsidered* (1990); and Leonard Dinnerstein, *Natives and Strangers* (1990). The Cuban example is mentioned in Nancy Mirabal, "The Afro-Cuban Community in Ybor City and Tampa," *OAH Magazine of History* (Summer 1993).

The most recent views on the Leo Frank case are detailed in Jacquelyn Dowd Hall, "Private Eyes, Public Women: Images of Class and Sex in the Urban South, Atlanta, Georgia, 1913–1915," in *Work Engendered,* ed., Ava Baron (1991); and Nancy McLean, "The Leo Frank Case Reconsidered: Gender and Sexual Politics in the Making of Reactionary Populism," *Journal of American History* (December 1991). Americanization efforts and violence is the subject of David Chalmers, *Hooded Americanisms* (1965); and Kathleen M. Blee, *Women of the Klan* (1991).

David Roedigger and Eric Lott offer a broad analysis of the making of working-class white identity; see, respectively, *The Wages of Whiteness* (1991), and *Love and Theft* (1993). In addition to previously cited works, see also David Montejano, *Anglos and Mexicans in the Making of Texas, 1836–1986* (1987); Mario T. Garcia, *Mexican Americans* (1989); Susan E. Keefe and Amado M. Padilla, *Chicano Ethnicity* (1987); and Alfredo Mirande, *The Chicano Experience* (1985). Donald A. Grinde and Quintard Taylor, "Red vs Black: Conflict and Accommodation in the Post Civil War Indian Territory, 1865–1907," *American Indian Quarterly* (Summer 1984), and Alvin M. Josephy, *Red Power* (1971), tender useful treatments of Native Americans. For Asians, see Takaki's *Strangers from a Different Shore.*

A broad discussion of the power dynamics of race are noted in John Hope Franklin and Alfred A. Moss,

Jr., *From Slavery to Freedom* (1988). The best single study of the *Plessy* case is Charles A. Lofgren, *The Plessy Case* (1987). On Mississippi during the age of Jim Crow, see Neil McMillan, *Dark Journey* (1990). The history of Jim Crow is revealed in C. Vann Woodward, *The Strange Career of Jim Crow* (1974). Randy Roberts's *Papa Jack* (1983) remains the best social history of Jack Johnson and his times. Benjamin Mays's recollection of the riotous conclusion to the Johnson-Jeffries bout is provided in his autobiography *Born to Rebel* (1971). Race and gender dynamics are the focus of Ellen DuBois and Vicki L. Ruiz, eds., *Unequal Sisters* (1990). To understand the effects of border crossings for Mexican migrants see George Sánchez, *Becoming Mexican American* (1993). The rise of pre–World War I black leaders is reviewed in John Hope Franklin and August Meier, eds., *Black Leaders in the Twentieth Century* (1982). See also August Meier, *Negro Thought in America, 1880–1915* (1966); Louis Harlan, *Booker T. Washington: The Making of a Black Leader, 1865–1901* (1972), and *Booker T. Washington: The Wizard of Tuskegee, 1901–1915* (1983); and David Levering Lewis, *W. E. B. Du Bois: Biography of a Race* (1993). The literature on Garvey is voluminous. Consult Lawrence Levine for a general overview of Garvey and his uses of race, "Marcus Garvey and the Politics of Revitalization," in *Black Leaders in the Twentieth Century* (1982). And the contours of African American migration are noted in Joe William Trotter, ed., *Black Migration in Historical Perspective* (1992). The poem referenced in the text can be found in the National Urban League Papers at the Library of Congress.

The autobiographical literature includes several references to color and the power dynamics of race. For example, read Lillian Smith, *Killers of the Dream* (1949); Helen Jackson Lee, *A Nigger in the Window* (1978); and Alice Dunnigan, *A Black Woman's Experience* (1974).

In addition to the volumes previously cited, for an understanding of the relationship between racial ideology and work the following books are useful: Earl Lewis, *In Their Own Interests* (1991); Carol Marks, *Farewell—We're Good and Gone* (1990); and John Bodnar, Roger Simon, and Michael P. Weber, *Lives of Their Own* (1982). The history of Mexican workers can be ascertained from reading Erasmo Gamboa, *Mexican Labor and World War II* (1990); Emilio Zamora, *The World of the Mexican Worker in Texas* (1993); Clete Daniels, *Chicano Workers and the Politics of Fairness* (1991); and Vicki Ruiz, *Cannery Women, Cannery Lives* (1987).

Several books aided my understanding of race, culture, and music. Among the selected volumes are Eileen Southern, *The Music of Black Americans* (1983); Houston A. Baker, *Blues, Ideology, and Afro-American Literature* (1984); Lawrence Levine, *Black Culture and Black Consciousness* (1979); and Michael Harris, *The Rise of Gospel Music* (1992). On parallels within the Chicano community, read Sánchez, *Becoming Mexican American*. Nathan I. Huggins has written the most useful overview of the Harlem Renaissance, *Harlem Renaissance* (1971). It should be read along with David Levering Lewis, *When Harlem Was in Vogue* (1979). The writing of race onto a nonracial terrain is developed in Toni Morrison, *Playing in The Dark* (1992). The movies of the 1930s are reviewed in Carlos Clarens, *Crime Movies* (1980). As for the Amos 'n' Andy show, see Melvin Patrick Ely, *The Adventures of Amos 'n' Andy* (1991).

The new politics of race began during the 1940s. To understand that period one should read a number of the books already cited. For the Asian American experience a good starting point is Takaki's *Strangers from a Different Shore*. Supplement that reading with Evelyn Nakano Glenn, *Issei, Nisei, War Bride* (1986); Yuji Ichioka, *The Issei* (1988); and Karen Isaksen Leonard, *Making Ethnic Choices* (1992). The postwar changes in the black communities are discussed in Richard Kluger, *Simple Justice* (1977); William Julius Wilson, *The Declining Significance of Race* (1980); Aldon Morris, *The Origins of the Civil Rights Movement* (1984); and Reynolds Farley and Walter Allen, *The Color Line and the Quality of Life in America* (1989). On television and race during the Cold War period, read George Lipsitz, *Time Passages* (1990).

Suburbanization and the claiming of white ethnic identities undergirded the shift to identity politics. The process of suburbanization is delineated in Kenneth Jackson, *Crabgrass Frontier* (1985). The connection between ethnic identity, race, and housing is the topic of Hillel Levine and Lawrence Harmon, *The Death of an American Jewish Community* (1992). Michael Novak, *The Rise of the Unmeltable Ethnics* (1972), first drew the nation's attention to this population. Questions of social mobility and integration had been raised a decade earlier in Nathan Glazer and Daniel Patrick Moynihan, *Beyond the Melting Pot* (1963). The issues were just as raw in the late 1980s when Waters and Blauner interviewed subjects about their racial and ethnic views: see, respectively, Mary C. Waters, *Ethnic Options* (1990); and Bob Blauner, *Black Lives, White Lives* (1990). Nonetheless, as Richard Griswold del Castillo reported in *La Familia* (1984), Mexican Americans, for instance, were not opposed to marrying members of other racial groups.

State hostilities were an important part of the shift in emphasis. On the rise of "Black Power" and racial pride among nonwhites, see William L. Van Deburg, *New Day in Babylon* (1992). A pan-Asian consciousness is discussed in Yen Le Esperitu, *Asian American Panethnicity* (1992). Native American social and cultural actions are the topics of essays in William George Cronon and Jay Gitlin Miles, eds., *Under an Open Sky: Rethinking America's Western Past* (1992). Kenneth O'Reilly examines the FBI's hostile responses to social change in *Racial Matters* (1989). Within the academy, Molefi Asante helped frame the debate over Afrocentricity in a number of books; for a sense of his general view, read *The Afrocentric Idea* (1987). At the same time, another group of nonwhite scholars have asked a different set of questions about race and America. Among them are Evelyn Brooks Higginbotham, "African-American Women's History and the Metalanguage of Race," *Signs* (Winter 1992); and Patricia Williams, *The Alchemy of Race and Rights* (1991). For the conflict between blacks and Asians that threatened any hope for a people-of-color coalition, examine Ivan Light and Edna Bonacich, *Immigrant Entrepreneurs: Koreans in Los Angeles, 1965–1982* (1988).

The Hill-Thomas controversy is the topic of two important books of essays. For a sense of the varied and complicated reactions that were nonetheless racialized, see Robert Chrisman and Richard Allen, ed., *Court of Appeal* (1992) and Toni Morrison, ed., *Race-ing Justice, En-gendering Power* (1992).

Finally, a number of scholars have challenged the architects of identity politics. The list includes Cornel West, Henry Louis Gates, Jr., Adolph Reed, Stephen Carter, and Randall Kennedy. Although they espouse different personal politics, indicative of the group that believes race is a social construction and eschews identity politics are Kwame Anthony Appiah, *In My Father's House* (1992); and Shelby Steele, *The Content of Our Character* (1991). Arthur Ashe's poignant reminder of race's powerful hold can be read in Ashe and Arnold Rampersad, *Days of Grace: A Memoir* (1993).

ETHNICITY AND IMMIGRATION

Rudolph J. Vecoli

Ethnicity has been a major force shaping life in the United States in the twentieth century. As a source of group identity and solidarity, it has influenced both private and public spheres, from choice of marriage partners to rates of social mobility to the formulation of foreign policies. Ethnicity is essentially a form of collective consciousness that presumes a common past and prospective future with "one's own kind." Milton Gordon's definition is simple yet serviceable: "A sense of peoplehood." In its most intimate form, ethnicity is based in cultural lifestyles, communal arrangements, and shared memories and values. Politicized ethnicity, however, mobilizes its followers behind slogans and symbols that have little to do with—and in support of causes which are far removed from—everyday lived ethnicity. Because its reach extends far beyond the circle of face-to-face acquaintances, ethnicity partakes of what Benedict Anderson has termed "imagined communities." Joined with aspirations for political self-determination and statehood, it becomes full-blown nationalism.

During the first half of the nineteenth century, race had been used ambiguously to denote the conjoined influence of history, environment, and ancestry in producing such specific national characters as the German "race." Under the influence of Social Darwinism, and particularly eugenics, the idea of race took on a scientific cast; mental and physical differences of particular segments of humankind were thought to be biologically determined. The ideology of racialism employed this concept to construct a hierarchy of races and to justify relationships of dominance and subordination among groups. Decades before Hitler carried these doctrines to their logical and deadly extreme, this ideology held sway among educated Americans. Although anthropologist Franz Boas challenged "scientific" racism prior to World War I, cultural explanations of human differences did not make headway until the 1920s. Through the influence of sociologists such as Robert Ezra Park, the terms *nationality group, cultural group,* and *minority* gradually replaced *race* in scholarly discourse.

Although Caroline Ware had written about American immigrant groups under the rubric "Ethnic Communities" in the *Encyclopedia of the Social Sciences* in 1933, the term "ethnicity" itself did not come into currency until the 1960s. Since then it has become a key concept in discussions of the formation of group identities within the context of American pluralism. While certain definitions have emphasized its source in a "primordial" human need for belonging, or in "traditional" folk cultures fated to be eroded by forces of modernity, in this essay ethnicity is conceived of as a cultural construction and (in agreement with Werner Sollors) race as "merely one aspect of ethnicity." Key agents of ethnicization, the process whereby a sense of peoplehood is generated, are ideologues who articulate symbolic representations that bridge ethnicity as lived experience and ethnicity as ideology. Not simply a "collective fiction" created by poets, prophets, and politicians, ethnicity is fabricated from the stuff of common experiences and cultural resources and is expressed through shared worldviews, behavioral repertoires, and institutional structures.

The history of ethnicity in the United States in the twentieth century is then not a tale of vanishing cultures, but an account of how various segments of the population created, sustained, and adapted distinctive peoplehoods out of their American experiences. Theories of modernization predicting the demise of ethnicity with increasing rationalization, urbanization, and secularism have proven as mistaken under capitalist as under socialist regimes. At the end of the twentieth century, ethnicity in the world at large and in the United States in particular remains a fundamental force in determining the course of human events. This essay will explore the reasons why attachment to one's own kind among Americans has demonstrated such amazing resilience and tenacity.

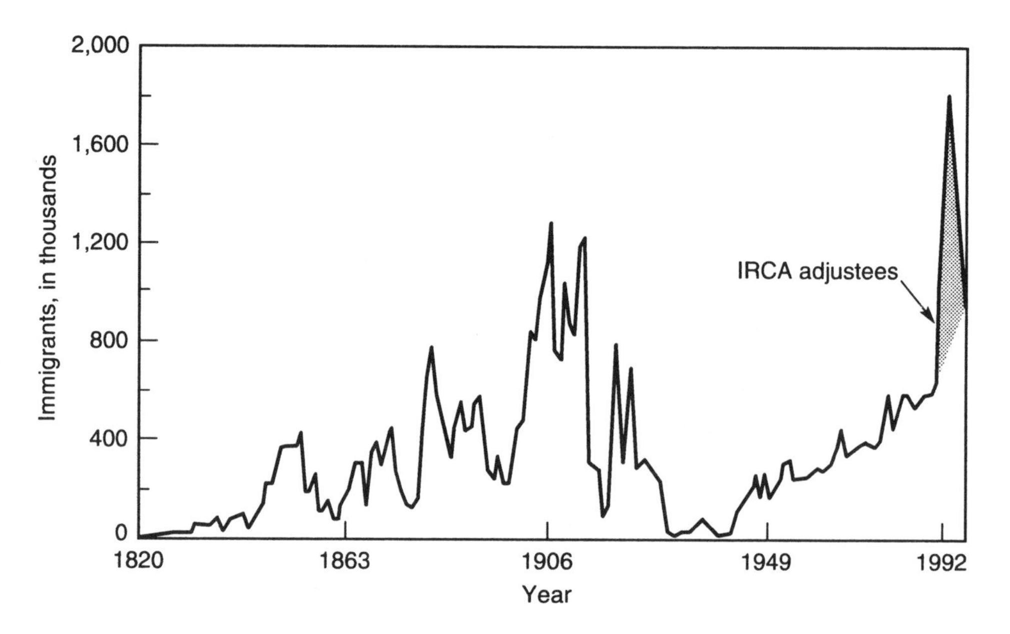

Figure 1. Immigration to the United States, 1821–1993. Most adjustees under the Immigration Reform and Control Act (IRCA) of 1986 were already living in the United States when they were counted as immigrants; most entered prior to January 1982. (Source: *1993 Statistical Yearbook of the Immigration and Naturalization Service,* [forthcoming]. Adapted from Philip Martin and Elizabeth Midgley, *Immigration to the United States: Journey to an Uncertain Destination, Population Bulletin* [September 1994].)

ETHNICITY AND IMMIGRATION AT THE TURN OF THE CENTURY

Two centuries of successive waves of migration, military conquest, and political expansion (entailing the conquest of indigenous inhabitants) had by 1900 produced a plural society distinguished by its diversity. As reported in the census of that year, almost 14 percent of the population was foreign born; if one added in the immigrants' children, over a third of the population was of "foreign stock." Another 12 percent was composed of "Negro, Indian, and Mongolian" native born. Native whites of native parentage constituted just over 50 percent of the total population. Although the latter were predominantly of northern and western European origins, immigrants from all continents had contributed to the peopling of the country. (See figure 1.)

The ethnic complexity of America, however, was not captured by such abstract categories. Those labeled "Indians" by Europeans, for example, comprised hundreds of tribes with distinctive languages, religions, and customs. African Americans, though subjected to brutal deracinating experiences of forced migration and slavery, had blended various origins and regional experiences into specific black cultures. Even a European nationality such as German was fragmented into religious groupings (Roman Catholic, Lutheran, Reformed, and Jewish) as well as along lines of regional dialects and cultures. The fusion over time of such particularistic solidarities into encompassing American Indian, African American, or German American peoplehoods was itself the product of ethnicization. Ethnicity thus was not imported in immigrant trunks; it was a product of the increasing diversity and segmentation of American society.

Among the identities that crystallized in the course of the nineteenth century, the most important—because the most powerful—was an Anglo-American (or Yankee) ethnicity. As Kathleen Conzen has observed, Anglo-Americans were involved in a process of dual construction, defining not only their own identities but other people's as well. From their early encounters with Indians and Africans, they established "whiteness" as an essential marker of difference—and superiority; thus race and color became basic ethnic categories. As immigration increased, Yankees noted significant differences among European newcomers. The greater the likeness to the Anglo-American type (e.g., British Protestants), the more readily they were accepted and assimilated; but those, like Irish Catholics, whose religion or culture clashed with Yankee ideals were viewed pejoratively as "others." As the gatekeepers to opportunity,

Anglo-Americans exercised the power of inclusion and exclusion according to an increasingly complex calculus of ethnic differentiation.

Fresh from military victory over decrepit Spain, adorned with the trappings of empire, and enjoying a period of sustained prosperity, turn-of-the-century Anglo-Americans espoused an optimistic, bumptious ethnonationalism that attained the status of a civil religion. Among its major tenets were belief in moral and material progress, capitalism, and America's civilizing mission in the world. Yankee ideologues, such as Henry Cabot Lodge, justified imperialism abroad and hegemony at home in terms of Anglo-Saxon superiority. Racialism not only informed public policies with respect to foreign affairs and immigration, it also provided the rationale for increasing segregation in the North as well as the South. Affronted by the obnoxious presence of southern and eastern Europeans, upper- and middle-class Anglo-Americans reserved social and public spaces for themselves. Exclusive neighborhoods, clubs, watering places, private schools, and university quotas established boundaries that defined the precincts of the dominant group and excluded others. Symptomatic of a rising ethnic consciousness among Anglo-Americans was the formation in the 1880s of ancestral organizations such as the Society of Mayflower Descendants and the Sons and Daughters of the American Revolution.

A self-conscious Anglo-American ethnonationalism thus confronted the heavy immigration of the first years of the century. In 1904, Henry James, having returned to the United States after an absence of twenty years, pondered "the great 'ethnic' question." "What meaning," he asked, "can continue to attach to such a term as the 'American' character?—what type, as a result of such a prodigious amalgam, such a hotch-potch of racial ingredients, is to be conceived as shaping itself . . . in the cauldron of the 'American' character?"

Because it was viewed as involving no less than the definition of the "American character," immigration policy was a hotly contested issue in the decade preceding World War I. Not only were immigrants arriving at the unprecedented rate of a million a year, their origins had changed radically. Rather than the northern and western Europeans ("old immigrants") of the first wave, eastern and southern Europeans ("new immigrants") now predominated (see figure 2). To many Anglo-Americans, such as sociologist E. A. Ross, the "new immigrants" posed a dire threat to the nation's political, cultural, and biological integrity. In response to this threat, the Dillingham Commission (1907–1911) conducted an exhaustive study reported in forty-two volumes. Among these, *A Dictionary of Races and Peoples* (1911), a concoction of ethnology and stereotypes (the entry for Sicilians, for example, observes that they are "excitable, superstitious, and revengeful"), provided a rationale for imposing restrictions on the "new immigration." It was clear that the commission had eastern and southern Europeans in mind when it called for the exclusion of those "who by reason of their personal qualities or habits, would least readily be assimilated, or would make the least desirable citizens." Asians, of course, were totally unacceptable to the commission, which endorsed the policy established by the Chinese Exclusion Act of 1882. While immigration controls were gradually tightened, the nativists' objective of rigorous restriction was not realized until the 1920s. (For table of immigration legislation, see table 1.)

Not all Anglo-Americans were of one mind on this issue. Countering the xenophobia of the restrictionists, proponents of a liberal immigration policy cited Christian and democratic ideals of universal brotherhood. Emma Lazarus's sonnet, "The New Colossus" (1883), with its welcoming (if patronizing) reference to "your tired, your poor,/Your huddled masses yearning to breathe free,/The wretched refuse of your teeming shore./Send these, the homeless, tempest-tost to me," resonated with the hallowed concept of America as an asylum for the oppressed. David, the Jewish protagonist of Israel Zangwill's *The Melting Pot* (1909), gave a reassuring response to Henry James's query: "America is God's Crucible, the great Melting Pot where all the races of Europe are melting and re-forming! . . . into the Crucible with you all! God is making the American." Zangwill's play was enormously popular with Anglo-Americans such as President Theodore Roosevelt because it confirmed their belief in the efficacy of American institutions to transform even Lazarus's "wretched refuse" into worthy and productive citizens. The "melting pot" henceforth served as the symbol of a progressive assimilationist ideology.

Underlying such ideological commitments to a liberal immigration policy was the economic reality of an expansive American capitalism that relied upon the peasant-proletarians of Europe, French Canada, and Mexico as a reserve army of labor. By 1910, the majority of workers in the country's basic industries were either immigrants or the children of immigrants. Reflecting swings in the business cycle, the labor market recruited foreign workers by the millions when needed and sent them back home during dull times. As many as a third of all immigrants—and, in the case of certain nationalities such as Italians

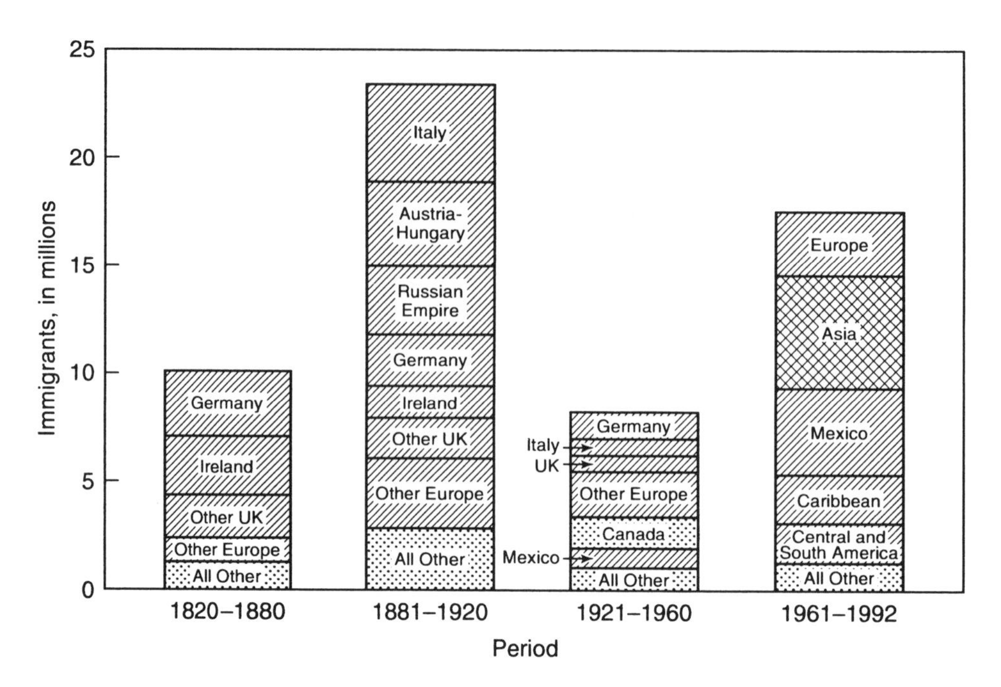

Figure 2. Regions and Countries of Origin of Immigrants to the United States, 1820–1992. (Source: *Statistical Yearbook of the Immigration and Naturalization Service* [various years]. Adapted from Philip Martin and Elizabeth Midgley, *Immigration to the United States: Journey to an Uncertain Destination, Population Bulletin* [September 1994].)

and South Slavs, over 50 percent—remigrated. Given their single-minded objective to work and save money, such "birds of passage" were hardly aspiring Americans.

Industrial capitalism created the material and social environments to which both immigrants and natives had to adapt. Paradoxically, work in factories, mills, and mines made for both assimilation and ethnicization. Employers often applied ethnic stereotypes in the recruitment and management of their labor forces: Slavs were "oxlike men," suited for heavy work; Italians and Jews, physically weak and clannish; Finns, rebellious and socialistic, and so forth. Managerial practices contributed to the hardening of ethnic categories. While labor gangs and departments were sometimes segregated according to ethnicity, many companies favored a "judicious mix" on the assumption that racial, cultural, and linguistic differences made workers' resistance more difficult. Preferential hiring practices and work assignments (no "white" man would deign to take a "dago" job) engendered group rivalries. Strikes pitting workers of different backgrounds against each other often resulted in long-lasting animosities. In workplace argot, epithets such as "bohunk," "kike," "kraut," "mick," "nigger," "polack," and "wop" became designators of ethnicity. Naming and name-calling were basic elements in the process of ethnicization.

At the same time, the organization and technology of production, the tempo and discipline of work, were acculturating experiences. The shopfloor, the saloon, and the neighborhood provided common ground where newcomers could be assimilated into a working-class culture under the tutelage of experienced native and immigrant workers. Did industrial migrants acquire a working-class consciousness in the process? The relationship between ethnicity and class has been a problematic issue in American social history. Marxist historians have been wont to attribute ethnicity to a false consciousness that prevented workers from acting upon their true interests as proletarians. Ethnicity and class, however, were not necessarily exclusive, competing expressions of identity and solidarity. Rather, given a rough congruity between social structure and ethnic hierarchy in the twentieth century, class and ethnicity have often reinforced each other.

In broad strokes one might portray a "vertical mosaic" of early-twentieth-century industrial America: an upper class of white old-stock Protestants, salted with an occasional British immigrant (such as Andrew Carnegie); a middle class that was a composite of Anglo-Americans and northwestern

Table 1. LANDMARK IMMIGRATION POLICY LEGISLATION

Title	Date Enacted	Description
Act of 3 March 1875	1875	Established the policy of direct federal regulation of immigration by prohibiting entry to criminals and prostitutes and any Asian person without his or her free and voluntary consent.
Chinese Exclusion Act	1882	Suspended immigration of Chinese laborers (not students, teachers, merchants, tourists) to the U.S. for ten years; provided for deportation of Chinese illegally in the U.S.; barred Chinese from naturalization. Chinese exclusion laws were renewed in 1892 and 1902 and repealed 17 December 1943.
Immigration Act of 1891	1891	The first comprehensive law for national control of immigration, establishing the Bureau of Immigration under the Treasury Department to administer all immigration laws (except the Chinese Exclusion Act). Also added to the inadmissible classes were persons likely to become public charges, those suffering from contagious diseases, and persons convicted of certain crimes.
Immigration Act of 1903	1903	Extensive codification of existing immigration law added to the list of inadmissible immigrants and provided for the exclusion of aliens on the grounds of proscribed opinions (e.g., anarchists or persons who believed in the overthrow of the U.S. government).
Naturalization Act of 1906	1906–1907	Made acquisition of citizenship more difficult.
Immigration Act of 1917	1917	Codified all previous exclusion provisions and added the exclusion of illiterate aliens from entry; created a "barred zone" (known as the Asia-Pacific triangle), natives of which were inadmissible.
Emergency Immigration Restriction Act (Quota Law)	1921	The first quantitative immigration law; limited the number of aliens entering the U.S. to 3 percent of the number of foreign-born persons of that nationality who had lived in the U.S. in 1910; exempted those who had resided continuously for at least one year preceding their application in one of the independent countries of the Western Hemisphere.
National Origins (Johnson-Reed)	1924	The first permanent limitation on immigration, establishing the national-origins quota system; set the annual quota of nationalities under the law at 2 percent of the number of foreign-born persons of such nationality resident in the U.S. in 1890 (total quota: 164,667). System established from 1 July 1929 to 31 December 1952 fixed quota for the Eastern Hemisphere at 150,000 and established family preferences within it. Wives and unmarried children (under 18) of U.S. citizens and natives of Western Hemisphere countries were permitted to come without reference to quota. Established system for issuing immigration visas by American consular officials abroad.
Act of 14 June 1940	1940	Permanently transferred the Immigration and Naturalization Service from the Department of Labor to the Department of Justice.
Act of 29 April 1943	1943	Provided for the importation of temporary agricultural laborers to the U.S. from North, South, and Central America. The program served as the legal basis for the Mexican *bracero* program, which lasted through 1964.
Displaced Persons Act	1948	First major expression of U.S. policy for admitting persons fleeing persecution; permitted the admission of up to 205,000 displaced persons during the two-year period beginning 1 July 1948 (chargeable against future years' quotas).

Table 1. LANDMARK IMMIGRATION POLICY LEGISLATION (*Continued*)

Title	Date Enacted	Description
Immigration and Nationality (McCarran-Walter) Act	1952	All immigration laws brought into one comprehensive statute. All races made eligible for naturalization; sex discrimination eliminated with respect to immigration; established quota preference for skilled aliens. Broadened the grounds for exclusion and deportation of aliens. Repealed the ban on contract labor (see Act of 30 March 1868) but added other qualitative exclusions.
Immigration and Nationality Act Amendments	1965	Abolished the national-origins quota system, eliminating national origin, race, or ancestry as a basis for immigration. Established Eastern Hemisphere ceiling of 170,000 and Western Hemisphere ceiling of 120,000, except for immediate relatives of U.S. citizens and certain special immigrants. Established 20,000-per-country limit within numerical restrictions for Eastern Hemisphere, applied in 1976 to Western Hemisphere. Established seven-category preference system for relatives of U.S. citizens and permanent resident aliens in U.S. and for persons with special occupational skill.
Refugee Act	1980	First omnibus refugee act enacted by Congress; established procedures for consultation with Congress by the president on numbers and allocation of refugees for each fiscal year. Defined refugees according to United Nations' 1967 protocol on refugees; established category of asylees; provided comprehensive program for domestic resettlement of refugees and for the adjustment of the status of refugees and asylees to immigrants.
Immigration Reform and Control Act	1986	Authorized legialization of illegal aliens who had resided in an unlawful status since 1 January 1982. Established sanctions prohibiting employers from knowingly hiring illegal aliens. Increased immigration by authorizing adjustments for Cubans and Haitians who had entered the U.S. without inspection prior to 1 January 1982, increasing number of immigrants admitted from dependent areas, and creating a small additional number for aliens from countries adversely affected by 1965 law.
Immigration Act of 1990	1990	A major overhaul of immigration law increasing total immigration under an overall flexible cap. Ratio of employment-based immigrants to family-sponsored immigration increased. All grounds for exclusion and deportation revised. Bar against admission of Communists as nonimmigrants and exclusion of aliens on foreign-policy grounds repealed. Attorney general authorized to grant temporary protective status to aliens of countries subject to armed conflict or natural disasters. Created new temporary-worker admissions categories. Recodified 32 grounds for exclusion into 9 categories.

SOURCE: Adapted from *Encyclopedia of the United States Congress* (1995), pp. 1098–1099.

Europeans; and a wage-earning working class that included the full spectrum of ethnic groups, but was heavily weighted with African Americans, Mexican Americans, and European and Asian immigrants. The industrial labor force was itself divided into distinctive strata according to skill levels and ethnicity. Skilled workers tended to be Yankees, British, Irish, German, and Scandinavian; semi-skilled or machine tenders were increasingly eastern and southern Europeans (and French Canadians in New England); while the ranks of unskilled laborers were preponderantly filled by "new immigrants" in the Northeast and Midwest, African Americans in the South, and Mexicans and Asians in the West. This segmentation along skill lines reinforced attitudes of ethnic difference and superiority. In the words of David Montgomery, "The dominance of the skilled crafts blended all too easily with a national ideology that proclaimed the supremacy of the white race." Employers and labor leaders referred to unskilled southern and eastern Europeans as "black men." Such congruency between social stratification and ethnicity not only reflected differentials in terms of cultural advantages, but also blatant discrimination in the functioning of opportunity structures. Until World War II, immigrants and their children, as well as African Americans and Indians, were largely confined to a working-class status.

Prior to the 1930s, the American labor movement, reflecting these skill and ethnic fissures, was dominated by a narrow trade union ideology and racist and nativist sentiments. The American Federation of Labor (AFL) primarily represented the aristocracy of labor: skilled, native or "old immigrant" European workers. With few exceptions, AFL unions did not attempt to organize the unskilled, black, or foreign born. From the 1890s on, Samuel Gompers and other union leaders, influenced by racialism, vigorously advocated immigration restrictions directed at Asians and eastern and southern Europeans. Not surprisingly, immigrant-based labor and socialist movements mounted a major challenge to Gompers-style trade unionism. German socialists in particular were instrumental in the formation of both the Socialist Labor Party and the Socialist Party of America. Even socialists, however, were guilty of nativism and racism. A leading German-American socialist, Victor L. Berger, advocated restrictions on Asian and southern and eastern European immigrants because he believed they threatened "white civilization." Although foreign language federations affiliated with the American Socialist Party, it failed to realize the potential for recruitment among immigrants, in part because of xenophobic attitudes among American Socialists.

In the pre–World War years, the Industrial Workers of the World, a syndicalist organization, mobilized masses of immigrant workers in large-scale strikes. Meanwhile, unions such as the Amalgamated Meat Cutters and Butcher Workmen of North America, the Amalgamated Clothing Workers of America, and the United Mine Workers of America successfully organized the foreign born. In such struggles, ethnic and class solidarities sustained a high level of morale and commitment among a multiethnic labor force; foreign-born anarchists and socialists emerged as leaders of their countrymen, while ethnic fraternal organizations, businessmen, and churches supported the strikers. If the singing of the "Internationale" in a dozen different languages demonstrated the possibility of working-class solidarity, such multiethnic coalitions proved ephemeral. Employers' strategy to divide and conquer by exploiting ethnic antipathies did in fact work more often than not.

Just as the intersection of ethnicity and class shaped the American vertical mosaic, so it largely determined the cultural contours of the American landscape, rural and urban. Contrary to general belief, neither immigration nor ethnicity has been primarily an urban eastern phenomenon. In 1900, the states with the largest percentage of foreign born (over 50 percent) were North Dakota and Minnesota; New York lagged behind in tenth place with only 38 percent. Over 50 percent of the foreign born lived in places with populations of less than 25,000. Germans, Norwegians, Swedes, and Dutch, heavily involved in agriculture, gave a distinctive ethnic coloration to great swaths of land, particularly in the Upper Mississippi Valley. Drawn to rural industrial occupations like lumbering and mining, Cornish, Swedes, Poles, Finns, and Italians were scattered in camps and villages in Pennsylvania, West Virginia, and the Great Lakes region, while Irish, French Canadians, Greeks, and Hungarians made their homes in mill towns clustered about factories in New England, New York, and New Jersey.

A distinction is sometimes made between plural societies where ethnicity is based on territoriality and the United States where it is alleged ethnic groups lacked an attachment to a particular soil. While immigrants failed to establish homogeneous colonies bounded by political frontiers (the dream of a "German state" of Wisconsin was not fulfilled), through chain migrations they did realize high degrees of residential concentration. Despite the fabled mobility of the American people, patterns of spatial distribution of ethnic populations have remained surprisingly stable throughout the twentieth century: Irish and French Canadian concentrations in New England; Italian and Jewish in the Middle Atlantic states; German and Scandinavian in the Midwest; Slavic in the industrial heartland from Pennsylvania west to Illinois; old-stock Americans (black and white) in the South; Mexicans in the Southwest; and Asians on the Pacific Coast. A perusal of *We the People: An Atlas of America's Ethnic Diversity* (1988), based on 1980 census data, vividly illustrates how territoriality has been an important factor in the persistence of ethnicity.

Among the defining characteristics of American cities in the twentieth century are high proportions of migrant populations, foreign and native, and an urban ecology of differentiated zones of commerce, industry, and residence. While significant differences have existed among various cities in terms of ethnic mix, segregated housing patterns were a common feature. Housing covenants (applied to Asians, Jews, and Italians, as well as to African Americans), real estate markets, and social pressures combined to maintain clearly demarcated neighborhoods. If few districts were "ethnically pure," the areas in which particular groups preponderated were quite distinct. Such urban residential patterns both reflected and reinforced the construction of specific ethnicities.

By the turn of the century, immigrants were commonly associated with urban slums and their attendant ills. A genre of muckraking literature, beginning with Jacob Riis's *How the Other Half Lives* (1892), exposed the congestion, sanitation, and health conditions in tenement districts. Such descriptions often depicted the denizens of the slums as morally squalid as well as poor—hence responsible for their own misery. The term *ghetto,* first applied to Jewish districts in Europe and then America, evokes the Anglo-American view of ethnic enclaves as exotic, noxious, and dangerous. From the "Little Dublins" or "Little Italies" of the past to the barrios and "'hoods" of the 1990s, the association of such areas with crime, immorality, and filth stigmatized their residents.

While such "ascribed ethnicity," to use Ewa Morawska's term, was imposed from the top down, the process of ethnicization occurred from the bottom up. Country folk with little sense of nationality, most immigrants initially identified themselves in terms of family and place of origin. As they established niches in particular occupations, pioneers recruited family and friends through chain migrations. These nuclei in time became neighborhoods serving as a buffer against insecurity, culture shock, and hostile strangers. Mutual aid societies among *paesani* and *landsleit* were formed, saloons and groceries established, and synagogues and churches erected. Such small-scale communities became building blocks for a more encompassing ethnicity. Working with and living among others engendered a sense of peoplehood among those who shared a familiar language, religion, and culture. Immigrants quickly learned a basic rule of American pluralism: strength lies in numbers. Whether defending neighborhood turf, cultivating business clientele, or trading votes for jobs, ethnic solidarity served as the organizing strategy.

Transcending kinship and neighborhood, an ideological ethnicity articulated a sense of peoplehood free of constraints of time and space, bridging both oceans and past and present. As an imagined community, ethnicity required symbolic representations of "our people," thus the importance of rhetoric and rituals, of flags and uniforms, of music and poetry. Such representations, however, had to resolve the dilemma of being an alien minority situated within an Anglo-American society actuated by its own jealous ethnonationalism. While Navahos, Finnish socialists, Hutterites, and Hasidic Jews might defy pressures for Anglo-American conformity, the more common ethnic strategy was to accommodate assimilationist demands while retaining as wide a sphere of autonomy as possible. In delineating their peoplehoods, ethnic groups invented mythic histories highlighting episodes, heroes, and qualities compatible with Anglo-American ideals. Thus the insistence of Scandinavian Americans on the primacy of Leif Ericson, and the equally vociferous insistence of Italian Americans upon Cristoforo Colombo, as discoverer of the New World. Von Steuben, Kosciusko, and Lafayette, all Revolutionary War heroes, served as ethnic surrogates in the American pantheon. In the negotiation of their ethnicities, marginalized groups sought to reconcile the dualism of hyphenated identities.

Janus-faced, immigrants continued to look backward to the politics and cultures of their lands of origin at the same time they looked forward to America. Old World influences affected the process of ethnicization in the United States. If the typical immigrant was semi-literate and apolitical, an elite of clergymen, political exiles, and educated adventurers was the bearer of high culture and political and religious doctrines. Self-anointed leaders, they exploited, elevated, and mobilized their countrymen by establishing churches, mutual aid societies, labor groups, and newspapers. Free of repression by state churches and thought police, immigrant communities became battlegrounds among contending theologies and ideologies. Preachers, nationalists, and radicals engaged in heated, sometimes violent, debates. Publications and refugees from abroad kept immigrant groups in a state of uproar over homeland politics, monarchists versus republicans, clericals versus free thinkers, high church versus low church, conservatives versus socialists.

Anglo-Americans, puzzled and annoyed that "ignorant foreigners" should engage so passionately in Old World polemics, were especially alarmed when the rhetoric turned revolutionary. Contemporaneous with mass emigration in the lands of origin, social upheavals fueled movements of opposition to monarchy, landlordism, and capitalism. Recurring repression caused leaders and rank-and-file to flee to this

"Free Country" (a term radicals applied sardonically). Although its influence varied from group to group, such radical yeast fermented under the auspicious conditions of American industrial exploitation. Through labor organizations, cooperatives, theatrical groups, and publications, socialists created countercultures that competed with nationalist and religious ethnicities for the loyalty of the immigrants.

Whatever the degree of "institutional completeness," migrants could not live entirely unto themselves within their ethnic enclaves. Willy-nilly they came into contact, sometimes collision, with others as a part of everyday life. Few escaped incorporation into the hurly-burly of the American economy. Certain groups drew upon Old World skills and entrepreneurial traditions, while others exploited chance opportunities to create niches for themselves in certain trades. The Chinese laundryman, the Greek confectioner, and the Italian barber became characteristic ethnic types. Through rotating loan associations or other forms of mutuality, immigrants accumulated capital to launch modest business enterprises. Over time, ethnic economies in which entrepreneurs and employees shared the same backgrounds emerged—Italians in construction, Germans in brewing, Japanese in truck farming. Such economic autarchy strengthened ethnic bonds by reducing interaction with outsiders, but at the same time generated intraethnic class conflicts between owners and workers, as among Jews in the clothing industry. Economics on the whole, however, made for interethnic encounters in the marketplace that were as often hostile as they were harmonious.

If American democracy did not function in accordance with textbook maxims, the vote nonetheless has served to empower marginalized groups in twentieth-century America. Naturalization for the immigrant and the ballot for the native born were key points of entry into the public sphere; for that reason, denial of the former to Asians and of the latter to African Americans condemned them to an inferior status. Although the acquisition of citizenship became more difficult after the Naturalization Act of 1906, access to the ballot gave European Americans a major advantage in their struggle for advancement. While they might sell their first votes for a glass of beer, in time they learned the value of the franchise. Irish Americans, who dominated the politics of most northern cities, served as tutors of the politically naive immigrants. In return for their votes, ward heelers provided help at a time when government acknowledged little or no obligation to aid the poor and the powerless.

While politics introduced the newcomers to America's civic culture, it was also a catalyst of ethnic consciousness and solidarity. The larger the vote, the greater the rewards in the form of patronage and public services. While ethnic bloc voting and the balanced ticket were condemned by the "good government" reformers (i.e., Anglo-Americans), they provided access to public officials for otherwise excluded elements of the population. Political contests became symbolic tests of strength among ethnic groups. The election of one's own to the city council or to Congress, regardless of character or party, was an occasion for community pride and celebration.

Since the mid-nineteenth century, ties between criminal activities and politics have been associated with recent immigrants and marginalized ethnic groups. As a form of business enterprise, criminal activity involved the provision of illicit goods and services (prostitution, bootleg liquor, drugs) that required the collusion of politicians and police. Immigrants learned that corruption was also an element of the civic culture. Organized crime, as Daniel Bell observed, served as a "queer ladder of mobility" for those denied access to legitimate careers because of ethnic and class barriers. A process of ethnic succession can be observed: the Irish, generally credited with being pioneers in organized crime, were followed by Jews, Italians, and Slavs, who in turn were succeeded by African Americans, Puerto Ricans, and Asians. The mass media, from yellow journalism to television, stigmatized certain ethnic groups as criminally inclined; Italian Americans in particular have been burdened with the albatross of the Mafia.

The relationships between religion and ethnicity have been intimate and complex in twentieth-century America. Given the constitutional doctrine of separation of church and state, the sphere of religious belief and practice has served as an umbrella under which groups have been relatively free to conserve their languages and cultures. Also, absent a state church, a competitive religious marketplace necessitated new styles of clerical leadership, greater lay participation, and enlarged institutional functions as compared to the Old Country. Among the first institutions established by new arrivals, places of worship served as a physical focus and community center for a neighborhood. A common faith and ritual, which transcended regional differences, provided the basis for an expanded definition of ethnic community. Venetians and Calabrians could belong to the same Italian parish, although not without difficulty. Conflicts, schisms, and mergers involving questions of theology, church polity, and cultural issues (e.g., language use) further complicated the picture. While the ancestral faith has been at the core of the peoplehood of Polish Catholics, Norwegian Lutherans, and Orthodox Greeks, an overarching ethnicity subsumed multiple religious affiliations among German Americans, Anglo-Americans, and African Americans. Meanwhile socialists and free-thinkers (e.g., Czech Americans, Italian Americans, and Jewish Americans) made of their nonbelief an ethnic marker. Lacking a simple congruency of church and peoplehood, varied patterns of ethnoreligiosity resulted as particular groups constructed their ethnicities.

Prior to World War I, Anglo-American ethnonationalism did not penetrate deeply into immigrant enclaves; in addition to linguistic and cultural barriers, the contradiction between ideology and reality was too great. The America of the immigrants differed drastically from that depicted in Fourth of July speeches. Anglo-American efforts to assimilate and civilize the immigrants had limited success at best. Christian Americanization—in which a number of denominations invested heavily for the civic as well as spiritual salvation of the foreigners—was almost a total failure. Settlement houses and social workers were effective insofar as they respected the cultural mores of the immigrants. The public school system, which was to be the primary instrument for the assimilation of the "little foreigners," had various outcomes depending largely upon the values of the ethnic groups. East European Jews, who perceived education to be a means of advancement, more often took advantage of the public schools; Poles, who wished to have their children instructed in the Polish language and Catholic religion, favored parochial schools; while Italians generally preferred to send their children to work. For most immigrant children, Americanization was more likely to take place in city streets, movie houses, and factories than in the classroom.

ETHNIC NATIONALISM, AMERICANIZATION, AND WORLD WAR I

Wars have been defining moments in the history of ethnicity in twentieth-century America. Although the United States did not enter World War I until April 1917, the European conflict from its inception in 1914 stirred deep and conflicting emotions among the country's diverse populations. President Woodrow Wilson (himself an Anglophile) asked Americans to be neutral in thought as well as deed, but as Randolph Bourne observed, "the war has set every one vibrating to some emotional string twanged on the other side of the Atlantic." While old-stock Americans constituted the largest single component, the foreign born and their children accounted for 35 percent of the total population of 100 million. Moreover, German-speakers totaled almost 9 million, while over a million persons spoke Italian, Polish, Yiddish, or French. In addition, speakers of Dutch, Greek, Czech, Slovak, Slovenian, Serbo-Croatian, Magyar, Lithuanian, and Finnish, each numbered over 100,000. Coming from the German, Austro-Hungarian, and Russian empires, the Balkans, and Italy, they were indeed vibrating to emotional strings plucked in their countries of origin.

During the war, nascent ethnic nationalisms blossomed into movements of patriotic support for their respective homelands. Immigrants and their children bought war bonds, lobbied, and prayed for victory of their respective countries, while a minority even returned to fight. German Americans, numerous, prosperous, and influential, vigorously protested the pro-Allies policy of the Wilson administration. Irish Americans, who saw the war as an opportunity to liberate the Emerald Isle from British rule, and Russian Jews, who welcomed the defeat of the Czarist regime, also favored the Central Powers, while Slavic groups from the multiethnic empires supported independence for their nationalities. Once Italy entered the war in 1915, Italian immigrants rallied to the Allied cause. While political and religious dissenters opposed the war, many immigrants were simply grateful to be on this side of the Atlantic.

Anglo-Americans reacted with alarm to this cacophony of ethnic nationalisms and feared that the melting pot had not worked. From 1915 on, a Preparedness Campaign promoted material and psychological readiness for war under the banner of "100 percent Americanism." The excoriation of hyphenism, particularly German-Americanism, as a form of disloyalty by Theodore Roosevelt and Woodrow Wilson inspired an aggressive Americanization crusade. Frances Kellor, a leading ideologue of the movement, observing that the melting pot had failed, called for a policy of aggressive assimilation. Federal and state governments, business and patriotic organizations, embarked upon intensive Americanization programs. Hard-line Americanizers demanded that use of foreign languages in workplaces, publications, schools, religious services, and even the home, be prohibited.

In this tinderbox setting, the debate over the future of ethnicity in American society intensified. Philosopher Horace Kallen fired the opening salvo in an article, "Democracy versus the Melting Pot" (1915), responding to E. A. Ross's rabidly anti-immigrant polemic, *The Old World in the New* (1914). Kallen argued against the necessity, indeed the desirability, of cultural assimilation, offering a vision of America as a federation of nationalities. While sharing a common citizenship in the republic, ethnic groups should maintain and foster their particular languages and cultures. In Kallen's vision of America, each nationality was an instrument in an orchestra that would perform the symphony of civilization. Among the adherents of Kallen's concept of cultural pluralism, Randolph Bourne hailed the promise of a "cosmopolitan America" that would serve as an example of a "world federation in miniature." Preservationists within ethnic communities, such as Norwegian American novelist Waldemar Ager, took up the cudgels against the melting pot. If advocates of 100 percent Americanism drowned out these voices, Kallen's conception of a democratic pluralist society would reemerge at a more propitious time.

With the entry of the United States into the war, vigilante organizations such as the American Protective League abetted state organs like the Minnesota Committee on Public Safety in ferreting out "disloyal" elements. From the lynching of a farmer who refused to buy Liberty Bonds to the stoning of dachshunds, the patriotic crusade against all things German ranged from the tragic to the absurd. The vehemence of the anti-German onslaught suggests that the war served as a pretext for Anglo-American retaliation against a rival ethnicity that had the audacity to challenge its hegemony. A flourishing German American culture never recovered from this concentrated barrage of vilification and repression.

Paradoxically, while the wartime psychology was intolerant of diversity in general, particular forms of ethnicity were encouraged. Immigrant groups whose homelands were aligned with the Allies, such as the Italians, or which represented stateless nationalities, such as the Poles, were allowed to manifest their Old World patriotism by raising funds, parading, and even enlisting in their national armies. George Creel, director of the Committee on Public Information, provided foreign language publications with boiler plate in their own tongues, while Four Minute Men adapted patriotic speeches to their ethnic audiences. Liberty Bond posters portrayed immigrants sympathetically against the background of the Statue of Liberty. Despite its Americanization rhetoric, the Wilson administration geared its propaganda to exploit the many ethnicities of the American people.

Social and economic changes engendered by the war affected the status of ethnic communities in American society in other ways. Universal military conscription, adopted in 1917, served as an agent of Americanization by bringing together men of all classes and nationalities. Although the military roughly replicated in its ranks of officers, noncommissioned officers, and enlisted men the class and ethnic hierarchy of American society, it did serve as an acculturative influence upon millions of young men, bringing them into contact with persons of other religions, cultures, and regions. Intelligence testing (applied for the first time on a massive scale) of military recruits, however, confirmed racialist assumptions regarding the "inferior mental capacities" of African Americans and southern and eastern Europeans. These findings not only sanctioned discriminatory treatment by the military, but were cited in the twenties in the eugenic brief for immigration restriction.

A booming war economy coupled with the interruption of European immigration created new employment opportunities for previously excluded ethnic groups. While southern and eastern Europeans moved into skilled jobs, growing numbers of African Americans and Mexican Americans entered the common labor stratum. When migrants from the South and the Southwest competed for jobs and housing, "race riots" erupted in East Saint Louis, Chicago, and Omaha. Northern industrial cities became even more ethnically diverse as blacks and Mexicans confronted established European ethnic groups.

Meanwhile, organized labor had achieved unprecedented strength based upon the war economy, favorable government policies, and newfound multiethnic working-class unity. In 1919, hundreds of thousands of workers participated in strikes in steel, meatpacking, textiles, and other industries in an effort to protect wartime gains, but hostile public authorities and an employers' "open shop" campaign overwhelmed dogged resistance by the strikers. U.S. Steel and other corporations exploited ethnic and religious antagonisms among workers and red-baited strike leaders as foreigners and "Bolsheviks."

Radicals—particularly foreigners—had been subject to mob violence and to government persecution under the wartime Espionage and Sedition Acts. During the "Red Scare," the Bureau of Investigation of the Department of Justice under the direction of J. Edgar Hoover pursued Bolsheviks with particular zeal. Radical publications were suppressed, labor organizers were beaten and lynched, and in a mass trial almost a hundred Wobblies (IWW members) were sentenced to prison. Many immigrant activists were deported, while some returned voluntarily to their countries of origin. A "Black Terror" of reaction, comparable to contemporary Fascism in postwar Italy, cowed those who dared oppose Anglo-American capitalist hegemony. This fierce repression crushed immigrant working-class movements and demonstrated that the radical option for ethnicity had been foreclosed.

FROM XENOPHOBIA TO CULTURAL DEMOCRACY, 1920s–1930s

Although World War I affirmed their dominance over both ethnic- and class-based opponents, Anglo-Americans felt increasingly besieged by alien forces. While modernization was the true enemy of their "traditional values," they responded with an intensified nativism. Henry Ford, typical of the small-town Yankee mentality, resorted to anti-Semitism to explain these threatening changes, for which he as much as anyone was responsible. From this sense of being embattled in defense of the American way of life stemmed various offensives against alien forces.

Immigration restriction was one response to a perceived threat from the supposedly defective genes and subversive ideas of the Old World. Congress responded to the postwar flood of immigrants with laws in 1921 and 1924 which imposed racially inspired quotas reducing the torrent to a trickle. The national origins system—which remained in effect until 1965—extended preference to northern and western Europeans, radically reduced southern and eastern European immigration, and completely excluded Asians, with the exception of Filipinos. One effect of the new immigration policy was the stabilization of the foreign-born population. Women now comprised an increasing percentage (and a majority since 1930) of the arrivals, indicative of family formation and permanency of residence in the United States.

Prohibition was another expression of xenophobia, pitting small-town and rural Protestants against urban Catholic and Jewish "foreigners." The enactment of the Eighteenth Amendment to the Constitution (1919) merely intensified the cultural war between "drys" and "wets" that split American society—and in particular the Democratic party. Although moonshining was a time-honored profession in the dry states of the South and West, the illicit production of alcoholic beverages became concentrated in the households of recent immigrant populations familiar with traditional modes of distilling alcohol. Gangsters, among whom Irish, Jews, and Italians were conspicuous, fought to control traffic in bootleg liquor, turning cities into battlefields. Chicago and Al Capone came to epitomize this era of lawlessness, a legend that Hollywood has exploited since the film *Little Caesar* (1930).

The spirit of the "Tribal Twenties," to use John Higham's term, was also expressed through a resurrected Ku Klux Klan, which, unlike the KKK during Reconstruction, had major contingents in the Midwest and West. Middle-class white Protestants, fearful that aliens were corrupting "their" country, marched in hooded robes and burned crosses from New England to the state of Washington; their targets were less likely to be African Americans than Roman Catholics and Jews. Such manifestations of bigotry elicited condemnation from liberal Anglo-Americans and militant resistance from these new Americans. Although achieving impressive political strength in certain states, by the late twenties the Klan had been driven from the streets and from public power.

The Sacco and Vanzetti case epitomized the ethnic and class conflicts of the twenties. Bartolomeo Vanzetti and Nicola Sacco, caught in the snares of the Red Scare, were convicted of a robbery and murder committed in South Braintree, Massachusetts, in 1920. It was widely held at the time—and has been since—that they did not receive a fair trial and that their conviction was due to prejudice against them as Italians and radicals. Despite a protest movement of international dimensions, Sacco and Vanzetti were executed on 27 August 1927. Their case became a symbol of the struggle between the Anglo-American establishment and an emerging ethnic working-class–progressive coalition.

Notwithstanding the xenophobic atmosphere of the twenties, outgroups made significant gains in their efforts at incorporation into American society. As immigrants and black migrants in northern cities gained the vote, they began electing mayors, state legislators, and even congressmen. By the 1920s, ethnic leaders such as Fiorello La Guardia, Anton Cermak, and Oscar De Priest were representing working-class and ethnic constituencies in city halls, state houses, and the national capital. The Democratic presidential candidacy of Alfred E. Smith, a Roman Catholic "wet," in 1928 signified the emergence of a new force in American politics. Despite Republican breakthroughs in the Anglo-American "Solid South," Smith's strong showing among urban working-class ethnics prefigured the victory of Franklin D. Roosevelt in 1932.

Although the prosperity of the twenties was uneven, workers on the whole enjoyed increased earnings and stable employment as compared with prewar years. Expanded access to factory jobs, higher productivity, and greater acculturation accounted for these modest gains. If this was not quite the "Promised Land," many immigrant families realized their aspirations: ownership of a house with a garden. Mass production and advertising meanwhile combined to create a culture of consumerism. While the foreign born, raised in conditions of scarcity, often resisted the new ethos, their children embraced this materialization of the American Dream.

Immigrant families now typically consisted of several generations. Already in 1900, native children of immigrant parents outnumbered the foreign born. Once they became wage earners, these young people not only increased family income, but were more susceptible to advertising and attuned to "American" tastes. Despite conflict with their parents, they adopted the latest fashions in clothing and leisure, and acquired the accoutrements of modern household technology (washing machines, refrigerators, radios) and automobiles. The appearance of American-born generations signified important transitions in the lives of ethnic families and communities.

Meanwhile, mass culture was transforming the lifestyles of old and new Americans alike. Motion pictures, radios, phonograph recordings, tabloid newspapers, and spectator sports disseminated standardized entertainments, images, and messages nationwide. Culture heroes—among them Rudolph Valentino, Babe Ruth, Knute Rockne, and Theda Bara—were role models for the second generation's ideas about "American" values, manners, and fashions. Ironically, the stars and impresarios (as in the case of Greek and Jewish movie moguls) of popular culture were themselves often immigrants or children of immigrants.

Participation in mass consumption and mass culture entailed substantial changes in the way in which new-stock Americans thought and behaved. To term this process "Americanization," however, is a misnomer, since old-stock Americans were undergoing analogous changes. Moreover, mass media could serve a variety of cultural tastes. Recordings in many different languages catered to a polyglot market, a multitude of publications served ethnic readerships, and radio programs—even motion pictures—were produced for ethnic audiences. Fans could express their ethnicity by choosing "their own kind" as favored movie stars, singers, and athletes. If baseball was the great American pastime, Jewish spectators still identified with Andy Cohen and Italians with "Poosh 'Em Up Tony" Lazzeri. The exclusion of African Americans from "white" baseball until Jackie Robinson played with the Brooklyn Dodgers in 1947 was another form of segregation that denied them full participation in American life. In sum, mass culture served contradictory functions: it integrated American society by providing common interests and experiences across class and ethnic lines; yet it also provided opportunities for the validation of particular ethnic identities.

Thinking about group differences underwent important changes in the 1920s. Franz Boas and his students championed the tenets of cultural anthropology, which were subversive of any regime based upon the alleged biological superiority or inferiority of races. Embracing a cultural interpretation of human differences, the Chicago school of sociology centered about Robert Ezra Park focused its studies upon immigrant communities in urban settings. W. I. Thomas set forth the essential thesis of the Chicago school in *Old World Traits Transplanted* (1921), a volume in the Studies of Methods of Americanization series sponsored by the Carnegie Corporation. Thomas contended that immigrants, displaced from familiar environments, experienced cultural confusion and breakdown, resulting in various forms of social pathology. To cope with this disorganization, they drew upon their Old World traits to create institutions and reestablish social order. Since immigrant cultural retention was a transitory phenomenon, the foreign born did not pose a long-term threat to the institutions or values of the United States. Moreover, coercive Americanization—by eliciting a counterethnic consciousness—actually retarded the assimilation process. Like Thomas, Park did not envision cultural pluralism as a permanent arrangement for American society; once ethnic communities had served their purpose as "decompression chambers," they would wither away. The implications for public policy were that Anglo-Americans should not only tolerate, but support, such ephemeral ethnic adaptations since the alternative was social chaos.

The social sciences thus encouraged melioristic programs for easing the transition of immigrants into American society. The Foreign Language Information Service (FLIS) of the Committee on Public Information became a private-sector organization in the twenties with the mission of interpreting the immigrant to American society and American society to the immigrant. International Institutes (II), first established under the aegis of the YWCA, served immigrants in more than fifty cities throughout the country. In addition to teaching English and citizenship, the institutes encouraged immigrant groups to celebrate traditional holidays, preserve their mother tongues, and cultivate their folk arts. While FLIS and II leaders cultivated ethnic cultures, they anticipated that in time the various groups would be absorbed into American society, bequeathing their "immigrant gifts" to the goddess of Liberty.

In assisting immigrant families, social workers, such as the nationality secretaries of the institutes, became keenly aware that the second generation particularly was suffering from cultural conflict. On a whole range of issues—dress, speech, courtship, work, and leisure—young people were receiving one message from parents and another from American schools and media. Social workers viewed this generational conflict between Old World familism and American individualism with alarm, associating it with increasing crime, promiscuity, and other forms of juvenile delinquency. Through agencies such as the institutes they sought to mediate generational disputes and strengthen families by valuing ethnic traditions. From this perspective, ethnicity was viewed as an important bulwark against broken families and wayward youth.

Not all American institutions appreciated the integrative value of immigrant cultures. Public schools, by and large, continued to view their mission as one of Americanizing immigrant children as quickly and thoroughly as possible. Not only did teachers rarely provide positive reinforcement for the language and cultural skills that students brought from home, but they often ridiculed and even punished such behavior. A young teacher in New Jersey, Rachel Davis DuBois, recognizing the destructive effects on the self-esteem of children, introduced curriculum and teaching methods that incorporated an appreciation of the ethnic backgrounds of students. DuBois's pioneering work gradually evolved into the intercultural education movement of the thirties. DuBois gained an influential ally in Louis Adamic, who had emigrated from Slovenia at age fourteen and become a successful American writer. In a widely cited article, "Thirty Million New Americans" (1934), Adamic identified the source of the "second-generation problem" as the self-hatred engendered among immigrant youth. The antidote, he prescribed, was the teaching of immigrant cultures and histories from elementary schools through the universities. Despite the efforts of such precursors of ethnic studies, educators by and large continued to subscribe to a pedagogy of Americanization.

Ethnic communities were most sensitive to the seduction of youth by American ways and resulting family strife. For the most part such issues were dealt with within the family, perhaps with the help of a priest or other respected counselor. The neighborhood gang became a means by which young men and women asserted their autonomy and mediated their contacts with the outside world. These "athletic clubs" also defended the neighborhood from marauding rival gangs and served as training grounds for political and criminal careers. Settlement houses, on the other hand, attracted upwardly mobile youths who aspired to escape from the ethnic enclave. Through parochial schools and cultural activities, fraternal and religious leaders sought to imbue in young people a sense of ethnic identity. Recognizing the allure of American popular culture, they also sponsored athletic teams, dances, summer camps, and other activities. If the children were to be Americanized, let it be under ethnic auspices.

While few ethnic leaders challenged head-on the idea of Americanization, they contended that the cultures introduced by the immigrants enriched America and should be incorporated into an all-American stew or salad (metaphors which now competed with the melting pot). Seeking to reassure Anglo-Americans, their rhetoric attempted to reconcile affection for land of origin with loyalty to adopted country ("We love Italy as our mother, and America as our bride"). Disillusioned with postwar developments in the Old World, they manifested less interest in the politics of the homeland and more in the status of their group in American society. Indeed, they urged their fellow ethnics to learn English, become citizens, and be good Americans, yet at the same time admonished them to preserve their attachment to the ancestral heritage.

The relative prosperity that Americans enjoyed in the twenties came to an abrupt end with the implosion of the economy following the stock market collapse of October 1929. Not all strata in the vertical mosaic were equally affected by this catastrophe. Anglo-Americans generally fared better than recent immigrants and African Americans, who as blue-collar workers, shopkeepers, and small farmers most sharply felt the impact of unemployment and mortgage foreclosures. For most new Americans, the thirties were a decade of privation and insecurity. Some gave up and returned to their homelands. Net immigration during the decade 1931 to 1940 reached the lowest point since 1820, less than 100,000.

In some ways, however, recent immigrants were better equipped than Yankees to cope with economic crisis. Vegetable gardens and backyard chicken coops supplemented family larders; extended families and neighbors helped those in need; corner groceries extended credit; while parish churches, political organizations, and fraternals provided relief. Yet as the depression deepened, families turned to government for work, food, and shelter. For some, the shame of dependency was too great; suicides increased. For many, memories of the Great Depression scarred their vision of the American Dream.

Ethnic workers played major roles in two of the most significant responses to the economic crisis: the New Deal and the Congress of Industrial Organizations. As Lizabeth Cohen has argued, industrial workers in the thirties made a new deal for themselves largely on their own initiative and out of their own resources. Politically, the shift of blue-collar ethnics to the Democratic party, which had begun in 1928, became a landslide for Franklin D. Roosevelt. Rather than turning to revolutionary alternatives, they became a pillar of the Roosevelt coalition, which dominated national politics in the thirties and beyond. Ethnic radical traditions were channeled into labor organizing as Wobblies, socialists, and Communists led mass strikes in basic industries. Since a substantial portion of the labor force was composed of immigrants and their children, the CIO leadership astutely based its strategy in ethnic institutions and neighborhoods. Popular culture and heightened class consciousness united workers across ethnic and racial lines. Meanwhile, citing the model of the Soviet Union—and drawing support and direction from Moscow—the Communist Party of the U.S.A. (CPUSA) gained followings among groups with radical traditions such as east European Jews and Finns.

Membership in the Democratic party and in a revitalized labor movement empowered millions of new Americans to participate fully in American society. Barriers of exclusion were demolished as sons and daughters of southern and eastern European immigrants gained union and political office. The career of Russian-born Sidney Hillman, who rose from the ranks of Jewish garment workers to become an adviser to President Roosevelt, exemplified this revolutionary assault upon the established ethnic and class hierarchy. Such gains by a multiethnic proletariat under the New Deal signified a loss of power on the part of southern whites, who feared the threat to the Jim Crow system of segregation, and Yankees, who feared the challenge to their privileged status.

Paradoxically, if working-class solidarity was a reality in the thirties so was heightened ethnic, racial, and religious conflict. Hard times evoked bigotry and hostility, which were expressed in the search for scapegoats. Nativist solutions to the Depression included mass deportation of Mexicans (including American citizens) and tightened restrictions on immigration. Despite the growing number of refugees from totalitarian regimes, xenophobia and anti-Semitism prevented the liberalization of immigration policies. Demagogues such as Silvershirt leader William Dudley Pelly, the Reverend Gerald L. K. Smith, and Father Charles E. Coughlin, who blamed Jews both for the economic crisis *and* communism, gained substantial followings among ethnic Catholics as well as fundamentalist Protestants.

Growing international tensions resulting from Fascist Italy and Nazi Germany's aggressions exacerbated intergroup relations in the United States. Smarting from World War I charges of disloyalty, few German Americans aligned themselves openly with Hitler by joining the German American Bund. Resentment of ethnic discrimination, however, made Italian Americans more susceptible to the appeal of Fascism. Since Anglo-Americans expressed admiration of Mussolini, Italian Americans could bolster their egos by identifying with *Il Duce.* A combative minority of Italian American anti-Fascists challenged the Blackshirts in print and on the streets. While Fascism served as a catalyst in the redefinition of Italian American identity in the thirties, it was also a source of bitter intragroup conflict.

More than any other foreign event of the thirties, the Spanish Civil War (1935–1939) divided Americans along ethnoreligious as well as ideological lines. Supporting the Franco-led Rebels were not only anticommunist conservatives, but also Irish, Slavic, and Italian Catholics, while the Loyalist cause attracted liberal Anglo-Americans and ethnics of various radical persuasions. The Loyalist Abraham Lincoln Brigade of volunteers from the United States was very much a rainbow division.

Intensified ethnic conflicts challenged the country's ideologues to imagine a vision of national unity transcending the all-too-vivid diversity. If racism persisted, the ideology of racialism lost its credibility in the face of the social science critique and the horrors of Nazism. Cultural democracy emerged as the guiding motif of progressive artistic and intellectual activities of the decade. In the writings of Carl Sandburg, the paintings of Ben Shahn, and the music of Aaron Copland, one finds an affirmation of the common people in all their variety. Under the aegis of New Deal programs such as the Federal Writers' Project, the lives of plain people, their folk music, tales, and humor were documented and published. A "history from the bottom up" perspective (a term first used by Caroline Ware in *The Cultural Approach to History,* 1940) informed a library of books dealing with farmers, workers, and a wide range of ethnic and racial groups. Novels and plays, paintings and murals, songs and symphonies explored and celebrated the lives of African Americans, Jewish Americans, Italian Americans, Slovak Americans, and others. Voices of ethnic diversity challenged Anglo-American hegemony in all the arts. While expressive of New Deal populism, the ethos of cultural democracy also reflected the influence of the Communist party among artists and intellectuals. With the adoption by the Communist International of the "United Front" strategy in 1935, the CPUSA subordinated the theme of class struggle to the struggle against fascism and sought to identify itself with democratic traditions, including ethnic pluralism.

An efflorescence of ethnic expression marked the emergence of a generation of gifted writers from working-class and ethnically diverse backgrounds (Richard Wright, Thomas Bell, Henry Roth, and Pietro Di Donato, to name a few). Among these, Louis Adamic stands out, not because he was the best writer, but because he was a single-minded advocate of an America in which all cultural heritages would be equally valued. Throughout the thirties, he campaigned for a new synthesis of the old and the new Americas, of Plymouth Rock and Ellis Island. Adamic was instrumental in transforming FLIS into the Common Council for American Unity (CCAU) in 1939 and in establishing the multiethnic journal *Common Ground* (1940–1949). Among its contributors were many new voices speaking for previously silent ethnicities, including Langston Hughes, Jade Snow Wong, Michael De Capite, George Papashvily, Frank Mlakar, and Marie Syrkin. The name change from FLIS to CCAU itself represented a redefinition of the organization's agenda to an all-inclusive conception of American diversity.

Many shared Adamic's worries about the ugly cleavages in American society against the backdrop of a world on the verge of global war. National organizations such as the National Conference of Christians and Jews disseminated messages of brotherhood, while many local community relations councils promoted intergroup harmony. Expressive of this quest for unity within diversity, the U.S. Office of Education in 1939 broadcast a series of radio programs narrating the stories of many ethnic groups under the title *Americans All*.

LOYALTIES TESTED AND ETHNICITIES REDEFINED: WORLD WAR II AND COLD WAR

When war came to Europe in 1939, Americans again engaged in acrimonious debate over the appropriate response of the United States. In the partisan alignments on foreign policy one could find the lineaments of the ethnic composition of the American people. As Samuel Lubell observed, bitter memories of World War I engendered a "politics of revenge" on the part of those groups that had suffered repression or disappointment. Not only German Americans, but Scandinavian Americans, Irish Americans, and Italian Americans, opposed the pro-Allied leanings of the Roosevelt administration. The isolationist America First movement was solidly based among the northern and central European Americans of the Middle West. One of its leading spokesmen, the celebrated aviator Charles A. Lindbergh, was the son of a Swedish-born congressman from Minnesota who had opposed U.S. entry into World War I. Interventionists, organized into the Committee to Defend America by Aiding the Allies, drew their primary strength from the Anglophile old stock of the East and South as well as from those ethnic groups whose relatives had suffered at the hands of Hitler and Mussolini. The Soviet invasion of Finland in 1939 left Finnish Americans, many of whom had communist sympathies, torn between ideological and national loyalties. Ethnic alignments on the European war expressed themselves politically in the election of 1940, when isolationists angry at FDR's pro-British policy deserted the Democratic party en masse.

The Japanese attack on Pearl Harbor on 7 December 1941 brought unity to the United States. America Firsters and ethnic leaders immediately vowed dedication to military victory over the Axis powers. World War II posed the issue of dual loyalties for Italian Americans and German Americans (for the second time). With few exceptions, they responded by professing their unqualified loyalty, by buying war bonds and sending their sons and daughters off to war. Compared to World War I, there was relatively little persecution of "disloyal" elements and violation of civil liberties, with one notable exception. Germans and Italians who were not naturalized were classified as "enemy aliens," but aside from a few thousand "extremists" who were incarcerated, they were for the most part subject to mild restrictions. Even this stigma was lifted from Italian noncitizens by a proclamation of U.S. Attorney General Francis Biddle (issued on Columbus Day 1942!) that declared them to be loyal to the United States. In addition to being important sources of manpower, their political clout protected Italian Americans and German Americans from punitive measures.

Japanese Americans fared very differently. A small population concentrated on the West Coast, long objects of racist prejudice and resented for their economic success, they presented an ideal scapegoat, easily identifiable and vulnerable. Certainly the attack by the Japanese on Pearl Harbor and their early military gains inflamed American opinion against the "Japs." In subsequent American propaganda (including Hollywood films), Japanese were caricatured as cruel and bestial. The decision of Secretary of War Henry L. Stimson and Assistant Secretary of War John J. McCloy (with President Roosevelt's approval) to forcibly remove nearly 120,000 Japanese Americans—two-thirds of them American-born Nisei—from the West Coast (the much larger Japanese American population of Hawaii was not "relocated") to concentration camps was justified in terms of "military necessity"; this massive violation of civil and human rights was due, however, essentially to racial prejudice. Acquiescence by the Congress, the Supreme Court, the press, the universities, indeed by the entire society (with few dissenting voices), may be attributed in part to war psychology, but it also demonstrated that racism had not disappeared from America.

Deprived of liberty and property for the "crime" of Japanese origins, imprisonment behind barbed wire represented a traumatic rupture in the lives of the internees. Families and communities disintegrated, and individuals chose different paths. While many young men seized the opportunity to enlist in the U.S. military, some chose repatriation to Japan. Nisei were permitted to take jobs or pursue studies in the Midwest; from these secondary relocations, nuclei of permanent communities were formed in Chicago, Minneapolis, and other cities. After the war, most eventually returned to the West Coast to pick up the pieces of their broken lives. The relocation camp experience remained a deep source of shame with which Japanese Americans (and Americans generally) have only come to grips in recent years. The third-generation Sansei, intent on recovering this grim chapter of their history, finally awakened the American conscience to this unacknowledged injustice. In 1988 Congress apologized to Japanese Americans and authorized payment of $20,000 to each camp survivor as a form of redress.

Other ethnic and racial groups prospered during the war as never before. After a decade of grinding depression, mobilization brought full employment, high wages, and government-supported collective bargaining. Military service and war industries drew younger generations out of ethnic enclaves, scattering them around the country and the world, throwing them together with all kinds of people, and opening them to new possibilities. Despite concomitant social problems such as increased housing shortages, juvenile delinquency, and rates of divorce, the morale of the American people was generally high because the war effort provided a sense of a common cause transcending class and ethnic boundaries.

The moral justification of the war against Nazism further undermined barriers of discrimination and prejudice. African Americans, who had made few gains under the New Deal, realized major breakthroughs, but not without struggle. A. Philip Randolph's threatened March on Washington to demand equal opportunities for jobs and desegregation of the armed forces resulted in the establishment of the Fair Employment Practices Committee by President Roosevelt (1941) which, while yielding few immediate gains, established the principle of equality of opportunity in the labor market. Government pressure and labor shortages opened new jobs to African Americans; even in the armed forces racial segregation began to break down. In retrospect, one can observe that the seeds of the civil rights movement of the fifties were sown during World War II.

Despite the pluralist rhetoric of "Americans All," war-engendered encounters among different segments of the population in manufacturing plants and military units made for some heightened ethnic tensions. Physical relocations with resulting disruptions of community ties created a psychology of insecurity that lent itself to expressions of hostility. Great numbers of black and white rural southerners responded to the demand for workers in centers of war production. Congestion in overcrowded, segregated housing, competition for public services and facilities, and workplace antagonisms erupted in "race riots" in Detroit, Harlem, and elsewhere. Meanwhile, Mexicans were being recruited under the *bracero* program to provide agricultural and railroad labor in the Southwest. In Los Angeles, barrios expanded with resulting conflicts over jobs and turf. In an expression of ethnic assertiveness, Mexican American youth, so-called "zoot-suiters," adopted a lifestyle and costume that antagonized Anglos. Skirmishes between them and servicemen culminated in attacks on young Mexicans and blacks. Notwithstanding American condemnation of Nazism, blatant expressions of anti-Semitism were also common in the United States during the war.

Ethnic hostilities tended to be viewed increasingly in "racial" terms, as pitting whites against Japanese Americans, African Americans, and Mexican Americans. Social scientists and social service agencies shifted their focus from the assimilation of immigrants to race relations as the latter became viewed as the more intractable problem confronting society. Gunnar Myrdal's *An American Dilemma* (1944), a monumental study that addressed the persistence of a caste-like status for "Negroes," predicted a gradual but steady assimilation of African Americans as white Americans struggled with the contradiction between democratic ideals and racial injustice. Contemporaneously, the Congress of Racial Equality, the National Association for the Advancement of Colored People (NAACP), and the Urban League, newly established or revitalized, mounted assaults upon the Jim Crow system in the South and discrimination in the North.

Since episodes of ethnic conflict threatened to undermine both morale and the moral basis of the war, the task of American propaganda was to create the illusion of a harmonious, united society. Rather than denying diversity, the Office of War Information chose the theme of an inclusive pluralism, in which all Americans, regardless of religion, race, or origin, worked and fought together for victory. Public recognition of contributions to the war effort, whether a bond drive, scrap collection, or ceremony honoring Gold Star Mothers (women whose sons had been killed in action), included a cross section of groups. Stories and films about American troops featured platoons composed of a spectrum of ethnic types identifiable by names and accents. The military exploits of the segregated Japanese American 442d Regimental Combat Team were highlighted to illustrate the theme of "united for victory." In such portrayals of diversity, attention was focused on the common patriotism rather than the cultural distinctiveness of the participants.

Military victory over the Axis powers did not bring peace. With hardly an interlude, the country moved from hot war to cold war. While the Soviet Union was now the external enemy, "subversives" (Communists and fellow travelers) were identified as the internal enemy. The ensuing "Red Scare" had significant repercussions on ethnic communities. Fraternal and labor organizations, many of a Slavic character, were placed by the attorney general on the list of communist "front organizations." Membership in such organizations was regarded as prima facie evidence of communist sympathies and thus possible grounds for denaturalization and deportation under the Alien Registration Act of 1940 and the Internal Security Act of 1950. Meanwhile, right-wingers utilized the provisions of the Taft-Hartley Act (1947) that required union officials to sign affidavits attesting that they were not (and had not been) Communists to purge the labor movement. The 1948 presidential campaign of Henry Wallace under the banner of the Progressive party, which opposed Truman's "Cold War" policies, represented a last hurrah of the ethnic-labor left wing of the Roosevelt coalition. Louis Adamic, who as chairman of the United Committee of South Slavic Americans had supported Tito and the Partisans, was a Wallace supporter. Questioned by the House Committee on Un-American Activities, labeled a "Commie" in the press, ostracized and boycotted, Adamic died under mysterious circumstances in 1951. McCarthyism thus created a mood of paranoia that marginalized leftists within ethnic and labor organizations.

Anticommunism served yet another function in the continuing struggle among ethnic groups for status and power. Whereas previous Red Scares had been directed by Anglo-Americans against foreigners, in this instance certain out-groups seized the opportunity to hoist the Yankees with their own petard. Of the hunt for communists in the State Department, it was said that Irish Catholic graduates of Fordham were now investigating Anglo-American graduates of Ivy League universities. Senator Joe McCarthy, himself an Irish Catholic who embodied the "Mick" street brawler image, won a populist following among many with class and ethnic resentments. A striking congruency existed between his strongholds and areas of America First isolationist sentiments. In the iconography of the anticommunist crusade, Alger Hiss, the archetypal WASP, was the big fish that Richard Nixon, always the outsider, figuratively mounted over the fireplace in the White House. Among other things, McCarthyism was an assault on the bastions of Anglo-American supremacy.

The Cold War also shaped U.S. immigration policy during the postwar decades. Millions of Europeans had been uprooted by the war, redrawn international boundaries, and massive population transfers. Initially the United States clung to its rigid quota system, but responding to various pressures, the Truman administration secured congressional approval of the Displaced Persons acts of 1948 and 1950 that admitted a total of 450,000 refugees—ethnic Germans, Jews, Poles, Ukrainians, and Baltic peoples—as well as granting special entry to other groups. Reflecting the Cold War climate, the Immigration and Nationality Act of 1952 erected barriers to the entry of potential subversives, while it reaffirmed the national origins quota system. The act also allocated 185 visas a year to Japan (and abolished the category of aliens ineligible for citizenship), thus repealing the last vestige of the longstanding Asian exclusion policy (Chinese in 1943 and Filipinos and natives of India in 1946 had been allocated quotas). Since the 1940s, U.S. immigration policy liberally extended asylum to refugees from communist countries, while often denying admission to persons fleeing rightist regimes on the grounds that they were merely economic immigrants. Special entry was granted to escapees following the Hungarian Revolution of 1956, Castro's ascent to power in 1959, and the fall of Saigon in 1974. While exiles from communist regimes collectively totaled some 2 million between 1945 and 1990, their influence exceeded their numbers. Often from their countries' upper classes, the newcomers realized quick adjustment and upward mobility. But committed to an eventual return, they maintained languages and cultures by establishing churches, schools, and publications. While they infused new life into established communities, the refugees' political agenda often clashed with that of second- and third-generation American ethnics. The recent history of many east European groups has been one of struggle among representatives of the various immigrant waves over definitions of peoplehood.

Politically conservative, Cold War refugees lobbied vigorously for tough policies with respect to communist regimes. Through their extraordinary presence as professors, journalists, and on the staffs of the CIA and State Department, east European and Cuban exiles influenced public opinion and policy in the direction of Cold War orthodoxy. The Assembly of Captive European Nations and a network of refugee organizations kept alive the charge of a Yalta betrayal against the Democratic party and persuaded the Eisenhower administration to adopt a policy of liberation. Influenced by such Cold War rhetoric, significant numbers of ethnic voters, particularly Slavic Americans, convinced that the Democratic party was "soft on communism," shifted over to the Republican column.

In the Cold War atmosphere of loyalty oaths, second-generation Americans repressed traces of ethnicity that might impugn their Americanism. After two decades of depression and war, they satisfied yearnings for economic and psychological security by dissolving into an anonymous middle class and indulging in an orgy of consumption. Riding the postwar economic boom, with an assist from the GI bill of rights, working-class ethnics in growing numbers pursued higher education, entered white-collar occupations, and moved to the suburbs. Meanwhile, city planners and developers accelerated the process of out-migration by bulldozing old urban neighborhoods to make way for high-rise buildings and highways. Not until urbanologists like Jane Jacobs (*The Life and Death of Great American Cities,* 1961) rediscovered the virtues of neighborhood was there a reevaluation of what had become known as "urban removal." By then numerous ethnic communities had been physically and socially demolished by federally funded projects.

While the cityscape was literally being leveled, the mental landscape of Americans was figuratively being bulldozed by the pervasive influence of television. More than radio or motion pictures, TV exerted a powerful influence for cultural homogenization, introducing directly into homes standardized myths, tastes, and values. Programs with ethnic themes were few, yet the underlying diversity of American life did at times appear on the tube. The televised hearings of the Kefauver committee on organized crime reinforced stereotypes of the Mafia and prepared the way for innumerable fictionalized portrayals of Italian American gangsters such as the long-running series *The Untouchables. Father Knows Best,* about a "typical" Anglo-American, suburban, middle-class family, perhaps best projected the fifties' hunger for security, normalcy, and material comforts. Its portrayal of a sanitized and de-ethnicized lifestyle appealed to those fugitives from inner-city ghettos searching for the "real America."

In retrospect, the decade of the fifties appears to have been a Never-Never Land. In a rapture of boosterism, many believed that America was embarked upon an upward spiral of growth and progress. Capitalism was a cornucopia that would shower its benevolence upon all, creating a homogenous middle-class society through a citizenship of consumption. Consensus historians labored to demonstrate that American history had been relatively conflict-free since Americans, it was said, essentially shared the same values. Class and ethnic differences in any case had been dissolved by what Frederick Lewis Allen called the "big change" in his 1952 book of the same title. Other authors wrote about Americans as a "people of plenty" (1958), and if they once had been "the uprooted" (1951), the pains of the immigrants had been justified by the gains of their children. Historians and sociologists agreed that nationality groups (ethnicity had not yet entered their vocabulary) were largely a thing of the past. Will Herberg, in *Protestant, Catholic, Jew* (1955), announced that nationality had been replaced by religion as the primary source of identity and community, as ethnic groups were absorbed into a "triple melting pot." If there was a problem it was that Americans were too much alike, complained David Riesman in *The Lonely Crowd* (1950), or they were too conformist, as in Sloan Wilson's *The Man in the*

Gray Flannel Suit (1955). But what of the Negroes? Hailing the Supreme Court school desegregation decision in *Brown* v. *Board of Education* (1954), liberal commentators believed with Myrdal that it was only a matter of time before blacks too would realize full assimilation into a colorblind middle class.

THE NEW PLURALISM, 1960s–1970s

If conformity was the keynote of the fifties, conflict was the leitmotif of the sixties. Black power, the Vietnam War, the student revolution, feminism, gay rights, these—and more—were the issues and causes that wracked the nation. Americans engaged in bitter debate in bars and in Congress, and in bloody battles in ghettos and on the campuses of the country. The causes of this "ungluing of America" were complex and profound, but certainly one was the collapse of Anglo-American hegemony. Popular confidence in the superior wisdom of the WASP establishment, eroded by the Depression and McCarthyism, crumbled with the unfolding tragedies in the jungles of Southeast Asia and the "mean streets" of Detroit. Plain Americans, confronted with moral dilemmas to which traditional elites appeared not to have answers, sought guidance and security in more personal and communal values. The transmogrification of the American Dream caused many to reconsider their previously assumed identity as just plain Americans.

Along with other myths of the civil religion, the melting pot came under attack as a sham for Anglo-American dominance. African Americans first challenged the assimilationist paradigm when they rejected the civil rights strategy of integration for the black nationalist goal of self-determination. Legal and direct action campaigns painstakingly dismantled the Jim Crow system, but the social and economic subordination of African Americans, in northern cities in particular, was not notably alleviated. Young militants questioned the efficacy of nonviolent resistance and the legal strategies of the Southern Christian Leadership Conference and the NAACP. Under diverse auspices, the Nation of Islam, the Black Panther party, and the Student Nonviolent Coordinating Committee, an African American ethnicity was articulated that affirmed Black Power as the basis for an autonomous community. The emergence of postcolonial independent nations in Africa served as a source of inspiration for American black nationalism. One consequence was a reinvention of black identity, its Africanization if you will, through the adoption of African names, dress, and rituals.

In the mid-sixties, frustrated by unfulfilled expectations and incited by the slogans of Black Power, ghettos exploded in uprisings that laid waste major urban areas. The so-called civil disorders in Harlem, Watts, Newark, and Cleveland culminated in a nationwide wave of uprisings following the assassination of the Rev. Dr. Martin Luther King, Jr. in April 1968. Insurrections characterized by widespread arson, looting, and armed resistance, they were finally suppressed by military force. In its report, the National Advisory Commission on Civil Disorders warned that America was becoming "two societies, one black, one white, separate and unequal" and called for strong remedial measures if this polarization was not to destroy the nation. The Kerner Report and its proposed remedies, however, were flawed by a reification of race as the primary (indeed, only significant) source of difference, ignoring the extraordinary ethnic and religious—not to mention economic and class—diversity that in fact continued to characterize the country.

Frightened by the sight of burning cities and bedeviled by a guilty conscience, the liberal political establishment beefed up "affirmative action" programs under the Civil Rights Act of 1964. Although the act guaranteed equality of opportunity in voting, education, housing, employment, and use of public accommodations, "regardless of race, color, religion, sex, or national origin," its subsequent implementation specified particular racial and ethnic populations as the beneficiaries of affirmative action programs. In 1977, the Office of Management and Budget promulgated *Directive No. 15: Race and Ethnic Standards for Federal Statistics and Administrative Reporting,* which established the following racial and ethnic categories: American Indian or Alaskan Native; Asian or Pacific Islander; Black; Hispanic; White. These categories egregiously mixed racial, cultural, and geographic criteria and ethnic groups with quite disparate cultures and histories. (The directive included the caveat that the classifications should not be interpreted as being scientific or anthropological in nature!) In this classificatory scheme, the category "white" (defined as persons having origins in Europe, North Africa, or the Middle East) promiscuously lumped together Mayflower descendants and the most recent arrivals from Poland or Iran. Further, all whites, regardless of education, income, or previous history of discrimination, were presumed to belong to the dominant racial group and thus not entitled to the protection of the Civil Rights Act. This quinquepartite division of the American people became the basis for federally mandated affirmative action that extended beyond government programs to educational institutions and businesses receiving federal grants or contracts. Other institutions, public and private, subsequently embraced these fictive categories in making decisions regarding employment, promotion, admissions, and grants.

While affirmative action had the well-intentioned purpose of correcting deeply rooted inequities, it became a divisive policy that polarized public discourse and further embittered relationships among groups. According to the principle of compensation for past injustices, members of a "protected class" (e.g., African Americans) were entitled to redress regardless of individual history and current circumstance. As affirmative action was aggressively implemented to include "goals and timetables" (quotas and deadlines), critics such as Nathan Glazer attacked this as "reverse discrimination." In actuality, affirmative action programs encountered stiff legal and social resistance from defenders of the racial status quo; while a minority of the intended beneficiaries gained access to hitherto foreclosed opportunities, the prospects of those who suffered most from prejudice and poverty were not significantly altered.

The politics of retrospective compensation served as a major catalyst for ethnicization in the sixties and seventies. Taking a page from the black nationalists' book, leaders of other minority groups proclaimed that they too had suffered at the hands of Anglo or white oppressors and demanded indemnification. Seeking to maximize their numbers and clout, ideologues espoused strategies of panethnicity, seeking to consolidate scattered, passive, and, at times, incongruous constituencies into national movements. Agents of ethnicization, they invented histories, symbols, and names (Native Americans, Chicanos, Hispanics or Latinos, and Asian Americans) for these newly imagined communities.

To the consternation of social scientists and policymakers, who had predicted the demise of European American groups, the phenomenon of "white ethnicity" burst upon the public scene. Bemused journalists and pundits devoted extensive coverage to what was described as a "white ethnic backlash" against African Americans. Suddenly the lives and histories of these communities became the object of TV specials, news stories, and foundation-sponsored studies. What such scrutiny discovered was that these "white ethnics" were really Polish Americans, Slovak Americans, Italian Americans, etc., who had somehow survived the melting pot. Emulating African Americans, they too demanded recognition and respect; if Black was beautiful, so was Ukrainian and Greek.

Despite erosion of ethnic neighborhoods, remnants of Poletowns and Little Italies persisted. Dense residential concentrations, family and social networks, and institutional infrastructures continued to demarcate these communities. In northern metropolitan areas, aging immigrants and their children often constituted the only substantial nonblack population left in the inner cities. They suffered similar problems as their African-American neighbors, a decaying urban infrastructure, inferior schools, crime, and poor public services; and as industrial workers, they confronted the insecurities posed by automation and deindustrialization. In addition, despite their loyalty, hard work and military service, they were still regarded as second class citizens, the butt of ethnic jokes; now they were berated as "hardhat racists."

Second- and third-generation working-class European Americans had willy-nilly assimilated racial prejudice as part of their acculturation. Given their ambiguous place in the vertical mosaic, race was an important distinction that established their superiority at least to the "colored." Living in proximity to black ghettos, the drugs, prostitution, and violence conflicted with their traditional values even though such pathologies were not absent from their own communities. African American demands for equality were viewed as encroaching on their jobs, homes, and schools. Forming cross-ethnic coalitions, European Americans mobilized vigilante groups and political organizations to defend their neighborhoods. The white ethnic movement also expressed class resentments against the presumed moral superiority of middle- and upper-class liberals who were viewed as patrons of black revolutionaries. Engaging in the politics of victimhood, white ethnic advocates calculated how prejudice and discrimination had disadvantaged their groups and demanded their own affirmative action.

European American neighborhoods appeared to be fertile ground for antiblack politics as dramatized by the presidential candidacy of George Wallace in 1968. Although Wallace failed to garner the anticipated blue-collar ethnic vote in northern cities, a growing shift to Republican ranks among Jews, Italians, and Poles alarmed Democratic politicians and liberal organizations. Formerly allied in progressive causes, Jews and African Americans increasingly clashed on political and economic issues. The "school wars" of 1967–1969 in New York City, which pitted the largely Jewish United Federation of Teachers against black and Hispanic community school boards, exacerbated this estrangement. Having prospered under the system of meritocracy, Jews strongly opposed affirmative action, while attacks on Israel by black militants threatened the very core of Jewish ethnonationalism.

These escalating conflicts moved the American Jewish Committee to initiate the Depolarization Project on Ethnic America, a strategy for building interracial coalitions among disadvantaged urban dwellers, black and white, Jewish and Catholic. Beginning with a conference at Fordham University in 1968, the AJC's Institute on Pluralism and Group Identity assembled ethnic leaders, community activists, and academics in cities across the country to dialogue and seek common ground. Despite modest accomplishments, such coalition strategies ultimately failed. African Americans, who viewed the white ethnic movement as an effort to divert the nation's attention from their agenda, were not interested in allying themselves with "honkies." Many European Americans could not overcome their fear and hatred of blacks. An inability to reorient political behavior from issues of race to issues of class doomed interracial coalition building.

Were European American ethnicities simply a reflex of black nationalism? Various writers have gone to great lengths to discredit the white ethnic revival as a smoke screen for racism, as a manifestation of class-based resentments, or as stemming from a guilt complex of second-generation ethnics who had "betrayed" their immigrant ancestors. While such factors may have played a part, the sixties witnessed a bona fide resurgence of European American ethnicities. Although the black movement served as a catalyst, the revival was fueled by multiple causes. In addition to racial conflict, the United States was riven by searing discords that challenged the values of all Americans. To the ambiguities posed by the Vietnam War, working-class ethnics responded with the unconditional patriotism they had been taught as apprentice Americans, sending their sons to fight in the jungles of southeast Asia. They reacted with moral outrage to antiwar protests and the hippie lifestyle with its flagrant sexuality and recreational drugs. Ironically when college students greeted white ethnic police and blue-collar workers with the epithet "fascist pigs," they alienated the very proletariat they aspired to radicalize.

The election of John F. Kennedy, the first (and only) Irish Catholic president (but also a graduate of WASP Choate and Harvard), had been a cause for celebration as the last bastion of Anglo-American exclusiveness surrendered to the new Americans. But the slaying of the Kennedy brothers brought this brief euphoria to an abrupt and tragic end. The Republicans adopted a political strategy of appealing to the racial and sexual fears of the "moral majority." Beginning in 1968, when many disgruntled white ethnics voted for Nixon, the movement to the Republican party became an avalanche by 1972. To many ethnic traditionalists, the Democratic party and its candidate, George McGovern, appeared to have been completely taken over by the potheads, bra-burning feminists, draft card–burning peaceniks, and Black Panthers. The Roosevelt coalition broke up on the rocks of such "cultural issues," bringing to power conservatives, both Republicans and Democrats, who were to dominate American politics for the balance of the twentieth century.

Another source of ethnicization for European and Asian Americans was the appeal of homelands in distress. Ethnic communities had long responded to crises in their ancestral countries with material assistance and lobbying for a responsive U.S. foreign policy. Since World War II, the American Jewish community, galvanized by the Holocaust, the birth of Israel, and Israel's recurring wars with Arab states, contributed billions of dollars and decisively influenced U.S. policy in the Middle East. In opposition, Arab Americans, an ethnicity that emerged out of the melding of several immigrant groups, mounted a vigorous movement for the liberation of Palestine. The invasion of Cyprus by Turkey in 1974 likewise mobilized Greek Americans to rush aid to the Cypriots and to establish an anti-Turkish lobby in Washington. Irish Americans, in a tradition extending back over a hundred years, supported the Catholic struggle in northern Ireland, even providing money and arms to the IRA. Meanwhile, mirroring the struggle in the homeland, Chinatowns were rent by clashes between supporters of the Nationalists and the Communists. Events abroad thus have been powerful catalysts of a heightened sense of peoplehood among many ethnic groups.

It was only natural that during the decade of liberation European Americans should come out of the closet with everyone else. Michael Novak's *The Rise of the Unmeltable Ethnics* (1972) touched a nerve with many second- and third-generation Americans who had been ashamed of their foreign-sounding names, immigrant ancestry, and non-Anglo behavior. When Novak told them it was O.K. to be ethnic, the oppressive weight of the melting pot was lifted off their shoulders. Moreover, as Anthony Smith and others have pointed out, the contemporary global surge in ethnicity expressed the need for an intimate sense of community in a postmodern, impersonal society. Symbols of peoplehood were refurbished or devised; institutions revitalized or established; festivals revived or invented. Nor was the "new ethnicity" limited to big cities or to recent immigrant groups; a quickening of ethnic life was manifest in small towns and rural areas and among persons generations removed from foreign soil.

The seventies appeared to be a decade of triumphant ethnicity, as the Vietnam War ground to a halt and the racial wars became skirmishes. For many Americans, the cultivation of their ethnic heritages became an avocation. Buttons and bumper stickers ("Kiss Me, I'm Slovak" and "Swedish Pride"), the study of ancestral languages and cultures, and visits to the Old Country were all affirmations of ethnic identities. Indicative of this mood was a newfound obsession of many Americans with a search for roots. Genealogy had long been the fashionable preoccupation of prideful old-stock Americans. Now, descendants of peasants from Finland, Sicily, and Ireland pored over old records in libraries and archives. Rather than a national patriotic celebration, as the nation's Centennial was in 1876, the Bicentennial in 1976 was observed with a cycle of conferences, workshops, and festivals exploring the varied cultural backgrounds of Americans.

Reflecting upon this phenomenon, the sociologist Herbert Gans coined the term *symbolic ethnicity* to indicate that rather than a reality affecting everyday life, ethnicity had become a voluntary, leisure-time activity—and further, that symbolic ethnicity was a final stage in a straight-line process of assimilation. Gans's conception posited an original or authentic ethnicity in which changes over time were taken as evidence of progressive assimilation. Essentialist and deterministic, Gans's concept of ethnicity is at odds with my view that ethnicity is culturally constructed and thus can change, wane, and revive. Obviously the ethnic revival did not signify a return to original Old World cultures, but as a synthesis of family traditions, shared memories, and new elements, it was no less authentic. To dismiss contemporary forms of ethnic identity as symbolic or nostalgic is to trivialize an important passage in the evolving definition of what it has meant to be American.

The legitimation of diversity in the seventies opened clogged channels of creativity, resulting in an outpouring of novels, films, plays, and poetry exploring the many American identities. Broadway, Hollywood, and Madison Avenue produced slices of ethnic life, ranging from commercials to sit-coms to serious dramas. While some exploited stereotypes, others delved into the delights, tensions, and contradictions of being ethnic. The literary and media events of the seventies were Mario Puzo's *The Godfather* and Alex Haley's *Roots,* both highly fictionalized family histories that reached vast audiences through film and television. Thus popular culture in its omnivorous fashion commodified ethnicity and naturalized it as part of the American way of life.

From the sixties on, African Americans led the attack upon Anglo-American bastions of education. When persuasion failed, demonstrations, sit-ins, and angry rhetoric resulted in the establishment of Black Studies programs and the appointment of African American faculty. Other minority groups followed suit, demanding inclusion in the curriculum, their own teachers, and recognition of their traditions. By the seventies, many institutions of higher education had departments or programs in Chicano, Latino, or Hispanic studies, American Indian studies, and Asian American studies as well. Often the result was not Rachel Davis Dubois's ideal of intercultural education, but a ghettoization of both subject matter and students. Demands from white ethnic groups for courses dealing with their histories were less successful; not only did they pose less of a threat to the consciences and fears of faculty, but a liberal bigotry prevailed in teachers' lounges and faculty clubs that tolerated Polish and Italian jokes while slurs against "people of color" were taboo.

In varying degrees the pluralist theme percolated through the American educational system from kindergartens to colleges. Curricula and textbooks were revised to represent the motley character of America, though often in token form. In certain states and localities, training in ethnic studies for teachers and incorporation of ethnic materials in the curriculum were mandated. Such educational innovations were sanctioned by the Ethnic Heritage Studies Program Act (EHSPA) of 1972, which declared: "In recognition of the heterogeneous composition of the Nation . . . it is the purpose of this [title] . . . to afford to students opportunities to learn about the nature of their own cultural heritage, and to study the contributions of the heritages of the other ethnic groups of the Nation." European American activists and organizations lobbied most vigorously for the act, whose original sponsor was congressman Roman Pucinski of Chicago. While Congress appropriated small sums of money in the seventies in support of the measure's provisions (funding ceased entirely in the eighties), the National Endowment for the Humanities, the National Historical Publications and Records Commission, and various foundations also funded projects that reflected the spectrum of American diversity. Although Congress acknowledged in the language of EHSPA that the United States was a "multiethnic society," the United States did not formally espouse a policy of multiculturalism as did Canada in 1971. While Canadians adopted the mosaic as symbolic of their country's diversity, the melting pot retained its status as the American national icon.

If the ethnic revival caught most by surprise, certain astute observers had noted the persistence of American pluralism prior to the Black Revolution. In the fifties, Nathan Glazer had called attention to the "ghost nations" deriving from the European immigrations; and it was he and Daniel Patrick Moynihan who challenged the assimilationist paradigm in *Beyond the Melting Pot* (1964). The point about the melting pot, they asserted, was that it had not happened; ethnicity rather than class continued to shape political and social behavior. Meanwhile Milton Gordon's *Assimilation in American Life* (1965) offered a more complex model of the absorption of immigrants into the mainstream and posed anew the question of whether assimilation had—or would ever—completely take place. A year later, Joshua Fishman's *Language Loyalty in the United States* (1966) argued that immigrant groups had not eagerly and easily dissolved into some generic American stew; rather their histories were characterized by sustained struggles to maintain languages and cultures.

On the heels of these pioneering works a virtual flood of writings over the past quarter century has portrayed and analyzed the multiethnic nature of American society in the past and present. Historians, social scientists, and humanists recovered the experiences of ethnic groups, celebrated the achievements of ethnic writers and artists, and traced the pervasive influence of diversity in all aspects of life. Pluralism became the paradigm of this new scholarship and ethnicity its key interpretive concept. These intellectual assaults upon the ideological foundations of the melting pot were informed and energized by the cultural politics of the times: a search for a useable past on the part of identity movements; the empowerment of subaltern elements; and the antiestablishment animus of the New Left. The "new social history" addressed the role of ordinary people rather than elites, listening to the voices of the "inarticulate" and crediting them with agency to influence their own fate. This reorientation of scholarship was also a consequence of the entry into the professoriat of a cohort of students recruited from ethnic and working-class backgrounds who broke a virtual Anglo-American monopoly on academia.

From the mid-seventies, however, critics from both the left and the right launched a counterattack against the new ethnicity and its academic exponents. Neo-Marxists contended that white ethnic identity was a smoke screen for racism and reactionary politics that obscured the realities of social class. Neoconservatives, alarmed by what they perceived to be the fragmentation of American society, accused pluralists of fomenting disunity. In a reprise of the consensus school of the fifties, they stressed that Americans were more alike than different. Such critics agreed in dismissing the ethnic revival of the seventies as largely factitious. The scholarly assault was joined by journalists who warned that programs of ethnic studies and bilingualism could lead to separatist movements and even civil war.

RETURN TO THE MELTING POT OR MULTICULTURALISM, 1980s–1990s

The cultural revolutions of the sixties and seventies culminated in the Thermidorian reaction of the eighties and nineties. It appeared to many Americans that family, state, and church were being undermined by sinister, even satanic, forces. A self-proclaimed "moral majority" rallied in opposition to abortion, gay rights, sex education, gun control, rock music, welfare, the Equal Rights Amendment, and "secular humanism." This anomalous coalition of Protestant fundamentalists, ethnic Catholics, and neoconservative Jews congealed about an ideological hodgepodge of social issues: law and order, anticommunism, and racism. Perhaps the overriding anxiety these disparate groups shared was fear of moral and social anarchy, exemplified by crime, street violence, and drugs associated with inner-city blacks. The Republican party skillfully orchestrated these phobias into a fundamental realignment of American politics and control of the White House—and in 1994 of the Congress. Many found an antidote to their angst in Ronald Reagan's flag-waving patriotism, anticommunism, and religiosity. The son of a hard-drinking Irish American, former actor Reagan played the role of the "cowboy," the rugged individual, without family or community, that is, without ethnicity. In his public pronouncements, he was wont to refer glowingly to the melting pot.

Under both Presidents Reagan and Bush, an aggressive posture abroad and a crusading moralism at home generated pressures for conformity to conservative ideas and mores. Ironically, their administrations coincided with two centennials intimately associated with the history of immigration. The observance of the Statue of Liberty's centennial in

1986 was the occasion for an extravaganza of show business and high-blown rhetoric; that of Ellis Island in 1992 was a more low-key affair. Since the Statue of Liberty–Ellis Island Centennial Commission was composed of corporate executives and media celebrities—chaired by Chrysler president and son of Italian immigrants Lee Iacocca—it was a foregone conclusion that the celebrations would evoke the myth of America as the Land of Opportunity. Thanks to the National Park Service and an advisory committee of historians, the restoration of the two monuments, including the creation of the Museum of Immigration at Ellis Island, was carried out with due respect for historical accuracy. However, immigrant success, patriotism, and assimilation were the main themes invoked by official spokespersons. In a sense, Adamic's aspiration of a synthesis of Plymouth Rock and Ellis Island was realized. Descendants of immigrants, particularly those of Ellis Island vintage, were just as good Americans as members of the Society of Mayflower Descendants—or so it seemed.

The 1988 presidential election, however, demonstrated that Anglo-American hegemony had not lost its potency to define insiders and outsiders. George Prescott Bush and Michael Dukakis could not have been better typecast: the Groton-Yale Yankee (despite his disguise as a "good old boy" from Texas) versus the second-generation, multilingual Greek American. Dukakis presented himself as the embodiment of the American Dream, the successful son of immigrants. The Bush campaign cleverly exploited Dukakis's ethnicity by portraying him as un-American, impugning his patriotism on the grounds that he was opposed to the recitation of the Pledge of Allegiance in the public schools.

Among the circumstances that accounted for the return to the melting pot mood, none was more important than the dramatic increase in immigration—and the racial and cultural character of the new arrivals. Following World War II, immigration had averaged between 250,000 and 300,000 a year, but the Immigration Act of 1965 radically altered the rules for entry. It eliminated national origins quotas; imposed annual caps of 170,000 for the Eastern Hemisphere and 120,000 for the Western; and established preferences favoring near relatives of U.S. citizens or resident aliens, persons with particular skills and talents certified to be in short supply in the United States, and refugees from communist countries or the Middle East. Signing the bill at the Statue of Liberty, President Lyndon B. Johnson asserted that while the law righted old injustices it would have few practical consequences. He was mistaken—as were his expert advisors. The annual volume of legal immigration increased steadily in the seventies, reaching over 600,000 by 1978. In addition to the multiplier effect of nonquota relatives of citizens, extraordinary numbers of refugees were admitted. To address the latter issue, Congress passed the Refugee Act in 1980, establishing an annual quota of 50,000 refugees—which, however, could be adjusted upward by the president after consultation with Congress. During the eighties, the number of refugees typically exceeded that figure: 125,000 Mariel boat people arrived from Cuba in the spring of 1980 alone.

Not since the early years of the century had immigrants arrived in such numbers, over 10 million legal entries between 1971 and 1990. Meanwhile, an unknown number of undocumented immigrants filtered through the country's porous borders—Mexicans, Central Americans, and Caribbean islanders, but also substantial numbers from China, Ireland, and eastern Europe. Concern that "we have lost control of our borders" resulted in the establishment of a Select Commission on Immigration and Refugee Policy in 1979 whose recommendations were incorporated in the Immigration Reform and Control Act (IRCA) of 1986: amnesty for illegal immigrants who had entered the country prior to 1 January 1982; stiff penalties for employers who knowingly employed undocumented immigrants; and special provisions for temporary agricultural migrant workers. Although over 3 million persons qualified for consideration for amnesty, employer sanctions failed for lack of effective enforcement, and the number of undocumented immigrants has not decreased since the enactment of IRCA.

Since the 1986 act failed to deal with legal immigration, Congress enacted the Immigration Act of 1990, which established a cap of 700,000 immigrants per year, maintained preferences based on family reunification, and expanded the number to be admitted because of extraordinary skills (including immigrants willing and able to invest $1 million in a new enterprise). The law also reserved 40,000 visas for natives of countries "adversely affected" by the 1965 act; thanks to Senators Edward Kennedy and Daniel Patrick Moynihan, 40 percent of these were designated for Irish nationals. Ethnic lobbying over immigration policy was particularly intense during these years. Jewish Americans assured that coreligionists from the Soviet bloc were granted refugee status, while Mexican Americans demonstrated new clout relative to policies concerning undocumented aliens.

The post-1965 immigration has shaken the American kaleidoscope and produced a dramatic reconfiguration of ethnicities. The historical pattern of a predominantly European immigration was reversed; the great majority were now arriving from Asia and Latin America. During the eighties, they accounted for 85 percent of the total number of immigrants, with Mexicans, Chinese, Filipinos, and Koreans the largest contingents. This newest immigration introduced unusual racial, cultural, and religious features into the American population. The range of skin hues was further expanded, a phenomenon referred to as the "browning of America"; the country's linguistic, musical, and culinary repertoire was spiced up; and exotic forms of worship enriched the religious spectrum. Although not technically immigrants, Puerto Ricans nonetheless contributed to the growing numbers of Spanish-speakers on the mainland. Of the 2 million migrants from the island, about half lived in the barrios of the New York metropolitan area. Meanwhile of the nearly 1 million Cuban refugees, over 50 percent settled in Florida, transforming Miami into a "Little Havana." In the Southwest, some 2 million Mexican immigrants reinforced an Hispanic population that dated back to the pre-conquest era. Following routes of migratory labor, Mexicans also settled in communities throughout the western and midwestern states. An additional 2 million immigrants came from Central and South America and the Caribbean islands, primarily to the East Coast.

Asian immigration was also distinguished by a broad diversity of cultures, languages, and religions. Chinese (almost a million) from Hong Kong, Taiwan, and southeast Asia, as well as mainland China, brought new life to the Chinatowns of San Francisco, New York City, and Chicago. Filipinos added significantly to their prewar numbers, growing to almost a million and a half, principally located in California. Following the fall of Saigon in 1975, a million and a quarter Vietnamese, Laotian, Cambodian, and Hmong refugees reached a safe haven in the United States. Koreans, who had not previously immigrated in large numbers, numbered over 800,000 by 1990, while Asian Indians constituted a new immigrant population of almost 700,000. A less noted influx from the Near East and Africa brought a million and a half Arabic and Persian speakers, and other linguistic/cultural elements from Lebanon, Jordan, Syria, Iran, Nigeria, and Ethiopia. With an estimated 3 million Muslims, and 500,000 each of Buddhists and Hindus, by 1990, the United States could no longer be referred to as a Protestant-Catholic-Jewish nation.

If in certain respects the circumstances and adjustments of the newest arrivals resembled those of immigrants of past eras, there were also striking differences. Rather than being concentrated in the bottom strata as turn-of-the-century immigrants had been, the foreign born were now conspicuously present at all levels of the vertical mosaic. A cosmopolitan technocratic elite moved to and from the United States without let or hindrance. As members of a transnational corporate culture, such persons hardly thought of themselves as immigrants. Others, with advantages of education and experience, integrated smoothly into middle-class American life, entering professions and businesses, residing in suburbia, and mingling with their native peers. But many immigrants of peasant-worker backgrounds experienced greater difficulties of adjustment and sought security with their own kind. Struggling for existence at the bottom of the ethnic-class hierarchy, they competed with disadvantaged natives for jobs, housing, and welfare.

The alleged success of Asian immigrants, touted as a model minority, became problematic upon close scrutiny. Important differences existed depending upon socio-economic backgrounds and countries of origin. Filipinos and Asian Indians, many of them engineers, doctors, and nurses, quickly established themselves professionally, while Hong Kong Chinese and Koreans, equipped with skills and capital, readily achieved prosperity in commercial enterprises. In contrast, many southeast Asians (e.g., the Hmong) often endured long periods of unemployment and dependency. In fact, the availability of cheap Asian and Hispanic labor stimulated a recrudescence of sweatshops in clothing manufacturing in New York and Los Angeles. The declining strength of the U.S. labor movement, as well as the antipathy of American workers toward the newcomers, denied these workers the protection of collective bargaining. Since the American economy no longer needed armies of workers to build railroads, mine coal, and tend machines, traditional entry level jobs were not available to the latest arrivals.

Reflecting varying socioeconomic positions, residences of immigrants ranged from exclusive high-rise apartments to public housing. Like their predecessors, the newcomers established distinctive neighborhoods in American cities. Despite misguided efforts by the United States government to disperse refugees about the country "to facilitate assimilation," families and clans reunited in particular locations. New ethnic districts with specialty food shops, churches, temples, mosques, cultural centers, and publications served the social and cultural needs of their inhabitants as had the Little Italies and Poletowns of the past. In the process, blighted urban areas were revitalized. Arriving immigrants, particularly Asians, alerted to the dangers of the inner city, showed a marked tendency to head directly for the suburbs.

The observation commonly made that Asians and Latinos clung more tenaciously to their cultures and languages than had immigrants of yesteryear carried the negative inference that they were more resistant to assimilation. "In the past, the United States has successfully absorbed millions of immigrants from scores of countries because they . . . enthusiastically embraced the American creed of liberty, equality, individualism, democracy"; but, asked Harvard professor Samuel P. Huntington, "Will this pattern prevail as 50 percent of the population becomes Hispanic or nonwhite?" In addition to an underlying racist assumption, such statements were based on the historically erroneous notion that Europeans eagerly dove into the melting pot. They also underestimated the capacity for cultural adaptation of the newcomers. Of necessity, the newest immigrants learned to accommodate their customs, cuisine, and ceremonies to the American environment. Old Country practices, such as child marriages or ritual slaughter of animals, which clashed with the values and laws of the United States, were gradually abandoned. Like earlier immigrants, the newcomers began to construct new ethnic identities, creating self-help and political organizations. Traditional divisions along clan lines (e.g., between "yellow Hmong" and "white Hmong") were transcended as they sought a larger solidarity as Hmong Americans, and more tentatively began to form coalitions with Vietnamese, Cambodians, and Laotians under the umbrella of a Southeast Asian panethnicity. As was true of former immigrants, ancient animosities and generational conflicts made the process of ethnicization tortuous. In all of this, their experience mirrored that of the Europeans who had proceeded them.

While the cumulative impact of an immigration of some 15 million since 1965 had profound consequences for the demographic and cultural future of the American people, forebodings about an "unprecedented immigrant invasion" were exaggerated. If the volume of recent immigration exceeded that of the early 1900s, the rate of immigration (the number of immigrants as percentage of population size), which was 10 per thousand between 1900 and 1910, only registered 3.5 per thousand in the 1980s. True, the number of foreign born reached an all-time high of almost 20 million in 1990, but they accounted for only 8 percent of the population as compared with 14.7 percent in 1910. In other words, the statistical impact of contemporary immigration has been of a much smaller magnitude than in the past.

The heightened nativism of recent years may have more to do with the visibility of the newcomers, their color, languages, and cultures, than with their numbers. While eschewing explicit racialism, advocates of tighter restrictions expressed anxiety that the immigrants posed a threat to the homogeneity of the United States. As Senator Alan Simpson of Wyoming, a leading congressional advocate of tighter controls, put it: "If language and cultural separation rise above a certain level, the unity and political stability of our nation will—in time—be seriously eroded." Given current immigration and birth rates, certain demographers predicted, minorities (persons of American Indian, African, Asian, and Latino ancestry) would make up half the American population by the year 2050 and the United States would cease to be "a predominantly white society rooted in Western culture." In such predictions, one heard echoes of Madison Grant's *The Passing of the Great Race* (1916), which warned of the imminent decline of the Anglo-Saxons before the onslaught of inferior, but prolific, races.

Bilingualism became a lightning rod for anxiety over the future of the republic. Bilingual programs in the schools, use of foreign languages in public business, printing public documents in any language other than English, were viewed with alarm as challenging the cultural and political integrity of the country. Alistair Cooke, himself an English immigrant, admonished: "But the day that the immigrant's mother tongue becomes the first language of any community or—God forbid—a State, the American experiment will be on its way to breaking up into a collection of feuding German republics, with several Quebecs in our future." A more credible critic of bilingual education, Richard Rodriguez, argued in *Hunger of Memory* (1982) that command of English was essential for the children of immigrants to escape from the ethnic ghetto and participate in the national culture.

Be that as it may, the movement against bilingualism was clearly animated by nativist fears that America would become an "incomprehensible Tower of Babel." With the growth of the Hispanic population, Spanish in particular came to be regarded as a threat to the primacy of the Anglo-American language. Innocent of the country's linguistic history, proponents of monolingualism asserted that earlier immigrants had speedily and gladly Anglicized, and that new immigrants must do likewise. U.S. English, an organization led for many years by former U.S. Senator S. I. Hayakawa, lobbied for a constitutional amendment making English the official language of the United States. While unsuccessful at the federal level, laws forbidding the use of other-than-English languages in certain public transactions have been enacted in nineteen states. Vigorous opposition was mounted by an "English Plus" coalition of Hispanic organizations, educators, and pluralists, which contended that coerced linguistic conformity violated the rights of non-English speakers and was in any case unnecessary given the overwhelmingly English-speaking culture. The struggle over language, symptomatic of a broader ideological and political conflict, was sure to continue.

As John Higham pointed out years ago, the intensity of nativist sentiment in the United States has fluctuated with the general health of the society. Contemporary xenophobia was, at least in part, an expression of angst generated by radical structural change in the economy. In recent decades, progressive deindustrialization transformed the character of the labor force. In the Rustbelt, the American Dream had proved illusory; rather than holding secure, high-paying jobs in steel mills or automobile factories, youngsters were flipping hamburgers at a minimum wage. The aspirations—steady work, job advancement, home ownership—that had inspired generations of immigrants and their children seemed to be beyond the reach of many Americans of all races and ethnicities. Meanwhile the reactionary politics of the eighties had resulted in a dramatic increase in the maldistribution of wealth. In 1993, the top 20 percent of households earned 48.2 percent of the income, while the bottom 20 percent earned 3.6 percent. Poverty was on the increase with almost 40 million below the poverty line (defined as $14,763 for a family of four). While more whites than people of color lived in poverty, a much larger proportion of blacks (perhaps one-third) were trapped in the underclass. More and more, the vertical mosaic appeared to consist of hermetically sealed compartments rather than a skyscraper of upward mobility. As in the past, frustration at blighted expectations found expression in attacks, verbal and physical, against vulnerable ethnic and racial groups. Lacking a class-based political party to provide an outlet and focus for their anger, the grandchildren of Italian or Polish immigrants blamed "gooks" and "greasers" for taking jobs away from "Americans"—and "niggers" on welfare or in prison for high taxes.

Most negatively impacted by deindustrialization, African Americans particularly expressed hostility toward recent immigrants whom they regarded as receiving preferential treatment in housing, jobs, and social programs. They especially resented Asians and Hispanics who leap-frogged over them into the professions or business. Koreans and Cubans were the particular targets of black street gangs in Miami, Philadelphia, and elsewhere. In the summer of 1991, African Americans and Hasidic Jews fought in the streets of the Crown Heights neighborhood of New York City. The Los Angeles riot (or insurrection) of May 1992, following the "not guilty" verdict in the trial of policemen accused of brutalizing Rodney King, resulted in fifty-four deaths and over a billion dollars of property damage. However, given the complex population mix of the City of the Angels, multiple ethnic hostilities were played out during the riot. Mexican American youth comprised a large segment of the rioters, and Korean-owned shops were a prime target of looters.

If nativism in the nineties was threatening many new immigrants, Vietnamese and Cubans still received a more cordial welcome than did Japanese or Greeks at the turn of the century. In contrast to the laissez-faire attitude of those days, public programs and voluntary agencies now provided assistance and social services to newcomers. Also, federal policies and Supreme Court decisions since the 1960s regarding bilingualism, voting rights, and affirmative action have legitimized ethnic pluralism. Compared to rabid xenophobic movements in European countries, exponents of ethnic hatreds have not attracted large followings among Americans. In 1992, the Rev. Pat Robertson and Pat Buchanan apparently alienated more voters than they attracted with their rhetoric about "religious and cultural wars," while Bill Clinton, who promised an administration that "looks like America," won the presidential election.

Yet, indicative of the volatility of the American temper, the mood of the country in the 1990s regarding race and immigration quickly turned ugly. The slogan "family values" dominated the political rhetoric of the congressional elections of 1994. Code words for opposition to abortion, homosexuality, gun control, crime, unwed teenage mothers, and welfare—issues with ethnic and racial overtones—tapped into a deep well of fear that extended far beyond the Christian Right—or the fans of Rush Limbaugh. Also, as Robert Suro observed, "The summer of 1994 marked a turning point in the history of immigration to the United States." Responding to angry voters, politicians rushed to offer proposals to curb illegal immigration and to limit access of legal immigrants to Medicare and other welfare benefits. Making immigrant-bashing the theme of his reelection campaign, Governor Pete Wilson of California even advocated a constitutional amendment denying citizenship to American-born children of illegal aliens. Fearing a repeat of the Mariel boat lift, the Clinton administration reversed the established policy of granting asylum to Cuban rafters, interning them at the Guantánamo Bay naval base. Meanwhile, the Commission on Immigration Reform, chaired by Barbara Jordan, recommended urgent action to curb illegal immigration. But it was the Save Our State (S.O.S.) campaign in California that put immigration at the top of the political agenda. Approved by a commanding majority, Proposition 187 would deny illegal immigrants public educational, welfare, or medical (except for emergencies) services, and require that providers report suspected illegal aliens to the Immigration and Naturalization Service. By endorsing Proposition 187—and making immigrants the scapegoats for California's problems—Wilson won a comeback victory in the gubernatorial election.

Meanwhile, an acrimonious controversy that had erupted between proponents of multiculturalism and guardians of the national heritage in the 1980s continued. In its broad sweep, multiculturalism was a movement to make American culture and institutions representative of the increasing diversity of society. In addition to race and ethnicity, gender and sexual orientation were identified as differences requiring educational and administrative remedies to fill past silences and to rectify past exclusions. The multicultural offensive sought to transform popular consciousness by exposing and rooting out racism and sexism. There was much that fair-minded Americans could agree with in the multicultural program. However, on many college campuses, "ideological multiculturalists," to use Richard Bernstein's term, launched an attack upon the European American canon and its white male exponents. Drawing upon Marxist, poststructural, and feminist theories, their strategy was to undermine what they viewed as the intellectual underpinnings of patriarchy, racism, and capitalism. The classics of Western civilization were to be replaced by works of women and persons of color or read as texts of western male hegemony. Multiculturalism in this form had significant successes at many universities, not only in terms of curriculum (e.g., required courses in the histories and cultures of the preferred groups), but through preferential treatment of female and nonwhite faculty and students as well as codes regulating behavior and speech deemed offensive to "minorities."

As defined by its extreme exponents, multiculturalism assumed an exclusive, dogmatic, and adversarial character. While employing the language of pluralism and diversity, advocates subsumed all significant differences under the categories of Race, Gender, and Class, devaluing other sources of ethnicity (e.g., religion, language, and culture). Paradoxically this movement dedicated to radical change embraced federally mandated racial and ethnic classifications—Black, Asian American, Hispanic, Native American, and White—as its intellectual paradigm. "White" or European American males were by definition the oppressors: their particular ethnicities suspect as covers for racism and chauvinism. By denying the full range of diversity and by reifying race, multiculturalists of this stripe confounded rather than clarified an understanding of American ethnicity.

Multiculturalism in its extreme version elicited vociferous opposition both on and off campuses. The attack upon the canon outraged conservative professors and pundits such as Allan Bloom and George Will, who fulminated at the "cult of political correctness." Neoconservatives such as William Bennett and Lynne Cheney, both of whom served as chairmen of the National Endowment for the Humanities (NEH), rushed to the defense of Western civilization. Underlying the angry responses were anxieties regarding the consequences of the emphasis on multiple histories and group identities. Arthur M. Schlesinger, Jr. articulated this concern in *The Disuniting of America* (1991), which warned that "the cult of ethnicity" threatened the "fragmentation, resegregation, and tribalization of American life." Embracing the melting pot as symbol of assimilation, Schlesinger called for an American history that would sustain a sense of national identity.

The debate over "who owns history?" reached a boiling point with the release in October 1994 of the *National Standards for United States History: Exploring the American Experience.* Funded by NEH and prepared in consultation with many historians and educators by the National History Standards Project (NHSP), the document was the culmination of several decades of revisionist progressive historiography. This "New American History," which emphasized social history rather than politics ("history from the bottom up") and formerly neglected elements (women, workers, racial and ethnic groups) at the expense of Great White Men, could not but be anathema to neoconservatives. Cheney led the charge, denouncing the standards for ignoring "traditional history" and "heroes," and focusing on "bad news" while neglecting the "good news" of American history. The historian Gary B. Nash, codirector of the NHSP, responded that the standards represented "balanced history" and were designed to involve students in active inquiry rather than rote memory. The clash over the standards constitute a battle in the ongoing struggle over multiculturalism, a struggle which, in the words of Earl Lewis, is over "power to define and lay claim to the 'true' history of America and the world."

If the polemics regarding multiculturalism often generated more heat than light, serious attempts continued to offer well-reasoned conceptualizations of ethnicity in American life. While calling for a reaffirmation of American peoplehood on the basis of "our egalitarian ideology 'American universalism'," John Higham recognized the need to accommodate the reality of diversity. In Higham's model of "pluralistic integration," while a dominant American core ensured the coherence of society, subordinate ethnic groups were free to maintain their distinctiveness, but with permeable boundaries that allowed free passage to individuals. Agreeing with Higham on "the democratic-egalitarian core" of American values, David A. Hollinger offered "cosmopolitanism" as an alternative to pluralism. Hollinger's cosmopolitanism espoused the idea of group affiliation as contextual and as subject to "revokable consent," while pluralism (according to Hollinger) was primordial and based on descent. In Hollinger's vision of "postethnic America," all Americans would be free to choose to be or not to be ethnic.

In theorizing about ethnicity, certain commentators differentiated between the ethnicity of people of color and the ethnicity of European Americans. Applying Herbert Gans's concept of symbolic ethnicity, Mary Waters (*Ethnic Options: Choosing Identities in America,* 1990) described the ethnicity of racial minorities as real, imposed, and costly while that of persons of European descent had become voluntary, painless, and contentless. Seeking to account for the tenacious attachment of European Americans to ethnic identities, she attributed it to a craving for community and to racism. Contemporaneously, Richard Alba (*Ethnic Identity: The Transformation of White America,* 1990) argued that since the objective bases of ethnicity of persons of European ancestry had largely disappeared, their particular cultural identities (e.g., as Italian Americans) were rapidly fading into the "twilight of ethnicity." However, Alba concluded that a new ethnic group was emerging: European (or white) Americans.

By and large, these writings subscribed to a simplistic notion of ethnicity as a response to negative external stereotyping, rather than as a positive expression of peoplehood. Moreover, the authors appeared to be out of touch with the raw realities of lived ethnicity in contemporary America. Some bore a distinct animus toward ethnic groups of European American origin. Waters, for example, gratuitously characterized traditional white ethnic groups as sexist, racist, clannish, and narrow-minded. Uncritically endorsing the Waters-Alba forecast, Hollinger welcomed the emergence of a "Euro-American bloc" because it replicated the "comparable erasures of diversity that victimize people within the other four, pseudo-primal categories." How the resulting "ethnoracial pentagon" would further Hollinger's vision of a postethnic America was not clear. Rather it appeared to be a prescription for permanent apartheid.

More even-tempered and even-handed, Werner Sollors, particularly in *Beyond Ethnicity* (1986), contended that throughout American history consent (i.e., achieved identity) had been more important than descent (i.e., ascribed identity). Ethnicity was to be understood not as a primordial force or hoary survival, but as a modern surrogate for the tightly knit kinship groups of yesteryear. Sollors further argued that ethnicity itself was a form of assimilation by which immigrants came to terms with America's melting pot culture. Yet confronted with the contemporary debate about multiculturalism, Sollors confessed to being nonplussed: Was multiculturalism itself responsible for the increase in racial and gender hostilities? Would multiculturalism engender greater tolerance or would it reach "an explosive crisis point"?

A more optimistic perspective was offered by Ronald Takaki, who reassured his readers that diversity was not to be feared. Rather, a multiculturalism that respected group differences would "bring us together." His *A Different Mirror: A History of Multicultural America* (1993) attempted such a pluralistic portrait, interweaving the histories of Irish and Jews, Chinese, Japanese, and Mexicans, Indians and Africans into "the story of our coming together to create a new society in America." If, like Higham, Takaki aspired to see America whole, for him its coherence did not come from the legacy of the Founding Fathers, but from the recurring encounters of races and ethnicities that resulted in redefinitions of national identity. For Takaki, it was not ethnic diversity that threatened the unity of America, but the hegemonic aspirations of "traditional Eurocentrism."

This sampling of voices suggests the range of

contrasting interpretations that swirled about the multiculturalism debate. Each carried its own ideological freight; each was committed to its own vision of American society.

TOWARD THE TWENTY-FIRST CENTURY

As the United States approaches the twenty-first century its future as an ethnically plural society is hotly contested. Is the United States more diverse than in the past? Is the unity of society threatened by its diversity? Are the centrifugal forces in American society more powerful than the centripetal? Such questions inspired Sheldon Hackney, chairman of NEH, to call for the project "A National Conversation on American Pluralism and Identity." "What unites us as a country," he asked, "and what [do] we share as common American values in a nation comprised of so many divergent groups and beliefs?" These issues are being debated not only in scholarly conferences and journals, but in the mass media. In a major 1993 piece entitled "The New Face of America: How Immigrants Are Shaping the World's First Multicultural Society," *Time* magazine put a positive spin on the subject; its cover featured a computer-generated image of a beautiful woman created from a "mix of several races." However, *Time* qualified its endorsement of diversity by insisting that newcomers accept "the host of values [that unite] Americans of every color and ethnic background." Contemporaneously *Newsweek* offered a more pessimistic view; illustrative of a story headlined "Immigration Backlash," its cover depicted the Statue of Liberty in water up to its nose, encircled by rafts and boats. The lead story, "America: Still a Melting Pot?" expressed anxiety and doubt about the outcome.

There was no gainsaying the reality of ethnic diversity in the America of the nineties. In addition to the 20 million foreign-born enumerated, the U.S. Census of 1990 reported on the ancestry or ethnic origin of Americans, regardless of the number of generations removed from country of origin. The 90 percent who reported at least one ancestry were classified in 215 ancestry groups. The largest ancestry group was German (58 million), followed by Irish, English, and Afro-American (all over 20 million); next came Italian, Mexican, French, Polish, American Indian, Dutch, and Scotch-Irish (each over 6 million); another 21 groups accounted for over a million each. Scanning the roster of ancestries, one was struck by the plethora of smaller groups with sizeable representations: Maltese, Basque, Rom, Wendish, Paraguayan, Belizian, Guyanese, Yemini, Khmer, and Micronesian, among others.

While the ancestry data appeared to verify the enormous range and vitality of ethnicity among Americans, the census report was careful to point out that the question "was not intended to measure the degree of attachment the respondent had to a particular ethnicity." Granting this qualification, the fact that only 5 percent of the respondents chose to identity themselves simply as "American"—and less than 1 percent as white—was telling. At a minimum, the data revealed not only the extremely diverse origins of the American people, but a consciousness of those origins on the part of the vast majority. On the face of it, they contradicted the assertions of the emergence of "unhyphenated whites" or European Americans as significant identities.

Granted that ethnicity remained a vital force, fears of political disunity and social fragmentation underestimated the centripetal forces that held American society together. Much more so than a hundred years ago, nationwide systems of economics, politics, mass communications, and popular culture connected Americans within functional and symbolic networks of relationships. Only a catastrophe of major proportions, it seemed, could disrupt such a highly integrated social order. Despite doomsayers who foresaw "The Coming Anarchy" in uprisings of the underclass and ethnic/racial conflicts, a right-wing reaction dedicated to the repression of differences of all kinds seemed to be more within the realm of possibility. If economic insecurity and identity anxiety continued to feed a politics of conformity, xenophobia rather than pluralism could pose the greater danger to American democracy.

As society has increasingly polarized into "haves" (who fear that what they have will be taken from them) and "have-nots," the resulting economic inequities have fueled ethnic and racial antagonisms. A harmonious pluralism requires not only that barriers to mobility within the vertical mosaic be removed, but that a decent, good life be within the grasp of all. Beyond that, a reinvention of our national identity is needed that will come to terms with our expanding diversity and define us as a multiethnic people in the context of a multiethnic world. If we are to make the transition to that world of the twenty-first century successfully, we must re-vision difference as a source of enrichment, not a menace. If a return to the melting pot is impossible, and the present too chaotic and contested for a new shared vision, then one has to look to the future for a compelling paradigm that will command the faith of all Americans because it embraces them in their manifold variety within a just society. In the twenty-first century, the United States will confront with more urgency than ever the question posed by Michel-Guillaume-Jean de Crèvecoeur more than two centuries ago: "What then is the American?"

SEE ALSO Race; Gender Issues; Class (all in this volume); Judaism and Jewish Culture; Catholicism; Nontraditional Religions (all in volume IV).

BIBLIOGRAPHY

For a sampling of the extensive literature, see Nathan Glazer and Daniel P. Moynihan, eds., *Ethnicity: Theory and Experience* (1975). Influential conceptualizations are in Anthony D. Smith, *The Ethnic Revival in the Modern World* (1981); and Benedict R. Anderson, *Imagined Communities: Reflections on the Origin and Spread of Nationalism* (1983). The case for cultural construction is made by Werner Sollors, *Beyond Ethnicity: Consent and Descent in American Culture* (1986); and Kathleen Neils Conzen et al., "The Invention of Ethnicity: A Perspective from the USA," *Journal of American Ethnic History* 12 (Fall 1992). *Harvard Encyclopedia of American Ethnic Groups* (1980), ed. Stephan Thernstrom, is the standard reference work; while Roger Daniels, *Coming to America: A History of Immigration and Ethnicity in American Life* (1991), is the most comprehensive and up-to-date history.

The classic work on nativism is John Higham, *Strangers in the Land: Patterns of American Nativism, 1860–1925* (1963). On Anglo-American ethnicity, E. Digby Baltzell, *The Protestant Establishment: Aristocracy and Caste in America* (1964), remains the key study. Class and ethnicity in the labor movement is the theme of Robert Asher and Charles Stephenson, eds., *Labor Divided: Race and Ethnicity in United States Labor Struggles, 1840–1970* (1989). Maps and text portray patterns of settlement in James P. Allen and Eugene J. Turner, *We the People: An Atlas of America's Ethnic Diversity* (1988); for ethnicity and urbanism, see David Ward, *Poverty, Ethnicity, and the American City, 1840–1925: Changing Conceptions of the Slum and the Ghetto* (1989). For transoceanic influences, Marianne DeBouzy, ed., *In the Shadow of the Statue of Liberty: Immigrants, Workers and Citizens in the American Republic, 1880–1920* (1988), is valuable. The role of ethnicity in politics is the subject of Samuel Lubell, *The Future of American Politics* (1952); and Steven P. Erie, *Rainbow's End: Irish-Americans and the Dilemmas of Urban Machine Politics, 1840–1985* (1988). On immigrant entrepreneurship, Ivan H. Light, *Ethnic Enterprise in America: Business and Welfare Among Chinese, Japanese, and Blacks* (1972), is insightful. For crime as a form of social mobility see James M. O'Kane, *The Crooked Ladder: Gangsters, Ethnicity and the American Dream* (1992). Attempts at Americanization are described in Allen F. Davis, *Spearheads for Reform: The Social Settlements and the Progressive Movement, 1890–1914* (1967); and Bernard J. Weiss, ed., *American Education and the European Immigrant, 1840–1940* (1982).

Nationalism and repression during World War I are chronicled in Frederick Luebke, *Bonds of Loyalty: German-Americans and World War I* (1974); and William Preston, Jr., *Aliens and Dissenters: Federal Suppression of Radicals, 1903–1933* (1963). For the influence of mass culture, see Andrew H. Heinze, *Adapting to Abundance: Jewish Immigrants, Mass Consumption, and the Search for American Identity* (1992); and Stuart Ewen, *Captains of Consciousness: Advertising and the Social Roots of the Consumer Culture* (1976). Interethnic solidarity during the Depression is the theme of Lizabeth Cohen, *Making a New Deal: Industrial Workers in Chicago, 1919–1939* (1990); but ethnic antagonisms are reported in Ronald Bayor, *Neighbors in Conflict: The Irish, Germans, Jews and Italians of New York City, 1929–1941,* 2d ed. (1988). For social theories regarding race and ethnicity, see Fred Matthews, *Quest for an American Sociology: Robert E. Park and the Chicago School* (1977); and Stow Persons, *Ethnic Studies at Chicago, 1905–45* (1987).

A pluralistic history of the war and postwar years can be found in Richard Polenberg, *One Nation Divisible: Class, Race and Ethnicity in the United States since 1938* (1980). The wartime ideology is best analyzed by Philip Gleason, in "Americans All," in his volume of essays (all of which are relevant) *Speaking of Diversity: Language and Ethnicity in Twentieth-Century America* (1992). On Japanese American internment, the essential work is Roger Daniels, *Prisoners without Trial: Japanese Americans in World War II* (1993). The role of the media in shaping stereotypes is analyzed in Allen L. Woll and Randall M. Miller, *Ethnic and Racial Images in American Film and Television: Historical Essays and Bibliography* (1987).

On African American movements, Harvard Sitkoff, *The Struggle for Black Equality, 1954–1980* (1981), and Manning Marable, *Race, Reform and Rebellion: The Second Reconstruction in Black America, 1945–1982* (1984), are excellent summaries. Panethnic movements are described in Joan W. Moore and Harry Pachon, *Hispanics in the United States* (1985); Murray L. Wax, *Indian Americans: Unity and Diversity* (1971); and William Wei, *The Asian American Movement* (1993). For "white ethnicity," Richard Krickus, *Pursuing the American Dream: White Ethnics and the New Populism* (1976), is thorough. The influence of Old Country politics is reported in Laurence Halley, *Ancient Affections: Ethnic Groups and Foreign Policy* (1985); and Abdul A. Said, ed., *Ethnicity and U.S. Foreign Policy* (1977). For the "white ethnic" response to policies stemming from the Civil Rights Act of 1964, see John Lescott-Leszczynski, *The History of U.S. Ethnic Policy and its Impact on European Ethnics* (1984). Ronald P. Formisano, *Boston Against Busing: Race, Class, and Ethnicity in the 1960s and 1970s* (1991), and Jim Sleeper, *The Closest of Strangers: Liberalism and the Politics of Race in New York* (1990), are perceptive analyses of racial conflicts. Among the attacks on "white ethnicity," the following are representative: Orlando Patterson, *Ethnic Chauvinism: The Reactionary Impulse* (1977); and Arthur Mann, *The One and the Many: Reflections on the American Identity* (1979). For a more sympathetic interpretation, see Peter Kivisto, ed., *The Ethnic Enigma: The Salience of Ethnicity for European-Origin Groups* (1989).

For different estimates of the salience of race in American society, see Andrew Hacker, *Two Nations: Black and White, Separate, Hostile, and Unequal* (1992); and William J. Wilson, *The Declining Significance of Race* (1980). Also by Wilson, *The Truly Disadvantaged: The Inner City, the Underclass, and Public Policy* (1987), analyzes the underlying causes of urban poverty and calls for non-race-specific responses. Barry Bluestone and Bennett Harrison, *The Deindustrialization of America: Plant Closings, Community Abandonment, and the Dismantling of Basic Industry* (1982), describes the impact of economic change on the Rustbelt. For post-1965 immigration, David Reimers, *Still the Golden Door: The Third World Comes to America* (1985), is the best study. See the *Population Bulletin,* especially Philip Martin and Elisabeth Midgley, *Immigration to the United States: Journey to an Uncertain Destination* 49 (September 1994), for current reports.

Richard Bernstein, *Dictatorship of Virtue: Multiculturalism and the Battle for America's Future* (1994), offers a critical analysis. Useful collections of essays are Paul Berman, ed., *Debating P.C.: The Controversy over Political Correctness on College Campuses* (1992); and Patricia Aufderheide, ed., *Beyond P.C.: Towards a Politics of Understanding* (1992). "Symbolic Ethnicity" is the title of an essay in Herbert Gans, ed., *On The Making of Americans* (1979); for recent applications of this concept, see the works by Mary C. Waters and Richard D. Alba. John Higham, *Send These to Me: Jews and Other Immigrants in Urban America* (1975), presents the model of "pluralistic integration"; but see also his essay, "Multiculturalism and Universalism: a History and Critique," *American Quarterly* 45 (June 1993). Writings by David A. Hollinger are "How Wide the Circle of the 'We'? American Intellectuals and the Problem of the Ethnos since World War II," *The American Historical Review* 98 (April 1993), and "Postethnic America," *Contention* 2 (Fall 1992). In addition to *Beyond Ethnicity,* see Werner Sollors, ed., *The Invention of Ethnicity* (1989), and his essay, "E Pluribus Unum: or, Matthew Arnold meets George Orwell in the 'Multicultural' Debate," John F. Kennedy–Institut für Nordamerikastudien, Freie Universität Berlin, Working Paper No. 53/1992. Ronald Takaki, ed., *From Different Shores: Perspectives on Race and Ethnicity in America* (1987), is a handy compendium of readings.

CLASS

Olivier Zunz

The recognition that inequality was a growing and pernicious dimension of American life signaled the start of the twentieth century. Concern with inequality began to pervade all aspects of public discourse, from muckrakers' exposés of corruption to speeches at party conventions. In 1890, the Farmers' Alliance charged that "there were 31,000 millionaires in the United States, all of them having accumulated their wealth by the 'robbery' of the people."

While their claims were exaggerated, they had ample reason to focus on increased inequality and its consequences for the American class structure. The day of the super rich had arrived. By the late nineteec nth century, Andrew Carnegie was worth $500 million. Scant decades later, John D. Rockefeller and Henry Ford would measure their wealth in billions. Although prominent "Social Darwinists" like William Graham Sumner maintained in *What Social Classes Owe to Each Other* (1883) that "It is not wicked to be rich" and justified wealth accumulated by hard work and self-denial, most Americans were uneasy with the extent of the new inequality, which was as visible in the plight of the working class and in the formation of a seemingly inassimilable underclass as it was in the appearance of a corps of millionaires.

Inequality has remained a motive for social action throughout most of the twentieth century because extremes of wealth and poverty are still with us and stay visible. Nonetheless, the lives of most twentieth-century Americans have been shaped by a no less significant phenomenon: the growth of a large middle class. Although a middle class had existed in the United States since the eighteenth century, the twentieth century witnessed a shift from a rural lower-middle class to an urban industrial middle class. A discussion of class in the twentieth century is therefore not just an argument about the great inequalities and labor conflicts that separated the robber barons from a growing working class, or about the periodic surge of an underclass, but a debate on the remarkable growth and metamorphosis of the American middle class, partly generated by the rise of corporate and bureaucratic structures. The formation of a large middle class, with an extraordinary capacity for expansion as well as internal segmentation, has facilitated the assimilation of newcomers, fostered social mobility, and eased tensions among parts of society.

Defining class defies common sense. Theoreticians of class have long recognized that the issue of consciousness—the sense of belonging to one group, of sharing some overarching ideas, and of behaving accordingly—is not necessarily related to the cohesiveness of that group. It is particularly important in studying the issue of class in twentieth-century America to recognize that there is little agreement about what constitutes membership in any given class. Class consciousness is only tangentially related to measurable reality. Thus three-quarters of the adult American population currently volunteer an identification with the middle class. But does this phrase have any meaning if so many disparate and unrelated segments claim this distinction, or if objective measures such as income or occupation suggest that many self-identified middle-class Americans belong instead to the working class? Conversely, we cannot ascribe specific objective or subjective boundaries to the working class when so many Americans aspire to upward mobility.

It has often been noted that Americans have been reluctant to think in class terms alone because they have been driven in different directions by multiple allegiances. Friedrich Engels recognized that a real obstacle to class consciousness was the diversity of the American ethnic fabric. As ethnic groups occupied distinct geographic and occupational clusters, the words *ethnicity, assimilation,* and *pluralism* remained as crucial to the discussion of American life as *class. Race* and *racism* were another set of terms that diminished the American perception of class as a shaping force in twentieth-century America.

In 1900, the map of the United States was dramatically divided by a color line. Most African

Americans lived south of the Mason-Dixon line, primarily as disfranchised sharecroppers. Southern class relations were plastered over with considerations of race just as northern class relations were saturated by considerations of ethnicity. Race was also a defining issue in the West, where Chinese and Japanese "sojourners" were denied civil rights and citizenship. Furthermore, as the history of women in the twentieth century shows, *gender* has also intersected with both perception and definition of class at all levels of the social structure.

Americans' treatment of class has also been affected by political rhetoric. Politicians, intellectuals, policymakers, social workers, social scientists, and other professionals who analyze class have often positioned themselves within the broad center of society, minimized the tension among classes, and stressed instead individual mobility and the multiplicity of groupings in American life within an ever-absorbing middle class. Depending on circumstances and vantage points, however, they have also engaged in capturing or weakening the center, emphasized the dangers of extreme inequalities, underscored the realities of class conflict and class consciousness, and pointed to many forms of exploitation. Similarly, ordinary Americans' perceptions of class-related issues, be they workers or managers, employed or unemployed, men or women, have been closely tied to changing economic circumstances, political climate, and mores.

But despite our frustrated yearning for clear definitions and precise boundaries, class is a large part of Americans' collective consciousness. The concept of class is central for understanding twentieth-century American history, for the process of inclusion in the United States has been class driven. Furthermore, class formation, social change, and class consciousness combine to create major divisions within society as well as powerful cultural, economic, and political agendas.

The key words different groups of Americans adopted to describe their circumstances, or that of others, were never devoid of class significance. Although Americans have been reluctant to resort to a rhetoric of class in the way that citizens of other modern industrial or postindustrial societies have, resolving class tensions has remained key to social integration in a democracy. Thus both Walter Lippmann and John Dewey, keen observers of the early twentieth century, addressed the future of American democracy by searching for the dynamic interaction of class, power, and diversity in American society and the connection between class formation and social integration. The young Walter Lippmann, in *Drift and Mastery* (1914), articulated first and most acutely the need for countervailing powers in conflict resolution: how big business should be countered by big labor and consumer groups. If for Lippmann American democracy was ultimately dependent upon a public's ability to listen to expert advice, for Dewey it could only survive through the participation of all citizens in the collective good. Dewey, whose influence as the quintessential pragmatist philosopher is being rediscovered today, stressed democratic participation and the cumulative enrichment that the recognition of diversity brought. Seen in this light, an open class structure becomes central to the realization of the social contract.

This essay will attempt to do justice to conflicting theories and select fairly among a myriad of relevant facts when analyzing each of four broad social groupings—the middle class, the working class, the elites, the underclass—that make up the American social fabric. The essay begins with the middle class and its significance for the twentieth century before turning to those theories and facts that concern the large American working class. Following that, it examines the often conflicting debates on elites and the underclass, and analyzes the intersection of class with ethnicity, race, and gender in American life.

THE AMERICAN MIDDLE CLASS

The American middle class is characterized by its belief in individual achievements and in freedom of association in an open society. These beliefs were best expressed by two giants of social thought. The French aristocrat Alexis de Tocqueville articulated the ideal of individualism in *Democracy in America* (1830–1835) and James Madison defined the American social contract in *Federalist* 10 (1787).

In America, Tocqueville found *homo democraticus.* In analyzing equality as he saw it affecting the course of American history, Tocqueville explained the ways in which Americans defined themselves as free individuals who willingly joined in voluntary associations. He contrasted America to Europe, where prescribed social hierarchies instead reinforced ascribed collective identities. Among Tocqueville's readers of the 1950s, Louis Hartz, who was also influenced by Marx, extended Tocqueville's thoughts by contending in his *The Liberal Tradition in America* (1955) that the absence of a feudal past had simply prevented the dialectic of class from being initiated in America and was the key to American exceptionalism.

Atomized individuals, however, do not constitute

society. One of the characteristics of the American middle class is that it comprises not a single, uniform group, but a multiplicity of groups, as James Madison observed. Responding to the concerns of many around him that "those who hold and those who are without property" form "distinct interests," Madison prescribed a society broken into so many "parties and interests" that no majority could "invade the right of other citizens." A continent-sized republic would not become the instrument of a single group and its government need not be feared as long as there were several groups competing for its favors. In effect, Madison described a country characterized by the endless ferment of small groups, combining and recombining, rather than one driven by class conflict. The Madisonian prescription proved an enduring formula for the ways in which middle-class Americans live and think of themselves. Many pluralist political scientists have argued that this view saved America from the Marxist projection of ever more bitter animosity between capital and labor.

Nineteenth-century individualism was a deeply felt economic reality as well as a philosophical commitment for many Americans who pushed back the frontier, acquired land, and were entrepreneurs in a growing market economy. The United States was to change drastically, however, in the late nineteenth and early twentieth centuries, from a society of individuals attached to local forms of life reinforced by a commitment to voluntary associations, to a society dominated by national institutions, big business, and big government. Twentieth-century middle-class Americans had to come to grips with an unprecedented system of mass production, mass distribution, mass communication, and intense social engineering that transformed their lives.

In living these big changes, middle-class Americans redefined the nineteenth-century idea of individualism within a strong civil society for their emerging mass society. They attempted to maintain a fluid social system by opening access to knowledge, jobs, and goods, giving equality of opportunity to an ever greater portion of the population. Mass society, however, has its homogenizing tendencies. As observers like David Riesman et al. in *The Lonely Crowd* (1950) and Robert Bellah et al. in *Habits of the Heart* (1985) have remarked, twentieth-century middle-class Americans mixed a new kind of individualism with a new kind of conformity. As their individual achievements were partly dampened by the bureaucratic structures of large organizations, they increasingly sought self-realization by rechanneling their individualism through these structures and through consumption. Their conformity was no longer generated by the fear of the unknown in unfamiliar surroundings or the solitude brought about by too much geographic mobility, as in Tocqueville's days, but instead by a significant homogenization of cultural forms that reached a climax by mid-century and has perhaps been declining since.

Although early-twentieth-century European theorists like José Ortega y Gasset in *The Revolt of the Masses* (1929) had seen in mass society the seeds of totalitarianism, as the mass would be an easy prey for unscrupulous and brutal leaders, their American counterparts viewed mass society more optimistically. The very people who, in the Progressive Era and beyond, promoted a new scientific ethos for America worried about the potential loss of individuality. In *The Public and its Problems* (1927), John Dewey called for the development of new "tools of social inquiry" to manage new institutional mechanisms for production, consumption, learning, and leisure. But Dewey also warned in *Individualism* (1930) that "quantification, mechanization and standardization" had "invaded mind and character, and subdued the soul to their own dye." Herbert Hoover, who exemplified the new engineering spirit of the twentieth century and thought of individualism in terms of equality of opportunity, worried in *American Individualism* (1922) that "a man in the mass does not think but only feels." While anxiety over the fate of individuals in a mass society was real, most observers kept faith in the individualistic ethos of middle-class Americans. By the 1960s, Edward Shils saw in American mass society a beneficial relationship where the mass of the population is integrated "into the central institutional and value systems of the society." Daniel Bell called the same process "the eclipse of distance."

The relevant facts and figures about the institutions of mass society are readily available. The large corporation, which has dominated the economy in the twentieth century, was already entrenched in the American landscape by World War I. As Alfred Chandler has shown in *The Visible Hand* (1977), the 200 largest U.S. manufacturing companies (measured in assets) in such fields as petroleum, rubber, machinery, food products, and transportation equipment that had reached dominance by 1917 retained it through the mid-1970s. By mid-twentieth century, the corporate reorganization of the country was a fait accompli. In 1948, the corporate sector held almost 60 percent of national income-producing wealth, and the largest 200 employers accounted for one of every five private nonagricultural jobs. Although many businessmen remained small and independent, their work life brought them into constant interaction with corporate and bureaucratic America.

Early in the twentieth century, the large corporations had begun to require great concentrations of office workers and proceeded to recruit them in many sectors of American society, including the children of working-class immigrants. Counting clerks, sales employees, managers, and professionals, the white-collar group as a whole grew to 37 percent of all U.S. workers by the 1950s. Furthermore, women, who were virtually absent from the clerical work force in 1870, made up a quarter of clerical jobs in 1900 and 62 percent in 1950. At the turn of the century, most working women were still employed as domestics, farm laborers, unskilled factory operatives, and teachers. By 1950, clerical tasks had emerged as the dominant category for women's work. Clerical workers also swelled the ranks of the federal bureaucracy.

The organizational transformation underway resulted also from the unprecedented expansion of the federal government as well as the growth of national professional associations, the systematization of knowledge in universities, and the ensuing certification process. The motivation for creating these national associations was to codify the academic requirements for entry into professionalized fields, to standardize methods, to disseminate information, and to influence public policy. Prominent physicians, lawyers, engineers, administrators, scientists, and professors would now gain recognition as leaders of large numbers of like-minded middle-class individuals. The incorporation of the economy therefore changed the constitution of the middle class from independent entrepreneurs to managers and white-collar workers as both growing corporations and the government created demands for new professionalized fields and drew heavily from the old middle class of small businessmen to fill their managerial ladders, and from the ranks of upwardly mobile, young native-born Americans of diverse ethnic origins to staff their offices.

Middle-class Americans therefore adapted to the new institutions of mass society but also molded the public and private bureaucracies they came to serve to their own image. Professionals were not simply pawns of the corporation. They learned how to protect their individuality from the dominant corporate economy by developing multiple loyalties as well as compromises between their employers' demands for service and the professional ethics promoted by their expanding professional organizations.

The number of middle-level managers grew very rapidly throughout the country, promoting a new work culture, and carrying an innovative organizational revolution into key sectors of society. The emergence and growth of salaried personnel on such a grand scale translated into lifestyles that came to dominate America's cultural scene. Organization began to symbolize both a way of life and the kind of people who advocated it. Managers promoted a more homogeneous social order through organizational principles capable of integrating people of various origins into the new American middle class. Through their program of job stability, easy access to suburban home ownership and consumer goods, middle-level managers promoted a relative simplification of America's cultural system—a simplification directly linked to their position in the new bureaucratic order of corporate America and big government.

By the middle of the twentieth century, both private and public sectors had generated those complex organizations that made America "modern" in the eyes of social scientists and that stimulated economists', sociologists', and psychologists' theories of modernization as well as inspiring William H. Whyte's *The Organization Man* (1956). It was these organizations that orchestrated the increasing standard of living that Americans experienced through fully two-thirds of the twentieth century. And it was from within these organizations that middle-class Americans defined their search for abundance as well as their formulae for coping with anomie, boredom, and stress.

The idea of the twentieth-century American middle class became closely tied to that of abundance. A rising standard of living was until recently its hallmark and softened class tensions. After a brief post-World War I recession, Americans of the twenties began to enjoy the benefits of mass production, mass consumption, and innovations in consumer credit. Only 8 percent of American households had washing machines in 1920, but by 1930 this number grew to 24 percent; 26 percent had cars in 1920, a percentage that soared to 60 percent in 1930. Earnings grew and unemployment declined. In 1914 dollars, employee income rose from $546 in 1910 to an average of $793 in 1929, just before the stock market crash, while unemployment declined from 5.9 percent to 3.2 percent.

The 1920s were also a time of freewheeling speculation. Everybody, including workmen, "ought to be rich" by investing in the market, claimed John Raskob, the Du Pont executive who managed Al Smith's campaign in 1928. Although his prescription must have sounded insane to the mass of working people who had to pool family incomes to make ends meet and who borrowed from credit unions just to pay for medical bills and coal, Raskob's pronouncement reflects the faith many held in the redistributive power of corporate capitalism and its potential for abolishing class divisions.

The middle class, as its standard of living rose, strengthened its position through acquisitive individualism. It expanded its reaches, welcoming an ever larger segment of sons and daughters of the working class. Laborers aspired to a comfortable middle-class existence. Social scientists, attuned to such shifts and to popular sensibilities, saw disciplined family budgets as a means to help workers achieve middle-class respectability, while marketing executives equated the middle class with the average consumer.

During the Depression, however, the middle class was rocked to its foundations. For the workers who had already experienced poverty, the Depression was a more dramatic replay of a known scenario, but for middle-class Americans who had shared in the prosperity of the twenties, the decade that followed was a period of great fear and adjustment as they wrestled with poverty. While millions turned temporarily to Huey Long's "Share Our Wealth Campaign" or the populist formulas of Dr. Francis Townsend or Father Charles Coughlin, most clung to an American way of life they wanted to reclaim.

War production and the subsequent postwar boom did restore the economy. In managing abundance again in the 1940s and 1950s, middle-class Americans—the "people of plenty," as historian David Potter called them—developed a new outlook on life. The consensus of the postwar era was echoed in the voices of social scientists who provided policymakers with the tools to manage abundance and offered the rest of the world a model for achieving it.

In *The End of Ideology* (1962), Daniel Bell suggested that Americans created new forms of political discourse to guide them in responding to abundance. The economy was growing vigorously, he felt, and the problems of production had been solved. The worst aspects of inequality had been alleviated, and economists like John Kenneth Galbraith argued, in *The Affluent Society* (1958), that Americans needed to develop an appreciation of their new tools. The shift in attitude Galbraith called for was best summed up by economist Walter Heller's pronouncement: "When the cost of fulfilling a people's aspirations can be met out of a growing horn of plenty—instead of robbing Peter to pay Paul—ideological roadblocks melt away, and consensus replaces conflict" (*New Dimensions of Political Economy,* 1967). Policymakers eventually accepted the idea that abundance would be permanent and that a new way of distributing income would have to be found, nineteenth-century methods being obsolete. Rather than foreseeing a country characterized by polarities, they saw a trend toward a congeries of middle classes, unionized workers among them, with only "vestigial classes" standing above and below. But such predictions, as we will see, did not materialize.

The sense of belonging to the middle class has been so powerful among twentieth-century Americans that social scientists have devised ways to measure its gradations in fine detail. It has become a staple of American sociology and survey research to divide up society on a continuum of "classes" according to such characteristics as education, income, patterns of friendship and associations, habits of consumption and the like. American sociologists, taking their cue from the work of German sociologist Max Weber, published posthumously in 1921 as *Economy and Society,* proceeded to quantify his ideas on class, status, and power, that is, to develop methods to measure such characteristics. Typically, they have concentrated on education, occupation, and income as the three most important indicators of status among upper- to lower-class white males. Ownership of stock or other assets adds little once the three main variables are accounted for. The socioeconomic level of one's acquaintances, however, whether friends, relatives, or neighbors, also plays a role in class identification. An important characteristic of these status continuum models (challenged by Marxists) is that no cleavages separate the population into distinct homogeneous groups. Sociologists usually point out that such detailed patterns of stratification were well ingrained in people's consciousness and easily identifiable among small-town residents, as W. Lloyd Warner attempted to show in his pioneering *Yankee City* (Newburyport, Mass.) studies in the 1930s. But sociologists insist that the strata are not hermetically sealed. They point instead to significant upward mobility, especially intergenerational mobility.

When David Potter identified major characteristics of American society in his remarkable *People of Plenty* (1954), he relied heavily on this sociological approach and argued that if "the American class structure is in reality very unlike the classless society which we imagine, it is equally unlike the formalized class societies of former times, and thus it should be regarded as a new kind of social structure in which the strata may be fully demarcated but where the bases of demarcation are relatively intangible." People move rather fluidly from level to level. This vision of stratification reached its highest level of popularity among social scientists after World War II, for it allowed them to talk at once about a very large and diversified middle class.

A class structure where dividing lines are hard to draw has had enormous psychological implications for twentieth-century Americans. Noting that the first popular article on psychoanalysis, "Diagnosis by Dream," appeared in *Good Housekeeping* in 1915, Marie Jahoda forcefully pointed to the connection between the class experience of middle-class Americans and the appeal of psychoanalysis. As she put it,

> Long before J. K. Galbraith popularized the phrase, America was an affluent society in which the belief that everybody could reach the top was widespread, almost universal. . . . In England before the war the ambitious working-class youngster knew that the class structure was holding him back. He could join a labor movement and find satisfaction in collective experience; though his individual fate was frustrating, he did not need to lose self-respect. Society was at fault, not he. His counterpart in the States, even in the relatively rare instance in which he joined a political movement, was confronted with the powerful ethos of his society: he believed in his heart that he had nobody to blame but himself.

Under such circumstances, psychoanalysis relieved the individual from full responsibility for his or her failures, which may have been beyond his or her control. But the social structure was not to blame.

A key point about the American middle class is indeed the ease with which one can gain membership in it in good times. Far more important than its internal divisions has been its expansiveness, facilitated by a low point of entry, a process C. Wright Mills understood well in *White Collar* (1951), although he attacked middle-class subservience and championed the entrepreneurial spirit. The working-class origins of many white-collar workers and frequent movements from blue-collar to white-collar work only underscore the constant process of middle-class re-formation. With the entry level low, it became easy for children of immigrants to enter the middle class. The spread of jobs in local government and the federal bureaucracy only accelerated the lower-middle-class entry into professionalized fields. So did the spread of mass education.

In the twentieth century, then, parts of the working class and of the middle class have slowly merged into a very large, loosely differentiated American middle class. How the lines between these two classes have blurred, in reality and/or in perception, is an important dimension of twentieth-century American history. The twentieth-century American middle class emerged from the amalgamation of a few key occupational categories that have grown large: the expansion of the professions, the corporate managers, and the white-collar workers. Foremen were increasingly brought into management while many small independent entrepreneurs and skilled workers continued to blur the "collar line."

The prerequisites for corporate and government clerical work were a solid foundation in English grammar and proficiency in writing, as well as the ability to comport oneself in accordance with the rules of conduct appropriate for offices. In a country that drew its working class mostly through immigration, these prerequisites for office work limited applicants to educated, native-born Americans or children of immigrants. This simple fact is of overriding importance. Immigrants could readily see that this expanding sector of the economy would be available to them only if they developed a better-than-working knowledge of their new country's language, in itself an act of assimilation. Securing a job in this sector, in turn, meant even further assimilation, for the rules were set entirely by and for native white workers. Although routine tasks on the assembly line were for unskilled immigrants with limited knowledge of English—foremen learned how to say "hurry up" in multiple languages—white-collar work remained the preserve of a more educated lower-middle class that sought respectability, including those immigrants who could operate well in both worlds, and most of their children.

This is not a universally accepted proposition. Sociologists like Harry Braverman have pointed instead to clerical proletarianization (*Labor and Monopoly Capital,* 1975). Braverman's thesis has been influential among historians and sociologists who argue that the growth of white-collar occupations generated a swelling of the working class as well as status anxiety. They point to the division of white-collar tasks into a series of standardized procedures, as in mail-order houses like Sears, as well as low salaries and absence of social protection as an indication that many white-collar workers in corporations had not attained middle-class status. We will return to that charge in a later discussion of the relationship between gender and class.

The availability of so many new white-collar jobs actually fostered the expansion of the American middle class and set in motion a complex process of class redefinition. Although the range of jobs and aspirations that contribute to the heading "white collar" was large, and the line between blue-collar worker and white-collar employee was diffuse in some areas, the educational prerequisite for a white-collar job and the hope of mobility account for the status that clerical work enjoyed even after it became standardized. White-collar work represented a well-tested source of improvement, and this understanding remained ingrained in the American middle class.

The spread of mass education has also encouraged the process of middle-class expansion. At the dawn of the twentieth century, only 8 percent of young Americans graduated from high school. In 1950 that figure had reached 50 percent; it was 75 percent in 1990. Early in the twentieth century, John Dewey had placed much hope in the power of education to foster an inclusive citizenry respectful of cultural differences and eager to infuse meaning into the learning process. Dewey saw culture as "the democratic password" (*The School and Society,* 1900). Although Dewey's unshakable optimism and belief in progress are not always to the taste of a late-twentieth-century reader, the mass education movement to which he contributed so much of his energies nurtured the expanding middle class.

Marxist revisionists have sought to disprove that mass education has fostered advancement for the majority, arguing instead that educational reforms have been the handiwork of capitalists who have used public education as a means to teach future workers those values that would minimize class tensions in the industrializing society. But if we contrast the history of American secondary education to that of other advanced nations, we see that the American system of education has been relatively free from selective tracks channelling some students at an early age into long-term educational careers while holding others to limited terminal curricula. Primary schools, with common charters and curricula, have provided a similar experience to all white students since the nineteenth century, although one in which African American children would not fully participate for most of the twentieth century. The comprehensive high school created during the years 1890–1920 was a normal extension of the nineteenth-century common school toward the forging of a shared culture.

The pattern of education in the United States, marked by limited stratification for white students, high enrollment, and a common curriculum, reflects middle-class assimilationist and individualistic values. Economic elites made repeated efforts to reverse this pattern by stratifying public education in the interest of their children. But they were barred from imposing their views by the extraordinary growth of a middle class of white-collar and skilled workers and by the powerful alliance of middle-class reformers, educational professionals, their political allies in city government, and working-class groups. As a result, vocational education given in separate institutions, designed directly to mediate between youth and the labor market, training them for jobs and guiding them neatly into their appropriate places in the labor market, has not flourished in America. Although the Smith-Hughes Act of 1918 provided federal funding for separate vocational schools, most vocational education remained within the comprehensive high school where all students could be brought together for some classes and extracurricular activities.

The growth of high school education in the first half of the century was followed by an equally impressive growth of postsecondary education after World War II. A student having followed the general curriculum could look forward to higher education. Between 1940 and 1970, enrollments in the nation's colleges rose from about 1.5 million to about 8.5 million, significantly exceeding the rate of population growth. And by 1991, overall enrollment in colleges and universities reached 14 million. Currently, roughly two-thirds of high school graduates (or about half of the age cohort) enter postsecondary institutions within seven years of earning their high school diploma.

Mass higher education, especially since the great expansion following World War II, has helped the sons and daughters of the working class achieve upward mobility. As educators have launched aggressive affirmative-action programs to attract minority students, mass education has also been a real avenue opened to those ethnic and racial minorities who were least prepared to do so. These large changes in postsecondary education drove a massive increase in enrollments in the institutions that had formerly educated the older social and professional elite. Furthermore, vocational education has also flourished within the growing network of junior colleges that prepare students both in practical subjects and in topics needed to transfer to universities.

For all these educational opportunities and general feeling of openness to newcomers, the American middle class is again on trial at the close of the twentieth century. Its ideals are questioned anew in ways reminiscent of the Great Depression when middle-class Americans had to reconcile their dignity with an eroding purchasing power. Facing a major restructuring in the world economy as well as a decline in the standard of living relative to other advanced nations for almost a quarter of a century, late-twentieth-century middle-class Americans have justifiably less confidence in the managers, experts, and technocrats that have come to symbolize twentieth-century managerial capitalism.

The technocrats who, by losing touch with economic reality, are also losing their employees' confidence, have often been described as a new ruling class. Whether engaged in industry or service, these technocrats have characteristics similar to other workers (they receive salaries) and the old moneyed class (they exercise control over vital resources and structure their own work environments). They have run economic production, military systems, and social-welfare programs. They have directed the flow of public resources and determined the ways in which they are used. But their outlook is premised on a particular sort of rationality (purposive rationality, means rationality, value-free rationality) that limits their political and cultural perspectives. As a result, technocrats are incapable of accounting for social and cultural factors when making crucial decisions. Efficiency, competitiveness, or "mastery," as Walter Lippmann called it, have often become hollow terms in their hands.

Furthermore, American technocrats have been slow to respond to the massive challenges a rebuilt Europe and Japan, and a newly vitalized East Asia, have brought to the American economy. Giant American corporations were successfully challenged by more flexible, post-Fordist production systems that made more efficient use of just-in-time production techniques and the information-processing revolution. The deindustrialization of large parts of the American economy since the 1970s has disturbed the traditional channels of mobility from manual to nonmanual work and has devalued the latter. Large, once apparently unassailable corporations have been downsizing, and the security associated with white-collar work has all but vanished. As the rich became richer in the 1980s under the Reagan and Bush administrations, inequality resurfaced as a forming influence on American life. According to figures reported by the economic historian Claudia Goldin in the *New York Times* (16 August 1992), by 1990, the richest 1 percent owned 36.3 percent of the national wealth—the highest level since the all-time peak of 42.6 percent in 1929, and a drastic departure from the century's lowest, 17.6 percent in 1976 (figure 1). Middle-class Americans find themselves, with reason, worrying about the many who are again left out and are unsure of their ability to offer a helping hand. Is the American middle class losing its integrating power, overtly dependent on economic conditions, as the twentieth century closes?

THE AMERICAN WORKING CLASS

As the leading industrial power for most of the twentieth century, the United States created a large working class comprising millions of unskilled, semiskilled, and skilled workers, immigrants and natives alike, in all parts of the country. The first vast stretch of land to industrialize extended from the Pennsylvania coal fields to the iron mines near Lake Superior. This industrial belt, created between the 1870s and the 1920s, reached the New South early in the twentieth century, where it expanded during World War I. Shipbuilding and explosives in particular helped southern cities. Southern textile factories, where employers could continue to employ a nonunionized labor force no longer available in the North, surpassed New England textile factories in the 1920s. After 1920, it was the West that transformed its primary-resource economy—mining, agriculture, and timber—into an industrial one. World War II, in turn, greatly boosted western industrialization and brought the West onto an equal footing with the East. During and after World War II, the federal government poured billions of dollars into military bases and military-production facilities in the urban West.

While the process of inclusion in the United States has depended on the formation in the twentieth century of a very large middle class, labor historians have generally insisted that the American's working-class cohesiveness and ethic of mutual help were equally important to American society, critical to the working class's long and difficult fight for recognition by the state and employers alike.

Most historians of the working class, influenced by one form or another of Marxism, have rejected the stratification models of non-Marxist scholars. They consider stratification useful only as a means to describe a social structure in fine detail, a different exercise entirely from analyzing class dynamics, and the higher-order principles of class consciousness and class conflict. For the fine and fluctuating occupational categories of stratification, they substitute a dualistic identification—membership in the business class or in the working class—and a dialectic of class relations. This is the procedure Robert and Helen Lynd used in their landmark study of Muncie, Indiana, *Middletown* (1929).

While Tocqueville pointed to the growing equality that would pervade modern societies, Marx instead stressed inequality and class conflicts (*Capital,* 3 vols., 1867, 1885, 1894). In traditional Marxist theory, the business class owns the means of produc-

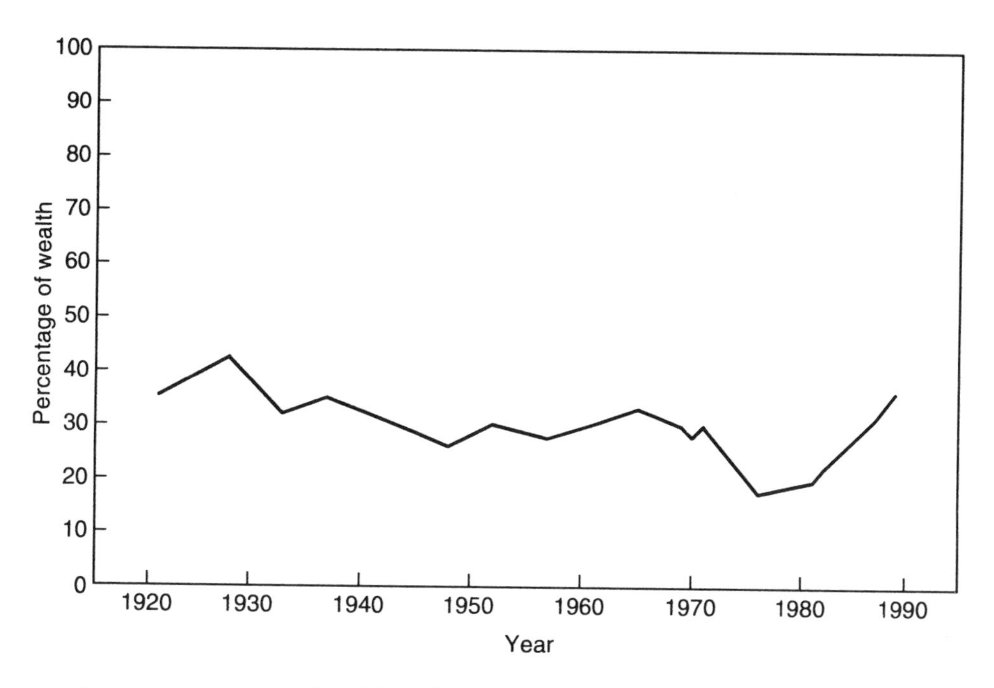

Figure 1. Percentage of wealth held by the top 1 percent of Americans, 1922–1990. (Adapted from *New York Times,* 16 August 1992; data from Claudia Goldin, Bradford DeLong, and Edward Wolff.)

tion and controls state power to exploit a growing proletariat of wage labor. Marxism, however, has undergone many revisions. Neo-Marxist labor historians who have written on the American working class have recently stressed cultural factors over economic factors in their descriptions of the American class experience. They have contrasted the working class's ethos of mutual help and solidarity with the middle class's ethos of acquisitive individualism, and assigned greater moral value to the former. Mutuality—that is, concerted, not individual action— labor historians argue, has been a real alternative to middle-class acquisitive individualism.

There are conflicting ways to interpret the history of the American working class and the fate of the "House of Labor." We must begin with German economist Werner Sombart's enormously influential 1906 essay, "Why Is There No Socialism in the United States?" Sombart answered his question by pointing to the American worker's superior purchasing power. American class consciousness was wrecked, he said, on "shoals of roast beef and apple pie" and on the remarkable openness of a society where a worker "mixes with everyone—in reality and not only in theory—as an equal."

Although much labor history has cast doubt on the validity of Sombart's theory and that of other generalizations about American exceptionalism, his ghost is not easy to exorcise. We now understand why it is inaccurate to explain the failure of radicalism in late-nineteenth-century America by single-mindedly pointing to a pervading countercurrent—the redistributive power of unlimited growth. There is no such simple relationship between collective action and standard of living, between contentiousness and consumption. Furthermore, tenacious habits of thrift, motivated by an acute sense of future need, effectively prevented the American working class from believing in the therapeutic ethos of consumerism until well into the 1920s.

The fact remains, however, that the primary beneficiaries of high wages were skilled workers who supported craft unionism and who were reluctant to make alliances with unskilled workers, often immigrants freshly arrived from eastern Europe or African Americans from the South. An older, better-established working class did not willingly unite with a newer mass of unskilled immigrants.

That is one reason why uniting the working class at election time was extremely difficult. Universal white-male suffrage had early on brought skilled American workers into the political process and engaged their loyalties in nonrevolutionary parties. Such loyalties broke only with difficulty in the face of independent workers' political organizations. In *City Trenches* (1981), Ira Katznelson discusses how political parties built networks of loyalties in ethnic neighborhoods while labor unions performed the same task in the workplace alone. "What needs to be explained," Katznelson notes, "is not the absence of class in American politics but its limitation to the arena of work." Stressing the separation of class and community, he points out that "what is distinctive about the American experience is that the linguistic, cultural, and institutional meaning given to the differentiation of work and community, a characteristic of all industrial capitalist societies, has taken a sharply divided form, and that it has done so for a very long time."

Only exceptional moments could help workers cross the boundaries that divided a growing working class. And even during these exceptional moments, radicalism's intellectual aspirations were generated in so many competing cultural systems that they could not in themselves unify the working class. But when Eugene Debs rallied 6 percent of the popular vote in 1912 behind his fifth bid for president as the Socialist party candidate, Socialists had reasons to hope that the moment had come. Debs led Socialists in a class struggle against ruthless employers who were building their own army of Pinkerton detectives, enforcing blacklists of unionized workers, playing on the ethnic divisions of the working class, as well as mustering the police and judicial power of the state behind them to better enforce their rule.

Debs's case is important, not only as a reminder of what might have been, but because the man from Terre Haute, Indiana, embodied a special American vision for his socialist dream. Debs did not derive his unbending determination to oppose class domination from Marx. Rather, he harkened back to Ralph Waldo Emerson, Henry David Thoreau, and Walt Whitman to promote a new social conscience. He came to believe that workers were denied their dignity as long as they were the subject of violence and inequities. Determined to bring about a new "brotherhood of man," Debs, like other American labor leaders, radicalized the very ideas on which the nation was born.

Yet at the time of Debs's electoral popularity, the programs for industrial unionism and revolutionary radicalism had only partially overlapped. For many unionized workers, the search for personal improvement was not necessarily synonymous with larger social reform. Herein lies one of the critical problems of the American working class: bread-and-butter labor unionism did not marry well with revolutionary goals. Despite his enormous power to inspire, Debs, and with him the Socialist party, failed to mend the basic skill division within the working class. He and others were unable to reconcile the more radical but still craft-conscious skilled workers with the radical "Wobblies," as the mostly unskilled Industrial Workers of the World were called. Debs's failure to choose between Samuel Gompers (American Federation of Labor) and "Big" Bill Haywood (I.W.W.) in the end meant being torn between two segments of the working class and becoming unable to talk in its name. The structural/stratification problem within the working class undercut revolutionary radicalism in the United States as much as any internal rivalries of the Left or the devastating blow the Wilson administration delivered in crushing the peace and radical movements during World War I.

It is wishful thinking to believe that radicalism would have fared better if only the great wave of populism and agrarian radicalism had intersected with the socialist movement. As Lawrence Goodwyn recognized in *Democratic Promise* (1976), "In 1892 . . . the Alliance organizers looked at urban workers and simply did not know what to say to them—other than to repeat the language of the Omaha platform." To be sure, dirt farmers in the Southwest supported the Socialists (16 percent of the Oklahomans voted for Debs in 1912), but their commitment to socialism was often weak. For many, it did not survive the first opportunity to participate in the market economy. Furthermore, not only did agrarian and industrial radicalism largely ignore each other, but farm workers came to account for a declining share of the working population: 39 percent in 1900, only 18 percent in 1940, not even 3 percent in 1980.

Sombart's working class, always present in discussions of American exceptionalism, was "job conscious" rather than "class conscious." And so, most of the time, was the labor movement dominated by craft-conscious, skilled workers. For a long time, the study of the working class was limited to the activities of organized labor, neglecting the majority of American workers. It is only since the 1960s that a new labor history has been promoting a larger vision of the American working class.

In his *History of Labor in the U.S.* (1918–1935), John R. Commons, who trained at Johns Hopkins with Richard Ely, defined the study of labor as the study of trade unionism and collective bargaining. He had good reasons to do so. By stressing institutions, Commons and his followers actually fought for the acceptance of collective action and collective bargaining by skilled workers, activities heretofore often considered an unacceptable intrusion into the laws of the market. Commons's best student, Selig Perlman, made the case for bread-and-butter unionism most forcefully in *A Theory of the Labor Movement* (1928).

In stressing labor unions only, the old labor history accepted the division between skilled and unskilled labor. By contrast, the new labor history, born with the New Left—in the civil rights movement and in the protest against the Vietnam War—and disappointed by an American working class that had turned conservative, sought, in Herbert Gutman's formulation, to break the "cocoon" that the previous generation had spun around American workers (*Work, Culture, and Society in Industrializing America,* 1976). The new labor history would bring back the entire working class as part of its inclusive vision of American history by linking the unskilled workers' subcultures to the larger national culture. Gutman and other new labor historians took their cues from the British historian E. P. Thompson, who had made a very strong case in *The Making of the English Working Class* (1963) that the proper usage of class is as a historical category, as a social process which evolves over time and is inseparable from the notion of class struggle. Thompson maintains that it is in discovering the need for class struggle that class consciousness emerges. His years of reflection on English history led him to conclude that "the wrong assumption is that classes exist and that they struggle because they exist. Instead they come into existence because of that struggle." As a consequence Thompson denied any value to literal quantitative measurement of the positivistic sociological tradition so important in stratification theory. In an article in *Social History* (1978), using an important distinction Karl Marx had made, he reserved the word "class" for a *Klasse für sich* (class for itself) discarding out of hand a *Klasse an sich* (class in itself). Following Thompson's lead, American New Labor historians downplayed economics and politics and turned instead to culture to identify class consciousness.

Labor historians therefore advocated the study of ethnic subcultures in American society as part of an attempt to shed new light on heretofore ignored sources of class consciousness and reaction to capitalistic exploitation. In their view, as ethnic subcultures and institutions provided an alternative to unionism, the study of ethnicity had the potential to provide a more encompassing vista than the study of unionism. The sometimes convergent histories of social and ethnic groups, however, have led some historians to confuse class and ethnicity and treat these two categories interchangeably. The more challenging task would be to analyze the impact of conflicting loyalties on twentieth-century class structure.

By turning away from labor institutions dominated by skilled workers, labor historians brought unskilled workers into the mainstream of American history. In so doing, they repaired the nineteenth-century schism between unskilled and skilled workers. The twentieth century actually added a new subject for their lens: the semiskilled operative—a product of Frederick Winslow Taylor's "scientific management" and Henry Ford's techniques of assembly line production. The semiskilled operative came to dominate the American working class numerically and changed its character. Thus, when discussing semiskilled workers, New Labor historians have focused on the workers' will to retain control of their work lives. David Montgomery especially has gone to great lengths to show workers' ability to maintain some autonomy on the shop floor in the face of oppressive production systems (*Workers' Control in America,* 1979; *The Fall of the House of Labor,* 1987).

The dramatic reduction of immigration in the 1920s also changed the composition of the working class and helped the labor movement overcome its most profound ethnic divisions. A much more homogeneous working class than in the nineteenth century, both in ethnic identity and in skill levels, organized the sit-down strikes of 1936–1937, joined the CIO, and finally gained full recognition in the New Deal.

Historians have studied the slow transition from a working class deeply divided along ethnic lines to a more homogeneous working class dominated by the semiskilled laborer, as it evolved from the 1910s to the 1940s in places as different as Detroit, a city quickly transformed by the automobile industry; Woonsocket, Rhode Island, a smaller New England textile center; and the diversified industrial metropolis of Chicago. In these and other detailed monographs, they have considered the whole array of evidence available to them, from demographic indicators (fertility, marriage patterns, residential concentration) to associational life, labor protests, consumerism, home ownership, religious commitments, and others.

In the nineteenth century, immigrants often experienced multiple channels of opportunity, some within their own group, some without. Conversely, class conflict was often a form of intra-ethnic conflict. By the time an Italian or Slav joined his fellow immigrants to work for Ford or other large conglomerates in cities like Detroit or Pittsburgh, many opportunities available within ethnic communities had been replaced by the concentration of resources into those large-center firms, as business historians call them, that were to dominate the American economy, virtually unchallenged, until the 1970s. In the process, as I have discussed elsewhere (*The Changing Face of Inequality,* 1982), ethnicity became a more distinctively working-class attribute. In smaller New England textile cities, the transition from ethnicity to class took longer than in cities dominated by heavy industries like Detroit. As Gary Gerstle put it in his study of Woonsocket, *Working-class Americanism* (1989), "in the first three decades of the twentieth century, a Woonsocket individual's ethnic identity shaped, to a large extent, his or her world of friends and acquaintances, his or her personal dreams, and his or her political ambitions." The strength of ethnic ties decreased in the 1920s in the face of external political and cultural forces that "shattered Woonsocket's cultural insularity." In the end, "external economic pressures (and the consequent decline of the city's cotton textile industry) pushed issues of class to the fore with ever greater urgency." As the Great Depression struck, class divisions had already superseded ethnic divisions. Lizabeth Cohen, in turn, maintains that in the large and very diversified industrial metropolis of Chicago, ethnic bonds remained sufficiently strong throughout the twenties and thirties for workers successfully to resist the assimilative pressures of welfare capitalism even longer. Only when the Depression struck did Chicago workers overcome their ethnic parochialism and finally unite in a mass movement to negotiate a "new deal" partly on their own terms (*Making a New Deal,* 1990).

These changes in individual and collective behavior contributed to integrating the working class more fully into the American political landscape. Although such labor leaders as the coalminers' John Lewis, the autoworkers' Walter Reuther, the clothing workers' Sidney Hillman, and their followers intimately knew the meaning of class struggle, their victories as well as the nationalism of World War II that shattered both radical unions and many ethnic identities brought an ever greater segment of the working class of mostly semiskilled workers into the fold of increasingly conservative unionism. So did the vast array of New Deal and post-World War II neo-Keynesian policies. As numerous social and economic surveys of the 1950s and 1960s have shown, workers subsequently joined the mainstream of American consumers with middle-class aspirations. Once there, it became more and more difficult to separate them from an ever-expanding middle class.

Furthermore, as the working-class outlook changed, so did the center of radicalism. While the old Left was closely identified with labor radicalism and the working class, the New Left turned against the New Deal political consensus. The separation between the old and New Left was slow and painful but ultimately unavoidable. As Jeffrey Goldfarb sums it up well in *The Cynical Society* (1991), old-fashioned Marxists intellectuals, who were committed to a view of historical progress, had found "the class agent that would enable them actively to take part in its teleology." That commitment had run its course by the 1960s. "New labor historians" began searching the American past for evidence of class consciousness outside the working class mainstream. More generally, the new radicals found little appeal in an American working class that had experienced *embourgeoisement* and was resisting both the antiwar and the civil rights movements. The Students for a Democratic Society (SDS) openly attacked the labor movement for being "too rich and sluggish," experiencing a "crisis of vision." If radicalism were to find a new "class" base, it would be by taking a whole new look at the bases of inequality in America.

HOW OPEN IS AMERICAN SOCIETY? THE DEBATES ON MOBILITY, ELITES, AND POWER

Horatio Alger's stories were immensely popular in their day. Nothing appealed more to the American imagination than rags-to-riches stories, even if they were not true. In fact, few American careers were as spectacular as Andrew Carnegie's famous rise from poverty to become the richest man in the world.

Historians have retraced thousands of ordinary people's careers in the twentieth century. Tracking Americans' movements and jobs in old census enumerations, city directories, and other vital statistics, and creating large computerized data bases to trace people's whereabouts, historians have documented in great detail the relationship between the geographic mobility of Americans who sought to improve their lot and their actual gains. Stephan Thernstrom concluded a decade of historical research on mobility in *The Other Bostonians* (1973) by pointing out that opportunities for advancement significantly offset the disadvantages many poor immigrants had initially suffered. The availability of these opportunities impeded "the formation of class-based protest movements that sought fundamental alterations in the economic system."

Mobility historians, in their debates, recognized the potential for serious social conflict in the history of ethnic, social, and racial entities. But because minorities were continually integrated into the majority, this conflict rarely materialized. By positing an ever present social mobility as the mechanism of social change, they suggested that mobility was at once an assimilation device and a safety valve.

There were dissenters. Some historians offered the sobering, although overdrawn, objection that mobility merely gave the illusion of advancement. Thus Daniel Rodgers saw Alger's heroes as emerging from a "magical web of coincidences" (*The Work Ethic in Industrial America, 1850–1920,* 1978). These historians' remarks had some basis in the economic history of the twentieth century. The transformation of the economy created a structural mobility that played a role perhaps more important than individual accomplishment in explaining intergenerational mobility. In a twentieth-century economy in which the business and bureaucratic sectors grew at an unprecedented speed, children of immigrants, perhaps through no special efforts of their own, worked at white-collar occupations more often than their fathers. Under such circumstances of structural mobility, the social theorist Anthony Giddens argued in *The Class Structure of the Advanced Societies* (1981) that the perception of "working class" and "middle class" in the twentieth century more closely came to reflect a manual-nonmanual dichotomy. Such a distinction had been blurred in the nineteenth century, when many entrepreneurial ventures were still propelled by people from the shop culture of tinkerers and manual workers.

Other dissenters, especially among advocates of the Great Society of the 1960s, found the American social system less open than was generally believed. Disturbed that the general prosperity that they witnessed had failed to extinguish poverty, they assessed the receptivity of the social system and pointed to the many obstacles to mobility that impaired people's chances in life. In the process, these historians became concerned primarily with issues of social justice. This may be why, as Hartmut Kaelble has shrewdly remarked in *Historical Research on Social Mobility* (1981), mobility ceased to interest American historians when it lost its radical appeal; that is, when studies revealed that ordinary Americans experienced periods of significant upward mobility more often than frustrations in their careers.

Others maintained that mobility was just another tool of the dominant class to assert its power. For New Left scholars, a worker who aspires to middle-class life does so against his class interest, and a middle-class worker who does not recognize that he or she had been denied all real power becomes another victim of false consciousness. Thus among New Left scholars, James Weinstein suggested in *The Corporate Ideal in the Liberal State, 1900–1918* (1968) that "false consciousness of the nature of American liberalism has been one of the most powerful ideological weapons that American capitalism has had in maintaining its hegemony."

It is therefore important in this essay to assess Marxist and neo-Marxist claims that the American middle class has been subservient to the interest of a dominant class. For as every American knows, the middle class accounts for the lion's share of American history. In dispensing with the middle class, Marxists have taken to the extreme the concept of false consciousness. How powerful, then, is the power elite?

THE POWER ELITE

Like the middle and working classes, the power elite also escapes easy definition but is nonetheless real. Most Americans, not just social scientists, agree that a national upper class exists. The idea of an upper class is most often associated with that of a power elite. Depending on the circumstances, that elite is defined narrowly, with reference to a single powerful interest group such as the American Medical Association, or more broadly, as when people evoke the power of "Wall Street" or that of "Washington insiders," or quite broadly, as when President Eisenhower coined the phrase "military-industrial complex." Although such abstractions say little about who the power brokers are and who benefits from what, they carry enough meaning to suggest that some Americans are controlling much more of American life than others, and that their doings escape most Americans' grasp and democratic control. Even though the United States was born "modern," that is, without guaranteeing elite status at birth as was the case in older aristocratic societies, aristocracies of money, power, and expertise do persist in the United States, a circumstance that contradicts Americans' yearning for equality of opportunity.

Agreement ends as soon as Americans ask three related questions: Is the American upper class cohesive? How large is it? Is it a governing class? Although perceptions of elite status and power are often associated, they cover different realities. One can be a member of a wealthy elite with little power beyond what money can buy. Conversely, people of modest background and wealth can wield considerable power because of their position in politics, government, science, business, or the professions.

The idea of the power elite owes much to C. Wright Mills's 1956 book of that name. Mills, a

Texan turned New Yorker, saw the world from the city where power was most concentrated during the apex of the "American century" in the 1950s. The fact that New York's elites were far more diverse than that of other cities, like Boston, could not have escaped Mills's attention, but that was beside the point. New York remained the uncontested capital of world finance from 1945 to 1973. It was from their Manhattan headquarters that New York-based banks and corporations expanded their operations throughout the world. And it was from the powerful New York-based Council on Foreign Relations that much of the postwar liberal international order emerged. New Yorkers also controlled mass culture. It was perhaps inevitable that Mills, who lived in New York at this time, translated such a concentration of resources into the idea of a cohesive power elite.

Mills and his followers, especially G. William Domhoff in *Who Rules America?* (1967), point out that the power elite became national in scope in the last half of the nineteenth century "coincident with the rise of the national corporate economy which was its economic base and the national transportation-communications network which made its cohesiveness possible." Although the New Deal did mark a shift with "the beginning of a more ethnically representative establishment," it did not drastically change the ways in which the power elite operated.

Power elitists believe that members of the "governing class" not only intermingle and intermarry, they are tied together by a number of institutions, such as stock ownership, trust funds, private schools, elite universities, clubs, resorts, debutante parties, and foundation and corporate boards. These ties make the upper class cohesive and national in scope. In addition, they remind us that the upper class, while not monolithic, owns a disproportionate amount of the country's wealth and contributes a disproportionate number of its members to the key decision-making groups in American civil society and the state.

Mills's concept of a cohesive power elite has survived the widespread recognition that the power elite is actually quite diverse. Thus Domhoff, prominent among Mills's followers, recognized that, despite the high level of intermingling within the upper class, different coalitions exist caused by the splits between business conservatives and business liberals, between big and small business, and between WASPs and Jews or Catholics. Although the power elite may control the executive branch, the cabinet, the federal judiciary, the CIA, and regulatory agencies (since the regulated have "captured" these agencies), it does not control the legislative branch. Domhoff points out that only a handful of senators and congressmen come from the upper class, hence the power elite's need to lobby Congress. Domhoff also disagrees with Mills's assertion that the military rose to a place of prominence in the power elite. Power elitists, however, generally align with the position Antonio Gramsci expounded in his *Prison Notebooks* (1929–1935) that a dominant group, however divided, exercises "political and cultural hegemony" over the whole of society by controlling the decision-making process of both civil and political society. In Martin Sklar's formulation, "the 'ruling ideology' is not necessarily the ideology of the ruling class but may be a cross-class, cross-strata outlook." Resorting once more to Gramsci's hegemony, Sklar includes in the ruling class even "socialists and labor leaders who believed in administered market and government regulation, hence legitimized the corporate-capitalist order" as well as experts who became "service savants" (*The Corporate Reconstruction of American Capitalism, 1890–1916,* 1988).

Others, who strongly disagree, argue that the upper class has actually lost its power to a variety of "interest groups" that contend for power on an almost equal footing. They also point out that, despite fluctuating levels of wealth concentration, stock has been more widely owned by ordinary Americans than power elitists are willing to admit. Furthermore, as business historian Alfred Chandler has convincingly shown, as family capitalism became less and less prominent over the course of the twentieth century, the people who controlled the large corporations were managers, not owners. Thus, as Daniel Bell has argued in *The Coming of Post-industrial Society* (1976), inheritance was no longer the key to becoming a member of the "ruling class." The people who have ruled American institutions have done so in the twentieth century because they had "technical skill rather than property, and political position rather than wealth." The ruling class, that is—according to Bell, "the power-holding group which has both an established community of interests and a continuity of interests"—is no longer the same as the "upper class"—those who have privileges and can pass these privileges down to their children. Other critics have pointed out that the Gramscian concept of hegemony, however attractive it may be, is not so easily implemented in real life. Thus Barry Karl and Stanley Katz have contended that American foundations, the very institutions which wealthy Americans have created to leave their mark upon their country, have largely escaped both their founders' and/or the state's control. Karl and Katz argue in a *Daedalus* article (Winter 1987) that foundations consciously remained "independent from both government and business" to insure that "neither politics nor profits would shape the direction of intellectual growth."

Others have maintained that there is no easy alliance between business and politics, for American businessmen consistently distrust the state. Although one can say that a weak state leaves plenty of room for elites emerging from business to make their influence deeply felt on national affairs, the fact remains that American businessmen have tended to support only limited government intervention in the domestic economy. They have consistently opposed, in David Vogel's words (*British Journal of Political Sociology*, January 1978), "any government policies that would centralize economic decision making or strengthen the authority of government over the direction of the business system as a whole." As a result, the New Deal saved the business system in spite of the virtually unanimous opposition of businessmen themselves.

The debate will continue between those who see too much power in the hands of a few and those who point out that because the power elite has been consistently splintered into many parts in a proper Madisonian fashion, it has posed no real threat to democracy. This is an essential debate. The polynucleated and shifting character of the American power elite should not be construed as evidence for denying its existence and potential for abuse.

THE UNDERCLASS

It is equally important not to lose sight of the other end of the social spectrum. The reemergence of a large underclass at the end of the twentieth century, outside the working-class mainstream, has led to a return to the worst apprehensions of the Progressive Era, when the country feared the continuous flow of presumably inassimilable immigrants and called for drastic immigration restrictions. The resurgence of the underclass in the late twentieth century has also revitalized the debate, not just on class, but on how the country can morally and economically afford to sustain the significant fraction of its population that lives on the margin of the economic system. A large permanent underclass threatens the very process of social integration as well as the resources of private and public welfare systems.

The word *underclass* carries significant negative connotations. Some commentators have suggested that it is a new name for what the Victorians called the "undeserving" poor, that is, people who presumably have only themselves to blame for their state of poverty. But when the ranks of undeserving poor swelled to include members of the middle class during the Great Depression, Americans learned the limits of Social Darwinism. How, then, can we justify a return to a "blame the victim" view of poverty? In fact, the return of that concept may be as destabilizing as the problem itself. As William Kornblum has argued in *Dissent* (Spring 1991), the underclass is not a separate class but a label for "those people who are trapped in a netherworld at the bottom of both the legal and illegal class systems."

The middle-class fears of inassimilable immigrants who live on the margins of the economic system have traditionally been alleviated by the mobility of the poor, the extraordinary ingenuity, resourcefulness, and agency that even the poorest among them have invested in their new country. Family strategies such as income pooling to provide an education for some children, investments in voluntary associations that secured a modicum of safety in case of industrial accidents or untimely death prior to the rise of the welfare state, home acquisition and mutual help among neighbors, and participation in labor unions all combined to produce intergenerational mobility and social integration.

In the 1960s, Americans reached a progressive consensus whereby, after a century of efforts by social workers of the Gilded Age, reformers of the Progressive years, and New Deal architects of the welfare state, policymakers finally saw it as possible to eradicate poverty in the land of plenty by fueling the engine of mobility. For a brief period, success seemed to be around the corner. Only six years after Lyndon Johnson declared the War on Poverty in 1964, the percentage of poor had decreased nationwide from 15 to 11 percent, although it was still 32 percent among African Americans and 23 percent among Hispanics.

The economic restructuring of the 1970s and 1980s, however, had serious negative consequences. Americans saw the relative decline of both their overall standard of living and their ability to respond to the societal problems the economic restructuring generated. Traditional channels of upward mobility in industrial employment have been drastically reduced. Entry-level industrial jobs, once the basic mechanism of social integration, have now left the country. To make things worse, in our postindustrial economy, the poor are concentrated in inner-city zones where no employment is found. And the few remaining jobs seem to be monopolized by recent immigrants whose modest success only ignites resentment and violence.

Most victims are African Americans. In the optimistic years of the War on Poverty, it seemed appropriate to reject the implications of Daniel P. Moynihan's 1965 report, "The Negro Family: The Case for National Action," for Moynihan argued that the black family was caught in a "tangle of pathology." The critics' furor was aroused by the word "pathology." They countered by arguing that matriarchy was not a cultural flaw but instead an alternative culture African Americans had developed as a strategy to overcome the worst effects of racism they had suffered first on the plantation and, then, in the ghetto.

Thirty years have passed. Although few have the temerity to resurrect the term "pathology," the inescapable fact is that the situation has deteriorated even further for the majority of African Americans, with an alarming number among them feeling, in New York journalist Ken Auletta's words (*The Underclass,* 1982), "excluded from society," rejecting "commonly accepted values," and suffering "from behavioral as well as income deficiencies." The underclass comprises not only drug dealers, alcoholics, street criminals, and the mentally ill but also men and women without jobs and skills, struggling welfare mothers, and children abandoned to the mean streets. William Julius Wilson has reported in *The Truly Disadvantaged* (1987) that between 1965 and 1980, "out-of-wedlock black births increased from 25 to 57 percent of all births; black families headed by women have increased from 25 to 43 percent." In 1987, up to 45 percent of black children were considered poor. Violent crimes have also increased in the inner city as poor neighborhoods are the place of a burgeoning and dangerous drug market; 46 percent of the inmate population was black in 1987. Poverty translates directly into death. In 1993, there were 19.5 deaths for every 1,000 black men in the lower income group as against 3.6 deaths in the higher income group. The inequality in death rates between rich and poor has actually more than doubled between 1960 and 1986.

Although most investigations of extreme poverty have concentrated on African Americans, Latinos, the fastest growing segment of the American population, have added their numbers to the current underclass. In 1990 the Census Bureau reported that 28 percent of Latinos were poor compared to 32 percent of African Americans. Proportionately more Puerto Ricans are likely to be destitute than African Americans.

While studies of the African American underclass have concentrated on the Rustbelt and pointed to increased segregation of the very poor in urban areas blighted by both deindustrialization and flight by middle-income families, recent studies of Latino communities in sunbelt cities, where a large part of the Latino population lives, show a more complicated pattern. Equally affecting the Latino and African American underclass is government disinvestment in community-based organizations providing health care, housing aid, and other forms of assistance. Organizations that flourished in the 1960s have now deserted the poorest urban areas of the country for lack of continuous funding. Sunbelt cities, however, have been less affected by deindustrialization than rustbelt cities. Furthermore, as Joan Moore and Raquel Pinderhughes correctly underscore in *The Barrios* (1993), "continual immigration" has sustained Latino communities and "a historically lower level of housing discrimination" has kept them more open. Today's poorest Latinos are less intensely concentrated in barrios than African Americans in ghettos. There seems also to be more mobility in and out of the barrios as well as more cross-class contacts among Latinos than among African Americans. The traditional processes of mutual aid among immigrants that have survived in Latino communities compensate in part for the fact that only their U.S.-born children are eligible for the full range of welfare benefits.

It is clear, then, that Americans have once again to face poverty anew. As Michael Katz forcefully puts it, the process by which we generate an underclass is part of the larger "degradation of civic experience, democracy, and the public sphere" in contemporary America. Americans, Katz rightly underscores in *The "Underclass" Debate* (1993), will collectively be diminished if they cannot reverse the trend.

CLASS DIMENSIONS OF ETHNICITY, RACE, AND GENDER

Although specific theories of class help us understand major divisions within the American social structure, class intersects with other defining characteristics of Americans: ethnicity, race, and gender.

Horace Kallen once forcefully made the distinction between ascription and achievement by contrasting ethnicity to other social attributes. As Kallen put it, "An Irishman is always an Irishman, a Jew always a Jew. Irishman or Jew is born; citizen, lawyer, or church-member is made" (1913). However perceptive this observation may be, it reflects only imperfectly the relationship between class and ethnicity in the American experience. For ethnicity is no more than class a fixed attribute inherited at birth and unchangeable. Like class boundaries, ethnic bonds are constantly redefined by the circumstances of life: migration, marriage, occupational mobility, and so on. Tuscans and Sicilians became Italian Americans after moving to this country and Bavarians and Prussians German Americans, but if they move to Texas they all become "Anglos." When asking about ethnic affiliations, survey researchers and census takers have often elicited conflicting answers from respondents themselves depending on how they phrased the question. Ethnicity is an emerging and changing category as well as an ascribed status.

Like the study of class, the study of ethnicity recognizes the dynamics of change and also involves the classification of individuals into categories. And as in class, over time some groups grow while others decline. Although traces of ethnicity may be long-lasting, sociologists have for a long time contended that ethnicity is essentially a temporary attribute, best understood in the context of the first generation. Because most immigrants entered this country at the bottom of the social ladder, sociologists usually identify ethnicity as a working-class attribute and work out the sequences of assimilation as workers/immigrants (or their children) improve their lot and are integrated into the larger society.

Assimilation also entails diffusion of the ethnic group into one of the three wider religious groups—Catholic, Protestant, Jewish—a pattern diagnosed as the triple melting pot in the 1940s by sociologists who saw religion as enlarging the boundaries of ethnic identities. These sociologists based their findings on increasing intermarriage not simply between different ethnic groups but rather within larger religious communities.

This assimilationist interpretation of the relationship between class and ethnicity has been considerably revised in the wake of the ethnic revival of the late 1960s. As long as the Cold War intensified pressures for national unity, the concept of the melting pot went unchallenged. In the 1960s, however, various groups of intellectuals rediscovered diversity in their crusade for cultural democracy. They understood the American nation as a plurality comprised of groups defined by skin color, religion, language, nationality, and class, and they rewrote American history accordingly.

Americans, ethnic historians have shown, often practiced pluralism as a form of mutual avoidance, a key concept for understanding the American class structure. The patchwork of ethnic groups in America erected boundaries that compartmentalized institutional and social life although individuals were also free to adapt their way of life to the norms of the larger community.

Most nineteenth- and many early-twentieth-century ethnic communities were sufficiently large and autonomous to provide their members with an alternative opportunity structure independent of the economic networks dominated by native white Americans. This alternative channel—reinforced by intra-ethnic family and associational life—was visible in the labor markets, in the organization of the neighborhoods, and in the acquisition of property, and was conducive to ethnic semi-autonomy. Ethnic communities coexisted with the larger society and strong intra-ethnic group channels for upward mobility were established within them.

Ethnic entrepreneurship, as documented in classic immigrant novels, in the immigrant press, in numerous public documents on the organization of work, and in studies of ethnic businesses, is a key to the cross-class social structure of many immigrant communities. In many cities, ethnic groups dominated particular industries, not only as general laborers but also as manufacturers and wholesalers (like the Russian Jews who came to dominate the New York garment industry previously dominated by German Jews). Class conflicts often turned into intra-ethnic conflict.

Furthermore, those members of the immigrant communities who were employed in white-collar occupations did not always have to enter the Anglo-Saxon world. Their rise could be contained within a social system based on complex intergroup relationships. To be sure, many immigrants who rose up the social ladder did not remain within the more restricted and incomplete opportunity structure of the ethnic group. The important point, however, is that they could elect to do so. In addition, communities often created channels for the political expression of mobility and independence.

The interpretation of ethnic history that became dominant in the 1960s and 1970s had more validity for the early decades of the twentieth century than it did for mid-century. Ethnic life, with its diversified social structure, was still extremely important in the first quarter of the twentieth century; but it receded with the immigration restrictions of the 1920s. Large-scale economic changes such as mass production, bureaucratization, mass consumption, and the creation of the welfare state also undercut ethnic autonomy. As Richard Weiss neatly summed it up in a *Journal of American History* article (December 1979), by the 1930s "it was clear that assimilationism or pluralism were idealized conceptions that were capable of only partial realization. The most ardent assimilationist had to recognize the fact of ethnic variety, however attenuated it might become. By the same token, the most ardent pluralist had to acknowledge that the retention of cultural diversity could not preclude a substantial conformity to general American norms."

The practice of history has its well-known ironies. The pluralistic theories that hardened in the 1960s anticipated real changes in the population and social structure. New waves of Asian and Hispanic immigrants entered the country in the 1970s and 1980s. Among the approximately 8.4 million immigrants who entered the country in the 1980s, 38 percent settled in California and 14 percent in New York State. New immigrants have changed the face of such huge metropolitan areas as Los Angeles–Long Beach, New York, Chicago, San Diego, Anaheim–Santa Ana, and Miami–Hialeah. These six urban areas absorbed 36 percent of all legally admitted immigrants in 1991. Over 14 percent were headed for Los Angeles alone. Large semi-autonomous ethnic communities are emerging anew. Americans are living through a significant resurgence of ethnicity as a real component of their history, an unexpected shift that gives new significance to the old debate between assimilation and pluralism. The pluralism of the 1960s was only a theory of society—a vision of what society should be. The meaning and significance of the multiculturalism of the 1990s remain open to inquiry. Will the same pluralist–assimilationist struggle, leading to inclusion of the new immigrants in the middle class, take place, or does the future hold a new and unforeseen pattern?

If white immigrants experienced a diverse opportunity structure, the situation of African Americans has been far more severe. The cohesiveness of immigrant communities suggests that their political autonomy, their socioeconomic autonomy, and their cultural autonomy compensated, at least in part, for the inequality and discrimination their members had to face. Immigrants, however, could integrate into the main society in ways that were closed to blacks. Blacks who had migrated from the South to work in northern factories during World War I did not hold on to their industrial jobs when the war emergency was over. They were the first ones to be fired in the postwar recession, and they would not reenter industrial jobs in large numbers until the next world war. The message they heard from the labor unions during the interwar years was too often discouraging: they were not welcome. Under these circumstances, their segregation into growing ghettos completed their isolation from the rest of society. No matter the efforts advocated by race leaders like Booker T. Washington to accommodate white prejudice, the color line dramatically limited opportunities for African Americans.

To some extent, therefore, African American elites turned inward in the 1920s. The New Negro would put his expertise to the service of his or her community: black doctors and nurses healing black patients in black hospitals, black lawyers rescuing black defendants, black educators teaching black students. Thus African Americans were torn between their desire to achieve equal rights and a better life through integration and the need to protect themselves by creating alternative channels of opportunity.

The ambiguities of race relations were further exacerbated by splits within the black community, for race is also subject to many variations in identity. Thus the early-twentieth-century sense of blackness in America still followed a Latin American model: light skin was seen as a sign of beauty and a source of prestige. Mulattoes benefited from their whiteness and formed, according to Joel Williamson, "clusters of affluence and influence in business, in the professions, and in the trades" (*New People,* 1980). But many were torn between their desire to be accepted in the white world and the "soul movement." Not until the second reconstruction did color distinction become less salient. The "black is beautiful" movement of the sixties was, partly, an attempt to devalue references to whiteness as a measure of status within the black community.

It is a common error in many studies of blacks in twentieth-century America to apply standard notions of occupational stratification, like those used by the census bureau, to lump 90 percent of the black population in the lower class. E. Franklin Frazier, one of the most important black sociologists of the 1920s and 1930s, made that point clearly in his comparative studies of black occupational structure after the great migration in northern cities (Boston, New York, Philadelphia, Cleveland, Seattle, and Chicago), southern cities (Atlanta, Birmingham, Houston, Memphis, New Orleans, and Richmond), and border cities (Baltimore, Cincinnati, and Washington, D.C.). Frazier asserted in the *American Journal of Sociology* (1929–1930) that the major occupational divisions in the census are just too vague to convey the finer sense of social structure that exists in black communities where small gains do count. Frazier also stressed the North-South dichotomy in occupational differentiation that was already clearly visible in the

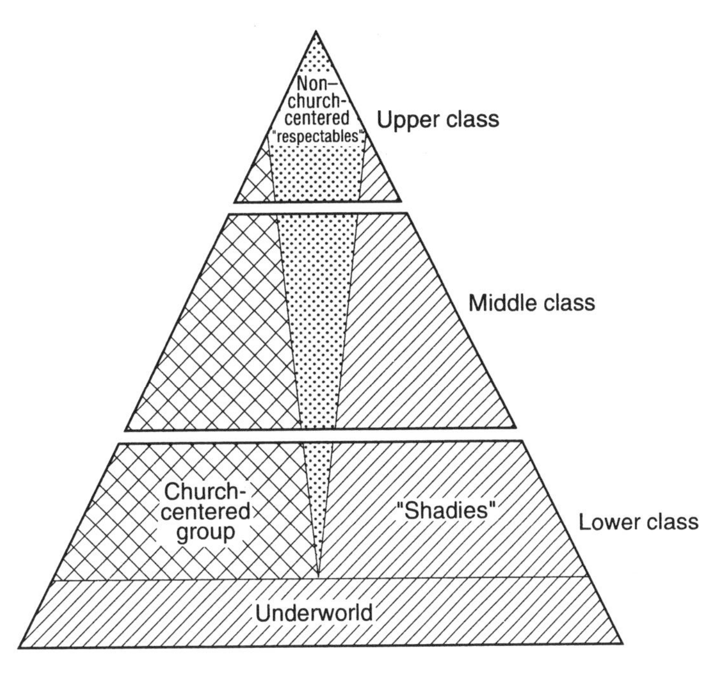

Figure 2. The system of social classes in Bronzeville. (Adapted from St. Clair Drake and Horace R. Cayton, *Black Metropolis*, 1945; repr. 1993)

1920s and 1930s. Southern cities showed a much smaller percentage of African Americans employed in public service and clerical occupations than northern cities.

But Frazier recognized that blacks were increasingly trapped in the northern ghetto. Seeing that successful blacks just could not escape from living with the lower occupational groups, Frazier entitled a section of his most important book, *The Negro Family in the United States* (1939), "In The City of Destruction" to underscore the power of segregation and the enormous obstacles blacks faced in shaping their destiny.

Frazier's studies were at least partly confirmed by St. Clair Drake and Horace Cayton's 1946 classic *Black Metropolis,* a study of the rapidly developing class structure among Negroes in "Bronzeville," the inner city of Chicago. Drake and Cayton estimated that after just a few decades of rural-to-urban migration, 5 percent of the African Americans in their study area were in the upper class, 30 percent in the middle class, and 65 percent in the lower class. But under the special conditions of racial segregation, the black upper class was penetrated by the leaders of the underworld (figure 2). Drake and Cayton therefore felt they had to separate the "true" leaders of the race from the "gentlemen racketeers." They also distinguished the honest lower-class majority living a decent life organized around churches and clubs from the "disorganized segment of the lower class" and the criminal underworld. Their study revealed the complex internal social differentiation within the castelike world of blacks in urban America.

In the 1920s, progressive observers still thought that blacks would follow the route that immigrants took to assimilation. Robert Park, once Booker T. Washington's secretary and the leading figure in the burgeoning field of urban sociology as well as Frazier's teacher, believed that blacks were just the last of the immigrants. But the American dream eluded them.

During the Depression, issues of race became closely linked to issues of class. The radical Left looked to the condition of American blacks as a product of the class struggle and attracted black intellectuals to fight the class war on behalf of all workers. Many young intellectual leaders of the black community such as Richard Wright accepted the challenge and adopted an economic interpretation of their people's problems. They saw the race issue as a manifestation of class conflict in a capitalist economy. Remedies could only be found in a union with white workers. They also assumed that discrimination would vanish with economic betterment.

But improvement was very slow in coming. By World War II, the majority of African Americans were still locked out of what Laurence Fuchs calls, in *The American Kaleidoscope* (1990), the American civic culture. As Fuchs succinctly put it:

> In 1940, only 1 out of 20 black males was employed in a white-collar occupation, compared to 1 out of 3 white males. Six of 10 employed black women worked as maids; one of 10 white women did so. In Chicago where blacks were 8 percent of the labor force, they were 22 percent of the unemployed. Government employment practices, local and national, were based to a large extent on caste. The five southern states in which African Americans were more than a third of the population employed not a single African American policeman. Blacks could not enlist in the Marines or in the Army Airforce. The Navy accepted them only in menial jobs. The Army was segregated, and no black officer was permitted to outrank any white man in the same unit. Every state in the South, where three-quarters of the African American population lived, as well as a number of states in the North outlawed intermarriage. Caste pluralism was enforced by law, by hiring practices, and by public discourse and social etiquette. Southern whites still called adult African Americans by their first names or "boy" or "girl."

Such was the situation in 1941 when A. Philip Randolph, the head of the Brotherhood of Sleeping Car Porters, threatened a march on Washington, D.C., to protest a government that drafted blacks into the armed services but maintained discrimination in defense industries and in government. President Franklin D. Roosevelt partly yielded to the pressure and banned discrimination in defense industries, but not in the armed services.

With the attention now focused on civil rights as much as on economic issues, there was hope again. The hope was that once the "formal structure of caste" would be dismantled, the disparity between creed and conduct in American life—exposed so timely by Gunnar Myrdal in his 1944 *An American Dilemma*—would disappear.

Shifting the strategy from economic meliorism to civil rights had major consequences for the African American social structure, if only because of the intensifying focus on race. That focus was perhaps sharpest when the Johnson administration initiated affirmative action programs in 1965. Counting by race, it was argued, was necessary to redress past injustices by reversing patterns of inequality until fair representation was achieved. As a result of affirmative action, significant portions of the black population did gain economically, not just in the professions but also in such occupations as bus driver, police officer, and health-care worker. Some surveys have reported a 12-percentage-point increase among blacks placing themselves in the middle class from 1952 to 1978. Much was there to justify William Julius Wilson's hope for *The Declining Significance of Race* (1978).

By the 1990s, however, we know that the results have been mixed and yielded to a dramatic separation between middle-class blacks and the underclass. Affirmative-action programs, designed to help educated blacks who could gain access to better-paying jobs, did nothing to help the disproportionate number of blacks at the low end of the labor market. As a result a new black middle class has grown significantly. But its members are estranged from the majority of African Americans and live in their own suburbs without having achieved integration into the white population. Demographers Douglas Massey and Nancy Denton have actually reported the sad fact that black segregation does not fall even when education and income rise (*American Apartheid,* 1993).

In other words, in addition to a persisting black-white dichotomy among middle-class Americans, one now witnesses the emergence of two separate black Americas, as African Americans are tragically swelling the ranks of the underclass. In our postindustrial society, traditional employment opportunities in unskilled and semiskilled industrial jobs have all but disappeared. And other ethnic groups—especially Asian immigrants—have fared better in mobilizing the resources of ethnic institutions and the economy's opportunity structure. In the 1992 race riot that destroyed large sections of South Central Los Angeles, rioters clearly targeted small Korean entrepreneurs as if they had stolen the American dream from the black and Latino underclass. And civil rights leaders, who had been prompt to rally behind the Watts rioters of 1965, remained helpless observers.

With ethnicity and race, gender enters the class debate in several important ways. By working in the home and rearing children, women have been the traditional guardians of class values. In the Victorian middle-class family, the mother maintained the cult of domesticity and took it on herself to perpetuate the system by passing on different values to her sons than to her daughters: worldly values to the former, domestic values to the latter. In working-class families, however, even though mothers rarely worked outside their own home, daughters did, and both mothers and daughters became a part of a larger family income strategy. Married women accepted piecework at home and rented rooms to boarders, while their daughters worked in factories. The "family economy"—the pooling of income among household members—and the recognition of its importance were the objects of several studies by newly formed state bureaus of labor statistics as early as the 1870s. Family-budget studies became a perennial feature of the federal Bureau of Labor Statistics in the 1890s and early twentieth century and were the basis for Carroll D. Wright's pioneering work in Massachusetts and Washington. The various ways in which household members combined their income was also Margaret Byington's major preoccupation in *Homestead* (1910), the volume she wrote in connection with the landmark *Pittsburgh Survey* (1909), which the Russell Sage Foundation funded.

At the dawn of the twentieth century, the class position of most women was clearly determined by that of their husband or father. In a male-dominated society, education was better invested in sons who would eventually determine the class status of their own households. In Russian-Jewish immigrant families aspiring to middle-class status, young men were often sent to school while their sisters were sent to work. As a result of such expectations, sociologists who studied the class position of Americans rarely bothered to interrogate women; when they did, they found that women borrowed their class status from the male breadwinner.

The massive entry of lower-middle-class women in the office work force did not initially alter this principle. The common belief that feminization of office work signaled the "de-skilling" of white-collar workers, to borrow Harry Braverman's phrase, is at best misleading. The degradation and subsequent proletarianization of white-collar work means little unless understood within the larger framework of gender relations. For we should replace the initial movement of women into the clerical labor force within the context of male class domination that lasted virtually uncompromised until World War II. In this context, women accepted the middle-class taboos that centered around marriage and childrearing for women and effectively set a time limit on the business positions they held. Young women's stint in the workplace was to be transitory, an interlude before marriage. Although systematization of tasks and discrimination in the workplace reflected gender stereotyping, they were made more bearable because they were temporary. In the meantime, the young women and their families benefited from the enlarged income without threatening men in their lifelong careers.

But there were cracks in the system early on. The relationship between work and family, and with it the class position of women, changed under the pressures of consumerism. Male dominance was challenged by women's changing expectations of family life and personal fulfillment. The middle class was especially sensitive to the pressures and potential for greater disappointment when a modicum of luxury became the anticipated norm. While the rise in the standard of living generally enhanced family life, it also created new pressures in the homes of those who could not afford the fruits of abundance. Even during the Depression, American women went to work not just because of necessity but also because of heightened expectations. Failing to meet new expectations wreaked havoc in many homes. It is no accident that the emergence of the affluent society paralleled the skyrocketing of the American divorce rate.

To achieve prosperity, more married women worked outside the home. As the family income increased, girls as well as boys were sent to school. Meanwhile, welfare institutions began caring for the indigent and the elderly. The modern family adapted to new forms of opportunity and relinquished its bargaining and its welfare functions to unions or the state. The modern nuclear family became a more specialized unit, devoted to the expressive and childrearing functions and adapted to the educational and career movements of its individual members.

Feminist critics of the welfare state have argued that twentieth-century social policies merely reproduced male interests and "patriarchal" relationships just as neo-Marxists have argued that the state merely reproduces capitalist relationships that benefit the dominant class. But as Theda Skocpol has shown in *Protecting Soldiers and Mothers* (1992), well-organized women reformers in the United States with a "gender consciousness" were quite effective at pushing for gender-specific labor laws and child labor laws that would ultimately free women from the dominant patriarchy. Furthermore, even though post-World War II prosperity made the once familiar one-male-wage-earner family possible, the trend of increasing participation of married women in the work force, itself greatly accelerated by the war emergency, never stopped.

Even when the ideal of the male provider dominated in the fifties, female employment quickened. By 1960, as William Chafe reports, "twice as many women were at work as in 1940, and 40 percent of all women over 16 held a job" (*The American Woman,* 1972). Over half of married women worked in 1985. The increasing participation of women in the labor force, declining family size, the growing number of women who live in households without men, and changing attitudes about sexual divisions of labor and power in the family all combine to give women an

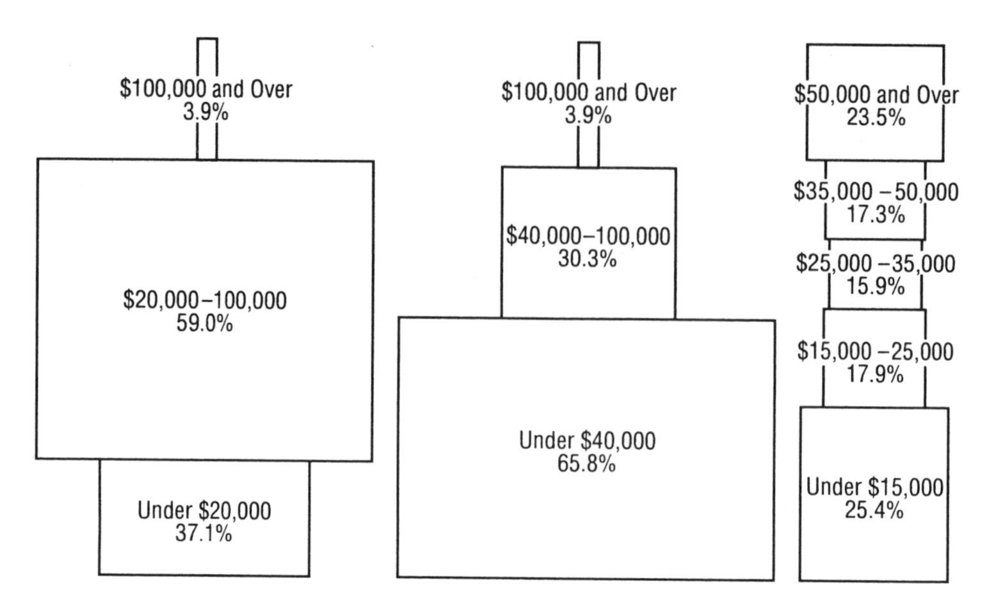

Figure 3. Classes and income levels. Three ways of defining social class by income level produce three ways of seeing the structure of American society: is the country mainly middle class (left), predominantly poor (middle), or characterized by merging income levels? (Adapted from Andrew Hacker, "Class Dismissed," *New York Review of Books* [7 March 1991]; data from Bureau of the Census, 1989.)

increasing role not only in their own class position but in that of their family members as well.

The history of women and class in the twentieth century is therefore that of a slow shift from borrowed class, where women had no autonomous class status, to shared class. With men and women sharing in determining the class structure, we will have to rethink the very meaning of individualism when applied to issues of class and mobility. Measuring male achievements or failures alone is a practice of the now defunct "fraternal social contract."

THE 1990s AND BEYOND

Americans are undergoing a major restructuring of their class relations. The late twentieth century seems not a culmination of century-long trends but a time for new beginnings. American class relations, embedded as they have been in ethnic, racial, and gender identities, are changing under the pressures of a new economic structure and world order as well as altered expectations (figure 3).

Early-twentieth-century industrialization fostered the growth of both a very large middle class and a large working class. As business historians have explained, huge center firms, which capitalized on economies of scale and scope, dominated the American economy and accounted for the massive demand in both white-collar and blue-collar jobs. They also became the backbone of middle-class financial security both in employment and in retirement. Although class tensions that culminated in the 1930s were real, next to ethnic and racial ones, they eased as an ever larger part of the working class moved into the middle class. With the growing post-World War II American prosperity sustained by the Pax Americana, it seemed that class tensions would continue to recede as long as an integrative, expansive, and ever-widening middle class flourished.

But the postwar days, when the United States provided a large part of the world with both the goods for reconstruction and the money to buy those goods, are long gone. Giant American corporations have been drastically downsizing since the mid-1970s as they are responding not only to aggressive European and Japanese competition but also to a new technological revolution. The very economies of scale and scope that once justified the continuous concentration of resources in giant firms are no longer operating in the late-twentieth-century global economy. Adjusting to the more flexible post-Fordist production techniques, new market conditions, and the loss of monopoly in information processing, American business bureaucracies have had to overhaul both the white-collar and blue-collar sectors that had grown too large.

While the American economy ran a trade surplus in 1993 in high-tech, leading-edge industries, it was still handicapped by a large trade imbalance in most traditional sectors. Goods formerly manufactured in the United States are now made elsewhere. High-paying blue-collar industrial jobs have declined as factories move to developing areas of the world where the labor force is significantly cheaper. American labor unions that had once stood for high wages have lost their bargaining power. Only 11.8 percent of private sector employees were unionized in 1993 as opposed to 35 percent in 1953. For many Americans, these blue-collar jobs were the point of entry into the middle-class world of high-volume consumption, easy access to home ownership, and intergenerational access to higher education. Thus the economic bases of the mid-twentieth-century class structure have been greatly altered, especially since the mid-1970s. Whether the middle class will survive the current restructuring as it survived that of the Great Depression is an open question.

The mid-twentieth-century trend toward an ethnically homogenizing population has also collapsed under the pressures of new immigration. Immigrants now find low-paying jobs in the service sector while their predecessors of the early twentieth century found jobs in industry. Like their predecessors, however, they compete with still-impoverished African Americans. As more African Americans falter in the competition, the society experiences renewed racial tension and a new level of class polarization. In that respect, the late twentieth century resembles the early twentieth century a good deal more than it does the mid-twentieth century. As in the Progressive Era, late-twentieth-century Americans will have concurrently to face diversity and new levels of inequality.

In the unpredictable circumstances of the 1990s, one thing remains likely. The class debate in twentieth-century America, that has been largely an exchange among Madisonian, Marxist, and Tocquevillean perspectives, will continue. Madisonian pluralists want a social system that primarily maximizes freedom of association, Marxists want one that guarantees social justice, and Tocquevilleans stress individual opportunity. As the twentieth century closes, Americans must continue to meet the challenge of maintaining balance among these essential perspectives.

See Also Gender Issues; Race; Ethnicity and Immigration; Social Welfare (all in this volume); Wealth and Poverty (volume III).

BIBLIOGRAPHY

Some general histories of the early twentieth century present a distinct interpretation of class relations. For the period before World War II, Richard Hofstadter's *The Age of Reform: from Bryan to F. D. R* (1955) charts the Progressive impulse as originating in an old middle class that feared losing its status under the pressures of social and economic conditions. Robert H. Wiebe, in *The Search for Order, 1877–1920* (1967), stresses instead the role of a new bureaucratic middle class. The reader will find an excellent treatment of the reformist impulse in Paul S. Boyer, *Urban Masses and Moral Order in America, 1820–1920* (1978); while Alan Dawley, *Struggles for Justice: Social Responsibility and the Liberal State* (1991), emphasizes patterns of inequality. William Miller, "The Realm of Wealth," in John Higham, ed., *The Reconstruction of American History* (1962), is a succinct essay on wealth distribution. Richard Hofstadter's *Social Darwinism in American Thought,* rev. ed. (1959) is still important. On rural areas and the South, one should consult, in addition to C. Vann Woodward's classic *Origins of the New South, 1877–1913* (1951); Jonathan M. Wiener, "Class Structure and Economic Development in the American South, 1865–1955," *American Historical Review* 84 (October 1979): 970–1006; and especially Edward L. Ayers, *The Promise of the New South: Life after Reconstruction* (1992).

New Left historians like J. Weinstein and M. Sklar, whose work is discussed in the essay, have centered their critique of capitalism on the concepts of false consciousness and hegemony. To restore a sense of human agency to our understanding of the making of corporate capitalism and the formation of the new middle class in the early twentieth century, see Olivier Zunz, *Making America Corporate, 1870–1920* (1990).

Important books on class issues during the Depression and the coming of the New Deal order are Alan Brinkley, *Voices of Protest: Huey Long, Father Coughlin, and the Great Depression* (1982); and Steve

Fraser and Gary Gerstle, eds., *The Rise and Fall of the New Deal Order, 1930–1980* (1989). How the middle class weathered the Great Depression is well analyzed in Warren Susman, *Culture as History: The Transformation of American Society in the Twentieth Century* (1984).

The most significant books on the class structure of postwar America, especially the fifties and early sixties, written by economists, sociologists, and political scientists who were close to events and engaged in forecasting, are cited in the essay. For the 1970s and beyond, see Daniel Bell, "The World and The United States in 2013," *Daedalus 116* (Summer 1987): 1–31; and "Downfall of the Business Giants," *Dissent* (Summer 1993): 316–323. To understand the changing class structure of a "global" city in the 1980s, see John H. Mollenkopf and Manuel Castells, eds., *Dual City: Restructuring New York* (1991).

On the economic foundations of class, see, in addition to Chandler's work, Adolf A. Berle and Gardiner C. Means's classic *The Modern Corporation and Private Property* (1932). See also Stuart Bruchey, *Enterprise: The Dynamic Economy of a Free People* (1990); Frank Levy, *Dollars and Dreams: The Changing American Income Distribution* (1987); and Thomas K. McCraw, *Prophets of Regulation: Charles Francis Adams, Louis D. Brandeis, James M. Landis, Alfred E. Kahn* (1984), for insights on the class dimensions of the regulatory movement. James M. Fallows analyzes the restructuring of the world economy in the 1980s in "America's Changing Economic Landscape," *The Atlantic* (March 1985): 47–68.

The characteristics of mass society are analyzed by Hannah Arendt in *The Origins of Totalitarianism* 2d enl. ed. (1958), and by such neo-Marxist scholars of the Frankfurt school as Theodor W. Adorno and Herbert Marcuse. See Adorno's "Freudian Theory and the Pattern of Fascist Propaganda" (1951), in Andrew Arato and Eite Gebhardt, eds., *The Essential Frankfurt School Reader* (1978); and Marcuse's *One-Dimensional Man: Studies in the Ideology of Advanced Industrial Society* (1964). American sociologists like Edward Albert Shils in *Center and Periphery: Essays in Macrosociology* (1975), and Daniel Bell have been significantly more optimistic about their own mass society.

Most discussions of class and interest-group politics are by political scientists who always return to the classic text by James Madison. For a historical study profoundly influenced by the political pluralism of Robert Dahl's *Who Governs? Democracy and Power in an American City* (1961), see David C. Hammack, *Power and Society: Greater New York at the Turn of the Century* (1982). The key books remain those of David Bicknell Truman, *The Governmental Process: Political Interests and Public Opinion* (1951); Grant McConnell, *Private Power and American Democracy* (1966); and Theodore J. Lowi, *The End of Liberalism: Ideology, Policy, and the Crisis of Public Authority* (1969).

On the classic problem of the United States' class structure as an exceptional case among nations, see, in addition to Louis Hartz's and David Potter's books mentioned in the essay, Seymour Martin Lipset, *The First New Nation: The United States in Historical and Comparative Perspective* (1963); and Michael Kammen, "The Problem of American Exceptionalism: A Reconsideration," *American Quarterly* 45 (March 1993): 1–43. One will find a concise and brilliant comparative treatment of Tocqueville's *Democracy* and Marx's *Capital* in François Furet's *In the Workshop of History* (1984); see also Walter Nugent, "Tocqueville, Marx, and American Class Structure," *Social Science History* 12 (Winter 1988): 327–347.

On individualism, social stratification, and mobility, there is a rich literature in sociology and social history. Sociologists have often applied Max Weber's ideas on the relationship between class, status, and power: see Robert W. Hodge and Donald J. Treiman, "Class Identification in the United States," *American Journal of Sociology* 73 (March 1973): 535–547; Milton M. Gordon, "Social Classes in American Sociology," *American Journal of Sociology* 55 (November 1949): 262–266; and Peter Michael Blau, Otis Dudley Duncan, and Ralph Dahrendorf, *The American Occupational Structure* (1967).

Social historians have put greater emphasis on patterns of mobility. In addition to Stephan Thernstrom's work discussed in the essay, see Richard Weiss, *The American Myth of Success: From Horatio Alger to Norman Vincent Peale* (1969); and Margo Anderson Conk, "The Language of Class in Twentieth-Century America," *Social Science History* 12 (Winter 1988): 349–376.

On the nature of American elites, one should still read Thorstein Veblen, *The Theory of the Leisure Class: An Economic Study of Institutions* (1899). Digby E. Baltzell, *Philadelphia Gentlemen: The Making of a National Upper Class* (1958), is an important case study. On businessmen in American politics and society, one should still turn to Sigmund Diamond, *The Reputation of the American Businessman* (1955). See also Martin Shefter, ed., *Capital of The American Century: The National and International Influence of New York City* (1993), for an interesting study of the concentration of power in one place.

On the concept of authority and the role of

experts on the class structure of an industrializing society, see David A. Hollinger, *In the American Province: Studies in the History and Historiography of Ideas* (1985); Samuel Haber, *The Quest for Authority and Honor in the American Professions, 1750–1900* (1991); Thomas L. Haskell, ed., *The Authority of Experts: Studies in History and Theory* (1984); and Jürgen Habermas, *The Structural Transformation of the Public Sphere: An Inquiry into a Category of Bourgeois Society* (1989).

The reader who wants to learn more about the American middle class could turn to John S. Gilkeson, *Middle-Class Providence, 1820–1940* (1986), a case study of associational life. Loren Baritz, *The Good Life: The Meaning of Success for the American Middle Class* (1988), offers alternative viewpoints on middle-class ideals. See also Andrew Hacker, "The Imperial Middle," *New York Review of Books* 38 (March 7, 1991): 44–46. Amid a growing literature on white-collar workers, see Jürgen Kocka, *White Collar Workers in America, 1890–1940: A Social-Political History in International Perspective* (1980); and two case studies by Cindy Sondik Aron, *Ladies and Gentlemen of the Civil Service: Middle-Class Workers in Victorian America* (1987); and Susan Porter Benson, *Counter Cultures: Saleswomen, Managers, and Customers in American Department Stores, 1890–1940* (1986). On middle-class lifestyles and consumerism, one should turn to Daniel Horowitz, *The Morality of Spending: Attitudes toward the Consumer Society in America, 1875–1940* (1985); John F. Kasson, *Amusing the Millions: Coney Island at the Turn of the Century* (1978); Richard Wightman Fox and T. J. Jackson Lears, *The Culture of Consumption: Critical Essays in American History, 1880–1980* (1983); Stanley Lebergott, *Pursuing Happiness: American Consumers in the Twentieth Century* (1993); and Kenneth T. Jackson, *Crabgrass Frontier: The Suburbanization of the United States* (1985). For stimulating discussions of what sociologists sometimes call status anxiety, see Barbara Ehrenreich, *Fear of Falling: The Inner Life of the Middle Class* (1989); and Richard Sennett and Jonathan Cobb, *The Hidden Injuries of Class* (1972). On psychoanalysis and status anxiety, see Marie Jahoda, "The Migration of Psychoanalysis: Its Impact on American Psychology," in Donald Fleming and Bernard Bailyn, eds., *The Intellectual Migration: Europe and America, 1930–1960* (1969), 420–445.

For the new labor history of the "people," not just institutions, see, in addition to the work of Herbert Gutman and David Montgomery, the essays assembled by Daniel J. Leab in *The Labor History Reader* (1985); Michael H. Frisch and Daniel J. Walkowitz, eds., *Working-Class America: Essays on Labor, Community, and American Society* (1983); David Brody, *Workers in Industrial America: Essays on the Twentieth-Century Struggle* (1980); Roy Rosenzweig, *Eight Hours for What We Will: Workers and Leisure in an Industrial City, 1870–1920* (1983); and Nelson Lichtenstein, *Labor's War at Home: The CIO in World War II* (1982). The most stimulating biographies of labor leaders are Nick Salvatore, *Eugene V. Debs: Citizen and Socialist* (1982); and Steve Fraser, *Labor Will Rule: Sidney Hillman and the Rise of American Labor* (1991). For an essay on paternalism in the textile industry, see Jacquelyn Dowd Hall et al., *Like a Family: The Making of a Southern Cotton Mill World* (1987).

One will find recent debates on Marxism and the American class structure in Erik Olin Wright et al., *The Debate on Classes* (1989); and Ira Katznelson, *Marxism in the Cities* (1992). On working-class life in the 1970s, see David Halle, *America's Working Man: Work, Home, and Politics Among Blue-collar Property Owners* (1984); see also Michael Goldfield, *The Decline of Organized Labor in the United States* (1987).

In addition to the work by Cohen, Gerstle, and Zunz on the relation between class and ethnicity, John Bodnar's *The Transplanted: A History of Immigrants in Urban America* (1985) links the findings of the new labor history with those of the new ethnic history. Richard Jules Oestreicher is sensitive to ethnic cultures in his history of the Knights of Labor, *Solidarity and Fragmentation: Working People and Class Consciousness in Detroit, 1875–1900* (1986).

On assimilation and the American class structure, see Milton M. Gordon, *Assimilation in American Life: The Role of Race, Religion, and National Origins* (1964). Among immigration historians who have paid attention to the American class structure, see especially John Higham, *Send These To Me: Immigrants in Urban America*, rev. ed. (1984), and his essay "Multiculturalism and Universalism: A History and Critique," with comments by Gerald Early, Gary Gerstle, Nancy Hewitt, Vicki Ruiz, and rejoinder in *American Quarterly* 45 (June 1993): 195–256; among case studies, see Andrew R. Heinze, *Adapting to Abundance: Jewish Immigrants, Mass Consumption, and the Search for American Identity* (1990); and Roger D. Waldinger, *Through the Eye of the Needle: Immigrants and Enterprise in New York's Garment Trades* (1986). Among recent sociological studies, see Edward O. Laumann, *Bonds of Pluralism: The Form and Substance of Urban Social Networks* (1973); and Charles Hirschman and Morrison G. Wong, "Socioeconomic Gains of Asian Americans, Blacks, and Hispanics: 1960 – 1976," *American Journal of Sociology* 90 (November 1984): 584 – 607. The work of Lawrence Fuchs cited in the essay, especially the sections on the 1970s and 1980s, should be read in conjunction with Nathan Glazer and Daniel P. Moynihan's classic statement on the rediscovery of ethnicity in the 1960s, *Beyond the Melting Pot: The Negroes, Puerto Ricans, Jews, Italians, and Irish of New York City* (1963). On the ethnic context for the 1990s, see David A. Hollinger, "Postethnic America," *Contention* 2 (1992): 79–96.

Among historical studies of the making of northern ghettos, one should read Gilbert Osofsky, *Harlem: The Making of a Ghetto: Negro New York, 1890–1930* (1966); Allan H. Spear, *Black Chicago: The Making of a Negro Ghetto 1890–1920* (1967); and Kenneth L. Kusmer, *A Ghetto Takes Shape: Black Cleveland, 1870–1930* (1976). On leadership among African Americans, see John Hope Franklin and August Meier, eds., *Black Leaders of the Twentieth Century* (1982); and C. Eric Lincoln and Lawrence H. Mamiya, *The Black Church in the African-American Experience* (1990). For a turning point in the study of race relations, see Walter A. Jackson, *Gunnar Myrdal and America's Conscience: Social Engineering and Racial Liberalism, 1938–1987* (1990).

On the shifting grounds for African Americans in the more recent past, see Lynn Weber Cannon, "Trends in Class Identification among Black Americans from 1952 to 1978," *Social Science Quarterly* 65 (March 1984): 112–126; Diane and Linda F. Williams Colasanto, "The Changing Dynamics of Race and Class," *Public Opinion* 9 (January–February 1987): 50–53; Thomas J. Durant, Jr. and Joyce S. Louden, "The Black Middle Class in America: Historical and Contemporary Perspectives," *Phylon* 47 (December 1986): 253–263; and Charles Hammer, "Racially Changing Neighborhoods," *New Republic* 169 (September 15, 1973): 19–21.

In addition to the literature on the underclass already cited in the essay, Michael Harrington's *The Other America: Poverty in the United States* (1962), was a very influential early statement; see also Christopher Jencks and Paul E. Peterson, *The Urban Underclass* (1991); and Norman Fainstein, "The Underclass/Mismatch Hypothesis as an Explanation for Black Economic Deprivation," *Politics and Society* 15 (1986–1987): 403– 451.

On the democratic goals of education, one should supplement David B. Tyack, *The One Best System: History of Urban American Education* (1974); with Reed Ueda, *Avenues to Adulthood: The Origins of the High School and Social Mobility in an American Suburb* (1987); and Joseph F. Kett, *Rites of Passage: Adolescence in America, 1790 to the Present* (1977). Diane Ravitch, *The Revisionists Revised: Studies in the Historiography of American Education: A Review* (1977), and Richard Rubinson, "Class Formation, Politics, and Institutions: Schooling in the United States," *American Journal of Sociology* 92 (November 1986): 519–548, debate the issues of class and education with Marxist scholars. Martin Trow, "Class, Race, and Higher Education in America," *The American Behavioral Scientist* 35 (March–June 1992): 585–605, surveys the more recent history.

Interpreting the relationship between class and gender is still recent. Among the best studies are Linda Gordon, *Heroes of Their Own Lives: The Politics and History of Family Violence: Boston, 1880–1960* (1988); Elaine Tyler May, *Great Expectations: Marriage and Divorce in Post-Victorian America* (1980); Winifred Wandersee Bolin, "The Economics of Middle-Income Family Life: Working Women during the Great Depression," *Journal of American History* 65 (June 1978): 60–74; and Ruth Milkman, *Gender at Work: The Dynamics of Job Segregation by Sex during World War II* (1987). On the more recent past, see Nancy J. Davis and Robert V. Robinson, "Class Identification of Men and Women in the 1970s and 1980s," *American Sociological Review* 53 (February 1988): 103–112; and Carole Pateman, "The Fraternal Social Contract," in John Keane, ed., *Civil Society and the State* (1988), pp. 101–128.

FAMILY

Steven Mintz

Although economic issues such as the recession, jobs, the federal budget deficit, and foreign trade dominated public debate during the 1992 presidential campaign, another issue repeatedly aroused public concern: anxiety about the family and especially about the well-being of the nation's children. The Republican party embraced "family values" as a campaign theme, maintaining that many of the nation's social ills, such as poverty, crime, and drug abuse, resulted from a breakdown in family structure, moral standards, and parental responsibility. The Democratic party, in turn, accused the Reagan and Bush administrations of neglecting families, and advocated expanded federal programs in the areas of family leave, child health care, and preschool education to enhance the strength of the American family unit.

Anxiety about the family is, of course, nothing new. In virtually every decade of the twentieth century, Americans expressed fear that the family was failing to fulfill its critical functions adequately. At the turn of the century, rising divorce rates and plunging birth rates were seen as threats to family values. Other challenges stemmed from the family patterns of different immigrant groups and the effects of industrialization and urbanization on the family unit. The Depression and the world wars presented economic obstacles to holding the family together and opportunities for women to join the work force. During the 1950s, juvenile delinquency was a major source of anxiety, along with concerns about "Why Johnny can't read." By the 1960s, an array of controversies caught the public's attention, from the "generation gap" to premarital sex, a supposed link between fatherless ghetto homes and poverty and street crime, and the feminist demand for liberation from patriarchal family structures. In the 1970s and 1980s, Americans were troubled by the impact of divorce and maternal employment upon children and upon moral values—damage supposedly evident in the spread of single parenthood, unwed motherhood, abortion, and teenage pregnancy—all of which tarnished the ideal of the nuclear family.

Unfortunately, public discussion of families has tended to be based on misconceptions about the past. Lacking historical perspective, Americans continue to contrast today's families with a mythical "golden age." But the picture of the stable, intact families of earlier generations is a nostalgic, romanticized mixture of carefully selected memories and media images that shrouds the actual diversity, complexity, and problems facing American families earlier in this century.

The history of twentieth-century families embodies many of the broader themes of modern American history. For example, the expanding role of the government in the lives and welfare of the American public resulted in an ad hoc system of subsidies and welfare programs to stabilize and support families. The professionalization and diversification of education gave rise to a host of new specialists working in family-related areas as early as the 1920s, including juvenile and family court judges, pediatricians, marriage counselors, social workers, juvenile psychologists, childrearing experts, and gerontologists. During the early twentieth century, the mass media helped to popularize and institutionalize a set of family ideals known as the "companionate" family, emphasizing sexual fulfillment, intimacy, and companionship, which did not make an impact on society until the late 1940s and 1950s because of the interruption of the Great Depression and World War II. Beginning in the 1960s, popular culture promoted a set of cultural norms, stressing growth, self-realization, and personal fulfillment. Another ongoing trend is the long-term growth of American individualism, apparent in a decline in marriage rates and birth rates, an increase in divorce and out-of-wedlock births, the expansion of maternal employment outside the home, and the emergence of no-fault divorce and new definitions of children's rights. The notion of a stable family standard is an illusion: the twentieth-century American family has always been in flux as it has adapted to major societal upheavals, including economic depression, war, and a radical redefinition of gender roles.

THE "CRISIS OF THE FAMILY"

The last years of the nineteenth century and the first years of the twentieth witnessed an extraordinary outburst of anxiety about the American family. Magazine articles, newspaper editorials, and a wide array of social authorities decried an ever worsening "crisis of the family." Many Americans shared the fear of literary critic Chauncey Hawkins that "the family, that institution which we have long regarded as the unit of civilization, the foundation of the state," would not survive the "bold and uncompromising selfishness" of the age. The demise of the family was seemingly evident in a rapidly rising divorce rate, a sharply falling birth rate, a trend toward delayed marriage, and a growing number of "spinsters" and bachelors. This crisis was also apparent in mounting public debate over such issues as "race suicide," the "black plague" of venereal disease, women's changing roles, and the effects of the family patterns of the new immigrants, which were in turn responses to rapid industrialization and urbanization.

When journalists, sociologists, and other social observers pondered the causes of the late-nineteenth-century crisis of the family, they focused particular attention on a series of long-term social and economic developments that had stripped the family of many of its earlier functions, reduced its size, and deprived it of traditional supports. Contemporaries viewed industrialization and urbanization as the primary engines of change. By undermining the family economy—the economic interdependence that resulted from shared, family-centered employment such as a family farm—industrialization and urbanization weakened paternal authority and the influence of kin groups and loosened the bonds that had traditionally held families together.

An 1889 report revealed that the divorce rate in the United States was the Western world's highest. Around the turn of the century, the rate rose at a dizzying pace, climbing from 1 in every 21 marriages in 1880 to 1 in every 12 in 1900 and 1 in every 9 by 1916. In the face of the surging divorce rate, state legislatures across the country sought to stabilize marriage by reducing the statutory grounds for divorce from over four hundred to fewer than twenty in 1906. To further discourage divorce, a number of states prolonged the waiting period between divorce and remarriage, prohibited the guilty party in divorce suits from remarrying for a period of time, reduced judicial discretion in granting divorces, and required more adequate defense of divorce suits.

According to the studies of Joseph Kirk Folsom, Ernest W. Burgess, and other figures associated with the Chicago school of urban sociology, "the present instability of monogamous wedlock" reflected the collapse of the material conditions that had supported the traditional family. Earlier in American history, the family performed many functions that later were relegated to nonfamilial institutions. Not only had the family ceased to be a productive unit, but its roles in caring for the aged and educating the young were increasingly assumed by public institutions, ranging from schools and hospitals to insurance companies, public charities, and juvenile courts. At the same time, paternal authority was no longer reinforced by control of landed property or craft skills that could be transmitted to children. More isolated than its predecessors from the worlds of work, kinships, and community life, the stability of the modern middle-class American family rested on the tenuous basis of affection, compatibility, and mutual interest. As the sociologist E. A. Ross observed, "the old economic framework of the family has largely fallen away, leaving more of the strain on the personal tie."

The urban, industrial economy dramatically altered the family's internal dynamics. The demands of business meant that fathers spent more and more time away from home and took a less active role in family life. Moreover, industry assumed many of the functions that housewives had been accustomed to performing and, by defining work in terms of income, devalued household labor. The family's diminishing role in production, combined with the development of higher definitions of an acceptable standard of living, encouraged delayed marriage and lower birth rates, since children were no longer economic assets.

In 1900, total fertility of white American women stood at an average of 3.54, or 50 percent below the level of a century earlier. The falling birth rate prompted fears that the native population would be outbred by immigrants. President Theodore Roosevelt gave pointed expression to public concern by accusing the native-born middle class of committing "race suicide" and refusing to fulfill its fundamental duty, "the reproduction of the race." Partly in response to the plunging birth rate, late-nineteenth-century legislatures criminalized abortion, and prohibited the sale and distribution of birth-control materials.

Delayed marriage and growing numbers of men and women who chose not to marry, especially among the educated classes, cast further doubt on the family's future. In 1890, the age of marriage rose to its highest point yet, with the median age reaching 26.1 years for men and 22.0 years for women. Graduates of elite colleges married even later, with over a quarter of Harvard graduates and nearly half of the graduates of the seven sisters colleges still single between the ages of forty and fifty. Turn-of-the-century observers attributed these trends to a growing selfishness—"the latter day cult of individualism; the worship of the brazen calf of Self"—the spread of venereal disease, and psychological infirmities induced by "the high voltage of American civilization."

At the end of the nineteenth century, a growing number of physicians, clergy, and reformers identified prostitution and venereal disease as fundamental threats to the family unit. New medical studies contended that venereal disease had a devastating impact on the family, producing infections and even sterility in innocent wives and blindness and deformities in infected infants. Alarm over these dangers prompted lurid exposés of "white slavery" and sexually transmitted diseases (bearing such titles as *The Traffic in Souls, The Inside of the White Slave Traffic, The Sins of the Fathers,* and *Whatsoever a Man Soweth*) and investigations of prostitution by state and municipal vice commissions. Public concern over the "black plague" also stimulated new efforts to close brothels and abolish red-light districts; the passage of laws in seven states, starting with Michigan in 1899, requiring men to undergo a physical examination before they could receive a marriage license; and the introduction of courses in sex hygiene in nearly half of all secondary schools by the early 1920s. Equally important, the heated discussion of prostitution and venereal disease ripped through the "Victorian" veil of silence that surrounded public discussion of sexuality and family problems in the nineteenth century.

Perhaps the single greatest source of public anxiety about the family stemmed from the changing role of women. A declining birth rate freed a growing number of women to take an active role in the public sphere—in schools, workplaces, and places of entertainment. As more and more women attended high school and college, took part in mixed-sex leisure activities (such as dance halls, nightclubs, amusement parks, inexpensive theaters, and moving-picture houses), joined clubs, worked outside the home, and agitated for the vote, access to the professions, and even sexual freedom, an older nineteenth-century concept of "separate spheres" for men and women quickly broke down.

By 1910, 40 percent of college students were women. During the first decade of the twentieth century, the number of female wage earners grew 43 percent, and the number of female clerks, saleswomen, and factory workers climbed even faster. Whereas as late at 1870 half of all working women labored as domestic servants or washerwomen, by 1920, just 16 percent of women wage earners performed housework.

Growth in female employment was accompanied by increasingly independent living patterns for young women. As early as 1900, more than 35 percent of young urban working women lived outside of a family unit, in boardinghouses or single furnished rooms. Reformers responded to a perceived breakdown in traditional mechanisms of moral control by promoting municipal licensing of boardinghouses and creating a host of new organizations, including Girls' Protective Leagues and Travelers' Aid societies, as surrogate families and alternatives to "dangerous" and "immoral" amusements.

At the same time that the structure of the middle-class family was evolving due to changes in the economy and society at large, the concept of the American family was being challenged by the tide of immigration sweeping into American cities. Between 1877 and 1890, 6 million immigrants arrived in the United States; during the quarter-century before World War I, another 18 million immigrants entered the country. Unlike earlier immigrants, who came primarily from Britain, Germany, Ireland, and Scandinavia, the new immigrants came largely from southern and eastern Europe.

Despite the popular image of America as a melting pot in which diverse cultural traditions dissolved into distinctly American patterns, in actuality immigrant families differed markedly from native-born families in their allocation of family roles, internal dynamics, housing arrangements, and attitudes toward female and child labor. The new immigrants relied heavily on family and kinship ties to sustain them, settling in neighborhoods populated by people from the same home village or community who provided information about urban life, offered temporary housing, and assisted them in finding work. While they retained some of their ethnic patterns—a 1902 study found that the immigrant birth rate was 70 to 80 percent higher than that of native-born whites and blacks—they also had to invent ways of adapting to their working-class status in an industrial urban environment.

Immigrants were more likely to take boarders or

lodgers into their homes and their children were more likely to work. At a time when most middle-class families had only one breadwinner, relatively few working-class immigrant families could support themselves without the economic contributions of other family members. Typically, a male laborer earned just two-thirds of his family's income; the other third was earned by wives and children. Many married women contributed by performing work that could take place in the home, such as making embroideries, tailoring garments, washing laundry, or caring for boarders or lodgers. Children under the age of fifteen contributed 20 percent of the income of many working-class families.

Some immigrant groups, like the Irish and the Slavs, were willing to forgo their children's education rather than send married women into the work force. Other groups, particularly African Americans and Jews, tended to keep their children in school despite the lost earnings. Among many ethnic groups, it was common for daughters to leave school at an early age and enter work so that sons could continue their education. It was also customary for a daughter to remain unmarried so that she could care for younger siblings or her parents in their old age. In this concept of the "family economy," decision making was a byproduct of collective needs rather than individual preferences. The family functioned as a cooperative economic unit and all household members were expected to contribute to the material support of the family and to subordinate their personal wishes to larger family considerations. In this respect, the immigrant working-class families were upholding the traditional American family values that middle-class families were leaving behind. The difference was that many of them lived in abject poverty and some of the adaptations they made to their new environment as they attempted to grasp the American dream of prosperity were seen as threatening the fabric of American society.

PROGRESSIVE REFORM AND OTHER PRESCRIPTIONS FOR CHANGE

Progressive-era reformers associated a variety of social ills with immigrant family life: poverty, child labor, the physical and moral neglect of children (which reformers linked to an apparent increase in single-parent families and working mothers) and parental cruelty, "promiscuous" households containing boarders and lodgers, and neglect of proper hygiene—problems that demanded public intervention by specialists in child and family welfare or through state regulation. Convinced that many of society's most intractable social problems originated in dysfunctional homes, these reformers believed that it was necessary to expand the state's supervisory and administrative authority over the family, arguing that government should serve as an "overparent." In much the same way that industry had assumed many of the family's traditional productive economic functions, Progressive Era reformers believed that the state had to assume many of the family's welfare functions. During the new century's first decades, Progressive reform legislation played a critical role in restructuring immigrant working-class families according to middle-class norms.

Eager to end the exploitation of child laborers, many Progressive reformers agitated for compulsory school attendance laws, child labor laws, and an expanded number of years of schooling. To provide children with a more wholesome environment, cities established kindergartens and playgrounds. In addition, fearful that urban life had deprived the young of the opportunities to build character found in rural areas, reformers created new youth organizations, including the Boy Scouts, the Camp Fire Girls, and the YWCA to teach discipline, self-reliance, and the virtues of cooperation.

Beginning in the mid-1870s, newly formed societies for the prevention of cruelty to children brought problems of child abuse and neglect to public attention. Municipalities in New England, the Middle Atlantic states, and the Midwest empowered private societies to take children away from drunken, neglectful, and physically abusive parents and place them in public institutions, private shelters, or foster families. By the 1910s, there were 494 anticruelty societies in the United States. Ironically, legislation was based on laws preventing the abuse of animals, who were afforded protection earlier than children, since, it was argued, children were a man's property. Drawing on the old legal doctrine that the state had an obligation to protect children from "imminent harm," public agencies received new power to remove neglected and vagrant children from their parents, to construct industrial-training and reform schools, and to invoke criminal penalties against parents for abandonment, nonsupport, and contributing to the dependency or delinquency of a minor. Theodore Roosevelt, a proponent of an expanded state role in family affairs, wrote, "If this be Socialism, make the most of it!"

To provide care and supervision for neglected, delinquent, and vagrant children, philanthropic organizations, settlement houses, and private individuals established more than 450 charitable day nurseries in working-class neighborhoods by 1910. The nurseries not only provided custodial care for children whose mothers worked, they also sought to Americanize immigrant children through instruction in proper manners, eating habits, and personal hygiene. Many reformers viewed day nurseries as a "more humane and less costly substitute" for orphan asylums, where many working parents, lacking other forms of child care, temporarily placed children (in New York City alone, parents placed 15,000 children in orphanages in 1899).

A new view of children as wards of the state was nowhere more apparent than in the reconstruction of the juvenile justice system. In an effort to give special attention and rehabilitative opportunities to youngsters found guilty of crimes or status offenses, Illinois established the first juvenile court in 1899. By 1917, all but three states had enacted juvenile justice legislation. Within these separate tribunals, informal hearings were designed to replace adversarial proceedings, and diagnostic investigations, psychological assessment, and rehabilitation were to replace judgments of guilt or innocence and the imposition of punishment.

The campaign against cruelty toward children was accompanied by a new sensitivity toward other forms of domestic violence. Beginning in the 1880s, temperance reformers, feminists, and crusaders for social purity launched campaigns against drunkenness, wife beating, husbands' excessive sexual demands, and other "crimes against women." Three states—Maryland in 1882, Delaware in 1901, and Oregon in 1905—passed laws providing for the flogging of wife-beaters. In addition, the enactment of mothers' pensions in thirty-nine states during the Progressive Era represented an innovative attempt to help indigent, widowed, separated, divorced, and unmarried mothers to preserve their families.

The growing assertion of a special state interest in family welfare during the Progressive Era can also be seen in the establishment of the first family courts. Family courts were intended to provide a less formal and less adversarial forum than the criminal courts for a broad range of family problems, including desertion, divorce, child neglect and maltreatment, and juvenile delinquency. First in New York City in 1910, and then in many other municipalities and states, family court judges, assisted by a professional staff of psychologists, social workers, probation officers, and divorce proctors were charged with settling domestic conflicts, resolving marital disputes, and reconciling marriage partners.

A particular object of concern during the Progressive Era was the severe health problems besetting American families. At the beginning of the twentieth century, half of all parents experienced the death of a child (compared to just 4 percent today) and a quarter of all children lost at least one parent before reaching the age of fifteen (versus 5 percent today). Fewer than half of all American women experienced the "normative" female life cycle: marrying, bearing children, and surviving to age fifty with their marriage still intact (long enough to see a youngest child leave home). Most women died early, never married, had no children, or had their marriages prematurely disrupted by death, divorce, or separation.

To combat infant mortality, male doctors increasingly replaced female midwives, anesthetics replaced natural childbirth, and hospital delivery replaced home delivery. In 1910, half of all births in the United States were still attended by midwives, but increasingly midwives' clientele was limited to black and immigrant women. Before 1900 only poor and unwed mothers gave birth in hospitals. By 1935, 37 percent of all American women delivered their babies in hospitals and by 1945, the figure had reached 45 percent. Within hospitals, deliveries were increasingly performed by doctors trained in obstetrics. Accompanying the professionalization of childbirth care were other efforts to reduce childhood death rates, including the pasteurization of milk, improved garbage and sewage disposal, and attacks on such diseases as diphtheria and tuberculosis.

A heightened sense of public responsibility for the family was evident in a series of legal innovations. Eugenicist, racist, and nativist ideas led many states to impose physical and mental health requirements for marriage, require premarital medical tests, outlaw polygamy (in Idaho and Utah) and interracial marriages (primarily in the border states and the lower South), establish a waiting period before marriage, institute a higher age of consent, and adopt procedures for public registration of all new marriages (by 1907, twenty-seven states required registration). A growing number of states barred first-cousin marriages and other marriages between blood relations, and an increasing number of judges refused to accept the validity of common-law marriages.

In addition to these various reforms, tied together by a broad progressive outlook emphasizing efficiency, science, and professional expertise, experts in childrearing and household management advised homemakers about how they might apply the lessons of science and economics to the home. A new attitude toward childhood was apparent in the rise of the late-nineteenth-century child study movement, which sought to identify the distinctive features of children's emotional, physiological, and psychological development at each age. This growing sensitivity to children's unique needs and problems led physicians to establish a new branch of medicine—pediatrics—specifically devoted to infant and childhood diseases. By 1900, specialists in child nurture propounded a new ideal of scientific mothering based on the study of child development. Inspired by the growth of child psychology as an academic discipline that sought to trace the psychological and physiological stages of child development, professional childrearing specialists advocated strict feeding and sleeping schedules and early toilet training, and admonished mothers against fondling or playing with their children. Beginning in the 1920s, a reaction against such strict theories appeared, and childrearing experts began to emphasize delayed weaning and toilet training, attentiveness to children's needs, and an awareness of the necessity of fostering a secure and well-adjusted personality.

The late nineteenth century also witnessed the emergence of adolescence as a clearly defined stage of life. G. Stanley Hall, one of the nation's pioneer psychologists, helped formulate and popularize a modern conception of adolescence as a period of "storm and stress," rooted in the physiological and psychological changes associated with puberty. Among the factors that contributed to a recognition of adolescents as a clearly defined age group were the subjection of young people to longer periods of formal schooling—which meant that children spent less time at home under parents' supervision and increasingly acquired values from their peer groups—and growing public concerns over juvenile delinquency and child labor. Perhaps the most striking developments were a marked increase in the number of young people attending high school (by the 1920s, high school attendance had become the norm) and the appearance, as early as the mid-1910s, of a system of unchaperoned dating among high school students.

Old age, like adolescence, began to be perceived as a clearly delineated stage of life. By the turn of the century, old age was increasingly associated in the public mind with such problems as dependency, physical disability, mental debility, and a host of character problems including depression, bitterness, hypochondria, and an inability to absorb new ideas. A number of factors contributed to this negative perception of old age, including the increasing economic dependence of the elderly in an urban and industrial society, the increasing incidence of chronic degenerative conditions among the elderly as medical advances reduced the number of deaths caused by infections and epidemic diseases, and a cult of youth, which regarded the elderly as inflexible, unadaptable, and out of step with the times.

Increasingly, social workers, government policymakers, and businessmen regarded old age as a social problem. Old age homes began to appear during the late nineteenth century. During the Progressive Era, the first public commission on aging was established (Massachusetts, 1909), the first survey of the economic conditions of the elderly was conducted (Massachusetts, 1910), and the first old-age-pension system was enacted (Arizona, 1915).

Along with changes in perceptions of life stages came new efforts to restructure women's domestic roles in terms of the principles of efficiency, expertise, and professionalism. Since the 1840s, experts such as Catharine Beecher had called on women to apply rational business principles to housekeeping, but in the late nineteenth century, home economics and domestic science became specific courses of study in the nation's schools and universities. Spearheaded by the Congress of Mothers, the movement sought to introduce young women to the relevant teachings of bacteriology, biology, chemistry, child psychology, and economics.

As specialists in household management instituted new programs to train mothers in the new science of parenting plus home economics and domestic science, obstetricians transformed the birth process, and public health authorities combated infant and childhood diseases, reformers such as Margaret Sanger fought to make modern methods of birth control accessible to working-class women for the first time. Although psychologists and social workers launched ambitious programs of parent education and marriage counseling, legal reformers crusaded for new laws relating to marriage and divorce and for new institutions to serve maltreated children, and lawmakers enacted the first government programs in American history to provide financial aid to families with dependent children, few addressed the problems of poverty and its effects on the family in a more tangible way than Sanger.

There was no lack of other proposals to reform the family, some centering on overhauling old notions of marriage. The most radical prescriptions for change came from feminists like Ellen Key, pioneer sex researchers like Havelock Ellis, free-love advocates and anarchist sex radicals like Emma Goldman, and sex enthusiasts like Edward Carpenter. Key, a Swedish feminist, preached a scheme of "unwed motherhood"; Edith Ellis, wife of Havelock Ellis, advocated trial marriage and "semi-detached marriage," where each spouse occupied a separate domicile; still others advocated "serial marriage."

Proposals to reshape marriage were not, however, confined to free lovers, Greenwich Village bohemians, and anarchist sex radicals. A small but influential group of psychologists, educators, and jurists gave shape to a new conception of a "companionate family," in which husbands and wives would be "friends and lovers" and parents and children would be "pals." Convinced that the "old-style" family—idealized as a sacred refuge in a corrupt world but based on sexual repression, patriarchal authority, and hierarchy—was "unsatisfactorily adjusted to twentieth-century conditions," these experts sought to foster a new kind of family better suited to "modern society and industrial conditions."

Patriarchal authority was to give way to a new ethic of equal rights and responsibilities. Marriage, which was romanticized in Victorian morality as a way of overcoming man's animal nature, was instead to be a source of romance, emotional growth, and sexual fulfillment. The Victorian ideal of motherhood, which sentimentalized women as pious and virtuous figures and guardians of domestic morality, was to be replaced by a new ideal of womanhood emphasizing equality and mutuality in sexual gratification. And finally, the Victorian ideal of childhood, emphasizing innocence and insulation from the corruptions of the adult world, was to give way to a democratic ideal offering children greater freedom from parental control, greater latitude in expressing their feelings, and increased interaction with peers.

The achievement of this new companionate ideal entailed such reforms as access to birth control information, divorce by mutual consent for childless couples, and training for marriage and parenthood. After 1920, a growing number of reformers, convinced that the roots of marital breakdown lay in lack of communication, unsatisfactory sexual relationships, and psychological maladjustments created new programs in sex education, marriage reconciliation, and counseling services, and high school and college courses in family living.

Believing that the law's adversarial approach to divorce was harmful both to spouses and children, reformers also recommended changes in divorce proceedings, and greater availability of divorce on grounds of mental cruelty and incompatibility. New Mexico and Oklahoma revised their divorce statutes to allow divorce on grounds of incompatibility, and Arkansas, Idaho, and Nevada shortened residency requirements and liberalized divorce codes in order to attract couples seeking divorce. In many other states, judges diluted stringent divorce statutes. In 1931, only seven states specifically permitted divorce on grounds of mental cruelty, but judges in most other jurisdictions reinterpreted laws permitting divorce on grounds of physical cruelty to encompass such conduct as constant nagging, humiliating language, unfounded and false accusations, insults, and excessive sexual demands.

Sex education and improved methods of contraception were major goals of marriage reformers, who believed that an increase in the quantity and quality of sexual relationships would stabilize marriages and promote connubial affection. Robert Latou Dickinson, the nation's best known gynecologist, reported that "no single cause of mental strain in married women is as widespread as sex fears and maladjustments."

By the late 1920s the sexual attitudes and behavior of significant numbers of middle-class Americans had undergone far-reaching change. The first scientific sex surveys indicated that women who came to maturity after the turn of the century were much more likely than their mothers to engage in sex before marriage and outside it. Women who were born around 1900 were two to three times as likely to have premarital intercourse compared to women born before 1900. They were also more likely to experience orgasm.

Surveys of popular magazines indicate that approval of divorce, birth control, and premarital sexual intercourse rose sharply during the late 1910s and 1920s. Approval of "sex freedom" rose from just 13 percent in mass market magazines in 1918 to 40 percent in 1928. In 1931, the President's Committee on Social Trends reported that 66 percent of the opinions about birth control expressed in mass market periodicals were favorable. A shift in behavior accompanied changing attitudes. When Katherine Bement Davis published the first statistical study of contraceptive use in the United States in 1922, she found that nearly 75 percent of her subjects (1,000 college alumnae or women's club members) used some form of birth control. Contraceptive use was less common, though increasing, among working-class women.

Women used contraceptives despite the fact that before 1930 birth control devices could not be legally advertised or sent through the mails. The federal government, under the Comstock law, and twenty-two states, restricted access to contraceptive devices or birth control information. A 1936 appeals court decision, *U.S.* v. *One Package of Japanese Pessaries,* removed restrictions limiting doctors' access to contraceptive information and devices.

Among the most influential agents of change promoting the companionate ideal of the family were a number of new research institutions and advocacy organizations. The late-nineteenth-century crisis of the family produced a powerful institutional response. After the turn of the century, major foundations, including the Milbank Memorial Fund, the Rockefeller Foundation, and the Scripps Foundation began to fund programs in sex education and marriage counseling, as well as research on contraception and population problems. Such organizations as the Bureau of Social Hygiene, the National Research Council's Committee for Research on Problems of Sex, the Committee on Maternal Health, and the National Association of Marriage Counselors played a pivotal role in popularizing the new ideal of the companionate family, overcoming the opposition of the medical profession toward contraception, revising divorce statutes, and opening birth-control clinics and improving birth-control methods.

These organizations had distinct and conflicting agendas. Whereas Margaret Sanger's Committee on Maternal Health sought to promote female autonomy and separate sex from procreation, the Bureau of Social Hygiene sought to stabilize marriage by promoting sexual adjustment. The National Association of Marriage Counselors tended to emphasize the economic problems that underlay family problems and the importance of a healthy sex life to a strong marriage. The Committee for Research on Problems of Sex, which focused most of its resources on endocrinology and human sexual physiology, also funded pioneering studies of human sexual behavior by Lewis Terman and Katherine Bement Davis as well as the early research of John Rock and Gregory Pincas that would culminate decades later in the development of the birth control pill.

By the late 1920s, ethnic and working-class families had begun to superficially resemble middle-class families in structure and the allocation of family roles. As a result of rising real wages and the institution of seniority systems, a higher proportion of working-class families were able to withdraw wives and children from the labor force. In addition, ethnic differences in fertility rates declined, rates of intermarriage among ethnic and religious groups rose, and home ownership rates jumped sharply. But the Great Depression, followed by the deprivations of the war years, proceeded to unravel many of the advances of the Progressive Era as economic survival became the foremost challenge to the American family.

THE IMPACT OF THE DEPRESSION AND WORLD WAR II

During the Depression, unemployment, part-time work, reduced pay, and the demands of needy relatives tore at the fabric of family life, forcing many families to share living quarters with relatives, delay marriages, and put off having children. In Pennsylvania coal-mining towns, three or four families crowded together in one-room shacks and lived on wild weeds. In Arkansas, families were found living in caves. In Saint Louis, adults and children dug through garbage dumps for rotten food. In Oakland, California, whole families inhabited sewer pipes. And in Harlan County, Kentucky, families subsisted on dandelions and blackberries.

The Depression confronted families with a loss of support and sustenance. By 1933, American families had only 54 percent as much income as they had had in 1929 to purchase food and clothing, pay taxes, or repay debts. Average family income tumbled more than 40 percent, from $2,300 in 1929 to just $1,500 four years later. During 1932, the Depression's worst year, 28 percent of the nation's households did not have a single employed wage earner. But even those fortunate enough to hold jobs suffered drastic pay cuts and reductions in hours. Only one company in ten did not reduce wages, and by mid-1932, three-quarters of the nation's workers were on part-time schedules.

The Depression not only created poverty, it also brought preexisting poverty to public notice. A 1929 Brookings Institution study calculated that, prior to the Depression, nearly 60 percent of American families lived at or below a basic subsistence level of $2,000 a year. Even before the Depression began, a combination of social developments had contributed to an increase in poverty. Growth in the number of "broken" families—fractured by death, divorce, or desertion—had been underway throughout the 1920s. Members of single-parent families totaled 10.5 million in 1930. A rapid increase in the number of older Americans over the age of sixty-five during the 1920s—from 4.9 million to 6.6 million—also contributed to the growing incidence of poverty, as did an increasing number of the disabled (who numbered approximately 1 million in 1930). Joblessness was on the rise even before the stock-market crash, climbing from 1.5 million in 1926 to nearly 3 million in 1929. Tenant farming had been climbing since the start of the century (with 8.5 million tenant-farm families in 1930), and soil depletion, farm mechanization, boll weevils, and deflated crop prices pushed a million Americans off farms during the 1920s.

According to some Americans, the Depression had a salutary effect on the family. It encouraged family members to turn "toward each other with greater, more intelligent interdependence." The divorce rate actually declined, and families began to play new games like Monopoly together and to listen to the radio or go to the movies together. As a Muncie, Indiana, newspaper editorialized, "Many a family that has lost its car has found its soul."

Most observers, however, believed that the economic devastation of the 1930s wreaked havoc on families. Financial strain was responsible for a sharp drop in marriages and births. As the economy contracted, the marriage rate dropped off. In 1932, 250,000 fewer couples married than in 1929; altogether, 800,000 marriages were postponed or foregone due to the Depression. As the number of new households formed dropped, so did the birth rate, falling below the replacement level for the first time in American history. During the 1930s, Americans had nearly 3 million fewer babies than they would have had birth rates remained at the 1929 level. Hard times encouraged a growing public acceptance of birth control. During the Depression the number of birth-control clinics jumped from just 28 to 746. A 1936 court decision struck down federal restrictions on prescription of contraceptives, and the next year the American Medical Association recognized birth control as an area of legitimate practice. By the end of the Depression, every state except Connecticut and Massachusetts permitted doctors to provide birth-control devices.

The divorce rate fell (for the simple reason that fewer people could afford one), but rates of marital separation and desertion soared: at the end of the 1930s, over 1.5 million married couples were living apart. Child neglect was another product of the Depression. During its first two years, the number of children placed in custodial institutions rose 50 percent, while more than 200,000 vagrant children roamed the country.

Families sought to cope with economic hardship through creative economies: planting gardens, buying day-old bread, making their own clothing, and relining coats with old blankets. The economic crisis forced many families to "double up" by sharing their homes. As many as a sixth of all urban families shared apartments with other families.

Pooling incomes was an important buffer against loss of work. The 1930 census indicated that one-third of all American families had more than one wager earner and that a quarter had three or more income earners. Many children took part-time jobs, and wives earned supplementary income by taking in sewing, laundry, or dressmaking, setting up parlor groceries, and housing lodgers. To cut expenses further, social interaction with friends and neighbors was sharply curtailed.

Traditional roles within the family changed. Many unemployed fathers found their status lowered and a loss of power when they were no longer the family's economic provider and decision maker. The inability to support their families proved psychologically debilitating for many men; some became immobilized and stopped looking for work; some took their frustrations out in drink and became self-destructive or abusive to their families; still others walked out the door, never to return.

In contrast to men, many women found their status enhanced by the Depression. Despite the historic opposition to outside employment for married women, they entered the work force in large numbers. And just as unemployment eroded men's status, employment brought women more power. It changed the way they saw themselves and the way others saw them, and it redistributed authority within the family. The fact that many women brought home paychecks strengthened their voice in family decisions.

Certain groups were especially hard hit by the Depression. For the nation's growing number of senior citizens, a longer life span meant increased financial dependency. According to a government survey in 1937, less than 35 percent of elderly Americans were financially secure; nearly half had to rely on relatives for support.

African Americans suffered during the Depression with particular intensity. Even though black unemployment rates were consistently one-and-a-half times higher than the rates for whites, just 3 million African Americans—one out of four—received any public relief during the Depression. To survive, the nation's black families had to rely largely on their own financial and emotional resources.

The Great Depression caused a major revolution in government's role in securing the welfare of American families, as traditional means of coping with economic disaster proved to be totally inadequate. Public and private expenditures on relief in 1932 amounted to only $317 million, less than $27 for each of the nation's 12 million jobless. As part of

President Franklin Roosevelt's New Deal program, Washington enacted several thousand pieces of legislation that directly affected the welfare of the nation's families, ranging from farm relief and rural electrification to Aid to Families with Dependent Children.

A centerpiece of the New Deal's system of social welfare was the Social Security Act of 1935. The law set up two separate systems of social provisions: a contributory system of old-age insurance and federal grants-in-aid to support state-administered, needs-based programs for the nation's unemployed, blind and handicapped, dependent children lacking a wage-earning parent, and the indigent poor uncovered by the old-age insurance program. The Depression revealed the inadequacy of traditional family means of coping with economic disaster in an increasingly urban, bureaucratic society and underscored the fact that families were no longer able to protect themselves against adversity without government aid. It is this precedent for growing government involvement in family welfare that is the Depression's central legacy.

World War II continued to subject the nation's families to severe strains and dislocations. Family separation, an unprecedented tide of migration, and wartime rationing and shortages tested families with novel economic and psychological pressures. One-sixth of the nation's families suffered prolonged separation from fathers or sons. Five million "war widows" cared for children alone.

An increase in marriage and birth rates was one of the first visible social changes brought about by the war. In contrast to World War I, when the number of marriages actually declined, passage of the Selective Service Act in 1940 touched off a sharp rise in nuptials, ranging between 93 and 105 per 1,000 women aged seventeen to twenty-nine during the war (compared to 89.1 in the predepression years of 1925 and 1929). The rush to the altar was accompanied by the beginning of the baby boom. By 1943, the birth rate had risen to its highest level in twenty years. During the war, the population grew by 6.5 million, compared to just 3 million during the 1930s.

The war set hundreds of thousands of families in motion. Twelve million men and women left home for military service, while another 15 million Americans moved across state lines to find jobs in defense industries or to follow uniformed loved ones from one military base to another. This unprecedented reshuffling of the population pulled hundreds of thousands of families away from farms and small towns to large urban areas, where they faced severe housing shortages. Migrating families crowded into squalid trailer camps, shanty towns, and "foxhole houses"—excavated basements with tarpaper roofs—while 1.5 million families shared apartments with relatives, friends, or strangers.

The war was a powerful instrument of social change. The induction of millions of men into military service left thousands of jobs unfilled at home. Many of these jobs were "manned" by women workers. Between 1941 and 1945, female employment increased a staggering 57 percent, and for the first time in American history married working women outnumbered single working women. Altogether, nearly half of all American women worked at some point during the war. The middle-class taboo against a working wife or mother was temporarily repealed.

Throughout the war, public attitudes toward married women working were characterized by a deep ambivalence. Marriage counselors feared that employment of wives would generate marital friction and undermine husbands' self-esteem, while social workers blamed working mothers for a rise in juvenile delinquency and child psychologists linked maternal neglect to truancy, sleeping and eating disorders, regressive infantile forms of behavior, and "slower mental development, social ineptness, weakened initiative, and . . . [an inability] to form satisfactory relationships."

Although it is uncertain whether juvenile delinquency or child abuse represented greater problems in the United States in the 1940s than in the 1930s, social workers and psychologists were deeply troubled by the impact of the war on the nation's young people. Inevitably, wartime exigencies led to a relaxation of social restraints on the young. The number of teenagers who worked rose by 1.9 million, while the number attending school fell by 1.25 million. Frequent movement from one community to another and a weakening of parental authority contributed to a sharp rise in wartime rates of premarital pregnancy, illegitimacy, and venereal disease.

In adjusting to wartime conditions, American youth developed a new sense of identity. Adolescents began to create a distinctive teenage subculture, with its own garb, hairstyles, dance music, language, and values. Teenage boys, particularly in poorer communities, showed their disdain for social conventions by donning zoot suits, swinging yo-yos, participating in "bull sessions," and sporting penny loafers and blue jeans. Teenage girls, called "bobby-soxers" after the short socks they wore, held slumber parties, read new teen magazines like *Glamour* and *Seventeen,* and swooned over Frank Sinatra. The shared interests and values of these peer groups were distinct from those of the larger stateside adult population, which was caught up in wartime production work.

No families were more deeply affected by the war, however, than those of Japanese Americans. In the spring of 1942, 110,000 Japanese Americans—two-thirds of them U.S. citizens—were relocated from homes on the West Coast to detention camps. For these people, internment meant severe economic hardship, physical dislocation, and a sharp reordering of family roles. Tarpaper covered wooden barracks were partitioned into one-room family apartments eighteen by twenty feet in size, each containing six or seven people. Toilets, showers, and dining facilities were communal, precluding family privacy.

The camps tended to invert traditional roles and relationships within the Japanese American family. Men and women, regardless of age, worked at interchangeable jobs paying twelve to nineteen dollars a month. Within the camps, influence shifted from the older generation, the Issei, to the younger generation born in the United States, the Nisei.

The end of World War II produced severe problems of postwar adjustment. Housing was in extremely short supply, and many couples were forced to "double up" with relatives or occupy cramped one-room apartments. In addition, many hasty wartime marriages proved unstable, and as the war ended the divorce rate shot up. In 1946, American courts granted a record 600,000 divorces. Whereas in 1940, one marriage in six had ended in divorce, by 1946, the figure was one in four. Factors that contributed to the rising divorce rate included the strains of wartime separation, the suspicion of wartime adultery, and a new independence and self-sufficiency among women who had lived alone and earned independent incomes. One long-term effect of the dramatic postwar upsurge in divorce rates was to eliminate some of the social stigma surrounding divorce.

POSTWAR FAMILIES

During the 1950s, many American men and women reacted against the poverty of the Depression and the upheavals of World War II by placing renewed emphasis upon family life. The divorce rate slowed, young women married earlier than their mothers had, they had more children and bore them faster. The average marriage age of American women dropped to twenty, a record low. The fertility rate rose 50 percent between 1940 and 1950, producing a population growth rate approaching India's.

Women were encouraged to forsake higher education or a full-time career for emotional fulfillment as wives and mothers. Politicians, educators, psychologists, and the mass media all echoed the view that women would find their highest fulfillment managing a house and caring for children. Many educators agreed with the president of Barnard College, who argued that women could not compete with men in the workplace because they "had less physical strength, a lower fatigue point, and a less stable nervous system." Women's magazines pictured housewives as happy with their tasks and depicted career women as neurotic, unhappy, and dissatisfied. A 1952 advertisement for Gimbel's department store expressed the prevailing point of view. "What's college?" the ad asked. "That's where girls who are above cooking and sewing go to meet a man so they can spend their lives cooking and sewing." By "marrying at an earlier age, rearing larger families," and purchasing a house in the suburbs, young Americans believed, in the words of *McCall's* magazine, that they could find their "deepest satisfaction."

Although many Americans think of the 1950s family as a kind of ideal, it was in fact a historical anomaly unlike other families in this century before or since. During the preceding decades, couples married in their mid-or late twenties, the birth rate was declining, and the divorce rate was steadily rising. During the 1950s, in contrast, the marriage age dropped to a historic low, the birth rate rose sharply, and the divorce rate stabilized. After the 1950s, the marriage age returned to its historic norms, the birth rate resumed its downward drift, and the divorce rate its upward climb.

A postwar economic boom made it possible for millions of young adults to satisfy their desire to abandon cramped urban apartments for brick and frame houses located in America's burgeoning suburbs. In the ten years following 1948, 11 of the 13 million homes built in the United States were erected in the suburbs. By 1960, as many Americans lived in the suburbs as in central cities, and the suburban way of life began shaping the patterns and rhythms of many Americans, reinforcing the family orientation of postwar society.

Suburban populations during the 1950s were remarkably homogeneous, consisting primarily of newlyweds or young couples between the ages of twenty-five and forty, with few single adults, teenagers, blacks, or elderly or poor people. In addition, fewer suburban wives and mothers worked than their urban counterparts, contributing to the popular stereotype that families in the suburbs were child-centered and female-dominated. Because of the demands of commuting, fathers spent little time with their families. The result was a "matriarchal society, with children who know men only as nighttime residents and weekend guests." The fathers' absence forced mothers to assume the roles of both parents. Mothers chauffeured children to friends' homes, piano and dancing lessons, and the doctor. Quipped one humorist, a suburban housewife's life was "merely motherhood on wheels," delivering children first "obstetrically . . . and by car forever after."

Transience was a characteristic common to suburban family life. In the New York metropolitan area, less than 6 percent of the suburban population was living in the same house in 1960 as in 1955. Frequent movement from one house to another accentuated the rootlessness of suburban families, isolating individual families from relatives and neighbors.

During the 1950s, middle-class Americans began to pursue the "companionate" ideal that had been devised by marriage counselors, family psychologists, and legal experts in the 1920s. In the postwar economic boom, the luxury of mutuality and companionship could be enjoyed by millions of Americans. Marriage, wrote singer Pat Boone in a 1958 bestseller, was now a "fifty-fifty deal." In fact, partnership did not mean equality. A wife's primary role was to serve—her husband, her children, her church and community—and to maintain the home.

An essential element in the family ideal of the 1950s was a child-centered outlook, based to a large degree on the advice of Dr. Benjamin Spock. When he wrote his childrearing bestseller in 1946—targeted at war-weary parents who wanted to improve upon their own upbringing—Spock counseled them to dispense with the rigidities of traditional childrearing. Rejecting the idea of strict feeding and bathing schedules, Spock told parents to pick up their babies and enjoy them. His reassuring message was, "You know more than you think you do." Although Spock's book was often treated as a synonym for permissiveness in childrearing during the 1960s, in fact it emphasized the importance of discipline. Spock stressed that children needed firm leadership, but that discipline depended not on physical punishment or intimidation but upon the power of love, reason, and parental example. He taught parents that their actions carried enormous consequences for their children's future, that children's needs and desires had as much legitimacy as their own, that parental authority should be flexible rather than arbitrary, and that children needed to be involved in the formulation of rules intended to govern their behavior. Spock placed particular emphasis on the mother-child bond, arguing that creative individuals owed their talents to "the inspiration they received from a particularly strong relationship with a mother who had especially high aspirations for her children."

Despite Spock's warm and comforting language, childcare manuals of the 1950s had an undercurrent of anxiety. No previous generations of childcare books had ever expressed so much anxiety and fear about children's health, safety, and happiness. One source of concern was meningitis and polio, which crippled tens of thousands of children a year before the introduction of the Salk vaccine in 1955. Childcare experts were also more observant of children's psychological well-being, warning that defects in mothering could cause schizophrenia, homosexuality, and an inability to assume the commitments of adulthood. Another fear was that children, especially boys, were failing to develop an appropriate sex-role identity. Because fathers worked outside the home and provided little of the emotional and physical care of children, boys and girls were raised almost exclusively by women. It was thought that boys, therefore, were identifying with their mothers and failing to develop a firm sense of their masculinity, while girls needed fathers to encourage their femininity and make them feel adequate as love objects for men. In retrospect, it seems clear that the underlying source of the anxiety pervading postwar childrearing manuals lay in the fact that mothers were raising their children with an exclusivity and in an isolation without parallel in American history.

If the 1950s family has come to represent a standard of comparison against which Americans look at family life today, this is largely because of the influence of television. During the 1950s, family life was one of TV's main sources of drama and amusement. The most popular television personalities personified postwar family ideals: Jerry Mathers as the epitome of preteen mischief on "Leave It to Beaver"; Robert Young as the wrinkled-browed, all-knowing middle-class dad on "Father Knows Best"; and Donna Reed as the ideal, cookie-baking, doting mom. But, as historian Stephanie Coontz has emphasized, TV's family comedies were not documentaries. While television celebrated middle-class family bliss in fictional Springfields and Mayfields, a quarter of all American families—and half of all two-parent black families—lived in poverty, a third of all marriages ended in divorce, and nearly 2 million married men and women who could not or would not divorce lived apart from their spouses. Public opinion polls indicated that approximately one-fifth of all couples considered themselves unhappy in marriage, and another fifth reported only "medium happiness." The image of domestic tranquility celebrated in the popular media was, in part, a myth.

With the advantage of hindsight, it is clear that historical processes were underway in the 1950s that would contribute to major transformations in American family life during the 1960s. These included new definitions of women's roles and the identity of youth. A dramatic upsurge took place during the 1950s in women's employment as more and more married women entered the labor force; by 1960 the proportion of married women working outside the home was 1 in 3. The number of women receiving college degrees also rose, from just 24 percent in 1950 to over 35 percent a decade later. Meanwhile, beginning in 1957 the birth rate began to drop as women elected to have fewer children.

THE TRANSFORMATION OF CONTEMPORARY AMERICAN FAMILIES

Since 1960, ideals and role expectations that largely characterized the family for a century and a half have gone through a fundamental redefinition. But perhaps the most radical transformation was from the postwar to the contemporary family structure. One stunning fact dramatically illustrates the dimensions of change. As recently as 1960, 70 percent of all American households were nuclear families like Ozzie and Harriet Nelson's 1950s television creation, consisting of a breadwinner father, a housewife mother, and their children. Today, fewer than 15 percent of American households consist of a go-to-work dad, a stay-at-home mom, and two or more kids. Although none of the developments that contributed to this evolution is entirely new, what is novel is that they are much more pronounced than in the past and have penetrated all social classes and ethnic groups more deeply than ever before.

Divorce rates, on the rise since at least 1860, accelerated in the mid-1960s. Whereas only 12 percent of marriages contracted by women born between 1900 and 1904 ended in divorce, approximately 40 percent of the marriages of women born between 1940 and 1944 will end in divorce. As the divorce rate has climbed, the stigma attached to divorce has faded. In the 1960s, a divorce shattered Nelson Rockefeller's presidential aspirations; but by 1980, when Ronald Reagan became the first divorced person to be elected president, attitudes had clearly shifted.

Climbing divorce rates contributed to the rapid growth of single-parent families, what used to be known as "broken" homes. In 1960, just 8 percent of American children lived with their mother as their only parent: in the 1990s, that figure is 22 percent. Another 8 percent live with a mother and a stepfather, and an additional 5 percent live apart from both their father and mother, in foster care. Altogether, a third of the nation's children now live apart from their biological father.

Each year since 1976, over a million American children have experienced their parents' divorce—triple the number in 1950. Yet the 1990s' high divorce rate does not necessarily mean that marital instability has increased proportionately. While divorce rates have certainly risen, rates of death, desertion, and separation have fallen. As a result, the proportion of disrupted marriages remained roughly constant between 1910 and 1970 and only in the mid-1970s began to exceed the figure earlier in the century. Despite the rising divorce rate, the proportion of children living with at least one of their biological parents was actually higher in 1980 (95 percent) than in 1940 (90 percent), when many widowed or divorced spouses sent their children to live in orphanages or with relatives.

A shattering of traditional family norms has also been apparent, in the eyes of many Americans, in a declining marriage rate, delayed marriage, a falling birth rate, teen pregnancy and unwed motherhood, and the numbers of mothers in the work force. The marriage rate has dropped sharply since the 1950s, and as the number of nuptials fell, the age of marriage climbed. Since 1960, when the median age at marriage was twenty for women and twenty-three for men, the average has risen by over two years. At the same time, the ratio of children per mother declined by 50 percent, from nearly 3.5 children during the 1950s to 1.8 in 1990, which is below the natural population replacement level.

In addition, at century's end marriage and childbearing have become increasingly discrete events. In the 1990s, 27 percent of all children are born out of wedlock, four times the percentage of just twenty-five years ago. Few developments of the past quarter century have provoked more controversy than the destigmatization of out-of-wedlock childbearing. As recently as the mid-1960s, illegitimate children were called "bastards" and possessed fewer legal rights than those born to married parents. White women often dealt with unwed pregnancies in one of two ways: "shotgun" weddings or adoption. In the early 1960s, over half of young women who conceived out of wedlock married the father before the child was born, compared to just 27 percent in the late 1980s. Other unmarried white women who became pregnant entered maternity homes and put their children up for adoption. Nearly 20 percent of white children born out of wedlock were put up for adoption—six times the rate in the 1990s. African American and Hispanic women were much less likely to relinquish children born out of wedlock, relying instead on informal adoption or upon extended families to raise their children.

Each year, nearly a million teenagers become pregnant and almost half a million have babies. In 1950, 5 out of every 1,000 white teenagers had children out of wedlock; by 1988, the figure had climbed to 25 per 1,000. Yet despite extensive publicity about an epidemic of teenage pregnancies, pregnancy rates among teenagers have actually declined sharply, falling by about one-third from the mid-1960s until the early 1990s. The proportion of births to unmarried teenage mothers has increased—two-thirds of all 1989 births were out of wedlock, up from one-third in 1970—but this reflects a decline in the marriage rate among teenagers and a drop in the number of children born to married couples. While the birth rate of unmarried white teenagers has risen slightly since 1970, the birth rate of unmarried black women has declined.

The postwar stereotype of the housewife-mother and breadwinner-father broke down as millions of married women joined the paid labor force. The influx of mothers into the work force was already well underway during the 1950s, but the rate increased during the 1960s and 1970s. In 1950, 25 percent of married women living with their husbands worked outside the home; in the early 1990s, the figure climbed to nearly 70 percent. The increase in working mothers has been particularly rapid among mothers of young children. In the 1990s, approximately 60 percent of mothers of preschool-age children hold jobs, compared to just 12 percent in 1950. Thus increasing numbers of children are cared for during the day by adults other than their parents. In the early 1990s, over two-thirds of all three-to-five-year-olds participated in a daycare, nursery school, or prekindergarten program, compared to one-fifth in 1970.

The driving force behind the changes that have taken place in American family life since the late 1950s lies in a far-reaching shift in values. Formerly, an overwhelming majority of Americans endorsed marriage as a prerequisite to well-being, social adjustment, and maturity. Men and women who failed to marry were denigrated as "sick," "neurotic," or "immoral" and couples who did not have children were deemed "selfish." A large majority of the public believed that an unhappily married couple should stay together for the sake of their children, that a woman should not work if she had a husband who could support her, that premarital sex was always wrong, and that an unmarried couple had to get married if they were expecting a baby.

During the 1960s and 1970s, cultural biases against divorce, working mothers, premarital sex, and out-of-wedlock births declined, encouraged by a sexual revolution, expanding job opportunities for women, the women's movement, and the growing popularity of psychological therapies stressing "growth," self-realization," and "fulfillment."

Economic changes played a major role in the emergence of a new outlook, for individuals who came of age during the 1960s and 1970s spent their childhoods during an era of unprecedented affluence. Between 1950 and 1970, median family income tripled. For the middle class, this increase led to opportunities in education, travel, and leisure, all of which helped to heighten expectations for fulfillment and personal happiness. For the working class and ethnic minorities, the portrayal of American affluence on television, in movies, books, and magazines also raised expectations, even though the same opportunities for fulfillment were not available.

New philosophies and psychological therapies promoting individual self-realization flourished in this atmosphere. Beginning in the 1950s, "humanistic" psychologies triumphed over earlier theories that had emphasized adjustment as the solution to individual problems. The underlying assumptions of these new "third force" psychologies (a name chosen to distinguish them from the more pessimistic psychoanalytic and behaviorist psychologies) were that a person's spontaneous impulses were intrinsically good and that maturity was not a process of "settling down" and suppressing instinctual needs but of achieving one's potential. Unlike the earlier psychology of adjustment associated with Alfred Adler and Dale Carnegie—which had counseled compromise, suppression of instinctual impulses, avoidance of confrontations, and the desirability of acceding to the wishes of others—the new humanistic psychologies of Abraham Maslow, Carl Rogers, and Erich Fromm advised individuals to "get in touch" with their feelings and freely voice their opinions, even if this generated feelings of guilt.

Another force for change in the family was the sexual revolution. Contemporary Americans are much more likely than their predecessors to postpone marriage, to live alone, and to engage in sexual intercourse outside of marriage. In the early 1990s, over

80 percent of all women said they were not virgins when they married, compared to less than 20 percent a generation ago. In addition, the number of unmarried couples living together has quadrupled since 1960, and nearly half of all Americans who married between 1980 and 1984 cohabited with a member of the opposite sex while they were single, compared to just 1 in 9 Americans married between 1965 and 1974.

The roots of these developments were planted in the early 1960s, when a new openness about sexuality swept the nation's literature, movies, theater, advertising, and fashion. This blossoming was due in large part to the introduction of the birth-control pill, a highly effective method of contraception, in 1960. Large numbers of women were suddenly able to choose to have sex without the complications of unwanted pregnancies. This unaccustomed freedom was reflected in a new era of public sexuality that included "singles only" weekends at resorts that acknowledged couples outside of marriage; "singles bars," where casual sex rather than friendship or marriage was often the goal of both men and women; the production of the musical *Hair,* which included nudity, on Broadway; the creation of the topless bathing suit; and displays of full frontal nudity in sexually oriented magazines and simulated sex in movies. As a result of all this, it became far easier and more acceptable to have an active social life and sex life outside of marriage.

Along with changes in traditional roles outside of marriage came changes in roles within marriage. The massive influx of mothers into the work force radically altered family roles and expectations. Major forces that propelled women into the work force included a rising cost of living coupled with elevated expectations of what constituted an acceptable standard of living, which together spurred families to seek a second source of income; increased control over fertility through contraception and abortion, which allowed women to work without interruption; rising educational levels, which led many women to seek employment for intellectual stimulation; and the women's movement, which articulated a powerful critique of the idea that childcare and housework were the apex of a woman's accomplishments or her sole means of fulfillment and attacked the societal expectations that women defer to the needs of spouses and children. As wives assumed a larger role in their family's financial support, they felt justified in expecting that husbands perform more childcare and housework.

While this portrait of the evolution of the contemporary American family applies in a general way to the whole population of the United States, the profile of low-income African American families living in urban areas is somewhat different. Of all the issues that have aroused concern about the contemporary family, the plight and problems of the inner-city family are perhaps the most significant. In 1965, the federal government released a confidential report by an obscure assistant secretary of labor named Daniel Patrick Moynihan entitled *The Negro Family: The Case for National Action,* which argued that an increasing rate of fatherless black families had become a major obstacle to black advancement. The black middle class had managed to create stable families, he wrote, "but for the vast number of the unskilled, poorly educated city working class, the fabric of conventional social relationships has all but disintegrated."

Moynihan supported his thesis with startling statistics. Nearly 25 percent of all black women were divorced, separated, or living apart from their husbands, three times the rate for whites. Illegitimacy among blacks had climbed from 16.8 percent in 1940 to 23.6 percent in 1963, while the white rate had only risen from 2 to 3 percent. The breakdown of the black family, Moynihan contended, had led to a sharp increase in welfare dependency, delinquency, unemployment, drug addiction, and failure in school.

The Moynihan report attributed the instability of the black family to the effects of slavery, Reconstruction, poor education, rapid urbanization, and thirty-five years of unemployment rates twice those of white Americans and wages half those of whites. The report concluded with a call for national action to strengthen the black family through programs of jobs, family allowances, and birth control.

The Moynihan report prompted a barrage of criticism for ignoring the strengths of the black family. By focusing on instability, weakness, and pathology, critics claimed, the Moynihan report ignored the strength and durability of the lower-class black kinship system—an extensive network of kin and friends supporting and reinforcing the lower-class black family. Moynihan's detractors also said that his report exaggerated the problems of illegitimacy and absent fathers, and overestimated the differences between black and white families. Contrary to the impression conveyed by the report, critics noted, the overwhelming majority of black families during the 1960s, 1970s, and 1980s included two spouses. In 1960, 75 percent of black children lived with two parents; a decade later, 67 percent did. The report's discussion of illegitimacy also distorted the facts, critics observed. Far from increasing, the black illegitimacy rate was actually declining: in 1960, 98 out of every 1,000 single black women gave birth to a baby; in 1980, only 77 did.

Yet despite civil-rights victories, enactment of Great Society programs, and establishment of affirmative-action programs, many of the issues identified in the Moynihan Report have intensified. The income gap between black and white families widened in the 1980s and early 1990s; fewer black Americans live in two-parent families in the early 1990s than in the 1950s; and the proportion of black children born to single women has climbed sharply. Most black children spend at least a portion of their childhood in a female-headed household, at or near the poverty level, having impermanent relationships with their father or father surrogates. In 1960, 20 percent of all black children lived in fatherless families; by 1985, the figure was 51 percent. In 1960, 75 percent of all black children were born to a married black woman; in 1985, the figure was less than 40 percent.

What needs to be emphasized is that divorce rates, single parenthood, and out-of-wedlock births have increased throughout American society since the 1960s. The trend has affected affluent whites as well as poorer blacks, and middle-class suburbs as well as inner-city ghettoes. Increases in single parenthood, divorce, and illegitimacy, however, have posed particular problems for poorer black communities, where rates of divorce, desertion, and single parenthood historically have been much higher than among other groups. In these neighborhoods, a majority of children now grow up without the support of an adult male.

There is no single explanation for family dissolution among the economically deprived. Recent scholarship has tended to dismiss the derogatory terms previously used to describe lower-class family patterns—like "pathology" and "disorganization"—and instead see the family patterns of the urban poor as a response to specific social, economic, and demographic realities. Rather than suggesting that the family patterns of the urban poor are inferior to those found among the middle class—using such emotionally charged concepts as "unwed mothers," "illegitimate children," and "deserting fathers"—scholars have adopted a more neutral vocabulary, referring instead to "multiple child care figures," "coparenting," and "exchange" relationships, and to intermittent relationships with fathers and father surrogates and have viewed these arrangements as the product of specific social circumstances. Thus, impermanent common-law unions among the poor reflect the economic uncertainty and instability of poor communities, as well as a higher level of adult mortality. Economic and demographic realities help explain why the urban poor tend to rely upon kinship connections and less upon marriage to share financial resources and provide care for children. Similarly, the prevalence of coparenting arrangements and informal child placement strategies among the urban poor reflect a desire to place children in households better able to care for them financially. And, finally, differences in sexual behavior (urban nonwhites experience coitus at a younger age than whites), reflect the fact that for many of the poor the birth of a first child and marriage have become separate events.

Many Americans feel that children, white and nonwhite, have suffered the largest losses in the transformation of the contemporary American family, and that the nation, which has long prided itself on its child-centered orientation, is slighting children's needs. They fear that today's children are caught between two difficult trends—decreasing parental commitment to child nurture and an increasingly perilous social environment, saturated with sex, addictive drugs, and alcohol—that make it more difficult to achieve a well-adjusted adulthood.

Throughout the century, authorities on the family have disputed the behavioral, psychological, and emotional consequences of divorce upon children. As early as the 1920s, a growing number of social workers and family sociologists such as Miriam Van Waters, Ethel Dummer, and Edward Reuter began to reject the prevailing view that children experienced the divorce of their parents as a devastating blow that stunted their psychological and emotional growth and caused maladjustments that persisted for years. They argued that children were better off when their parents divorced than when they had an unstable marriage, and that the adverse effects of divorce were generally of short duration.

Although the impact of divorce on children remains in dispute, certain conclusions do seem warranted. On the one hand, it appears that conflict-laden, tension-filled marriages have more adverse effects on children than divorce. Children from discordant homes permeated by tension and instability are more likely to suffer psychosomatic illnesses, suicide attempts, delinquency, and other social maladjustments than are children whose parents divorce. There is no empirical evidence to suggest that children from "broken" homes suffer significantly more health or mental problems, personality disorders, or lower school grades than children from "intact" homes. On the other hand, it is clear that divorce is severely disruptive, at least initially, for a majority of children.

Childrens' reactions to divorce vary tremendously, depending on their age, sex, the amicability or bitterness of their parents' interactions, custody arrangements, and, above all, their perception of their parents' marriage. Children who viewed their parents' marriage as unhappy tend to adjust more easily to divorce than those who regarded their home life as basically happy.

The emotional and psychological upheavals of divorce are often aggravated by a series of readjustments children must deal with, such as the loss of contact with the noncustodial parent. More than 9 of every 10 children are placed in their mother's custody, and recent studies have found that two months following a divorce fewer than half the fathers see their children as often as once a week, and after three years half the fathers do not visit their children at all.

Further complicating children's adjustment is the impact of remarriage. Roughly half of all mothers remarry within approximately two years of their divorce. These reconstituted families often confront jealousies and conflicts of loyalty not found in families untouched by divorce; at the same time, a number of researchers have found that most children favor remarriage.

For many children, the most disruptive consequence of divorce is economic. In the immediate aftermath of a divorce, the income of the divorced woman and her children falls sharply, by as much as 73 percent in the first year. Adding to the financial pressures facing children of divorce is the fact that a majority of divorced men evade court orders to support their children. Other sources of stress result from the mother's new financial responsibilities as her family's breadwinner, additional demands on her time as she tries to balance economic and child rearing responsibilities, and, frequently, adjustment to unfamiliar and less comfortable living arrangements.

The increase in divorce has contributed, in part, to an increase in child poverty. As a result of declining family size and rising family income (due, in part, to the influx of mothers into the work force), average family income per child has risen by over 50 percent since 1962. But if many children are significantly better-off economically than their counterparts three decades ago, others are not. After declining in the 1960s, the child poverty rate climbed in the 1970s and 1980s, reflecting the growth of income inequality in American society and the increasing number of children living in single-parent households, which are three times more likely than two-parent households to be poor. Between 1970 and 1989, the poverty rate among children under eighteen rose by 40 percent. In the early 1990s, a fifth of the nation's children are poor, as are almost a fourth of its preschoolers and half of its black children.

Another family issue that has been recognized as having an important impact is domestic violence, including wife beating, child abuse, and child abandonment. At the end of the 1960s, women's groups established a network of shelters for battered women and their children. Recent government statistics indicate that as many as 2 to 4 million women each year suffer serious injury at the hands of husbands or boyfriends—more than are hurt in auto accidents, rapes, or muggings—and other statistics show high rates of child abuse. Between 1976 and 1984, reports of child abuse and neglect rose from nearly 700,000 to 1.7 million annually, and since 1985 reports of child abuse and neglect have risen another 40 percent. Although reports of domestic violence have risen sharply in recent years, no one knows for sure whether the actual incidence of abuse has increased or if there are simply more people willing to report it than ever before, perhaps due to public awareness and professional acceptance of the dimensions of the problem.

The first organized response to domestic violence appeared in the late 1870s, when Societies for the Prevention of Cruelty to Children sprouted up in major cities to offer protection to victims of cruelty and child neglect. The tendency of the upper-class charity workers, inspired by ideals of Christian stewardship, was to blame the evils of alcohol for the problem; and indeed the disease of alcoholism and other drug addictions is still seen as a major factor in domestic violence. During the Progressive Era, however, professional social workers attributed the problem to poverty and unemployment. Public awareness declined during the 1930s and 1940s, probably due to the dire economic stress of the Depression and wartime, but concern resurfaced in the mid-1950s. In 1954, the Children's Division of the American Humane Association conducted the first national survey of child neglect, abuse, and exploitation. Three years later the U.S. Children's Bureau launched the first major federal study of child neglect, abuse, and abandonment. By the early 1960s, child cruelty had captured the attention of a growing number of radiologists and pediatricians who found bone fractures and physical trauma in children suggesting deliberate injury. After C. Henry Kempe, a pediatrician at the University of Colorado Medical School, published a famous essay on the "battered child syndrome" in the *Journal of the American Medical Association* in 1962, legal, medical, psychological, and educational journals began to focus attention on family violence. Growing professional concern about child abuse led to calls for greater state protection and services for abused and neglected children and their parents.

Another issue, which may not have as traumatic effect on children as divorce and domestic violence but probably affects more children, is the decreasing amount of time that parents spend with their children—which has dropped 40 percent over the past quarter century, from thirty hours a week to only seventeen—and the quality of care the children, especially the youngest, are receiving.

In large measure, the declining amount of time devoted to children reflects the rise of the working mother, for in the early 1990s, two-thirds of all mothers with children under eighteen worked outside the home. The most striking increase has taken place among mothers of preschoolers; over 60 percent of the mothers of children under six were in the labor force in the early 1990s; a quarter of these mothers worked full time year-round, the rest part time or full time for part of the year. In 1993, half of all infants—and a higher proportion of preschoolers—were regularly cared for by someone other than their parents: either in "family daycare," unlicensed care by a relative or nonrelative in another home, in their own home by a relative or nonrelative, or in a licensed daycare center or nursery school.

For much of the last four decades a bitter debate has raged about the effects of nonmaternal child care on children's psychological well-being, intellectual development, and social and psychological growth. An early salvo in this debate was fired in the 1950s, when English psychiatrist John Bowlby, who studied orphans in British institutions following World War II, argued that children deprived of an intense maternal relationship exhibited antisocial behavior and an inability to form intense relationships with significant others. Later commentators interpreted Bowlby's scholarship to mean that children needed a full-time mother in order to develop normally and that the family was superior to any other institution in raising well-adjusted young children.

As the number of children in nonmaternal care has increased, expert opinion on preschool care has grown more positive. Studies of the federal government's Head Start early education program found that children enrolled in the program were more likely to finish high school, stay off welfare, and avoid crime and teenage pregnancy. Other research emphasized the psychologically beneficial effects of a stimulating peer environment and the fact that children could assimilate information earlier than previously thought.

Most recently, debates have centered primarily on the effects of daycare upon infants. A highly controversial 1987 review of the scholarly literature by Jay Belsky, a professor of human development at Pennsylvania State University, suggested that infants who were cared for more than twenty hours a week by a surrogate were at risk for future psychological and behavioral difficulties, including elevated rates of insecurity and heightened aggression and noncompliance—points hotly contested by Belsky's critics. Nevertheless, growing concern for the psychological and emotional well-being of newborns helped promote the concepts of maternal and paternal leaves.

In conclusion, while there are clear links between family structure and poverty, there is no empirical evidence from the latter half of the twentieth century that changes in the family have directly contributed to an increase in behavioral, academic, or psychological problems. A variety of social indicators do appear to indicate a worsening of children's well-being—such as a doubling of juvenile crime rates and a tripling of teenage suicide and homicide since 1960, a substantial decline in college entrance examination scores, and sharp increases in drug and alcohol use and premarital sex. But no studies conclusively demonstrate that these trends result from an increase in marital instability or in the number of mothers working outside the home. If anything, these trends seem to have stabilized in the 1990s, even as family transformations continued unabated.

PUBLIC POLICY ISSUES AND THE REVOLUTION IN FAMILY LAW

Should the federal government help working parents take care of their children through subsidized daycare? Should parents have the right to take unpaid leave after the birth or adoption of a child? Should there be national standards governing staff qualifications, child-teacher ratios, and health and safety requirements in child-care centers? These are among the questions that the nation's legislatures have wrestled with as the nature of American family life has been revolutionized in the course of a generation, transforming the family into a political battleground.

One of the issues most hotly contested by conservative social analysts such as Charles Murray is whether state and federal social-welfare policies encouraged family dissolution and out-of-wedlock births. President Ronald Reagan voiced a common conservative viewpoint when he declared, "There is no question that many well-intentioned Great Society-type programs contributed to family breakups, welfare dependency, and a large increase in births out of wedlock." Murray argued that government welfare policies provided poor women with more purchasing power than a minimum-wage job while encouraging nonmarriage, illegitimate births, and nonwork. The belief that government welfare expenditures caused family breakdown rests on a close chronological correlation between rising welfare spending and dramatic increases in female-headed households and illegitimacy among the poor. In 1959, just 10 percent of low-income black Americans lived in a single-parent household; by 1980, the figure had climbed to 44 percent.

Did the growth of state services contribute to rising rates of illegitimacy and single-parent families or was it simply part of the trend of the whole society? The expansion of Aid to Families with Dependent Children in the late 1960s allowed many poorer mothers to care for children born outside of marriage. But the pregnant teenager going onto welfare quickly became a symbol of the alleged excesses of the Great Society programs of the early sixties. As teenage mothers bear about half of the children born out-of-wedlock, much public concern has centered on a fear that they and their children are doomed to lives of welfare dependency and poverty. In fact, the evidence on this point is mixed. On the one hand, unmarried mothers tend to be younger, poorer, less educated, and more dependent on welfare than those who are married at the time of the birth; and 40 percent of unmarried mothers end up as long-term welfare recipients compared to only 14 percent of divorced mothers. On the other hand, recent studies suggest that a majority of unwed teenage mothers succeed in pulling themselves and their families out of poverty by the time they reach their early thirties.

Studies by David Ellwood and Mary Jo Bane have found no correlation between the level of welfare payments and the incidence of out-of-wedlock births (although states with higher welfare benefits do tend to have slightly higher divorce rates and lower rates of remarriage). Between 1972 and 1980, for example, the number of black children in single-parent families jumped 20 percent, even though the number of black children on welfare declined. And even though welfare benefits fell in real terms during the 1970s and 1980s, the number of black female-headed families continued to climb.

The influential sociologist William Julius Wilson offered an alternate explanation emphasizing structural changes in the American economy, and arguing that increases in joblessness among poor black men have made marriage a less attractive option for poor black women. The number of marriageable black men capable of supporting a family fell after 1970, as the number of jobs in central cities requiring less than a high school education, particularly in manufacturing, decreased. In 1960, there were 70 employed black men aged twenty to twenty-four for every 100 black women in the same age group; by the early 1980s, the number of employed men had fallen to less than 50. The issue is still subject to debate, since other figures show that, in fact, the marriage rate among black men with steady jobs declined nearly as much as the rate among all black men, suggesting that noneconomic factors contributed significantly to the decline in black marriage rates.

In an attempt to address problems of poverty, illegitimacy, and single parenthood, in 1988 Congress enacted the first major overhaul of federal welfare laws in half a century. The new law requires states to set up educational, training, work, and childcare programs to help move welfare recipients into private jobs. It also requires absent fathers to contribute to the financial support of their children.

In the 1990s, the United States is a society deeply divided over what role government should take in strengthening American families. Conservative activists, fearful that climbing rates of divorce, single parenthood, and working mothers represent a breakdown of family values, launched a politically influential "pro-family" movement during the 1970s that has continued into the 1990s. They have sought to restrict or abolish access to abortion, blocked ratification of the proposed Equal Rights Amendment to the Constitution, censored eroticism on television and song lyrics on recordings, and limited teenagers' access to contraceptives and information on choices regarding pregnancy. Their position is that the government has a positive duty to define and enforce family norms and values, which precludes paying for programs, such as subsidized daycare, that might threaten those norms.

Liberals have approached family issues from a different tack. Unlike conservatives, they are more willing to use government social policies to try to help individual families. Some of the proposals they have made to assist families include expanded nutritional and health programs for pregnant women, federal subsidies for daycare services for low-income families, uniform national standards for child care centers, and a requirement that employers give parents unpaid leave to take care of a newborn or seriously ill child—a proposal which was adopted into law in 1993.

Even the meaning of what constitutes a family has been challenged. Up until the mid-1960s, certain largely unquestioned assumptions guided American family law. It was a basic, if generally unstated, premise that the nuclear family had a privileged status and that government could discriminate against nonnuclear families in granting benefits and establishing zoning restrictions. Similarly, it was taken for granted that the father, as "head and master" of his family, automatically gave his children his surname, determined the family's legal residence, was immune from lawsuits instituted by his wife, and was entitled to sexual relations with her. Other underlying legal assumptions were that marriages could only be dissolved on grounds of serious fault, that following a divorce young children were better off with their mothers (unless these women were unfit), and that states had the power to regulate private sexual behavior.

Since the early 1960s, all these assumptions have been questioned, as new notions of privacy rights, sexual equality, and children's rights initiated a revolution in the field of family law. The practical effect of this upheaval in family law has been a gradual erosion in the traditional conception of the nuclear family as a legal entity with its own special rights. For instance, in recent years courts have overturned older legal definitions of what constitutes a family. In cases involving zoning and public welfare, a number of influential court decisions declared that municipal, state, and federal governments cannot define "family" too restrictively, holding that common-law marriages, cohabitation outside of marriage, and large extended households occupying the same living quarters are entitled to protection against hostile regulation. In other cases, the Supreme Court ruled that government cannot discriminate against groups of unrelated individuals living together (for example, in hippie communes) in providing food stamps (while upholding zoning ordinances that limit occupancy of homes to members of families related by blood, marriage, and adoption) and that state legislatures cannot designate one form of the family as the preferred form. Meanwhile, courts and state legislatures have tended to weaken or overturn laws that assigned individual responsibilities on the basis of family membership, including laws that make children legally responsible for the support of indigent parents or statutes that hold parents accountable for crimes committed by their children.

At the same time that definitions of family grew broader and more pluralistic, courts became increasingly willing to intervene in ongoing marriages. Until recently, it was assumed that courts should not interfere in marital decision making except in cases of divorce or separation nor interfere with the parents' discretionary authority over the details of their children's upbringing except in cases involving neglect, abuse, delinquency, or child custody. These assumptions have recently been challenged, as the courts have increasingly stressed the equality of spouses and held that minors have independent rights that can override parental authority.

Invoking the principle that all individuals have rights to privacy, due process, and equal treatment under law, the courts have increasingly emphasized the separateness and autonomy of family members, holding, for example, that husbands cannot legally prevent wives from having an abortion, that a husband's home is not necessarily his wife's domicile, and that under certain circumstances husbands can be prosecuted for spousal rape. In decisions involving children's rights, a number of courts have ruled that parents do not have an absolute veto over whether a minor girl can obtain contraceptives or an abortion (while upholding statutes that require doctors to notify parents before performing an abortion). Two states—Iowa and Utah—now allow children to seek placement outside the parental home in instances in which a serious conflict exists with their parents, even if their parents are not guilty of abuse or neglect.

While judicial involvement in the decision making of ongoing families has increased, the nation's courts and state legislatures have shown a declining interest in enforcing sexual norms. Beginning in 1965, in *Griswold* v. *Connecticut,* the Supreme Court struck down state statutes prohibiting the prescription or distribution of birth control devices and the dissemination of contraceptive information. In *Eisenstadt* v. *Baird,* the high court extended access to contraceptives to unmarried persons. In 1973, in *Roe* v. *Wade,* the Supreme Court decriminalized abortion, and in 1976, in *Planned Parenthood* v. *Danforth,* the high court held that "competent" unmarried minors could decide to have abortions without parental permission. Intense political and legal controversy followed the court decisions striking down restrictive state abortion laws. A number of states, asserting a public interest in how abortions occur, proposed a variety of restrictions on abortion rights, including waiting periods and notification of minors' parents.

Since 1962, when Illinois became the first state to decriminalize all forms of private sexual conduct between consenting adults, twenty states have decriminalized private consensual sexual conduct. Judicial decisions in four other states invalidated statutes making such conduct a crime. Today, two-thirds of the states have repealed statutes prohibiting fornication, adultery, and cohabitation outside of marriage.

By far the most dramatic changes in family law involved divorce. Beginning in California in 1970, no-fault divorce statutes replaced laws that allowed divorce only on grounds of fault in every state. Instead of proving that a spouse was guilty of a serious marital offense, no-fault statutes allowed spouses to obtain divorce by mutual consent or on grounds of incompatibility or "irretrievable breakdown" of the marriage. Proponents of change—primarily lawyers and judges—argued that no-fault divorce would create less adversarial divorce proceedings, reduce perjury and legal charades, and bring the law into line with the social reality of sharply rising divorce rates.

Although advocates of divorce reform described the introduction of no-fault divorce statutes as a technical modification of existing laws rather than as a major legal reform, in fact the new statutes had far-reaching effects on such issues as alimony, child custody, child support, and the division of property. The new no-fault statutes undermined the traditional legal assumption that a wife had a right to lifelong support, to retain the marital dwelling, and to custody of her children. Under the new legislation, certain preferences that had generally worked to the advantage of women (who were often regarded as innocent victims by the courts) were eliminated. Temporary "maintenance" or "spousal support" replaced alimony; the principle of equal or equitable division of property replaced the distribution of property on the basis of fault; and the principle of gender neutrality in custody decisions and, in some cases, a presumption in favor of joint custody, replaced the older presumption in favor of mothers in disputes over young children.

One ironic consequence of the new statutes has been to contribute to an increasing number of poor divorced women and their children. Since most divorces involve families with small amounts of property to divide, child-support awards are often inadequate and compliance with child-support orders is low, and since many women, especially older women, find it difficult to obtain employment, the no-fault statutes—with their emphasis on equitable distribution of property, court-ordered child-support payments, and temporary maintenance to facilitate the entry of spouses into the labor market—have not, in practice, effectively aided many divorced women. In most instances, the household income of divorced women and their children tends to fall sharply after a divorce, while husbands' incomes rise.

The revolution that has occurred in the realm of family law since 1960 can be viewed from two very different perspectives. On the one hand, it is possible to regard this legal revolution in essentially positive terms, as a trend toward extending equality between men and women and parents and children, increasing personal freedom, and greater recognition of a right to privacy. Courts and state legislatures have eliminated certain historic legal preferences given to nuclear families and to fathers, made divorce less adversarial and more accessible, and granted wives and children greater access to courts in family disputes. And yet, at the same time, a disparate group that includes liberal and radical women's organizations and "profamily" conservative groups have viewed these changes from a much more negative perspective, arguing (in quite different ways) that this legal revolution has produced hardship for many women and children, undermined family stability, and intruded on family autonomy in decision making.

Nevertheless, there does appear to be a growing consensus, spanning the ideological spectrum, on the need for a national effort to assure the well-being of children. Among the measures that have been proposed are expanded tax credits for children, "family-friendly" workplaces with more flexible work hours, more rigorously enforced child-support obligations from absent parents, expanded access to high-quality daycare, increased financial support for impoverished single-parent households, and a reconstruction of divorce and child-custody proceedings to ensure that the interests of children are better represented.

Critics in both the public-policy arena and in the general public lack historical perspective when they worry that falling birth rates mean that individuals have grown too self-centered to have children, that increasing numbers of working mothers means that more and more children fail to get sufficient attention to their needs, that soaring rates of unmarried teenage motherhood consign growing numbers of women and their offspring to lives of poverty, unemployment, and dependence, and that high divorce rates and the trend toward delayed marriage spell the impending demise of the family as an institution. Public discussion has been distorted because the stereotypical white, middle-class postwar family was viewed as the baseline, when actually family patterns characteristic of that period were an aberration that obscured long-term trends toward lower birth rates, high divorce rates, delayed marriage—and a liberalization of family roles, restraints imposed on children, and sexual behavior.

Every social barometer indicates that the changes that have taken place in family life over the past three decades—particularly the increase in two-wage-earner and single-parent families—are unlikely to reverse themselves. According to a growing consensus, the challenge facing American society as the twentieth century ends is to provide a supportive environment for families based on current and long-term trends rather than past expectations in order to enhance their capacity to raise children to become healthy adults.

See Also Gender Issues; Class; Social Welfare (all in this volume); Wealth and Poverty (volume III).

BIBLIOGRAPHY

As recently as the mid-1960s, it would not have been possible to discuss the history of twentieth-century American family life based on any accurate data. Since then, the history of American families has attracted enormous attention from demographers, developmental psychologists, historical sociologists, and social historians. A number of historical surveys and overviews have recently appeared that summarize the major historical findings, including Stephanie Coontz, *The Social Origins of Private Life: A History of American Families, 1600–1900* (London: Verso, 1988), and *The Way We Never Were* (1993); Carl N. Degler, *At Odds: Women and the Family in America from the Revolution to the Present* (1980); Joseph M. Hawes and Elizabeth I. Nybakken, *American Families: A Research Guide and Historical Handbook* (1991); and Steven Mintz and Susan Kellogg, *Domestic Revolutions: A Social History of American Family Life* (1988).

Twentieth-century American families have only recently attracted intensive scholarly examination. On turn-of-the-century families, see Elaine Tyler May, *Great Expectations: Marriage and Divorce in Post-Victorian America* (1980). The impact of the Great Depression is assessed in Lois Scharf, *To Work and To Wed: Female Employment, Feminism, and the Great Depression* (1980); and Susan Ware, *Holding Their Own: American Women in the 1930s* (1982). On the impact of World War II, see Karen Anderson, *Wartime Women: Sex Roles, Family Relations, and the Status of Women during World War II* (1981); D'Ann Campbell, *Women at War with America: Private Lives in a Patriotic Era* (1984); and Susan M. Hartmann, *The Homefront and Beyond: American Women in the 1940s* (1982). Families of the 1950s are discussed in Andrew J. Cherlin, *Marriage, Divorce, Remarriage* (1981); and Elaine Tyler May, *Homeward Bound: American Families in the Cold War Era* (1988).

The dramatic upheavals that have occurred in American family life since 1960 are analyzed in Mary Jo Bane, *Here to Stay: American Families in the Twentieth Century* (1978); Andrew J. Cherlin, ed., *The Changing American Family and Public Policy* (1988); Sar A. Levitan et al., *What's Happening to the American Family? Tensions, Hopes, Realities* (1988); David Popenoe, *Disturbing the Nest: Family Change and Decline in Modern Societies* (1985); and Arlene Skolnick, *Embattled Paradise: The American Family in an Age of Uncertainty* (1991).

Valuable specialized studies that address the impact of changing patterns of sexuality upon the family are John D'Emilio and Estelle B. Freedman, *Intimate Matters: A History of Sexuality in America* (1988); and David M. Kennedy, *Birth Control in America: The Career of Margaret Sanger* (1970). On domestic violence, see Linda Gordon, *Heroes of Their Own Lives: The Politics and History of Family Violence* (1988); and Elizabeth Pleck, *Domestic Tyranny: The Making of American Social Policy against Family Violence* (1987). On divorce, see Frank F. Furstenberg, Jr. and Andrew J. Cherlin, *Divided Families* (1991); and Glenda Riley, *Divorce: An American Tradition* (1991). On teenage pregnancy, see Maris Vinovskis, *An "Epidemic" of Adolescent Pregnancy?* (1988).

A number of recent studies examine American families' changing demographic characteristics. These include Steven Ruggles, *Prolonged Connections: The Rise of the Extended Family in Nineteenth-century England and America* (1987); Rudy Ray Seward, *The American Family: A Demographic History* (1978); James A. Sweet and Larry L. Bumpass, *American Families and Households* (1987); Robert V. Wells, *Revolutions in Americans' Lives: A Demographic Perspective on the History of Americans, Their Families, and Their Society* (1982), and *Uncle Sam's Family: Issues in and Perspectives on American Demographic History* (1985).

Changes in the definition and timing of the life stages and major life-cycle transitions are described and analyzed in Howard P. Chudacoff, *How Old Are You? Age Consciousness in American Culture* (1989); John Demos, *Past, Present, and Personal: The Family and the Life Course in American History* (1986); and Tamara K. Hareven, ed., *Transitions: The Family and the Life Course in Historical Perspective* (1978).

On changes in the experience of childhood, see Harvey J. Graff, ed., *Growing Up in America: Historical Experiences* (1987); Joseph M. Hawes and N. Ray Hiner, *American Childhood: A Research Guide and Historical Handbook* (1985); N. Ray Hiner and Joseph M. Hawes, eds., *Growing Up in America: Children in Historical Perspective* (1985); and Vivian A. Zelizer, *Pricing the Priceless Child: The Changing Social Value of Children* (1987). On changes in adolescence and young adulthood, see Paula S. Fass, *The Damned and the Beautiful: American Youth in the 1920's* (1977); William Graebner, *Coming of Age in Buffalo: Youth and Authority in the Postwar Era* (1989); Joseph F. Kett, *Rites of Passage: Adolescence in America, 1790 to the Present* (1977); and John Modell, *Into One's Own: From Youth to Adulthood in the United States, 1920–1975* (1989). On old age, see Andrew W. Achenbaum, *Old Age in the New Land: The American Experience Since 1790* (1978), and *Shades of Gray: Old Age, American Values, and Federal Policies since 1920* (1983); David Hackett Fischer, *Growing Old in America* (1977); Carole Haber, *Beyond Sixty-Five: The Dilemma of Old Age in America's Past* (1983); and Tamara K. Hareven and Kathleen J. Adams, eds., *Aging and Life Course Transitions: An Interdisciplinary Perspective* (1982).

The literature on ethnic and class differences in family experience is vast. On ethnic, working-class, and immigrant family life, see John Bodnar, *Immigration and Industrialization: Ethnicity in an American Mill Town, 1870–1940* (1977), *The Transplanted: A History of Immigrants in Urban America* (1987), and *Workers' World: Kinship, Community, and Protest in an Industrial Society, 1900–1940* (1982); John Bodnar et al., *Lives of Their Own: Blacks, Italians, and Poles in Pittsburgh, 1900–1960* (1981); Richard G. Del Castillo, *Familia: Chicano Families in the Urban Southwest, 1848 to the Present* (1984); Richard Erlich, ed., *Immigrants in Industrial America, 1850–1920* (1977); Tamara K. Hareven, ed., *Family and Kin in Urban Communities, 1700–1930* (1977), and *Family Time and Industrial Time: The Relationship between Family and Work in a New England Industrial Community* (1982); Theodore Hershberg, ed., *Philadelphia: Work, Space, Family, and Group Experience in the Nineteenth Century* (1981); Judith Smith, *Family Connections: A History of Italian and Jewish Immigrant Lives in Providence, Rhode Island, 1900–1940* (1977); and Virginia Hans-McLaughlin, *Family and Community: Italian Immigrants in Buffalo* (1977).

On African American families, see Andrew Hacker, *Two Nations: Black & White, Separate, Hostile, and Unequal* (1992); Christopher Jencks, *Rethinking Social Policy: Race, Poverty, and the Underclass* (1992); Christopher Jencks and Paul E. Peterson, eds., *The Urban Underclass* (1991); Kenneth L. Kusmer, *A Ghetto Takes Shape: Black Cleveland, 1870–1930* (1976); Charles Murray, *Losing Ground: American Social Policy, 1950–1980* (1984); Lee Rainwater and William L. Yancey, *The Moynihan Report and the Politics of Controversy* (1967); Carol Stack, *All Our Kin: Strategies for Survival in a Black Community* (1974); and William Julius Wilson, *The Truly Disadvantaged: The Inner City, the Underclass, and Public Policy* (1987).

Part 2

POLITICS

INTRODUCTION

Robert Dallek

In a best-selling book, the *Washington Post* journalist E. J. Dionne told us *Why Americans Hate Politics.* Hating politics is an unfortunate and possibly even dangerous development in the life of the nation. For in America, our constitutional democracy has put politics—the art of the possible or pragmatic arrangements to accommodate the enormous variety of competing groups and influences—at the center of the nation's well-being. The system has worked reasonably well for over two hundred years. But it may be that the country occasionally needs reminding of why and how the American style of politics has been a largely constructive influence.

The articles in this part of the Encyclopedia do just that. This is not to suggest that they are a patriotic celebration of the American system of politics. To the contrary, they are analytical, scrupulously objective, essays that dissect the country's political ideologies, its parties and interest groups, its governmental practices at the federal, state, and local levels, and its bureaucratic and social welfare systems.

Stuart McConnell's essay depicts American nationalism as characterized by three influences. First, unlike Europeans in the twentieth century, Americans did not identify the nation with specific cultural characteristics or the product of "organic groupings with deep roots in shared language, race, and history" or exclusively with the state, as was the case in Fascist Italy and Nazi Germany. Rather Americans traditionally identified America with the universalist principles of egalitarianism and democracy, describing the nation as exceptional or a country apart from other countries. In the last decades of the century the American sense of nationality has been eroded by an emphasis on discrete groups—be they women, blacks, Catholics, southerners, or almost any other specifically defined identity—which includes little concern for a shared sense of nationality by all the groups. McConnell's essay is a richly conceived analysis of how the varieties of American national identity have evolved during the century. No one reading this article will doubt that the subject of American nationality is as complicated and intriguing a part of American history as anything in the nation's past.

James Kloppenberg's discussion of political ideas and movements complements McConnell. It is through our political ideas, Kloppenberg asserts, that citizens "reformulate their conceptions of what America is and what Americans ought to do." His essay is, first, an argument for taking political ideas seriously. The suspicion that behind every politicians' rhetoric is nothing more than calculated personal advantage is an expression of the belief that "political discourse is a charade." Kloppenberg believes otherwise; he makes a most compelling case for the continuing importance of political ideas in American life. Second, he urges that we abandon liberalism and communitarianism as the categories through which we can best comprehend twentieth-century American politics. If we are to understand the complexities of political debate in the United States, we need to return to earlier ways in which Americans thought about the country's political life—specifically, as a contest between freedom and community or between individualism and larger social commitments.

Graham Wilson's discussion of parties and interest groups is a demonstration of what Kloppenberg is getting at. But Wilson's essay is more than that; it is also a description of how the political parties and various special interests have developed and changed over the last hundred years. Further, it is an explanation of how America pioneered and succeeded at the conduct of mass politics. Those who doubt the viability of the American political system will find considerable comfort in what Wilson has to say.

The next five articles—Bert Rockman on the presidency, Joel Aberbach on Congress, Mary Dudziak on the courts, Michal Belknap on the Constitution, and Harry Scheiber on federalism and the states—contribute to the huge literature on all five subjects. They provide overviews of where each of these institutions have been during the last hundred years, how they evolved, and where they may be going in the immediate future.

Rockman sees the presidency as a distinctly limited office constrained by a variety of other institutions and influences. The idea that the chief executive is somehow much more powerful than he was a hundred years ago is, in Rockman's estimate, a grand illusion. Indeed, as he puts it, "The history of the American presidency in the twentieth century . . . is a history of the growth of the illusion of our president's power." Rockman brings considerable evidence to bear to support his unconventional conclusion. As for Congress, Aberbach sees it as an institution characterized by fits and starts. Its power and influence in the twentieth century have expanded and contracted with changes in the times and the people who served in the two houses. Most of all, Aberbach sees the Congress as a reflector of the country's strengths and weaknesses and a major force, through its deliberations and decisions, on the life of the nation. As for the future, he anticipates more of the same. "The resurgence of Congress in the latter third of the twentieth century," he says, "demonstrates that Congress should never be counted out. It may cede influence at times, and it may often appear rudderless, but the American system of separate institutions sharing powers gives it both the means and the incentive to fight back."

Mary L. Dudziak and Michal Belknap have contributed probing essays on the legal and constitutional history of the twentieth century. Dudziak focuses on the courts and the unique role in the American system, one that steadily enlarged as the twentieth century witnessed judicial attempts to regulate the boundaries of the legislatively established regulatory state. Dudziak's tracings of judicial history focus on both doctrinal issues and the political struggles over judicial nominees. Her last section affords a glimpse into the everyday life of courts, the kind that Americans of the late twentieth century were exposed to with regularity, if not insight.

Michal Belknap's article surveys the ever-evolving Constitution. He examines the growth of governmental power at the beginning of the century, the steady accumulation of presidential power through wars and depression, and the expansion of national power as the twentieth-century nation-state replaced the more fragmented constitutional arrangements of earlier periods. Finally, Belknap explores the contentious issues of civil rights and civil liberties, and how struggles involving them have mirrored conflicts in the political and social arenas of American life.

Harry Scheiber sees a similar development for the American federal system. He describes the many far-reaching changes that have affected the states during the century, but he also emphasizes the extent to which state governments have survived as centers of significant power. Scheiber believes that this situation reflects the extent to which the public sees "special value in the decentralization of decision-making authority in government." The strength of Scheiber's article lies in its succinct description of the changes and continuities in federalism during the century. His article also shows convincingly that government and politics in America are ever-evolving institutions with deep roots that sustain national and local stability.

The last three articles—on the cities and the suburbs, the social welfare system, and bureaucracy or "the bureaucratic state"—underscore some of the greatest difficulties the country struggles with in its national political life. Jon Teaford compresses a vast amount of material about the transformation of America's cities and the rise of its suburbs into a brief but comprehensive account. Here is a succinct overview of how the cities and their outlying regions were transformed and how they changed into something that cannot be described as either city or suburb. "At the end of the twentieth century," Teaford says, "the United States had moved beyond city and suburb to a new form of settlement that was not exactly either."

Edward Berkowitz describes the great changes that transformed America's twentieth-century welfare system from a set of heterogeneous local and private company practices to a national public-insurance system. The rise of social welfare experts in the employ of local, state, and national governments ensured not only an economic safety net for the least affluent members of the society but also the growth of a welfare bureaucracy that has become the target of widespread antagonism from middle class taxpayers unsympathetic to the country's dependent poor. More specifically, Berkowitz shows how welfare changed from a system chiefly designed to aid the elderly to one designed to aid families with dependent children. His essay is a splendid synthesis of a controversial and complex subject that has generated more stereotypes and clichés than almost any other public issue in twentieth-century America.

The expanding role of foundations has been a significant, yet overlooked, aspect of twentieth-century public policy. Indeed, we tend to think of governmental interventionism as the exclusive means for dealing with public needs. But as far back as the early nineteenth century, Tocqueville noted the American practice of forming associations to deal with common, public problems. Before World War II, as Barry Karl demonstrates in his essay on foundations and public policy, private foundations acted in the virtual absence or limited role of federal expenditures in such fields as health, education, welfare, and science. By mid-century, foundations continued to seed new social programs, but their limited resources made a governmental role in ongoing responsibility and activity inevitable. By the 1990s, as the nation seriously debated the proper scope and wisdom of government intervention, the private foundation was resurrected as an alternative, though the burgeoning scale of public problems left in uncertain whether private groups would be able to provide the necessary resources.

Herman Belz's article on the bureaucratic state is a logical sequel to Berkowitz's discussion of welfare. As Belz clearly demonstrates, while the formal arrangements of American government have changed little over the centuries, "the nature, scope and purpose of government in the United States have changed profoundly." And the greatest alteration has been the rise of the administrative or bureaucratic state. Why and how this has come to pass is the burden of Belz's analysis. He describes four phases to the process: national economic regulation instituted between 1887 and 1920; the rise of bureaucratic governance in the years 1920 to 1960; the democratization of the system and the introduction of new social regulation between 1960 and 1980; and the conservative attempt at bureaucratic reform since 1980. The causes and results of these changes form the heart of Belz's important discussion of one of the most significant developments in twentieth-century American political life.

NATIONALISM

Stuart McConnell

Among the most striking features of the American scene is a recurring invocation of *the nation,* coupled with significant confusion as to the concrete meaning of the term. State actions are said to be in "the national interest." Economic proposals will help "the national economy." Large public expenditures will provide for "national defense." Yet when we ask what sort of nation this is, we typically meet with blank stares. Few Americans would equate the nation with the state—it is not the "state economy" or "state defense" they wish to fund or fight for. Nor is American *nationalism* usually defined in explicitly cultural terms, periodic outbreaks of nativism notwithstanding. If the American nation is not simply state power or cultural baggage, what is it?

Americans' general lack of interest in the study of nationalism stands in marked contrast to the vogue of the subject in Europe, where it intensified in the late 1980s with the reemergence of the national question in Eastern Europe. There are at least three reasons for this disparity. In the first place, the movement that brought the United States into being, unlike most European movements of the eighteenth and nineteenth centuries, did not invoke nationalist arguments but rather the universal principles of egalitarianism and democracy. In principle, if not in practice, *American* was from the first a voluntary identity rather than something pegged to specific cultural characteristics. Thus, despite a history of racial exclusion that has been at least as central to the development of the United States as the concept of democracy, Americans have rarely framed their nationalism in racial or ethnic terms. Instead, academic specialist and advertising copywriter alike have been prone to stress "American institutions," or, more ethereally, "the American Dream."

Second, the political events of the twentieth century have forced Europeans to think more intensely about what nations actually are. It took the carnage of two world wars fought among nation-states, both involving a Germany openly committed to a romantic ideal of nationality, to debunk the romantic idea that nations are natural, organic groupings with deep roots in shared language, race, and history. Since then, and particularly since the appearance of nationalist movements in non-Western countries in the 1950s and 1960s, writers on nationalism have worked to attribute the phenomenon to something other than innate cultural characteristics. By contrast, scholars of the United States have tended to accept as natural such exceptionalist categories as American history or American literature without much thought (though sometimes the process is more conscious, as with the post–World War II construction of American Studies as a separate field).

Third, American historians of the last two decades or so have been more interested in studying discrete groups within American society than in examining the United States as a whole. From this perspective, such broad concepts as the nation can only be mystifications—tools used by one group against another. If, as Karl Marx wrote, "the workers have no country," the presumption of much recent scholarship seems to be that southerners, women, ethnic minorities, local politicians, Catholics, and a host of other groups have no country either, or at least no country in common.

Yet if the nation is only a mystification, it is a remarkably widespread one. It provides the basis of the modern political map; it justifies unprecedented expenditures on weapons; in many parts of the world, it represents the most powerful roadblock to a worldwide economic system that long ago ceased troubling itself about national boundaries. We neglect it at our peril. And in many nation-states, including the United States, an unexamined or vaguely defined nationalism can lead to something far worse: the identification of the nation with the state, to the exclusion of all else.

THEORIES OF NATIONALISM

Because nationalism is a notoriously plastic concept, some caveats and definitions are essential. First, nationalism must be separated from another loyalty with which it is often confounded in everyday speech, namely *patriotism*. Patriotism is itself troublesome to define, since it is employed popularly in two quite disparate ways. On the one hand, its literal meaning—the love of one's ancestral soil—describes the affection people feel for a particular place or group, an almost primitive attachment that requires neither a modern state nor a developed capitalist economy. Many early writers on nationalism, such as Carlton Hayes, Hans Kohn, and Elie Kedourie, distinguished a presumably ancient patriotism from modern nationalism in exactly these terms. On the other hand, Frank De Roose points out that patriotism more commonly denotes loyalty to a political community, not a locality or a kin group. An American exhibits patriotism by expressing loyalty to the political institutions set forth in the Constitution, to the federal system, to the principles of democracy, and so forth. Patriotism is not loyalty to the state as such, for as De Roose notes, it is possible to use patriotic rhetoric of this sort against particular actions of the state (arguing as did opponents of the Nixon administration that the bombing of Cambodia was unconstitutional, for example). But it is something more than sentimental localism.

Nationalism is loyalty to neither land nor political community, though historically it has attached itself to both. In fact, the chief task of the nationalist propagandist from the late eighteenth century onward was to conflate the fundamental loyalties of family and kin, on the one hand, and political institutions on the other, with the nation. But the loyalties of the nationalist attach to different objects than do those of the patriot. In pure form, nationalism has only two characteristics: (1) the identification of a particular group as a nation, and (2) the demand that the group have either a state of its own, or a sphere of autonomy within a state controlled by others. Some writers have been reluctant to generalize much beyond this basic definition because the experience of nationalism has varied so much from era to era and place to place. Yet at least three other features of nationalism seem so widespread that they should be added to this basic definition. First, in more cases than not, nations insist on linguistic and/or cultural homogeneity (though sometimes a homogeneity that is artificially manufactured, as in many newly independent former colonies, or in early modern France as described by Eugen Weber). Second, in almost every case, nations insist on their own boundedness (national citizens are not allowed dual loyalties to other nations) and predominance (national citizens are expected to subordinate whatever other loyalties they may have to their national loyalties). Third, in Europe at least, and probably in the rest of the world as well, the rise of nationalism has accompanied industrialization and the rise of capitalism.

It is the historical relation of nationalism to industrial capitalism that is the main point of contention among writers on the subject, and the most important to explicate for the American case. Early theory, best exemplified by the work of Hayes and Kedourie, held that nationalism originated in the thought of the Enlightenment, took political form in the French and American revolutions, and was subsequently spread over the globe by colonization and Western intellectual tutelage. Nationalism was thus an intellectual phenomenon with no necessary relation to capitalism. Under this reading, the only thing distinctive about the ideology of early American nationalism was the weakness of monarchical resistance to it.

More recent scholarship attributes nationalism to the worldwide rise of industrial capitalism, though there is little consensus on the nature of the linkage. From the functionalist side, Ernest Gellner argues that nationalism is the inevitable result of industrial society's need for a labor pool that is flexible, mobile, and literate—all attributes that are best produced by monolingual educational systems under the protection of states. Scholars in the Marxist tradition, by contrast, see nations as covers for class interests: some, such as Eric Hobsbawm, believe that nationalism served only to legitimate the rising bourgeoisie of the early modern period, while others, such as James Blaut, contend that nationalism has been bourgeois in some times and places but proletarian in others. Roman Szporluk maintains that nationalism predated industrialism, and, rather than being formed by industrial change, was one of the two major interpretive frameworks (Marxism being the other) through which people understood that change. John Breuilly stresses the prior emergence of the state, arguing that nations originated as cultural bridging mechanisms, aimed at reconciling the newly separate public (state) and private (market, family, religious) spheres. Benedict Anderson suggests that the "imagined communities" of nationalism arose as substitutes for traditional religion and as ways of consolidating the large vernacular markets required by print capitalism. And Daniel Segal disputes the notion that nationalism originated on the continent of Europe, declaring that the construction of American and European identities must be traced to the racial hierarchies of Europe's colonial empires.

Although these writers disagree on many points,

it seems clear that nationalism originated neither as the awakening of a dormant group consciousness nor as a mystification perpetrated by intellectuals. Rather, it was the social and cultural expression of a new economic system's need for mobile and interchangeable labor. It was also one of several ways—as it has turned out, the chief way, with Marxism being equally important for much of the nineteenth and twentieth centuries—in which that labor explained the new state of affairs to itself, a process greatly facilitated by the new vernacular culture of print. By the mid-nineteenth century, nationalism was the dominant language of political argument and the new basis of legitimacy in state after state. Above all, the nation came to represent an identity that superseded or absorbed important alternative loyalties—locality, class, race, ethnicity, religion. Tied to the educational and training apparatus that now held the key to material well-being, buttressed by the armed might of the state, it became a difficult identity to resist.

From this perspective, American nationalism might be viewed as an unremarkable case study in a fairly uniform international process of capitalist industrialization. In fact, however, the expansion of capitalism was a wildly uneven process, and the nationalist movements that arose in conjunction with it have varied a great deal. What in one place and time (revolutionary France, for example) was a coherent bourgeois ideology with an explicit program appeared elsewhere as a confused amalgam of ethnicity and class (the Soviet Union of 1917–1920), a residue of colonial administration (post–World War II India), or revolutionary resistance to colonialism (post–World War II Vietnam). Moreover, nationalism in one place was often constructed with reference to nationalism in some other place—the Jacobin revolution of slaves in Haiti, for example, caused revolutionaries in Paris to reconsider what they meant by "French." Thus while virtually all modern nations have the general characteristics set forth above—possession of or demand for state sovereignty, homogeneity (usually cultural or linguistic), boundedness, functional relation to industrial capitalism—each nation also combines them in historically contingent and unpredictable ways. Each nation is a case unto itself.

For the United States, one must consider that the elements driving the development of nationalism in Europe—the modern state, expanding capitalism, print culture—were all in place in America long before 1776. While these global factors may be enough to explain the colonists' British nationalism (their fealty to Magna Carta, the Empire, and the English language, for example), they cannot explain the colonists' growing sense of themselves as distinct, as "Americans." For the origins of that sense, we must look elsewhere—perhaps to the unique system of racial classification stressed by Segal, colonial political institutions, the economy of slavery. Whatever its origins, American nationalism was undoubtedly multiple—that is, it looked different depending on such things as one's class position and place of residence—and changing throughout the nineteenth century, and remained so even after the advent of self-conscious nationalist groups in the 1890s.

This essay, then, proceeds from two assumptions. First, while the United States was subject to the same forces that helped create nation-states elsewhere in the world—state centralization, industrialization, mass politics—American nationalism, like nationalism elsewhere, was the product of a unique chain of historical contingencies and ought to be considered in that light. Second, American nationalism was neither timeless nor unitary, but changing and subject to multiple readings. Rather than taking in the whole sweep of United States history in an effort to identify that which is "typically American," one ought to examine the ways in which different groups have used terms like *American* and such symbols as the national flag, with particular attention to those groups that self-consciously identify themselves as nationalists. For these purposes, the years around the turn of the century, which saw the birth of many enduring nationalist groups and symbols, are a logical starting point.

IMAGINING THE NATION

To appreciate the changes that began in the 1890s, it is worth remembering that for most of the nineteenth century the United States was a nation of localities. Regiments for the Civil War had been locally raised and locally officered; historical societies remained local or statewide in scope; economic and social life was dominated by the sorts of local luminaries whose autobiographical sketches fill the hefty pages of many a civic history. Locally significant events, such as the transfer of Connecticut regimental flags from the Arsenal to the State Capitol (1879) or the fiftieth anniversary of the Mormons' arrival at the Great Salt Lake (1897), were celebrated with great gusto.

The institutions and symbols of nationalism were correspondingly weak. The national state intruded upon local life chiefly through the post office and quadrennial presidential campaigns (although the latter were organized largely at the state level). Whereas a large city such as New York might have as many as a dozen daily newspapers, national mass media were nonexistent. Colleges did not usually offer courses in specifically American history, and as late as 1889 most schoolhouses did not fly flags or offer any sort of patriotic instruction. There was no national anthem; the closest approximation, a song known as "The Star-Spangled Banner," was sufficiently obscure that when a patriotic group requested it at an 1898 flag-raising at Columbia University, the university's president, Seth Low, replied that he was not sure the student band knew the tune.

All of this began to change during the 1890s. In public education, students engaged in military drill, while patriotic bodies such as the Grand Army of the Republic, a Union Army veterans' group, vied with each other to censor textbooks and encourage the teaching of American history. National hereditary associations, including the Sons of the American Revolution (1889) and the Daughters of the American Revolution (1890), were founded and took on projects such as the renovation of Mount Vernon and the preservation of Independence Hall. The Pledge of Allegiance to the American flag was created, Flag Day was invented and recognized by law in a number of states, a campaign was launched to make "The Star-Spangled Banner" the national anthem, and, between 1897 and 1905, the new American Flag Association helped pass laws in twenty-nine states barring desecration of the flag. By 1898, more than 35,000 schoolrooms posted the flag, the Declaration of Independence, or both; the Pledge of Allegiance was administered regularly in more than 26,000 of them.

What caused the nationalistic onslaught that began in the last decade of the nineteenth century? Clearly it was not the rise of a powerful national state. None of these campaigns originated from official quarters, and the state apparatus itself remained almost absurdly small (about 130,000 people staffed it in 1883, most of them in the postal service or in federal customs houses). Nor was the nationalism of the 1890s the product of an overtly nationalist political party, as it sometimes was in Europe. Instead, it was a cultural reaction among native-born, middle-class white people to three important developments of the decade: massive immigration, continued industrial unrest, and an overseas war.

More than 4.8 million immigrants arrived in the United States during the 1880s. Not only was this an unprecedented number, but these new immigrants, as they have been styled, were increasingly from southern and eastern Europe. Before the Civil War, the ratio of northern and western European immigrants to southern and eastern European immigrants had been about 500:1. Between 1890 and 1894 it was only 2:1, and by 1910 to 1914, it would be less than 1:4. Few of the new arrivals spoke English and most of them were Catholics or Jews. The number of Catholics in the United States had reached 6,259,000 by 1880; that number would more than triple by 1920. The number of Jews skyrocketed from 250,000 in 1880 to 2 million in 1910.

The differences of language, religion, and culture between the new immigrants and the predominantly English-speaking, Protestant native-born whites led some members of the latter group to think seriously for the first time since the 1850s about what being American entailed. One result was the rise of nativism. Groups such as the American Protective Association (1887) worked to defend the state against "foreign" influences. The first bills demanding a literacy test for immigrants were introduced in 1896, and the head tax on immigrant entry was raised substantially. In the realm of culture, Social Darwinism and quasi-scientific racism became fashionable, with books such as the Rev. Josiah Strong's *Our Country* (1885) purporting to show that the newcomers were actually interlopers on a nation that in its heart was "Anglo-Saxon." President-to-be Theodore Roosevelt warned of "race suicide" if native-born Americans failed to outbreed the immigrants.

The picture of the nation that these nativists drew was that of an extended kinship group. "American" was to be defined not simply by allegiance to political institutions, or even by language (though there was an increased stress on the teaching of both in the public schools). Instead, it was a racial or a blood tie, the possession of those already in the United States and theirs to preserve or modify. This possessory interest was clearest in the hereditary societies, which made the kinship tie literal—true Americans were those descended from American Revolutionaries. But it was also visible in the host of monuments, centennials, preservation efforts, and commemorative activities that swept the middle classes. Michael Kammen has even gone so far as to argue that the late nineteenth century was the era in which the United States first "acquired a memory."

The second factor feeding the new nationalist frenzy was industrial unrest, which peaked in the depression years of 1893 to 1897. For half a century, industrialization had been opening a wide class gulf in the cities between the prosperous middle classes and workers in the new mass industries, a gulf made wider by ethnocultural tensions. When violent strikes shook Carnegie Steel's Homestead works in

1892 and the Pullman Palace Car Company in 1894, many feared an insurrection. A long-established ideology of sameness, predicated on the equality of independent freehold farmers, had always defused such situations before, but it no longer could explain away the manifest inequalities of power and wealth appearing in the cities. Instead, an ideology of sameness that was predicated on the equality of "Americans" offered a new kind of resolution: loyalty to the nation would supersede social class. The patriotic author of *The Volcano under the City* (1887), for example, called workingmen "the community's real bulwark against disorder," while an 1892 editorial in the *National Tribune,* a newspaper aimed at military veterans, lauded the National Guard—then engaged in smashing the Homestead strike—as "the agent of the whole people, organized to carry out the will of the people by insuring obedience to the law." When the Essex Institute of Salem, Massachusetts, opened its new historical museum in 1907, a local newspaper commented approvingly that its displays would inspire workers with "respect for American ideals and American institutions" lest they "swell the columns of socialism, militant laborism, and other worse isms."

Although this brand of nationalism was often linked with nativism, it did not require the blood ties that obsessed the nativists. Instead, it typically emphasized English-language training, acceptance of American institutions, and the liberal idea of individual advancement rather than group solidarity—ideas popularly expressed in the pluck-and-luck novels of Horatio Alger. By recasting the residents of the United States as English-speaking, individual "nationals," standing above more parochial cultural ties, such an ideology functioned in much the same way as Gellner suggests other nationalist ideologies did during industrialization: by creating a mobile, interchangeable, monolingual work force. This homogeneous vision would be invoked repeatedly to defuse class conflict in the United States in the twentieth century.

The third great spur to nationalism at the turn of the century was the United States' short war with Spain in 1898. Here the crucial factor in the construction of national identity was not class, but race. American troops in Cuba were surprised at the blackness of their allies, and in Washington official justifications of the war tended to stress the backwardness of the peoples to be liberated. President William McKinley, for example, said in a speech to Methodist clergymen that it was the duty of Americans "to educate the Filipinos, and uplift and civilize and Christianize them," while Sen. Albert Beveridge told Congress that God "has made us adepts in government that we may administer government among savage and senile peoples." The American flag, Grand Army of the Republic chaplain Frank C. Bruner told an audience of veterans in 1898, would "make the nations who have been blackened by superstition and darkness, brighter and more beautiful."

What made Americans alike, in this jingoist vision of national sameness, was that they were "civilized." In Segal's terms, hierarchy was externalized—Americans could consider themselves equals of one another because they were "civilized" relative to their Spanish enemies, and also, as it turned out, relative to the people of the United States' newly acquired colonies. While not exactly a code word for "race," "civilization" came to connote a hierarchical system of cultural classification in which what the jingoists called "the darker peoples" were inevitably placed at the bottom. At the World's Columbian Exposition at Chicago in 1893, for example, black Dahomeyans recently subdued by the French were put on display as "primitives." Similarly, scholarly studies of African and South Pacific peoples were mostly exercises in quasi-biological classification.

Internally, the emphasis on a crusading white civilization helped to heal the divisions between white northerners and white southerners, though it did so largely at the expense of African Americans. During the fighting in Cuba and the Philippines, newspapers in both sections fondly recounted the enthusiasm of former Confederates for Old Glory and proclaimed the sectional divide a thing of the past. While more than 10,000 black soldiers served in the war, they did so under white officers and in segregated units. In the Philippines, where a vicious struggle between United States troops and dark-skinned Filipino guerrillas continued long after the Spanish surrender, African American troops came to question the whole notion of a war for "civilization." Meanwhile, the 1890s saw a rash of lynchings directed at blacks, as well as the creation of the Jim Crow system of legalized segregation across the South. The process reached its logical conclusion in 1913, when Woodrow Wilson, a southerner elected with northern votes, segregated the federal civil service.

In the years around the turn of the century, then, immigration, industrialization, and empire combined to make white, middle-class Americans imagine the nation in ways that would resonate for the rest of that century and into the next. Some defined American nationalism in ethnic terms, against newcomers with different cultural or linguistic backgrounds; some in economic terms, against proponents of alternatives to capitalism, or against those who resisted the continued integration of the national economy; some in imperial terms, against the "lesser" races of the world. Different people combined these definitions in different ways; the point is that by 1910 more Americans were posing questions in national terms that previously had been ignored or treated as local matters.

FEDERAL MACHINERY AND WAR MACHINERY

Nowhere was the new national outlook more apparent than in the quintessential middle-class reform impulse of the early twentieth century, progressivism. While notoriously diffuse (and never a really coherent movement such as abolitionism or populism), progressivism was nonetheless a new way of thinking about social problems that was fundamentally national and systematic. In politics, Progressives tended to frame their solutions—such as the Federal Trade Act (1914) and the so-called Progressive Amendments to the Constitution (sixteenth to nineteenth amendments, 1913–1920)—in national terms. When Lincoln Steffens structured his muckraking *The Shame of the Cities* (1904) as a series of local exposés, it was only to show the pervasiveness of corruption and the need for a nationwide attack on it. "I was not writing about Chicago for Chicago, but for the other cities," he explained, "so I picked out what light each had for the instruction of the others." Even the Progressives' terminology was national: Theodore Roosevelt called his economic program New Nationalism; Herbert Croly, perhaps the most cogent American political theorist of the Progressive years, entitled his influential book of 1909 *The Promise of American Life*.

In the realm of social theory, older conceptions of organic nationalism gave way to a new stress on national organization and efficiency. Whereas late-nineteenth-century thinkers had drawn on Hegel to argue that the American nation was a living organism with an indivisible "national will," Walter Lippmann wrote in *Drift and Mastery* (1914) that the nation was (or rather, should be) a master organization: because there was "no real cohesion for America" in the multitude of ethnic groups now occupying it, it was time to stop being "a nation of villagers" and to create a new unity based on "science." The people of his generation, had "the vast opportunity of introducing order and purpose into the business world, of devising administrative methods by which the great resources of the country can be operated on some thought-out plan." The new metaphor for the nation was not the human body, but rather the machine. This was a philosophy with obvious implications for the role of the national state, a role that would expand dramatically during World War I.

In their racial and ethnic aspects, Progressive concepts of the nation were somewhat less consistent. On the one hand, the vogue for science and system could easily blend with nativism, leading to quasi-scientific attempts to specify "American racial characteristics." In 1906 and 1907, for example, *Munsey's Magazine* ran a series of articles on "leading races" of the United States that included "The Americans in America." The author, Herbert N. Casson, asked: "Is there an American race, with characteristics that are definitely its own; and what individuals, if any, may be fairly said to represent it?" The answer was provided in "definitions of Americanism by eminent race students." Similarly the pioneer Progressive sociologist Edward A. Ross argued in *The Old World in the New* (1914) that Anglo-Saxon Americans needed to keep "sub-normal and low-grade people shut up in their own country." By the 1920s, this sort of thinking would lead to severe immigration restriction, and, at its extremes, to the eugenics movement.

On the other hand, the Progressive vision of society as an organization, a machine that ran because its parts meshed smoothly, could support assimilationism. The same *Munsey's* series that investigated "racial characteristics" concluded that the democratic institutions of the United States would eventually homogenize them. A blunt attempt to speed this process was the graduation ceremony of Henry Ford's "English School" for employees in the 1910s. There, as Werner Sollors describes it, graduates dressed in "foreign costumes" descended into a gigantic representation of a melting pot and emerged dressed in American clothes and waving American flags. More benign were social settlements such as Jane Addams's Hull House in Chicago, where members of the new profession of social work tried to help immigrants cope with American life. No one worked harder to defend immigrant cultures than Addams, who at heart was an internationalist rather than a nationalist. But some of her ventures—such as the Hull House Labor Museum, where immigrant women demonstrated the skills and crafts of their native lands—were really mummifications of these cultures, while the overall settlement project of "adjustment" was an exercise in assimilation.

The outbreak of World War I slowed the flow of immigrants from Europe, but it greatly intensified the discussion of nationalism, especially after the

United States entered the war in 1917. Most obviously, the war accelerated the consolidation of the national state. New agencies such as the Council on National Defense and the War Industries Board managed production and labor, controlled prices, and censored press accounts of the war. Campaigns promoting war bonds and meatless days declared that all Americans were united in a democracy of sacrifice. The Committee on Public Information (CPI) churned out anti-German propaganda.

The activities of the CPI in particular clearly showed a second major change wrought by official wartime nationalism, for in building support for itself the state mercilessly attacked those it perceived as enemies or dissenters. No longer was assimilation assumed to be a natural or gradual process; instead, the government demanded "100-percent-Americanism." In 1915, the Fourth of July was celebrated as Americanization Day under the slogan, "Many Peoples, But One Nation"; in 1918, a CPI-sponsored celebration featured immigrants in native costume performing patriotic exercises. The Sedition Act (1918) provided fines and twenty-year jail terms for those who interfered with the military draft or otherwise "encouraged disloyalty."

More ominously, German Americans were persecuted, and socialists and anarchists were jailed as subversives. Across the country, Germania Halls became Lincoln Halls, sauerkraut became "liberty cabbage," German-language teaching was banned because it inculcated "un-American ideas," and Boston Symphony Orchestra conductor Karl Muck came under suspicion for failing to play "The Star-Spangled Banner" before concerts. The most prominent Socialist, Eugene Debs, went to jail; Emma Goldman, who in 1908 had written *Patriotism: A Menace to Liberty,* was deported in 1919; the leading socialist newspaper, the *Appeal to Reason,* was denied the use of the mails and effectively driven out of business.

After the Armistice in 1918—and after revolution in Russia and major strikes in the United States—the 100-percent-Americanizers turned their full fury on economic radicals. Vigilante veterans attacked socialist newspapers and rallies, states passed laws banning the red flag, and Attorney General A. Mitchell Palmer led a series of raids that resulted in the arrests of more than 6,000 supposed subversives and the deportation of about 500 persons. Although Americanization programs continued to be aimed at assimilating immigrants, they now were couched in the language of antibolshevism.

The brand of nationalism sponsored by the government during the war and espoused widely during the Red Scare years of 1919–1920 demanded deep cultural fusing, not just the surface acquiescence of earlier assimilationists. Multiple or divided loyalties were suspect. As Kansas City Chamber of Commerce president Samuel Wilson put it in an *American City* article of 1918, there were "only two classes of citizens—those who are Americans and those who should be interned." Nor was simple allegiance to American institutions enough; indeed, such institutions were sometimes pictured as impediments to true national unity. A 1919 cartoon in the Philadelphia *Inquirer,* for example, showed a sinister Bolshevik hiding under the Stars and Stripes (and, presumably, constitutional guarantees), while Palmer warned that "free expression of opinion is dangerous to American institutions." Instead, Americanism became intertwined to an unprecedented degree with loyalty to the national state.

The official initiatives of 1917–1919 represented the national state's first deliberate attempt to create a sense of American nationality and to stifle alternatives to it. Reactions to this new state activism reflected both excitement and unease. Progressive intellectuals such as Lippmann hoped that the war would lead to the sort of expert national management they had long championed. Businessmen and conservative trade unionists such as Samuel Gompers saw in the official rhetoric of national harmony the promise of an end to class conflict. Even John Dewey, who would soon come to rethink his position, argued that the war could create "instrumentalities" that would enforce war discipline and curb American individualism. But others feared the rise of a centralized state, and of the mechanisms designed to ensure loyalty to it. "The State is a jealous God, and will brook no rivals," warned Randolph Bourne in "The State" (1919). "Its sovereignty must pervade every one, and all feeling must be run into the stereotyped forms of romantic patriotic militarism which is the traditional expression of the State herd-feeling." Bourne denounced Dewey and other intellectuals for unthinkingly supporting the war.

Although the immediate postwar years were dominated by a repressive 100-percentism, they also saw the development of intellectual resistance to homogeneity. Dewey, for his part, struggled toward a definition of nationalism that did not entail endorsement of the Red Scare hysteria. In "Americanism and Localism," a short piece that appeared in the *Dial* in 1920, Dewey pointed out that the newspapers most shrill in their calls for "Americanization" of immigrants, at the same time "fairly shriek with localism." Most people, he suggested, were "chiefly concerned with what goes on in their tenement house, their alley, their factory, their street," and had little idea of what "American" might mean in trans-local terms. "The only things that seem to be 'nation-wide,'' he concluded, "are the high cost of living, prohibition, and devotion to localisms." American nationalism was experienced chiefly through local and community life; its essence was variety, not some deep cultural unity.

As Merle Curti once observed, Dewey's endorsement of local diversity had been anticipated by the philosopher Josiah Royce, who in *Race Questions, Provincialism, and Other American Problems* (1908) had argued that localism, far from being a hindrance to national loyalty, was its essential building block. It also owed something to William James, whose stress on the multiplicity of experience called into question unitary concepts such as the nation of the 100-percenters (though James's own musings on nationalism, in his 1910 essay *The Moral Equivalent of War,* suggested that unifying loyalties might serve good purposes if turned to nonviolent projects such as road-building and swamp reclamation).

The most notable proponents of diversity between 1914 and 1920, however, saw the key to American national identity not in local variety, but in ethnic pluralism. In a Fourth of July oration of 1915, "True Americanism," Louis Brandeis told his audience that "America has believed that each race had something of peculiar value which it can contribute to the attainment of those high ideals for which we are striving." Similarly Randolph Bourne declared the existence of "Trans-National America" (1916), a "cosmopolitan" place that could justly call itself "the first international nation."

The most developed pluralist position was that of Horace Kallen, who penned the first of his several writings on nationalism, "Democracy Versus the Melting Pot," in 1915. Kallen argued that the United States was best understood as a federation of ethnic groups. "Democracy," he wrote in *Culture and Democracy in the United States* (1916), "involves not the elimination of differences but the perfection and conservation of differences." Like Dewey and Bourne, Kallen was reacting to the wartime calls for national homogeneity. But, as John Higham points out, Kallen's notion of a pluralistic national identity also sprang from his own struggle, as a son of Jewish immigrants, to define his relation to America. He was interested at least as much in preserving a distinct Jewish identity as in redefining American national identity. Thus, as Philip Gleason notes, in spite of his pluralistic outlook Kallen remained committed to a form of racialism: different cultures needed to be maintained in order to preserve the romantic "racial" characteristics of each. Moreover, Kallen's vision of pluralism was limited to the realm of culture; he was perfectly willing to concede the necessity of a national state and national political institutions. In politics, at least, a sort of supernational identity remained in the form of overarching American institutions—a view not too dissimilar from the more benign assimilationism of the prewar period.

In sum, prewar conceptions of American nationalism—conceptions that grew out of the nativism, industrialism, and imperialism of the 1890s—played through the war and Red Scare years in complicated ways. One could find the ethnocultural concept of nationality employed by 100-percenters who insisted on a "pure" Americanism, but also by pluralists such as Kallen and Brandeis, who thought of each ethnic group as unique and valuable. The rapid centralization of the state could imply national integration of the sort favored by Lippmann, or it could mean only a set of national political institutions, underneath which the localism admired by Dewey would continue to flourish. Even "civilization," the stock in trade of Americanizers and war propagandists, turned up occasionally in the rhetoric of the pluralists. (Bourne, for example, spoke of the "forward-looking drive of a colonial empire" as an admirable American trait, and maintained that it was still proper to rank nations on the basis of their cultural achievements: "Let us speak, not of inferior races, but of inferior civilizations.") The most important developments of the war years, however, were the entry of the national state into the business of Americanization, and the resistance to this development on the part of some Americans, who began to develop a pluralist conception of American national identity.

THE VARIETIES OF NATIONALIST EXPERIENCE

If one looked only at the middle-class whites who dominated public debate from the Progressive years through the 1920s, one might conclude that American nationalism developed in the early twentieth century in relatively smooth tandem with the centralization of the state, the main disagreement being between pluralists and assimilationists. But the language of Americanism was used by other groups as well, and in markedly different ways. In the first quarter of the twentieth century, important countertraditions were current among African Americans, immigrants, and industrial workers. Members of these groups interpreted American nationalism primarily through what John Bodnar has called "vernacular memory"—that is, memory based on firsthand experience and small-scale group life—rather than through the "official memory" fostered by school history texts and Americanization campaigns.

When African Americans thought about the term *American,* for example, it was impossible not to be brought up short before the United States' long history of racial exclusion and violence. From the seventeenth century onward, the same American institutions that had bridged gaps between disparate groups of white people had usually done so by marginalizing blacks. The Constitution provided for equality of standing among white voters; it also institutionalized slavery. The public schools educated children of immigrants and the native-born together but rigidly segregated black students. The Spanish-American War brought northern and southern whites together only by allowing them to assert their racial superiority over "lesser peoples." Because American so often had been defined by whites in terms of what it was *not*—not slave, not black, not "uncivilized"—enthusiasm for a specifically American nationalism among blacks was distinctly limited.

Instead, many blacks experienced life in the United States as a strange feeling of simultaneous inclusion and exclusion, a feeling W. E. B. Du Bois described as "twoness" and wrote about in *The Souls of Black Folk* (1903):

> It is a peculiar sensation, this double-consciousness, this sense of always looking at one's self through the eyes of others, of measuring one's soul by the tape of a world that looks on in amused contempt and pity. One ever feels his twoness,—an American, a Negro; two souls, two thoughts, two unreconciled strivings; two warring ideals in one dark body, whose dogged strength alone keeps it from being torn asunder.

This sense of double identity was also visible in the writings of immigrants (and sometimes, as with Kallen, those of their children). But the rigid black-or-white distinctions established in American society during the era of slavery made twoness especially powerful among African Americans. Perhaps no one felt dual loyalties more strongly than did black soldiers, who returned from a war to make the world safe for democracy only to find that the Red Scare had triggered one of the worst racial panics in United States history. Seventy-eight black people were lynched in 1919—ten of them veterans, some still in uniform.

In the 1920s, some African American leaders argued that the wartime sacrifices of black troops mandated social equality and declared the existence of a "New Negro." Here, as during Reconstruction, the language of Americanism was invoked on the African American's behalf. "The Negro reaches out as yet to nothing but American wants, American ideas," wrote Alain Locke in "The New Negro" (1925); "so the choice is not between one way for the Negro and another way for the rest, but between American ideals progressively frustrated on the one hand and American ideals progressively fulfilled and realized on the other." Similarly, W. E. B. Du Bois's "The Black Man Brings His Gifts" suggested that "American" was a multiracial construct. In this piece of short fiction, which appeared in the *Survey* in 1925, the white residents of a small town in Indiana try to design a historical "America's Making" pageant, but discover they cannot do so without taking into account such things as black labor under slavery or the black roots of jazz music.

The 1920s, however, also saw the development of black nationalism and separatism in the form of Marcus Garvey's Universal Negro Improvement Association (UNIA). Garvey, a Jamaican immigrant, argued that it was futile for blacks to expect equal standing with whites in the United States. Instead, he worked to lead African Americans back to Africa and to create a separate black economic infrastructure through such ventures as the Black Star Navigation Line and the Negro Factories Corporation. "To be a Negro is no disgrace, but an honor," he wrote, "and we of the UNIA do not want to become white." By 1923, the UNIA had several hundred thousand members, a reflection of the disgust and fear many blacks felt in the wake of postwar racial violence. Although the UNIA foundered after Garvey was convicted of mail fraud and deported in 1927, it was noteworthy as the first in a string of black nationalist movements that would culminate in the Black Power initiatives of the late 1960s and early 1970s.

Garveyism was also unique in its call for political and economic separatism. Advocates of the New Negro were not alone in invoking American ideals on behalf of their group; Kallen, Brandeis, and other ethnic pluralists were similarly committed to a broad Americanism that sheltered ethnic diversity. By contrast, there was no real parallel to the angry separatism of the Garveyites among other excluded groups. True, immigrant residents of the United States sometimes indicated that they still considered themselves foreign nationals—by returning to Italy or Germany in response to military draft calls during World War I, for example, or by limiting the use of the term *American* to English-stock residents of the United

States, as did German-language newspapers in Chicago. But unlike Europe, where irredentist nationalisms tore the existing political map apart after 1914, the United States saw no moves for geographical separation other than Garveyism.

The singular strength of black nationalism in the 1920s was in large part the logical result of three centuries of American thinking about race. For whites, Americanness had always been constructed in part as nonblackness, from John Adams's eighteenth-century complaint that "Providence never designed us for Negroes" through the booming of American "civilization" at the time of the Spanish-American War. Garvey simply turned the tables, offering a version of black national identity that was constructed in terms of nonwhiteness. Like his economic program, which stressed self-sufficiency and hard work, Garvey's racial ideology gained some of its strength from the familiar bipolar terms in which it was couched.

Because Garveyism assumed the fixity of race as a category, it spoke the same language as nativism and white racism, both of which were gaining strength in the 1920s. When President Warren Harding delivered a prosegregationist address at Birmingham, Alabama, in 1921, Garvey sent him a congratulatory telegram: "All true Negroes are against social equality, believing that all races should develop on their own social lines." Similarly, because Garvey viewed Ku Klux Klansmen as no different from other whites (except in their candor), he was willing to meet with them, a tactic that brought him a deluge of criticism from the integrationist National Association for the Advancement of Colored People (NAACP).

White Americanizers of the 1920s had other targets, of course. The Klan agitated against Jews and Catholics as well as African Americans. The National Origins Act of 1924 virtually shut Africans and Asians out of the country, but it was only minimally kinder to southern and eastern Europeans. The period was one in which native-born whites tried to define American nationalism in increasingly narrow and exclusionist terms. But whereas the ethnic pluralists and the proponents of the New Negro fought back by contesting the term *American,* Garvey took the nativists at their word and posited a counternationalism based on blackness.

A second alternative sense of American nationality could be seen in the commemorative activities of immigrants. Under heavy pressure during the 1920s to acquit themselves as patriots, most immigrants nonetheless managed to maintain their own traditions and, at the same time, to interpret the visions of the Americanizers in their own ways. As John Bodnar points out, this involved overcoming not only the nationalism offered by the native-born, but often that of assimilation-minded ethnic leaders as well. Thus when Norwegian Americans gathered for the Norse-American Centennial at Saint Paul, Minnesota, in 1925, they celebrated not only the American patriotism and citizenship emphasized by their leaders, but also the renewal of personal ties and the need to preserve Norwegian ethnic culture. Similarly, some of the first statues raised by ethnic groups in Cleveland's Cultural Gardens in the 1930s honored Frédéric Chopin and Johann Wolfgang von Goethe, who could serve both as international culture heroes and as champions of specific ethnic homelands.

Recent works in labor history by Roy Rosenzweig and Gary Gerstle have shown how many industrial workers also had their own ideas about what being an American meant. Sometimes the workers' nationalism was a modified version of previous ethnic national notions, as in the rough-and-tumble version of Americanism that emerged from the Irish Fourth of July in Worcester, Massachusetts. Sometimes it was simply allegiance to another homeland, as in the dedication of early Woonsocket, Rhode Island, textile workers to *la survivance*—the preservation of French Canadian nationality. Often working-class nationalism drew on the ideals of equality and justice in the Bill of Rights, a vision that appealed to native-born workers and immigrants alike. As Joseph Schmetz, a Woonsocket organizer, put it in 1936, unionization would allow workers to "be as American men and women should be, possessors of self-respect in an industrial democracy." Finally, as Lizabeth Cohen has argued, the experience of corporate welfarism in the 1920s led many workers by the 1930s to embrace a vision of moral capitalism, under which the national state would ensure economic security for all workers. In any case, by the time of the Great Depression a wide variety of working-class Americanisms existed but had yet to find political voice.

A final alternative may be found in the stubborn sense of locality to which Americans of many different backgrounds continued to cling. As Bodnar demonstrates, participants in official ceremonies of the 1930s were often more interested in commemorating the pioneer—symbol of independence and self-sufficiency, and often a figure of genealogical interest—than in remembering the civic-mindedness and self-sacrifice of the officially sanctioned hero, the patriot. Local historians insisted on the authenticity of dubious vernacular historical monuments. The George

Washington "birthplace" at Wakefield, Virginia, reports Michael Kammen, "had been reconstructed on the wrong location and on the basis of no reliable documentation as to the appearance of the eighteenth-century original." When the National Park Service entered the business of historical commemoration in the 1930s, it often found it had to acquiesce to existing local conceptions of what was considered significant.

The New Deal years saw the flowering of some of the alternative visions that had been promulgated in the 1920s. While black separatism did not survive the demise of Garveyism, pluralist conceptions of Americanism among African Americans and other minority groups did gain some breathing space in the 1930s. In part they survived because of the tenacity of ethnic, class, and local loyalties. But they also flourished because the racialism so characteristic of official nationalism in the 1920s was greatly toned down during the ensuing decade.

There were at least three reasons for the moderation of racial notions of nationality in the 1930s. In the first place, the National Origins Act of 1924 defused the issue somewhat by reducing the flow of new immigrants to a trickle. The number of newcomers was limited to 164,447—less than 15 percent of the number who arrived annually in the years just before World War I. The immigration quotas set by the act would not be substantially expanded until 1965.

Second, "scientific" racism was largely discredited during the 1930s, partly by new work in cultural anthropology and partly by the horrendous uses to which racist theories were being put by fascist parties in Europe. Here the key figure was Franz Boas, whose students had been at work debunking the "naturalness" of races and nationalities since before World War I; Boas himself testified against the 1924 immigration act. The relativizing of nationalism was also among the projects of Carlton Hayes, whose *Historical Evolution of Modern Nationalism* (1931) was the first substantial scholarly analysis of the phenomenon by an American writer. Like most later theorists of nationalism, Hayes was concerned primarily with Europe, and as a champion of the Catholic Right he opposed what he called the integral nationalisms of fascism and the Action Française because they were secular, not because they were irrational or discriminatory. Still, Hayes pointed out the man-made character of all nationalisms. "Human beings are social animals and do appear equipped with traits which render it possible and necessary for them to live in groups," he observed, "but the groups do not have to be nationalities."

Finally, the Democratic party, which came to power in 1932, built its electoral majority on a trans-ethnic coalition; it could ill afford to indulge in ethnocentrism. Drawing votes from urban Catholics as well as southern Protestants, blacks as well as whites, the Democrats reconfigured politics along class rather than ethnic lines. Indeed, as Cohen and others have argued, the central achievement of the New Deal may have been its success in transforming the consciousness of working-class immigrants from that of ethnics, concerned primarily with cultural preservation, to that of workers with a class agenda.

The alternative Americanism of laborers also found partial fulfillment in the New Deal. In West Virginia, miners organized themselves under the slogan "The President Wants You to Join the Union" and displayed banners that combined images of Franklin Roosevelt with the logo of the United Mine Workers union. In Washington, Roosevelt's national radio addresses fused the rhetorics of nation and class to an extent not seen before, deploring the existence of "one-third of a nation ill-housed, ill-clad, ill-nourished," and adding "freedom from want" to the list of "essential human freedoms." To the left of Roosevelt, even the Communist party, which had been practically read out of any role in defining Americanism during the Red Scare, made nationalist overtures. Political activists announced that "Communism Is Twentieth-Century Americanism," while a Popular Front textbook, *Building America,* treated the story of the country as the story of work.

If the 1930s saw the easing of ethnocentrism and the partial embrace of working-class Americanism, they also witnessed a rediscovery of American folk culture and local life. Post office murals and theater productions of the Works Progress Administration (WPA) showcased American themes and scenes from local history; Appalachian music and southern slave narratives were held up as indigenous cultural forms; painters such as Thomas Hart Benton and photographers such as Dorothea Lange depicted ordinary people in specific American settings. In these and many other works, the United States was envisioned as a congeries of localities, each with its own peculiarities, much as John Dewey had suggested it ought to be.

What knit these places together was not ethnocultural similarity or devotion to capitalism (indeed, the depression-ravaged 1930s produced a certain amount of unity in misery). Instead, there was a new appreciation of the diversity of American local life. At the same time, authors, artists, and politicians alike began to stress what might be called infrastructural linkages: common highways, common mass media experiences (primarily through the radio), and, most important, common participation in the greatly expanded activities of the national state.

The overland journey, for example, became a popular metaphor that described the connections between Americans as a trip from one place to another. In 1938, a wagon train reenacted the migration of pioneers from Ipswich, Massachusetts, to Marietta, Ohio, with patriotic celebrations at every stop along the way. New York and Virginia began the practice of erecting road markers and naming highways to commemorate historical events. Writers and artists such as Constance Rourke, Zora Neale Hurston, Edward Weston, Edmund Wilson, and John Dos Passos traversed the country in search of source materials, emerging with both pictures of regional diversity and narratives that integrated it. Most enduringly, John Steinbeck used Route 66 in *The Grapes of Wrath* (1939) as a device to capture both the particular migration experience of the Joads and the national scope of the Depression.

Similarly, popular national radio programs—such as *American School of the Air* and *Major Bowes' Original Amateur Hour,* which featured a special "Honor City" each week, for example—pulled listeners together in an electronic village. The new radio networks themselves, the National Broadcasting Company (consolidated in 1927) and Columbia Broadcasting System (consolidated in 1928), functioned as powerful tools for national integration almost no matter what they broadcast.

Most attempts to rediscover and then integrate the alternative Americanisms of ethnic groups, laborers, and localists, however, went on under the aegis of the national state. From the theater projects and state historical guides of the WPA to national labor legislation and the nationwide radio fireside chats of the President, the flowering of diversity in the 1930s was at base a state-sponsored affair. Most obvious of all was the National Recovery Administration (NRA), whose Blue Eagle campaign and "We Do Our Part" slogan were designed to demonstrate corporate loyalty to the national recovery plan. The Blue Eagle campaign looked and sounded much like a World War I propaganda drive. But even those projects most devoted to recovering the multiplicity of national experience often had national aims in mind—the WPA state guides, for example, usually related local historical events in ways that emphasized their national significance.

By 1941, then, nationalist visions that in the 1920s had been associated only with particular ethnic, labor, and local constituencies had largely joined the mainstream. They had done so, however, only through close association with an increasingly powerful national state. At the same time, the 1930s saw the rapid rise of commercial mass media, which in the decades to come would exert homogenizing pressures of their own.

FROM WORLD WAR TO COLD WAR

As Philip Gleason has observed, it is hard to exaggerate the importance of World War II as "the central event in shaping Americans' understanding of their national identity for the next generation." More than 16 million women and men served in the United States armed forces at some point during the war. The state economic apparatus, already enlarged by the New Deal, expanded even further with the creation of such agencies as the War Production Board, the National War Labor Board, and the Office of Price Administration. Overseas, a series of treaties and informal commitments began the process of turning the United States into a global military power.

The federal bureaucracy had expanded during wars before, of course, but this time it had come to stay. Federal employment grew from 14 to 18 percent of the work force between 1948 and 1970, compared with a prewar level of 10 percent; active-duty military personnel never again totaled less than 1.4 million, or about five times as many as had been enlisted in 1937. The military, in fact, remained on a quasi-war footing for most of the next forty-five years, prompting Dwight Eisenhower's famous 1960 warning about a permanent military-industrial complex. Between 1940 and 1990, the United States would evolve from a nation deeply suspicious of standing armies, to one with 400 military installations and half a million troops overseas.

As it had in 1917–1918, the government during World War II launched propaganda campaigns designed to pull the population together and stigmatize "disloyalty." Much more so than during World War I, however, official propagandists directly addressed the ethnic and class fault lines in American society, and attempted to tie participation in the war to personal experiences such as marriage and family. The typical war film pictured a foxhole populated by one member of every ethnic group from every region of the country. Public campaigns urged workers to "Be American!" by purchasing war bonds and striving to increase industrial production.

Gary Gerstle points out that the kind of Americanism promoted by government propagandists during the war was new in that it stressed cultural pluralism. The United States was said to be fighting against the racist totalitarianism of the Nazis, and for the right of everyone in the world to life, liberty, and the pursuit of happiness, regardless of race, creed, or nationality. This vision required an American society tolerant of differences. As one advertisement in a Woonsocket, Rhode Island, labor newspaper put it in 1944, "The more Americans fighting each other at home, the fewer [Hitler] will have to meet on the field of battle."

Gerstle also observes that the officially sponsored pluralism of the war years differed significantly from earlier visions. First, unlike the calls of Horace Kallen and others for equality among diverse groups, wartime pluralism was a call for equality among individuals. The scenes of interethnic harmony in films and advertisements, for example, were always situated in training camps and on battlefields, far from the homes and communities that might have reinforced older group loyalties. At the same time, the new emphasis on racial and ethnic tolerance subtly obscured the working-class Americanism that had loomed so large in the rhetoric of the New Deal. Far from being the basis of a new kind of national identity, the interest of labor was treated as just another unseemly division in American life, like ethnicity and race. The only entity to which individuals might legitimately pledge their loyalties was the national state, which was seen as the protector of pluralism, the place where diverse individuals converged.

The official embrace of pluralism during World War II also completed the intellectual process that had begun with the debunking of "scientific racism" in the 1930s. Racism now appeared to be an aberration from the individualism and equality before the law that were the essence of American identity, rather than something deeply embedded in that identity and largely constitutive of it. The new intellectual climate allowed Gunnar Myrdal to pose race as *An American Dilemma* (1944), as did Ruth Benedict, Ashley Montagu, and a number of other authors.

The great omissions from the wartime calls for national unity were Japanese Americans. While German Americans were treated with considerably more leniency than during World War I, more than 112,000 Americans of Japanese ancestry were placed in barren internment camps. Although the 442d Regimental Combat Team, made up entirely of Japanese Americans, distinguished itself in Europe, war films never pictured Japanese Americans in the intercultural foxhole. Instead, the Japanese became the objects of vicious racist caricature in both film and the popular press.

Moreover, despite the triumph of pluralism at the ideological level, it still had a long way to go in practice even for non-Japanese Americans. The government did take some steps to implement the pluralist vision, outlawing discrimination in federal hiring and partially integrating the armed forces. But African American GIs continued to experience discrimination even in such petty matters as segregated seating for bus rides and training films. At Fort Hood, for example, Jackie Robinson was court-martialed (and acquitted) for resisting segregation in bus seating. Among civilians, race riots between blacks and whites in Detroit and New York City in 1943 killed thirty-nine people. In Los Angeles, dozens of Mexican Americans were injured in the zoot suit riots of 1943. It would take the mass action of the civil rights movement in the 1950s and 1960s to bring about institutional change.

On the surface, then, what the wartime propagandists offered was a pluralist, individualist Americanism, which came together as a unity only in loyalty to the national state. As Robert Westbrook notes, however, a state whose ruling ideology is that of liberal capitalism must entice its citizens to war by appealing to loyalties other than pure statism. State loyalty must somehow be linked with individualism—a difficult trick—or at the very least with the elemental loyalties of family and kin. The propaganda of World War II made such linkages in two ways: first, in its paeans to American pluralism, which equated the defense of individualism with the defense of the United States; second, in a conscious attempt to connect the war effort with the defense of the home.

On the latter score, the employment of a new strategy of gender was vital. Because the liberal capitalist state lacked a coherent philosophy of obligation, Westbrook argues, it tried during World War II to "colonize" the potent appeals of home and family through "the cultural construction of women as icons of prescribed male obligation." With Hollywood firmly under the supervision of the war authorities, not only war films but such things as pinup photos and show tours portrayed the America for which men were fighting as the America of "the girl next door," the America of the home. Film stars such as Rita Hayworth and Betty Grable were cast as archetypes of wives and sweethearts at home, with pilots sometimes pasting their images over the official insignia of planes. Advertisements idealized the American home, centerpiece of the American way of life to which the veteran would return: a home full of material goods—everything from electric irons to new refrigerators. At the same time that official propaganda was stressing the new role of women in industrial production—most famously through the fictional character of Rosie the Riveter—commercial advertisements tended to show women as loyal housewives, dreaming of the material prosperity that would follow the war. As tools of gendering American nationalism, Rosie the Riveter disappeared in 1945, but Rita Hayworth and the happy housewife did not.

The wartime campaigns for national unity depended heavily on the new mass media. The national audiences for Hollywood films and network radio programs that had developed by 1940 were evidence for the existence of a relatively homogeneous nation, an audience that mass marketers in the 1940s and 1950s would work to homogenize even further. Whereas John Dewey had found that even the most nationally inclined papers of the mid-1920s "screamed with localisms," the new mass media had no locality (a point Dewey himself made regarding the popular *Saturday Evening Post,* which, he said, was really designed for rootless people "in transit" from one locality to another). With their huge budgets, cartelized managements, and national scope, the radio networks and Hollywood studios were perfect vessels for the national message.

Of course, there is no way to know with certainty whether the Americans who read about Rosie the Riveter or viewed "Why We Fight" films interpreted them in the same local, particularistic, terms with which they had greeted earlier attempts at the creation of a national culture. But locality and ethnicity undoubtedly decreased in significance during the war years, and would continue to do so through the 1950s. The greatest growth industry of postwar social science, in fact, would be the study of alienation and anomie, of rootlessness. The only alternative to the particularisms of class, ethnic group, and locality, on the one hand, and anomie on the other, seemed to be the sort of state-sponsored pluralism so loudly trumpeted during the war.

Consequently, the postwar decade in intellectual life was marked by histories and social theories that emphasized American commonalities and downplayed differences—the so-called consensus school. Writers such as Louis Hartz, David Potter, Daniel Boorstin, and Will Herberg conceived of Americanism in unitary terms: Americans had a "national mind" or a "national character"; they were a "people of plenty" who shared a "liberal tradition" or a "secular religion." Immigration studies focused anew on assimilation; labor histories pictured the United States in exceptionalist terms, as a place where class consciousness and socialism had failed to develop. In *American Nationalism* (1957), Hans Kohn emphasized the uniqueness of American nationalism, which he viewed as loyalty to institutions or to an ideology, in contrast to the statism and ethnocultural loyalties of Europe. Although these writers offered quite detailed explications of the divisions and complexities within American society, they all assumed that national identity had an underlying essence that could be specified.

As David Hollinger has indicated, postwar theorizing about American identity was part of a broad intellectual context of the 1940s and 1950s that favored universalism. Religious studies pointed toward ecumenicism; the Kinsey reports of 1948 and 1953 made sweeping generalizations about sexual behavior; internationalist movements ranged from Esperanto to Wendell Willkie's call for a worldwide coalition of farmers. But while Americans spoke in universalist terms, their generalizations usually stopped short of relativizing their own institutions. Other nations had classes; the United States had the American way of life. Other nations had ingrained racial hatreds; the United States, with a nationalism that was essentially ideological or institutional, had only an American dilemma. The same authors who saw Americanism as unitary also saw it as unique in the world—a stance that has come to be known as American exceptionalism.

The difference between this sort of exceptionalism and early-twentieth-century exaltation of unique American institutions was that after 1945 exceptionalism played to a world audience. The United States had emerged from World War II in an unparalleled position of military and political dominance. In 1947 it produced 47 percent of the world's steel and 62 percent of the world's oil, drove 75 percent of the world's automobiles, controlled the world's most powerful armed forces, and possessed a monopoly on the atomic bomb. While Americans might continue to think of their national development as exceptional, they no longer had the option of isolationism.

The result was that from 1945 through the late 1960s, official ideologists proclaimed both American exceptionalism *and* the universal applicability of American values and institutions. Although the United States had been uniquely favored by history, citizens of the newly designated developing nations were told, there was hope for the rest of the world as well—provided it copied the American model. Thus when the United Nations formed in 1945, it resembled a United States of the World, complete with a ratified constitution (charter), a one-nation-one-vote deliberative assembly, and a separate International Court of Justice. Similarly, the new field of developmental economics arose to explain how the conditions of American prosperity could be duplicated elsewhere.

The equating of American nationalism with American political and economic institutions was also a gambit in the developing Cold War between the United States and the Soviet Union. The celebration of the American way of life that had begun during World War II intensified during the 1950s, with the Soviet Union held up as an ominous counterexample. The film *Red Nightmare,* for example, envisioned the Soviet takeover of a small American town and the repression that would follow; by way of contrast, the California shopping center sponsoring the film was careful to note its own abundance of free parking. In 1959, Vice President Richard Nixon lectured Soviet Premier Nikita Khrushchev directly on the superiority of American domestic appliances as they stood in the middle of an American model kitchen on display in Moscow. The new Other against whom Americans were to define themselves was a political and economic one.

Americanism-as-not-communism was given concrete form by the separate investigations of Sen. Joseph McCarthy and the House Un-American Activities Committee (HUAC). As a result of these investigations 2,200 government employees lost their jobs; many in Hollywood, the universities, and private industry saw their careers derailed. The loyalty demanded by the anticommunists was of a type different even from that of the 100-percenters after World War I. It was not loyalty to an ethnocultural group. It was not loyalty to the national state—if anything, the McCarthyites exhibited a kind of petit bourgeois suspicion of state centralization. It was not loyalty to constitutional principles, for which McCarthy daily demonstrated his contempt. Instead, anticommunist Americanism was framed in terms of its hatreds, in terms of what it was not: not the New Deal; not communism.

The ideological nationalism of the 1950s, however, whether expressed positively as American exceptionalism or negatively as anticommunism, was a thin soup. Unlike the nationalism of the first Red Scare, it was not rooted in "nature" or biology. The Other against whom it defined itself was a shadowy figure half a world away; indeed, anticommunism seemed to save most of its fire for home-grown dissidents. And while it could trace its intellectual roots back to the antiradical Americanism of the 1890s, the world in which antiradicalism operated had been complicated considerably since then by the rise of alternative nationalisms, the New Deal's innovations in state regulation, even by the internationalization of the economy.

At the same time, the thinness of Cold War nationalism reflected a growing sense of the paradox of advanced capitalism as it had come to exist by the late 1950s. On the one hand, the imperative of capitalism was to individualize, to sunder group loyalties at every level of society. In theory, these were to be replaced with sovereign individuals: the free laborer, the bold entrepreneur, the independent consumer. At the extreme of free-market ideology, there was little space for the sense of "groupness" that nationalism required—unless one defined American nationalism itself in paradoxical terms, as an aversion to groupness (as Daniel Boorstin did in 1953, in *The Genius of American Politics*).

On the other hand, the handmaidens of advanced capitalism were mass distribution and mass marketing, processes that required a high degree of homogeneity among consumers. Thus even as the mass marketers freed the individual from older but "divisive" group loyalties (to race, class, region, or ethnic group, for example), they substituted a more inclusive—but less substantial—loyalty to a consumerist American way of life. The result was a Cold War nationalism framed in terms of loyalty to consumer capitalism itself, defined against an overseas communist Other who was framed as a sort of anticonsumer.

Contemporaries were quite aware of how unsatisfying the new formulations were. Vance Packard's *The Hidden Persuaders* (1957) exposed advertisers' manipulations of consumers, while David Riesman's *The Lonely Crowd* (1950) and William H. Whyte's *The Organization Man* (1956) expressed widespread fears of rootlessness and conformity. None of these authors, however, was ready to argue for the supremacy of some group smaller than the nation, or to define Americanism in terms other than those set by consumer capitalism. Those positions awaited developments in the 1960s and 1970s.

FROM CONSENSUS TO CONFLICT TO CONSTRUCTION

Even the brittle ideological nationalism of the early Cold War years would look substantial compared with what followed. In his inaugural address of 1961, John F. Kennedy told his listeners to "ask not what your country can do for you; ask what you can do for your country"—a fair summation of the Cold

War imperatives of consensus and unity. By the end of the decade, the terms of Kennedy's challenge would be nearly reversed, as Americans increasingly thought of themselves as members of groups rather than as citizens of a nation. At the same time, the creation of an ersatz, commercial nationalism proceeded apace. By the 1970s, the flag was being used to sell everything from automobiles to beer, while televised national sporting events had become unifying rituals of the first order. Although the whimpering end of the Cold War in 1989 took away the communist Other against whom Americanism-as-consumerism had been defined, it hardly eliminated American industry's need for a homogeneous national market.

There was no single point at which Cold War nationalism broke down. Rather, it accumulated strains in the years between 1960 and 1980 until it had few adherents left, especially among Americans born since World War II. But three developments in particular sped its disintegration: the rise of the civil rights movement, the failure of the United States war effort in Vietnam, and the continuing globalization of the American economy.

Beginning with the Supreme Court decision in *Brown* v. *Board of Education* (1954) and the bus boycotts of 1955, African Americans forcefully reasserted their rights to civil equality. In the early years of the civil rights movement, leaders such as Martin Luther King, Jr., employed the conventional language of pluralism under law and American institutions. The integration of lunch counters, King wrote in 1963 in his "Letter from a Birmingham Jail," would bring "our nation back to those great wells of democracy which were dug deep by the founding fathers in their formulation of the Constitution and the Declaration of Independence." What the civil rights protestors sought was consensus and harmony: "[W]e who engage in nonviolent direct action are not the creators of tension," King wrote. "We merely bring to the surface the hidden tension that is already alive. We bring it out in the open where it can be seen and dealt with."

Even these rather conservative sentiments were outside the bounds of Cold War nationalism. King was denounced on the right as a communist and became the object of a lengthy Federal Bureau of Investigation surveillance. At Birmingham in 1963, police dogs were set on a nonviolent march of black schoolchildren, while another march at Selma in 1965 was stayed by a court order. When more radical black nationalist groups, such as the Black Panthers, arose after 1965, they were infiltrated and attacked by local police.

As the civil rights movement met with white resistance, it was pushed, as Garveyism had been in the 1920s, toward separatism and black nationalism. The transition was epitomized by the career of the slogan "Black Power." Chanted during an interracial civil rights march at Jackson, Mississippi, in 1966, Black Power originally meant economic or political power, manifested in such things as the bus boycotts or the Civil Rights Act of 1964. But it very quickly became a slogan of younger black militants in the Student Nonviolent Coordinating Committee (SNCC), and of Black Muslims, who favored a separatist approach. "The political philosophy of black nationalism means we must control the politics and politicians of our own community," Muslim leader Malcolm X said in 1964. "They must no longer take orders from outside forces." By 1968, Black Power had come to stand for African American economic and political autonomy. By the 1980s it would be the ideological touchstone of a wide variety of movements, ranging from the Rev. Louis Farrakhan's Nation of Islam to a secession referendum in Roxbury (a predominantly African American section of Boston) to a black-initiated proposal to resegregate Milwaukee's public schools.

The civil rights movement ushered in what might be called the age of group consciousness, as Americans of different ethnicities, genders, sexual orientations, and generations all found independent voices. Some, like King, began their protests by appealing to one of the alternative traditions of Americanism. The early outbursts of youth culture in the Free Speech movement at Berkeley and among the members of Students for a Democratic Society (SDS), for example, were essentially jeremiads, calling Americans back to "American values we found good—principles by which we could live as men," in the words of the original SDS manifesto of 1962, the Port Huron Statement.

But most of the social movements of the 1960s and early 1970s, like the civil rights movement, sooner or later assumed an adversarial stance. "America" was defined as the enemy, or as a mystification perpetrated by some more powerful group. Black Power was followed by Red Power among Native Americans, La Raza Unida among Chicanos, Gay Pride among homosexuals, by ethnic revivals among older immigrant groups. The revived women's movement declared that "sisterhood is powerful" and lobbied for an amendment to the Constitution that explicitly recognized the rights of women. Students spelled out their differences from their elders in such works as *The Student as Nigger* (1969) and

The Strawberry Statement (1969). Nor were African Americans any longer unique in their desire to separate from the body politic. Both the American Indian Movement (AIM) and the women's movement developed substantial separatist wings, while self-sufficient communalism gained favor among the young.

Beginning with changes in the civil rights movement, then, the late 1960s saw the rise of movements that grounded personal identity almost wholly in the experiences of specific groups. What was important was not the nation, but the solidarity and autonomy of one's ethnic group, neighborhood, generation, or gender community. As Philip Gleason points out, the real innovation of the 1960s was not the concept of group rights—the pluralists of the 1910s had demanded those—but the way in which group experience came to be seen as normative. Things were to be judged according to how they affected the group and its interests, not on some broader basis.

The notion of group identity as normative was mirrored in intellectual life, where universalism entered a steep decline. According to David Hollinger, a key text here was Thomas Kuhn's *The Structure of Scientific Revolutions* (1962), which argued that science received its authority from particular professional communities, not from any cross-cultural ability to generalize. If even science was culture-bound, every other realm of human endeavor must be equally contingent, temporal, and community-based. Through the 1970s and 1980s, scholars revisioned the United States as an assemblage of more or less autonomous communities: ethnic communities, local communities, professional communities, communities of readers, and so forth. The result was a conception of American social life as a collection of tribal experiences.

The decline of universalism did not bode well for sweeping theories of nationalism, and in fact most academic work on the subject through the 1980s was done outside the United States. When American scholars approached the subject at all, it was usually in the debunking mood expressed by the title of Lawrence Friedman's 1975 book, *Inventors of the Promised Land.* Concepts such as the American character and the American mind fell into disrepute; the words *nation* and *nationalism* were ceded to the political Right. Instead, studies of distinct communities and cultures abounded. By the late 1980s, the hottest reform movement in higher education was multiculturalism, an attempt to create texts and curricula that represented the diversity of American experience.

Meanwhile, the war in Vietnam made a mess of the Cold War version of nationalism, pointing up the inequities in American society while at the same time showing the weakness of anticommunism as a unifying ideology. The military draft, for example, sent thousands of poor, often minority, youths to fight, while their better-off peers took student deferments or lay low in National Guard units. The war also caused rampant price inflation that produced different kinds of inequities: adjusted for inflation, the average worker's take-home pay, which had been rising steadily since 1954, stood still from 1965 to 1969.

As the war in Vietnam continued to go badly and its cost mounted, more Americans came to question the official rationale that this was a war against communism. Works such as Frances Fitzgerald's *Fire in the Lake* (1972) humanized the monolithic communist Other by showing the complexities of Vietnamese history. Indeed, antiwar activists did best when they cast the conflict in personal rather than ideological terms: by reading the names of the dead during the 1969 national moratorium, for example. Such gestures inevitably turned attention away from the Vietnamese enemy and toward the continuing divisions in American society. As Muhammad Ali put it in refusing induction to the Army in 1967, "No Vietnamese ever called me nigger."

The American withdrawal from Vietnam in 1973 ended not only the easy conflation of anticommunism with Americanism, but also the American political and economic hegemony established by World War II. In the 1970s, the limits of American power became apparent, first with a series of price shocks administered by Middle Eastern oil producers, then with the penetration of the United States domestic market by Germany and Japan, followed by the long captivity of American hostages in Iran and Lebanon. The United States no longer could portray itself as an exception to the rules of world history, with unique institutions whose export would cure the ills of the rest of the globe. It was one nation among many—just as each ethnic, racial, generational, and gender group within it was coming to be seen as one autonomous unit of a collection.

By the time of the Bicentennial in 1976, every Cold War indicator of national consensus was being read instead as evidence of conflict. Whereas historian Louis Hartz in 1954 had seen Americans united in devotion to liberal capitalism, liberal ideology now was pictured as serving only one class. In the same year, David Potter had seen the key to American identity in the country's exceptional abundance; critics now stressed the unequal distribution of that abundance and the ways in which it had been extracted from "economic colonies" at home and overseas. The welter of American interest groups seemed to have nothing in common beyond allegiance to the national state, and even the state had been tainted by the Vietnam debacle.

The Bicentennial itself was a perfect illustration of what President Jimmy Carter in 1979 would call the national malaise. Although the federal government sponsored a few extravaganzas, such as a Fourth of July concert and fireworks display in Washington, there was nothing like the Centennial Exhibition that had riveted the nation's attention in 1876. Instead, as John Bodnar notes, most money and planning authority for the celebration was shifted to localities, which proceeded to memorialize ethnic heroes, bury time capsules filled with local mementos, or erect Bicentennial park benches and fire hydrants. On the left, a Peoples' Bicentennial Commission arose to denounce the whole affair as a corporate conspiracy. Only national advertisers seemed to enter fully into the spirit of the occasion, embracing the Bicentennial as a way to sell products.

The commercial flavor of the Bicentennial was no accident, for by the 1970s the mass marketers who paid the costs of the big media—television above all—were at the height of their power. While it might have been possible to craft a separate product and message for every one of the newly self-conscious groups making up American society, sheer economic logic drove national advertisers and broadcasters in the direction of homogeneity. Consequently, they rang the national chimes loudly even as the national polity seemed to be disintegrating. America was addressed as if it were a person ("Go ahead, America, pile it on," began one advertisement for an artificial sweetener; America was said to be watching ABC; Sears was "where America shopped"). National symbols such as the flag were worked into network and product logos. Sporting events were structured as national championships, and became television spectacles (with appropriate national product tie-ins) that outdrew all but the most important political speeches. If the cultural nation was splintering, the commercial nation had never been so united.

The decline of cultural nationalism and the rise of its ersatz commercial shadow both continued through the 1980s. In many ways, the eight-year presidency of Ronald Reagan complemented both trends. Enormously popular while in office, Reagan combined vintage Cold War rhetoric (the Soviet Union was an "evil empire," while the United States stood for "families") with minimal overseas commitments. He employed a Madison Avenue invocation of the nation ("Morning in America") during his 1984 reelection campaign, and promoted abstract symbols of patriotism such as the flag, but did not seriously attempt to break an interest-group deadlock in Congress that resulted in eight consecutive deficit budgets.

Intellectual life followed a similar path. Communities and cultures continued to be studied as the essential molders of identity, with nationalism something to resist or demystify. But whereas debunkers in the 1970s had demystified nations in order to show that some form of group identity was more fundamental—class position, ethnic background, gender—the postrevolutionary depression of the 1980s produced a new style. Postmodernists, or deconstructionists as the new thinkers were often called, treated all social categories as historically contingent constructions. The nation might be a fiction, but so were ethnic groups, genders, classes, and even (or especially) the self.

The postmodern view that all are alienated, and that meaning and reality float, may appear at first glance to be the ultimate in revolutionary skepticism. But as J. G. A. Pocock argues in an important short essay, "Deconstructing Europe," postmodernism, while purportedly a challenge to the hegemony of mass-market capitalism, is actually its twin, or even its accomplice. "The marketers of images instruct us that we have no selves other than those they choose to impose on us," Pocock noted: "The deconstructionist intellectuals, if they are not willing to stop somewhere and make a stand, tell us exactly the same thing." Without some grounding, in other words, whether in a nation or in some smaller group, the self is at the mercy of image manipulators.

Under this dystopian view, deconstruction is likely to produce an internationalism whose only use for nations is as a marketing tool. In Japan, for example, American film stars, including Gene Hackman, Madonna, and Sylvester Stallone, have been used to sell products on television even though they speak not a word in the advertisements—what sponsors want is to associate their products with the generalized image of the American. Similarly, Disney World lures visitors to Florida with simulated "international" restaurants.

Alternatively, nationalism may disappear into some kind of socialist or corporatist internationalism. This development is eagerly anticipated by theorists such as Benedict Anderson, Ernest Gellner, and Eric Hobsbawm, who stress nationalism's connection to the rise of industrial capitalism. The puzzlement evident in their analyses, however, and the compulsion each author feels to offer yet another demonstration of the artificial character of nationalism, are testimony to the staying power of real-world nation-states. If nationalism is simply a stage in worldwide capitalist development, they seem to ask, when may we expect its disappearance?

In part, nationalism persists because of sheer institutional inertia. In theory, the call for multiculturalism may be a demand for a more fluid, less uniform national identity. But in practice, the bureaucratic structures of such things as affirmative action programs and college curricula (Are South Asians an ethnic minority? How many "area studies" programs should be created?) have often forced its advocates to reify ethnocultural groups in order to achieve anything. Nor should the power of the national state to justify itself be underestimated, as the propaganda experience of the world wars demonstrates.

Nationalism also persists because of what Bodnar calls its vernacular side, a local and personal sense of connectedness that is stubbornly resistant to homogenization. The Vietnam Veterans Memorial, dedicated in 1982, has become a place to commemorate the fallen comrades whose names (more than 50,000 in all) are emblazoned on its walls. The memorial does not celebrate the state or the anticommunist cause. Yet it is not a monument to internationalism either—the names of dead Vietnamese do not appear. Rather, it gains its power from the connections visitors draw between their own memories and the national history it materially represents.

In the American case, nationalism has been a concept of many uses. It has been appropriated by the state in wartime propaganda and in the Blue Eagle campaigns of the 1930s. It has been conflated with ideology, as in the Cold War nationalism that followed 1945. It has been invoked by nativists from the 1890s onward and by pluralists from Horace Kallen to Martin Luther King. This is not to suggest that the American nation is an empty vessel into which anyone can pour any kind of meaning, for historically some versions have been dominant, some groups privileged. Nor is it to posit an essential Americanism that has somehow survived the twists and turns of exploitation by various groups. Rather, the history of American nationalism in the twentieth century has been a history of arguments among differently empowered social groups about what the nation is. Americanism has been the subject and object of arguments, not a position from which any one group has argued.

As a framework for intellectual argument and personal identity, nationalism seems likely to last for some time. To date, attempts at international culture and even international economic regulation have been tentative at best. And despite the confidence of theorists such as Hobsbawm that "the owl of Minerva . . . is now circling around nations and nationalism," ready to dissect their decline, we have seen such prophecies before. The "international mind," Randolph Bourne wrote in 1916, "will be essential to all men and women of good-will if they are ever to save this Western world of ours from suicide." In the three quarters of a century since then, the world has managed to stave off suicide. But Bourne's "higher cosmopolitan ideal" of a "new spiritual citizenship . . . of the world" remains elusive.

SEE ALSO Political Ideas and Movements; Parties and Interest Groups; Congress; The Courts (all in this volume).

BIBLIOGRAPHY

Early theoretical works on nationalism include Carlton J. H. Hayes, *The Historical Evolution of Modern Nationalism* (1931); Hans Kohn, *American Nationalism* (1957); and Elie Kedourie, *Nationalism* (1960). More recently, Benedict Anderson's *Imagined Communities: Reflections on the Origins and Spread of Nationalism* (1983), explains nationalism as shared mythology brought on by the rise of print capitalism in early modern Europe. John Breuilly, *Nationalism and the State* (1982), draws evidence from nationalist movements around the world to argue that nations are constructed for the purpose of obtaining state power. Ernest Gellner, *Nations and Nationalism* (1983), offers a functionalist approach that stresses the centrality of industrialization. From the Marxist side, Eric Hobsbawm, *Nations and Nationalism since 1780: Programme, Myth, Reality* (1990), is an engaging analysis that emphasizes the rise of bourgeois hegemony in the nineteenth century; James Blaut, *The National Question: Decolonizing the Theory of Nationalism* (1987), is a Leninist interpretation that stresses nationalism's revolutionary potential. For an intellectual historian's contention that nationalism predates industrialization, see Roman Szporluk, *Communism and Nationalism: Karl Marx versus Friedrich List* (1988). Two essays by Daniel Segal argue for the connections between race and American nationalism: "Nationalism, Comparatively Speaking," *Journal of Historical Sociology* 1 (September 1988); and, with Richard Handler, "How European Is Nationalism?," forthcoming in *Social Analysis*. An occasional paper published by the University of Illinois Program in Arms Control, Disarmament, and International Security (1990), Frank De Roose, "The Study of Patriotism," offers lucid definitions of different types of loyalty, while David Potter, "The Historian's Use of Nationalism, and Vice Versa," in his collection of essays *The South and the Sectional Conflict* (1968) posts some needed warnings. David Kertzer, *Ritual, Politics, and Power* (1988), examines the use of symbols in the construction of national identities. Wilbur Zelinsky, *Nation into State: The Shifting Symbolic Foundations of American Nationalism* (1988) is an excursion in cultural geography whose title is also its thesis.

The most important study of popular American patriotism yet to appear is John Bodnar, *Remaking America: Public Memory, Commemoration, and Patriotism in the Twentieth Century* (1992), which looks in detail at such things as local historical celebrations and ethnic commemorations. Also useful in spots is Michael Kammen's sprawling, anecdotal overview of popular history and memory, *Mystic Chords of Memory: The Transformation of Tradition in American Culture* (1991). Merle Curti, *The Roots of American Loyalty* (1946), remains an important history of intellectual attitudes toward nationalism.

For the period before 1930, important studies include Robert Rydell, *All the World's a Fair: Visions of Empire at American International Expositions, 1876–1916* (1984), a treatment of the imperial pretensions of those events; William Tuttle, *Race Riot: Chicago in the Red Summer of 1919* (1970), a riveting monograph whose introductory chapter ties together most of the major events of the Red Scare; William Preston, *Aliens and Dissenters: Federal Suppression of Radicals, 1903–1933* (1963), which contains an account of the official repression of 1917–1920; and William Pencak, *For God and Country: The American Legion, 1919–1941* (1989), the only serious study of that influential ultrapatriotic organization. In intellectual history, many of the wartime essays of Randolph Bourne on American nationalism are conveniently collected in Carl Resek, ed., *War and the Intellectuals: Essays, 1915–1919* (1964), while John Higham's "Ethnic Pluralism in American Thought," in *Send These to Me: Jews and Other Immigrants in Urban America* (1975), offers a good look at that doctrine and especially at Horace Kallen's use of it.

Three valuable analyses of working-class nationalism before World War II are Gary Gerstle, *Working-Class Americanism: The Politics of Labor in a Textile City, 1914–1960* (1989), a model study of changing notions of Americanism among French Canadian immigrant textile workers in Woonsocket, Rhode Island; Roy Rosenzweig, *Eight Hours for What We Will: Workers and Leisure in an Industrial City, 1870–1920* (1983), which includes fascinating material on the distinctly Irish Fourth of July; and Lizabeth Cohen, *Making a New Deal: Industrial Workers in Chicago, 1919–1939* (1990), which traces the evolution of an ethnic working class into a political, state-oriented working class in the 1930s. For black nationalism, a useful starting point is Judith Stein's exploration of the broad ramifications of Garveyism, *The World of Marcus Garvey: Race and Class in Modern Society* (1986). Philip Gleason has provided two stimulating meditations on the connections between ethnicity and national identity: "American Identity and Americanization," an essay in the *Harvard Encyclopedia of American Ethnic Groups* (1980); and *Speaking of Diversity: Language and Ethnicity in Twentieth-Century America* (1992). Werner Sollors, *Beyond Ethnicity: Consent and Descent in American Culture* (1986), is especially good on ethnic literature.

The construction of the American way of life during the 1940s is covered in John Morton Blum, *V Was for Victory: Politics and American Culture during World War II* (1976). For anti-Japanese American sentiment during the war, see John W. Dower, *War without Mercy: Race and Power in the Pacific War* (1986); and Roger Daniels, *Concentration Camps USA: Japanese Americans and World War II* (1972), the best short history of the wartime internments. Robert Westbrook explores the gendering of loyalty in "I Want a Girl, Just Like the Girl that Married Harry James: American Women and the Problem of Political Obligation in World War II," *American Quarterly* 42 (December 1990); while Elaine Tyler May, *Homeward Bound: American Families in the Cold War Era* (1988), explores the connections between gender and national politics in the 1950s.

The best short overview of the breakup of Cold War consensus is Richard Polenberg's *One Nation Divisible: Class, Race, and Ethnicity in the United States since 1938* (1980). Intellectual histories of the same developments include "A Time of Troubles," John Higham's epilogue to the revised edition of his *History: Professional Scholarship in America* (1983); and David Hollinger, "How Wide the Circle of the We? American Intellectuals and the Problem of the *Ethnos* since World War II," in Ronald G. Walters, ed., *Science and Social Reform in Modern America* (1993).

Stuart Ewen, *Captains of Consciousness: Advertising and the Social Roots of the Consumer Culture* (1976), offers a stimulating, if somewhat tendentious, introduction to the rise of mass marketing. Two recent essays are also worthy of note: J. G. A. Pocock, "Deconstructing Europe," *London Review of Books,* December 19, 1991, a rumination on nationalism and deconstruction; and Michael Walzer, "What Does It Mean to Be an 'American'?" *Social Research* 57 (Fall 1990), a restatement of the pluralist argument that incorporates developments since the 1960s.

POLITICAL IDEAS AND MOVEMENTS

James T. Kloppenberg

In his inaugural address on 20 January 1993, William Jefferson Clinton declared categorically, "our greatest strength is the power of our ideas." But what are our ideas? Clinton himself identified democracy, freedom, responsibility, sacrifice, and religious conviction—the same themes he invoked throughout his campaign for the presidency. But the pundits were not impressed. Calls for sacrifice and responsibility, they assured savvy listeners and readers, mean only higher taxes and increased government spending.

It is tempting to deny any connection between theorists' ideas and political reality; but they are related to the changing social and political contexts in which they appeared, the circumstances of their articulation. Of course, many factors shape public policy, including political institutions, social and cultural pressures, economic conditions, legal traditions, religious, ethnic, racial, and gender identities and conflicts, the nature and content of communications technology, international pressures and opportunities, and, doubtless, others. But for both the producers and the consumers of political discourse, ideas have been and continue to be constitutive of political consciousness. Encountering, or engaging in, political discourse provides the occasion for citizens to reflect on their preferences and occasionally to reformulate their conceptions of what America is and what Americans ought to do. Such activities proceed within historical horizons which ought to be kept in focus.

Two features of contemporary American intellectual life complicate the historical analysis of political ideas in the twentieth century. First, a pervasive cynicism threatens to undercut any effort to take seriously the role of ideas in political life. The public suspects that hidden beneath politicians' lofty rhetoric lies personal calculation. Many scholars insist that language is merely strategic. Viewed from either perspective, political discourse appears less likely to express deeply held convictions than to reflect judgments concerning which symbols can be manipulated to greatest effect. Now that the electorate's responses to candidates' comments can be electronically monitored during the course of a campaign, as they were throughout the 1992 presidential debates, each individual voter's reactions to word choices, quips, inflections, and facial expressions can be measured instantly. Candidates' presentations can be calibrated to the preferences of targeted segments of the population, rendering ever greater both the potential rewards for shrewd strategists and the risks run by those who express, naively, their genuine convictions. Taking ideas seriously runs counter to the popular and the scholarly suspicion that political discourse is a charade.

Second, contemporary debates in political theory tend to revolve around the categories of "liberalism," with its focus on individual rights, and "communitarianism," with its focus on social responsibility. Neither of these categories, however, adequately captures the complexities and dynamism of twentieth-century political debate in the United States. Such simplifications only reproduce the complementary demonologies of political partisans. In order to understand our political ideas, it is necessary to escape such unsatisfactory conceptual frameworks and return to the very different terms in which earlier generations of American thinkers conceived of the relation between freedom and community.

LOOKING BACKWARD: POLITICAL IDEAS IN HISTORICAL PERSPECTIVE

Late-nineteenth-century thinkers inherited from their predecessors a rich and complex mixture of ideas drawn from diverse sources and leavened by historical experience. From the Revolutionary era they derived ideals of virtue that blended together Christian notions of sinfulness and salvation, the public spiritedness and autonomy joined in the ideal of republican citizenship, and the concern for responsible individual freedom that was central to early liberal theory. From the antebellum years they inherited the Jacksonians' celebration of a boisterous democratic politics for white males, together with the formal exclusion of blacks and the less formal but equally significant creation of a separate, domestic sphere for white women. But earlier, more universal ideals did not disappear. Abolitionists, woman suffragists, labor radicals, and Whigs continued to invoke the standards of Christian, republican, and liberal justice against proclamations of the sanctity of white men's rights. Thanks largely to Lincoln's legacy, such ideals continued to resound powerfully in post–Civil War American political discourse.

Confronting a new, urban industrial world, and the excesses of the era that Charles Warner and Mark Twain christened "The Gilded Age," late-nineteenth-century American political thinkers slipped into varieties of Manichean thinking. Conservative champions of the ideas that have come to be known as Social Darwinism gloried in the mysterious process whereby progress emerged miraculously from conflict. Ranging from the romantic guild ideal of the Knights of Labor to the diverse forms of agrarian protest that coalesced into the Populist crusade, and from Henry George's single tax to Edward Bellamy's magical post-industrial utopia, radical thinkers gravitated toward what Walter Lippmann, writing in *Drift and Mastery* in 1914, termed "the panacea habit of mind." All these thinkers shared Bellamy's nostalgic yearning for the world America had left behind. Like Bellamy's protagonist, Julian West, they were "looking backward" even as they envisioned futures in which harmonious communities would replace the strident competition of their world. Those who were to follow them looked toward the future rather than the past.

PROGRESSIVE DEMOCRACY: AN AGE OF REFORM, 1900–1917

When Theodore Roosevelt succeeded the assassinated William McKinley as president in 1901, he brought a new spirit of activism to the national political scene. In response to the widespread perception of corruption in the public and private spheres, a perception that would be sharpened by the disclosures made by muckraking journalists in the first few years of the new century, various social, economic, and political reforms had been bubbling up from the local and state levels since the 1890s. When Roosevelt ascended to the presidency, he used that "bully pulpit" to bring to national attention the reformist views he shared with many Progressives. Although historians have discovered too many varieties of progressivism to make possible a simple characterization of a broad-based movement, it is clear that a diverse array of new political ideas and reform proposals appeared in the first two decades of this century.

Several streams fed the flow of Progressive thinking. The new social sciences, which emerged in the post–Civil War era and began to take shape around the turn of the century as the distinct disciplines we know today, contributed not only a wealth of new information, but also a new way of thinking about social life. Sociologists Franklin Giddings, Albion Small, Charles Cooley, and E. A. Ross replaced atomistic individuals with selves constructed through the process of social interaction, and earlier ideas of independence with the concept of interdependence. Economists John Commons, E. R. A. Seligman, and Richard T. Ely called for historical analysis to replace the false timelessness of classical economics.

Ely drew on a wide range of social scientific research to advance arguments concerning economics, politics, and social reform. His *Outlines of Economics* went through six editions, and in the early decades of the twentieth century it was outsold, among economics books, only by Adam Smith's *The Wealth of Nations*. In his widely read *Socialism and Social Reform* (1894), Ely marshaled evidence from several social sciences in support of a typical Progressive reform agenda. The United States could find a "golden mean" between stasis and revolution, Ely argued, only if the nation took three steps. First, Americans must reduce the "waste" in their competitive economic system by achieving full employment and "wholesome" working conditions. Second, Americans must reduce the "extremes" of wealth and poverty by shaping distribution so that "all shall have assured incomes, but that no one who is personally qualified to render service shall enjoy an income without personal exertion." Third, Americans must commit themselves to "abundant public provision of opportunities for the development of our faculties," primarily by developing educational and recreational facilities. In his discussion of the design and implementation of such plans for what is now called the welfare state, Ely stressed the need for democracy and decentralization, two recurrent themes in American Progressive and social democratic discourse. He also emphasized another common theme, the consistency between Progressive reform and Americans' religious and ethical ideals. Religion, Ely insisted, is an "independent force, often sufficient to modify and even to shape economic institutions." Society "is not an automaton. That society has some option, some choice, and conscience to which an appeal can be made, is a fact, if there is any such thing as a fact at all." For many social scientists of Ely's generation, evidence derived from empirical research went hand in hand with ethical commitment, and together they bolstered the case for democratic economic, social, and political reform.

Ely's style of argument points toward the second source feeding Progressive political thinking, the Social Gospel movement. A reformist impulse swept through American Protestantism from 1890 to 1915, spreading gradually from moderate preachers such as Washington Gladden to more radical figures such as William Dwight Porter Bliss, who helped create the Society of Christian Socialists and also edited the comprehensive *Encyclopedia of Social Reform*. Most partisans of the social gospel combined, as did Ely and Bliss, a passion for social research with a commitment to social change, and they conceived of both within the framework of their Christian religious faith. The most creative theorist of the social gospel was Walter Rauschenbusch, whose most important book, *Christianity and the Social Crisis* (1907), sold fifty thousand copies and was translated into eight languages. In *Christianizing the Social Order* (1912), Rauschenbusch singled out Ely as one of the "pioneers of the social gospel" whose spirit had "kindled and compelled" Rauschenbusch's own reformist sensibility. In his writings Rauschenbusch passionately denied the adequacy of competition as a principle for social organization, contrasting it to the principle of cooperation governing interaction in homes, schools, and churches. Reform could come only through steady, gradual democratic progress keyed to the ethical and religious ideal of cooperative life. But Rauschenbusch, perhaps more realistically than some of his Progressive allies, cautioned his readers against expecting too much from society even if it were reformed: suffering, conflict, and tragedy, he warned, would persist as an inevitable part of the human condition.

That nonutopian spirit likewise infused the work and the writings of Jane Addams, who shared with social scientists and social gospelers a commitment to reform, and whose example inspired the third source of progressivism, the social settlement movement. As Addams explained in *Twenty Years at Hull-House* (1910), she established Hull House in Chicago in 1889 in order to provide herself and other young women with an opportunity to provide useful service. Her religious faith, combined with a faith in democracy that she considered complementary to her Christian principles, undergirded her commitment to working with the poor. Unlike many other—usually male—Progressives who preferred the universalistic approach of social insurance, women such as Addams valued the hands-on approach that was to become standard among social-work professionals later in the twentieth century. But central commitments nevertheless linked social-settlement workers with other Progressives. Together with social scientists such as Ely, who was a frequent visitor to Hull House, Addams believed that "the dependence of classes on each other is reciprocal." Together with social gospelers such as Rauschenbusch, she believed that "the things which make men alike are finer and better than the things that keep them apart, and that these basic likenesses, if they are properly accentuated, easily transcend the less essential differences of race, language, creed and tradition."

Their common humanity might also enable individuals to transcend differences of gender, at least according to some feminists who believed that the ultimate triumph of "the woman movement" would result in unprecedented levels of social cooperation. Charlotte Perkins Gilman, the most creative and influential American feminist theorist, argued in *Women and Economics* (1898) that women's dependence on men had debased both sexes and had robbed society of the contributions independent women could make. Building on Gilman's influential arguments, some feminists sought to expand women's separate sphere to encompass the entire public realm, thereby bringing to political life the virtues of selflessness and sacrifice that had unfortunately been cordoned off from politics. In *The Man Made World, or Our Androcentric Culture* (1911), Gilman herself made such arguments explicit in an extended prescription for social reforms that complemented her earlier diagnosis of her culture's sickness. "The mother instinct," Gilman declared, "is one of unmixed devotion, of love and service, care and defense, with no self-interest." If that instinct could be brought to public life, citizens might develop "an intelligent interest in [their] social nature." As women leave the home and bring with them to public life "the principle of loving service," the male "habit of dominance and mastery" will be replaced. When women participate in politics, "Democratic government is no longer an exercise of arbitrary authority from those above, but is an organization for public service of the people themselves—or will be when it is really attained. In this change government ceases to be compulsion, and becomes agreement; law ceases to be authority and becomes co-ordination."

So complete would be the transformation from competition to cooperation, Gilman concluded, that "a flourishing democratic government [could] be carried on *without any parties at all*."

That confidence in the capacity of citizens to transcend their individual differences was a hallmark of much Progressive thinking. Although it was consistent with all four sources already discussed, the ideal of the public interest also drew heavily on the fifth source of Progressive political thinking, the philosophy of pragmatism. In his reconceptualization of experience, William James broke down the dualisms that had undergirded empiricist as well as rationalist philosophy, dualisms that had thereby contributed indirectly to the abstract and dogmatic theorizing characteristic of laissez-faire liberalism and revolutionary socialism. Proclaiming a radical theory of knowledge, James abandoned the philosophical quest for certainty, placing all ideas within their historical contexts and urging that an attitude of constant experimentation replace the search for timeless truths. Hermeneutical understanding, historically sophisticated and self-consciously aware of its provisionality, replaced certainty as James's standard for human knowledge.

The contribution of pragmatism to the Progressive-era search for a public interest that would transcend particularity is reflected in the writings of other feminists as well. The educational pioneer Lucy Sprague Mitchell studied with James while she was at Radcliffe, and later with John Dewey at Columbia. In her work as the first female dean at the University of California, and as founder of what was to become the Bank Street College of Education, she applied the principles of pragmatism to social reform. The too-little-known feminist philosopher Jessie Taft likewise attempted to apply pragmatic philosophy to social and political criticism. She studied at the University of Chicago with George Herbert Mead, and her book, *The Woman Movement from the Point of View of Social Consciousness* (1916), may have been the first philosophy dissertation written on feminist theory. She argued, as Gilman had done, that the purpose of the woman movement was less to emancipate women than to enable all people to "feel within themselves as their own the impulses and points of view of all classes and both sexes." Taft believed that women, especially women educated in pragmatism and the social sciences, had a particularly clear view of social conflict because of their marginality. For that reason they could see that the fundamental transformation of gender roles, not mere institutional reforms or the achievement of woman suffrage, was a necessary precondition to effecting permanent social and political change.

Such feminists were not alone in advancing political arguments from pragmatist foundations. W. E. B. Du Bois, who studied philosophy at Harvard, described himself as "a devoted follower of James at the time he was developing his pragmatic philosophy." Du Bois credited James with turning him away from "the sterilities of scholastic philosophy to realist pragmatism," and Albert Bushnell Hart with saving him from "the lovely but sterile land of philosophic speculation" and turning him toward "the social sciences as the field for gathering and interpreting that body of fact which would apply to my program for the Negro." Du Bois's program, and the means he suggested for its achievement, bore a striking resemblance to the ideas of Gilman and Taft. As he wrote in *The Souls of Black Folk* (1903),

> The history of the American Negro is the history of this strife—this longing to attain self-conscious manhood, to merge his double self into a better and truer self. In this merging he wishes neither of the older selves to be lost. He would not Africanize America, for America has too much to teach the world and Africa. He would not bleach his Negro soul in a flood of white Americanism, for he knows that Negro blood has a message for the world. He simply wishes to make it possible for a man to be both a Negro and an American, without being cursed and spit upon by his fellows, without having the doors of opportunity closed roughly in his face. This, then, is the end of his striving: to be a co-worker in the kingdom of culture.

In that spirit Du Bois undertook to edit *Crisis,* the periodical published by the newly formed National Association for the Advancement of Colored People. In its early years he was the only African American to serve as a national officer of the organization. His faith in the prospects for racial harmony would fade, but during the prewar years he shared the progressives' confidence in the possibility of cooperative reform.

The mercurial Walter Lippmann and the stolid Herbert Croly were two other prominent progressive theorists inspired by pragmatism. Eventually their confidence in reform, too, would falter, but prior to World War I they helped articulate progressive ideas in a series of important books and in *The New Republic,* the journal they founded in 1914 together with the reform-minded economist Walter Weyl. Both Lippmann and Croly had studied with James at Harvard, and both shared the common Progressive belief that pragmatism provided a fruitful method for thinking about political as well as philosophical problems. In his first book, *A Preface to Politics* (1913), Lippmann mocked those who set to work on politics "with a few inherited ideas, uncriticized assumptions, a foggy vocabulary, and machine philosophy." Instead Americans needed the flexibility only pragmatism and democracy together could provide. In *Drift and Mastery* (1914), Lippmann explained why radical philosophy and radical politics fit together. Now that our culture has lost confidence in authority, we must "substitute purpose for tradition." Just as the community of scientific inquiry reaches provisional agreement through testing hypotheses, so a democratic community must proceed through constant experimentation. The precise shape of the culture created by that process could not be delineated in advance. In *Drift and Mastery* Lippmann endorsed the full range of economic, social, and political reform measures advocated by most Progressives: "a minimum standard of life below which no human being can fall is the most elementary duty of the democratic state." Yet he emphasized that the democracy he had in mind could not be reduced to particular programs. "The day is past, when anybody can pretend to have laid down an inclusive or a final analysis of the democratic problem. Everyone is compelled to omit infinitely more than he can deal with; everyone is compelled to meet the fact that a democratic vision must be made by the progressive collaboration of many people."

If Lippmann's idea of "mastery" seemed vague, its imprecision was no worse—and no less deliberate—than was Croly's call for a "democratic St. Francis" at the conclusion of *The Promise of American Life* (1909). Due largely to Theodore Roosevelt's enthusiastic endorsement of its call for a "new nationalism" to supplant the old shibboleths of small-scale democratic individualism, *The Promise* established Croly as the most influential theorist of Progressivism. Whereas in *The Promise* Croly appeared to teeter unsteadily between science and mysticism, challenging every citizen to become "something of a saint and something of a hero," in *Progressive Democracy* he rooted his political ideas firmly in the philosophy of pragmatism. The resemblance between Lippmann's idea of mastery and Croly's conception of democracy as cooperative problem-solving derives from their shared reliance on pragmatism. Democracy, Croly wrote, "assumes the ability of the human intelligence to frame temporary programs which will provide a sufficient foundation for significant and fruitful action. It anticipates that as a result of such action a progressive democracy will learn how to be progressively democratic."

Although that formulation initially appears circular, it reflects instead Croly's incisive understanding that a genuinely democratic politics depends on a genuinely democratic culture, a culture not afraid of change. Croly urged Americans to unshackle their imaginations from the "presumably permanent body of constitutional law" and have the courage to experiment with "a social program which will not make any corresponding pretensions to finality." The only "permanent element in the life of the community will be derived," Croly concluded, from "the democratic faith and ideal." Croly never doubted that conflicts faced in that spirit could be resolved.

All the sources of Progressive political thinking—social science, the social gospel, social settlements, feminism, and pragmatism—came together in the life and work of John Dewey. Dewey was the towering figure of twentieth-century American political thought, and his development, along with Lippmann's, provides a thread connecting many of the central debates that have occupied those involved in shaping American political discourse. Although Dewey is best known as a philosopher, his ideas cannot be separated from the broader cultural ferment of progressivism. He first established his reputation with his writings in psychology; in his work on education he applied ideas about experience and interaction from psychologists and sociologists. From his early address, "Christianity and Democracy" (1892), to his unconventional *A Common Faith* (1934), Dewey grappled with the consequences of religious faith for politics. During his years at the University of Chicago around the turn of the century, Dewey was involved with the activities at Hull House. When he moved to Columbia University in New York in 1904, he became affiliated with Lillian Wald's Henry Street settlement. Dewey dedicated his most strident call to political radicalism, *Liberalism and Social Action* (1935), to the memory of Jane Addams. According to his daughter, Jane M. Dewey, whose biography of her father appeared in Paul Arthur Schlipp's *The Philosophy of John Dewey* (1939), Dewey enthusiastically supported "every cause that enlarged the freedom of activity of women," and Dewey attributed to the influence of Jane Addams his central, abiding conviction that "democracy is a way of life, the truly moral and human way of life, not a political institutional device."

Consistent with that belief, Dewey's political writings yoked together epistemological, psychological, sociological, and especially ethical arguments to sustain a program for democratic reform. For Dewey democracy was, from first to last, an ethical project. As he wrote in *The Ethics of Democracy* (1888), and reiterated tirelessly throughout his career, "Democracy is an ethical ideal. . . . Democracy and the one, the ultimate, ethical ideal of humanity are to my mind synonyms." But the precise meaning of democracy would for that very reason necessarily remain both fuzzy and elastic, since its shape could emerge only from the efforts of all citizens working together. That conception of democracy as a cooperative undertaking was doubtless the source of Dewey's great appeal; his apparent blindness to the pervasiveness and persistence of power was the principal reason his critics judged his political ideas naive.

Given the emphasis on flexibility that linked him with such Progressives as Croly and Lippmann, Dewey's views on particular issues shifted in ways that can be characterized as supple or opportunistic. Unlike Croly and Lippmann, both of whom endorsed Roosevelt in 1912, Dewey judged both Roosevelt and Wilson too timid and voted instead for Eugene Debs. By 1916, however, he admitted admiring Wilson for the reforms passed during his administration. Writing in *The New Republic* in 1916, Dewey acknowledged that Wilson "has appreciated the moving forces of present industrial life and has not permitted the traditional philosophy to stand in the way of doing the things that need to be done." Against all odds, Wilson had freed the Democratic party from nostalgia and reoriented it toward progressivism. "A party which is in effect as nationalistic as the Republican, but which allies its nationalism with the interests of the masses and not of the privileged pecuniary classes, is what, in my judgment, this country most needs." Roosevelt's New Nationalism, which emphasized accommodating and regulating concentrations of private power by counterposing public power, was widely believed to have been inspired by Croly. Wilson's New Freedom, which emphasized decentralization of all power, was widely believed to have been inspired by "the people's attorney," Louis Brandeis, who feared that concentrations of power in large-scale organizations, either private or public, necessarily threatened democracy. When the assumed dichotomy between Croly's and Brandeis's agendas seemed to dissolve in practice, Dewey, committed as a Pragmatist to revising his views on the basis of experience, shifted his allegiance—and his hopes for democratic reform—to Wilson in 1916. The events that were to unfold during Wilson's second term would prompt Dewey, together with many other Progressives, to think again.

AMERICAN INDIVIDUALISM: RETHINKING DEMOCRATIC CULTURE, 1918–1932

World War I brought Progressive democracy to an end. The sources of prewar reformist ideas seemed to run dry, as the Progressives' enthusiasm for democracy soured into disillusionment. A more careful look back at those sources, though, indicates that the developments of the 1920s flowed directly from submerged elements already present in Progressive political thinking.

First, social science, which some Progressives had seen as a weapon to be wielded for the cause of democratic reform, had from the beginning attracted others for a quite different reason, because it promised new and sophisticated techniques that could be used to achieve more effective social control. The study of politics in particular shifted from the broad nineteenth-century focus on culture and zeroed in on institutions and administration. The resulting discipline of political science employed different tools of analysis to reach a different objective: the successful management, or adjustment, of social and political conflicts that were assumed to be inevitable.

Second, the religious enthusiasm that fed the social gospel could lead away from radical Progressive reforms and toward the affirmation of more conservative positions in theology and politics. The fateful division of American Protestantism into its liberal and fundamentalist/Pentecostal wings in the 1920s marked the beginning of a division that would give religious arguments a very different resonance for American Progressives and Social Democrats than they ever had before.

Third, the spirit of voluntarism and democratic idealism that motivated many early settlement-house workers was from the outset at odds with an equally deep-seated moralism that saw the purpose of reform as the assimilation of outcasts into American middle-class culture. As social work developed into a profession, new notions of providing "services" to "clients" supplanted the earlier reformist ideals of Jane Addams and her generation.

Fourth, the broad-ranging cultural critique of early-twentieth-century feminism narrowed to concentrate on winning the vote. The rationale for woman suffrage shifted from the insistence on women's rights as human beings to the claim that women's unique sensibilities would transform and purify American public life. The "new woman" of the 1920s, although liberated from constraints of many kinds, was scarcely the new woman that thinkers such as Addams, Gilman, and Taft had envisioned.

Finally, pragmatism was transformed by social scientists in the 1920s from a robust philosophy into something unrecognizable. Psychologists inspired by John B. Watson and political scientists following the lead of Arthur Bentley and Wesley Clair Mitchell detached James's and Dewey's functionalism from its ethical and democratic foundations and christened the result behaviorism. In the words of Lord Kelvin, which William F. Ogburn had chiseled into stone on the wall of the Social Science Research Building at the University of Chicago, "If you cannot measure, . . . your knowledge . . . is meager." Drawn to that conception of knowledge, or bewitched by the lure of power, social scientists developed sophisticated technologies of behavioral modification and management, techniques antithetical to the voluntarism that was at the heart of pragmatism. The science of behaviorism dispensed with one of the pragmatists' most important insights, their understanding of the normative dimension of all human experience and activity. Behaviorists instead flattened the rich complexity of James's and Dewey's ideas into scientistic methods of conditioning, administration, and social engineering. Such methods were suited to managing well-adjusted workers and soothing happy consumers instead of contributing to the creation of the autonomous democratic citizens James and Dewey envisioned.

The anesthetizing effect of these developments was intensified by the consequences of the postwar Red Scare and its lingering aftereffects. The populace seemed lost in the mindless celebration of an American culture that had turned its back on the democratic potential of progressivism and embraced its most antidemocratic manifestations. Many writers went into exile; many political thinkers turned away in disgust. Harold Stearns's *Civilization in the United States* (1922) brought together commentators who shared Stearns's contempt for a barbaric civilization overwhelmed by vulgar materialism. In 1922, the *Nation* ran a series of articles, "These United States," in which such writers as H. L. Mencken, Sinclair Lewis, Sherwood Anderson, and William Allen White competed to produce the most savage satire. They offered a state-by-state survey of the crass, smug, ugly, conformist, dogmatic, lethargic, provincial, ignorant, and, worst of all, contented American people. In this desolate landscape, filled with hicks and yokels, what had happened to that hardy perennial of American political discourse, "the people," and who could lead them out of this wilderness and toward the promised land?

In 1922, a reviewer for the *New York Times* hailed the appearance of just such a prophet, whose new book ranked "among the few great formulations of American political theory. It bears much the same relation to the problems of the present and the future that the essays of Hamilton, Madison, Jay, and Noah Webster bore to the problems that occupied men's minds when the Constitution was framed." The book under review was Herbert Hoover's *American Individualism.* Hoover contrasted the ideology of American individualism with its principal competitors around the world, including communism, socialism, syndicalism, and autocracy. He also distinguished American individualism from capitalism and from the individualism of European democracies, insisting in good Progressive fashion that laissez faire was irresponsible, and that individualism without equal opportunity was repressive. The only individualism worth having—American individualism—must combine personal initiative with a deep spiritual commitment to the value of public service and the importance of cooperation. Instead of celebrating an entrepreneurial or consumerist ethos, Hoover celebrated regulation, equality, and responsibility. But of course that Progressive conception of responsible individualism contained a multitude of diverse possibilities, which Hoover himself embodied. As the great engineer and the savior of Belgium, Hoover had been in 1920 the preferred presidential candidate of democratically inclined Progressive intellectuals and corporate capitalists alike, the darling of those drawn to strikingly inconsistent notions of a "Progressive" America. *American Individualism* too was a Rorschach test: it invited and received a wide range of enthusiastic responses from across the political spectrum.

Among Hoover's admirers was Walter Lippmann, who had tried, along with Franklin D. Roosevelt, to persuade the Democratic party leadership to nominate Hoover for the presidency in 1920. Lippmann had also served (rather more quietly) in the American war effort as a part of the Inquiry, the group Wilson charged first with plotting strategy and then with plotting the boundaries for the new nations that were to spring forth from the Treaty of Versailles. Lippmann himself wrote most of Wilson's Fourteen Points. Also like Hoover, Lippmann derived from his wartime experience a new perspective on public life, which he presented in *Public Opinion* (1922), a book as celebrated in its day as *American Individualism.* The people, Lippmann lamented, could no longer be trusted to perform the tasks democracy demanded of them. Individuals are separated from the complex modern world by the "fictions in their heads." They inhabit artificial "pseudo-environments," which are kept in order thanks to the comforting but distorting "stereotypes" that help them make sense of an otherwise incomprehensible reality. In place of Jefferson's faith in idealized, "omnicompetent" citizens, the "dogma of democracy," America needed a "specialized class" of experts, operating with the security of lifetime tenure, to provide reliable information on issues of public policy. After mounting a devastating critique of the public's capacity to exercise sound critical judgment, Lippmann concluded *Public Opinion* by suggesting that a reformed educational system, by inculcating a passion for scientific inquiry, would enable the public to exercise sound critical judgment. Only readers unpersuaded by his diagnosis, however, could have faith in Lippmann's remedy. Lippmann's former allies could only shake their heads.

Reviewing *Public Opinion* in the *New Republic*, John Dewey applauded Lippmann's dissection of the problems besetting American democracy. But by focusing attention on the role of public advisers, and suggesting "the enlightenment of administrators and executives" as the solution, Lippmann had missed the point. Dewey insisted, as he had done before the war, that the challenge lay in creating citizens capable of the active and intelligent participation that American democracy clearly lacked. In *The Public and Its Problems* (1927), perhaps the clearest statement of his political ideas, Dewey responded to Lippmann's challenge. Dewey began by denying fashionable behaviorist and naturalist conceptions of social science, insisting that normative questions of meaning and value are inescapable in all human inquiry. Because man is a social and historical being, philosophy and politics alike must remain flexible, attuned to cultural change. Dewey advanced three arguments that, in other forms, would attract a great deal of attention when applied by critics to later versions of rights-based liberalism. First, Dewey wrote, "The idea of a natural individual in his isolation possessed of full-fledged wants, of energies to be expended according to his own volition, and of a ready-made faculty of foresight and prudent calculation is as much a fiction in psychology as the doctrine of the individual in possession of antecedent political rights is one in politics." Questions of desire, and conceptions of interest, are historical rather than timeless.

Second, Dewey continued, the idea of community needs to be demystified and understood as a part of everyday experience.

> Events cannot be passed from one another, but meanings may be shared by means of signs. Wants and impulses are then attached to common meanings. They are thereby transformed into desires and purposes, which, since they implicate a common or mutually understood meaning, present new ties, converting a conjoint activity into a community of interest and endeavor. Thus there is generated what, metaphorically, may be termed a general will and social consciousness: desire and choice on the part of individuals in behalf of activities that, by means of symbols, are communicable and shared by all concerned.

Community is not something elusive or romantic; it is forged by individuals through the imperfect process of communication and brought to life through their active participation in joint endeavors.

Third, Dewey challenged the idea of a democracy administered efficiently and benevolently by elites who claim to know better than the public what needs to be done.

> No government by experts in which the masses do not have a chance to inform the experts as to their needs can be anything but an oligarchy managed in the interests of the few. And the enlightenment must proceed in ways which force the administrative specialists to take account of the public's needs. The world has suffered more from leaders and authorities than from the masses. The essential need, in other words, is the improvement of the methods and conditions of debate, discussion and persuasion. That is *the* problem of the public.

The democratic project involves widespread participation and critical reflection on the constitution of desires, the communication of ideas, the construction of communities, and the shaping of public policy. That democratic ideal derives, Dewey pointed out, from the experience of individuals in their families, their homes, and their neighborhoods; only if we can find ways to extend those experiences to the broader local, state, and national levels can we create a genuinely democratic culture.

As *American Individualism, Public Opinion,* and *The Public and Its Problems* illustrate, the problems addressed by Progressive political thinkers did not disappear in the 1920s. Instead, given the consolidation of power in new private and pubic hierarchies, and the attendant triumph of technocratic values and managerial strategies, those problems changed shape.

The alienation exhibited by many American intellectuals in the 1920s reflects their dissatisfaction with the direction in which public life appeared to be developing. But when viewed in a comparative perspective, and placed next to the alternatives being offered by European champions of fascism, corporatism, and communism, the distinctive frameworks of Progressive thought remain evident beneath the different solutions proposed by Hoover, Lippmann, and Dewey.

With the onset of the Depression, those frameworks began to fade from view. Hoover's presidency was overwhelmed when his reliance on voluntary cooperation collided with the reality of conflict in conditions of scarcity. Lippmann's *A Preface to Morals* (1929) called for a return to asceticism, stoicism, and "disinterestedness." Although the book was published before the stock market crashed, its phenomenal success reflected the uncanny appropriateness of its counsel at a moment when political activity seemed pointless and despair offered a more attractive alternative. Dewey, almost alone, kept the democratic faith. In *The Quest for Certainty* (1929), he updated the history of ideas he had offered a decade earlier in *Reconstruction in Philosophy* (1920), insisting that Western culture would escape its dead ends of dogmatic philosophy and authoritarian politics only when it finally discarded the discredited effort to achieve and enforce certain knowledge. Whereas Lippmann had come to see in that loss of certainty the melancholy acknowledgment of finitude, for Dewey the loss promised at last the prospect of a new culture designed and built by ordinary people to replace what had been imposed on them from above.

To redeem that promise was the goal of Dewey's *Individualism Old and New* (1930). Dewey believed, as Hoover did, that American individualism differed from earlier, European varieties because it sprang from a different tradition, which "contains within itself the ideal of equality of opportunity and of freedom for all, without regard to birth and status, as a condition for its effective realization of that equality." Although it was the "spiritual element of our tradition" that distinguished this new individualism from the old, in "the pecuniary culture characteristic of our civilization" that "spiritual factor . . . is obscured and crowded out." Dewey believed that emphasis on an ethic of voluntary service did not go far enough. Again the answer lay in democratic participation. We must use "the realities of a corporate civilization to validate and embody the distinctive moral element in the American version of individualism: Equality and freedom expressed not merely externally and politically but through personal participation in the development of a shared culture." The differences between Hoover's and Dewey's ideas are clear enough, but the resonances are nevertheless striking. They shared a common confidence that America's political tradition contained resources rich enough to restore hope where cynics saw only grounds for despair. Both identified that hope with versions of an enlarged individualism. The roots of that idea stretched back beyond the "self-interest properly understood"—individualism refined from egoism by participation in political associations—that so impressed Tocqueville to the ethically charged amalgamation of religious, republican, and liberal ideas in the eighteenth century.

LIBERALISM AND SOCIAL ACTION: THE PARADOXES OF THE NEW DEAL, 1933–1948

The choice between Hoover and Franklin D. Roosevelt in 1932 struck most intellectuals as unappetizing. A surprising number joined the Committee of One Hundred Thousand, a somewhat optimistic title for what was nevertheless an impressive collection of writers who supported the Socialist party candidate, Norman Thomas. Among those affiliated with the committee were many of the critics who had been alienated from politics in the 1920s; John Dewey was one of its officers. Both the *Nation* and the *New Republic* endorsed Thomas. During the campaign Hoover seemed lost, Roosevelt inconsistent. But after his victory Roosevelt enlisted bright young intellectuals to design and administer the programs of his New Deal, and many skeptical radicals quickly became fans. Henry Wallace, Rexford Tugwell, Harold Ickes, and Charles Merriam all brought great energy and an apparent—and, to many, inspiring—commitment to social-democratic politics. Many writers thought they could make out distinctly communitarian overtones in the rhetoric of the early New Deal, and they waited with eager anticipation to assess the consequences of this new departure.

They did not have to wait long. For a variety of complex institutional and political reasons, the New Deal failed to live up to those early expectations, and the ideal of a national-planning state faded. In place of Wallace's and Tugwell's solidaristic rhetoric came more sober reformist calls from Thurmond Arnold and Felix Frankfurter, in the spirit of Louis Brandeis, for decentralizing and regulating the economy. The tacking and veering of the New Deal, although necessitated by choppy political waters, satisfied few political commentators.

Radicals felt themselves pushed further toward varieties of socialism and communism, both of which attracted more enthusiastic support among more intellectuals than at any time before or since. Dewey's student Sidney Hook tried valiantly, if vainly, to forge a philosophical alliance between Marxism and pragmatism. But as Max Eastman (among others) pointed out, one could not at the same time both claim to know the plot of history and deny that history has a plot. For young writers such as Irving Howe, the appeal of communism in the early 1930s lay precisely in the confidence it inspired, an invigorating change from the rudderless alienation that so many intellectuals felt in the previous decade.

Conservative reactions to the New Deal predictably ranged from alarm to horror. Hoover abandoned all vestiges of his early interest in cooperation between the private and public spheres. In *The Challenge to Liberty* (1934), Hoover branded the New Deal's tentative experiments with economic planning a dangerous threat to freedom. Lippmann too tried to sever his ties to his progressive past, but he failed to make a clean break. In *The Good Society* (1937), he admitted that America needed to construct a system of social insurance, that the current distribution of wealth was unacceptable, and that government spending would be required to rebuild America and restore economic growth. Despite the resemblance between that program and Roosevelt's, Lippmann saw in the New Deal an ominous foreshadowing of collectivism. The apocalyptic tone of his critique suggested that something odd was happening to American social commentary, an amplification of hopes and fears whose echoes would persist for several decades. Further raising the volume were the raucous appeals of Louisiana Senator Huey Long, Father Charles Coughlin, and Dr. Francis Townsend, who capitalized on personal magnetism to advance a variety of programs hard to place on the political spectrum.

Awakening from the slumber of isolationism, Americans were startled to see that Europe was again slouching toward war. From the mid-1930s onward, American political ideas cannot be understood without reference to European developments. In the 1920s, the idea of planning was discussed openly by politicians as moderate as Hoover and Roosevelt; by the 1940s it was anathema. In the early 1930s, the Soviet Union represented to many Americans an intriguing experiment in social engineering; by the end of the decade it was the scene of the purge trials and the source of the insurance policy (the Nazi-Soviet Pact) that freed Hitler to unleash his panzers on Poland. In tandem, fascism and communism changed everything, and as a result America too began to look quite different.

Dewey's progress through the 1930s illustrates that change. In 1934, he joined the editorial board of *Social Frontier,* a periodical committed to the idea that "an age of collectivism is opening." In 1935, he published *Liberalism and Social Action* in which he extended his earlier arguments for radical democratic politics and proclaimed that "the cause of liberalism will be lost for a considerable period if it is not prepared to go further and socialize the forces of production." Three years later, explaining "What I Believe" in *Forum* magazine, Dewey admitted "a change in emphasis," acknowledging that he had lost his enthusiasm for central economic planning. In *Freedom and Culture* (1939), Dewey stressed the oppressive weight of the Soviet state and contended that Stalin had obliterated any prospects for democracy that communism might once have contained. Also in 1939, Dewey joined with Hook and others to form the Committee for Cultural Freedom. In their founding manifesto, they linked Hitler's Germany with Stalin's Soviet Union, formally repudiating the popular front against fascism that had attracted many American radicals prior to the purge trials and the Nazi-Soviet Pact. Dewey continued to criticize Roosevelt, but his focus shifted from his earlier impatience with the moderation of the New Deal to concern about Roosevelt's inclination to strengthen the power of the federal government.

If Dewey's growing wariness about collectivism reflected an increased sensitivity to developments in Europe, it also reflected an increased sensitivity to developments closer to home. Besides backing Norman Thomas in 1932, Dewey had supported the state senate campaign of fellow New Yorker Reinhold Niebuhr, who won 4 percent of the vote as the Socialist party candidate. Their political alliance disguised Dewey's and Niebuhr's profoundly different perspectives on politics. In *Moral Man and Immoral Society* (1932), Niebuhr singled out Dewey to illustrate his broader contention that liberals placed unwarranted faith in reason. Because they refused to acknowledge irrationality, liberals such as Dewey overlooked the pervasiveness of sin and the consequent persistence of power. Until Americans confronted conflict realistically, Niebuhr concluded, plans for democratic reform would go nowhere.

Niebuhr's prominence reflected the return of religious voices to the discourse of American reform, as did the appearance of Dorothy Day's *Catholic Worker* and the spread of the Catholic Worker movement. Both Niebuhr and Day scorned the easy pieties of liberalism and hearkened back to sterner, more demanding versions of Christianity that stressed human sinfulness and divine justice. Particularly after the combined impact of the events of the 1930s, and his brother H. Richard's turn toward the astringent theology of Karl Barth, Niebuhr rejected radical politics and called instead for repentance. In *The Nature and Destiny of Man* (1940), he stressed even more emphatically the gulf dividing humanity from God. Religious voices from the Left thus joined the larger chorus denouncing the New Deal, and liberalism more broadly, for its facile confidence in progress and its refusal to admit the intractability of the problems facing American culture.

Intractable those problems proved to be, not least because of the straitjacket that Republicans and Southern Democrats wrapped around the New Deal's few bold initiatives. The constraints imposed by federalism, the separation of powers, and the two-party system, to say nothing of Roosevelt's own instinctive caution, conspired to limit his latitude. Yet given the obvious political perils of social democracy, Roosevelt's continued gestures in that direction are difficult to understand unless he genuinely sought reform. When he commissioned the National Resources Planning Board to draw up blueprints for an extensive, democratically administered welfare state, he hoped they would chart a path between Americans' longstanding distrust of state power and their desire for social-welfare programs to ensure equal opportunity for all citizens.

An obscure young graduate student named Hubert H. Humphrey, writing a thesis in politics at Louisiana State University in 1940, understood clearly the limitations within which Roosevelt was forced to operate. Humphrey noted the gap that separated the radical experimentalism of Dewey's pragmatism from the prudence of the New Deal. In "The Political Philosophy of the New Deal," an essay whose title would have struck many contemporaries—as indeed it strikes later critics—as delicious if unconscious comedy, Humphrey offered a judicious and incisive assessment of Roosevelt's presidency: "The pragmatism of the New Deal stops at the gateway of immediate fundamental change in either the political or economic order." Anticipating and dissolving a later debate, he declared that "the New Deal is neither revolution nor counterrevolution." Instead, it represents "American democracy working within the political and economic limitations of established government and private enterprise." Humphrey understood that Americans were not about to abandon the Constitution or capitalism, despite the severity of the Depression, and for that reason Roosevelt had no choice but to make haste slowly.

Within those boundaries, Roosevelt's desire for change was strong. But by the time the NRPB Report was available in 1943, the solidaristic language of Roosevelt's early initiatives had been tarnished by the perceived failures of the experiments with communitarianism and statism in Europe, as well as by the failures of his own administration. Roosevelt had learned a lot. He knew that Henry Wallace had become a political liability for various reasons, including his association with the discredited idea of economic planning, and he was prepared to sacrifice his vice president. FDR knew that his scheme for social security was politically safe only because all workers "earned" the benefits they would receive, and he knew that only the plan's contributory principle distinguished social security from other "handouts" that came with stigmas attached.

Thus when Roosevelt sought to make the NRPB Report the basis for his 1944 state of the union address, the dramatic speech in which he pledged "economic security, social security, moral security" for all Americans, he felt compelled to frame his unfamiliar agenda in the familiar vocabulary of individual rights. He labeled his plan a second Bill of Rights, even though the policies he outlined would have shifted American politics decisively toward economic and social democracy. Roosevelt tried to justify his proposals for full employment, a minimum income, antimonopoly legislation, universal housing, universal health care, and insurance against old age, sickness, accidents, and unemployment—the full social-democratic agenda—in terms of their contribution to protecting individual rights. Whereas earlier American champions of such programs had argued in terms of equality or justice, by 1944 the language of rights was the only viable language available. As it turned out, even draped in the ill-fitting robe of rights, Roosevelt's plan for American social democracy failed to command assent. But he had taken a fateful step by abandoning the Progressives' ideals of justice and equality. When he stated his most far-reaching call for change in terms of individual rights, Roosevelt shifted the terms of debate and inadvertently sealed the fate of such social democratic initiatives, for himself and for those reformers who followed him. After World War II, calls for reform in American politics, if they were to be effective, would have to be demands for civil rights rather than pleas for social or economic justice. In the history of American political discourse, the difference has proved to be decisive.

THE END OF IDEOLOGY: CELEBRATING CONSENSUS, 1949–1963

Many of the political thinkers who resisted the nostrums of Dr. New Deal willingly swallowed the remedies of Dr. Win-the-War. Intellectuals who embraced the Allied cause had reason to celebrate America's contributions, and the celebration continued when the war ended. Particularly when the world soon again seemed hostile, and the United States found itself facing, as enemies in a Cold War, the world's two largest (if hardly the most powerful) nations, it made sense to rally around the American flag, or at least to appreciate that it was still flying: the world's first constitutional democracy, after all, had survived to become its oldest.

The war had done wonders for America. Unprecedented government spending not only lifted the economy out of depression, at last, it persuaded policymakers that Keynesian strategies could deliver lasting prosperity. Without the pressure of scarcity, conflicts could be postponed forever, both planning and regulation could be avoided, and the effects of economic concentration and political lethargy could be endured happily by consumers growing steadily more affluent. Learning those lessons dramatically altered policymakers' views of the American cultural landscape. Both the first and second New Deals looked less like noble failures than wasteful expenditures of scarce political resources. Keynes had triumphed over both Croly and Brandeis.

Even Reinhold Niebuhr pocketed his scorn for American liberalism. No book better reflected the overwhelming impact of America's wartime experience than *The Children of Light and the Children of Darkness* (1944). Niebuhr simply divided the world in two. The children of darkness included Nazi, Fascist, and Stalinist "moral cynics," who admitted no law beyond their own evil wishes. The children of light, by contrast, knew that self-interest must be disciplined. In their number Niebuhr enlisted practically everyone else, including Locke and Rousseau, Adam Smith and Marx, utilitarians, and even "educators" (by which he appeared to mean Deweyans). Beneath the shadow cast by totalitarianism, all other political theories appeared to Niebuhr more similar than different, and many other writers shared that judgment. Although Niebuhr himself remained critical of the distance separating America from its democratic aspirations, as *The Irony of American History* (1952) showed, Americans' revulsion toward the defeated children of darkness led most political thinkers to identify their culture with the children of light.

Consistent with such Manichean formulations, those who gloried in the triumph of American democracy found pragmatism unattractive. Compared with the alternatives of natural law, toward which thinkers such as Lippmann had been leaning even before World War II, ascetic Christianity of the sort Niebuhr embodied, and the clear evidence from the natural and behavioral sciences that they could deliver results, the pragmatists' counsel of moderation premised on the awareness of uncertainty seemed pale and unsatisfying. Dewey confronted the challenge in a new preface to his *Reconstruction in Philosophy,* which was published in a new edition in 1948. Denying charges that moral relativism lay beneath the savage outbreaks of totalitarianism, Dewey warned that those who invoked religious, moral, political, or economic absolutes themselves fed a dangerous intolerance that could stifle dissent. Within a few years, that warning would appear prophetic, as Senator Joseph McCarthy's charges of communist conspiracies would ignite a bonfire of intolerance.

In the late 1940s on all sides of this controversy, though, partisans agreed that America embodied the essential principle necessary for democracy. For champions of Aristotelianism and Christian neo-orthodoxy, that principle was fidelity to unchanging ideals. For champions of science and social science, that principle was hardheaded empiricism. For champions of Deweyan pragmatism, the principle was a democratic commitment to inquiry. Despite their deep disagreements, all of them identified American culture, as they understood it in their very different ways, as the standard by which other nations, and other political systems, could be judged—and found wanting. The threat of totalitarianism loomed so ominously that Americans took shelter in what they judged most familiar. When European émigré Hannah Arendt proclaimed authoritatively, in *The Origins of Totalitarianism* (1951), that totalitarianism was utterly unprecedented, and that it dissolved all existing political categories, she seemed to validate Americans' impulse to celebrate the culture that had vanquished that threat.

An early indicator of the powerful dynamic at work in postwar American culture was the formation of Americans for Democratic Action in 1947. While sharing a domestic agenda more progressive than that of the Democratic party, ADA founders emphasized their strident anticommunism to distinguish themselves from Henry Wallace's more sympathetic view of the Soviet Union. Truman's upset election in 1948 heartened hard-boiled reformers such as those in the ADA; some even hoped Truman's Fair Deal would at last redeem the promise of Roosevelt's second Bill of Rights. But Congress greeted Truman's version of an expansive welfare state with the same distrust Roosevelt's had met. Lacking support from the diverse coalitions of labor, farmers, and professionals that enacted similar social legislation elsewhere in the industrialized world during these years—Roosevelt complained that England's Beveridge Plan should have been called the Roosevelt Plan because of its resemblance to the report of his NRPB—American social democrats were defeated by the combination of contentment and the fear of collectivism. Political writing in the postwar years reinforced both of those impulses.

Joining Niebuhr in the ADA were ex-New Dealers, labor leaders, and two writers who would become prominent commentators in the postwar years, Arthur Schlesinger, Jr., and John Kenneth Galbraith. In *The Vital Center* (1949), Schlesinger shrewdly appropriated for himself and his moderate allies the American tradition of reform. Chastened realism, commitment to individualism and voluntary associations, and confidence in America's can-do spirit characterized the vital center. To its left as well as its right lay totalitarianism, tyranny, and oppression. Although Schlesinger admitted that industrialization had brought not only affluence but anxiety, alienation, fear, and even despair, he counseled readers to abandon utopianism and place their faith in America's free society.

Galbraith provided one of the most compelling and influential explanations of America's success in *American Capitalism: The Theory of Countervailing Power* (1952). Although the economy had grown in the ways that Brandeis, for example, had feared, and was now dominated by oligopolies, these economic mammoths had proved in practice to be stabilizing rather than threatening forces. The countervailing powers of big firms, big labor, and of different segments of the economy contributed to achieving a rough equilibrium. Since the system worked, government should exercise restraint in regulating it. Galbraith himself later revised and even rejected this argument, notably in *The Affluent Society* (1958), and even more forcefully in other volumes that followed. But in the 1950s his analysis proved irresistible to many social scientists, because it provided an economic analysis that bolstered the prevailing political theory of pluralism.

Earlier political theorists, including especially James Madison and Alexis de Tocqueville, had emphasized the salutary consequences of individuals' participation in a variety of voluntary organizations. According to pluralists writing in the 1950s, membership in various groups alleviates the potentially destabilizing effects of industrialization and disenchantment associated with the breakdown of stable communities. In addition to providing individuals with the means to escape—or at least cope with—the anomie of life in modern society, such groups also contribute to political stability. Multiple group memberships, because they cut across the lines of religion, class, race, and ethnicity, enable elites to manage, rationalize, and moderate political conflict. David Riesman argued in *The Lonely Crowd* (1950) that the strength of group identifications reduced chances of political turmoil in America, even though that peace was purchased at a considerable cultural price. In contrast to the autonomy prized by earlier generations of Americans, modern Americans found satisfaction through others' eyes: they were "other directed" rather than "inner directed." According to Robert Dahl in *A Preface to Democratic Theory* (1956), political power, concentrated in other systems, was in America uniquely diffuse. Whereas conflicts typically emerge from the clash between an overbearing majority and an oppressed minority, in the United States, as Dahl put it, "minorities rule." In addition to offering a description of how American pluralism worked, Dahl offered American practice as the criterion for democratic culture. Dahl, like Galbraith, later changed his mind, but in the 1950s his writings seemed to demonstrate that pluralism assured both order and a rough approximation of justice.

American politics works, pluralists believed, because Americans agree about essential issues and squabble, albeit sometimes boisterously, only about relatively insignificant differences. They agree about the rules of the game, even when they disagree about how it should be played. The widely read and celebrated historian Daniel Boorstin baptized this consensus *The Genius of American Politics* (1953), and he argued that it was made possible by Americans' admirable ignorance of political theory. Rather than arranging themselves into doctrinaire, ideologically sophisticated, programmatic political parties, as Europeans seemed always to do, Americans accommodated themselves to an imperfect world, clustered around the political center, and disputed questions of policy rather than fundamental—and dangerously divisive—questions of principle. The historian David Potter attributed American consensus to the richness of the nation's resources and the ingenuity of those who exploited them. Together, abundance and technology could explain the distinctive American character: Americans were a *People of Plenty* (1954). Although he came to denigrate consensus, not to praise it, Louis Hartz offered a portrait of *The Liberal Tradition in America* (1955) that paralleled other pluralist accounts but differed sharply in its disappointed, sometimes bitter tone. Lacking a feudal past, Hartz argued, America developed neither a political Right that could cherish aristocracy nor a political Left that could vow to destroy it. Lacking a revolution worthy of the name, America developed neither nostalgic reactionaries nor romantic utopians. Since Americans were born equal, they concerned themselves only with freedom. Blessed with abundant land and resources, Americans were blinded by their own good luck; their "national irrational liberalism" prevented them from understanding the tragic fate of other people in the world.

Although Hartz's narrative of American liberalism now seems too flat and too static, and his argument seems to depend more on epigram and allusion than evidence or even analysis, his conceptualization of American liberalism had a deep and lasting effect on scholarly debate and, more indirectly, on political discourse. For if only discussions of liberty, and considerations of rights, had a legitimate place in the American political tradition, then conservatives and radicals alike were justified in claiming that discussions of equality required stepping outside the fundamental American consensus. Conversely, when challenges were launched from extremes against the middle, liberal pluralists felt confident in dismissing them. McCarthyism presented an obvious test case for pluralist theory and social scientists proved worthy of the challenge. From an interdisciplinary seminar at Columbia University in the early 1950s emerged an ambitious, collaborative attempt to explain the phenomenon, a book edited by the sociologist Daniel Bell and first published as *The New American Right* (1955). The contributors distinguished between "class politics," which was rational, grounded in economic interest, limited in aspirations, and for all of those reasons typically American, and "mass politics," which was irrational, grounded in psychological maladjustment, utopian, and thus un-American. Whereas the former politics was pluralist, the latter—of which extremist, reactionary McCarthyism was a perfect example—tended toward dogmatism at best and toward totalitarianism at worst. Studies of McCarthy's support have since demonstrated that his appeal was actually consistent with old-fashioned rural conservatism. But while such evidence may undercut the liberal pluralists' explanation, it highlights the powerful appeal of consensus as an analytical construct. Any political upheaval that the center could not contain must be irrational. For the historian Richard Hofstadter, one of the contributors to *The New American Right,* what was true of McCarthyism was also true of Populism and Progressivism. In *The Age of Reform* (1955), Hofstadter portrayed the Populists as irrational, xenophobic, and anti-Semitic; the Progressives as members of an old middle class anxious about losing their status. Both groups indulged in mass political actions best understood as futile, ceremonial gestures against modernity. The New Deal, by contrast, relied on balancing legitimate group interests; it was a model of pluralist accommodation.

If competition among interest groups exhausted the sphere of legitimate political activity, what role was left for political ideas? Disillusioned by the failures of communism, instructed by the findings of liberal-pluralist social science, and impressed by the apparent consolidation of social democracy in Western Europe, a group of intellectuals gathered in Milan in 1955 for a conference sponsored by the Congress for Cultural Freedom and quietly subsidized by the CIA. From their discussions, Daniel Bell was inspired to construct a bold interpretation of what had been happening. When the resulting book was published, it bore the title *The End of Ideology: On the Exhaustion of Political Ideas in the Fifties* (1962). Bell described members of his generation as "twice born." They had passed from their first youth, their radicalism in the 1930s, only to emerge from the sobering realities of war and totalitarianism still, or rather again, young, but transformed. They had learned from experience the folly of all "total ideologies" and the real potential of pragmatic social democracy. Their outlook was a chastened skepticism, their political ideas a combination of pluralism, decentralization, and support for mixed economies and more comprehensive welfare states. Beyond that, Bell concluded, his generation was not prepared to go. But incisive as Bell's argument was, and consistent as it was with some of the most widely held political ideas of its day, his timing could hardly have been worse. Almost as soon as the end of ideology was announced, ideology returned with a vengeance.

WHOSE JUSTICE? WHICH RATIONALITY? CONFRONTING DIVERSITY, 1963–1993

In the closing pages of *The End of Ideology,* Bell noted that the lessons learned by his generation assumed special importance because "a new Left with few memories of the past is emerging." As he suspected, members of that New Left resisted his counsel; that they had few memories of the past is less clear. They distanced themselves from the old Left, the more doctrinaire Left of the 1930s, but they drew heavily from other traditions in the American past. Thoreau provided particular inspiration, not only his essay on civil disobedience but his example of living the simple life at Walden pond. When Students for a Democratic

Society (SDS) distributed a recommended reading list in 1961, it included (among other things) the Declaration of Independence, Dewey's *The Public and Its Problems,* and Bell's *The End of Ideology.* In 1962, Tom Hayden wrote the Port Huron Statement, which was to become the manifesto of the New Left, while consulting *The Public and Its Problems.* A year earlier he had traveled from the University of Michigan to New York City, where he met Daniel Bell, discussed *The End of Ideology,* and explained his own hopes for democratic renewal. From its architects' perspective, SDS stood in a proud tradition of radical democratic action. "Participatory democracy" served the New Left as rallying cry and shorthand political theory; its lineage could be traced directly to Dewey's responses to Lippmann's *Public Opinion.* But as its successes and failures would both reflect, the commitment to local democracy continued to present the same challenges familiar from the progressive period: those opposed to change also took seriously the call to participation. Egalitarian democrats had to decide what to do when "the people" did not share the priorities of those who sought to inspire them.

If Dewey was the New Left's grandfather, more proximate influences included C. Wright Mills, the radical sociologist whose critique of American culture stood in sharp contrast to the celebrations of consensus in the postwar years; religious and existentialist philosophers who decried the meaninglessness of lives without commitment; and the electrifying examples of those involved in the civil rights movement, whose lives seemed to embody such commitment. According to Hayden, an interview with Martin Luther King, Jr., at the Democratic Party National Convention in 1960 was the transforming moment of Hayden's life, because it convinced him to put away his journalist's pen and become a political activist. A beating Hayden received from a white man a year later, while he was in Mississippi helping to register black voters, brought home to him, as similar experiences did to many, the obstacles facing radicals who were committed to social change as well as democratic participation. The civil rights movement drew on many sources. The tradition of civil disobedience from Thoreau and Mohandas Gandhi provided a strategy. American theologians such as Rauschenbusch and Niebuhr linked religious faith and political action. The scholarship and activism of black writers such as the sociologist E. Franklin Frazier provided insight into African American culture. The writings and example of Du Bois, whose Marxist-inspired radicalism in the 1930s led to a prison sentence in 1951 and then exile in Ghana, alerted black Americans to potential contacts, and support, in the third world. In Frantz Fanon's *The Wretched of the Earth* (1961), and in his other writings, they found a contemporary voice passionately condemning oppression. Perhaps the most important sources, though, were biblical stories of bondage and liberation, which King and other civil rights leaders used repeatedly, and the secular tradition of individual rights, which drew on American liberalism and appealed to the central value proclaimed by American political writers in the postwar period.

By far the most significant political ideas of the civil rights movement came from King and from Malcolm X. Although their ideas are usually presented as a study in contrast, their trajectories before their assassinations point toward another conclusion. King's eloquent "Letter from the Birmingham Jail," which was printed in the *Christian Century* on 12 June 1963, and the concluding pages of *The Autobiography of Malcolm X* (1964), suggest such a convergence. King defended his strategy of nonviolent civil disobedience, much as Niebuhr did in *Moral Man and Immoral Society,* by denying the moral force of unjust laws. He admitted the vulnerability of standing "in the middle of two opposing forces in the Negro community." On the one side stood complacent blacks, those either demoralized and "adjusted to segregation" or relatively comfortable and "insensitive to the problems of the masses." On the other side were those driven by "bitterness and hatred" who came "perilously close to advocating violence"; in their vanguard were various militant groups, especially the Black Muslims led by Elijah Muhammad. "I have tried to stand between these two forces," King wrote, "saying that we need emulate neither the 'do-nothingism' of the complacent nor the hatred of the black nationalist. For there is the more excellent way of love and nonviolent protest." King likened the struggle for civil rights to other struggles for justice being fought around the world. He placed himself and his allies in a long tradition of "extremists" fighting for justice, a tradition stretching from Old Testament prophets through Jesus and early Christian martyrs to Jefferson, Lincoln, and the heroes produced by the civil rights movement itself. He concluded with the two most powerful arguments in his arsenal, appealing to shared religious convictions and the American tradition of natural rights:

> We will win our freedom because the sacred heritage of our nation and the eternal will of God are embodied in our echoing demands. . . . One day the South will know that when these disinherited children of

> God sat down at lunch counters they were in reality standing up for what is best in the American dream and for the most sacred values in our Judeo-Christian heritage, thereby bringing our nation back to those great wells of democracy which were dug deep by the founding fathers in their formulation of the Constitution and the Declaration of Independence.

The Autobiography of Malcolm X begins as a book smoldering with anger, becomes a book of rage, and ends as a book aspiring to brotherhood. Malcolm's impatience with moderation during the years of his most intense radicalism prompted him to dismiss the utility of civil disobedience and mock King's confidence that appeals to assumed common ideals would lead to racial justice. King might have a dream, but singing spirituals and invoking the ghost of Lincoln would never make it a reality or end black Americans' long nightmare. The great March on Washington in 1963 Malcolm described as a "circus," "a monumental farce," which only encouraged blacks to continue waiting for whites to give them what he believed they would have to take for themselves.

After his break with Elijah Muhammad in 1964, however, and as a result of his experiences on trips to the Middle East and Africa, Malcolm X began to see things differently. While he remained committed to separatism as a strategy for blacks seeking to alter their subservient status in white America, and he remained cynical about any progress blacks could achieve through the help of a southern white "fox" such as Lyndon Johnson, Malcolm began to see beyond division the dim prospect of cooperation. He realized, as he put it, "that the white man is *not* inherently evil," as he had been taught by Elijah Muhammad, "but America's racist society influences him to act evilly. The society has produced and nourishes a psychology which brings out the lowest, most base part of human beings." Proceeding along their distinct paths, blacks and whites working to end racism

> might be able to show a road to the salvation of America's very soul. It can only be salvaged if human rights and dignity, in full, are extended to black men. Only such real, meaningful actions as those which are sincerely motivated from a deep sense of humanism and moral responsibility can get at the basic causes that produce the racial explosions in America today.

Although the approaches to justice would remain different—as his strategy remained different from "King's nonviolent marching"—nevertheless the "goal has always been the same."

But the language of rights, necessary and even shrewd as it might have seemed strategically, proved to be a cul-de-sac. Activists had nowhere to turn once the Civil Rights Act of 1964 and the Voting Rights Act of 1965 were enacted. Many rejected moderation for more violent strategies to effect change. Attention shifted from King's Southern Christian Leadership Conference to the more militant Student Non-Violent Coordinating Committee, and after 1966 to the still more militant Black Panthers. By 1968 even King had lost patience. Radicalized by America's escalation of the Vietnam War and by the limited success of the civil rights movement, by the time of his death King had started a Poor People's Campaign that looked beyond political liberalism toward a more expansive social democracy. It had become apparent that the problems facing black Americans were cultural as much as political, rooted in a racism that proved stubbornly resistant to change.

Feminists faced a similar problem. The second wave of American feminism began with the publication of Betty Friedan's *The Feminine Mystique* in 1963. By challenging the ideology of domesticity, Friedan offered a rationale for changes that were already underway in American culture. Large numbers of women, many with college educations, were postponing marriage or at least childbearing, and entering the work force. They were refusing to play the parts scripted for them by their male-dominated culture and justified by social scientists' arguments for women's separate sphere, such as those advanced by Ferdinand Lundberg and Marynia Farnham in *Modern Woman: The Lost Sex* (1947). Such disaffected women formed the core supporters of the National Organization for Women (NOW), which was founded in 1966 to support enforcement of the antidiscrimination clause of the 1964 Civil Rights Act. Patterning their efforts on the New Left and the civil rights movement, the women's movement faced some of the same strategic and cultural problems.

Like black activists, women splintered into more and less militant camps. The upper-middle-class professionals of NOW did not seek so much to change the American system as to be permitted to enter it and succeed by its rules. A more radical feminism, announced by Kate Millett in *Sexual Politics* (1970), challenged the adequacy of the NOW approach. Moderate and radical feminists disagreed about philosophical as well as strategic issues. Radical feminists questioned the long-standing assumption, accepted by earlier champions as well as critics of feminism, that because women are biologically different from men, they are destined to play different cultural roles as well. Earlier feminists grounded their arguments on women's special nature, arguing that women's unique gift for nurturing would help to purify male-dominated culture. Radical feminists, borrowing a phrase from the New Left, insisted that "the personal is the political," by which they meant that questions of power infect all social relations. For that reason gender must be examined critically. Assumptions about women's difference effectively legitimated their subjection inside as well as outside the family. Gender, such feminists argued, is a complex cultural construction rather than a brute biological fact. When feminist theorists showed that basic concepts such as "authority" and "the public" contain implicit gender biases, they concluded that considerations of gender must henceforth be central to all discussions of political ideas. Such arguments have proved profoundly unsettling for male thinkers across the political spectrum, and their ultimate effect on political discourse remains impossible to assess.

Like black activists since the mid-1960s, however, feminist theorists have been hamstrung by their own preferred discourse of rights. Couching their demands for change in the vocabulary of rights has been doubly dangerous for women, since it carries an implicit challenge to the ethic of service that has been a profoundly powerful force in American culture since early in the nineteenth century. When feminists call for the right to work, their critics—female as well as male—fear the abandonment of children. When feminists call for the right to choose abortion, their critics—female as well as male—fear a selfish disregard for human life. Because no other group in American culture has been assumed to embody the ethic of care, no other group has faced equivalent responses when it demanded its rights. Finding ways to defuse those conflicts, as the feminist legal theorist Joan Williams has argued, remains the principal political challenge women face as they try to resolve our culture's "gender wars."

Together with the New Left, feminism had the additional misfortune of arriving on the American scene at the same time, and for some of the same reasons, as the counterculture. When egocentric male or female hedonists mouthed the same slogans of commitment to high ideals that their own commitment to self-indulgence only mocked, they managed to make those few who were genuinely devoted to political activity appear foolish. With friends like the hippies of San Francisco's Haight-Ashbury district, feminists and the New Left were guaranteed plenty of enemies. When feminists' demands became amalgamated in the public mind with the bottomless desires of consumer culture, it was difficult to invest them with the same moral purpose attached to the civil rights movement. Guilt by association is unfair but difficult to suppress. Widespread public reaction against the perceived self-indulgence of cultural radicals helped fuel one of the most powerful developments of recent American politics, the resurgence of conservatism.

Champions of conservative ideas have had a rough time in America. Ever since the eighteenth century, when in the wake of the Revolution most Loyalists left the country and aristocrats who remained had to learn to speak the language of republicanism, American public discourse has prized equality above privilege. The American economic system has rewarded innovation and relentlessly subverted tradition in its march forward. Lacking a coherent case for hierarchy and stasis, conservatives have learned from experience that they are most convincing when they invoke the Constitution as their ally and portray their opponents as un-American. The perceived threat of communism made such arguments plausible in the 1920s and the 1950s, and the enthusiasm of many radicals in the 1960s for Fanon, Fidel Castro, Mao Zedong, and Ho Chi Minh lent added force to such claims. Civil rights activists were widely characterized as communist sympathizers. The New Left was pilloried for its passionate opposition to America's anticommunist crusade in Vietnam. Feminists were accused of betraying the sacred ideals of motherhood and domesticity.

The political triumph and consolidation of New Deal liberalism left the Right without much in the way of a positive political alternative. Opposing the power of big government seemed one attractive option. According to Frederick von Hayek's influential *The Road to Serfdom* (1944), a steep downward path led directly from economic planning to totalitarianism. But as the New Deal, and then postwar social scientists and the Democratic administrations of John F. Kennedy and Lyndon Johnson, abandoned planning and embraced Keynesian fiscal policy, the federal government became a less convincing bogeyman. To complicate matters, most conservatives rather liked the Defense Department. Moreover, opinion polls indicated widespread support for such programs as social security. Conservative thinkers instead sought to exploit public anxieties about civil rights, the New Left, and feminism. In the pages of William F. Buckley's magazine the *National Review,* a wide variety of conservatives targeted the radicalism of such groups and, even more fervently, railed against the excesses of the counterculture.

The rebirth of American conservatism is inexplicable without Herbert Marcuse, Angela Davis, and Abbie Hoffmann, who were from conservatives' perspectives the king, queen, and clown prince of the 1960s revolution. When radicals challenged all cultural as well as political authority, when they defied civility and sang the praises of pleasure, when they championed drugs, sex, and subversive music, even many who considered themselves liberals began to be alarmed. The *Public Interest,* a journal founded by and for mainstream social scientists in 1966, gradually changed from a source of progressive ideas on public policy to a source of warnings about the dangers of cultural and political excess. Many of the journal's principal contributors, including Daniel Bell, Irving Kristol, Nathan Glazer, and Seymour Martin Lipset, had moved from 1930s radicalism through 1950s liberalism and had arrived, with Bell, at the end of ideology. In response to the irrationality and utopianism of 1960s radicals, however, the *Public Interest* slid from chastened liberalism into what came to be known as neoconservatism. Kristol in particular became increasingly suspicious of radicalism and increasingly sympathetic toward capitalism.

Successful exploitation of racial, religious, and cultural anxieties lay behind the conservative resurgence that dominated American presidential politics from 1968 to 1992. Voters feared that the Democratic party had been captured by a combination of uncouth radicals, racial minorities, and elitist technocrats, which together fed conservative uneasiness about cultural change and right-wing populist resentments toward sophisticated cosmopolitans. But this new conservatism lacked a coherent body of ideas. At least for Ronald Reagan, its central value seemed to be the sanctity of the free-market economy, and through his most lasting legacy, a massive national debt, he hoped to guarantee that the federal government would be unable to mount expensive programs of the sort Reagan and his allies opposed. But as always, as the economy swept forward in the 1980s it eroded the traditional values and destroyed the traditional communities that conservatives claimed to cherish. Conservatives also claimed to value the principle of liberty, but they worried that the practice of freedom, especially by women, too often led to self-indulgence.

In *The Cultural Contradictions of Capitalism* (1976), Daniel Bell tried to explain why things seemed to be falling apart. Bell argued that the principles behind the market (functional rationality), the polity (equality), and the culture (self-fulfillment) had become hopelessly inconsistent. He called for a renewed religiosity and a renewed sense of civic responsibility as the solution, but from his reading of Max Weber he seemed aware that the very cultural contradictions he hoped such virtues would resolve militated against their return. A decade later, in the widely read *Habits of the Heart: Individualism and Commitment in American Life* (1985), Robert Bellah, Richard Madsen, William Sullivan, Ann Swidler, and Steven Tipton likewise urged Americans to reach beneath their obsession with "expressive individualism" for the buried religious and civic republican resources that together could redeem American culture.

There are signs that the secular, rights-based discourse that has dominated American politics since the New Deal may be changing. When John Rawls's *A Theory of Justice* (1971) appeared, it was hailed as providing a persuasive statement of the blend of individualist and egalitarian principles underlying the liberal welfare state. Rawls tried to imagine what principles of justice would be chosen by free and equal individuals who came together artificially blind to their own abilities and values. In such circumstances, he argued, individuals would opt for two principles to ensure "justice as fairness." First, all individuals would enjoy as extensive a set of equal rights as would be compatible with the existence of such rights for everyone. Second, any inequalities would be attached to positions and offices open to everyone, and such inequalities would have to benefit the least advantaged members of the society. But Rawls's robust conception of individual rights, and his "thin theory of the good," did not command universal assent. Libertarians such as Robert Nozick wanted even firmer guarantees for individual rights. Communitarians such as Michael Sandel worried that Rawls undervalued community. Feminists such as Susan Okin complained that Rawls's theory of justice—like the theories of his critics and his defenders—was gendered male. Others disputed Rawls's procedures, wondering where such abstract individuals, bereft of history or culture, learned to reason as American professors of philosophy would do.

Oddly enough, just before Rawls's *Theory of Justice* was published, philosophers had been lamenting the sorry state of political theory. Overshadowed by the mass of empirical studies that dominated the discipline of political science, and buried under proclamations of the end of ideology, by 1970 political theory appeared to have vanished. Such reports, as it turned out, were exaggerated; the last two decades have witnessed a resurgence of interest in political theory. Although it is difficult, as well as risky, to attempt a historical assessment of contemporary developments, it seems clear that both Rawls's version of rights-based liberalism, and his deductive style of argument, now represent only one choice among many.

One of the most arresting developments is the relative decline of enthusiasm for a universal science of politics or a universal theory of justice. Political thinkers, including Rawls himself, increasingly admit that they are writing from premises, and according to procedures, that derive from, and are suitable for, our culture rather than all cultures. The arguments of historians of science such as Thomas Kuhn, philosophers from the tradition of hermeneutics such as Charles Taylor and Paul Ricoeur, cultural anthropologists such as Clifford Geertz and James Clifford, and poststructuralist theorists such as Jacques Derrida and Michel Foucault have all alerted political theorists to the ubiquity of interpretation, which has made them wary of claims to certainty.

American political theorists are now more inclined to stress the incommensurability of different ideals. Michael Walzer argued in *Spheres of Justice: A Defense of Pluralism and Equality* (1983) that our conceptions of rights and obligations do not extend beyond the "shared understandings" of our own cultural tradition. Alasdair MacIntyre has examined that problem in a series of important books, notably *Whose Justice? Which Rationality?* (1988) and *Three Rival Versions of Moral Enquiry* (1992), in which he contrasted distinctive liberal and Nietzschean traditions to his preferred Aristotelian/Thomist tradition of moral reasoning. As such studies illustrate, we have come a long way from consensus.

In this climate, the renewal of the philosophy of pragmatism is hardly surprising. Renewed emphasis on the centrality of questions of meaning, and the provisional status of all interpretations, returns thinkers to the arguments that Dewey made repeatedly concerning the inescapability of normative considerations in all inquiry. Renewed emphasis on the inadequacy of rights talk, and growing awareness of the difficulties involved in moving toward justice from a lopsided concern with individualism returns thinkers to the arguments Dewey made repeatedly concerning the social nature of experience and the need to recognize the inseparability of individuals and communities.

But pragmatism is currently moving along several different axes. Richard Rorty, the most widely read and controversial of contemporary pragmatists, insists in *Contingency, Irony, and Solidarity* (1989) that philosophy cannot provide philosophical foundations for political arguments. Rorty stresses the need to protect a precious private realm within which individuals may pursue their own ideals or passions without causing pain to any others. Cornel West yokes his pragmatism to the traditions of Marxism and Christianity in *The American Evasion of Philosophy: A Genealogy of Pragmatism* (1989), offering what he calls a "prophetic pragmatism" that aspires to make common cause with oppressed minorities in America and elsewhere. Joan Williams and Thomas Grey, writing in *Pragmatism in Law and Society* (1991), advance varieties of feminist and pragmatic legal theory that rule out all essentialist arguments and look to earlier as much as contemporary pragmatists for inspiration. Richard J. Bernstein, although sympathetic with much of the postmodernism that Rorty champions, accurately points out in *The New Constellation: The Ethical-Political Horizons of Modernity/Postmodernity* (1992), that Rorty's dichotomy between the public and private spheres is inconsistent with Dewey's pragmatism. In a passage that deftly summarizes the situation in political theory as well, Bernstein acknowledges that cacophony prevails today in philosophical writing. "Philosophy has been decentered. There is no single paradigm, research program, or orientation that dominates philosophy. The fact is that our situation is pluralistic." Given that diversity,

> the pragmatic legacy is especially relevant, in particular the call to nurture the type of community and solidarity where there is an engaged fallibilistic pluralism—one that is based upon mutual respect, where we are willing to risk our own prejudgments, are open to listening and learning from others, and we respond to others with responsiveness and responsibility.

During the last century the United States has become a multicultural society, and it will continue to become more rather than less diverse. Political discourse will continue to revolve around the central issue of accommodating differences. Our current political environment does not provide very effective ways of solving that problem. As Mary Ann Glendon argues persuasively in *Rights Talk: The Impoverishment of Political Discourse* (1991), contemporary political argument locks us into polarized positions that make compromise and even conversation increasingly difficult. Compared with political discourse in other industrial democracies, she argues that our rights talk is distinctive because of "its starkness and simplicity, . . . its exaggerated absoluteness, its hyperindividualism, its insularity, and its silence with respect to personal, civic, and collective responsibilities." As Bernstein points out, Dewey's conception of pragmatic democracy offers an escape from those dead ends.

The recognition of difference and uncertainty,

and awareness of the need to balance rights against responsibilities, might alter the terms in which we talk about politics. E. J. Dionne, in *Why Americans Hate Politics* (1992), describes the "false choices" that distort our political perception and blind us to what we share as Americans. No one, he correctly points out, really wants—or needs—to choose between feminism and the family, between reform and traditional values, or between racial justice and individual accountability. Our fondness for stark dichotomies has led us to transform practically all the difficult political issues we face into questions of constitutional law. The more we focus attention on such either/or formulations as the right to choose *or* the right to life, the presence *or* absence of prayer in school, affirmative action *or* meritocracy, the more rigidly we lock ourselves into a politics of false choices.

The alternatives that Bernstein, Glendon, and Dionne suggest will not automatically resolve such problems. But they return us to the more promising approach of earlier generations of political thinkers, who understood that rights talk obscures more than it clarifies. As Dewey in particular understood, we must examine critically how we as individuals develop our preferences and interests, how we understand and communicate political ideas, how we construct the small and large communities that we prize, and how we can shape public policy on the basis of our experience and our aspirations rather than according to the false choices we are fed.

The problems of politics are perennial, and every provisional solution we attempt will generate a new set of problems. It is difficult now to muster Dewey's confidence that all problems can be resolved neatly through participation and cooperative community building; we know how deeply conflicts divide us. Yet democracy, like the "engaged fallibilistic pluralism" that Bernstein recommends, remains attractive precisely because no final answers are available to political questions. The search for justice will continue to require, as it has for the last century, political ideas that refine the delicate balance between freedom and equality, between rights and responsibilities. Our culture will not escape that condition. Perhaps together pragmatism and democracy will help cure us of our desire for a cure.

SEE ALSO Nationalism; Parties and Interest Groups; The Presidency (all in this volume).

BIBLIOGRAPHY

The books cited in the article itself provide the best entry into twentieth-century American political ideas. An anthology that contains selections from a number of the thinkers discussed, as well as comprehensive bibliographies, is David A. Hollinger and Charles Capper, eds., *The American Intellectual Tradition,* 2d ed. (1992). Two recent interpretations of American political thought are Christopher Lasch's brilliant *The True and Only Heaven: Progress and Its Critics* (1991); and John P. Diggins's mordant, encyclopedic *The Rise and Fall of the American Left* (1992). Although his understanding of the role of ideas and how we should understand them differs sharply from my own, Daniel T. Rodgers, *Contested Truths: Keywords in American Politics* (1987), is a provocative interpretation of political discourse. On the strange career of democratic theory, see the indispensable analysis by Edward A. Purcell, Jr., *The Crisis of Democratic Theory: Scientific Naturalism and the Problem of Value* (1973), which encompasses the entire period from the 1890s to the 1960s.

Among recent studies of Progressive Era thought, different interpretations are available in James T. Kloppenberg, *Uncertain Victory: Social Democracy and Progressivism in European and American Thought, 1870–1920* (1986), which emphasizes the connection between philosophy and political theory for selected thinkers on both sides of the Atlantic; Robert Crunden, *Ministers of Reform: The Progressives' Achievement in American Civilization, 1889–1920* (1982), which stresses the importance of religion; and Dorothy Ross, *The Origins of American Social Science* (1991), which highlights the role played by the ideology of American exceptionalism. Splendid biographies on central Progressive theorists include David W. Levy, *Herbert Croly of "The New Republic"* (1985); Ronald Steel, *Walter Lippmann and the American Century* (1980); Philippa Strum, *Louis D. Brandeis: Justice for the People* (1984); and the outstanding study by Robert Westbrook, *John Dewey and American Democracy* (1991), which, given Dewey's centrality and his longevity, also provides a remarkably comprehensive guide to twentieth-century political discourse. A sympathetic treatment of some of Dewey's critics is Casey Nelson Blake, *Beloved Community: The Cultural Criticism of Randolph Bourne, Van Wyck Brooks, Waldo Frank, and Lewis Mumford* (1990).

Three fine studies on feminist theory are Rosalind Rosenberg, *Beyond Separate Spheres: Intellectual Roots of Modern Feminism* (1982); Nancy Cott, *The Grounding of Modern Feminism* (1987); and Ellen Fitzpatrick, *Endless Crusade: Women Social Scientists and Progressive Reform* (1990). Still valuable are two older works: on settlements, Allen F. Davis, *Spearheads for Reform: The Social Settlements and the Progressive Movement, 1890–1914* (1967); and on suffrage, Aileen S. Kraditor, *The Ideas of the Woman Suffrage Movement* (1965). On individual feminists, see Mary Jo Deegan, *Jane Addams and the Men of the Chicago School, 1892–1918* (1988); Ann J. Lane, *To Herland and Beyond: The Life and Work of Charlotte Perkins Gilman* (1990); and Joyce Antler, *Lucy Sprague Mitchell* (1987).

Reliable overviews of the interwar period include Arthur Ekirch, *Ideologies and Utopias: The Impact of the New Deal on American Thought* (1969), which stresses the positive achievements of liberal reform; the more critical but still sympathetic study by R. Alan Lawson, *The Failure of Independent Liberalism, 1930–1941* (1971); and Richard Pells's comprehensive and detailed account, *Radical Visions and American Dreams: Culture and Social Thought in the Depression Years* (1973). On critics outside the mainstream, see the graceful studies by Daniel Aaron, *Writers on the Left* (1961); and Alan Brinkley, *Voices of Protest: Huey Long, Father Coughlin, and the Great Depression* (1982).

Two outstanding collections of essays provide a wealth of material on the interaction among ideas, institutions, and political pressures in shaping the New Deal and the postwar American welfare state: Steve Fraser and Gary Gerstle, eds., *The Rise and Fall of the New Deal Order* (1989); and Margaret Weir, Ann Shola Orloff, and Theda Skocpol, eds., *The Politics of Social Policy in the United States* (1988). On pluralism and its consequences for social and political theory, see Michael Paul Rogin's brilliant *The Intellectuals and McCarthy: The Radical Specter* (1967). A thorough overview is Richard Pells, *The Liberal Mind in a Conservative Age: American Intellectuals in the 1940s and 1950s* (1985). Richard Wightman Fox, *Reinhold Niebuhr: A Biography* (1985), provides an excellent, nuanced portrait of one of the most influential thinkers of the century. Howard Brick, *Daniel Bell and the Decline of Intellectual Radicalism* (1986), traces its subject's development through the writing of *The End of Ideology.*

An outstanding analysis of the ideas of the New Left is Jim Miller, *"Democracy is in the Streets": From Port Huron to the Siege of Chicago* (1987). Other accounts include Maurice Isserman, *If I Had a Hammer . . . The Death of the Old Left and the Birth of the New Left* (1987); and Todd Gitlin, *The Sixties: Years of Hope, Days of Rage* (1987). Among the many studies of the civil rights movement, of particular value for the study of ideas are Richard H. King, *Civil Rights and the Idea of Freedom* (1992); Taylor Branch, *Parting the Waters: America in the King Years, 1954–1963* (1988), which pays particular attention to the role of religious leaders; and, on the movement's more militant wing, Clayborne Carson, *In Struggle: SNCC and the Black Awakening of the 1960s* (1981). On second-wave feminism, see Sara Evans, *Personal Politics: The Roots of Women's Liberation in the Civil Rights Movement and the New Left* (1979); and Alice Echols, *Daring to be Bad: Radical Feminism in America, 1967–1975* (1985).

Until recently, significant political ideas were likely not to come from the discipline of political science; to understand why, see David Ricci, *The Tragedy of Political Science: Politics, Scholarship, and Democracy* (1984); and the comprehensive review essay by John S. Dryzek and Stephen T. Leonard, "History and Discipline in Political Science," *American Political Science Review* 82 (1988): 1245–1260. Recently, however, things have changed. A number of outstanding collections provide evidence of the renewal of political theory in American scholarship: Michael Sandel, ed., *Liberalism and Its Critics* (1984), provides an overview of the debate over Rawls's *A Theory of Justice.* Amy Gutmann, ed., *Democracy and the Welfare State* (1988), includes thoughtful reflections on the ethics and the political status of social welfare programs in America. The contributors to Nancy Rosenblum, ed., *Liberalism and the Moral Life* (1989), challenge the assumed identification of liberalism with a narrow and shallow possessive individualism. Cass R. Sunstein, ed., *Feminism and Political Theory* (1990), reprints essays originally published in *Ethics* on a wide array of topics related to feminism. Jane J. Mansbridge, ed., *Beyond Self-Interest* (1990), harvests recent work from leading social scientists who agree about the inadequacy of the common view that human behavior is driven by self-interest. David Held, ed., *Political Theory Today* (1991), provides an up-to-date survey of the richness and diversity of work currently being undertaken from a variety of critical perspectives.

For students of political ideas, the work of Richard J. Bernstein is of special importance. In *The Re-*

structuring of Social and Political Theory (1976), he masterfully explained how and why the value-free empiricism of mainstream social science collapsed in the 1960s and 1970s; in *Beyond Objectivism and Relativism: Science, Hermeneutics, and Praxis* (1983), and in *Philosophical Profiles: Essays in a Pragmatic Mode* (1986), he explored the alternatives of hermeneutics and pragmatism and their implications for political theory. Two theorists whose work points in a similar direction are William Sullivan, one of the contributors to *Habits of the Heart,* who was explicit about his debts to Dewey in his *Reconstructing Public Philosophy* (1982); and William A. Galston, who argued in *Justice and the Human Good* (1980); and in a collection of essays, *Liberal Purposes: Goods, Virtues, and the Diversity in the Liberal State* (1991), that liberals need not claim to be neutral about what constitutes the good, and what liberal virtues are—such proclamations of neutrality have impoverished liberal discourse and weakened progressive politics. Mary Ann Glendon extends her earlier analyses of family law and comparative law in *Rights Talk* (1991), in which she examines the impoverishment of American politics that has resulted from a narrow focus on absolute rights to the exclusion of other considerations such as civility and justice.

Perhaps the best way to follow the development of contemporary political ideas is by reading such journals as *Political Theory, Dissent, Ethics,* the *American Prospect,* the *Public Interest, Commonweal, Commentary, Tikkun,* and especially the *Responsive Community,* which includes on its editorial board, among others, Robert Bellah, William Galston, Mary Ann Glendon, Jane Mansbridge, and William Sullivan, some of the most intriguing political thinkers currently at work.

PARTIES AND INTEREST GROUPS

Graham K. Wilson

If, as seems reasonable, one of the basic requirements for a country to be called democratic is that all its adult citizens have the right to vote, then the United States became a democracy only recently. It was 1920 before women gained the suffrage with the adoption of the Nineteenth Amendment; and it took the 1965 Voting Rights Act to secure in practice the right to vote that had been systematically denied most blacks in the South for nearly all of American history. Yet throughout the nineteenth century the United States was one of the most advanced countries in regard to a democratic form of government. By 1824, all but three states had removed property qualifications for white males, whereas Great Britain did not extend the suffrage to all males irrespective of property qualifications until the passing of the 1918 Representation of the People Act. Even if the United States did not have a completely democratically constituted electorate, it was more extensive, and U.S. politics were more popular, than in any other country throughout the nineteenth century.

TECHNIQUES OF MASS POLITICAL ACTION

Not surprisingly, therefore, the United States has been seen as the pioneer of techniques of mass political action. Alexis de Tocqueville came to the United States from France in the 1830s specifically to observe democracy in action. Since he believed that the spread of democracy to other countries was inevitable, it was natural for him to examine the American experience for the dangers implicit in democracy and the safeguards that must be mounted against them. Whatever the limitations on democracy in nineteenth-century America, politics in the United States involved more participation by a higher proportion of the citizenry than in any other country because American political parties had found ways by the 1830s to recruit and mobilize millions of voters. The British Liberal and Conservative parties, for example, did not develop a structure and machinery for reaching beyond Westminster and into the country as a whole until the late nineteenth century.

Americans seem to have formed interest groups to tackle problems as instinctively as the British turned to a public-spirited aristocrat or the French to the state (as one of the most famous sections of Tocqueville's *Democracy in America* described). Perhaps the proclivity for interest group politics went back even further, to the founding of the Republic. In one of the most famous of the *Federalist* papers (No. 10) James Madison had predicted that interests would flourish in the free polity the Founders were creating. Like Tocqueville, Madison did not believe that clash of interests would undermine the public interest, but that the multiplicity of contending interests would itself hold their abuses in check, allowing Americans to enjoy both liberty and responsible government.

An assessment of the party and interest group system is central to an evaluation of the degree to which the promise and performance of American democracy coincide. Critics of American politics at home and abroad have been quick to note that the fact that the United States pioneered techniques of mass politics does not mean that, from a democratic perspective, such techniques were or are beyond reproach. Nineteenth-century political parties in the United States are remembered more for graft, corruption, spoils, and the influence of bosses who controlled the party apparatuses at the local level than for promoting quality democracy by offering voters meaningful choices. Indeed, as Stephen Skowronek has argued, the very development of the American state was circumscribed by the centrality of spoils in the American party system; movements to increase the quality and professionalism of the civil service were impeded by the parties' needs to reserve as many jobs as possible with which to reward supporters.

The interest group system has also prompted troubling questions. To some, it seemed biased toward the rich, providing representation for special interests such as corporations but not general interests such as consumers. Interest groups damaged the general interest either because they could influence public policy by using means that scarcely seemed democratic—such as making strategic campaign contributions—or simply because, whatever techniques were used, the interest group system allowed vocal minorities excessive influence. Thus the interest group system can be seen as reducing rather than increasing the overall representativeness of the political system.

Several major attempts have been made in the twentieth century to reform the party and interest group systems. In the case of parties, the main reforms have been attempts to increase opportunities for participation (notably in primary elections to choose candidates), to reduce the corrupt practices of offering jobs and contracts in return for supporting the party, and recurring attempts to unite different parties around contrasting ideologies. In the case of interest groups, reformers have attempted to end the purchasing of favorable public policy through campaign contributions or private gifts and to increase the equality of access of interest groups to policymakers, thus reducing the domination of the interest group system by the wealthy and powerful.

The frequent attempts to reform parties and interest groups have made change endemic in the party and interest group systems. But the party and interest group systems would be changing anyway because they reflect a society that is in flux. For example, the farm vote has been sought by politicians throughout the century, and farmers' organizations have always been a major component of the interest group system; but farmers and their families, once a quarter of the population, are today little more than one-fiftieth of the population. The proportion of the workforce employed in the manufacturing industry has also fallen, if not so precipitously. Naturally, these socioeconomic changes have consequences for parties and interest groups, which together constitute the connective tissue that links state and society. In addition, trends toward "cause" groups that seek to promote a public policy not directly related to members' occupations or economic self-interests and "producer" groups that promote public policies to the economic advantage of members (usually united in a common occupation) have had periods of popularity.

Yet the first impression that strikes the observer of political parties and interest groups throughout this century is continuity. Prominent in American politics at the outset, interest groups remain so today. In contrast to the situation in most democracies, the same two parties, the Republicans and the Democrats, dominate politics at the end of the century as at the beginning. From time to time third parties have been a significant presence in presidential elections: Theodore Roosevelt, running as a Progressive in 1912, won 27 percent of the popular vote; Gov. George Wallace of Alabama won 13 percent of the popular vote in the 1968 election; and H. Ross Perot won 19 percent in 1992. Presidential third parties have always faded, however, while at the subnational levels, third parties have succeeded in controlling politics in only two states (the Progressives in Wisconsin and the Farm-Labor party in Minnesota in the 1930s). The workings of the plurality electoral system used in the United States and the ability of the loosely structured parties to incorporate third parties have ensured their demise.

Beneath the level of the apparent continuity in the party—and in some respects, the interest group—system, significant changes have indeed occurred. It is relatively easy to identify the major changes, but not to assess their significance. While reformers have sought to make the parties more democratic, some observers believe they have simply become less significant: candidates for office can raise money, campaign, and win votes without much help from a political party. Others believe that American political parties make a better contribution than ever before to the quality of democracy in the United States by offering ordinary citizens more opportunities to participate in choosing their candidates for office and voters more meaningful choices in elections. A similarly optimistic view can be taken of developments in interest group politics, which most commentators deem more inclusive than ever before. Environmentalists, consumer advocates, women's organizations, and campaigners for the advancement of every racial or ethnic minority have joined business, agriculture, and labor in being represented effectively in Washington. Can we therefore portray the development of parties and interest groups in twentieth-century America as advancing the democratic ideals that America proclaims? Or have attempts to reform political parties and interest groups amounted to a devoted but futile pursuit of a democratic Holy Grail?

POLITICAL PARTIES IN THE EARLY TWENTIETH CENTURY

Three great waves of reform have shaped the contemporary party system: the Progressive movement, the

New Deal, and the post-1960s protest movements. In order to appreciate their impact we need to remind ourselves of the situation at the start of this century, the structure of politics at the accession of President William Howard Taft. At that time, American political parties were characterized by four features that would not be evident by the end of the century.

First, the parties as organizations were dominated by either machines or somewhat less centralized structures that David Mayhew has called traditional party organizations (TPOs) that differed from machines in that they had no single leader. Both machines and TPOs used the perquisites of office—contracts, jobs, and variances from laws or regulations—to reward their supporters. Those who voted for the TPO or machine were given jobs, contracts, or simply better services such as clean streets without potholes; those who failed to support the machine or TPO were not rewarded. "To the victor belongs the spoils" was an organizing principle of American politics. Sometimes the spoils took the form of "honest graft" that could be distributed without breaking the law; sometimes a measure of illegality was involved. The support that was garnered through the spoils system was used by machines and TPOs to develop a monopoly on the capacity to nominate successfully candidates for office within the area controlled by the TPO or machine.

It would be a caricature of early-twentieth-century politics to say that it consisted entirely of the machinations of TPOs and machines. TPOs were never strong in Milwaukee or Minneapolis, but were common along the eastern seaboard, where they were the norm in the large cities, and farther west in such cities as Kansas City and Pittsburgh. Although primarily an urban phenomenon, machines and TPOs were sometimes found in rural areas. Their strength was greatest at the local level, for party organizations rested in most places on the spoils system, but the leaders of these local organizations were also highly influential in choosing candidates for national office. In national elections, particularly presidential elections, contests between the parties were fierce and close throughout most of the late nineteenth century; the machines or TPOs maintained their monopolies only locally. When the balance of power between the parties shifted clearly in favor of the Republicans after the 1896 election, however, it did so for reasons that went beyond the comparative strength of Republican and Democratic machines.

A second feature of American political parties was that they derived support from voters who were not recipients of spoils by appealing to regional, ethnic, and religious loyalties. Social class had no clear relationship to partisan allegiance. As national politics, in contrast to our own age of television, was mostly experienced indirectly through highly partisan newspapers or persuasion by machines and TPOs, both candidates and issues were usually muted in their impact. Most people voted—and turnout was extremely high by the standards of the late twentieth century—on the basis of habit rather than after evaluating carefully the qualities and policies of the candidates. Voting as they had shot in the Civil War, the South was loyal to the Democrats and the Upper Midwest to the Republicans. Republicans were likely to gain support from white Anglo-Saxon Protestants (WASPs) and Democrats from "hyphenated Americans" such as Irish Americans. When there were religious differences among immigrants (as with the Germans), Protestants were likely to vote Republican and Catholics were likely to vote Democratic. The famous charge in the 1884 election that the Democrats were the party of "rum, Romanism, and rebellion" may not have affected the outcome of that particular election, but it did encapsulate the spirit of much partisan politics.

Third, the political parties stood for no clear general principles. The Republicans had been the high-tariff party since the Civil War, but even on that issue the difference between the two parties was a matter of degree and the Democrats had an important high-tariff contingent. After the demise of the Radical Republican plan for thoroughgoing reconstruction in the South, intense ideological divisions disappeared from party competition, except in the election of 1896 when the Democrats captured the Populist vote by nominating William Jennings Bryan but then suffered a massive defeat. Thereafter, reformers and conservatives could be found in both parties. When Progressives set out to tackle the obvious problems of a newly urbanized and industrialized society, it was far from clear which party offered the most congenial home.

Fourth, the national parties exerted no strong discipline. The price of keeping the parties together nationally has always been a willingness to allow state parties and legislators to follow their constituents' opinions rather than attempting to coerce them into following a party line on key issues. A partial exception to this generalization existed in the House of Representatives, where Speaker Joseph Cannon enjoyed considerable power to reward those who followed his leadership and punish those who did not. The exception (for once) really does prove the rule; in 1910 Cannon's power was broken by a revolt against him. The consequences of the revolt were immense. From 1910 until 1975 the House joined the Senate in following doggedly a seniority principle that allocated the most powerful posts without regard to the wishes of the party leaders. Professional legislators dominated the House, and, in contrast to the pattern in the nineteenth century, served multiple terms; they could be cajoled, but not commanded, by their leaders. Outside Congress, the parties existed nationally once every four years when the powerful local leaders came together at national nominating conventions to choose a candidate on whom they could all agree. Procedures at conventions protected regional minorities; until 1936, the Democrats required a presidential candidate to obtain the support of two-thirds of the delegates to receive the nomination. In 1924, the Democrats took over one hundred ballots to discover an undistinguished candidate whom they could all support. American parties were, in short, loose confederations.

Perhaps surprisingly, the American political parties of the early twentieth century have had their defenders. The party organizations, it has been argued, sped the assimilation of new immigrants as they courted their votes. Local party organizations helped immigrants become citizens so that in due course the organization would receive its just reward—their votes. Party organizations also provided help for the poor or unemployed in a period when governments did not. The familiar story of the ward leader who brought a chicken to a family fallen on hard times or found a job for the unemployed worker has a degree of truth. The self-interest of party bosses providing such help may have been less important than the fact that some help was provided. They were probably more sympathetic to the needs of working-class neighborhoods and more willing to provide them with services than the professional city managers with whom reformers hoped to replace them. The parties also served a national purpose, binding together the recently fractured Republic. The Democrats' alliance between the South and large northern cities, for example, saved the South from being permanently isolated after the Civil War. The speed with which the South was given a pivotal position within the Democratic party, and through the party in Congress, has few parallels in the history of defeated rebellious regions round the world; not even the equally misplaced generosity of the British handing power in South Africa to the Boers they had just defeated quite matches the treatment of the South.

Yet American political parties have been more criticized than admired. For some, the simple corruption of party organizations was sufficient reason to dislike them; the exploitation of public office for private gain is rarely an attractive sight. For others, the failing of the parties was that their need for extensive patronage inhibited the development of effective state capacities. A competent bureaucracy could not be developed while politicians distributed jobs as rewards to incompetent but loyal supporters. Finally, the lack of ideological consistency within the parties that made it as likely that a conservative would be a Democrat as a Republican or a liberal a Republican rather than a Democrat prevented the parties from playing what could have been their most valuable role: offering voters the simplified but meaningful policy choice without which mass democracy cannot be attained. For most political scientists, parties have had a crucial role to play in mass politics by offering voters a simplified but meaningful choice of policy approaches. Voters do not have to examine every candidate's policies, but can make simple, generally accurate assumptions about the policy implications of an election. Thus voters can assume that by voting for one party they are voting for better government services and higher taxes, while voting for the opposing party means supporting a reduction in both taxes and services. Early-twentieth-century American parties manifestly failed to fulfill this important role because of their ideological heterogeneity. Both Republicans and Democrats could be progressive supporters of regulating powerful corporations, for example; both Republicans and Democrats could be defenders of the economically privileged.

REFORMING THE POLITICAL PARTY SYSTEM

The first major wave of reforms directed at the political parties was associated with the Progressive movement. Like many of the important movements in American politics, it was not a single organization; although a Progressive party contested the 1912 presidential election as a third party, Progressives were also found in the ranks of the Democratic and Republican parties. Progressives, like environmentalists in the later twentieth century, are best thought of as a social movement that mobilized people in many different settings—cities, states, and nationally—to demand changes in politics. Even the start and end of the Progressive era are hard to state exactly; the movement's influence is evident in the 1880s yet it can be argued that many of the reforms of the New Deal have been associated with Progressive reformers. The period in which the Progressives were most important, however, was roughly the twenty years preceding the entry of the United States into World War I.

A vigorous debate has raged among historians about the character of the Progressives. For some, the Progressives were insecure members of the professional classes, trying to protect the traditional values of American politics against the corruption produced by mass immigration and the party bosses who based their power on the new citizens. For others, the Progressives represent a noble response to the mounting problems of a nation that was increasingly urban, not rural, and industrial, not agrarian. In a sense, both interpretations are correct. Progressives championed a wide variety of reforms in different settings, and the character of these reforms naturally varied somewhat from place to place. Progressives did try to wrest power from local politicians who represented the immigrant hoards in order to secure economical government by replacing corrupt machine politicians with professional city managers. But Progressives also championed reforms that restrained the worst excesses of giant corporations and robber barons by promoting government regulation of business in the public interest.

Space does not permit a lengthy discussion of the complex phenomenon of progressivism. What is of concern here are the consequences of progressivism for the party system. There were two. First, at local, state, and national levels, the Progressives promoted the development of the career civil service. For Progressives, a career civil service brought merit and competence to government, freeing it from the bloated number of political appointees chosen for their political loyalty, not their ability. For the parties, such reforms took away their lifeblood, their ability to reward their supporters. Second, the Progressives struck at the power of party bosses to control politics by promoting the adoption of primaries in which ordinary citizens, not party activists, would choose their party's nominees. These reforms occurred gradually in the late nineteenth and early twentieth centuries; the proportion of merit civil service appointees grew slowly in this period, as Stephen Skowronek describes, as professional class reform organizations enlisted the support of presidents, particularly those not seeking reelection, to push civil service reform through Congress. Primaries were not adopted in every state or for every type of election; less than one-third of the delegates to presidential nominating conventions in the 1920s were selected in primaries. But the Progressives had introduced primaries into presidential nominating politics and made them the dominant form of candidate selection in subpresidential contests. Primaries had to be secured state by state, for it is state legislatures that determine whether primaries are used or not, through the tireless efforts of Progressive reformers.

The rules governing primaries varied considerably from state to state. The most important variation concerned whether voters had to be declared supporters of the party in whose primary they wished to vote in advance of the election, could declare their affiliation on primary election day, or could participate without declaring a permanent affiliation to the party. Where the Progressives were strongest—as in Wisconsin—the criteria for being allowed to vote in a primary election were the least onerous. All forms of primary produced, however, a shift in power away from the party bosses or enthusiasts who previously controlled nominations. At the local level, Progressives tried to remove the influence of party organizations by stipulating that elections should be nonpartisan. In some cities, an extreme example of Progressive reform entailed the appointment of managers to replace elected mayors. Administration would replace politics.

The impact of the Progressives was limited in time and place. The Progressive impulse faded (though did not entirely disappear) after 1924, when Sen. Robert La Follette lost his bid for president. But the Progressives' impact on the political parties endured. The spoils system never recovered its full strength. And though the number of states holding primaries to choose delegates to the presidential nominating conventions declined between the 1920s and the 1970s, primaries remained an important feature of American elections through which nearly all candidates for subpresidential offices were selected. Even in presidential politics, the minority of states that held primaries to select delegates to the presidential nominating conventions provided a means by which the party leaders' grip on power could be challenged.

President Franklin D. Roosevelt's New Deal program became the instrument of change in the 1930s and 1940s. The Progressives had taken aim at the party system trying consciously to correct its defects; the impact of the New Deal was less direct, though considerable. Several features of the New Deal moved the American party system somewhat closer to the state that reformers desired. For one thing, it provided some definition of party ideologies. Before the New Deal, as we have noted, reformers might find either the Republicans or the Democrats more congenial; after the New Deal, the Democrats were established as the left-of-center party of reform, while the liberal wing of the Republican party declined until by the end of the century it had virtually disappeared. The New Deal—especially by laying the foundations of the American version of the welfare state—established the Democrats as the natural party for those who wished to bring about social reform.

For another, defining the Democrats' position attracted certain segments of the population as a power base. Before the New Deal, there had been little class basis for the divisions of support between the Democrats and Republicans; after the New Deal, social class became a powerful influence on voting behavior, as blue-collar workers (especially if they were union members) were likely to favor the Democrats. Although we do not think of American politics primarily in class terms, between the New Deal and the 1970s, working-class voters generally favored the Democrats, sometimes by very wide margins. In the 1948 presidential election, for example, blue-collar voters supported Truman by a three-to-one margin, a larger margin of working-class support than the British Labour party receives. Even when Republican candidate Dwight D. Eisenhower ran strongly among blue-collar voters in 1952 and 1956, they remained more likely to vote Democratic than voters in general, so that the Republican share of the working-class vote was always lower than the Republican share of the vote in general. Indeed, since the New Deal, unions and their confederation, the AFL-CIO (American Federation of Labor–Congress of Industrial Organizations) have been the largest source of support and money for the election campaigns of liberal Democrats and particularly important in assisting Democratic challenges to Republican incumbents.

Whether the unions have received as much in return as they could have hoped for is doubtful. The AFL-CIO has been much more successful as an interest group when it has been part of a coalition working for a program, such as Medicare, that extends beyond union members; when it has attempted to secure changes in labor law that might halt the precipitous decline of union strength Democrats whom the unions have helped in elections have failed to support the reform. Since World War II even when liberal and moderate Democrats have had a majority in Congress, proposals to amend labor legislation in favor of the unions have failed.

The New Deal created a pattern of electoral politics that endured almost half a century and greatly favored the Democrats; almost twice as many Americans thought of themselves as Democrats than as Republicans until the 1980s. Yet the New Deal did not transform the Democrats into an American social democratic party. In fact, older elements of the party were temporarily strengthened by the New Deal. Party organizations had more patronage to distribute because the New Deal programs brought extra resources to local governments. One of the most famous machines in the country, the Chicago machine associated with Mayor Richard Daley, was not established until the 1930s under Anton Cermak. Party bosses remained strong enough to play a major role in presidential electoral politics throughout the 1960s; at the local level, the power of bosses such as Chicago's Mayor Daley or Brooklyn's Meade Esposito lasted into the 1970s. In addition, although the South lost control over Democratic presidential candidates with the repeal of the two-thirds rule for nominating conventions in 1936, southerners held a disproportionately large share of committee chairs in Congress due to the seniority system. In consequence, the region benefited handsomely from public policy. Programs such as agricultural subsidies or the Tennessee Valley Authority (TVA) were structured so that the South gained more than any other region. The military build-up of World War II and the Cold War brought vast federal spending to the South. Nor did the importance of ethnicity end with the New Deal. The old tribal sense of loyalty—that people like us are Democrats (or Republicans) endured. The New Deal brought new elements—particularly organized labor—into the Democratic party, but it did not remove the old.

In the long term, however, the New Deal did transform the parties by changing the social order. New Deal agricultural policies aided the mechanization of agriculture that changed the South by ending the need for cheap labor from black Americans, thus driving them north. New Deal welfare programs reduced the value of the relief that party organizations provided in times of hardship. The long period of prosperity that Keynesian economics (introduced into the United States during the New Deal) helped ensure reduced the attractiveness of the public service jobs the parties controlled.

The New Deal also created profound tensions within the Democratic ranks. Liberal reformers and party bosses made strange bedfellows. Those attracted to the Democratic party as the representative of the underdog were bound to quarrel with southern politicians fiercely attached to racial discrimination. Indeed, by the end of the second Roosevelt term, the informal, conservative coalition of Southern Democrats and Republicans had appeared in Congress, and it has remained a feature of congressional politics ever since. When the conservative coalition appears, it generally wins. Southern Democrats have been the crucial swing bloc on most issues of domestic policy. The wonder of the Democratic party is not that it tends to fragment but that it has endured at all. As Rep. Morris Udall (D-Ariz.) once remarked, when Democrats form a firing squad, they form it in a circle.

The Democrats not only endured but prospered for four decades after their victory in the 1932 presidential election. They controlled Congress in all but four years of those four decades, and held the presidency for all but twelve. What held the diffuse and often mutually antagonistic groups in the Democratic party together? Perhaps underlying all their differences was a greater willingness than Republicans displayed to use the power of federal government to advance domestic goals. Even Southern Democrats generally favored federal spending on programs such as agriculture and housing, so long as the benefits did not in general go to blacks. The New Deal created a "broker state" that allowed the Democrats to achieve some unity by forming coalitions with each other to achieve their objectives. Thus northern urban liberals could obtain southern support for the food stamp program in return for voting for cotton subsidies. The Democratic party was an institutionalized set of deals; it worked best by trying to avoid noticing the contradictions within it (which was why the congressional Democratic caucus rarely met in the 1950s and 1960s).

The final wave of reform to shape the political party system resulted from the impact of the post-1960s protest movements, which forced the Democratic party to acknowledge its internal differences. Liberal critics of American involvement found that, although they could mobilize enough strength to dissuade Lyndon Johnson—the Democratic president who had committed large numbers of American troops to Vietnam—from seeking renomination in 1968, the structure of the party allowed the president to bestow the nomination on his chosen successor, Vice President Hubert Humphrey. Liberal activists could secure victories in those states that held primaries for candidates such as Senators Eugene McCarthy and Robert Kennedy (who was murdered immediately after triumphing in the California primary) while Hubert Humphrey failed to win a single primary. But the "regulars" of the party organizations that selected most delegates to the presidential nominating convention in Chicago—only a quarter of delegates were selected in primaries—were set against the liberals' heroes. Matters were not helped when the Chicago police of the archetypal party boss, Mayor Richard Daley, engaged in what an inquiry termed subsequently a "police riot," during which antiwar protestors (and, much less wisely from the Democrats' point of view, journalists) were beaten and tear-gassed.

In the face of a media backlash and public disapproval, and in an attempt to unify the party, the regulars agreed to a commission to examine methods of delegate selection, chaired first by Sen. George McGovern of South Dakota, then (as McGovern began to campaign for the presidency) by Rep. Donald Fraser of Minnesota. As a result of this appeasement, the McGovern-Fraser Commission unleashed one of the major waves of reform in twentieth-century party politics. The major enduring consequence (although not fully intended) was to accelerate a trend toward using primaries as the normal mode of selecting delegates to presidential nominating conventions. The commission had proposed elaborate rules for Democrats (naturally it had no control over Republican practices) to use in delegate selection if they did not use primaries that were designed to allow for full and fair participation by party supporters. Many states decided to simplify matters by switching to a primary system. In consequence, the proportion of delegates selected in primaries grew from about one-third in 1968 to three-quarters in 1980. The grip of party organizations on party nominations that had been loosened somewhat by the Progressives had been ended.

The McGovern-Fraser reforms were not limited to encouraging the growth of primaries. The commission's call for quotas of delegates to nominating conventions for women, blacks, and young people in order to reflect the voting public encouraged the tendency for the Democrats to be identified with a more restrained foreign policy, less conventional lifestyles, feminism, and the racial minorities with whom President Lyndon Johnson had already aligned the party with the civil rights legislation of the 1960s. The party of Woodrow Wilson and Franklin Roosevelt gained the image of being weak, almost pacifist in foreign policy. The party of the racist, segregated South became identified with civil rights. The party of the urban, often Catholic, immigrants, became identified with issues such as abortion rights.

POLITICAL PARTIES IN THE LATE TWENTIETH CENTURY

These changes were not always popular with the Democrats' blue-collar constituency. Far from commanding the loyalty of working-class Americans, the

Democrats saw Republican presidential candidates Richard Nixon (in 1972) and Ronald Reagan (in 1984) capture a majority of the working-class vote. Although Watergate and recession denied the Republicans the presidency in 1976, thereafter the Democrats' image of being unpatriotic on foreign policy questions and devoted to causes such as the interests of racial minorities and feminism lost them the White House. Indeed, even a Republican candidate from an upper-class, patrician background, George Bush in 1988, could claim with some success to understand working-class Americans better than his Democratic opponent. Republicans, not Democrats, gained control of the symbols that mobilized the nation in presidential elections. Democrats continued to dominate in congressional elections, in which candidates could tailor themes to suit their constituencies, but had difficulty in defining themes around which they could unite voters across the nation in presidential contests.

The twenty-five years after the entry of the United States into the Vietnam War witnessed a remarkable recovery by the Republican party, although to some degree their success must be credited to the Democrats' errors. As late as the early 1970s, it was debatable whether or not the Republican label brought a candidate more harm than help: less than a quarter of the population identified with the Republican party. Yet, with the exception of the post-Watergate election of 1976, Democratic prospects for electing another president were poor. Republican political strategies had paid off. Some of these strategies were primarily organizational: the Republicans learned faster than the Democrats how to utilize computerized direct mail, television campaigning, polling, and direct fundraising. Republicans also benefited from carefully exploiting the divisions in the Democratic party by emphasizing so-called wedge issues. Reminders that many Democratic politicians supported racial quota programs in hiring, for example, helped strip away working-class support for the Democrats, as blue-collar workers sensed that affirmative action would likely redress longstanding racial inequities at their expense and in violation of widely held notions of justice. Republican appeals to white southerners, working-class Democrats offended by their increasing tax burden as well as by affirmative action to help minorities, and Catholics and fundamentalist Christians opposed to allowing pregnant women to choose to have an abortion peeled away Democratic support in presidential elections like the skins of an onion. President Bush even attempted to detach blacks, the most heavily Democratic population group, with actions such as nominating Clarence Thomas to the Supreme Court. In presidential politics, the New Deal Democratic majority gave way to a loose Republican coalition of "right-to-lifers," those opposed to tax increases, and southern whites and working-class Americans who felt that Democratic presidential candidates did not share their values. The coalition was not agreed on common values, let alone a common philosophy, but it was large and cohesive enough to secure a string of victories for Republicans in presidential elections.

Republicans, however, were frustrated by their inability to turn this lead in presidential politics into a congressional majority until the 1994 midterm elections. Many explanations of this failure have been advanced. The great advantages of incumbency—"credit claiming" for good things that happen to the district, name recognition, greater ability to attract campaign contributions, the freedom to use the perquisites of office such as free mailings to bolster support all play a part. Some have argued that district boundaries were drawn to disadvantage the Republicans. But Republicans have held the Senate only briefly since World War II (1947–1949, 1953–1955, 1981–1987, 1994–) and gerrymandering cannot be blamed for their lack of success in the Senate. (See table 1 for the balance of parties in Congress and the White House.)

Nor were the advantages of incumbency alone sufficient to explain Republican failure to win control of the House until 1994. The House has seen considerable turnover through retirement in recent decades; if incumbency was the only factor disadvantaging their candidates, Republicans would have won a majority in the House on the basis of the frequent "open seat" elections that occur when the incumbent retires or dies. The number of open seat contests in the House has varied from twenty-one to forty-nine in elections since 1945, clearly enough to create a Republican majority over a few elections if incumbency were the only problem they faced.

The Democrats' lock on Congress for most of the period since World War II remains a puzzle, therefore. Perhaps congressional Democrats were able to adapt to their diverse constituencies whereas one presidential candidate could not unite them. Perhaps voters believed Democrats were better at representing their localistic interests than Republicans or they like control of national institutions divided between the parties. In all events, the Republican failure in congressional elections up to 1994 made "divided government" seem the norm in the late twentieth century: the Republicans would hold the presidency and the Democrats would control the House and usually the Senate. The 1994 elections produced a continuation of divided government with, for the first time since 1948, the Republicans holding Congress and the Democrats the White House. How this unexpected situation arose is discussed below.

The term "congressional party" seemed an oxymoron in the years since the emergence of the conservative coalition in the late New Deal. Indeed, congressional party leaders enjoyed few powers with which to impose discipline on members of their congressional party after the fall of the "tyrannical" Speaker Cannon in 1911; congressional rules and traditions were designed to prevent party leaders from exerting power. The seniority system, for example, ensured that the powerful chairmanships of congressional committees were awarded according to a criterion (longest continuous service on the relevant committee) that insulated the chairman from the control of party leaders. In the 1950s and 1960s, Democrats in Congress minimized meetings of their party caucuses because tensions between southerners and northerners, and conservatives and liberals, were likely to be exacerbated in any meeting.

The period after 1974 witnessed a resurgence of the importance of party institutions in Congress. Revisions of party rules allowed the Democratic caucus in the House to strip away committee chairmanships from those who had irritated their fellow Democrats by their conservativism or treatment of more junior colleagues. Under Jim Wright and Tom Foley, the Speaker became a major figure again—a trend the Republican Speaker, Newt Gingrich, was to take even further after the 1994 elections (as we shall see below). The parties in both the House and the Senate (the least-changed chamber) became both more united ideologically and more in conflict with each other. For better or worse, the spirit of partisanship was greater in Congress in the 1980s and 1990s than it had been for many decades.

THE CLINTON VICTORY AND THE DEMOCRATS' RECOVERY OF THE WHITE HOUSE

The presidential election of 1992 was therefore doubly astonishing; it caught most political scientists—and politicians—by surprise. The Republicans had seemed to have "a lock" on the presidency; commentators noted that if their presidential candidate carried the states that had voted Republican in every election since 1968, they had an electoral college majority in the bag. The Republicans had apparently impregnable bastions of presidential support in the West and South (unless the Democrats nominated a candidate from that region). Moreover, in addition to the usual advantages of incumbency, George Bush, the first American president since Truman in 1945 to win a war, seemed invincible the year before the election. Considering Gov. Bill Clinton's triumph, had the Republican presidential majority that had existed since 1968 (except in the aftermath of Watergate) shattered or was the 1992 result the consequence of unusual circumstances?

Governor Clinton had not seemed an extraordinary candidate in the 1992 campaign. Indeed, in the spring when Clinton had been damaged by reports of his extramarital affairs and evasion of the draft as a young man, many Democrats had assumed they had once again succeeded in picking a candidate who was bound to lose. The economic downturn or recession was perceived by many commentators as the explanation for President Bush's difficulties; a much publicized sign in the Clinton campaign headquarters that was the suggested answer to every question—"It's the economy, stupid!"—summarized this perspective on the campaign. The psychological impact of the economic downturn was perhaps even greater than its size warranted because the regions and groups hit (such as California and professionals) were used to constantly rising living standards.

Yet the British Conservative party had shown earlier in 1992 that it was possible for a government to be reelected in the midst of a recession if it campaigned adroitly. This President Bush had failed to do: his campaign, like his presidency, lacked clear themes. He failed to capitalize on obvious weaknesses in the Clinton campaign, such as the irreconcilability of Clinton's promises on taxation, spending, and the deficit. Instead, the Republicans loudly proclaimed the themes that had worked so well for them in the past of patriotism, "family values," and hostility to homosexuals, affirmative action, and those who were "soft on crime." In the midst of a recession that some interpreted as part of a long-term economic decline of the United States such themes seemed suddenly trivial and out of line with people's deepest concerns. Perhaps the many years of Republican success, followed by Bush's popularity after the Gulf War, had lulled him into a false sense of security. In any event, Bush received the lowest share of the vote for an incumbent since President Taft in 1912.

The 1994 midterm elections came as a staggering

Table 1. DIVIDED GOVERNMENT: PRESIDENTS AND CONGRESS, 1897–1995[a]

			Senate			House		
President	Congress		Maj	Min	Other	Maj	Min	Other
McKinley, R	**55th**	**1897–99**	**47 R**	34 D	7	**204 R**	113 D	40
McKinley, R	**56th**	**1899–1901**	**53 R**	26 D	8	**185 R**	163 D	9
McKinley, R	**57th**	**1901–03**	**55 R**	31 D	4	**197 R**	151 D	9
T. Roosevelt, R								
T. Roosevelt, R	**58th**	**1903–05**	**57 R**	33 D		**208 R**	178 D	
T. Roosevelt, R	**59th**	**1905–07**	**57 R**	33 D		**250 R**	136 D	
T. Roosevelt, R	**60th**	**1907–09**	**61 R**	31 D		**222 R**	164 D	
Taft, R	**61st**	**1909–11**	**61 R**	32 D		**219 R**	172 D	
Taft, R	62d	1911–13	**51 R**	41 D		228 D	161 R	1
Wilson, D	**63d**	**1913–15**	**51 D**	44 R	1	**291 D**	127 R	17
Wilson, D	**64th**	**1915–17**	**56 D**	40 R		**230 D**	196 R	9
Wilson, D	**65th**	**1917–19**	**53 D**	42 R		**216 D**	210 R	6
Wilson, D	66th	1919–21	49 R	47 D		240 R	190 D	3
Harding, R	**67th**	**1921–23**	**59 R**	37 D		**301 R**	131 D	1
Coolidge, R	**68th**	**1923–25**	**51 R**	43 R	2	**225 R**	205 D	5
Coolidge, R	**69th**	**1925–27**	**56 R**	39 D	1	**247 R**	183 D	4
Coolidge, R	**70th**	**1927–29**	**49 R**	46 D	1	**237 R**	195 D	3
Hoover, R	**71st**	**1929–31**	**56 R**	39 D	1	**267 R**	167 D	1
Hoover, R	72d	1931–33	**48 R**	47 D	1	220 D	214 R	1
F. Roosevelt, D	**73d**	**1933–35**	**60 D**	35 R	1	**310 D**	117 R	5
F. Roosevelt, D	**74th**	**1935–37**	**69 D**	25 R	2	**319 D**	103 R	10
F. Roosevelt, D	**75th**	**1937–39**	**76 D**	16 R	4	**331 D**	89 R	13
F. Roosevelt, D	**76th**	**1939–41**	**69 D**	23 R	4	**261 D**	164 R	4
F. Roosevelt, D	**77th**	**1941–43**	**66 D**	28 R	2	**268 D**	162 R	5
F. Roosevelt, D	**78th**	**1943–45**	**58 D**	37 R	1	**218 D**	208 R	4
F. Roosevelt, D	**79th**	**1945–47**	**56 D**	38 R	1	**242 D**	190 R	2
Truman, D								
Truman, D	80th	1947–49	51 R	45 D		245 R	188 D	1
Truman, D	**81st**	**1949–51**	**54 D**	42 R		**263 D**	171 R	1
Truman, D	**82d**	**1951–53**	**49 D**	47 R		**234 D**	199 R	1

setback to Democratic hopes that the election of President Clinton had ended the party's post-Vietnam travails. The Republican share of the national vote in the elections for the House of Representatives—just under 54 percent—was their best performance since 1946. Perhaps some loss of seats by the Democrats was inevitable, as in most midterm elections. However, the heavy midterm elections usually befall a party six years after it has captured the White House (as in 1956, 1966, 1974), not two. The national mood was sour, reflecting disappointment that the end of the Cold War and of the recession of the early 1990s had not resulted in world peace or more rapidly rising living standards. But the rapid economic growth that had in fact started in the last year of the Bush administration provided an odd backdrop to heavy losses for the President's party.

Undoubtedly, some of the congressional Democrats' misfortune was their own doing; apart from the defeat of conspicuously corrupt members such as Dan Rostenkowski (chairman of the Ways and Means Committee), Democrats had proved unwilling to undertake necessary reforms of Congress when they had the opportunity. Much of the blame for the Democrats' difficulties, however, belonged to the President. The ineptitude of President Clinton during his first two years in office had done much to worsen the old vulnerabilities of the party that it had hoped his election had ended. An emphasis on unimportant but controversial issues, such as allowing avowed homosexuals to serve in the military, and a series of nominations of people associated with exactly the causes—such as affirmative action, gay rights, and left-wing cultural values—that had cost the Democrats the support of socially conservative working-class voters destroyed Clinton's support among those whom he had won back from the Republicans in 1992. Through political errors rather than through whole-hearted commitment to these controversial policies, Clinton attached to the Demo-

Table 1. DIVIDED GOVERNMENT: PRESIDENTS AND CONGRESS, 1897–1995[a] (*Continued*)

President	Congress		Senate			House		
			Maj	Min	Other	Maj	Min	Other
Eisenhower, R	**83d**	**1953–55**	**48 R**	47 D	1	**221 R**	211 D	1
Eisenhower, R	84th	1955–57	48 D	47 R	1	232 D	203 R	
Eisenhower, R	85th	1957–59	49 D	47 R		233 D	200 R	
Eisenhower, R	86th	1959–61	64 D	34 R		283 D	153 R	
Kennedy, D	**87th**	**1961–63**	**65 D**	35 R		**263 D**	174 R	
Kennedy, D	**88th**	**1963–65**	**67 D**	33 R		**258 D**	177 R	
L. Johnson, D								
L. Johnson, D	**89th**	**1965–67**	**68 D**	32 R		**295 D**	140 R	
L. Johnson, D	**90th**	**1967–69**	**64 D**	36 R		**247 D**	187 R	
Nixon, R	91st	1969–71	57 D	43 R		243 D	192 R	
Nixon, R	92d	1971–73	54 D	44 R	2	254 D	180 R	
Nixon, R	93d	1973–75	56 D	42 R	2	239 D	192 R	1
Ford, R								
Ford, R	94th	1975–77	60 D	37 R	2	291 D	144 R	
Carter, D	**95th**	**1977–79**	**61 D**	38 R	1	**292 D**	143 R	
Carter, D	**96th**	**1979–81**	**58 D**	41 R	1	**276 D**	157 R	
Reagan, R	97th	1981–83	**53 R**	46 D	1	243 D	192 R	
Reagan, R	98th	1983–85	**54 R**	46 D		269 D	165 R	
Reagan, R	99th	1985–87	**53 R**	47 D		252 D	182 R	
Reagan, R	100th	1987–89	55 D	45 R		258 D	177 R	
Bush, R	101st	1989–91	55 D	45 R		260 D	175 R	
Bush, R	102d	1991–93	57 D	43 R		266 D	166 R	1
Clinton, D	**103d**	**1993–95**	**57 D**	43 R		**258 D**	176 R	1
Clinton, D	104th	1995–97	53 R	47 D		230 R	204 D	1

[a] Division in each house of Congress between the majority party, the principal minority party, and other members (independents and members of minority parties) at the beginning of each Congress. When the majority party is the party of the President, it is printed in boldface. When the majority party in both houses is the party of the President, the President's name and the number of the Congress are also printed in boldface.
Abbreviations: D, Democratic; Maj, majority party; Min, principal minority party; R, Republican.
SOURCE: Adapted from *Encyclopedia of the American Presidency* (New York: Simon & Schuster, 1994), pp. 383–384.

crats precisely the "McGovernite" image he had been chosen to destroy. In consequence, white males across the nation deserted the Democrats in droves in 1994, and a large majority of white Southerners of both sexes backed the Republicans against the party of the President from Arkansas.

The Democrats' loss of control of the Senate was bad enough, ending their hopes that they could adopt major reforms such as national health insurance. It was the loss of the House, however, that was the crueller blow. As we have seen, House Democrats had been able to use the advantages of incumbency to overcome the disadvantages of having an unpopular Democrat running for President. Even President Reagan at his most popular had been unable to break the Democrats' grip on the House. Led by the then Minority Whip (later Speaker) Newt Gingrich (Georgia) the Republicans overcame these advantages.

Gingrich's strategy was twofold. First, he made the campaign much more nationally focused than is usually the case in House elections, reversing the well known dictum of the former Democratic Speaker of the House, Tip O'Neill, that "all politics is local." One step in the tactic was to have Republican candidates sign a "Contract with America" on the steps of the Capitol specifying the policies they would advance if elected. Although the contract had many "escape" clauses, it represented a large step toward the national party manifestos common in parliamentary democracies but unknown in congressional elections in the United States. While most Americans did not read the contract, the focus of the campaign was shifted to national issues where the Republican positions were popular.

Gingrich's second tactic was to undermine the value of incumbency. The proud boasts of incumbent Democrats that they had won valuable government programs for their districts were rendered worthless or even damaging by labeling all such expenditures "pork." When the Republicans also kept up unremitting attacks on the "professional politicians" who allegedly dominated Washington, being an incumbent became a disadvantage, not an advantage. Most unusually, 35 of the 53 seats that Democrats lost were lost by incumbents Representatives seeking reelection; the conventional wisdom had been that the Republicans had their best chance in the open-seat contests with no incumbent running.

The Republican gain of over fifty seats in the House and the capture of control of both chambers in Congress for the first time since 1954 was impressive enough. Republicans hoped that the 1994 election also marked their escape from the status of minority party. In states such as Ohio, where the Republicans made considerable gains, Democrats could hope to recover in future elections if they were more astute politically. In contrast, the Republicans' victories in the South seemed more significant, moving that part of the country away from the Democrats for good in a regional version of the long-awaited realignment. Strikingly, many of the Republican victors in the South had been Democrats early in their political careers; they had decided that they could pursue their political careers more successfully in the Republican Party than in the Democratic Party. The Democrats' leader, President Clinton, was so unpopular there that he did not campaign south of the Mason-Dixon line. All but one of the six top Republican leaders in the new Congress were Southerners, and the exception, Senate majority leader Robert Dole, was from the border state of Kansas.

The Republicans brought major changes to the party system in Congress. No Speaker since Cannon had acquired as much power as Speaker Gingrich. Departing from the seniority system that had been developed in the House as an antidote to the power of the Speaker, Gingrich appointed as committee chairmen those whom he thought best capable of advancing the Republican agenda. Many house Republicans had received help from Gingrich in the election, and the two-thirds of them who had been elected for the first time in 1992 or 1994 thought that it was Gingrich's leadership that had brought them out of the wilderness and into the majority.

Yet, in the Senate, the Republicans were more clearly divided. The minority leader, Robert Dole (Kansas), was both more moderate and much less powerful than Gingrich. A conservative Republican, Trent Lott (Mississippi), was elected to be Dole's deputy (Republican whip) but neither could prevent a liberal Republican, Mark Hatfield (Oregon), from becoming chairman of a powerful committee under the seniority rule. Divisions in the Republican Party over issues such as the desirability of holding organized prayer in public schools threatened to undermine the effectiveness of the party in Congress. The most important threat to their aspirations to be the securely majority party, Republicans could reflect, was the fickleness of the voters. In an era when a President (Bush) could go from record popularity to defeat in eighteen months, no party could be confident of keeping its following from one election to the next.

THE PARTY SYSTEM AT THE CENTURY'S END

The comparison noted earlier between the 1912 and 1992 Presidential elections was apposite for another reason. H. Ross Perot received the largest share of the popular vote won by a third-party candidate, 19 percent, since Theodore Roosevelt's candidacy in 1912. This success was all the more extraordinary given Perot's many weaknesses as a candidate. He had withdrawn from the race in July and only reentered in October; his vice presidential candidate was so unqualified that he may even have attracted some support out of sympathy. Perot was ignorant of many issues and, most dismaying of all for many, displayed highly undemocratic attitudes toward his critics and reporters. And yet he received one-fifth of the vote.

It is tempting therefore to see in Perot's success a measure of the decline of the hold of parties on the loyalties of voters, which had been noted by many political scientists for at least two decades before the Perot phenomenon. In the early 1960s, the dominant view in electoral studies, the so-called Michigan school, had argued that most voters nearly always voted in line with a loyalty to a party ("party identification") that was acquired early in life and remained stable. Candidates, issues, and such short-term influences as the state of the economy were much less important than partisanship as influences on political behavior.

By the 1970s, the Michigan school's emphasis on party identification had been abandoned by most voters (though not by the Michigan school itself). Not only did voters choose candidates less frequently on the basis of their proclaimed partisanship (particularly in presidential elections), but both their willingness to proclaim a partisanship and the stability of that partisanship were less than had once been thought customary. Many more voters than in the past regarded themselves as Independents, not Republicans or Democrats. Citizens also seemed to change their partisanship more frequently than the Michigan school's emphasis on the stability of partisanship had suggested. These trends were apparent in the patterns of voting in elections, as well as in response to the questions asked by political scientists in survey research. The long period of divided government, in which the Republicans controlled the presidency and the Democrats the Congress, followed by the period after 1994 in which this division of the institutions was reversed, could not have occurred without one aspect of voters' reduced loyalty to parties, namely their increased willingness to split their tickets in voting for the president and the Congress. The diminished importance of party in terms of appeals to the electorate was also evident in the way in which many Republican (and also some Democratic) candidates made no mention of their party in their commercials or literature. The weakened power of party loyalty was also evident in the enormous fluctuations in the standing of the parties in the 1990s; President Bush went from record approval ratings in the opinion polls to defeat in eighteen months; President Clinton's standing declined very rapidly after he took office, and, as we have seen, his party was humiliated by the voters in the next midterm elections. Neither party could count on stable support from the voters.

Yet it would be wrong to interpret these developments as showing a simple, across the board decline in the political parties. In terms of their organization nationally and importance in Congress, the parties could be described better as changed, or even strengthened, rather than as weakened. Both parties developed major institutional capacity at the national level to raise funds and provide advice or services to their candidates. For example, both the Democratic and Republican National Committees were important sources of funds and assistance for their candidates in the 1992 elections, the Democrats having finally caught up with the Republicans in these regards after twelve years of trying. The Republicans had moved very successfully to build up the Republican National Committee's ability to assist candidates after their heavy losses in the 1974 and 1976 elections; the Democrats found it more difficult to build up party organization and fundraising at first, perhaps because of their greater ideological diversity and the ability of their incumbent legislators to raise money directly. In the end, however, the Democrats could not ignore the incentives in campaign finance legislation to develop party fundraising to take advantage of "soft" money that parties were allowed to raise and spend beyond the limits specified for candidates. Thus both the Republicans and Democrats ended the century with stronger national (and probably state) organizations than hitherto whereas parties at the local level were much weaker than the machines or, to revert to Mayhew's terminology, typical party organizations of earlier in the century.

The parties could also claim to be doing more than ever before to help the American political system attain democratic goals. Although, as we have seen, the Democrats lost traditional supporters because of their internal reforms, those reforms (and their counterparts in the Republican party) did enhance American democracy significantly. The growth of primaries, for example, allowed ordinary voters a greater chance to participate in the selection of presidential candidates than ever before, even if most voters did not avail themselves of the opportunity. Although Republican—as well as Democratic—controlled state legislatures moved to adopt presidential primaries in the early 1970s, the impetus for change had come from within the Democratic party. Instead of being chosen primarily by party bosses at nominating conventions, presidential candidates were chosen in primary elections in which millions of ordinary Republicans and Democrats could participate.

A second way in which the parties have come to contribute better to the quality of American democracy lies in their increased ideological differentiation and consistency. American political parties often used to be criticized as offering voters the choice between Tweedledum and Tweedledee. Such criticism has lost its plausibility. The choice between Ronald Reagan and Walter Mondale in 1984, for example, offered Americans a greater and clearer ideological choice than major European political parties typically offer voters. Changes in the patterns of support for the parties have also made the parties more united. As recently as the 1960s, American political parties at the national level were very odd coalitions that each contained liberals and conservatives; a Republican liberal such as Jacob Javits (New York) would be far to the left of many Southern Democrats. By the 1990s, the Democrats were the more liberal party throughout the nation. Even Southern Democrats, newly dependent on solid support from black voters as Republicans there generally captured the support of a majority of whites, have been forced to be more liberal than in the past, particularly on race. Liberals in states once tied to the Republicans by ethnic or historical factors (as in Wisconsin or Minnesota) became Democrats.

In consequence, the parties in Congress became more cohesive. The liberal wing of the congressional Republican party, once significant particularly in the Senate, had practically vanished by the 1990s. The proportion of roll calls in Congress in which a majority of one party opposes a majority of the other in the 1980s and early 1990s was at an unusually high level. Party unity scores in Congress—the proportion of votes in which legislators vote with their party against the other—rose dramatically in the late twentieth century. American parties are both more sharply distinguished ideologically and more unified than before.

It might seem therefore that American political parties are serving democratic purposes better. Yet, ironically, this development might have been accompanied by a reduction in the significance of the parties in the minds of the voters, as the willingness of so many Americans to back H. Ross Perot in 1992 seemed to indicate. Parties engage the loyalty of many fewer voters, a large proportion of whom regard themselves as independents; of those who do identify with a party, a large proportion are prepared to defect to its rival's candidate, particularly in presidential elections. The primary system was influenced by party regulars meeting in conventions and caucuses, but power may have passed not only to ordinary voters but to the media who shape their perceptions. The more open system based on primaries of nominating presidential candidates may have transferred power from the bosses, not to ordinary voters, but to the journalists, the "boys [and now also 'girls'] on the bus" who interpret the candidates to the public. Campaigning has become vastly more expensive, and candidates raise the majority of their money either directly from the public or from the political action committees (PACs) of interest groups, not from political parties. Representatives and senators use the advantages of incumbency to build their own support, working as individual political entrepreneurs whereas once they might have been more dependent on their party. In brief, while the parties at the highest levels—as national organizations, in Congress or in presidential elections—might have become ideologically more distinct and unified, they might be less effective as organizations linking government to the people. In most parts of the United States today, parties at the local level are little more than loose networks of like-minded enthusiasts who coalesce around candidates.

Nor did the "new politics" of late century produce more elevated political debate than in the past. Voters might have become more independent and politically volatile, but were not transformed into attentive, deliberative citizens. Late-twentieth-century voters proved to be highly susceptible to manipulation by the use of symbols. The campaign consultants whom all major candidates employed proved capable of as distasteful campaigning with the aid of television as any old-time party boss, even if the manipulations and smears were more subtly delivered. Attempts to impugn the private lives of opponents, to appropriate national symbols such as the flag for one party, and meaningless slogans (such as Reagan's 1984 claim that "It's morning in America") were at least as common late in the century as early in it. Reform had changed parties, but it had also weakened them. Other participants in electoral politics—the media, campaign consultants, PACs, and advertising agencies—were the beneficiaries. This was scarcely the situation that reformers had sought to create.

INTEREST GROUP POLITICS IN THE EARLY TWENTIETH CENTURY

A discussion of political parties can proceed without much concern about definitions; we all know roughly what they are. In contrast it is always necessary to define interest groups. An interest group is an organization, with a defined membership, that seeks to influence public policy by lobbying government officials. Interest groups are therefore distinct from the interests in society they seek to organize and represent; retired people are thus the interest that an interest group, the American Association of Retired People (AARP), seeks to organize and represent. This distinction, which may seem pedantic, is important because, whereas interests have always been important in American politics, interest groups have not. In the 1896 election, for example, Mark Hanna raised millions from business for the Republicans to help defeat the menace of William Jennings Bryan and populism. But business interest groups were poorly organized at the time.

American politics has long been thought to be congenial to interest groups. Most political scientists have believed, like Tocqueville, that Americans are more willing than most peoples to join or form groups. The comparative weakness of class consciousness and of debates between ideologies (often misinterpreted as the absence of ideology in the United States) left interest groups more opportunity to swing votes than in other democracies. A blue-collar hunter, for example, is potentially more open to arguments from the National Rifle Association to support a right-wing candidate because he does not have the same strong attachment to a Labour or Social Democratic party as his counterpart in western Europe. Party competition has given certain interests—such as the farm bloc in the 1948 presidential election or the "Moral Majority" in the late 1970s—the opportunity to claim that though they are a minority of the population, they cast the decisive votes in the election. The fragmentation of American government has also helped interest groups by increasing the number of access points to decisionmakers to the point where a well-organized group can usually find leverage somewhere. When the National Association for the Advancement of Colored People (NAACP) was ignored by Congresses dominated by Southern Democrats and by President Eisenhower (who was instinctively hostile to integration), it could still find a sympathetic hearing in the courts. Both the executive branch and Congress traditionally have been structured so that the interests most affected by government policies have had considerable influence over the agencies or congressional committees that devise them. The Agriculture Department and the congressional agriculture committees, for example, have been seen as dominated by rural interests rather than by the consumers or taxpayers who pay for the programs.

Interest groups were certainly prominent in the politics of early-twentieth-century America. The power of economic interests was very evident near the turn of the century. But interest group politics was dominated by cause groups. The Progressive movement spawned many interest groups that campaigned on such issues as civil service reform. The most obvious examples of interest groups in this period were those campaigning for Prohibition and women's suffrage, movements that had been active in the nineteenth century. Both ultimately achieved their goals by amending the federal Constitution (the Eighteenth and Nineteenth Amendments). The suffrage movement had overcome the dispute over tactics that had divided suffragists and developed an organization, the National American Woman Suffrage Association (NAWSA), that could claim to be the best organized interest group of its day. By 1917, NAWSA had 2 million women members in forty-four state auxiliaries; the organization raised $750,000 a year.

Although less evident, economic groups had already started to appear, making a surprisingly halting start and needing government encouragement to grow at the national level. Farmers had organized the Grange movement in the 1870s, which influenced the adoption of railroad regulation in the states and later by the federal government with the creation in 1887 of the Interstate Commerce Commission. The Grange movement, however, declined rapidly thereafter. The organization that established permanent preeminence in representing farmers was the American Farm Bureau Federation (AFBF). The AFBF spread through the nation with the help of county extension agents, who encouraged farmers to join in part to reduce the opportunity for more radical farm organizations to succeed. By the 1920s, the Farm Bureau had launched a campaign for a stable relationship between farm income and national income, a concept known as parity; though initially unsuccessful, the campaign prepared the way for New Deal agriculture programs.

Employers were also slow to develop interest groups to represent them, perhaps because they had been used to living in such a favorable political climate. The privileged political status of business, protected by a solicitous judiciary, a Senate often labeled "the rich man's club," and politicians at all levels eager for campaign contributions, at first made organizing a business interest group superfluous. Challenges from the nascent labor organizations and Progressive reformers encouraged some development of business groups. So did the White House. The creation of the Chamber of Commerce followed urging from President Taft that business organize to make its voice heard more effectively in Washington.

American unions developed more slowly than their counterparts in northern Europe, and have never been as successful in recruiting members. As in Britain, the first successful attempts to form enduring labor unions were among skilled craft workers. The formation of the American Federation of Labor in 1887 marked a conscious choice by labor organizers to emphasize respectability. Only the more skilled, higher status and higher income workers were unionized. Although the AFL became a significant organization, by World War I it had settled into complacency, making few if any attempts to organize the vast majority of less skilled, lower paid workers. In contrast, unions represented only a small minority of workers.

Samuel Gompers, the leader of the AFL, limited his political agenda to matters of direct concern to labor. Some of these concerns, such as restricting Asian immigration in order to protect high wages, were scarcely examples of issues that a social democratic labor organization would espouse. Gompers eschewed identification with either political party, believing correctly that ties of ethnicity, region, and religion would overwhelm any calls from union leaders for workers to identify with either party and would instead weaken attempts to recruit union members.

THE EFFECTS OF THE NEW DEAL ON INTEREST GROUP POLITICS

The New Deal transformed the politics of interests, reversing the situation at the start of the century. After the New Deal, writers on interest groups thought naturally in terms, not of mass-membership cause groups, but of producer groups such as farmers, unions, and employers. Mass-membership interest groups remained active but the interest group system became dominated by producer groups.

The New Deal mobilized groups in a variety of ways. Most obviously, the New Deal raised the stakes that producer groups had in national politics. The federal government, which until 1940 spent a smaller proportion of national income than did state governments, became a force important to every producer interest. Prevailing judicial doctrine ceased to buffer employers from regulation. Whereas in the infamous *Lochner* decision (1905), the Supreme Court had denied the authority of the state of New York to protect bakers from working excessive hours, by 1942 the Court was asserting the right of federal government to control the amount of grain that could be grown on a farm even if not a gram of the grain left the farm (*Wickard* v. *Filburn,* 1941). In the early stages of the New Deal, the National Recovery Administration (NRA) attempted to develop codes covering every aspect of industrial production in order to stabilize production and limit cost cutting. As the New Deal gave way to military mobilization, the federal government assumed the role it has played ever since of being the country's largest consumer. In brief, federal government became an incomparably more important actor in the economy and society; as such it attracted much more attention from interest groups.

But the New Deal did more. It actively promoted the development of producer groups. The farm bureaus spread further as county extension agents were better able to encourage farmers to join now that they had the power to distribute (or withhold) federal farm subsidy payments. The NRA encouraged a dramatic surge in the number of trade associations (interest groups representing employers in a single industry) because it needed trade associations to work with it in developing its Blue Eagle codes of good practice. Above all, the Wagner Act placed the power of the federal government behind attempts to unionize less skilled workers. Although the 1930s witnessed a surge of spontaneous militancy, and the motives of the proponents of the National Labor Relations Act (the Wagner Act) may have included a desire to inhibit the spread of more radical labor organizations, without the act, the wave of militancy would have left no enduring institutional legacy. The National Labor Relations Board (NLRB) conducted secret ballots so that workers could choose freely to join a union, and obliged employers to bargain in good faith with the unions. The NLRB thereby allowed the impetus to organize to coalesce into America's first experience with mass unionism. The new unions, linked in the Congress of Industrial Organizations (CIO), were well aware of how much they owed their existence to government; in consequence they were much more politically committed and active than the old AFL unions. Yet in spite of these dramatic developments, in the end the New Deal produced an incomplete mobilization of economic interests. No single employers' group emerged in the United States; the Chamber of Commerce, the National Association of Manufacturers, and various other organizations contended for the title.

When Raymond Bauer et al. conducted the most important investigation of interest groups in the 1950s, they found that trade associations were generally underfinanced, poorly staffed, and little respected. Farmers' organizations were badly divided; after 1948, the AFBF abandoned support for New Deal subsidy programs to press for a return to the free market, while the National Farmers' Union, the Grange, the National Farmers' Organization, and dozens of groups representing producers of single commodities pressed for their retention. Union membership peaked at about 35 percent of the workforce in the early 1950s and declined thereafter until it reached about 16 percent by the 1990s. Although the AFL and CIO merged in the 1950s, the constituent unions continued to feud over politics, and major unions such as the United Auto Workers (UAW), the Teamsters, and the United Mine Workers (UMW) spent long periods outside the organization.

The contrast with other democracies was acute. In most other democracies, a single organization spoke for employers. Sometimes these organizations became partners of government, not merely interest groups. In France and Japan, for example, the employers' groups (the Patronat and the Keidanren) participated in planning that transformed their economies. In Sweden, Austria, Norway, and the Netherlands, the employers' organization was joined by the labor union federation in working with government to design social and economic policy. Even in Britain, where trends toward government sharing power with economic groups were weaker, single-interest groups such as the Trade Union Congress,

National Farmers' Union, and the Confederation of British Industry were recognized as the authoritative voices of the sectors they represented. No producer group in the United States achieved such authority. Why did the New Deal result in what seems in comparative perspective an untidy and incomplete mobilization of economic interests?

In the first place, government pulled back from the most detailed forms of intervention associated with the early New Deal. The NRA's attempts to govern in detail every industry were generally agreed to have failed before the Supreme Court declared them unconstitutional: the American economy was too vast and varied for the task. The collapse of the NRA resulted in a major decline in the number of trade associations represented in Washington. In place of detailed intervention in industry, the United States edged toward a half-hearted Keynesianism in which the federal government by and large tried to steer the macro economy, not specific industries. (It is interesting to recall, however, that Richard Nixon did not announce his conversion to Keynesianism until the early 1970s, by which point its days were numbered.) Even mobilization for World War II was accomplished with greater reliance on business cooperation and less reliance on government controls than had been attempted in World War I. After 1945, with rare and brief exceptions, the federal government avoided attempts to run incomes policies intended to limit inflation in full employment by limiting wage increases. The absence of incomes policies had important implications for the interest group system, for, to be successful, incomes policies require tripartite bargaining among government, unions, and employers. Governments that wish to use incomes policy as a technique of economic management generally have to work closely with employers' organizations and unions.

The federal government remained a dramatic presence in the economy as the proportion of gross national product it spent grew to levels once associated with European welfare states, but it avoided taking part in anything approaching economic planning for individual sectors. This bypassed the need governments in other democracies experienced to work closely with economic interest groups in order to make and implement such plans. When the federal government did become closely involved in individual sectors, as in the defense industry and agriculture, the results did not encourage emulation; private interests seemed more adept at using the federal government to their own advantage than the federal government seemed at planning those sectors.

Federal policy switched gradually from encouraging to discouraging membership in labor unions. The most important change came with the Taft-Hartley Act, adopted by a Republican Congress over President Truman's veto in 1947, although its full effects were not felt for some time. The act contained two particularly important provisions for the long-term future of labor unions. First, states were allowed to enact "right to work" laws that prohibited the closed shop. Second, "sympathy" strikes or actions were forbidden. Unions were thus unable to use strength in one sector (such as manufacturing) to force an employer such as a retail store to recognize a union by stopping deliveries unless a union was recognized. These two provisions of the act helped to limit unions to regions and industries in which they were already strong. As industry migrated south and west, and as employment shifted out of industries in which unions were already strong, the share of the workforce unionized declined. Although Taft-Hartley mobilized unions politically—even the former AFL unions—to an unprecedented degree, it ensured that unions would not attain the same importance in the United States as in many other democracies. Indeed, in spite of the enormous importance of unions in supporting liberal Democrats and such general liberal causes as civil rights and Medicare, their inability to secure changes in labor law added to their long-term demise. In the Reagan years, employers with unionized workforces faced fierce competition from both overseas and from American employers with nonunionized workforces; moreover a sympathetic, antiunion NLRB helped them defeat their unions and persuade their workers to leave unions.

A further reason why the New Deal did not lead to a more complete mobilization of producer groups is that many of the groups were able to focus their attention on very limited sectors of government; the fragmented institutions of American government allowed interests to protect their favorite programs adequately even though their interest groups seemed unimpressive organizations. For example, wheat and dairy farmers did not need to influence the entire Congress or even the entire agriculture committees to achieve many of their objectives; the subcommittees of the agriculture committees and the relevant agencies within the Agriculture Department would suffice. Even though labor unions could not secure a revision in their favor of the labor laws, their friends (usually Democrats) on the House and Senate Labor committees were able to prevent further antiunion legislation from reaching the floor. Partnerships among defense contractors, the armed services, and members of the armed services committees of Congress were advantageous to all partners. The legislators representing western ranchers helped assure that the fees paid for grazing their cattle on federally owned land were kept at modest levels by the Interior Department's Bureau of Land Management and the number of cattle that could be grazed per acre at immodest levels. Most of these interests faced little serious opposition from other groups on these issues. No consumer groups questioned the dairy program with its lavish encouragement to dairy farmers in Florida and California; no environmental group raised questions about whether or not Interior Department land in the West was being ruined by overgrazing. Narrowly defined interests, unopposed by other groups, were able to protect the interests of their members even though the groups impressed observers more by their weaknesses than their strengths. In the new American state characterized by Theodore Lowi as one dominated by "interest group liberalism," groups could succeed without achieving high levels of organization.

Finally, New Deal interest group organization was not more complete because the level of intergroup conflict was quite low. Until the late 1960s, it was plausible to celebrate or bemoan the end of ideology. Groups that tended to disagree usually did so to a limited degree. Unions and employers, for example, disagreed on a large number of issues, including labor law, social welfare issues, and health insurance. Yet the intensity of conflict was quite low. Large corporations, particularly once Taft-Hartley had helped to limit the potential growth of American unions, prided themselves until the Reagan years on their acceptance of unions; strident antiunionism, confined politically to the far right of the Republican party, was a hallmark of unsophisticated Main Street business. The lavish defense contracts and often ludicrous agricultural subsidy programs were rarely attacked. Programs that benefited particular interests but that wasted significant resources from the viewpoint of society as a whole were readily tolerated.

Such programs were accepted because the American economic machine seemed to produce ever increasing prosperity effortlessly. It was taken for granted that the economy as a whole and individuals' incomes would increase steadily in real terms. Foreign competition was an insignificant problem for all but a few industries (such as textiles); indeed, American corporations dominated the world for a generation after World War II. A society that had attained unprecedented prosperity did not need to worry about squandering a few hundred millions on enabling Florida and California farmers to keep dairy cattle in what, without federal aid, would be unsuitable territory.

We should not imagine, however, that all major policy questions were settled by interest group pressure, or even that interest groups invariably controlled policy questions that concerned them. In spite of many suggestions to the contrary, there is no evidence that American foreign policy was based on the articulated wishes of powerful interests, such as corporations. (Whether American foreign policy served the interests of capitalism in general is a different question.) Even on issues on which interest groups were indeed very active, politicians were able to use a variety of techniques to preserve their freedom of action. Sometimes one group could be set off against another, as when the American Medical Association and the AFL-CIO were on opposite sides of the debate over whether to introduce Medicare.

Even when groups could not be balanced against each other, insulation from group pressure was available. Congress used techniques such as having voice votes rather than recorded votes, closed committee hearings to which lobbyists were not admitted, and the delegation of difficult decisions to committees such as Ways and Means composed of the most senior, most electorally secure legislators to escape from interest group pressure. It was by no means unusual for legislators to praise privately the action of a committee chair or committee in turning down an interest group request while gaining political capital by attacking it publicly. Destler has argued that it was precisely the ability of strategically placed politicians to "take the heat" for turning down demands for protectionism from interest groups that made it politically possible for the United States to maintain a liberal international trading system. On one side were crusaders for clean air, clean water, and the protection of the public; on the other side were greedy business executives bent on maximizing profits and prepared to use any means to protect their interests. The contrast was epitomized by the conflict between the ascetic Ralph Nader and General Motors over the safety of the Corvair; GM's response to Nader's claims that their car was unsafe at any speed was to employ private detectives to inquire into Nader's abstemious private life in the hope of finding embarrassing material about him. In the light of such incompetence, it is scarcely surprising that even while Nixon was president, business found that regulatory measures it disliked were passing Congress by huge margins.

Confidence in business was reduced further by the Watergate affair. Although business executives felt that they were victims of Nixon's Committee to

Re-Elect the President (CREEP) in that they were coerced into making illegal campaign contributions, the public was more likely to blame business for corrupting politics with large, secret, and illegal campaign contributions whose existence became widely known only as a result of inquiries into the Watergate affair.

Watergate also seemed to threaten business with a more hostile political environment as many of the most pro-business politicians were weakened in the aftermath of Watergate. It was not unreasonable to suppose after Watergate that the Republicans could expect to lose the next two presidential elections. The Democrats could anticipate victory in 1976 and the retention of the White House in 1980. Even more worrying for business was the transformation in Congress that was an indirect consequence of Watergate. The 1974 midterm elections punished the Republican party heavily for the sins of its president (even though, ironically, Nixon had kept considerable distance between himself and the party). The Watergate babies, as the freshmen were known, provided reformers with the support they needed to make major changes in the power structure, particularly in the House. The most important changes included attacks upon the seniority system and a reduction in the power of committee chairmen. Both of these reforms reduced the disproportionate power of conservative, pro-business southern Democrats. As critics of business gathered strength, business felt that its allies were being weakened. Bryce Harlow, who had worked as an aid to Nixon responsible for congressional liaison and in a similar capacity for Proctor and Gamble, warned that there was a danger that business would be "rolled up and thrown in the garbage can."

Other developments were propelling business into greater political involvement. The 1970s marked the end of American international dominance. Years of continuing trade deficits culminated with the forced devaluation of the dollar in 1971. Basic industries such as steel or automobiles faced increasingly effective challenges from foreign competitors. The automobile and steel industries soon joined the textile industry, long an unusually effectively represented industry in Washington in seeking protection from foreign competition. Furthermore, the value of government contracts, which are rarely truly open to foreigners, increased along with foreign competition. If Chrysler had lost part of its automobile market to the Japanese, its sales of tanks to the government were more important than ever. In spite of, or even perhaps because of, the growing number of regulations that covered federal contracting, corporations needed lobbyists to reinforce politically the technical appeal of their products. In brief, the deteriorating commercial position of American corporations reinforced their need to become more active politically.

The pressures on corporations resulted in a massive political mobilization. If the major feature of interest group politics between roughly 1968 and 1974 was the rise of the public interest group, the major feature of the period from 1974 to 1980 was the rise of business interest groups. Corporations realized that their resources allowed them to copy every one of their opponents' tactics. Just as environmentalists could bring law suits seeking court orders for force agencies to produce stricter regulations, so could corporations bring suits to block regulations. Just as the number of public interest organizations and lobbyists in Washington had grown rapidly, so could business increase the number and quality of its organizations and lobbyists. The Chamber of Commerce, once almost a laughingstock in Washington, became instead one of its most admired practitioners of interest group politics. The largest corporations formed the Business Roundtable to represent their concerns as opposed to those of small-scale business. Many trade associations representing specific industries were rejuvenated. Most large corporations felt that even if organizations to which they belonged had improved their performance considerably, it was still desirable to open their own embassies in Washington, employing their own lobbyists instead of relying on business organizations or occasional visits by staff from headquarters.

The most visible and controversial aspect of the increase in business political activity was the growth of business political action committees (PACs). As we noted earlier, PACs were pioneered by unions, and it was unions who pressed for legislation that legalized PACs. Fearing that the Supreme Court was about to declare union campaign contributions in violation of the hitherto unenforced campaign-finance legislation, unions sought speedy confirmation from Congress of the legality of their contributions. In order to make the legislation less controversial and therefore more likely to pass quickly, the phrase "or corporations" was added whenever unions were mentioned. No one expected that corporations would make much use of their new power.

Thus unintentionally was a behemoth created. Corporate campaign contributions soon outstripped those of labor. Just as most large corporations found it best to have their own lobbyists in Washington, so their lobbyists also found it best to reinforce the wisdom of their arguments with a contribution from a PAC. Corporate PACs were given a valuable advantage. Like union PACs, corporations were allowed to pay the operating expenses of their PACs out of general revenue. Whereas PACs promoting a cause spend a very high proportion of their income—sometimes close to 100 percent—on fund-raising expenses (such as the costs of direct mail), corporate PACs can use every cent contributed by stockholders or executives as campaign contributions. Rarely among the largest fundraisers, business PACs were prominent among the largest donors.

The 1970s therefore witnessed an interest group arms race. As new interest groups such as the environmentalists made their presence felt, so other groups such as business felt obliged to mobilize. In turn, environmentalists were spurred on to greater efforts by what they naturally saw as evidence of a business political offensive.

One important interest had particular problems keeping pace with this arms race, however. In retrospect, the 1970s witnessed the last chance for American unions to secure changes in their legislative environment without which they were doomed to decline. Perhaps because of the great age of many union leaders, including the octogenarian president of the AFL-CIO, George Meaney, unions were very slow to adapt to changes in the broader political environment. In particular, unions failed to develop a strategy for maintaining their influence within the Democratic party in the face of the decline in the power of the party "professionals," the growth in the number and importance of presidential primaries, and the emergence of a generation of liberals whose concerns such as Vietnam or the environment made them indifferent or even hostile to unions. In 1972, the majority of unions and the AFL-CIO were "neutral for Nixon" refusing to support the liberals' successful nominee for Democratic presidential candidate, Sen. George McGovern. In 1976, having realized that unions had predictably gained little from recent Republican administrations, the AFL-CIO and most unions endorsed a Democratic nominee, Gov. Jimmy Carter, over whose selection they had enjoyed little influence. Similarly in Congress, the new, highly educated liberal Democrats elected from districts containing a high proportion of white-collar voters neither loved nor feared unions as had many of their predecessors. Labor had expected confidently to secure passage of labor legislation to its advantage while the Democrats held both White House and Congress. It failed. Although unions continued to employ many able lobbyists and to be the major source of money for liberal Democrats, they had lost their special position in Democratic party politics.

With the exception of labor, however, the late 1960s and 1970s was a period of tremendous growth for interest groups. A new interest group system was created that was more plural and inclusive than the old. Whereas in the old system only a few or a single interest existed in a policy area (e.g., grazers or ranchers in the federal land use policy area), now there were typically a number of different and often conflicting interests. Whereas the old interest group system had been composed largely of producer groups, now public interest groups were equally noticeable. Other factors, several of which we have mentioned in passing were also to have a powerful influence on the interest group system.

INSTITUTIONAL CHANGE

The 1970s were a decade of unusually extensive institutional change. These changes disrupted many of the institutional ties that had been a part of the old interest group system.

The extensive reforms in the Democratic party in the early 1970s disrupted the unofficial alliance between most national labor unions and the Democratic party. With some exceptions (such as the United Auto Workers), unions found both primaries and mass participation caucuses used to select delegates as in Iowa not to their advantage. Unions found it difficult to mobilize members to play a role in primaries or caucuses, and disliked being required to choose openly one candidate to endorse; after all, nearly all candidates for the Democratic nomination have had a good record from labor's viewpoint. Labor leaders deplored the passing of the old Democratic party structure, in which, they felt, the professionals who ran the party gave the views of union leaders the respect that labor deserved in view of its contributions to Democratic campaigning.

The congressional reforms of the 1970s weakened the grip of committee chairmen and even whole committees. For decades, committee chairmen had been treated with great deference, particularly by junior legislators who were expected to follow an apprenticeship before exerting power vigorously. But when House Democrats gathered after the 1974 elections, the newly elected Watergate babies made clear their rejection of such traditions. Four committee chairmen, both conservative and liberal, who seemed condescending or insensitive to junior representatives were removed from office. The refusal of the Democrats to follow automatically the dictates of the seniority system in choosing committee chairs sent shock waves through Congress. Committee chairmen who kept their jobs realized that this was the age of the common Representative; rank in Congress was no longer determined solely by seniority but ultimately by the votes of one's colleagues, including the votes of the most junior freshmen. Legislators were similarly less deferential to expert committees than in the past. Committees such as Appropriations and, most clearly of all, Ways and Means, that expected never to lose on the floor found that bills they had approved were being rejected or amended.

The greater unpredictability of the policy process that resulted was increased by a breakdown in the boundaries that defined the roles of committees. Overlapping or even competing committees claimed jurisdiction over the same policy, such as energy conservation. Interest groups could no longer be confident that the traditional committee would retain control over a policy area, or that if it did, its decisions would prevail on the floor.

Institutional arrangements that had facilitated the old interest group politics were also disrupted by what at first glance seems to be a contradictory development—the attempts to exert greater central control in the executive branch and in Congress. Central agencies in the executive branch made stronger efforts to evaluate and control the work of line agencies or departments. President Reagan made the Office of Management and Budget stronger not only by encouraging it to cut domestic expenditures but by giving it additional powers over regulatory agencies within the executive branch. Similarly in Congress, the 1974 Budget and Impoundment Control Act created opportunities to cut across the institutional boundaries of subgovernments. The reconciliation process created under the act, used for the first time effectively to impose the Reagan budget cuts of 1981, imposed spending limits on classes of expenditure within which the Appropriations committees were forced to operate. The Congressional Budget Office provided analysis of expenditure that emphasized a central perspective rather than an agency or committee view.

The latter part of the century also saw an increase in interest group activity in the courts. The courts had always been an arena in which interest groups contended. A variety of changes in the 1960s and 1970s made the courts even more significant. First, the courts invited more cases in by relaxing the rules governing standing to sue. In perhaps the most vivid demonstration of this new leniency, a group of law students who enjoyed walking in woods were allowed to sue the Interstate Commerce Commission for setting freight rates at a level the students thought so high that the transportation of waste paper for recycling would be discouraged; the students argued less recycling would result, and therefore an increase in the use of timber to make paper. Given such a relaxed interpretation of standing to sue, almost any interest group could find a way into court.

Second, courts proved more willing to impose their views on agencies. Inspired by political scientists who portrayed the federal bureaucracy as captured by interest groups or prone to taking only symbolic action, judges felt freer than since the New Deal to make policy. For example, judges were happy to pronounce on whether scientific evidence that suggested that benzene caused leukemia was or was not good enough to support a regulation limiting exposure to benzene in the workplace.

Third, Congress invited courts to make policy in important areas, particularly on issues that were potentially embarrassing to Congress. The wave of regulatory legislation passed in the 1960s and 1970s provided for interests displeased with new regulations promulgated by agencies (such as those from OSHA on workplace safety and health) to challenge them in the federal appeals courts. Far from displeasing Congress, judicial activism allowed Congress to hand over to the unelected federal judges difficult issues such as how much extra expenditure employers should be obliged to make in order to save additional lives. When Robert Bork was nominated (unsuccessfully) to the Supreme Court by President Bush, his arguments in favor of legislative rather than judicial determination of controversial issues such as abortion fell on very stony ground among the members of the Senate Judiciary Committee.

The changed role of the courts provided interest groups with both opportunities and challenges. Environmentalists could file suits arguing that proposed new regulations were too lax; corporations could file suit arguing that regulations were too strict. But neither environmentalists nor corporations could assume that any deal they had made with the Environmental Protection Agency would be honored as public policy. The interest group that had lost in negotiations with the agency could be expected to try its luck in the courts. Once again, the political battleground had been expanded, and the capacity of interest groups to operate in a more restricted arena eroded.

In general, therefore, across a wide range of institutions, the boundaries of policy areas became less clearly defined, generally obliging interest groups to spread themselves more widely and therefore less effectively over the political system. If the quintessential old interest group politics took place in subgovernments composed of a stable grouping of interest groups, congressional committees, and the relevant executive branch agency, the new interest group politics took place in a less predictable institutional environment, one in which different Congressional committees, other executive branch agencies, or even individual legislators on the floor of the House or the Senate might become important actors.

CHANGES IN INTELLECTUAL FASHION

Several other developments weakened the old interest group system. First, the increase in the popularity of neoclassical economics in the last three decades of the century as a way of looking at the world generated much criticism of accommodations that had been made between interests and the state. As we have seen, the old interest group system produced subgovernments that typically secured a subsidy or protection from a policy area for the interest group that dominated the subgovernment. Thus airlines were protected from competition, farmers received subsidies, workers in federally funded projects were paid higher wages and corporations doing business with the federal government, particularly defense contractors, made handsome profits. Until the 1960s, many of these payments, such as farm subsidies, were seen as desirable corrections for the failures of markets. Thereafter the tide of criticism rose. By the late 1970s, liberal Democrats such as Sen. Edward Kennedy were advocating re-regulation of industries such as the airline industry, and were doing so using free-market rhetoric once associated with conservatives. The fruits of the settled, secluded arrangements enjoyed by interest groups in subgovernments were questioned increasingly by economists and policy analysts influenced by neoclassical economics. For such critics, subgovernments had produced privileges for interest groups, not necessary adaptation to market failure.

The upsurge in neoclassical economic thinking prompted not only criticism of the arrangements made in subgovernments but also the development of techniques to evaluate their cost. In particular, central budgeting agencies used with growing frequency techniques derived from neoclassical economics such as cost benefit analysis that were intended to highlight the costs of government programs to society. In the past, arrangements made in subgovernments could escape wider scrutiny because their full cost to society was not known. New techniques of policy analysis highlighted those costs.

THE DECLINING POLITICAL ECONOMY

A profoundly important change in the constraints on the interest group system came, however, from the decline in the fortunes of the American political economy. We noted earlier that the unprecedented prosperity and economic dominance of the United States following World War II had facilitated the creation of a postwar settlement between the major producer groups. Large corporations were able to afford steady increases in real wages, while society as a whole could absorb without pain increased government expenditure, readily financed out of economic growth. In the early 1970s, the rising economic challenge to the United States from Europe and Asia brought an end to American dominance and to steady increases in living standards. Indeed, average wages actually *declined* from the early 1970s onwards. The decline of the American economy had a substantial impact on interest group politics. Large corporations, facing intensified competition from abroad and nonunion producers at home became much more hostile to unions. This hostility was evident industrially as corporations employed specialists to try to persuade employees to leave unions and strip recognition from them. Big business also joined small business in the campaigns to prevent labor-law reform in the 1970s and became interested in rolling back welfare programs whose costs had caused them little concern before. In brief, the easy prosperity that had underpinned the postwar compromise between producer groups had gone, and with it went the compromise. Conflict between producer groups became much more intense. New groups were also affected by the intensification of conflict. Corporations were also encouraged to resist more vigorously proposals for stricter regulations whose costs would fall on them. In short, while the opportunities for interest group conflict had increased, the economic resources available to accommodate compromise had diminished.

THE NATURE OF THE NEW INTEREST GROUP SYSTEM

There is no doubt that the new interest group system is more diverse in the range of interests it includes and more prominent than the old. Groups representing interests such as women, environmentalists, and consumers have come into existence to challenge the old supremacy of producer groups. New techniques of interest group politics such as PACs are much more visible than old, discreet campaign contributions. Two subjects of concern for political scientists and commentators in the late 1970s were the supposed dangers of *single-issue* interest groups that, as the term suggests, were focused on a single issue such as abortion, and *overload,* the supposed danger to the political system arising from ever more demands being placed on governments by ever more interest groups, while the capacity of governments to meet those demands diminished during the economic crises of the 1970s.

Pluralists had celebrated the number and vitality if interest groups in the United States; perhaps we now had too much of a good thing. The failure of President Carter to secure reform of the tax system he had labeled a moral outrage, or adoption in full of the energy program he called the moral equivalent of war were ascribed by many including Carter to the excessive power of interest groups. Conservative single-issue groups were widely if probably incorrectly given credit for the defeat of prominent liberal Democrats in the 1978 and 1980 congressional elections, prompting many to wonder if a legislative career would be ended by an "incorrect" vote on a single issue. If so, the prospects for Congress making difficult but necessary decisions were more remote than ever.

ASSESSING THE IMPORTANCE OF INTEREST GROUP POLITICS

A claim that interest groups play a more conspicuous role than ever in American politics is often taken as synonymous with a claim that interest groups are more powerful than ever. They are not synonymous, however.

Interest groups in late-twentieth-century America were both more visible and less powerful. Both producer and non-producer groups have suffered some highly visible reverses since 1981. Indeed, a remarkable feature of the years since 1981 has been a series of policy changes that have involved important defeats for interest groups. The Reagan budget cuts, the comprehensive tax reform of 1986, "fast track" procedures for approving trade negotiations and deregulation of a number of industries were all measures that took important benefits or protections away from interest groups and were naturally therefore opposed by them. Tax reform had been considered a classic example, particularly after the failure of Carter's initiative, of a reform that would be to the general advantage but would never pass because of the opposition of powerful interests that benefitted from tax concessions or allowances. Yet pass it did in spite of energetic lobbying against it by corporate lobbyists whose firms stood to lose significantly under the proposal. Nor were producer groups the only ones to suffer reverses. The National Rifle Association finally lost its ability to defeat all gun-control measures in the House, while the antiabortion groups were unable to make any progress on proposals for a constitutional amendment to prohibit abortion even though they had the support of President Reagan.

Why were interest groups, though so visible, not more successful? There are several reasons.

First, the Reagan years provided an example of a rare phenomenon in American politics, an administration unified by an identifiable set of coherent, ideological principles in domestic policy that can secure a majority in Congress for them. Whether or not Reagan had a mandate for his program from the American electorate, he behaved as though he had, and even his opponents seemed to believe the claim. The Reagan agenda cut across policy communities and subgovernments, disrupting long-established compromises between agencies, Congress, and interest groups as the administration pressed for tax and expenditure cuts. Using new institutional procedures such as the reconciliation procedures in Congress skillfully, the Administration managed to keep political attention focused on the totality of its package, not on the component pieces that mattered to individual interest groups. Perhaps interest groups could have won more fights had each and every expenditure cut or tax change been considered on its merits. However, interest groups seemed less able to defeat measures assembled into a coherent broad package that could be debated more in terms of general strategy or principle than in terms of specific measures.

Second, as we have seen, political parties became somewhat more important in the 1980s and 1990s than they had been immediately before. The modest revival in the fortunes of political parties enabled them to provide resources to candidates that previously candidates had obtained from, among other sources, interest groups. Campaign contributions are an obvious example. Although strong interest groups are often allied with strong political parties (the Swedish LO *[landsorganisationen]* and the Social Democratic party being an obvious example), in two-party systems parties are necessarily obliged to be more general than interest groups in their appeal and concerns. The modest revival of political parties therefore reduced the influence of interest groups. For example, the increase in party cohesion in Congress in the 1980s made it more difficult for lobbyists to persuade legislators to defect from their party's position.

The most important check on the importance of interest groups, however, were the changes in institutions and interest groups that we have described. The institutional changes that we have described served to make interest groups more visible yet possibly less effective. The changes that undermined subgovernments forced interest groups to compete for influence more openly across a wider variety of institutions.

Yet the greater visibility of interest groups did not necessarily translate into greater power. Highly visible contributions from PACs naturally fueled fears of excessive interest group influence. But, to take one example, publicly disclosed contributions from business PACs may buy less influence than secret contributions did in the past. The changes that had produced more, and more varied interest groups have indeed given greater reality than before to the hopes of the Founders about how interest group power can be contained without surrendering liberty. In *Federalist* No. 10, Madison had argued that although a proliferation of interest groups was inevitable under liberty, they could counteract each other. By canceling each other out, contending interests would allow the polity ultimately to focus on the public good rather than private advantage. In the old interest group system, Madison's argument had seemed unpersuasive. Encompassing interests such as the protection of the environment seemed impossible to organize, while sectional interests such as the trucking industry were more effectively represented. Vast sections of American society, particularly the poor, had no representation within the interest group system. Many interest groups within subgovernments faced no opposition; no critical interest group challenged their arguments.

The explosion of interest group activity in the 1970s changed the situation significantly. Many interest groups found for the first time that they did indeed have an opponent. The PAC system offered candidates the possibility of support from a wide variety of interest groups; a candidate, particularly an incumbent, threatened with the loss of support from a PAC could be confident of replacing its contribution with another. This is not to say that all sectors of society were represented or represented equally effectively by interest groups. It is to say that interest groups were much more likely to counteract each other than in the past. If the dominant form of interest group activity in the 1950s was to participate in a subgovernment in which few interests were involved, in the 1990s interest groups were more likely to face opponents. Conflict between interest groups necessarily reduces their influence.

Modern interest group politics is therefore less stable than in the past. Subgovernments and policy networks have been disrupted by the frequent intrusions of groups who were not part of the old system. The institutional setting for interest group politics is also less clearly demarcated and stable than in the past; congressional committees and executive agencies that were once stable allies of interest groups have less autonomy now themselves. Interest groups have to adapt to this less certain world by making alliances and forming coalitions that are much more temporary than in the past. Interest groups have always formed coalitions. The Farm Bureau and the Chamber of Commerce often cooperated. Now, however, interest groups more regularly form temporary coalitions, such as the coalition that opposed the 1986 tax reform, with the expectation that the coalition will dissolve within a few months. Indeed, a fast-growing profession emerged in Washington in the 1980s, the contract lobbyists, who were hired precisely in order to form and coordinate such coalitions.

Ironically, the new interest group system is strangely familiar. While considerable inequalities in interest group resources remain, the new interest group system is closer to pluralist ideals. When pluralism dominated the study of interest groups in the United States, the interest group system in practice was far from pluralist; now that pluralism as an academic doctrine is less popular, it is closer to reality. A wide variety of interests contend with each other, form temporary alliances, and often by opposing each other reduce the danger of excessive interest group power. The interest group system continues to reproduce inequalities in the broader society so that, for example, corporations have more resources than environmentalists. But at least we have seen the number and range of interests included in the interest group system expand considerably. Madison would be pleased.

THE SIGNIFICANCE OF THE AMERICAN EXAMPLE

This essay began with the observation that the United States as one of the most democratic nations in the nineteenth century had pioneered certain techniques of mass politics. Both mass political parties and mass membership interest groups existed in the United States long before universal male suffrage was achieved in countries such as Britain. Do American interest groups—or political parties—still offer a lesson to other democracies?

On one level, the answer is definitely yes. The United States continues to lead the world in political techniques such as television commercials. The British Labour party's image-building political broadcasts about its leader from 1983, Neil Kinnock, have numerous precursors in the movies about presidential nominees shown at American party conventions. American political parties were far ahead of European ones in their use of opinion polling, the use of the media, and campaign managing. The record for American interest groups is more mixed. Nonproducer groups such as Friends of the Earth in the United States have been more sophisticated in fund-raising, publicity seeking, and recruiting than European equivalents. However, American producer groups rarely match the technical expertise of their equivalents in other democracies; most European employers' organizations have greater standing in economic and policy analysis than the competing employer groups in the United States.

Apart from questions of political technique, few overseas have seen much to emulate in American political parties. Their corruption, the undemocratic nature of machines, the lack of ideological commitment, and disunity have seemed at best a bizarre spectacle to most foreign observers. More Americans (if only a minority) have wanted to copy the programmatic parties of other democracies than have citizens of those countries wanted to copy American. But there are in fact two aspects of American political parties that deserve closer attention from foreigners. First, the contemporary primary system, for all its weaknesses, does seem to have solved the problem of how to attain internal party democracy without handing over power to the most extreme or dogmatic party members. Those in, for example, the British Labour party, who have wrestled unsuccessfully with this problem might find in the American primary system something that might be fruitfully adapted to British conditions. Second, at a time when the fissiparous forces in many countries have never seemed stronger, the role of the old catch-all American political parties in preserving national unity surely has relevance. There is a strong temptation in the United States to see the country's political history as lighting the way for other nations. In spite of the many obvious failings of this tendency, it might well be that many nations can achieve unity and democracy only with catch-all political parties of a type as puzzling to outsiders because of their apparent ideological contradictions as American parties have been. A party system that helps avoid the disintegration of a nation is not without its advantages.

The vitality and success of cause groups in the United States will encourage emulation elsewhere. The American women's movement enjoys a prominence and strength not equaled in other democracies. Consumer, environmental, and safety groups are all unusually strong in the U.S. In contrast, many observers, such as Robert Reich, have seen in the fragmented pattern of producer groups in the U.S. a real barrier to economic growth. Weak and divided producer groups have been unable to work in partnership with government in securing growth as they have in other countries, most obviously Japan, France, and Sweden. Relations between government and economic interests have often rested on mutual suspicion and antagonism that has made solving obvious problems more difficult. For example, the United States has experienced more conflict and less progress in occupational safety and health policy than Sweden because of conflict between interest groups, and between interest groups and government. The producer interest group system in the United States has seemed inefficient and backward in reconciling the goals of government and private interests.

Yet by the end of the century the signs were not that the United States would move toward a Swedish or Japanese style economic interest group system but that those systems would decay. The fast-changing economies of the late twentieth century are unsuited to attempts at economic planning or partnership between government and economic interests. Economic interests became more diversified so that their interest groups had difficulty maintaining cohesion. Economic interest group systems that tried to base interest group representation on relatively few large blocs such as farmers, employers, and workers found that those blocs had crumbled. The interest group system of the United States, which had never come close to building such a simplified, cohesive interest group system, looked less like an outdated relic and more like a precursor of future systems for other democracies.

SEE ALSO Nationalism; Political Ideas and Movements; The Presidency (all in this volume).

BIBLIOGRAPHY

The reader interested in political parties should begin with Leon Epstein's *Parties in the American Mold* (1986) which introduces all the major controversies as well as providing a wealth of information. David Mayhew's *Placing Parties in American Politics* (1986) provides a careful reconstruction of the types of party organization found around the United States in different historical eras. Nelson Polsby explores the challenge of institutionalization in Congress to party leaders in his article "The Institutionalization of the House of Representatives" *American Political Science Review* 62 (March 1968): 144–168. Byron Shaffer explores recent party reforms in *Quiet Revolution: The Struggle for the Democratic Party and the Shaping of Post-Reform Politics* (1983). Walter Dean Burnham has done more than anyone to promote historically informed writing on political parties; a good introduction to his approach can be found in William Nisbet Chambers and Walter Dean Burnham (eds.), *American Party Systems: Stages of Political Development* (1975). Stephen Skowronek has made a notable contribution to both history and political science in his study *Building a New American State* (1982) that traces the importance of parties in limiting the development of the American state.

The literature on voting behavior is vast. The most influential work is Angus Campbell, Philip E. Converse, Warren E. Miller, and Donald E. Stokes, *The American Voter* (1960). Many scholars, while accepting their account as accurate for an earlier era, argue that their stress on party identification as an influence on voting is outdated; the case is presented by Norman Nie, Sidney Verba, and John R. Petrocik, *The Changing American Voter* (1979) and by Martin Wattenberg, *The Decline of American Political Parties 1952–1980* (1984).

See Graham Wilson, *Interest Groups in the United States* (1981) and *Interest Groups* (1990) for my own arguments on the American interest group system. David Vogel presents a cogent analysis of fluctuations in the relative power of business in the United States in *Fluctuating Fortunes* (1989). We are all the poorer for the untimely death of Jack Walker, whose article "The Origins and Maintenance of Interest Groups in America" *American Political Science Review* 77, 2 (1983): 390–406, typifies his scholarship and insights. Kay Lehman Schlozman and John Tierney provide a picture of interest groups late in the century in *Organized Interests and American Democracy* (1986). The definitive account of interest groups at mid-century can be found in Raymond Bauer, Ithiel de Sola Pool, and Lewis Anthony Dexter, *American Business and Public Policy* (1963). David Truman's *The Governmental Process* (1951), and V. O. Key's *Politics, Parties and Pressure Groups* (1942) remain classics. No one, however, will ever displace Alexis de Tocqueville's *Democracy in America,* of which, fortunately, there are many editions in print.

THE PRESIDENCY

Bert A. Rockman

The evolution of the American presidency in the twentieth century highlights rather than overshadows the constitutional ambiguities of the presidential office in American government. Contemporary mythologies regarding the office are reflected in aphorisms such as the one Harry Truman reputedly had displayed on his desk, "The buck stops here." They are reflected as well in clichés such as that frequently evoked about the U.S. presidency being the most powerful elective office in the world. Such maxims are at odds with much of American history. They are certainly inconsistent with the structure of government bequeathed by the American Constitution.

In fact, Truman was wrong. The buck did not stop at his desk or those of his predecessors or successors. It was never meant to. The buck stops nowhere in the American system, certainly not in any given office. Similarly, the notion of the presidency as "the most powerful elected office in the world" has far more to do with the powerful position of the United States in the world than it has with the position of the presidency within the American system of government.

Why have these mythologies been generated? The answers may well lie in the desire to find the center in a political system founded to deny the existence of such a center. Despite Alexander Hamilton's arguments for more powerful central authority especially embodied in the executive, the American system, institutionally and in the prevailing political culture, has not treated that argument kindly. That, of course, does not solve the problem of authority in the American political system; rather it exacerbates it.

DEMOCRACY AND THE PROBLEM OF AUTHORITY

Americans, like citizens of other democracies, are profoundly ambivalent about authority, an understandable result of democratic politics that tells us that government should be effective, yet also responsive to popular preferences and accountable to the people for its actions. It is unlikely that Americans are unusual in simultaneously craving both decisive leadership and popular responsiveness. The Ross Perot mania that attracted nearly one-fifth of the voters in the 1992 presidential election surely testifies to a significant demand for powerful, yet responsive, leadership. While this demand is endemic to any political system, what makes America different is its salience, the consequence largely of a system constituted to limit the empowerment of any given authority. While the constituted arrangements of the American political system have remained basically stable, they now operate within a modern political context that frequently craves leadership that is at once powerful and responsive. This situation leads to a condition that some refer to as an impossible presidency. It often leads to oscillations between an imperial presidency and an imperiled presidency.

These conflicts about authority are broadly of three sorts. The first kind of conflicts are those that set the parts of the system against the whole. The president presumes to act as an advocate for the whole, or at least wishes to be so portrayed. The second kind set the center against a fragmented political and institutional structure wherein the presidency becomes identified as the center that must hold and galvanize a highly fragmented political system. If no one is exclusively empowered to pull this off, the president is at least more favorably situated than any other political leader to command attention and to galvanize action. The third, which is of course intimately related to the other two, pits the desire for direction against the convenience of the status quo. Fragmentation plays to the status quo because it raises the costs of action.

The American political system celebrates pluralism. It does so both institutionally and in its democratic creed. The system provides numerous opportunities for various interests to gain access but makes it difficult for any to prevail. It is generous in granting toeholds but far more resistant to granting footholds. The democratic creed in America similarly stresses grassroots participation and the permeability of government. Although Americans vote less than their counterparts elsewhere do, in other ways they participate more. The opportunities to do so are greater and the expectation that action may be efficacious is also greater.

One way, of course, in which power presumably can be legitimately invested in a central authority (the president) is when powerful groups are perceived to block the paths of popular access or influence. Behind the 1992 Perot campaign, for example, was the image engendered by the candidate that special interests thwarted the public will, which only the president (Perot) could execute.

Of course, it is natural for incumbent presidents and even presidential aspirants to believe—or, more cynically, merely to encourage the belief in others—that only they can stand above the tugs and pulls of politics and of special interests clamoring to buy and exercise influence. Thus, a largely twentieth-century version of how to marry the democratic creed to the quest for centralizing political authority is that only the president can roust the undemocratic money-changers (special interests) from the democratic temple. In that supposition lies the popular mythology that "the buck stops here," meaning, of course, with the president.

A similar conflict of authority is struck by the architecture of the American political system. The American system devolves authority outward through the separation of powers and downward through federalism. Everywhere a president turns, there is someone else with legitimately invested authority to potentially impede the path a president might prefer.

Beyond the broad architectural design, however, there is even more fragmentation and power diffusion than meets the eye. Not only is the formal authority to govern diffused, but there is little to pull it together and more to make it even more centrifugal. American political parties lack the controlling mechanisms to ensure that presidential majorities are fulfilled, though in recent years they have become increasingly cohesive. Some institutions, such as the U.S. Senate, defy the ability of majorities to work their will. The Senate was not designed to be a majoritarian body and its rules give great advantages to cohesive minorities and even to individual senators.

In his classic book, *Congressional Government,* written over a hundred years ago, Woodrow Wilson, a notable political scientist as well as future U.S. president, argued that "this division of authority and concealment of responsibility are calculated to subject the government to a very distressing paralysis." Wilson continued, "Policy cannot be either prompt or straightforward when it must serve many masters. It must either equivocate, or hesitate, or fail altogether." The logic of reform, given this diagnosis, seems transparent. Centralize and empower the president. This, of course, has happened less constitutionally than it has by presidents' defining new prerogatives for themselves and finding a relatively high degree of compliance in the courts for such empowerment. In large part because of the mythology that surrounds the modern presidency, many of its incumbents have sought to assume as theirs that which the Constitution has not so clearly given. In the absence of institutional alterations to enhance presidential power, the tale of the modern presidency has been to assert prerogative whenever possible to enhance its authority in a system that denies exclusive empowerment.

Modern politics makes it difficult for a president to stand there and do nothing when problems mount, regardless of whether that is an acceptable intellectual alternative or not. Moreover, except in the rare instance of a tragic succession in the presidency, modern presidents seek slogans that emphasize change to define their administrations. The slogans imply that they have the ability to right whatever wrongs a preceding administration was charged with. Hence, Theodore Roosevelt gave us "the square deal," while his cousin, Franklin Roosevelt, dished out a "new deal." There have been "fair deals" (Truman), "great crusades" (Eisenhower), "new frontiers" (Kennedy), "great societies" (Johnson), "new beginnings" (Reagan), and even ill-starred "new foundations" (Carter). Upon Kennedy's assassination, Johnson importuned Congress to "let us continue." But once Kennedy's unfinished agenda began to make headway through Congress, Johnson chose to unveil the "great society."

The slogans are, as slogans inevitably are, devoid of serious meaning. Some, such as Reagan's "new beginnings," are even tautological. But their existence implies presidential vision to create a more attractive world. Without the ability to inspire such a vision, a president will inevitably be perceived as the object of events rather than their master. It is hard, as George Bush learned, to say that doing nothing is often better than doing something even if that is an intellectually defensible posture. Whatever its intellectual worth, when things go sour the view that the status quo is the better if not the best of possible worlds is not likely to yield many votes for any president who adheres to it. Despite the slogans about new beginnings and the like and our tendency to define political history in terms of presidential administrations, the facts are that no president is a free agent. Few policies begin just because there is a new occupant of the White House. The legacies of past policies inevitably weigh heavily on the present. It is entirely understandable that presidents would wish themselves not to be so burdened. It is, indeed, fully understandable that if they are to be held responsible for the present that they should seek to rid themselves of constraints woven into their choices from the past. In this regard, presidents in the modern era, especially, having inherited choices that limit their present discretion, have incentives to be radical. To be radical in a system designed to deny that very instinct may sometimes mean, to be charitable, stretching the Constitution.

In general, the story of the modern presidency lies in the tension between the powers that presidents actually possess and the accountability to which they are held. Not very surprisingly, modern presidents often try to enhance the one while seeking to limit the other. Divided government, which since the 1954 elections has been such a frequent part of the American political landscape, plays directly to presidential efforts to try to accumulate power while seeking to avoid blame for unfavorable conditions. Under divided government, presidential motivation to take unilateral actions against which Congress must react is at its peak. Accompanying that is an equal motivation on the part of the president and the Congress to blame each other for the resulting stalemate.

While the constituted political arrangements in the United States largely have been constant throughout American history, the meanings attached to them have not. These have been transformed over time. To understand the meanings provided during the twentieth century, we need to trace some of the developmental ambiguities influencing the U.S. presidency in the preceding century.

DEVELOPMENTAL AMBIGUITIES

The modern presidency as we have come to think of it in the twentieth century is an instrument of political leadership and of political mobilization. It is an operation, not just a person. Although presidents in the modern era have means to mobilize through instant and direct communication that their nineteenth-century counterparts could not imagine, the irony is that the instruments for political change may have been more substantial in the nineteenth than in the twentieth century. Political change, for example, was more complete than tends to be the case now. New political coalitions seemed to be more decisive in their impact. The link between mass political change and elite political behavior seemed clearer. Political shifts at the mass level in terms of electoral preference were accompanied by elite political shifts that resulted in more cohesive party-based voting within Congress, majorities available to move in new directions, and considerable change even in committee chairs. Describing the pre–Civil War realignment of 1854–1860, for example, the political scientist David Brady argues in his book, *Critical Elections and Congressional Policy Making* (1988), that it "resulted in a new two-party system characterized by a cohesive new party committed to changing the shape of the American political landscape . . . [and] to an industrial future for America."

While the realignment of the 1890s seeped into the twentieth century, the major realignment of the twentieth century was that associated with Franklin Roosevelt's New Deal. One explanation proffered for the relative incompleteness of political change in the twentieth century in contrast to the nineteenth is that congressional seats have become more resistant to massive sweeps of change. As a consequence, the winds of electoral change in the twentieth century must carry greater force with them to produce institutional effects similar to those of the preceding century. The professionalization of Congress and the ability of many members to hold onto their seats regardless of shifts in the broader political context means that members of Congress and the president have fundamentally different electoral incentives regardless of any political vision they may share in common. The supposed coattails effect, in other words, is now of little consequence. Presumably, one reason for this is that members of Congress learn to nurture their constituencies in ways that make them as electorally invulnerable as possible. Their electoral incentives are eminently local. When that presents a problem in supporting an incumbent president, there is surely strong incentive to withhold such support. The consequence is a dampening effect on political change and a constraint on the ability of presidents, when they are so inspired, to generate policy change and successfully exert political leadership.

Although the nineteenth-century president, on the surface, had a more appealing political context in which to work—governments that were more frequently unified and only occasionally divided, greater congressional responsiveness to national political changes, electorates that for a variety of reasons were more party responsive, and parties that monopolized more of the political action—there also were strong inhibitions against the exercise of presidential leadership stemming from that context.

For example, even while parties had a greater hold on political life than they now do, the nineteenth-century conception of the presidency was fundamentally, if not always uniformly, different from the present. The Whig conception of the office—a conception that emphasized the preeminence of Congress rather than the presidency as the leading instrument of governance—tended to dominate nineteenth-century thinking about the presidency. While strong presidencies did exist in the nineteenth century—those of Jefferson, Jackson, and Lincoln, to name a few—these presidencies coincided with rare opportunities provided by a combination of changing political coalitions and unusually demanding circumstances. Jefferson's presidency, in essence, coincided with the beginning of the demise of the Federalists, great opportunities for territorial expansion, and a willingness to exert party leadership in an era before the parties and politicians became professionalized. Jackson's ascendancy too coincided with another fundamental political shift marking the identity of the Jacksonian Democrats with their populist agrarian base and battles against the Bank of the United States. Lincoln, of course, was faced with the largest crisis of all, the breakup of the Union, and with a new political party and coalition representing the burgeoning industrial base of the American Northeast.

For the most part, however, presidents did not lead their parties. They were often led by them. The party, in this conception, represented a president's peers, not his shock troops. Especially as the parties themselves became more professionalized with party bosses of varying reputations, presidential candidates had to survive their scrutiny. Presidents were expected to get along with the party bosses because they mostly owed their positions to them. The key to this relationship was not leadership but trustworthiness. This is in sharp contrast to contemporary expectations that the president's party should be a mere extension of his wishes. The conditions of party insider dominance in the presidential nomination process extended, if erratically, into the twentieth century. In sum, presidents were not in command of their parties but were expected to be a part of them.

Similarly, nineteenth-century presidents generally operated within a context of powerful congressional leaders whose writ, at least in the House, was far more extensive than it was after the revolt against Speaker Joseph Cannon early in the twentieth century. Senators, too, were not directly elected until a constitutional amendment permitted that in 1917. Hence, senators often were themselves major party bosses or their agents.

Indeed, the relative position of the two institutions in the nineteenth century—Congress and the presidency—is suggested by the level of media attention given the two branches. A content analysis of newspapers between 1820 and 1876 undertaken by two political scientists, Samuel Kernell and Gary C. Jacobson, revealed that in articles covering affairs of government Congress rather than the president tended to dominate the coverage. This seems to reflect the relative dominance of Congress as the principal governing instrument, especially in the postbellum era. The rise of professionalization in politics, evidenced by the corresponding rise of party organizations and machines, the lengthening of the congressional career, and the ascendancy of party luminaries, actually tended to eclipse the president's role. Presidents were more likely to be instruments of their party than parties were to be instruments of presidential command.

In sum, despite the seeming advantages of nineteenth-century presidents—more frequent and complete sweeps of political change, stronger party organization, even a more complete patronage system—these advantages were readily countermanded by equally, and perhaps more powerful, constraints. Among such constraints were those of the very conception of the role of the presidency itself, its relationship to the Congress as a governing instrument, its relatively limited visibility (in comparison to now) because of the limited means for reaching the public of the day, and, especially, the powerful role of political party bosses and organizations in selecting the president and in influencing presidential conduct.

TRUMPETING IN THE TWENTIETH CENTURY

Political eras are never discrete events. At any given historical moment many different, even seemingly irreconcilable, political tendencies coexist. Parties, at least organizationally and in the electoral domain, were never so powerful as at the beginning of the century. Newly enfranchised immigrants provided the means to sustain political machines in locales that immigrants flocked to.

Yet, the old order was clearly changing much to

the benefit of presidential power. Three factors appear to be tied into this change. One is the rise of the United States as an imperial power beginning to exercise global reach and certainly exercising proprietorship over the Americas. Second is the appeal and rise of progressivism as a political movement and political reform in general. Third, and inevitably a consequence of the changes in the American role in the world and of the movement for political reform, is the effort to grapple with a new political philosophy about the role of public authority and, in particular, that of the federal government.

The imperial competition among the European powers that ultimately ushered in the Great War of 1914, or as we later came to know it, World War I, brought with it newcomers. One of those was the German Reich, recently unified. Another was the Japanese Empire, which had emerged from its isolationist cocoon under the Meiji Restoration. The Japanese defeat of Russia in 1905 marked it as a new competitor in the marketplace for the world's spoils. A third new entrant to the world's power sweepstakes was the United States, reunified after a long and bitter civil war, only half a decade before the unification of the German Reich. The industrial might of the United States and its enormous power resources became manifest toward the end of the nineteenth century as American interests and the reach of older imperial powers such as Britain and Spain collided.

While armed hostilities did not take place with Britain, they did with Spanish forces, notably in Cuba and, to a degree, in the Philippines, where the major hostilities were with indigenous forces. If, as the historian Charles Tilly observed, "wars are statemakers," they also magnify the power of central leaders within the state. Reputedly, William McKinley

President William McKinley (1897–1901). As the president speaks, members of the press take notes. PRINTS AND PHOTOGRAPHS DIVISION, LIBRARY OF CONGRESS

President Theodore Roosevelt (1901–1909). PRINTS AND PHOTOGRAPHS DIVISION, LIBRARY OF CONGRESS

was browbeaten into declaring war against Spain after being egged on by the hawks of the day. But neither Theodore Roosevelt nor Woodrow Wilson would be quite so reluctant. Although both Roosevelt and Wilson engaged in "gunboat diplomacy," only Wilson actually led the country into full-scale war. Wars generate power for the executive. They activate the commander-in-chief role of the American president. This was so even when Congress was more in the habit of actually issuing declarations of war and when presidents had little standing army to call upon, depending instead upon the national mobilization of the state militias.

It was, in fact, this process of national mobilization of the various state-based forces, which were mostly ill-organized and ineptly prepared, that led to efforts to modernize and rationalize the American military. A self-respecting global pretension had to have a self-respecting and well-organized military force. So, in its way, military mobilization, as it often is, was a precursor to modernizing the state over which presidents would govern.

As America's reach into the world had challenged existing institutions and organizational practices, so too had the gilded age of corruption, party machines, and patronage spurred a wave of reform. To be sure, political reform was uneven. Its influence was strongest in the upper Midwest and on the West Coast. As the challenge to America's fragmented military organization induced a compelling need to modernize and centralize military operations, the challenges to American political institutions compelled an effort simultaneously to rationalize, democratize, and insulate government. Obviously, not all of these values are consistent with one another.

While the motives of Progressive reformers are open to debate—and undoubtedly they were varied—the products are more clear. Parties were an evil. The connection between the voice of the governed and the governors was corrupted by party machines, with their focus on corralling graft and getting patronage jobs for their supporters. Intermediary organizations, parties and lobbies, were viewed as self-interested and corrupt. To democratize government, a direct voice (referenda, recalls, primary elections, initiatives) was the preferred vehicle for registering public sentiment. To professionalize government, the ragtag army of patronage hacks was to be replaced by professional and tenured civil servants. At the federal level, the Pendleton Act of 1883 launched a merit-based career civil service while retaining a smaller force of political appointees at the top of the ladder. The professionalization of government strengthened its executive hand. In *The American Presidency: Origins and Development, 1776–1990* (1990), Sidney M. Milkis and Michael Nelson argue that the professionalization of administration was central to the idea of "directing the development of American industrial society." In Theodore Roosevelt's view, according to Milkis and Nelson, attention to administrative management was necessary both "to foster economic efficiency and . . . to bolster the power of the increasingly active federal government." Strengthening the executive, in brief, was a means to rationalizing and strengthening the American state to confront the new industrial order and the concentrations of power it represented. From this standpoint, a professional administration would be a more effective presidential tool than an administration largely composed of party hacks.

In addition, as is usually the case, war served to strengthen the role of the president in the American political system. Future struggles regarding delegated presidential power in the New Deal period were presaged by the extraordinary emergency powers granted to Wilson as a wartime leader. Especially important was the Lever Food and Fuel Control Act of 1917, which essentially granted the president the

President William Howard Taft, 1909–1913. PRINTS AND PHOTOGRAPHS DIVISION, LIBRARY OF CONGRESS

President Woodrow Wilson (1913–1921). PRINTS AND PHOTOGRAPHS DIVISION, LIBRARY OF CONGRESS

authority to regulate most commercial transactions. This was an extraordinary endowment of executive power. Not quite two full decades later in 1935, these issues would be joined again by the U.S. Supreme Court in the case of *Schechter* v. *United States,* which invalidated the discretionary authority granted to the executive (the National Recovery Administration) by Congress to regulate the economy. The crises of wartime under Wilson provided the rationale for the enhanced presidential discretion that Franklin Roosevelt sought to combat the Great Depression and to organize the state, as Wilson also had wished, to respond to the needs of a modern economy and society.

Political reform was the means for developing the American state. The development of the American state, on the one hand, was essential to counter the growth of monopoly power in the private sector and to regulate the social dysfunctions of unrestricted capitalism. On the other, it was necessary to make America's mark on the world. These ideas came together under the heading of the "new nationalism."

Enhancing the ability of the American state to tackle both concentrations of private power and to regulate capitalism's negative externalities meant two things. First, it required a more expansive federal presence than had been the case throughout the preceding century. Second, it required a vigorous presidency able to assert the authority of the federal government. It required, in a cliché that resonates to the present, an ability to overturn a politics of special and partial interests and replace it with a politics focused on national interests legitimized by the people.

The conception of the presidential role seems to have changed fundamentally in this period as part of the quest for a new polity and active government. Teddy Roosevelt referred to his office as the bully pulpit. Woodrow Wilson was viewed as a president whose concept of legitimating himself in the American political order was to appeal to its democratic rather than republican propensities. In *The Rhetorical Presidency* (1987), Jeffrey Tulis shows, for example, that in the twentieth century, presidents have targeted their speeches to the general public six times as frequently as they did in the nineteenth century and about one-fourth as frequently to the Congress. In Tulis's view, this phenomenon originated in Wilson's idea of the president as a leader-interpreter who could employ rhetoric to educate the public to his goals. To do so, required simplification, even arousal. But only the president, in Wilson's understanding, had the claim of being a nationally elected official and, therefore, the legitimacy to engage the public in this way.

Wilson's ill-fated campaign on behalf of American involvement in the League of Nations illustrated the rhetorical presidency in action. If it is not inevitable, it is certainly likely that a rhetorical presidency will be one that frequently is in contest with the Congress. Such a presidency will demand more from the political system than its political resources normally give it. In that, there is likely to be tension between president and Congress.

President Warren G. Harding (1921–1923) PRINTS AND PHOTOGRAPHS DIVISION, LIBRARY OF CONGRESS

BACK TO "NORMALCY"

After the failure of Wilson's campaign on behalf of sustained American involvement in world affairs, his debilitating stroke, and the general postwar desire to return, in Warren G. Harding's immortal words, "to normalcy," the political alignment interrupted by the Wilson years was regenerated. The crusading zeal for political and social reform came to a halt, and with that also came a loss of inspiration to utilize the presidency as a central energizing force. Neither Harding nor Calvin Coolidge were political leaders or individuals of sufficient stature around whom one would seek to advance a theory of presidential leadership. They filled the office rather than led from it. But this was entirely compatible with the prevailing political coalition of the time and with Harding's and Coolidge's conceptions of the office. Because of the lopsided Republican electoral and congressional majorities, these were opportune times for political leadership. Yet if the window was open, there was no agenda to go through it.

Nonetheless, rationalizing the administration of the federal government was, to some extent, inevitable. The Budget and Accounting Act of 1921, for example, continued a process of making the president more of a chief executive within the executive branch. It did not, and could not however, make the president the exclusive or even necessarily preeminent authority on fiscal matters. But it did provide the presidency with new instruments.

Although the Hoover presidency was the most tarnished because its history has been under the shadow of the Great Depression, a recent quantitative analysis of policy change by two political scientists, Michael S. Lewis-Beck and Peverill Squire, suggests that the actual policy differences between the Hoover and Roosevelt presidencies may have been overdrawn in some renditions. Although some historians had noted important continuities between Hoover and Roosevelt, these two scholars present a provocative thesis and amass a systematic quantitative analysis of the continuity/disruption question. They also make note of a well-developed revisionist Hoover history that portrays him as a progressive humanitarian. The validity of their argument, which appears in the *Journal of Politics* (February 1991), no doubt will attract much legitimate debate as to what the real nature of change was between the presidencies of Herbert Hoover and Franklin Roosevelt. They do offer the

President Calvin Coolidge (1923–1929). PRINTS AND PHOTOGRAPHS DIVISION, LIBRARY OF CONGRESS

President Herbert C. Hoover (1929–1933). Photograph taken during the 1938 campaign. PRINTS AND PHOTOGRAPHS DIVISION, LIBRARY OF CONGRESS

provocative thought, however, that "a great share of the supposed Hoover-Roosevelt differences rests on symbols rather than substance."

Without directly entering into the debate that Lewis-Beck and Squire invite, two important observations are generated. The first is that despite presidential efforts to sell their administrations as offering bold new initiatives, much of what any presidential administration does is repackage proposals and ideas from the past. The second is that all initiatives are overtaken by powerful events. Continuity and contingency are, thus, useful lenses through which to look at change and stability across presidential administrations. When looked at through these lenses, we are led to view more skeptically any tendency to look at history discretely through the term(s) in office of any presidential administration. We also should be led to reassess as well the actual impact of any administration's policy proposals. In sum, like geological evolution, history is a continuous process rather than a discrete process. Despite most presidents' proclamations about change and bold new directions, there are powerful continuities that connect presidencies.

Despite these continuities, it is still quite natural to see particular presidencies as occupying pivotal moments in history and, indeed, influencing that history. Partly because of the unprecedented length of its incumbency, the powerful events (depression and war) forcing it to respond, and the rhetorical and symbolic skills of the incumbent, the presidency of Franklin Roosevelt is frequently cited as a pivotal one. This, of course, may have had as much to do with the changes occurring in American society as with anything happening in the White House. Still, the Franklin Roosevelt presidency typically is regarded—for reasons that are not always clear—as the first modern American presidency. Whether in lore or in fact, the administration of Franklin Roosevelt brought with it significant changes in the presidential role and in the public conception of the presidency.

FDR AND THE EMERGENCE OF THE MODERN PRESIDENCY

Crisis and powerful events can fuel leadership capacity. It is better, of course, for a leader to inherit a

President Franklin D. Roosevelt (1933–1945) PRINTS AND PHOTOGRAPHS DIVISION, LIBRARY OF CONGRESS

crisis than to have it occur while in office. The inheritance feeds hope that decisive action might generate positive results. Overall, the conditions under which the presidency of Franklin Roosevelt came into power and sustained its hold on power were of this nature. As a consequence, it is doubtful that any presidency has matched Roosevelt's for its long-term impact on American life and on American government.

The economic crisis inherited by the newly elected Roosevelt administration in 1933 provided it initially with the slack to invoke emergency powers, to expand the scope of regulation in the American economy, and eventually to set forth a program of social reform, putting into place a social insurance state. All of this would fall under the handy slogan of the New Deal. The growth of executive activity simultaneously expanded American government, especially its bureaucratic apparatus, and energized the executive. The president came to be regarded as the fulcrum of leadership within the government, perhaps expanding the role of the presidency beyond its normal capabilities.

Later, when the United States entered World War II, the perceived role of the president and the administrative state over which he presided grew apace. The combination of social and economic reform and a commitment to military readiness produced what Walter Dean Burnham has called "the warfare-welfare state." The decades of the 1930s and 1940s contributed massively to changing Washington from a small backwater capital to a larger capital city. The growth in the Washington metropolitan area during these two decades was unprecedented. Something had changed. More of the locus of governing activity was centered in the federal government in Washington. And more of the locus of authority was being vested in the executive.

Two scholars of American constitutional law suggest the importance of the courts in altering the received view of executive authority. In their book *The President, Congress, and the Constitution* (1984), Christopher Pyle and Richard Pious remark that "since 1937, the Supreme Court has embraced the Hamiltonian–New Deal view of the Constitution as preeminently a source of authority, and only secondarily as a set of limitations. . . . During the Roosevelt and Truman administrations, particularly, but under all administrations since 1935, the Court has acceded to the view that even the most general delegations of authority are constitutionally acceptable so long as Congress oversees." Beyond this fundamental alteration in the discretionary power granted the executive, the 1936 Supreme Court decision in *United States* v. *Curtiss-Wright Export Corporation* designated the president as the sole organ of the nation in its conduct of foreign affairs. In this view, essentially one person is granted the authority to act "until and unless overwhelming political opposition can be mounted against him in Congress" (Pyle and Pious).

Strictly speaking, nothing in either the Constitution or in statutory empowerment changed. What did change, of course, was a quite fundamental view of the relationship between executive and legislative authority, a view that conceived of the relationship much like a tennis match in which only one of the players serves while the other is placed in a position only to react. In this juridical alteration, presidents came to be granted significant discretionary authority through the executive branch. The nature of that balance as rendered through court decisions of the Roosevelt era continues to be pertinent today. In a later era, often featuring divided government, the altered balance would provide enterprising presidents with the means to do that which seemed legislatively impossible to do.

The balance between the executive and legislative

branches ironically is in practice determined by the courts. But big government intensifies the struggles between the branches if for no other reason than that there is more to fight over.

It is impossible, of course, to know how much government would have expanded in the absence of the Great Depression and the New Deal response to it. Under one conception, most changes would likely have occurred regardless of either the crisis of the times or the Roosevelt presidency. Just as the burgeoning rail system required regulation in the 1880s, the advent of recent technologies such as radio required regulation of the airwaves in the 1930s. A different conception, however, is that the New Deal administration at the very least hastened many of the activities of government and fostered its growth. Above all, the New Deal opened up new lines of social and political conflict in the United States, more than ever defining the parties along a business-labor rift.

By most accounts, when Franklin Roosevelt entered the White House few plans had been clearly formulated. Doing something, however, beat doing nothing, in view of the circumstances. The New Deal was not constructed in a vacuum. The crisis brought to the surface ideas about the role of government and about social reform that had been bottled up for some time. Roosevelt's presidency in the midst of a severe crisis provided opportunity for these ideas to be debated and for some of them to be put in place. The so-called brain trust—a set of youthful policy intellectuals serving Roosevelt as advisers—provided the basis for a continuing linkage between the presidency and an outside world of policy intellectuals. Roosevelt advertised his administration as an experimental one. No context could be more commodious for any set of policy advisers eager to audition their ideas.

The ideas provided direction to the Roosevelt presidency. They assured that the Democrats would be transformed as the party of labor, of social reform, and of government intervention. If the favorite expression of the Clinton administration some sixty years later is "reinventing government," much of the New Deal period would be spent inventing government or at least inventing new things for government to do. The ideas stemming from the Roosevelt presidency survived almost wholly intact through the administration of Lyndon B. Johnson (1963–1969), himself a young member of Congress from Texas during the New Deal period. Despite some efforts to modulate the tenets of the New Deal ideology, the Democratic presidencies of Jimmy Carter (1977–1981) and of Bill Clinton (1993–) still borrow heavily from New Deal conceptions of the responsibilities of government, though these have been revised to accord with the prevailing and more skeptical moods of recent times.

While the ideas of the New Deal invested the Roosevelt presidency with policy energy and governing purpose, they also enabled the Democrats to build a new political coalition that was attracted to them. The Democrats were principally the party of southern whites, of agrarian interests, and increasingly of immigrant ethnic and religious minorities in the nation's big cities. Through the New Deal, the party was able to add labor, intellectuals, and, over time, African Americans (a previously strongly Republican group) to its coalitional structure. Above all, a new generation of voters inducted into the electorate in the 1930s cast their lot with the New Deal and the Democratic party.

For several decades the new coalition would mesh uneasily with the old, producing fissures that ultimately would loosen the Democrats' grip on the presidential electorate. Economics provided the basis for coalescence while race would provide the basis for its rupture. Yet, throughout the Roosevelt period, the new political alignment assured the Democrats both the presidency and large congressional majorities, giving them an unparalleled opportunity to create and to institutionalize policies. A small smattering of those policies indicates something about the depth of the Rooseveltian revolution: the introduction of a social security pension system, assistance to families with dependent children, the granting to labor unions of collective bargaining rights and the setting up of the National Labor Relations Board to certify the rights of labor, generating numerous regulatory agencies to oversee a variety of commercial activities ranging from the airlines to the securities and futures markets.

As with all fundamental political alignments, the New Deal alignment would erode with time. Its apogee was reached in the election of 1936 when Roosevelt's massive landslide was accompanied by a huge congressional landslide as well. Roosevelt's own majorities would be less impressive in the election of 1940 and would dim further in the election of 1944. Congressional majorities also would decline somewhat. More important, political fissures would begin to appear in the Democratic coalition as southern conservatives joined Republicans after 1938 in opposing New Deal initiatives. The war effort that began in Roosevelt's third term provided an interlude before a significant Republican resurgence in the 1946 congressional elections.

In sum, the Roosevelt years were momentous ones for American government, American politics, and the presidency itself. For American government, the New Deal period greatly expanded the role of the federal bureaucracy, essentially creating much of it. It produced a form of the social insurance state and an expectation that government would regulate the economy as a whole and its various sectors. The combination of the positive state domestically to respond to the crisis of the Depression and the mobilization state to meet the crisis of war enlarged the role of Washington, of the federal bureaucracy, and of the president. None of this happened because of constitutional change or even statutory change. A great deal of it happened because of the powerful currents of events and of political change. Big government arose as a solvent for problems that had newly made it onto the agenda. But the agenda of the Roosevelt presidency also enabled Roosevelt to build a political coalition that, to a greater or lesser degree, would hold for at least a generation.

The close connection between the New Deal agenda and its accompanying political support base meant also that the issues comprising this agenda would provide a continuing basis of political cleavage in the United States. Democrats would become the party associated with big government, the social insurance state, social welfare, and, above all, labor. The Republicans, in turn, would become increasingly identified as the party preferring markets to government intervention, the party of business and financial interests, and the party critical of government-supplied welfare. Eventually, Republicans bought into the social insurance state—usually after opposing initiatives generated by Democrats—because of its great popularity. The political realignments of the New Deal continue to echo in contemporary politics, even if more faintly.

As Congress later became more conservative toward the New Deal and its successors, an institutional rift also would come into play along ideological lines. Pro–New Dealers became fond of the executive and of presidential power. Anti–New Dealers sought solace in Congress. Such tendencies came most prominently into play during Truman's presidency and especially during Kennedy's.

The notion that there were actually four parties became part of the lore accompanying this institutional division. Presumably, there was a Democratic presidential party and a Democratic congressional party as well as a Republican presidential party and Republican congressional party. According to the lore, articulated most powerfully by the presidential scholar James MacGregor Burns in the early 1960s, both presidential parties were hamstrung by their more provincial and conservative congressional parties. Presidential-congressional tensions were manifest even during the height of the New Deal, but they would loom much larger in the decades ahead as the presidency became the repository of liberals' dreams and the Congress that of conservatives. In short, both institutions were to become ideological magnets. The Roosevelt presidency, however, defined the office for a time as the leadership role through which social change could be realized.

Social and technological changes do not conveniently fit into any president's administration. Often, changes that occur earlier are brought to fruition only later. For example, one of the aspects of the modern presidency, noted previously as the rhetorical presidency, was associated with Woodrow Wilson. But Wilson did not have the advantages of commercial radio, the introduction of which brought new possibilities to presidential efforts to generate political support. Although the first commercial radio station came onto line in 1920, the initial significant use of this medium by a political figure has been associated with Franklin Roosevelt. The "fireside chat" became a means of communicating directly to the nation. The medium of radio provided a president who could master it with a comparative advantage over his political rivals in the Congress. The president could speak for the presidency, get his definition of problems and solutions out front, and advertise himself as the spokesperson for the national interest against more parochial or self-serving interests. The new instrument of mass communications was a precursor of things to come when radio would be supplemented, if not largely supplanted, by television. No president could ever escape from being interpreted by others, but direct means of communication allowed a president to get his story out. How well future presidents got their stories out would depend on the quality and clarity of their story and their ability to communicate it. But the availability of the new technology of radio and Roosevelt's skills at telling his story enabled him to become the first mass communicator among presidents.

A second technology that began to flower during the Roosevelt presidency had more ambivalent consequences for presidents. This was the technology of modern survey polling. This technology allowed a form of continuous examination of presidential political health that had been unknown heretofore. For presidents, the critical question was whether people approved or disapproved of how the president was doing his job. Reputedly, increases or decreases in a president's standing with other political actors in the

President Harry S. Truman (1945–1953). PRINTS AND PHOTOGRAPHS DIVISION, LIBRARY OF CONGRESS

American system flowed from the nature of their approval ratings. Thus, unlike the radio, which was a tool for presidents to use, the continuous examination of presidential standing with the public could provide presidents with advantages or disadvantages depending upon how well they actually were doing. In Roosevelt's case, when ratings were taken more sporadically than they are today, his popular approval by current standards was astronomical.

Technology wedded to the large political and governmental changes occurring during the Roosevelt presidency combined to create the modern presidency—a role for which the expectations of leadership normally go beyond its political possibility.

THE ONSET OF THE COLD WAR AND THE WANING OF THE NEW DEAL

Not long after the end of World War II, a different kind of war began: Cold War between the Soviet Union and its erstwhile Western allies from the victorious coalition that brought World War II to an end. The emergence of Marxist-Leninist states in the areas of Soviet occupation, the civil war between insurgent communist forces and the government in Greece, the blockade of Berlin, communist insurgencies in Asia, and the development of the Soviet Union as a nuclear power created a need for permanent readiness in national security. Hence, a national-security state was generated shortly after the end of World War II in response to the perception of Soviet threat.

The Truman administration was faced with the growth of Soviet power after World War II and a common belief that all communist insurgencies were orchestrated through Moscow. The communist victory in 1949 in the Chinese civil war and the hot war on the Korean peninsula that began in 1950 further fed fears of worldwide Soviet communist dominance.

The national-security state created a sense of permanence to military, intelligence, and covert operations. New agencies and staffs were set up and new departments created. The military generated a new branch through the Air Force, the Defense Department replaced the old War Department, a Joint Chiefs structure emerged across the military services, and the National Security Council came into being.

The immediate post–World War II period, in fact, represented a major effort to modernize American federal government. This was as true domestically as in national security affairs. Consider the Administrative Procedures Act (1946), the Congressional Reorganization Act (1946), the Full Employment Act (1946), and the National Security Act (1947). For the executive branch, new organizations came into being. For the presidency, more staff organizations were added and more professional advisers were mandated. The Council of Economic Advisers was added through the Full Employment Act with the daunting task of advising the president as to how to bring about full employment. The National Security Act created the National Security Council and gave it the responsibility to coordinate security policy. The Administrative Procedures Act followed upon the Executive Reorganization Act of 1939, each providing for a larger discretionary role for the president and, in general, more discretionary authority for the executive in a train of logic that originated at least as early as Woodrow Wilson's wartime efforts to enhance executive authority. Despite these efforts, the issue of discretionary authority in the executive continues to be a contested one, although presidents have accrued advantages over time in this struggle.

Although modernization and rationalization of government in the postwar world was a primary theme, an important subtheme was to provide the organizational basis for the national-security state and institutionalize it. In that sense, this period of intense

Cold War conflict was to the national-security state what the New Deal was to the social-insurance state.

In one sense, the national-security state enhanced executive power inasmuch as it placed a greater premium on secrecy, discretionary activity, and the ubiquitous cover of national security for a multitude of activities. With the nation's security seemingly at stake, less public and political quibbling was likely to be tolerated.

In a quite different sense, however, the national-security state eroded executive power, claiming two sets of victims: the agencies charged with carrying out American foreign policy and, often, presidents themselves, especially Democrats. In 1947, for example, President Truman found it necessary (politically at least) to institute loyalty procedures for federal employees. In an effort to promote themselves and tarnish the Fair Deal successor to the New Deal, a number of officials, past and present, high or otherwise, were singled out as either agents of Soviet espionage or as security threats to the country. The most notorious cases were those of Harry Dexter White and Alger Hiss, each accused of being communist agents. After the communist regime gained power in China in the fall of 1949, State Department officials associated with China (the so-called China hands) came under attack as sympathizers, if not outright agents, of the new communist Chinese regime. Taking advantage of this charged atmosphere, Sen. Joseph McCarthy, a Republican from Wisconsin, joined in the fray and achieved great notoriety as the leading hunter of communist subversives in government. During the Eisenhower presidency, the military would be added to the targets of the McCarthyite rampage through the executive.

The anticommunist hysteria was brought to a boil especially after Senator McCarthy's famous speech of February 1950 in Wheeling, West Virginia, in which he claimed that there was a known number of subversives in the federal government. It placed the Truman administration irretrievably on the defensive. The later military stalemate in Korea, the charges of communist subversion in the government, the emergence of a postwar Soviet empire in Europe, the attainment of nuclear weapons by the Soviet Union, the communist success in China, and the seemingly successful march of communism in Asia all contributed to marked declines in the political fortunes of the Truman administration and to the displacement of domestic-policy concerns by national-security concerns.

In fact, the displacement began much earlier when it became clear that the anticipated post–World War II arrangements would not hold. The domestic-policy agenda to sustain the legacy of Franklin Roosevelt was placed in great distress by the 1946 electoral comeback of the Republican party, which gained majorities in both chambers of Congress for the first time in eighteen years. During these years, the Truman administration forged a bipartisan coalition with Sen. Arthur Vandenberg, the Republican chair of the Foreign Relations Committee. Together, they helped enact legislation that brought the United States directly into a sustained leadership role as head of the anticommunist alliance. A consensus had emerged on behalf of the national-security state and a U.S. leadership role in world affairs. This largely displaced Truman's domestic Fair Deal agenda, however.

The 1948 elections are famous for Truman's upset victory over the Republican candidate, Thomas E. Dewey. But they also brought back Democratic majorities to Capitol Hill. By the time they had done so, however, at least two significant facts had set in. First, as noted, the Cold War (just as World War II had) took precedence over Truman's Fair Deal agenda. Second, New Deal political alignments had weakened further at both the elite and mass-public level. Running in a four-person race, Truman won a minority of the popular vote, a pattern for Democrats that continues to the present with the exception only of Lyndon Johnson's 1964 landslide victory and Carter's narrow 50.1 percent. (See table 1.)

The Democratic party's patchwork coalition had begun to be pulled apart by the midpoint of Roosevelt's second term. Later events ripped it further. Race, for example, came to be an issue that tore the Democrats' fabric. Court decisions in the 1940s, the effects of wartime mobilization, the movement of African Americans into the New Deal political coalition, and decisions by the Truman administration to desegregate the armed forces and to offer a civil rights bill moved southern Democratic politicians (elected then by almost exclusively white electorates) to coalesce frequently with Republicans in opposition to the Truman administration. Increasingly, many members of the party's southern wing were Democrats in name rather than in deed. The conservative coalition of Republicans and southern Democrats which came into being after the 1938 elections hardened. The seniority of southern Democrats in the Congress and, therefore, their hold on committee chairmanships made even nominal Democratic control of the Congress far from a safe bet to provide support for Democratic presidents' liberal policy proposals. In essence, then, while the Cold War waxed, the New Deal waned.

The purported consequence of this turn of events

Table 1. PRESIDENTIAL ELECTIONS, 1896–1992

Year	Candidate[a]	Running Mate	Popular Vote[b]	Popular Percentage[c]	Electoral Vote
1896	William McKinley (R)	Garret A. Hobart	7,114,000	51.0	271
	William J. Bryan (D)	Arthur Sewall	6,517,000	46.7	176
	Others		317,000	2.3	0
1900	William McKinley (R)	Theodore Roosevelt	7,220,000	51.7	292
	William J. Bryan (D)	Adlai E. Stevenson	6,358,000	45.5	155
	Others		396,000	2.8	0
1904	Theodore Roosevelt (R)	Charles W. Fairbanks	7,629,000	56.4	336
	Alton B. Parker (D)	Henry G. Davis	5,085,000	37.6	140
	Others		409,000	3.0	0
	Eugene V. Debs (S)	Benjamin Hanford	403,000	3.0	0
1908	William H. Taft (R)	James S. Sherman	7,679,000	51.6	321
	William J. Bryan (D)	John W. Kern	6,411,000	43.1	162
	Others		336,000	2.6	0
	Eugene V. Debs (S)	Benjamin Hanford	421,000	2.8	0
1912	Woodrow Wilson (D)	Thomas R. Marshall	6,301,000	41.9	435
	Theodore Roosevelt (BM)	Hiram W. Johnson	4,128,000	27.4	88
	William H. Taft (R)	Nicholas M. Butler	3,486,000	23.2	8
	Eugene V. Debs (S)	Emil Seidel	901,000	6.0	0
	Others		239,000	1.6	0
1916	Woodrow Wilson (D)	Thomas R. Marshall	9,132,000	49.3	277
	Charles E. Hughes (R)	Charles W. Fairbanks	8,549,000	46.1	254
	Others		270,000	1.5	0
	Allan L. Benson (S)	George R. Kirkpatrick	586,000	3.2	0
1920	Warren G. Harding (R)	Calvin Coolidge	16,154,000	60.3	404
	James M. Cox (D)	Franklin D. Roosevelt	9,147,000	34.1	127
	Eugene V. Debs (S)	Seymour Stedman	920,000	3.4	0
	Others		455,000	2.1	0
1924	Calvin Coolidge (R)	Charles G. Dawes	15,725,000	54.0	382
	John W. Davis (D)	Charles W. Bryan	8,387,000	28.8	136
	Robert M. La Follette (Pr)	Burton K. Wheeler	4,831,000	16.6	13
1928	Herbert C. Hoover (R)	Charles Curtis	21,431,000	58.2	444
	Alfred E. Smith (D)	Joseph T. Robinson	15,016,000	40.8	87
	Others		364,000	1.0	0
1932	Franklin D. Roosevelt (D)	John N. Garner	22,822,000	57.4	472
	Herbert C. Hoover (R)	Charles Curtis	15,762,000	39.7	59
	Norman Thomas (S)	James A. Maurer	885,000	2.2	0
1936	Franklin D. Roosevelt (D)	John Nance Garner	27,752,000	60.8	523
	Alfred M. Landon (R)	Frank Knox	16,679,000	36.5	8
	William Lemke (Union)	Thomas C. O'Brien	892,000	2.0	0
1940	Franklin D. Roosevelt (D)	Henry A. Wallace	27,243,000	54.7	449
	Wendell Willkie (R)	Charles L. McNary	22,334,000	44.8	82
1944	Franklin D. Roosevelt (D)	Harry S. Truman	25,612,000	53.4	432
	Thomas E. Dewey (R)	John W. Bricker	22,018,000	45.9	99
1948	Harry S. Truman (D)	Alben W. Barkley	24,104,000	49.6	303
	Thomas E. Dewey (R)	Earl Warren	21,971,000	45.1	189
	J. Strom Thurmond (Dixiecrat)	Fielding L. Wright	1,619,000	2.4	39
	Henry A. Wallace (Pr)	Glen H. Taylor	1,157,000	2.4	0
1952	Dwight D. Eisenhower (R)	Richard M. Nixon	33,937,000	55.1	442
	Adlai E. Stevenson (D)	John Sparkman	27,315,000	44.4	89
1956	Dwight D. Eisenhower (R)	Richard M. Nixon	35,589,000	57.4	457
	Adlai E. Stevenson (D)	Estes Kefauver	26,036,000	42.0	73
	Walter B. Jones	none	—	—	1
	Others		704,000	1.2	0

Table 1. PRESIDENTIAL ELECTIONS, 1896–1992 (continued)

Year	Candidate[a]	Running Mate	Popular Vote[b]	Popular Percentage[c]	Electoral Vote
1960	John F. Kennedy (D)	Lyndon B. Johnson	34,221,000	49.7	303
	Richard M. Nixon (R)	Henry Cabot Lodge	34,109,000	49.6	219
	Harry F. Byrd	none	—	—	15
1964	Lyndon B. Johnson (D)	Hubert H. Humphrey	43,130,000	61.1	486
	Barry Goldwater (R)	William E. Miller	27,178,000	38.5	52
1968	Richard M. Nixon (R)	Spiro T. Agnew	31,785,000	43.4	301
	Hubert H. Humphrey (D)	Edmund S. Muskie	31,275,000	42.7	191
	George Wallace (AI)	Curtis E. LeMay	9,906,000	13.5	46
1972	Richard M. Nixon (R)	Spiro T. Agnew	47,170,000	60.7	520
	George McGovern (D)	R. Sargent Shriver	29,170,000	37.5	17
	John Hospers (Ln)	none	—	—	1
	Others		1,378,000	1.8	0
1976	Jimmy Carter (D)	Walter F. Mondale	40,831,000	50.1	297
	Gerald R. Ford (R)	Robert Dole	39,148,000	48.0	240
	Ronald Reagan	none	—	—	1
	Others		1,577,000	1.9	0
1980	Ronald Reagan (R)	George Bush	43,904,000	50.7	489
	Jimmy Carter (D)	Walter F. Mondale	35,484,000	41.0	49
	Other		1,407,000	1.6	0
	John B. Anderson (NUC)	Patrick J. Lucey	5,720,000	6.6	0
1984	Ronald Reagan (R)	George Bush	54,455,000	58.8	525
	Walter F. Mondale (D)	Geraldine A. Ferraro	37,577,000	40.6	13
	Other		621,000	0.7	0
1988	George Bush (R)	Dan Quayle	48,886,000	53.4	426
	Michael Dukakis (D)	Lloyd Bentsen	41,809,000	45.6	111
	Lloyd Bentsen	none	—	—	1
	Other		900,000	1.0	0
1992	Bill Clinton (D)	Al Gore	44,908,000	43.0	370
	George Bush (R)	Dan Quayle	39,102,000	37.5	168
	Ross Perot (I)	James B. Stockdale	19,741,000	18.9	0

[a] All candidates who received electoral votes are shown. Other candidates are not shown when they received no electoral votes and their share of the popular vote was less than 1 percent.
[b] General election results are rounded to the nearest thousand.
[c] Percentages are rounded to the nearest tenth. Percentages do not add to 100.0 because of rounding.
Party abbreviations: AI, American Independent; BM, Bull Moose (Progressive); D, Democratic; I, Independent; Ln, Libertarian; NUC, National Unity Campaign; Pr, Progressive; S, Socialist.
SOURCE: Adapted from *Encyclopedia of the American Presidency* (New York: Simon & Schuster, 1994), pp. 1716–1718. For elections from 1896 to 1960: Svend Petersen, *A Statistical History of the American Presidential Elections* (1968). For elections from 1964 to 1988: Richard M. Scammon and Alice V. McGillivray, *America Votes 18: A Handbook of Contemporary American Election Statistics* (1989). For the election of 1992: *Congressional Quarterly* (23 January 1993):190.

was that the executive reach would be grander in foreign policy than in domestic policy, where presidents would face more resistant forces. This would tend to frustrate Democratic presidents whose ambitions on behalf of an activist domestic agenda and an activist president were typically larger than those of their Republican counterparts. For conservatives, extending the presidential reach seemed to be justified when it meant expanding the national-security state. For liberals, on the other hand, enlarging presidential power was desirable for furthering the goals of the social insurance state and for social and economic reform.

THE EISENHOWER INTERLUDE

Until Richard Nixon managed to top his record for disapproval in the performance of his job, President Truman in the last year of his presidency had reached a low of 23 percent approval. The fragmentation of the Democratic coalition into a treaty of electoral convenience, the stalemated Korean War, scandals

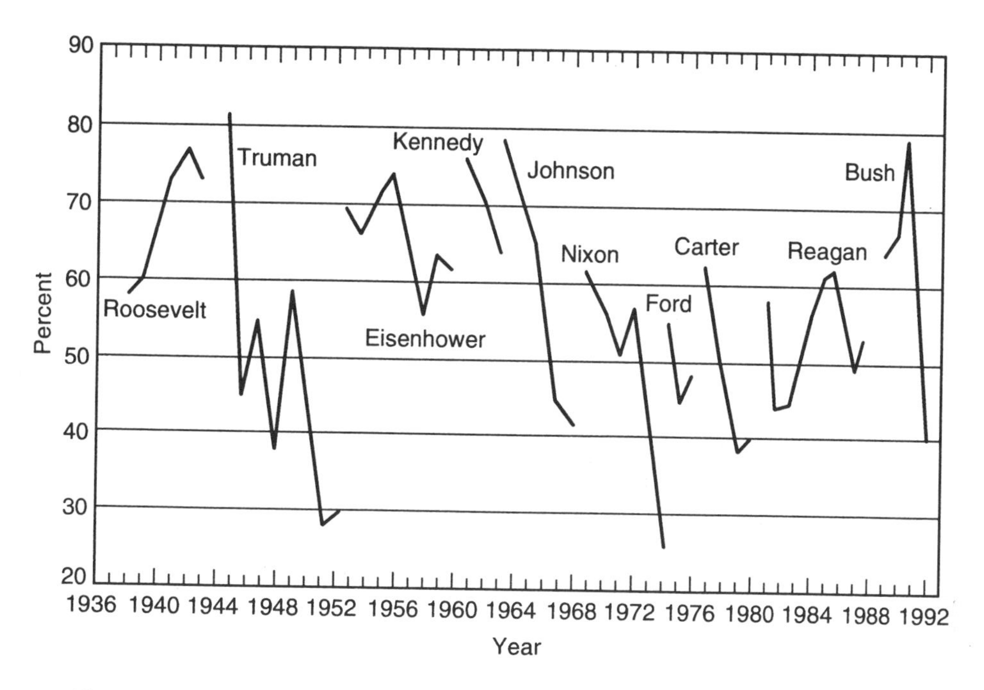

Figure 1. Public Approval of the President. Percent of those approving of the president's performance in office is averaged by year. Respondents were asked, "Do you approve or disapprove of the way [last name of president] is handling his job as president?" (Sources: *Encyclopedia of the United States Congress* [1994], p. 1592; *The Gallup Opinion Index* [October–November 1980], pp. 13–38; *The Gallup Report* [July 1988], pp. 19–20; Gallup Poll, "Reagan Regaining Public Confidence," press release, 9 October 1988; Gallup Library; Harold W. Stanley and Richard G. Niemi, eds., *Vital Statistics on American Politics,* 3d ed. [1992], p. 279.)

and corruption within the administration, charges of subversion from within, the seeming loss of ground in the world, and a two-decade grip on the White House by Democrats all contributed to weakening the popular base of the Truman presidency. Truman also suffered then from something his reputation later would capitalize on, namely, his ordinariness. Many years later, Truman would be perceived as a little man who made big decisions and was not afraid to make them. When Truman fired World War II commander of Pacific forces Gen. Douglas MacArthur for insubordination during his command of United Nations (mostly U.S.) forces in Korea in 1951, however, Truman's ordinariness was a far greater liability than a virtue.

General MacArthur's counterpart in the European theater was Gen. Dwight D. Eisenhower, a military leader who embodied the traits of teamwork more than MacArthur. MacArthur's imperial style was countered by Eisenhower's popular and more politic characteristics. After the war, Eisenhower became president of Columbia University and then commander of the new North Atlantic Treaty Organization (NATO) forces. In the meantime, Democrats hungering for a more plausible nominee than Truman appeared to be in 1948 made overtures to Eisenhower to challenge Truman for the party's presidential nomination. Eisenhower's acceptance of the challenge to enter the political arena came four years later in 1952 when he accepted the Republican party's nomination for president. If Eisenhower, known as Ike, was not the imperial MacArthur, he also was not the poker playing, Hawaiian-shirt-wearing Harry Truman.

Eisenhower's two-term presidency, from 1953 to 1961, took on an aura of nonpartisanship. That is, of course, something of an exaggeration. No one was likely to think of Eisenhower as a New Dealer. By contrast, though, with Franklin Roosevelt's jibes at "economic royalists" or Harry Truman's zest for anti-Republican invective, Eisenhower sought less to arouse the opposition of Democrats than to reconstruct his own party into what he called modern Republicanism. By this, Eisenhower certainly meant that he wanted the Republican party to support America's newfound global responsibilities. He wanted in this regard to loosen the grip of the party's Main Street (isolationist) faction and strengthen its

President Dwight D. Eisenhower (1953–1961) PRINTS AND PHOTOGRAPHS DIVISION, LIBRARY OF CONGRESS

Wall Street (global involvement) faction. First and foremost, of course, Eisenhower wanted to strengthen Republican commitments to security guarantees through multilateral security pacts for which NATO was the model. Second, however, Eisenhower wanted a continued bilateral and also multilateral commitment to foreign assistance and development without which parts of the world would become ripe for communist insurrection. On the domestic side, modern Republicanism apparently came to mean an acceptance of the New Deal legacy that had been institutionalized, while opposing its further expansion.

Eisenhower's first election was accompanied by a Republican takeover of both chambers of Congress—the last time that has happened (the Republicans again gained control of both houses in the 1994 midterm elections). Although Eisenhower won the nomination against what his allies regarded as the old-guard midwestern isolationist wing of his party (the Main Street wing), he would be challenged again when Republicans controlled the Congress. A number of key committee chairs were representatives of the Republican old guard.

The continuity of the McCarthyite investigations, in fact, was largely abetted by Republican control of the Congress. Through the Government Operations Committee, McCarthy continued baiting the administration in power despite its changed political character. Other Republican luminaries of the McCarthyite genre in the Congress, such as William Jenner, Chair of the Senate Internal Security Committee, and Harold Velde, Chair of the House Un-American Activities Committee, also embarrassed the administration of their own party. After McCarthy was censured for his conduct in the Senate following the televised Army-McCarthy hearings in 1954, the McCarthyite forces significantly lost their bite. But in the next congressional elections in 1954, the Republicans also lost their marjorities.

The Army-McCarthy hearings and the damaging aftermath for McCarthy was a product of the latest full-scale development in mass communication, namely the popularity of television. The tube could bring to life events in a way that even radio lacked. Eisenhower was not a personality, yet he adapted to this new medium. Although he was widely regarded as of heroic stature, he appeared more like the national grandfather on television. His prepared speeches lacked the kind of animation that television can highlight, and his off-the-cuff remarks were often laden with dense and ungrammatical constructions. In spite of this—or perhaps because of it—Eisenhower became the first president to have a television consultant. Although one Eisenhower television speech has, in lore at least, been given credit for helping to rally support behind pending legislation (the Griffin-Landrum Labor Management Reform Act), Eisenhower's younger and more photogenic successor, John F. Kennedy, would take fuller opportunity of what television might do for him.

Eisenhower was a great political success, winning two terms by wide margins. However, his reelection in 1956 was the first time a president had been elected with an opposition Congress. The nature of his impact beyond the unquestionable level of his personal political success is thus debatable. Indeed, the Eisenhower presidency has become a focus of precisely such scholarly debate. Two particularly contrasting points of view are expressed by the political scientists Richard E. Neustadt and Fred I. Greenstein, approximately twenty-two years apart. In his seminal book, *Presidential Power* (1960), Neustadt pictured Eisenhower as an amateurish politician, essentially incapable of cashing in his considerable political assets. More than two decades later, Greenstein, who had the advantage of having plowed through the Eisenhower archives, saw a different kind of president. In *The Hidden-Hand Presidency* (1982), Eisenhower became not a political amateur but a master at the arts of concealment. In Greenstein's rendition, the key to Eisenhower's concept of his presidency was not policy activism or polarizing partisanship, but instead legitimacy. By the notion of legitimacy, Greenstein meant that high public approval of the president as a representative of the whole nation was vital. This, naturally, was a very different concept from Neustadt's notion of public approval being merely a means to a policy-activist end. For in Greenstein's version of Eisenhower, public approval was the end, not a means. Eisenhower chose, in Greenstein's account, to emphasize the chief-of-state role of the presidency at the expense of its more overt political functions, such as party leader and political head of the executive.

For a presidency often unsympathetically portrayed as one of unrelieved blandness, Eisenhower's presidency today remains one about which there is exceptional debate. Of course, Eisenhower inherited substantial legacies. The New Deal was here to stay even without New Dealers to maintain it. Given Eisenhower's very conservative economic views, this was a victory of conservative temperament over conservative ideology. The national-security state was also inherited via the Cold War. It too was not likely to disappear, and during the Eisenhower years of intense competition with the Soviet Union it was built up yet further. It is unclear just exactly what Eisenhower's views of all this were, but in a speech given at the close of his administration, Eisenhower warned darkly of a growing military-industrial complex that was a new force with which American democracy would have to contend.

Like most presidents during most times, the Eisenhower presidency found itself reacting to rather than dictating events. The civil rights revolution began to bloom in the 1950s in the aftermath of the Supreme Court's *Brown* v. *Board of Education* decision of 1954 in which the Court unanimously declared school segregation unconstitutional. Eisenhower's own views were essentially segregationist. Yet the

The Army-McCarthy Hearings. Sen. Joseph R. McCarthy gestures toward the map as army counsel Joseph Welch holds his head. OFFICE OF THE HISTORIAN OF THE U.S. SENATE

administration responded to threats to federal authority in Little Rock in 1957 and sent in federal troops to protect the students who were integrating the high school there. At no time did Eisenhower seek to capitalize, as a number of his Republican successors successfully would, on the growing disillusionment of white southern voters with the national Democratic party.

Similarly, the *Sputnik* satellite that the Soviets launched to take a symbolic lead in the race for space grandeur moved Democrats in Congress to pass the National Defense Education Act (NDEA), which provided a clear federal presence in support of the nation's universities. Whatever Eisenhower actually may have thought, the administration agreed to this rather revolutionary policy.

Yet another such grand policy initiated during the Eisenhower administration was the Federal Highway Act, designed to tie together the nation's transportation infrastructure into a network of connecting interstate highways. No doubt, this was an inevitable response to the growing traffic on outmoded highways, but it was given justification, just as the NDEA later would be, on national-security grounds.

In the popular sociology of the 1950s, conformity and organization were regarded as stultifying influences on creativity. William Whyte's *Organization Man* (1956) decried the growth of organizational conformity. Such films as *Executive Suite* (1954) explored the deadening impact of the big-business culture, while *Rebel without a Cause* (1955) portrayed the adults of the 1950s as slavish and hypocritical adherents to conformity and safety in contrast to youthful, if troubled, idealism. Among the popular critics of the day, the Eisenhower presidency was perceived to be in complete conformity with the culture they so disdained.

In large part, this disdain stemmed from the temperamental conservatism of the Eisenhower presidency. It offered no visionary conception of social progress, and cared more for the interests of business than of labor (whose voting members however were not nearly so unsympathetic to Eisenhower). It reinforced the national-security state that, in the language of sociologist C. Wright Mills in a landmark book of that decade, *The Power Elite* (1956), closely intertwined big corporate interests with military and bureaucratic interests.

From a more micro perspective, the modus operandi of the Eisenhower administration was organization and teamwork. Indeed, Richard Neustadt, in his book *Presidential Power,* disdained the Eisenhower style of emphasizing collectively organized choices as naive and ineffective, placing the president in the position of acting on behalf of least-common-denominator solutions. The emphasis on organization and staffing was perceived to epitomize blandness and conformity rather than boldness or questioning. In contrast to Franklin Roosevelt's skeptical eye and efforts to wire the system to respond to his objectives, the Eisenhower style seemed to emphasize the virtues of trust which, according to Neustadt, placed the president in prime position to become the agent of assorted bureaucratic interests within his administration. In the popular lore, the Eisenhower administration seemed to be a microcosmic reflection of the organizational conformity that was being attacked by the intelligentsia in the broader society. As such, it was perceived by its critics as lacking in ideas and ideals and uninterested in providing galvanizing leadership for the country. The organizational and staffing prowess of the Eisenhower administration came later to be regarded as virtues. At the time, however, it was viewed by its critics as the tired style of an uninspired administration.

NEW DEALERS FOR A NEW ERA

The president who succeeded Eisenhower was in many ways his antithesis as a political personality. Whereas Eisenhower spent his career in the military, gaining appreciation for the politics of organizations and for staff responsibilities, John F. Kennedy was a youthful politician (the second youngest president to enter the White House), whose career was spent entirely in the Congress, a largely individualistic enterprise. Kennedy brought style and zest into the White House and the enthusiasms of the political literati.

At the dawn of the space age, the then-Democratic nominee in his acceptance speech at the Democratic National Convention spoke of the New Frontier. The New Frontier was a slogan designed to conjure up images of energy and exploration as befit Kennedy's commitment to American leadership in the Cold War space race with the Soviet Union. In reality, the New Frontier was a combination of older New Deal economic and social policies and a commitment to ratchet up American capabilities to do battle with the Soviet Union around the globe (the creation, for example, of special forces and counter-insurgency tactics) and beyond (the space race).

As the first president born in the twentieth century, with strikingly good looks, wit, and charm, Kennedy was a president tailor-made for the twentieth century. Where Eisenhower relied on formal and collegial processes with considerable delegation of authority, Kennedy preferred highly informal one-

President John F. Kennedy (1961–1963). PRINTS AND PHOTOGRAPHS DIVISION, LIBRARY OF CONGRESS

on-one meetings with advisers. Whereas Eisenhower gave credence to the cabinet as an institution, Kennedy found cabinet proceedings stultifying, preferring instead to deal with cabinet members individually. Where Eisenhower preferred formal organization of the White House with a chief of staff, Kennedy reverted to the style of Franklin Roosevelt, placing himself at the center through which competing streams of advice had to flow. And where Eisenhower was still not comfortable with the new medium of television, Kennedy milked it for all its worth. He was the first president to have his press conferences on live television, altering the balance between electronic and print media and their respective reporters.

Despite Kennedy's efforts to resuscitate the New Deal agenda, he confronted a Congress that was not overly sympathetic to the liberal economic and social policies of the national Democratic party. Kennedy himself won election by a razor-thin margin over the incumbent vice president, Richard M. Nixon. In the same election, the Democrats lost twenty seats in the House from the lopsided majority they had gained in the 1958 congressional elections. Worse yet, from the White House's perspective, the early 1960s represented the high water mark of domination by the conservative coalition in Congress (most Republicans and most southern Democrats) so that nominal Democratic majorities meant less than they seemed. In addition, southern Democratic dominance of committee chairs was at its peak and so was the ability of these chairs to bottle up legislation they did not like.

While Kennedy's style and image was one of youthful dynamism, underneath he was a cautious and calculating politician. He knew he did not have the numbers in Congress to do much that was controversial and so he did not propose much. Mostly in 1961, mild proposals to stimulate the economy or to provide pork-barrel largesse (known as development assistance) were acceptable. Kennedy's main efforts early in the administration were devoted to getting the funding to conduct the space race and to developing flexible-force structures for military intervention and counterinsurgency tactics in peripheral Cold War theaters. One of these areas of turbulence and insurrection—that brewing in Southeast Asia—eventually came to overwhelm Kennedy's successor, Lyndon B. Johnson. In the following year, Kennedy's principal focus was to gain legislative approval to connect the United States more intimately to a world trading system. But one of the main features of social insurance reform the administration had sought, universal health insurance for the elderly, went down to a narrow defeat in the Senate.

In the grip of the Cold War, the Kennedy presidency espoused a posture of active response to what were perceived as Soviet challenges. The Kennedy inaugural address articulated the challenge and commitment in both elegant and unmistakable terms. The Kennedy administration was given much to respond to. American involvement in the North Vietnamese–sponsored insurgency in South Vietnam was gradually growing as North Vietnamese–sponsored activities themselves grew. A more sudden crisis over the status of Berlin and Western access to it bubbled up after a summit meeting between Kennedy and Soviet leader Nikita Khrushchev in Vienna. This led to a partial mobilization of reserve forces and the movement of additional U.S. troops into Berlin itself. A potential face-off between U.S. and Soviet troops across the recently installed Berlin Wall loomed with fearsome consequences. The growing Soviet presence in Cuba also challenged the administration, both tactically and politically. That particular challenge led to perhaps the defining moment of the nuclear era. By the fall of 1962, the Kennedy administration was under attack for failing to respond to an apparent Soviet arms buildup in nearby Cuba. By mid-October, signs of that buildup included Soviet nuclear installations. After a tense confrontation, the Soviets bowed to American demands to eliminate the missile sites it had constructed in Cuba. The outcome of the Cuban missile crisis and the decision processes within the Kennedy administration were subsequently lauded and served to buoy Kennedy's political prospects.

The aftermath of the Cuban missile crisis seemed to defuse some of the most intense tension of the Cold War and may have helped lead to a breakthrough agreement with the Soviet Union on a partial nuclear test ban treaty—the first agreement on arms control of the Cold War era.

In 1963, the civil rights revolution, which had been fomenting since the Supreme Court's 1954 school desegregation decision and which turned into high gear during the 1960s, had reached a new stage. The Kennedy administration had been faced with a delicate balancing act between the demands for federal intervention in the South and sweeping civil rights action, on the one hand, and the political need to hold the support of southern Democrats on the other. The legislative route for major civil rights activity also bumped up against the ability of southern senators to resist floor action through filibuster, effectively killing off other efforts to achieve federal civil rights legislation. Now, however, shocking scenes from Birmingham, Alabama, which portrayed peaceful civil rights protesters being set upon by police dogs and fire hoses, forced Kennedy to act. Far-reaching civil rights legislation was proposed a few months later to bring the authority of the federal government into regulating such areas as accommodations, employment, and education.

Kennedy's death by assassination in November 1963 preceded the ultimate passage of the omnibus civil rights bill and the successful effort to invoke cloture in the Senate against the predictable filibuster. The civil rights pressures and the commitment of a Democratic president on behalf of a pro–civil rights stand laid the foundations for a major regional shift in political alignment. Voting for Democrats in the South no longer provided the means by which white domination could be maintained. When Barry Goldwater, who opposed passage of the civil rights bill, became the Republican standard-bearer in 1964 against Lyndon Johnson, nearly all Goldwater's electoral votes came from southern states.

The Voting Rights Act of 1965, which moved the federal government directly into regulation and enforcement of minority voting rights, reinforced powerfully the realigning direction that had been set. The cycle of protests and violence again sprang the federal government into action. The huge Democratic congressional majorities that came into office in the wake of Lyndon Johnson's landslide victory over Goldwater in the 1964 election made the task of responding somewhat easier than it had been. Republicans in 1964 had made inroads into the southern states' congressional delegations, loosening the grip of southern Democrats on the levers of congressional power and strengthening the liberal forces among Democrats in Congress. Passage of the voting rights bill, therefore, clearly marked the Democrats as the party of federal intervention in the South. Eventually, when African Americans took advantage of the bill's provisions and became a powerful voting presence in the South, they overwhelmingly aligned with the Democrats. Two consequences derived from this. First, Democratic politicians increasingly needed the support of African Americans and found that they could not afford to alienate this base of support. Second, African Americans' and whites' political alignments clearly were moving in opposite directions; the former toward the Democrats and the latter toward the Republicans. As a further consequence, the South became increasingly Republican, most obviously at the presidential level but also increasingly at the congressional level. In addition, each party's coalitions and their elites became progressively less diverse. Republicans became more conservative and Democrats more liberal.

Lyndon Johnson was clearly different in style from the more youthful Kennedy. Johnson had been a master of congressional politics. Kennedy was Harvard; Johnson was Southwest Texas State. Kennedy was privileged; Johnson grew up under more austere circumstances. Despite these differences and the personal animosities that ensued between Johnson and the Kennedy supporters, Johnson successfully transformed the New Frontier into the Great Society. Both, of course, were direct descendants of the New Deal.

Unlike Kennedy, Johnson had far more favorable political circumstances through which to move a massive program of economic stimulation, social reform, and vintage social-insurance programs. Kennedy's sudden death gave impetus toward passage to those of his proposals still under congressional consideration, particularly a big tax-cut economic-stimulus package and the civil rights bill. Johnson proved to be the master of the moment in successfully shepherding Kennedy's unfinished agenda through Congress. The election of 1964 enabled even more to happen. The big majorities in Congress and presi-

Heirs of the New Deal. Eleanor Roosevelt with Democratic candidates John F. Kennedy and Lyndon B. Johnson at a campaign rally in New York, 5 November 1960. PRINTS AND PHOTOGRAPHS DIVISION, LIBRARY OF CONGRESS

dential commitment to a liberal agenda produced a flurry of legislation not seen since the heyday of the New Deal.

Johnson's presidency began hopefully but ended badly. A confluence of circumstances brought the hopeful beginning to the sad ending in which, challenged by multiple candidates within his own party, Johnson chose not to run for reelection in 1968. Despite the flurry of social programs, civil rights improvements, and other ameliorative governmental policies, the years 1965–1968 saw riots in many of America's central cities. The Watts riot in Los Angeles in the late summer of 1965 helped destroy the illusion that social amelioration necessarily bought social peace. Moreover, the general growth of black militancy clearly cut against whatever grain of sympathy white Americans held for the conditions under which the black minority had been subjected. In addition to rising militancy among African Americans and the impact of that on widening the political cleavage between whites and blacks, the country's growing commitments in Vietnam provided another source of social unrest and discontent.

During the 1964 campaign, Johnson tried to distance himself from Goldwater's hawkish stance and pledged that in Vietnam "American boys would not be sent to fight wars that Asian boys should fight." Whatever Johnson knew or did not know at that point, he reneged on that pledge by the summer of 1965. Initially, discontent with the U.S. involvement in the war was centered on major university campuses where nascent black militancy and feminism also emerged as streams of discontent. University campuses became hotbeds of rebellion in nearly every way from social mores to clashes with the authorities. Hence, a cleavage opened up between the seemingly

President Lyndon B. Johnson (1963–1969) with Dr. Martin Luther King, Jr. NATIONAL ARCHIVES

President Richard M. Nixon (1969–1974) with Vice President Spiro Agnew. PRINTS AND PHOTOGRAPHS DIVISION, LIBRARY OF CONGRESS

privileged radicals in the nation's universities and the mainstream of the society. As the war dragged on, however, and especially after the North Vietnamese Tet offensive in 1968, the population as a whole began to think the war was a great mistake.

Johnson's presidency basically lay in ruins—a consequence of avoidable errors of judgment and of uncontrollable social changes. Johnson's popularity had plummeted severely and the public's distrust of its governing authorities began a secular rise over the next quarter century. Furthermore, the Vietnam quagmire also began a long process of restoring greater congressional involvement in foreign policy. That process culminated during the Nixon presidency, when divided government reemerged and hostilities ensued between a Congress seeking to stake out its role and a president seeking to preserve his turf.

PRESIDENTIALISM ASCENDANT—AND DESCENDANT

The close election of Richard Nixon in the 1968 election (along with a Democratic Congress) brought a new (if recycled) face into the White House amidst a host of old problems. One of those problems remained the American commitment in Vietnam—and how to get out of it without appearing to have been defeated. A second problem was the growing racial divide in the country. The close Nixon victory apparently would have been a landslide without the third-party candidacy of George Wallace, who won 13 percent of the popular vote and four states. Wallace's campaign agenda, built on the politics of resentment, was three-pronged. Through code, the Wallace campaign fired out against whites' resentments of blacks; less subtly, it attacked the growth of governmental mandates and the bureaucrats who were administering them. More generally, it excoriated the utilization of presumably unaccountable judicial and administrative means essentially to federalize and regulate what heretofore had been matters of local choice. Finally, Wallace's campaign attacked violators of social mores and unrest on university campuses.

Nixon's political challenge in the face of Wallace's continuing appeal and probable return as a candidate in 1972 was how to eradicate Wallace as a threat to his reelection prospects. This challenge led Nixon to adopt what came to be known as the southern strategy. The southern strategy was designed to place the administration in opposition to court-ordered mandates or administrative edicts such as forced busing to desegregate schools. More broadly, the southern strategy was to create an alliance in the South among whites that could cross class boundaries. Nixon needed to look as sympathetic to southern whites as possible if he was to obviate a 1972 race by Wallace, or at least blunt the effects of a Wallace candidacy.

While Nixon promoted the southern strategy on the one hand, on the other his administration in its early years sought also to co-opt potential black opposition. Internally, the Nixon administration appointed a fairly significant percentage of African Americans. Approximately 13 percent of its domestic political appointments in 1970, for example, were African American. In policy terms the Nixon administration produced agreements for minority set asides in federal contracts. Whatever its reasons, the Nixon administration pursued neither an unabashed southern strategy nor an overt policy of outreach toward the African American minority.

In fact, the early part of the Nixon administration was a period of considerable policy initiative. Demands from new coalitions were filtering into the political process, environmentalists among them. Nixon spent a good bit of political capital on pollution control, creating a new agency (the Environmental Protection Agency) and a White House advisory unit (the Council on Environmental Quality). Even more capital was spent, especially inside the Republican party base, but this time to little avail, when the administration proposed a guaranteed minimum annual income and later a health care program. Neither of these became law.

From a managerial perspective, the Nixon presidency sought to centralize the operations of its administration to an unprecedented degree. Among its actions, it created the Office of Management and Budget from the old Bureau of the Budget to extend the reach of the White House into the agencies that acted in its name. Within this new presidential agency, the Nixon presidency also created a new line of political appointees to give direction to the operations of its career officials. The White House staff also expanded, even more in importance than size. During the first Nixon administration, the White House staff frequently mirrored functions being performed in the agencies. The idea was to provide White House oversight of these activities. In some instances, as in foreign policy, the president's national security adviser brought in an enlarged and highly talented National Security Council staff designed to create the back-up for a foreign policy that largely ignored the secretary of state and much of the State Department.

One of the key features of the Nixon presidency, then, was its emphasis on trying to run the government from the White House. Nixon White House domestic policy adviser John Ehrlichman summed up the White House view of its appointees in the executive branch when he asserted that the "appointees go off to marry the natives" in their departments, therefore becoming departmental advocates to the president rather than the president's agents in the departments.

Because of the events that caused the Nixon administration to disintegrate, the American public gained more information about Nixon's feelings and thinking with his White House intimates than with any other president. While we cannot be certain how Nixon compares with other presidents in this respect, there is no doubt that he had a paranoid style, continuously suspicious of the motives of others and of their desires to frustrate him. The distrust fueled Nixon's obsessions with secrecy and with having full policy control in the White House.

One of the continuing problems leading to Nixon's distrust was his inability to achieve an acceptable agreement to end U.S. involvement in Vietnam. The Nixon White House, as had the Johnson administration before it, believed the protests against the war constrained its prospects for ending it. Nixon's response was to compile "enemies lists" and to try to delegitimize the protesters. The war, however, continued to dog the administration and direct U.S. military involvement came to an end only in 1973 during Nixon's aborted second term.

Essentially, the Nixon administration can be characterized in three stages. The first was its policy activism stage in which it produced a number of new policies, many of which seemed to reflect a political environment in which policy activism and governmental solutions were still regarded as the norm. A second stage came as Nixon headed closer to the election and in the aftermath of the election. At this point, the costs of the policy activism were becoming apparent and placing constraints on the budget. The administration clearly wanted to put its own house in order and sought to have appointees likely to fall in line with its wishes. The Nixon White House also became less likely to reconcile with constituencies it believed it had no chance of winning from the

President Gerald R. Ford (1974–1977). PRINTS AND PHOTOGRAPHS DIVISION, LIBRARY OF CONGRESS

Democrats. It also became more openly hostile toward Congress—a pattern that would be revived under succeeding divided governments. The third stage was the Watergate crisis, which actually was a protracted period beginning approximately two months after Nixon's second inauguration when the cover story began to unravel and continuing until his unprecedented resignation from office in August 1974. The Watergate period reinvigorated congressional challenges to presidential prerogative in committing troops abroad, setting the budget, and impounding appropriated funds. Unintended as it may have been, institutional reform and the assertion of congressional authority against a presidency perceived to have grown to imperial dimensions was a major byproduct of the Nixon era.

After Nixon's forced resignation on 9 August 1974, his appointed vice president, Gerald R. Ford (himself a replacement for Spiro Agnew, who had resigned), assumed office. A longtime former House minority leader, Ford made entreaties to Congress. Ford operated from a weakened position, especially after pardoning Nixon not long after he came to the presidency. The big news of the Ford interregnum was less what Ford did than what Congress did in the aftermath of the 1974 congressional elections. The 1974 elections augmented the Democrats' majorities in both chambers of Congress. But by bringing in so many new members exactly at a time when Congress was seeking to strengthen its grasp on the reins of government, it produced an enormous amount of internal change in the means by which Congress—principally its Democratic majority—operated. The Democratic majority in the House of Representatives strengthened the role of the Speaker, the party caucus, and, above all, weakened the seniority system to make committee chairs more responsive to the majority.

After the crash of the Nixon presidency, Ford's great virtue was that he was normal. As such, he was a perfect stopgap president. Yet Ford essentially was held hostage to the robust Democratic majority in Congress. On a per annum basis, Ford vetoed legislation at a near record pace while congressional majorities also set a record for overrides (see table 2). With diminished popularity, a nagging recession, rapidly growing governmental expenditures (much of it the product of Johnson's Great Society entitlement programs), and a challenge to renomination from his party's right wing in the form of Ronald Reagan, a former two-term governor of California, Ford was highly vulnerable when the election season of 1976 came around.

Ford lost a close election to a political unknown, Jimmy Carter, after he had narrowly secured the Republican nomination. Carter, a one-term Georgia governor, came into office with a malleable set of political ideas. A new southern Democrat who promoted good race relations, Carter was otherwise nondescript as a political personality. He was what the minds of many different beholders perceived him to be. One thing, however, that he was not was a doctrinaire New Dealer.

Three characteristics of Carter stood out. First, he was what presidential scholar Erwin Hargrove, in *Jimmy Carter as President: Leadership and the Politics of the Public Good* (1988), described as a "collective goods president." By this Hargrove meant that Carter was interested in having government act on problems that affected everyone and that were vital to the nation's future. Carter's first big legislative proposal, his energy bill, reflected this concern. Alternatively, Carter seemed less interested in problems whose solution benefited any particular constituency. This feeds into a second characteristic of Carter: he was a remarkably apolitical politician. His first flap in office was to veto a set of water projects without prior consultation. Like Nixon before him, Carter had little regard for Congress as a body nor did he have much respect for politicians as a class of people.

Table 2. VETOES, 1897–1995

President	Vetoes: Regular	Vetoes: Pocket	Vetoes: Total	Vetoes Overridden
McKinley	6	36	42	0
T. Roosevelt	42	40	82	1
Taft	30	9	39	1
Wilson	33	11	44	6
Harding	5	1	6	0
Coolidge	20	30	50	4
Hoover	21	16	37	3
F. Roosevelt	372	263	635	9
Truman	180	70	250	12
Eisenhower	73	108	181	2
Kennedy	12	9	21	0
Johnson	16	14	30	0
Nixon[a]	26	17	43	7
Ford	48	18	66	12
Carter	13	18	31	2
Reagan	39	39	78	9
Bush[b]	29	17	46	1
Clinton	1	0	1	0

[a] Two of Nixon's "pocket vetoes," overruled in the courts, are counted here as regular vetoes.

[b] Bush claimed to pocket veto two bills (H.R. 2712 in 1989 and H.R. 2699 in 1991), but actually returned them to Congress, which attempted to override the veto on the first bill; these vetoes are counted here as regular vetoes because they were returned to Congress. Congress argued that two other pocket vetoes by Bush (of H.J. Res. 390 in 1989 and S. 1176 in 1991) were invalid and that the bills became law. Because the National Archives did not recognize those bills as enacted law, they are counted here as pocket vetoes.

SOURCE: Adapted from *Encyclopedia of the American Presidency* (New York: Simon & Schuster, 1994), p. 1553. Data from U.S. Senate, Office of the Secretary, *Presidential Vetoes, 1989–1991* (1992), pp. viii–ix.

This meant that he was going to have difficulties with Congress and, indeed, with his own party, which had great difficulty figuring him out. It also meant that all his political foibles (which were indeed many) would be magnified. A unified government fell far short of resembling a party government. A third characteristic of Carter was his modest life-style. Unlike Nixon, who sought to outfit the White House guard with plumage and who was otherwise disposed to an imperial presidential style, Carter was known instead for his miserliness with public perquisites, carrying his own suitbag, and not having "Hail to the Chief" played upon his entrances.

Indeed, Carter came to office essentially running against the imperial style associated with the disgraced Nixon presidency. Carter delivered on decency but was widely believed to be incompetent. Such a charge is, of course, remarkably vague. A key Carter problem, though, was that, as an outsider, he had few links inside Washington to shore him up when the going got rough. And the going got rough early. Carter's collective-goods proposals were hacked apart, while he failed to satisfy many in his party either on economic or social welfare proposals (where he was regarded as too conservative) or in foreign policy (where he was regarded as too softheaded). Carter fell between the liberals in his party and the neoconservatives, many of whom eventually felt more comfortable with his successor, Ronald Reagan.

President Jimmy Carter (1977–1981) ARCHIVE PHOTOS

The flow of events and the flow of ideas were moving in currents favorable neither to the Democratic party nor to the Carter administration. Carter's popularity had begun to sink below critical levels by the fall of 1977, levels from which it would never again rise for any sustained period. The loss of seats in the 1978 congressional elections gave Republicans even greater hope for 1980. The stagflation that gripped the country (and the world) in 1979–1980 sent prices, interest rates, and unemployment soaring. The late 1970s witnessed an explosion of ideas associated with conservatives, the Republican party, and free-market, low-tax advocates. Like Gerald Ford in 1976, Carter faced a challenge from a more popular figure within his own party, Sen. Edward Kennedy of Massachusetts, the youngest brother of the slain president. Like Ford, Carter narrowly survived this challenge. But it was all for naught as Carter suffered a big defeat in the 1980 presidential election, winning just 40 percent in a three-person race.

Carter was the fourth president in succession who was reputed to be a failed president and the fifth president in a row who failed to serve two full terms. What had caused this? Presidents of different styles and different levels of experience ultimately could not pass tests of popular legitimacy no matter what they might have accomplished during their tenure in office. Some analysts of American politics pointed to the breakdown of connective tissue between presidents and their fellow party members in Congress, the result of citizens' disassociative voting choices. Other analysts began to talk of governmental overload or the rise of single-issue interest groups, which increase the demand on government without any adjustment in its governing capacity. Others pointed to the complexity of public problems, the narrowed space with which to negotiate solutions and the limited resources available for them. Yet others pointed to a political process easily infiltrated by outsiders, short-term political passions, and little connection to the concerns of average citizens. Finally, some commentators argued that what was missing was leadership and vision in the Oval Office. Whatever the causes, books began to appear with titles such as *The Impossible Presidency.*

President Ronald Reagan (1981–1989) PRINTS AND PHOTOGRAPHS DIVISION, LIBRARY OF CONGRESS

CONFIDENCE RESTORED: THE REAGAN PRESIDENCY

In the midst of the doom and gloom that surrounded the end of the Carter years, Ronald Reagan became the Republican presidential nominee in 1980 at the age of sixty-nine. Reagan was the candidate of the growing right wing of the Republican party. But unlike Barry Goldwater, who failed massively in the 1964 election, Reagan was running against a highly vulnerable incumbent in bad times rather than, as Goldwater had, against an incumbent at the top of his game. The public personae of the two candidates also differed. Goldwater was viewed as simple but gruff; Reagan as simple but amiable.

Reagan's election margin was sufficient in size, especially in the electoral college, that he could lay claim to the mythical mandate. Especially important to the success of the Reagan presidency is that the 1980 election gave the Republicans control of the Senate for the first time in thirty-six years. Even though Democrats retained nominal control of the House, the Republicans gained thirty-three seats and could put together a working majority with conservative Democrats. Above all, the Reagan administration came into office with firm ideas about what it wished to achieve and how to gain control of the government so as to be in a position to achieve its substantive objectives.

The substantive aims of the Reagan administration were quite straightforward. It wanted lower marginal tax rates, less governmental expenditure and regulation, more for defense, and a confrontational stance toward the Soviet Union around the world. To achieve its goals and to institutionalize them, the Reagan administration paid a great deal of attention to the process of appointments in the executive branch and to the federal bench. It learned from the belated efforts of the Nixon administration to exercise such authority that it should seek immediately to wrest control of the mechanics of government. Appointees and court nominees were carefully vetted for their allegiance to relevant parts of the Reagan program. Having control of the Senate for six years gave the administration an advantage in getting controversial nominees through the confirmation process. Civil servants, whose influence had been on the decline for a while, were moved farther away from policy decisions and given more exclusively managerial functions. The Office of Management and Budget and the White House directly imposed greater internal regulation of government to decrease the level of regulation by government. In sum, the Reagan administration knew what it wanted and what it took to ensure that its legacy would be enduring.

The first year of the Reagan administration was the key to its policy success. In that first year, the administration began a massive growth in defense expenditures that would not level off until midway into the second term. It also managed to get its two-pronged economic program through—an approximately 4 percent cut in projected expenditures and a sizable multiyear income tax cut that also was indexed for inflation. By achieving these legislative goals, the impossible presidency seemed possible after all. One by-product of these achievements, however, was a massive structural growth in the federal deficit.

The voluminous growth in the federal deficit changed the terms of public conversation from "what government can do" to "what government cannot do." The size of the deficit—whose causes are more complex than being merely the consequence of the deeds of 1981—discouraged proposals for new program expenditures or for nonmandated growth in old programs. Perhaps one of the most enduring legacies of the Reagan administration was to change the terms of policy conversation and restrict future expenditure commitments.

The economy eventually turned around by the end of the first quarter of 1983. In the meantime, while inflation was being squeezed out of the economy through the austere monetary policies of the Federal Reserve (supported by the Reagan administration), the recession got worse and unemployment hit its highest mark since the Great Depression. As unemployment soared, Reagan's popularity plummeted. The economic turnaround that began in 1983 provided the longest skein of economic growth in the twentieth century and Reagan's political prospects prospered accordingly. In 1984, Reagan won reelection carrying all but his opponent's home state. On the domestic front, tight controls over government regulation of business and opposition to tax increases to deal with the budget deficit were the hallmark policies of the Reagan administration.

The powerfully held convictions of Ronald Reagan and many of his appointees were at the center of clashes between the executive and other branches of government, including the courts. Clashes between Congress and the executive grew more frequent after the Democrats regained control of the Senate in the wake of the 1986 elections. The federal government had been experiencing divided government in some form or other for a significant proportion of the second half of the century. Aside from the later stages of the Nixon administration, however, conflicts over prerogatives had been generally more tempered. By temperament, Eisenhower chose not to fling challenges to congressional authority. Moreover, he had good working relationships with the Democratic Senate leader Lyndon Johnson and House Speaker Sam Rayburn. Of critical importance was that the Democrats were then still divided between their southern and northern wings, and many of the southern Democrats were a part of the conservative coalition. By virtue of the times, Nixon's early agenda was a relatively liberal one for a Republican president and tension between the Nixon administration and Congress (despite Nixon's personal contempt of congressional politicians) was not great until later in the administration when Nixon abandoned his earlier stances and Congress limited Nixon's ability to conduct the Vietnam War. But now the Reagan administration made little pretense of accommodation and saw the executive as a means by which it could govern through secret operations as in the Iran-contra episode, the promulgation of administrative law, or by tying the government itself into regulatory knots. Congress, however, had become a body better equipped to do battle with executive authority—Nixon's legacy from the 1970s. Above all, the parties had become more clearly polarized against one another. As a result, the 1980s were a time of strong clashes between the White House and the Democrats in Congress.

In spite of these clashes, which were generally of greater interest to political analysts than to the public, the Reagan years restored both the country's confidence in itself as well as in the presidency. Reagan's optimism and upbeat style played well once the economy picked up steam, and the country's heavy investments into the military seemed to induce a new leadership in the Soviet Union to seek an end to a Cold War that was rapidly bankrupting it. Reagan's professional background as an actor helped him to maximize the symbolic nature of the office he held. Finally, while Reagan entered office with the lowest public approval rating of any president since such ratings have been recorded, his approval ratings over the course of most of his administration fared very well by contrast with his immediate predecessors. Reagan was the first president since Eisenhower to serve two full terms and the first since Eisenhower (Kennedy excepted) to leave with the approval of more than half of the public.

Like most presidents who have made a substantial mark, Reagan was aided by having big problems to solve and favorable political conditions in which to do so. Ideas important to the Reagan administration's goals had become fashionable. The opposition Democrats had been largely placed on the defensive during much of the Reagan presidency. The election of 1980, like that of 1964, produced rare clear signals and a working majority in Congress for the first two years. A Republican Senate enabled the Reagan presidency to follow through on its executive and judicial appointment strategies with minimal interference. But what ultimately made it work, given these conditions, was a president passionately and unmistakably committed to a particular vision of America and the world.

LEADING INTO THE 1990s

George Bush, who had been Reagan's chief opponent for the 1980 Republican presidential nomination, was then selected as Reagan's vice president. Reagan and Bush presented stark contrasts. Reagan was the ultimate outsider; Bush had a well-traveled governmental résumé. Reagan was a conviction politician; Bush's political history was filled with identity problems. As Reagan's vice president, however, Bush came to conclude that his chances for the Republican presidential nomination in 1988 required him to seem like the natural successor to Ronald Reagan. Bush's leading opponent for the Republican nomination was Senate minority leader Bob Dole, a fiscal conservative often at odds with the Reagan administration's tolerance for large budget deficits and intolerance for taxes. Bush portrayed himself as a ready follower of Reagan's economic doctrines during the primary season and in his acceptance speech at the 1988 Republican national convention when he uttered the now memorable statement: "Read my lips. No new taxes."

Despite having a relatively high public disapproval rating ("negatives" in the parlance of campaign managers), Bush handily defeated the Democratic candidate, Gov. Michael Dukakis of Massachusetts, who shortly after the Democrats' convention held a seventeen-point lead over Bush. Bush's campaign was meant to associate himself with Reaganesque symbols—opposition to taxes, emphasis on the symbols of patriotism and strong defense, and social conservatism.

The world that had begun to change significantly under Ronald Reagan changed even more under George Bush. Movement toward the end of the Cold War and extensive liberalization within the Soviet Union and some of its allies radically surged forward in the first year of the Bush presidency. Poland and Hungary cast away most of their communist leadership. The Berlin Wall came down and East Germany eventually became extinct, unifying with the German Federal Republic in 1990. By the end of the year, Romania and Bulgaria also threw off their old leadership and political structures. Later even remote Albania did so. Europe was in the throes of a democratic springtime. At this stage, most of the international news was good and Bush, who claimed long international experience and expertise, prospered. His good fortune was also a continuing function of the country's prosperity, which by 1990 was coming to an end, containing within it the seeds of destruction of Bush's reelection prospects.

President George Bush (1989–1993). PRINTS AND PHOTOGRAPHS DIVISION, LIBRARY OF CONGRESS

In contrast to Reagan, when Bush came into office he offered a spirit of moderation to his administration, frequently appointing centrists and highly experienced executives. He also sought to reach out early to Congress. Indeed, there was an era of good feeling for much of the first half of Bush's term. At one point, the most Democratic constituency of all—African

Americans—gave him a nearly 45 percent approval rating. In short, for most of his administration, and certainly over the first two and a half years, Bush had exceptionally high public approval ratings in spite of a generally actionless administration. Bush's approval ratings soared to an all-time high in 1991 shortly after the decisive American-led victory in the Gulf War against Saddam Hussein's forces.

However, a real turning point may have occurred a few months earlier when the Bush administration cut a deal with Democratic congressional majorities to reduce the deficit by placing caps on spending categories and increasing taxes. Bush had difficulty bringing Republicans into the Congress, especially the House, and was held responsible by his party's Reaganites for the lack of success in the 1990 congressional elections. The budget summit illustrated the continuing problem of achieving significant deficit reduction and the strong stance of the Republican party against tax increases. Equally, of course, Democrats were more inclined to go the tax-increase route and more likely to resist expenditure reduction. It also put Bush in a defensive position vis-à-vis his party's right wing.

When the recession continued through 1991, Bush's popularity fell and Democratic hopes soared. Toward the end of the year, Democrats gained an unexpected Senate win in a special election and sensed that Bush was vulnerable. In 1991, and especially in 1992, clashes between the White House and Congress under Democratic majorities heated up. Again, issues of executive prerogative as well as policy were at stake. C. Boyden Gray, the Bush administration's legal counsel, had an especially expansive view of executive prerogative among other things, issuing findings that defined the executive interpretation of congressional statutes. The shoe was now on the other foot. The anti–New Dealers were compatible with a powerful, maximizing presidency, while the inheritors of the New Deal legacy found refuge in Congress. The federal judiciary, by this time, also was overwhelmingly appointed by Presidents Reagan and Bush and its prevailing concepts of executive-legislative authority were preponderantly favorable to the executive.

In 1992, Bush turned increasingly to the right wing of his party (even denouncing his own budget deal) in order to mollify what he perceived to be his core constituency. Along with the sluggish economy and the loss of confidence in his leadership, this turn to the right also may have hurt his chances among swing voters. In any event, Bush became a one-term president in spite of the fact that overall he ranks

President Bill Clinton (1993–). THE WHITE HOUSE

fourth among the last ten presidents in average popular approval ratings. Here, presumably, was another failed presidency.

The winner of the 1992 election, Bill Clinton, was from a political generation for which Vietnam, not World War II, was the defining crisis. Like other Democrats, Clinton brought with him large policy ambitions, and for the first time in thirteen years the country had unified party government. How relevant that is remains to be seen in light of the issues that remain to be resolved. Matters of financing deficit-reduction or footing the costs for health-care reform set the parties against one another but also produce less cohesion among the Democrats than the Republicans. Unified government, even under the conditions of greater party cohesion that exist today, is no guarantee of presidential success. This is particularly so in view of the mixed signals (a fairly typical outcome) sent by the 1992 election, in which Clinton won a minority of the vote and Democrats lost ten seats in the House and gained none in the Senate.

Early public evaluations show the Clinton presidency has not been able to expand its minority support base. It has had the lowest public approval ratings of any presidency so early in its term. Does this signal yet another failed presidency? And, if so, why? Has the presidency become impossible again?

LEADERSHIP IN HARD TIMES

The history of the American presidency in the twentieth century is a history of growth in its visibility and role in the political system. The separation of powers implies there is no center, only competing sources of authority. Yet modern means of communication and expectations about leadership inevitably place the president at the center of a system in which one can with limited resources at best cajole, but certainly not command, responsiveness. When presidents have tried to create that responsiveness on their own, they have courted trouble.

Leadership is hard everywhere. In spite of President Clinton's early troubles, he still fared better than the French president (François Mitterand), the Canadian prime minister (Brian Mulroney), the British prime minister (John Major), and the German chancellor (Helmut Kohl), perhaps combined. Problems that require adjustments in standards of living to achieve longer-term betterment are not popular anywhere. Nor is economic slowdown good for politicians' fortunes. How much of this is new to the twentieth century is questionable. After all, presidents were tossed out in bad times during the nineteenth century as well.

No ready formula exists for presidential success. Although, to be sure, the criterion of success is elusive, presidents as varying in temperament as Roosevelt, Eisenhower, and Reagan have generally been regarded as successful, Johnson, Nixon, and Carter as over- or underreaching with disastrous results.

As with all great moments of leadership, policy opportunities must arise to be exploited. There must be a problem or set of problems generally recognized for which available solutions can be agreed upon. There also must be political opportunity. This means amassing large majorities on behalf of some set of solutions, whether through partisan majorities or a far-reaching consensus—on the whole, a difficult proposition, given the design of the American system. On the leadership side, there must be exploitation of the available opportunities, and clearly presidents have been given more tools technologically to mobilize support. But utilizing these tools only rarely proves to be effective.

The great irony, of course, is that the presidency has become a more important, more visible, and certainly more imperial office than in the nineteenth century. Much of this has to do with the growth of the state itself and especially the perception of presidential responsibility for macroeconomic conditions and peace or war. Yet for all this growth in importance and visibility, it is not clear that the office is any more powerful in 1993 than it was in 1893. Importance and visibility have increased demands on the president for leadership; but to lead, the president must in the end cajole and persuade. The history of the American presidency in the twentieth century, then, is a history of the growth of the illusion of our presidents' power.

SEE ALSO Political Ideas and Movements; Parties and Interest Groups (both in this volume).

BIBLIOGRAPHY

The most important general book on the relationship of the presidency to the political system in which a president operates is Richard E. Neustadt, *Presidential Power and the Modern Presidents: The Politics of Leadership from Roosevelt to Reagan* (1960, 1990). In addition, another central work from a nineteenth-century perspective on the role of the executive in relation to the fragmented structures of power at work in the American system is Woodrow Wilson, *Congressional Government: A Study in American Politics* (1885). A useful work that contrasts the power of the president in the American system with that of chief executives in other large modern democracies is Anthony King, "Foundations of Power," in *Researching the Presidency: Vital Questions, New Approaches,* ed. George C. Edwards III, John H. Kessel, and Bert A. Rockman (1993).

A valuable general history of the presidency is Sidney M. Milkis and Michael Nelson, *The American Presidency: Origins and Development, 1776–1990*

(1990). A more specialized history of interbranch relations and the executive power is Christopher H. Pyle and Richard M. Pious, *The President, Congress, and the Constitution: Power and Legitimacy in American Politics* (1984).

A work dealing with the relative public salience of the president and Congress in the nineteenth century is Samuel Kernell and Gary C. Jacobson, "Congress and the Presidency as News in the Nineteenth Century," in *Journal of Politics* (1987). Two works that overlap the nineteenth and twentieth centuries focus on the issues of rationalizing the federal executive and the military, on the one hand, and the capability of the federal government to make powerful shifts in policy, on the other: Stephen Skowronek, *Building a New American State: The Expansion of National Administrative Capacities, 1877–1920* (1982); and David W. Brady, *Critical Elections and Congressional Policy-making* (1988).

One of the more interesting works connecting the presidencies of Theodore Roosevelt and, especially, Woodrow Wilson to the instrument of popular appeal as a means of legitimizing presidential leadership is Jeffrey K. Tulis, *The Rhetorical Presidency* (1987). Two especially useful books that connect the quest for administrative reform and presidential leadership from the beginning of the twentieth century to close to mid-century are Barry D. Karl's *Executive Reorganization and Reform in the New Deal: The Genesis of Administrative Management, 1900–1939* (1963) and his *The Uneasy State: The United States from 1915–1945* (1983). An article that examines the extent to which continuity or discontinuity marked the New Deal presidency of Franklin Roosevelt from that of his predecessor is Michael Lewis-Beck and Peverill Squire, "The Transformation of the American State: The New Era–New Deal Test" *Journal of Politics* 53 (1991): 106–121.

Two noteworthy books on the presidency of Franklin Roosevelt focus, respectively, on the constraints influencing FDR's leadership strategies and on the dissolution of the New Deal coalition in Congress: James MacGregor Burns, *Roosevelt: The Lion and the Fox* (1956); and James T. Patterson, *Congressional Conservatism and the New Deal: The Growth of the Conservative Coalition in Congress, 1933–39* (1967, 1981). A book that follows up on the idea of a disconnection between parties in Congress and the presidency is James MacGregor Burns, *The Deadlock of Democracy: Four Party Politics in America* (1963); see also in this regard, Morris P. Fiorina, *Retrospective Voting in American National Elections* (1981).

On the Eisenhower presidency, *The Hidden-Hand Presidency: Eisenhower as Leader* by Fred I. Greenstein (1982) is a much-discussed revisionist interpretation of Eisenhower's presidency from the stereotype then prevalent. Stephen E. Ambrose, *Eisenhower,* vol. 2 (1983), also is an excellent if less clearly focused history of Eisenhower's presidency. Two books that reflected the scholarly disdain for the society and the culture in which Eisenhower governed are C. Wright Mills, *The Power Elite* (1956); and William H. Whyte, *The Organization Man* (1956).

A good history of the Kennedy presidency is Herbert S. Parmet, *JFK: The Presidency of John F. Kennedy* (1983).

Important changes in the nation's political alignments and reflected in Congress stemming from the 1964 presidential election are traced in David W. Rhode, *Parties and Leaders in the Postreform House* (1991). A more general trend toward a nationalization in politics stemming from the 1960s and 1970s is argued in William M. Lunch, *The Nationalization of American Politics* (1987).

Two political biographies of Nixon and histories of his presidency worth attention are Stephen E. Ambrose, *Nixon,* vols. 2 and 3 (1987); and Herbert S. Parmet, *Richard Nixon and His America* (1990).

For an excellent analysis of Jimmy Carter's conception of his presidency and style of operations, one should consult Erwin C. Hargrove, *Jimmy Carter as President: Leadership and the Politics of the Public Good* (1988).

Several anthologies focusing on the Reagan presidency are worth looking at: B. B. Kymlicka and Jean V. Matthews, eds., *The Reagan Revolution?* (1988); Charles O. Jones, ed., *The Reagan Legacy: Promise and Performance* (1988); and Larry Berman, ed., *Looking Back on the Reagan Presidency* (1990). For an anthology on the Bush presidency, see Colin Campbell and Bert A. Rockman, eds., *The Bush Presidency: First Appraisals* (1991).

CONGRESS

Joel D. Aberbach

In a document both simple and ambiguous, the founders of the American state established a system of separate institutions sharing powers and created the conditions for unending institutional conflict in U.S. government. Fearing that the legislative branch might aggrandize its power, the framers of the Constitution divided the Congress into two houses—the Senate and the House of Representatives—with different representational bases and, initially, with different modes of election. The stage was set for a governing system that has lasted for more than two hundred years, at once enduring and adaptable.

As the branch of national government closest to the nation's eligible electors, Congress tends to reflect the country's strengths and weaknesses. As a result, even if it is not always admirable, Congress is endlessly fascinating to observers of the American scene. Rogues and heroes, reflective individuals and hotheads, bigots as well as paragons of tolerance and understanding have all served, and anecdotes about them enliven the discussions of aficionados of the Congress. So much of our national life is reflected in and shaped by congressional deliberations and decisions, however, that inevitably the focus of this essay must be narrowed. The history of Congress in the twentieth century is examined here by looking at four interrelated topics: (1) the changing power and place of Congress in the American political system; (2) areas of challenge and how Congress has met them, including the national budget, congressional oversight of the executive branch, and the power to make war; (3) changes in who Congress represents and how it is organized; and (4) the future of Congress.

THE CHANGING POWER AND PLACE OF CONGRESS IN THE AMERICAN POLITICAL SYSTEM

In the late nineteenth century, Congress was widely acknowledged to be the dominant branch of government. Woodrow Wilson's classic book, *Congressional Government,* described Congress as the prominent and controlling force in American national government:

> The legislature is the aggressive spirit. . . . [It] has entered more and more into the details of administration, until it has virtually taken into its own hands all the substantial powers of government. . . . I know not how better to describe our form of government in a single phrase than by calling it a government by the chairmen of the Standing Committees of Congress.

While Congress may have been dominant in this period, its core weaknesses remained. Lord Bryce, a well-known British observer of the United States in the late nineteenth century, noted Congress's many limitations: among them that it was divided into two houses, had a decentralized committee structure, lacked unifying leadership, and was incapable of producing "general or continuous legislative policy." Yet, as James Sundquist argues in *The Decline and Resurgence of Congress* (1981), by the turn of the century Congress was able to achieve a historic high point in internal discipline and strong leadership. In fact, Sundquist points out, as early as 1891 the historian Albert Bushnell Hart had already observed the rise in influence of the Speaker of the House and predicted that the holder of that position was "likely to become and perhaps is already, more powerful, both for good and evil, than the President of the United States."

However, the congressional weaknesses Bryce identified eventually triumphed. The House rose in revolt against Speaker Joseph Cannon in 1910. Cannon had exercised the powers of his office vigorously, assigning members to committees, appointing and removing committee chairs, referring bills to committee, and dominating, in his role as chair of the Rules Committee, the flow of bills to the floor and the terms of debate itself. A virtual dictator, Cannon was forced from the Rules Committee chairmanship in 1910 and thus lost a significant amount of his influence over the legislative agenda. When the Democrats took control of the House in 1911, Champ Clark, the new Speaker, was denied the authority to make committee assignments, and had his power of recognition curtailed. A major legacy of the revolt was an increase in the power of committee chairs. Seniority, not the Speaker, now determined who chaired committees, including the Rules Committee. Speakers, in fact, were forced to rely on personal resources to be effective.

In an important way, the revolt against Speaker Cannon marked the culmination of a transition from a Congress of transient officeholders to an institutionalized Congress of Washington-oriented professionals. Nelson Polsby's classic 1968 article describing the institutionalization of the House reported enormous turnover in the House after each election in the eighteenth and nineteenth centuries. Thus, even though the highest incidence of turnover in the House in the twentieth century—37.2 percent in Franklin Roosevelt's landslide election of 1932—was double the twentieth-century median, it showed a decrease from elections in the two previous centuries, where 50 percent turnovers were not uncommon. In addition, the seniority of those chosen Speaker increased dramatically from a mean of six years served before 1899 to a mean of twenty-six after that date. Polsby uses this and other evidence to conclude that "one important feature in the development of the U.S. House of Representatives has been its differentiation from other organizations in the political system, a stabilization of its membership, and a growing specialization of its leaders to leadership of the House as a separate career."

Institutionalization of the House and related but less stark changes in the Senate (which did not have guaranteed direct election of its members until the Seventeenth Amendment was ratified in 1913) were byproducts of profound social and economic changes which transformed the United States. Turnover decreased because the national government, which initially was not all that important, became the focal point of efforts to adapt to and control the forces which were transforming American life. Congress was the place to be for an ambitious politician because it was where major battles would be fought over policies to confront the consequences of rapid industrialization, new modes of transportation, the emergence of the United States as a world power, and the like. One could make a profitable political career in Washington (literally in many cases as well as figuratively), and one could reach the city and return home with greater ease than before, making long-term tenure in the Congress much more attractive than it once had been.

Lawrence Dodd develops this argument in his stimulating essay, "Congress and the Quest for Power" (1977), examining some of the events that dramatically altered the nature of power in the American political system. The Civil War, Dodd notes, clearly established "the supremacy of the national government over the states and . . . the hegemony of the national government in political affairs." In addition, the industrial revolution "helped create an interdependent economy based on interstate commerce, thus expanding the power potential of the national government by confronting it with social and economic decisions of considerable magnitude that lay within its constitutional mandate." With the power to regulate interstate and foreign commerce, its influence over treaties and ambassadorial nominations, the ability to authorize and appropriate defense expenditures, and the authority to declare war, Congress exercised more control over the lives of individual citizens in the twentieth century than it had previously.

Between 1910 and 1915 disaffected members of Congress who wanted a more equitable arrangement of congressional power successfully overthrew both the Speakership and the party caucus, dispersing congressional power to the standing committees. The decentralized congressional committee system, however, had important effects on the position of Congress relative to the presidency. The higher visibility afforded the presidency by the new nationwide system of mass communications, the increasing importance of international relations, the growth of the administrative state, and the increasing lack of congressional constraints allowed the presidency to assert itself in filling the growing need for coherence in national policy which the now decentralized, committee-dominated Congress could not possibly provide. It is important to understand that many elected to Congress preferred a system that left them free to operate as political entrepreneurs seeking reelection to office, the furtherance of particular policy goals (usually favoring their constituencies and in the jurisdiction of their committees), and the like. Consequently, Congress slowly ceded more and more power to the president and the institutions of the executive branch. Although it certainly did not cede all power and has often asserted or reasserted itself through specific actions or general reforms, its struggle has always been hampered by the conflicting goals of its members. They do not want to play second fiddle to the executive; but their individual aspirations inhibit their efforts to generate collective strength through centralized organization or its ally, strict party discipline.

Dodd argues provocatively that in broad historical perspective there is a cyclical pattern in Congress's internal organizational dynamics and its external relations to the president. Members of Congress seeking national prominence decentralize power and create committee government. What follow are "severe problems of congressional decision making, presidential assumption of legislative prerogatives, and an eventual presidential assault on Congress itself," to which Congress reacts by reforming its internal structure.

> [S]ome reform efforts will involve legislation that attempts to circumscribe presidential action; other reforms will attempt to break specific points of deadlock by further decentralization and dispersal of congressional authority; eventually, however, problems of internal congressional leadership and coordination will become so severe that Congress will be forced to undertake centralizing reforms. As Congress moves to resolve internal structural problems and circumscribe presidential power, presidents begin to cooperate so as to defuse the congressional counterattack. . . . As the immediate threat to congressional prerogatives recedes, members of Congress (many of whom will not have served in Congress during the era of institutional crisis) become preoccupied with their immediate careers and press once again for greater power dispersal within Congress and removal of centralizing mechanisms that inhibit committee and subcommittee autonomy. Decentralization reasserts itself and Congress becomes increasingly leaderless, uncoordinated, insulated, unresponsive, unable to control executive agencies. Tempted by congressional weakness and hounded by cries to "get the country moving," the executive again asserts itself and a new institutional crisis eventually arises. A review of American history demonstrates the existence of this cycle rather clearly, particularly during the twentieth century.

Dodd overstates his case somewhat, but his basic point has much to commend it. The twentieth-century Congress has been the home of career politicians. While they want their institution to be powerful so that they can be players in the central political dramas of the nation, they also have an abiding interest in the decentralization of power within Congress so that they can bring benefits to their constituencies (both geographic and interest-based) and claim credit sufficient to ensure reelection. Our system of single-member constituencies with nominations made at the district level (and since the Progressive era, nominations increasingly secured through district-based primary elections) encourages support for decentralization because each individual in the Congress benefits from a system allowing him or her to exercise individual influence.

What we have is a complex interplay of factors that has produced a Congress whose committee system yields substantial policy expertise and narrowly focused influence, but gives it little ability to deal with larger cross-cutting issues requiring coordination. For that, Congress would (except perhaps in periods of crisis) need centralized leadership with tools to bring a broader perspective to bear and discipline members to accept the broader perspective. The individual needs of members of Congress find their most congenial expression in a decentralized system of committee government. When presidents encroach on its position in the policy system, Congress initiates reforms that have a centralizing thrust to protect the institution. But since members of Congress reserve to themselves sufficient prerogatives so that the influence of central leadership in the Congress is restrained, the reforms contain the seeds that eventually compromise or undermine whatever centralizing mechanisms are put into effect. And the memories of those in Congress, particularly the cohort of members elected after the events that stimulated the reforms, are likely to be short and the temptations to enhance individual influence great enough so that the forces of decentralization regain the upper hand. That, in turn, frustrates activist presidents and gives them an opening to pursue a more assertive stance.

In short, there is a tension between the individual goals of members of Congress and their desire to serve in a strong institution. Their institutional concerns win out when the Congress is sufficiently challenged by the president, but the victory is incomplete and undermined over time since Congress's responses to outside challenges contain the seeds (and sometimes full-grown plants) that sooner or later allow individual interests to reassert themselves. The tension between individual goals and institutional concerns, or as Dodd puts it "the implicit tension between the quest for power by individuals and the necessity of maintaining the external authority of the institution," is a key to understanding congressional history and the declines and surges of congressional power in the twentieth century. It is particularly crucial to understanding Congress's fitful and usually flawed efforts to centralize institutional power and coordinate policy.

THE NATIONAL BUDGET

Of all the powers of Congress, the power of the purse is arguably the most important. Historically, the key to the power of legislatures has been centered on budget issues. From the Magna Carta to the American Constitution and beyond, control of the power to tax and spend has been a defining element of limited government.

In the area of the budget, as Donald Kettl notes in *Deficit Politics: Public Budgeting in Its Institutional and Historical Context* (1992), "the Constitution split power, clearly but not cleanly, between the president and the Congress." The president was in charge of spending money, but Congress was given the power to raise it. And only the House of Representatives, the one branch the original Constitution specified was to be elected directly by the people, could originate bills for raising revenue, an additional check on both the president and the indirectly elected Senate. Further, the president could spend money only on programs enacted by Congress, "as Congress enacted them." Until 1921, "Congress was the clear center of the budgetary process. Individual agencies submitted their spending requests directly to Congress, which decided agency by agency how much to approve. There really was no 'budget' in the sense of a coordinated plan detailing how much money was to be raised and how it was to be spent. Budgeting was largely an ad hoc affair, with the 'budget' simply the accumulation of individual congressional decisions."

The stimulus to change this system came from growth in the federal budget that taxed the ability of Congress to deal with the agencies and their requests for ever more money. As Allen Schick points out in a 1983 essay, during the half-century from 1870 to 1920 "federal expenditures soared from less than $300 million to more than $3 billion." Congress responded by passing the Budget and Accounting Act of 1921, one of the landmark pieces of legislation in the nation's history. In this act, according to Schick, "Congress willingly turned the financial controls [of the government] over to the president."

The Budget and Accounting Act of 1921 created the General Accounting Office (GAO), an important congressional support agency with a mission to audit federal expenditures. In provisions of even greater significance, it mandated that the president submit an annual budget and set up the Bureau of the Budget within the Treasury Department to assist in this endeavor. Agencies could no longer submit requests for funds directly to the Congress; they now had to go through the president, who would formulate a comprehensive federal budget and submit it to Congress.

It is important to note, as Schick does, that "Congress did not adopt the proposal that it bar itself from appropriating more than the amounts recommended in the president's budget." It thus reserved a great deal of power for itself. But the president now had the ability to set the agenda through the comprehensive budget, with Congress in a reactive posture. Agencies submitting requests to the president would have to justify them in terms of the budgetary guidelines received from the Bureau of the Budget, which would act as agent for the president. The policies of the president could determine what went into the budget, which agency requests would be allowed and which not, and the like. The budget the president submitted would give him the opportunity to state a framework for federal policy and action.

At first, the system did not cause stress between the president and Congress. As Schick says, "The president willingly served Congress because his interests were closer to those of the legislative branch than to those of the executive agencies. No less than Congress, the White House felt helpless in the face of agency expansion." However, the situation grew more complex with the rapid expansion of the government accompanying the New Deal and World War II. The president, Schick notes, became "chief executive in his own right, not merely as the agent of Congress." President Roosevelt was in many ways a master of relationships with the Congress, but, as Sidney Miklis provocatively argues, "the Roosevelt administration deliberately rejected the doctrine of responsible party government, requiring stronger linkages between the President and Congress, and adopted instead a program dedicated to executive responsibility, in which a refurbished presidency would be delegated responsibility to govern."

The Roosevelt administration aggressively pursued increased presidential influence. The Bureau of the Budget was moved from the Treasury and became the keystone of the newly established Executive Office of the President. Its staff was expanded. It became the agency for "legislative clearance." Roosevelt shaped what was inherent in the original budget act of 1921 and added to it so that the president now had primacy in setting the government's agenda in fact as well as in form, with the budget as the key statement of presidential policy.

Congress acceded to all this, but of course retained its own vigorous institutions for authorizing programs, reviewing budget proposals, and appropriating money. Increasingly uneasy about the flow of budgetary power (and policy influence) to the presidency by the close of the war, Congress passed the Legislative Reorganization Act in 1946. Among other goals, the act sought to reorganize the budgetary process. Not too surprisingly, the reorganization was sufficiently weak and ineffective that it quickly failed. As Schick notes, one provision of the act, Section 138, "provided that the members of the House and Senate Appropriations and the tax committees were to constitute a joint committee each year and recommend a legislative budget. [Yet], Section 138 did not provide for a permanent budget committee or staff; nor did it provide a means for enforcing the legislative budget." Abandoned after unsuccessful attempts to implement it in 1947 and 1948, Congress tried a more modest approach to the legislative budget in 1950. This, too, was discarded, as the Appropriations subcommittees worried that consolidating all appropriations into a single bill would centralize power in the full committee.

The next major attempt by Congress to reform the budget process came in reaction to the "administrative presidency" strategy of Richard Nixon. Nixon, as Richard Nathan points out in *The Plot That Failed: Nixon and the Administrative Presidency* (1975), gave up trying to make his mark through legislation passed by the Congress and instead sought to rule through administrative mechanisms. He had a four-pronged strategy which consisted of (1) appointing presidential "loyalists" who had no independent standing and therefore could be manipulated and, if necessary, dismissed at will to high-level positions in the agencies; (2) using presidential reorganization powers to downgrade or eliminate programs the White House opposed; (3) writing regulations in a manner to further presidential objectives regardless of the views of Congress or, for that matter, the manifest intent of the relevant statutes; and (4) impounding funds appropriated by Congress as a means to undermine programs the president did not want.

Impoundment had been used by presidents as far back as Jefferson, but only occasionally and under informal rules which preserved an important congressional voice. Congress, especially the relevant committees, was consulted. Funds were usually released when they could be spent in a useful or effective manner. Nixon's impoundments were aggressive challenges to Congress. He argued that chronic budget deficits and the declining economic situation in the country were a result of undisciplined behavior by Congress and that only the president, acting alone if necessary, could bring coherence to federal policy and put the country on the right path.

Congress reacted forcefully. It passed the Congressional Budget Act of 1974, which put strict limits on what a president can do when he does not wish to spend money appropriated by Congress. In addition, the act gave Congress new powers and responsibilities in the budget process. It established budget committees in both houses and charged them with developing a congressional budget. (Previously the president proposed a budget under authority granted by the 1921 budget act and Congress acted on the proposal it received through decisions recommended by individual committees.) The new budget committees were to recommend revenue and expenditure targets for the budget as a whole and to allocate targets to the relevant committees in each chamber. A scorekeeping system was set up so that Congress would know whether or not the targets were being met, and a process established to allow Congress to "reconcile" the amounts spent and revenues raised with the ceilings set by the congressional budget resolution.

Of special note is the fact that the congressional budget resolution mandated by the 1974 budget act is a concurrent resolution passed by both houses. It does not require the signature of the president. In short, the law positions Congress to play a role parallel to the president in the budget process.

One of the most important changes brought about by the 1974 act was the establishment of the Congressional Budget Office (CBO), a congressional staff arm which provided Congress with a body of experts to counter the president's staff in the Office of Management and Budget (the old Bureau of the Budget, renamed and reorganized under the Nixon administration, and now commonly known as OMB). CBO has emerged as the most respected source of budget information and analysis in Washington. High professional standards were set by CBO's initial director, Alice Rivlin, while OMB suffered a decline in its reputation due to its tendency since Nixon to serve the interests of particular presidents rather than the institutional interests of the presidency. OMB's budget projections, for example, were often done with an eye to serving the political needs of the president.

However successful the new budget process may have been in improving the balance between presidential and congressional power in budgeting, it did not solve the nation's deficit problem and indeed has more often than not failed to yield a completed budget. In fact, according to David Kettl, "With a more even balance [between the president and Congress] . . . it became harder to pass any budget at all. Since passage of the Budget Act in 1974, Congress completed all of its work on the budget only twice, for the 1977 and 1989 budgets. In most other years, the process became entangled in conflict."

One can argue that the conflict Kettl describes is due at least as much to intense disagreements about public policy in an era of divided government as it is to the new process, and it has clearly been the case that, as Louis Fisher states, "multiple budgets have opened the door to escapism, confusion, and a loss of political accountability." But it is also true that Congress, much in accord with the Dodd thesis on the flawed nature of congressional reform efforts, designed the budget reform so that it would not do too much damage to the opportunities individuals and preexisting committees had to get what they wanted. In doing so, the act restricted the budgeting power of Congress as a collective institution. As a result, the effectiveness of the act was necessarily limited and opportunities were provided by the nature of the reform's convoluted design for a resurgence of presidential influence in budgeting.

What the Congressional Budget and Impoundment Control Act of 1974 did was to build a new process and create new organizations to implement that process, while at the same time leaving the existing structures and processes in place. Congress did not abolish the existing revenue and appropriations committees, for example. It left the House Ways and Means Committee, the Senate Finance Committee, and the House and Senate Appropriations committees as major actors. In fact, to ensure that the new Budget Committee in the House did not threaten the existing committees too much, the act provided that the House Budget Committee would have five members from the Appropriations Committee and five from the Ways and Means Committee and fifteen (later seventeen) members of other House committees. In addition, as Smith and Deering note, "Each member's service was limited to four years out of any ten-year period, a limit that was extended to six years in 1979. Consequently, Budget members [in the House] do not have the opportunity to develop long-term chamber influence by virtue of membership on the committee or the prestige that might come from that influence." The same membership and service limitations do not apply in the Senate, but it shares with its House counterpart the need to deal with the existing revenue and appropriations committees, a lack of jurisdiction over programs, and the disadvantages, due to the congressional budget process's high level of aggregation, of not being able to take much positive action on behalf of constituents or colleagues.

The verdict is not yet in on the change in the budget process since 1974, but Kettl's summary statement is probably fair: "With authorizations made for longer periods, appropriations covering less of the budget, and budget resolutions rendered meaningless by last-minute summits, congressional budgeting is scarcely a textbook example of an ordered process." Kettl pithily describes the process as a "simultaneous centralization and decentralization" by which he means the following: the influence of congressional leaders has been increased through their important role in the summits frequently used to reach budget agreements, yet, at the same time, with the shrinking of funds available for discretionary spending, the power of the appropriations committees has been enhanced by their control over the little that remains, and "the increasing violation of Congress's budget schedule has weakened the budget committees."

As of the last decade of the twentieth century, Congress has "reformed" the budget process and regained some of the influence it had before the flowering of executive budgeting power brought about by the Budget and Accounting Act of 1921 and the administrative mechanism of Richard Nixon. But weaknesses in the budgetary process emerging from the reform that ultimately derive from the reticence of a member-centered legislative body to yield too much authority to central leaders make the future level of influence of Congress in this area uncertain. The Constitution ensures that Congress will always be important in budgeting, but problems built into the reformed process ultimately invite a renewed presidential challenge.

CONGRESSIONAL OVERSIGHT OF THE EXECUTIVE

Congressional review of the actions of federal departments, agencies, and commissions, and of the programs and policies they administer—congressional oversight in Washington jargon—was not a major concern prior to the emergence of a powerful government in the United States. As the dominant branch of administration for much of the nineteenth century, Congress initiated and drafted most legislation. Allen Schick notes the extent of its involvement as follows: "Individual positions and their salaries were itemized in law; post roads were plotted by Congress; tariff schedules were enacted for hundreds of imported goods; pensions were voted for designated soldiers and their survivors." Indeed, Woodrow

Wilson, in *Congressional Government*, charged Congress with entering "more and more into the details of administration until it has virtually taken into its own hands all the substantial powers of government."

However, it became increasingly difficult for Congress to control policy and administration as the government began to grow in the second half of the nineteenth century (200,000 civilian employees were added between 1861 and 1901, according to James Q. Wilson's classic essay "The Rise of the Bureaucratic State," and only 52 percent of them were in the postal service, heretofore the major source of growth in federal employment), and especially when growth continued at a rapid rate in the first part of the twentieth century (federal civilian employment was nearly half a million by 1925). While it certainly is true that Congress became more "institutionalized" during this period (and along with the increased tenure in office that marked this institutionalization came increased policy expertise), the scope of Congress's control tasks eventually overwhelmed the legislative body.

After ceding much of its influence over the bureaucracy to the president in the Budget and Accounting Act of 1921, Congress worked cooperatively with Republican presidents of the 1920s in a mutually satisfactory effort to control the bureaucracy. But the election of Franklin D. Roosevelt and the expansion of U.S. government brought about by the New Deal and World War II eventually put great stress on the relatively tranquil congressional-executive relationship that existed in the twenties. Roosevelt shaped modern government and the office of the presidency in ways redistributing power between the branches in a manner clearly favoring the president. Indeed, after discussing the increase in the size of government under Roosevelt (a doubling of federal employees from the start of the New Deal to the beginning of World War II and a further expansion during the war) and the successful effort to build up an Office of the President capable of formulating and executing national policy, Schick states, "The president gained more than the institutional wherewithal to conduct the business of government; no longer was presidential leadership seen as a usurpation of congressional power but as an appropriate and expected role."

Many in Congress chafed under this new regime. Efforts to redress the balance began soon after the war with the passage of the Legislative Reorganization Act of 1946. The act rationalized the jurisdictions of congressional committees and reduced their numbers, provided additional staff to the standing committees of Congress so that they would be in a better position vis-à-vis the executive branch, and mandated "continuous watchfulness" over the executive agencies by congressional committees. Roger Davidson and Walter Oleszek, in *Congress against Itself* (1977), describe the assumptions and goals of the reforms as follows: "The reformers of 1936 believed that strengthening the committee system strengthened Congress itself. That was necessary because congressmen were concerned about the growing power of the executive branch and recognized the imperative of reestablishing Congress' role as a coequal branch of government."

Consolidating and strengthening the committees, however, failed to solve, indeed even exacerbated, a host of problems in the Congress. Since senior southern (and usually conservative) Democrats chaired most of the committees, younger and more liberal members were dissatisfied with their opportunities to influence policy. Chairs were able to control what legislation reached the floor (with the conservative Rules Committee in the House as another hurdle for progressive legislation that did get through). The nature and extent of committee reviews of what went on in the executive branch was largely determined by the whims of committee chairs. In the view of many, inside Congress and out, the most parochial members had control of what Congress did or, equally important, did not, do.

Scholars who studied congressional oversight of the executive in the period after the Legislative Reorganization Act of 1946, especially those who held the dominant view of the day that extensive congressional review would interfere with the activities of the nationally elected (and therefore less parochial) president and the administration he should control, were leery of increased congressional oversight. They felt that neither the president nor even administrators should be too encumbered because they represent the public interest far better than the narrow, insulated Congress with its rigid, unrepresentative committee structure and its parochial makeup. This perspective did not deny an oversight role for the Congress—indeed one scholar of the period, Joseph P. Harris, went so far as to suggest that Congress's parochial nature made it fit for little else—but it emphasized that Congress "should not become excessive or encroach upon the executive function."

The excesses of Senator Joseph McCarthy's investigations of the State Department and the army during the communist scare days of the early 1950s made this view seem perfectly reasonable. Indeed, as a result, reasonable people worried that any increase in congressional oversight capabilities could pose a threat to liberal democracy, one that went beyond the inconveniences to administration which congressional investigations—with their tendencies to irresponsible headline seeking, attention to particularistic concerns, and the like—might ordinarily be expected to cause.

The 1960s, however, saw the rise of a different set of concerns. Events of this decade increased the interest of members on both sides of the aisle in a more active oversight role for Congress. The programs of the Great Society increased the scope of government (and the import of the president and the executive branch), directly stimulating the concern of many Republicans that Congress should be a more frequent and vigorous overseer. As the Vietnam War increased in intensity and cost, and as public approval of it fell, Democrats were also more and more concerned about spending priorities and, like Republicans, sensitive to criticisms of Great Society programs. President Johnson's deceptiveness about the war also made Congress more and more suspicious of him, and increasingly sensitive to the growth of what came to be called the "imperial presidency." The effect was to reawaken concern about Congress's role in government. This concern was further stimulated by the actions of President Richard M. Nixon who, lacking a majority in Congress, eventually devised his "administrative presidency" strategy. Nixon impounded funds, harassed civil servants in programs favored by congressional committees, and prosecuted the Vietnam War as he saw fit, essentially ignoring Congress when it would not do what he wished.

One of Congress's responses to these challenges was to press itself to do more oversight. The 1970 amendments to the Legislative Reorganization Act contained a set of provisions designed to encourage oversight: most committees were required to issue biennial reports on their oversight activities; standing committees were authorized to employ additional staff so that they could more effectively monitor executive branch activities; the Congressional Research Service of the Library of Congress was strengthened and the General Accounting Office was given formal authority to do program evaluation. In 1974 the House made additional changes to spur oversight and also made an enfeebled attempt to coordinate committee oversight plans. Senate concern to strengthen oversight was apparent in the work of the Commission on the Operation of the Senate which reported in 1976 and in activities connected to "Sunset" legislation which would have mandated periodic review of programs by Congress.

A recent study documented the hearing and meeting activity of congressional committees for the first six months of each odd-numbered year from 1961 to 1983, years when concerns about oversight as Congress's "neglected function" were clearly articulated and which witnessed heightened levels of congressional conflict with the president as well as a dizzying array of internal congressional reforms. A simple analysis of data on the aggregate number of "days" congressional committees spent on oversight reveals a rather clear picture. The average number of days of hearings and meetings committees devoted to oversight during the first six months of each year in the period from 1961 to 1965 was 149, rising to 192 in the years from 1967 to 1971, 290 in 1973, and 587 in 1983. In short, there was a marked but modest increase in oversight activity evident in the data starting in 1967. This was followed by larger increases in 1973 (to 290 days) and 1975 (to 459 days). The average from 1975 on was 477 days of oversight by congressional committees in the first six months of each year, more than three times the 1961–1965 average. Oversight started to climb in 1967 when tension between President Johnson and Congress heightened. It then took off in the seventies as the struggle between President Nixon and Congress intensified and as Congress, ever more conscious of real and potential threats to its influence over the executive branch and of public discontent with government, made significant internal changes to encourage oversight.

Among other things, what Congress did internally was to increase staff resources and decentralize committee decision making, thereby making subcommittees more autonomous than before. This proved especially important for oversight because subcommittee chairs and staff have greater time, opportunity, and incentive to build expertise—and, therefore, to seek out information aggressively about the executive branch—in their narrow areas of jurisdiction than full committee personnel do. There was no corresponding increase, however, in the coordination of congressional oversight activity. Congressional committees now "speak" much more often to the executive than they did in the era prior to the increase in oversight and they often speak quite forcefully (especially in defense of favored programs within their jurisdictions), but they do not necessarily speak with one voice or even in one language. And there lies another illustration of the problems of the late-twentieth-century Congress.

To take one example, the House's Select Committee on Committees (known as the Bolling Committee, after its chair) was established in the 93d Congress (1973) to evaluate the committee system then in operation and propose reforms. One change suggested was to have an oversight agenda coordinated by the leadership. Fear of centralized control and all that might go with it led to the watered-down version actually adopted that required each House committee to draw up an oversight plan at the beginning of each Congress, with the Government Operations Committee (a major oversight unit in the House) to play a role in coordinating the plans. The Government Operations Committee, for fear of treading on the toes of other committees, did nothing more than compile the documents given to it. Whatever is left of the responsibility for coordination now rests with the Committee on House Administration which reviews committee budget requests.

Another example, this one drawn from the Senate, was the Sunset proposal that Congress place a termination date on authorizing statutes so that it is forced to review programs and agencies periodically. Sunset reached its high point in 1978 when the Senate passed a version of it prior to adjournment, secure in the knowledge that it would die since the House would not act before the end of the session. What was most interesting for our purposes about the debate over Sunset was the strong opposition to a proposal put forward by Senator Edmund Muskie of Maine. Muskie was the chair of the subcommittee of the Senate Governmental Affairs Committee which had jurisdiction over the Sunset bill, but he also served as Chair of the Senate Budget Committee at the time. Muskie proposed that Congress reauthorize programs and activities on the basis of groupings by budget functions and subfunctions. If done this way, Congress could then have examined and compared federal programs in an entire functional area rather than piecemeal. This would have increased the power potential of the Budget committees in each House since all programs in each budget function would then have been subject to meaningful comparative examination and would therefore have been more vulnerable to possible consolidation or even termination. Had Muskie's proposal been enacted, the Budget committees could have acted more effectively as central arms to coordinate programs and policy, an uninviting prospect to many members of Congress.

The Sunset case is an illustration of the fact that the more a reform opens the possibility of centralized control of the oversight agenda and the more comprehensive the reviews it encourages, the more resistance it is likely to meet in Congress. Members of Congress want the institution to be powerful, especially when faced by outside threats, but members want to surrender as little of their own power as possible to facilitate this.

MAKING WAR

As in many other areas, the Constitution is not entirely clear on the power to make war. Congress is given power to "declare war," "raise and support armies," and "provide and maintain a navy" (Article I), but the president is named "commander in chief" in Article II. For the most part, the latter authority has given presidents a distinct advantage in war making throughout our history, and particularly in the second half of the twentieth century when there have been no formal declarations of war and modern technology has made it possible for presidents to deploy forces with great rapidity.

Robert Katzmann points out in "War Powers: Toward a New Accommodation" (1990) that presidents have regularly committed U.S. military forces to combat without a declaration of war by Congress. In fact, as he notes, Congress has declared war only four times—the War of 1812, the Spanish-American War, World War I, and World War II—and passed a joint resolution to authorize a fifth (the Mexican-American War). Decisions to go to war, he concludes quite convincingly, has been an area dominated by the executive branch.

The Vietnam War was a watershed event in the ongoing debate over war powers. Acting on reports from President Johnson about aggressive action by North Vietnam against American naval forces, Congress adopted the Tonkin Gulf resolution in 1964. James Sundquist describes the resolution and its complex politics in his *Constitutional Reform and Effective Government* (1992):

> The resolution was broad enough to authorize a full-scale war in alliance with South Vietnam, but Johnson had assured leading legislators that he had no such intention. When, within three years, Johnson had cited the resolution as authority for plunging half a million American troops into Southeast Asia, many of those who had voted for the resolution felt betrayed, particularly J. William Fulbright, who as chairman of the Foreign Relations Committee had pushed the resolution through the Senate. And they felt doubly so when Fulbright's committee developed evidence that Johnson had misrepresented the facts about the Gulf of Tonkin incident, that perhaps the United States had actually provoked the encounter to provide grounds for seeking the congressional action.

Tensions created by these feelings of betrayal were exacerbated by comments made by administration officials in subsequent congressional hearings. Under Secretary of State Nicholas deB. Katzenbach, for example, told the Foreign Relations Committee in 1967 that "the expression of declaring a war is one that has become outmoded in the international arena." When Richard Nixon, Johnson's successor as president, continued to prosecute the war, particularly after opposition in both Congress and the country had increased significantly beyond the level that existed during the Johnson administration, sentiment within Congress crystallized around the need for some formal mechanism to limit presidential war powers.

The House and Senate were deadlocked about what to do, with the House generally taking a less assertive view of congressional powers when it came to war making. President Nixon, his own worst enemy in this as in so many other instances, finally provoked passage of the War Powers Resolution of 1973 with his decision to bomb Hanoi, the capital of North Vietnam, in December of 1972, coupled with his continued bombing of Cambodia after March of 1973 when all U.S. troops had been withdrawn from South Vietnam and the American role in the war seemed to most everyone finally to be at an end. As James Sundquist notes in his excellent treatment of the subject, *The Decline and Resurgence of Congress* (1981):

> The undeclared presidential war in Cambodia provided a realistic backdrop for renewed consideration of the War Powers Resolution. No one could say that the Congress had acquiesced in the bombing of that small, remote country. By May, both houses had explicitly rejected it. Yet it went on. It was plain, as Senator Javits had said on introducing his bill in January, that for the Congress to rely solely on its powers to cut off funds was unsatisfactory, that the power of the purse was a "clumsy, blunt, and obsolescent tool."

The War Powers Resolution was enacted over President Nixon's veto in November 1973. Nixon by this time was severely weakened by Watergate and subsequent events. However, Sundquist (1992) points out, because of continued House opposition to specifying precisely the circumstances under which the president "could order the armed forces into hostilities without prior approval by the Congress, . . . the Senate's proposed restrictions [such as specific statutory authorization or an emergency caused by attack upon the United States or its forces] were made advisory." The resolution, as passed, says that the president has to consult with Congress, whenever possible, prior to sending troops into situations where hostilities are ongoing or imminent, report to Congress in writing within forty-eight hours after the commitment of troops, and withdraw the troops within ninety days if Congress does not grant specific authorization for their continued presence within sixty days after the report is submitted or required to be submitted.

With one exception (President Ford who appeared to accept the War Powers Resolution in reporting to Congress on the *Mayaguez* incident of 1975), presidents subsequent to Nixon have complied with the reporting requirements of the resolution (twenty times from 1973 to the spring of 1993) without acknowledging a legal obligation to do so. And Congress has never required withdrawal of troops under the resolution. It is, therefore, not surprising that many take the view that the War Powers Resolution has not been a great success. As Robert Katzmann notes, "Presidents have refused to invoke the law in ways that could limit their freedom of action; indeed, they have not even conceded its constitutionality. Congress, for its part, has been reluctant to challenge the president." And, as Katzmann also observes, "it would be hard to make the case that the War Powers Resolution has deterred chief executives bent on engaging troops."

Yet the reporting requirements of the War Powers Resolution have been grudgingly adhered to and the resolution itself has been a symbol of congressional assertiveness and probably has made presidents at least somewhat more cautious than before in committing U.S. troops. In the case of Desert Storm in 1991, for example, although President Bush had a UN Resolution (678) to support a decision to go to war with Iraq after 15 January, it was considered politically risky to do so without congressional authorization. Congress solved the problem by voting to authorize use of U.S. forces pursuant to the UN resolution. As with budgeting and oversight, Congress may not have done as much as it could—in the case of the War Powers Resolution because of the great advantages enjoyed by presidents in foreign affairs, particularly when it comes to war powers, and the great reluctance of many members of Congress to run the risks of second-guessing the president in the early days of a deployment of American troops—but Congress almost certainly is in a stronger position today than it was before the reforms of the 1970s.

WHO CONGRESS REPRESENTS AND HOW IT IS ORGANIZED

In a well-known article published in 1965, Samuel P. Huntington argued that "during the twentieth century Congress gradually insulated itself from the new political forces which social change had generated and which were, in turn, generating more change. Hence the leadership of Congress lacked the incentive to take the legislative initiative in handling emerging national problems." Power had become so dispersed among officials, committees, and subcommittees that Congress was incapable of establishing national legislative priorities. The signs of insulation included increasing length of members' tenure in office, the role of seniority in determining who would hold key leadership roles in Congress, and the provincialism of members of Congress who tended to be oriented to local interests and, prior to the Supreme Court decisions in *Baker* v. *Carr* (1962) and *Wesberry* v. *Sanders* (1964), to come disproportionately from districts dominated by rural and small-town interests. The seniority system, Huntington argued, would mean that the leadership of Congress would be unrepresentative for years to come after the Court decisions of the early 1960s mentioned above. Huntington did not mention the race or sex of those in Congress when he talked about representativeness, but the Congress of the mid-sixties had very few women and only a small number of people from the nation's racial minorities.

There is little doubt that the Congress of 1965, the year Huntington's article was published, did not look much like the population of the United States. However, big changes were in the offing. The Voting Rights Act of 1965, the many social and political movements that were in part stimulated by the civil rights movement of the late fifties and sixties as well as by the political turbulence that surrounded the Johnson and Nixon administrations, the tide of immigrants sweeping into the nation in the latter part of the twentieth century, the movement of population to the Sunbelt, and the impact of Supreme Court decisions on districting had a profound effect on Congress.

Since passage of the Voting Rights Act in 1965, there has been a striking increase in the number of black members of the House of Representatives. As late as the 90th Congress in 1967, there were but five African Americans in the House (1.1 percent of the membership). By 1993, the 103d Congress, there were thirty-eight black representatives (8.7 percent of the membership) (table 1). And, significantly, sixteen of these members were from the eleven states of the Old Confederacy and an additional four from Border States. The 103d Congress also had nineteen Hispanics (including two delegates), a Native American and two Asians in the Senate, and seven Asians and Pacific Islanders in the House.

Changes in the number of women in Congress is equally impressive (table 2). In 1965, the year Huntington's essay was published, 2.5 percent (eleven) of the representatives were women. After the 1992 election, the figure stood at 11 percent (forty-eight members)—more than a four-fold increase. There were also six female senators following the 1993 election.

The profile of religious affiliation among members of the House of Representatives and the Senate has also changed over the years (tables 3 and 4). The number of Roman Catholic representatives rose from 87 (overwhelmingly Democrats) in 1963 to 118 in 1993, with most of the increase in the number of Republicans. In the Senate, the number of Roman Catholics rose from eleven in 1963 (ten of whom were Democrats) to twenty-three in 1993 (less than two-thirds Democrats). There were but nine Jewish members of the House in 1963, rising to thirty-two in 1993. There were two Jewish Senators in 1963 and ten in 1993. The most notable decline over time is in the number of Methodists and Presbyterians.

In brief, the Congress elected by the people of the United States in November 1992 (which met for the first time in January 1993) may not have been perfectly representative of the American public in demographic terms, but it was a far cry from the insulated Congress of the 1960s and before. It is a fair guess that, if one could have gathered them together for the occasion, the average member of the 89th Congress (seated in 1965) would have been amazed by a quick look at the members of the 103d Congress on their first day in session in 1993.

Not only has the demography of Congress undergone a change over time, but the regional composition of the House and the size and nature of the party delegations in both houses have also changed. The South gained seats steadily, starting with the 1970 census, and after the 1990 census had 125 seats, close to 30 percent of the total. (It had 104 seats, roughly 24 percent of the total, in 1960.) The Pacific Coast also gained, going from twenty-one in 1924 to sixty-nine in the 1992 election. Losers, particularly since 1960, include the Mid-Atlantic, the Plains, and the Midwest states.

Had the voting pattern of the southern electorate remained unchanged from earlier years of the century, the significance of the gain in the number of southern seats in the House would have been quite different from what the data show (table 5). The combination of many northern Republicans moving to the South and many white southerners changing their voting habits in national elections as blacks started to vote in large numbers after the Voting Rights Act has changed the composition of the

Table 1. BLACKS IN CONGRESS, 41ST–103D CONGRESSES (1869–1993)[a]

	House		Senate	
Congress	D	R	D	R
41st 1869	—	2	—	1
42d 1871	—	5	—	—
43d 1873	—	7	—	—
44th 1875	—	7	—	1
45th 1877	—	3	—	1
46th 1879	—	—	—	1
47th 1881	—	2	—	—
48th 1883	—	2	—	—
49th 1885	—	2	—	—
50th 1887	—	—	—	—
51st 1889	—	3	—	—
52d 1891	—	1	—	—
53d 1893	—	1	—	—
54th 1895	—	1	—	—
55th 1897	—	1	—	—
56th 1899[b]	—	1	—	—
71st 1929	—	1	—	—
72d 1931	—	1	—	—
73d 1933	—	1	—	—
74th 1935	1	—	—	—
75th 1937	1	—	—	—
76th 1939	1	—	—	—
77th 1941	1	—	—	—
78th 1943	1	—	—	—
79th 1945	2	—	—	—
80th 1947	2	—	—	—
81st 1949	2	—	—	—
82d 1951	2	—	—	—
83d 1953	2	—	—	—
84th 1955	3	—	—	—
85th 1957	3	—	—	—
86th 1959	3	—	—	—
87th 1961	3	—	—	—
88th 1963	4	—	—	—
89th 1965	5	—	—	—
90th 1967	5	—	—	1
91st 1969	9	—	—	1
92d 1971	13	—	—	1
93d 1973	16	—	—	1
94th 1975	16	—	—	1
95th 1977	15	—	—	1
96th 1979	15	—	—	—
97th 1981	17	—	—	—
98th 1983	20	—	—	—
99th 1985	20	—	—	—
100th 1987	22	—	—	—
101st 1989	23	—	—	—
102d 1991	25	—	—	—
103d 1993	37	1	1	—

[a] Does not include Eleanor Holmes Norton, a nonvoting delegate who represents Washington, D.C.
[b] After the Fifty-sixth Congress, there were no black members in either the House or Senate until the Seventy-first Congress.
SOURCES: Norman J. Ornstein, Thomas E. Mann, and Michael J. Malbin, *Vital Statistics on Congress: 1991–92* (Congressional Quarterly Press, 1992), table 1-16, p. 38; *Congressional Quarterly Special Report,* 16 January 1993, p. 12.

southern congressional delegations. Where over 90 percent of the House seats in the South were held by Democrats in 1960, the percentage fell to 68.2 percent in 1972 and was down to 61.6 percent after the 1992 election. Figures for the border states are a similar 88.1 percent and 65.6 percent for the respective years. Where once New England was a Republican bastion, in 1992 63.6 percent of its House seats were held by Democrats. In fact, the only region with fewer than 50 percent of its seats held by Democrats in 1992 was the Rocky Mountain region. Where in 1960 the difference between the percentage figures for the region with the highest percentage of seats held by Democrats (the South with 94.2 percent) and the region with the lowest percentage (the Plains States with 16.1 percent) was 78.1, that figure dropped to 19.8 in 1992 (the Border States were high with 65.6 percent and the Rocky Mountain states were low with 45.8 percent).

Similar figures could be run out for the Senate (table 6). Suffice it to say, that where once the South had a solid contingent of Democratic senators (100 percent), by 1992 the percentage had dropped just below 60, lower than that in three—Border, Mid-Atlantic, and Midwest—of the other major regions.

The key fact is that regional differences in the party composition of Congress have waned in the last half of the century, particularly since passage of the Voting Rights Act of 1965. This means that the significance of the gain in House seats by the South is much different than it would have been had blacks not started to participate in large numbers. Rather than increased domination of the House Democratic party by southerners, there has actually been a decrease in southern Democrats. (Southern Democrats were 37.5 percent of all House Democrats in 1960. This percentage was down to 29.7 in 1992, even with the larger southern delegation.)

And the political leanings of the southern Democrats are different from what they once were. A study by Kenny J. Whitby and Franklin D. Gilliam analyzing the voting behavior of white southern members

Table 2. WOMEN IN CONGRESS, 65TH–103D CONGRESSES (1917–1993)[a]

Congress		House D	House R	Senate D	Senate R	Congress		House D	House R	Senate D	Senate R
65th	1917	—	1	—	—	84th	1955	10	7	—	1
66th	1919	—	—	—	—	85th	1957	9	6	—	1
67th	1921	—	2	—	1	86th	1959	9	8	—	1
68th	1923	—	1	—	—	87th	1961	11	7	1	1
69th	1925	1	2	—	—	88th	1963	6	6	1	1
70th	1927	2	3	—	—	89th	1965	7	4	1	1
71st	1929	4	5	—	—	90th	1967	5	5	—	1
72d	1931	4	3	1	—	91st	1969	6	4	—	1
73d	1933	4	3	1	—	92d	1971	10	3	—	1
74th	1935	4	2	2	—	93d	1973	14	2	1	—
75th	1937	4	1	2	—	94th	1975	14	5	—	—
76th	1939	4	4	1	—	95th	1977	13	5	—	—
77th	1941	4	5	1	—	96th	1979	11	5	1	1
78th	1943	2	6	1	—	97th	1981	10	9	—	2
79th	1945	6	5	—	—	98th	1983	13	9	—	2
80th	1947	3	4	—	1	99th	1985	13	9	—	2
81st	1949	5	4	—	1	100th	1987	12[b]	11	1	1
82d	1951	4	6	—	1	101st	1989	14	11	1	1
83d	1953	5	7	—	1	102d	1991	19	9	1	1
						103d	1993	37	11	5	1

[a] Includes only women who were sworn in as members and served more than one day.
[b] Includes Sala Burton, who died after being sworn into the 100th Congress, and who was replaced by another Democratic woman, Nancy Pelosi.
SOURCES: Norman J. Ornstein, Thomas E. Mann, and Michael J. Malbin, *Vital Statistics on Congress: 1991–92* (Congressional Quarterly Press, 1992), table 1-17, p. 39; *Congressional Quarterly Special Report,* 16 January 1993, p. 12.

of the House from the 91st (1969) to the 100th (1987) Congresses found fundamentally altered policy preferences. Incumbents had become more liberal over time, and newly elected southern Democrats were more liberal than their predecessors, changing congressional voting patterns in a profound way. In a similar vein, Kenneth Shepsle describes what he calls the "Northernization of the South" in his provocative piece on the changing Congress of the modern period. "Not only," he says, "did southern representation among Democrats decline numerically, but also the behavior of southern legislators became less distinctively southern." Citing figures from a study by David W. Rohde, he presents the following summary comparison of the behavior of northern and southern Democrats in Congress:

> Consider first their party loyalty. Between 1969 and 1973 the average difference between northern and southern Democrats on *Congressional Quarterly* party unity scores was 36 percentage points; northerners voted with the Democratic majority 84 percent of the time, southerners 48 percent of the time. Between 1975 and 1979 the difference shrank to 27 points and between 1981 and 1985 to 21 points; the difference fell to 14 points in 1986, when southern Democrats voted with their party 76 percent of the time. Between 1969 and 1986 southern party loyalty had increased 34 percentage points, whereas the northern increase was only 5 points.

The increase in partisanship in Congress, especially the House, has gone so far that some are concerned about its impact on Congress as an institution. Thomas Mann and Norman Ornstein, two noted scholars based in Washington, for example, said in testimony delivered to the Joint Committee on the Organization of Congress in February of 1993 that the ideological consolidation within the parties due to such developments as the rise of the Republican party in the South "has reduced the incidence of cross-party coalitions in committees and on the floor, thereby diminishing opportunities for minority party members to leave an imprint on legislation." They worry that "Congress today suffers from an intense and destructive partisanship, especially in the House, that discredits the institution in the eyes of the public and diminishes the quality of life within it."

Huntington's 1965 essay emphasized the dispersion of power within Congress, a feature of Congress that has been much affected by reforms put into place since he wrote. The 1970s, in particular, saw an upheaval in the rules of the House—changes in the

Table 3. RELIGIOUS AFFILIATIONS OF REPRESENTATIVES, 88TH–103D CONGRESSES (1963–1993)

	88th (1963)			89th (1965)			90th (1967)			91st (1969)			92d (1971)		
Affiliation	D	R	Total	D	R	Total	D	R	Total	D	R	Total	D	R	Total
Catholic	72	15	87	81	13	94	73	22	95	72	24	96	77	24	101
Jewish	8	1	9	14	1	15	14	2	16	15	2	17	10	2	12
Protestant															
Baptist	38	10	48	33	9	42	30	12	42	30	13	43	32	10	42
Episcopal	23	22	45	29	25	54	25	25	50	22	27	49	27	22	49
Methodist	48	30	78	46	23	69	37	32	69	34	32	66	33	32	65
Presbyterian	28	40	68	30	26	56	27	37	64	26	38	64	26	41	67
All other	41	58	99	62	43	105	43	54	97	44	56	100	49	49	98
Total	258	176	434	295	140	435	249	184	433	243	192	435	254	180	434

	93d (1973)			94th (1975)			95th (1977)			96th (1979)			97th (1981)		
Affiliation	D	R	Total	D	R	Total	D	R	Total	D	R	Total	D	R	Total
Catholic	69	30	99	88	22	110	95	24	119	93	23	116	81	38	119
Jewish	10	2	12	17	3	20	20	3	23	18	5	23	21	6	27
Protestant															
Baptist	33	12	45	37	10	47	36	10	46	33	10	43	28	13	41
Episcopal	25	25	50	29	21	50	26	22	48	29	22	51	25	27	52
Methodist	30	33	63	40	23	63	36	24	60	32	26	58	26	30	56
Presbyterian	25	35	60	25	25	50	23	22	45	25	27	52	18	28	46
All other	50	55	105	55	40	95	56	38	94	47	45	92	44	50	94
Total	242	192	434	291	144	435	292	143	435	277	158	435	243	192	435

	98th (1983)			99th (1985)			101st (1989)			102d (1991)			103d (1993)		
Affiliation	D	R	Total	D	R	Total	D	R	Total	D	R	Total	D	R	Total
Catholic	87	37	124	82	43	125	81	39	120	85	37	122	77	41	118
Jewish	24	5	29	24	6	30	26	5	31	26	6	33[a]	26	5	32[a]
Protestant															
Baptist	30	8	38	27	9	36	33	10	43	35	12	47	38	13	51
Episcopal	23	19	42	22	22	44	22	21	43	24	17	41	18	17	35
Methodist	35	22	57	35	27	62	38	25	63	38	24	62	31	23	54
Presbyterian	24	25	49	22	25	47	16	26	42	15	27	42	20	26	46
All other	44	49	93	41	50	91	44	49	93	44	44	88			
Total	267	165	432	253	182	435	260	175	435	267	167	435[a]			

[a] Totals include Bernard Sanders, Independent-Vermont.
Party abbreviations: D, Democratic; R, Republican.
SOURCES: Norman J. Ornstein, Thomas E. Mann, and Michael J. Malbin, *Vital Statistics on Congress: 1991–92* (Congressional Quarterly Press, 1992), table 1-14, pp. 34–35; *Congressional Quarterly Special Report,* 16 January 1993, p. 13.

Senate were much more modest—that in many ways made it a different place from the institution that existed in the sixties. These reforms cut in two directions simultaneously: increasing decentralized power through measures to make subcommittees stronger and increasing centralized power through a revival of the Democratic caucus and a strengthening of the leadership. The losers were the full committees and their chairs and those who held positions of power purely as a result of the rigid seniority system previously in place.

The changing membership of Congress chafed under the restrictions of the system built up after the revolt against Speaker Cannon in 1910 and cemented into place by the Legislative Reorganization Act of 1946. They were frustrated by the oligarchs who controlled the committees, perpetuating the political triumphs of the previous generation. As Roger Davidson notes, "In 1973, the average House committee chairman was sixty-six years old and had almost thirty years of congressional service behind him; the average Senate chairman was sixty-four years old and

Table 4. RELIGIOUS AFFILIATIONS OF SENATORS, 88TH–103D CONGRESSES (1963–1993)

	88th (1963)			89th (1965)			90th (1967)			91st (1969)			92d (1971)		
Affiliation	D	R	Total	D	R	Total	D	R	Total	D	R	Total	D	R	Total
Catholic	10	1	11	12	2	14	11	2	13	10	3	13	9	3	12
Jewish	1	1	2	1	1	2	1	1	2	1	1	2	1	1	2
Protestant															
Baptist	10	2	12	9	3	12	7	4	11	6	3	9	5	3	8
Episcopal	7	8	15	8	7	15	8	7	15	5	10	15	4	13	17
Methodist	15	8	23	15	7	22	15	8	23	14	8	22	13	7	20
Presbyterian	7	4	11	8	3	11	8	4	12	8	5	13	10	6	16
All other	17	9	26	15	9	24	14	10	24	14	12	26	13	12	25
Total	67	33	100	68	32	100	64	36	100	58	42	100	55	45	100

	93d (1973)			94th (1975)			95th (1977)			96th (1979)			97th (1981)		
Affiliation	D	R	Total	D	R	Total	D	R	Total	D	R	Total	D	R	Total
Catholic	10	4	14	11	4	15	10	3	13	9	4	13	9	8	17
Jewish	1	1	2	2	1	3	4	1	5	5	2	7	3	3	6
Protestant															
Baptist	5	3	8	6	3	9	6	3	9	6	5	11	3	6	9
Episcopal	6	11	17	6	9	15	6	11	17	5	12	17	5	15	20
Methodist	13	5	18	11	5	16	13	7	20	13	6	19	9	9	18
Presbyterian	8	6	14	10	7	17	9	5	14	10	2	12	8	2	10
All other	15	12	27	15	9	24	14	8	22	11	10	21	10	10	20
Total	58	42	100	61	38	99	62	38	100	59	41	100	47	53	100

	98th (1983)			99th (1985)			101st (1989)			102d (1991)			103d (1993)		
Affiliation	D	R	Total	D	R	Total	D	R	Total	D	R	Total	D	R	Total
Catholic	9	8	17	11	8	19	12	7	19	12	8	20	15	8	23
Jewish	4	4	8	4	4	8	5	3	8	6	2	8	9	1	10
Protestant															
Baptist	4	6	10	4	7	11	4	8	12	4	8	12	4	7	11
Episcopal	4	16	20	4	17	21	7	13	20	6	12	18	4	11	15
Methodist	10	8	18	9	7	16	9	4	13	9	4	13	7	5	12
Presbyterian	8	2	10	8	1	9	7	2	9	7	2	9	5	3	8
All other	7	10	17	7	9	16	11	8	19	11	9	20			
Total	46	54	100	47	53	100	55	45	100	55	45	100			

Party affiliation: D, Democratic; R, Republican.
SOURCES: Norman J. Ornstein, Thomas E. Mann, and Michael J. Malbin, *Vital Statistics on Congress: 1991–92* (Congressional Quarterly Press, 1992), table 1-15, pp. 36–37; *Congressional Quarterly Special Report,* 16 January 1993, p. 13.

had twenty-one years of experience. Not only did such a situation squander talent in the mid-seniority ranks, but it eventually generated frustration and resentment."

Members of the House set about to solve their problem by enacting a series of decentralizing reforms designed to reduce the power of committee chairs and increase the influence of other members. A majority of committee members were empowered to call a meeting if the chair refused, decreasing control by chairs over the agenda. And, beginning in 1971, the House Democratic caucus stipulated that no member could chair more than one legislative subcommittee, providing opportunities for a younger generation of liberal nonsouthern members to become subcommittee chairs. Other innovations included a subcommittee "bill of rights," giving each standing committee's Democratic caucus the authority to select subcommittee chairmen, and the establishment of a more equitable subcommittee assignment process.

Subcommittees were given the right to have their

Table 5. DEMOCRATIC PARTY STRENGTH IN THE HOUSE, BY REGION, 1924–1992*

Region	1924	1936	1948	1960	1972	1978	1980	1982	1984	1986	1988	1990	1992
South													
Percent	97.1	98.0	98.1	94.2	68.2	71.3	64.5	71.2	62.9	66.4	66.4	66.4	61.6
Seats	104	101	105	104	107	108	107	116	116	116	116	116	125
Border													
Percent	58.7	95.2	88.1	84.2	77.1	77.1	67.6	76.4	73.5	67.6	67.6	67.6	65.6
Seats	46	42	42	38	35	35	34	34	34	34	34	34	32
New England													
Percent	12.5	44.8	39.3	50.0	64.0	72.0	64.0	66.6	58.3	62.5	58.3	69.6	63.6
Seats	32	29	28	28	25	25	25	24	24	24	24	23[a]	22[a]
Mid-Atlantic													
Percent	26.7	68.0	48.9	49.4	53.8	63.8	53.8	58.3	56.9	56.9	58.3	56.9	54.5
Seats	90[b]	94	92[c]	87	80	80	80	72	72	72	72	72	66
Midwest													
Percent	16.9	78.3	43.7	40.7	38.4	55.3	51.2	55.0	56.2	57.5	58.8	61.2	58.1
Seats	83[d]	83[e]	87	86	86	85	84	80	80	80	80	80	74
Plains													
Percent	15.4	44.8	16.1	19.4	33.3	40.0	36.0	54.2	45.8	45.8	50.0	54.2	54.5
Seats	39[f]	29[g]	31	31	24	25	25	24	24	24	24	24	22
Rocky Mountain													
Percent	28.6	93.3	75.0	73.3	42.1	47.4	36.8	33.3	29.2	37.5	37.5	45.8	45.8
Seats	14	15	16	15	19	19	19	24	24	24	24	24	24
Pacific Coast													
Percent	19.0	80.0	37.1	51.2	57.9	66.1	56.1	62.3	60.6	59.0	59.0	60.6	63.8
Seats	21	30[h]	35	43	57	56	57	61	61	61	61	61	69

* Numbers refer to the Congress that followed the election. Number of seats is total for all parties in the region (exceptions noted below). Does not include vacant seats. Discrepancy in the number of regional seats before and after 1980 is caused by post-1980 redistricting.

[a] Excludes one seat held by an Independent from Vermont.

[b] Excludes one seat held by a Socialist from New York.

[c] Excludes one seat occupied by a representative from New York who was a member of the American Labor party.

[d] Excludes one seat held by a Socialist from Wisconsin.

[e] Excludes seven seats held by Progressives from Wisconsin.

[f] Excludes two seats occupied by representatives from Minnesota who were members of the Farmer Labor party.

[g] Excludes five seats occupied by representatives from Minnesota who were members of the Farmer Labor party.

[h] Excludes one seat held by a Progressive from California.

SOURCES: Norman J. Ornstein, Thomas E. Mann, and Michael J. Malbin, *Vital Statistics on Congress: 1991–92* (Congressional Quarterly Press, 1992), table 1-2, pp. 10–11; *Congressional Quarterly Special Report,* 7 November 1992, p. 3571 (corrected for California).

own staff. Legislation had to be referred to them. All standing committees, except for the Budget Committee, were required to establish subcommittees—a decision aimed at the powerful House Ways and Means Committee, which did not have them. Committee members were empowered to determine the number and jurisdiction of subcommittees, and the party caucus was given the power to elect committee chairs by secret ballot. In effect, says Kenneth Shepsle, "Full committees and their chairs thus had their wings clipped. A chair was now beholden to the committee caucus, power had devolved upon subcommittees, and standing committees were rapidly becoming holding companies for their subunits."

At the same time that these decentralizing reforms were being enacted, the House was also strengthening its central institutions by increasing the power of the Democratic caucus and the Speaker. Reminiscent of earlier days, the Speaker's role was enlarged with new powers to appoint members of the Rules Committee, the Democratic Committee on Committees, and the whip system. The Speaker could refer bills simultaneously or sequentially to more than one committee, create ad hoc committees, and set time limits for their deliberations. The changes gave the Speaker, and to a degree his colleagues in the leadership (the majority leader and the whip), significant new tools to use in controlling the flow of legislation, making members beholden to the Speaker for their committee assignments, and expediting the passage as well as influencing the shape of legislation.

Table 6. DEMOCRATIC PARTY STRENGTH IN THE SENATE, BY REGION, 1924–1992*

Region	1924	1936	1948	1960	1972	1978	1980	1982	1984	1986	1988	1990	1992
South													
Percent	100.0	100.0	100.0	100.0	68.2	72.7	54.4	50.0	54.5	72.7	68.2	68.2	59.1
Seats	22	22	22	22	22	22	22	22	22	22	22	22	22
Border													
Percent	50.0	100.0	80.0	60.0	50.0	70.0	70.0	70.0	60.0	60.0	60.0	60.0	60.0
Seats	10	10	10	10	10	10	10	10	10	10	10	10	10
New England													
Percent	8.3	50.0	25.0	41.7	58.3	58.3	50.0	50.0	50.0	50.0	58.3	58.3	58.3
Seats	12	12	12	12	12	12	12	12	12	12	12	12	12
Mid-Atlantic													
Percent	37.5	75.0	37.5	25.0	37.5	50.0	50.0	50.0	50.0	50.0	50.0	50.0	62.5
Seats	8	8	8	8	8	8	8	8	8	8	8	8	8
Midwest													
Percent	10.0	88.9	20.0	70.0	60.0	80.0	60.0	60.0	70.0	70.0	70.0	70.0	80.0
Seats	10	9[a]	10	10	10	10	10	10	10	10	10	10	10
Plains													
Percent	0.0	66.7	16.7	25.0	58.3	41.7	25.0	25.0	33.3	50.0	50.0	58.3	58.3
Seats	11[b]	9[c]	12	12	12	12	12	12	12	12	12	12	12
Rocky Mountain													
Percent	50.0	93.8	75.0	75.0	43.8	37.5	31.3	31.3	31.3	37.5	37.5	37.5	37.5
Seats	16	16	16	16	16	16	16	16	16	16	16	16	16
Pacific Coast													
Percent	16.7	50.0	33.3	80.0	60.0	60.0	40.0	40.0	30.0	40.0	40.0	40.0	50.0
Seats	6	6	6	10	10	10	10	10	10	10	10	10	10

* Number of seats is total for all parties in the region (exceptions noted below).
[a] Excludes one Progressive from Wisconsin.
[b] Excludes one senator from Minnesota who was a member of the Farmer Labor party.
[c] Excludes two senators from Minnesota and one senator from Nebraska who were members of the Farmer Labor party.
SOURCES: Norman J. Ornstein, Thomas E. Mann, and Michael J. Malbin, *Vital Statistics on Congress: 1991–92* (Congressional Quarterly Press, 1992), table 1-4, pp. 12–13; *Congressional Quarterly Special Report,* 16 January 1993, p. 175.

The Democrats initially felt that they needed a stronger leadership in the early 1970s to challenge Richard Nixon. The struggles in the eighties between the Democratic House and the administration of Ronald Reagan made a stronger leadership seem even more essential. In addition, the budget deficits of the eighties had a profound impact on congressional politics. Lawrence Dodd and Bruce Oppenheimer (1989) provide an excellent summary of the shift of internal power in Congress in the 1980s:

> Just as subcommittee government was becoming firmly entrenched, the nation elected Ronald Reagan. The president pushed through giant tax cuts without a concomitant reduction in spending, and the country faced massive federal deficits, which blocked new programs and new spending. Seemingly overnight, the rationale for subcommittee government was gone: without money to spend, there was less need for a highly specialized system of subcommittees. Instead of the extensive legislative agenda of the past, the House moved to what many members refer to as the "four bill" system. In an average year there may be only four important domestic legislative vehicles—the budget resolutions, continuing appropriations, supplemental appropriations, and the reconciliation package of spending cuts that the budget dictates. . . . In the new system, [committee] power is concentrated . . . in the membership of a few elite committees, primarily those dealing with money.

The pressures of increasingly severe budget austerity have clearly undermined much of the influence the reforms of the seventies gave to subcommittees, at least when it comes to creating new programs. The leadership, especially in the House, and the money committees have gained influence as Congress has struggled to deal with an unfamiliar situation—an inadequate resource base for government and limited immediate prospects for rectifying the situation. The unanswered question is how stable this situation will be.

Dodd and Oppenheimer argue that "it took fiscal

austerity and the Reagan presidency for the majority party leaders to use fully the powers given them by the reforms [of the 1970s]. While the Reagan revolution undercut the subcommittee reforms, it breathed new life into the powers of the Speaker and party leadership." Barbara Sinclair, a leading contemporary scholar of Congress, takes this argument a step further in her 1992 article on "The Emergence of Strong Leadership in the 1980s House." She says that since "only the party leadership possess the coordination capacity required to put together and pass" legislation centering on questions of basic priorities such as reconciliation bills and budget resolutions, the 1980s political climate encouraged the Democratic committee leaders and members to pull together to pass legislation to advance their goals. And further, she concludes, "only a strong party leadership could provide [the necessary] help."

In addition, Sinclair argues, the costs of strong leadership declined in the 1980s. Democrats in Congress became more homogenous ideologically, and deficits made the differences that did exist among members seem less important since there was less that could be done anyway. What she calls the "freelance policy entrepreneurship" practiced by liberals in the 1970s was much less feasible in the climate of the 1980s.

Sinclair's view is that the increased ideological homogeneity of the Democrats is likely to persist and that most of the institutional changes of the 1970s could well endure for some time. But she also believes that the political environment of the 1980s "which made Democrats badly need their leadership's help to pass legislation may change in the short term." In that event, the decentralizing forces still very much in place (such as subcommittees with the "rights" granted to them in the 1970s and ready access to skilled staff, and entrepreneurial members who must build strong support in their districts for themselves as individuals and pay court to constituency and interest groups for campaign contributions) could fairly quickly undermine the strong leadership that grew up in the eighties. In other words, consistent with the pattern of congressional reform we have seen at other times over this century—incomplete and often inconsistent efforts to centralize power and coordinate policy—even the House, which has made many changes in its formal rules which strengthen the leadership, could easily slip back into a much more decentralized mode of operation if the U.S. economy (or the government's revenue generating system) returns to something like its former robust state.

WHITHER CONGRESS?

A member of Congress at the turn of the century returning to Washington in the early years of the 1990s would find many changes. The members are a much more diverse lot. Women and minorities, literally invisible in the chambers of Congress at the beginning of the century, are now much in evidence. Black Democrats from the South can be seen interacting comfortably with white Democrats from the same region. Race-baiting speeches are unheard of. Rural influence has declined substantially. California now has the largest state delegation, and the regional distribution of representatives in the House reflects massive changes in population distribution.

Likewise, a returning member who had served at mid-century would also find many changes. Committee barons are now a subject for nostalgic discussion among old hands and Congress buffs. The rich and powerful nation that stood poised to lead the free world through the Cold War is still powerful and remains rich by most standards, but its government is deeply in debt and its legislative politics have been much affected by this fact. Leaders, especially in the House, have many more formal powers than they had before, and in both chambers the force of traditional southern conservatism, if not totally spent, is much reduced.

The results of Congress's struggles over the years to find its role in the face of a growing administrative state and of a presidency with vastly greater powers than it enjoyed at the turn of the century would also be apparent. Congress, which had a relative handful of employees in 1900, had more than 23,000 in the late 1980s. "Committee staffing," a definitive work on congressional statistics notes, "has grown steadily since the turn of the century, but the most dramatic increases occurred in the 1970s" as congressional subcommittees proliferated and Congress sought to counter the administrative assertiveness of President Nixon. With the assistance of its large staff, Congress is now a vigorous overseer of the executive branch. It also has a new budget process (enacted in 1974), which is an attempt to make Congress a more significant player in a budget game greatly changed since passage of the Budget and Accounting Act of 1921 and further modified when Richard Nixon sought to expand executive power through aggressive impoundment of appropriated funds in areas where he had policy disagreements with Congress. Congress has asserted itself in foreign policy as well, even attempting to find a greater role for itself with regard to war powers.

All this has taken place against a backdrop of political ambivalence. Members of Congress, career politicians who must secure their own nominations and build sufficient support in their districts to ensure reelection, want an institution strong enough to guarantee the influence and results they need to survive in office and flourish. For this, they want a system that enhances their visibility and importance to the constituents and groups whose support they desire. They are, therefore, reluctant to surrender individual prerogatives much beyond what they believe is necessary to secure the institution against excessive losses of influence to the president.

In a century during which the federal government has become the central focus of a large administrative state—the very reason, of course, that many are drawn to seek election to the House and Senate—Congress has struggled with the often conflicting pressures to provide for its members' individual needs, while maintaining institutional power and addressing the periodic pressures from the president and the larger society for more coherent and coordinated policy. What Congress has done in response is to enact a set of reforms (both substantive and procedural) that often promise to increase the centralization of congressional decision making and improve coordination. The reforms, however, tend to be incomplete or flawed due to member ambivalence about yielding too much power over areas that can affect their political survival. Congressional oversight, for example, is vigorous but uncoordinated, and often done to protect programs favored by committee members. And the revised budget process is jerry-built on traditional congressional institutions, rendering it much less effective than it might have been.

In the latter years of the twentieth century, we have witnessed a major reinvigoration of central congressional leadership, especially in the House. Faced with an unprecedented peacetime debt, a skeptical public, the fallout from intense struggles to protect legislative prerogatives against Presidents Nixon and Reagan, and overwhelming budget constraints, party leaders have been given significant tools and leeway to coordinate.

Few, however, think that the current situation means that strong party leadership of the type that existed in the House as the century dawned is about to return. As Barbara Sinclair says,

> So long as members' reelection chances remain more dependent on their own behavior than on the decisions of party leaders, members will refuse to give their leadership power sufficient to coerce. By the same token, however, so long as members continue to need help in attaining their policy goals, they will expect their leaders to provide it and, so long as they continue to be reasonably homogeneous in their policy preferences, they will, much of the time, behave in such a way as to make it possible for party leaders to do so.

The situation in the early 1990s is one in which members can do relatively little because resources are so scarce. Major changes (tax increases or significant program cuts) would be necessary to furnish the additional resources needed for new initiatives, and these can only be provided through effective central leadership and the kind of omnibus bill packaging that can supply members with protective cover when they do the necessary unpleasant things. But an eventual return of vigorous economic growth, or an immediate tax increase that provided significant additional revenue, or a combination of the two, could easily make members feel less need for strong leaders. In that circumstance, especially, a serious regional split over a controversial issue such as trade policy or, in a period of Democratic control of both branches, a split between congressional and presidential wings of the party, could erode party consensus sufficiently to undo the current pattern of strong leadership.

Many of the issues concerning congressional leadership will be vigorously debated—though, if history is any guide, not resolved—by the Joint Committee on the Organization of Congress that began work in the 103d Congress (1993). A report prepared as input to the Joint Committee's work put the matter squarely: "Lacking the ability to discipline rank-and-file members effectively, and with their own status vulnerable to challenge, party leaders in Congress are not in an enviable position." The authors of the report recommend a series of changes ranging from the establishment of a Majority Agenda Committee in the House to allowing the Speaker of the House or the Democratic Steering Committee controlled by the Speaker to declare a committee chair vacant at any time during a Congress. (Little, significantly, is said in the report about the Senate, which is traditionally much more decentralized and difficult to lead.)

The outcome of the Joint Committee's deliberations will be raw material for the analyst of the twenty-first-century Congress. Barring radical changes in congressional rules and procedures or a major shift in election financing (toward party control of the bulk of funds for congressional candidates), or perhaps even a change in nominating procedures giving party leaders significant influence over nominations for seats in the House and Senate, the odds are that many of the problems of leadership, coordination, and congressional relations with the president that marked the history of Congress in the twentieth century will be familiar a century from now. But the resurgence of Congress in the latter third of the twentieth century demonstrates that Congress should never be counted out. It may cede influence at times, and it may often appear rudderless, but the American system of separate institutions sharing powers gives it both the means and the incentive to fight back.

THE 1994 ELECTION

The midterm election of November 1994 struck Congress like an earthquake. Republicans won control of the House of Representatives for the first time in forty years. They also regained control of the Senate. Newt Gingrich of Georgia became Speaker of the House and his "Contract with America," signed by over 350 Republicans in September, was the blueprint for the changes Republicans promised the election would initiate.

The election shook the Democrats nationally and at all levels of government, but the results in the South were particularly stunning. Republicans won a majority of southern House seats for the first time since the end of Reconstruction, signaling a new phase in the long developing realignment of that region. The depth of the change can be seen in the fact that Republicans gained control of the House delegations from Georgia, North Carolina, and South Carolina. And not a single Republican incumbent was defeated anywhere in the United States.

Aside from the implications of the election results for public policy, the Republican victory in the House created the conditions for a wave of changes in the rules. Term limits were set for committee and subcommittee chairs who could serve for no more than three consecutive terms (six years) before they must be replaced. Most committees were restricted to five subcommittees, and control of staff hiring was given to the chairs of the full committees. (Prior to the change, subcommittee chairs had the formal authority to hire a staffer for their units.) Absentee voting in the committees was prohibited, depriving chairs of one of their most valuable tools for controlling the outcome of committee votes. Committee staff levels were reduced. And three committees were eliminated (Post Office and Civil Service, District of Columbia, and Merchant Marine and Fisheries), although the House stopped short of a major overhaul of its committee structure.

On balance, most analysts would subscribe to the evaluation of Thomas E. Mann, director of governmental studies at the Brookings Institution in Washington, who described the changes as leading to "a recentralization of power within the majority party in the House." Subcommittee power was restricted, but committee chairs also lost influence. Speaker Gingrich, even though his own term was limited to eight years, was the clear winner in the early going.

These changes will be grist for the mills of future historians. They may signal a long-term shift in the way the House is run, or they may be undercut over time. Significantly, House Republicans failed in their initial effort to win the two-thirds majority necessary to adopt a constitutional amendment limiting congressional terms. Senior Republicans resisted this change. It will be interesting to see whether their more junior colleagues begin to chafe under the restrictions imposed by some of the new rules. Such a reaction would not shock anyone who knows the history of the twentieth century Congress.

SEE ALSO The Courts; The Presidency; The Constitution; Federalism and the States (all in this volume).

BIBLIOGRAPHY

An overview of congressional history can be found in Congressional Quarterly's *Origins and Development of Congress* (1992). Joel H. Sibley, ed., *The Congress of the United States: 1789–1989* (1991), is a multivolume series containing a comprehensive collection of articles on the evolution and behavior of Congress over its history. Woodrow Wilson's *Congressional Government: A Study in American Politics* (1885) is a classic study of Congress in the late nineteenth century; and James Bryce, *The American Commonwealth* (1891), is a comprehensive work on American government and politics as seen by a European observer. James L. Sundquist, *The Decline and Resurgence of Congress* (1981), offers a sweeping review of Congress's ups and downs. Norman J. Ornstein, Thomas E. Mann, and Michael J. Malbin, *Vital Statistics on*

Congress: 1993–1994 (1994), is the latest in a series of books providing data on changes over time in Congress's members, committees, workload, and the like.

There are many excellent textbooks covering Congress and its politics. Among the best are Roger H. Davidson and Walter J. Oleszek, *Congress and Its Members* (1994); Charles O. Jones, *The United States Congress* (1982); and William J. Keefe and Morris S. Ogul, *The American Legislative Process* (1993).

Other, somewhat more specialized, but still sweeping, historical treatments of Congress are also important reading for those wishing to understand the evolution of Congress in the twentieth century. Joseph Cooper and David W. Brady, in "Toward a Diachronic Analysis of Congress," *American Political Science Review* 75 (1981), review research on Congress that treats change over time as a major factor. Lawrence C. Dodd and Bruce I. Oppenheimer, eds., *Congress Reconsidered* (1977, 1981, 1985, 1989, 1993), provides a set of essays on changes in Congress. Each edition has fresh material for students of Congress. David W. Brady's *Critical Elections and Congressional Policy Making* (1988) is a historical and statistical analysis of the conditions under which the majority party in the House is able to legislate major policy changes. Joseph Cooper and David W. Brady, "Institutional Context and Leadership Style: The House from Cannon to Rayburn," *American Political Science Review* 75 (1981), describes and analyzes the transition in House leadership from Cannon to Rayburn. Lawrence C. Dodd, "Congress and the Quest for Power," in Lawrence C. Dodd and Bruce I. Oppenheimer, eds., *Congress Reconsidered* (1977), presents a particularly interesting cyclical theory of legislative-executive relations. Nelson W. Polsby's "The Institutionalization of the U.S. House of Representatives," *American Political Science Review* 62 (1968) is a now classic analysis of changes in career patterns which have shaped the modern House.

The evolving role of Congress in budgeting is key to understanding its powers. Donald F. Kettl, *Deficit Politics: Public Budgeting in Its Institutional and Historical Context* (1992), presents an overview of U.S. government budgeting. A comprehensive review of budget reform is provided by Allen Schick, *Congress and Money: Budgeting, Spending, and Taxing* (1980). Louis Fisher, "Federal Budget Doldrums: The Vacuum in Presidential Leadership," *Public Administration Review* 50 (1990), is an article by a leading Congressional Research Service expert on government institutions. Hugh Heclo's "OMB and the Presidency: The Problem of Neutral Competence," *The Public Interest* 38 (1975) is an analysis of presidential attempts to "politicize" the Office of Management and Budget. And every student of budgeting should read Aaron Wildavsky's *The New Politics of the Budgetary Process* (1992).

Congressional efforts to oversee the executive have been a subject of increasing importance with the growth of the administrative state in the twentieth century. James Q. Wilson, "The Rise of the Bureaucratic State," *The Public Interest* 41 (1975), is a brief history and analysis of the growth of the U.S. bureaucracy. Allen Schick, "Politics through Law: Congressional Limitations on Executive Discretion," in Anthony King, ed., *Both Ends of the Avenue* (1983), is an excellent treatment of executive-legislative relations. Joel D. Aberbach, *Keeping a Watchful Eye: The Politics of Congressional Oversight* (1990), presents a longitudinal (over time) analysis of congressional review of policy and administration. Joseph P. Harris, *Congressional Control of Administration* (1964), surveys congressional behavior in supervising the bureaucracy. John F. Bibby, "Congress' Neglected Function," in Melvin R. Laird, ed., *The Republican Papers* (1968), is an oft-cited lament about the role of Congress in oversight. James Davidson's "Sunset—A New Challenge," *The Bureaucrat* 6 (1977) is an account by a congressional staffer of the philosophy behind the Sunset proposals of the 1970s.

The war powers of Congress have been a controversial subject. They are covered in several of the general treatments of Congress mentioned above. Two studies cited in the text will be of particular interest to readers of this essay. Robert A. Katzmann, "War Powers: Toward a New Accommodation," in Thomas E. Mann, ed., *A Question of Balance: The President, the Congress, and Foreign Policy* (1990), provides a good overview of the War Powers Resolution. And Larry Berman and Bruce W. Jentleson, "Bush and the Post–Cold War World: New Challenges for American Leadership," in Colin Campbell, S.J., and Bert A. Rockman, eds., *The Bush Presidency: First Appraisals* (1989), contains an account of the relationship of President Bush and Congress.

Who Congress represents, how it is organized, and efforts to reform it have been matters of great concern in this century. Samuel P. Huntington, "Congressional Responses to the Twentieth Century," in David B. Truman, ed., *The Congress and America's Future* (1965), is a now classic article on the role of Congress at mid-century. Barbara Sinclair, *The Transformation of the U.S. Senate* (1989), looks at changes in the Senate from a closed, inward-looking institution to a more open and outward-looking body. Richard F. Fenno's *Congressmen in Committees* (1973), is a pioneering work on the nature of congressional committees. Steven S. Smith and Christopher J. Deering, *Committees in Congress* (1990), presents a comprehensive analysis of the role and development of congressional committees. Barbara Sinclair, "House Majority Party Leadership in an Era of Legislative Constraint," in Roger H. Davidson, ed., *The Postreform Congress* (1992), provides an account of why the leadership of the contemporary House is more comprehensively involved in the legislative process than its postwar predecessors. Sinclair, "The Emergency of Strong Leadership in the 1980s House," *The Journal of Politics* 54 (1992), is an analysis of the increased influence of the central leadership in the 1980s House. Lawrence C. Dodd and Bruce I. Oppenheimer, "Consolidating Power in the House: The Rise of a New Oligarchy," in Lawrence C. Dodd and Bruce I. Oppenheimer, eds., *Congress Reconsidered* (1989), look at leadership in the House in the 1980s. Roger H. Davidson and Walter J. Oleszek, *Congress against Itself* (1977), provide the definitive account of the House reforms of 1974. Roger H. Davidson, "Subcommittee Government: New Channels for Policy Making," in Thomas E. Mann and Norman J. Ornstein, eds., *The New Congress* (1981), is an excellent analysis of the role of subcommittees in the postreform period. Kenny J. Whitby and Franklin D. Gilliam, Jr., "A Longitudinal Analysis of Competing Explanations for the Transformation of Southern Congressional Politics," *The Journal of Politics* 53 (1991), examine changes in the behavior of white southern members of the House of Representatives. Kenneth A. Shepsle, "The Changing Textbook Congress," in John E. Chubb and Paul E. Peterson, eds., *Can the Government Govern?* (1989), looks at changes in Congress in the modern era. James L. Sundquist, *Constitutional Reform and Effective Government* (1992), presents an analysis of the American constitutional system and of ideas for reforming it. Thomas E. Mann and Norman J. Ornstein, *A First Report of the Renewing Congress Project* (1992), contains suggestions for reforming Congress in the 1990s. And the same authors, in testimony before the Joint Committee on the Organization of Congress, 16 February 1993 (mimeographed), provide a cogent overview of many of the problems of the contemporary Congress.

Other valuable pieces cited in the text or of widespread interest should also be noted. David R. Mayhew, *Congress: The Electoral Connection* (1974), presents an analysis of congressional behavior based on the premise that reelection is a member's principal motivation. His work is the basis for much of the contemporary interpretation of the nature of Congress. Morris P. Fiorina, *Congress: Keystone of the Washington Establishment* (1989), provides a view of Washington politics in which Congress is central. Sidney M. Miklis, "E. E. Schattschneider, The New Deal, and the Rejection of the Responsible Party Doctrine," *P.S.: Political Science and Politics* 25 (1992), is an article drawn from *The President and the Parties: The Transformation of the American Party System since the New Deal* (1993). Richard P. Nathan, *The Plot That Failed: Nixon and the Administrative Presidency* (1975), presents a view of the administrative presidency from the perspective of an academic who served in President Nixon's administration. Finally, students of the Congress should also be familiar with the following major studies: R. Douglas Arnold, *The Logic of Congressional Action* (1990); Gary P. Cox and Mathew D. McCubbins, *Legislative Leviathan* (1991); Richard F. Fenno, *Home Style* (1978); D. Roderick Kieweit and Mathew D. McCubbins, *The Logic of Delegation* (1991); John W. Kingdon, *Congressmen's Voting Decisions* (1981); and Keith Krehbiel, *Information and Legislative Organization* (1991).

Thanks are due to Mara Cohen for her excellent research assistance on this project.

THE COURTS

Mary L. Dudziak

The twentieth century began with the courts at the center of a debate about their role in containing the scope of government power. The Supreme Court, perhaps ironically, powerfully acted to limit the authority of other branches of the federal government in the name of local autonomy and the free market. As the century progressed, the Supreme Court stepped up to the brink, then backed away from a constitutional crisis over its role, conceding the expanded role of the federal government in economic affairs in the New Deal period. Conflicts over the role of the courts in reining in government power reemerged in different forms throughout the century, affecting the nature of constitutional theory, court doctrine about judicial restraint, and the politics of active federal involvement in broadening areas of American life, as well as cultural understandings of the role of the courts in American society. Although the scope of judicial power and the nature of judicial review would be a source of constant tension during the twentieth century, the courts played an increasingly prominent role in American politics and culture as the century progressed.

The turn of the century found state and federal courts in the midst of a more intrusive review of legislative action than they had previously engaged in. Although the power of judicial review had long been established, the Supreme Court struck down few acts of Congress or state statutes before the 1880s. But from the 1880s through the early decades of the twentieth century, the Court found itself increasingly at odds with legislative action.

The motivating force behind turn-of-the-century judicial activism was, in part, jurisprudential. In the late nineteenth century, laissez-faire economic theory influenced judicial theories about such constitutional norms as liberty and property rights. Informed by the belief that a free market would lead to optimal social good, and also that liberty in economic and property relations was a fundamental value, the courts were hostile to legislative reform efforts that restricted freedom in the marketplace. The methodology of laissez-faire judicial theory was formalism. Judges deduced a set of rules that they could then mechanistically apply to enforce limits on legislative action. While there was great judicial creativity in applying formalist principles, the method bore with it the ideology of detached, nondiscretionary judging.

Another reason for the clash between the courts and the legislatures was the growth of the regulatory state. At the turn of the century state legislators and Congress enacted new solutions to a new set of urban and industrial problems. The judiciary saw it as their role to set the boundaries of expanding legislative and executive power.

THE LOCHNER ERA

Lochner v. *New York* was the defining case of this era. Decided by the Supreme Court in 1905, *Lochner* involved a challenge to a New York statute that limited the number of hours bakers could work to ten hours a day and sixty hours a week. The ten-hour day had been a hard fought victory of the labor movement, along the way toward their ultimate goal of an eight-hour day. While unionized bakers in New York in the late 1880s were able to bargain for a ten-hour day, nonunionized immigrant bakers often worked twelve- to fourteen-hour shifts. The state argued that such hours were harmful to bakers' health, presenting evidence that long hours inhaling flour dust led to lung disease and a short life expectancy for many in the industry.

Unmoved by these arguments, Justice Rufus W. Peckham, writing for the majority, found that the statute violated the "right of contract" between workers and employers, which was a form of liberty protected under the due process clause of the Fourteenth Amendment. Under Peckham's theory of substantive due process, states did not have the power to interfere with the freedom of individual workers and employers to bargain in an unregulated marketplace unless there was some reason that the workers were particularly at risk. In this case, the New York statute was not an appropriate exercise of the state's police power to protect public health, for "wholesome bread does not depend upon whether the baker works but ten hours per day or only sixty hours a week," and the bakers' trade was not so unhealthful as to require legislative intervention. Justice John Marshall Harlan's dissent, relying on treatises on occupational disease, questioned the latter assumption, while Justice Oliver Wendell Holmes, in perhaps his most famous dissent, claimed that the majority based its decision on a particular view of economic theory, and "the Fourteenth Amendment does not enact Mr. Herbert Spencer's Social Statics."

Even as the Court decided *Lochner,* competing theories about the wisdom of regulating the workplace, and of the nature of judicial action, challenged laissez-faire economics and formalism. Progressive reformers argued that our democratic system was based on fairness as well as liberty, and fairness required recognition of the fact that individuals were not on an equal footing in the marketplace. At the same time, Roscoe Pound criticized legal formalism as engaged in by "legal monks who pass their lives in an atmosphere of pure law from which every worldly and human element is excluded." He called for a "sociological movement in jurisprudence" which would be more sensitive to the application of legal rules to actual human conditions. Theodore Roosevelt echoed Holmes's *Lochner* dissent in a 1912 defense of reform legislation, arguing "we, the people, have the constitutional as well as moral right to try these experiments if we soberly determine to try them." In spite of this opposition, in the years after *Lochner* the federal courts played an active hand in limiting much of what state legislatures and Congress could do.

The Supreme Court's approach was criticized in the substantive due process cases for not taking into consideration the inequalities in bargaining power between workers and employers. In *Coppage* v. *Kansas* in 1915, the Court made clear that it would be inappropriate for the courts to remedy such differences in status. In *Coppage,* the Court struck down a state law that prohibited employers from forcing their employees not to join labor unions. Such a statute, the Court reasoned, interfered with the personal liberty protected by the due process clause, a right "as essential to the laborer as to the capitalist, to the poor as to the rich." Justice Pitney wrote for the Court that "wherever the right of private property exists, there must and will be inequalities of fortune." It would be "impossible to uphold freedom of contract and the right of private property without at the same time recognizing as legitimate those inequalities of fortune that are the necessary result of the exercise of those rights."

As important as they seemed to the Court, the principles of freedom of contract could be moderated when other important societal values were at stake. In *Muller* v. *Oregon* in 1908, the Court upheld a statute limiting the number of hours women could work. In *Lochner* the Court had suggested that workers who needed special protection might be subject to state regulation, in spite of the general rule of freedom of contract. Women were such a group. Perhaps influenced by the social science amicus brief filed by Louis Brandeis chronicling women's physical inferiority to men and the negative impact on women's childbearing capacity of long factory hours, the Court found that the state had a legitimate interest in protecting this weaker group of workers. Important to the justification for state regulation of women's labor contracts was the impact of work on women's ability to breed healthy babies. As a result, in *Muller,* a eugenic interest in maintaining and improving "the race" outweighed freedom of contract.

For many working-class women, the result in *Muller* was helpful, even though the reasoning in the opinion was based on women's inequality. At a time when few women's industries were unionized, most women workers lacked power to change labor conditions on their own. Further, because so many women, married and single, faced the double shift of work at home as well as at the factory, many women desperately needed relief from lengthy hours. Still, the distinction between *Lochner* and *Muller*—that protective legislation was permissible for women but not for men—limited women's opportunities, particularly in traditionally male jobs, and reinforced the sex segregated nature of the labor force. Further, because the ultimate demise of *Lochner* in the 1930s would not be coupled with an abandonment of *Muller,* sex distinctions in workplace regulations would be upheld by courts for many years to come.

Notwithstanding the *Muller* decision, early in the century the Supreme Court's interest in protecting women workers had its limits. In 1923 in *Adkins* v. *Children's Hospital,* the Court, perhaps less sympathetic to women's protective legislation due to the passage of the woman suffrage amendment in 1920, struck down a minimum wage law for women on the basis that low wages were not as detrimental to women's health and morals as long hours.

Reformers were frustrated by the Supreme Court's limitations on states' ability to pass legislation addressing conditions in the workplace. When they turned to federal legislative action, however, the Court placed limits on Congress's legislative power as well. Beginning in the late nineteenth century, motivated by angry voter concern over the power of big business and the dangers of factory life, Congress used its power under the Commerce Clause to regulate the economy in new ways. Some laws, such as the Sherman Antitrust Act of 1890, involved direct congressional regulation of business activity. Others, such as the Interstate Commerce Act of 1887, delegated regulatory power to administrative agencies. In decisions beginning in the 1890s, the Court placed limits on Congress's power under the Commerce Clause in certain contexts, while enabling legislative flexibility in others. In *United States* v. *E.C. Knight Co.* (1895), the Court ruled that the Sherman Act could not be applied to a virtual monopoly of the sugar refining market because that activity was manufacturing, not commerce. Commerce related more narrowly to the buying and selling of goods, and their transportation. Other activities that did not *directly* affect commerce were, in the Court's view, beyond the scope of congressional power. In spite of *E.C. Knight*'s formalist analysis, the court adopted a more functional approach to the commerce power in other areas. It held in the *Houston, East and West Texas Railway Co.* v. *United States* (1914), for example, that even purely intrastate railroad rates could be regulated by the federal government if those rates affected Congress's ability to effectively regulate interstate rates. Although *E.C. Knight*'s more narrow definition of the scope of the commerce power was departed from in other important turn-of-the-century cases, its distinction between commerce and manufacturing would later be relied upon to limit congressional power over workplace regulations in an area of particular public concern: child labor.

While freedom of contract was the central question in the cases involving state statutes, questions of government power—federalism and the role of the courts in limiting federal legislative excesses—were the central concerns in the commerce power cases. In attempting to regulate new areas of American life, from labor conditions to lottery tickets, Congress took on issues that had traditionally been handled by state legislatures. Viewing the Tenth Amendment as placing limits on the degree of federal intrusion into local affairs, the Supreme Court struck down many statutes in the name of federalism. The Court's decisions were not neatly consistent. Throughout the early years of the twentieth century, however, state autonomy remained a constitutional value, and federalism an enforceable limit on congressional action, even if its invocation seemed to turn on the Court's preferences for a particular legislative policy.

In a case that became the focus of particularly harsh criticism of the Court, in 1918 the Court ruled that Congress exceeded its authority under the Commerce Clause, and usurped a power reserved to the states when it passed a statute regulating child labor. The Child Labor Act struck down in *Hammer* v. *Dagenhart* prohibited goods from being shipped in interstate commerce if they had been produced in factories that employed children under the age of fourteen, or if children between the ages of fourteen and sixteen worked more than eight hours a day or six days a week or at night. The Court had previously ruled in *Champion* v. *Ames* in 1903 that Congress had the power to prohibit shipment of such a pestilence as lottery tickets in interstate commerce. In the child labor case, however, the Court said that the goods produced by the children were not harmful, whereas lottery tickets were. The Court felt that Congress was really trying to regulate local labor conditions, and that was up to the states and not the federal government. As Justice Day saw it,

> The far-reaching result of upholding the act cannot be more plainly indicated than by pointing out that if Congress can thus regulate matters intrusted to local authority by prohibition of the movement of commodities in interstate commerce, all freedom of commerce will be at an end, and the power of the States over local matters may be eliminated, and thus our system of Government be practically destroyed.

In *Hammer* v. *Dagenhart* the Court protected a particular vision of government and of federalism that was at odds with the more activist vision of congressional reformers. Congress was, after all, not trying to destroy "our system of Government" when it passed progressive reform legislation. It simply had a different conception of what the nature of that government was.

POLITICS AND THE COURT BEFORE THE NEW DEAL

Popular criticism of the courts escalated during the presidential campaign of 1912. Theodore Roosevelt made the federal and state courts a campaign issue, condemning "every strained construction of the Constitution which declares that the nation is powerless to remedy industrial conditions which cry for law." Roosevelt urged that "the people themselves must be the ultimate makers of their own Constitution, and where their agents differ in their interpretations of the Constitution, the people themselves should be given the chance after full and deliberate judgment, authoritatively to settle what interpretation it is that their representatives shall thereafter adopt as binding." He called for an easier means of amending the Constitution, and for recall of judges by the electorate.

In the context of the campaign, a national debate about the Constitution and judicial power focused on three issues: first, two pending constitutional amendments providing for a federal income tax and for direct election of senators; second, the popular recall of judges, and whether that would undermine the independence of the judiciary; and third, whether "the people" were a higher authority than the Constitution. Republican incumbent president William Howard Taft opposed Roosevelt's proposals, declaring that his party supported "the Constitution as it is, with such amendments adopted according to its provisions as new conditions thoroughly understood may require." It was ultimately Woodrow Wilson who won the 1912 election, but in the following years, Roosevelt renewed his pledge to "overthrow those who perverted the Constitution," while Taft formed a "Constitutional League" dedicated to preserving the Constitution as it was.

The Constitution and the role of the courts continued to be a subject of popular debate. Even as some critics warned against constitutional "fetishism," opposing organizations were formed to further different ideas of constitutionalism, with fundamentally different conceptions of the role of the courts. Charles A. Beard's Committee on the Federal Constitution hoped to bring the Constitution "under a more democratic control." The following year the National Association for Constitutional Government was formed to campaign against such changes as popular recall of judges, and to "Secure a popular realization of the vital necessity of preserving the nation's basic law unimpaired." Whether or not the Constitution was "fetishized," instruction in it was at least popularized. By 1923, twenty-three states had laws requiring instruction in the Constitution, and by 1931 that number had nearly doubled.

Former president and now Chief Justice Taft argued in 1922 that the Court's activism in striking down federal statutes had "made the Court a stormy petrel in the politics of the country, and has promoted serious attempts to change and minimize the constitutional function and power of the Court." In the next two years alone, eleven bills were introduced in Congress to curb the power of the Supreme Court. Following a Court decision striking down a tax on child labor in 1922, Sen. Robert M. La Follette proposed a constitutional amendment that would allow Congress to override Court decisions by repassing them by a two-thirds majority, complaining that "we cannot live under a system of government where we are forced to amend the Constitution every time we want to pass a progressive law." The court-curbing proposal was a key part of La Follette's 1924 presidential campaign plank. The proposal was attacked by the American Legion and other groups, and La Follette ultimately was soundly defeated in his presidential bid. During the same period, Sen. William E. Borah offered a plan to require a seven-to-two majority before the Court could declare an act of Congress unconstitutional. Although supported by major newspapers, the proposal was not adopted. The most serious challenge to the Court would await the New Deal period and the growing concern in the Depression years that the courts stood in the way of essential government action.

THE NEW DEAL PERIOD AND THE JUDICIAL REVOLUTION OF 1937

The popular debate on the courts early in the century may well have primed the nation for the constitutional crises that would follow. The tensions over the role of the Supreme Court came to a head following the election of President Franklin Delano Roosevelt. Roosevelt took his election in 1932 as a mandate for federal government activism to pull the country out of depression. Upon assuming office, he proposed creative measures to regulate the economy.

Roosevelt's New Deal legislation ran into trouble in the Supreme Court. In the first major blow, codes of fair competition established under the National Industrial Recovery Act (NIRA) were overturned in *A.L.A. Schechter Poultry Corp.* v. *United States* (1935) on the theory that although the poultry sold by Schechter had moved across state lines, the working conditions of employees who processed and sold the chickens locally only affected interstate commerce "indirectly." As a result, Congress had exceeded its power and usurped the authority of the state. Because the NIRA was a key New Deal measure, its demise suggested that other New Deal programs were also in jeopardy.

An important 1936 case made matters worse. *Carter* v. *Carter Coal* invalidated the Bituminous Coal Conservation Act of 1935, which regulated pricing and labor conditions in coal mining, relying again on the formalist distinction between matters that directly and indirectly affected commerce. Under *Carter Coal,* the magnitude of effect on interstate commerce did not bring matters within congressional power if their effect on commerce were nevertheless "indirect," as was, in the Court's view, the mining of coal. If allowed to stand, *Carter* and the narrow approach to the commerce power it reflected would greatly restrict Congress's hand in regulating labor conditions, threatening in particular the important National Labor Relations Act of 1935. Meanwhile, the Court invalidated the Agricultural Adjustment Act in *United States* v. *Butler* (1936), finding that Congress had exceeded its taxing and spending powers and thereby "invaded the reserved rights of the states," when it taxed producers of agricultural commodities in order to raise funds to pay farmers to reduce production. Following these decisions FDR angrily complained that the Court was issuing "horse and buggy" decisions in a machine age.

While the Supreme Court was harshly criticized by supporters of FDR's New Deal programs, the President did not make the Court an issue in his 1936 reelection campaign, although the Republicans did raise the specter of more liberal FDR Court appointments. The President waited until after the election returns were safely in, and then proposed a plan to reshape the federal courts. In a message to Congress on 5 February, Roosevelt suggested that the aged members of the Supreme Court were simply not able to keep up with their work. "At the present time the Supreme Court is laboring under a heavy burden," he stated. "Part of the problem of obtaining a sufficient number of judges to dispose of cases is the capacity of the judges themselves. This brings forward the question of aged or infirm judges." Roosevelt proposed that for every member of the federal judiciary who did not retire within six months of his seventieth birthday, the president would nominate an additional judge. Under the proposal, the Supreme Court could not be expanded beyond fifteen justices. Since six members of the Court at that time were over seventy, the proposal would potentially give Roosevelt the ability to expand the Court to fifteen members.

Although the initial reaction in Congress seemed sufficiently favorable to ensure its passage, the "court-packing" bill, as it was quickly dubbed, soon encountered stiff opposition. Roosevelt attempted to reorient the debate about the bill in a radio address to the nation on the eve of Senate Judiciary Committee hearings on the proposed legislation. He argued that the courts had interfered with the efforts of Congress and the president to rehabilitate the economy and protect the nation from economic difficulties. "I want to talk with you very simply," he implored, "about the need for present action in this crisis—the need to meet the unanswered challenge of one-third of a nation ill-nourished, ill-clad, ill-housed." He declared that "we have . . . reached the point as a Nation where we must take action to save the Constitution from the Court and the Court from itself." Yet even as Roosevelt's appeal now went to the heart of his concerns about the Supreme Court's disposal of his New Deal legislation, still he invoked the smokescreen of age. The President argued that his plan would bring younger judges into the court system, "men who have had personal experience and contact with modern facts and circumstances under which average men have to live and work." The plan would save the Constitution from "hardening of the judicial arteries."

The nation seemed not to be moved by Roosevelt's appeal. Following his address, the deluge of letters to the editor of *The New York Times* ran seven-to-one against the proposal. Meanwhile, Chief Justice Charles Evans Hughes notified the Judiciary Committee that the Supreme Court was "fully abreast of its work," and that additional justices would actually make the Court less efficient. On 18 May, Justice Willis Van Devanter announced his retirement, which lessened sympathy for Roosevelt because he now had the chance to shape the Court with his own appointment. Then, on 14 June, the Senate Judiciary Committee issued a report rejecting the plan as a dangerous proposal that "violates every sacred tradition of American democracy." The report called for a repudiation of the plan so strong that "its parallel will never again be presented to the free representatives of the free people of America."

By the time Congress turned against the court-packing plan, the plan itself was no longer needed. On 29 March 1937, the Supreme Court upheld a minimum wage law for women in *West Coast Hotel* v. *Parrish,* reversing its 1923 decision in *Adkins* v. *Children's Hospital.* The *West Coast Hotel* decision represented a particularly dramatic turnaround, for only a year earlier, in *Morehead* v. *New York ex rel. Tipaldo,* the Court had relied on *Adkins* and struck down a New York minimum wage law for women on the basis of freedom of contract. Both the *Tipaldo* case and *West Coast Hotel* were decided by five-to-four votes. The difference in outcome was due to a switch by Justice Owen J. Roberts, who voted to strike down the minimum wage law in *Tipaldo,* and to uphold it in *West Coast Hotel.* Although Roberts cast his vote in the case before the court-packing plan was announced, the vote was characterized as a "switch in time" that "saved nine," and was greeted with joy in Congress. Then, as the Supreme Court continued to back down from its activist role in striking down economic regulation, the crisis over the Court ebbed.

West Coast Hotel was followed quickly by a reversal in the area of congressional power under the Commerce Clause in the landmark case of *NLRB* v. *Jones & Laughlin Steel Corp.*, a five-to-four decision handed down on 12 April 1937. *Jones & Laughlin* upheld the National Labor Relations Act of 1935, finding that Congress had power to regulate the labor conditions of employees for a large steel corporation, even if those employees were engaged in production, and not directly in the shipment of goods in interstate commerce. Departing from the reasoning in *Schechter* and *Carter Coal,* though without directly overturning those cases, the Court adopted an analysis of the scope of Congress's power under the Commerce Clause that turned on the impact of economic activity on interstate commerce, rather than the formalistic categories that governed many previous rulings. Once economic impact became the touchstone of commerce power analysis, Congress could more fully regulate the economy and the labor market.

If the turnabout of 1937 made it seem as if Court decisions were simply a matter of politics, this perspective was not a new one to the American public. Popular culture through the Progressive Era projected an image of a politicized Court that favored the wealthy and big business. Turn-of-the-century utopian novels *Waiting for the Signal* by Henry O. Morris and *President John Smith* by Frederick Upham Adams even included revised constitutions restricting the scope of judicial power. The constitution in *President John Smith* withdrew court jurisdiction over "laws passed by the people of the United States." Meanwhile, defense lawyer Clarence Darrow published a series of short stories in the Chicago *Evening American* attacking the Court's laissez-faire jurisprudence in 1902. Because novelists and other writers had portrayed the Court as championing the rights of the wealthy over those of the poor, the Court's reversal brought it more in line with the outcomes favored by these popular critics, even if its method reinforced public skepticism about the judicial process.

The Court's thin majorities in the 1937 cases would then be consolidated with changes in its membership. Beginning in 1937, Roosevelt would find that what he was not able to accomplish through legislation, he would ultimately be able to accomplish through filling Supreme Court vacancies. The first to go was Justice Van Devanter. Because Van Devanter had been a staunch opponent of New Deal legislation, replacing him with the more liberal Hugo Black would have an important impact. As only the first of eight Court appointments Roosevelt would be able to make in his four terms in office, the President would have ample additional opportunity to shape the direction of the Court. Only George Washington filled more seats on the high Court.

Politics were also at play in the selection of then Senator Black. Robert Jackson recalled that Roosevelt wished to humiliate the Court and the Senate "at a single stroke by naming Black," who had been one of the Court's "most bitter and unfair critics." Yet the Senate and the Court were not the only ones humiliated when rumors circulated during the confirmation process that Black had been a member of the Ku Klux Klan during the 1920s. After Black's confirmation, when it became clear that Black had in fact been a Klan member, Roosevelt disavowed any prior knowledge of it, and Black went on national radio to explain himself. Yet Black left a note "for posterity" in his private papers indicating that, in fact, he and FDR had discussed Black's Klan involvement over lunch before the confirmation. According to Black, FDR said that "there was no reason for my worrying about having been a member of the Ku Klux Klan. He said that some of the best friends and supporters he had in the State of Georgia were strong members of the organization."

In 1938, George Sutherland, another conservative anti–New Deal justice, stepped down. Roosevelt replaced him with Solicitor General Stanley Reed. That same year, liberal justice Benjamin Cardozo died. One of the intellectual leaders of the Court was replaced by another, as Cardozo's seat was filled by Harvard law professor Felix Frankfurter.

In 1939, Brandeis retired and was replaced by William O. Douglas. Douglas was a staunch civil libertarian, and became the longest serving justice in the history of the Court. Also in 1939, conservative Pierce Butler died and Attorney General Frank Murphy took his place. Murphy was criticized for lacking judicial temperament, yet he would go on to write passionate opinions in defense of civil liberties. Finally, in 1941 James McReynolds, the last of the conservative "Four Horsemen," stepped down, as did Chief Justice Charles Evans Hughes. With the appointment to the Court of Senator James Byrnes and Attorney General Robert Jackson, Roosevelt had fully reshaped the Court with two remaining appointments during his presidency to make.

THE ROLE OF THE FEDERAL COURTS IN MATTERS OF STATE LAW

In 1938, the Court continued its retreat from an activist posture in a case that questioned whether federal courts hearing cases involving state law claims brought by citizens of different states should follow state court interpretations of state law or interpret state law independently. The Court's ruling on this matter in *Erie Railroad Co.* v. *Tompkins* was of such significance that in 1942 Justice Black called it "one of the most important cases at law in American legal history."

Cases involving purely state law claims can be heard in federal court when the plaintiff and defendant are from different states, subject to particular rules established by Congress. Under the Judiciary Act of 1789, the "rules of decision" in such cases were to be "the laws of the several states." In *Swift* v. *Tyson* in 1842, the Supreme Court ruled that decisions by state courts were not part of state "laws" under the statute, and further that there was a distinction between matters of local law, such as those involving real property, and matters of "general law," including such things as commercial transactions. The federal courts under *Swift* had the authority to decide for themselves questions of general law, and before long the scope of general law questions had grown to include over two dozen doctrinal areas, including property rights and employer-employee relations.

By the turn of the century, *Swift* had come under heavy criticism, with Justice Field predicting in 1893 that the doctrine would "die among its worshippers." The doctrine soon came into conflict with the understanding of the nature of law and of judicial decisions held by a new generation of judges and legal scholars. Legal realists believed that judges did not simply discover preexisting law, but that the act of judging was a creative process. When a judge ruled in a case, the judge *made* law, and the judge's own experiences and ideas had a powerful and inevitable impact on the way the judge would rule. This understanding of the judicial process made independent federal court interpretations of matters of state law highly problematic. The federal courts were making state law.

In the 1928 case *Black and White Taxicab Co.* v. *Brown and Yellow Taxicab Co.*, which concerned a taxi company's contract with a railroad for the exclusive right to provide taxi service at a railroad station, the Court disregarded thirty-five years of Kentucky state court rulings that exclusive contracts were contrary to public policy and unenforceable. The Court instead upheld the contract as a matter of general law. Justice Holmes, joined by Justices Brandeis and Stone, dissented, arguing that the *Swift* rule was "an unconstitutional assumption of powers by the Courts of the United States" because it allowed federal courts to make law in areas beyond the scope of federal government authority.

It would not be until 1938, in the midst of the retreat from judicial activism and changes in the Court's membership that *Swift* would finally be discarded. The vehicle for its demise was *Erie Railroad Co.* v. *Tompkins,* a tort case brought by a man who was hit by something protruding from a passing railroad train as he walked along by the tracks. Under state law, Tompkins would have found it more difficult to recover, but the lower courts applied general law principles, and found the railroad liable for negligence. The Supreme Court overturned *Swift,* finding that newly uncovered evidence regarding the Judiciary Act of 1789 suggested that it had been interpreted incorrectly, and more importantly that the *Swift* doctrine was unconstitutional. Hereafter, in diversity of citizenship cases the federal courts would look to state court decisions as well as state statutes. According to the Court's opinion in *Erie,* "whether the law of the state shall be declared by its Legislature in a statute or by its highest court in a decision is not a matter of federal concern. There is no federal general common law." *Tompkins*'s fate under state law was then determined on remand to the Second Circuit Court of Appeals, and he did not prevail.

The legal scholar Charles Alan Wright later wrote that "It is impossible to overstate the importance of the Erie decision," which "goes to the heart of the relations between the federal government and the states, and returns to the states a power that had for nearly a century been exercised by the federal government." The importance of the case was lost on the nation's press, however. *The New York Times* only covered it eight days later after Justice Stone wrote columnist Arthur Krock encouraging him to write about *Erie.* Krock began the first of two columns on the case by suggesting that the Supreme Court needed a publicity agent.

CONSOLIDATING A NEW MAJORITY

Following the judicial revolution of 1937, the dissenters now found themselves in the majority, and faced the challenge of turning a dissenting tradition into a ruling constitutional doctrine. The critics of excessive judicial intervention in legislative decision making did not wish the Court's role to retreat to a minimalist position in all areas, however. In the area of economic regulation, the path was clear: the Court adopted a posture of deference to legislative judgment. It was more difficult, however, to carve out a justification for more intrusive judicial review in civil rights and civil liberties cases, which the Court felt needed greater scrutiny. Justice Stone faced the task of suggesting a justification for treating cases involving individual rights more carefully than cases involving economic regulation in the unlikely case of *United States* v. *Carolene Products* in 1938. In that case, the Court upheld regulation under the commerce power of the sale of milk combined with coconut oil as pure milk. In the celebrated footnote four of *Carolene Products,* Justice Stone suggested that the Court's announced rule of deference to the legislature would not always apply. "More searching judicial scrutiny" might be appropriate when the legislation was the product of political process failure, such as when the legislature had restricted voting, assembly, and other "political processes which can ordinarily be expected to bring about repeal of undesirable legislation." In addition, Stone suggested that greater scrutiny might be needed in cases involving religious, national, or racial minorities, raising the question of whether "prejudice against discrete and insular minorities may be a special condition, which tends seriously to curtail the operation of those political processes ordinarily to be relied on to protect minorities."

This theory gave a more focused judicial activism a majoritarian basis. If the legitimacy of democratic government rested on popular sovereignty, the Court had a duty to step in to ensure that all of "the people" could have their voices heard. This seed planted by Stone in the *Carolene Products* footnote was obscured for a time, but would fully blossom during the Warren Court era. The process-based theory implicit in footnote four eventually gave rise to a body of constitutional theory, and gave liberals an effective response to conservative critiques of the countermajoritarian nature of judicial review.

In the late 1930s and early 1940s, several changes in Supreme Court personnel helped to consolidate a liberal majority. The dramatic expansion in protection for individual rights and ratification of seemingly boundless federal regulatory power that would follow in the ensuing years cannot be explained simply in terms of changes on the Court, however. Of central importance were the new domestic and international responsibilities the federal government took on as the nation edged into World War II.

In November 1942, while the nation was fighting "the good war" in Europe and Asia, the Supreme Court handed down an opinion that embraced a breathtaking expansion of congressional power under the Commerce Clause. *Wickard* v. *Filburn* involved the Agricultural Adjustment Act of 1938, which allowed the Secretary of Agriculture to set quotas for wheat and various other crops as a way to stabilize prices. Roscoe C. Filburn, an Ohio dairy farmer who grew wheat for consumption on his own farm and for sale, exceeded his allotment of 222 bushels, and was fined. He brought suit claiming that the act was unconstitutional as applied in his case. The central question considered by the Supreme Court was whether the scope of the commerce power was so broad that Congress had the authority to regulate the wheat Filburn grew for his own consumption. Finding that consumption of home-grown wheat was "the most variable factor in the disappearance of the wheat crop," the Court reasoned that although Filburn's own impact on interstate commerce might be trivial, taken together with other farmers engaged in similar practices, there was a cumulative effect on interstate commerce from home-grown and consumed wheat that was substantial enough that Congress had power to regulate it. Only five years after the Court upheld Congress's power to regulate a massive steel corporation in the New Deal era case *Jones & Laughlin,* the Court's action in *Wickard* v. *Filburn* was a dramatic step toward even greater federal power. And if Filburn's home-consumed wheat was within the purview of Congress's regulatory authority, federal legislative power under the Commerce Clause seemed limitless.

Wickard is generally seen as within the line of progression of post–Court-packing-plan cases, and therefore presumably a logical extension of the "realist" analysis in *Jones & Laughlin,* with its search for economic impact. More was at stake in this case than wheat farmers' cumulative economic impact on the national economy, however. The nation was at war, and the Roosevelt administration was keeping a watchful eye on the production of essential commodities. In 1941, Secretary of Agriculture Claude P. Wickard gave a radio address entitled "Wheat Farmers and the Battle for Democracy." Wickard announced that "because of the uncertain world situation, we deliberately planted several million extra acres of wheat this year." A package of farm loans and production quotas were needed to maintain prices so that "Farmers should not be penalized because they have provided insurance against shortages of food." Agricultural programs, of which production quotas were a part, "protect all farmers," Wickard urged. "Since the second world war began, commodity loans have stood between wheat producers and the economic blitzkrieg."

World War II—and the perceived need for broad federal power to deal with domestic difficulties that can attend international crises—provided the context for the Court's mid-century embrace of such expansive federal power. With its "cumulative effects" test, enabling Congress to reach even activities that, by themselves, affected interstate commerce only trivially, *Wickard* decimated the remnants of New Deal era federalism. The Court firmly embraced the regulatory state. As the nation emerged as a world power, and its economy as well as its national security was increasingly interdependent with its world neighbors, effective government now required no less.

Domestic imperatives were equally on the agenda in the early 1940s, as the Supreme Court undid some important *Lochner*-era handiwork. A critical case was *United States* v. *Darby* (1941), which tested the constitutionality of the Fair Labor Standards Act under Congress's Commerce power. The act prohibited shipment in interstate commerce of goods produced by workers whose wages and hours did not meet federal standards. It also directly forbade the employment at substandard wages or excessive hours of employees engaged in production of goods for interstate commerce. The statute directly challenged two of the Court's commerce power doctrines. First, production was supposed to have occurred *before* interstate commerce began, so it was beyond the scope of Congress's power over interstate commerce. Second, under *Hammer* v. *Dagenhart,* the child labor case, if the goods produced in violation of federal labor standards were not themselves harmful, shipment of the goods could not be banned. The Court overturned *Hammer,* allowing shipment of goods to be prohibited. Then, looking to the impact of labor practices on interstate commerce, the Court found that production employees could be regulated. For good measure, the Court added that the Tenth Amendment posed no bar to the statute, for "the amendment states but a truism that all is retained which has not been surrendered." The Court's economic impact analysis in *Darby* was similar to that used in *Jones & Laughlin,* yet the circumstances were markedly different. Darby operated a lumber mill, and was not a massive corporation firmly embedded in interstate commerce, as was Jones & Laughlin Steel Corporation. As a result, beyond the doctrinal development in *Darby,* the case signaled that Congress's regulatory power could reach the average employer-employee relationship as long as the business had some impact on interstate commerce. As the building of interstate highways and improvements in train and air travel nationalized the marketplace, it would ultimately be difficult to argue that any business was not in some important way touched by interstate commerce. As a result, *Darby* marked doctrinally an extension of regulatory authority that the increasingly national economy may have made inevitable.

Wartime federal power would not always be in service of beneficent ends. As the nation reacted in fear to the bombing of Pearl Harbor in 1942, FDR signed Executive Order 9066 ordering the removal of persons of Japanese heritage, including Japanese American U.S. citizens, from the West Coast. The reason for the order was a fear that Japanese Americans would sabotage the war effort, making military operations on the coast vulnerable to attack. The result was that whole families were uprooted, taking only what they could physically carry, and were sent to rudimentary camps in desolate and isolated parts of several western states.

The ultimate justification for the imprisonment of all persons of Japanese heritage was ultimately race-based. Even for those persons who had never set foot on Japanese soil, U.S. Army General John DeWitt argued that their primary loyalty was to the Emperor of Japan. The government claimed that there was no reliable way to distinguish the loyal from the disloyal in a timely way. Relying on the government's arguments, the Court upheld the internment program in *Korematsu* v. *United States* in 1944.

In an eloquent dissent, Justice Robert Jackson acknowledged the necessities of military power during wartime, but questioned the role of the Court in legitimating such acts. Once the Court validated the race discrimination in this case, "the principle lies about like a loaded weapon ready for the hand of any authority that can bring forward a plausible claim of an urgent need." The Court's role in the internment was therefore more lasting. By placing its stamp of constitutionality on this exercise of military power, the Court equated this harsh act with justice. In so doing, Jackson suggested, the Court functioned as an arm of the military. Further, its legitimation of such discriminatory action made it more likely that such an injustice could happen again.

Wartime hysteria seemed to play into the *Korematsu* ruling. In less charged circumstances, the Court was able to mediate wartime passions and to protect civil liberties. After ruling in *Minersville School District* v. *Gobitis* (1940) that the First Amendment rights of schoolchildren were not violated when they were required to salute the United States flag, the Court reversed itself in *West Virginia State Board of Education* v. *Barnette* (1943). As communities closed ranks in support of the war, and patriotic symbols abounded as images of the fight for democracy, the Court reminded the nation that democracy encompassed the freedom to dissent. Justice Jackson wrote for the Court that "if there is any fixed star in our constitutional constellation, it is that no official, high or petty, can prescribe what shall be orthodox in politics, nationalism, religion, or other matters of opinion or force citizens to confess by word or act their faith therein."

The scope of power the Court would concede to the federal government was, of course, not without its limits. President Harry S. Truman came up against those limits in 1952. When a steel strike threatened to halt production in the midst of the Korean War, Truman seized the steel mills to keep them open, arguing that continued steel production was essential to the country's national defense. The Court quickly heard an appeal from the steel companies, and found the president's order to be unconstitutional. In sharp contrast to the careful unanimity the Court was maintaining in race relations cases, in this important decision the six members of the majority each wrote separately, relying on a variety of separation of powers arguments. Underlying each of their approaches, though, the Justices shared a common concern about the implications of unbridled executive power. Truman himself seemed unlikely to be a threat, at least to Justice Frankfurter. "It is absurd to see a dictator in a representative product of the sturdy democratic traditions of the Mississippi Valley," Frankfurter wrote in his concurrence. However, "the accretion of dangerous power does not come in a day. It does come, however slowly, from the generative force of unchecked disregard of the restrictions that fence in even the most disinterested assertion of authority." In striking down the president's power to seize the steel mills, the Court saw itself as protecting the nation from a greater harm than labor unrest: the excessive concentration of power in the hands of a leader.

Faith in federal power to protect against the exigencies of wartime had guided the Court through World War II. In the postwar years, as McCarthyism gripped the country and as the Cold War grew hot in Asia, the fears about dangers of excessive executive authority—fears, essentially, about Stalinism—gripped the consciousness of the nation and the Court, helping to move the Court away from pragmatic accommodation of government action, and toward judicial limitations on executive branch encroachment.

THE WARREN COURT

Perhaps the most dramatic debate over the role of the courts in the twentieth century was the debate over court decisions on racial segregation in the schools. In the same year that the Supreme Court stepped back from close scrutiny of economic legislation and announced, in footnote four of *Carolene Products,* the possibility of a process-based justification for greater judicial activism in cases involving minority rights, the Court began the process of chipping away at *Plessy* v. *Ferguson*'s doctrine of separate-but-equal. Decided in 1896, *Plessy* provided the constitutional basis for the system of segregated education in the South. In 1938, in *Missouri ex rel. Gaines* v. *Canada,* the Supreme Court did not question the constitutionality of racial segregation per se, but invalidated Missouri's practice of sending black students out-of-state to go to law school since legal education was not offered to them in the state. It was the first time that the Court had looked seriously at the equality side of the separate-but-equal formula. During the 1940s, the Court struck down impediments to the right to vote, at the core of footnote four's theory of judicial review. Then in 1950, in *Sweatt* v. *Painter* and *McLaurin* v. *Oklahoma,* the Court found that legal education and graduate education could not be equal under the conditions of segregation at issue in those cases. *Plessy* seemed to be on its way out, yet a formidable constitutional barrier remained in the way: federalism and the states' traditional role in public education. Although the Court had ratified a dramatic extension of congressional power over matters previously thought to be of local concern, and invalidated particular discriminatory state practices involving higher education, it was another matter for the federal courts to interfere with public elementary and secondary schools.

Although some members of the Supreme Court clearly wished that the issue would not visit them so soon, the NAACP brought a series of cases in four states and the District of Columbia challenging the constitutionality of racially segregated public education. The cases reached the Court and were argued in the spring of 1953, consolidated as *Brown* v. *Board of Education.* As the nation waited for an announcement of the ruling, a divided Court opted for delay. The Court called for reargument, asking the parties to address the question of whether the framers of the Fourteenth Amendment intended to invalidate public school segregation.

In the intervening months before the Court again considered the *Brown* case, a human tragedy and a personal triumph in the lives of two men profoundly affected the course of the litigation. On 8 September 1953, Chief Justice Fred Vinson died of a heart attack. He was replaced by Governor Earl Warren of California, a skillful politician who had been promised a spot on the high court as an inducement to withdraw from consideration for the 1952 Republican presidential nomination. As California attorney general in 1942, Warren had been a strong supporter of the internment of Japanese Americans, so his record did not suggest particular sensitivity to race discrimination. Nevertheless, in the spring of 1954 it was Warren who pulled the Court together behind a unanimous ruling against segregated schools.

The Court's decision in *Brown* was, in many ways, a simple moral judgment: racial segregation was wrong. The difficulty for Warren in writing the opinion was the question of why it was the Court's job to make that moral judgment and to enforce it on local school systems. In a footnote of the *Brown* opinion, Warren relied on social science evidence to support the finding that racial segregation was harmful to children. The evidence was useful not only because, at the time, it seemed powerful, but because reliance on modern scientific evidence also provided a means of arguing that the Court had learned something new about conditions of segregation, and that new knowledge required a different interpretation of the Fourteenth Amendment's guarantee of equality, justifying a departure from past rulings.

Yet southern supporters of segregation had argued that "stateways can't change folkways," that legal change was not the way to alter cultural practices in the South. The most effective response to that argument came in a finding from the lower court in Topeka, Kansas, and quoted in the Supreme Court's ruling in *Brown*. Not only was segregation harmful to black children, but "the impact is greater when it has the sanction of the law." As Justice Jackson had argued in *Korematsu,* it was a greater harm when law legitimated discriminatory practices. And this harm from the law itself was clearly something within the Court's competence to remedy.

As it turned out, the denial of legal legitimacy was all that the Court accomplished in *Brown,* at least initially. In 1955 in *Brown* v. *Board of Education II* the Court denied the plaintiffs in the cases before it a remedy, calling instead for "all deliberate speed" in the enforcement of *Brown*. Justice Frankfurter had hoped that delay in ordering a remedy would enable the Court to avoid provoking a constitutional crisis and violence in the South. Instead, both followed.

The second great twentieth-century national crisis over the role of the courts developed in the aftermath of *Brown*. Southern politicians stood in the schoolhouse door, claiming that their states' rights had been violated, and wrapping their resistance in the cloak of the Constitution. Southern members of Congress submitted a manifesto arguing that the Supreme Court had subverted the Constitution. Federalism became a way for cultured people to argue that the southern states were right, without having to mention the words "race" or "segregation."

The apex of the constitutional crisis occurred in Little Rock, Arkansas, in 1957–1958. The Little Rock school board had decided that it should comply with *Brown,* and drew up a desegregation plan that involved sending nine black children to all-white Central High School in the fall of 1957. Arkansas governor Orval Faubus, who had discovered that it was easier to get reelected as a segregationist than as a moderate, called in state troops and ordered them to bar the children from entering the school. As a white mob ringed the high school, it eventually required federal troops sent in by President Eisenhower to enable the "Little Rock Nine" to go to school.

Meanwhile, the school board had requested permission from the federal district court in Arkansas to delay implementing its desegregation plan due to the disorder. In *Cooper* v. *Aaron* in 1958, the Supreme Court reasserted its authority, first articulated in *Marbury* v. *Madison* in 1803, that "it is emphatically the province and duty of the judicial department to say what the law is." That meant that "the federal judiciary is supreme in its exposition of the law of the constitution." The Court's *Brown* decision was therefore the supreme law of the land, under the Constitution, and state government officials were bound to follow it. Quoting Chief Justice John Marshall in *United States* v. *Peters,* the Court admonished that "If the legislatures of the several states may, at will, annul the judgments of the courts of the United States, and destroy the rights acquired under those judgments, the constitution itself becomes a solemn mockery."

The Supreme Court could order the state of Arkansas to desegregate its schools, and President Eisenhower could enforce the order with federal troops, but the Court's power had important limits. The Court could not order the state of Arkansas to operate a public school system. In the fall of 1958, the state closed down its public school system. State autonomy prevailed, at least temporarily, at the expense of children's education. Eventually, the courts forced reopening of the schools, declaring the closing unconstitutional in 1959.

Meanwhile, the school desegregation cases were only one area in which the Warren Court expanded the constitutional rights of individuals. From *Baker* v. *Carr* (1962), establishing one person, one vote as a constitutional rule, to *Miranda* v. *Arizona* (1966), requiring police officers to notify arrested persons of their rights, the Supreme Court, amid plenty of controversy, engrafted a new image of liberty and equality into the law. As individual rights expanded, so did opposition to the Warren Court in general, and to Chief Justice Warren in particular. "Impeach Earl Warren" signs appeared along highways throughout the South. Members of Congress sponsored legislation designed to cut back on the Court's jurisdiction over particular areas. Even other judges got behind the anti-Warren effort. In 1958, thirty-six chief justices of state supreme courts signed a resolution critical of the Warren Court.

Although the impact of *Brown* as a legally enforceable precedent was muted by southern resistance, the Court's ruling had a different kind of impact whose power was immeasurable. In 1960 in Greensboro, North Carolina, four black students decided that the time had come for them to be served at the segregated lunch counter at Woolworth's. From Rosa Parks's decision a few years earlier in Montgomery, Alabama, not to give up her seat on the bus to a white man to the Freedom Riders' organization of integrated bus trips into the deep South in the face of certain and brutal violence, *Brown* was, for many, a symbol of hope and a source of empowerment that helped energize a civil rights movement that would ultimately be of much greater importance in dismantling the legal structure of racial inequality.

While civil rights activists reacted to *Brown* in the streets, legal scholars reacted in the nation's law reviews, touching off a debate about the nature of judicial power. Some scholars supported the outcome in *Brown* v. *Board of Education,* but were uncomfortable with the way the Court got there. In an influential 1961 article, "Toward Neutral Principles of Constitutional Law," Herbert Weschler implied that *Brown* was more politics than law because it was not based on neutral, generalizable principles. Weschler's suggestion for an alternative basis for *Brown* was freedom of association.

While such scholars as Charles Black responded to Weschler by defending *Brown* as appropriately applying principles of equality to victims of discrimination, others expanded the critique of *Brown* to an attack on judicial activism in general. Titles like Lino Graglia's *Disaster by Decree,* and Raoul Berger's *Government by Judiciary* appeared on the bookshelves. A more temperate, and ultimately more influential, voice in this debate was that of Alexander Bickel, a former Frankfurter law clerk and protégé, and a Yale law professor. In 1962, Bickel published a book that would become the bible of advocates of judicial restraint—*The Least Dangerous Branch: The Supreme Court at the Bar of Politics.* Bickel's title was borrowed from Alexander Hamilton, who had written in *The Federalist* that the judiciary was the least dangerous of the branches of government because it had "neither FORCE nor WILL, but merely judgment." This branch, Bickel wrote, had become "the most extraordinarily powerful court of law the world has ever known." Yet the courts played a problematic role in our political system. A democracy is based on majority rule, yet each time a court strikes down a statute, it acts counter to the will of the majority. Because of this "counter-majoritarian difficulty," Bickel argued that the courts should not play an activist role in striking down unwise popular enactments. He shared Frankfurter's fondness for what he called the "passive virtues"—the exercise of court power in a restrained way so as to conserve the court's authority.

Bickel's analysis of the countermajoritarian difficulty set the terms of debate over the role of the courts for the remainder of the twentieth century. Conservative scholars found in Bickel a justification for narrow theories of judicial power and constitutional interpretation. Liberals such as John Hart Ely took Bickel as their starting point and, turning to footnote four of *Carolene Products,* crafted a theory of judicial activism limited to contexts where the majoritarian political process was likely to fail. Even Bruce Ackerman in the 1980s and 1990s, in trying to cast off Bickel's hold on constitutional theory by rejecting his premise, acknowledged the hold countermajoritarian theory had on constitutional analysis.

In the early 1970s, Bickel's book was also required reading in the Nixon White House. As the Supreme Court, now under the leadership of Chief Justice Warren Burger, began to put more teeth into school desegregation remedies in the early 1970s, upholding a cross-town busing order in *Swann* v. *Charlotte-Mecklenburg Board of Education* in 1971, and as school desegregation moved north in the Denver case of *Keyes* v. *School District No. 1,* busing became a hot political issue, and with it the role of the courts. In 1972, with *Newsweek* magazine reporting that only 2 percent of the country supported busing, and facing a strong challenge in the Republican primaries from school desegregation opponent George Wallace in the South, Nixon went on television to call for a moratorium on court-ordered busing. The courts were, again, a campaign issue.

Although school desegregation was a particular focus of post-*Brown* criticism of the federal courts, the Warren Court's reapportionment and criminal justice cases had also come under fire. In the spring of 1964, Alabama Governor George Wallace broadened his critique of the Supreme Court to include the Court's criminal justice cases. According to Wallace, the Court was responsible for a rise in "crime in the streets," for "the court system has now ruled that you can hardly convict a criminal." Moving beyond sectional concerns, Wallace helped to nationalize court-bashing. Barry Goldwater, the 1964 Republican presidential nominee, picked up on this theme, criticizing the Court for having "abandoned the principle of 'judicial restraint.'" He charged that "Of all three branches of Government, today's Supreme Court is least faithful to the constitutional tradition of limited government and to the principle of legitimacy in the exercise of power." Goldwater proposed a package of reforms, including the appointment of more conservative judges and a constitutional amendment that would "give back to the states those powers absolutely necessary for fair and efficient administration of criminal law." Meanwhile, complaining about Court interference with legislative power, Sen. Russell B. Long of Louisiana said that the Supreme Court rarely interfered with presidential power because the president "might send Marines down there and put some of those screwballs in jail."

THE POLITICS OF SUPREME COURT APPOINTMENTS

During the second half of the twentieth century, Supreme Court nomination battles provided a context for political struggles over the role of the courts. Controversy over Court nominees was, of course, not new. Justice Brandeis, considered a "rabid" social reformer, and the first Jew to join the Court, was narrowly endorsed by the Senate Judiciary Committee before being confirmed by a 49-to-22 Senate vote in 1916. John J. Parker failed to secure Senate confirmation in 1930, amid allegations of racism and antilabor sentiment. Later in the century confirmation battles more directly implicated the executive branch because nominees were at times explicitly selected to further the presidents' political agendas. In addition, after 1939, it became common for nominees to testify at their confirmation hearing. The added factor of televising hearings toward the end of the century enabled the nation to look in on the process more closely. (See tables 1 and 2.)

A mix of ideology, politics, and patronage informed Supreme Court appointments. The president did not, of course, act alone in appointing justices. The Senate's confirmation was required, and senators often played a role in offering names or screening out potential appointees. The Senate's role was greater at the lower court level. As David O'Brien has described it, "The appointment process has become essentially a bargaining process in which the influence of the Senate is greater in regard to lower-court judgeships and that of the President is greater in regard to the Supreme Court."

While the Supreme Court appointments by Presidents Truman, Eisenhower, and Kennedy were met with little controversy, Lyndon B. Johnson's and Richard Nixon's experiences were quite different. President Johnson's nominee for Chief Justice, Associate Justice Abe Fortas, withdrew amid charges of cronyism and judicial impropriety due to his close involvement with LBJ while on the Court in the waning days of the Johnson administration.

In 1967, Solicitor General Thurgood Marshall was the subject of controversy of a different kind. The former NAACP counsel during that organization's struggle to desegregate schools was the first black Supreme Court nominee. While Marshall's nomination was widely praised, it ran into predictable and protracted opposition in the South. Yet when the vote finally came after a two-and-one-half-month delay, Marshall was confirmed by an ample margin, receiving favorable votes from six southern senators—a sign that the politics of race were changing, even in the South.

In some ways President Nixon invited controversy by attacking the Court in his 1968 campaign, signaling that ideology would play an important role in his Supreme Court appointments. Picking up on George Wallace's argument that the federal courts were responsible for increased "crime in the streets," Nixon's 1968 campaign focused on "law and order." He attacked the Supreme Court and its liberal rulings protecting the rights of defendants as standing in the way of government crime-fighting efforts. As an antidote to the liberal bench, Nixon promised to appoint "strict constructionists who saw their duty as interpreting law and not making law. They would see themselves as caretakers of the Constitution, not super-legislators with a free hand to impose their social and political viewpoints upon the American people."

Nixon's first appointee was Warren Burger to fill the position of chief justice. Burger's ideology fit well

Table 1. SUPREME COURT JUSTICES[a]

President	Justice	State from which Apptd	Birth Date	Service Dates	Death Date
25 McKinley, R	58 Joseph McKenna, R	Calif.	1843	1898–1925	1926
26 T. Roosevelt, R	59 Oliver Wendell Holmes, Jr., R	Mass.	1841	1902–1932	1935
	60 William R. Day, R	Ohio	1849	1903–1922	1923
	61 William H. Moody, R.	Mass.	1853	1906–1919	1917
27 Taft, R	62 Horace H. Lurton, D	Tenn.	1844	1909–1914	1914
	63 Charles E. Hughes, R	N.Y.	1862	1910–1916	1948
	64 *Edward D. White, D	La.	1845	1910–1921	1921
	65 Willis Van Devanter, R	Wyo.	1859	1911–1937	1941
	66 Joseph R. Lamar, D	Ga.	1857	1911–1916	1916
	67 Mahlon Pitney, R	N.J.	1858	1921–1922	1924
28 Wilson, D	68 James C. McReynolds, D	Tenn.	1862	1914–1941	1946
	69 Louis D. Brandeis, R[b]	Mass.	1856	1916–1939	1941
	70 John H. Clarke, D	Ohio	1857	1916–1922	1945
29 Harding, R	**71 William H. Taft,** R	Conn.	1857	1921–1930	1930
	72 George Sutherland, R	Utah	1862	1922–1938	1942
	73 Pierce Butler, D	Minn.	1866	1922–1939	1939
	74 Edward T. Sanford, R	Tenn.	1865	1923–1930	1930
30 Coolidge, R	75 Harlan F. Stone, F	N.Y.	1872	1925–1941	1946
31 Hoover, R	**76 *Charles E. Hughes,** R	N.Y.	1862	1930–1941	1948
	77 Owen J. Roberts, R	Pa.	1875	1930–1945	1955
	78 Benjamin N. Cardozo, D	N.Y.	1870	1932–1938	1938
32 F. D. Roosevelt, D	79 Hugo L. Black, D	Ala.	1886	1937–1971	1971
	80 Stanley F. Reed	Ky.	1884	1938–1957	1980
	81 Felix Frankfurter, I	Mass.	1882	1939–1962	1965
	82 William O. Douglas, D	Conn.	1898	1939–1975	1980
	83 Frank Murphy, D	Mich.	1890	1940–1949	1949
	84 James F. Byrnes, D	S.C.	1879	1941–1942	1972
	85 *Harlan F. Stone, R	N.Y.	1872	1941–1946	1946
	86 Robert H. Jackson, D	N.Y.	1892	1941–1954	1954
	87 Wiley B. Rutledge, D	Iowa	1894	1943–1949	1949
33 Truman, D	88 Harold H. Burton, R	Ohio	1888	1945–1958	1965
	89 Fred M. Vinson, D	Ky.	1890	1946–1953	1953
	90 Tom C. Clark, D	Texas	1899	1949–1967	1977
	91 Sherman Minton, D	Ind.	1890	1949–1956	1965
34 Eisenhower, R	**92 Earl Warren,** R	Calif.	1891	1953–1969	1974
	93 John M. Harlan, II, R	N.Y.	1899	1955–1971	1971
	94 William J. Brennan, Jr., D	N.J.	1906	1956–1990	
	95 Charles E. Whittaker, R	Mo.	1901	1957–1962	1973
	96 Potter Stewart, R	Ohio	1915	1958–1981	1985
35 Kennedy, D	97 Byron R. White, D	Colo.	1917	1962–1993	
	98 Arthur J. Goldberg, D	Ill.	1908	1962–1965	1990
36 L. B. Johnson, D	99 Abe Fortas, D	Tenn.	1910	1965–1969	1982
	100 Thurgood Marshall, D	N.Y.	1908	1967–1991	1993
37 Nixon, R	**101 Warren E. Burger,** R	Va.	1907	1969–1986	1995
	102 Harry A. Blackmun, R	Minn.	1908	1970–1994	
	103 Lewis F. Powell, Jr., D	Va.	1907	1972–1987	
	104 William H. Rehnquist, R	Ariz.	1924	1972–1986	
38 Ford, R	105 John Paul Stevens, R	Ill.	1920	1975–	
39 Carter, D					

Table 1. SUPREME COURT JUSTICES[a] (*Continued*)

President	Justice	State from which Apptd	Birth Date	Service Dates	Death Date
40 Reagan, R	106 Sandra Day O'Connor, R	Ariz.	1930	1981–	
	107 *William H. Rehnquist, R	Va.	1924	1986–	
	108 Antonin Scalia, R	Va.	1936	1986–	
	109 Anthony M. Kennedy, R	Calif.	1936	1988–	
41 Bush, R	110 David Souter, R	N.H.	1939	1990–	
	111 Clarence Thomas, R	Va.	1948	1991–	
42 Clinton, D	112 Ruth Bader Ginsburg, D	D.C.	1933	1993–	
	113 Stephen G. Breyer, D	Mass.	1938	1994–	

[a] Chief Justices are shown in bold face. The Justices' party designations are nominal party affiliations at appointment. States from which Justices were appointed are usually, but not neccessarily, the Justices' birth states.
[b] Though many consider Brandeis a Democrat, he was a registered Republican when nominated.
Abbreviations: D, Democrat; I, Independent; R, Republican.
* Associate Justice promoted to Chief Justice.
SOURCE: Adapted from *Encyclopedia of the American Presidency* (New York: Simon & Schuster, 1994), pp. 900–901. Prepared by Henry J. Abraham.

with Nixon's agenda. He had publicly attacked the Warren Court and the expansion of individual rights. "Too many law professors for a long time gave uncritical applause to anything they could identify as an expansion of individual 'rights,'" he said, "even when that expansion was at the expense of the rights of others." The nominee was quickly and easily confirmed.

Hoping to pay back political debts to southern supporters, as well as to appoint another person who would bring a conservative ideology to the high court, Nixon turned to Clement Haynesworth of South Carolina for the next vacancy. Haynesworth was a Fourth Circuit Court of Appeals judge who was strongly supported by Sen. Strom Thurmond. Haynesworth's record was closely scrutinized by the Senate, and many senators did not like what they saw. Although the Democrats charged Haynesworth with judicial improprieties, most stark was his conservative record in civil rights cases, particularly those involving segregation. Liberals charged that he was a "laundered segregationist" who would slow down the progress of Warren Court reforms. The combination of criticisms led the Senate to reject the nomination.

Next, Nixon nominated Judge Harrold Carswell of Florida. Allegations of racism would dog this nominee as well. Carswell had made a campaign speech in the 1940s in which he argued that "segregation of the races is proper," and he expressed his "firm, vigorous belief in the principles of white supremacy." Carswell also had a competence problem, however. Rated only "qualified" by the American Bar Association (not "highly qualified"), one of his supporters defended him by saying that Carswell disagreed with "those who criticize your opinions by comparing them to a plumber's manual." Duke law professor William Van Alystyne testified that there was "nothing in the quality of the nominee's work to warrant any expectation whatever that he could serve with distinction" on the Court. When another scholar called Carswell mediocre, Carswell supporter Sen. Roman Hruska responded, "there are a lot of mediocre judges and people and lawyers. They are entitled

Table 2. UNSUCCESSFUL SUPREME COURT NOMINATIONS

Nominating President	Nominee	Approximate Date of Nomination	Outcome
Hoover, R	John Parker, R	21 March 1930	Rejected (39–41)
L. B. Johnson, D	Abe Fortas, D[a]	26 June 1968	Withdrawn
Nixon, R	Clement F. Haynsworth, Jr., R	18 August 1969	Rejected (45–55)
	G. Harrold Carswell, R.	19 January 1970	Rejected (45–51)
Reagan, R	Robert H. Bork, R	2 July 1987	Rejected (42–58)
	Douglas H. Ginsburg, R	20 October 1987	Withdrawn

[a] Johnson nominated Associate Justice Fortas to be Chief Justice; the nomination was withdrawn in the face of Senate opposition.
Abbreviations: D, Democrat; R, Republican.
SOURCE: Adapted from *Encyclopedia of the American Presidency* (New York: Simon & Schuster, 1994), p. 1425. Prepared by John Massaro.

to a little representation, aren't they?" After weeks of floor debate, the nomination was defeated.

With Carswell's loss, Nixon abandoned his southern strategy, and turned instead to Chief Justice Warren Burger's good friend, Harry Blackmun of Minnesota. Easily confirmed, Blackmun would at first so closely mirror Burger's votes that the two were called the "Minnesota Twins." In time, however, Blackmun would become more independent and more liberal, authoring the Court's famous *Roe* v. *Wade* opinion upholding the right to abortion in 1973, against a vigorous dissent joined by his friend Warren Burger. Blackmun's liberalism would be somewhat overemphasized in the 1990s as the Court moved to the right and liberal and moderate justices resigned, leaving Blackmun on the left of a court of conservatives.

A NEW CONSERVATIVE CRISIS?

Toward the end of the twentieth century, in the late 1980s and early 1990s, the federal courts seemed to be veering toward another conservative crisis. Liberal critics of the Supreme Court claimed that the right wing of the Court was on an activist mission to rewrite federal law, particularly in the area of civil rights. Supreme Court rulings that generated the most widespread political reaction were in the area of abortion rights, where the Court began to uphold state abortion regulations that under the earlier caselaw would have been unconstitutional.

As a reaction to this conservative trend, beginning in the 1970s, civil rights litigants turned with increasing frequency to state courts, bringing claims under state constitutional law. As a result, the growing hostility of the federal courts to civil rights claims ultimately spawned a body of state constitutional law that was often more protective of individual rights. By the 1990s, some state courts had found broader protection for individual rights in the context of public funding for abortions and inequality of government expenditures in public schools, among other areas.

Helping to fuel the controversy over abortion and the federal courts, President Ronald Reagan instituted an antiabortion "litmus test" for judicial appointees. Seeing the courts as a means to achieve a conservative social agenda over time, the Reagan administration sought staunch conservatives who were also young, and therefore likely to have a long-lasting impact on the courts. President George Bush followed a similar strategy. The Reagan and Bush court appointments had a profound effect on the lower federal courts as, by 1992, approximately 70 percent of lower court judges were Reagan and Bush appointees.

There was a limit to what could be accomplished, however, as demonstrated by the defeat of Supreme Court nominee Robert Bork. Nominated in July 1987 to fill the vacancy created by the resignation of Justice Lewis F. Powell, Bork was immediately opposed by a broad coalition of civil rights groups due to his conservative views. In testimony before the Senate Judiciary Committee, Bork advocated judicial restraint, and a theory of constitutional interpretation based on the constitutional text and the intentions of the framers. Bork believed that *Roe* v. *Wade* was not authorized by the framers' intentions, and also that the right to privacy in the use of birth control articulated in *Griswold* v. *Connecticut* was something the framers had not contemplated, and therefore something the Constitution did not protect. Bork's widely televised testimony provoked a strong, negative public reaction. Some commentators likened the Bork hearings to a national teach-in on the Constitution, with a final public referendum in favor of a constitutional right to privacy. Bork was ultimately defeated in the Senate by the widest margin of votes in the history of the confirmation process.

The political climate on abortion rights profoundly affected the selection of subsequent Supreme Court nominees. Chastened by the rejection of Robert Bork, Reagan and Bush turned to nominees who seemed to have no track record on reproductive rights. Anthony Kennedy in 1988 and David Souter in 1990 were confirmed easily, the latter with such a sparse paper trail that he was called the "Stealth candidate" after the radar-evading Stealth bomber. However, when Justice Kennedy sided with Court conservatives in an opinion severely undermining *Roe* v. *Wade* in 1989, members of the Senate became more staunchly critical of the strategy of picking silent candidates, and vowed that they would be more diligent in ferreting out the views on privacy and abortion rights of future Supreme Court nominees.

In this context, in 1991, George Bush nominated Clarence Thomas to fill a vacancy created by the retirement of Justice Thurgood Marshall. The selection of Thomas, a conservative black Court of Appeals judge who formerly served as chair of the Equal Employment Opportunity Commission, in part reflected a sense that it was important for a black person to fill the seat of the only black justice ever to serve on the Supreme Court. President Bush also rightly calculated that it would be more difficult for liberals to mount an effective challenge to a black appointee. Compounding the opposition's difficulties, in the

Senate Judiciary Committee hearings Thomas took the stealth strategy a step further than other nominees, claiming never even to have discussed the landmark abortion rights case *Roe* v. *Wade.*

Ultimately it would not be abortion or a conservative ideology that would be the greatest hurdle to the Thomas nomination. Rather it was a charge of sexual harassment brought by Anita Hill, a black woman who was a former Thomas subordinate at the EEOC. A second set of Senate hearings was held to air the Hill allegations. The spectacle proved more dramatic than the Bork hearings, riveting the nation's attention. With both Thomas and Hill as powerful witnesses, the controversy ultimately turned on the question of which one to believe. Judiciary Committee chair Joseph Biden declared that doubt should be resolved in favor of the nominee, and with public opinion polls suggesting that the public sided with Thomas, the committee and the full Senate approved the nomination. Although Thomas gained a seat on the high court, he was not to find a place in the hearts of most Americans. By the end of his first Supreme Court term, his harshly conservative opinions led the *New York Times* to call him "The Youngest, Cruelest Justice," and polls a year after the hearings suggested that public sentiment now favored Anita Hill, who had become the nation's new civil rights heroine.

As the Thomas hearings ended, a presidential campaign began. The 1992 election year's primary focus was on the nation's struggling economy. A consistent, though minor, theme was the role of the courts in protecting the right to abortion. The potential power of the courts as a campaign issue was undercut in June 1992 when a new coalition of Justices—O'Connor, Kennedy, and Souter—voted to uphold most aspects of a Pennsylvania statute restricting access to abortion, but not to overturn *Roe* v. *Wade.* With the symbol, if not the reality, of access to abortion protected, the courts' role in protecting reproductive rights faded as a campaign issue.

THE FUNCTIONING OF THE COURTS

The substantive direction of court rulings was not the only factor to provoke a crisis over the courts in the twentieth century. There were periodic outcries, though often confined within the judiciary and the political process, over the volume of cases and the courts' capacity to handle them. Perhaps the loudest of these, a supposed "liability crisis" in the late twentieth century, suggested broad cultural ramifications of an excess in cases prompted by a "litigious society." As newspaper columnist Jack Anderson described it in the 25 January 1985 *Washington Post,* "massive, mushrooming litigation has caused horrendous ruptures and dislocations at a flabbergasting cost to the nation."

Although the cry was not always so plaintive, caseload concerns arose at different junctures. In 1891, Congress acted to relieve the Supreme Court's post–Civil War docket congestion that had resulted in two- to three-year delays of pending appeals through the establishment of nine circuit courts of appeals to hear most appeals from federal district courts.

In 1906, Roscoe Pound sounded the alarm for court reform in a speech before the American Bar Association. In response to Pound's call, the ABA formed a special committee to propose solutions to the delay and "unnecessary cost" in the court system. From the committee's report, according to Felix Frankfurter and James M. Landis, came "all contemporary movements for judicial reform." Wisconsin was the first state to act, establishing a judicial council in 1913 as a clearinghouse for information about the judicial process in the state and to distribute state judges according to needs of particular areas.

World War I placed court reform on the back burner, but also increased its importance by leading to a postwar surge of litigation. Wartime contract cancellations and Prohibition-related petty criminal cases swamped the courts in the early 1920s. Concerns about court congestion led to unsuccessful efforts to organize a joint House-Senate committee on court reform. In the meantime, the federal courts were so understaffed that "thousands of persons accused of crime must lie in jail for a year or two years, if they are unable to discharge themselves by giving bond, awaiting trial, and . . . in many parts of the United States it is utterly impossible to secure the trial of a civil case within a year or two years." Congress accommodated the particularly overcrowded docket in New York by modifying the otherwise geographic structure of the federal judiciary, allowing judges from other areas to sit on New York cases.

One proposal to relieve overcrowding was the appointment of a number of judges who could move from one jurisdiction to another as docket pressures required. However, such a "flying squadron of judges" conflicted with the local representation and community ties that members of Congress hoped for in judges. Other important reforms would go further, as Congress placed court reform squarely on its agenda. In 1922, Congress passed a more limited assignability provision, allowing the transfer of judges from one area to another when the chief judge of the receiving jurisdiction certified that there was a need for more judges. The same bill created a judicial council, and established many new judgeships. The judicial council would consist of an executive committee of judges headed by the chief justice of the U.S. Supreme Court. According to Frankfurter and Landis, the 1922 Act marked "the beginning of a new chapter in the administration of the federal courts." Rather than simply responding to docket pressures with an increase in judges, the establishment of the judicial council would bring centralized administration to the federal courts.

In 1925, responding again to concerns about overcrowded dockets, Congress passed the Judges Bill, which set the basic structure of the federal judicial system for the rest of the century, and gave the Supreme Court more control over its docket. The act greatly reduced the cases eligible for mandatory appeal to the Court, making the courts of appeals the courts of last resort in many federal cases. Most cases would now come before the Court on a discretionary writ of certiorari. This meant that the Supreme Court could choose to hear only those cases it believed were of national importance.

The significant increase in federal district court caseloads in the 1920s and 1930s fell off with the end of Prohibition. By the 1950s, however, the courts were again overcrowded. In a speech before the American Law Institute in 1958, Chief Justice Earl Warren expressed concern about a backlog of more than 5,000 new civil cases in the federal district courts. According to Warren, whereas the criminal caseloads took "only a minor portion of the court time," the number of civil cases had "skyrocketed since 1941," increasing from 38,000 to 62,000 civil filings between 1941 and 1957. During the same period, the number of federal trial judges had increased by a much smaller percentage, from 200 to 250. Because of this the average number of civil cases handled by federal trial judges had increased by 37 percent. Sounding the alarm, Warren claimed that "delay and the choking congestion in the federal courts today have created a crucial problem for constitutional government in the United States." To resolve this crisis, Warren recommended the appointment of additional judges, and also suggested a limitation on federal court jurisdiction in cases based on diversity of citizenship and federal question jurisdiction.

Concern about the judicial workload increased in later years, so that in 1973 Judge Henry J. Friendly focused an entire chapter of his *Federal Jurisdiction* text on the "Causes of Explosion in Federal Litigation." According to Friendly, much of the increased pressure on court dockets resulted from new causes of action originating in both Congress and the federal courts, as well as a liberalization of standing rules. The Civil Rights Acts of 1964 and 1968 and the Voting Rights Act of 1965, for example, created new statutory rights that resulted in new litigation. Meanwhile the Supreme Court expanded its reading of Fourteenth Amendment rights. The protection extended by the Court for the rights of criminal defendants increased appeals of criminal convictions.

The growth of regulatory agencies, and with it judicial oversight of agency actions, also put pressure on court dockets. Congress responded to concerns about overcrowded dockets by increasing the number of federal judgeships from 279 in 1953 to 647 in 1983, yet, as appeals to federal circuit courts rose, from 3,446 in 1940 to 23,200 in 1983, the increase in judgeships did not keep pace. Moreover, Judge Alvin B. Rubin argued that it was not the number of cases itself that was the problem. It was their complexity.

Chief Justice Warren Burger sought to relieve the Supreme Court from docket congestion by proposing a U.S. Court of Appeals for the Federal Circuit, made up of two judges from each circuit, to resolve conflicts between circuits, and an Intermediate Court of Appeals to review petitions for certiorari and to select cases the Supreme Court would hear. Meanwhile in California, where federal court backlogs resulted in long waiting periods for litigants, some opted to "rent-a-judge" to avoid the crowded federal court system. In one form of alternative dispute resolution, parties would pay retired judges to resolve their cases. While favored by many corporations due to the speed and confidentiality afforded by this process, rent-a-judge was also criticized for creating a two-tiered system of justice in which the wealthy could have their cases heard in a timely manner, while the poor had to wait.

One obvious response to docket congestion was to increase the number of judges, and as a result the federal judiciary steadily expanded during the 1980s. Some judges, however, looked askance at their increasing ranks. The greater number of judges, it was argued, would lead to a decline in the quality of the federal bench. And because prestige was a form of nonpecuniary compensation, Judge Richard Posner argued that declining prestige resulting from an expanded judiciary would reduce judges' overall compensation.

Another response to burgeoning workloads was increased reliance on judicial law clerks. Law clerks were usually recent law school graduates who would work for a judge for a year or two before beginning law practice. In the second half of the twentieth century the federal courts steadily expanded the number of law clerks assigned to judges. By the 1980s, district judges had two, court of appeals judges had three, and Supreme Court Justices had four. Judges began to rely on their clerks to draft opinions, a practice widely adopted yet widely deplored.

In the 1980s and 1990s, concern focused on more than simply the volume of caseloads. According to some analysts, there was a "liability crisis" growing out of excessive damage awards given to plaintiffs. The nation had become a "litigious" society, with individuals all too ready to sue to gain legal redress for any and all of life's misfortunes. As U.S. Senator Mitch McConnell put it in 1986, "Hardly a day goes by that we do not hear or read of the dramatic increase in the number of lawsuits filed, or of the latest multimillion verdict, or of another small business, child care center, or municipal corporation that had its insurance canceled out from under it." McConnell placed the blame on the fact that the Nation had a "mad romance . . . with the civil litigation process." In a 1991 speech before the American Bar Association, Vice President Dan Quayle called for reform, claiming that the entire civil justice system was "in danger of spinning out of control."

But was there really a liability crisis? Social psychologist Michael Saks argued in an influential 1992 *Pennsylvania Law Review* article that the crisis was all smoke and mirrors—there simply was no hard data to support the assumption that litigious tort plaintiffs were driving up insurance premiums. According to Saks, although there was data on the number of civil cases there was insufficient evidence available to assess the nature of damage awards in civil suits in the federal and state courts, and how the awards had changed over time. The result was that policymakers were working with "a picture of the litigation system built of little more than imagination." Yet the impression of money-hungry lawyers and their greedy clients soaking the national economy remained, as journalists made the so-called crisis front-page news. Meanwhile, social scientists found that legitimate victims of torts and discrimination actually chose not to sue most of the time.

Still, as legislatures considered reforms that would cap jury awards and otherwise reduce what were seen as excessive verdicts for plaintiffs that pushed insurance premiums too high, the courts found their own ways to limit the volume of litigation. Through changes in the Federal Rules of Civil Procedure in 1983, parties could be assessed the attorney's fees of their opponent if they filed a "frivolous" case, a rule that plaintiffs' attorneys feared would deter novel or potentially difficult claims. Burdens of proof under Title VII of the Civil Rights Act of 1964 that had long rested with defendants were shifted by the Supreme Court to plaintiffs, making it much more difficult for victims of discrimination to prevail, and therefore discouraging Title VII plaintiffs from bringing actions. The Court also placed greater procedural barriers in the way of prisoner habeas corpus appeals, particularly for those involving defendants who were sentenced to death. The Supreme Court cut back on its own docket congestion by simply taking fewer cases in the 1990s.

STATE COURT ORGANIZATION

Although the federal courts in general, and the Supreme Court in particular, received a disproportionate amount of attention in the press and in the political process, the state courts received a disproportionate share of the business. In 1984, for example, the number of cases filed in federal district and appellate courts totaled approximately 335,000. That same year there were over 62 million state court filings, meaning that over 99 percent of all cases were brought in state courts.

Approximately 80 percent of all litigation in 1984 was heard in state courts of limited jurisdiction. These included juvenile and domestic relations courts, traffic courts, justice of the peace courts, and small-claims court. Although these courts were the forum in which most Americans experienced the legal system directly, they were regarded as the weakest link in the American judicial system. The American Judicature Society reported in 1975 that "the sheer volume of cases in relation to personnel, the generally poor quality of judicial and nonjudicial personnel, low salaries, inadequate facilities, weak administration . . . simply underscore the shortcomings of courts of limited jurisdiction and the myriad problems which must be overcome to compensate for generations of neglect." These courts tended to be more informal and unpredictable, and tended not to record their proceedings. Presiding judges were not always required to have legal training. In 1966, only four out of over four hundred current and former justices of the peace in Virginia had law degrees, 71 percent had never attended college, and 18 percent had never graduated from high school. The statistics in the states of Oregon and Pennsylvania were similar. A California judge without legal training defended his fitness for office as follows: "I don't know anything more about the law than a hog does about the 4th of July, but I know what's right and wrong." Although in 1974 the California Supreme Court ruled that judges without legal training violated litigants' due process rights, the U.S. Supreme Court and nine state supreme courts upheld lay judging.

The next step up in most state court systems was state trial courts of general jurisdiction. In addition to cases that originated in these courts, the courts would hear appeals from courts of limited jurisdiction. Judges in these trial courts had law degrees, and the courts were sufficiently well funded, at least toward the end of the century, that court proceedings could be recorded. It is in these courts that state trials involving serious criminal and civil matters were held.

All states had courts of last resort, often called a state supreme court and sometimes called a state court of appeals. Early in the century, in 1911, thirteen states had an intermediate appellate court between state trial courts and the state supreme court. That number had grown to thirty-six by 1986. The primary impetus for the establishment of another layer of state courts was to relieve state supreme courts of some of their workload.

As with the federal courts and review of congressional action, state courts were slow to use the power of judicial review to overturn state statutes until the twentieth century. Early in the century, however, state courts played an active role in reviewing legislative action. During a particularly active period, in the five years from 1903 to 1908, state courts across the country found as many as four hundred state statutes to be unconstitutional. Nevertheless, the critique of courts as countermajoritarian would generally not have the same resonance in the state court systems because state judges were often elected, or had some tie to the electoral process.

During the early years of the nation, state legislatures played a prominent role in judicial selection. Judges were almost universally appointed, but not by the executive alone. State legislatures had either a legislative veto over appointments, or themselves had the power to appoint. In the mid-nineteenth century, informed by the principles of Jacksonian democracy, many states changed to popular election of judges. In the late nineteenth century, a call for nonpartisan elections was a focus of early bar association efforts.

Although nonpartisan elections were intended to diminish political party influences over judicial selection, bar association leaders at the beginning of the twentieth century decried the use of any popular elections for judges. In an address before the American Bar Association in 1906, Roscoe Pound argued that "putting courts into politics, and compelling judges to become politicians, in many jurisdictions has almost destroyed the traditional respect for the bench." Reform efforts coalesced in the formation of the American Judicature Society in 1913. The purpose of the Society was the "improvement of justice," and it focused on developing a system of judicial selection that would be better than popular election. In 1914 the Society's research director, Albert Kales, proposed a system that had elective and appointive elements. An elected chief judge would appoint a state's judges, choosing at least every other one of them from a list of highly qualified candidates prepared by a judicial commission composed of judges. These appointees would then periodically be either ratified or rejected by the electorate.

Variations on Kales's proposal were suggested by bar leaders in a number of states in the 1920s and 1930s, and such an approach was endorsed by the American Bar Association in 1937. Although often called the "Missouri" plan due to that state's adoption of "merit" appointments in 1940, California was the first state to adopt a judicial selection system incorporating some of the proposed reforms in 1934. In California, the governor would submit a candidate's name to a commission on judicial appointments, which would essentially ratify the governor's choice. The judge's name would then either be approved or disapproved in a referendum at the next gubernatorial election. By further reducing the governor's role in judicial selection, Missouri's system was intended to be more merit-based. In Missouri, members of a judicial nominating commission would submit three names to the governor, who would pick one of the three. The judge's name would then be submitted to the electorate after one year on the bench. Missouri judges served fixed terms: six years for trial court judges and twelve years for appellate court judges.

Although reform efforts continued, it would be sixteen years after the adoption of the Missouri plan before another state would follow. Alaska enacted its version of the Missouri plan in 1956, followed by Kansas's adoption of the system for supreme court justices only in 1958. More states adopted it in the 1960s and 1970s, at least for some levels of courts, so that by 1978 Henry Glick wrote that the Missouri plan was "the most popular" judicial selection plan, "winning acceptance in more and more states. . . . In the past thirty years, every state which has changed its method of judicial selection has adopted some version of the Missouri Plan."

THE COURTS IN AMERICAN LIFE

For all the public debate about judicial power, the role of the courts in American life in the twentieth century has also been a very personal one. Countless individuals regained their liberty, faced incarceration, sought to right wrongs they had suffered, began and ended marriages, gained and lost custody of children, became citizens of the United States, and faced other tragic and joyous turning points in their lives within the doors of American courtrooms.

At the same time, trials were often community events, although the nature of community experience varied greatly among social groups and across the century. When early-nineteenth-century circuit riding judges arrived in a community on horseback, court day would be a focus of community life. The same could be true in the twentieth century, although urban life redefined the nature of communities. In *Bread Givers* (1925), Anzia Yezierska's novel of turn-of-the-century Jewish immigrant life in New York, the trial of the narrator's father for striking a bill collector became a community event, with the community defined by neighborhood and ethnicity. "It was like a holiday all over the block when they had Father's trial. The men stopped their work. The women left their cooking and washing and marketing, and with babies on their arms, and babies hanging on to their skirts, they crowded themselves into the court to hear the trial." When the narrator's father prevailed, for weeks "everybody was telling everybody over and over again, as you tell fairy tales," about the immigrant's victory over the landlord's bill collector.

By the middle of the twentieth century, the experience of the courtroom was increasingly brought to American homes by the medium of television. Television both broadened the scope of the "community" interacting with the court and privatized the experience, as Americans watched *Perry Mason* and *Divorce Court* in the 1950s and 1960s alone or in small groups in their living rooms.

In the 1980s and 1990s, the American public seemed captivated by the legal system. Courtroom scenes had long been portrayed on television dramas; however, in the late 1980s a new phenomenon came to the small screen. *The People's Court* brought individuals with actual disputes before a studio audience. They would make their case to the robed and white-haired Judge Wapner, in real life a retired trial judge. "Litigants" would argue over their differences, and face the outcome of their case, all for public amusement. *The People's Court* became so popular that in 1989 a *Washington Post* survey reported that although less than 10 percent of the public could name the chief justice of the United States Supreme Court, more than 25 percent were familiar with Judge Wapner.

The popularity of televised justice led, in the early 1990s, to cable television coverage of prominent criminal trials. For days in 1992, viewers could tune in for the lurid details of the trials on rape charges of William Kennedy Smith (the nephew of Sen. Edward Kennedy) and boxer Mike Tyson. While the juries determined the fate of the defendants (Smith acquitted, Tyson convicted) instant telephone polling enabled the news programs to broadcast the verdict of public opinion. A new cable service, Court TV, was established to bring additional trials to living rooms across the country. The courts had become a form of mass entertainment.

Trials in particular communities would often set the bounds of the "law" on the local level. And the system of actual law enforcement had aspects to it that the formal law on the books did not acknowledge. This was particularly true in the area of race. While criminal law formally established crimes without regard to the race of the perpetrator or victim, race had a major impact on the operation of the criminal justice system. Early in the century, the role of race would be quite overt, so that, for example, in some southern agricultural communities unemployed blacks would be arrested for vagrancy at harvest time and then compelled to work off the fine through being leased to an employer. In what William Cohen has called the system of involuntary servitude that lingered through the Progressive-Era South, the courts essentially served as a broker in the appropriation of involuntary labor.

A notorious double standard applied in the prosecution of violent crimes. White juries in the South as late as the 1960s regularly declined to find guilty whites who killed or brutalized blacks. At the same time, black defendants were at times denied the opportunity for a trial, and instead were taken from prison by a lynch mob. Even when the most overt forms of racism in the criminal justice system eased following the civil rights movement, social scientists still uncovered a race-based difference in death sentences. Defendants were more likely to receive the death penalty if they killed a white person rather than a black person.

Concerns about racism in the criminal justice system permeated urban communities from the 1960s on, and occasionally led to violent outbursts. Widely publicized incidents of police brutality, and the trials of police officers charged with brutalizing persons of color, served as flashpoints for massive riots.

But even as justice in American courtrooms seemed out of reach for persons of color, activists appealed to the image of the court and the ideal of justice. When black farm laborers were jailed in Arkansas in 1922 because of their attempts to organize a farm labor union, journalist Ida B. Wells-Barnett did not take their case to court, but to the forum of public opinion. "I appeal to the people of Arkansas," she wrote, "as the judge and jury," urging the people to bring justice to the men who had been wrongly accused. For Wells, the image of the court provided a rhetoric to move her readers to bring about a result that the "justice" system itself would fail to accomplish.

"The people" have acted as judge and jury in different ways. In Arkansas in 1922, public pressure eventually led to the prisoners' release. In later years, community outrage following verdicts in racially charged cases signaled a rejection of the verdict and disbelief in the fairness of the justice system by particular groups in society. In 1992, four white Los Angeles police officers were acquitted in the beating of Rodney King, a black man, although a guilty verdict was widely expected, partly due to a home videotape of the brutal beating that had been shown repeatedly on television news programs. When the predominately white jury did not convict the officers, South Central Los Angeles erupted in anger. The burning and looting equalled that of the Watts riots in 1965, which had also been triggered by charges of police brutality. The extensive foreign news coverage of the 1965 verdict and riots echoed the sentiment of critics of the King case. Even at this late date, they editorialized, justice in the American court system served whites, but not persons of color.

In South Central Los Angeles in 1992, as in the halls of Congress in 1937 during the court-packing controversy, the role of the courts in American society was hotly disputed. The truth of any conclusion about the courts' capacity to act justly depended more on the perspective of the speaker than on the consistency of any abstract theory of judicial review. At the same time, the courts' role in American culture was greater than even activist constitutional theorists would argue for; their impact was broader and deeper, touching even the way individuals imagined their own possibilities. Beside the flicker of hope engendered by *Brown* v. *Board of Education* or the crushing blow of the Rodney King verdict, concepts of federalism and judicial power seemed a small thing.

SEE ALSO Nationalism; The Presidency; The Constitution; Federalism and the States (all in this volume).

BIBLIOGRAPHY

The political and doctrinal history of the U.S. Supreme Court in the twentieth century is effectively surveyed in Alfred H. Kelly, Winfred A. Harbison, and Herman Belz, *The American Constitution: Its Origins and Development,* vol. 2, 7th ed. (1991). Most of the century is also covered in David P. Currie, *The Constitution in the Supreme Court: The Second Century, 1888–1986* (1990); and Alpheus Thomas Mason, *The Supreme Court from Taft to Burger,* 3d ed. (1979). Helpful works covering particular time periods include Herbert Hovenkamp, *Enterprise and American Law, 1836–1937* (1991); William F. Swindler, *Court and Constitution in the Twentieth Century: The Old Legality, 1889–1932* (1969); Robert H. Jackson, *The Struggle for Judicial Supremacy: A Study of a Crisis in American Power Politics* (1949) (on the court-packing controversy); Paul Murphy, *The Constitution in Crisis Times, 1918–1969* (1972); Bernard Schwartz with Stephan Lesher, *Inside the Warren Court* (1983); and Vincent Blasi, ed., *The Burger Court: The Counter-Revolution that Wasn't* (1983). Also informative on many twentieth-century political struggles that came before the Supreme Court is David M. O'Brien, *Storm Center: The Supreme Court in American Politics* (1986). See also Kermit L. Hall, ed., *The Oxford Companion to the Supreme Court of the United States* (1992).

Erwin C. Surrency, *History of the Federal Courts* (1987), details the structure and jurisdiction of the federal courts; while Peter Graham Fish, *The Politics of Federal Judicial Administration* (1973), covers the history of federal court administration. On lower federal courts, see Richard J. Richardson and Kenneth N. Vines, *The Politics of Federal Courts: Lower Courts in the United States* (1970). Charles Alan Wright, *Law of Federal Courts,* 5th ed. (1994), is an accessible treatise on the legal doctrines governing the federal courts. On state courts, see Robert A. Kagan, Bliss Cartwright, Lawrence M. Friedman, and Stanton Wheeler, "The Business of State Supreme Courts, 1870–1970," *Stanford Law Review* 30 (November 1977): 121–156; and Kagan et al., "The Evolution of State Supreme Courts," *Michigan Law Review* 76 (May 1978): 961–1005.

The process of appointing Supreme Court Justices is described in Henry J. Abraham, *Justices and Presidents: A Political History of Appointments to the Supreme Court,* 3d ed. (1992). A helpful discussion of lower federal court appointments appears in Rayman L. Solomon, "The Politics of Appointment and the Federal Courts' Role in Regulating America: U.S. Courts of Appeals Judgeships from T.R. to F.D.R.," *American Bar Foundation Research Journal* (Spring 1984): 285–343. State judicial selection is discussed in Harry P. Stumpf, *American Judicial Politics* (1988).

Felix Frankfurter and James M. Landis, *The Business of the Supreme Court: A Study in the Federal Judicial System* (1927), explores increasing federal court caseloads during the early twentieth century, and suggests reforms. Richard Posner, *The Federal Courts: Crisis and Reform* (1985), argues that the federal courts are currently overloaded, and relies on economic analysis in proposing reforms. The "liability crisis" is discussed in Marc Galanter, "The Life and Times of the Big Six; Or, The Federal Courts Since the Good Old Days," *Wisconsin Law Review* 1988 (1988): 921–954; and Michael J. Saks, "Do We Really Know Anything About the Behavior of the Tort Litigation System—and Why Not?" *University of Pennsylvania Law Review* 140 (April 1992): 1147–1292.

There is an extensive social science literature on the courts, including Sheldon Goldman and Austin Sarat, eds., *American Court Systems: Readings in Judicial Process and Behavior* (1978). For a comparative analysis of courts, see Henry J. Abraham, *The Judicial Process: An Introductory Analysis of the Courts of the United States, England, and France,* 6th ed. (1993).

Influential and different approaches to the question of judicial review appear in Alexander Bickel, *The Least Dangerous Branch: The Supreme Court at the Bar of Politics,* 2d ed. (1986); Raoul Berger, *Government by Judiciary: The Transformation of the Fourteenth Amendment* (1977); John Hart Ely, *Democracy and Distrust: A Theory of Judicial Review* (1980); and Bruce Ackerman, *We the People: Foundations* (1991). A particularly insightful historical treatment of the topic is Robert Cover, "The Origins of Judicial Activism in the Protection of Minorities," *Yale Law Journal* 91 (June 1982): 1287–1316.

The courts and popular culture are discussed in Michael Kammen, *A Machine that Would Go of Itself: The Constitution in American Culture* (1986); and the work of Maxwell Bloomfield, including "The Supreme Court in American Popular Culture," *Journal of American Culture* 4 (Winter 1981): 1–13. For a discussion of the effect of television, see David A. Harris, "The Appearance of Justice: Court TV, Conventional Television, and Public Understanding of the Criminal Justice System," *Arizona Law Review* 35 (Winter 1993): 785–827.

THE CONSTITUTION

Michal R. Belknap

The Constitution suffers from a split personality: in establishing the federal government and structuring the relationship between the central authority and the states, it both confers and limits governmental power. The demands of these dual roles have constantly pulled the nation's frame of government in opposite directions, infusing its development with more than a little inconsistency. When Justice Sandra Day O'Connor described America's fundamental charter as a "coherent succession" whose "written terms embody ideas and aspirations that survive more ages than one," she was only half right. The Constitution does embody certain aspirations and ideas that generation after generation of Americans have agreed are central to this country's governmental system. These are, however, conflicting desires for a government possessing sufficient power to meet all the demands the nation places upon it, that is also effectively constrained from encroaching upon the fundamental rights of the people. The first of these objectives generates pressure to expand governmental authority, while the second gives rise to demands to limit it. The tension between them has made the history of the Constitution anything but a coherent succession.

Certainly that has been true in the twentieth century. Most Americans in 1900 viewed the Constitution primarily as a collection of judicially enforceable limitations upon the authority of government. To some people that meant the Constitution was safeguarding individual rights; to others it meant that the national charter was thwarting the essential exercise of governmental authority. The next several decades witnessed a struggle to tap the full potential of the Constitution's power-granting provisions, and thereby to invest Congress and the Executive with the capacity to meet the economic, diplomatic, and military challenges the country faced.

As governmental power expanded, it increasingly threatened the liberties of the people. In the 1930s the Supreme Court began to place more emphasis on the provisions of the Constitution that protect individual rights. Even as it came to read the document's power-granting clauses more broadly, the Court insisted with growing vigor that public officials, whose authority it was expanding, respect individual liberties. Over time both the scope and number of the rights that legislators and bureaucrats were forbidden to invade expanded, and rights became the focus of constitutional jurisprudence. The more rights judges recognized, and the more rigorously the judiciary enforced them, the more limitations the judiciary imposed on the politically responsible branches of government. By the last decade of the twentieth century, conservatives were complaining loudly about judicial interference with efforts to combat what they perceived as social problems, ironically echoing the complaints of early-twentieth-century liberals about judges thwarting the popular will and the effective use of public power. Far from a coherent progression, the constitutional history of the twentieth century appears to have been a circular journey, at the end of which the inherent conflict between authority and rights is no closer to resolution than when the trip began.

GOVERNMENTAL POWER BEFORE 1900

By the 1990s the Constitution had largely realized its potential as a source of governmental power, accomplishing the overriding objective of those who wrote it: to enhance the capacity of government to govern. The Constitution was the product of concerns about the weakness of the central authority created by the Articles of Confederation in 1781. That government lacked authority to tax and the capacity to deal effectively with either foreign nations or domestic crises. The Constitutional Convention assembled in Philadelphia at the request of delegates to an earlier meeting in Annapolis in 1787, who recognized that something had to be done "to render the constitution of the federal government adequate to the exigencies of the Union." The Philadelphia convention accomplished what these conservative nationalists regarded as essential: drafting a document that gave the central government an executive and a judiciary and vastly enhanced the authority of its legislature.

Yet, throughout most of the nineteenth century the convention's creation was not particularly potent. During John Marshall's tenure as Chief Justice (1801–1835), the Supreme Court sought to invigorate the Constitution, interpreting its power-granting provisions quite broadly. In *Gibbons* v. *Ogden* (1823) the Court announced that Article I's "commerce clause," which empowers Congress to regulate interstate and foreign commerce, gave the national legislature plenary power over all commercial intercourse that concerned more states than one. In *McCulloch* v. *Maryland* (1819) Marshall declared that although nothing in Article I explicitly empowered Congress to charter a bank, authority to do so could be inferred from its enumerated powers because a bank was a necessary and proper means of carrying those powers into execution.

The Marshall Court also took an expansive view of its own authority. In such cases as *Martin* v. *Hunter's Lessee* (1816) and *Cohens* v. *Virginia* (1821), it held that the judicial article (Article III) and the clause in Article VI making the Constitution the supreme law of the land gave the Supreme Court the authority to review the decisions of the highest courts of the various states on constitutional questions and required state courts to comply with its rulings. In *Marbury* v. *Madison* (1803) Marshall declared that his Court had the power to invalidate acts of Congress which conflicted with the Constitution, although nothing in Article III explicitly gave it this authority. The power of judges to rule on the constitutionality of legislation and to refuse to enforce statutes they deemed in violation of the Constitution came to be known as judicial review. (See table 1.)

While the Marshall Court interpreted expansively the power-granting provisions of the national charter, its decisions often aroused virulent opposition. Except during a brief period of euphoric nationalism just after the War of 1812, strict constructionism and states' rights were the prevailing constitutional dogmas of the early nineteenth century. Pointing to the silence of the Constitution concerning these subjects, Presidents James Madison, James Monroe, and Andrew Jackson all insisted the federal government lacked the authority to build roads and canals. Besides preventing the creation of a national system of internal improvements, strict constructionism contributed to Jackson's decision in 1832 to do away with the national bank that Congress had chartered in 1816. South Carolinians also resorted to strict constructionist arguments when they disputed the authority of Congress to levy a protective tariff. They added that should the national legislature adopt such an unconstitutional measure, the states might lawfully nullify it.

The nullification controversy South Carolina provoked in 1832–1833 was only one of many manifestations of an increasingly militant southern commitment to the theory of states' rights. The South came to view that doctrine, and ultimately the more extreme notion of state sovereignty, as essential to the preservation of slavery. Southerners believed that keeping the states strong and the national government weak would safeguard the "peculiar institution" against outside interference. Thus, (although accepting a broad definition of federal admiralty jurisdiction), they came to regard such potential sources of congressional power as the commerce clause with suspicion. Sectional politics precluded effective utilization of these grants of authority.

The outbreak of the Civil War revived interest in exploiting more fully the power-granting provisions of the Constitution. After secession removed scores of southerners from Congress, the national legislature enacted the sort of internal improvement and banking legislation the South had long denied Congress had the authority to adopt. President Abraham Lincoln demonstrated even more dramatically the Constitution's potential as a source of governmental strength and energy. He validated the arguments of northern legal writers, such as Timothy Farrar and Sidney George Fisher, who contended that southerners had wrongly pictured the national charter as essentially a framework of negative restraints on authority when in fact it contained numerous positive commandments for the government to act effectively. By preserving the Union Lincoln confirmed that far from being the failure some pessimists claimed, the Constitution was, as the likes of Farrar and Fisher insisted, adequate to meet even the extreme demands of secession and civil war. The President welded together the clauses in Article II making him the commander in chief of the army and navy and charging him "to take care that the laws be faithfully executed," forging from them a broad presidential war power. In Lincoln's hands the commander in chief clause, which the Framers apparently had intended only to ensure civilian control of the armed forces, became an authorization for the chief executive to exercise virtually limitless authority on the home front during a military conflict. By

Table 1. DECISIONS OF THE SUPREME COURT OVERRULED AND ACTS OF CONGRESS HELD UNCONSTITUTIONAL, 1789–1988; AND STATE LAWS AND MUNICIPAL ORDINANCES OVERTURNED, 1789–1988

Year	Court	Supreme Court Decision Overruled	Acts of Congress Overturned	State Laws Overturned	Ordinances Overturned
1789–1800	Pre-Marshall				
1801–1835	Marshall Court	3	1	18	
1836–1864	Taney Court	6	1	21	
1865–1873	Chase Court	3	10	33	
1874–1888	Waite Court	11	9	7	
1889–1910	Fuller Court	4	14	73	15
1910–1921	White Court	6	12	107	18
1921–1930	Taft Court	5	12	131	12
1930–1940	Hughes Court	14	14	78	5
1941–1946	Stone Court	24	2	25	7
1947–1952	Vinson Court	11	1	38	7
1953–1969	Warren Court	46	25	150	16
1969–1986	Burger Court[a]	50	34	192	15
1986–	Rehnquist Court[b]	5	4	29	3

[a] In *Immigration and Naturalization Service* v. *Chadha* (1983), the Burger Court struck down a provision for a "one-house" legislative veto in the Immigration and Naturalization Act but effectively declared all one- and two-house legislative vetoes unconstitutional. While 212 statutes containing provisions for legislative vetoes were implicated by the Court's decision, *Chadha* is here counted as a single declaration of the unconstitutionality of congressional legislation.

[b] The Court's ruling in *Texas* v. *Johnson* (1989), striking down a Texas law making it a crime to desecrate the American flag, invalidated laws in forty-eight states and a federal statute; it is counted here, however, only once.

SOURCE: David M. O'Brien, *Storm Center: The Supreme Court in American Politics,* 2d ed. (New York: W. W. Norton, 1990), p. 60.

resorting to extraordinary measures in a successful effort to save the Union, Lincoln demonstrated the potential of the presidency and created precedents for the exercise of presidential power that would significantly influence constitutional development in the twentieth century.

Besides revealing the previously untapped potential of Article II, the Civil War resulted in the addition to the Constitution of three amendments, all ratified during the Reconstruction period that followed the fighting. These appeared to enhance the authority of the national government considerably. The Thirteenth Amendment prohibited slavery and involuntary servitude. The Fourteenth declared all persons born or naturalized in the United States to be citizens of both the United States and of the states in which they resided and forbade those states to deny citizens the privileges and immunities of citizenship, to deprive persons of life, liberty, or property without due process of law, or to refuse anyone subject to their jurisdiction the equal protection of the laws. The Fifteenth Amendment prohibited both states and the national government from withholding or abridging the right to vote because of race, color, or previous condition of servitude. In addition to their substantive guarantees, each of these Reconstruction amendments contained an enforcement section, which empowered Congress to enforce its other provisions "by appropriate legislation."

To this day historians and legal scholars continue to debate just how much additional power those who wrote and ratified these amendments (especially the Thirteenth and Fourteenth) intended to confer upon the national legislature and the federal judiciary. The Republicans who controlled Congress during the Civil War and Reconstruction seem to have believed initially that by simply ending slavery they would invest the freedmen with the same fundamental rights enjoyed by all other free persons. When the white South refused to treat free African Americans as legal equals, Congress responded by enacting a civil rights statute, designed to compel southern states to afford equality before the law. The Republicans went on to amend the Constitution to require states to secure to all their residents the fundamental rights of national citizens. The framers of the Fourteenth Amendment apparently did not intend to deprive the states of their traditional role as the regulators and guardians of such rights. They did, however, view national citizenship as primary and were prepared to give Congress and the federal courts ample authority to ensure that the southern states would not deprive any American citizens of their basic rights, or allow freedmen to be deprived of those rights by private individuals whose violence and intimidation these states would not control.

Those who wrote and ratified the Thirteenth, Fourteenth, and Fifteenth Amendments and the legislation that Congress enacted effected a potentially revolutionary increase in the powers of the national government. The implications of what they had done profoundly disturbed many northerners, among them a majority of the justices on the Supreme Court. Although recognizing that the Reconstruction amendments contained additional guarantees of human rights, the Court proved unwilling to accept the vast expansion of federal power that full implementation of those guarantees entailed. In the *Slaughterhouse* cases (1873) the Court spurned the claims of white butchers that Louisiana had violated the Thirteenth and Fourteenth Amendments by granting to one company a monopoly on the livestock slaughtering business in New Orleans. Taking note of the indisputable fact that these provisions had been adopted to liberate the slaves and safeguard their freedom, the majority denied that the recent additions to the text of the Constitution had significantly altered traditional federalism. In order to avoid making the national Constitution a limitation on the regulatory authority of the states, the Court disregarded the apparent intent of the Republicans in Congress who wrote the privileges and immunities clause. The *Slaughterhouse* majority held that part of the Fourteenth Amendment did not prohibit the states from interfering with the fundamental rights of their citizens (including the right to pursue a lawful calling). Rather, the privileges and immunities clause protected only a very short list of relatively inconsequential privileges (such as the right to travel to Washington, D.C.) that arose directly out of those citizens' relationship with the national government. As other parts of the Constitution already safeguarded those rights, the Court was, in effect, saying this addition to the document had not changed it at all.

After utterly and permanently debilitating the privileges and immunities clause in *Slaughterhouse,* the Supreme Court eviscerated the rest of the Fourteenth Amendment by developing the "state action doctrine." In such cases as *United States* v. *Harris* (1883) and the *Civil Rights Cases* (1883), the Court declared that the due process and equal protection clauses limited only what state governments could do. Hence, the enforcement section of the Fourteenth Amendment did not empower Congress to legislate against private interference with the exercise of the rights those clauses guaranteed. By the mid-1880s a conservative Supreme Court, bent on preserving the essence of the pre–Civil War constitutional order, not only had invalidated a good deal of Reconstruction civil rights legislation but also had deprived the federal judiciary and the national legislature of much of the power they might have derived from the Reconstruction amendments.

The Court also restricted congressional authority under Article I. In two dubiously reasoned 1895 opinions, which conflicted with one of its own earlier decisions, the Court ruled that Congress could not impose an income tax without apportioning the levy among the states on the basis of population. Because doing that was utterly impracticable, federal taxation of incomes had to await the addition of the Sixteenth Amendment to the Constitution in 1913. The Supreme Court also read the commerce clause restrictively, taking the position in *United States* v. *E. C. Knight Company* (1895) that it did not empower Congress to outlaw monopolies in manufacturing, no matter how large a share of the national market for a particular product they controlled. Production was a local activity, and the Tenth Amendment reserved authority over it to the states. *Knight* was consistent with language in earlier opinions, and both the way the Justice Department argued the case and Chief Justice Melville Fuller's desire to encourage state regulation of corporations probably influenced the outcome. But the Court had clearly limited the capacity of Congress to combat the growing concentrations of economic power that were agitating the American people. Coming as they did in the same year as *In re Debs* (1895), in which the Court declared federal courts possessed inherent power to enjoin strikes that interfered with interstate commerce or the mail, *Knight* and the income tax decision struck many people as manifestations of class bias.

The Supreme Court added to its reputation as a protector of property by using the Fourteenth Amendment to restrict the regulatory power of the states. During the last three decades of the nineteenth century, it gradually accepted the argument that the due process clause of the Fourteenth Amendment imposed substantive as well as procedural limitations on state authority. The Court took the position that if a state legislature enacted a statute that interfered in an arbitrary or unequal way with the property or liberty of some of that state's citizens, it deprived them of their liberty or property without due process of law. "Substantive due process" became a device that judges used to invalidate what they considered unreasonable legislative restrictions on vested property rights or the freedom of employers to contract with their employees on any terms they chose. In its infamous *Lochner* v. *New York* (1905) decision, for example, the Supreme Court struck down as a violation of the Fourteenth Amendment a statute that limited the number of hours that bakery workers might be required to labor. Rulings like *Lochner* were the exception rather than the rule. In 83 percent of the cases it decided between 1887 and 1910 in which a state statute was challenged under the due process clause, the Court sustained the law. Yet, substantive due process arrogated tremendous discretionary power to the judiciary and made judicial notions of reasonableness the ultimate test of what states could do in the exercise of their police power. Since the Fifth Amendment, which applied to the national government, contained a due process clause identical in wording to the one in the Fourteenth Amendment, what judges considered reasonable became a limitation on the regulatory authority of Congress as well.

GOVERNMENTAL POWER IN THE PROGRESSIVE ERA

Although the hostility to paternalism that predominated in the United States during the decades after the Civil War fostered the development of substantive due process and other limitations on governmental interference with entrepreneurial liberty, by 1900 political pressure for the increased use of public power in the economic realm was rising rapidly. Demands for greater governmental regulation of business arose not only from consumers and political critics of the "trusts" but even from many businessmen. Desires to ameliorate the sometimes painful consequences of competition and to enhance economic efficiency combined with widespread anger at the political abuses of large enterprises and a growing concern for social justice to rouse legislators to action. The result was laws designed to tighten governmental control over railroads and other corporations and to improve the health, welfare, morals, and wages of workers. Such statutes poured out of statehouses across the country between the late 1890s and American entry into World War I in 1917. Congress also enacted a substantial amount of legislation on these subjects during this progressive era.

Members of Congress and state legislatures had to worry not only about finding legal solutions to the economic and social problems confronting a mature industrial society but also about whether the Constitution would permit them to implement their ideas. Reactionary judges in some states, most notably New York and Illinois, used the due process clause of the Fourteenth Amendment to invalidate reform legislation, such as the workers' compensation statute that the New York Court of Appeals struck down in *Ives* v. *South Buffalo Railway Co.* (1911). Outrage over rulings of this type fueled demands for constitutional change that would make it possible for the people to recall judges, their decisions, or both. In 1912 even former president Theodore Roosevelt endorsed the recall of judicial decisions. Only Colorado adopted the concept, however, and just seven states embraced the recall of judges.

During the Progressive Era, despite the attention which rulings such as *Ives* and *Lochner* received, courts ruled in favor of most regulatory and protective legislation alleged to violate liberty of contract or some other variant of substantive due process. The United States Supreme Court was no exception. It rejected Fourteenth Amendment challenges to state laws requiring employers to participate in workers' compensation systems and setting maximum hours for female laborers and for men employed by private contractors on public works projects. An evenly divided Court also affirmed an Oregon decision holding constitutional a minimum wage law for women. In *Wilson* v. *New* (1916) the Supreme Court even spurned a Fifth Amendment due process challenge to congressional legislation imposing the eight-hour day and related wage regulations on the railroad industry. Only when organized labor was the beneficiary of a statute was the Court likely to prove receptive to a due process attack upon it. In *Adair* v. *United States* (1908) and *Coppage* v. *Kansas* (1915), for example, it invalidated federal and state laws prohibiting yellow dog contracts. Although sometimes invalidating protective legislation on equal protection grounds, the Supreme Court generally sustained such laws if the beneficiaries were unorganized workers. Congress trusted the Court enough by 1914 to empower it to review decisions of state judges who used the federal Constitution to invalidate laws enacted by their own legislatures.

That the Court should have found favor with Congress is hardly surprising, for at the height of the Progressive Era it not only largely stopped using substantive due process to constrain federal and state legislative authority, but also interpreted the power-granting provisions of the Constitution expansively. This was particularly true of the commerce clause. While not repudiating *Knight,* the justices began to carve out exceptions to that decision's dichotomy between local activities and interstate commerce. In 1908 the Court invalidated legislation abolishing common law defenses for railroads being sued in tort by their employees, holding the statute unconstitutional because it covered shop workers as well as men employed on trains that actually traveled from one state to another. In the *Northern Securities Case* (1904), however, the Court rejected the contention that the commerce clause did not give the federal government the power to prevent the creation of a holding company linking competing railroads together because stock transactions, such as the one that had created the combination, were not part of interstate commerce. In *Swift & Co.* v. *United States* (1905) it held that Congress could regulate the buying and selling of cattle in stockyards, despite the localized nature of the transactions, because those stockyards were part of a "stream of commerce" along which beef flowed from ranches to retailers.

Besides taking a more expansive view of what constituted interstate commerce, the Supreme Court also held that the regulatory authority of Congress included the power to prohibit entirely the shipment of disfavored items from one state to another. The Court first articulated this position in *Champion* v. *Ames* (1903), a case in which it upheld by a 5-to-4 vote a statute that forbade interstate traffic in lottery tickets. Rejecting the contention that regulation did not extend to complete prohibition, Justice John Marshall Harlan's opinion reflected judicial sympathy for congressional efforts to stamp out the "moral pestilence" of lotteries. Because the restraint the statute imposed on interstate commerce seemed reasonable to him, it was constitutional. When Congress prohibited the interstate transportation of women for immoral purposes, the Supreme Court, equally sympathetic to the purpose of that law, held that the Commerce Clause authorized its enactment as well. In addition, the Court upheld the Pure Food and Drug Act of 1906, which banned shipment from one state or territory to another of adulterated food and drugs.

What the Supreme Court was doing was allowing Congress to use the commerce clause to enact measures comparable to state legislation adopted to protect the public's health, safety, and morals. The authority to adopt such laws, known as the police power, was not one that Article I explicitly gave to Congress. Indeed, by reserving to the states and to the people all powers not delegated by the Constitution to the federal government, the Tenth Amendment arguably withheld this authority from the national legislature.

Congress managed to develop the functional equivalent of the states' police power out of the commerce clause and the authorization to tax contained in Article I. Wishing to eliminate artificially colored oleomargarine as a competitor to butter, for example, it imposed a prohibitively high levy on that product. In the Harrison Act of 1914, while taxing dispensers of narcotics a mere $1, Congress required them to comply with extremely detailed regulations concerning the distribution of drugs. Rather obviously, neither of these measures was designed to raise revenue. Nevertheless, in *McCray* v. *United States* (1904) and *United States* v. *Doremus* (1919) respectively, the Supreme Court upheld them as valid exercises of the congressional power to tax.

PRESIDENTIAL AND CONGRESSIONAL POWER DURING WORLD WAR I

The Court did refuse to sanction federal proscription of child labor. With that one exception, however, whether interpreting the taxing clause or the commerce clause, during the first two decades of the twentieth century the Court generally read the Constitution in a way that enhanced the authority of the national government. This was especially true in cases arising out of World War I. Justices seemed to share with the president and Congress a conviction that the Great War, like the Civil War before it, required the full exploitation of all the energy and strength the national government could draw from the Constitution.

Woodrow Wilson met the challenges of modern warfare with what some critics characterized as presidential dictatorship. The powers of the presidency had lain largely dormant during most of the last third of the nineteenth century. William McKinley (1897–1901) managed to revitalize the office somewhat, but his successor, Theodore Roosevelt, was the first chief executive since the Civil War who possessed both the determination and the ability to exploit its potential. With his flair for the dramatic, TR turned the presidency into a "bully pulpit" and made it the focal point of the constitutional system. Roosevelt viewed himself as a steward of the people, having both the obligation and the power to take any action required by the national welfare that was not prohibited by the Constitution or federal law. His successor, William Howard Taft, vigorously condemned Roosevelt's expansive conception of presidential authority, but Wilson's understanding of the office was much closer to TR's than to Taft's.

A former political science professor, who had long believed that the president should lead Congress the way the British prime minister led Parliament, Wilson began implementing these views immediately after taking office in 1913. America's entry into the war four years later afforded enhanced opportunities for the sort of presidential leadership that Wilson favored. Sometimes he relied on the inherent powers of his office, using these, for example, to create the powerful War Industries Board, which oversaw economic mobilization, and the Committee on Public Information (or Creel Committee), which used propaganda to arouse public support for the war effort. Far more often than Lincoln, however, this president worked his will through Congress, asking for and obtaining congressional authorization for his actions before he took them. He persuaded the legislature to delegate sweeping authority to draft men into the armed forces, regulate food production, set fuel prices, license businesses, seize railroad, telegraph, and telephone lines, take over factories, censor the mails, and even imprison critics of government policies. Wilson secured enactment of legislation giving him a virtual blank check to reorganize executive agencies for the duration of the military conflict. Furthermore, he squelched efforts by several senators to set up a congressional joint committee to oversee his conduct of the war.

While the need for centralized direction of the national military effort impelled Congress to sanction a spectacular expansion of presidential power, the legislative branch itself exercised far broader authority during World War I than it ever had before. Mobilizing the country's economic and human resources for combat required massive and unprecedented federal intervention into private activity. For example, the Lever Act, which Congress adopted in August 1917, declared the food and fuel industries to be affected with a public interest and subjected them to extensive federal regulation. That law authorized the chief executive, among other things, to license the production and distribution of foodstuffs, to set prices for wheat and coal, to requisition supplies for the military, and even to take over factories, mines, and other businesses whose output he considered essential to the war effort. A few members of Congress criticized the Lever Act as an unconstitutional invasion of powers reserved to the states by the Tenth Amendment. Most, however, accepted the argument that the federal war power justified not only this law but any other legislation that had a reasonable relationship to the national military effort.

The war power on which Congress relied was not mentioned anywhere in the Constitution. All Article I explicitly did was authorize the national legislature to declare war, raise and support armies, make rules for the land and naval forces, and provide for the calling forth of the militia. Yet, senators and representatives viewed these discrete grants of authority as somehow collectively empowering them to do a vast array of things not permissible in peacetime. For example, on 21 November 1918, for the alleged purpose of conserving manpower and increasing the efficiency of war production, Congress enacted legislation prohibiting the manufacture and distribution of alcoholic beverages. Peacetime prohibition required adding the Eighteenth Amendment to the Constitution. Although an armistice actually had terminated the fighting ten days before Congress passed the War Prohibition Act, legislators assumed that the extraordinary authority which the war gave them remained operative during a period of demobilization after combat ended. Thus, they relied upon "emergencies growing out of the war" as justification for imposing rent control on the District of Columbia in October 1919, before the technical legal end of hostilities, but nearly a year after the guns had fallen silent in France.

Although both the president and Congress exercised extraordinary power during World War I, the Supreme Court did not oppose their acquisition of additional authority. Most of the critical war measures never came before the Court, but it found constitutional justification for all of those that it reviewed. In the *Selective Draft Law Cases* (1918) the Court unanimously upheld a statute mandating compulsory military service. Finding authorization for this law in the clauses empowering Congress to declare war and raise and support armies, the justices rejected without discussion the contention that it imposed involuntary servitude in violation of the Thirteenth Amendment. The "war power of the United States" seemed to the Court to provide sufficient constitutional justification for 1916 legislation authorizing the president to seize and operate the nation's railroads in wartime. It upheld that law in *Northern Pacific Railway Company* v. *North Dakota* (1919), despite the fact that the statute cavalierly swept aside state controls on intrastate rail rates. The Supreme Court also denied that the War Prohibition Act invaded the police powers of the states. The Court found ample justification for that law in the federal war power, which according to Justice Louis Brandeis, did not lapse when the fighting ended, but remained available so long as Congress thought an emergency continued to exist. The District of Columbia rent control law also won approval as a war measure, although four justices did dissent from that ruling.

While denying that the other branches had exceeded their authority under the Constitution's affirmative grants of power, the Supreme Court also controverted claims that Congress and the Executive had violated restrictions contained in the Bill of Rights. The high tribunal held that neither the portion of the Lever Act authorizing the president to fix coal prices nor the regulations Wilson had issued to enforce it violated the due process clause of the Fifth Amendment. No more protective of free speech than of liberty of contract, the Court affirmed in *Schenck* v. *United States* (1919) the constitutionality of provisions of the Espionage Act of 1917 that criminalized expression tending to affect adversely recruiting or the draft.

United States v. *Cohen Grocery Company* (1921) was a rare victory for individual rights over the perceived necessities of modern warfare. *Cohen* struck down a vague section of the Lever Act, that made it unlawful "to exact excessive prices." The Court invalidated this provision for failing to provide an ascertainable standard of guilt or adequately inform those prosecuted under it of the nature of the charges against them.

JUDICIAL RESTRICTION OF GOVERNMENTAL POWER, 1918–1936

Although in cases arising out of World War I the Supreme Court repeatedly found neither internal nor external limitations on the constitutional powers of the national government, its attitude changed significantly during the 1920s. The first important indication that postwar constitutional interpretation would be different came in cases involving federal legislation designed to eliminate child labor throughout the country. Congress had passed a law for that purpose in 1916, which prohibited the shipment in interstate commerce of products made in factories where children under sixteen worked more than eight hours a day or six days a week. In *Hammer* v. *Dagenhart* (1918) the Supreme Court invalidated this measure, which it viewed as an attempt to regulate manufacturing and, therefore, considered an unconstitutional invasion of powers reserved to the states. When Congress responded to *Dagenhart* with a 1919 law that required any mine or factory employing child labor to pay an excise tax equivalent to 10 percent of its net profits, the Court struck down that measure too, ruling in *Bailey* v. *Drexel Furniture Company* (1922) that, rather than the tax it purported to be, it was really a penalty, designed to enforce rules that violated the Tenth Amendment. The inconsistency between these decisions and earlier rulings sanctioning congressional development of a de facto federal police power under the aegis of the taxing and commerce clauses was obvious. Advocates of children's rights sought to invest the national government with the authority the Supreme Court insisted it did not have, and their proposed Child Labor Amendment passed Congress in 1924. Opposition from manufacturers' associations and certain religious groups defeated it in most states, however, and the Depression, which left many families in need of whatever money their children could earn, ensured the Child Labor Amendment would never become part of the Constitution.

While William Howard Taft was chief justice (1921–1930), the Supreme Court continued to manifest the sort of probusiness bias exemplified by its child labor rulings. This did not mean that the Court took a consistently narrow view of the power-granting provisions of the Constitution. For example, in *Myers* v. *United States* (1926) former president Taft ruled that the authority to fire subordinate members of the executive branch was inherent in the presidential office. The Chief Justice took an equally expansive view of the powers of Congress under the commerce clause. In *Stafford* v. *Wallace* (1922) he relied on the stream of commerce principle to uphold legislation giving the secretary of agriculture broad powers to regulate the business practices of packers and stockyards. The Taft Court similarly affirmed the constitutionality of a federal statute regulating grain futures exchanges and drew on Progressive-era precedents sanctioning regulatory prohibitions of interstate shipment to uphold the Motor Vehicle Theft Act of 1919. A ruling that Congress might not employ its taxing power to control the local dealings of boards of trade did little to limit federal power, for Taft hinted in his opinion that the legislature could accomplish its objectives under the commerce clause, a suggestion on which it promptly acted.

Indeed, the Taft Court actually enhanced the authority of the national government significantly by declaring in *Massachusetts* v. *Mellon* (1923) that when making grants-in-aid to the states, Congress might attach conditions to the money. This ruling made the congressional spending power a potentially important means of enhancing Washington's control over the states. Because the Supreme Court also declared in *Missouri* v. *Holland* (1920) that by entering into treaties with other countries, the national government could obtain the authority to adopt legislation that would otherwise violate the Tenth Amendment, its rulings during the 1920s actually served to raise substantially the level of potential federal power.

Simultaneously, however, the Court made vigorous use of the negative prohibitions in the Constitution to limit what Congress and the states could do with their authority. During the decade that Taft was chief justice, the Supreme Court declared unconstitutional nearly three-fourths as many state laws as it had invalidated in its entire previous history. It struck down federal statutes too. Between 1921 and 1933 the Court held unconstitutional 14 acts of Congress, along with 148 state laws placing governmental restraints on business activity, and 12 municipal ordinances. Substantive due process was the basis for most of these decisions. While rejecting in *Euclid* v. *Ambler Realty Company* (1926) the contention that one new form of governmental control over private property—zoning—violated the due process clause, the Court repeatedly struck down regulatory measures that offended the probusiness sensibilities of a majority of its members. It invalidated everything from a law requiring arbitration of labor disputes in key industries to one setting minimum sizes for bread loaves sold at retail. In *Adkins* v. *Childrens Hospital* (1923) the Court struck down as violative of due process a federal statute establishing minimum wages for women in the District of Columbia. This decision was so at odds with Progressive-era precedents that even Chief Justice Taft dissented.

Had the 1920s witnessed a major campaign to increase governmental supervision of business, such rulings could have made the Constitution a major impediment to the implementation of the popular will. In an era of unprecedented prosperity for which businessmen received most of the credit, however, neither public officials nor voters displayed much interest in enhancing the role of government in the economy. The Republican administrations in Washington endeavored to turn publicly owned enterprises over to private entrepreneurs and to put in charge of regulatory agencies, such as the Federal Trade Commission, men responsive to the wishes of the very interests these bodies were supposed to monitor.

The Great Depression, which descended on the country at the end of 1929, triggered demands for the sort of massive governmental intervention that hardly anyone had seemed to want during the 1920s. The states responded to the economic crisis with a variety of measures, ranging from mortgage moratoriums to wage and price controls. Congress also legislated furiously, especially after Franklin D. Roosevelt assumed the presidency in 1933. Supporters of Roosevelt's New Deal pointed to the commerce clause and to the congressional power to tax and spend as authority for a wide-ranging attack on problems created and revealed by the Depression. New Dealers also argued that, like World War I, the economic crisis somehow gave both the president and Congress additional power, which they would not have had in the absence of a national emergency. Legislators adopted measures patterned on wartime models, and Roosevelt persuaded them to make sweeping delegations of authority to him, as their predecessors had to Woodrow Wilson.

While the White House and Congress viewed the Depression as analogous to World War I, the Supreme Court did not. In *A. L. A. Schechter Poultry Corp.* v. *United States* (1935) the Court announced, "Extraordinary conditions do not create or enlarge constitutional power." In *Schechter* the Court held unconstitutional the National Industrial Recovery Act. This early New Deal measure had initiated governmental coordination of the economy by authorizing businessmen in various industries to draw up codes of fair competition. When approved by the president, these codes had the force of law. The NIRA also gave the chief executive the power to license enterprises as a means of forcing them to desist from unfair price, wage, and trade practices. The act was unconstitutional, the Court declared, because Congress had delegated too much of its authority to others and also because the commerce clause did not authorize the national legislature, even in an emergency, to enact a measure that regulated local as well as interstate enterprises. Neither did that constitutional provision empower Congress to control labor-management relations in coal mines. In *Carter* v. *Carter Coal Company* (1936) the Court utilized the distinction between production and commerce to strike down a New Deal law that attempted such regulation.

The Supreme Court interpreted restrictively not only the commerce clause but also Congress's spending power. In *United States* v. *Butler* (1936) it invalidated the Agricultural Adjustment Act, a statute that sought to raise crop prices by paying farmers to take land out of cultivation. Justice Owen Roberts reasoned that since congressional regulation of agricultural production would violate the Tenth Amendment, and since this law coerced farmers into limiting output by imposing conditions they must meet in order to receive federal money, it was nothing more than an indirect way of achieving an unconstitutional objective.

By early 1937 the Supreme Court had struck down virtually every New Deal measure that came before it. Its only concessions to the Roosevelt administration were rather narrow rulings that Congress could set aside clauses in private contracts requiring payment in gold and sell surplus electric power generated by Tennessee Valley Authority dams. The laissez-faire thinking that dominated the Court produced not only restrictive interpretations of the power-granting provisions of the Constitution, but also rulings that employed some of its negative prohibitions, such as the due process clauses and the takings clause of the Fifth Amendment to wipe out federal and even state regulatory measures.

JUDICIAL ENHANCEMENT OF GOVERNMENTAL POWER, 1937–1990s

On 5 February 1937 an irate President Roosevelt introduced legislation to increase the size of the Supreme Court. He wanted to add new members who shared his views about the need for vigorous governmental action to combat the Depression and who were willing to interpret the Constitution in such a way as to make this possible. The Court promptly executed an about-face. Most scholars now agree that the so-called "switch in time that saved nine" was inspired less by Roosevelt's "Court-packing plan" than by his landslide reelection victory in 1936, which convinced Justice Owen Roberts and Chief Justice Charles Evans Hughes, who held the balance of power on a divided bench, that the New Deal enjoyed overwhelming popular support. Whatever the cause, the effect was a change in the Supreme Court's approach to the powers of other governmental bodies that was sudden, dramatic, fundamental—and permanent. On 29 March 1937, in *West Coast Hotel Company* v. *Parrish* the Court upheld by a 5-to-4 majority a Washington state law setting a minimum wage for women. This statute was indistinguishable from a New York one it had struck down less than a year earlier as a violation of the due process clause. Never again would the Supreme Court invalidate any economic regulatory measure on substantive due process grounds.

Parrish was the harbinger of a series of decisions reflecting an equally significant change in judicial attitude toward the powers of Congress. First came a group of early April rulings affirming the constitutionality of the National Labor Relations Act, a 1935 New Deal statute that subjected employer-employee dealings to sweeping federal controls, even in manufacturing and other productive industries. In the most important of these cases, *National Labor Relations Board* v. *Jones & Laughlin Steel Corporation,* Chief Justice Hughes declared that the commerce clause gave Congress the power to regulate activities that might "be interstate in character when separately considered, if they have such a close and substantial relation to interstate commerce that their control is essential or appropriate to protect that commerce." Hughes insisted that under America's "dual system of government" some matters continued to be within a sphere reserved exclusively to the states, and he denied that the Court was subjecting all economic activity to congressional control.

Subsequent rulings revealed, however, that there remained few, if any, judicial limitations on the regulatory authority of Congress. As conservative justices retired and were replaced by Roosevelt appointees, the Supreme Court became ever more committed to the notion that the judiciary should defer to legislative judgments where economic matters were concerned. In *United States* v. *Darby* (1941) the Court overruled *Hammer* v. *Dagenhart* and announced that it was "no objection to [an] assertion of the power to regulate interstate commerce" that what Congress was doing resembled an "exercise of the police power of the states." *Wickard* v. *Filburn* (1942) went even further, declaring Congress might regulate even purely local activities that exerted "a substantial economic effect on interstate commerce." The fact that an individual's own impact on the national economy was minimal did not "remove him from the scope of federal regulation where . . . his contribution, taken together with that of many others similarly situated" was substantial. Thus, according to the Court, the commerce clause empowered Congress to limit the amount of wheat a farmer could grow for consumption on his own land because if many farmers supplied their own needs the aggregate effect on the market demand for wheat would be significant.

Virtually any law the national legislature claimed was an exercise of its commerce power survived judicial review, even statutes directed at activities as seemingly local in character as loan sharking and strip mining. Justices went so far as to permit Congress to use the commerce clause to get around one of the Court's own rulings. According to the *Civil Rights Cases* (1883), the Fourteenth Amendment gave the national legislature no authority to ban racial discrimination by privately owned businesses. Yet, when Congress passed a public accommodations act in 1964 in purported reliance on its commerce power, the Supreme Court upheld that law, even as applied to a neighborhood restaurant in Birmingham, Alabama, whose only connection with interstate commerce was the purchase of meat from a supplier who in turn had bought it in another state. Only twice after 1936 did the Supreme Court hold Congress had exceeded the authority given it by the commerce clause. *National League of Cities* v. *Usery* (1976) declared unconstitutional a requirement that state and local governments comply with federal wages and hours legislation. But this limitation survived only until the Court formally reversed *National League of Cities* in *Garcia* v. *San Antonio Metropolitan Transit Authority* (1985). In *New York* v. *United States* (1992) the Court went no further than to declare that Congress might not command states that made no provision for the disposal of low level radioactive waste to take title to all such waste generated within their borders.

While essentially eliminating judicially enforceable constraints on the commerce power, the Supreme Court did the same thing with other congressional powers as well. In two May 1937 decisions upholding the unemployment compensation and old age insurance provisions of the Social Security Act of 1935, the Court effectively repudiated *United States* v. *Butler.* It rejected the idea that imposing conditions on recipients of federal payments or the beneficiaries of federal tax credits was coercive and somehow violative of the Tenth Amendment. There was no coercion, the Court maintained in 1937 and later, even if those prodded by financial self-interest to do something Congress could not command them to do were state governments. Conditional grants became perhaps the most important means by which Washington expanded its de facto police power during the second half of the twentieth century. Congress used them to induce state and local governments to adopt and implement policies that the Constitution gave the national legislature no authority to mandate, governing matters such as the education of the developmentally disabled.

The Supreme Court repeatedly upheld such uses of the congressional spending power. It did so even when Congress required the states to legislate in particular ways on matters left to them by the Constitution. Thus, in *South Dakota* v. *Dole* (1987) the Court affirmed the constitutionality of legislation that pressured states into raising their minimum drinking age to twenty-one by threatening them with loss of some of the federal highway funds they would otherwise have received. The Court insisted in Dole that policy choices concerning teenage drinking remained "the prerogative of the states not merely in theory but in fact." In *New York* v. *United States,* however, even while declaring emphatically, "The Federal Government may not compel the states to enact or administer a federal regulatory program," the Court acknowledged that Congress might use its spending power to "urge a state to adopt a legislative program consistent with federal interests." The fiscal problems of state governments left them with little real choice but to implement congressional policy, even in areas once considered to be within their own exclusive control.

The Supreme Court proved equally unwilling to limit the uses Congress could make of its taxing power. As early as 1928 the Court affirmed the constitutionality of protective tariffs, although these often produced little revenue. In 1937 it upheld a tax on firearms rather obviously designed for regulatory purposes rather than to raise money. In 1953 it did the same with an occupational tax on gamblers, the main purpose of which seemed to be to compel bookies to register with the government.

These decisions all demonstrated the willingness of the post-1937 Supreme Court to allow Congress to define the extent of its own powers. *Katzenbach* v. *Morgan* (1966) offered a dramatic demonstration of how far the Court would carry such deference. *Morgan* sustained a statute, enacted pursuant to the authority granted Congress by the enforcement section of the Fourteenth Amendment, that forbade states to require immigrants from Puerto Rico to be able to read English in order to vote. The Court had previously ruled that English literacy tests did not violate the equal protection clause. Because the statute supposedly implemented that clause, the Court seemed to be taking the position that Congress could alter the meaning of the Fourteenth Amendment while purportedly enforcing it. Although *Morgan* was in many respects an unusual case, it reflected the predominant judicial outlook during the last half of the twentieth century: the only limitations on the powers of Congress were political.

The Supreme Court proved almost as reluctant to fence in presidential power as to constrain the authority of the legislative branch. From the late 1930s onward the United States found itself embroiled almost constantly in international crises, and as World War I had demonstrated, the presidency was the part of the government best equipped to deal decisively and effectively with such emergencies. During World War II, the Cold War, the Korean Conflict, and Vietnam, Congress, as it had in 1917–1918, delegated vast amounts of power to the president. Although the Supreme Court invalidated the National Industrial Recovery Act in part because of that law's excessive delegation of legislative authority to the executive, a year later in *United States* v. *Curtiss Wright Corp.* (1936) it asserted that what would be impermissible in domestic legislation could be constitutional in the realm of foreign affairs. After all, the president was the "sole organ" of the federal government in the field of international relations. Because the Court also announced that where external affairs were concerned the powers of the national government were not limited to those conferred by the Constitution, *Curtiss Wright* conceded an awesome amount of authority to the presidency.

In later litigation the Supreme Court expressed itself in a somewhat more restrained fashion, but it exhibited no greater willingness to limit presidential freedom of action in foreign affairs. In 1981 Presidents Jimmy Carter and Ronald Reagan agreed, as part of a deal to obtain the release of hostages held in Tehran, to terminate legal proceedings against Iran brought by Americans in this country's courts. The Supreme Court upheld their action. Obviously uncomfortable with recognizing a presidential prerogative to ride roughshod over the property rights of U.S. citizens, it went out of its way to find some sort of congressional sanction for what the presidents had done. But the Court was unwilling to hold that Carter and Reagan lacked the power to act.

The Court was no more willing to rule that presidents who commenced armed hostilities on their own initiative had exceeded their authority. Although Article I says that Congress shall have the power to declare war, no declaration of war preceded presidential commitment of American forces to Korea, Vietnam, or numerous smaller conflicts in the second half of the twentieth century. During the increasingly unpopular Vietnam War, numerous litigants asked the Supreme Court to decide whether it was unconstitutional for a president to go to war without congressional authorization, but the Court repeatedly refused even to hear these cases.

It did check one wartime presidential action on the home front. Confronted with the threat of a steel strike during the Korean War, President Harry Truman had responded by seizing the nation's steel mills, relying for authority on the inherent powers of his office. In *Youngstown Sheet & Tube Company* v. *Sawyer* (1952) the Court held Truman had acted illegally. The multiple opinions in that case disclosed, however, that most of the justices had ruled against the president only because he had refused to follow procedures for dealing with strikes that imperiled the national interest laid out in recently enacted congressional legislation. All but three seemed to think that in the absence of this statute, Article II would have given the commander in chief sufficient authority to do even something as drastic as placing the entire steel industry under government control.

As the *Youngstown* opinions revealed, the Supreme Court was extremely reluctant to reject presidential claims concerning the sweep of the authority conferred by Article II. *United States* v. *Nixon* (1974) evinced the same reluctance. There the Court confronted a president claiming that he could not be compelled to reveal confidential communications with his aides. The text of the Constitution makes no mention of such an "executive privilege," and there was more than a little reason to suspect that Richard Nixon was asserting its existence to hide his involvement in criminal wrongdoing. By the time of the decision, Nixon was on the verge of being impeached. Yet, rather than holding that there was no such thing as executive privilege, the Supreme Court recognized the existence of such a presidential prerogative and ruled against Nixon only on the ground that in this case that privilege must yield to the needs of the criminal courts for the information he was trying to withhold.

As *United States* v. *Nixon* illustrates, by the second half of the twentieth century, the Supreme Court had become extremely reluctant to dispute the claims of other branches of the federal government concerning the existence and scope of their powers. Generally, it afforded them substantial autonomy, leaving to the political process the job of ensuring that they did not exceed their authority. To be sure, in *Immigration and Naturalization Service* v. *Chadha* (1983) the Court did hold that it was unconstitutional for Congress, when delegating power to the executive, to retain the right to overrule individual exercises of the delegated authority. The rationale for that decision, however, was that the "legislative vetoes" that Congress was incorporating into a growing number of statutes violated the Constitution's procedural requirements for the enactment of a law and also impinged upon the prerogatives of the president. Rarely did the Supreme Court hold that the legislature lacked some substantive power that it claimed to derive from the Constitution. *Powell* v. *McCormack* (1969)—in which the Court ruled that Article I did not empower the House to refuse to seat, because of his allegedly improper conduct, someone who had been elected as a representative and satisfied the constitutional age, citizenship, and residence requirements—was a quite exceptional ruling. Since the Supreme Court professed to be, and was widely regarded as, the ultimate authority on the meaning of the Constitution, the consequence of its deferential posture was the virtual demise of internal constitutional constraints on the authority of the president and Congress.

This did not mean that the powers of the legislative and executive branches were unlimited. Congress and the president could and did restrain each other. For example, before Nixon resigned in August 1974, the House Judiciary Committee voted to impeach him for withholding from it material he claimed was protected by executive privilege. Congress disputed the claims of numerous commanders in chief that they possessed the authority to plunge the country into armed conflict without prior congressional authorization. By passing the War Powers Resolution in 1973, the legislature endeavored to preclude presidents from taking such action except in emergencies. Should legislators attempt to exercise power the chief executive believed they did not possess, he could thwart them with his veto, and if overridden, he could simply refuse to carry out the offending measure. Nixon, who considered the War Powers resolution unconstitutional, tried unsuccessfully to veto it, and his successors, who agreed with him that the Resolution impermissibly restricted presidential authority, often ignored it. But before launching Operation Desert Storm in 1991, George Bush sought authorization from Congress to use force against Iraq. Bush had deployed 400,000 troops to the Persian Gulf in reliance on nothing more than his authority as commander in chief, but the political risks involved in actually going to war without enlisting the support of the legislative branch had become too great for any president to ignore.

INDIVIDUAL RIGHTS

While the president and Congress restrained each other, the Supreme Court protected human rights. Although unwilling to enforce internal limitations on the power-granting provisions of the Constitution, the Court began to demonstrate around 1938 an increasing commitment to employing its negative prohibitions for the protection of the individual. When the justices abandoned their traditional role as censors of economic and social legislation, the United States was relatively homogeneous politically and for the moment isolated from foreign dangers. Operating in a climate affordable for the growth of civil liberties, the Supreme Court began to fashion constitutional rights, which in the past had been little more than an alternative means of fencing in the regulatory authority of government, into shields protecting human beings from governmental power. Rights eventually became the main focus of constitutional jurisprudence.

One reason for this development was the growing size and pervasiveness of government. In the United States, as in other modern industrial nations, the more services the public demanded from the state, the larger and more centralized the state became. The federal bureaucracy, which had already grown large enough by the 1920s to inspire some comment and concern, exploded during the New Deal era. Even many people who applauded governmental activism in combating the Depression viewed uneasily the proliferation of administrative agencies that this made necessary. Years of conservative rule, during which the power of the state had been repeatedly used against them, made trade unionists and radicals suspicious of government. On the right, opponents of the New Deal worried about Roosevelt's enhancement of presidential authority and his mobilization of an army of bureaucrats to carry out his liberal policies. Americans of all political persuasions needed only to gaze across the Atlantic at the totalitarian regimes of Nazi Germany, Fascist Italy, and Stalin's Soviet Union during the 1930s to witness dramatic demonstrations of the dangers posed by uninhibited statism. At the very time that the Supreme Court was enhancing governmental power, a feeling that people needed protection from government was spreading.

In 1938 the traditionally conservative American Bar Association created a Committee on the Bill of Rights. That committee joined with the National Lawyers Guild, set up a year earlier as a liberal alternative to the ABA, and the American Civil Liberties Union, which had been defending pacifists, radicals, and labor since World War I, to form an increasingly influential civil liberties lobby. Civil libertarians found sympathizers in the Roosevelt administration, and especially in the United States Department of Justice, where Attorney General Frank Murphy created a Civil Liberties Unit in 1940.

They also elicited a sympathetic response from the Supreme Court. Having abandoned its traditional role as a censor of economic legislation, the Court needed a new agenda. Justice Harlan Fiske Stone supplied one with a footnote that he added to his opinion of the Court in *United States* v. *Carolene Products* (1938). This case involved a 1923 federal statute that prohibited the shipment in interstate commerce of "filled milk," a compound in which the natural butterfat had been replaced with vegetable oil. Predictably, the Court spurned a substantive due process challenge to the law, deferring to the judgment of Congress that this legislation served to prevent fraud and to protect public health.

But in footnote 4 of his opinion, Stone declared:

"There may be a narrower scope for operation of the presumption of constitutionality when legislation appears on its face to be within a specific prohibition of the Constitution, such as those in [the Bill of Rights]." He suggested that "more exacting judicial scrutiny under the 14th Amendment" might also be appropriate when the Court confronted legislation that restricted "those political processes which can ordinarily be expected to bring about repeal of undesirable legislation." Because prejudice against "discrete and insular" racial, national, and religious minorities tended to "curtail those political processes ordinarily to be relied upon to protect" minority groups, laws directed at them also might "call for a correspondingly more searching judicial inquiry." What Stone was advocating was a constitutional double standard: complete judicial deference to legislative judgments on matters of economic regulation, but vigorous judicial protection of civil rights and civil liberties.

Footnote 4 reflected the "preferred freedom" approach that Justice Benjamin Cardozo had taken a year earlier in *Palko* v. *Connecticut* (1937). Cardozo believed the Fourteenth Amendment protected all of those rights "so rooted in the traditions and conscience of our people as to be ranked as fundamental"—but no others. Thus, in *Palko* he declared that the "liberty" which that amendment forbade states to take away from any person without "due process of law" embraced some of, but not all, the liberties enumerated in the Bill of Rights. Freedom of expression enjoyed the protection of the Fourteenth Amendment while the right to be free from double jeopardy did not, because unlike the latter, the former was part "of the essence of ordered liberty."

INCORPORATION OF THE BILL OF RIGHTS

Besides articulating the idea that some constitutional values stood on a higher plane than others, Cardozo's *Palko* opinion provided a theoretical framework for the nationalization of the Bill of Rights. This trend, one of the most important in twentieth-century constitutional history, expanded greatly both the power of the Supreme Court and the significance of those constitutional guarantees. The first eight amendments had been added to the Constitution following a ratification struggle in which Antifederalist opponents of the document written by the Philadelphia Convention argued that the powerful national government it created would be a threat to liberty, in part because the Framers had failed to include a bill of rights. Not surprisingly, in *Barron* v. *Baltimore* (1833) the Supreme Court held the Bill of Rights did not apply to the states.

Because the guarantees contained in the first eight amendments applied only to the national government, for a long time they were of little consequence. Throughout most of the nineteenth century that government was comparatively inactive. While political dissenters, racial minorities, small religious groups, and criminal defendants often had their rights violated, it was generally state and local authorities who were responsible for these violations. Consequently, as Paul Murphy notes, "The constitutional and legal historian looks virtually in vain during the years prior to the Civil War for federal precedents interpreting the Bill of Rights protections."

At first the addition of the Fourteenth Amendment to the Constitution did little to change this situation. Whether those who wrote and ratified that amendment intended by doing so to make the Bill of Rights applicable to the states is a question which historians, judges, and legal scholars have long debated. The evidence is inconclusive. Some proponents of the Fourteenth Amendment stated that its privileges and immunities clause would have this effect, and the congressional debates contain references to reversing the effect of *Barron* v. *Baltimore.* On the other hand, some of those who made such statements seemed to lack a clear understanding of what was in the Bill of Rights. Moreover, although the first eight amendments contained provisions (most notably the Fifth Amendment's requirement that criminal defendants be charged by grand jury indictment) inconsistent with procedures used in some of the states, those states ratified the Fourteenth Amendment without hinting that it might compel them to change what they were doing. In all likelihood, most of the Republicans who voted for this amendment intended it to secure against state infringement a group of fundamental rights that was vaguely defined even in their own minds. These rights probably included many (but not all) of the privileges already protected from the federal government by the Bill of Rights, and some other unspecified liberties as well.

The objective of the authors of the Fourteenth Amendment was not realized for decades. Reluctant to acknowledge the massive alteration of the American federal system affected by the Civil War and the Reconstruction amendments, the Supreme Court refused at first to accept the very substantial departure from traditional federalism that interpreting the Constitution as mandating state compliance with fundamental rights would necessarily have entailed. The narrow reading the Court gave the privileges and immunities clause in the *Slaughterhouse Cases* left that part of the Fourteenth Amendment protecting almost nothing, and in *Hurtado* v. *California* (1884) eight of nine justices spurned the argument that the due process clause applied the Bill of Rights to the states. Holding that this provision did not compel state compliance with the Fifth Amendment's grand jury indictment requirement, the Court adopted reasoning exempting the states from all the demands of the first eight amendments.

The high tribunal acknowledged, however, that the due process clause forbade states to interfere with "those fundamental principles of liberty and justice which lie at the base of all our civil and political institutions." Ironically, by accepting the concept of substantive due process during the decades after 1884, the Court laid the basis for eventual repudiation of the *Hurtado* doctrine. Initially, only property rights received the protection of the Fourteenth Amendment, but by 1923 the Court had decided that the liberty which it safeguarded against arbitrary legislative interference included such noneconomic freedoms as the right of parents to choose the language in which their children would be educated. The Court first departed from the reasoning of *Hurtado* in 1897, when it held that the due process clause required the states to pay just compensation for private property taken for a public purpose, just as the Fifth Amendment compelled the federal government to do. In the 1908 case of *Twining* v. *New Jersey,* the Court conceded that some of the specific personal rights mentioned in the first eight amendments might be "safeguarded against state action, because denial of them would be a denial of due process of law." Finally, in *Gitlow* v. *New York* (1925) Justice Edward Sanford indicated he and his colleagues now assumed the "freedom of speech and of the press–which are protected by the First Amendment"—were "among the fundamental personal rights and 'liberties' protected by the due process clause . . . from impairment by the states."

Thus, the Court "incorporated" those guarantees into the due process clause. During the 1930s and 1940s the high tribunal also made the Sixth Amendment's right to counsel and the First Amendment's bans on establishing religion and interfering with its free exercise applicable to the states. Justice Hugo Black argued passionately that the due process clause embraced all other provisions of the Bill of Rights as well, but he could never persuade a majority of his colleagues to accept this "total incorporation" position. Instead, the Court opted for the approach Cardozo had championed in *Palko,* reading into the due process clause only those rights it considered so fundamental as to be "implicit in the concept of ordered liberty." This process of "selective incorporation" accelerated after Earl Warren became chief justice in 1953. By the time Warren retired in 1969 the Court had made applicable to the states all the provisions of the Bill of Rights except the grand jury indictment clause, the Second Amendment's guarantee of the right to keep and bear arms, the Third Amendment's proscription of quartering soldiers in private homes in time of peace, the Seventh Amendment's guarantee of jury trials in civil cases in which the amount in controversy exceeded $20, and the Eighth Amendment's prohibition of excessive bail. In 1971 the Court suggested that if confronted with a case that squarely raised the issue, it would rule the bail provision had been incorporated too. In addition, several justices believed that the Fourteenth Amendment required the states to respect certain rights not explicitly enumerated in the Constitution, as they thought the Ninth Amendment commanded the federal government to do.

Incorporation not only broadened the reach and significance of the Bill of Rights but also changed its essential nature. The first eight amendments had been added to the Constitution in 1791, along with the Ninth and also the Tenth, which reserved to the states and to the people all powers not delegated by the document to the federal government. The purpose of these ten amendments was to protect a majority of the people from a possibly unrepresentative national government. The Fourteenth Amendment had a different focus; it was designed to shield vulnerable individuals and minorities from dominant social majorities. When the provisions of the Bill of Rights were incorporated into the due process clause, that became their role as well.

FREEDOM OF EXPRESSION

The Supreme Court began employing those provisions to protect the vulnerable even before it completed the process of selective incorporation. Between 1919 and 1969, in cases involving seditious speech and advocacy of illegal action, the Court rendered the First Amendment's guarantees of freedom of expression far more protective of individual dissenters and far less protective of the community than originally had been the case. Prior to 1917, claims of individual rights seldom prevailed if officials invoked the demands of public safety or social control against them. Most Americans believed that civil liberties enjoyed legal protection only when exercised by citizens who used their rights constructively; therefore, the community could withhold these privileges from the undeserving. This view prevailed during World War I, when Congress adopted the Espionage and Sedition Acts, under which dissidents who criticized the government and its policies could be punished.

The Supreme Court affirmed convictions obtained under those laws, in the process rejecting constitutional attacks upon the statutes. Although the First Amendment declares that "Congress shall make no law . . . abridging the freedom of speech, or of the press," the Court was unwilling in 1919, and has remained unwilling ever since, to accept the absolutist position that "no law" means no law. Upholding the Espionage Act in *Schenck* v. *United States* (1919), Justice Oliver Wendell Holmes, Jr., declared that when the country is "at war many things that might be said in time of peace are such a hindrance to its effort . . . that no Court could regard them as protected by any constitutional right." Wartime advocacy of draft resistance posed a "clear and present danger" of substantive evil, and consequently Congress might suppress it without violating the First Amendment. Holmes's approach differed little, if at all, from the "remote bad tendency" test employed by most other judges in cases involving World War I dissenters, under which any expression that might tend to provoke a violation of the law was considered to be beyond the protection of the Constitution.

Although formulated to justify a repressive ruling, the "clear and present danger test" that he announced in Schenck came to be regarded as quite protective of freedom of expression. Beginning in *Abrams* v. *United States* (1919), Holmes (whose thinking had been changed by Harvard professor Zechariah Chafee, Jr., and other legal academics) joined with Justice Louis Brandeis to file a series of separate opinions, most of them dissents, in which they argued that punishing anarchists, communists, and other radical critics of American government and society for their speech violated the First Amendment, unless the words these dissidents used created an imminent danger of some serious violation of the law. By 1940 a majority of the Supreme Court had abandoned the bad tendency approach and accepted the clear and present danger test, using it to overturn even contempt judgments lower court judges had imposed for comments seemingly intended to coerce the judiciary.

Amid the anticommunist hysteria of the McCarthy era, the Court retreated temporarily, placing its emphasis on preventing claims of individual rights from unduly restricting the capacity of government to protect the community. In *Dennis* v. *United States* (1951), it modified the clear and present danger rule, holding that if the evil advocated were great enough (for example, a communist attempt to overthrow the government), speech might be suppressed, even though the evil was very unlikely ever to occur. During the libertarian 1960s, a decade of social ferment, punctuated by militant protests against racial discrimination and the Vietnam War, the Supreme Court swung back in the other direction. In *Brandenburg* v. *Ohio* (1969) the Court announced that the "constitutional guarantees of free speech and free press" prohibited government from proscribing advocacy of force or violation of the law, unless the advocacy was "directed to inciting or producing imminent lawless action and is likely to incite or produce such action." *Brandenburg* freed a Ku Klux Klan leader, who had talked of taking "revengement" on Congress, the president, and the Court itself.

That decision was among numerous manifestations of a growing judicial tendency to use the First Amendment to protect individuals and minority groups whose expression defied the standards and values of society. This trend was particularly evident during Earl Warren's chief justiceship. The Warren Court extended constitutional protection to a good deal of sexually explicit expression. Moreover, in *New York Times* v. *Sullivan* (1964) the high tribunal subordinated civility in public discourse to uninhibited discussion of civic issues by injecting the First Amendment into the law of libel. The Court held that public officials could recover damages from newspapers that made false and defamatory statements about them only by proving that the statements had been made with knowledge that they were false, or with reckless disregard for their possible untruth. Although *Sullivan* fostered wide open discussion of public issues, it also contributed, as Kermit Hall observes, to a "decay of community values associated with first amendment law since the 1930s."

The phenomenon Hall criticizes continued under Warren's more conservative successors, Warren Burger and William Rehnquist. In *Cohen* v. *California* (1971), for example, the Burger Court (1969–1986) ruled that punishing a young man for wearing a jacket with "Fuck the Draft" emblazoned across the back violated his rights under the First and Fourteenth Amendments. Under Burger the Supreme Court repeatedly held that even profanity was constitutionally protected, so long as it was used to communicate ideas. In *Texas* v. *Johnson* (1989) the Rehnquist Court (1986–) (over the objections of the chief justice) invalidated a statute that prohibited desecrating the American flag.

Flag desecration was, of course, conduct, rather than "speech" in the traditional sense of the word. Since holding in 1940 that there was a First Amendment right to engage in peaceful labor picketing, however, the Court had been treating some kinds of conduct as constitutionally protected expression. In *United States* v. *O'Brien* (1968) the Warren Court accepted the argument that draft card burning, a popular form of protest against the Vietnam War, was symbolic speech. It upheld a law punishing that form of communication, but in *Tinker* v. *Des Moines School District* (1971) invalidated a prohibition on the wearing of black arm bands to protest the war. Although Justice Hugo Black argued passionately that only pure speech enjoyed the protection of the First Amendment, the Court continued to view it as shielding some conduct as well. The Burger Court struck down a state law that had been used to punish a man who taped a peace symbol on an American flag, and the Rehnquist Court held unconstitutional both state and federal laws proscribing flag desecration, as well as a municipal ordinance punishing cross burning. It even treated nude dancing as a form of expression.

Justifying its ruling in *Texas* v. *Johnson,* the Court explained, "If there is a bedrock principle underlying the First Amendment, it is that the Government may not prohibit the expression of an idea simply because society finds the idea itself offensive or disagreeable." Nor, according to the justices, might government use its power to compel unwilling individuals to endorse the beliefs of the majority. Despite the patriotic fervor inspired by World War II, the Court ruled in *West Virginia Board of Education* v. *Barnette* (1943), that it was unconstitutional for public schools to require students to salute the flag. More than four decades later in *Wooley* v. *Maynard* (1977), while holding that New Hampshire might not punish individuals who covered up the state motto ("Live Free or Die") on their license plates, the Court reaffirmed its opposition to governmental compulsion directed at forcing an individual to become an instrument for "fostering public adherence to an ideological point of view he finds unacceptable." The First Amendment, said the Court, protected "the right to refrain from speaking" because, like the right to speak freely, this right was part of a broader concept: "'individual freedom of mind.'"

There were some free speech decisions in the last half of the twentieth century that served to advance the interests of the community. These included a few rulings around 1960 upholding internal security measures and a series of cases in the 1970s and 1980s striking down governmental restrictions on advertising by professionals, such as pharmacists and attorneys. Most of the Supreme Court's freedom of expression rulings, however, defended the autonomy of the individual against the power of the state.

FREEDOM OF RELIGION

For a long time, most decisions involving the First Amendment's religion clauses also defended the autonomy of the individual against the power of the state. In the nineteenth century the Supreme Court had declined to use these to prevent government from imposing majority values on nonconforming minorities. In *Reynolds* v. *United States* (1878), for example, the Court held that application of a federal law prohibiting polygamy to a Mormon, whose religion required him to engage in the practice, did not violate the free exercise clause. Its attitude began to change in the late 1930s, however. While continuing to adhere to a dichotomy it had created in *Reynolds* between religious belief, which the free exercise clause protected from governmental interference, and religiously motivated conduct, which it did not, during the 1940s the Court invalidated numerous restrictions on the proselytizing activities of Jehovah's Witnesses as violations of freedom of expression.

After World War II, confronted by a rising tide of legislation providing governmental financial assistance to parochial schools and authorizing religious instruction for public school students, the Court turned its attention to the establishment clause. This provision, *Everson* v. *Board of Education* (1947) announced, had erected a "wall of separation" between church and state. For a time, though, the Court sanctioned what appeared to be fairly substantial breaches in that wall, upholding both state funding of transportation to parochial schools and off-campus religious instruction of public school students during school hours. Under Earl Warren, however, the Court aligned itself with liberals and civil libertarians who considered cooperation between church and state an infringement on the rights of the individual, holding that both prayer and Bible reading in public schools violated the establishment clause. Its decisions in *Engel* v. *Vitale* (1962) and *Abington School District* v. *Schemp* (1963) ignited a firestorm of criticism and sparked unsuccessful efforts to amend the Constitution to sanction what the Court had forbidden.

The Burger and Rehnquist Courts proved somewhat more willing to tolerate collaboration between government and religion. They held, for example, that tax exemptions for churches were constitutional; that states could provide some types of assistance to religious colleges and to parochial school students and their parents; and that Christmas nativity scenes on public property did not violate the establishment clause if they were part of displays that included enough secular objects to nullify their religious character. Burger even declared it was permissible for a state legislature to employ a chaplain. Yet, the Burger and Rehnquist Courts insisted the power of government might not be used, either coercively or through endorsement, to promote the religious views of the majority. While not all their decisions were consistent with their rhetoric, *Wallace* v. *Jaffee* (1985) held that a law requiring a daily "moment of silence," which its sponsors acknowledged was intended to promote voluntary prayer in the Alabama public schools, violated the establishment clause. In *Lee* v. *Weisman* (1992) the Court ruled that invocations and benedictions at public school graduations were unconstitutional because peer pressure might compel those who found them objectionable to participate.

The Supreme Court also used the free exercise clause to protect minorities. Beginning in the early 1960s, if an individual could show that some regulation interfered with her religious practices, that regulation could survive constitutional scrutiny only if the government came forward with a very important justification for the rule and for applying it to her. Thus, *Sherbert* v. *Verner* (1963) held that South Carolina might not deny unemployment compensation to a Seventh Day Adventist because she refused to work on Saturday. *Wisconsin* v. *Yoder* (1972) forbade a state to enforce its compulsory attendance laws against Amish parents who refused to send their children to high school. In *Employment Division* v. *Smith* (1990), however, the Rehnquist Court by a 5-to-4 vote rejected the reasoning of both of its two immediate predecessors. Justice Antonin Scalia interpreted the free exercise clause as permitting government to prohibit, without justification, conduct mandated by an individual's religious beliefs, so long as the prohibition was generally applicable and did not target religion. Although *Smith* affirmed the right of a state to enforce its drug laws against Native Americans who used peyote in religious ceremonies, spokesmen for mainstream churches joined civil libertarians in denouncing the decision, and Congress enacted legislation to overturn it.

RIGHTS OF CRIMINAL DEFENDANTS

The judicial reluctance to shield individual liberty from the power of the state which *Smith* reflected appeared most often during the last quarter of the twentieth century in criminal cases. These required judicial interpretation of the Fourth Amendment, which prohibits unreasonable searches and seizures; the Fifth Amendment, which bans double jeopardy and compelled self-incrimination; the Sixth Amendment, which guarantees those accused of crime the rights to a speedy and public trial before an impartial jury, to confront the witnesses against them, and to be represented by an attorney; and the Eighth Amendment, which forbids cruel and unusual punishment and excessive bail and fines. By incorporating these provisions from the Bill of Rights, the Warren Court transformed state criminal procedure into a branch of federal constitutional law. At the same time, convinced that the disadvantaged elements in society, especially racial minorities, must be protected from overbearing police and prosecutors, the Court interpreted the Fourth, Fifth, Sixth, and Eighth Amendments in ways that substantially augmented the rights of those accused of crimes.

Some of the Warren Court's criminal procedure decisions, especially *Gideon* v. *Wainwright* (1963), requiring states to supply attorneys to all persons charged with felonies who could not afford to hire their own lawyers, elicited favorable reaction. Others, most notably *Mapp* v. *Ohio* (1961), which made evidence obtained through unreasonable searches and seizures inadmissible in state criminal trials, and *Miranda* v. *Arizona* (1966), which required police to warn suspects of their rights before attempting to interrogate them, inspired widespread criticism, especially from law enforcement officials and conservative politicians. Richard Nixon excoriated the Warren Court's criminal procedure rulings, blaming these decisions for the nation's rapidly rising crime rate.

Nixon's victory in the 1968 presidential election marked the beginning of the end for judicial expansion of the rights of criminal defendants. Nixon and fellow Republican presidents Ronald Reagan and George Bush appointed to the Supreme Court justices committed to preserving "law and order" and convinced that "legal technicalities" should not permit the guilty to evade punishment. The torrent of narcotics that flooded the United States during the

1980s and 1990s, and a wave of violent crime associated with it, persuaded many Americans to accept the view that individual rights must be sacrificed to win the "war on drugs."

Such thinking substantially reduced judicial willingness to restrain governmental power for the protection of those accused of crime. The reaction that began in the late 1960s did not undo entirely what the Warren Court had wrought, however. State criminal procedure remained subject to federal supervision. The Court invalidated all existing death penalty laws in *Furman* v. *Georgia* (1972), and allowed the states to reinstate capital punishment only if they complied with standards it approved in *Gregg* v. *Georgia* (1976). Under Burger and Rehnquist, the Supreme Court qualified and created exceptions to major criminal procedure decisions from the Warren era. For example, in *Harris* v. *New York* (1971), the Court held that although a prosecutor was prohibited from using a statement obtained from a defendant who had not been given the warnings required by *Miranda* as proof of guilt, if the accused took the stand and told a different story, such a confession was admissible to impeach his credibility. In *Moran* v. *Burbine* (1986) the Court upheld the use of a confession obtained after a waiver of *Miranda* rights, secured by police who withheld from the suspect the information that his lawyer was readily available and misinformed the attorney about whether the suspect would be interrogated. *United States* v. *Leon* (1984) recognized an exception to the "exclusionary rule" created by *Mapp,* holding illegally seized evidence could be used in court if the officers who obtained it had acted in good faith reliance on a warrant, even though the warrant later proved to be defective. In 1987 the Court held that an FBI agent who had carried out an unlawful search could not be sued for damages if he had reasonably believed that what he was doing was lawful. While sanctioning inroads into principles laid down by the Warren Court, the Rehnquist and Burger Courts did not reverse *Miranda, Mapp,* or *Gideon.* The rights recognized by those decisions, although more limited than they had once been, still provided vulnerable individuals with some protection against abuses of governmental power.

EQUAL PROTECTION

Under Rehnquist and Burger, the Supreme Court continued to play the role that Justice Stone had envisioned for it in his *Carolene Products* footnote. Stone, of course, had suggested the need for judicial activism not only to enforce the specific constitutional prohibitions but also to eradicate legislation that restricted participation in the political process and laws that discriminated against discrete and insular minorities. The extremely activist Warren Court answered his call to eliminate those constraints on the democratic process that kept government from fairly representing all of the people. In *Baker* v. *Carr* (1962) the Court ruled that malapportionment of state legislatures, which often gave a small fraction of the population control of a state's government, posed a legal problem which judges could resolve. In *Reynolds* v. *Sims* (1964) Warren declared that the equal protection clause required states to apportion both houses of their legislatures on the basis of population. In 1968 the Court went on to hold that even members of local governing bodies, such as county boards of supervisors, must represent substantially equal numbers of constituents.

Although its reapportionment decisions promoted majoritarianism, the thrust of most of the equal protection jurisprudence the Supreme Court developed after 1938 was the protection of discrete and insular minorities. While eliminating all constitutional constraints on economic regulation, the Court grew increasingly protective of defenseless groups within society, ones peculiarly vulnerable to the enhanced governmental power wielded by majorities. As Robert Cover has observed, "Minorities . . . became a special object of judicial protection [after] Stone's *Carolene Products* footnote, which was written at almost the exact moment when majoritarianism became the dominant constitutional perspective."

During the late 1930s and early 1940s the Supreme Court utilized the First Amendment's guarantee of free speech to shield the Jehovah's Witnesses, a small and unpopular religious group, whose often abrasive proselytizing inspired repressive measures by local officials and state legislatures. The Court moved even more decisively to safeguard and enhance the rights of African Americans, long this country's most discrete and insular minority. A 1938 decision held that Missouri had violated the equal protection clause by providing legal education to whites but not to blacks. During World War II the Court ruled that for the Democratic party in the one-party South to exclude African Americans from its primaries constituted a violation of the Fifteenth Amendment. In *Shelley* v. *Kraemer* (1948) it held judicial enforcement of racially restrictive covenants in real estate deeds violated the Equal Protection Clause. The Court also handed down two decisions in 1950 that made it virtually impossible for southern state universities to operate separate graduate programs for blacks and whites.

Then in *Brown* v. *Board of Education* (1954) the justices electrified the nation with a ruling that public school segregation violated the equal protection clause. *Brown* provoked prolonged and sometimes violent opposition in the South. It also initiated several decades of bitter school desegregation litigation in federal courts throughout the country. Largely because of "white flight," *Brown* and its progeny failed truly to integrate American education. *Brown,* did, however, provide a precedent that both lower courts and the Supreme Court itself could use to declare unconstitutional the segregation of every type of public facility from courthouses to bathing beaches. Determined to enhance the rights of African Americans, judges manipulated constitutional doctrine and even constitutional language to achieve that objective. The Supreme Court attenuated the established rule that only state and local governments can violate the Fourteenth Amendment by holding that where there was limited public involvement in otherwise private discrimination (as where a restaurant that rented space from a municipal parking authority refused to serve African Americans), the equal protection clause applied. Although the Fourteenth Amendment clearly did not bind the federal government, in another case the Court held that the due process clause of the Fifth Amendment required Washington to do everything that the equal protection clause demanded of states and their subdivisions. The Supreme Court even forbade the use of governmental power to enforce the white South's taboos against interracial sexual relationships. In *McLaughlin* v. *Florida* (1964) the Court struck down a law that prohibited cohabitation between unmarried whites and blacks, and in *Loving* v. *Virginia* (1967) it ruled that miscegenation statutes violated the equal protection clause. The high tribunal eventually concluded that all laws intentionally classifying people on the basis of race are inherently suspect and must be invalidated unless necessary to achieve a compelling governmental interest, a test that only a few affirmative action measures managed to pass.

While eager to invalidate legislation that disadvantaged racial minorities, the Supreme Court was slow to react to discrimination against women. Although a majority of the population, females, like blacks, for a long time were denied the right to vote. Even after the Nineteenth Amendment enfranchised women in 1920, they remained in many respects in a subordinate position. Men continued to control most institutions of government and business, and female workers often received lower pay than their male counterparts. Many statutes, reflecting a Victorian view that men and women belonged in separate spheres, discriminated blatantly on the basis of gender. The women's liberation movement of the 1960s challenged this state of affairs, but not until *Reed* v. *Reed* (1971) did the Supreme Court hold that any law violated the equal protection clause because it treated men and women differently. Although Justice William Brennan argued that sex, like race, should be viewed as an inherently suspect basis on which to classify people, and should trigger the same strict judicial scrutiny, he failed to persuade a majority of his colleagues. In *Craig* v. *Boren* (1976) the Court held that while gender classifications would receive more than routinely rigorous review, a substantial relationship to an important (rather than compelling) governmental interest was enough to make them constitutional. Justice William Rehnquist opposed going even that far, at least when the law in question disadvantaged men rather than women. He wrote opinions upholding statutes that required only males to register for the military draft and subjected only men to punishment for statutory rape. While purporting to follow *Craig,* Rehnquist rested such rulings on what he and the members of his majorities viewed as "real differences" between the sexes.

Although rhetorical inconsistency plagued the Supreme Court's gender discrimination decisions, there was a pattern to them. The Court almost always invalidated measures that disadvantaged women (the principal exception being a disability insurance system that denied benefits for pregnancy and childbirth, which it rather implausibly insisted did not discriminate on the basis of gender). On the other hand, if a state or the federal government discriminated against men, the Court might or might not invalidate its action, depending upon how a majority of the justices felt about the policy embodied in the challenged law. Convinced that there were valid reasons for excluding women from combat, the Court upheld a draft for men only. On the other hand, it ordered a nursing school to admit a male applicant because the justices believed its "females only" policy reinforced undesirable sexual stereotypes. A measure that gave women a benefit not available to men would pass constitutional muster if it was genuinely remedial in nature, compensating them for the effects of past societal discrimination. Thus, for example, a tax exemption for widows but not widowers was constitutional because of the greater financial difficulties commonly faced by women who lost their spouses. On the other hand, policies that merely reflected outmoded notions about the proper roles of the two sexes, such as requiring divorcing husbands to pay alimony but never requiring divorcing wives to do so, even if they had higher incomes than their ex-spouses, would not pass constitutional muster.

The cases that revealed the most about the Supreme Court's perspective were ones, such as *Califano* v. *Goldfarb* (1977), brought by survivors of female workers who had received fewer benefits than survivors of men would have received. Although those who actually suffered as a result of this form of unequal treatment were generally widowers, the Court was always careful to characterize it as discrimination against the dead women. The rationale of the *Carolene Products* footnote would not support judicial activism on behalf of men, who were the historically dominant group and still controlled the machinery of government.

On the other hand, that rationale did suggest that the Supreme Court should protect from abuse by majoritarian government such traditional victims of discrimination as illegitimates and aliens. Beginning in *Levy* v. *Louisiana* (1968), the Court invalidated under the equal protection clause laws that burdened illegitimate children by, for example, denying them governmental survivors' benefits that other children received. *Clark* v. *Jeter* (1988) announced that measures that discriminated against illegitimates would receive the same intermediate level of judicial scrutiny as ones that classified on the basis of gender, meaning they would be upheld only if they were substantially related to an important governmental interest. After about 1970 the Supreme Court also subjected many measures disadvantaging aliens to rigorous examination. Because of the power that the Constitution grants Congress over immigration and naturalization, the Court consistently upheld federal legislation that treated aliens differently than citizens. But while allowing states to exclude aliens from policy-making positions and some other government jobs, it rigorously scrutinized and almost always invalidated under the equal protection clause state laws that conditioned receipt of economic benefits on U.S. citizenship. The Court refused to permit states to exclude even *illegal* aliens from their public schools.

PROTECTING INDIVIDUAL AUTONOMY

Besides subjecting to heightened scrutiny under the equal protection clause measures that disadvantaged such minority groups as aliens, illegitimates, and African Americans, the late-twentieth-century Supreme Court (while denying it was doing so) also used that provision to extend special protection to other targets of prejudice, such as the mentally retarded. In addition, the Court employed both the equal protection clause and the due process clause to build a kind of constitutional fence around an area of individual autonomy and personal choice into which the state might not intrude. The Court began erecting this barrier against governmental power in *Griswold* v. *Connecticut* (1965), a case striking down a statute that forbade even married couples to use contraceptives. This law was invalid, *Griswold* held, because it violated the right to privacy. The Constitution does not explicitly mention such a right, but a majority of the justices, although disagreeing among themselves about its source, were sure that a right to privacy existed and was protected against state interference by the due process clause.

Eight years later in *Roe* v. *Wade* (1973), the Supreme Court ruled that state laws that prohibited abortion violated this right to privacy. In one of the most controversial decisions of the twentieth century, the Court held that during the first trimester of pregnancy the decision concerning whether or not to have an abortion must be left entirely to the woman and her doctor. During the second trimester, a state might regulate abortion only to protect the mother's health. Not until after a fetus attained viability could government prohibit termination of the pregnancy.

The Court subsequently ruled that the Constitution did not require either states or the federal government to pay for abortions, even for indigent women, who received free medical care for childbirth. These funding decisions made it clear that what *Roe* had created was not a right to an abortion, but a right of personal choice. For a time the Court struck down any regulation that seemed designed to make it more difficult for a woman to decide to terminate her pregnancy. During the late 1980s and early 1990s, however, as justices appointed by Presidents Reagan and Bush (both avowed opponents of abortion) joined the Court, judicial tolerance of restrictive regulations increased. After *Webster* v. *Reproductive Health Services* (1989), in which a plurality endorsed significant reformulation of *Roe* and Justice Scalia demanded it be overruled, reversal of the controversial ruling appeared imminent. Instead, in *Planned Parenthood of Southeastern Pennsylvania* v. *Casey* (1992) the Court, while reinterpreting its 1973 decision to forbid only regulations that placed an "undue burden" on a woman's right to choose, nevertheless held that "*Roe v. Wade* should be retained and once again reaffirmed."

Although the plurality opinion in *Casey* claimed

the doctrinal basis of *Roe* was substantive due process rather than the right to privacy, the decision made it clear that, however the Supreme Court might characterize what its rulings protected, a majority of the justices remained committed to shielding an area of personal choice and individual autonomy from governmental intrusion. A variety of decisions in the 1970s and 1980s demonstrated that commitment. For example, the Court struck down legislation specifying which members of extended families might live together and forbidding divorced parents to remarry unless they could prove to a judge that they were meeting their child support obligations. It even appeared to recognize the right of a competent but terminally ill patient to choose to die. Although denying constitutional protection to the intimate relations of homosexuals, the Supreme Court repeatedly placed beyond the power of government matters that most people regarded as personal.

Increasingly, the Supreme Court took the position that when government intruded into extremely personal matters, it was impinging upon a liberty interest protected by the due process clause. In other words, it resurrected substantive due process. Now, though, rather than using that long-discredited doctrine to thwart governmental regulation of the economy, the Court made it a barrier shielding individual autonomy from the power of the state.

THE CONTINUING CONFLICT BETWEEN RIGHTS AND POWER

Critics insisted there was no real difference between what the Supreme Court had done prior to 1937 and what it was doing now. "The present generation," wrote Raoul Berger in 1977, "applauds a Court which read its libertarian convictions into the Fourteenth Amendment, forgetting that for generations the Court was harshly criticized because it had transformed laissez faire into constitutional dogma." Like the economic substantive due process decisions of an earlier era, as Richard Epstein was quick to point out, *Roe* v. *Wade* prevented state governments responsive to the wishes of their citizens from implementing what the majority regarded as a reasonable solution to a pressing social problem. Viewed from his perspective, protecting personal autonomy meant using claims of individual rights to trump the will of the majority and thwart the use of governmental power to serve what the people regarded as the public interest.

Although Epstein was a law professor, he and Berger articulated views also expressed by politicians and ordinary citizens. During the 1960s the Warren Court became a target of fierce political attack. Its rulings prohibiting racial segregation, banning religious exercises in the public schools, and requiring reapportionment of state legislatures inspired complaints that the Court was invoking the Constitution to keep the majority from working its will through the democratic institutions of government. While the Warren Court's decisions in race cases probably enjoyed the support of most Americans outside the South, and its reapportionment rulings outraged self-interested politicians more than the people, there was an element of truth in allegations that it was antimajoritarian. Those who criticized the Court on that basis could point to *Lucus* v. *Forty-Fourth General Assembly* (1964), in which it ruled that a state could not apportion even one house of a two-house legislature on a basis other than population, even if a majority of its voters elected to do so.

In enhancing the rights of those accused of crime, the Warren Court certainly was not doing what a majority of Americans desired. Nixon's victory in 1968, along with the strong showing of third-party candidate George Wallace, who also stressed "law and order" in his campaign, represented at least in part, a repudiation of the judicial decisions Nixon had condemned. The results of the 1968 election indicated Americans wanted public power used to curb crime and restore order in the streets. By arming criminal defendants with a host of rights that police and prosecutors must respect or forfeit the opportunity to punish them, the Warren Court appeared to be rendering government impotent. Judges seemed to be thwarting the use of governmental power to combat a crime wave that terrified many people. That perception inspired public hostility toward the Court.

"The moral imperialism of the Supreme Court did not end with Chief Justice Warren's resignation," observed Robert Bork, a conservative law professor and jurist, whom President Reagan tried unsuccessfully to appoint to the high tribunal. "The Courts headed by Chief Justice Warren Burger and Chief Justice William Rehnquist, while perhaps less relentlessly adventurous than the Warren Court, displayed a strong affinity for legislating policy in the name of the Constitution." Bork found particularly offensive judicial enhancement of privacy rights.

He strongly condemned *Roe* v. *Wade,* and so did demonstrators in the streets. Fired by moral fervor against abortion, conservative protesters demanded the power of government be used to halt a practice they considered murder. Even if they had the votes to outlaw abortion, however, they could not do so because the judiciary would not let them. Champions of the "right to life" felt victimized by what Bork condemned as "the imposition of moral relativism upon legislatures by judges," something he thought was "more accurately described as the belief that the only valid and trustworthy morality is the judges'."

Voicing a common conservative complaint, Bork protested that Americans were "increasingly governed not by law or elected representatives but by an unelected, unrepresentative, unaccountable committee of lawyers applying no will but their own." From the other end of the political spectrum, Ronald Dworkin praised the rights-centered jurisprudence developed by the Supreme Court during the second half of the twentieth century. Yet, ironically the complaints of Bork and his fellow conservatives echoed those of liberals two generations earlier. Like critics of judicial interference with New Deal economic regulation, they objected to judges limiting what government could do. In the 1930s the Supreme Court had accomplished such limitation by reading the power-granting clauses of the Constitution narrowly. Now the Court was doing the same thing by interpreting its rights-protecting provisions broadly. The end result was the same: judicial restriction of majority rule.

Even Bork conceded this was something that was an inescapable feature of America's Madisonian constitutional system. The first principle of such a system was self-government, which meant that in wide areas of life majorities were entitled to rule, simply because they were majorities. But equally fundamental to the American constitutional system was the conviction that there were "some things majorities must not do to minorities" and some spheres in which "the individual must be free of majority rule." The clash between these two conflicting principles was the central theme of twentieth-century constitutional history.

Nor is the friction between power and rights likely to disappear. As quick to excoriate government for failing to serve their every need as to condemn it for interfering in their lives, Americans like to have things both ways. The Constitution, as Chief Justice Hughes once observed, is what the Supreme Court says it is. But the Court constantly reinterprets the written document, and in giving new meaning to its words, judges respond to (even if they do not always follow) the demands and desires of the populace. For that reason, the Constitution will always reflect the ambivalent attitudes of the people it serves. Neither wholly a source of power nor wholly a guardian of rights, it will remain in constant tension with itself.

SEE ALSO The Presidency; Congress; The Courts; Federalism and the States (all in this volume).

BIBLIOGRAPHY

There are two excellent surveys of twentieth-century American constitutional history: Alfred H. Kelly, Winfred A. Harbison, and Herman Belz, *The American Constitution: Its Origins and Development,* vol. 2, 7th ed. (1991); and Melvin I. Urofsky, *A March of Liberty: A Constitutional History of the United States,* vol. 2 (1988). Also helpful is Leonard W. Levy, Kenneth L. Karst, and Dennis J. Mahoney, eds., *American Constitutional History,* 2d ed. (1989), which contains essays focusing on constitutional developments during various time periods in the twentieth century and on the work of the Supreme Court during the administrations of each twentieth-century chief justice. Paul L. Murphy, *The Constitution in Crisis Times, 1918–1969* (1972), is a superb book, which unfortunately was written before much of the manuscript source material from the latter part of the period with which it deals became available. Less thoroughly researched is Loren Beth, *The Development of the American Constitution, 1877–1917* (1971), a book that nevertheless offers insightful analysis of developments during the era it discusses. Kermit L. Hall, ed., *United States Constitutional and Legal History,* 20 vols. (1987), is a huge collection, which contains the most important articles on the subject published down to the time of its release.

For those seeking a detailed account of the work of the Supreme Court, William F. Swindler's *The Court and Constitution in the Twentieth Century,* 3 vols., has much to offer: *The Old Legality, 1889–1932* (1969), *The New Legality, 1938–1968* (1970), and *The Modern Interpretation* (1974). David P. Currie,

The Constitution in the Supreme Court: The Second Century, 1888–1986 (1990), although excessively legalistic in its approach, also provides a good overview of developments during the twentieth century. John E. Semonche, *Charting the Future: The Supreme Court Responds to a Changing Society, 1890–1920* (1978), is a solid, if somewhat pedestrian, history of the Court during the period with which it deals. Alexander M. Bickel and Benno C. Schmidt, Jr., *The Judiciary and Responsible Government, 1910–21,* Oliver Wendell Holmes Devise History of the Supreme Court of the United States, vol. 9 (1984), is quite detailed, but unfortunately somewhat fragmented, due to the fact that Schmidt had to finish a book Bickel was writing when he died. For a brief but insightful overview of the Court throughout its entire history, see William M. Wiecek, *Liberty Under Law: The Supreme Court in American Life* (1988). Although designed mainly for use by lawyers and law students, Lawrence H. Tribe, *American Constitutional Law,* 2d ed. (1988), is a brilliant analysis of Supreme Court decisions and constitutional doctrine which can be quite helpful to persons in other disciplines as well. John Nowak and Ronald Rotunda, *Constitutional Law,* 4th ed. (1991), another book intended for the same audience, offers fewer novel insights but provides good chronological accounts of doctrinal development in particular areas of constitutional law. Stanley I. Kutler, ed., *The Supreme Court and the Constitution: Readings in American Constitutional History,* 2d ed. (1984), is a historically organized casebook, which contains most of the major twentieth-century decisions.

Many of these involve the Fourteenth Amendment, so understanding the origins and purposes of that provision is crucial to comprehending twentieth-century constitutional controversies. Among the most helpful of the works on that subject are Harold M. Hyman and William W. Wiecek, *Equal Justice under Law: Constitutional Development, 1835–1875* (1982); Michael Kent Curtis, *No State Shall Abridge: The Fourteenth Amendment and the Bill of Rights* (1986); and William W. Nelson, *The Fourteenth Amendment: From Political Principle to Judicial Doctrine* (1988). By far the best explanation of how the Supreme Court came to use the Fourteenth Amendment to apply the Bill of Rights to the states is Richard C. Cortner, *The Supreme Court and the Second Bill of Rights: The Fourteenth Amendment and the Nationalization of the Bill of Rights* (1981). Melvin I. Urofsky, "Myth and Reality: The Supreme Court and Protective Legislation in the Progressive Era," *Yearbook of the Supreme Court Historical Society, 1983* (1983): 53–72, is quite informative concerning the Court's use of the Fourteenth Amendment's due process clause to censor economic legislation. James W. Ely, Jr., *The Guardian of Every Other Right: A Constitutional History of Property Rights* (1992), is brief but perceptive discussion of that and other property rights issues throughout American history.

There is a vast body of literature that deals with constitutional rights in general, as well as with the role of the Supreme Court in enforcing them. Many of the most important articles on the subject are collected in Paul L. Murphy, ed., *The Bill of Rights in American Legal History,* 20 vols. (1990). Akil Reed Amar, "The Bill of Rights as a Constitution," *Yale Law Journal* 100 (March 1991): 1131–1210, is excellent on the original purpose of the Bill of Rights. Paul L. Murphy, *World War I and the Origins of Civil Liberties in the United States* (1979), elucidates the context within which the Supreme Court began the development of a body of constitutional law protecting freedom of expression; while Kermit L. Hall, "Justice Brennan and Cultural History: *New York Times* v. *Sullivan* and Its Times," *California Western Law Review* 270 (1990–1991): 339–359, offers an unusual perspective on a landmark freedom of the press decision. Robert M. Cover, "The Origins of Judicial Activism in the Protection of Minorities," *Yale Law Journal* 91 (June 1982): 1287–1316, explains the significance of the *Carolene Products* footnote. David J. Bodenhamer, *Fair Trial: Rights of the Accused in American History* (1992), is a good short survey of the evolution of the constitutional criminal procedure; while Donald G. Nieman, *Promises to Keep: African-Americans and the Constitutional Order, 1776 to the Present* (1991), offers a concise but thorough overview of the development of racial equal protection law.

The subject of governmental power has received far less attention in recent decades than has the topic of constitutional rights, and most of the significant writing on the subject has appeared in law reviews. An exception is Richard C. Cortner, *The Jones and Laughlin Case* (1970), which delivers more than its title promises, providing a good overview of the development of commerce clause doctrine down to 1937. Richard Epstein, "The Proper Scope of the Commerce Power," *Virginia Law Review* 73 (1987): 1387–1455, offers a critical assessment of developments in the same area. For insights into the thinking about the sources of governmental power that underlay the New Deal and the significance of the rejection of those ideas by the Supreme Court, see Michal R. Belknap, "The New Deal and the Emergency Powers

Doctrine," *Texas Law Review* 62 (August 1983): 67–109. For informative discussions of the development of presidential power, see Arthur M. Schlesinger, Jr., *The Imperial Presidency* (1973); and the classic by Edward S. Corwin, *The President: Office and Powers, 1787–1957,* 4th ed. (1957).

The tendency of the contemporary Supreme Court to limit the governmental power that majorities can wield by creating and enforcing new constitutional rights is the target of Robert H. Bork's sharply critical *The Tempting of America: The Political Seduction of the Law* (1990). In the same vein are Richard A. Epstein, "Substantive Due Process by Any Other Name: The Abortion Cases," *Supreme Court Review* 1973 (1974): 159–185; and Raoul Berger, *Government by Judiciary: The Transformation of the Fourteenth Amendment* (1977), a book that combines law office history with railing against judicial activism. For a contrasting reaction to the development in recent years of a rights-focused jurisprudence, see Ronald Dworkin, *Taking Rights Seriously* (1977).

FEDERALISM AND THE STATES

Harry N. Scheiber

The federal structure of the American governmental system has been transformed over the course of the twentieth century, as have virtually all America's basic institutions. Yet there are remarkable evidences today of resilience and continuity in American federalism—not only in the survival of the state governments as centers of significant power, but also in the persistent responsiveness of the American public to the notion that there is special value in the decentralization of decision-making authority in government. Hence the historical record of federalism in the twentieth century is one mainly of innovation and change, yet with important elements of continuity and traditionalism.

THE "FEDERAL CREED" AND THE OLD FEDERALISM

The annals of the Republic's history before 1900 were replete with celebrations of the virtues of federalism—the unique design of authority that distributed power formally between a national government and its constituent states, the latter organized as constitutional polities with certain elements of "sovereignty." Thus the Framers celebrated federalism as a structure that would allow republican governance to be effective over a vast area and for a large population—"a novelty and a compound," as James Madison averred, which would also serve as a bulwark of individual liberty and assure a salutary diffusion of political power in many centers. The brilliant French observer of American democracy in the 1830s, Alexis de Tocqueville, contended that federalism gave vitality to the great tradition of localism, and was crucial to the development of private associations that were a key institutional expression of the exuberant individualism of the young Republic's people. Moreover, he wrote, "the federal form . . . allows the Union to enjoy the power of a great republic and the security of a small one."

It was common in American political rhetoric of the nineteenth century, even after the Civil War, to speak of federal design as "the ark of the covenant," a phrase that Chief Justice William Howard Taft would invoke many years later in a Supreme Court decision upholding some traditional states' prerogatives against intrusions by the central government. By using the religious imagery of the covenant, the champions of federalism and decentralized power gave vivid expression to what may be termed a "federal creed" that informed much of political discourse in the nineteenth century.

This creed—a key element of what many scholars refer to as the American "civic religion," the leading feature of which was reverence for the Constitution—expressed an abiding skepticism of centralized power, with its potential for imposing a stifling uniformity or even outright despotism; and it romanticized federalism as a political design that assured the fullest possible flourishing of citizen participation in public decision making, government "close to the people," and fostering of community. The political motto of the 1960s, "Resist Authority," had its precursor in the rhapsody to federalism penned by Walt Whitman in *Leaves of Grass:*

> To the States or any of them or any city of the States,
> Resist much, obey little.
> Once unquestioning obedient, once fully enslaved,
> no nation state, city of this earth, ever afterward
> resumes its liberty.

Perhaps the most extravagant praise on record of American federalism was voiced by a British commentator, Lord Acton, who proclaimed in his *Lectures on Modern History* that it was owing to the principle of federalism that the United States had "produced a community more powerful, more prosperous, more intelligent, and more free than any other which the world has ever seen!" If Acton's claim was extreme, still he captured the essence of what probably most Americans who enjoyed voting rights before 1900 instinctively believed (or at least habitually accepted) was a core truth about the virtues of decentralized authority under federalism.

Even after the states' rights challenge to nationalism from the slave states had ended in a bloody civil war, faith in the virtues of localism, "grass roots" political power, and autonomy for the states in vital areas of governance remained a dominant theme in American politics and American law. Virtually every public policy decision from the Founding era to the century's close was debated, accordingly, at two levels: first, with respect to what, if anything, should be done by government; and second, with respect to what level of government—state or federal—was the appropriate one, in constitutional as well as practical terms, to undertake responsibility. The U.S. Supreme Court reinforced this aspect of political behavior in a variety of post–Civil War decisions that reaffirmed the dignity and authority of the states. The Court's view was encapsulated in the famous phrase from *Texas* v. *White* (1869), to the effect that indissolubility of the Union did not imply in any way "the loss of distinct and individual existence, or the right of self-government, of the States. . . . The Constitution, in all its provisions, looks to an indestructible Union, composed of indestructible States."

Woodrow Wilson thus was on solid ground when he contended in his book *Constitutional Government in the United States* (1908) that "the question of the relation of the states to the federal government is the cardinal question of our constitutional system." This was so, Wilson argued, not only because the traditional federal creed placed state versus federal power in so central a position in constitutional theory. Each generation was required to debate the federalism question anew, he wrote: as "the life of the nation" changed, new issues would constantly arise; and as the problems calling for government action assumed unprecedented configurations and dimensions, the specific character of policy choices would require a reconsideration of what was the appropriate and legitimate distribution of powers between the central government and the constituent states.

The prevailing bias, when such reconsideration was forced upon Americans in the political process, was almost always toward maintenance of state "sovereignty" in some form. Almost entirely absent, in the nineteenth century, was any hint that the states and their prerogatives should be subordinated wholesale to the national will and supremacy of the central government; and never did the abolition or consolidation of states or the redrawing of state boundary lines enter seriously into political discussion. The virtues of federalism were taken as more or less axiomatic: The burden of proof, as it were, fell upon reformers who argued against state sovereignty and for a nationalization of powers, involving the imposition of national standards on activities in areas of policy where no governmental action had formerly been evident, or in areas where the states had been in control. This was true whether the reformers in question were, say, the politicians who championed Radical Reconstruction after the Civil War and pressed for nationalization of civil rights, or, later, the business leaders, agrarians, and others who supported national railroad regulation and federal antitrust measures in the 1880s and 1890s.

It is not surprising, therefore, that turn-of-the century federalism—as manifested both in constitutional doctrine and in working government arrangements—offered a picture of highly decentralized authority in many of the most important areas of policy. Its most extreme effects, which revealed the darkest side of federalism in action, were in the ability of the southern states to maintain elaborate systems of repressive segregation and discrimination against their African American citizens. By the 1880s, as the result of Supreme Court decisions that severely limited the reach of Reconstruction-era legislation, the definition of civil rights in race relations had become part of the virtually exclusive province of the state governments. Similarly, on the Pacific Coast, coalitions of farmers, urban workers, and other elements of the electorate who despised Mexican and Chinese minorities enacted harshly discriminatory labor and land-ownership legislation; only later did the federal courts intervene to give some measure of equal protection. The states also enjoyed virtually unchallenged authority in regard to family relations, labor law, the law of commercial transactions, property, and criminal justice. The principles and implementation of taxation, and control of local government, also remained within exclusive state control. Even in areas of policy where federal authority had begun to intrude on realms formerly almost exclusively in the hands of the states, the states still played a large role in setting their own policy agendas. This robust constitutional autonomy remaining with the states was not uniformly exercised as an instrument for maintenance of the status quo, or for conservative retrenchment; on the contrary, during 1900–1915 it provided a broad stage and bright political lights for Progressive governors and their reform administrations. It was precisely because so much of Americans' basic institutions and day-to-day lives were under the immediate and controlling influence of the states that state-level Progressivism was of such vital significance.

CENTRALIZING TRENDS AND THE PROGRESSIVE-ERA CHALLENGE

Although the American political system remained highly decentralized—both as to formal constitutional authority and as to the locus of real power in the political system—still, there was significant "drift" toward centralization from the Civil War to the Progressive years. One source of such centralization as did occur consisted of congressional initiatives, embodied in new legislation that invaded areas of policy formerly left largely or entirely to the states. The most important elements of legislative centralization included the establishment of the national banking system and introduction of a uniform national currency during the Civil War years; the forging of a subsidy and promotion policy for transcontinental railroads in 1862; and enactment of the Interstate Commerce Act of 1887, which established the first federal administrative agency for regulation of a national business interest, and of the Sherman Antitrust Act in 1890, the first national law for corporate regulation outside the transport sector. In the 1890s, Congress also instituted federal control over lotteries and liquor traffic; enacted national irrigation legislation; and initiated federal cash-grant programs for agriculture, augmenting the Morrill Act land grants (1862) for the founding of agricultural and mechanical colleges in all the states. Besides, there was the legislation for comprehensive federal oversight of governance in the former Confederate states during the Reconstruction era—an episode that formally ended in 1877 and was followed by the notorious resurgence of conservative Democratic party rule in the South.

The second major dimension of centralization had its source in initiatives by the federal judiciary. Building upon the Thirteenth, Fourteenth, and Fifteenth Amendments and also upon expanded jurisdiction given to them by Congress, the federal courts exercised censorial authority over state legislation with respect to state law in fields such as taxation, eminent domain, and—ultimately with the farthest-reaching impact—the regulation of business practices, labor relations, and civil rights. Dominated by an ideology of property-minded conservatism, the Supreme Court also struck down some major federal legislation, most notably an income tax voted by Congress in 1893; subsequently, it also invalidated federal legislation to regulate labor relations on interstate railroads. In one of its most controversial decisions of the era, the Court in 1894 upheld granting of federal injunctions requested by the Cleveland administration to break up a national railroad strike and cripple the railway brotherhoods. Withal, the major thrust of the Court's decisions in this era was to expand federal judicial power, and as such to extend the reach of centralized authority over the states.

The politics of the Progressive Era gave major impetus to the shift within the federal system toward more concentrated authority in Washington, displacing areas of policy formerly left to the states. Theodore Roosevelt and Woodrow Wilson, despite their differences in ideology, were both important for the challenges that they posed to the conventional wisdom—the old federal creed—concerning the alleged absolute evils of centralization and the virtues of localism.

Although Progressivism was in its origins, at least, a state-centered movement, the positions taken by Roosevelt as president on issues such as food and drug regulation, antitrust, labor relations, and forest conservation and management, served with unprecedented intensity to bring issues of federalism and allocation of authority to the fore in national politics. Roosevelt shrewdly claimed legitimacy for his position by referring to the "original intent" of the Framers and to the classical Hamiltonian strain in American political history—a strain of thought and practice clearly opposed to the limited-government and states' rights orientation of the old federalism creed. Thus in an address at the Pennsylvania state capitol in 1906, Roosevelt declared that the view on which the nation had been organized by the Framers and verified by the administration of George Washington and the Supreme Court under John Marshall was the concept that the state and national governments together "composed only one uniform and comprehensive system of government and laws; that is, whenever the States cannot act, because the need to be met is not one of merely a single locality, then the National Government, representing all the people, should have complete power to act."

The key to Roosevelt's appeal was his contention that national authority was legitimated when the states were unable to act effectively in addressing a major policy question that required government action. For many years, the Populists and reform elements in both major parties had contended that the reach of the states' authority was inadequate to deal effectively with the problems of business regulation caused by the hectic industrial expansion and rise of great financial empires in the late nineteenth century. Roosevelt and others took up this theme as an argument for extended national authority. Thus even relatively conservative voices conceded, as did Elihu Root in a widely noticed speech in 1906, that "our whole life has swung away from the old state centers and is crystallizing about national centers," requiring a reappraisal of the orthodoxies in the old federal creed. "The people move in great throngs," Root declared, and "the old lines between the states and the old barriers which kept the states as separate communities are completely lost from sight." As the historian William Graebner has shown, however, Root's essential conservatism was evident in what he proposed as the solution to the problem of nationalized business institutions and labor organization: he preferred to see the states cooperate by creating new uniform codes of law for business and labor regulation, rather than to have outright centralization of power and an imposed uniformity by congressional action.

Other reformers, however, were far less solicitous of traditional state prerogatives. Thus in his book *The Promise of American Life,* published in 1909, Herbert Croly assaulted outright the traditional federal creed, condemning it as an "erroneous and misleading tradition [that] must yield before the march of a constructive national democracy." The view of "the majority of American politicians and newspapers," that all centralization was evil and contrary to American constitutional ideals, Croly declared, was misguided and must be abandoned. Theodore Roosevelt took up this theme with increasing conviction, both as president and then in his role first as a critic of his successor, William Howard Taft, and then in his Bull Moose presidential campaign of 1912. Roosevelt stressed that the states were entirely unable to provide "adequate supervision and control over the business use of the swollen fortunes of today. . . . Only the Nation can do this work. To relegate it to the States is a farce, and is simply another way of saying that it shall not be done at all."

That the nation's political leadership, and no doubt the public at large, was increasingly receptive to such arguments became evident when Congress strengthened the national railroad regulatory laws, introduced federal food and drug industry regulation, and sent to the states a federal income tax amendment that would provide the foundation for subsequent expansion of federal power in future years. By the time of the 1912 election campaign, the question of the old federal creed and its continuing legitimacy had become a leading public issue.

As the Democratic presidential candidate, Woodrow Wilson necessarily remained sensitive to the party's traditional base in the "solid South," intransigently committed to states' rights; and Roosevelt attacked him for being held in thrall to sectional prejudices against the kind of activism by the national government that was indispensable in a modern industrial order. Finally Wilson was forced, in a campaign speech in New Haven, to provide a strong rejoinder: "The Democratic party," he contended, "does not stand for the limitation of powers of government, either in the field of the State or in the field of the Federal Government." It was only Roosevelt's proposal to place increased federal authority in the hands of administrative agencies to which he objected, Wilson said; he was not opposed on principle to "the utmost exercise of the powers of the government," whether national, state, or local, when conditions warranted it.

Throughout the remainder of the 1912 campaign, and then in Wilson's first presidential administration, when his domestic reform program was debated and largely enacted, he found himself a prominent and active agent in the process of "redefinition" of federalism on which he had written so tellingly only a few years earlier. The convergence of Wilson's ideas on federalism—or his rhetoric, at least—with Roosevelt's in 1912 marked a significant watershed in the nation's politics. It introduced to prominence in national political and legislative discourse the idea that the distribution of responsibilities between the national government and the states ought to be based upon a pragmatic, realist standard as to congruence and appropriateness—rather than being based upon immutable doctrines embodied in formal constitutional constructs, especially as they were handed down by a Supreme Court majority that often had set itself against most of the major popular reforms of that era. A new counterweight to the old federal creed was now firmly established in political rhetoric and constitutional thought: the proposition that centralized government and national initiatives were imperative if the problems of a nationalized, industrialized, and urbanized society were to be addressed effectively.

The federal system, although not yet transformed as it would be in later decades, was significantly and permanently altered during the national Progressive Era. Thus Congress in 1913 expanded the scope of federal administrative law, previously embodied only in railroad regulation, to establish the Federal Reserve System for the control of banking and currency. (A novel and precedent-setting feature of the Federal Reserve Act was the creation of regional administrative districts for purposes of a nationally centered regulatory regime; and the debates in Congress indicated that the writers of this legislation fully recognized that they were engaged in fashioning a new model of federal-state relationships.) During the Roosevelt, Taft, and Wilson administrations, Congress also introduced federal authority with respect to maritime and railroad labor relations, interstate commerce in goods illegal under state laws, provision of credit to the farm sector, competitive trade practices, and, as noted earlier, oversight of food and drug processing. Ironically, however, the Progressive centralizing legacy was also manifest in a policy that ultimately proved to be unpopular and largely unenforceable: the national prohibition of alcoholic liquors, under terms of a constitutional amendment that swept away all state authority in a traditional field of state regulation.

By 1917, when America's entry into the European war ended the national Progressive period, important new responsibilities had thus been undertaken by the national government. The war itself, however, though disruptive to the nascent progressive coalitions and ultimately to the advancement of progressive legislative programs, would ultimately have a larger significance for federalism. The vastly expanded federal control of the economy during the war period—involving nationalization of the railroads, allocation of production priorities, and intervention in labor relations and pricing—would serve in the 1930s as the model for New Deal reformers of how government could respond to implement comprehensive and uniform national policies in the extreme conditions of a national emergency.

The enhancement of the national government's role that was advanced by pre–1917 Progressive legislation did not represent a wholesale centralization of policy responsibilities. On the contrary, despite the incursions on their autonomy in some fields, the state governments continued to have wide control over their policy agendas. Thus in criminal justice, family and inheritance law, property law, public education, control of local governance, and a wide range of other fields, the states still were dominant. The result was not only continuing state activity of importance to the society and its institutions, but also a very great diversity of policy, practice, and—as some scholars would argue—even local or regional "legal cultures." Each state had its own mix of policies. Some, especially those in the Northeast and Midwest, took the lead in expanding public education and instituting public health and industrial safety programs, and new consumer-oriented regulations of business interests. Other states, most notoriously those in the Deep South, had a very different policy profile, resisting higher taxes and expanded public services. Undisturbed state-level control of discriminatory and segregationist policies—and even the punishment, or, typically, nonpunishment, of racially motivated lynchings of black citizens—continued to represent the extreme in "states' rights," and for many nationalist reformers represented the ultimate stigma of the old federalism.

Most of the states did expand their educational systems, undertook road-building programs as the automobile became more popular, and introduced new regulations affecting corporations, labor, railroad operations, and public health. In consequence, state and local expenditures and the size of state bureaucracies expanded. After 1910, this expansion accelerated: state government spending was $188 million in 1902, rose to $388 million in 1913, and reached $1.4 billion in 1922. Local spending meanwhile rose from under $1 billion to $4.6 billion. The combined expenditures of state and local governments were consistently about twice the level of federal spending throughout the entire period from 1870 to World War I. Especially significant, however, was the fact that the entire sum of governmental expenditures even in 1917 was less than 6 percent of gross national income. In sum, while there were some important changes in the distribution of responsibilities between the federal government and the states, and while bureaucracies and expertise were both gaining increasing prominence in both the state and federal governing establishments, the age of big government in America was still in the future.

The years from the end of World War I to the New Deal's commencement in 1933 marked a period of retrenchment and consolidation, rather than of dramatic change, in the federal versus state balance. Immediately after the war, upon returning the railroads (which had been nationalized during the war emergency) to private enterprise, Congress further extended national authority over basic transport policy and structure. New congressional measures during this period also brought hydroelectric-power siting on the public lands under administrative control of the Federal Power Commission (1920), and instituted federal regulation of radio broadcasting. A small but controlling federal presence was also established in the new field of aeronautics.

The Sheppard-Towner Act, which Congress enacted in 1921, inaugurated federal cash grants-in-aid to the states for support of infant and maternity care. Because this program required matching appropriations by the state governments, Sheppard-Towner was denounced by conservatives and states' rights champions as an unwarranted encroachment on state and local authority. A challenge to the program's constitutionality, culminating in *Massachusetts* v. *Mellon* (1923), was significant on two counts: first, it drew from the Supreme Court the opinion that an individual taxpayer had no standing to sue in such a case, and, second, it drew a dictum from the Court to the effect that grants of aid did not constitute compulsion, hence could not be viewed as violative of federalism principles. With programs of aid to highway construction, education, and agricultural research dominating expenditures, Congress continued throughout the 1920s to expand grants in aid. Total appropriations rose from $11 million just before the war to $93 million in 1925.

Otherwise, the 1920s decade was notable mainly for the mixed record of the Supreme Court in constitutional adjudication concerning federalism questions. Although in the matter of Sheppard-Towner and in a few other areas of policy, the Court upheld the authority of Congress to trench on "sovereign" prerogatives of the states, on other issues the Court took a different stance. The most notable decisions invalidating nationalization measures were decisions concerning the power of Congress to legislate against commerce in products of child labor. In *Hammer* v. *Dagenhart* (1918), the Court had declared that control of child labor was "a purely local matter in which federal authority does not extend," and contended that to permit congressional regulation in this area would permit "our system of government [to] be practically destroyed"! Then, in 1922, in *Bailey* v. *Drexel Furniture Co.,* the Court again overturned a federal statute—this one imposing a tax upon products of child labor—also on grounds that it unconstitutionally invaded state powers protected by the Tenth Amendment. Building on early jurisprudence regarding the state police power and its limitations, the Court also elaborated the concept of "business affected with a public interest" to distinguish types of business activity it would permit the states to regulate (because of their "public" aspects) and types of business deemed strictly private, hence not regulable. The Court did not uniformly disapprove regulatory legislation, but it did strike down state laws across a broad enough range of policy areas that charges of "government by judiciary"—in this instance, at the expense of state autonomy—were frequently voiced in political and legal debate.

THE NEW DEAL REVOLUTION IN FEDERALISM AND PUBLIC POLICY

The crisis of the Great Depression opened the way to major changes both in constitutional law and the structure of real power in the federal system. As a candidate for president in the 1932 campaign, Franklin D. Roosevelt occasionally attacked President Herbert Hoover for excessive expansion of the federal bureaucracy; and on one occasion he explicitly denounced "a dangerous tendency, on the part of the national government, to encroach . . . more and more upon state supremacy." It was not long after taking office, however, that President Roosevelt put aside such rhetoric, offering instead the theme that the national emergency required an entirely new approach, founded upon a pragmatic view of constitutional flexibility in the face of dire necessities. Indeed, in his first inaugural message, Roosevelt declared that the uniquely "simple and practical" character of the federal Constitution meant "that it is possible always to meet extraordinary needs by changes in emphasis and arrangement without loss of essential form." As the specific nature of programs and policies that Roosevelt proposed to meet the emergency were spelled out in the following weeks, it became clear that far more than "matters of emphasis and arrangement" were at stake. What the New Deal would mean, it now became evident, was a thorough transformation of constitutional governance—and in particular a basic redistribution of power between the national government and the states, within the inherited framework of American federalism.

Nearly every substantive policy introduced under the New Deal banner, not only in the Hundred Days of 1933 but also throughout the first two Roosevelt administrations, contributed to the multifaceted governmental and constitutional transformation of that era. Agriculture became a managed sector of the economy, as did manufacturing for a short time through the application of the National Industrial Recovery Act (NIRA). First the NIRA and later the Wagner Act established a dominant federal presence in regulation of labor relations, again expanding significantly the overall reach of federal administrative discretion. In the late 1930s national control of economic relationships was further augmented with wage and hours legislation. The Tennessee Valley Authority, instituted in 1933, was the first regional development program sponsored by the national government; and it was only a small part of an increasingly comprehensive, active program of federal conservation, reclamation, and management of natural resources. In the fields of banking and finance, securities marketing, transportation, and communications, too, Congress authorized a vast expansion of the federal role, exercised through administrative agencies charged with the duty of defining "the public interest." From the first days of the New Deal, the funding of extensive new public works programs provided federally financed employment for those out of work; within a few years, the Works Progress Administration grants for employment relief were being complemented by smaller-scale federal spending in the fields of public housing, experimental agricultural communities, farm-tenant and migrant programs, and expanded medical and relief aid for the indigent. Beginning in 1935 with Congress's enactment of the Social Security and unemployment compensation systems, the modern welfare system—a system mandated from the center, although the states retained some discretion on unemployment and disability benefits, and played a part in administration—was set in place.

It was no exaggeration, then, in light of the scope of the innovations in governance and policy toward which New Deal initiatives pointed from the beginning, for Roosevelt to argue that the entire "modern movement for social and economic progress through legislation" was at stake when the Supreme Court intervened in 1935 and 1936 to invalidate NIRA and the agricultural program, two key measures of the Hundred Days.

The full array of New Deal initiatives was reflected in a massive rise in the national government's expenditures: federal spending increased from $2.6 billion in 1929 to nearly $9 billion by 1939. The 1939 expenditure was greater than the combined 1939 state and local expenditures ($8.5 billion), whereas a decade earlier federal spending had been only one-third that of state and local spending.

A new pattern of intergovernmental administrative and fiscal relationships emerged during the New Deal era with respect to the use of grants-in-aid to the states. This pattern was aptly termed "the New Federalism" by some analysts but later was more commonly known as "Cooperative Federalism," to denote the involvement of both levels of government—and, at times in novel ways, the sub-state local governments as well—in the provision of services to the public. With welfare and relief programs accounting for some 80 percent of the expenditures, grants-in-aid rose from $193 million in fiscal year 1933 to some $2.3 billion two years later. The peak figure for the decade, $2.9 billion, was reached in 1939. Whether in education, health, agriculture, welfare and relief, transportation, or other areas of assistance, the grant-in-aid programs included more and more special features that gave Cooperative Federalism its unique character. The most dramatic essential feature was the proliferation of conditions attached to the new grants by Congress (e.g., requiring the states to submit plans deemed acceptable by federal authorities in advance of release of funds). An entirely new aspect of federal aid to the states was the creation of "demonstration program" grants, which was designed to test experimental ideas but was also subject to political manipulation and favoritism. Another was "project grants," made, for example, in the fields of airport construction or public housing, not on the basis of population-driven formulas but rather according to executive discretion. As a consequence of the growth in grant programs and these new features of their administration, some analysts argued that there was a strong skewing effect with respect to state-level policy decisions. State legislators and governors, it was argued, naturally tended to favor the programs that might qualify for federal aid, at the expense of other priorities.

In some federal programs, new types of governmental subunits were created for administrative purposes. A well-known example was in administration of the federal grazing programs on public lands in the West, as established by the Taylor Grazing Lands Act: the district officers enjoyed wide discretion in allocating grazing permits, but, as political scientist Grant McConnell persuasively argued in his book *Private Power and American Democracy,* the grazing authorities tended to be dominated by the larger cattle-ranching interests—and even were required to consult systematically with the private cattlemen's associations that represented the largest-scale operators. By dint of their new role in administration of this program fashioned in Washington and entirely bypassing the established structures of state and local government, a local cattle-ranching elite was thus empowered to exploit national resources in a manner that excluded consideration of interests other than their own. Under the rubric of localism and district self-governance—a rubric consciously fashioned to capture the alleged democratic and grass-roots virtues of the old federalism creed for a new program—the federal grazing program was effectively shaped to sustain the status quo in the cattle regions of the West. Like federalism in its earlier, more conventional permutations, McConnell argued, the new structural arrangements created by many New Deal programs became instruments of influence for local elites.

Definition and pursuit of the larger "public interest" became problematic in such structures. Similarly, how the public interest should be articulated and pursued became a core issue in the operations of the new "alphabet soup" of new federal regulatory agencies charged with oversight of key segments of the economic system.

Ineluctably, nearly all the New Deal initiatives were challenged on constitutional grounds and became the subjects of important Supreme Court decisions. While the cases regarding federal law were in progress, however, the Court signaled the beginnings of a constitutional transformation respecting the authority of the state governments with two decisions in 1934 regarding the state police powers. In the first, *Nebbia* v. *New York,* the justices announced a basic reversal of doctrine with respect to the distinction between businesses affected with a public interest and strictly private businesses; thus fell one of the longest-standing doctrinal instruments that the Court had used to strike down various state regulatory measures in the past. The second blow to conservative due-process doctrine was struck in *Home Building and Loan Association* v. *Blaisdall* (1934), when the Court upheld as constitutional a state moratorium on payments of interest on mortgages. Chief Justice Charles Evans Hughes's opinion for the majority, stating that "while emergency does not create power, [it] may furnish the occasion for the exercise of power," was a new doctrinal charter for extraordinary state interventions in crises—and also a source of great alarm to property-minded conservatives. Subsequently, the Court moved for a time to the right, striking down a state minimum-wage statute and other state regulatory measures. In 1937, however, another shift occurred in the Court's posture, this one more enduring: the majority in *West Coast Hotel* v. *Parrish* upheld minimum wage regulation in the state of Washington and explicitly overruled earlier doctrine regarding due process and economic regulation.

When New Deal congressional statutes were challenged, the Supreme Court at first took a conservative stance and invalidated key measures. The Court variously invoked the principles of federalism, especially as embodied in a sweeping interpretation (and rephrasing) of the Tenth Amendment as limiting the national government to "expressly enumerated powers"; in application of a broad and conservative reading of due process requirements against regulatory legislation; and in a restrictive reading of the commerce clause to invalidate national laws that encroached on traditional state prerogatives.

The Court's intransigence was encapsulated in the dramatic language of Justice Owen J. Roberts in the majority opinion in *United States* v. *Butler* (1936), declaring unconstitutional the federal processing tax on agricultural commodities that had been enacted in 1933 as part of the basic New Deal farm program. To admit the legitimacy of such a deployment of the taxing or spending power, Roberts contended, would be to permit "total subversion" of the powers reserved under the doctrines of federalism to the states. The result would be a constitution undermined, "the independence of the individual states obliterated, and the United States converted into a central government exercising uncontrolled police power in every state of the Union, superseding all local control or regulation of the affairs or concerns of the states." In an eloquent dissent, Chief Justice Harlan Fiske Stone, joined by two other justices, denounced the kind of activism in which the Court's majority was engaged. ("Courts are not the only agency of government that must be assumed to have capacity to govern," he wrote.) Stone also presented a different view of federalism, however, a view that reflected the crisis-driven, pragmatic approach that had become the hallmark of New Deal constitutional argument. No matter how compelling the constitutional imperatives associated with "an indestructible union of indestructible states," Stone declared, the preservation of both the states and the union itself might ultimately depend upon the Court's recognizing that "language, even of a constitution, may mean what it says: that the power to tax and spend includes the power to relieve a nationwide economic maladjustment by conditional gifts of money."

There ensued the extraordinary Court-packing fight, in which Roosevelt, given new confidence by his landslide victory in the 1936 election, directly assaulted the Court and called for its enlargement and reformation. Frustrated in the short run, the president was soon the victor. A switch in alignment established a new majority in 1937 on the side of the New Deal constitutional view, and subsequent liberal appointments virtually assured the achievement of what came to be known as the "constitutional revolution" of the period. It was a revolution amounting, some analysts argued, to amendment of the Constitution without recourse to the formal amending process. Others regarded it as, instead, a return to older and more supportable constitutional doctrine, contending that the real revolution in the Court's posture had occurred in the years of conservative hegemony from the 1880s to 1936, when such doctrines as economic due process and "liberty of contract" had held sway. More narrowly, the Court may be said to have departed in restrictive 1934–1936 decisions from its own main line of precedents of more recent vintage on the power of Congress to use taxation as an instrument of regulation, and even from some nationalistic commerce clause precedents set down by the conservative Taft Court.

However that may be, the Court produced a series of decisions beginning in 1937 that clearly established a new constitutional jurisprudence. Each of the foundation stones of the old federal creed, as they had been deployed by the Court during 1934–1936, now gave way. The Tenth Amendment, for example, was read by the new Court majority as being merely "declaratory." The amendment, they ruled, "states but a truism" and would no longer be read as a limitation upon federal legislation independently of other provisions of the Constitution. The commerce clause came in for similar reinterpretation, culminating in the *Wickard* v. *Filburn* (1942) decision, when the Court affirmed what it declared to be the view once taken by Chief Justice John Marshall—that any restraints upon "the embracing and penetrating nature of this power [to regulate commerce]" properly should come from political and not judicial process. A few years later, in *American Power and Light Co.* v. *S.E.C.* (1947), the Court flatly declared the commerce power to be "as broad as the economic needs of the nation." (This phrase echoed the Court's language in *Southern Railway Co.* v. *United States,* a 1911 decision in which it had upheld a congressional statute requiring minimum safety standards of all railroad cars on systems that crossed state lines, stating that while Congress had no authority to regulate "intrastate commerce as such, . . . its power to regulate interstate commerce is plenary.")

By the *Wickard* ruling and other decisions respecting the welfare, taxing, and spending power as well as the commerce clause authority of Congress, the Court indeed established during 1937–1942 the basis for the national government to exercise virtually a plenary regulatory power over every aspect of the national economy. In striking down the National Recovery Act in *Schechter Poultry Corp.* v. *United States* (1935), the majority had declaimed against any validation of federal power "to embrace practically all the activities of the people." Such an interpretation of the Constitution, the Court said, would mean "that the authority of the State over its domestic concerns would exist only by sufferance of the federal government." Within five years, however, the boundaries of what the Court was willing to recognize as "domestic concerns" of a purely intrastate nature had virtually dissolved.

In the heat of the fight with the Court in 1936–1937, President Roosevelt had denounced the justices' quixotic deference to "horse-and-buggy" concepts of federalism and national power. From other quarters in the New Deal camp came less restrained condemnations of the federal creed. For example, in 1934 Karl Llewellyn, the leading theorist of the academic school of jurisprudence called Legal Realism, scoffed at the inherited system of federal power distribution as "inane," declaring that "utter reconstruction" of government authority and structures was required. More generally, the depth and urgency of the Depression crisis placed under irresistible pressure a constitutional orthodoxy that was seen as crippling the nation's capacity to respond—and to survive without social chaos and political disintegration. In the economic and social fields, at least, pragmatism and a robust view of national authority won the day in regard to federal constitutional theory and governmental practice alike.

Paradoxically, while the Court was fashioning a plenary national police power, it had also begun to extend dramatically the realm of federal constitutional restraints over state action in the areas of civil liberties and civil rights. By 1940 the Court's new liberal majority had set in place the doctrinal foundations for federal judicial enforcement of Bill of Rights freedoms and Fourteenth Amendment equal protection requirements against the states. The "preferred freedoms" doctrine, set forth by Chief Justice Harlan Fiske Stone in his celebrated footnote to *United States* v. *Carolene Products* (1938), and the Court's articulation of a doctrine of freedoms "implicit in the concept of ordered liberty" (*Palko* v. *Connecticut* [1937]) that was relevant to the constitutionality of state criminal procedures, formed the keystone of the arch. By the decade's close, on the eve of World War II, the Court had also begun to deploy the Fourteenth Amendment's guarantees against racial discrimination in the field of public higher education (*Missouri* v. *Canada* [1938]). Persuaded that an active pursuit of civil liberties and civil rights objectives ought to be undertaken, Roosevelt in 1939 authorized establishment of a Civil Liberties Unit in the Justice Department's criminal division; and for the first time since Reconstruction, what Attorney General Frank Murphy announced as "a program of vigilant action in the prosecution of infringement of [federally guaranteed] rights" became a central concern of the national government. Within two years, with the decision of *U.S.* v. *Classic,* the government had successfully prosecuted against election fraud and coercion by a local official in New Orleans. The Court also began to act vigorously in extending a qualified protection to labor against antipicketing statutes, and it had begun to enlarge in other respects the scope of free speech protection it would enforce against the states.

In *Chambers* v. *Florida* (1940), the Court explicitly required the elements of "a fair trial" in state proceedings. Thus it had taken at least the first steps toward establishing the "incorporation" doctrine in the area of criminal procedures—that is, the doctrine that the Fourteenth Amendment "incorporated" the procedural protections in the Bill of Rights, and hence could be enforced against the states. The Court was deeply divided in the 1940s over the question of incorporation and the Bill of Rights. Building upon the reasoning in *Gitlow* v. *New York* (1925), in which the Court had declared that the Fourteenth Amendment incorporates certain "fundamental personal rights and liberties," and so protects them against adverse state actions, Justice Hugo L. Black played a leading role in trying to bring the entire range of Bill of Rights guarantees into the category of what was "fundamental."

In a long series of divided decisions, Black was opposed most intransigently by Justice Felix Frankfurter, who stood for highly selective incorporation—and that on a parsimonious basis at best, even in cases where he admitted that the actions of state authorities were offensive to basic notions of fairness. Frankfurter especially deplored the extension of Fourteenth Amendment protection in criminal process, contending, for example, in his dissent in *Adamson* v. *California* (1947) that the amendment was not intended as "the basis of a uniform code of criminal procedure," and that to apply it as such would undermine both state constitutional responsibilities and the effective vitality of state agencies. Frankfurter argued further that Black's expansive approach to incorporation admitted excessive discretion and so violated the principle of judicial self-restraint, which New Deal liberals had uniformly insisted must be honored in matters of economic regulation—and which Frankfurter insisted should be no less faithfully respected in cases regarding federalism and Bill of Rights issues. To these criticisms, Black rejoined that it was selectivity as an approach to incorporation, and not the comprehensive incorporation that he advocated, which would permit the Court too much room for subjective judgments, with the result, as he wrote in dissent in *Adamson*, that the Court would "frustrate the great design of a written Constitution" as the sole "point of departure" for defining basic rights.

This ongoing dispute over how far incorporation could properly reach state action would become, in the postwar years, one of the central issues that the Court had to confront.

"COOPERATIVE FEDERALISM" IN THE POSTWAR ERA

The march of centralization continued with full force after World War II. This was true both of constitutional doctrine and the distribution of governmental responsibilities, and it was for a long time a linear course of centralization—at least until challenged in the 1980s by the Reagan administration. Thus it is easy to lose sight of the fact that the central domestic issue of American politics, from 1945 through at least the end of the first Eisenhower administration in 1956, was whether the New Deal economic and social programs should be dismantled with the end of economic emergency conditions, or instead made permanent.

During the World War II years, the conventional issues of federalism were altogether suspended, as were many other aspects of normal American life and its institutions; but not long after the war's end, the debate over the future of federal-state relations entered a period of remarkable ferment.

Among the conservative opponents of the New Deal, there was discontent with the new, vastly enlarged role of the government in the federal system. They detested the new giantism in the national government because it was costly and required continued high taxes, because it involved an extensive regulatory apparatus and was supportive of organized labor in ways that threatened the once-accepted "economic liberty" prized by business interests, and because it had abandoned the traditional premises of individualism to embrace many of the precepts of a social-welfare state. Southern segregationists and their political allies from scattered areas of the regions outside the South had their own reasons for wishing to see the old federal creed restored to full vigor. Their worst fear for the future of states' rights seemed fully confirmed in 1947 when President Harry S. Truman proposed a major legislative program of civil rights enforcement. Indeed, Truman's posture on the issue inspired the third-party "Dixiecrat" movement, formed by the Democratic party's southern conservative wing, in the presidential election the next year. This placed a federalism issue, albeit in the role of framing the race question, at front and center in national politics.

The intimate association of states' rights with the segregationist cause merely validated and reinforced the dismissive and contemptuous view of the old federal creed that had become interwoven into the new competing, liberal creed to which the New Deal's champions subscribed. This new liberal creed enshrined the majoritarian concept of "liberal democracy" (Franklin Roosevelt's own term) at the core of the pragmatic view that constitutional principles—which were regularly termed "shibboleths" when deemed to be obstacles to the government's meeting contemporary needs—must give way to overwhelming electoral majorities such as Roosevelt's in 1936. In that respect, the liberal idea had been vindicated, or at least reflected in the fullness of its vision, by the new constitutional jurisprudence of a liberal Supreme Court.

The new creed also embraced, however, powerful "statist" arguments for the virtues of positive government. In regard to programs of social welfare, for example, the strongest proponents of the new liberal orthodoxy would argue that the new programs ultimately supported individualism in its best sense by assuring minimum levels of dignity and material sustenance to those who had been deprived of them: the more such programs, the better. The liberal creed also rejected the assumption that less government meant greater prosperity and freedom. James Landis, New Deal administrator and an important voice of the new liberalism, put it bluntly, declaring: "Efficiency in the processes of governmental regulation is best served by the creation of more rather than [fewer] agencies." Also embedded in the New Deal liberal creed was an acceptance, by the end of the 1930s, of a permanently enlarged fiscal role for the national government in order to make more effective the purposeful use (on Keynesian principles) of deficits and surpluses. In this respect, too, the traditional view of what was virtuous in governmental operations, part of the same tradition as the federal creed, was challenged head-on. Finally, the new liberal view embraced the emergent enthusiasm for federally guaranteed civil rights, culminating in Truman's proposals for a legislative program that would push beyond the limited and tentative gains made earlier in the federal courts. In sum, the New Deal liberal creed emerged as a faith in positive government that found little to criticize in any aggregating of power at the center.

Equally important, none of the new creed's concerns or substantive precepts was sympathetic, even superficially, to traditional claims regarding the virtues either of the states or of the federal design itself. Instead, the division of authority was generally regarded as inefficient and obstructive, insufficient to the purposes of a national economy with national economic and social institutions, and the source of unnecessary jurisdictional disputes and fragmentation of policy. In the liberal view, the states had failed not only as a matter of inappropriateness, but also as a matter of political lack of will, outright corruption, and antimajoritarian institutions and behavior.

The New Deal liberal view regarded the states as subunits that, at best, might continue to play a useful role as agents of new and expanding federal programs. At worst, as the states were seen by many liberals, however, they were beyond redemption for reasons that went beyond the civil rights issues. These new liberals deplored the states for their dependence on regressive taxes, their notorious malapportionment of legislatures with resultant disfranchisement of urban majorities in favor of entrenched rural interests, and their deficiencies in the quality of administration and justice. Making it worse still, as many liberals saw the states, was the dominance in so many of them (including, but not exclusively, the Solid South states) of a single party—leading to further, perhaps irremediable, erosion of responsible government.

Such a dismal reading of the states as disgraceful liabilities to democratic government was not confined only to the most ardent and committed advocates of a new New Deal approach, such as Landis (already quoted) or Thurman Arnold, who contended that Americans needed above all a new "religion of government" to finally overcome and supercede the inherited Jeffersonian suspicion of governmental power. While granting that decentralization had important virtues, for example, the political scientist David Fellman wrote in a penetrating essay, "The Future of the States" (1945) that "federalism has the result of giving the country too many laws and too many variations of law on the same subjects. . . . No less important, it has permitted and even encouraged the festering of local tyrannies and injustices." Insufficient appreciation of either "the implications of democracy or the institutional needs of a modern society," Fellman contended, in many instances lay behind attacks upon strong centralized government. In this as in so many other instances in the nation's history, arguments for the virtues of federalism were being used as a smoke screen for other causes such as segregation, opposition to business regulation, or simply a generalized hostility to government.

At the same time, as only very few Washington-oriented New Deal leaders or liberal intellectuals were prepared to admit, there were signs of change in some state governments. These signs, which were often overlooked or unappreciated in the immediate postwar years, included introduction of the merit system into areas of civil service formerly left for political appointments, upgrading of expertise in the state bureaucracies, and a spreading interest in tax reform. Still, the intractability of the structural and political ills of the states could not be denied. Nor was it a surprise to any of the liberal critics of the states that in subsequent decades the sources of reform came as much from the federal government as from any impulse to change and improve within the states themselves.

Thus it was the desegregation decisions of the Supreme Court that set in motion the processes that attacked the worst injustice associated with states' rights. It was the federal courts that also made the first great steps, beginning in 1961, to effect fundamental reform in the law enforcement and criminal justice procedures of the states. The reapportionment decisions, beginning in the mid-1960s, finally broke the cake of custom and the legal barriers that had long prevailed to sustain rural minorities in power in many state legislatures. And the continued expansion of federal social and economic programs brought the states into new administrative or other sharing roles—accompanied by congressionally mandated requirements for planning, for professionalization of staffing qualifications, for auditing—that gave major impetus to structural reform in the states.

Moreover, although the effects upon them of centralization were indisputable, the states, despite erosion of their relative power vis-à-vis Washington, continued to expand the range and deepen the intensity of their involvement in many areas of policy. Expansion of higher education and public health, for example, went forward vigorously in many states in the postwar decades. Regulatory agencies were professionalized and given new functions; state and local programs heavily funded by the national government, as in road-building, public housing, and airport development, retained much room for discretion (albeit at the sufferance of the federal agencies) at the local level, and they employed expanding bureaucracies of state officials. Many states undertook reform of tax programs, mainly to enhance revenues but often also to achieve a more progressive tax structure. A favorite cause of liberal commentators and frequent source of their disdain for the states, the need to strengthen gubernatorial powers and to introduce research and planning capabilities in legislative and agency staffing, also received intensive attention by state-level reformers in the postwar years. In sum, while dramatic change was being undertaken or forced upon the states, as with civil rights or reapportionment, a larger process of reappraisal, restructuring, and reform was beginning to answer some of the most strident indictments in the new liberal critique of the states' ability to govern efficiently and justly.

On the national stage, however, the outcome of the continuing confrontation between inherited ideas about federalism and the new liberal creed still remained uncertain. In the early months of his presidency, Dwight D. Eisenhower gave numerous reasons for fresh hopefulness to those who wanted to see the march toward centralization of power reversed. The Republican platform in 1952 had condemned the Democrats for having "weakened self-government" in America, charging that "they have violated our liberties by turning loose upon the country a swarm of arrogant bureaucrats and their agents who meddle intolerably in the lives and occupations of our citizens." Although never an outright champion of segregation policies, Eisenhower was privately critical of the Warren Court's decisions and he publicly distanced himself from demands for expanded federalization of civil rights. His rhetoric was replete with rhapsodic language drawn from the lexicon of the old federal creed—a significant element of the strength of his appeal in the Old South, where he broke the traditional hegemony of the once-solid Democratic party. Eisenhower also ardently supported the return of control over offshore oil resources to the coastal states (including the oil-rich waters of Texas and California, two politically crucial states in which he had made appeals on this issue during the 1952 campaign). The offshore waters issue carried symbolism that went beyond electoral college votes, making it a question of deep interest to proponents of states' rights. The legislation that Eisenhower signed, turning control of the offshore resources back to the states, marked an overturning of a Supreme Court decision in 1947 in which the justices had given a ringing endorsement to the concept of "paramount claims" of the national government to supremacy in such matters.

In all these respects, but also in the way that he continually deplored excessive governmental size, costliness, and complexity, Eisenhower maintained the public prominence of federalism issues. To those who feared that with much further centralization the states would become "hollow shells, operating primarily as the field districts of federal departments and dependent on the federal treasury for their support," Eisenhower appeared to be the last best hope for traditional federalism. True to this posture, Eisenhower called upon Congress in March 1953 to create a Commission on Intergovernmental Relations to report on the status of American federal-state relations. Centralization of powers, Eisenhower declared, had recently proceeded "at a speed-defying order and efficiency" without regard to effects upon "the basic structure of our Federal-State system of government." The effects had been higher taxes, confusion of responsibilities, and an excessive growth in the grant-in-aid programs—the latter so greatly expanded, the president pointed out, that they were accounting for fully one-fifth of state expenditures.

At the heart of Eisenhower's concerns was the issue of what, since his time, has become known as the "sorting-out" question—the systematic allocation of policy responsibilities between the nation and the states. That this allocation might be rational and efficient, on agreed criteria of appropriateness, is a vision as old as the Republic; indeed, Eisenhower's concern echoed many passages in *The Federalist* and in the ratification debates of 1787 and 1789.

Congress established the commission, as the president requested, and it produced a widely ranging report that reviewed state-local-federal relationships and called for better coordination and cooperation. In 1959 Congress created a permanent commission, the Advisory Commission on Intergovernmental Relations (ACIR), with membership composed mainly of elective officials and others from all levels of government. The ACIR has served since then as a prominent forum for an exchange of views, and some of its staff reports became valuable sources of data and analysis of various reform ideas. The most notable of its achievements was the lead role it took in advancing in the late 1960s what became known as the revenue sharing plan. At several junctures in its history, the ACIR has shown an anticentralist bias, but probably its chief importance rests in the continuing contribution it has made for good or otherwise, from its founding until 1981, in stressing the pragmatic, administrative, or technocratic side of federalism issues. In this respect, it reflected and in some measure influenced the dominant tendency in social scientific studies of government.

Indeed, it became commonplace by the late 1960s to speak of "intergovernmental relations" (IGR) rather than of "federalism," in definition and analysis of federal-state-local relations. Especially with regard to the study of the grant-in-aid programs by the ACIR and other analysts, typically much more was said of budgeting concepts, planning criteria, and managerialism than of basic issues of power and constitutionality. Words like coordination and oversight were in; sovereignty was definitely out, and even responsibility seemed to be pushed into the background. In that sense, although the ACIR was the immediate offspring of Eisenhower Republicanism's concern with restoring the virtues of federalism, it bore also the genetic markings of New Deal pragmatism and its approach to government in all its aspects—including the matter of the federal design.

The course of the ACIR's history mirrored the larger trends both in federal-state relationships and in political discourse, at least until Ronald Reagan's presidency. Contrary to much of his rhetoric, and doubtless in ways that ran against his deep personal preferences, Eisenhower presided over a continuing expansion of the national government's role in the working system of governance. The interstate highway program, inauguration of unprecedented federal aid to education (both under the political umbrella and formal rubric of "national defense priorities"), and a dramatic expansion of the Social Security retirement, disability, and unemployment programs all were enacted with Eisenhower's approval during the 1950s. At the same time the Supreme Court forced the government's hand with its school desegregation decisions: few moments in the history of the national government's demonstration of its supremacy exceeded in dramatic intensity or long-term social impact Eisenhower's sending of federal troops to the steps of Little Rock's Central High School to enforce its desegregation in 1957.

Profoundly disappointing to states' rights constitutionalists, especially the defenders of racial discrimination and segregation who were in their camp, the deeper political trends of the Eisenhower years represented an extension of what had been happening to American federalism since 1933. Thus federal government expenditures, which had been just over 10 percent of the gross national product in 1940, rising to 14.3 percent in 1950, increased again to 18.4 per cent in 1960. State and local expenditures of their own funds meanwhile were stable, at about 8.5 percent, throughout the period. While the federal "fisc" (revenue base) was solidly based on the income tax, augmented by corporation and Social Security taxes, many states were struggling with rising debt-to-revenue ratios and bumping up against the practical (or political) limits of their property and sales tax rates.

On the administrative side, the centralizing trends were magnified by the increasing frequency with which congressional programs for grants to the states required formal planning and imposed other management and auditing requirements. The Eisenhower years witnessed no slowing in Congress's resort to the grant-in-aid model of aid to the states as an instrument for effecting national policies across a broad range. By 1961, some forty major grant programs were funneling federal dollars to state and local governments. On a per capita basis, federal aid to the states more than doubled between 1944 and 1952; and during the Eisenhower years, it rose still further, from $16.47 per capita in 1952 to $38.86 in 1960. Not only the vision of clear criteria for "sorting out" functions, but also the hope for consensus as to their actual application, seemed to be all-but-unattainable objectives against the pressures for more government born of rising expectations. But further, even in regard to narrow managerial considerations, there was increasing complaint from the beneficiaries of the aid flow—governors, mayors, and other state and local officials—that a chaos of independently designed, organized, and administered programs was imposing inefficiencies and confusion upon their agencies. Thus, within even the narrow province of management and public administration, there was malaise with what had become the perdurable problems of complexity in the development of the new-style "cooperative federalism."

THE GREAT SOCIETY AND NIXON'S "NEW FEDERALISM"

In the 1960s, a period of Democratic party control of the White House and dominance of Congress by the liberal coalition, there was an acceleration of virtually all the trends that had frustrated the hopes of liberalism's critics in the Eisenhower years. Although Vietnam War–related events overshadowed some of the domestic changes of the period in their impact on the nation's political culture and direction of social change, the scope and effects of domestic policy innovations were great; and they gave a new configuration to the continuing process of centralization in American federalism.

The constitutional jurisprudence of the Warren Court reinforced other movements affecting the federal-state power balance. A series of decisions expanded the imposition of federal Bill of Rights requirements on the states in law enforcement and criminal justice. In *Gideon* v. *Wainwright* (1963), the Court resolved one of its longest-running and most bitter divisions in regard to Fourteenth Amendment "incorporation" doctrine: overruling its earlier decision in *Betts* v. *Brady* (1942), the justices now declared that the Sixth Amendment guarantee of right to counsel in criminal cases was to be applied to the states. The new judicial activism extended into new areas, as when in *Griswold* v. *Connecticut* (1965) the Court articulated a "right to privacy" with broad implications for the federal role in monitoring the ordering of the rules of family life and sexual behavior. Other Warren Court decisions pushed further the reapportionment and school desegregation doctrines of the previous decade. In this period, the federal courts began to exercise a direct oversight function in regard to consent orders and injunctions affecting the operation of local and state government institutions. This move toward affirmatively requiring certain kinds of governmental responses and policies was especially alarming to conservatives, who regarded judicial interference of this sort as perhaps the worst threat yet to state autonomy.

Responses were not confined to the conventional political arena: academic commentary critical of the Court was common, and even the august (and once dedicatedly apolitical) Conference of Chief Justices, composed of the highest-ranking state judges, rallied to assert the values of traditional federalism against the Court. In the last analysis, however, the "states' rights" being defended consisted of their power to maintain racial segregation and discrimination, to refuse recognition in state courts of rights of defendants that in some instances had been afforded for three-quarters of a century in federal trials, to enforce antisubversion laws and other statutes in areas that the Court ruled had been preempted by congressional legislation, and to engage in arbitrary denial of employment, welfare, and other benefits previously controlled without federal interference by the states. Another constitutional revolution had taken place, again with the effect of nationalization of rights and (by that token) centralization of power within federalism.

The new domestic policies put into place in the Kennedy and Johnson years set in motion changes that had equally far-reaching potential. Most important in this regard were the civil rights statutes enacted by Congress and vigorously enforced by a Justice Department that was also mobilized to enforce desegregation rulings by federal district courts throughout the South. The new determination with which the national government enforced policies for racial equality was soon matched by the forcefulness with which Johnson advanced his Great Society programs for social welfare, economic development, education, and health. The accommodation of New Deal innovations, and the effective political detente by which the "moderate" sector in American politics had effected it since 1948, proved but a prelude to far-reaching Great Society policy innovations.

The Great Society domestic programs that went forward in the 1960s, even as the Vietnam conflict was escalating with its extraordinary ramifications for American society, had several distinguishing features. First was the high degree of reliance upon the grant-in-aid instrumentality for delivering the new services and establishing the new structures that new legislation mandated. The number of programs skyrocketed, from 130 in 1960 to more than 400 by the end of Johnson's administration in 1969. The volume of grants rose rapidly, and by 1972 had reached nearly $40 billion, four times the 1964 level. There was also an increase in degree of complexity, as project grants and categorical grants were augmented by broadly defined block grants; and there was a major shift away from former concentration of grant funding in highways and toward social services, education, hospital construction, and community development. Meanwhile, the inauguration of Medicare established a new individual entitlement program with potential for enormous future growth, further shifting the locus of policy determination and the center of fiscal leverage toward Washington.

The states and local governments served in effect as a complex and fragmented delivery system for the Great Society programs of the Johnson era. An exceptional feature of these programs, notable especially in the War on Poverty community-action programs, was the way in which new (often participatory) structures were set up de novo and entirely outside existing governmental structures. Often they were controlled by leaders of grass roots groups, including radical elements, who previously had enjoyed little voice in the political process. The president had promised that a new style of government, which he termed "Creative Federalism," would bring change; but few predicted that it would take this form, amounting (as many state and local elective officials complained) to Washington's financing of a virtual revolution against the political establishment.

Johnson's view of how Creative Federalism would work had been rather more consensual and benign. He sought program designs, he said, that would institute "an expanded partnership" of all levels of government, but also with active involvement of private-sector institutions in the delivery of grant-aided services and benefits. "The cooperation of the state and the city, and of business and of labor, and of private institutions and private individuals," Johnson declared, all would be relied upon. In this sense, he translated consensus politics into a bold new concept of intergovernmental relations and consensus federalism.

Enthusiasts for the Great Society hailed this vision as one that finally put to rest the ancient rivalry of the states with the federal government, and that at the same time also brought business, the labor unions, and other private institutions into the expanded consensual apparatus of governing. One commentator, the journalist Max Ways, euphorically proclaimed that "the overall degree of centralization or decentralization" had now been rendered "seldom an interesting or even useful question." No need to worry about concentrations of power at the center, he argued, or about the autonomy of local decision making: "It is possible to think of vast increases of federal government power that do not encroach upon or diminish any other power. Simultaneously, the power of states and local governments will increase, . . . and the power of individuals will increase."

The notion that considerations of power could magically be rendered obsolete did not long survive the Johnson years. Criticism came not only from opposition leadership, on the Republican side, on grounds that the new programs were too numerous, too expensive, and the source of an overbearing and stifling uniformity; but also from the administration's friends in Congress and in the country, even those most supportive of Johnson's program objectives, who were concerned that the hydra of grant programs and proliferating policy initiatives was strangling the effectiveness of governance. Along with the ACIR, therefore, these political allies called for a technocratic approach to improve coordination, eliminate unnecessary duplication and overlap, and assure clarity of policy goals—and, by that means, restore clearer lines of responsibility. Thoughtful observers on all sides also recognized that the rich incentives and the multiplication of restraints associated with the grant programs had given new urgency to the problem of skewing of priorities and political decision making in many states. More generally, there was concern that while the federal government in the 1960s was enjoying a steady rise in tax-based revenues, the state and local governments were experiencing serious fiscal strain. Increasingly, both administration officials and critics of the Johnson programs began to think about instituting a more effective system to move funds on a wholesale basis from Washington to the states and local governments. From their preliminary proposals came to the fore a captivating new idea that was called General Revenue Sharing—an approach to federal aid that would be championed and made a central feature of Richard M. Nixon's domestic program when he succeeded Johnson in the White House.

The claims of the Great Society and creative federalism evoked expressions of a much deeper skepticism and concern, however, from many critics on all points in the political and ideological spectrum. The tone for some of the criticism was set in constitutional discourse, especially in the dissenting Supreme Court opinions in some of the most controversial Fourteenth Amendment, loyalty and security, and civil liberties cases in which the Court authorized sweeping new limits on the autonomy of the states. Like the dissenting justices, critics in the academic community rejected the pragmatic and technocratic versions of how the federal design ought to be evaluated. Thus Robert McCloskey, a constitutional scholar, insisted upon the continuing relevance of fundamental political values, even in swiftly changing times. "The idea that governmental purposes and societal needs are something less than coterminous," he wrote, "may still have some merit in America." McCloskey insisted that whether "local vitality" ought still to be maintained at least "as an alternative to static uniformity," but also at another level as an effective barrier to "tyranny" from the center, remained an important question. Critics who took this perspective, but who also were sympathetic with many programmatic goals of the regulatory and welfare state, had the special burden of finding ways to dissociate themselves from the racial segregationists who welcomed any expression of views that carried a states' rights message.

Equally vocal criticism of centralizing tendencies came from the political left, a quarter in which there was no reverence for any element of the traditional federal creed but in which the New Deal liberal creed and the Great Society were condemned for not being radical enough in their approach to reform. Radical community organizers such as Saul Alinsky took up the cause of "power to the people" in a vein that was entirely alien to the rhetoric and ideological orientation of localism as expressed in the federal creed. They were inspired by the radical strain in the American political past as well as by the more recent example of civil rights activism. Curiously enough, they were often financed and given a pulpit by the Great Society community-action programs. Their criticism of the mainstream establishment gained new prominence when it became increasingly interwoven with the anti–Vietnam War protests that shook the American political stage, against the background of the Robert Kennedy and Martin Luther King, Jr., assassinations, and the urban arson and riots that followed.

The Nixon administration's record on the matter of federalism defies easy categorization. He promised in his 1968 campaign to tame the growth of federal power and proliferating programs of federal aid; and in fact as president he did pursue the goal of reducing federal influence by attacking social welfare programs, by openly encouraging political opposition to court-ordered desegregation and supporting critics of the Supreme Court's activism, and by throwing his influence behind successful congressional initiatives to substitute General Revenue Sharing for some of the key federal categorical aid and demonstration programs. At the same time, however, Nixon was greatly augmenting federal *executive* power—most notably, in relation to federal aid, by the executive impoundment of funds appropriated by Congress, a tactic that paled in significance when compared with what was later learned of Nixon's more sinister abuses of executive authority, including sordid uses of the Federal Bureau of Investigation (FBI), the Central Intelligence Agency (CIA), and other agencies.

Nixon used the term *new federalism* to describe the domestic program proposals he presented in August 1969. He proposed to link the fundamental reform of intergovernmental relations with a parcel of innovations that would restructure welfare, manpower training, and poverty relief. The capstone of the New Federalism plan was revenue sharing, a program of grants-in-aid on very general terms, designed to free the states from excessive oversight and constraining conditions imposed from Washington. Revenue sharing did achieve some of its administrative goals in full measure, but it soon became apparent that there was a trade-off: in many states and localities the distribution of funds "without strings" led immediately to financing of expanded programs for the suburban middle class, while bringing cutbacks in aid to programs that reached the poor and the urban centers. Simultaneously, Nixon-era tax reform legislation embodied a shift that increased the share contributed to government revenues by the regressive Social Security tax while diminishing the share contributed by corporate income taxes—a feature of the Nixon record that led political critics to argue that the new federalism and proposed welfare program changes in fact constituted a counterrevolution that was successfully reversing key income-redistributive elements of the New Deal–Great Society programmatic legacy.

Paradoxically, Nixon did lend his support, reluctantly or otherwise, to environmentalism—a powerful new movement in American politics that within a few years would do much to advance the longer-term process of centralization within federalism. During the Johnson administration, there had been an important expansion of federal regulatory power activity in the fields of consumer protection and occupational safety and health. In the Nixon years, regulation of activities that threatened the environment came under vastly expanded federal agency supervision, dramatically centralizing power in an area of policy that previously had been left almost entirely to the states. Despite what became an extended effort under Nixon's presidential successors to deregulate in the transport, communications, and antitrust fields, these newer areas of social and environmental regulation remained securely in the federal government's control.

An interesting feature of the political battles that resulted in the Revenue Sharing Act of 1972 and its reauthorization in 1976 was the extraordinary strength demonstrated by the so-called public interest groups such as the mayors' and governors' conferences, the organized groups of state legislators and county executives, and the like. They had emerged as, in effect, public sector pressure groups. In their role as voices for the interests of public entities, these groups complemented the influence of another element that was increasingly visible in policy debates: the collection of bureaucrats with common professional training and policy responsibilities—what one analyst termed functional communities of specialist civil servants—who had become informal subsystems of interests within the federal structure. These expertise-based relationships cut across state-federal-local boundaries; and the specialist communities spoke with special authority on matters of policy in which they often allied themselves with particular private sector interests. Nixon had a shrewd understanding of the power that such bureaucrats could exercise, and he vowed to reduce their influence and recapture for the White House fuller control over the federal bureaucracy. After the Watergate scandal and Nixon's resignation, however, the specialist communities survived in full vigor as a major force in government—not only as influential voices in policy discussion but also at times as powerful obstacles to innovation. In that respect, the Nixon "counterrevolution" was unsuccessful.

CONTEMPORARY FEDERALISM: THE LAST QUARTER CENTURY

During Gerald Ford's brief presidency and the Carter administration, changes in the operation of federalism were less dramatic than in the previous two decades. The rate at which new grant-in-aid programs were inaugurated slowed, although their number still increased from 400 in 1970 to 540 in 1980. Both Ford and Jimmy Carter sought to consolidate and reduce the grant programs; and Carter was determined to reverse the revenue-sharing policy—which he denounced as "just a bunch of hokum" designed to undermine social reform—and restore fuller federal control over the policy goals and administrative constraints on the programs. Measured in constant dollars, federal grant aid peaked in 1978, but as of 1980 the flow of aid dollars from Washington still represented fully one-fourth of all state and local outlays.

The Carter administration also tightened up standards for affirmative action by government contractors and public institutions receiving federal aid, and it adopted strict enforcement standards to assure compliance with new mandates in federal statutes requiring states to comply with historic preservation, air pollution, age or gender discrimination, and disabled access requirements. At the receiving end of the grant-in-aid flow, state and local officials joined in a chorus of complaints that the new mandates (whether attached as conditions to aid or instead required irrespective of federal assistance) imposed heavy financial burdens that further skewed priorities in allocation of available revenues. The term *overload* became increasingly prominent in the rhetoric of federalism and intergovernmental relations, among analysts and practitioners who were concerned with excessive complexity (and perplexity) in the administration of governance. All this became grist for Ronald Reagan's political mill in the 1980 presidential elections.

The most influential changes in power relationships within American federalism in the Ford and Carter period were generated, however, by forces other than presidential or congressional initiatives. In the realm of constitutional law, for example, the Supreme Court was reopening some key issues governing the relationships of Washington with the states; and as the Nixon appointments to the Court had their effect on the pattern of decisions, important new doctrines emerged. For example, in *National League of Cities* v. *Usery* (1976), the Court astonished most observers by reviving the Tenth Amendment as a check upon the reach of congressional authority to regulate the terms of employment for state and local workers. The *Usery* decision marked the first time in nearly forty years that the Court had found a constitutional limitation upon congressional regulation of the economy. When Congress exercised regulatory authority, the Court ruled, the interests of "the States *as States*" required special deference. Throughout the majority opinion, vintage rhetoric of the old federal creed was prominent, and conservatives rejoiced in the idea that a keystone of the arch of New Deal liberalism was being put in jeopardy. The *Usery* doctrine inspired numerous additional challenges to federal regulation of state administration and policy, until, having decided that the doctrine was "unworkable in practice," a new majority of the Court again changed course in the 1985 *Garcia* v. *San Antonio Metropolitan Transit Authority* case. In the interim, however, the Court's willingness to reopen basic questions of state sovereignty gave new hope to conservatives who wished for further applications of the Tenth Amendment and perhaps similar judicial exhumation of long-discarded tenets of the old federal creed.

Of even greater potential effect on relationships within the working federal system was the direction of the Court's decisions in the area of criminal process. Since the beginnings of due-process Fourteenth Amendment "incorporation," the expansion of federal judges' authority to grant hearings and injunctive relief to prisoners and defendants—especially when they had not exhausted their rights in the state courts or were in process of prosecution or trial—had been a question that seriously divided liberal and conservative opinion. The trend in the Court since the early 1960s had been toward expansiveness of interpretation of the Fourteenth Amendment, of federal jurisdiction, and of the specific terms of civil rights statutes. Hence special importance was attached to the *Younger* v. *Harris* decision (1971), in which the majority opinion was written by Justice Hugo Black, who for three decades had been the principal architect of Fourteenth Amendment "incorporation doctrine." To the surprise of many observers, Black declared in *Younger* that federal judges must defer to the jurisdiction of state courts while actions were pending in them. Although some ambiguities remained as to the circumstances in which the *Younger* restraints would stay the hand of federal courts, Black's rhetoric left no doubt as to the shift it signaled in the Court's basic posture on centralized power. Ours is a "country . . . made up of a Union of separate state governments," he declared; the imperatives of a federal design required that the claims of the states to engage in their "legitimate activities" unhampered must be recognized. "Our Federalism," Black continued, did not mean "blind deference to 'States' Rights' any more than it means centralization of control over every important issue in our National Government and its courts." In subsequent years, the phrase "Our Federalism" became a slogan with tremendous appeal to those who believed centralization had gone too far; and for the Court, *Younger* marked the beginning of a retreat from vigorous judicial activism in the oversight of state judicial processes.

The doctrine called "adequate and independent state grounds" was another prominent area of constitutional law in which new developments in the 1970s had a major impact on federalism. The appellate courts in California, Hawaii, Massachusetts, and other states had begun to find in the provisions of their own state constitutions—provisions that were often cast in language identical to that of the federal Bill of Rights—an adequate basis for extending their citizens' civil rights and liberties; that is, these courts held their own state officials to higher standards than the Supreme Court had required in interpreting the national Constitution. The federal courts' deference to state courts in matters of their own law left ample room, therefore, for the elaboration of new doctrines of the right of privacy, and for the application of higher standards than federal courts were applying as to the rules restricting search and seizure practices, governing the admissibility of evidence in criminal trials, and for protection of activities defined as free speech. The independent state grounds doctrine was welcomed by liberals, who in this instance—contrary to the position they customarily took on matters of state autonomy versus federal oversight—praised the state courts' role as a means of providing an additional bulwark for individual rights and liberties against arbitrary uses of governmental power. Justices Stanley Mosk of the California Supreme Court and Hans Linde of the Oregon Supreme Court provided intellectual leadership in the development of the new doctrine. Ironically, however, the most influential theorist of independent state grounds was Justice William Brennan, who on the Supreme Court had made little secret of his view that state law enforcement and courts were much less likely than their federal counterparts to protect basic constitutional rights. Brennan called upon the state courts to fill the breach when the "federal half" of citizens' protection failed, as the federal judiciary became more conservative and hence more inclined to accept the implications of Justice Black's version of "Our Federalism."

While these departures in constitutional law were giving new coloration to the continuing political debates on federalism issues, the outcome of these debates would also be profoundly influenced by changes in the fiscal condition of the nation's government. Whereas in the Great Society years, liberal reforms and advocates of new revenue sharing ideas had been casting about for creative ways to apply the rising revenues of the national government, by the end of the 1970s federal deficits had become chronic. The deteriorating fiscal situation of the federal government immediately had its effect on grant-in-aid programs, which peaked in dollar amount in 1978. The decline continued, and between 1978 and 1985 the flow of aid to the states decreased by nearly one-fifth relative to the states' own revenues. During the same period, the comparable decline relative to local governmental revenues was 41 percent. An alarming upward shift in the inflation rate beginning at the same time, and lasting into the early 1980s, further dampened federal aid programs. No longer did anyone believe that the congressional cornucopia had unlimited capacity; the euphoric fiscal assumptions of the Great Society planners clearly were no longer credible.

Meanwhile political developments in the states also portended major changes in the operations of government, with major implications for federalism. Until the late 1970s, voters in most states seemed to accept as axiomatic the proposition that modern industrialization, urbanization, and social developments required growth in public services roughly commensurate with the growth of population and collective wealth. A deep skepticism about the efficacy of public sector activity began to gather strength, however, in what became a rising conservatism evident in the politics of even states such as California with dominantly liberal records. Politicians in both parties—the best known nationally were a Republican governor, Ronald Reagan, and his Democratic successor in California, Jerry Brown; another was Jimmy Carter as governor of Georgia—had throughout the 1970s given voice to this skepticism about the problem-solving capacity of government.

While the new antigovernmentalism focused at first upon bureaucratic inefficiency, it found a new target as it spawned a popular tax revolt, beginning in California in 1978, that resulted in enactment of stringent new limits on state government financing. And so at the very time when the volume of federal grants-in-aid was beginning to decline, the fiscal capacity of many states to maintain or expand their services was severely diminished. This change in basic capacity was disguised for a time by inflation and economic growth, but severe problems had begun to plague state finances by the mid-1980s in many areas of the country.

Meanwhile, many political leaders were framing campaigns on a strategy of running against government itself—a tactic that Reagan successfully brought to the national arena in his 1980 presidential election victory. The disillusionment with government to which he appealed so successfully meanwhile was further nourished by the public's angry reaction to rising crime rates, deterioration of urban environments, and the larger pattern of changing social and moral values. All these elements of the political environment were unsettling and destabilizing; and among the highly visible uncertainties in the new situation was the question of whether conservatives could successfully challenge and even reverse the long-term process of centralization that had prevailed for long.

That conservatives were prepared to place this federalism issue at the top of the political agenda became clear from the very first days of Ronald Reagan's presidency. In his presidential primary campaigns four years earlier, Reagan had called for the "systematic transfer of authority and resources [from Washington] to the states." This objective was kept at the forefront in 1981, as Reagan formulated his legislative agenda. He resorted once again to the label "New Federalism" (the phrase used earlier by Nixon, but largely forgotten by the public when Reagan revived it) to characterize his basic strategy of divesting the national government of specific major responsibilities that would be devolved upon the states. Reagan's program of "swaps," trade-offs of responsibilities, so as to effect a clear-cut sorting-out of functions between the states and Washington, quickly proved to be one that would oblige the states to provide service in costly areas of activity without giving them adequate long-term funding to carry the costs. Massive political opposition to his wholesale proposals emerged, with the nation's mayors and state governors in the forefront. Commenting upon the way in which so many state and local politicians who long had inveighed against preemption and restrictions now lined up to defeat the devolution plan, Senator Richard Lugar observed:

> It is interesting that after all the rhetoric about [the values of] local decision making and the ability of cities and states to deliver services, when the time came to "put up or shut up" a lot of people decided that, even though programs might be better off at the local level, now was not the time, not under these circumstances, and not with cutbacks of money.

The coalition of forces that emerged—much the same one that had pushed through revenue sharing in the 1970s—now defeated Reagan's "swap" program, which would have involved the national government's assuming full fiscal responsibility for Medicaid in return for the states' taking over exclusive responsibility for food stamp and family aid programs. Also defeated was Reagan's even less attractive proposal to initiate straight "turnbacks" of another thirty-five federal programs covering education, social services and community development, and transportation—but again, with proposed funding assistance that would have fallen far short of real costs. The success with which state and local interests coalesced across party lines bore eloquent witness to the accuracy of James Madison's prediction in the *Federalist* 46, that "ambitious encroachments" by the national government upon state authority would be perceived by the states as a common threat, and would lead every state government to "espouse the common cause."

Despite the defeat of Reagan's swap-and-turnback proposals, his presidency did bring about some important changes in federal-state relationships. First, the administration reduced the number of grant programs by one hundred, consolidating many of them into nine block-grant categories and altogether eliminating another sixty programs. Also achieved were a final end to revenue sharing and absolute reductions in the dollar amount of grants, with most of the cuts coming in social programs that were important for the support of services to the poor and to urban areas. While thus diminishing the flow of aid and consequently reducing the federal role in certain program areas, the Reagan administration also instituted changes in program administration. Some of those changes were aimed at simplification of programs, elimination of formal restrictions on use of money, and expanded authority for the states. In the view of the administration's critics, however, the more common result of administrative changes was the appointment of ideologically committed conservatives who provided centralized oversight every bit as stringent as had prevailed earlier—only now with a view toward seeing that state and local administration of programs did not frustrate conservative policy priorities.

Second, Reagan's legislative priorities and administrative policies were intended uniformly to reduce federal regulatory agencies' interference with private business interests. The antiregulatory thrust had the stated dual purpose of restoring the range of entrepreneurial freedom and of cutting back the federal presence in overall government activity. Federal preemption of regulatory power, at the expense of state authority, through specific provisions of congressional statutes had been a feature of national law for a century. Although Reagan singled out preemption as a target in speeches that attacked the "bloated federal bureaucracy," again political rhetoric and the actual uses of power were often starkly inconsistent. In fact, his administration continued to take significant regulatory power away from the states; the difference from earlier periods was that federal agencies now intervened to supplant stringent state regulations with more lenient federal regulations. In some instances, as in medical appliance regulation, the standard that the federal agencies formally adopted was a "no-standard standard," that is, an entire displacement of regulatory authority. It seemed curious for an administration that claimed to be devoted to restoring states' rights and older ideals of federalism to thus be systematically curtailing an important area of state authority.

In sum, when faced with the dilemma of choosing between giving deference to state autonomy under the rubric of "federalism values" or, instead, advancing free-market policies, the free-market objective consistently won out. The principles of federalism were consistently suborned to the objectives of privatism and of antigovernmentalism. Moreover, while conservative leaders and groups welcomed the Reagan administration's rhetorical deference to the old federalism creed, at the state level these same forces were usually aligned in favor of new constitutional limitations on state taxing authority.

As the tax revolt spread across much of the country, the states were caught in a fiscal bind. Federal grants-in-aid were declining, direct federal funding of other government services (except those related to the military) were being cut, and the states' own financial capacity to fill the gap was being undermined. The swiftness with which the federal grant-in-aid flows had been pumped up and then turned back, moreover, made governmental finances generally more volatile and rendered rational program planning very difficult. One dour commentator (the present writer) suggested the term "Whiplash Federalism" to describe the new system, or lack of it; another, referring to the way in which the states were so suddenly thrown back on their own resources after having become reliant on revenue sharing, called the new status of federal-state relations "Fend-for-Yourself Federalism."

A third front on which the Reagan administration sought to reverse the trend toward centralization was in constitutional law. As we have noted, the Supreme Court had already moved in some areas of adjudication toward a posture more solicitous of state claims and interests than the Court had taken since the late New Deal years. The Justice Department under Reagan effected a striking shift in the role of government lawyers in constitutional litigation and in interpretation of statutes. Attorney General Edwin Meese conducted a strident public campaign against the entire jurisprudence of Fourteenth Amendment incorporation to enforce nationalized civil rights and liberties. Making "original intent" of the Framers in 1787 the rallying cry, Meese and a committed ideological coterie of academics and political allies successfully pressed for appointment of conservative judges who could be counted upon to be activist in conservative causes (defense of property rights against regulation, upholding of new regulations that curbed use of federal funds for abortions, imposition of affirmative action standards, and the like) but who would be sure to exercise judicial self-restraint in matters where liberal objectives had for many years been advanced by the courts.

The Solicitor General fairly consistently appeared before the Supreme Court during the Reagan years to argue on the side of the states in a procession of cases in which state or local authorities resisted applications of the First and Fourteenth Amendments as barriers to their policies in areas touching religious freedom, civil rights and desegregation, and criminal due process. Ironically, however, Meese and others who were so ardent in the cause of restoring states' rights were largely opposed to the independent state grounds doctrine in the state courts, a cause that had won new popularity with liberals. The expressed ideal of the Reagan New Federalism, to leave more discretion with the states, did not extend to appreciation of state rulings that favored criminal defendants, trenched on private property rights, or enlarged the scope of privacy and antidiscriminatory doctrines under state law.

The Reagan administration also instituted a litigation policy of "nonacquiescence" in all instances when a federal district court in Social Security cases decided against government efforts to heighten requirements for eligibility and deprive individuals of benefits. This unprecedented strategy—by which the administration regarded each adverse court decision as applying only to that particular case or court, and having no general applicability—led several federal judges to threaten Justice Department officials with contempt citations. Although the government lawyers had to back off from this kind of resistance to judicial authority, the episode served as a vivid reminder that the "federalism value" embodied in suspicion of unbridled discretion in use of political power was not the controlling ideal in many crucial aspects of the Reagan administration's operations.

Most of the Reagan policies concerning federal-state relations were continued in the administration of George Bush. The states continued to be troubled by fiscal uncertainties, the continuing effects of the tax revolt, and the leveling-off of federal aid; and the national treasury meanwhile was burdened with a colossal level of debt, as the result of unrestrained defense spending and massive income tax cuts in the Reagan years. The pincers effect upon overall government financing thus put enormous pressure on Congress and state legislatures alike to cut back in individual entitlement programs, welfare, and other areas of spending—not only those that had originated with the Great Society programmatic innovations, but also many that had been at the core of the post–New Deal political detente that dated from the Truman-Eisenhower years.

Reagan had promised a sea change in federalism when he took office in 1981, and to many observers it appeared that he had accomplished it not by ideological persuasiveness so much as by his success in selling the American public on fiscal and tax policies that crippled the capacity of their governments to provide public services at the level considered minimal in most other advanced industrial societies in the late twentieth century. His attorney general had campaigned with great ideological ardor for restoration of a system in which "the states would retain the bulk of power and responsibility for governing society." Certainly that had not been achieved by 1992, when another three-way presidential contest, reminiscent in this respect of the 1912 campaign, raised fundamental questions about the role of government in American life. Rather, there had been a serious diminution in the stability and in the fiscal and administrative capacity of the public sector at all levels.

A comparison of the federal system in the 1990s with the system as it stood at the end of Franklin Roosevelt's presidency in 1945 suggests some important areas of fundamental change but also areas of continuity. The most striking departure is in the area of civil rights. Even in the Reagan-Bush years, the federal courts continued to accept cases challenging discriminatory or arbitrary procedures in the management of local schools, state prisons and jails, and other institutions of local government; and the Voting Rights Act was enforced and, after a struggle, extended. Affirmative action programs not only survived in most public institutions but also presented a new standard of private behavior in many institutions formerly beyond the reach of government guarantees. The Disabilities Act signed by George Bush similarly extended the reach of national guarantees of individual rights.

A second aspect of contemporary federalism that manifests a difference from the system as it was in 1945 is the vastly expanded role of federal agencies in the fields of social and environmental regulation, as opposed to the older regulatory regime that consisted largely of control over corporate structure, competitive practices and pricing, and labor relations. In most aspects, the newer regulatory initiatives have taken the form of direct federal control. But in coastal and offshore resources management, occupational health and safety, air pollution, and some other major areas of policy, there has also been an extended effort to involve the states or newly created regional bodies (as in marine fishery management) that serve as hybrid agencies for cooperative intergovernmental administration of national policies.

Third, the new ferment in constitutional law has decisively reopened issues that seemed to be effectively closed, if not by 1945, then (as in the case of criminal due process) certainly by the late 1970s. The Court has introduced new uncertainties or rejected old ones in numerous areas of law that vitally touch the rights of citizens and the prerogatives of state autonomy. Among the principal areas affected is criminal process and federal habeas corpus doctrine, in the *Younger* decision and its progeny. Other prominent matters include the constitutionality of state antisodomy laws; the shifting position of the Court on such key economic-doctrinal issues as the interpretation of Tenth Amendment constraints or the terms on which states may impose land-use restrictions on private property owners; and a shift in the 1970s and afterward toward giving the states increased latitude in financing public religious displays or giving state aid to private sectarian schools. The most volatile and politically dangerous constitutional issue of the early 1990s, however, concerned the policy of the states with regard to abortion rights. Constant reevaluation of federalism issues has always been a mainstay of the Court's docket, but the present range of uncertainties on key matters makes the last years of the twentieth century especially significant in constitutional law.

There are also themes that have proved to be persistent and durable in the record of modern American federalism. There is still a manifest persuasiveness in the notion, central to the old federal creed, that government close to the people is a good thing; it survives in the rhetoric of American political leaders across a wide spectrum, and it continues to exercise strong influence in constitutional adjudication. The survival of the states as political entities must also be recognized. The states retain important areas of discretionary power—still largely controlling, to take only one example, the field of family law. Hence there is substantial variation from state to state in the substance of law; the nation is, from that standpoint, now as in earlier eras of its history a mosaic of jurisdictions rather than monochromatic and monolithic. The robustness of independent state grounds doctrine in the courts reinforces the strength of potential state differences and of overall diversity.

Skeptics might contend that the states retain their discretion, and exhibit such diversity in important areas of law and policy, only because the national government has stayed its hand. It is a system, they contend, not of "true" federalism in which important state powers are entirely beyond the reach of federal power; rather, it is a system of "permissive" federalism in which state autonomy is exercised only by sufferance, not by right. Even if it is merely by sufferance, however, the states enjoy enough latitude in the policy realms that have been left to them that interstate competition remains a serious problem for public policy in the nation's governance. Thus the states still often engage in what Justice Louis Brandeis deplored as a "competition in laxity," by which they impose low or nil regulations, or offer costly tax subsidies and other incentives, in order to attract industrial investment and employment away from states that have higher regulatory standards or more expensive public services. On the positive side, states also compete with one another, in some instances, by offering superior educational and cultural facilities, or a better quality of life enforced by environmental regulation. In either case, only viable entities can engage in such competition; the states are not so lacking in influence or power as might be implied by considering only the strength and scope of the new federal establishment.

The vigorous coalitional behavior of state officials when confronted with the Reagan swap and turnback programs indicated, further, that the "structural elements" of federalism—by which the states protect their interests through the ordinary political process, rather than needing to depend on the courts—do truly serve as an instrument of action and protection for state concerns. Also relevant to an assessment of the state of contemporary federalism is the fact that, despite the impact of emergent (often crushing) fiscal burdens in the 1980s and early 1990s, the quality of state bureaucracies and delivery of services by state and local governments is generally regarded as vastly superior to anything the nation had experienced before the late 1950s. Whether stability and efficiency of state governance will survive the impact of term limits upon elective officials, a favorite conservative innovation in the early 1990s, remains an open question.

Although centralization has prevailed, withal, in the twentieth century, the United States is not yet a unitary country. It is a nation of fifty-one distinctive constitutional entities. Significant, and not merely trivial, areas of power and authority do remain with the states. Moreover, the rhetorical appeal of the old liberal creed and its tenets of localism, diversity, and diffused power has proven remarkably resilient in the politics of the post–World War II era. Issues of power, centralized and decentralized—and the question of what difference it makes that governmental functions are distributed among many entities in a complex system—thus remain significant in American political discourse more than two hundred years after the nation's founding.

SEE ALSO Nationalism; The Constitution; The Presidency; Congress; Political Ideas and Movements; Parties and Interest Groups (all in this volume).

BIBLIOGRAPHY

Samuel H. Beer, *To Make a Nation: The Rediscovery of American Federalism* (1993), though principally concerned with the intellectual history of federalism theory, provides a stimulating introduction to contemporary debates on the relative merits of centralization and decentralization. W. Brooke Graves, *American Intergovernmental Relations: Their Origins, Historical Development, and Current Status* (1964), is a magisterial work that remains the standard authority on its subject. Alfred W. Kelly, Winfred A. Harbison, and Herman Belz, *The American Constitution: Its Origins and Development* (6th edition, 1985), offers a survey of constitutional history that includes excellent analysis of federalism issues for each period of significant change. Similarly, Paul L. Murphy, *The Constitution in Crisis Times, 1918–1969* (1972), is an overview and analysis that treats due process, equal protection, and other constitutional issues that have shaped the law of federalism in modern constitutional development. Robert G. McCloskey, *The Modern Supreme Court* (1972) provides a cautious and often-skeptical view of centralized power, judicial activism, and the modern Supreme Court. These constitutional studies should be read against the broader history of change in law and society, as set forth, for example, in the classic work by James Willard Hurst, *Law and the Social Order in the United States* (1977).

Harry N. Scheiber, "Federalism and the American Economic Order, 1789–1910," *Law and Society Review* 10 (1975): 57–118; "American Federalism and the Diffusion of Power," *University of Toledo Law Review* 9 (1978); 619–680; "State Law and Industrial Policy in American Development, 1790–1987," *California Law Review* 75 (1987): 415–444 provide analyses of federalism that document the case for stages of centralization. Many key issues in the history and law of federalism are examined by authors representing a variety of interpretive views, in *Power Divided: Essays on the Theory and Practice of Federalism,* edited by Harry N. Scheiber and Malcolm M. Feeley (1989); and *Federalism and the Judicial Mind: Essays on American Constitutional Law and Politics, ed. Scheiber* (1992). The historical views in Morton Grodzins, *The American System: A New View of Government in the United States,* edited by Daniel Elazar (1966) are embedded in an overarching interpretation of both historic and modern federalism as "non-centralized," a view contrary to the interpretation in the present article and in other writings of the present author, viz., that there has been a persistent long-term tendency toward the progressive centralization of power in the system.

The Annals of the American Academy of Political and Social Science has published numerous important scholarly symposia on federalism issues, most recently in Volume 509 (May 1990), "American Federalism: The Third Century," edited by John Kincaid. *The United States Constitution: Roots, Rights, and Responsibilities,* edited by A. E. Dick Howard (1992), includes essays on numerous aspects of the U.S. constitutional heritage that intersect with federalism issues. Michael Kammen, *A Machine That Would Go of Itself: The Constitution in American Culture* (1994), covers broad evidentiary ground in reviewing the history of popular veneration for the Constitution. David Fellman, "The Future of the States" (1945) is one of many interesting scholarly and polemical essays reprinted in the insightfully edited work, *The State of the Union: Commentaries on American Democracy,* edited by Robert Dishman (1965). *A Nation of States: Essays on the American Federal System,* edited by Robert W. Goldwin (1963), though now dated, is still of interest for ideas on federalism theory and historic practice.

George F. Break, *Financing Government in a Federal System* (1980) is the standard source on the history of intergovernmental fiscal relations through the

Johnson years; it is the keystone volume in the Brookings Institution series, *Studies of Government Finance,* which includes many more specialized volumes that provide ongoing data and analysis on intergovernmental fiscal relationships. Lawrence J. O'Toole, Jr., *American Intergovernmental Relations* (2nd edition, 1993), contains important reprinted essays on the history, theory, and practice of federalism in the United States that constitute a useful sampling of the literature.

Morton Keller, *Regulating a New Economy: Public Policy and Economic Change in America,* 1900–1933 (1990) provides an interpretation of the larger policy context in which federalism issues arose during the Progressive period and until the beginning of the New Deal. Donald J. Pisani, *From the Family Farm to Agribusiness: The Irrigation Crusade in California and the West, 1850–1931* (1984), analyzes, in the framework of a detailed regional case study, the complex influences and operation of federalism in the history of farming and irrigation development. Alan Brinkley, "The New Deal and the Idea of the State," in *The Rise and Fall of the New Deal Order, 1930–1980,* edited by Steve Fraser and Gary Gerstle (1989) is an excellent source on the liberal New Deal creed.

Grant McConnell, *Private Power and American Democracy* (1966), is a brilliantly original analysis of how the institutions of modern federalism have contributed, through devolution, to entrenchment of local elites and other antidemocratic effects. James Patterson, *The New Deal and the States: Federalism in Transition* (1969), remains, despite the appearance of some more recent monographs on aspects of 1930s innovations in governance, the most incisive work on its subject. For the special configuration of the politics and practice of federalism in one region, see Harry N. Scheiber, "Federalism, the Southern Regional Economy, and Public Policy Since 1865," in *Ambivalent Legacy: A Legal History of the South,* edited by David J. Bodenhamer and James W. Ely, Jr. (1984), 69–105. A valuable regional study on the 1930s is Richard Lowitt, *The New Deal and the West* (1984).

William Anderson, *The Nation and the States: Rivals or Partners?* (1955), was an influential work in its day and remains useful as a snapshot view of intergovernmental relations in the 1950s. Deil Wright, *Understanding Intergovernmental Relations* (2nd edition, 1982) offers provocative analysis of modern grants-in-aid and related issues of administrative and fiscal federalism. David B. Walker, *Toward a Functioning Federalism* (1981), is focused on managerial and fiscal aspects of federalism, mainly on 1950–1980, but also contains a summary historical introduction that does not ignore constitutional law.

Michael D. Reagan, *The New Federalism* (1972), provides an interesting commentary on theories of federalism and is also a standard contemporary source on the policy issues that led to Nixon-era adoption of revenue sharing. The U.S. Advisory Commission on Intergovernmental Relations, *Emerging Issues in American Federalism* (1984), includes commentary by political leaders, among them Sen. Richard Lugar, whose contribution is quoted in the present essay, and by academics. Richard Nathan, *The Plot That Failed: Nixon and the Administrative Presidency* (1975) is a White House insider's retrospective view. In James L. Sundquist, *Making Federalism Work: A Study of Program Coordination at the Community Level* (1969), the reader will find a probe in depth into the "coordination problem" that is at the heart of modern "shared-program" administration.

The preemption issue in the Reagan years is treated well by Joseph F. Zimmerman in "Frustrating National Policy: Partial Federal Preemption," in *The Nationalization of State Government,* edited by Jerome J. Hanus (1981), 75–104; and Susan Bartlett Foote, "Regulatory Vacuums: Federalism, Deregulation, and Judicial Review," *University of California at Davis Law Review* (1982): 113–139. Harry N. Scheiber, "International Economic Policies and the State Role in U.S. Federalism: A Process Revolution?" in *States and Provinces in the International Economy,* edited by Douglas M. Brown and Earl H. Frey (1993), examines the increasingly high-profile recent state claims in policy-making for international trade and investment.

A symposium in *William & Mary Law Review* 22 (1981), "State Courts and Federalism in the 1980s," provides an excellent starting point for study of adequate and independent state grounds in modern constitutional law. Charles Black, in *Perspectives in Constitutional Law* (1963) and other writings, raised important questions about the constitutional imperatives that he believed must be taken as derivative from acceptance of a federal structure. An influential and provocative contemporary analysis of how federalism is related to judicial review and judicial politics is in Jesse H. Choper, *Judicial Review and the National Political Process: A Functional Reconsideration of the Role of the Supreme Court* (1980).

CITY AND SUBURB

Jon C. Teaford

Twentieth-century American urban development is a story of deconcentration and dispersion. At the beginning of the century big cities were largely confined to the northeastern quadrant of the nation, yet by the 1990s the deserts of Nevada and Arizona and the swamps of Florida boasted metropolitan areas that rivaled the older centers of the Great Lakes and Atlantic seaboard. Whereas urban America had once stopped at the Mason-Dixon Line and the Mississippi River, in the course of the twentieth century it expanded to the nation's southern and western rims. Urbanization spread throughout the United States, and at the close of the century metropolitan life was characteristic of every region.

Decentralization was also the prevailing trend within each individual metropolitan area. In 1900 city dwellers crowded within a five-mile radius of a central business district that was the unchallenged focus of the local economy and a common center for the diverse residents of the polyglot metropolis. Ninety years later millions of people populated former cornfields, potato patches, and orange groves dozens of miles from any traditional downtown and patronized outlying shopping malls that catered to a single race and class. In southern California, Florida, northern Virginia, and elsewhere, houses, stores, factories, and office buildings spread over hundreds of square miles, resulting in amorphous zones of population without any unifying center.

The American metropolis of the 1990s was, then, far different from its counterpart a century earlier. In fact, the old city and the new seemed hardly the same social species. The one was focused and frosty; the other was multicentered and more likely to be sunny and warm. In the course of a single century, Americans transformed urban life and created a new pattern of settlement unknown to their grandparents.

THE NEW CENTURY, 1900–1919

As evident in table 1, in 1900 urban life was a frostbelt phenomenon. Of the twenty most populous American cities, only one, New Orleans, was in the former Confederacy, and only one, San Francisco, was west of Minneapolis. With 3.4 million inhabitants, New York City was by far the largest metropolis, followed by Chicago with 1.7 million, Philadelphia with 1.3 million, and Saint Louis, Boston, and Baltimore each having between 500,000 and 600,000 residents. Los Angeles ranked thirty-sixth in the nation with a population of 102,000. It was approximately the same size as Fall River, Massachusetts, and Scranton, Pennsylvania, and it was less than half as populous as Jersey City. Miami was a remote village in the swamps with fewer than 1,700 inhabitants, and the obscure desert outpost of Phoenix could claim only 5,500 souls. At the turn of the century, the Northeast, comprising the Atlantic seaboard region north of the Potomac River, together with the Midwest, accounted for 86 percent of all Americans living in cities of 25,000 or more. Outside of the northeastern quadrant of the nation, one found few cities and only a small proportion of America's urban dwellers.

This was largely because the industrial, commercial, and transportation foundations that underlay urban growth were firmly rooted in the Northeast and Midwest but either nonexistent or shaky in the South and West. People congregated where they could make money, and nowhere were the opportunities for advancement so great as in the Northeast and Midwest. Here were the industries that attracted millions of immigrants in search of jobs. Here were the transportation facilities capable of distributing the wealth of the nation. Consequently, here too were the greatest cities.

The preeminence of the Northeast and Midwest was especially evident in manufacturing. The area stretching from Pennsylvania to Illinois was the chief source of coal in the United States, and the upper Great Lakes region was the principal supplier of iron ore. With excellent access to both of these vital resources, Pittsburgh, Cleveland, Detroit, Chicago, and Milwaukee emerged as the leading centers of metal working and iron and steel production. Proximity to

Table 1. TWENTY LARGEST CITIES IN THE UNITED STATES, 1900

Rank	City	Population	Rank	City	Population
1	New York	3,437,202	11	Pittsburgh	321,616
2	Chicago	1,698,575	12	New Orleans	287,104
3	Philadelphia	1,293,697	13	Detroit	285,704
4	Saint Louis	575,238	14	Milwaukee	285,315
5	Boston	560,892	15	Washington	278,718
6	Baltimore	508,957	16	Newark	246,070
7	Cleveland	381,768	17	Jersey City	206,433
8	Buffalo	352,387	18	Louisville	204,731
9	San Francisco	342,782	19	Minneapolis	202,718
10	Cincinnati	325,902	20	Providence	175,597

the forests of the upper Midwest boosted Chicago and Grand Rapids to the front ranks of the furniture industry, and abundant water power contributed to New England's early lead in textile manufacturing. Located at the center of the nation's richest agricultural area, Chicago also grabbed the lion's share of meat packing and the manufacture of farm implements. New York City assumed first place in the apparel industry, but each of the major cities of the Northeast and Midwest had shops and factories that assembled ready-to-wear clothing. At the turn of the century, manufacturing was, then, heavily concentrated in the cities of the Northeast and Midwest, with the three largest centers of New York, Chicago, and Philadelphia together accounting for 22 percent of the nation's total value of manufactured products. In contrast, such future sunbelt giants as California, Texas, and Florida had little or no coal, the vital substance fueling industrial development in the late nineteenth century, and they contributed relatively little to the nation's manufacturing wealth. By 1900 the value of New York City's industrial production alone surpassed by 50 percent the combined figure for all of the former Confederate states, and Chicago and Philadelphia each boasted a larger manufacturing output than the total for the Pacific Coast states.

Transportation advantages further contributed to the economic dominance of the northeastern and midwestern cities. In 1900 the railroad reigned supreme as the chief means of transport and the Northeast and Midwest enjoyed the densest web of rail lines in the United States. Illinois and Pennsylvania led the nation in railroad mileage, each having almost twice the trackage of the much larger state of California. As the greatest railroad hub in the world, Chicago was a natural center of distribution, and it was not surprising that the mail order houses of Montgomery Ward and Sears, Roebuck maintained their headquarters there. Chicago dominated inland commerce, but New York City was queen of overseas trade. Gotham handled about half the nation's imports and exports, and the value of foreign trade at this preeminent port was almost ten times that of the entire Pacific Coast.

Not only did the South and West lack the manufacturing and transportation advantages of the East and Midwest, they also lacked the necessary customers. Dixie was an economically backward region without a pool of cash customers equal to that in the prosperous territory to the North. Mail order houses could not flourish in a land of illiterate sharecroppers who could not read the catalog or pay for the watches and shoes advertised in its pages. Nor were farm implement manufacturers likely to prosper in a region where human hands remained the chief tools of agriculture. Although wealthier than the South, the West was sparsely populated and those cities that did exist west of the Rockies were too far removed from the nation's principal markets to compete effectively with the more favorably located cities east of the Mississippi. Urban centers in the remote West could not match their midwestern or northeastern counterparts in any contest for a share of the national market, and the poor South's regional market as yet nurtured relatively little trade or industry.

In the Northeast and Midwest, however, urban development was far advanced by the close of the nineteenth century, and the manufacturing belt stretching from Boston to Milwaukee had spawned one city after another. Yet there was no megalopolis with urban areas sprawling outward and flowing into one another. Instead, early-twentieth-century American cities were concentrated hubs, and no one had any problem determining the respective boundaries of Washington and Baltimore or where Boston ended and Providence began. The chief means of transportation within the city was the streetcar, and consequently the overwhelming majority of residents were confined to the area covered by the web of streetcar lines. Some of the wealthy traveled on commuter railroads to homes beyond the last streetcar stop. But for the average urban dweller the cost of these long commutes was prohibitive. The poorest urbanites could not even afford frequent streetcar trips and thus most often lived in the crowded core within walking distance of their jobs. In the 1890s Boston had pioneered underground transportation, and during the first decade of the twentieth century, New York City and Philadelphia opened their first subway lines. Faster than the surface cars, subway trains permitted more people to move farther from the heart of the city. By the standards of the late twentieth century, however, the typical American metropolis was a compact hub from which few city workers wandered far.

Overcrowding and congestion were, in fact, perceived as among the principal problems of the turn-of-the-century city. Teeming slums troubled the national conscience, and nowhere were the urban poor so tightly packed as the Lower East Side of Manhattan, the first American home of thousands of European immigrants. Every northeastern and midwestern city attracted a polyglot array of newcomers from abroad, but New York surpassed them all; in 1900, 37 percent of its population was foreign-born, and it was home to more Italians, Irish, Germans, and Russian Jews than any other city in the nation. On the Lower East Side this diverse mass of humanity crowded into notorious tenements. One ward in that area housed an average of 700 people per acre, most of them in five- or six-story buildings which covered 80 to 90 percent of their narrow lots. Most rooms lacked windows or adequate ventilation and exposés of tenement plumbing made ample use of such words as slime and stench. In the minds of many native-born Americans such living conditions seemed hardly conducive to proper assimilation or Americanization. Such neighborhoods would supposedly breed social ills that might threaten the American way of life. Other cities were not so crowded as New York, but in Chicago, Philadelphia, and elsewhere many middle-class observers were appalled by the living conditions of the poor newcomers.

Congestion also plagued the central business districts. The streetcar lines converged on downtown, making it the most accessible area in the city and the best place to locate a business seeking to serve customers and clients from throughout the metropolis. Consequently, stores and offices crowded in the core, driving the price of land so high that only skyscrapers could provide an adequate return on the owner's investment. These tall buildings, however, transformed streets into dark canyons and their thousands of workers flooded the sidewalks and streetcars at rush hour. When plans for a 909-foot skyscraper were disclosed in 1908, one concerned citizen complained to the *New York Times* that the armies of people doing business in such a structure would engulf downtown streets. "To accommodate such a crowd, the people would have to walk in three layers, one above the other," he argued, "while the roadways would not hold the delivery wagons, automobiles, and carriages of people going to the structures." That same year the distinguished architecture critic Montgomery Schuyler concluded in the pages of *Architectural Record:* "It is abundantly evident that something just has to be done about the skyscrapers if our cities are to remain, or to re-become habitable." Yet six years later in lower Manhattan construction began on the world's largest office building, a mammoth structure described as a "city within a city" capable of accommodating 10,000 to 15,000 workers.

An increasing number of middle-class reformers sought to remedy the conditions of the congested city. During the first two decades of the century, Lawrence Veiller led the crusade against the evils of overcrowded tenements and secured state legislation that required builders of new tenements to ensure more light and air for tenants as well as provide safer fire escapes and a private toilet for each apartment. In Chicago the City Homes Association emulated Veiller's efforts and also proved successful in obtaining tougher building and safety codes. Moreover, in each of the largest cities philanthropic builders were constructing limited-dividend model tenements offering higher-grade housing for the poor than that provided by profit-hungry developers. Yet the relatively few model structures erected brought relief to only a small minority of the lower class, and overworked or corrupt inspectors were not always able or willing to enforce the laws and ordinances sponsored by Veiller and his ilk.

Meanwhile, many middle-class reformers regarded the settlement house as a solution to the problem of city slums and as a means of closing the social gap between the comfortable and the poor, the native-born and the immigrant. Settlement houses were community centers in slum neighborhoods, offering recreational and educational opportunities otherwise not available in such districts. For example, Hull House in Chicago, directed by Jane Addams, maintained a kindergarten, offered meeting space for social clubs and labor groups, organized classes on such practical matters as cooking and sewing as well as discussion groups on Dante and Browning, and provided a coffeehouse and a gymnasium as wholesome alternatives to the neighborhood saloon. The staff of middle-class men and women lived in the settlement house and thus came into contact with the poor who took advantage of its programs. This mingling of the middle and working classes was expected to enlighten the affluent, uplift the deprived, and generally bridge the social chasm dividing urban America.

The crusade for better housing and the settlement house were only two of the many reform initiatives aimed at improving the early-twentieth-century city. Devotees of the playground movement sought to create open spaces for recreation in the crowded cities, believing that these playgrounds would help build both the bodies and character of urban youths. Public health reformers not only fought for improved medical care for the poor but expressed an unfailing belief in the need for more fresh air and sunshine and a reprieve from the pall of smoke suffocating urban areas. Advocates of the city-beautiful movement were troubled less by the city slums and more by the disorder and ugliness of the central business district. They dreamed of opening up the city with broad boulevards, plazas, and civic centers and of imposing a uniform cornice line, thereby eliminating the jagged skyline of the skyscraper-plagued metropolis. In the minds of an increasing number of Americans, city planning was a panacea for the physical ills of the city. In 1909 believers in planning held their first national conference, and the first textbook on the subject appeared that same year.

In every major city during the first two decades of the century, Americans were calling for change. Virtually everyone seemed to view the city as a problem. Urban America not only appeared to suffer from crowding, ugliness, and class conflict but also from political corruption, vice, and the effects of alcohol abuse. Newspapers carried stories of bribed politicians, preachers pronounced damnation on the swarms of urban prostitutes, and parents feared the impact of the city saloons on their sons and daughters. In the late nineteenth century, many commentators had claimed that urbanization was undermining the vitality of the human race and seriously threatening the health and character of future generations. During the early twentieth century, fewer observers regarded the city with such pessimism but still the focus was on urban faults. Some better form of human settlement seemed necessary.

Many Americans believed that the suburbs offered this better form. In his study *The Growth of Cities in the Nineteenth Century*, published in 1899, Adna Weber expressed the emerging belief in the advantages of dispersed settlement along the urban fringes. "The 'rise of the suburbs,'" Weber observed, "furnishes the solid basis of a hope that the evils of city life, so far as they result from overcrowding, may be in large part removed." The suburbs offered "a modified concentration" of population and "the advantages of both city and country life." As streetcar lines extended outward and electric interurban railroads began to offer cheaper, more frequent commuter service, the deconcentration of the metropolitan population appeared to be a definite possibility. And those troubled by the existing city found it a most appealing possibility.

During the late nineteenth century, suburban communities had developed around outlying commuter rail stations, but in the first two decades of the twentieth century suburbia grew even more alluring and attracted an increasing number of residents. In 1910 the federal census bureau recognized that urban Americans were moving beyond central-city boundaries and for the first time attempted to define metropolitan districts and record the combined population of each major city and its suburbs. "It is a familiar fact that, in some cases, the municipal boundaries give only an inadequate idea of the population grouped about one urban center," the census bureau explained, "and as regards the large cities in very few cases do these boundaries exactly define the urban area." Thus the federal government's statisticians were giving official notice that suburbia existed and that henceforth it was necessary to consider fringe areas beyond the city limits as increasingly significant elements of the metropolitan whole.

As yet central cities considerably overshadowed their suburbs, with the fringe areas accounting for only 23 percent of the population of the nation's twenty-five largest metropolitan districts. In some areas the outlying share was considerably smaller with the periphery contributing less than 10 percent of the metropolitan population of Cleveland, Minneapolis–Saint Paul, Detroit, and Milwaukee. But during the second decade of the twentieth century a growing body of real estate developers was buying suburban tracts and drafting the blueprints for ideal communities to house upper-middle-class Americans seeking a residential refuge from the city. Outside of Cleveland the Van Sweringen brothers were planning Shaker Heights; to the south in Columbus King Thompson was laying out Upper Arlington; farther west Kansas City's J. C. Nichols was creating his

Country Club district, including his Mission Hills subdivision beyond the municipal limits in adjacent Kansas. Suburbanization did not yet appear to threaten seriously the central cities, but smart investors realized that land on the periphery could prove a gold mine.

One metropolitan area already seemed to offer a vision of the decentralized future. That was Los Angeles, a booming metropolis where dispersion was the norm. The outward thrust of population in southern California was in part owing to Henry Huntington's Pacific Electric Railway, which offered a web of interurban lines that rapidly conveyed passengers miles from the city center. As early as 1905 the Huntington system operated nearly 500 miles of track, and at its peak it could boast of 1,164 miles of lines reaching into four counties. Along these lines Huntington and other real estate entrepreneurs laid out residential subdivisions where southern Californians could realize their dream of a single-family home. According to proud Californians, in Los Angeles even a family of modest means could enjoy the benefits of a modest bungalow and yard. In a 1916 issue of *Sunset* magazine, a Los Angeles booster contrasted working-class housing in southern California with the typical tenements of eastern cities, which she characterized as "dingy, crowded, devoid of fresh air and sunshine, ill-smelling, unhealthful." "Go north, go south, go east, go west, or to any point between on both urban and interurban lines," this enthusiast wrote of Los Angeles, "and just inside the city limits or outside up to the ten-cent limit, you will find climbing the hillsides, slipping along the valley, stretching across the plain until they join fields still planted in grain, street after street of cozy homes—miles and miles of homes for one man and his family. These are the tenements of Los Angeles."

With its unparalleled network of electric railroads, Los Angeles was, then, a sprawling metropolis, affording residents a degree of elbow room unknown in the older, more congested hubs of the East. Between 1900 and 1920 the city's area grew from 43 square miles to 364 square miles. By the latter date Los Angeles had the largest area of any city in the United States, though in population it ranked only tenth in the nation. Moreover, despite the city's success in annexing vast tracts, the number of independent suburban municipalities increased markedly, with thirty communities in Los Angeles County incorporating between 1903 and 1917. Thus seven miles north of the center of Los Angeles, Glendale opted for incorporation as a separate municipality in 1906, as did nearby Burbank in 1911, and the soon-to-be-famous suburb of Beverly Hills in 1914. Into these and a score of other outlying communities the expansive population of Los Angeles was flowing.

Reinforcing this dispersed pattern of metropolitan settlement was the growing popularity of the automobile. Southern Californians became devotees of the automobile earlier than most Americans, and by 1915 Los Angeles had one automobile for every 8.2 residents as compared with a national average of one for every 43.1 persons and Chicago's figure of one for every 61.0 inhabitants. Like the electric railways, the Model T Ford enhanced the mobility of southern Californians and freed them from the necessity of living close to the urban core. At the beginning of the century, Los Angeles boosters also claimed that their hometown had a higher ratio of telephones to the population than any other area in the world, and in 1905 one writer called it the "auto-phone" city. It was a city where people no longer had to congregate in order to communicate person-to-person or needed to cluster within a short streetcar ride of one another. Los Angeles was embracing the modern technology of the automobile and the telephone, both devices that enabled people to live apart but remain in contact with one another. As the preeminent auto-phone city in the world, Los Angeles could, then, sprawl across the valleys and hills with abandon.

Not only was the southern California metropolis anticipating the suburban age to come, its rapid growth was a sign that the South and West were beginning to catch up with the Northeast and Midwest in the race for urban prominence. During the first two decades of the century, the population of Los Angeles rose from 102,000 to 577,000, the fastest rate of increase of any American city of 100,000 or more inhabitants. Moreover, the population of neighboring Long Beach soared from 2,000 to 56,000 and the number of San Diego residents grew from 18,000 to 74,000. Clearly southern California was booming and Los Angeles was the destination for thousands of migrants from the East. By 1920 it had already surpassed such industrial hubs as Buffalo and Milwaukee and it was almost as large as Pittsburgh, the nation's perennial steel capital.

Los Angeles's success, however, was built on a foundation quite different from that of Pittsburgh. Sunshine rather than steel girded its growth, and oil rather than coal fired its economy. For decades the Los Angeles Chamber of Commerce had trumpeted the glories of its Mediterranean climate, blue skies, and beautiful scenery. Many first came to Los Angeles as tourists but the sunshine and warmth convinced them to become residents. Early movie producers found the sunny climate especially appealing since it enabled them to shoot outdoor scenes year-round, something that was impossible in often cloudy and frigid New York. Others were making money from the oil deposits that underlay the Los Angeles basin. By 1919 California ranked first among the states in number of barrels of oil pumped, and petroleum refining together with tourism and movie production were among Los Angeles's leading industries.

Sunshine and oil were a fortuitous combination for a twentieth-century city. In the new century oil rather than coal was to fuel economic growth and such amenities as climate were to assume new significance in a nation that was becoming increasingly leisure-oriented. Cities in California, Texas, and Florida that possessed one or both of these commodities were to be the urban dynamos of the century. With its overcast skies and sooty coal, an urban hub like Pittsburgh was doomed to fall behind.

Los Angeles was, then, a city pointing to the future. It was pioneering a pattern of dispersed settlement that was to become increasingly commonplace. Moreover, it was the first of the sunbelt urban centers to enter the top ranks of the nation's cities. Twentieth-century American urban development was basically to be a process of "Los Angelesization." Those cities that enjoyed the same assets as the California metropolis were to grow the fastest and prosper the most. And metropolitan areas throughout the nation were to come to look increasingly like Los Angeles.

CHANGING FORTUNES, 1920–1945

From the close of World War I to the end of World War II the pace of urbanization in the South and West accelerated. During the 1920s the five metropolitan areas with the highest rate of population increase in the nation were Miami, Los Angeles, Oklahoma City, Houston, and San Diego, all centers of oil or sunshine. Eighteen of the twenty-five fastest growing metropolises of the decade were in the states of the former Confederacy plus Oklahoma and California. During the 1930s the top three in terms of population increase were Corpus Christi, Texas, Miami, and Houston, and twenty-two of the leading twenty-five were in the Confederacy or California. In addition, by 1940 the city of Los Angeles had more than 1.5 million inhabitants and ranked fifth in the nation, surpassed only by New York, Chicago, Philadelphia, and Detroit. The term *sunbelt* was not coined until the 1960s, but already signs of phenomenal urban growth were all too apparent along the nation's southern rim.

Nowhere was the growth so extravagant as in Miami. With its population soaring from less than 30,000 in 1920 to over 110,000 in 1930 and 172,000 ten years later, this tropical boomtown was an overnight sensation. During the Florida land boom of the early 1920s Miami was the "Magic City," where tracts of swampland skyrocketed in value. Normally sober souls became infected with what one journalist called the "Florida boom bacilli" and invested their hard-earned savings in real estate schemes. Real estate developers huckstered their wares on page after page of the *Miami Herald,* so that by 1925 that newspaper printed more columns of advertising than any other in the nation, including the dailies in giant New York and Chicago. That same year the *Nation* magazine described "mighty Miami" as a city whose population was rising so rapidly that it would "take two federal censuses to count it" and whose wealth was "increasing at such a rate that depositors in its banks ha[d] to stand in line as long as one does to obtain a ticket to the world's championship baseball series."

Other cities along America's southern fringe were also worthy of such hyperbole. In 1923 alone, Los Angeles builders constructed 400 new factories, 800 mercantile buildings, 130 schools, and 60 hotels, as well as 700 apartment buildings and 25,000 other residential structures. As in Miami, land prices soared, and again in the boom year of 1923 more than 18 square miles were subdivided in the city of Los Angeles, an expanse equal to 40 percent of the area of San Francisco. By 1925 an author in *Outlook* magazine was referring to Los Angeles as "the magic mecca of Southern California," whose development had been "extraordinary, incredible, magical." Three years later a commentator in *Harper's* wrote of Los Angeles's "mushroom growth, its sprawling hugeness, its madcap speed, its splurge of lights and noise and color and money." According to this observer, "Suburbs where retiring people once settled quietly to raise lemons or squabs are now small replicas of the metropolis."

The breakneck pace of Houston's development was only slightly less impressive. With 292,000 inhabitants in 1930, it was the second largest city in the former Confederacy, surpassed only by the traditional urban leader in the South, New Orleans. Boosters labeled the Texas city the "little New York of the South" and during the 1930s some of its citizenry expressed their pride as well as a considerable degree of exaggeration when they tagged Houston "the city depression missed." The city did not escape hard times after the crash of 1929 but it did rebound handsomely and deserved yet another popular sobriquet, the "oil capital of the world."

World War II brought unprecedented growth to still other emerging urban centers in the South and West. The federal government pursued a conscious policy of dispersing defense industries throughout the nation, and this meant new industry in areas where little had existed before. In fact, federal agencies charged with procuring aircraft and ships awarded more than half their contracts to businesses located west of the Mississippi River, and some little-known desert towns attracted thousands of industrial workers. For example, at peak production Consolidated Vultee Aircraft Corporation employed over 6,000 workers in Tucson. Meanwhile, Goodyear Aircraft and Alcoa both opened plants in Phoenix, and in Las Vegas, a town of only 8,000 residents in 1940, a government magnesium plant maintained a payroll of 13,000 employees during the war years.

For aircraft contractors and military decisionmakers, the region's sunshine and warm climate were major assets. The cloudless skies of the arid Southwest made it ideal for training pilots and testing airplanes. Thus by 1942 six air bases clustered around Phoenix; El Paso, Albuquerque, Tucson, Las Vegas, and Reno also attracted air training fields. Sunny southern California established itself as the center of aircraft manufacturing with over 200,000 local workers engaged in the industry. Although it accounted for only 2.5 percent of the American population, the Los Angeles area produced 10 percent of the nation's defense matériel and Californians assembled one-fifth of all airplanes built in the United States during World War II.

Cities in the Northeast and Midwest also shared in the defense bounty of World War II, but during the previous two decades many of these older hubs had not seemed as dynamic as their sunnier counterparts in the South and West. The thriving midwestern automotive centers of Detroit, Flint, and South Bend were among the fastest growing metropolitan areas of the 1920s, but twenty of the twenty-five districts with the most sluggish population growth were also in the Midwest and Northeast. New England especially appeared to have passed its prime with four of Massachusetts's nine cities of over 100,000 inhabitants actually losing population during the prosperous decade.

The figures for the depressed 1930s were even worse. The central cities of Philadelphia, Cleveland, Saint Louis, and Boston each recorded a humiliating drop in population, and all but one of the thirty-one cities over 100,000 inhabitants that lost population were located in the Northeast or Midwest. Again the statistics for urban New England were gloomy, but during the 1930s stagnation spread westward and the once-flourishing industrial hubs of Akron, Toledo, Flint, and Grand Rapids suffered losses.

Some of this decline was due to the inability of the older central cities to annex additional territory as they became surrounded by suburban municipalities. Philadelphia's municipal limits had not changed since the 1850s and Saint Louis had not absorbed any new territory since the 1870s. Yet even the data for metropolitan areas, including both central city and suburbs, showed that the urban Northeast and Midwest was not advancing at the pace of the South and West. The national average for population increase in metropolitan areas was 9.3 percent, but sixty-five of the seventy-nine metropolitan areas in the Northeast and Midwest either grew at a slower pace or, in the case of seven districts, actually lost population. The number of inhabitants in the Boston, Cleveland, and Philadelphia metropolitan districts inched upward less than 2 percent.

Opportunity clearly seemed to be shifting to the South and West, leaving behind the aging centers of the nation's northeastern quadrant. During the 1930s the number of industrial wage earners in the nation dropped 6 percent and the hard-pressed industrial areas of Akron, Toledo, and Albany-Schenectady-Troy recorded a decline of approximately 40 percent. Yet in the Los Angeles area there were 25 percent more wage earners in 1939 than in 1929 as the California metropolis showed remarkable resiliency in the face of a sluggish national economy. Elsewhere along the nation's southern rim the Depression's wounds also healed relatively quickly. By 1935 ten new hotels were under construction in Miami Beach, joined by forty additional hostelries the following year. In 1937 Houston stood fifth in the nation in building activity, though it probably ranked only twenty-second or twenty-third in population.

These were ominous facts for the chambers of commerce and business leaders of the metropolises of the Northeast and Midwest. In the eyes of too many Americans, Saint Louis, Cleveland, and New York appeared older and dingier, and in the urban core decay had supplanted dynamism. By the late

1930s and early 1940s warnings of urban decline were appearing in the columns of newspapers, the speeches of mayors, and the reports of civic bodies. The Saint Louis city plan commission declared the Missouri's chief metropolis was "fast becoming a decadent city" and the mayor of Boston announced that "unless prompt measures are taken the contagion will spread until virtual decay and destruction of the whole city has taken place." Meanwhile, *Forum* magazine published articles with such grim titles as "Saint Louis: A City in Decay" and "Cleveland: A City Collapses."

Urban experts diagnosed the chief ill of the city as blight. By blight these commentators meant the depreciation of property values and the spread of slums. Gray areas of empty warehouses and obsolete commercial structures appeared to be encroaching on the big-city downtowns and an increasing number of neighborhoods were slipping into decay. Within the central business districts too many theaters, hotels, and stores were being demolished to make way for parking lots, and the streets were not as crowded with shoppers as in past years. There was good reason to avoid the central cities, for heavy palls of smoke engulfed these areas, especially during the winter when every furnace was burning sooty bituminous coal. In the particularly dirty cities of Pittsburgh, Saint Louis, and Cincinnati, the smoke was so thick on the worst days that residents could not see across the major streets. Sunshine and new construction seemed to characterize Miami and Los Angeles. By contrast, the venerable hubs of the Northeast and Midwest were acquiring an unfavorable image as cities of smoke and slums.

Responding to these ills, an increasing number of urban leaders called for vigorous government action. As early as 1929, the social critic Stuart Chase argued in the pages of *Harper's* that "a perfectly ruthless civic will must operate" if great cities were to be redeemed. "Tear down a square mile here, a square mile there," wrote Chase. "Obliterate this reeking slum. Double the width of this street; abandon and build on that one." A decade later this bulldozer prescription for aging hubs was attracting many more adherents. By the beginning of the 1940s, in one city after another there were downtown associations, planning groups, committees on blight, and forums on urban reconstruction, all calling for major government programs of demolition and rebuilding.

These groups won some legislative victories. In 1941 the New York, Illinois, and Michigan legislatures each passed urban redevelopment laws offering incentives to private companies willing to rebuild the rotting urban core. The laws allowed private developers to exercise the states' power of eminent domain to condemn slum properties, and many of the state redevelopment statutes enacted during the 1940s granted private investors a tax exemption on redeveloped tracts. Yet what the states, the cities, and private developers wanted was federal aid to give an added boost to the rebuilding of urban centers. In the 1930s Congress had authorized public housing programs that entailed the clearance and redevelopment of slum areas. Big-city mayors, however, were looking for much more, and by the early 1940s they were eagerly eyeing the possibility of raiding the federal treasury and carrying home the loot necessary for local redevelopment.

Contributing to the malaise in older central cities was the growing popularity of the automobile. As thousands of motor vehicles clogged thoroughfares in urban areas throughout the nation, municipalities not only needed funds to clear slums but also to build highways and parking facilities. With the relatively narrow streets and their lack of parking, aging downtown districts especially seemed in danger of becoming obsolete if swift action were not taken. Residential neighborhoods, however, also faced the blighting effect of the exhaust fumes, noise, and safety hazards which accompanied heavy traffic. Meanwhile, the burgeoning army of motorists were angry about traffic jams at rush hour and the slow pace of stop-and-go driving on city streets. Consequently, by 1940 New York City's great highway builder Robert Moses had already begun construction of a network of limited-access parkways crisscrossing the nation's largest metropolis, and that same year Chicago's city council debated the creation of a sixty-three-mile expressway system, including four eight-lane depressed highways radiating from the central district. Similar schemes for urban freeways were beginning to appear on the drawing boards of transportation planners throughout the country.

Social planners, however, were more concerned with the central cities' poor and dependent populations. Restrictive federal immigration laws enacted in the 1920s reduced the flow of newcomers from abroad, but between 1917 and 1945 impoverished migrants from the rural South moved into the urban slums of the Northeast and Midwest at an unprecedented pace. In 1910 blacks constituted only 1.9 percent of the population of New York City, 2.0 percent of Chicago's total, and 1.2 percent of Detroit's residents. Yet because of the increased northward migration of African Americans, by 1940 the figure was 6.1 percent for New York, 8.2 percent for Chicago, and 9.2 percent for Detroit. Moreover, in the Midwest the body of poor whites moving in from the South was even larger than the number of black newcomers. Although the migrants were of different races, they shared a common poverty, and in the minds of some urban dwellers they were an added burden to the already troubled cities of the Northeast and Midwest. In 1941 one Cincinnati business leader, Walter S. Schmidt warned: "During the past decade there has been a loss of approximately 6 percent of the substantial population, which has been supplanted by negroes, migrants from the Kentucky and Tennessee mountains, and persons seeking the relief bounty of the City."

The "substantial population" that was disappearing from Cincinnati and other older central cities was largely moving to the suburbs. During the 1920s and 1930s the suburban migration accelerated as the automobile enabled more Americans to move farther from the urban core. And in the vanguard of the outward migration were members of the upper middle class who found new homes in sylvan, sheltered municipalities beyond the central-city limits. Posh suburbs laid out during the first two decades of the twentieth century attracted thousands of new homeowners during the 1920s and 1930s. Thus the population of the Van Sweringens' Shaker Heights soared from 1,616 in 1920 to 23,393 in 1940; the number of inhabitants in King Thompson's Upper Arlington rose from 620 to 5,370 during the same period; and Beverly Hills, the nation's most famous suburban municipality, went from a population of 674 in 1920 to 26,823 in 1940. South of Miami, real estate entrepreneur George Merrick founded Coral Gables in 1921 and lured buyers to his sunny suburb by boasting of its forty miles of waterfront. By 1940 Coral Gables could claim 8,294 residents, many of them living in the Mediterranean-style pseudo-haciendas that proved so popular in both Florida and California during the interwar years.

Nationwide there was ample evidence that the centrifugal movement of population was growing markedly. According to the federal census bureau, during the 1920s the nation's suburban population rose 39 percent whereas the increase for the central cities was only 19 percent. In the following decade the suburbs recorded a 17 percent rise and the central cities continued to lag behind, their combined population growing 6 percent. By 1940 almost one-third of the nation's metropolitan residents lived in suburbs and every year this share was rising.

In the typical metropolitan area scores of suburban municipalities clustered around the central cities. During the single decade of the 1930s, the number of municipalities in suburban Saint Louis County almost doubled, increasing from twenty-one to forty-one. Moreover, most of these suburbs fought vigorously to preserve their independence and thwart any designs of proponents of annexation to the central city. When confronted by a proposed consolidation of all of the municipalities in Saint Louis County with the central city of Saint Louis, county officials and suburban newspapers responded with deafening protests. One patriotic judge evoked memories of German aggression in World War I, reminding suburban voters, "We sacrificed our men and money to preserve local self-government for Belgium and France." A similar proposal for the consolidation of Milwaukee and its suburbs met with equally fervent denunciations. One outlying resident argued that "we located our home outside of Milwaukee to better our living conditions and to obtain more comforts and lower taxes," and he did "not now care to yield to some fancy schemes Milwaukee had concocted." Proposals to unite city and suburb met with repeated defeat as Americans cast their ballots in favor of a continued fragmentation of America's metropolises.

Thus an increasing number of the more affluent metropolitan citizenry no longer lived, voted, or paid taxes in the central city. This departure of the urban elite troubled some metropolitan leaders, for they feared that the urban hub might become disproportionately poor and troubled. In a typical comment from the early 1940s, Leverett S. Lyon, a spokesperson for the Chicago Association of Commerce, warned of the "withdrawal from the city of many of the brains and voices best suited to help it help itself." Suburbanization appeared to be robbing Chicago, Milwaukee, Saint Louis, and a long list of other central cities of their "best" citizens, those who could contribute the most in terms of cash and supposedly in terms of civic leadership.

Although affluent suburbs attracted the greatest attention, the outward migration of the interwar years included urbanites wearing blue collars as well as those in white. Across the country the lower middle class and working class purchased lots in subdivisions that offered fewer amenities than Shaker Heights or Beverly Hills but also imposed fewer restrictions. For example, west of Detroit the Folker Company developed the community of Garden City, where it sold "farmlets" 147 feet wide and 135 feet deep to auto workers eager to grow fruits and vegetables in their spare time. Advertised as the "Sun Parlor of Detroit," Garden City, like wealthier suburbs, boasted fresh air and blue skies, but it also had an ample share of mud and standing water since many of its streets were unpaved, uncurbed, and sewerless. In sharp contrast to the smooth asphalt drives of the high-class suburbs, a typical Garden City thoroughfare was simply graded, ditched, and spread with cinders. The Van Sweringens, Thompson, and other developers of elite subdivisions imposed tight restrictions on the buyers of lots to ensure that only tasteful and expensive dwellings adorned their communities. The Folker Company, however, was not so demanding. In Garden City some working-class purchasers avoided expensive foundations and built frame cottages on wooden posts sunk into the ground while others lived in their garages until they saved enough money to construct a house.

Chicago's western suburbs of Berwyn and Elmwood Park were one step above Garden City but bore no resemblance to Beverly Hills. Here thousands of small brick bungalows lined the streets, providing middle-income families with the pleasures of a detached dwelling and a modest yard. These pleasures clearly proved attractive to many, for during the 1920s Berwyn's population more than tripled, soaring from 14,150 to 47,027.

For the rich and the not-so-rich suburbia held a magnetic attraction. In the minds of many Americans, the belief persisted that a better alternative to the traditional congested city could be created along the metropolitan fringe. In *The Suburban Trend,* the most significant study of suburbanization published in the 1920s, Harlan Paul Douglass referred to the suburbs as "the most promising aspect of urban civilization." The congested hub was supposedly destroying civilization, leading Douglass to conclude: "A crowded world must be either suburban or savage." Like Adna Weber a quarter century earlier, Douglass and many of his contemporaries felt that the traditional city was not the answer to the problem of life in a densely populated world. Instead, the outskirts appeared the hope of future decades.

Existing suburbs, however, fell far short of the dreams of many idealists. Certainly they did not satisfy the followers of the Garden City Movement led by the British utopian Ebenezer Howard. Howard advocated the building of new self-contained communities away from the existing urban hubs. Combining the advantages of town and country, these proposed garden cities would have a full complement of shops and factories, but they would also be of limited size and encircled by green belts of fields and forests. Unlike most American suburbs, they were not designed to enrich private real estate speculators nor were they intended to contribute to the urban sprawl mindlessly engulfing the countryside. Founded in 1923, the Regional Planning Association of America embraced Howard's dream, and at the close of the 1920s some members of the association laid out the model satellite community of Radburn in northern New Jersey, seventeen miles from Manhattan. Intended to be a garden city of 25,000 population, Radburn welcomed its first residents during the inauspicious year of 1929. The ensuing economic depression forced the project into bankruptcy after only a small portion of it had been completed. Radburn's innovative plan, which emphasized the segregation of people from traffic, won numerous admirers, but during the bleak years of the early 1930s it did not spark many imitators.

With private developers hard-pressed if not bankrupt during the depression decade, those Americans who dreamed of creating suburban utopias had to turn to the federal government for financing. The result was the Roosevelt administration's Greenbelt program, headed by the idealistic Columbia University professor Rexford Tugwell. A believer in the Garden City ideal, Tugwell expressed his aims in 1935 when he wrote in his diary: "My idea is to go just outside centers of population, pick up cheap land, build a whole community and entice people into it. Then go back into the cities and tear down whole slums and make parks of them." This task proved a difficult one, and the Greenbelt program actually produced only three small towns: Greenbelt, Maryland, just north of Washington, D.C.; Greenhills, Ohio, outside of Cincinnati; and Greendale, Wisconsin, in the Milwaukee metropolitan area. Without factories or major businesses, these communities were largely commuter suburbs for the lower middle class. Yet their ample open spaces and surrounding greenbelts ensured a semirural ambience that Ebenezer Howard would have found appealing. Expressing a Garden City advocate's characteristic enthusiasm for the sylvan and verdant, John P. Schroeder, an official of the program who moved to Greendale, observed: "We are living close to nature and shall adjust ourselves to her for our benefit; we are able to recover our lost affinity to the soil." Many Americans, however, regarded the notion of government-built suburbs as communistic and the Roosevelt administration dared not build any more of its model communities. At the close of the 1930s Tugwell's plan for fashioning new towns for evacuees from the crowded inner city had been placed on hold.

For hard-headed real estate developers as well as visionary professors, suburbia thus remained a fertile field for realizing dreams. In the opinion of many

Table 2. POPULATION OF THE TEN LARGEST CITIES IN THE UNITED STATES, 1950 AND 1980

1950			1980		
Rank	City	Population	Rank	City	Population
1	New York	7,891,957	1	New York	7,071,639
2	Chicago	3,620,962	2	Chicago	3,005,072
3	Philadelphia	2,071,605	3	Los Angeles	2,966,850
4	Los Angeles	1,970,358	4	Philadelphia	1,688,210
5	Detroit	1,849,568	5	Houston	1,595,138
6	Baltimore	949,708	6	Detroit	1,203,339
7	Cleveland	914,808	7	Dallas	904,078
8	Saint Louis	856,796	8	San Diego	875,538
9	Washington	802,178	9	Phoenix	789,704
10	Boston	801,444	10	Baltimore	786,775

observers, the central cities were on the skids, and some Americans were not willing to mourn their misfortunes. The older urban centers were supposedly the unpleasant products of the explosive and rapacious industrialization of the nineteenth century, and by the interwar period it seemed that Americans might well create a better existence beyond the central-city limits. In any case, it was increasingly clear that suburbia represented the wave of the future.

THE TRIUMPH OF THE SUNBELT AND SUBURBIA, 1945–1980

During the post–World War II era, the longstanding trend toward dispersion and deconcentration produced such dramatic changes that not even the most obtuse observer could miss them. Sunbelt cities surged ahead in population growth and economic development, pushing aside the older hubs of the Northeast and Midwest. Likewise, suburbia swallowed ever larger expanses of territory and received millions of new residents who abandoned the aging central cities. The suburbs, in fact, became the American norm and not simply a fringe area accommodating the urban overflow.

Census figures recorded the changes transforming the nation. As seen in table 2, between 1950 and 1980 the central cities of the northeastern quadrant suffered sharp population losses and slipped behind in the rankings of American cities, whereas sunbelt centers joined the list of the nation's top ten urban giants. For example, Dallas more than doubled in population between 1950 and 1980 and rose from twenty-second position to seventh place. Meanwhile, San Diego absorbed more than one-half million additional residents and climbed from thirty-first place to eighth rank. Most dramatic was the rise of Phoenix from ninety-eighth position to ninth place, its population soaring from 107,000 in 1950 to 790,000 thirty years later. Meanwhile, the beleaguered central city of Cleveland lost more than one-third of its residents and plummeted from seventh to eighteenth rank; Pittsburgh's population also decreased by one-third, causing the city to fall from twelfth to thirtieth position; and Saint Louis suffered an almost 50 percent decline, dropping from eighth to twenty-sixth place. As late as 1950 the former Confederate states, together with the states west of the Rockies, accounted for only one of the nation's top ten cities. By 1980 five of the ten largest cities were in this once peripheral zone.

The figures for metropolitan areas (see table 3) reveal that the relative position of the Northeast and Midwest was not quite so grim as the central-city data seemed to indicate. Because the census bureau redefined its area, metropolitan New York appeared to lose population, but elsewhere in the nation's northeastern quadrant growth was evident. Yet again these older metropolises could not match the rapid rise of their counterparts in the South and West. Dallas–Fort Worth tripled in population and rose from fifteenth to eighth largest metropolitan area. The population of metropolitan Houston, Atlanta, and San Diego each increased threefold as well, whereas the number of inhabitants in Phoenix and its suburbs soared almost fivefold from 332,000 in 1950 to 1,509,000 in 1980. At mid-century two of the ten largest metropolitan areas were in the South and West; thirty years later these regions contained four of the top ten.

During the postwar era the urban South and West had clearly arrived, and the signs of their new

Table 3. POPULATION OF THE TEN LARGEST METROPOLITAN AREAS IN THE UNITED STATES, 1950 AND 1980

1950			1980		
Rank	Metro. Area	Population	Rank	Metro. Area	Population
1	New York	12,911,994	1	New York	9,120,346
2	Chicago	5,495,364	2	Los Angeles	7,477,503
3	Los Angeles	4,367,911	3	Chicago	7,103,624
4	Philadelphia	3,671,048	4	Philadelphia	4,716,818
5	Detroit	3,016,197	5	Detroit	4,353,413
6	Boston	2,369,986	6	San Francisco–Oakland	3,250,630
7	San Francisco–Oakland	2,240,767	7	Washington	3,060,922
8	Pittsburgh	2,213,236	8	Dallas–Fort Worth	2,974,805
9	Saint Louis	1,681,281	9	Houston	2,905,353
10	Cleveland	1,465,511	10	Boston	2,763,357

maturity were everywhere. Perhaps the ultimate symbol of the success of southern and western cities was their acquisition of major league baseball teams. In 1950 no major league teams existed west of Saint Louis or south of Washington, D.C., but in 1957 both Los Angeles and San Francisco broke the monopoly of the Northeast and Midwest by acquiring the Dodgers and the Giants. Los Angeles's mayor gloated, "Now Los Angeles is major league in every sense of the word." The *New Yorker* magazine also recognized that the arrival of the Dodgers in southern California represented a significant rite of passage for the sprawling metropolis. "It's the first time Los Angeles ever had a chance to become *anything*," a long-time resident told the eastern magazine. Baseball awarded big-league status to other southern and western cities as well, and by 1980 nine of the twenty-six teams in the National and American leagues were in the South and West. On the sports pages and in the census returns the message was the same. The metropolitan gap between the northeastern quadrant and the South and West was fast closing. Urban America no longer clustered north of the Potomac and east of the Mississippi. Big cities were as characteristic of Florida as New York, as typical of Texas as Pennsylvania.

In the postwar era, as during World War II, defense industries fueled much of the metropolitan growth in the Sunbelt. Southern California remained the hub of the aircraft industry and was in the forefront of aerospace technology. Every boost in defense spending meant thousands of new jobs for Los Angeles, and bellicose rhetoric in Moscow was sweet music to cash-conscious California entrepreneurs. Owing to the Korean War, employment in Los Angeles's aircraft industry rose from 66,000 to 167,000 between 1950 and 1953. Moreover, continuing Cold War tensions brought the figure to 213,000 by 1957. At that time the aircraft industry accounted for almost one-third of the factory workers in Los Angeles County.

Meanwhile, Arizona's emerging cities were winning many of the military contracts for electronic components. Low humidity was necessary to the manufacturing of electronics equipment and that was something the sunny, arid Southwest had in abundance. In 1948 Motorola decided to locate its military electronics operations in Phoenix, and by 1960 the company had three plants in the desert metropolis and a payroll of 5,000 workers. During the 1950s Sperry Rand's aviation electronics division joined Motorola in Phoenix, fostering further growth in Arizona's booming capital.

Sunshine and dry weather not only attracted electronics firms, they continued to draw the dollars of tourists. By the 1940s smog plagued the Los Angeles basin, calling into question the validity of the phrase "sunny California." Yet the Sunbelt did not lose its appeal for vacationers, who crowded the beaches of Florida, flocked to Phoenix, and sampled the pleasures of San Diego. In fact, the development of air conditioning and its widespread adoption in the South and West made these regions even more attractive to visitors from the Northeast and Midwest. Now one could enjoy the sunshine without being unduly bothered by the heat.

Special attractions enhanced the tourist appeal of certain burgeoning sunbelt metropolitan areas. For example, gambling spurred the phenomenal rise of Las Vegas. In 1946 mobsters Meyer Lansky and Bugsy Siegel opened the Flamingo Hotel in the Nevada desert community, and the optimistic Siegel predicted: "In ten years, this'll be the biggest gambling center in the world." Siegel proved correct, and by the close of the 1950s such lavish hotel-casinos as the Desert Inn, Sands, Sahara, and Dunes had joined the Flamingo along Las Vegas's famed Strip. Boosted by the dollars of millions of suckers, Las Vegas grew from a small town of less than 25,000 people in 1950 to a metropolitan area comprising 463,000 inhabitants thirty years later. The sunbelt city of Orlando benefited not from gambling but from the magic of Walt Disney. In 1971 Disney World opened on a forty-three-square-mile tract south of Orlando. With an area twice the size of Manhattan, the giant theme park dwarfed all competitors and by 1980 it was drawing 13.8 million visitors annually. The biggest tourist attraction on earth, Walt Disney World proved an unprecedented boon to Orlando's economy and ignited a population explosion. During the single decade of the 1970s the population of the Orlando metropolitan area soared almost 55 percent, from 453,000 to 700,000.

In Texas oil continued to be the vital tonic promoting an exhilarating urban growth. Its oil refineries, petroleum processing plants, and offices for four hundred oil and gas firms confirmed Houston's right to the title of energy capital of the United States. During the postwar era the Texas metropolis also became a major center for the petrochemical industry, its total chemical production soaring 600 percent from 1940 to the late 1960s. By the early 1980s a boasting *Texas Monthly* could confidently assert: "Houston has shoved New York aside to become the center of the international oil business."

Much of the labor at Houston's refineries, Florida's hotels, and Los Angeles factories came from Latin America. Whereas the cities of the Northeast and Midwest had been the meccas for immigrants in the nineteenth and early twentieth centuries, the Sunbelt was the new port of entry for foreigners in search of jobs. And the arrival of millions of people from Mexico and Cuba boosted the population figures of metropolitan areas all along the nation's southern rim. By 1980, 36 percent of the population of the Miami metropolitan area was foreign-born as were 22 percent of the inhabitants of greater Los Angeles. Only about 4 percent, however, were foreign-born in the once-polyglot metropolises of Pittsburgh and Milwaukee. In Cleveland and Buffalo, Poles, Italians, Hungarians, and Germans had each staked out their share of the turf seventy or eighty years earlier, but by 1980 the foreign-born constituted only 6 percent of the total population of these metropolitan areas. During the postwar era New York City continued to serve as the gateway to America for many newcomers. But for thousands of Hispanics the great urban melting pot was not Gotham or any other northern center but rather Los Angeles or Miami.

Oil was the preeminent fuel of the late twentieth century, and Houston was the oil capital; airplanes had supplanted railroads as the preferred mode of intercity transport and Los Angeles was the center of aircraft manufacturing; air conditioning had taken the discomfort out of sunshine and rendered Florida and Arizona tolerable in the summer; Latin America was the new source of immigrants and Hispanics naturally disembarked at the cities along the nation's Latin rim. A multitude of factors were all pointing to success for the sunbelt cities. Thus Miami, Phoenix, San Diego, and other southern metropolises were figuratively as well as literally taking their place in the sun. By 1980 the urban axis of America had tilted even further to the south and west, increasing the flow of people and money to regions that only fifty years earlier had been notable for their lack of big cities.

This southward and westward flow of population and commerce took its toll on the older hubs of the Northeast and Midwest. During the post–World War II era the central cities of these regions were especially hard-hit and the worst forebodings of prewar pessimists seemed to come true. Decade after decade of population losses were discouraging enough, but the accompanying departure of jobs and businesses exacerbated the sense of despair. Moreover, decaying neighborhoods and racial clashes added to central-city woes. By the 1960s politicians, journalists, and social scientists were all talking of urban crisis, and all the signs of this crisis seemed to be concentrated in the aging central cities of the nation's northeastern quadrant. Southern California suffered its share of slums and race riots, but it also had explosive population growth, the fantasy of Disneyland, the glamor of Hollywood, and the glitz of Beverly Hills. Increasingly dismal Saint Louis, Detroit, and Cleveland lacked these compensating features.

In one older central city after another the signs of decline were readily evident. Throughout the postwar era manufacturing firms moved out of obsolete multistory, inner-city plants, and from 1947 to 1967 New York City alone lost 175,000 factory jobs. Moreover, the pace of decline was accelerating, for from 1967 to 1977 Gotham registered a loss of almost 286,000 manufacturing employees, a 32 percent decrease in a single decade. Elsewhere the story was the same. From 1967 to 1977 the number of manufacturing workers in Philadelphia dropped 40 percent, in Boston the size of the industrial work force declined 36 percent, and Pittsburgh recorded a 35 percent decrease in its factory employment. Superannuated factories were not the only white elephants on the central-city real estate market. Equally obsolete were the giant downtown movie palaces that gradually closed their doors during the postwar era. By the 1970s the extravagant theaters had more gilded cupids and plaster gargoyles than live customers. People simply did not turn to downtown any longer for their recreation.

Central business district retailing also seemed on the road to extinction. Gradually the big downtown department stores were either going out of business or cutting back their floor space and personnel. When adjusted for inflation, downtown retail sales between 1967 and 1977 plummeted 48 percent in Baltimore and 44 percent in both Saint Louis and Cleveland. Downtown had too much traffic and too little parking, so fewer of the increasingly auto-borne American population were buying their clothes, furniture, and housewares in the central business district. In the auto age of the second half of the twentieth century, the downtown emporiums were anachronisms, and declining sales figures reflected this fact of metropolitan life.

Scores of new office buildings did rise in the older central cities, changing the skylines of New York, Chicago, and Pittsburgh. During the 1970s Chicago secured the honor of having the world's tallest office building when the Sears Tower opened. Meanwhile New York City's gargantuan 110-story World Trade Center also welcomed its first tenants, and every city of any size celebrated the groundbreaking of lesser skyscrapers. The central-city office sector thus survived and seemingly flourished. Yet during these same years the nation's traditional hubs of capitalism faced the loss of corporate headquarters. From 1956 to 1974 the number of Fortune 500 headquarters in New York City fell from 140 to 98, in Chicago the figure declined from 47 to 33, and in Pittsburgh from 22 to 15. Just as America's urban population was becoming more evenly dispersed throughout the nation so were its corporate offices. High-powered business decisionmakers increasingly were found in Los Angeles, Dallas, and Houston as well as numerous suburban communities. No longer were Wall Street and Park Avenue so significant in determining America's business future.

All the varied symptoms of commercial decline added up to bad news for central-city tax collectors. With property assessments increasing at a slower pace than inflation and wage-tax receipts threatened by the loss of jobs, many of the central cities of the Northeast and Midwest faced periodic fiscal crises that further damaged their already blemished reputations. For example, virtually every economic recession seemed to send New York City to the brink of fiscal debacle. Gotham's rulers fought desperately to cover deficits in the late 1950s, mid 1960s, and mid 1970s, and this last financial crisis proved especially serious. To save the city from bankruptcy in 1975, agencies of the state of New York assumed control of municipal finances, depriving the nation's greatest urban center of a large measure of its self-government. The economist Robert Zevin said of the hard-pressed city: "New York is not quite dead, but death is clearly inevitable." Just as New York City's fiscal problems were receding from the headlines, Cleveland's imminent bankruptcy began to attract national attention. In 1978 Cleveland defaulted on it debt payments, the first major municipality to suffer this embarrassment since the 1930s. During the 1970s Boston also struggled with a "financial emergency," Detroit seemed perpetually strapped for cash, and Buffalo came precariously close to following the shameful path of New York City and Cleveland to fiscal collapse.

Money problems were not the only urban woes winning ample media coverage during the postwar decades. Racial tensions and a seeming rise in the level of violence in the central cities proved an indelible blot on the image of urban America. During the late 1940s, 1950s, and early 1960s, poor blacks continued to migrate to northern cities, joined by impoverished Puerto Ricans in the Northeast and disadvantaged southern whites in the Midwest. By 1970 Newark and Washington, D.C., had black majorities, and African Americans constituted more than 40 percent of the populations of Detroit, Baltimore, and Saint Louis. The expansion of blacks into formerly white neighborhoods repeatedly sparked resentment among whites and frequently led to violence. In 1949 rioting broke out among whites in Chicago's Englewood neighborhood when rumors spread that some visiting blacks were planning to move into the district. When a black family moved into one of Chicago's all-white public housing projects in 1953, whites likewise reacted violently, and rock throwing, window breaking, and incidents of arson continued for two years. From 1945 through 1954 Chicago experienced at least nine such race-oriented riots.

During the 1960s racial conflict attracted greater attention as many inner-city blacks rebelled against the legacy of racism and especially expressed their anger at the supposedly biased behavior of the white police. For example, police incidents ignited rioting in New York City in 1964, Cleveland in 1966, and both Newark and Detroit in 1967. The Motor City disturbance proved the most costly, resulting in forty-three deaths and $50 million in property damage.

Racial conflict was only one element in the emerging equation of violence with the central city. Crime rates soared, and Detroit was becoming synonymous not only with the automobile industry but with murder. New York City was the unchallenged mugging capital of America, and seemingly every Manhattan resident could tell of the time they were robbed in the street or the subway. During the 1970s rampant arson left acres of ruins in the South Bronx, transforming this district of New York City into an internationally renowned symbol of urban decay. The booming sunbelt city of Las Vegas actually had a higher murder rate than Gotham and usually ranked first in the nation in crime. But in vibrant, flashy Las Vegas, and in other sunbelt cities as well, there was not the combination of crime and decay that proved so debilitating to the reputation of the older central cities of the Northeast and Midwest. In growth-conscious America perhaps the greatest crime of all was decline.

Urban leaders, however, did not quietly submit to this onslaught of blight and decay. Instead, they continued to pursue the course fixed in the late 1930s and early 1940s and in 1949 secured passage of federal urban redevelopment legislation. Under the 1949 law Washington would contribute two-thirds of the net cost of purchasing and clearing slum properties with local governments providing the other one-third. On the cleared land, private developers would supposedly construct handsome new apartment buildings to house decent, taxpaying citizens, as well as commercial structures providing jobs for city dwellers and revenues for municipal treasuries. Over the next quarter-century federal urban renewal produced mixed results. Some projects proved successful, offering beleaguered cities hope for a better future. Others took decades to complete, becoming objects of local derision. And still others were monumental flops, attracting too few tenants and angering too many creditors.

Perhaps more important to the reconstruction of the older central cities was the development of new highways. Milwaukee, Chicago, Cleveland, and Baltimore were streetcar cities in an automobile age. Their thoroughfares were obsolete and their leaders firmly believed that these cities needed to adapt to the new era through the construction of limited-access freeways linking downtown with the outskirts. Consequently, in the late 1940s and early 1950s Philadelphia initiated construction of the Schuylkill Expressway, Detroit laid out the John Lodge and Edsel Ford expressways, Pittsburgh's Penn-Lincoln Parkway opened to traffic, and Chicago began clearing a path for the Congress Expressway. Passage of the Federal-Aid Highway Act of 1956 stepped up the pace of freeway construction, for this measure authorized the building of an interstate highway system that was to include 5,000 miles of expressways in metropolitan areas. The federal government paid 90 percent of the cost of this highway network, with the states and localities contributing only the remaining 10 percent. Washington clearly was dedicated to the realization of expressway systems in America's urban areas and was willing to provide the all-important cash necessary to reconstruct the transportation infrastructure of outdated central cities.

By the late 1960s and early 1970s, however, urban expressway plans faced growing opposition. Like urban renewal projects, the highway programs often seemed to destroy more than they created, and an expanding army of neighborhood activists were marching on city halls to protest the prospect of bulldozers leveling their homes to make way for new freeways. Americans wanted to speed along limited-access highways, but they did not want those highways to pass through their living rooms. Moreover, evidence was mounting that urban freeways were not channeling shoppers and theater-goers into the core and thus were not contributing to the revitalization of downtown. Dissatisfied with this superhighway option, an increasing number of urban Americans supported the alternative of new or improved mass transit systems. In 1973 Congress enacted legislation permitting cities to trade their share of interstate highway money for funds to build mass-transit facilities. With this new source of cash, blueprints for expansive subway systems abounded, inspiring new hope in Buffalo, Baltimore, Detroit, and Saint Louis. In every major city there was talk of high-tech trains speeding commuters to shops and offices. Some rapid transit systems were built, and again the results were mixed. Too often costs far exceeded original estimates whereas the number of passengers fell short of expectations. More people were willing to vote for such projects than were willing to ride on the finished product. In the end, most Americans continued to prefer the comfort and convenience of their own automobiles, and they also continued to avoid driving downtown.

The brick and asphalt programs of urban renewal

and highway development not only failed to meet expectations, they also did not confront the nagging problems of the city's poorest residents. Social programs were needed to aid the growing number of slum dwellers, and in the 1960s the federal government again answered the urban call for help. In 1964 the administration of Lyndon Johnson launched a much-publicized "war on poverty"; among the weapons in this war were the Community Action and Model Cities initiatives, both aimed at empowering the urban poor to help themselves. Popularly elected representatives from slum neighborhoods were supposed to participate in the making of policy to combat poverty, and the federal government was to put up the money to implement the desired programs. Yet in many urban areas the Johnson administration initiatives produced more friction than action. Factions led by self-appointed spokespersons of the poor fought for control of the policymaking community councils, and mayors balked at the idea of shifting power to grass-roots ghetto rebels. Social democracy did not necessarily blossom amid the ruins of the decaying cities, and by the beginning of the 1970s enthusiasm for social reform in the slums had waned. Some defended Community Action and Model Cities, but no one seriously argued that the war on poverty ended in unconditional victory.

In any case, by the early 1970s a majority of Americans lived far from the urban core and inner-city poverty was only something they read about in the newspapers or saw on an occasional television news special. Migration to the suburbs continued unabated during the postwar decades, resulting in the further segregation of America's metropolitan population. The comfortable and affluent increasingly inhabited the suburban rings, and many of them rarely left this fringe area. They shopped there, and a good proportion of suburbanites worked along the periphery as well. The problems of the inner city were not part of their lives; they were residents of a new city beyond the boundaries of the troubled core.

Every decade saw a rise in the suburban population until in 1970 the number of suburbanites actually surpassed the number of people living in America's central cities. That year 54 percent of the nation's metropolitan population resided beyond the central-city limits; central cities accounted for only 46 percent of the total. According to a 1975 estimate, suburbanites constituted more than three-fourths of the population of the Washington, Boston, Pittsburgh, and Saint Louis metropolitan areas. The suburban growth rate was especially marked in the late 1940s and the 1950s with the nation's fringe population rising 48.5 percent during this latter decade. Millions of tract houses went up in former pastures and meadows, offering city dwellers the opportunity to partake finally in the suburban dream.

The most famous of the postwar suburban developers were the Levitt brothers. In 1947 they launched their first Levittown, a community of Cape Cod cottages in Hempstead, Long Island, just twenty-nine miles from Manhattan. To encourage home ownership, the federal government guaranteed long-term, low-interest mortgages, and thus refugees from the crowded city were able to purchase a Levitt-produced home for as little as $90 down and $58 per month. The Levitts could construct 150 of the look-alike houses each week, mass-producing them at the rate of one every sixteen minutes. But even at this pace they could hardly keep up with the demand. In 1952 they founded a second Levittown, this one in Bucks County, Pennsylvania, north of Philadelphia. Then in 1958 a third Levittown of 10,000 houses arose to the east of the City of Brotherly Love in Burlington County, New Jersey.

Even more noteworthy than the residential development in suburbia was the growth in retailing along the metropolitan fringe. Before World War II suburbanites bought their groceries and drugs in neighborhood stores, but for most other purchases they continued to trek downtown. A survey of Shaker Heights, Ohio, households in the 1930s found that more than 50 percent of the respondents shopped at the downtown Cleveland department stores at least once a week. During the 1920s Kansas City's J. C. Nichols had created the first auto-oriented outlying shopping center, Country Club Plaza. Yet Nichols's retailing center spawned relatively few imitators prior to the 1940s. In the postwar era, however, the shopping center set amid a sea of parking lots became a ubiquitous feature of suburbia. In 1955 there were 1,000 shopping centers in the United States, two years later the number had risen to 2,000, and by the 1970s a trade directory listed almost 19,000.

In 1956 Southdale Center outside of Minneapolis inaugurated a new era in retailing, for Southdale was the first completely enclosed shopping mall. During the following two decades huge enclosed malls anchored by major department stores appeared in metropolitan areas throughout the country. Soon after its opening in 1971, Woodfield Mall in the Chicago suburb of Schaumburg was claiming to be the "world's largest shopping center under one roof." With 220 stores on three levels, it attracted busloads of shoppers from as far away as Ohio, and in 1976 the *Chicago Tribune* called it "the Super Bowl of retailing." Southern California's South Coast Plaza challenged Woodfield's claim to supremacy. Opened in the early 1970s, South Coast could boast eight department stores, three hundred shops, and more sales than any other mall in America. Millions of shoppers strolled through South Coast Plaza, Woodfield, and similar suburban malls each weekend. By 1980 retailing was primarily a suburban pursuit and relatively few shoppers still headed downtown.

Factories were also becoming more characteristic of the suburbs than the central city. In the postwar era most manufacturers preferred sprawling single-level plants for their assembly-line operations as well as ample loading space for the growing number of trucks and expansive parking lots for the convenience of their auto-borne employees. Thus they needed large, open tracts of land along the metropolitan fringe instead of congested central-city sites. Throughout the postwar era the migration of manufacturing to the suburbs continued. Between 1947 and 1954 Detroit's suburbs experienced a 220 percent rise in the number of factories, and during this same period the inventory of manufacturing plants in suburban Chicago doubled. In metropolitan areas across the nation, suburbs gained from the industrial obsolescence of the central cities. Between 1958 and 1963 manufacturing employment fell 11 percent in Philadelphia but rose 19 percent in its suburban counties, declined 6 percent in New York City but climbed 14 percent in Gotham's suburbs, dropped 9 percent in Saint Louis but increased 9 percent in the city's environs.

Not only were factory jobs migrating to suburbia, so was a share of the nation's office employment. The office sector remained vital in the central cities, yet in the 1960s and 1970s there were signs that the metropolitan fringe was even capturing a growing proportion of America's stenographers, clerks, and executives. For example, in 1959 the city council of the Saint Louis suburb of Clayton repealed its five-story limit on building height, and within the next decade ten- and twenty-story towers transformed the community into an office center rivaling the downtowns of many larger cities. By 1966 the *St. Louis Post Dispatch* could report that Clayton's skyline "no longer blended into the county's amorphous urban sprawl, but now appeared more like a little Tulsa or perhaps an Omaha, than just another incorporated outskirt of St. Louis." In 1975 for the first time the level of office construction in the nation's suburbs exceeded that in the central cities. Moreover, this was not a momentary aberration. By the end of the 1970s many more Claytons were springing up in outlying areas, challenging the outdated stereotype of suburbia as a quiet residential haven.

In fact, during the three decades following World War II Americans transformed suburbia. No longer was it merely an anteroom housing the excess population of the central city. It was the focus of shopping, living, and employment. Urban geographers estimated that in 1973 suburbia first surpassed the central cities in number of jobs. The pattern of dispersion evident throughout the twentieth century had resulted in metropolises where the central cities no longer dominated the local economy.

BEYOND CITY AND SUBURB, SINCE 1980

During the last decades of the twentieth century older central cities showed some signs of vitality that brought cheer to the hearts of their boosters. Festival marketplaces in Boston and Baltimore attracted throngs of happy consumers to the central business district as did new multilevel downtown shopping malls in Philadelphia, Milwaukee, and Saint Louis. Downtown skyscraper construction boomed throughout the 1980s, adding gleaming high-rises to every major skyline. Cities built gigantic new convention centers or expanded their old ones, and spendthrift conventioneers contributed their cash to the tills of shops and restaurants in the central business districts. Glitzy Hyatt hotels were the symbol of the seeming upturn in urban fortunes. They announced to passersby that people were coming downtown, having fun there, and spending money.

Especially in the 1980s the prevailing outlook was rosy and the rhetoric upbeat. Some inner-city neighborhoods were becoming fashionable again, and there were actually growing fears that gentrifying yuppies might displace some of the central-city poor. Mayors were proclaiming their cities as comeback miracles and some pedants declared that the urban crisis was over. Cleveland did not look or feel quite so down-at-the-heels, Detroit leaders put on a happy face despite the persistent slide of their city's fortunes, and lucky Pittsburgh claimed to be in the midst of its second postwar renaissance. In fact, "renaissance" was the urban cliché of the decade. It was the word on every mayor's lips and on every page of the optimistic prose issuing from chamber of commerce offices.

By the early 1990s, however, economic recession and a sobering second look at urban problems stilled much of the hype. Both New York City and Philadelphia suffered new fiscal crises and faced renewed threats of higher taxes and reduced services. Well-publicized crimes of violence in New York City also aroused past misgivings about the quality of life in the nation's largest metropolis. In 1990 *Time* magazine printed a cover story titled "The Decline of New York" in which it reported on "the rotting of the Big Apple." That same year *New York* magazine prepared a special issue on "How to Save New York," and the media in general fell upon the stricken city, exposing its manifold faults. At the beginning of the 1990s, the urban expert George Sternlieb expressed the grimmer outlook that was reemerging when he observed in the *New York Times:* "There was a momentary euphoria in downtown monument building in the 1980s, but those monuments are beginning to look like tombstones surrounded by the old crumbling cities." For a half-century the aged central cities had been on an emotional roller coaster, with sharp descents of despair followed by periodic ascents of optimism. The early 1990s appeared to be one of the down slopes.

At the close of the twentieth century, however, the changing fortunes of the central city seemed of peripheral significance to the nation as a whole. The urban hubs simply did not matter as much as they had eighty or ninety years earlier. In the 1980s and 1990s, as in the 1960s and 1970s, the real news was taking place along the metropolitan fringe. The migration of business to outlying areas was creating what were variously called postsuburban cities, urban villages, or technoburbs. They were such a new phenomenon that no one could agree what to call them. Yet everyone agreed that they existed. They were suburban business centers that, in many cases, had developed around a giant regional shopping mall. Like central-city downtowns they boasted high-rise office buildings and luxury hotels, yet they were less compact than the traditional central business districts. They were built for the automobile, and the sidewalks that existed in the office parks or on the hotel grounds were for the sole purpose of linking the buildings to the parking lots. Walking was simply a means of getting to one's car. Most of these suburban downtowns developed around freeway interchanges where there was auto access to a maximum number of people within the metropolitan area. These business hubs were, then, the ultimate adaptation of metropolitan America to the automobile.

These suburban downtowns were developing in every major metropolitan area during the late twentieth century. By 1988 the *Washington Post* was able to identify thirteen such commercial centers in the environs of the nation's capital. Perhaps the most notable of these was Tysons in northern Virginia. Using the "traditional measures of a downtown—jobs, office space, and shopping," the *Post* concluded that Tysons was "bigger than Miami." Meanwhile, the Atlanta metropolitan area also boasted at least a half dozen such downtowns that rivaled or surpassed the city's central business district. The Perimeter Center commercial zone sprawled outward from the interchange of I-285 and Georgia 400 in the northern suburbs. In 1988 it already contained 16 million square feet of commercial office space, as compared with downtown Atlanta's 13 million square feet. Moreover, it was one of the region's most popular shopping areas. A resident of the prestigious northern Atlanta suburb of Dunwoody told a *Los Angeles Times* reporter: "I haven't gone downtown by choice in the past seven years. Perimeter Center has everything I used to have to go downtown . . . for." With two large shopping malls near the intersection of I-285 and I-75, the Cumberland-Galleria area was yet another suburban downtown serving the Georgia metropolis. It recorded $547 million in retail sales in 1982, as compared with only $246 million in Atlanta's central business district, and by the late 1980s Cumberland-Galleria also had 14 million square feet of commercial office space.

In Washington, Atlanta, and other metropolises as well there was no longer any one dominant center. Instead, the typical American metropolis was developing multiple nuclei, most of them scattered around the outer ring of settlement. Metropolitan America was increasingly an amorphous sprawl without a single focus. Freeways were the arteries of life and commerce but there was no heart.

This was especially true in the growing number of metropolitan areas that had nothing resembling a central city. Most of these were counties once classified by the census bureau as suburban but that had escaped from the orbit of an older central city and had become identified as independent metropolises. According to the census bureau, Nassau and Suffolk counties on Long Island made up a separate metropolitan area by the 1980s and were no longer simply a collection of bedroom communities for New York City commuters. In 1990 Nassau-Suffolk was the nation's tenth largest metropolitan area, with over 2.6 million inhabitants, yet as its name implied it included no central city or single dominant hub. It was an almost continuous stream of population served by a multitude of shopping centers hugging the highways. Likewise, in 1990 Orange County, California, was the nation's sixteenth largest metropolitan area with 2.4 million people. Although the census bureau designated it the Anaheim–Santa Ana–Garden Grove metropolitan area, the county actually contained seven municipalities with over 100,000 population, none of them the preeminent focus for metropolitan life in the region. Census officials applied the hyphenated name simply for lack of a better alternative. With their housing and commerce dispersed across hundreds of square miles, such hyphenated metropolises defied traditional notions of the city. Whereas at the beginning of the twentieth century streetcar lines radiated from a strong city center, in late-twentieth-century Orange County a lattice of freeways overlaid the region, carrying residents in every direction but not toward any common hub.

Tysons, Perimeter Center, Nassau-Suffolk, and Orange County all offered compelling evidence that the traditional concepts of central city and suburb were increasingly obsolete. The central city was no longer central to metropolitan life and in some metropolises no community existed with even a historical claim to being central. At the same time, the largely independent suburbs were no longer "sub" to the "urb." The very name Perimeter Center was a contradiction in terms indicative of the fact that traditional notions no longer applied. The center was on the perimeter, the periphery was central to the commerce of the metropolis.

Thus by the close of the twentieth century the Los Angelesization of America's metropolises appeared to be well advanced. Just as the automobile and the telephone allowed southern Californians to spread throughout the Los Angeles basin as early as 1915, so these same inventions, together with computer terminals and fax machines, permitted the deconcentration of urban settlement and business in metropolitan areas throughout the nation by the 1990s. The map of urban America had changed radically in the course of the century. Not only was metropolitan life no longer confined to the northeastern quadrant of the United States, many urban centers also were no longer truly centers but rather unfocused expanses of population. At the end of the twentieth century, the United States had moved beyond city and suburb to a new form of settlement that was not exactly either.

SEE ALSO Consumption; The Infrastructure (both in volume III); Mass Media and Popular Culture (volume IV).

BIBLIOGRAPHY

Adna Ferrin Weber, *The Growth of Cities in the Nineteenth Century: A Study in Statistics* (1899), offers an excellent view of ideas on urbanization prevalent at the beginning of the twentieth century. William H. Wilson, *The City Beautiful Movement* (1989), considers a significant planning movement of the early twentieth century and its impact on Harrisburg, Kansas City, Denver, Dallas, and Seattle. For a classic account of settlement house work at the beginning of the twentieth century, see Jane Addams, *Twenty Years at Hull-House* (1910). David Ward, *Poverty, Ethnicity, and the American City, 1840–1925: Changing Conceptions of the Slums and the Ghetto* (1989), is a distinguished work by a historical geographer. The best history of the early-twentieth-century migration of blacks to northern cities is James R. Grossman, *Land of Hope: Chicago, Black Southerners, and the Great Migration* (1989). A widely acclaimed and imaginatively written account of the mid-twentieth-century black migration to the cities is Nicholas Lemann, *The Promised Land: The Great Black Migration and How It Changed America* (1991). Robert M. Fogelson, *The Fragmented Metropolis: Los Angeles, 1850–1930* (1967), offers a useful history of Los Angeles during its formative era.

For a classic analysis of suburbanization during the 1920s and its problems and possibilities, see Harlan Paul Douglass, *The Suburban Trend* (1925). John R. Stilgoe, *Borderland: Origins of the American Suburb, 1920–1939* (1988), offers an account of the emergence of the nation's suburbs during the interwar period. William S. Worley, *J. C. Nichols and the Shaping of Kansas City: Innovation in Planned Residential Communities* (1990), is a detailed study of the goals, methods, and achievements of a major suburban real estate developer. For a discussion of the processes of municipal incorporation, annexation, and consolidation along the metropolitan fringe, see Jon C. Teaford, *City and Suburb: The Political Fragmentation of Metropolitan America, 1850–1970* (1979). Kenneth T. Jackson, *Crabgrass Frontier: The Suburbanization of the United States* (1985), is the highly regarded standard history of the suburban movement in America. The best account of the impact of the automobile on the city and the response of urban government to this transportation innovation is Scott L. Bottles, *Los Angeles and the Automobile: The Making of the Modern City* (1987). The leading study of the Roosevelt administration's suburban communities program is Joseph L. Arnold, *The New Deal in the Suburbs: A History of the Greenbelt Town Program, 1925–1954* (1971).

For an authoritative account of the development of federal urban policy during the mid-twentieth century, see Mark I. Gelfand, *A Nation of Cities: The Federal Government and Urban America, 1933–1965* (1975). Gerald D. Nash, *The American West Transformed: The Impact of the Second World War* (1985), includes some helpful chapters devoted specifically to the impact of World War II on western cities. Roger W. Lotchin, ed., *The Martial Metropolis: U.S. Cities in War and Peace, 1900–1970* (1984), is a useful collection of essays on the impact of American military policies and defense spending on the development of American cities. Both Bradford Luckingham, *The Urban Southwest: A Profile History of Albuquerque, El Paso, Phoenix, and Tucson* (1982), and Richard M. Bernard and Bradley R. Rice, eds., *Sunbelt Cities: Politics and Growth since World War II* (1983), deal with southern and western cities that boomed in the post–World War II era.

The most influential work on urban planning and urban revitalization in the second half of the twentieth century is Jane Jacobs, *The Death and Life of Great American Cities* (1961). Richard M. Bernard, ed., *Snowbelt Cities: Metropolitan Politics in the Northeast and Midwest since World War II* (1990), is a collection of essays by urban historians on political developments in aging northeastern and midwestern cities during the second half of the twentieth century. Jon C. Teaford, *The Rough Road to Renaissance: Urban Revitalization in America, 1940–1985* (1990), also deals with efforts to revive older central cities and the problems these cities faced in the second half of the twentieth century. Teaford's *The Twentieth-Century American City* (2d ed., 1993) is a concise survey of the history of cities in the United States during the entire twentieth century.

Robert Fishman, *Bourgeois Utopia: The Rise and Fall of Suburbia* (1987), is a superb account of suburban development with an especially insightful chapter on the "technoburbs" of the postsuburban age. Rob Kling, Spencer Olin, and Mark Poster, eds., *Postsuburban California: The Transformation of Orange County since World War II* (1991), is a collection of essays on the economy, culture, and politics of one of the nation's best-known postsuburban metropolises. A highly useful survey by a distinguished urban geographer is Peter O. Muller, *Contemporary Suburban America* (1981).

SOCIAL WELFARE

Edward D. Berkowitz

During the twentieth century, American social welfare policy changed from a heterogenous set of local and company practices to a national system of social insurance. Between 1911 and 1920, under the influence of Progressive reform, states began experimenting with pensions for dependent children and elderly residents. Most states also passed laws that required employers to pay compensation to employees injured on the job. As a result, corporations operating in national product markets invested in safety devices in an effort to reduce industrial accidents. Some went further and paid compensation to employees during lay-offs and pensions at retirement in order to retain a skilled work force with a long-term commitment.

As more of these laws and practices were instituted control over social welfare benefits was removed from generalists and placed in the hands of experts, promoting the growth of new professions. Social workers supplanted politicians as dispensers of public assistance. Industrial commissioners, often trained as economists, usurped the role of judges in awarding benefits to injured workers. Personnel officers took the place of foremen in supervising company safety procedures. Whether money was routed through government agencies or private enterprise benefits programs, professional administrators were increasingly responsible.

The process of innovation in social welfare policy continued during the New Deal. Passage of the 1935 Social Security Act—establishing old-age federally administered retirement pensions—proved to be the single most important event in the history of American social welfare policy. Elderly citizens who had worked in industrial and commercial establishments received benefits as a matter of right; unlike requirements for public assistance or welfare, an extensive investigation of their assets by local authorities was not necessary. After 1950, this retirement program, known as old-age and survivors insurance or simply social security, became America's largest and most generous social welfare program.

Social welfare expenditures grew substantially in the last half of the century, particularly for social insurance. As table 1 shows, the nation spent 8.8 percent of its gross domestic product (GDP) on social welfare in 1950 and 19.1 percent of its GDP on social welfare in 1975. During these years, social security expanded from a program that paid limited retirement and survivors benefits to one that included disability and health insurance or Medicare. Social security expenditures (old-age, survivors, disability, and hospital insurance) rose from $11 billion in 1960 to $352 billion in 1990. (After 1972 benefit levels were indexed to the rate of inflation.) Medicare expenses increased thirteenfold between 1970 and 1990. Although welfare expenditures failed to keep pace with social security, they increased from $4 billion in 1960 to $104 billion in 1990.

During those years, welfare changed from a program that paid benefits mainly to elderly people to one that aided families with dependent children (AFDC). In 1936, 534,000 people were on the AFDC rolls; in 1990, more than 11.5 million people received AFDC in a given month. Unlike the growth of social security, policymakers tended to view the growth of welfare with alarm. Beginning in 1956, they sought means of substituting work for welfare.

THE POOR LAW TRADITION

At the beginning of the twentieth century, a set of "poor laws" that had been in place since the seventeenth century guided social welfare policy in the United States. In 1700 a person who sought aid appeared before local officials known as vestrymen and asked to be granted money from local tax funds. In 1919 the only difference in the procedure was that, instead of requesting aid from vestrymen, a person instead sought assistance from county commissioners. Even though the persistence of these laws indicated that social provision in America remained relatively unaffected by such developments as indus-

Table 1. PUBLIC SOCIAL WELFARE EXPENDITURES, IN BILLIONS OF DOLLARS, 1950–1990

Item	1950	1960	1965	1970	1975	1980	1985	1988	1989	1990
GDP[a]	267	507	671	986	1,511	2,664	3,971	4,810	5,170	5,460
Total social welfare expenditures	23	52	77	146	289	493	732	887	957	1,045
Social insurance	5	19	28	55	123	230	370	434	468	511
Public aid	2	4	6	16	41	73	98	120	129	146
Health and medical programs	2	4	6	10	17	27	39	53	57	62
Veterans programs	7	5	6	9	17	21	27	29	30	31
Education	7	18	28	51	81	121	172	219	239	258
Housing	0.02	0.02	0.03	0.07	3	7	13	17	18	19
Other	0.4	1	2	4	7	14	14	15	17	18
Social welfare as percentage of GDP	8.8	10.3	11.5	14.7	19.1	18.6	18.4	18.4	18.5	19.1

[a] Gross domestic product in current dollars.
SOURCE: Social Security Administration, *Annual Statistical Supplement* (1992), Table 3.A1.

trialization and urbanization, the early twentieth century marked a period of substantial innovation. New policies emerging at the federal and local levels of government and within individual corporations signaled a shift from the old poor law to a new notion that social problems could be prevented.

Despite the fact that the poor laws remained on the statute books, local officials began to modify traditional practices. In the nineteenth century, it became standard for each county or other local government entity to erect a poor house. Creation of these facilities meant that the location of relief shifted from a person's home to a special domicile in which the person receiving aid became, in effect, a ward of the state. Conditions within poor houses rapidly became controversial. Beginning in 1863, boards of state charities, although possessing no binding power over local practices, quickly became forces for reform.

One mission of these state boards was the removal of certain people from county poor houses and their relocation in other specialized institutions. Among those for whom residence in the poorhouse was considered inappropriate were veterans of the Civil War, people judged to be insane or "feeble-minded," and children. Nearly all states created special institutions for people in these categories, a process that began in the nineteenth century and continued in the twentieth. After the Civil War, for example, New Jersey had established a soldiers' home as a refuge for indigent disabled soldiers on the basis that it was unfair to treat our nation's veterans like common paupers. By the end of the nineteenth century, New Jersey also ran two state insane asylums and a training school for people who were mentally retarded. Early in the twentieth century, the state established a tuberculosis sanitarium and devoted substantial attention to the problem of removing children from poor houses and placing them in orphanages.

Although the general trend in the early twentieth century was to remove people from poor houses and to place them in state-run special institutions or to aid them in their homes, actual practice varied greatly from place to place. The lines between state and local and public and private authority were not firmly drawn. In North Carolina, where there were twenty-three orphanages in the 1920s, seventeen of them were private charitable endeavors, run by various religious denominations and four different fraternal organizations. The state did not administer an orphanage at all, but instead subsidized two private institutions, one of which was maintained by the Masons. In theory, the State Board of Charities and Public Welfare had the right to inspect local orphanages; but in practice, such inspections were seldom performed, and spokesmen for the private charities defeated efforts to give the state the power to license, and hence to close, local orphanages, preventing close regulation of acceptable conditions.

The poor house, at the cutting edge of social policy innovation in the nineteenth century, was condemned as old-fashioned and dangerous in the twentieth. By the 1920s, each county poor house in North Carolina had been officially renamed the County Home for the Aged and Infirm. The change indicated what the historian Michael Katz has described as the "transformation" of the poor house from "family refuges to old age homes."

Reporting on poor relief in various states in the 1930s, a series of investigators uniformly condemned the bad conditions and lack of professional standards in the management of poor houses and in the operation of local relief programs more generally. As late as the 1920s, nearly half of the ninety county homes in North Carolina did not yet have electricity: candles were still as the primary means of illumination. Three almshouses in New Jersey were located in decrepit structures that had been built during the American Revolution.

Twentieth-century commentators criticized more than the physical structure of poor houses. Whereas in the nineteenth century, the ordeals of poor house life were believed to strengthen a person's character, in the twentieth, social welfare professionals took as an article of faith that those ordeals undermined an individual's morals and encouraged maladaptive behavior. From 1900 to the 1930s, state boards filled their reports with tales of moral depravity drawn from local poor house records. The North Carolina State Board of Charities and Public Welfare reported in 1922 on the case of a man who was sentenced to the county chain-gang. He turned out to be too "feeble-minded" to repair the local roads, and so, in a telling policy action, he was placed in the county poor home for the remainder of his sentence. There he met a "feeble-minded woman thirty years old, herself born in the county home." Their union produced a child. "Fortunately, it died," reported the state board in a poignant commentary on the status of people with mental retardation. The implication was that segregation of the feeble-minded in a lax environment without proper supervision contributed to the degeneracy of society.

Throughout the South, poor houses were racially segregated. Institutions large and well-appointed enough to provide two living rooms, one for white people and one for colored people, were considered more advanced and humane than integrated poor houses. Southern authorities regarded racial segregation as an adjunct of privacy. Southern commentators, even the ones trained at such elite schools of social welfare as the University of Chicago, made few linkages between their critiques of poor house practices as backward and local and the practice of racial segregation.

The major alternative to the poor house was to provide what authorities referred to as "outdoor relief." The recipient of outdoor relief did not have to live in a poor house. Although nineteenth-century authorities had made concerted efforts to eliminate such relief, it never disappeared from local practice and increased in popularity by the end of the century. Cities, in particular, tended to favor outdoor over indoor relief for families in need. As with other social welfare practices, the provision of outdoor relief involved complicated linkages between private and public authorities. Cities tended to have their own budgets for indoor relief that supplemented programs run by the county. Some utilized the services of public welfare administrators. Others relied on private agencies, such as the Salvation Army or the local Charity Organization Society, to dispense relief.

Social welfare commentators, trained in social work schools, condemned the provision of outdoor relief in the early twentieth century every bit as much as they criticized poor house practices. One commentator, writing on the situation in the South during the 1920s, referred to "widespread pauperization of the recipients of aid unscientifically administered and hopelessly insufficient in amount" and to "political exploitation of the poor funds" and "graft." County commissioners remained "ignorant of the law."

At the heart of the critique was the commentator's notion of "pauperization," a process in which able-bodied people turned themselves into paupers by losing their sense of initiative and coming to rely on public aid. Not only did this process undermine their productivity and self-esteem, it also consigned them to a low standard of living. The amount they could receive through public aid was considerably lower than what they could make from working. The antidote to pauperization was the proper investigation of applicants by trained professionals who became known as social workers.

PROGRESSIVE-ERA ALTERNATIVES TO THE POOR LAW TRADITION

Beginning in 1911, with the passage of mothers' pension legislation in Missouri and Illinois, states took an important step away from the association between pauperization and outdoor relief. By 1919, the laws were on the books of thirty-nine other states, and by 1931, all but Georgia and South Carolina had adopted similar legislation. Typically, the law provided financial relief to mothers caring for children under sixteen years of age from a fund that included joint contributions from state and local revenues that was administered by state authorities who worked closely with local authorities. The idea behind the law was to move social provision into the home and community so that children would not be forced to grow up in a poor house. It was hoped that without that stigma they could develop normally, attend local schools, and meet other children in a wholesome atmosphere.

The number of people aided by such laws remained small throughout the period between 1920 and 1935. To protect against the perceived evil of pauperization, local authorities examined applicants closely for signs of moral weakness. In most states, only so-called "gilt edged" widows qualified for aid. In June 1931, for example, the laws gave financial aid to about 250,000 children; nearly all of these cases involved white widows. Once on aid, applicants did not have to submit to repeated investigations. At least in theory, they could work with a social worker or local official on a plan to better themselves.

The widow of a young farmer who died of cancer in the spring of 1925 provides an example of a prime candidate to receive aid. Her husband's death had left her with three small children and few financial resources. The woman tried to run the farm by herself but found it, in the words of the official case record, "overtaxing." In the time-honored manner of the poor law, the woman took her case to the county superintendent of welfare. He decided that, rather than sending the woman to the county poor house, she fit the criteria to receive aid from the mothers' aid fund. He helped to relocate the woman and worked with her on a plan to become self-sufficient by learning to make and repair drapes. The state director of mothers' aid approved the county superintendent's request and granted the woman twenty-five dollars a month. In less than a year, the woman was self-supporting. Here then was a way to smooth the hard edges of the poor law and to substitute professional supervision for the haphazard, demoralizing conditions of the poor house.

The creation of mothers' pension laws in the Progressive Era illustrated a general softening of the poor law tradition in the twentieth century. In 1911 New Jersey state authorities restricted the definition of "pauper," so that those who received public assistance would not lose their right to vote. As late as 1930, most New Jersey municipalities limited aid to "totally dependent people" who had lived in the municipality for five or more years and owned no real property; some localities expected applicants for relief who owned cars to surrender their license plates to local authorities. Yet in 1924 the state amended its law to allow relief to go to people who owned homes.

Conditions in the larger cities, such as Newark, never resembled those in the smaller municipalities. In Newark authorities received so many applications for relief and were so ill-equipped to handle them that they frequently granted aid without extensive investigation. As described by one contemporary in 1931, the scene in the Newark Poor and Alms Department was chaotic. A policeman acted as a receptionist, referring applicants to an interviewer who, as often as not, was a city employee on temporary assignment. The interviewer, who could be a plumbing inspector or an attendant at the public bath, would ask a few questions regarding name, address, and length of residence of the applicants; but little effort went into verifying such facts as the number of children in the family or the amount of money in the family's bank account. The applicant was asked to return in a few days for a voucher good for three dollars a week in groceries sold by participating merchants. Although the procedure often scared applicants, many of whom could barely speak English, and yielded very small relief payments, it did not operate in a punitive manner. Nor did it uphold strict, nineteenth-century poor law standards, such as limiting aid to those who had lived in Newark for five years. Under pressure of economic, social, and political circumstances, the poor law system had been converted into something approaching a mass system of relief.

Creation of special monetary grants to the indigent elderly, similar to the pensions for widows caring for small children, occurred in eleven states during the 1920s and fourteen more in the early 1930s. In the Massachusetts version people had to prove that they had lived in the state for twenty or more years and were seventy years of age. Pensions averaged twenty-five dollars a month at the end of 1932, with counties and localities contributing two-thirds of the funding (only North Dakota and Delaware relied exclusively on state funds). With the exception of Alaska, no state or territory paid more than a dollar a day.

All the laws contained stringent restrictions about who could be aided, and most permitted a great deal of discretion by local government authorities. A person or married couple who obtained an old age pension enjoyed the freedom to spend it in any way that they wished. Those on the rolls regarded their grants as lifetime entitlements, rather than a conditional gratuity from the state. Getting on the rolls was, however, far from a certainty, even for the poorest elderly residents of a particular community.

Even as the poor law continued on its erratic course early in the twentieth century, other developments provided a source of real innovation in social welfare policy. Corporations that operated in national markets and maintained business operations in scattered locations discovered how ineffective it was to deal with local authorities in matters of social welfare policy. If nothing else, the rules often differed from place to place. At the same time, these corporations faced the problem of maintaining a productive and healthy work force and sought means of reducing turnover among their employees. With this motivation, corporations developed practices that married the provision of social welfare services with normal business operations. The result was a series of innovations that became known as welfare capitalism.

A good example of welfare capitalism in operation was the campaign to promote safety in the work place. The safety movement stemmed from the more general Progressive reform agitation at the turn of the century and consisted of a series of interlocking government agencies, such as the Bureau of Labor Statistics, and private organizations, such as the National Safety Council. The focus tended to be on states rather than the federal government and on companies rather than on an industry or the economy.

Stated in the simplest terms, the movement tried to interest employers in making an investment in safety. Its line of development followed that of scientific management more generally. At first, the movement centered on the installation within individual plants of mechanical devices, such as guards on machinery that kept workers from getting entangled in the machinery and losing limbs. Called "safety engineering," this phase of the movement took place between 1907 and 1920 and corresponded with the time and motion studies of Frederick W. Taylor and other scientific management pioneers. Gradually, however, the focus shifted to the psychology of the individual worker, and creating a greater awareness of safe working procedures. Prominent in the 1920s, this approach coincided with the work of Elton Mayo and other industrial psychologists. A further development was to promote the safety function within the organization by appointing executives in charge of safety procedures.

Throughout each of these phases, the emphasis was on changing the working environment of individual companies rather than on the passage of an overarching safety law. In this respect, safety advocates differed in their methods and orientation from other Progressive reformers. The companies most responsive to safety propaganda, like those engaged in welfare capitalism more generally, tended to be large companies in oligopolistic product markets. Such companies did not have the luxury of hiring labor on a daily basis from what classical economists envisioned as an infinite pool of workers available at the market price. Instead, these companies had to nurture and train a labor force whose members often remained with the company for a substantial amount of time. The safer the workplace, the more productive would be the work force.

The activities of the U.S. Steel Corporation illustrate how safety campaigns operated within individual companies. From the moment of its creation in 1901, U.S. Steel became the largest and potentially the most hazardous corporation in the world. Steel making already had a reputation as a highly dangerous occupation, and U.S. Steel also owned mines. The corporation began its active involvement in the safety movement in May 1906. Judge Elbert Gary, the chairman, told the managers of the subsidiary companies that the board of directors would appropriate money for accident reduction. In April 1908, the company created a central committee on safety that served as a clearinghouse for safety information among the 143 manufacturing plants. This committee eventually formulated recommendations for safe production procedures that, according to company officials, produced beneficial results. Between 1910 and 1927, for example, the accident frequency rate in the steel industry dropped nearly 74 percent. U.S. Steel boasted in the 1920s that its safety program saved a million dollars a year.

Investments in safety lessened the vulnerability of companies to industrial accidents and reduced their potential liability from suits brought by injured workers. In this manner, the safety movement helped to pave the way for state workers' compensation laws. These laws imposed a legally sanctioned payment on an employer for every accident that occurred in the workplace and mandated the purchase of insurance by employers to cover the costs of industrial disability. Passage of the laws increased a company's incentive to invest in safety. If a company knew that its workers' compensation premiums and hence its operating costs could be lowered by reducing the number of accidents in its workplace, then it might begin a conscious campaign to make the workplace safer.

One motivation behind workers' compensation laws, therefore, was to enforce higher safety standards on the laggards in competitive product markets. These laggards, according to the safety proponents, acted as parasites, drawing more from the community than they returned by way of wages and other payments. In connection with the famous Pittsburgh survey of industrial conditions, sponsored by the

Russell Sage Foundation and conducted between 1908 and 1913, Crystal Eastman, a lawyer and social investigator, tried to estimate the "social loss involved in one year's work-accidents in Allegheny County." She arrived at a figure of $5.2 million, which she then compared to the much lower amount that Pittsburgh employers paid for compensation and medical expenses. She believed that smaller companies needed to bear more of the "true" costs of industrial accidents, and that workers' compensation laws provided a mechanism for bringing about this result.

During the Progressive Era, reformers both complained of a lack of access to social welfare benefits and worried about an excess of benefits for injured workmen who sued their employers and won large settlements from sympathetic juries. Court-administered industrial accident compensation systems often failed to grant any compensation or provide grants that bore little relationship to "the gravity of injury or need," wrote the social insurance expert I. M. Rubinow in 1913. At the same time, Rubinow noted, "we are startled by the very large and undoubtedly sometimes even excessive amounts of damages awarded." Tenuously uniting employers concerned about excess and employees concerned about access, reformers between 1911 and 1919 succeeded in creating workers' compensation laws in forty-three states. Such laws were intended to provide steady but unspectacular compensation to the victims of industrial accidents. They were administered in many states by agencies that claimed both legislative and judicial powers to make rules and settle disputes. With the passage of compensation laws, workers injured in the course of employment no longer needed to win a legal suit before they could receive financial recompense. Instead, they received a financial payment, based on their rate of pay and the severity of their disability, and reimbursement for their medical care directly from the state workers' compensation agency. In the nineteenth century, settlement of the matter had hinged on the question of who was at fault for the accident. Workers' compensation laws, at least in theory, eliminated the concept of fault and replaced it with the notion of objective need.

Workers' compensation laws exemplified an American version of social insurance. Entitlement to benefits under the poor law, a direct inheritance from feudalism, stemmed from a person's membership in the local community; entitlement to social insurance, although connected with paternalistic states or employers, stemmed from a person's job. Such insurance provided protection against contingencies that might interfere with the practice of that job—injury, layoffs, sickness, and old-age—and was far more compatible with industrial capitalism.

The passage of new social insurance laws and the maintenance of workers' compensation laws proved a difficult undertaking in the years between 1911 and 1935. Although business and labor could agree on the need for workers' compensation, considerable controversy attended other forms of social insurance. Neither business, concerned about costs, nor labor, concerned about the adequacy of benefits and control of their provision, wanted the state to intervene in the labor market and compel employers to provide health insurance. Nor did organized medicine trust the competence of state authorities to regulate medicine in the interest of either the profession or of the public. The Progressive-Era campaign for state-administered health insurance failed resoundingly. In the United States, unlike in other countries that experimented with social insurance in the late nineteenth and early twentieth centuries, a pervasive mistrust of the state undercut support for broad social spending measures.

Whenever possible, Progressive reformers tried to insulate the agencies administering workers' compensation from political pressure. As a result, the new agencies, often called industrial commissions, faced constant challenges to their jurisdiction. Lawyers contested compensation cases and discovered means of removing the cases from the new agencies to the courts. During the first year of the workers' compensation law in Maryland, 7.2 percent of claims were contested; in 1933, 20.2 percent of the claims were contested. At the same time, the number of hearings increased from 273 to 1,776 per year. Employers and employees used the legislature to gain their advantage, depending on the political circumstances of the moment; the legislatures regarded the new agencies not as removed from traditional politics but as objects of political patronage.

FEDERAL SOCIAL WELFARE

In the Progressive Era, much of the action in social welfare policy, whether with the traditional poor law or the campaigns to create new social insurance or widows' pension laws, remained at the state and local levels of government. The federal government continued to administer Civil War pensions, the nation's largest and most pervasive social welfare program. As the sociologist Ann Shola Orloff has detailed, during the 1880s and 1890s "the pension system was changed from a provision for compensation of combat injuries and war deaths to the functional equivalent of an old-age and disability pension for a politically important segment of the U.S. electorate." In 1890, veterans' pensions already consumed 34 percent of the federal budget. Because of the loose way in which the benefits were administered and the rising percentage of Union army veterans who availed themselves of them, expenditures for these old-age and disability benefits did not peak until around 1912. After 1906, for example, the law was amended to allow any Northern veteran (Confederate veterans were excluded) over sixty-two years of age to collect a pension. At that point, 90 percent of surviving Union veterans were on the pension rolls. The cost of old-age pensions for Civil War veterans amounted in 1913 to more than $160 million per year.

Consequently, the highest level of expenditures for Civil War pensions coincided with the height of Progressive reform agitation. I. M. Rubinow, the social insurance expert, complained that "it is a matter of common knowledge not only that pensions are obtained upon fraudulent representations of past services . . . but what is economically more important, a large proportion of the amount goes to individuals who have no need whatsoever of financial assistance." The sociologist Theda Skocpol has termed the system of Civil War social benefits a "kind of precocious social security system for those U.S. citizens of a certain generation and region who were deemed morally worthy of enjoying generous and honorable public aid."

Unlike social insurance and poor law provisions, veterans' pensions reflected the patterns of national politics, favoring northern Republicans rather than southern Democrats, and old-stock Americans rather than recent immigrants. Notions of economy ruled poor law administration, and efficiency predominated in social insurance. Veterans' pensions, by way of contrast, were administered such that the widest possible distribution of benefits became the desired norm. Progressive reform was in part a revolt against the enmeshment in local politics of the poor law and the national politics of veterans' pensions. Of course, Civil War pensions were self-limiting in the sense that they were tied to the members of a particular generation and its dependents. Although the process took more than one hundred years, the members of this generation and their survivors eventually died. The program ended. In the meantime, national government began to be more involved in social welfare provisions.

Three new federal laws created toward the end of the Progressive Era dealt with the areas of health, education, and welfare. In the field of health, Congress passed the Sheppard-Towner Act of 1921, providing prenatal and child health centers in hopes of reducing infant and maternal mortality rates. As in nearly all of the federal social welfare laws of the era, the legislators expected most of the aid to go to rural areas rather than to the urban areas. Cities were underrepresented in Congress and were considered to be "ahead" of the rural areas in the availability and quality of social welfare services. In the field of education, Congress initiated federal support for vocational education in 1917 and created a federal vocational rehabilitation program in 1920, allowing handicapped individuals to receive counseling and training in order to join the labor force and get a job. These programs expanded upon but did not conflict with the basic responsibilities of the state and local governments; they neither usurped the local poor laws or education systems nor condoned the use of the poor house.

Most of the laws owed their origins not so much to the forces of partisan politics as to the organized activities of groups that came into existence in the Progressive Era. Networks of female reformers were particularly influential. The social welfare workers Florence Kelley and Lillian Wald helped to create the federal Children's Bureau in 1912. Both were associated with the late-nineteenth- and early-twentieth-century settlement house movement, which, as Allen Davis has noted, served as a "spearhead" for Progressive reform. Housed in what soon became the Department of Labor, the Children's Bureau responded to a broad, if vague, mandate "to investigate and report upon all matters pertaining to the welfare of children and child life." The Bureau acquired a reputation as a "woman's agency," in part because of the nature of its mission and in part because its leaders were women. Julia Lathrop, formerly associated with Chicago's Hull House (the most prominent of the nation's settlement houses) and the Illinois State Board of Charities, served as the first head of the Children's Bureau. Lathrop and her fellow female employees of the Children's Bureau became the leading advocates of the Sheppard-Towner Act.

In this way, Lathrop and other women helped to shape part of what some recent historians have described as a "maternalist" welfare state. In addition to the Sheppard-Towner Act, the "maternalist" welfare state also included a series of state laws, passed in the Progressive Era, that established minimum wages and maximum hours for women in the labor force. The appeal of such laws to Progressive reformers lay in their direct response to what many considered to be the exploitation of women workers through low wages. In addition, the laws protected the health and welfare of American children.

The Progressive Era was a time of extreme sensitivity to racial and ethnic diversity. Hence, some legislators responded well to the argument that minimum wages and other protective labor legislation for women helped to perpetuate the American race at a time of massive immigration. Motherhood, argued the social gospel minister Walter Rauschenbusch in his 1914 book *Christianizing the Social Order,* was a function "higher than the production of goods." "If we desire to have the children of the coming generations strong and well-born," wrote Jeanne Roberts in a popular magazine in 1912, "we must give the working women healthy conditions surrounding their labor and pay them a minimum wage."

Because the maternalist welfare state agenda solved practical problems in the development of social welfare policy in America, it fared better than efforts to pass unemployment, old-age, and health insurance. In the first third of the century, the courts took constitutional strictures seriously. The reservation of "nondelegated" powers to the states blocked federal legislation. The prohibition of the states and the federal government from "depriving any person of life, liberty, or property without due process of law" cast doubts on the constitutionality of minimum wages. In effect, the courts, through the process of judicial review, exercised veto power over the actions of state and federal legislatures. Laws aimed at protecting the health and welfare of women could more easily be rationalized as constitutional than could similar laws that applied to both men and women. Judges used a common law notion, inherited from England, called the police power to uphold laws that protected the health and safety of women. In addition, laws aimed at women conferred benefits on a group that began to vote in federal elections in 1920. Hence, the Sheppard-Towner infant and maternal health law was also a response to the demands of a group with newly acquired political power.

The new federal laws, whether part of the maternalist welfare state or not, followed the rules of local, rather than national, administration. Each of the new programs operated through a system in which the federal government gave money to the states. This grant-in-aid structure enabled the state and federal governments to share the costs of the program and allowed the states to operate the programs. The federal supervisory offices remained small; for example, eight federal employees supervised the infant and maternal health programs, and an average of six people worked in the federal vocational rehabilitation office during the 1920s. Although the federal government paid cash to the states, the clients received services in-kind, usually in the form of advice or training. None of the programs could be described as an entitlement; instead, each exercised great selectivity in its clients, with the result that none served a high percentage of the people eligible for aid. During the 1920s, for example, the number of people successfully rehabilitated through vocational rehabilitation never rose above 6,000 in any one year. Funding was limited, as one might expect from a federal government that spent only twenty-five cents per capita on social welfare expenditures (independent of veterans' pensions) in 1928. As a result of all these factors, the programs were quite fragile. In 1929, for example, Congress refused to renew the Infant and Maternal Health Program. It did not operate between 1929 and 1935.

THE SOCIAL SECURITY ACT

In the 1930s, New Deal reformers had a chance to enact a new national social welfare law. Their thinking was shaped by the Progressive-Era critique of demeaning and restrictive poor laws and expensive and poorly administered veterans' pensions. The new law would strive to treat its beneficiaries with dignity, to include all industrial workers within its scope, and keep future costs within manageable limits. Unlike veterans' pensions, the new law would be administered by social insurance experts, not politicians anxious to satisfy voters. The occasion of a new social welfare law also gave reformers a chance to resurrect the infant and maternal health program by reviving the Sheppard-Towner Act and to strengthen the vocational rehabilitation program.

Passed in 1935, the new, omnibus social welfare law became known as the Social Security Act. Like many landmark pieces of legislation, its passage was a near thing. President Franklin D. Roosevelt slipped it through a window of political opportunity that opened in the middle of the Depression and closed very soon afterward. By seizing the moment, the President changed the nature and the administrative design of American social welfare benefits. Social security substituted a national system of monetary benefits, administered by the federal government, for the existing locally oriented system.

Beginning in 1930, the Depression slowly altered the face of America. Brutal in its force, it strained local systems of social provision to their limits. First the cities, then the states, and, after 1933, the federal government supplemented traditional poor relief with what came to be called unemployment relief. Some states, such as New York and New Jersey, created new sources of funds that the localities spent in aid of people who were unemployed as a result of the Depression. The New Jersey legislature passed a law in the fall of 1930 that allowed counties and municipalities to sell special bonds. The funds raised could be used to employ needy residents on public works projects. A year later, the state legislature created the Emergency Relief Administration to provide state funds for municipal work relief projects.

When Franklin D. Roosevelt became president in March 1933, he asked Harry Hopkins, a social worker with whom he had worked as governor of New York, to begin a national program of emergency relief that combined federal and state funds. Looking for a more permanent and less costly solution than the dole, Roosevelt also asked industrial and labor leaders to meet together and, in effect, to agree on measures that would aid economic recovery. This attempt at industrial self-regulation, which recapitulated many of the themes of welfare capitalism, became known as the National Recovery Administration (NRA). When it failed to produce the sustained recovery for which Roosevelt had hoped, he began to explore other social welfare measures, including social insurance. In other words, the President tried first to work through the poor law and welfare capitalist traditions before he contemplated the other items on the Progressive agenda.

In early summer 1934, Roosevelt decided to have his administration prepare an economic security bill that would cover both old-age and unemployment compensation. As a first step, he created the Committee on Economic Security, composed of cabinet members and cabinet-level advisers. While committee members debated broad points of policy, the hard staff work that supported their efforts fell to a special group recruited from outside of the government. These experts, assisted by an additional group of government technicians, made a comprehensive study of the field.

Roosevelt chose Frances Perkins to chair the Committee on Economic Security. By appointing her, the President practically guaranteed that the committee would be stacked with social insurance experts from top to bottom. Perkins, the secretary of labor, had devoted her career to the administration of social insurance programs. She had served on New York's Industrial Board, as a member from 1919 to 1924 and as chairman from 1924 to 1929. This board settled disputes in workers' compensation and established rules governing the program. Then in 1929, as governor of New York, Franklin Roosevelt appointed her Industrial Commissioner, an administrative position similar to secretary of Labor at the federal level.

For help in staffing the Committee on Economic Security, Perkins turned to other social insurance experts. Chief among them was Assistant Secretary of Labor Arthur Altmeyer, who headed the group of government technicians. Altmeyer came from Wisconsin, where he had been secretary of that state's Industrial Commission and administered its workers' compensation and unemployment compensation programs. As a result of Perkins's and Altmeyer's efforts, the Committee on Economic Security staff contained few people who were concerned with relief or welfare; nearly all of the administration's advisers were interested in the expansion of social insurance.

Social insurance, to which the staff was intellectually predisposed, also met pragmatic political needs. It depended on the taxing power of the federal government, which was explicitly sanctioned by the constitution; it relied on payroll taxes, which provided a source of revenue independent of income and other taxes. As a consequence, a social insurance program might hope to overcome the federal government's notorious inability to raise money for social projects. Finally, social insurance filled part of a hole in Roosevelt's program that was created by the demise of the National Recovery Administration. Although it would not help with such things as regulating the hours of work or wage levels, it could provide the foundation for a universal retirement program. It could also guarantee partial wages to laid-off employees.

As former state administrators, Perkins and Altmeyer held no particular brief for the federal administration of social welfare programs. The experience with veterans' benefits remained fresh in their minds and made them wary of leaving complex tasks to the oversight of Congress. Therefore, the President and his advisers entrusted many responsibilities to the states. They decided that the states should run the new social insurance program to protect against the risk of unemployment. In addition, they recommended that the federal government should make grants to the states for a host of other purposes. These included public health activities, child welfare services, services for crippled children, and vocational rehabilitation.

Each of the committee's recommendations was

incorporated first into its report and then into the Social Security Act itself. No groundswell developed in support of these recommendations because they did not offer major relief to the victims of the Depression. The work of the Committee on Economic Security, concerned with such matters as social insurance and infant mortality, bore little relationship to the urgent business of coping with the consequences of the Depression. To aid people in distress, states continued to depend on their old poor laws, supplemented by federal emergency public works programs.

Even President Roosevelt's allies had their doubts about the work of the Committee on Economic Security. Union officials could not abandon their tradition of hostility toward the central government. They considered things such as retirement pay the province of collective bargaining rather than government mandate. Union leaders, fearful that industrialists would get the better of the bargain, provided the President with only limited support on social security.

Despite these problems, President Roosevelt and the Committee on Economic Security persevered. In an action that would have far-reaching consequences, the committee and its staff drafted a social insurance plan that involved collecting payroll taxes from employers and employees to finance retirement pensions for workers over sixty-five. Unlike the other programs that the committee recommended, this one made no provisions for state or local administration. It was to be run by the federal government, with the cooperation of private employers. This old-age insurance program, or social security as it became known, developed into the nation's most important and successful social welfare program.

The question of public policy toward the elderly did not preoccupy the Committee on Economic Security. As it turned out, however, the problems of the elderly were unavoidable in 1934. Just as the Committee on Economic Security began its work, some elderly citizens formed a powerful alliance. Led by Francis Townsend, the citizens demanded that anyone over the age of sixty be paid a flat pension of $200 a month from the federal Treasury on condition that the recipient retire from the labor force and spend the entire amount of money within each month. Although the committee staff members recognized the appeal of the Townsend plan, never for a moment did they entertain the thought of endorsing it. If they were to design an old-age pension plan, they would do so on their own terms. Inevitably, that meant a social insurance program. The Townsend agitation therefore helped to put the question of old-age pensions on the political agenda but did nothing to influence the content of the social security program. Unlike the Townsend plan, social security was not conceived as an aid to economic recovery. Instead, it was part of a long-range campaign to enact the agenda of Progressive reform and replace local poor laws with a national system of social insurance.

Committed as the members of the Committee on Economic Security were to social insurance, they also recognized the need for pensions based not on future contributions but on present need. Someone already old in 1934 could not rely on contributory social insurance; nor could someone who worked outside of the commercial and industrial labor force that was the traditional focus of Progressive reform. The solution, as the staff members perceived it, was for the federal government to aid in the expansion of state old-age pensions. As matters stood in 1935, old-age pensions existed in twenty-eight states, and more than 180,000 people received them. The federal government, by supplying matching funds to the states, could make the pensions available in all of the states and raise the benefit levels. The federal government could also enforce other desirable norms, such as requiring that the pensions operate in an entire state rather than only in certain counties. The new federal grants-in-aid to the states would be consistent with the campaign to divorce public aid from the poor house and make state old-age pensions less subject to political abuse.

As a consequence of the committee's actions, the Roosevelt administration advocated a complex strategy for the provision of old-age security. In the short run, it expected that elderly people in need would receive aid from state welfare authorities. At the same time, a new program, federally administered and funded by payroll taxes, would be initiated. Over time, this federal old-age insurance program would remove the burden of paying old-age pensions from the states. There would be a transformation of public policy from a humane but nonetheless traditional reliance on the poor law to a new emphasis on social insurance. When the transformation was complete, the elderly would receive pensions upon the condition of retirement, without having to prove that they were financially needy and without having to surrender any of their assets. Because the new social insurance pensions depended solely on working, rather than on working for one employer, they would be perfectly portable. No matter how many times people changed jobs, they would not lose their social security protection. Because the new pensions would be funded through payroll taxes, they would be less of a burden on local and federal revenues than would state pensions.

In January 1935, President Roosevelt presented Congress with an omnibus social welfare measure that combined programs covering children, the unemployed, and the elderly in a single legislative package. It was by far the most comprehensive social welfare bill that any president had ever requested. Because the legislation sought to establish two new forms of federal taxation, Congress handled it as it did other forms of tax legislation. Hence, the Committee on Ways and Means in the House and the Committee on Finance in the Senate held lengthy hearings on the legislation in the winter and spring of 1935.

Congress shared few of the predilections of the Committee on Economic Security. Indeed, few of the congressmen understood the complicated logistics of the large piece of legislation. In 1935, however, congressional sentiments mattered far less than they did in other eras. It was one of the few times in American history when a president with a definite legislative agenda could bend Congress so easily to his will. When the President decided to put the Economic Security Act near the top of his political agenda, he practically ensured its passage. What the political scientist Christopher Leman describes as a "big bang" of activity ensued.

Congress did leave its imprint on the law. In particular, it made sure that old-age insurance covered only industrial and commercial workers, not farmers or businessmen. It also deleted sections of the bill that suggested to southerners that black welfare recipients would have to be paid as much as white ones. It added a provision that permitted the federal government to subsidize pensions for the blind. Other features of the bill, such as the design of unemployment compensation programs or the size of payroll taxes in 1957, concerned them far less. If Congress had voted on old-age insurance and unemployment separately, it would have defeated them. These measures became law only as part of a large package.

In August 1935, President Roosevelt signed the Social Security Act into law. Among many other things, the bill established a federal-state unemployment insurance program and, most importantly, created an old-age insurance program. In other words, the 1935 Social Security Act, although it lacked provisions for disability and health insurance, laid the basis for this country's modern social welfare system. It put the federal government in the pension business and the states in the unemployment compensation business. It solidified the grant-in-aid programs of the Progressive Era and the twenties, and it initiated new grant-in-aid programs in public health and child welfare.

THE DEVELOPMENT OF SOCIAL SECURITY, 1935–1950

For all that social security represented a policy breakthrough, few politicians rushed to endorse it in its early years. Between 1935 and 1950, the development of social security reflected the internal dynamics of the program more than the influence of external political events. Once created, the program became largely invisible, responding only to the problems inherent in its design and those created by the effect of the economy on its performance.

At first, the fiscal discipline that a contributory old-age insurance program required clashed with the needs of an economy that was in a deep depression. Social security, as it was planned by the President's advisers, took more money out of the economy in the form of payroll taxes than it returned in the form of retirement pensions. In 1937, for example, the program collected $765 million and paid out $1 million in benefits; two years later, it collected $360 million and paid out $14 million. During these years, it reduced the amount of money in people's pockets, further depressing the moribund economy.

The plan was for payroll taxes to begin in 1937 and for the first regular benefits to be paid in 1942. Starting in January 1937, workers had 1 percent of the first $3,000 of their wages deducted from their paychecks. Employers contributed an equal amount. People would contribute for five years without any real assurance of getting the money back.

This situation created a political liability. During the nation's most severe depression, it was impolitic for a social welfare program to collect more in revenues than it spent in benefits. The Republicans played upon this vulnerability in the 1936 campaign. Alfred Landon, the Republican presidential nominee, criticized the program as "unjust, unworkable, stupidly drafted and wastefully financed."

As early as 1937, a consensus had begun to emerge in favor of changing the old-age insurance program so that its expenditures more nearly matched its revenues. Senator Arthur Vandenberg, an influential Republican politician, recommended that the payments of benefits begin sooner than 1942, that the initial benefits be more generous, and that payroll tax increases scheduled for 1940 be postponed. Ultimately, the financing issues were debated in a special

Social Security Advisory Council established in 1937 by Vandenberg and Arthur Altmeyer, the chairman of the Social Security Board. The creation of the council marked the beginning of a pattern in which social security was discussed in closed forums, or in executive sessions of committees of Congress, rather than in open public debate.

The late-Depression changes in social security illustrated the tensions between politics and program management. When the program was an idea, an abstraction, as it was in 1935, the politicians could dismiss many of its potential problems. The social security program before Congress in 1935 had no effect on any worker or employer until after the next election, and it was not the center of congressional debate. Soon after the election, the abstraction of 1935 became the tax of 1937. When social security acquired the potential to create problems for its sponsors, such as President Roosevelt, the feeling grew among both Republicans and Democrats that something needed to be done about it.

The design of the program eased the political dilemma. Simply by raising the level and type of benefits and by initiating benefits sooner than planned, one could solve the problem. In 1938, social security officials proposed, and the advisory council accepted, recommendations that, when adopted by Congress, radically changed old-age insurance. In particular, the advisory council recommended that benefits be paid to the survivors of deceased workers. That was the essence of the 1939 amendments. Old-age insurance became old-age and survivors insurance.

Despite the importance of the 1939 changes, they attracted far less attention than did the passage of the Social Security Act in 1935. Social security policy had become a matter of technical adjustment. Large questions of social policy were subsumed by small details in program design.

Although the 1939 amendments marked a significant step in the creation of social security, the program still lacked crucial elements that kept it from becoming the country's major old-age security program. One was broad coverage. In 1939, the program still failed to cover farmers, the self-employed, and others outside of the industrial or commercial labor force. Another was benefits that matched the rising cost of living. A program created in the Depression needed to be modified for a time of prosperity. After delaying the reform of old-age insurance through the war years and through the postwar conservative resurgence, Congress remedied these defects in 1950.

As late as 1940, veterans programs and state programs, such as welfare and workers' compensation, continued to dwarf social security. Workers' compensation payments exceeded social security payments by a factor of six; veterans programs cost fifteen times as much as social security. As late as 1950, more than twice as many people were on the state welfare rolls receiving old-age assistance or pensions than were receiving retirement benefits from the federal government under social security. The average monthly welfare payment was $42 in 1949, compared with an average social security benefit of $25.

Welfare predominated over social security because it was more widely available and offered its recipients higher benefits. Congress, for its part, appeared ready to accept welfare over social insurance. In the 1940s, although distracted by the war and the problems of postwar adjustment, Congress managed to raise federal aid to the elderly for welfare (state pensions) and to reduce the percentage of the labor force covered by social security. Tax levels for social security remained stagnant throughout the decade, even though the law called for the tax rate to rise. Congress refused to raise taxes for something that appeared to have little popular support. As if to underscore this lack of popularity, proposals to create an integrated social insurance system, uniting old-age insurance, unemployment compensation, and health insurance in one federal system, failed to pass.

With social security in what might be called a crisis of inactivity, Congress proceeded as it had in passing the 1939 amendments. It appointed an advisory council to study the situation and produce concrete recommendations. This council met in 1948. At the time, Congress was under Republican control and not predisposed to pass legislation requested either by the Social Security Administration or President Truman.

The 1948 council accepted the agenda for the expansion of social insurance that federal bureaucrats placed before it. The council members recommended a major expansion of the program so that it reached self-employed businessmen and those permanently employed on farms. They also advocated a major rise in the level of benefits, so that dollar value of old-age insurance benefits was as high or higher than the value of state old-age pension (welfare) benefits.

Report or no report, Congress continued to oppose social security expansion. This situation changed in 1949 after the Democratic victory in the 1948 elections. The new Democratic Congress acquiesced in the expansion of social security. For one thing, it served as a means of continuing a New

Deal institution in postwar America. For another, it did not force legislators to make many hard choices. An expansion of social security did not imply a cutback in welfare. So long as the elderly continued to receive the same level of support from the government, it did not matter much whether this support came from welfare or social security. In addition, the political situation had changed somewhat with the creation of collective bargaining agreements in such large industries as steel and automaking. These agreements guaranteed pensions to workers that included social security payments. As a consequence, an increase in social security lessened the burden on large employers, reducing their resistance to an increase in social security taxes.

In 1950, Congress substantially modified the social security program, and in direct response the social security system began to grow. Eight million workers, most of whom were self-employed, were brought into the system, and average benefits were increased by about 80 percent. In February 1951, for the first time, the number of old-age and survivors insurance beneficiaries exceeded the number of people receiving state old-age assistance. It was a moment of epochal importance in the history of America's social welfare policy. After 1950, social insurance, not the poor law, defined America's approach to old-age security.

SOCIAL WELFARE IN THE 1950s

Social security's triumph over welfare came just in time to withstand the challenge posed by the election in 1952 of Dwight D. Eisenhower, the first member of his party to be president since the passage of the Social Security Act. Conservatives, who had been waiting for the right president, expected a responsive audience for their ideas. They were sorely disappointed.

Right before the election of 1952, Congress, acting largely on its own initiative, decided to raise the level of social security benefits. That began a long tradition of election year increases in the program. Congress enacted no major social security amendments in the eleven years between 1939 and 1950. Then, in only two years, it amended the program again. In the 1940s, war provided a pretext for inaction on social security; in the 1950s, Congress did not allow the Korean War to interfere with liberalizing the program. Republicans joined Democrats in the effort.

Legislators justified their action by the fact that wage levels had risen faster than expected between 1950 and 1952. In this manner, postwar prosperity became harnessed to the cause of social security expansion. Social security expansion came to enjoy bipartisan support. Table 2 details the growth of social security.

Conservatives tried unsuccessfully to counter the trend. Right after the election of 1952, the Chamber of Commerce circulated a social security plan to its members. This plan, enthusiastically adopted by the chamber, took as its major premise that social security was peculiarly vulnerable to expansion. Every time a new group entered the system, such as the self-employed in 1950, large surpluses developed because, in the beginning, workers always paid more into the program than they received in benefits. Surpluses, according to the conservatives, led to liberalized benefits that eventually would have to be supported by higher taxes. Hence, conservatives believed that the bureaucrats in charge of social security were engaged in a shell game, using early surpluses to mask the true costs of expansion. To expose the shell game, it was necessary to reveal the true costs of social security. That could only be done by eliminating the state welfare programs for the elderly, making social security coverage universal, and paying social security benefits to all the elderly, regardless of whether they had paid into the system. The chamber plan would be funded through payroll taxes. At first, the program would be sustained by the surplus in the trust funds. As the surplus diminished, payroll taxes would be set to bring in only enough money to pay for current pensions. Any rise in the benefit levels would require an immediate increase in the tax rate. Consequently, the option of expanding coverage and running a further surplus would be eliminated.

Opponents of the chamber proposal argued that, by combining earned and unearned benefits, the proposal would lead to flat pensions financed through payroll taxes. Workers would pay for minimal pensions through social security and for better pensions through private pension plans that did not require them also to support the poor. Eventually private pensions would supersede public pensions, and the social security program would die.

The opponents of the chamber plan triumphed. Although pushed by proponents of the Chamber of Commerce plan and by conservatives within his own party to abandon social security, President Eisenhower endorsed the program instead. Responding to the stockbroker E. F. Hutton's characterization of social security as tyranny, the President wrote that "it would appear logical to build upon the system that has been in effect for almost twenty years rather

Table 2. GROWTH OF OLD-AGE AND SURVIVORS INSURANCE, 1940–1965

Year	Minimum Retirement Benefit at Age 65	Annual Maximum Taxable Earnings	Average Monthly Amount for Retired Workers	Contribution Rate (Percent) Employer and Employee
1940	$10.00	$3,000	$22.71	1
1941	10.00	3,000	22.72	1
1942	10.00	3,000	23.64	1
1943	10.00	3,000	24.50	1
1944	10.00	3,000	24.61	1
1945	10.00	3,000	25.11	1
1946	10.00	3,000	25.42	1
1947	10.00	3,000	26.21	1
1948	10.00	3,000	27.14	1
1949	10.00	3,000	28.39	1
1950	10.00	3,000	29.03	1
1951	20.00	3,600	37.54	1.5
1952	20.00	3,600	39.65	1.5
1953	25.00	3,600	56.76	1.5
1954	25.00	3,600	56.98	1.5
1955	30.00	4,200	69.74	2
1956	30.00	4,200	67.36	2
1957	30.00	4,200	67.59	2
1958	30.00	4,200	74.47	2
1959	33.00	4,800	81.46	2.25
1960	33.00	4,800	81.73	2.75
1961	33.00	4,800	80.17	2.75
1962	40.00	4,800	78.80	2.875
1963	40.00	4,800	80.30	3.375
1964	40.00	4,800	81.24	3.375
1965	44.00	4,800	82.69	3.375

SOURCE: Social Security Administration data.

than embark upon the radical course of turning it completely upside down and running the very real danger that we would end up with no system at all." In 1954 his administration added to the growing social security consensus by sponsoring a major extension to cover agricultural workers.

Despite the widespread approval of social security, social welfare policy was in a state of ferment in the 1950s. At issue was the nation's approach to welfare dependency. Just as Progressive reformers worried about the pauperization of outdoor relief recipients, so a new generation of post-Progressive reformers grew concerned about the demoralizing effects of welfare. So long as welfare went mainly to the elderly, as it did between 1935 and 1957, such concerns receded to the background. In 1957, however, for the first time, more people received aid to families of dependent children (AFDC), the successor to Progressive-era mothers' pension laws, than received aid to the elderly. During the 1950s, social insurance expenditures more than doubled as a percentage of GDP and public assistance expenditures, considered as a percentage of GDP, actually declined. Still, the number of people in the AFDC caseload rose by nearly 800,000 people from 1950 to 1960. This rise, coming at a time of prosperity and in an era when the number of children receiving survivors' benefits from social security increased by 1.3 million, troubled many observers. They wondered just who entered the AFDC caseload and how the federal government should respond.

Between 1957 and 1962, a discussion took place that divided the inheritors of the Progressive legacy in social welfare policy. It occurred in schools of social work and in government agencies administering social programs. Some, such as former Social Security Commissioner Arthur Altmeyer, regarded the unrestricted payment of monetary benefits and the right of needy persons to assistance as the essential aspects of the Progressive legacy. The state had no right to intervene in the family life of welfare recipients or to require that women on welfare accept a job outside of the home. Others, such as North Carolina's chief welfare administrator Ellen Winston, believed that therapeutic casework lay at the heart of the Progressive legacy. The state had an obligation to offer rehabilitative services to families. "From an examination of the AFDC caseload," wrote Wilbur Cohen, a professor of public welfare administration of the University of Michigan in 1958, "it appears that a high proportion of the caseload has multiple problems of a psychological and social nature." Such people needed to be approached "with active vigorous services of a preventive and rehabilitative nature." The trouble was that the two aspects of the Progressive legacy conflicted with one another. Rehabilitation, if not carefully managed, could undermine a family's basic right to a welfare benefit.

The fact that a growing percentage of the people on AFDC were black added a troubling racial dimension to the problem. Work and rehabilitation requirements for mothers on welfare were perceived by Arthur Altmeyer and other authorities as punitive measures aimed at blacks. Altmeyer worried about the way that some states tightened their residence requirements for the receipt of AFDC and took new steps to ensure that aid was not paid to children in an "unsuitable home." In Louisiana, the governor defined a home with an illegitimate child as unsuitable. Other localities, such as Oakland, California, initiated midnight raids on the homes of welfare beneficiaries to make sure that no man was living in the house.

The discussion about whether welfare beneficiaries should be rehabilitated even spilled into public policy governing social security. At issue was whether or not to expand the program so as to pay benefits to people who became disabled before they reached retirement age. Proponents of social security expansion argued that many other countries, such as England and France, ran disability insurance programs. Such a program, they asserted, would meet a real need in America. Those who favored the rehabilitation approach said that people with disabilities needed, above all else, the services necessary to facilitate their participation in the labor force. Aid conditioned upon withdrawal from the labor force impeded rehabilitation. The country should regard prosperity as a force to draw more people into the work force, not as a means of paying for more leisure.

In 1956, the proponents of social security expansion defeated the advocates of rehabilitation. As a result, Congress initiated a disability insurance program that allowed workers to receive a disability pension at age fifty. In 1960, true to the incremental style that governed policy making for social security, this program became modified so as to permit workers of all ages and their dependents to receive both social security and a disability pension. By 1972, disability insurance recipients received subsidized medical care as well. After 1956, therefore, social security became known as old-age, survivors, and disability insurance.

SOCIAL WELFARE POLICY IN THE 1960s

When the Kennedy administration arrived in 1961, it concentrated on passing items on an agenda of social welfare initiatives developed by Senate liberals in the late 1950s. The central idea behind the new projects was for the federal government to close gaps that separated the nation's performance from its potential. In particular, the Kennedy administration pushed federal aid to education and the expansion of social security to cover medical care costs for the aged. In marked contrast to the items on the New Deal agenda, the new items took the form of investments in human capital, rather than protections against economic catastrophe. In these respects, they more closely resembled programs of the Progressive Era and the 1920s than those of the 1930s.

In 1965, after Kennedy's death, Johnson's election landslide, and the Civil Rights Act's passage, the pieces fell in place for a major expansion of the American administrative state. One again a president with a firm agenda met an acquiescent Congress. In another of the nation's "big bangs" of legislative activity, Congress cleared aid to elementary and secondary education and Medicare from the agenda. Behind these high visibility items, Congress also expanded existing programs, such as vocational rehabilitation. Further, it tied incidental concerns, such as "special education" or the education of the handicapped, to the new major legislative vehicles.

In addition, Congress increased the rehabilitation features of welfare programs. It built on legislation, first passed in 1962, that allowed the federal government to pay three-quarters of the costs of state rehabilitative services for welfare beneficiaries. The doubts and uncertainties of the 1950s concerning the efficacy of rehabilitating welfare beneficiaries tended to be resolved in favor of increased state intervention. Scandals continued in the administration of local welfare programs. The association between the receipt of welfare benefits and a rise in the rate of illegitimacy caused growing dismay. Despite these problems, Congress had firm faith in the ability of professionals to "cure" dysfunctional families and restore the economic productivity of the heads of those families.

The years between 1963 and 1973, in particular, marked an era of unprecedented federal generosity. A nation that spent 10.3 percent of its GDP on public social welfare expenditures in 1960 devoted 14.7 percent to such expenditures in 1970, even though the GDP itself nearly doubled (in nominal terms).

As much as anything else, the passage and implementation of Medicare defined the social welfare style of the era. With the accomplishment of disability insurance in 1956, attention in social security policy-making circles had shifted to health insurance. Advocates for the expansion of social security argued that Medicare, hospital insurance for social security beneficiaries, was, in the words of Kennedy's assistant secretary of health, education, and welfare, Wilbur Cohen, not "new," but rather "a means of filling a gap in the floor of protection provided by monthly cash benefits under the social security program." Nor did Cohen believe that the proposal for Medicare amounted to socialized medicine. The administration proposal, as Cohen noted, did not cover physicians' services, nor did it allow the government to supervise either doctors or hospitals.

Between 1961 and 1965, first the Kennedy and then the Johnson administrations tried hard to gain congressional passage of Medicare. In 1962 the administration lost a close vote in the Senate. In 1964 the measure cleared the Senate only to be vetoed in a conference committee by the powerful Ways and Means chairman, Wilbur Mills.

After these false starts, Medicare became law in 1965, the heyday of the Great Society. Throughout the long legislative process, administration officials tried to reassure doctors and members of the public that the federal government would not interfere in medical practice. Before the 1965 congressional session, Cohen, Nelson Cruikshank of the American Federation of Labor–Congress of Industrial Relations, and Social Security Commissioner Robert Ball drafted the administration's Medicare bill. It included an explicit guarantee of freedom of choice of physician and hospital. Bills were to be paid just as they were under private Blue Cross arrangements. Indeed, the federal government even invited hospitals to designate Blue Cross or other private entities to receive Medicare bills and act as an intermediary between the hospital and the federal government.

As finally enacted, Medicare formed part of a broad health package that included three major items. The first was Medicaid, or subsidized medicine for welfare recipients. The American Medical Association brought this proposal to Wilbur Mills, who inserted it into the law. The second item was hospital insurance, or Medicare, intended for social security retirees. Medicare was the part of the bill that Cohen, Ball, and Cruikshank had drafted. The third item was known as Part B of Medicare. It defrayed the cost of doctor's bills for social security beneficiaries. Part B was optional. Elderly citizens paid for it through deductions in their social security paychecks. Part B also received a subsidy from general revenues. Unlike Part A of Medicare, therefore, Part B did not depend solely on contributions from workers and their employers. The optional features of Part B made it more palatable to Republicans. Indeed, John Byrnes, ranking Republican on the Ways and Means Committee, had proposed something similar in January 1965.

The scope of the legislation surprised nearly everyone. As Wilbur Cohen explained to the President, Congressman Mills simply turned to Cohen one day early in March and asked him to consolidate all the various proposals before the committee. "The effect of this ingenious plan is, as Mr. Mills told me, to make it almost certain that nobody will vote against the bill when it comes on the floor of the House." Indeed, few people did. In the days of the Great Society, the federal government had the financial means to adopt simultaneously what were previously competing alternatives.

In the case of Medicare, Lyndon Johnson did not use his power to dictate to Congress. Instead, he accepted its legislative handiwork on an issue that, prior to the big bang of 1965, had generated considerable controversy. The result was an expensive and complex piece of legislation. It allowed varying degrees of state, local, and federal control and showed considerable deference toward the political power and professional prerogatives of organized medicine and hospital administrators.

Soon after 1965 the window of legislative opportunity closed. Although Congress maintained existing programs and the level of federal funding increased, legislators proved reluctant to create new programs. In part, this reluctance reflected the growing costs of maintaining the programs already in place. As an example, Medicaid ultimately became the most costly of the nation's welfare (as opposed to social insurance) programs. Between 1966 and 1980 Medicaid costs doubled every four years. In 1980, Medicaid cost $30.4 billion at all levels of government, compared with $14.6 billion for AFDC.

The growth of public assistance programs, primarily AFDC, was a continuing concern after 1965. As the 1960s advanced, urban riots, the continued growth in the welfare rolls, and the substantial increase in black welfare recipients as a percentage of the total caseload all tended to increase public dissatisfaction with the welfare program and with the rehabilitation approach. During the decade, the unemployment rate was halved, AFDC recipients increased by almost two-thirds, and AFDC money payments doubled. As early as 1962, many states, including New York and Pennsylvania, spent more for welfare than for highways.

Congress responded, over the objections of President Johnson, with legislation in 1967 that froze the level of federal expenditures for welfare grants to families with illegitimate children. The legislation also permitted states to discontinue welfare grants for people who refused to join work training programs "without good cause." John Gardner, Johnson's secretary of HEW, protested these actions, as did such urban-based politicians as New York mayor John Lindsay and Sen. Robert F. Kennedy, all to no avail. An approach to welfare that emphasized the requirement that women on welfare should work had begun to replace the more permissive rehabilitation approach.

Liberals tried to counter the growing emphasis on work requirements with work incentives. In 1967, the Johnson administration and Congress negotiated changes in the law. Known as work disregards, they were designed to encourage welfare recipients to work by allowing them to keep some of their earnings without a reduction in their welfare payments. The 1967 social security amendments also established a rule that permitted welfare recipients to keep the first thirty dollars that they earned per month, as well as one third of the remainder. This rule signaled a change in welfare policy, away from psychologically oriented social services and toward more tangible economic incentives.

SOCIAL WELFARE IN THE 1970s

Less conflicted than Johnson about the benefits of welfare payments, Richard Nixon entered office with the view that the welfare rolls demanded immediate attention. Nixon referred to welfare as a "mess," a description that lingered over the course of the next two decades. He pointed with despair to the growing welfare caseload in urban areas. New York City had half a million people on the rolls in 1965, and 875,000 on the rolls in the middle of 1968. As Nixon began his presidency, the total reached a million. Resolving to encourage work among potential welfare recipients and to discourage illegitimacy and promiscuity, Nixon opted in August 1969 for comprehensive reform. He proposed to replace AFDC with a guaranteed income, payable to all families with children. His Family Assistance Plan promised to pay $1,600 to a family with four children, along with a $720 work disregard and a 50 percent marginal tax on earnings. That meant that a person could earn $720 and still receive the guarantee; for earnings above $720, the government reduced the family's payment by fifty cents for every dollar earned. Nixon accompanied this plan with rules to extend the food stamp program, so that welfare recipients would spend no more than 30 percent of their income on food.

In making these recommendations, Nixon explicitly rejected the service approach to welfare with its emphasis on social work. "The best way to ameliorate the hardships of poverty is to provide the family with additional income—to be spent as that family sees fit," the President said.

The Family Assistance Plan met with a hostile reaction in the Senate. Liberals such as Sen. George McGovern (D-S.D.) thought the guaranteed income contained in the plan was too low and that it was unfair to demand that mothers with children work. Conservatives such as Sen. John Williams (R-Del.) believed that a guaranteed income, even with work requirements, would be prohibitively costly and reduce the level of labor force participation. Williams pointed to what the experts in the field, who were growing in number and in econometric sophistication, called "notch effects." The existence of these effects, which phased out public housing and medical benefits at given levels of income, made it extremely difficult to design a welfare reform plan in which working mothers received more than nonworking mothers.

In October 1972, the President managed to salvage only a new program for the elderly, blind, and permanently and totally disabled from his proposals. Congress left AFDC intact. Supplemental Security Income (SSI), as the new program was called, allowed the federal government to take over the existing state programs in these categories. It put the federal government behind an absolute guarantee of $210 a month for an elderly couple on welfare. Unlike the AFDC program, SSI was administered by the Social Security Administration, which enjoyed a wide reputation as a competent agency. SSI, in effect, separated the administration of welfare for the worthy poor from welfare for mothers with dependent children.

During the 1970s, welfare became a hotly contested topic, as experts debated the fine points of program design and the public questioned the utility of paying welfare mothers not to work. Both the deterioration of the national economy and changes in the black family influenced the discussion. As the sociologist William Julius Wilson has reported, "in 1965 nearly 25 percent of all black families were headed by women and by 1980, 43 percent were."

President Carter, in particular, highlighted welfare reform. He worked to pass a new version of a guaranteed income, but achieved as little success as had Nixon. Carter, whose Program for Better Jobs and Incomes appeared in 1977, hoped to guarantee a higher income for the disabled, blind, and elderly people who were not expected to work and a lower income for able-bodied adults. These able-bodied adults were expected to supplement their welfare grants with jobs that the government would guarantee them, either in the private sector or in public service. Skeptics inside and outside of Congress doubted the ability of the federal government to provide sufficient jobs to those in need of them.

Indeed, the deteriorating economy of the 1970s substantially undermined the social welfare approaches of the 1960s. In the 1960s, Congress had been able to accompany inducements to change local policies with substantial grants-in-aid. In 1974 and 1975, when gross domestic product (GDP) declined and unemployment surged to 8.5 percent, the federal government lacked the financial means to engage in similar largesse. A common solution was simply to mandate responsibilities, such as making public buildings accessible to the handicapped, on employers, states, and localities. Mandating kept the policy focus on Congress. It also satisfied a growing constituency of "consumers" and public interest lawyers of congressional sympathy with their objectives. It did not affect existing programs and added no new strains to the federal budget.

The stagflation of the 1970s even affected the social security program. Indeed, when the rate of economic growth slowed in the 1970s, the system was in crisis almost by definition. At such times, social security had constant or increasing costs and, decreasing income. Further, the political system that had done so much to preserve the program also limited the available options. Congress could not easily increase payroll taxes or augment the program's income with general revenues. Raising taxes in a recession made little economic, let alone political, sense, and general revenues violated the rule that the system had to be self-supporting. The only other option was to cut benefits. Nearly all the benefits—whether for early retirement or for free health insurance for those with end-stage renal disease—reflected a political consensus that protected them against cuts.

During the 1970s, economic conditions proved strikingly unfavorable for the social security program. In 1972, after legislating a large increase in the benefit level, Congress decided to index future benefit increases to the rate of inflation. Between 1973 and 1975 unemployment and inflation increased to such an extent that the gross national product (GNP), expressed in real dollars, declined. The effects on the social security program were immediate. In 1974, the total assets in the Old Age and Survivors and Disability Insurance trust funds at the end of the year reached a high of nearly $46 billion. These assets declined steadily until 1981, when the figure was less than $25 billion. Inflation and rising disability rolls—the number of disabled workers rose from 350,384 in 1970 to 592,049 in 1972—increased costs. Unemployment decreased revenues. As these impersonal statistics implied, economic downturn meant a serious crisis in the social security program.

THE REAGAN ERA AND BEYOND

In 1981, President Reagan, facing the most severe crisis in the social security program's history, turned for help to the old device of an outside advisory council. Within the council, Robert Ball helped to cement an agreement between Democrats such as Rep. Claude Pepper (Florida) and Republicans such as Sen. Robert Dole (Kansas). The two sides agreed that the program would skip a cost of living adjustment, thus lowering benefits. This agreement formed the core of a package of benefit cuts and tax increases that became the basis for the Social Security Amendments of 1983. The 1983 law bailed out the program and left it in a secure position to face the future.

Shortly after the 1983 amendments, other factors turned in social security's favor and increased its financial solvency. The smaller Depression cohort began to retire and the larger baby-boom cohort remained in the labor market. The disability rolls began to recover, in part because administrators made it harder for workers to qualify for disability benefits. And by the end of Reagan's first term, the economy entered a long and sustained boom, with low inflation. Large surpluses began to accrue. That spawned a new round of political debate over government's ability to prefund the retirement of the baby boom. As the surpluses piled up, politicians began to consider using them for new projects, such as the creation of long-term insurance.

The program was not free of all its problems. Medicare, in particular, continued to pose complex dilemmas, as health care costs continued to rise, and as the entire health care financing system threatened to unravel.

Welfare interested President Reagan far more than did social security. He had made welfare reform a priority of his tenure as governor of California, and his interest in the subject continued during his presidency. In 1981, he persuaded Congress to make substantial cuts in AFDC, by changing the work-disregard formula and limiting welfare grants to 150 percent of a state's "standard of need." Unlike his immediate predecessors, Reagan disapproved of a guaranteed income and instead stressed purifying the welfare rolls and removing them of ineligible recipients. He believed that able-bodied welfare recipients should do public service jobs to pay off their grants. He favored state administration of welfare over federal administration.

In 1988 the President collaborated with congressional leaders, such as Daniel P. Moynihan (D-N.Y.) and with the National Association of Governors in sponsoring what became the Family Support Act of 1988. The law established comprehensive state education and training programs. It mandated transitional child care and medical assistance benefits and compulsory coverage of two-parent families for at least six months of each year. The law also contained a strong child support enforcement provision.

By the 1990s, it became clear that social security was the century's major innovation in social welfare policy. Few people suggested a return to the traditional poor law system, with its means tests, social workers, and great variations from place to place. Instead, they worked hard to try to preserve the social security and Medicare programs so as to meet the challenges of the next century.

Between 1900 and 1965, the nation had defined a distinctive approach to social welfare. Using the historian's expression for the reform era between 1900 and 1920, one might describe the approach as progressive. Legacies of this approach included an emphasis on occupationally oriented social welfare and the creation of programs in aid of economic growth and labor force participation. The approach relied on professional expertise, and featured a strong suspicion of democratic political processes.

The stagflation of the 1970s severely undermined this approach. Increasingly, that decade, almost as much as the 1930s, came to be regarded as the century's watershed: it was then that the nation learned the limits of the federal government's ability to solve social problems through the expansion of social insurance programs and grants-in-aid to the states. Further, it was no longer clear that professionals, whether they were economists, doctors, social workers, or vocational rehabilitators were the best interpreters of individual and collective needs.

Indeed, as the century ended, the nation sought to preserve the best of the Progressive legacy and to restore the illusive sense of community that marked the best aspects of nineteenth century society. Reform, whether of the welfare system or of health care finance, once again emphasized economy and the primacy of the local community.

SEE ALSO Wealth and Poverty (volume III); Race; Class (both in this volume).

BIBLIOGRAPHY

Among the excellent contemporary studies on the poor law are Roy M. Brown, *Public Poor Relief in North Carolina* (1928); and Douglas H. MacNeil, *Seven Years of Unemployment Relief in New Jersey 1930–1936* (1938). The contemporary classic on social insurance is I. M. Rubinow, *Social Insurance* (1916). An indispensable contemporary account of welfare capitalism is Don D. Lescohier and Elizabeth Brandeis, *History of Labor in the United States, 1896–1932,* vol. 3, *Working Conditions* (1935).

The best overviews of social welfare policy in the twentieth century are Michael B. Katz, *In the Shadow of the Poorhouse: A Social History of Welfare in America* (1986); James Patterson, *America's Struggle Against Poverty, 1900–1980* (1986); Walter I. Trattner, *From Poor Law to Welfare State: A History of Social Welfare in America,* 3d ed. (1984); and Margaret Weir, Ann Shola Orloff, and Theda Skocpol, eds., *The Politics of Social Policy in the United States* (1988). The first embodies the social history approach, the second perceptively blends intellectual and policy history, the third details the traditional liberal approach, and the fourth reports on the findings of the new historical sociology work in the field.

Good insights into veterans' pensions and the early phases of America's welfare are provided by Theda Skocpol, *Protecting Soldiers and Mothers: The Political Origins of Social Policy in the United States*

(1992). Also useful are the essays by Morton Keller and Ellis Hawley in Donald Critchlow and Ellis Hawley, eds., *Federal Social Policy: The Historical Dimension* (1988).

On workers' compensation, see Edward Berkowitz, *Disabled Policy: America's Programs for the Handicapped* (1987). An interpretation of the social welfare programs of the 1920s can be found in Berkowitz and Kim McQuaid, *Creating the Welfare State: The Political Economy of Twentieth Century Reform* (1992).

The Social Security Act is perhaps best explained by W. Andrew Achenbaum, *Social Security: Visions and Revisions* (1987), a scholarly and definitive account. Edward Berkowitz, *America's Welfare State* (1991), looks at the growth of the program. Berkowitz, ed., *Social Security after Fifty: Successes and Failures* (1987), contains interpretive essays on the development of the program. Martha Derthick, *Policymaking for Social Security* (1979), is a classic account of the manner in which social security has been governed. William Graebner, *The History of Retirement: The Meaning and Function of an American Institution* (1980), examines the links between the needs of the economy and the development of social security. So does Jill Quadagno, *The Transformation of Old Age Security: Class and Politics in the American Welfare State* (1988), an intriguing and richly interpretive work. Eric Kingson and Berkowitz, *Social Security and Medicare: A Policy Primer* (1993), provides a nuts-and-bolts guide to the program.

On the development of disability insurance and Medicare, see Alice M. Hoffman and Howard S. Hoffman, *The Cruikshank Chronicles: Anecdotes, Stories, and Memoirs of a New Deal Liberal* (1989), an interesting portrait of a leading advocate of social security expansion. Sherri David, *With Dignity: The Search for Medicare and Medicaid* (1985), explains the passage of Medicare. Paul Starr, *The Social Transformation of American Medicine* (1985), is a magisterial account of the development of public policy toward medical care. Deborah Stone, *The Disabled State* (1983), analyzes the role of disability in the welfare state. James Sundquist, *Politics and Policy* (1965), chronicles the legislative battles over Medicare.

The history of public assistance can be followed in Stuart Butler and Anna Kondratas, *Out of the Poverty Trap* (1987), a conservative interpretation of events. David T. Ellwood, *Poor Support: Poverty in the American Family* (1988), presents a contrasting liberal view. Michael B. Katz, *The Undeserving Poor: From the War on Poverty to the War on Welfare* (1989), writes with a sense of outrage that the poor have not been treated better. Theodore R. Marmor, Jerry L. Mashaw, and Philip L. Harvey, *America's Misunderstood Welfare State: Persistent Myths, Enduring Realities* (1990), do a nice job of defending the status quo. Peter Marris and Martin Rein, *Dilemmas of Social Reform: Poverty and Community Action in the United States* (1973), explain the origins of the service approach. Gilbert Y. Steiner, *Social Insecurity: The Politics of Welfare* (1966), is the definitive account of the development of public policy toward welfare reform. Steiner, *The State of Welfare* (1971), is a useful account of subsequent events. William Julius Wilson, *The Truly Disadvantaged: The Inner City, the Underclass, and Public Policy* (1987), perceptively explores the connections between welfare and race.

Important supplemental perspectives come from Daniel Levine, *Poverty and Society: The Growth of the American Welfare State in International Comparison* (1989); and Stanley Wenocur and Michael Reisch, *From Charity to Enterprise: The Development of American Social Work in a Market Economy* (1989).

FOUNDATIONS AND PUBLIC POLICY

Barry D. Karl

Although the creation of charitable trusts to provide for such needs as the education of the poor have been part of philanthropy for centuries, the broadening of those purposes to include a much wider range of public services became part of nineteenth-century Anglo-American practice. Middle-class citizens of modest means joined together with their wealthier bourgeois contemporaries to take over responsibilities once confined largely to religious institutions and aristocrats. As the state churches and public governments were transformed into the modern state in the eighteenth and nineteenth centuries, the popular citizenry created their own private systems of public management, as alternatives or supplements to the state, and often as critics. In the United States traditions of federalism divided functions among state, city, and federal governments, with sizable shared responsibilities that drifted into areas of management where the responsibilities of the state and of private associations of citizens serving one another were virtually indistinguishable. Tocqueville in his earliest visits to the new nation lauded the American practice of forming associations to meet public needs for tending common problems rather than depending on government bureaucracies.

INVENTING FOUNDATIONS

In the first decades of the twentieth century, Americans whose extraordinary wealth had developed from the post–Civil War expansion of natural resource exploration, industry, and transportation began to form new associations called foundations. Their common commitment to the general public welfare and the uses of science to benefit it combined with their different conceptions of the stewardship of wealth to produce a national system of private philanthropy. The intersection of that system with the growing public awareness of national needs in areas like education, medicine, and poverty created a dual system for funding what later generations would call public policy. The character of that system was complicated by the shadow of the Civil War. A national system would have required a cultural and racial integration no postwar Congress would have approved. The dual national system placed the new philanthropic foundations in a curious position, both private and public, both charitable and (from the perspective of the sciences that based their perception on method) revolutionary and progressive.

Three foundations established between 1907 and 1913—Russell Sage, Carnegie, and Rockefeller—are generally taken as the beginning point. While dollar comparisons are misleading, and not easy to calculate accurately given the fact that donors contributed additional sums between the initial gifts and their deaths ten or twenty years later, one can figure the foundations of the first three donors as constituting something over $200 million by 1920. During that time span federal expenditures in fields involving health, education, welfare, and scientific research ranged from nonexistent to very limited. Military pensions, health benefits, training and research combined with modest programs in regulatory economics, natural resource exploration, census study, immigration, and public health constituted the federal government's commitment to policy programs.

Almost a century later, there are 6,334 foundations listed in part 1 of the Foundation Center's *Foundation Directory, 1993.* It is important to note that foundations included in that volume of the directory constitute less than a fifth of the number of philanthropic foundations that exist in the United States. Inclusion in part 1 is dependent on the foundation's holding assets of at least $2 million or yearly grants of at least $200,000. Their combined assets at the time of the creation of the 1993 directory were $151,181,502,000 and their total giving $8,395,479,000. One should add to that $134,868,000 in low-interest loans they are allowed to make to organizations engaged in activities related to their philanthropic programs. Of those six thousand plus foundations, one thousand provided 60 percent of foundation grants given in 1993. Those one thousand hold $119 billion in assets and give $6 billion annually. Of that one thousand, no more than twenty-five, and probably fewer than that, are known as "the big foundations" or "the golden donors"—subjects of a continuing literature (chiefly two books by Waldemar A. Nielsen), national magazines that discuss them periodically, congressional hearings approximately once in a decade, and articles in the few newspapers that maintain surveillance.

In addition to those foundations described in the first volume of the directory, part 2 of the directory covers another 4,327 foundations whose combined assets were $3,581,296,000 and whose total giving came to $393,742,000 (exclusive of loans), with a range of grants from $50,000 to $200,000. Beyond the foundations dealt with in the directory and its supplement there exists a world of foundation philanthropy based on organizations that use the legal form simply to operate as little more than checkbooks for donors, convenient means of utilizing present law to maintain traditional charitable operations for individuals whose private resources, however limited they may be, are still sufficient to justify the method. Yet all are descendants of the original three and all are engaged in some form of influence on what we consider public policy in its broadest sense, from the care of the poor and the sick to the maintenance of art museums, opera companies, and symphony orchestras. The fact that the latter cultural institutions, once the private preserve of wealthy local elites, are now often the joint responsibility of both local and federal support agencies suggests the remarkable broadening of public policy that has taken place over the last decades of this century.

The modern philanthropic foundation, for all its novelty, can be located clearly in the ancient history of charity. Since charity is recognized in both religious and secular law as inherently public, to distinguish charitable acts from private acts of benevolence is one of the most important and oldest elements of the world of public policy. As an innovation in the history of charity, however, the philanthropic foundation added factors that had not been part of traditional charity, despite many common areas of concern. Chief among them was the optimism generated by the belief that scientific research and the systematic application of its discoveries would so improve the prospects of human development as to render the need for traditional charity unnecessary. By focusing on the institutions capable of furthering scientific research and those intended to distribute its solutions to social problems to the public at large, the makers of the great industrial fortunes (who had benefited so remarkably from late-nineteenth-century industrial expansion) could end the social ills that had made life tragic for all of human history: poverty, disease, war, famine, ignorance.

The incorporation of the general purpose foundation in the United States left the determination of direction to trustees and the succession of managers who served at their pleasure. In British law comparable charitable trusts required trustees to exercise the powers articulated for them by donors and thus serve as managers or administrators with legally defined responsibilities. The American foundation could be established without a specific purpose stated in its charter of incorporation that was binding on trustees. Therefore, foundations added to the history of charity a continuing concern with defining their programs of giving and managing the direction of philanthropy as their perception of the changing needs of society around them seemed to require.

The creators of the new foundations, the trustees they selected, and the staffs responsible to donors and trustees were the means of defining the world of social and intellectual problems and funding, even sometimes directing, the search for solutions. Thus, while foundations provide less than 10 percent of the total amount of money Americans give to charity, their influence on the history of policy making must be understood apart from their status as charitable trusts.

Foundations' status as charities has been a continuing source of debate in the American world of politics and policy, where the largest and most familiar programs of charity are associated with religion, which the First Amendment separates from the state. Many factors contributed to the invention of these distinctive institutions. Perhaps the most predominant characteristic of the modern foundation is its interest in research, which fits well with the large-scale concerns of the more enlightened policymakers of the new century as well as with the rapidly growing community of social scientists. The federal government's commitment to practical problems and short-term, politically viable solutions for them divided the territory of social policy with relative clarity. Until well into the twentieth century education at all levels was local and/or private, while the federal government restricted its attention to issues of practical training that affected the military services where scientific study held a limited, even if significant, position. As communities came to understand the necessity of training new generations to cope with the problems of a world dominated by ongoing technological transformations, however, theory and practice had to come together.

At the end of the nineteenth century, a dispersed system of collegiate education was in place to provide a nationwide network of research scholars in various fields. The emergence of a national system for propagating and developing new ideas required a financial structure that had not existed in colonial and frontier America. The establishment of the philanthropic foundation joined with the creation of private endowments for colleges and universities to provide such a structure.

Before foundations came into being, institutions like the Peabody Fund (1867), the Carnegie Institute at Pittsburgh (1900), the Carnegie Institution in Washington (1901), the Carnegie Endowment for International Peace (1910), and Rockefeller's Sanitary Commission (1909), Institute for Medical Research (1901) (now Rockefeller University), and General Education Board (1903) were directed toward almost specific purposes. All were efforts to find ways of coping with a recognizable and definable set of problems, ranging from education and the physical well-being of southern Negroes to medicine in China in particular and education in general. Carnegie began devoting his resources to building public libraries in 1901; but he was explicit in his belief that the founding of universities was not an efficient use of his supposedly limited philanthropic funds. The Russell Sage Foundation (1907), founded by Sage's widow, Margaret Olivia Sage, was an intermediary form between the specific funds and the general interest in social research that characterized the later period. Her husband's philanthropic interests during his lifetime were minimal, but she guided the foundation she insisted bear his name only into research in social welfare, the condition of the urban family, and the status of industrial labor, rather than centering attention on the funding of research in colleges and universities. It should be pointed out that while it is important to consider her foundation as the first modern foundation, those who advised her in the establishment of it pointed to the existence of what they referred to at the time as "foundations." The Milbank Memorial Fund, created two years earlier and with comparable funding, operated initially largely in carrying out the interests of its donor, Elizabeth Milbank Anderson. New research hospitals were also classified as foundations. The use of the designation "foundation" rather than "fund," "trust," "institution," or "board" did not make the difference initially that it seemed to make later, although we note that Carnegie called his last creation a corporation, and Eli Lilly named his institution an endowment.

Each of the corporations founded by Rockefeller reflected the interests of John D., Sr. The Rockefeller Foundation (1913) and the Carnegie Corporation of New York (1911), however, each founded with the general purpose of serving the good of humankind, reflected a common emphasis on research, education, and the products of technological change, even though the interpretations of their respective founders may have differed considerably. By refusing to define what each of them meant by the various versions of human welfare or the good of mankind, they in effect defined it as unpredictable and beyond the scope of prophesy, secular or religious.

THE NATIONALIZATION OF PRIVATE PHILANTHROPY THROUGH THE 1920s

Despite the absence of federal funding for policy programs, both Carnegie and Rockefeller assumed that the private institutions they were creating would work jointly with the federal government. Both men had previously been given charters by Congress for their earlier philanthropic corporations, following lines set up by the formation of the Smithsonian Institution. Established by Congress in 1846 as a private institution, the Smithsonian had a Board of Regents consisting of the vice president, the chief justice of the Supreme Court, three members each of the House and Senate, and nine citizens appointed by Congress. The Carnegie Institution in Washington not only bore a similar name, but included on its board of trustees the president and vice president of the United States and other federal officials as ex-officio members. Rockefeller's general education board had also been granted a federal charter. Yet when Rockefeller went to Congress for a charter for his foundation, Congress, caught up in the Progressive Era's protestations against trusts and large accumulations of wealth, rejected his offer. President William Howard Taft agreed. Both Rockefeller and Carnegie went to state legislatures to incorporate their foundations.

It is perhaps useful to point out here that the private resources wealthy philanthropists were eager to devote to education, scientific research, and social welfare were far greater than those the federal government was willing to direct toward such interests and would remain so until World War I, the New Deal, and World War II. While similar programs concerned with education, health, and even housing had been included in the management of the First World War, they were dismantled immediately after the war. The reluctance of the federal government to compete with or even match such private funding was a product of the still strong commitment to states' rights, and a surreptitious way of dealing with the fact that southern states did not want to offer social services to blacks even on a supposedly separate but equal basis.

Foundation donors, thus, did not think initially of a sharp distinction between their activities as private and those of the federal government as public. Even in the aftermath of the rejection of the Rockefeller federal charter, foundation trustees and executives maintained behind-the-scenes relations with national government, as well as with local governments, at the same time that they guarded jealously their status as private institutions. But Woodrow Wilson's decision to base government's management in World War I on so-called volunteers from business, industry, and social service agencies—rather than following the British model of a more professionalized war cabinet—brought managers from American industry into government as "dollar-a-year" administrators to work alongside government bureaucrats, bringing new changes to the role of wealthy private citizens in government. More important, the need of such men for staff chosen from both lower level business echelons and academia led those managers who could afford it to fund staffs for themselves, which distinguished them from the ranks of wartime volunteers who could not afford to be so generous.

The war established a pattern, however inadvertent it may have been, that has continued to characterize the role of private philanthropy in its relation to public policy. In the years between the two world wars that relationship was not only open but celebrated by its leaders as the future of the new "volunteer capitalism." A new generation of philanthropic leaders committed to professionalizing their foundation management began applying some of the conceptions of wartime management they had helped establish in government agencies. Aware of the need for staffs of experts who could bring their specialized knowledge to the service of a wider range of philanthropic management, they searched in academic institutions for new personnel to co-opt into their system.

John D. Rockefeller, Jr., became the first full-time professional in the Rockefeller philanthropies, serving first (and briefly) as head of the foundation and then moving out of the orbit of the foundation itself to help direct such other Rockefeller philanthropic interests as the building of Williamsburg, Virginia. By the 1920s he was inclined to oversee the Foundation by helping to select others to control the institution as well as by guiding the Foundation's policies from behind the scenes toward projects that reflected various aspects of his personal interests. Those interests could range from art and art museums to the building of Rockefeller Center as a privately funded, quasi-public works project for business, and ultimately after World War II to the gift of land for the United Nations building.

One can see in the 1920s the beginnings of what was destined to become one of the major shifts in foundation control as foundations began to select university presidents and other academic administrators as foundation presidents. The connection that had come to exist between the Rockefellers and the University of Chicago through its initial founding by John D. Rockefeller led to the choice of most University of Chicago figures as foundation executives. At the same time, a Rockefeller executive like Beardsley Ruml returned to the University of Chicago as the institution's first dean of social sciences. James Angell, Ruml's Chicago mentor during his student years at the university, had become president of the Carnegie Corporation of New York and then president of Yale.

Another important innovation in the war years was reflected in the founding in 1917 of the Julius Rosenwald Fund. A clothing business executive in New York and Chicago whose purchase of a one-fourth interest in Sears, Roebuck and Company made him president of the company by 1910, Rosenwald developed such ideas as profit-sharing and savings for employees. An opponent of Zionism, he wanted his fund to benefit American interests, most particularly programs for schools for blacks in the South and more adequate housing for blacks in northern cities. Again, as with other philanthropists, he asked for and received aid for his programs through tax support in the communities he benefited, and matching funds from other donors. An opponent, too, of perpetual foundations, he placed an ending point to his fund: twenty-five years after his death. His fund paid for the construction of more than five thousand schools in fifteen southern states. His personal contributions to the city of Chicago included the building of the Museum of Science and Industry and major gifts to the University of Chicago. He also played a significant role as a donor in Chicago reform politics, chiefly as backer of some of the new Progressive-era social science reports on crime and corrupt government.

The attractiveness of the foundation form spread well beyond the world of great wealth and surprisingly quickly after the big foundations were put in place by their donors, although not without an interesting connection. Frederick H. Goff, president of the Cleveland Trust Company, and not incidentally Rockefeller's Cleveland lawyer, was instrumental in forming the Cleveland Foundation (1914) out of a collection of local charity organizations. It began a movement that would, through the 1920s, be repeated in many leading cities, touching on and influencing principles used to build various forms of Community Chest to unite local charities under a single umbrella agency. Community foundations, however, took the charitable responsibility a step beyond the distribution of funds to existing organizations. They offered potential donors of relatively modest means a way of banding together to assure administration of their funds both as they would have administered them themselves and as a trustee group would direct, bringing a continuing interest in the welfare of the community to bear on the long-range use of funds.

Several factors characterized foundation contributions in the 1920s, chiefly a new emphasis on the social sciences and their relation to new developments in government policy making. While medicine remained strong in Rockefeller interests, John D. Sr.'s early concern with economic policy and education for economic understanding achieved new research status with the formation of the National Bureau of Economic Research. The establishment of the Social Science Research Council in 1923 was a step in the direction of building a new view of the modern social sciences as well as a new set of relationships between the growing generation of policy-oriented social scientists and foundation managers. Ruml had gone from a short stint under Angell, who had brought him to Carnegie, to the Rockefeller Foundation where he headed the Laura Spelman Rockefeller Memorial. Originally an extension of the Rockefeller family concerns with the traditional problem of caring for widows and children, under Ruml's leadership the Memorial became the central funding source for research in the social sciences. The relation between foundations and the academic community formed in the 1920s was established quickly and decisively in the first five years of the decade.

Edward S. Harkness, the son of one of Rockefeller's business partners, Stephen Harkness, and a friend of John D. Jr.'s, formed the Commonwealth Fund in 1919, which he did not wish to bear the family name. Among the fund's initial interests was American law, which the fund began to study under the leadership of Max Farrand, but the foundation moved into the field of medicine and hospitals. Medicine would continue to be the refuge of philanthropists under attack for interventions in more obvious social and political policies. A committed Anglophile, Harkness created a British fund whose purpose was the bringing of young and promising British civil servants to the United States for periods of training, a kind of reverse Rhodes scholarship. As part of his love of British education, he gave money for building the house systems at Harvard and Yale. Although his gifts came not from the Commonwealth Fund but from his personal fortune, he continued to stipulate that his name not be on any of the houses built by his money. It was not until after his death, when Harvard built its dormitory for graduate students, that the Harkness name began to appear on buildings he had helped fund.

It is tempting to divide the 1920s into two five-year episodes. The first five years were, in some respects, a period of readjustment not only to the war experience that had shaped some foundation practices but to the inevitable transformation in leadership as the original donors either died or stepped aside in favor of a younger generation of managers. The chief impact of the war was in the size of foundation grants. The war had enveloped American philanthropy in unanticipated ways. The Red Cross, a modestly sized private agency before the war, mushroomed as a result of wartime national and international responsibilities. The same was true of war relief activities for those organizations that accepted the mandate of emergency relief to war-damaged Europe. Herbert Hoover's role in coordinating the acceptance and distribution of at least some of the relief contributions enhanced his reputation, both among those who saw him as the source of food for war and postwar Europe, and those who thought him a dictator in the making who could not be trusted to be a collegial manager of the various ad hoc groups assembled to deal with the problems of war and postwar relief. As secretary of commerce throughout the 1920s and as president at the era's end, Hoover would go on to attempt a major liaison between private philanthropy and public policy.

If the first half of the postwar decade was one of consolidation and organization, the second half witnessed the effort to apply those organizations to the solution of social problems. Again, foundations were deeply involved, although in different ways. The Social Science Research Council (SSRC) and the National Bureau of Economic Research (NBER) were formed to promote the generation of new social science ideas; the Institute for Public Administration (IPA), the Brookings Institution, and in 1931 the Public Administration Clearing House (PACH) were formed to apply such research to the ongoing problems of government operations. In what may have been an effort to keep the Rockefeller name out of sensitive political areas, the Laura Spelman Rockefeller Memorial spun off the Spelman Fund, which financed work in public administration.

The whole city planning movement, with its related fields of modern public services, housing, and budget finance, helped produce a self-awareness among a new generation of practitioners in the various new fields of urban studies. The Spelman Fund was one of several sources that helped establish new organizations to work side by side with the somewhat older organizations that had grown out of the city planning movement of an earlier era. The founding of the Public Administration Clearing House in proximity to the University of Chicago (it was housed in buildings adjacent to the university but never intended as part of its quadrangular pattern of buildings or under the control of its trustees and administration) was a center for such organizations. Headed by Louis Brownlow, who had come directly out of the city manager movement, PACH provided a generation of "practitioners" in government management with the academic environment that came to characterize much of the new urban academia in the field of public administration. The Maxwell School at Syracuse University, like Harvard's Littauer Center, aspired to be an educational center for practitioners, providing potential government administrators with the academic background—and credentials—that would enable them to reform American government at all levels.

Thus, although medicine and medical research would remain the most common objects of philanthropic support, the social sciences in the 1920s were rapidly becoming a leading interest. Borrowing from the reasoning that had spurred interest in medical research earlier in the century, social science enthusiasts were prepared to go beyond consideration of social problems as a new species of disease and to focus on more basic research in the nature of social organization and all of its elements: economic, sociological, political, and even anthropological. While the problems were certainly not new, approaching them as symptoms of disease rather than as evidence of moral failure, which had been the first reform approach, could now be expanded into a larger and richer understanding of the nature of society itself and the application of new methodological techniques to understanding it. Although still focused on the possibility of cure, rather than punishment, as the answer to problematic social behavior, thereby continuing the initial optimism of disease theory, the new social sciences advanced concepts of discovery and frontier on a new level. Despite the fact that this optimism was not universally accepted in the growing community of serious social scientists—some of whom were much more concerned with the need to establish objective methodological standards and to discover and analyze more sophisticated data without regard to application let alone political purpose—there was no question that the relation between theory and practice was used to sustain the support of donors.

Perhaps the high point of open and publicly acclaimed foundation involvement in the federal government came during the Hoover administration. Part of Hoover's program for his government was built on his belief that all federal advisory systems, like the backing for programs in old age pensions, unemployment insurance, and health care, would come from private resources. He set all his cabinet secretaries searching for such funding, using himself and his White House as his prime example. His Committee on Social Trends, which he appointed in 1929, and its monumental report, *Recent Social Trends,* which appeared in 1933, was funded by the Rockefeller Foundation. The report, based on research undertaken by joint groups of academics and government bureaucrats, remains even today the most thorough single study ever undertaken of the state of American society. Although many of its ideas and several of its recommendations were to become part of New Deal organization, it was forgotten for many years after its virtual inundation by the Roosevelt transition.

One can see interesting transformations in other areas. The Carnegie focus on libraries had become, in the postwar period, a concern with the staffing of libraries with trained professionals. The founding of a Graduate Library School at the University of Chicago seemed to the Carnegie Corporation a logical step in the modernization of what had become a Carnegie tradition of public library development. The intermixture of foundation direction and personal philanthropy was also manifested in the religious interests of John D. Jr. and his wife, Abby Aldrich Rockefeller, and the University of Chicago was once again their medium. The establishment of the Oriental Institute at Chicago was based in part on their desire to further scholarship to study the origins of Western Christianity in the Middle East through advances in the exploration of the archeology of that ancient region of the world. Coupled with sophisticated scholarly analysis of Biblical texts, archeological research could explore scientifically the origins of Western religion.

The decade of the twenties thus rested on an optimism that was, in essence, progressivism scientifically conceived to provide a new, supposedly objective, unbiased, value-free knowledge that had no ideological base. Later critics would accuse their scholars and their earlier medicine researchers of shielding themselves from reality to provide their donors with knowledge they would find acceptable within the context of their obvious commitment to capitalism; but it would be difficult to find either concealment or self-delusion in what the new scholars wrote. That generation of academics, many of them from small town religious and political backgrounds not unlike Rockefeller's, was not looking for revolution. They were looking for the perfection of a social order they felt had been handicapped by ignorance of the sciences they were beginning to understand. Their historical perspective often saw the original thrust toward democracy formed in the Revolution and articulated by the Jacksonians as having been thwarted temporarily by the excesses of a late-nineteenth-century entrepreneurial energy that could now be harnessed to work for the good of all Americans.

They did not predict the Crash and the Depression. Despite acceptance of the later critiques of business attitudes in the 1920s, their relation to the foundations that funded them and the universities that employed them spoke to a different prophecy. Franklin Roosevelt was their prophet and the New Deal the fulfillment of their prophecy. Capitalism under rational, scientific control could be made to work.

FOUNDATIONS AND THE FEDERAL GOVERNMENT, 1930s–1940s

By the 1930s the federal government and many state governments had grown accustomed to calling on the Brookings, IPA, and PACH, all privately funded and privately managed, for advisory services the governments could not themselves afford. One of those services was the very provision of personnel who, sometimes with salary support from foundations, helped run New Deal programs in various areas. The support of program advice and development was carried on without public acknowledgment lest fire be drawn to the foundation donors themselves who could be accused of policy manipulation.

The mid-1930s also marked a turning point in the federal government's approach to tax policy and foundations. The emergence of new foundations, potentially of large proportions, was destined to place names like Henry Ford, Eli Lilly, and Robert Wood Johnson at the forefront of American foundations in the years after World War II. Inheritance taxes had been part of political debate for years and had in fact been enacted as part of the taxes that funded the costs of World War I, but they became part of the permanent taxing process in 1935. The establishment of a foundation became a method of sheltering the wealth of estates, giving the money to public programs, in a sense, without giving it to the government. As far as congressional criticism was concerned, issues of tax avoidance seemed to take precedence over the potential political power of money, except for the oddly singular fear on the part of Congress that foundation money would be used for lobbying purposes. The same tax legislation untangled the authority of corporations to give to charitable causes and ultimately to set up corporate foundations, although the road to that form of independence, fought by stockholders and their lawyers, remained rocky. Not until after World War II would that path be cleared, and even then it was difficult to see it as a philanthropic instrument corporations were willing to commit themselves to without some of the old reservations. The line between a company's public relations and its responsibility to the community's welfare remained unclear.

It would be wrong to take tax shelter as the sole purpose of foundation establishment, attractive though it was. Some of the fortunes of which we speak were so large as to leave more than adequate resources to heirs, even after taxes (which did not exist significantly in the years of Rockefeller and Carnegie). William Danforth of Saint Louis had interests that were complex. A business devoted to such products as chicken and animal feed could be said to need farmers educated in the new technologies of agriculture in order to assure the viability and modernization of civilization's oldest profession in an industrial age. Danforth originally sought to promote his business interests, perhaps. But his intense religious commitments combined with the mid-twenties continuation of the concern with the sustenance of farming as a whole way of life to produce the educational ideas that he sought to develop through the foundation that still bears his name. Danforth's grandson, William, as president of Washington

University, was involved in the transfer of large amounts of Danforth Foundation capital to Washington University and other Saint Louis academic centers; but that was in 1973 and again in 1986 after the Danforth Foundation had already made a major contribution to the 1960s revolution in graduate education.

One should also point out the use of foundation money to aid in the internationalization of American academic interests energized by World War I. The Rockefeller Foundation's concern with the establishment of research programs in many of the countries of Europe and Asia moved well beyond the early interest in health care delivery—the training of doctors and nurses—and into more advanced research in diseases, physical science, even mathematics in eastern Europe. The possibility that scientific research in the Soviet Union might help direct or redirect the ideological interests of its social and political managers had not been ignored in the 1920s and continued, albeit with a great deal of frustration, in the Stalinist period. The establishment of International Houses on major university campuses was intended to bring foreign students into contact with American students, with the hope that their social relationships would lead to greater understanding of one another.

Study of foreign societies in Asia as well as Europe were intended to help structure programs in the United States, although the rise of Hitler in Germany created conundrums foundations found difficult to handle. On the one hand although they themselves, like many American educators and intellectuals in the 1920s, had been given to various degrees of the same selective anti-Semitism that marked all of American culture—Jewish intellectuals were acceptable only when they met the very highest standards—they nonetheless became concerned with the migration of German scientists, scholars in a range of fields in the social sciences, artists, literary figures, and musicians to the United States in the years before American entry into the war. But it would appear that academic utility and quality governed the direction of generosity if not the degree. Neither government nor foundations addressed the humane issues of the Holocaust.

The Carnegie Corporation of New York had shifted its interests in Europe even immediately after World War I from Germany to France and had continued Andrew Carnegie's concern with the British Empire and the older African settlements. The Commonwealth Fund remained committed to the British Empire. It was an interesting era of highly specialized internationalization that was to have its most important effects in the years after World War II. Thus, even before American entry into the war, the loose system of foundation, academic, and government relations had been formed.

When Albert Einstein signed the famous letter of the atomic physicists informing Franklin Roosevelt of atomic experiments in Europe and the United States that could result in a new potentially devastating weapon, Einstein, a recent Jewish immigrant from Hitler's Germany, was already housed at the institution that had backed his migration, the Princeton Institute for Advanced Study—a newly formed, privately funded but administratively independent adjunct to the university, under the direction of former Rockefeller executive Abraham Flexner. Einstein mentions other physicists, most of them recent émigrés, who were engaged in the same work, and points to the possibility that private universities, industry, and government might engage in cooperative work to build an American version of the weapon before German scientists and their government reached the same dangerous end.

The subsequent work of physicists at Columbia and the University of Chicago is, of course, well-known now but the degree of involvement of foundations, either directly or indirectly, in the steps that led up to those historic events is not, and may not be as clearly traceable as one might wish. The imposition of secrecy once the wartime American government took control obscured such relationships and their history while it began contacts among government, universities, and individual academics that formed models for interaction after the war. The involvement of foundation personnel from trustees through staff in the war effort assured that individuals would and did move back and forth.

In any case, the ground for cooperation between university scientific research and the federal government had been laid. Studies in the fields of political science, history, and economics were also part of the training programs that spread across the country to produce courses for officers-in-training for work abroad—not in combat, but in the various forms of occupation and citizen retraining that were expected to follow the war. They were also part of a large-scale cooperative enterprise that used the products of foundation funding of research of the previous decades not only in problem solving for the war but in the postwar world. Meetings associated with the names of estates of the wealthy in New Hampshire and Washington, D.C., brought the same kind of leadership from academia, industry, banking, and government that had been brought to the Dartmouth College campus by the Rockefeller Foundation, acting through the Social Science Research Council, in the 1920s and 1930s. With or without congressional backing and even against the possibility of congressional opposition the plans were laid. Economic policy toward the Soviet Union also began to take shape.

Part of the problem faced by policymakers rested on the continuing limitations of knowledge. The relationship between the gathering and creating of knowledge on the one hand and the application of knowledge on the other had been an intensifying issue in the academic world ever since the establishment of that world in ancient times. The building of universities had inherited and continued the conflict. In the United States the conflict had seemed exacerbated at times by the shortages of knowledge generated by an ever changing, ever expanding society. Foundations had vacillated between research and application from their very beginnings. Sold on research but promised application by an academic community inherently in need of funds for its own developments in pure research, donors observed the war demonstrating the possibility of support by the federal government. Since many of the donors and their foundation staffs were part of wartime administration, the relation between foundations and government was a more sophisticated continuation of the practices of the government of World War I. In both cases government's essential commitment to the politics of action and accomplishment and recurrent suspicions of knowledge and the ideological sensitivities felt by both political and bureaucratic leaders would only briefly suggest limits on what government could or would be willing to do.

Beginning perhaps with the GI bill of rights (the Serviceman's Readjustment Act of 1944) and its rejuvenation of an academia suffering both from the years of depression and the effects of the war, American universities and colleges could begin to see before them an entirely new source of expansion. Some even looked forward to freedom from the restrictions placed on them by foundation managers and trustees. As Don K. Price pointed out, scholars had found military managers more open to their belief in experiment, less insistent than foundation managers that they, too, understand the basic issues involved in the research they were funding, and therefore unlikely to ask the questions that raised issues of practicality. Price, a colleague and disciple of Brownlow's, helped lead the Hoover commissions of the Truman and Eisenhower years in their programs for executive reorganization and capped his career with the deanship of Harvard's public policy program. Few of his generation appreciated the increasingly complex relation between public policy and both public and private funding as he did.

It is worth pointing out that the GI bill of World War II and its successors in the aftermaths of the Korean and Vietnam wars were obviously tied to war service rather than to the need for national support of higher education. What other advanced societies accepted as a national responsibility, Americans viewed as specific responses to specific conditions. Even federal support for elementary and secondary education followed similar one-shot agendas rather than permanently acknowledging national needs.

POSTWAR PLANNING AND OTHER INFLUENCES

Organizations that brought together businessmen, foundation officials, and government administrators in various combinations began during the war and followed the model created by the SSRC in the Dartmouth meetings of the prewar period and the general suggestions of Einstein in his prewar letter to Roosevelt. Indeed, one would be hard-pressed to find the beginnings of the various organizations as they progressed from meeting groups to incorporation. The Rand Corporation, whose origins are traceable, received its charter of incorporation in 1948 after such relatively informal beginnings. The Committee for Economic Development was a similar grouping of interested businessmen and other professionals that got together first in 1942 to begin postwar planning (at a time when leaders like Roosevelt himself were loathe to suggest that we were certain that we would be doing the planning).

While Rand joined such organizations as Brookings, IPA, and PACH as independently funded centers of policy study, its identification as what was beginning to be called a "think tank" seemed to open a new range of cooperation between government and policy research institutions staffed by specialists through contracts that were independent of direct influence and control by government bureaucrats. The influences that did in fact exist involved, among other things, the exchanges of personnel as the government policy advisers of an administration in power sought professional refuge in the aftermath of a change of party administrations and a new administration seeking staff looked for experienced personnel.

Eager to involve themselves as participants and agents, foundations tried to be careful not to commit themselves as creators of such groups, lest that commitment be looked upon as permanent (a problem the older foundations were already experienced at avoiding) but also in the interest of promoting the idea of cooperation among larger and more varied kinds of participants. The metaphor of "seed money" had long been one of the practices of foundations and individual philanthropists as a way of encouraging wider participation in projects chosen by the first donors, but in addition assuring that foundations would not be accused of the kind of pressured manipulation of policy they might in fact have been engaged in. Critics would see the donor's requirement of matching funds as a way of directing larger numbers of smaller gifts to meet the interests of the donors who initiated the projects, whether or not those interests were shared by the community as a whole.

While, as in World War I, the role of individuals from private industry and academia had been central to the war effort, it was clear that a new generation of such leaders had emerged. Much more convinced of the importance of relationships between public and private interests, they saw less threat, more control, and the possibility of a more cooperative world than their fathers had known. The trustees and staff of the Rockefeller Foundation were eager to educate the new Rockefeller family leader, John D. Rockefeller III, and scarcely gave him time to change from his uniform before they began inviting his visits and writing him of their hopes for the postwar foundation. His father, meanwhile, was expressing his own concerns. The foundation, he thought, may have been too focused on research, too little on application. The old debate was still there.

The foundations that moved into positions of authority in the immediate postwar years were in several significant instances the consequences of the tax reforms of the New Deal and even the war. The New Deal Wealth Tax of 1935, as it was called, was not quite the "soak the rich" tax both defenders and critics labeled it. The inheritance provisions were scaled back versions of demands that had been made as far back as the Populist and Progressive eras, when the very large fortunes of the post–Civil War period and the new industries that helped produce them had come under attack. By no means confiscatory, except possibly where the largest estates were concerned, the new taxes were sufficiently stringent to make wealthy individuals look for ways of ridding themselves of taxable resources before their deaths.

Increased taxation on inheritance and wartime "excess profits" had had parallel but different effects on foundation development. Henry Ford, Eli Lilly, and Robert Wood Johnson had all established their foundations initially, one presumes, to continue the particular forms of generosity each had practiced in varying degrees as well as to preserve their fortunes from the significant inheritance taxation that would follow their deaths (something the earlier foundation creators had not had to do). The tax legislation up to that point had enabled them to make their children wealthy and to protect their own resources for as long as they lived. But they were not required to state the purposes of their newly institutionalized philanthropy or the amounts they would distribute yearly, which had been part of what was by then a tradition of foundation practice. The wealth of foundations could accumulate as their own wealth had accumulated, but not subject to taxation. In keeping with the old tradition of not subjecting the property of religious or educational institutions to taxation, property given to foundations or purchased with foundation resources would also be relatively protected from taxation. The benefits donors themselves might take from resources now transferred to foundations, whose activities they might continue to influence as they had influenced their own philanthropic giving, was not clear. They could build, occupy, staff, and furnish such office space as they chose and as lavishly as they chose. That space could be used for whatever additional personal or even quasi-business purposes they might find useful; or at least it was not determined initially that they could not or under what circumstances they could. Whether family members could also make use of such benefits was also not clear. Later revisions of tax legislation would tighten up many of these "loopholes," but not without publicity that would disturb the older foundations and create interesting problems for the newer ones.

A second important change that came out of the war experience was a potentially enhanced relationship between corporations and possibilities for philanthropic giving. Corporations interested in such giving had been restricted by the courts to a no-man's-land between a limited support of such community needs as could be claimed were a benefit to employees and community interests that could be called advertising. The deductibility of contributions to cultural endeavors that were then claimed as advertising and deductible under the excess profits tax led to the funding of such cultural treasures as radio broadcasts of performances of the New York Philharmonic and the creation of an orchestra for Arturo Toscanini—special audience events that were probably not acceptable as profit-seeking occasions. Such activities had preceded the war but on a somewhat more restricted public service scale, such as Texaco's funding of the Saturday matinee radio broadcasts of the Metropolitan Opera. Yet such activities came much closer to advertising, even though they represented the sponsor's product less obviously, often only by stating the name of the company. They could still be defined as public relations and therefore did not violate the legal requirement that corporations prove the benefit of their gifts to the business interests of the corporation.

The court case that clarified the way for large-scale funding of colleges, universities, and other such institutions by corporations was *A. P. Smith* v. *Barlow* in 1953. Designed as a test case, the Smith company had made a gift to Princeton University in order to bring the issue to the attention of the courts. The specific instance reflected major national changes. Corporation managers were of a new generation, increasing numbers of them educated in the institutions they were now seeking to support. Aware, too, of the need to broaden audiences to expand the backing for the tastes and judgments they saw as necessary for the development of an American culture to stand alongside the great cultures of the world—most particularly the culture of the Soviet Union and the nations it was seeking to influence—they saw no alternative to some kind of democratizing of that culture. The judgment in the *Smith* case also makes crystal clear the role that the Cold War had begun to play in American intellectual life. If the United States was going to be able to defeat its ideological enemies in the world, it would have to have a public educated to understand the values of its "free" society and prepared to defend that society's democratic ideology. And if, according to the court, one could no longer rely on great fortunes to support that education—since the age of individual multimillionaires was presumably at an end, or so the court believed—then great corporations were going to have to take their place.

Whether corporations were to benefit more from the subsequent establishment of foundations of their own or the independent philanthropic activity many of them began to engage in as institutional public relations remained an open question. The issue of function was still there, although not in the *Smith* decision. Should corporations move outside their accustomed role of producing profit? Was public involvement beyond that a two-edged sword that might end up damaging the corporation in the public's eyes?

Corporations are still being urged to contribute more to philanthropy than their sense of business practice often seems to incline them to give, particularly in periods of business recession. And the distinction between traditional needs of community well-being—education, health, and poverty—and the newer conceptions of culture did not follow easily or according to traditional practices better understood in older societies of the world. Even in the years before *Smith* v. *Barlow* corporations could give to institutions like hospitals if they could show a direct benefit to the firm's employees. The new legal status of corporate giving extends that allowance considerably but still leaves the requirement that profit must come first. The definition of corporate community responsibility remains cloudy.

THE PROFESSIONALIZATION OF PHILANTHROPY, 1950s

Criticism of foundations grew in the 1950s. As the Ford Foundation vastly broadened its activities in keeping with its increased resources the search for distinctive purpose also expanded. Its ownership of approximately 90 percent of the stock of Ford Motor Company gave it a remarkable position in the foundation field. Yet its controversial role in promoting internationalism as postwar isolationist and anticommunist debates swept the country embarrassed some Ford automobile dealers, who perceived the Ford Foundation as promoting radical ideas. But that was a minor and somewhat familiar problem in the foundation world. Contributions from Rockefeller's Standard Oil, after all, had been seen by some as "tainted money," although U.S. Steel seemed to bear little of the burden as far as Carnegie's benefactions were concerned. For obvious reasons neither of the latter two foundations was named after the donor's business. Ford was.

Eli Lilly, founder of a pharmaceutical firm that bore his name, explicitly restricted the Lilly Endowment from engaging in medical research but set up a board dominated by Lilly executives and an endowment consisting entirely of stock in his company. The Robert Wood Johnson Foundation, by contrast, pressed an agenda focused on medicine, specifically health care delivery, despite the fact that the production of medical care products was Johnson and Johnson's business. Subsequent congressional legislation would restrict the ability of a foundation to influence fields that might ultimately affect the profits of the donor's company as well as the control of stock in that company.

After a period of relative postwar calm where

the issue of philanthropy was concerned, several committees of the House of Representatives began looking into the question of the role of foundations in their relation to public policy. Both the select committee headed by Congressman Cox (1952) and the special committee of Congressman Reece (1954) were moved largely by questions generated by the concern over communist influences on American intellectual groups. The Cox committee was content to point out that several of the groups to which foundations had contributed money were also on the attorney general's list of communist-influenced organizations, but that such organizations represented a very small proportion of foundation donees. Nor was there any reason to presume that foundations knew of such connections, where they did exist, at the time they made their grants.

The Reece committee took a much more critical tack. Its hearings suggested parallels with the investigations conducted by Sen. Joseph McCarthy, using questionable tactics to suggest serious communist influence, if not outright domination by Communists. This was a charge that appeared laughable to those inside the generally conservative foundation world but not to those who identified all forms of intellectual elitism with communist control and who in any case were not conversant with the practices of foundations. Years of private activity had protected foundations from public view, but they had left a lacuna in public understanding that could not be filled quickly amid the storm of criticism. To be sure, foundations had been subjected from the beginning to criticism of elitism and exclusivity, but the identification of intellectual elitism with communist radicalism went far off that particular mark. Foundations were, after all, the trustees of large amounts of money accumulated by the nation's leading capitalists, some of whose family members continued to take part in the making of foundation policy as well as in their own capitalist enterprises. Foundation trustees had been selected traditionally from the nation's business and banking leadership, and included as well retired judicial figures, women academics (not a very large group), and college presidents; this was scarcely what one could call a radical crew. The self-selecting character of foundation trustee membership assured that change would be slow.

Foundation staffs also continued to come from the same special groups—white males from eastern establishment educational institutions, often recommended to foundation presidents and trustees by college presidents or the trustees themselves. Rockefeller's use of the University of Chicago was possibly an exception because it was a Rockefeller creation; but the dominance of Yale, Harvard, and other eastern institutions is clear and continues even in the 1990s. Staff members of foundations made their own recommendations as well, thereby assuring a certain amount of inevitable cohesion and continuity.

While foundation staffs may not have had independent means themselves and served initially for relatively modest salaries, they were able to maintain a professional life-style that was scarcely proletarian. Membership in upper-class social clubs in New York, Boston, and Washington assured them that they would continue the patterns of behavior that they had known at Harvard, Yale, Princeton, and similar institutions that had produced the nation's intellectual and financial leadership much as Oxford and Cambridge had produced Great Britain's. Indeed, many of the wealthier among them contributed to the early-twentieth-century restructuring of American universities to imitate as closely as possible their British counterparts.

Foundation staff members moved cautiously and with a proper reluctance to consider associating with one another to protect themselves from populist attacks. The caution and reluctance stemmed from the fact that the location of the largest foundations in New York City brought on accusations of collusion in and of itself. Still, the utility of having a central library where anyone could find the available literature on foundations, as well as statistical data on practices and financial status of foundations, led to the creation of a center and library in 1956, the expanded publication of yearly reports of foundations, and, perhaps most important of all, the publication of successive editions of a directory that listed donors, personnel, purposes, amounts of capitalization, and addresses and telephone numbers of the largest foundations. The Council on Foundations offered an open forum for internal discussion and education of the growing community of foundations as well as of the interested public. This led ultimately to the publication of a journal, *Foundation News* (1959), and, in the 1960s, publications and research committees to study foundation activities. Regular meetings of the council and periodic meetings of foundation heads helped establish a foundation world that began to operate as an association for the professionalization of foundation interests and management.

The foundation world had become a planet of its own. It had produced a profession, even what some humorously considered a new species. What Dwight Macdonald called "a philanthropoid" in his book on the Ford Foundation (1956) had been institutionalized but in ways quite different from those Macdonald might have considered. While there existed no schools for the training of philanthropoids and no literature guiding them, both were not far off.

When Robert Bremner's *American Philanthropy* appeared in 1960 it spelled out what appeared to be the established pattern of the association of government and philanthropy in the building of social progress in the United States. It also predicted a future that seemed set, as indeed it was through the years of the Great Society. Foundations in particular and public needs and private philanthropy in general would fund pilot studies frequently through university research and propose private remedies that could be offered as experiments. Public agencies could adopt those that promised benefits and bring in to government personnel trained in their practice. John F. Kennedy's staffing of his New Frontier was a virtual model of the plan, to the extent that one could call it a plan. The expansion of existing government agencies and the creation of new ones to carry out such programs was not generally predicted, although it was so consistent with Progressive-era aims and practices that it is difficult to see why it was not. Such expansion was also characteristic of New Deal reform even though the temporary character of a large number of the agencies was not often mentioned as the New Deal became, it seemed, the model of what was rapidly emerging as the Great Society. Such programs could be tied to New Deal innovations like social security or to the older reforms dealing with child welfare and public health, but virtually everything one sees in the government programs of the Great Society, including the various developments in public housing, environmental quality, highway and automobile safety, and civil rights can be traced to prior government interests stimulated by private research interests privately funded. The inclusion of the arts and humanities in government programs was perhaps one of the more remarkable of the seemingly new developments, as was the creation of publicly funded radio and television; but, again, the mixture of private and public funding and the involvement of the growing number of foundations—some focused on specific medical conditions like heart disease and cancer, others with more general social and educational mandates—point to the complexity of the relationship between government and foundations.

GOVERNMENT, PRIVATE PHILANTHROPY, AND THE PUBLIC INTEREST, 1960s–1990s

As early as 1960 the expanded role of the federal government as the major donor to research in private institutions was beginning to be a subject of concern. President Eisenhower's farewell address raised the subject of the "industrial-military complex," warning the nation about the expanded role of American scientists and the impact of government funding on their research. In addition, a report issued in 1960 by the president of Harvard University raised the issue of federal dominance of private universities through the simple fact of overwhelming government funding and its effect on institutional independence. Cold War intellectual politics had created the federal government as an almost accidental and soon to be reluctant actor.

After Sputnik (the Soviet Union's artificial satellite) was launched in 1957, President Eisenhower appointed an official scientific adviser in the White House and Congress passed the National Defense Education Act (NDEA) of 1958, which poured unprecedented amounts of money into American higher education, both public and private. The concern with private education had been part of American foundation interest all along, but in 1955 the Ford Foundation contributed an unprecedented $560 million to private institutions. The Ford gift may be the single most critical factor in the salvation of private higher education in America after World War II, at least as important as the GI bill that preceded it. However accidental the forces behind NDEA may have been, the combination and the concern indicated, once again, a remarkable partnership between public and private interests.

President John F. Kennedy liberally staffed his administration with academics, to be sure, but among them two whose past and future connections with the foundation world were significant. John Gardner, president of the Carnegie Corporation, became his secretary of health, education, and welfare. McGeorge Bundy, dean of faculties at Harvard, became his national security adviser, and, after his departure from the Johnson administration, president of the Ford Foundation. Mrs. Kennedy sought private funding for major historic restorations in the White House and moved toward leadership in the national community of culture and the arts. It was a brief period of academic hegemony that was reflected as well in the recruitment of students from the nation's colleges for the Peace Corps and the use of social science literature and research in the beginnings of the programs that would be reflected in and joined by the Great Society where academics like Daniel Patrick Moynihan would begin their governmental careers. Moynihan had headed an urban studies program jointly based at Harvard and the Massachusetts Institute of Technology. He would later enter Congress as senator from New York.

When Congressman Wright Patman of Texas announced in 1964 that the J. M. Kaplan Fund was channeling money from the Central Intelligence Agencies to support anticommunist groups, he was touching the tip of a modest-sized iceberg that would shortly be revealed as the use by the CIA of major foundations, and even the creation of a foundation, to route CIA funds to support anticommunist causes in eastern Europe and Africa. One need not see these as shocking misuses of private philanthropy or public agencies. Similar symbiotic public/private relationships existed in heart and cancer research, public television, even art museums and symphony orchestras, where the promotion of interests by either government or private philanthropy led to quiet interpenetrations of the two in what was clearly perceived by all the parties involved as the larger public interest. In older western cultures where the line between public and private was never so precisely, if artificially, drawn as in the United States, the assumption that private organizations had the responsibility of joining with government to support agreed-upon national needs produced no such shock. Even Americans had called upon similar partnerships in the two world wars. The Bremner model, as we have called it, assumed it as essential to intellectual and governmental progress.

One could find similar interrelationships of private and public management in the very personnel of the governments and foundations of the 1960s and early 1970s. John Gardner returned to Washington to help found Independent Sector, a new interest group organization with a broader representation of its purpose. The Third or Independent Sector reflected a new terminology designed to place a new category of service organizations, called now "nonprofits," in a new relation to the other two service sectors: business and government. Third sector organizations were private, like business, and, like both business and government, depended on professionals to provide services to the public. But they did so without the need for profit, depending instead on contributions from donors, volunteers who were willing to provide services conjointly with professionals but not for pay, and recipients of services willing to pay fees to defray the costs of the services received or, when necessary, part of the costs for those recipients who could not afford to pay all or any of the costs of the services they received.

Nonprofit organizations also looked to foundations for financial support. Their search for sources of grants grew in the 1970s as the number of organizations expanded. That expansion was the result of the reform era generated by President Johnson's Great Society agenda. The concept of community self-help promoted the alliance of local organizations with property owners, local banks, and real estate companies to recapture urban areas affected by middle-class flight from the city and poverty. The most famous model continues to be Chicago's South Shore Bank, which, under the leadership of Ronald Grzywinski and reform-minded young colleagues in the banking community, solicited funds from foundations and public-interested investors to use banking facilities to revive a rapidly declining, formerly elite neighborhood on Chicago's south side.

The growing consciousness of poverty and its effect on urban minorities began to draw the interest of foundations. To that was added a new awareness of voting injustices as the center of problems involving inadequate representation of blacks and other minorities, including women and gays as members of both the work force and the private and public bureaucracies that managed it. Foundations financed groups of northern youths of both races that registered voters in the South in order to increase the presence of blacks and poor at the polls, transforming the racial character of southern politics. The sacrifice of safety and even lives of the northern volunteers indicates the genuinely revolutionary character of the endeavor.

Such activities were perhaps the single most important factor producing the congressional attacks on foundations that resulted in the Tax Reform Act of 1969. The debates that produced the legislation first considered provisions that would have limited foundations to a life span of forty years. Again, since foundations were not chartered by Congress, it is difficult to see how legislation could have done anything more than limit the tax deduction of foundations to that life span; but since Congress at the same time moved into consideration of a 50 percent limit on all charitable deductions by individuals to organizations other than foundations, thereby increasing the allowable amount from an original 30 percent, it is easy to see how complex the factors involved in American philanthropy and its relation to public policy had become. The requirement that foundations pay out a percentage of their earnings each year was designed to prevent foundations from using the resources given them by donors to increase those resources at the expense of their responsibility for contributing to the general welfare. Since the initial requirement of 6 percent was a deliberate effort to hold foundations to a distribution that would halt any internal growth of foundation resources on the threshold of the inflation that followed—and would therefore have meant a diminution of effective foundation resources for distribution—Congress subsequently reduced the percentage to 5 percent. The payout provisions, as they were called, nonetheless had the effect of pressing some foundations to expand their staffs to make possible a level of giving they had not engaged in before. That, and the greater visibility the debate gave to foundations, produced two different, if unintended, consequences. A new literature critical of foundations began to appear. Foundations, writers like Waldemar A. Nielsen argued, were not the Bremner-like intellectual adventurers they and their supporter claimed them to be, but rather a cautious, careful elite who followed well behind winds of change. Other more radical critics labeled them conservative supporters of the capitalist status quo using their funds to stimulate policy programs to counter more radical social change.

Such criticisms, whether or not one supported a tendency to lump together a vastly expanded number of organizations that increasingly represented a wide variety of positions, did call attention to the need to expand the range of personnel working in foundation philanthropy. Board memberships were made more inclusive of women and minorities who had not previously been represented. Groups were formed to monitor the number of women and minorities who held positions on foundation staffs as well as to sustain a concern with what was called the social responsibility or responsiveness of foundations.

It is difficult, perhaps, to understand the focus on foundations as the embodiment of the threat of uncontrolled philanthropy, given the fact that foundation giving in the 1960s still amounted to only 8 percent of charitable giving, while individual gifts to charities of various kinds represented half of American philanthropy. Such percentages ignore the fact presented at the very beginning of this essay that foundation giving is a highly organized and purposefully directed form of grant making, no more a gift than federal grants are gifts; while donations to religious and social welfare organizations are given to organized groups (qualified by the IRS to warrant tax exemption) that define their own direction and purpose to the individuals supporting them. The distinction is important. Foundations, when all is said and done, select the purposes they support and organize themselves to encourage those purposes on a scale and with an authority that few individuals can match. Most other forms of charitable organization must appeal to potential donors in the public for the financial support of purposes they articulate. The distinction is one that might argue, indeed, for a definition of the differences between foundation philanthropy and charitable giving, and of both from volunteer and not-for-profit services.

Such distinctions have not been part of the history of private and public philanthropy in recent American history. The reverse has been true. The Commission on Private Philanthropy and Public Needs, chaired by John H. Filer of Aetna Life and Casualty (and stimulated by the interest of John D. Rockefeller III and privately funded largely through his efforts in raising money from other philanthropists and philanthropic groups) was a major event in bringing together all of the private philanthropic and quasi-public, volunteer, and not-for-profit concerns under one umbrella. Study in scholarly detail projected effects of the so-called private sector activities as they had developed over the years. The use of professional economists, and the introduction of the field to economists, was a major refinement that had a great deal to do with changes in the character of nonprofit economic analysis itself, particularly a greater awareness of the utility of comparing costs and benefits of various forms of service. Academic and scholarly interest in philanthropy, volunteerism, and nonprofits generated research in sociology, philosophy, and public administration as well as economics.

The interactive role of government and private philanthropy, dramatized from time to time by such events as the brief excitement caused by the Department of Health and Human Services' contribution in the waning days of the Carter administration of funds earmarked for the elderly poor to a group of major private religious agencies for distribution, became a norm no one troubled over. Health and Human Services grants to private universities for social research ebbed and flowed with the social service interests of different administrations, as did grants from the Department of Education. More technological interests in science, defense, transportation, and industrial change did not bring criticism when they took the form of grants to private institutions for research; although criticisms of elitism surfaced from time to time, chiefly with regard to the general distribution of such funds to a few academic institutions rather than to all such institutions across the board. The government, too, used its funding powers to examine the employment of minorities and women by such institutions and to block funding where questions of civil rights were legitimately raised. Whether or not the federal government erred in funding a supercollider in Texas, where no such project had existed, rather than in institutions where research of that kind had been underway for many years, the politics of the issue took over. The Eisenhower Institute, a Washington-based privately funded policy organization, has distributed Justice Department funds to urban areas concerned with youth programs to deal with poverty and crime. While there is no particular outcry or even awareness, instance by instance, the practice seems embedded in the logic of American reform.

While there was a sizable literature on philanthropic foundations almost from their beginnings, professional historians did not enter the field until the mid-1950s. One reason was the fact that, as private corporations, foundations did not feel it necessary to open their papers to scholars. Another, perhaps subtler reason, is that historians were slow to recognize the significance of foundations in the shaping of American policy making. By the mid-1950s, however, understanding of the whole question of historical interest had begun to change, chiefly as a result of efforts led by the Russell Sage Foundation, which organized a conference at Princeton University and published a report of it in 1956. A subsequent article by the University of Wisconsin historian Merle Curti, the leading participant at that conference, opened the topic to the historical profession. He continued to write in the field, but the absence of available research materials from foundations themselves limited the scope and the depth of analysis historians could undertake.

The opening of the Rockefeller Archive Center in August 1975 in a Rockefeller mansion adjacent to the family estate, Pocantico Hills at North Tarrytown, New York, transformed the field as a subject of historical research. The result of discussions that had been going on in the Foundation for the previous two years, as well as a concern shared by John D. Rockefeller III and his father that the family's philanthropic activities were not well enough understood by the public, the founding of the archive broke through the pattern of privacy that had been shared by all foundations. While the protection was obviously part of the pattern, just as important was the practical difficulty in maintaining large quantities of records as the cost of floor space grew, the costs of alternatives like microfilming had to be calculated, and the complexities of access and professional management became clear. The simple fact of a move from one office location to another had already targeted old file cabinets as the first among disposables for foundations as for any business organization, and with little sense of the historic importance of the materials and a large sense of the cost in personnel and time of the process of sorting through them, the garbage heap was the simplest solution.

With the growing awareness of historical relevance, balanced, too, by the belief that publicity would benefit the reputation of a three-quarter-century old American policy institution, a number of other foundations followed Rockefeller's example, opening their papers for research; and the Rockefeller Archive Center itself began a process of selective collection of such materials, providing the collections with professional archival staffing to facilitate their use by scholars. Relevant papers in the growing presidential library system, the National Archives, the Library of Congress, and the virtually new practice of universities of collecting and preserving faculty papers as well as their own administrative papers and making them available for research quietly revolutionized the field.

In addition, the establishment of centers for the study of philanthropy and nonprofits at institutions like Yale, Duke, Case Western Reserve, the Graduate School of the City University of New York, and Indiana University at Indianapolis, as well as programs of interest in the field at several of the nation's law schools and business schools, assured a continuing concern in a growing range of professions. While foundations were by no means the central focus of such research programs, the attention to charity and philanthropy as a central part of policy life in America was clear. The formation of regional centers for discussion of charitable and philanthropic interest among the donor organizations themselves was also part of the period from the 1970s on. Groups like the Donor's Forum of Chicago, the New York Regional Association of Grantmakers, the Minnesota Council on Foundations, and similar relevant groups for both northern and southern California, assumed the importance of sources of communication and, in a somewhat subtler fashion, provided guidance as newcomers entered the field either as donors or as staff. One of the functions both of the academic centers and the professional associations of grantmakers was formed in response to the growing public awareness of private philanthropy in general and foundations in particular. Congressional criticism of foundations joined with the criticisms leveled by donees and their representatives to press foundations to respond to donee conceptions of public need rather than solely to their own determination of those needs. Organizations supporting research received their funding from many of the same sources supporting public programs and private institutions. The question of whether research and commentary critical of foundations and donors received the same attention as supportive work came in for its share of debate. After all, the impetus for the creation of the first institutions of communication and for the earliest of the research programs came from a sophisticated understanding by a generation of philanthropists faced with the congressional attacks of the 1950s and 1960s. Whether or not foundations wished to acknowledge it, they were indeed part of public debate over major issues of policy—social welfare, medical care, education, and academic research—that had once been their private preserve. Concepts like responsibility, responsiveness, and accountability were now public debate, even though governmental control of philanthropic activity still rested solely on the tax exemption. Forcing the IRS to become a quasi-policy institution may have been an unintended outcome of decisions made at the very beginning, but no one on either side of the public-private conflict seemed to want it to change.

Nonetheless, the role of the Internal Revenue Service expanded after the Tax Act of 1969. By the 1990s the categories covering trusts, charities and charitable trusts, and foundations included a range of categories that required more than twenty-five pages of instructions and a raft of forms devoted to each of those categories. What had begun as a simple information sheet, Form 990, asking that foundations identify their sources and amounts of funds, now covered the full range of possibilities—not only of sources, but of beneficiaries as well as foundation employee salaries, benefit plans, and a variety of other activities that could bring foundations into the category of ordinary business operations. Identified in the Internal Revenue Code by the number 501(c)3, the paragraph in the legislation, foundations are categorized as tax-exempt organizations and are therefore able to assure all donors that their gifts will be tax exempt. The identification is crucial both to the existence of such organizations and to their ability to raise funds, to expend funds, and to call for matching funds from other potential donors. It is the chief instrument of federal control over foundation philanthropy, in terms of both the very existence of the foundation and its activities in the policy world.

By the end of the 1970s the major foundations appeared to have given the whole field of foundation philanthropy an image of radicalism once again, as a result of the voter registration drives but also the programs that fed into the Great Society. The forming of so-called conservative think tanks and foundations to promote alternatives to such thinking was a logical outcome. Since foundations were initially formed to engage in programs the public would not have pressed its government to create, the adoption of those programs by government placed an aura of ideology on the private system that it may not initially have deserved, but now did. The issue, however, was not radicalism but federal control, and conservatism was now equated with private control. That did not protect philanthropy from an ideological focus some might wonder at if they peruse the history. Philanthropic names like Olin, Pew, and the Heritage Foundation, the latter hoping to counter the supposed liberal bias of think tanks like the Brookings Institution, emerged as part of a new ideological alternative.

Nonetheless, the establishment of the John D. and Catherine T. MacArthur Foundation in 1978 seemed a throwback to the earlier years. While not as large as the giant Ford Foundation, it was still the largest in almost two decades. It also reflected John D. MacArthur's view of the necessary independence of trustees, not only of staffs but of one another. Combining as his first trustees what he perceived to be the cream of the scientific, academic, and artistic minds of his day with old friends and business associates, he charged them with the responsibility of determining the future of his philanthropy for themselves. Echoing on a much larger scale the grants to individual scholars pioneered by the Guggenheim Foundation established in the 1920s to support individual talents in the arts and sciences rather than the institutions through which some of them worked, the foundation announced the MacArthur Fellowships. The foundation continues to take particular pride in its so-called genius grants to represent the most promising new minds of every present generation in all fields. Providing them with such benefits as their full salaries for five years, the grants were intended to free them from their dependence on their professional salaries for that period and enable them to be fully productive without having to teach (for those who were members of faculties) or to make their livings by whatever activity they normally depended upon. Members of university faculties did not have to give up their employment by their institutions; and institutions, while obviously proud of the attainments of men and women they had selected as faculty, had nonetheless to accommodate themselves to the possibility of doing without those very necessary services as faculty during the peak periods of their careers. The MacArthur Foundation also moved into a variety of areas ranging from international relations and arms control to elementary and secondary education and to the needs of its own Chicago community. It was a far-reaching mandate initially controlled by the trustees, who made their own determination of interests and needs as they saw them.

The older war materials and defense industries and the new electronics industry also spawned their share of foundations. The Howard Hughes Foundation, whose origins and purposes were almost, but not quite, as mysterious as the man for whom it was named, became a new, potentially large entry as early as 1954 when Hughes made his Medical Institute the sole owner of Hughes Aircraft. While not a foundation in the sense of a general purpose instrument of the kind created by Carnegie and Rockefeller, it was given a special category by the Internal Revenue Service. It nonetheless follows patterns of research and relation to academic institutions that had characterized other foundations. The 1985 sale of the company enabled the institute to double its support of research.

Smaller but still significant organizations were brought into existence, some in even more traditional form. When Vincent Astor died in 1959 after a lifetime of philanthropic activity that went counter to his famous family's traditional conservatism (he was a supporter of the New Deal, particularly housing programs for the poor) he left a foundation with $67 million in assets to be used for "the alleviation of human misery." The management of the foundation has continued to be the responsibility of his wife, Brooke, who has been one of New York City's leading philanthropists.

Changes in tax laws in the Reagan administration expanded the opportunities for giving. Individuals who did not itemize deductions on their tax returns could nonetheless list charitable gifts as deductions. Corporations were permitted to increase the allowable 5 percent to 10 percent. Since the vast majority had not yet reached the 5 percent limit, the new opportunity was a questionable gift to the world of philanthropy. The relation between philanthropy and public relations advertising had never been clear, and it seemed to some corporate managers much easier to continue to deal with contributions as public service promotion of the company name than to become involved in the institutionalization required by foundation philanthropy with its subsequent oversight by government. There was the fact, too, that philanthropy obviously came second to profits and reinvestment. Economic downturns were going to hit a company's philanthropic policies first and the presence of a foundation complicated the normal processes of retrenchment. While government policy encouraging corporate giving relieved corporations from legal threats from stockholders, there was still ground for objection from those who felt that they preferred to engage in their personal philanthropy on their own rather than having companies in which they had invested their resources do it for them.

Yet, there is no question that foundations in the years after World War II had become major vehicles for keeping alive the continuity of the liberal side of the New Deal, both in national and international affairs, that Congress had been unwilling to support or had supported only cautiously. Civil rights was a major example. So was international relations, particularly in those "underdeveloped," "developing," or "Third World" areas of the world newly pressed to the attention of American policymakers. Foundations could support research programs that would have drawn fire from congressional critics had government agencies engaged in such policy research.

It is perhaps a significant irony that one of the first calls from the White House of Ronald Reagan was for private philanthropy to take up the slack that would be generated by the planned withdrawal of government from the programs of the Great Society. Yet, if we follow the Bremner model of 1960, even if modified to suit more recent perceptions of that history, it is clear that the expansion of government responsibility for new social programs had been initiated in significant part by foundations and private philanthropy. They had proudly helped generate the ideas that were essential to many of the reforms. They had been aware from the beginning that their resources, large as they might be perceived as being, were nowhere near what society needed. They did not consider permanent commitments that limited future programs from proper use of their initial mandates. Government had joined in to aid and expand programs foundations had proposed in the first place. To ask foundations and charities to move back in to support programs they could not continue without government help has raised some important questions. The idea, at the very least, distorts the history of the partnership between public and private entities that has been central to American historical development. If one insists on a sharp separation between public and private, one must redefine a multitude of relationships between the two that have been central to the development of public policy.

FOUNDATIONS AT THE END OF THE TWENTIETH CENTURY

As the century approached its end, the foundation as a legal form has generated a wider range of philanthropic activity than had been envisioned by Rockefeller, Carnegie, and Mrs. Sage. Contrary to the future predicted by the *Smith* case, large donors whose wealth came from new, major industries as varied as cosmetics and electronics established foundations. Individuals with lesser but still significant resources were setting up foundations in their own names and the names of their families to perpetuate not only their philanthropic interests but their money. Popular stars in both the sports and entertainment fields were establishing foundations to minister to various causes, particularly protecting the welfare of children and fighting specific diseases like AIDS. The foundation form extended the possibilities for public relations both for the public reputations of donors and for the attraction of additional funding. Those who still chose to be critical of philanthropists for their power to direct sources of smaller funds by the use of their larger resources could continue to criticize without seriously affecting the process.

Other, less dramatic, medical conditions pressed families and interested doctors to join together to form organizations like the older ones that had dedicated themselves to finding cures for polio, cancer, and heart disease. Many of them used publicity as one of their main instruments, following the older "stamp" campaigns pioneered by those seeking treatment for tuberculosis (broadened now to include all lung diseases). Television campaigns helped generate individual donations for multiple sclerosis, using a popular star to lead the program. In the case of polio, where the success of experimental research had obviated the need for continuing support, interested backers of a fund-raising system that had, for a quarter of a century, built up a significant name, the March of Dimes, decided to transfer its interests to cognate research fields in birth defects rather than lose a well-known title and association. Originally associated with President Franklin D. Roosevelt, whose face had been put on the coin as a tribute both to him and to the organization he had helped found to fight polio, the March of Dimes aided in efforts to democratize philanthropy in much the same way that Community Chests had by encouraging children in the public schools to put pennies in envelopes as their contribution to public services. (Managers of the postwar March of Dimes might often have wished that he had called it "March of Dollars" when it was clear that inflation was pricing their name out of the fundraising market.)

In an action that also reflected change in purpose and direction, the Markle Foundation, originally established in the era of full-time medical school professional staffs first recommended by the Rockefeller Foundation's Abraham Flexner to help support the careers of young doctors who could no longer depend on fees for service, transferred its focus to public television and communication in general when the intervention of government in payment for medical care through Medicare and Medicaid changed the status of the underpaid physician at every level of medical care. Government support for the building of hospitals generated a similar rethinking of the role of private philanthropy for what had been the major interest of several foundations, including the Commonwealth Fund of New York, but earlier government hospital funding had ended most such programs a decade before Medicare. The Great Society revolution had widespread effects on the status of foundations, different in each case, but no less profound. The legal form had become part of an American tradition of public policy and of the sequestration of wealth in the hands both of private holders and the succession of private foundation boards and administrators who would manage its distribution. One could certainly argue that Markle's impact on public communication has certainly outstripped in long-term utility the effects of the full-time staffing of the nation's research hospitals.

Perception of the problems and the issues at the end of the century were different from those at the beginning as far as the world of foundations and public policy was concerned. If one applied the standard of "cure" so beloved of the first foundation philanthropists and the programs they supported, for instance in the field of medicine where diseases once conquered could reappear and the side effects of new cures could turn out to be as dangerous as the diseases themselves, the success of the whole enterprise could be questioned, particularly by those committed to evaluating research programs by the same standards used for political programs. Could one determine whether or not they "worked?" Shortsighted though such evaluations tended to be, they reflected a pragmatism that continued to provide fuel for attacks on research. Still, the impulse to consider philanthropy an ongoing process that would respond to change as it occurred could be used to underscore the revolutionary reality that had produced the new instruments of philanthropy.

The center of the criticism was bound to remain. Poverty was still there, some thought worse. The same could be said of crime, illiteracy—one could list the issues and document perceived failures. Even though both the private and the public institutions of policy making were essentially the same, their relation to one another had changed. What had begun as a policy world—clearly divided between public responsibilities and private ones—had moved by the middle of the century to a national partnership where governmental programs and private programs shared shifting responsibilities. If the shifts appeared to develop with some kind of decadal rhythm, they still seemed, by the beginning of the 1990s, set by habits of experiment, expansion, and withdrawal. As foundations moved to aid government in the formulation of its programs, one could see the edges of dispute once again beginning to form. The Robert Wood Johnson Foundation helped organize and support meetings for Hillary Rodham Clinton's committee planning health care reform, and moved from there to the seemingly revolutionary idea that foundations could provide network television with support for programs on health care. Foundations, government, and now a major for-profit industry found themselves in an alliance for good that was undoubtedly destined to be perceived rather differently when critics from both public and private camps took a careful look at what was happening. The underlying continuity, nonetheless, may be clearest in the persistence of personnel at every level, from top leaders to the managerial bureaucracies trained in the system by public and private universities, who move from universities to government and from there to foundations. The paths may reverse the lines as well, as shifting careers move individuals among the three institutional entities.

Yet, what seems to be happening in the 1990s appears to be a more long-range change as the United States takes part in a worldwide revolution against the public controls advocated by a century of social reform that began in the 1870s and started to crumble in the 1970s. The industrial unrest that produced socialism and progressivism idealized central government as the best and most reliable representative of public will. The growth of trained managerial staffing to replace corrupt political officialdom, whether that staff be called civil servants or bureaucrats, depended on educational systems and concepts of responsible management for those systems to teach to each new generation of managers. By the latter part of the century those ideals were under attack for what they had not achieved, in and of themselves. Faith in automatic government progress had ended. Government, it seemed, was no different than many of the framers of the Constitution had suspected it of being: potentially corrupt and ineffective. The dream of changing it had, at least for a time, come to an end. Returning control to private hands had become, once again, an ideal. How long that would remain the ideal was anybody's guess. In any case, the idea that foundations would pioneer programs that could then be adopted by government seemed to be changing. Exactly how and with what consequences was unclear.

By the last decades of the twentieth century, it was also clear that the purposes for which foundations had been created in the first place had changed. Prior to World War I, foundations stood alone in their engagement in national concerns. There was little overlap with the federal government except perhaps for fields like public health and military research. From the New Deal on, the federal government played an uncertain role in areas once the exclusive province of private philanthropy and local government, the latter two intertwined and continuing to reflect a suspicion of federal control. The American unwillingness to accept the centralized national government Herbert Croly had recommended to them in 1909, on the threshold of the twentieth century's first major reform era, had not changed by the end of the century. The role of citizen associations in American life pointed out by Tocqueville early in the nineteenth century became part of the ideology the administration of President George Bush called "A Thousand Points of Light." Yet philanthropic foundations as we have known them are scarcely Tocqueville's citizen associations. The light they reflect has been no minor flicker; nor has it been the burst of a nova. Characterizing its significance remains an important historical task.

SEE ALSO Patronage of the Arts (volume IV); Class (volume I).

BIBLIOGRAPHY

This essay is based on and condensed from a forthcoming book on the subject by the author.

While the literature is large and growing, there are a few basic materials that serve as bibliographical source centers, historical analyses, and examples of current direction.

While the literature from foundation managers themselves is now old—Raymond B. Fosdick's *The Story of the Rockefeller Foundation* appeared in 1952 but followed a literature compiled by others like himself from the Carnegie and Russell Sage Foundations—it was the culmination of a process of self history most practiced by Rockefeller Foundation interests, but represented more extensively in the writings of F. Emerson Andrews, a member of the Sage group for many years. Frederick Keppel's *The Foundation* (1930) summarized the first eight years of his nineteen years as president of the Carnegie Corporation of New York. In 1947 the remaining members of the first generation of managers of the Russell Sage Foundation, John M. Glenn, Lilian Brandt, and F. Emerson Andrews, published a history of that foundation's first four decades.

That literature was paralleled by a critical literature that included Edward Lindeman's *Wealth and Culture* (1936); and Dwight Macdonald's *The Ford Foundation* (1955). Professional historians did not enter the field until the calls by the University of Wisconsin's Merle Curti took effect. His "The History of American Philanthropy as a Field of Research" appeared in the *American Historical Review* 62 (1957): 352–363, summarizing and amplifying the *Report of the Princeton Conference on the History of Philanthropy* (1956), an assemblage of historians who examined the question of the future of philanthropic study as an historical field. Even so, the critical literature vastly outnumbered and outshone the work of professional historians. Waldemar Nielsen's *The Big Foundations* (1972) was followed by *The Golden Donors* (1982), establishing Neilsen as one of the most articulate of the populist critics of foundations. Marion Fremont-Smith's *Foundations and Government* (1965), remains the classic in the field of foundation legal and governmental history. Her *Philanthropy and the Business Corporation* (1972) deserves a similar place.

Robert Bremner, *American Philanthropy* (1988), contains a helpful chronology and bibliography. Peter Dobkin Hall has been one of the leading commentators on the full range of not-for-profit history in the United States. His *Inventing the Non-profit Sector and Other Essays on Philanthropy, Voluntarism, and Non-profit Organizations* (1992) brings together a number of the perspectives he has represented in the field. Steven Wheatley's study of the origins of the Flexner report on medical education, *The Politics of Philanthropy* (1982), and Kathleen McCarthy's work *Noblesse Oblige* (1982) and her more recent *Women's Culture* (1991), like Ellen Lagemann's studies of the Carnegie philanthropies, *The Politics of Knowledge* (1989), are excellent approaches to individual foundations, donors, and their projects by professional historians. Special notice should be given Robert E. Kohler's *Partners in Science, Foundations and Natural Scientists 1900–1945* (1991), which treats the approaches taken to a particular set of disciplines by the first foundations. Daniel M. Fox, *Power and Illness: The Failure and Future of American Health Policy* (1993), is a thoughtful work by someone whose experience both in government and as president of the Milbank Foundation provides him with special insight. Daphne Niobe Layton, *Philanthropy and Voluntarism: An Annotated Bibliography* (1987), is the fullest bibliography of writings on the subject. The ongoing *Philanthropy Studies Index* now provides current listings of materials.

The Marxist perspective, specifically of those Marxists who have adopted the Gramscian view of intellectuals in the hegemonic order as ideological servants to powerful monied interests, has been best represented in the work of Robert Arnove and his colleagues in *Philanthropy and Cultural Imperialism* (1980); and Donald Fisher in *Fundamental Development of the Social Sciences* (1993).

Joint and individual writings by Barry D. Karl and Stanley N. Katz offer background on foundation philanthropy itself: "The American Philanthropic Foundation and the Public Sphere, 1890–1930," *Minerva* 19 (1981): 236–270, and "Foundations and Ruling Class Elites," *Daedalus* 116 (Winter 1987): 1–40, are the major examples. See also Barry D. Karl, "Philanthropy, Policy Planning, and the Bureaucratization of the Democratic Ideal," *Daedalus* 105 (Fall 1976): 129–150.

A number of universities now maintain centers for the study of philanthropy. The more prominent ones are at Yale, The Graduate School of the City University of New York, Duke University, Case Western Reserve University, and Indiana University at Indianapolis. The Aspen Institute maintains important research programs in the field and funds study by other scholars. The Foundation Center of New York and Independent Sector in Washington, D.C., are the major continuing sources of research data and publication. The Center's directory is part of a major collection of publications providing a wide range of information collected and collated to give varying perspectives on both the contemporary and historical scenes. The Foundation Library (and its counterparts in the regional centers that maintain libraries for local users and researchers) remains one of the chief sources for understanding of both national and regional foundation philanthropy. Most publish regular commentaries and reports on topics of interest to donors in general and foundations in particular. The Rockefeller Archive Center at Pocantico Hills, New York, holds not only all Rockefeller family and Foundation archives, but those of a number of the other foundations as well. Its newsletter appears regularly with information about research at the center. *The Chronicle of Philanthropy* provides current running commentary and news concerning the entirety of the philanthropic sector.

BUREAUCRACY

Herman Belz

Although the formal structure of American government has changed relatively little since the ratification of the Constitution over two centuries ago, the nature, scope and purpose of government in the United States have changed profoundly over the course of the twentieth century. This transformation is best described as the bureaucratization of government and the formation of the modern administrative state. So familiar is the phenomenon of bureaucratic governance that it is often assumed to be the form that constitutional government takes in modern America. But is bureaucratic government wholly consistent with the constitutional principles on which the United States was founded? Although historical analysis cannot answer this question, it can clarify the issue by examining the legitimacy of the administrative state as it has actually operated since the late nineteenth century.

This essay provides an account of bureaucracy in American national government and politics in the twentieth century. It begins with a discussion on the meaning of bureaucracy in terms relevant to constitutional analysis and considers the ends and purposes of bureaucratic government, as well as the organizing forms, principles, and procedures of the administrative state. Following an examination of the design of the Constitution with respect to the public administration is an analysis of the formation of the administrative state during four periods: the origins of national economic regulation in the late nineteenth and early twentieth centuries (1887–1920); the establishment of bureaucratic governance in the New Deal era (1920–1960), the democratization of administrative management and the enactment of new social regulation (1960–1980); and the reform of the regulatory welfare state by conservative critics of bureaucracy (1980–1989).

CONCEPTIONS OF BUREAUCRACY

Although in recent years public-choice scholars have advanced a theory of public administration that views the free market as a regulatory institution, most writers on the administrative state adhere to the traditional hierarchical concept of bureaucracy based on the theories of Max Weber. This view defines bureaucracy as a command-and-control system of organization and policy making that is the central mechanism of modern government. In Weber's approach, bureaucracy is an organizational means for maintaining the legal, economic, and technical rationality inherent in modern civilization. Administration, defined as the management of affairs, may not necessarily require the formation of bureaucratic institutions, but in modern political society a correspondence between these two concepts has usually been assumed. Hence the *administrative state* and *bureaucracy* are regarded as equivalent terms. The bureaucratic or administrative state is conventionally described as consisting of hierarchical institutions emanating from a single, dominant center of authority. In bureaucratic institutions decision making is entrusted to experts, recruited according to merit who perform specialized functions and act in an impartial, rational, and nonpolitical manner.

From the bureaucratic perspective good government is efficient and economical government, and efficiency is assumed to result from hierarchical ordering. In the classic Weberian formulation, bureaucratic administration is the exercise of control based on knowledge that takes the form of rational decision making in accordance with fixed, objective rules. In theory, bureaucratic rules and regulations eliminate or radically restrict the exercise of discretion by office holders. In the actual conduct of affairs in a government or business organization, however, informal adaptation of bureaucratic rules and procedures occurs, which reintroduces the element of discretionary action. Out of the Weberian concept of bureaucracy, moreover, social scientists in the twentieth century have formulated a variety of organization and management theories that place considerable emphasis upon discretion. These theories, gathered under the rubric of public administration, are based on concepts such as human relations, leadership, motivation and self-actualization of the individual, management by objectives, and rational choice in decision making. Bureaucratic organization can thus assume a variety of forms under a number of different rationales. None of these rationales is rigidly Weberian although they retain elements of hierarchy and centralization and are intended to increase the productivity of the organization, as Weber claimed rational bureaucracy would do. In this more catholic understanding of the concept, it may be said that bureaucratic organization is a pervasive and inevitable feature of modern mass society, that it is instrumental in fulfilling the diverse ends of a vast array of public and private institutions and associations.

In twentieth-century American political history bureaucracy has been significant above all as the defining element in the creation of the administrative state. In government, generally bureaucratic forms can serve a variety of ends depending on the function of the particular institution, but in the historical context of late-nineteenth-century industrialization and the succeeding transformations that produced twentieth-century postindustrial society, the bureaucratic state served the fundamental political purpose of abolishing the laissez-faire state of the nineteenth century. By the 1960s there could be no doubt about the existence in American political culture of what the political scientist Stephen Skowronek referred to as "a sense of the state." This term described a widespread popular belief that a sovereign national government, possessing coercive power, operated beyond the control of citizens and was capable of regulating—and to a considerable extent did regulate—virtually every aspect of their existence.

In political discourse the word *bureaucracy* expressed this pejorative and threatening sense of the state. In a related and more precise legal and constitutional sense the bureaucratic or administrative state signified the exercise of broad discretion in the making of public policy. Aside from the importance attached to discretion in post-Weberian organizational theory, discretion is essential to administration, in the basic sense that general rules always need to be modified and adjusted as they are applied to particular circumstances. Innocuous as discretion may be in quotidian administrative practice, in highly charged political moments discretion can mean the ability to act outside or in disregard of established laws. Traditionally the statesman is thought of as one who exercises discretion in this extraordinary sense, taking political action for the common good. In the contemporary administrative state, however, it has become common legislative practice to confer broad discretionary policy-making authority on legions of government bureaucrats. The executive officers and subordinate administrators who possess discretionary power in the modern state are free to follow the dictates of prudence and practical reason; yet, in the elaborate and often obscure regulatory labyrinths that constitute the bureaucratic state, public officials may also act on the basis of self-interest, ideology, and political partisanship, despite public administration theory to the contrary. In considering the relationship between bureaucracy and constitutional government, moreover, it is apparent, as the political scientist J. Roland Pennock observed, that discretion exercised without limits is tyranny.

Although bureaucracy is usually discussed in organizational and procedural terms, a constitutional perspective requires consideration of the ends and objects of the administrative state. If the leading purpose of the nineteenth-century laissez-faire state, as historical consensus holds, was to protect individual liberty and property rights, then the principal end of the twentieth-century administrative state has been to limit property rights and economic liberty. Whether policies that limit property ownership and use have been motivated by a deliberate and perhaps punitive intention to redistribute the wealth of the possessing classes, as critics have contended, is a controversial question that continues to divide scholars. In the alternative view, favored by supporters of the administrative state, the reason for restricting economic liberty was the need to place individual liberty on a firm foundation in the age of industry by seeking the ideal of distributive justice. While it is difficult to assign clearly defined motive and intent in analyzing historical developments of the magnitude of the administrative state, it is clear that redistribution of wealth as a basis for guaranteeing programs of social welfare and security has been a major result of bureaucratic governance.

The concept of "regulation in the public interest" is the outstanding symbol and rhetorical touchstone of the bureaucratic state that serves to describe it in a substantive sense. Regulation, defined as controlling or directing something according to a rule, can be viewed as the essential activity of government everywhere and always. In twentieth-century America regulation signifies the rejection of the assumptions concerning the nature, scope, and purpose of government in relation to individual liberty and property rights that provided the framework of the laissez-faire state. Whether the purposes and methods of bureaucratic regulation further signify contradiction and repudiation of the basic principles of American constitutionalism has been a deeply contested issue in American politics for over a century.

Although the Constitution does not contain the word *administration,* the framers anticipated the need for public administration and made provision for it in the fundamental law. The concept of the separation of powers, the organizing principle of the new government, is evidence of this foresight. Under the separation of powers the legislative department makes the laws and the judicial department interprets or decides their meaning in matters pertaining to individual rights. The executive branch enforces the laws and is the most obvious source of an administrative capacity under the Constitution.

In *Federalist* 72, Alexander Hamilton expressed the assumption underlying the widely held view that the chief executive is primarily responsible for the conduct of administration. Hamilton wrote:

> The administration of government, in its largest sense, comprehends all the operations of the body politic, whether legislative, executive, or judiciary; but in its most usual and perhaps in its most precise signification, it is limited to executive details, and falls peculiarly within the province of the executive department.

Hamilton's belief that the executive is the source of unity, energy, and vigor in government provides further justification for the concept of executive control of administration. The pertinent constitutional provisions that support what might be called the presidential supremacy theory of public administration are in Article II, vesting the executive power in a president. Article II, section 3 states that the president "shall take Care that the Laws be faithfully executed" and section 2 authorizes him to require "the Opinion, in writing, of the principal Officer in each of the executive Departments, upon any Subject relating to the Duties of their respective Offices"; and grants the president the power to appoint ambassadors, public ministers and consuls, Supreme Court judges, and all other officers whose appointment shall be established by law.

Strong as the president's claim to control administration may be, it is not exclusive. Under the system of checks and balances that the framers built into the separation of powers, the Senate shares the power of appointment. Congress may by law vest the appointment of such inferior officers as it thinks proper in the president alone, in the courts, or in the heads of departments (Article II, section 2). And, most important, Congress can by statute create executive departments and independent agencies, determine their purpose, the scope of their authority and specific duties, and the method of appointment and tenure of office. Congress can further influence the conduct of administration by controlling the funding of departments and agencies through its appropriations power and by its power of investigation.

That the modern administrative state and its regulatory functions are rooted in the framers' fundamental law is suggested by the presence in the Constitution of the concept and the language of regulation. Congress legislates rules of action for civil society that constitute regulation, and is given power specifically to make rules for the "government and regulation" of the military forces of the United States. More significant, Congress has authority to "regulate" commerce with foreign nations, among states, and with the Indian tribes (Article I, section 8). The existence of these provisions in the text of the Constitution does not necessarily confer legitimacy on the modern administrative state, however. The provisions need to be understood in the light of concepts of limited government and individual rights, which have been eroded if not repudiated in the era of bureaucratic governance.

The framers established limited government in several basic senses. First, the national government was limited to certain ends or objects, including protection of national security, conduct of foreign affairs, and regulation of commerce for the promotion of economic development. Second, the national government was limited by the delegation of specific legislative powers, with powers not delegated being reserved to the states or the people. A division of sovereignty was thus provided for between the central government and the state governments, a third conception of limited government. The separation of powers as the organizing principle of the national government was still another means of limitation.

It is a hallmark of the twentieth-century administrative state that for all practical purposes it is not limited by these several principles and institutional arrangements. On the contrary, through its taxing, spending, commerce, and national security powers, the federal government can act on virtually any matter that arises in the nation's social and economic life. Under the older idea of limited government, a federal law or executive action was valid if it was rationally related to a legitimate constitutional object or end. In the administrative state, by contrast, legal inquiry focuses on whether a legitimate federal power, enumerated or implied, exists as the basis for a statute or government action. If it does, it can be used for any purpose whatever. By this means the national government becomes a government of unlimited ends. The single most important source of authority in the federal regulatory arsenal is the commerce power, which has been used to serve a multitude of social reform purposes removed from the framers' original intention of fostering commerce and the production of wealth in a free market regulated by common-law rules. The commerce power can even be used to interdict the production of goods produced by labor the conditions of which are not in conformance with national standards, as the Supreme Court held in *United States* v. *Darby* (1941), and to regulate the production of agricultural goods not intended for interstate exchange, as the Court ruled in *Wickard* v. *Filburn* (1942). In view of these doctrines of constitutional law, which have been legally entrenched since the New Deal, a persistent question in American politics has been whether the bureaucratic state is subject to effective limitation.

Historical evidence legitimating the functions of the modern administrative state can more readily be found at the level of state rather than federal government activity in the nineteenth century. Although the state police power, in accordance with English common-law precedents, was in theory limited to policing conduct based on force or fraud, it was often used to regulate property rights and economic liberty under the judicial rationale of promoting the good of the community as a whole. Regulation was nevertheless subordinate to the purposes of economic development and should be understood in the context of distributive, interest-group politics. Seldom did regulation take the form of statutory restriction applied to all firms or an entire industry in a jurisdiction. State legislatures typically regulated economic activity by means of corporate charters specific to individual firms. On the whole, government regulation was the exception; private individuals regulating themselves through market exchange under common-law rules was the dominant method of adjusting and reconciling private economic interests.

Of course the market as a regulatory institution required the exercise of government power, as in the imposition of sanctions to prevent fraud or to enforce contracts. Therefore, the laissez-faire state and the administrative state can be seen as essentially similar in that both depend on government power; the latter simply makes greater use of governmental sanctions in defining the duties and obligations of property ownership and in protecting the enjoyment and use of property that characterize economic liberty. It is important to note, however, that fundamentally different purposes define the growth of bureaucratic institutions in the twentieth century. Instead of protecting individual liberty and property rights in order to expand economic productivity, the administrative state tends to restrict the economic liberty and property rights of certain classes in order to redistribute wealth to disadvantaged classes. *Class legislation,* the term that describes this transfer process, was the bête noire of the laissez-faire state. The bureaucratic state in contrast regards class legislation, intended to equalize opportunities for all citizens, as an essential feature of good government.

Historians have been slow to recognize the distinctive ends of bureaucratic governance. In part this is because it has taken decades for the political, social, and economic consequences of the administrative state, both intended and unintended, to be experienced and understood. These realities were partially obscured by the political rhetoric of the founders of the regulatory state. In the name of a "new individualism," for example, progressive proponents of regulation claimed that limiting the number of competitors in a given market would foster competition, or that fixing prices and wages at a "fair" level would create economic opportunity and benefit the community as a whole. By the middle of the twentieth century the concept of positive liberty was offered as justification for the regulatory welfare state. In contrast to the negative liberty of laissez-faire, which in protecting people against government left them vulnerable to rule by private corporations, the positive liberty of the bureaucratic state consisted of government programs that conferred on individuals the capacity to exercise fundamental civil rights. In the wave of regulatory reform that swept through American society in the 1960s and 1970s, the concept of civil rights was expanded to include employment, housing, education, medical care, and minimum social welfare benefits. The concept of welfare "entitlements" for "protected classes," as distinguished from equal opportunity for individuals, expressed the inner logic of the administrative state at the end of the twentieth century.

In each of the periods of reform that have produced the bureaucratic state, regulation of social and economic affairs has been equated with defense of the public interest against the selfish demands of special interests. Yet studies of the origins and development of administrative agencies show that a principal purpose and effect of regulatory policy has been to protect existing economic interests against market competition. Frequently this result followed from the so-called capture of regulatory commissions by the interest groups they were intended to regulate. Moreover social-welfare regulation, intended to secure positive liberty for the victims of laissez-faire liberty, appeared to make protected-class individuals, the beneficiaries of entitlement programs, dependent on government. By the 1970s the consequences of regulatory intervention were the object of scholarly investigation by historians, political scientists, and economists, whose findings increased public skepticism about the efficacy and utility of regulation as the characteristic activity of the administrative state. The emergence of an explicitly antibureaucratic impulse in national politics in the 1970s, followed by Supreme Court decisions in the 1980s that questioned key institutional mechanisms of the administrative state (e.g., the legislative veto), signified serious doubt about the legitimacy of bureaucratic governance.

If in its regulatory and redistributive functions the administrative state tends toward a government of unlimited ends, its reliance on centralized authority contradicts the separation of powers and federalism as organizing principles of limited constitutional government. Since the late nineteenth century political reformers have criticized these two principles as obstacles to enlightened administration of the nation's social and economic problems. The favored techniques of bureaucratic governance have been centralization of authority in the national government and delegation of legislative power to the executive. By these means discretionary policy-making authority is conferred on executive departments and administrative agencies, in potential contradiction to the rule of law as expressed in legislative statutes and judicially defined due process of law.

In the Progressive and New Deal eras the administrative state developed in the form of executive centralization. Since the 1960s the bureaucracy has proven amenable as well to congressional and judicial management. The structure of bureaucratic politics changed when Republican presidents Richard M. Nixon in the 1970s and Ronald Reagan in the 1980s used the New Deal model of executive administrative management to limit the expansion of the regulatory welfare state. Congress was then forced to assert its power over administration to defend bureaucratic governance. Reviving the antiexecutive strain in the American political tradition, congressional committee heads appealed to the separation of powers principle to justify efforts to control administration in the executive branch. In the period of divided government in the 1980s, when the Democratic party controlled one or both houses of Congress and the Republican party held the White House, the ideal of concentrated power and unity in administration was thus frustrated.

After a century of development, the specific reasons for the creation of the administrative state remain controversial. The received historical interpretation views bureaucracy as an inherent attribute of modernity, and the regulatory state as the inevitable response to changes in the social environment caused by industrialization. In this view government regulation was required to deal with problems of economic instability, monopolistic privilege, and social injustice that resulted from the failure of the laissez-faire market. Discretionary administrative management of social problems was necessary because the legislature lacked the knowledge, experience, and ability to make rules that would adjust the conflicting interests of industrial society. In social science terms, the demand for government regulation arose when changes in the social environment produced a disequilibrium between behavior and institutions, leading to the reform of social institutions in several areas at the same time. Moreover, in this perspective bureaucratic solutions, occurring in periodic waves of regulation, are cumulative. Government decisions to intervene benefit particular interests and create a presumption that new problems require more intervention, producing a ratchet effect that makes it difficult to stop regulatory expansion.

An alternative and more recent interpretation argues that bureaucratic intervention, far from inevitable, results from deliberate political decisions to restrict individual liberty and property rights with a view toward redistributing wealth according to standards of justice based on the subjective judgment of government administrators. Although rationalized by public-interest rhetoric, regulation in this respect serves the interests of specific groups and classes, including the class of government bureaucrats. In the language of public-choice theory, bureaucratic regulation is driven by the rent-seeking purposes of private parties intent on excluding competitors from the market; by politician-lawmakers trying to win votes by distributing benefits or transferring them from one group to another; and by government officials pursuing their self-interest in the form of larger budgets, expanded staffs, and broader policy-making discretion. Without denying the existence of disinterested political action and government action for the public good, this interpretation focuses on the pursuit of self-interest and market advantage as the dynamic element in the growth of the administrative state. It takes as its basis Adam Smith's insight that people—including public officials—are more prodigal with the wealth of others than with their own.

Although there is evidence to support both of these views of the administrative state, the cumulative knowledge derived from historical scholarship shows that features of the more recent interpretation were also relevant and occurring in the past. This requires understanding historical actors as they understood themselves, and recognition of the actual consequences of their thoughts and actions. In the light of these general considerations, this essay includes analysis of the ends and purposes of regulatory intervention, and the structures, forms, and procedures that define bureaucracy as a governmental type in twentieth-century American politics and constitutionalism.

REGULATING CORPORATIONS AND COMPETITION, 1880–1920

The first of several waves of regulation that created the federal administrative state began in the late nineteenth century when Congress passed two seminal laws that interjected the national government into the economic market. The Interstate Commerce Act of 1887 mandated "reasonable and just" charges in the railroad industry, a business that affected the entire economy. The act created the Interstate Commerce Commission (ICC), the prototype of the independent regulatory agency that was to typify bureaucratic governance. The second statute was the Sherman Antitrust Act of 1890, an economy-wide regulation intended to prohibit monopolies and unlawful combinations in restraint of trade. In the complex interplay revealed between private interests, public authority, and public-interest ideology, these measures illustrate the nature and purpose of the bureaucratic state in its incipient stage.

Government regulation of the railroads was intended to enforce market competition in an industry that was inherently not well suited to regulation by free-market competition. The construction and operation of railroads in its most efficient form tended toward a number of natural monopolies, linked in a national system by pooling or cartel arrangements, and facilitated by practices such as long- and short-haul rate discrimination. Even under monopolistic conditions rail charges were lower than those from alternative modes of transportation. This fact was of little consolation to shippers, businessmen, farmers, and consumers, however, who demanded that the national government force the railroads to operate competitively for the benefit of the diverse interests that depended upon them. At the same time, many railroads sought federal regulation to avoid destructive competition and costly and inconsistent state laws regulating intrastate transportation carriers. These contradictory purposes were embodied in the Interstate Commerce Act.

The act mandated *reasonable* and *just* rates—without defining the terms—and declared unjust charges illegal. It prohibited numerous specific practices, including pooling of traffic and earnings, rate-fixing agreements, rebates, and long- and short-haul rate discrimination. The act also served the interests of the railroads by creating a commission, without rate-setting powers, to promote cartels or associations within the industry to prevent excessive competition and encourage economic efficiency. The statute also authorized the ICC to permit railroads, in special circumstances, to discriminate between long- and short-distance charges. In effect it invited collusion among the railroads by requiring the announcement of uniform rates from which it was illegal to deviate, and by not prohibiting the companies from setting rates.

Originally assigned to the Interior Department, the ICC was removed from the executive branch and made an independent regulatory commission in 1889. In twentieth-century administrative law the meaning of agency independence has been almost as obscure as the meaning of reasonable and just rates. In a formal sense it means that an agency is not subject to exclusive or preponderant control by any of the three branches of government. In the case of the ICC, Congress established the mission, powers, jurisdiction, and operational budget of the agency, and the tenure and salaries of its members; the president appointed commissioners with Senate confirmation, who could be removed only for cause; and ICC decisions and orders were enforceable in court and subject to judicial review. In these respects the commission was assimilated into the separation-of-powers system.

In a more significant constitutional sense, however, the creation of the ICC confuted the separation of powers by conferring on the commission a combination of the functional powers of the three branches. It could make rules of conduct and issue orders declaring practices or rates illegal in a legislative manner. It could hold hearings, gather evidence, and make determinations in a judicial manner about whether rules were observed in particular cases. The chief purpose of the ICC, however, was to enforce and administer the act of Congress regulating transportation. Neither a court nor a legislature, the commission primarily had executive and administrative responsibilities, yet it was independent of the executive branch—an arrangement that was not consistent with the tripartite structure of the U.S. Constitution.

Political considerations, more than a new conception of good government, explain this anomaly. In contemporary understanding, the ICC was viewed as an information-gathering and advisory body intended to mediate between the government—especially Congress—and the varied interests involved in railroad policy making. The congressional orientation of this first independent regulatory commission, evident also in the creation of later ones, became apparent when Congress, controlled by Democrats, removed the ICC from the executive branch two days before the inauguration of President Benjamin Harrison, a Republican. The purpose of the change apparently was to limit executive control of the agency. In the perspective of the administrative state, the political meaning of agency independence has usually been to insulate the regulatory commission from presidential control, making it more amenable to congressional influence.

A bellwether of the regulatory movement, the ICC's early history is instructive for understanding what the administrative state does, and how bureaucratic governance raises questions of constitutional legitimacy. In its first decade the commission tended to support the purposes that lay behind the railroads' tendency to form cartels, advocating a limited amount of pooling and permitting long- and short-haul rate discrimination in some situations. The ICC also attempted to set maximum rates after declaring a rate unjust, but the Supreme Court invalidated agency rate setting as an exercise of legislative power in violation of the separation of powers and the doctrine of nondelegation of legislative power (*Cincinnati, New Orleans, and Texas Pacific Ry. Co.* v. *I.C.C.* [1896]).

In the Progressive period the commission responded to the demands of antirailroad interest groups. It received congressional backing against the courts in the form of legislation that gave it the power to set maximum rates and that partially insulated it from judicial review (Hepburn Act of 1906; Mann-Elkins Act of 1910). Statutory limitation of judicial review of agency actions signified the weakening of constitutional guarantees of property rights, and the strengthening of the federal government's power to interfere with private economic decision making. With its expanded powers the ICC aligned itself with political forces demanding greater government regulation of railroad corporations. It denied rate increases that would have enabled the railroads to generate sufficient profits to make improvements in service and operations. Although the railroad companies could still set rates, the ICC, on its own initiative rather than upon complaint, could suspend rates, conduct an investigation, and set new ones. According to the transportation historian Albro Martin, the expansion of commission powers in effect deprived the railroads of the ability to make intelligent rate decisions.

In 1916 Congress, via the Adamson Act, imposed coercive regulation on the railroad industry by limiting railroad workers in interstate commerce to eight hours of work per day without any reduction in pay. The Supreme Court affirmed this act, rejecting the argument that it was an uncompensated taking of property in violation of the Fifth Amendment (*Wilson* v. *New* [1917]). The Adamson Act presaged complete government control of the railroad industry during World War I, which occurred when President Woodrow Wilson created the U.S. Railroad Administration under a delegation of legislative power from Congress. In the Transportation Act of 1920 Congress restored the railroads to private management, although the ICC continued to regulate the rates, issuance of railroad securities, expenditure of proceeds, and construction, use, and abandonment of facilities.

In standard historical accounts and in public administration writings, regulation of the railroads—and of the economy in general—is necessitated by the failure of the market to regulate the varied interests involved in economic development in a fair and effective manner. Reliance on independent commissions is viewed as a principled, quasi-constitutional decision to remove a controversial political issue from the legislative arena, committing it to neutral, scientific, administrative management in the public interest. According to the standard accounts, Congress lacked the knowledge, information, and expertise needed to govern the railroads, a major and complex sector of the economy. It might be suggested, however, that Congress abdicated its deliberative, policy-making function by creating an independent commission. As the early history of the ICC shows, the establishment of bureaucratic agencies did not separate politics from administration, as proponents of regulation assumed, but rather created a new forum in which interest-group conflict could occur. The main finding of recent scholarship is not that well-conceived, public-interest reform projects such as the ICC went awry because the agencies were captured by the interests they were supposed to regulate. Rather, in the case of the ICC, it promoted economically inefficient policies that prevented market forces from operating to the benefit of both the railroads and the public they served.

The railroad question formed part of the larger problem of regulating large-scale corporate organizations. To deal with the new form of economic association, popularly known as the "trust," the Sherman Antitrust Act, the second foundational statute of the administrative state, was enacted in 1890.

In the Sherman Act Congress used the traditional method of regulation by statutory command and law enforcement because it viewed the policy of the English common law toward the maintenance of economic competition as less intrusive into business affairs and more compatible with traditional ideas of limited government than the regulatory commission approach. Subsequently, Congress used both law enforcement and administrative management to deal with the problem of corporate competition. It passed new antitrust laws, spanning the period from the Clayton Act of 1914 to the Antitrust Improvement Act of 1976, and it created the Federal Trade Commission in 1914 as a bureaucratic agency to enforce these statutes. In 1933 Congress established an executive agency for this purpose, the Antitrust Division in the Department of Justice.

The contribution of antitrust policy to the development of the administrative state lay more in the area of regulatory theory and ideology than in bureaucratic institutions and forms. Under the potent symbol of antitrust regulation, the federal government—in the name of free-market competition—effectively imposed command-and-control rules of action that restricted the economic liberty of business firms. This paradoxical development lies at the heart of much of the controversy surrounding the legitimacy of the bureaucratic state in the twentieth century.

The social and political protest in the 1880s that led to antitrust legislation has often been taken at face value as proof of market failure. The trusts were perceived as ruthless predators threatening the economic liberty, equality of opportunity, and political freedom of poor and middle-class citizens. In economic terms, however, the development of trusts reflected the operation of the market. As productive capacity rose in consequence of technological advances, imbalance existed between systems of production and distribution. Industry segmentation also occurred as some types of industries, such as steel and oil, gravitated toward large size while others did not. Under the circumstances, larger and more successful firms combined to limit plant output, maintain price levels, and discourage market entry. Smaller, less efficient firms viewed this situation as a monopolistic power wielding unfair advantage. From the standpoint of consumers generally, corporate combination was efficient, resulting in expanded output and declining prices. In political terms, groups and firms adversely affected by the economic changes of the 1880s, invoking the antimonopoly rhetoric of the American political tradition, demanded government intervention in the market to prohibit concentrations and mergers. The conflict between economic interests that resulted in the Sherman Act, and that foreshadowed the politics of the administrative state, should not be taken as evidence of market failure justifying government intervention into private economic decision making for the public interest.

The Sherman Act, in its own words, declared illegal "every contract, combination in the form of trust or otherwise, or conspiracy in restraint of trade or commerce among the states or with foreign nations." If taken literally, this language possessed sweeping and radical potential for government regulation of the free market. The act was not intended to have that effect, however, and is best understood as an exercise in symbolic politics that in practical terms was to be given a reasonable interpretation in the light of existing common-law rules marking out acceptable and unacceptable restraints of trade. It is doubtful that Congress meant to outlaw economic mergers and corporate combinations categorically, because these new forms of organization sometimes were economically efficient and socially constructive. The act was inherently ambiguous. On the one hand it reflected interest-group tactical maneuvering, justified in the rhetoric of republican economic liberty. On the other hand it expressed the desire to promote economic efficiency defined as expanded output of goods at lower prices. The act was designed to restrict the trusts in some way, but vague enforcement provisions that were left to judicial definition precluded any clear expectation of its practical impact.

The Supreme Court's interpretation of the Sherman Act was consistent with congressional intent, broadly conceived. Adhering to the basic distinction between commerce and manufacturing that was recognized in constitutional law, the Court held that the act did not reach or render illegal a combination of sugar producers (*United States* v. *E. C. Knight Co.* [1895]). While the Court decided that agreements to fix prices or output and to divide markets were illegal per se, it clarified the fact that enforcement of the act required the application of a "rule of reason," meaning that it prohibited restraints on trade that were unreasonable (*Standard Oil Co. of New Jersey* v. *United States* [1911]). Because large corporations might be the result of superior performance and efficiency, size alone or market share was not evidence of illegality.

Antitrust ideology—the idea, in essence, that large-scale capitalist organizations are a threat to economic and political liberty—became a staple of Progressive and later New Deal regulatory intervention. Its proponents professed the goal of maintaining free-market competition, but at some point events showed the regulatory process to be in reality an attempt by government to decide how private property and economic resources should be allocated and used. In broader perspective, the questions surrounding the regulatory process concerned the nature of legitimate business practices and the relationship between individuals and groups in economic production and exchange. The ultimate issue was the identification of reasonable principles and means for producing wealth in a liberal republican polity. In the early twentieth century proponents of regulation believed that these questions should be removed from private decisionmakers and decided by government, through the imposition of rules that restricted market exchange.

To some extent these questions were debated in the election of 1912. Republican President William Howard Taft had a genuine commitment to judicial enforcement of the antitrust laws that left room for self-regulation by private decisionmakers in the market. Democrat Woodrow Wilson supported statute-regulated competition, and Progressive Theodore Roosevelt supported regulation by administrative commission. Although Wilson won, the enactment of the Clayton Antitrust Act and the Federal Trade Commission Act left the policy debate unresolved. The Clayton Act defined a number of corporate practices as illegal, but only in circumstances where they substantially reduced competition or created a monopoly. The act did not state criteria for determining these effects. Similarly, the Federal Trade Commission Act authorized an administrative agency to prevent unfair methods of competition, but did not define the meaning of *unfair.* In both cases it was clear only that government would decide the legal meaning of uncompetitive, monopolistic, or unfair practices. In doing so, moreover, administrators and judges would not apply fixed formal rules equally to all parties in a general and prospective manner, as the rule of law under limited government required. Rather, they would resolve and adjust conflicts among competing interests in an expedient and discretionary way. Because the courts at this time still largely adhered to laissez-faire principles, progressive reformers looked especially to an administrative commission to provide informal advice to help corporations conduct their affairs within the limits of the law.

Redefining key symbols of the American political tradition, progressive reformers used the rhetoric of individual rights, equality of opportunity, and competitive entrepreneurial liberty to obscure the nature and tendency of administrative regulation as a form of class legislation.

Equating bigness per se with unlawful monopolistic practices, progressives advocated policies such as government-legalized price-fixing to protect the market position of small firms against larger competitors. In general they advocated control of market entry through government licensing requirements to protect existing firms. These policies, examples of "regulation in the public interest," in fact reflected political decisions to confer benefits on some private groups at the expense of other groups and the public at large. Contrary to progressive regulatory theory, in a genuine free-market system consumers benefit from increased output and lower prices. Competition in terms of price is fundamental to the market, and unrestricted entry into competition—which carries the risk of failure and subsequent exit—is essential.

EXECUTIVE CONTROL OF ADMINISTRATION, 1920–1960

Reformers rationalized government interference in private economic decision making—the characteristic activity if not the end of the bureaucratic state—as an inevitable consequence of social complexity of modern industrial organization. To gain acceptance for this policy proponents conceived a new type of scientific and nonpolitical government administration as a way to improve an allegedly defective constitutional system. To guide this transformation progressive intellectuals introduced public administration as a new branch of political science and posited administrative law as a new field of jurisprudence. In the writings of scholar-reformers such as Henry Jones Ford and Herbert Croly, legislatures were identified with corrupt special interests, and courts with guarantees of property rights giving corporations legal immunity against regulation. Reformers proposed to bypass these institutions by appealing to the executive as the source of authority and the center of intelligent design in constructing the administrative state.

Reformers relied on the traditional understanding that administration of government, by reasonable inference from the text of the Constitution, could be considered an executive function, as Hamilton had said in *The Federalist*. Nevertheless, progressive reformers believed good government, in the form of the administrative state, required the superseding of if not the formal abrogation of the separation-of-powers principle. Theodore Roosevelt energized presidential power under Hamiltonian teaching by claiming that problems of administrative organization and management were executive matters. Woodrow Wilson broke even more decisively from previous constitutional practice and made the modern presidency the effective basis of the bureaucratic state.

Wilson was the author of seminal works on the theory of public administration that attacked what he disparagingly called the "literary theory" of the American Constitution. He criticized in particular the separation of powers, which he viewed as the major obstacle to effective modern government. Wilson said that by dividing power and setting the political branches against each other, the separation of powers obscured clear lines of responsibility and prevented the emergence of political leadership needed to deal with exigent national problems. To elicit such leadership Wilson and the founders of public administration reconceptualized the nature of American government and the role of the executive power.

Instead of the tripartite constitutional design, theorists of public administration posited two functions of government: to express the popular will and to execute it. The key to the new approach to governance was that the will of the people should emerge through presidential leadership. Drawing power from the people as the living constituent force of the nation, rather than from the formal Constitution, the chief executive acts as national opinion leader. Shaping and interpreting the popular will through his rhetorical ability and actions, and backed by a responsible or programmatic party, the executive forms opinion into legislative measures stating general policy objectives. Expert administrators under executive control then implement and adapt the ends of policy to specific situations by means of regulatory rules and orders. The work of administrative management is to be done in an expedient and discretionary way, yet also in a nonpolitical way. The underlying assumption is that politics can be separated from administration. In the words of progressive theorist Frank J. Goodnow, the administrator's "mission is the exercise of foresight and discretion, the pursuit of truth, the gathering of information, the maintenance of a strictly impartial attitude." According to Woodrow Wilson, through the building of an administrative state American government can be made "a straightforward thing of simple method, single unstinted power, and clear responsibility."

While proponents of public administration questioned the separation of powers structure, incremental changes occurred, as a result of statutes and judicial decisions, that began the shift of policy-making power to executive officers that would characterize the twentieth-century bureaucratic state. In a constitutional sense this change modified and ultimately rejected the separation-of-powers principle that Congress may not delegate its legislative power to the executive.

In traditional constitutional theory the deliberative and discretionary lawmaking function is assigned to the legislative branch, and the nondiscretionary law enforcement or administrative function to the executive branch. Although this arrangement is tempered by checks and balances that give each branch a partial agency in the exercise of the other's power, by plain inference the controlling principle is that Congress may not abdicate its duty to deliberate and make policy; may not, that is, delegate legislative power to the executive branch or to private parties. To be sure, the cooperation that is necessary between statutory rule making and administration required a degree of modification of the rule in practice. Thus Congress in the nineteenth century occasionally delegated limited discretionary authority to the executive to find and declare specific facts that activated certain provisions of a statute; to fill in the details of legislation; and to exercise discretion in accordance with standards set by the legislature. The Supreme Court upheld these grants of power as consistent with the separation-of-powers principle. From the standpoint of those who wanted to create an administrative state, however, these measures were precedents that supported policy making by executive agencies and independent regulatory commissions. It was significant, moreover, that judges who were known as constitutional conservatives upheld these governmental innovations (*Field* v. *Clark* [1892]; *Buttfield* v. *Stranahan* [1904]; *United States* v. *Grimaud* [1911]; *J. W. Hampton, Jr., and Co.* v. *United States* [1928]). Without abrogating the nondelegation doctrine, the Court reconciled the desire to experiment with bureaucratic techniques with the constitutional principle of the separation of powers.

Significant steps toward bureaucratic governance were taken during World War I as Congress delegated vast discretionary authority to the executive. The

Selective Service Act gave the president discretion to conscript an army; the Trading with the Enemy Act authorized him to license trade with Germany and to censor mail, cable, and radio communications with foreign states; and the Army Appropriations Act of 1916 empowered him to take over and operate common carriers in time of war. The most far-reaching delegation was conferred by the Overman Act of 1918, which gave the president authority to redistribute functions in the executive branch and signified the abandonment of all ordinary restraints on the delegation of legislative power to the executive. Enacted under a Democratic administration, these measures inspired later New Deal planners of the administrative state.

Despite wartime bureaucratization under Democratic auspices, the drive for executive control of administration was in general a bipartisan undertaking. This can be seen in the Budget and Accounting Act of 1921, which was approved by Republican President Warren Harding as the culmination of efforts begun by Taft and supported by Wilson to provide the executive with budget authority to strengthen his administrative management role. Prior to this seminal measure no formal budget process existed. Congress passed spending and revenue bills separately, without knowing the total amount it was spending, and executive departments and agencies submitted budget requests directly to congressional committees. The Budget and Accounting Act, described by the public administration scholar Herbert Emmeri as "the greatest landmark of our administrative history except for the Constitution itself," created a Bureau of the Budget in the Treasury Department with a line of responsibility direct to the president. Budget requests were directed from the departments and agencies to the president for revision and submission to Congress. Although in passing this act Congress in effect conceded the need of the legislative branch for discipline from the executive in fiscal matters, it protected its authority by creating the General Accounting Office to conduct audits of executive department and agency spending.

The bipartisan nature of the building of the administrative state is further apparent in the career of Republican President Herbert Hoover. A progressive engineer and administrator of food relief during World War I, Hoover as secretary of commerce in the 1920s promoted techniques of administrative management to expand and rationalize the productive and distributive potential of American industry. Rejecting the stricter laissez-faire, limited government philosophy of President Calvin Coolidge, he encouraged the formation of trade associations for the exchange of information about materials, production, marketing, and advertising that permitted corporations to maintain prices at a satisfactory profit level while eliminating costly competition. As president during the Depression, Hoover interjected the government farther into market operations, proposing public works appropriations, tax reductions, and expansion of credit facilities to stimulate economic activity. While he was more aware than other progressives of the danger of bureaucratic coercion, his conception of industrial self-government under benign government supervision was in the mainstream of progressive scientific management ideology on which the administrative state was based.

The New Deal administration of Franklin D. Roosevelt also moved in the direction of greater federal involvement in private economic decision making. Although generally content to apply the received theories of progressive public administration, New Deal liberals were more forthright than earlier reformers in repudiating the tenets of laissez-faire political economy. Their enthusiastic embrace of direct government regulation of economic life by administrative experts marked the decisive establishment of the bureaucratic state.

In the context of the Great Depression, the first task of the New Deal administration was to promote industrial and commercial recovery. To this end President Roosevelt employed an experimental strategy that departed from the precepts of limited government. More clearly than their Wilsonian predecessors, New Deal reformers challenged the private power of corporations and questioned the free market as a system of social regulation. Contending that corporations were in reality public institutions that held workers in a condition of industrial serfdom, they proposed to subject large business firms to democratic accountability and control. The New Deal Congress enacted regulatory statutes, such as the far-reaching National Industrial Recovery Act (NIRA), that took economic decision-making power away from private property owners and conferred it on government administrators under executive control. In actual implementation the NIRA, to take the most radical example of Roosevelt's reconstruction of the political economy, delegated lawmaking power to private businesses and trade associations by allowing them to draft codes of fair competition. But the president and the National Recovery Administration, his executive creation, retained the authority to approve and prescribe the industry codes. The fundamental assumption of the New Deal regulatory regime, even after modifications were forced upon it by a resistant legislature and judiciary after 1936, was that government officials knew the standards of justice under which fair price and wage systems would be established, the proper level of industrial production to be set, and the right number of competitors to be allowed entry into the market. The government, through the federal executive, should order national economic priorities and direct private economic interests.

Purporting to "constitutionalize" private economic power, the New Deal proposed to redefine individual liberty with reference to the social security and welfare requirements demanded by modern industrial society. The programmatic logic of the regulatory welfare state appeared in the argument, announced first in Franklin D. Roosevelt's address to the Commonwealth Club of San Francisco in 1932, for a revised social contract between the people and the government that would recognize the realities of modern industrial organization. Positing an economic bill of rights as the centerpiece of a new "economic constitutional order," the Democratic candidate said the government should guarantee everyone the right to a comfortable living and the opportunity to possess through his own work a portion of the plenty that the nation possessed, sufficient to meet his needs. In liberal ideology this heralded a "new individualism," which required organized planning under an energetic executive and strict limitations on corporate property rights. Closely related in the revised liberalism of the administrative state was the concept of class legislation, the bête noire of laissez-faire constitutionalism. Illustrated in both the National Industrial Recovery Act and the National Labor Relations Act of 1935, class legislation gave certain groups legal privileges and immunities for pursuing their special interests relative to other groups and the public in general.

Programmatic liberalism required new governmental forms to overcome the constitutional guarantees of individual liberty and property rights that were an obstacle to government regulation of social and economic life. For this purpose the New Deal relied on administrative agencies and independent regulatory commissions. Although these governmental instruments had been developing for half a century, they were still of questionable constitutionality, and they had evolved in a more or less haphazard way without effective subordination to presidential control. The constitutional strategy of the New Deal therefore was to expand the executive's authority over the rapidly growing federal bureaucracy, a process that Congress carried out by creating numerous statutes that delegated legislative power to the executive branch. In political terms, the transformation of liberalism and the centralization of bureaucratic governance was a Democratic party affair. Mindful of the local, interest-oriented nature of the party system, however, Roosevelt ultimately aspired to create a presidential party that would transcend pluralistic partisanship in the name of enlightened public administration.

The long-range design and structure of the liberal bureaucratic regime assumed more specific form after 1936 when judicial opposition to the New Deal clarified the fundamental challenge to the constitutional order implicit in Roosevelt's reconstruction project. Trying to preserve laissez-faire and limited government, the Supreme Court in a series of decisions declared the substance of New Deal liberalism unconstitutional. Specifically, it violated the constitutional principles of states' rights, the commerce clause, the nondelegation doctrine under the separation of powers, and due process of law. In 1937 President Roosevelt proposed a plan of judicial reform that effectively induced the Court to adopt a more favorable view of New Deal legislation. At the same time, Roosevelt proposed to reorganize the executive branch as a way to establish presidential control of the bureaucracy.

Rapid expansion of the federal bureaucracy in the 1930s provided the occasion for placing executive reorganization high on the political agenda of Roosevelt's second administration. Among the more important government agencies created since 1933 were the National Recovery Administration, Agricultural Adjustment Administration, Tennessee Valley Authority, Federal Deposit Insurance Corporation, Home Owners Loan Corporation, Securities and Exchange Commission, National Labor Relations Board, Social Security Administration, Federal Emergency Relief Administration, and Works Progress Administration. To provide justification for executive control of this proliferating apparatus of government, Roosevelt in 1936 created the President's Committee on Administrative Management, headed by the public administration expert Louis Brownlow. The Brownlow committee was intended to find ways to institutionalize Roosevelt's political advantage and strengthen his ability to bring the government under unified managerial control.

The recommendations of the Brownlow committee can be viewed as a point of convergence of the two lines of development that have been observed in the formation of the administrative state since the late nineteenth century. These are the substantive tendency of government regulation to supersede market regulation and the procedural-institutional tendency of bureaucratic governance to come under presidential control. Rejecting the idea that executive reorganization should reduce the size and expense of government, as previous presidents believed, the Brownlow committee redefined administrative efficiency to mean enhanced executive policy making and delivery of government services aimed at providing social security and redistributing wealth. Oblivious to the antiexecutive tradition in American political thought, the Brownlow committee recommended a system of centralized, top-level, presidential management that it claimed would merely carry out policies established by Congress. In a manner that in retrospect appears disingenuous, the committee insisted that executive reorganization would not undermine the separation of powers, but rather would strengthen the role of Congress by creating mechanisms for holding the executive accountable.

The Brownlow committee proposed major changes in the executive branch to make the president's legal authority over administration more commensurate with his political responsibility for national policy. The most significant recommendations were to enlarge the White House staff; create the Executive Office of the President; transfer the Bureau of the Budget from the Treasury Department to the Executive Office of the President; and give the president control of accounts, with Congress having a post-audit responsibility over government expenditures. The fiscal power of the president would thus be greatly enhanced, with the power of the General Accounting Office reduced and prior controls over spending made internal to the executive branch. Other recommendations were to create two new executive departments (Social Welfare and Public Works), give the president authority to define their duties, and bring the independent regulatory commissions into the executive departments, which were subject to presidential control. These several proposals expressed the consensus not only of the Brownlow committee, but also of the public administration community in general that the whole executive power of the United States was conferred upon the president.

Taken in conjunction with President Roosevelt's judicial reform plan, the report of the Brownlow committee provoked strong opposition in Congress, and most of the recommendations were rejected. Nevertheless the strength of Roosevelt's attack on the old order, reinforced by the substantial constitutional authority of the presidency even in its unreconstructed form, was sufficient to secure a compromise that gave the chief executive significant new powers. In the Executive Reorganization Act of 1939 Congress accepted several of the proposals, thereby laying the foundation for the modern presidency. The act created the Executive Office of the President, expanded the White House staff, shifted the Bureau of the Budget to the Executive Office of the President, and authorized the president to transfer agencies from one executive department to another. No authority to abolish agencies was conferred, and the independent regulatory commissions were protected from executive interference. The Reorganization Act inaugurated a gradual process of congressional approval of the substance of the Brownlow report that extended over two decades. Equally important, the presumption of executive supremacy in administration underlying the report steadily gained adherents in the academic and media culture, establishing a basis in public opinion for the expansion of presidential government in the post–World War II period.

As it had been a consequence of World War I, bureaucratic centralization was also a consequence of World War II. The principal instrument of foreign and domestic policy making was the delegation of legislative power to the executive, which was used in statutes such as the Selective Service Act of 1940, the Lend-Lease Act, the War Powers Acts of 1941 and 1942, the Emergency Price Control Act, and the War Labor Disputes Act. Under authority provided by the Executive Reorganization Act of 1939, President Roosevelt created the Office of Emergency Management as a legal cover for scores of boards and commissions, and as a coordinating agency for industrial production and economic mobilization. Although it is often thought that the New Deal preserved capitalism, government-business relations in World War II assumed a command-and-control form—with government allocating resources and setting prices—that was far removed from the traditional understanding of free-market economic decision making under limited constitutional government.

The regulatory state was confirmed and consolidated on a bipartisan basis after World War II. Statutes such as the Taft-Hartley Act of 1947, which limited the powers of labor unions, reflected the waning of programmatic liberalism, but other measures and events signaled the growing acceptance of the bureaucratic state. These included the Administrative Procedure Act (A.P.A.) and the Employment Act of 1946, the report of the Hoover commission on government organization in 1949, and the two-term presidency of Dwight D. Eisenhower in the 1950s.

The Administrative Procedure Act in part reflected conservative criticism of regulatory disregard of individual rights. Administrative agencies routinely performed adjudicatory functions that challenged and superseded the judicial guarantees of liberty and property of constitutional law. In 1940 critics of bureaucracy passed the Logan-Walter bill, giving any individual or corporation with substantial interest in the effects of any administrative rule the right to go into court and challenge its constitutionality. President Roosevelt vetoed this measure, but his administration accepted the proposition that bureaucratic rule making and adjudication raised genuine civil liberties concerns. This view was expressed in the Report on Administrative Procedure, issued by Attorney General Robert Jackson in 1941. While insisting on the superiority of administrative agency policy to private rights and interests under administrative law, Jackson conceded the necessity of introducing more effective due process safeguards for parties subject to administrative regulation.

The Administrative Procedure Act of 1946 embodied the renewed concern for individual rights provoked by bureaucratic governance, even as it confirmed the basic principles of the administrative state. These principles were the delegation of legislative power to the executive, and the primacy of informal "adjustment of interests" (i.e., political bargaining) over formal guarantees of individual rights. Within this framework the A.P.A. was intended to constitutionalize the bureaucracy by introducing rule-of-law procedures, in order to give private parties "a means of knowing what their rights are and how they may protect them."

The Administrative Procedure Act classified rule making and adjudication functions as formal or informal. Formal rule making and adjudication involved a trial-like hearing on the record; informal procedure, which public administration lawyers preferred, required notice of a proposed rule in the *Federal Register* and opportunity for comment by affected parties. These provisions constituted what Congress considered "an outline of minimum essential rights and procedures," drawn from a judicial rule-of-law model of governance, that administrative agencies were obliged to follow. The act also placed limits on the extent to which the powers of government could be fused or combined in the actions of administrative agencies. Fact-finding was separated from policy determination both in rule making and adjudication. The A.P.A. thus used the concept of separate functions of government to reform the regulatory regime that was premised on the alleged inadequacy of the separation-of-powers principle.

The Employment Act of 1946 further institutionalized the liberalism of the administrative state. Although it omitted key liberal symbols such as "full employment" and "guarantee," the act stated in effect that it was the responsibility of the federal government to create and maintain conditions of maximum employment opportunity, and to promote maximum employment, production, and purchasing power. These ends were to be pursued with the cooperation of industry, agriculture, labor, and state and local governments "in a manner calculated to promote free competitive enterprise and the general welfare." The act created a Council of Economic Advisers to assist the president in formulating and recommending national economic policy.

Still another indication of bipartisan acceptance of the bureaucratic state was the report of the Commission on the Reorganization of the Executive Branch, appointed by the Republican Congress in 1947 and chaired by former president Herbert Hoover. Adapting the premise of the Brownlow committee that the government needed more centralized executive management, the Hoover commission recommended a presidential secretariat to provide staff assistance to the chief executive. President Truman endorsed the report, and Congress adopted many of its proposals, including a renewal of executive reorganization authority, an expanded White House staff, and the creation of the Department of Defense and the General Services Administration. Although the Hoover commission used the older rhetoric of economy and efficiency in government, its report affirmed both the executive-supremacy model of bureaucratic governance and the progressive theory of neutral public administration based on the separation of politics and administration.

The Eisenhower administration maintained the bureaucratic state and the politics of interest-group liberalism established by the New Deal. Policy making in the liberal regulatory regime was carried on within triangular systems of distributional coalitions comprising administrative agencies, private interest groups, and congressional committees. Government agencies looked to interest groups for technological expertise and advice in rule making; interest groups appealed to the agencies for advance advice and favorable resolution of policy disputes; and both turned to Congress for protection against outside interference, including occasional efforts by the White House to assert executive control. President Eisenhower, after at first advocating the restoration of legislative and executive balance, adopted the conventions of presidential government. He used the Bureau of the Budget to coordinate a legislative program, relied increasingly on the White House staff for administrative management, and utilized the National Security Council, created by Congress in 1947, to set foreign and domestic policy. The National Security Council, Council of Economic Advisers, and Bureau of the Budget formed the nucleus of the policy-making machinery by which the president tried to control the regulatory state in the era of the Cold War.

THE SWING TO CONGRESS AND THE COURTS, 1960–1980

A new stage in the development of the bureaucratic state began in the 1960s, which saw the introduction of social regulation of a far more comprehensive scope than that of earlier reform legislation. In the Progressive and New Deal eras regulation was justified by market failure and directed at specific problems such as entry and exit, market share, prices and production levels, and services. The purpose of regulation typically was to secure or retain a competitive advantage for a particular interest group, notwithstanding the public interest rhetoric that was used to justify legislative or administrative policy making. The regulations of the 1960s and 1970s were more universal, categorical, and results oriented in the sense that they mandated specific outcomes. The general intent of the new social regulations were to reduce if not eliminate risk in the areas of public health, employee and consumer safety, and environmental protection. As reformers turned their attention to the quality of life in an era of material affluence, concern for risk became the basis for a fundamental transformation in public opinion that shifted responsibility for injury and dependency from the private sector to the government. Blame and fault were attributed to society rather than to individuals, and the concept of social costs replaced the notion of personal responsibility.

The sources and causes of this change in the regulatory regime are a matter of scholarly controversy. Some regard it as a popular manifestation of continued faith in the ability of an activist federal government to solve the nation's social and economic problems. According to this interpretation, change occurred because reformers perceived the flaws and inadequacies of pluralistic democracy and resolved to complete the New Deal revolution by guaranteeing social and economic equality for previously excluded racial, ethnic, and sex groups. Others view the burst of reform activity starting in the 1960s as a periodic manifestation of the inherent instability in American politics caused by the aspiration of new generations of Americans to fulfill the nation's democratic ideals. Still another and more critical view of post–New Deal social regulation sees it as an expression of the hostility to the free market and private economic decision making that is inherent in the nature of the bureaucratic state.

The wave of social regulation that defined post–New Deal liberalism began with the Civil Rights Act of 1964. From a regulatory standpoint, the most important provisions of the act prohibited discrimination in the operation of public accommodations and facilities and federally funded activities, and guaranteed equal employment opportunity to individuals irrespective of race, color, religion, national origin, or sex. Contrary to the stated intentions of its authors, the Civil Rights Act promptly resulted in government regulation of the labor market that to a considerable extent redefined equal opportunity in terms of proportional employment for racial and ethnic minority groups. Administrators in the Equal Employment Opportunity Commission and the Office of Federal Contract Compliance, two new regulatory agencies, led the way in designing affirmative action programs that identified a number of minority groups as victims of past societal discrimination entitled to compensatory preference in employment.

The civil rights movement galvanized liberal reform energies that demanded an imposing array of regulatory controls to improve the quality of American life. Under Presidents Johnson, Nixon, Ford, and Carter, social regulation was adopted dealing with environmental protection, worker safety, consumer protection, transportation safety, fair packaging and labeling, energy conservation, and fair housing. Regulatory activity far exceeded that of previous reform eras. Approximately two hundred of the four hundred regulatory statutes passed since 1900 were enacted in the post-1960 period. More than a score of regulatory agencies were created, and from 1970 to 1980 the number of personnel in federal administrative agencies increased from 30,000 to 90,000 and the number of pages in the *Federal Register,* a barometer of regulatory activity, increased from 20,000 to 90,000.

The variety of the new social regulations is apparent in the following list: the Traffic Safety Act of 1966, Flammable Fabric Act of 1967, Age Discrimination in Employment Act of 1967, Truth in Lending Act of 1968, National Environmental Policy Act of

1969, Clean Air Act of 1970, Economic Stabilization Act of 1970, Equal Employment Opportunity Act of 1973, Federal Energy Administration Act of 1974, Employee Retirement Income Security Act of 1975, Energy Policy and Conservation Act of 1975, Energy Conservation and Production Act of 1976, Surface Mining Control Reclamation Act of 1977, Marine Protection Research and Sanctuaries Act of 1977, National Energy Conservation Policy Act of 1978, Natural Gas Policy Act of 1978, and Public Utilities Regulatory Policies Act of 1978.

Instead of focusing on specific practices in discrete industries as earlier regulations had, the new social regulation typically imposed economy-wide performance standards on business and industry. Although the goals of the regulations were valid, the social benefits, in terms of injury and harm prevented, were often hard to measure. In addition, there were costs and unintended consequences that had predictable negative effects on economic productivity and efficiency. For example, the goals of environmental statutes were expressed in comprehensive and systematic terms that if taken literally would require the complete elimination of injury or risk. To achieve a completely clean environment would require extremely high standards of performance by industrial firms. Compliance with environmental standards is expensive and affects economic production, expansion, and innovation. Estimates of the general cost of regulatory compliance in the economy as a whole in the 1980s were approximately $400 billion annually or 3.5 percent of the GNP. Although some administrative agencies seemed determined to try, it was especially difficult and expensive to achieve zero risk or injury because compliance costs rise exponentially as the goal is approached. Furthermore, social regulation at times had irrational consequences, as when rules that restricted conduct in one area caused people to change their behavior and risk greater injury in another.

Although the social purpose was different, the new regulations produced economic effects not unlike those of earlier government interventions. The imposition of economy-wide performance standards affected individual firms differently, proving beneficial to some and injurious to others with respect to market position. At times interest-group aggrandizement appeared to drive the regulatory process, despite claims of scientific justification for a given policy. When, for example, the use of ethanol was approved as a sound environmental protection measure, it was not hard to discern that there was pressure from midwestern corn traders to support the policy. In order to accommodate the new social regulation, firms were required to spend more on lobbying activities. Hence they became politicized on an individual-firm basis rather than as part of a trade association.

As it asserted new social purposes, so the regulatory reformism of the 1970s assumed institutional forms different from those of the New Deal administrative state. The most significant change was the rejection, after decades of uncritical acceptance by liberal elites, of presidential supremacy as the organizing principle of bureaucratic governance. This alteration in outlook occurred when liberals realized, after the election of Richard M. Nixon in 1968 and Ronald Reagan in 1980, that conservatives could use the model of presidential government for antiregulatory ends. Rediscovering the constitutional sources of legislative control of administration, liberal lawmakers and bureaucrats revived the doctrine of the separation of powers as a means to challenge executive control of administration. They wrote regulatory statutes with a view toward congressional supervision of agency policy making. The legislation also included an expanded judicial role in administrative policy making and opportunities for citizen participation in the regulatory process.

The most novel structural change in the post–New Deal administrative state was the emergence of the judiciary as a partner with Congress in policy making and bureaucratic oversight. In the early twentieth century the courts had occasionally resisted government intervention in the market and restricted the authority of independent regulatory commissions. After the constitutional crisis of 1937, however, the judiciary acquiesced in regulatory interventions, accepting the pragmatic adjustment of interests under administrative law as compatible with constitutional guarantees of property rights. In the name of judicial restraint, the courts deferred to legislative and administrative policy making. This deference was expressed in the Administrative Procedure Act of 1946, which denied judicial review where the action of an agency was committed to the agency's discretion by law. Silently overruling the invalidation of legislative delegations in *Schechter* v. *United States* (1935), the Supreme Court approved the delegation of legislative power to the executive, assuming that agencies correctly found the facts and properly interpreted the statutes they were charged with enforcing.

Responding to political protest that among other things attacked impersonal and irresponsible bureaucracy, the federal judiciary in the 1960s began to democratize the forms and procedures of the administrative state. In place of the progressive theory of deference to administrative agency expertise, courts adopted a pluralistic model of policy making in which the public interest is seen to emerge from the clash of interest-group demands in the regulatory arena. Consistent with this approach, courts made decisions liberalizing the rules of standing, the necessity for a decision, and exhaustion of remedies that had the effect of expanding the scope of public participation in the regulatory process. Under this judicial dispensation, private groups were allowed to initiate litigation challenging agency policy or forcing an agency to adopt rules that implemented a regulatory statute. Courts also interpreted the "notice and comment" language of the Administrative Procedure Act to require agencies to announce their goals and priorities, as well as the facts and methods on which they based their rules. And they permitted private groups to present data, question other groups, and rebut evidence.

Regulatory statutes in the 1970s incorporated citizen participation features in the system of bureaucratic governance. Noteworthy examples included the requirement of Environmental Impact Statements, which brought private groups into the decision-making process of the Environmental Protection Agency, and the Intervenor Funding Program of the Federal Trade Commission, which subsidized the involvement of public lobby groups in agency rule making. Congress established such procedures in order to create a documentary record of agency actions that could be used to enforce regulatory statutes in court. Participatory reforms were also designed to make bureaucratic institutions more representative, and to enlist the judiciary in administrative policy making. Politically the reforms were intended to create obstacles to executive control of bureaucratic policy making, thereby preventing the capture of regulatory commissions by the business interests they were supposed to regulate.

In addition to inaugurating procedural reforms, the judiciary played a part in administrative policy making. In employment discrimination, for example, courts and civil rights agencies jointly developed affirmative action policies to enforce the Civil Rights Act of 1964. In the area of welfare administration the courts revised basic definitions of key terms such as *family* and *parent,* and established the legal meaning of *entitlement* as the right to benefits adequate to meet individual needs. Through creative statutory interpretation the judiciary revised social welfare policy in general to establish a comprehensive welfare class that replaced the limited categories of public assistance provided by congressional legislation. Furthermore the courts imposed a stricter standard of judicial review on administrative agencies, requiring a demonstration of the substantive rationality of regulatory policy in relation to the authorizing statute. Notwithstanding their lack of scientific expertise, courts were prepared to declare agency policies unsound or incorrect on substantive rather than procedural grounds. Depicted by regulatory reformers as unelected representatives of the people against bureaucratic elites, the courts justified their regulatory intervention in the name of the rule of law.

Complementing judicial activism in the post–New Deal liberal regulatory state was the expanded role of the legislative branch. In contrast to earlier reform eras, Congress rather than the executive supplied the political energy and directed the planning and administration of the regulatory movement of the 1970s. Indeed, the purpose of regulatory policy making was now to limit presidential influence. This institutional restructuring of the administrative state was the outcome of the change in bureaucratic politics caused by President Nixon's attempt to control the post–New Deal regulatory regime.

The politics of administration in the Nixon era was based on long-standing partisan and ideological hostility between the new Republican president and the Democratic party, which retained control of Congress and was well represented in the bureaucracy. At the outset of his administration Nixon asked Congress for authority to reorganize the executive branch. Congress agreed, and permitted the appointment of a presidential advisory commission, headed by corporate executive and defense contractor Roy Ash, that would try to do for the Republican president what the Brownlow committee had done for Franklin D. Roosevelt. The Ash commission submitted a plan for executive branch revision intended to strengthen presidential managerial capacity over the civil service, and Congress approved the plan in 1970.

The Nixon reorganization plan made two major changes in bureaucratic organization. The Bureau of the Budget was renamed the Office of Management and Budget and was transformed into a more exclusively presidential agency intended to serve a top-level managerial function for the executive branch. The plan also created a Domestic Policy Council to coordinate and enhance White House influence on policy making in the executive departments. Both reforms were intended to make the president's policy-making authority more commensurate with his political responsibility as national leader. In order to promote conservative policies, Nixon at first tried to use a legislative strategy. When Democratic control of Congress frustrated this endeavor, the president decided to use the Domestic Policy Council to create a parallel bureaucracy in the White House that could effect policy change. Nixon further impounded funds for more than one hundred government agencies in order to achieve budgetary savings. This strategy exacerbated tensions between the executive and career administrators, who turned to Congress for protection and support. In 1971 plans for further executive reorganization were rejected by Congress amidst widening perceptions of presidential aggrandizement. In this context the Watergate burglary, the subsequent cover-up by the White House, and related revelations of executive abuse appeared as the logical culmination of Richard Nixon's personal corruption and quest for power.

President Nixon's near impeachment and his resignation from office in 1974 severely damaged the presidency, and discredited the theory of executive control of administration that had been the leading principle of the bureaucratic state for half a century. In reaction against Watergate and the dangers of what was now called the "imperial presidency" by liberals, who had previously hailed a strong chief executive, Congress reasserted its authority over policy making and administration. The Budget and Impoundment Control Act of 1974 and the Ethics in Government Act of 1978 were the most important of several measures affecting the structure of the bureaucratic state that attempted to redress the imbalance between the executive and legislative branches that had developed since the New Deal.

Intended to recover authority long since conferred on the executive, the Budget and Impoundment Control Act created the Congressional Budget Office and House and Senate Budget committees to prepare legislative budget recommendations. The act restricted impoundment of funds, requiring the president to inform Congress and secure approval for intended deferrals and rescissions. Effective in serving liberal reform purposes, the budget act prevented the executive from unilaterally reducing the expenditure of appropriated funds and facilitated increased federal spending in support of entitlement programs and social regulation.

The Ethics in Government Act created the office of special prosecutor as a safeguard against executive power. Based on a separation-of-powers rationale, the law was intended to prevent corruption of the prosecutorial function and the administration of justice because of conflict of interest in the executive branch. Covering about seventy top-level executive offices, the act provided for the appointment of a special prosecutor (later renamed special counsel) by a federal court, upon the recommendation of the attorney general, to investigate alleged wrongdoing by named individuals. The special prosecutor could be removed only for cause and hence was relatively immune to presidential influence. The law questioned the traditional view that criminal prosecution was an executive function under the separation-of-powers principle, in effect creating an executive office outside the executive branch. The special prosecutor was not directly accountable to Congress or to any other institution or authority. In the context of the executive-legislative conflict that produced the act, however, and that was a prominent feature of politics in the 1980s when the statute was frequently applied, a special prosecutor was more likely to be responsive to congressional opinion than to executive branch concerns.

Another instrument of congressional power over administration in the aftermath of Watergate was the legislative veto. First used in 1932 as a procedure for reorganizing the executive branch, the legislative veto was a means of delegating legislative power to the executive. In statutes conferring lawmaking authority, Congress typically required the executive department or agency to submit its rules and regulations for legislative consideration; if not rejected by one or both houses of Congress within a specific period of time the regulations would go into effect. This arrangement accommodated the desire of the executive to exercise discretionary policy-making power, and of Congress to retain control of administrative rule making without passing new legislation.

The legislative veto was sparingly used until the 1970s, when it became a favored technique of congressional control of administration. From 1970 to 1975 Congress passed eighty-nine statutes with legislative veto provisions, dealing with an array of subjects from immigration to public works to federal salaries. The device was so appealing to members of Congress that a proposal was introduced in the late 1970s to amend the Administrative Procedure Act to provide for a general legislative veto. This proposed "generic" veto, which gained serious support, would have covered all new regulations and permitted either legislative chamber to require executive agencies to reconsider existing rules. Although it was not adopted, the proposed A.P.A. amendment raised basic questions about the place of the separation of powers in the administrative state.

DEREGULATION AND THE REAGAN REVOLUTION, 1980–1989

The social regulation of the 1970s prompted a reaction on behalf of individual liberty and property rights, decentralization of policy making and regulatory authority, and free-market entrepreneurialism. Partly evident in the Nixon and Ford administrations, these classical liberal tenets—now considered bedrock principles of conservatism—were revived in the election of President Ronald Reagan in 1980. Although conservative hopes and liberal fears that the "Reagan revolution" would restore limited government were vastly exaggerated, important changes nevertheless occurred in the policies and institutional structure of the administrative state in the 1980s.

Deregulation was the political catchword of Republican partisans seeking to reform the post–New Deal regulatory regime. Although the call for deregulation carried ideological overtones, it rested on a factual basis in the form of economic studies showing the costs and unintended consequences of government regulation. Revisionist thinking in economics gradually led to a reconsideration of the free market as a regulatory system and provided the intellectual framework for critical reexamination of command-and-control regulation. Concepts such as price as a regulative mechanism, managerial costs, and allocative and productive efficiency were used to analyze the effects of regulation. Moreover the "public-interest" justification of regulation appeared less persuasive in the light of historical studies showing that the main effect—and often the apparent purpose—of Progressive and New Deal regulation was to confer economic benefits on some groups at the expense of others. Advocates of deregulation did not question the traditional assumption, accepted by even the strongest judicial proponents of laissez-faire constitutionalism, that regulation for health and safety purposes was consistent with free-market competition. Yet regulatory policy increasingly came to be seen as politically motivated government intervention based on arbitrary and irrational standards that restricted competition and impeded the pursuit of economic efficiency and consumer satisfaction.

Regulatory reform could be approached in several ways. The most prominent was deregulation, which allowed private individuals and firms to engage in an activity on market terms and make economic decisions. The concept of *privatization* was used to describe other approaches, including discontinuance of government programs, sale of public assets such as public lands and airport facilities, and contracting out for services by private firms at public expense but under market conditions. Regulatory reform could also proceed by introducing economic incentives into public policy in a regulatory framework.

In the reassessment of regulatory policy, developments in antitrust economics were seminal. Except for the New Deal's brief fling with cartelization and corporatism in the National Industrial Recovery Act, the antitrust laws had long assumed an iconic status in the ideology of regulatory intervention. Although historically, under the judicial rule of reason, the main effect of antitrust enforcement was to promote corporate mergers, the official government position in the post–New Deal era was that antitrust activity was justified by market failure and was intended to restore competition. The criterion of unlawful conduct in antitrust policy was market concentration regardless of intent, and under the theory of economic structuralism that guided the enforcement process corporate concentration and market dominance were equated with anticompetitive conduct. In the 1950s, however, neoclassical economists began to argue that market dominance reflected efficiency and superior performance, and that consumer welfare, measured in expanded output and lower prices, was the goal of antitrust policy. The assumption underlying antitrust revisionism—and deregulation in general—was that the market is a more rational and efficient system of social regulation than government fiat.

By the 1970s, in fields where regulation was plainly protectionist (e.g., transportation), deregulation appealed even to public-interest lobby groups. In areas such as consumer and environmental protection the idea of a compromise between the competing purposes of social justice and economic productivity began to be considered, in the form of cost-benefit analysis of the effects of regulation. Accordingly steps toward deregulation were taken in the latter part of the decade. Market-oriented measures passed by Congress during the Carter administration included the Airline Deregulation Act of 1978 and the Motor Carrier Act, Railroad Transportation Deregulation Act, and Depository Institutions Deregulation and Monetary Control Act of 1980. Moreover, in the Paperwork Reduction Act of 1980 Congress created the Office of Information and Regulatory Analysis to ensure that agencies conducted cost-benefit analyses of major regulations.

Reagan's election on a platform attacking government intervention and urging the release of private economic energies raised the political stakes of regulatory revision. The clearest indication of the direction in which the Reagan administration wished to move government-business relations was antitrust policy.

The Antitrust Division of the Department of Justice rejected the traditional liberal policy of enforcing the antitrust laws to achieve social and political goals rather than economic efficiency for the benefit of consumers. Advocating competition, the division initiated enforcement proceedings only when efficiency gains were obtainable and interpreted the antitrust laws to apply to horizontal price-fixing or cartel arrangements that reduced output. Mergers that resulted in lower prices and increased competitiveness were encouraged. The Federal Trade Commission pursued the same policy with even greater vigor, to the point of becoming virtually a deregulatory agency and provoking criticism that it had abandoned its statutory responsibilities. Supported by economic studies of the negative effects of the traditional liberal policy, the Reagan administration withstood congressional opposition and succeeded in discrediting antitrust as a basic feature of the regulatory state.

In other respects the deeply entrenched structure of the liberal regulatory regime, built on mutually rewarding relationships among bureaucratic agencies, congressional committees, and interest and issue groups, proved resistant to change. Some regulatory revision occurred in civil rights, environmental protection, employee health and safety, and other areas, but the Reagan administration's aggressive efforts provoked numerous lawsuits, by public-interest lobby groups against administrative agencies, which tied up regulatory reform in the courts. The drive for deregulation also spurred a revival of regulatory activism in Congress, which in 1985 passed a series of reauthorization statutes extending environmental protection programs. From a constitutional standpoint the Reagan policies presented the ironic spectacle of a conservative president using the New Deal model of executive centralization to stop or reverse the expansion of bureaucratic intervention in the society.

Although the Republican administration achieved some of its goals through statutory means, as in the appropriations act of 1981 and the tax reform act of 1986, legislative options were limited by Democratic control of one or both houses of Congress during Reagan's two terms. Accordingly, President Reagan relied principally on the tools of administrative management to advance his policy ends.

The Reagan administrative strategy operated through centralization of policy making in the White House Domestic Policy Council and Office of Management and Budget (OMB). It also imposed controls on the bureaucracy by means of appointments, budgetary manipulation, and regulatory supervision. More than previous chief executives, President Reagan appointed political officials farther down the bureaucratic chain of command who were ideologically committed to shaping policy along White House lines. He used the Senior Executive Service, an executive branch reform of the Carter administration, to shift career officials to serve policy ends. (Reagan made about three thousand appointments in cabinet, White House, Senior Executive Service, and top-level noncareer agency positions.) The administration also curtailed bureaucratic policy making by cutting agency budgets. The main instruments of administrative policy making, however, were executive orders to reform the regulatory process in the ninety-one federal agencies that were authorized to issue regulations in the 1980s.

Executive Order 12291, issued in 1981, gave the Office of Management and Budget authority to require agencies to submit a cost-benefit analysis of proposed regulations. Within the scope of their statutory mandate, agencies were directed to assess the budgetary impact of new regulations in order to limit bureaucratic power, cut costs, and improve efficiency. Considered one of the most important changes in the administrative state since the Budget and Accounting Act of 1921, Executive Order 12291 attempted to subject bureaucratic rule making to a discipline of efficiency and economic accountability. In 1985 President Reagan extended executive control of administration by issuing Executive Order 12498, which required agencies to submit proposed regulations to the OMB for review and approval in a substantive sense. This order was not confined to budgetary matters, but rather limited agency discretion and was intended to bring policy making in the bureaucracy within the framework of White House policy.

The Reagan executive orders reflected a widely held view that bureaucratic decision making was confused, uncoordinated, and largely under the control of permanent staff in the agencies. The orders rested on the premise that the executive has the constitutional authority to supervise the conduct of administration both in a procedural and substantive sense. Politically the directives reflected the fact that, despite the post-Watergate reaction against executive power, the president was still expected to provide vision and leadership for the nation. The Reagan executive orders were nevertheless criticized by defenders of the regulatory state, who accused the administration of refusing to enforce statutes that it did not like. Critics argued that the president's power to see that the laws are executed does not authorize him to demand specific policy results.

President Reagan's resort to policy making by administrative management revealed the essential ambiguity of the modern regulatory regime. Administrative bodies are created by Congress, which in a general way determines the nature and scope of their mission and exercises operational oversight through the appropriations process. At the same time, the agencies as law enforcement institutions are executive in nature and subject, within reasonable limits, to executive discretion and discipline. The bureaucracy thus exists on an uncertain middle ground where it is the object of contention between the legislative and executive branches. This was a vulnerable position during the period of divided government in the 1980s.

The efforts of the Reagan administration to reform the regulatory state met powerful opposition in Congress, the bureaucracy, and the private sector. Having spent millions of dollars to comply with regulations, many businesses resisted proposals to change rules to which they had become accustomed. In some instances career administrators protested regulatory revision as lawless disregard of binding precedents or statutory requirements. The major opposition to change came from Congress, which under Democratic control showed aptitude and ambition to engage in detailed supervision of the federal bureaucracy.

Extending or updating the social regulation of the previous decade, Congress passed laws spelling out agency mandates in more explicit terms to reduce the scope of administrative discretion. Lawmakers attacked vulnerable bureaucrats, blocked the president's budget rescissions, and used oversight hearings to challenge Reagan administration policies in a substantive sense. Acting in the time-honored manner of the legislative branch, Congress furthermore used the appropriations process to influence the conduct of administration. It passed appropriations acts containing scores of specific policy determinations that in effect, given the cumbersome and inflexible nature of the budgetary process, were immune from executive veto. Typical of congressional micromanagement of administration were the elimination of minor agencies that disagreed with legislative policy; denial of funds for the purpose of compiling the record of a particular department's communications with Congress; and proscription of cost-benefit analysis by the Office of Management and Budget in reviewing certain controversial government programs. Congress influenced administrative policy making by compelling testimony in oversight hearings and by stipulating the actions of administrators in committee reports. And lawmakers invented a variety of informal devices to replace the legislative veto when the Supreme Court, in the first of several controversial cases dealing with the administrative state, declared it unconstitutional.

The legislative veto, a symbol of the post–New Deal regulatory regime, was considered by the Supreme Court in *Immigration and Naturalization Service* v. *Chadha* (1983). The justices declared the device to be legislative in purpose and effect, and thus subject to Article I, section 7 of the Constitution. This required every bill passed by the House of Representatives and the Senate to be presented to the president, and if disapproved to be repassed by a two-thirds vote of both houses. The decision vindicated the principle of the separation of powers, although perhaps more in a theoretical than a practical sense. The Reagan administration initiated no further litigation to invalidate scores of legislative vetoes contained in other statutes, and the committees of Congress fashioned informal arrangements with executive agencies that served as substitutes for the legislative veto.

In *Morrison* v. *Olson* (1988), the Supreme Court rendered another key decision affecting the structure of the administrative state. It affirmed the office of independent counsel, the most significant institutional development in the post-Watergate revision of the presidency. The Court held that the independent counsel was an "inferior officer" in the sense of Article I, section 2 of the Constitution; therefore the appointment could be made by the judicial department as provided in the Ethics in Government Act of 1978. The fact that executive power to prosecute crimes was conferred on the independent counsel, the Court asserted, did not prevent the president from discharging his constitutional duty to take care that the laws are executed. No violation of the separation of powers was therefore involved. At the time of the decision in *Morrison* v. *Olson* the office of independent counsel was prosecuting alleged criminal conduct by White House officials in the Iran-Contra affair. In this heavily charged political atmosphere the Court prudently acquiesced to Congress by upholding the constitutionality of the office that was cooperating with lawmakers in attacking the Reagan administration.

THE PERSISTENCE OF REGULATION

After a century of evolution, the institutions of the administrative state appeared to be a permanent part of the American polity. If this conclusion is correct, the drive for deregulation in the 1980s, contrary to much of the political rhetoric surrounding it, should not be considered a fundamental challenge to the commitment to bureaucratic intervention established by the New Deal. It should be viewed instead as a phase in the normal process of regulatory reform that was, in effect, a course correction based on renewed appreciation of the significance of private property and economic liberty in a balanced and well-ordered regime. Regulation will in all likelihood continue to be the major activity of contemporary government. It is human nature for people to be averse to risk, just as it is almost inconceivable that politicians will forgo the rewards that accrue when government intervenes to satisfy the needs and wants of citizens. Because health, safety, and the environment raise genuine problems from the standpoint of adequate regulation by the market, these matters will continue to be the object of public policy. Regulation will also persist because interventionist statutes and policies have created interests and forms of property that exert political pressure to maintain the status quo. Bureaucrats, public-interest lobbyists, corporate managers, and other groups that benefit from the existing order will resist reforms that would seriously disrupt the regulatory state.

Although regulation may be a permanent feature of postindustrial society, it is not clear what forms it will take. Government coercion under the command-and-control model of intervention, the approach favored in Progressive and New Deal regulation, has been shown to be economically inefficient and politically arbitrary. For example, no reasonable grounds exist for government to determine the number of firms that should compete in the market, although proponents of regulation still seem to assume that it is valid for the government to do so. As the advantages of the free market for regulatory purposes have been recognized in the 1980s and 1990s, experiments have been undertaken using private economic incentives within a public regulatory framework. In environmental policy the government has set the total amount of acceptable pollution and then sold pollution rights to private firms on a market basis. The same concept has been used in land use with the creation of transferable development rights. Some recent Supreme Court decisions reviving constitutional protection of property rights have reinforced the tendency toward limitation of regulatory intervention that is inherent in free-market principles. The Court has held that in some circumstances state and local regulation of land use constitutes a taking of private property for a public purpose without just compensation, in violation of the Fifth and Fourteenth Amendments (*Nollan* v. *California Coastal Commission* [1987]; *Lucas* v. *South Carolina Coastal Council* [1992]).

If the market has proved more adaptable and socially effective than the founders of the administrative state thought possible, the same may be said of the separation of powers principle against which the bureaucratic initiative was directed in the early twentieth century. Even in the heyday of presidential government in the New Deal, the tripartite constitutional structure was an effective obstacle to centralized executive sovereignty. Indeed the modern presidency was decisively shaped by the reassertion of the separation principle when Franklin D. Roosevelt was forced to accept limitations on presidential reconstruction of the American regime in the Court-packing and executive reorganization conflicts of 1937. A case can be made, moreover, that bureaucracy has been constitutionalized by being integrated into the system of separated powers and checks and balances. This was one of the major purposes of the Administrative Procedure Act of 1946, clarifying the renewed concern for constitutional limitations that the New Deal provoked. In recent years rival theories of public administration have contended either that bureaucracy is a fourth branch of government, equal in legitimacy and authority to the executive, legislative, and judicial branches, or that it is legitimate only when subordinated to the three branches established by the Constitution. The controlling principle in any case is that administrative discretion in policy making should be limited by a combination of political accountability and judicial oversight, toward the goal of maintaining constitutional balance and limited government.

Although the administrative state has apparently demonstrated its permanence, the belief of Progressive reformers that politics can be separated from administration has proved illusory. Public administration has become a political process for representing interests, which is as pluralistic as is the political culture from which it springs. The political nature of administration and its discretionary authority, widely acknowledged yet also regarded as a discordant element in liberal democracy, require that the bureaucracy be subject to the discipline of constitutionalism. Whether at any given moment due subordination of administrative agencies to the rule of law exists will always be a matter of political judgment, and hence controversial. Although the judiciary has an important part to play in keeping the bureaucracy accountable, the principal responsibility—in accordance with the design of the Constitution—falls on the executive and legislative branches and takes the form of conflicts between them for control of administration.

If administration in an abstract sense means the management of affairs, in practice it requires the adjustment of interests in specific situations in ways that often contradict the logic of centralized command-and-control regulation. For a variety of reasons, the New Deal model of centralized bureaucratic governance became more politically problematic in the 1960s. Opposition to the federal bureaucracy was a popular theme in the 1970s, which was reinforced by the politics of divided government in the 1980s. President Reagan, guided by the imperative for national leadership that has shaped every executive administration since the New Deal, tried to manage the bureaucracy in order to achieve the policy goals that his election signified. Although only marginally successful in a programmatic sense, his efforts at regulatory reform reopened the question of the nature and scope of the bureaucratic state in relation to limited constitutional government. This issue seems certain to remain central to the politics of the administrative state into the twenty-first century.

SEE ALSO The Presidency; Congress; The Courts; Federalism and the States (all in this volume).

BIBLIOGRAPHY

The relationship between bureaucracy and constitutionalism is analyzed from different philosophical points of view in John A. Rohr, *To Run a Constitution: The Legitimacy of the Administrative State* (1986); James O. Freedman, *Crisis and Legitimacy: The Administrative Process and American Government* (1978); and Vincent C. Ostrum, *The Intellectual Crisis in American Public Administration* (1974). Outstanding recent studies of the origins of the modern regulatory state are Herbert Hovenkamp, *Enterprise and American Law, 1836–1937* (1991); and Stephen Skowronek, *Building a New American State: The Expansion of Administrative Capacities, 1877–1920* (1982). Business-government relations in the evolving framework of regulatory reform are examined in Thomas K. McCraw, *Prophets of Regulation* (1984); Morton Keller, *Regulating a New Economy: Public Policy and Economic Change in America, 1900–1933* (1990); and Robert Higgs, *Crisis and Leviathan: Critical Episodes in the Growth of American Government* (1987).

The best accounts of the New Deal regulatory regime are Sidney M. Milkis, *The President and the Parties: The Transformation of the American Party System since the New Deal* (1993); and Theodore J. Lowi, *The End of Liberalism: The Second Republic of the United States* (1979). For a fair-minded analysis of Richard M. Nixon's contribution to the post–New Deal presidency, see Richard P. Nathan, *The Administrative Presidency* (1983). Ronald Reagan's achievements in restoring executive authority in the 1980s are described in James P. Pfiffner, ed., *The Managerial Presidency* (1991); and Marshall R. Goodman and Margaret T. Wrightson, *Managing Regulatory Reform: The Reagan Strategy and Its Impact* (1987). The post-Watergate administrative state is the subject of Richard A. Harris and Sidney M. Milkis, eds., *Remaking American Politics* (1989); and Gordon S. Jones and John A. Marini, eds., *The Imperial Congress: Crisis in the Separation of Powers* (1988).

Recent trends in administrative law are analyzed in Martin Shapiro, "APA: Past, Present, Future," *Virginia Law Review* 72 (1986); and Jeremy Rabkin, *Judicial Compulsions: How Public Law Distorts Public Policy* (1988). An illuminating study of changing concepts of political economy in the management of the regulatory state is Marc Allen Eisner, *Antitrust and the Triumph of Economics* (1991). Judicious reflections on the development of the regulatory project of the twentieth century are offered in Hugh Heclo, "General Welfare and Two American Political Traditions," *Political Science Quarterly* 101 (1986); James Q. Wilson, "The Rise of the Bureaucratic State," *The Public Interest* No. 41 (1975); and Bruno Leoni, *Freedom and the Law* (1961).

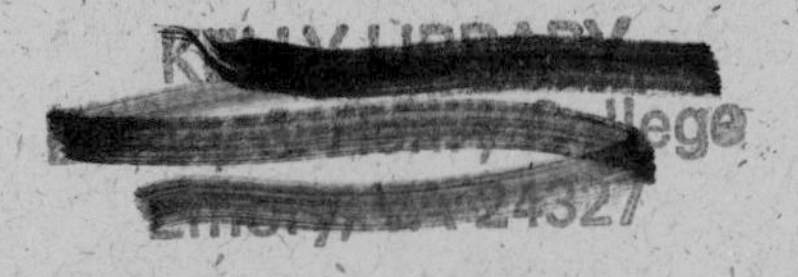